America Votes 32

ELECTION RETURNS BY STATE

RHODES COOK

2015–2016

Los Angeles | London | New Delhi
Singapore | Washington DC | Melbourne

FOR INFORMATION:

CQ Press
An Imprint of SAGE Publications, Inc.
2455 Teller Road
Thousand Oaks, California 91320
E-mail: order@sagepub.com

SAGE Publications Ltd.
1 Oliver's Yard
55 City Road
London, EC1Y 1SP
United Kingdom

SAGE Publications India Pvt. Ltd.
B 1/I 1 Mohan Cooperative Industrial Area
Mathura Road, New Delhi 110 044
India

SAGE Publications Asia-Pacific Pte. Ltd.
3 Church Street
#10-04 Samsung Hub
Singapore 049483

SAGE Editor: Laura Notton
Editorial Assistant: Tamara Tanso
Researchers: John Engelken, Jeanine Marie
Database Leads: Roylene Kulesza, Christopher Wozniak
Database Team: Sal Hewavita, Andre Messier
Production Editor: Tracy Buyan
Typesetter: Hurix Systems Pvt. Ltd., India
Proofreader: Sally Jaskold
Cover Designer: Michael Dubowe
Marketing Manager: Jennifer Bourque

ACKNOWLEDGMENT: Richard M Scammon
The publishers of *America Votes* wish to recognize the creator and long-time editor of *America Votes*, the late Richard M. Scammon. He brought his keen perceptions of the American electorate and his in-depth knowledge of U.S. voting patterns to his more than 40 years of work on the *America Votes* series. Scammon founded and directed the nonprofit Elections Research Center and was widely considered the most prominent American elections expert during his long career as a government official, advisor to presidents, and analyst of voting trends and developments. His love of elections was rooted in his lifelong commitment to democracy and his belief that the voice of one is always bested by the voice of the many.

Printed in the United States of America.

ISSN: 0065-678X
ISBN: 978-1-5063-6898-6

17 18 19 20 21 10 9 8 7 6 5 4 3 2 1

Contents

List of Maps

Introduction

The 2016 election was surreal, strange, and unique. For starters, the presidential contest between Republican Donald J. Trump and Democrat Hillary Clinton reflected a strong mood for change and rejection of the status quo. Trump, a brash political newcomer, surprisingly defeated Clinton, who in the minds of many boasted one of the best political resumes of any presidential candidate in recent American history.

Yet beyond the presidential level, it was a status quo election. Republicans held the Senate, the House of Representatives, and a large majority of the nation's governorships, with only modest shifts in the partisan numbers at any of the three levels.

Taken together, it was a banner election for the Republicans, giving them control of both ends of Pennsylvania Avenue for the first time since 2006, as well as furthering their dominance at the state level. Yet for a Republican Party seemingly built more for opposition than governance, the 2016 election recalled the old adage: "Beware what you wish for, you may get it."

2016: Republicans Rule the Roost

Little went wrong for the Republicans in 2016. They won the White House, maintained control of the Senate and the House of Representatives, and lengthened their advantage in the states, where they finished 2016 with nearly two-thirds of the nation's governorships. The chart below reflects partisan seat totals immediately before and after the 2016 general election. The pre-election House totals include Democratic vacancies in Hawaii and Pennsylvania, and a Republican seat in Kentucky, which are each credited to the party that held them before they became vacant. Two independent senators who caucus with the Democrats are listed in the "Other" column, Angus King of Maine and Bernard Sanders of Vermont. There is one independent governor, Bill Walker of Alaska.

	Pre-election			Postelection		
	Rep.	Dem.	Other	Rep.	Dem.	Other
Governor	31	18	1	33	16	1
Senate	54	44	2	52	46	2
House	247	188	0	241	194	0

An Election Like None Other

There is little doubt about it. The 2016 presidential election was like none other in American history. Russian hackers, the FBI director, even *Access Hollywood,* a television show devoted to the goings-on in the entertainment industry, all played significant roles.

But throughout the year, the spotlight was firmly trained on Trump, who confounded virtually everyone in the nation's political community by not only capturing the Republican nomination, but the White House as well.

Trump was a totally different breed of candidate than what politicians and the media were used to. He burst onto the political scene in 2015 as a brash New York real estate developer, the star of a reality TV show, and a political novice, albeit a savvy and very wealthy one. He belittled his rivals, railed against the media, debunked the credibility of both major parties, and questioned the legitimacy of the American electoral process itself.

Trump was easy to underestimate, running his campaign by his own rules. Still, signs of Trump's eventual success were evident early, as he breezed through the crowded Republican primary field, while Clinton struggled to surmount the upstart populist candidacy of Sen. Bernard "Bernie" Sanders of Vermont on the Democratic side.

In one of the more skillful feats of recent times, Trump —who liked to flaunt his great wealth—was able to sell himself to "forgotten" working-class Americans as a consummate deal-maker who would put his skills to work for them. "I am your voice," he proclaimed.

His campaign was wrapped up in a nationalistic veneer, with the slogan: "Make America Great Again." And being a political newcomer, Trump was able to run as an outsider, an agent of change in a year where many voters felt the country was on the wrong track.

In contrast, Clinton touted an impressive political resume: First Lady of the United States (as wife of former President Bill Clinton), senator from New York, and secretary of state under Barack Obama.

Clinton allied herself closely with Obama, who was leaving office with both a presidential approval rating above 50% and an economy in much better shape than when he had taken office nearly eight years earlier.

Counting the 2016 Vote

Republicans dominated the electoral scene in 2016 by making their votes count in a way that the Democrats did not. Republican Donald J. Trump lost the nationwide popular vote for president to Democrat Hillary Clinton by nearly 3 million, but he carried the all-important electoral vote. In Senate races, Republicans had an aggregate deficit of 11 million votes, but were able to stay in control of the Senate by winning 22 of the 34 seats that were up in 2016. (The GOP nationwide Senate vote deficit was due in large part to the Republicans' inability to advance a Senate candidate to the general election in California. There, under the state's unique election rules, two Democrats competed in the general election). In the House, Republicans were able to make a modest 1.4-million advantage in the nationwide congressional vote count and turn it into a solid 47-seat advantage. The totals below are based on official returns from the 2016 presidential election in all 50 states and the District of Columbia, House elections in the 50 states, Senate contests in 34 states, and gubernatorial races in 15 states (with three of the elections for governor held in 2015, and 12 in 2016, including a special election for governor in Oregon). No blank or void ballots are included in the totals below.

Office	Total Vote	Republican	Democratic	Other	Rep.-Dem. Plurality	Percentage of Total Vote		
						Rep.	Dem.	Other
President	136,667,388	62,984,824	65,853,510	7,829,054	2,868,686 D	46.1%	48.2%	5.7%
Governor	22,430,964	11,185,865	10,596,760	648,339	589,105 R	49.9%	47.2%	2.9%
Senate	95,321,149	40,423,868	51,536,671	3,360,610	11,112,803 D	42.4%	54.1%	3.5%
House	128,377,310	62,977,071	61,753,341	3,646,898	1,224,467 R	49.1%	48.1%	2.8%

Clinton was also mounting a history-making candidacy. If elected, she would have become the nation's first female president. But an agent of change she was not.

There was a negative undertone to the entire campaign, due in no small part to the unpopularity of the two nominees. Clinton's trustworthiness took a beating with the disclosure of her use of a private email server as secretary of state, an issue that was magnified by hackers, apparently Russian, who to the embarrassment of the Democrats fed their information to WikiLeaks for publication. Other hacks into emails of the Democratic National Committee and the Clinton campaign operation further undermined the Democratic effort.

Clinton appeared to be weathering the assault until less than a fortnight before the election, when FBI Director James Comey turned a bright spotlight on the issue by indicating that the FBI was looking into a glut of newly discovered Clinton emails. Comey announced a week or so later that no incriminating evidence had been found, but it was an "October surprise" that many Democrats felt cost them the election.

As for Trump, his unorthodox candidacy was a magnet for concerns that revolved around his boorishness, doubts about the depth of his knowledge of major issues, and head scratching about his "soft spot" for Russian strong man Vladimir Putin. His campaign seemed on the verge of extinction in early October when a decade-old tape from *Access Hollywood* surfaced that featured Trump in his own words bragging about his techniques as a sexual predator. Some Republican officeholders briefly suggested that he quit the ticket, until polls showed that Trump remained a viable challenger.

2016: Close House Races

There has been a declining number of highly competitive House races in recent years, with less than 5 percent of the nation's congressional elections (21 of 435) decided in 2016 with less than 52 percent of the total vote. It was a significant drop from just six years ago, when 55 House contests were won with less than 52 percent. An asterisk (*) indicates an incumbent.

Republicans (10)	2016 Winning Percentage	Democrats (11)	2016 Winning Percentage
Claudia Tenney, N.Y. 22	46.5%	Carol Shea-Porter, N.H. 1	44.3%
Jason Lewis, Minn. 2	47.0%	Jacky Rosen, Nev. 3	47.2%
Will Hurd, Texas 23*	48.3%	Ruben Kihuen, Nev. 4	48.5%
Martha Roby, Ala. 2*	48.8%	Ann McLane Kuster, N.H. 2*	49.7%
Don Bacon, Neb. 2	48.9%	Richard M. Nolan, Minn. 8*	50.3%
Don Young, Alaska AL*	50.3%	Timothy J. Walz, Minn. 1*	50.3%
Darrell Issa, Calif. 49*	50.3%	Tom O'Halleran, Ariz. 1	50.7%
Mike Coffman, Colo. 6*	50.9%	Joshua S. Gottheimer, N.J. 5	51.1%
Kevin Yoder, Kan. 3*	51.3%	Ami Bera, Calif. 7*	51.2%
Jeff Denham, Calif. 10*	51.7%	Stephanie Murphy, Fla. 7	51.5%
		Charlie Crist, Fla. 13	51.9%

The House Since 1990: A Political Weathervane

For much of the 20th century, Democrats relied on large majorities in the South to control the House of Representatives. But nowadays, it is the Republicans' overwhelming advantage in the region that provides their critical House margin. The GOP finished the 2016 election holding nearly three-quarters of all Southern House seats, which represent 45 percent of the Republicans' entire complement in Congress' lower chamber.

	South				West			Midwest			East				Total House			
	R	D	I		R	D		R	D		R	D	I		R	D	I	
1990	44	85	0	D	37	48	D	45	68	D	41	66	1	D	167	267	1	D
1992	52	85	0	D	38	55	D	44	61	D	42	57	1	D	176	258	1	D
1994	73	64	0	R	53	40	R	59	46	R	45	54	1	D	230	204	1	R
1996	82	55	0	R	51	42	R	55	50	R	39	60	1	D	227	207	1	R
1998	82	55	0	R	49	44	R	54	51	R	38	61	1	D	223	211	1	R
2000	81	55	1	R	43	50	D	57	48	R	40	59	1	D	221	212	2	R
2002	85	57	0	R	46	52	D	61	39	R	37	57	1	D	229	205	1	R
2004	91	51	0	R	45	53	D	60	40	R	36	58	1	D	232	202	1	R
2006	85	57	0	R	41	57	D	51	49	R	25	70	0	D	202	233	0	D
2008	80	62	0	R	35	63	D	45	55	D	18	77	0	D	178	257	0	D
2010	102	40	0	R	43	55	D	65	35	R	32	63	0	D	242	193	0	R
2012	108	41	0	R	39	63	D	59	35	R	28	62	0	D	234	201	0	R
2014	111	38	0	R	41	61	D	61	33	R	34	56	0	D	247	188	0	R
2016	109	40	0	R	39	63	D	61	33	R	32	58	0	D	241	194	0	R
Net Change in GOP Seats, 1994–2016	+ 36				– 14			+ 2			– 13				+ 11			

SOUTH - Alabama, Arkansas, Florida, Georgia, Kentucky, Louisiana, Mississippi, North Carolina, Oklahoma, South Carolina, Tennessee, Texas, Virginia.

WEST - Alaska, Arizona, California, Colorado, Hawaii, Idaho, Montana, Nevada, New Mexico, Oregon, Utah, Washington, Wyoming.

MIDWEST - Illinois, Indiana, Iowa, Kansas, Michigan, Minnesota, Missouri, Nebraska, North Dakota, Ohio, South Dakota, Wisconsin.

EAST - Connecticut, Delaware, Maine, Maryland, Massachusetts, New Hampshire, New Jersey, New York, Pennsylvania, Rhode Island, Vermont, West Virginia.

Not surprisingly, each candidate went after the other with gusto. Trump repeatedly brought up Bill Clinton's own checkered history with women and referred to Clinton's wife as "crooked Hillary." Meanwhile, she dismissed Trump as unqualified to be president, and described half of his supporters as belonging in a "basket of deplorables."

Still, as the campaign headed to the finish line, it was regarded as Clinton's election to lose. National polls showed her narrowly, but consistently, ahead. So did those in most of the battleground states. The big question was whether Clinton would be joined in the nation's capital by a Democratic Senate.

But what was widely expected to be a good election for Democrats turned out on November 8 to be a great one for Republicans. For the first time in a dozen years they won both ends of Pennsylvania Avenue, taking the White House and maintaining control of both the House and the Senate. The GOP also strengthened its hegemony in the states, where they emerged from the 2016 election with control of nearly two-thirds of the governors and state legislatures.

Democrats were left with a handful of consolation prizes. Clinton won the popular vote by nearly 3 million, thanks to a gigantic advantage of more than 4 million votes in California, and Democrats scored modest gains in both the Senate (two seats) and the House (six seats). But in both congressional chambers, they remained stuck in the minority.

Democrats Fall Short

For Democrats, it was an election squandered. The party had a plethora of opportunities in 2016 to win control of the Senate, where 24 of the 34 seats at stake were held by Republicans. And in presidential election years of late, Democrats have been able to run with the wind at their backs, swept along by an electorate much larger and more racially diverse than that in midterm elections, which Republicans have come to dominate.

2016: Defeated Incumbents

Of the governors, senators, and U.S. representatives who lost their bids for re-election in 2016, most were Republicans. That included the one governor, two senators, and nine of the 13 House members who lost their primary or general election. Still, their losses were not enough to threaten GOP control of the Senate and the House of Representatives, or dominance of the nation's governorships. The chart lists the gubernatorial, Senate, and House incumbents defeated in the 2016 primaries and general election, the number of full terms they had served in that office at the time of their loss in 2016, the percentage of the total vote they had received in the previous general election (2010 for senators, 2012 for governors, and 2014 for House members), and their percentage of the total vote in the 2016 general election (for those who were not sidelined by the primaries).

	Number of Full Terms	Previous Election Percentage	2016 Election Percentage
GOVERNORS			
Primaries (0)			
General Election (1)			
(1 Republican)			
Pat McCrory, R-N.C.	1	54.6%	48.8%
SENATORS			
Primaries (0)			
General Election (2)			
(2 Republicans)			
Kelly Ayotte, R-N.H.	1	60.0%	47.8%
Mark Kirk, R-Ill.	1	48.0%	39.8%
REPRESENTATIVES			
Primaries (5)			
(3 Republicans, 2 Democrats)			
Corrine Brown, D-Fla. 5	12	65.5%	—
Renee L. Ellmers, R-N.C. 2	3	58.8%	—
Chaka Fattah, D-Pa. 2	11	87.7%	—
J. Randy Forbes, R-Va. 4*	7	60.2%	—
Tim Huelskamp, R-Kan. 1	3	68.0%	—
General Election (8)			
(6 Republicans, 2 Democrats)			
Brad Ashford, D-Neb. 2	1	48.9%	47.7%
Robert Dold, R-Ill. 10	2	51.3%	47.4%
Scott Garrett, R-N.J. 5	7	55.4%	46.7%
Frank C. Guinta, R-N.H. 1	2	51.7%	43.0%
Cresent Hardy, R-Nev. 4	1	48.5%	44.5%
Michael M. Honda, D-Calif. 17#	8	51.8%	39.0%
David W. Jolly, R-Fla. 13	1	75.2%	48.1%
John L. Mica, R-Fla. 7	12	63.6%	48.5%

Note: An asterisk (*) indicates that J. Randy Forbes was re-elected in 2014 in the Virginia 4th District, but after mid-decade redistricting in the state Forbes unsuccessfully sought renomination in 2016 in the Virginia 2nd District. A pound sign (#) denotes that Michael M. Honda lost his re-election bid to a fellow Democrat, Ro Khanna.

Clinton did become the sixth Democratic candidate in the last seven presidential elections to win the popular vote, but a half dozen battleground states that were carried by Obama in 2008 and 2012 went for Trump, enough to give the Republican a solid 304–227 win in the Electoral College.

The remaining seven electoral votes, a historically large number, were cast by "faithless" electors, five Democrats and two Republicans. A variety of individuals received their votes, including former Secretary of State Colin Powell, Ohio Gov. John Kasich, former Rep. Ron Paul of Texas, Sen. Sanders, and Faith Spotted Eagle, an anti-pipeline activist from the Sioux tribe. (Powell received three electoral votes; the others, one apiece.)

The six states that switched from Obama in 2012 to Trump in 2016 included Florida, plus a quintet of states strewn across the Frost Belt: Iowa, Michigan, Ohio, Pennsylvania, and Wisconsin. Iowa, Florida, and Ohio had last voted Republican for president in 2004. Michigan, Pennsylvania, and Wisconsin had not chosen GOP electors since the 1980s.

Altogether, the six states possessed 99 electoral votes, which, combined with those in reliably Republican states across the South, the agricultural Midwest, and the Mountain West, were more than enough to give Trump a solid Electoral College victory.

Iowa and Ohio swung decisively to Trump, favoring him by margins of 9 and 8 percentage points, respectively. Florida was much closer, going Republican by 1.2 percentage points. Michigan, Pennsylvania, and Wisconsin went down to the wire, all decided in Trump's favor by margins of less than 1 percentage point. The latter three were considered part of the Democrats' "blue wall," which, combined with loyal Democratic states in the Northeast and West, plus a handful of scattered others (Illinois, Minnesota, and Virginia), were enough in the recent past to give Democrats an electoral vote majority. If Clinton had carried Michigan, Pennsylvania, and Wisconsin—as Bill Clinton, Al Gore, John Kerry, and Obama had done before—she would have won more than the 270 needed to take the White House, even with the five "faithless" Democratic electors.

But in a problematic decision, the Clinton team spent valuable time in the final stages of the 2016 campaign trying to pick off some demographically enticing, though traditionally Republican, Sun Belt states, such as Arizona and Georgia. Unfortunately for Clinton, the offensive forays did not pay off and came at the expense of holding Michigan, Pennsylvania, and Wisconsin. The three fell to Trump by a combined margin of less than 80,000 votes.

A Case Study: Michigan

Trump won Michigan by barely 10,000 votes out of more than 4.7 million cast (a margin of just two-tenths of a percentage point).

Democratic presidential candidates from 1992 through 2012 had carried the Wolverine State with margins ranging from 165,000 votes for Kerry in 2004 to nearly 825,000 for Obama in 2008. Four years later, Obama won the state by nearly 450,000 votes over native son Mitt Romney.

Throughout 2016, Michigan was expected to be in the Democratic column again. Why then, did it get away? First, Clinton fell far short of matching Obama's 2012 margin in heavily Democratic Wayne County, which is anchored by the predominantly African American city of Detroit. Obama had carried the county by more than 380,000 votes in his re-election race, a margin more than 90,000 votes larger than Clinton's.

Second, Clinton failed to match Obama's showing in the Detroit suburbs. Both Democrats swept Oakland County with its pockets of affluence. But unlike Obama in 2012, Clinton lost the more blue-collar Macomb County, the quintessential home of Ronald Reagan Democrats. The result: A nearly 70,000-vote suburban edge for Obama over Romney shrank to a 5,500-vote advantage for Clinton over Trump.

Even then, Clinton could have easily carried Michigan if she had shown a modest measure of appeal in the rest of the state. In 2012, Obama and Romney had battled to a draw in the rural areas, small cities, and industrial centers outside Detroit and its suburbs. But in 2016, Trump crushed Clinton by more than 300,000 votes in this terrain, just enough to carry the state.

Trump's formula for success was not unique to Michigan. Clinton's inability to reassemble the Obama coalition in its entirety and Trump's unusual strength in rural counties and blue-collar bastions turned out to be common themes in the battleground states.

Third-Party Impact

Nearly 6 percent of all ballots cast in the 2016 presidential election were for someone other than Trump or Clinton, the highest level of non-major party ballot activity since Ross Perot made his two presidential runs in the 1990s.

Altogether, votes for third parties, independents, and write-ins totaled nearly 8 million of the almost 136.7 million presidential votes cast. That far eclipsed Clinton's nearly 2.9-million vote advantage in the popular vote.

Most of the third-party votes (nearly 4.5 million) went for the Libertarian ticket of Gary Johnson and William Weld (two former Republican governors), who posted by far the highest vote total ever for the ambitious third-party.

Green Party candidate Jill Stein drew nearly 1.5 million votes, second only in party annals to the nearly 2.9 million collected by Ralph Nader in 2000.

And independent Evan McMullin, who presented himself as a polite, low-key, anti-Trump conservative, received more than 700,000 votes, although his late-starting candidacy was on the ballot in only 11 states. (He did not enter the race until three months before the election.) Ultimately, nearly a quarter million of McMullin's votes came from his home state of Utah, where he won more than 20 percent of the vote. The other votes cast in the 2016 presidential election basically went for an array of smaller third parties and write-ins.

The third-party vote was large enough in 2016 that it could have acted as a balance of power in a number of battleground states.

In Florida, which Trump carried by 112,911 votes, the combined total for third-party, independent, and write-in candidates approached 300,000.

In Pennsylvania, which Trump won by 44,292 votes, the total for the non-major candidates was almost 270,000.

In Wisconsin, where the Trump margin was 22,748 votes, the vote that did not go for either Trump or Clinton was nearly 200,000.

In Michigan, which Trump carried by just 10,704 votes, the number of ballots cast for Johnson, Stein, McMullin, and friends reached 250,000.

Given the millions of votes that they received, third-party and independent candidates could have played a major role in determining the outcome of the 2016 election. Yet unlike Nader, who in the razor close election of 2000 is believed to have taken votes primarily from the Democrats, it is harder to make the case that Clinton was critically wounded in 2016 by the third-party vote. The election day national exit poll showed that if the race had been restricted to Clinton and Trump, with no other options, the popular vote result would have been largely what it was: a virtual wash.

The Methodology

The thirty-second edition of *America Votes* follows the same format as other recent editions in this series. The introductory text and variety of summary tables that accompany it seek to tie together basic elements of the 2016 election cycle. The section that follows presents national tables on voter turnout as well as the aggregate vote by state for president, Senate, and House in 2016. A gubernatorial table features results from elections for governor in 2015 and 2016.

The turnout table uses voter registration and "citizen" voting-age population figures compiled by the Census Bureau. In the latter, the millions and millions of non-citizens age 18 years and older are not included, giving a truer sense of the voter turnout rate than if all persons of voting age were included.

The overview material also features a summary of special elections held between the general elections of 2014 and 2016 that filled vacancies in the 114th Congress. There is also a list of changes in the congressional membership of the 115th Congress that occurred between the 2016 general election and August 18, 2017. Tables with the presidential vote by state from 1960 through 2012 follow. The overview material concludes with state-by-state results from the 2016 Democratic and Republican presidential primaries, including tables at the end of this section with the aggregate primary votes for candidates in both major parties.

The heart of the volume, 51 chapters—one for each state and the District of Columbia—follows this introductory material.

Each state chapter begins with a list of the current governor, senators, and representatives, followed by tables with the statewide vote for president, governor, and senator from the end of World War II (1945) to the present. A map of the state shows its counties, major population centers, and congressional districts for members of the House in the 115th Congress. Other maps are included in states with at least one particularly large population center that features multiple congressional districts. County-by-county tables of presidential, gubernatorial, and Senate elections follow the maps. All these tables are for the 2016 general election, with the exception of gubernatorial contests in Kentucky, Louisiana, and Mississippi, which were held in 2015.

In all cases, the county tables for presidential elections feature three columns of votes (Republican, Democratic, and Other, the latter of which includes the aggregate vote for third-party, independent, and write-in candidates). The same format is used in the county tables for gubernatorial and Senate elections, except those contests in which a third-party or independent candidate received at least 10 percent of the vote. Each non-major party

candidate that reached that threshold has their own vote and percentage of the vote columns. All the county tables include 2010 population figures from the Census Bureau.

After that, in each state chapter, is the vote for the House of Representatives arranged by congressional district. The implementation of the 2010 Census for redistricting purposes led to changes before the 2012 election in district boundaries in all states with more than one House member. In addition, there has been mid-decade redistricting in several states, with lines changing in Florida, North Carolina, and Virginia before the 2016 election. House results for elections before 2012 (or whenever the district lines were last changed) are not included for any state except those with a single House seat.

The conclusion of each state chapter consists of two parts. The first is a notes section containing a breakdown of votes cast in 2016 for each federal office and governor in the general election for third-party, independent, and write-in candidates. The total of scattered write-in votes is listed in states where they were included in the official returns. For those major party candidates who also ran on a third-party ballot line, which was possible in Connecticut, South Carolina, and most notably New York, votes are aggregated as Democratic or Republican.

The second part of the conclusion of each state chapter deals with primary elections. It opens with an explanation of who could vote in the state's primary in 2016 as well as voter registration totals at the time of the primary election. The latter is broken down by party in the 30 or so states where voters register by party. This material is followed by Democratic and Republican primary results for president, governor, senator, and House, as well as the results for runoff elections in states, mainly in the South, that held them.

The lone exceptions to this format were in California and Washington, which in recent elections have held "top two" primaries (for governor, senator, and representative) in which candidates from all parties ran together on one ballot, with the top two, regardless of party, advancing to the general election. Louisiana has held a variant of this, with the same format as California and Washington, with the exception that the leading vote-getter could win election outright if he or she received a majority of the vote in the first round.

In the six New England states, where town government is often accented, tables list the vote for president, governor, and senator by larger cities and towns as well as by counties. In Rhode Island, the results are listed for all cities and towns.

The *America Votes* series is compiled from official results obtained from each state and the District of Columbia. Although complete accuracy is always the goal, it can prove elusive in a work such as this. On occasion, states may belatedly report changes in their vote totals that occur after publication of this volume. And human nature being what it is, there is always an example or two (or three or four) of self-inflicted errors. The goal is always to keep these to a minimum. In light of the desire to make these reference volumes as useful as possible to readers and researchers, corrections of data are always welcome as are suggestions for new material.

The creation of each edition in this series has always taken a fair-sized army of dedicated and talented people. Outside of CQ Press, a special tip of the hat is due Richard Winger and Robert Yoon. Winger, the publisher of a political newsletter, *Ballot Access News*, pointed out corrections that needed to be made to pre-2014 editions of *America Votes*. Yoon, a former CNN director of political

research, spearheaded the creation of "CNN Election Night in America Research Guide 2016" that proved invaluable in compiling the presidential primary results in this edition of *America Votes*.

Within the SAGE family, Andrew Boney, the Acquisitions Editor at CQ Press, once again efficiently guided work on this edition with his patience, good humor, and considerable expertise. Andrew was the Washington-based cornerstone of this edition. But creating each edition of *America Votes* can be likened to piecing together a massive jigsaw puzzle, which required able assistance, which was provided by David C. Felts, Sal Hewavita, Roylene Kulesza, Andre Messier, Laura Notton, Tamara Tanso, and Chris Wozniak. Very special thanks goes to John Engelken and Jeanine Marie for their heroic efforts in collecting and curating many of the voting returns for this election cycle.

Rhodes Cook
September 2017

Errata

America Votes 31

The following corrections should be noted for the previous edition, *America Votes 31*, covering the 2013–2014 election cycle.

Page 1. In the 2014 Voter Turnout table, the first note at the bottom should read that Oklahoma and South Carolina each held two Senate elections on November 4, 2014 (not 2015).

Page 3. In the 2014 Senate Elections table, the Hawaii race should have been designated as a special election with "(S)."

Page 46. In the California Postwar Vote for Governor table, the Democratic candidate in the 1974, 1978, 2010, and 2014 elections was "Brown, Edmund G. Jr." In the California Postwar Vote for Senator table, the Democratic candidate in the 1982 election was "Brown, Edmund G. Jr."

Page 71. In the Connecticut primary table, the last name of one of the Republican governor candidates should be spelled "McKinney."

Page 84. In the Florida General Elections: Other Votes section, governor candidates Glenn Burkett and Farid Khavari should be designated as "No Party Affiliation."

Page 103. In the Hawaii Postwar Vote for Senator table, the 2014 contest should have been designated as a special election with "(S)."

Page 105. In the Hawaii primary table, the second set of races should be labeled on the left-hand side as Senator.

Page 121. In the Illinois primary table, Sherry Procarione should have been designated as a "write-in" in the Republican Senate primary. In the 5th District Republican primary, Fredrick K. White should have been designated as a "write-in."

Page 155. In the Louisiana Postwar Vote for Senator table, the first 2014 line should be deleted since it features results from the first round primary. Complete results for that event are found in the Louisiana primary table on page 158. The second 2014 line was the decisive vote, a runoff election. It should be designated with two asterisks (**). Meanwhile, the two asterisks (**) associated with the 2010 Senate line should be deleted.

Page 244. In the New Jersey 3rd District, the last name of the House member should be spelled "MacArthur (R)."

Page 314, In the Rhode Island Postwar Vote for Governor table, the Plurality column on the 2010 line should be "R#" to designate that the winner (Lincoln D. Chafee) was an independent candidate.

Page 405. In the Wisconsin Republican gubernatorial primary, Steve R. Evans received 94 votes as a write-in, while the number of scattered write-ins totaled 1,293. In the Wisconsin Republican 7th District primary, John Schiess received 2 votes as a write-in.

America Votes 30

The following correction should be noted for *America Votes 30*, covering the 2011–2012 election cycle.

Page 125. In the Florida General Elections: Other Vote section, Randall Terry in the 20th District should be designated as "No Party Affiliation."

America Votes 22 (1996 edition)

Page 403. In the Ohio General Elections: Other Vote section, there should be the following entry: "CD 17: 21,685 Natural Law (Cahaney)."

UNITED STATES
VOTER TURNOUT 2016

State	2016 Voting Age Population	Registration 2016 General Election	Percentage Voting Age Registered	Presidential Vote	Presidential Vote as Percentage of		House Vote	Senate Vote	Governor Vote
					Voting Age Population	Registered Voters			
Alabama	3,651,000	2,526,000	69.2%	2,123,372	58.2%	84.1%	1,889,685	2,087,444	—
Alaska	502,000	358,000	71.3%	318,608	63.5%	89.0%	308,198	311,441	—
Arizona	4,585,000	3,145,000	68.6%	2,573,165	56.1%	81.8%	2,412,064	2,530,730	—
Arkansas	2,116,000	1,456,000	68.8%	1,130,676	53.4%	77.7%	1,068,577	1,107,522	—
California	24,890,000	16,096,000	64.7%	14,181,595	57.0%	88.1%	13,414,018	12,244,170	—
Colorado	3,895,000	2,893,000	74.3%	2,780,247	71.4%	96.1%	2,701,561	2,743,029	—
Connecticut	2,483,000	1,763,000	71.0%	1,644,920	66.2%	93.3%	1,575,183	1,596,276	—
Delaware	669,000	487,000	72.8%	443,814	66.3%	91.1%	420,682	—	425,812
Florida	14,428,000	9,604,000	66.6%	9,420,039	65.3%	98.1%	8,837,426	9,301,820	—
Georgia	7,048,000	4,892,000	69.4%	4,114,732	58.4%	84.1%	3,772,862	3,898,605	—
Hawaii	974,000	530,000	54.4%	428,937	44.0%	80.9%	412,873	416,562	—
Idaho	1,150,000	790,000	68.7%	690,255	60.0%	87.4%	681,594	678,943	—
Illinois	8,970,000	6,665,000	74.3%	5,536,424	61.7%	83.1%	5,241,767	5,491,878	—
Indiana	4,795,000	3,298,000	68.8%	2,734,958	57.0%	82.9%	2,658,367	2,732,546	2,719,968
Iowa	2,292,000	1,657,000	72.3%	1,566,031	68.3%	94.5%	1,515,555	1,541,036	—
Kansas	2,029,000	1,438,000	70.9%	1,184,402	58.4%	82.4%	1,173,736	1,177,922	—
Kentucky	3,246,000	2,253,000	69.4%	1,924,149	59.3%	85.4%	1,765,376	1,903,465	973,692
Louisiana	3,353,000	2,446,000	73.0%	2,029,032	60.5%	83.0%	1,470,199	884,007	1,152,864
Maine	1,038,000	830,000	80.0%	747,927	72.1%	90.1%	744,574	—	—
Maryland	4,158,000	3,114,000	74.9%	2,781,446	66.9%	89.3%	2,707,745	2,726,170	—
Massachusetts	4,967,000	3,660,000	73.7%	3,325,046	66.9%	90.8%	2,940,688	—	—
Michigan	7,332,000	5,434,000	74.1%	4,799,284	65.5%	88.3%	4,670,905	—	—
Minnesota	3,985,000	3,055,000	76.7%	2,944,813	73.9%	96.4%	2,860,432	—	—
Mississippi	2,170,000	1,725,000	79.5%	1,209,357	55.7%	70.1%	1,182,273	—	725,207
Missouri	4,486,000	3,333,000	74.3%	2,808,605	62.6%	84.3%	2,750,079	2,802,641	2,803,046
Montana	790,000	581,000	73.5%	497,147	62.9%	85.6%	507,831	—	509,360
Nebraska	1,336,000	1,008,000	75.5%	844,227	63.2%	83.8%	788,453	—	—
Nevada	1,975,000	1,371,000	69.4%	1,125,385	57.0%	82.1%	1,078,497	1,108,294	—
New Hampshire	1,012,000	763,000	75.4%	744,296	73.5%	97.5%	716,777	739,140	724,863
New Jersey	5,958,000	4,165,000	69.9%	3,874,046	65.0%	93.0%	3,463,311	—	—
New Mexico	1,396,000	916,000	65.6%	798,319	57.2%	87.2%	780,126	—	—
New York	13,751,000	9,142,000	66.5%	7,721,442	56.2%	84.5%	7,116,422	7,396,305	—
North Carolina	6,960,000	5,194,000	74.6%	4,741,564	68.1%	91.3%	4,598,458	4,691,133	4,711,014
North Dakota	564,000	424,000[1]	75.2%	344,360	61.1%	81.2%	338,459	342,501	339,601
Ohio	8,499,000	6,128,000	72.1%	5,496,487	64.7%	89.7%	5,218,355	5,374,164	—
Oklahoma	2,746,000	1,861,000	67.8%	1,452,992	52.9%	78.1%	1,133,244	1,448,047	—
Oregon	2,929,000	2,147,000	73.3%	2,001,336	68.3%	93.2%	1,911,865	1,952,478	1,946,046
Pennsylvania	9,596,000	6,909,000	72.0%	6,165,478	64.3%	89.2%	5,743,978	6,051,856	—
Rhode Island	766,000	538,000	70.3%	464,144	60.6%	86.3%	431,519	—	—
South Carolina	3,598,000	2,575,000	71.6%	2,103,027	58.4%	81.7%	2,039,462	2,049,893	—
South Dakota	612,000	437,000	71.4%	370,093	60.5%	84.7%	369,973	369,656	—
Tennessee	4,872,000	3,251,000	66.7%	2,508,027	51.5%	77.1%	2,391,061	—	—
Texas	17,378,000	11,724,000	67.5%	8,969,226	51.6%	76.5%	8,528,526	—	—
Utah	1,969,000	1,398,000	71.0%	1,131,430	57.5%	80.9%	1,114,170	1,115,608	1,125,035
Vermont	488,000	351,000	71.9%	315,067	64.6%	89.8%	295,334	313,809	315,295
Virginia	5,829,000	4,399,000	75.5%	3,982,752	68.3%	90.5%	3,782,428	—	—
Washington	5,104,000	3,906,000	76.5%	3,317,019	65.0%	84.9%	3,141,035	3,243,317	3,245,282
West Virginia	1,425,000	913,000	64.1%	714,423	50.1%	78.3%	686,349	—	713,879
Wisconsin	4,354,000	3,323,000	76.3%	2,976,150	68.4%	89.6%	2,773,662	2,948,741	—
Wyoming	427,000	304,000	71.1%	255,849	59.9%	84.2%	251,776	—	—
District of Columbia	512,000	420,000	82.1%	311,268	60.8%	74.1%	—	—	—
Total	224,059,000	157,596,000	70.3%	136,667,388	61.0%	86.7%	128,377,310	95,321,149	22,430,964

Source: Registration and voting age population (VAP) figures were provided by the U.S. Census Bureau. VAP figures are based on estimated numbers of citizens of voting age in each state (and nationally) at the time of the November 2016 general election. Figures do not account for felony or other forms of disenfranchisement. They also do not account for those living outside the United States and those naturalized in 2016, both of which are enfranchised but not counted in the Census enumeration of age-eligible citizens.

Notes: Does not include special elections or elections for non-voting delegates. The gubernatorial vote includes 2015 elections in Kentucky, Louisiana, and Mississippi. Includes vote totals for general election Senate and House races in Louisiana; does not include runoff votes in the 3rd and 4th districts.

1. North Dakota does not require voter registration.

2

GUBERNATORIAL ELECTIONS 2015 AND 2016

State	Total Vote	Republican Vote	Republican Candidate	Democratic Vote	Democratic Candidate	Other Vote	Rep.-Dem. Plurality	Total Vote Rep.	Total Vote Dem.	Major Vote Rep.	Major Vote Dem.
Delaware	425,812	166,852	Bonini, Colin	248,404	Carney, John C. Jr.	10,556	81,552 D	39.2%	58.3%	40.2%	59.8%
Indiana	2,719,968	1,397,396	Holcomb, Eric	1,235,503	Gregg, John R.	87,069	161,893 R	51.4%	45.4%	53.1%	46.9%
Kentucky (2015)	973,692	511,374	Bevin, Matt G.	426,620	Conway, Jack	35,698	84,754 R	52.5%	43.8%	54.5%	45.5%
Louisiana (2015)	1,152,864	505,940	Vitter, David B.	646,924	Edwards, John Bel		140,984 D	43.9%	56.1%	43.9%	56.1%
Mississippi (2015)	725,207	480,399	Bryant, Phil	234,858	Gray, Robert	9,950	245,541 R	66.2%	32.4%	67.2%	32.8%
Missouri	2,803,046	1,433,397	Greitens, Eric	1,277,360	Koster, Chris	92,289	156,037 R	51.1%	45.6%	52.9%	47.1%
Montana	509,360	236,115	Gianforte, Greg	255,933	Bullock, Steve	17,312	19,818 D	46.4%	50.3%	48.0%	52.0%
New Hampshire	724,863	354,040	Sununu, Chris	337,589	Van Ostern, Colin	33,234	16,451 R	48.8%	46.6%	51.2%	48.8%
North Carolina	4,711,014	2,298,880	McCrory, Pat	2,309,157	Cooper, Roy	102,977	10,277 D	48.8%	49.0%	49.9%	50.1%
North Dakota	339,601	259,863	Burgum, Doug	65,855	Nelson, Marvin E.	13,883	194,008 R	76.5%	19.4%	79.8%	20.2%
Oregon (S)	1,946,046	845,609	Pierce, Bud	985,027	Brown, Kate	115,410	139,418 D	43.5%	50.6%	46.2%	53.8%
Utah	1,125,035	750,850	Herbert, Gary R.	323,349	Weinholtz, Mike	50,836	427,501 R	66.7%	28.7%	69.9%	30.1%
Vermont	315,295	166,817	Scott, Phil	139,253	Minter, Sue	9,225	27,564 R	52.9%	44.2%	54.5%	45.5%
Washington	3,245,282	1,476,346	Bryant, Bill	1,760,520	Inslee, Jay	8,416	284,174 D	45.5%	54.3%	45.6%	54.4%
West Virginia	713,879	301,987	Cole, Bill	350,408	Justice, Jim	61,484	48,421 D	42.3%	49.1%	46.3%	53.7%
Total	22,430,964	11,185,865		10,596,760		648,339	589,105 R	49.9%	47.2%	51.4%	48.6%

Notes: The gubernatorial vote includes 2015 elections in Kentucky, Louisiana, and Mississippi as well as the special gubernatorial election (S) in Oregon (2016). No independent or third-party candidate drew even 10 percent of the vote. Louisiana has a blanket primary election system for many offices, including governor. All candidates, regardless of party, appeared together on the October 24, 2015, ballot. Since no candidate received more than 50 percent of the vote, a runoff was held November 21, 2015, between the top two vote recipients, John Bel Edwards (D) and David B. Vitter (R). The result of the runoff is included here.

SENATE ELECTIONS 2016

| State | Total Vote | Republican | | Democratic | | Other Vote | Rep.-Dem. Plurality | Percentage | | | |
| | | Vote | Candidate | Vote | Candidate | | | Total Vote | | Major Vote | |
								Rep.	Dem.	Rep.	Dem.
Alabama	2,087,444	1,335,104	Shelby, Richard C.	748,709	Crumpton, Ron	3,631	586,395 R	64.0%	35.9%	64.1%	35.9%
Alaska	311,441	138,149	Murkowski, Lisa	36,200	Metcalfe, Ray	137,092	101,949 R	44.4%	11.6%	79.2%	20.8%
Arizona	2,530,730	1,359,267	McCain, John S. III	1,031,245	Kirkpatrick, Ann	140,218	328,022 R	53.7%	40.8%	56.9%	43.1%
Arkansas	1,107,522	661,984	Boozman, John	400,602	Eldridge, Conner	44,936	261,382 R	59.8%	36.2%	62.3%	37.7%
California*	12,244,170			12,244,170	Harris, Kamala D.		12,244,170 D		100.0%		100.0%
Colorado	2,743,029	1,215,318	Glenn, Darryl	1,370,710	Bennet, Michael F.	157,001	155,392 D	44.3%	50.0%	47.0%	53.0%
Connecticut	1,596,276	552,621	Carter, Dan	1,008,714	Blumenthal, Richard	34,941	456,093 D	34.6%	63.2%	35.4%	64.6%
Florida	9,301,820	4,835,191	Rubio, Marco	4,122,088	Murphy, Patrick	344,541	713,103 R	52.0%	44.3%	54.0%	46.0%
Georgia	3,898,605	2,135,806	Isakson, Johnny	1,599,726	Barksdale, Jim	163,073	536,080 R	54.8%	41.0%	57.2%	42.8%
Hawaii	416,562	92,653	Carroll, John S.	306,604	Schatz, Brian	17,305	213,951 D	22.2%	73.6%	23.2%	76.8%
Idaho	678,943	449,017	Crapo, Michael D.	188,249	Sturgill, Jerry	41,677	260,768 R	66.1%	27.7%	70.5%	29.5%
Illinois	5,491,878	2,184,692	Kirk, Mark Steven	3,012,940	Duckworth, Tammy	294,246	828,248 D	39.8%	54.9%	42.0%	58.0%
Indiana	2,732,546	1,423,991	Young, Todd	1,158,947	Bayh, Evan	149,608	265,044 R	52.1%	42.4%	55.1%	44.9%
Iowa	1,541,036	926,007	Grassley, Charles E.	549,460	Judge, Patty	65,569	376,547 R	60.1%	35.7%	62.8%	37.2%
Kansas	1,177,922	732,376	Moran, Jerry	379,740	Wiesner, Patrick	65,806	352,636 R	62.2%	32.2%	65.9%	34.2%
Kentucky	1,903,465	1,090,177	Paul, Rand	813,246	Gray, Jim	42	276,931 R	57.3%	42.7%	57.3%	42.7%
Louisiana**	884,007	536,191	Kennedy, John Neely	347,816	Campbell, Foster		188,375 R	60.7%	39.4%	60.7%	39.4%
Maryland	2,726,170	972,557	Szeliga, Kathy	1,659,907	Van Hollen, Chris Jr.	93,706	687,350 D	35.7%	60.9%	36.9%	63.1%
Missouri	2,802,641	1,378,458	Blunt, Roy	1,300,200	Kander, Jason	123,983	78,258 R	49.2%	46.4%	51.5%	48.5%
Nevada	1,108,294	495,079	Heck, Joe	521,994	Masto, Catherine Cortez	91,221	26,915 D	44.7%	47.1%	48.7%	51.3%
New Hampshire	739,140	353,632	Ayotte, Kelly	354,649	Hassan, Maggie	30,859	1,017 D	47.8%	48.0%	49.9%	50.1%
New York	7,396,305	2,009,355	Long, Wendy	5,221,945	Schumer, Charles E.	165,005	3,212,590 D	27.2%	70.6%	27.8%	72.2%
North Carolina	4,691,133	2,395,376	Burr, Richard M.	2,128,165	Ross, Deborah K.	167,592	267,211 R	51.1%	45.4%	53.0%	47.1%
North Dakota	342,501	268,788	Hoeven, John	58,116	Glassheim, Eliot	15,597	210,672 R	78.5%	17.0%	82.2%	17.8%
Ohio	5,374,164	3,118,567	Portman, Rob	1,996,908	Strickland, Ted	258,689	1,121,659 R	58.0%	37.2%	61.0%	39.0%
Oklahoma	1,448,047	980,892	Lankford, James	355,911	Workman, Mike	111,244	624,981 R	67.7%	24.6%	73.4%	26.6%
Oregon	1,952,478	651,106	Callahan, Mark	1,105,119	Wyden, Ron	196,253	454,013 D	33.4%	56.6%	37.1%	62.9%
Pennsylvania	6,051,856	2,951,702	Toomey, Pat	2,865,012	McGinty, Katie A.	235,142	86,690 R	48.8%	47.3%	50.8%	49.3%
South Carolina	2,049,893	1,241,609	Scott, Tim	757,022	Dixon, Thomas	51,262	484,587 R	60.6%	36.9%	62.1%	37.9%
South Dakota	369,656	265,516	Thune, John	104,140	Williams, Jay Henley		161,376 R	71.8%	28.2%	71.8%	28.2%
Utah	1,115,608	760,241	Lee, Mike	301,860	Snow, Misty K.	53,507	458,381 R	68.2%	27.1%	71.6%	28.4%
Vermont	313,809	103,637	Milne, Scott	192,243	Leahy, Patrick J.	17,929	88,606 D	33.0%	61.3%	35.0%	65.0%
Washington	3,243,317	1,329,338	Vance, Chris	1,913,979	Murray, Patty		584,641 D	41.0%	59.0%	41.0%	59.0%
Wisconsin	2,948,741	1,479,471	Johnson, Ron	1,380,335	Feingold, Russell D.	88,935	99,136 R	50.2%	46.8%	51.7%	48.3%
Total	95,321,149	40,423,868		51,536,671		3,360,610	11,112,803 D	42.4%	54.1%	44.0%	56.0%

Notes: All Senate elections were for full six-year terms and held in November 2016. The plurality is the difference between the top two vote recipients, regardless of party or independent status. Two third-party candidates, both from Alaska, drew more than 10 percent of the vote: 90,825 Joe Miller (Libertarian) 29.2 percent; 41,194 Margaret Stock (Non Affiliated) 13.2 percent.

* In California's jungle primary, the top two vote recipients, Kamala Harris and Loretta Sanchez, were both Democrats. Harris received 7,542,753 votes to Sanchez's 4,701,417 (or 61.6 percent to 38.4 percent).

** Louisiana's results listed are from the December runoff election, where the race was decided.

HOUSE OF REPRESENTATIVES ELECTIONS 2016

State	Seats Won Republican	Seats Won Democratic	Total Vote	Republican	Democratic	Other	Rep.-Dem. Plurality	Percentage Total Vote Rep.	Percentage Total Vote Dem.	Percentage Major Vote Rep.	Percentage Major Vote Dem.
Alabama	6	1	1,889,685	1,222,018	621,911	45,756	600,107 R	64.7%	32.9%	66.3%	33.7%
Alaska	1	0	308,198	155,088	111,019	42,091	44,069 R	50.3%	36.0%	58.3%	41.7%
Arizona	5	4	2,412,064	1,264,378	1,034,687	112,999	229,691 R	52.4%	42.9%	55.0%	45.0%
Arkansas	4	0	1,068,577	760,415	111,347	196,815	563,903 R	71.2%	10.4%	87.2%	12.8%
California	14	39	13,414,018	4,682,033	8,624,432	107,553	3,942,399 D	35.6%	64.3%	35.2%	64.8%
Colorado	4	3	2,701,561	1,288,618	1,263,791	149,152	24,827 R	47.7%	46.8%	50.5%	49.5%
Connecticut	0	5	1,575,183	568,134	990,139	16,910	422,005 D	36.1%	62.9%	36.5%	63.5%
Delaware	0	1	420,682	172,301	233,554	14,827	61,253 D	41.0%	55.5%	42.5%	57.6%
Florida	16	11	8,837,426	4,733,630	3,985,050	118,746	748,580 R	53.6%	45.1%	54.3%	45.7%
Georgia	10	4	3,772,862	2,272,460	1,498,437	1,965	774,023 R	60.2%	39.7%	60.3%	39.7%
Hawaii	0	2	412,873	85,626	316,265	10,982	230,639 D	20.7%	76.6%	21.3%	78.7%
Idaho	2	0	681,594	447,544	208,992	25,058	238,552 R	65.7%	30.7%	68.2%	31.8%
Illinois	7	11	5,241,767	2,397,436	2,810,536	33,795	413,100 D	45.7%	53.6%	46.0%	54.0%
Indiana	7	2	2,658,367	1,442,989	1,052,901	162,477	390,088 R	54.3%	39.6%	57.8%	42.2%
Iowa	3	1	1,515,555	813,153	673,969	28,433	139,184 R	53.7%	44.5%	54.7%	45.3%
Kansas	4	0	1,173,736	694,240	317,635	161,861	376,605 R	59.2%	27.1%	68.6%	31.4%
Kentucky	5	1	1,765,376	1,248,140	516,904	332	731,236 R	70.7%	29.3%	70.7%	29.3%
Louisiana	5	1	1,470,199	966,185	473,835	30,179	492,350 R	65.7%	32.2%	67.1%	32.9%
Maine	1	1	744,574	357,447	386,627	500	29,180 D	48.0%	51.9%	48.0%	52.0%
Maryland	1	7	2,707,745	962,088	1,636,200	109,457	674,112 D	35.5%	60.4%	37.0%	63.0%
Massachusetts	0	9	2,940,688	451,121	2,344,518	145,049	1,893,397 D	15.3%	79.7%	16.1%	83.9%
Michigan	9	5	4,670,905	2,243,402	2,193,980	233,523	49,422 R	48.0%	47.0%	50.6%	49.4%
Minnesota	3	5	2,860,432	1,334,686	1,434,590	91,156	99,904 D	46.7%	50.2%	48.2%	51.8%
Mississippi	3	1	1,182,273	680,810	449,896	51,567	230,914 R	57.6%	38.1%	60.2%	39.8%
Missouri	6	2	2,750,079	1,600,524	1,041,306	108,249	559,218 R	58.2%	37.9%	60.6%	39.4%
Montana	1	0	507,831	285,358	205,919	16,554	79,439 R	56.2%	40.6%	58.1%	41.9%
Nebraska	3	0	788,453	557,744	221,069	9,640	336,675 R	70.7%	28.0%	73.0%	27.0%
Nevada	1	3	1,078,497	498,104	508,113	72,280	10,009 D	46.2%	47.1%	49.5%	50.5%
New Hampshire	0	2	716,777	316,149	336,575	64,053	20,426 D	44.1%	47.0%	48.4%	51.6%
New Jersey	5	7	3,463,311	1,541,631	1,821,620	100,060	279,989 D	44.5%	52.6%	45.8%	54.2%
New Mexico	1	2	780,126	343,124	436,932	70	93,808 D	44.0%	56.0%	44.0%	56.0%
New York	9	18	7,116,422	2,530,440	4,476,756	109,226	1,946,316 D	35.6%	62.9%	36.1%	63.9%
North Carolina	10	3	4,598,458	2,447,326	2,142,661	8,471	304,665 R	53.2%	46.6%	53.3%	46.7%
North Dakota	1	0	338,459	233,980	80,377	24,102	153,603 R	69.1%	23.8%	74.4%	25.6%
Ohio	12	4	5,218,355	2,996,017	2,165,413	56,925	830,604 R	57.4%	41.5%	58.1%	42.0%
Oklahoma	5	0	1,133,244	781,691	305,222	46,331	476,469 R	69.0%	26.9%	71.9%	28.1%
Oregon	1	4	1,911,865	730,894	1,026,851	154,120	295,957 D	38.2%	53.7%	41.6%	58.4%
Pennsylvania	13	5	5,743,978	3,096,576	2,625,157	22,245	471,419 R	53.9%	45.7%	55.2%	45.9%
Rhode Island	0	2	431,519	141,324	263,642	26,553	122,318 D	32.8%	61.1%	34.9%	65.1%
South Carolina	6	1	2,039,462	1,193,711	800,801	44,950	392,910 R	58.5%	39.3%	59.8%	40.2%
South Dakota	1	0	369,973	237,163	132,810		104,353 R	64.1%	35.9%	64.1%	35.9%
Tennessee	7	2	2,391,061	1,493,740	814,181	83,140	679,559 R	62.5%	34.1%	64.7%	35.3%
Texas	25	11	8,528,526	4,877,605	3,160,535	490,386	1,717,070 R	57.2%	37.1%	60.7%	39.3%
Utah	4	0	1,114,170	710,656	356,290	47,224	354,366 R	63.8%	32.0%	66.6%	33.4%
Vermont	0	1	295,334		264,414	30,920	235,004 D	0.0%	89.5%	0.0%	100.0%
Virginia	7	4	3,782,248	1,843,010	1,859,426	79,812	16,416 D	48.7%	49.2%	49.8%	50.2%
Washington	4	6	3,141,035	1,404,890	1,736,145		331,255 D	44.7%	50.0%	44.7%	50.0%
West Virginia	3	0	686,349	445,017	224,449	16,883	220,568 R	64.8%	32.7%	66.5%	33.5%
Wisconsin	5	3	2,773,662	1,270,279	1,379,996	123,387	109,717 D	45.8%	49.8%	47.9%	52.1%
Wyoming	1	0	251,776	156,176	75,466	20,134	80,710 R	62.0%	30.0%	67.4%	32.6%
Total	241	194	128,377,310	62,977,071	61,753,341	3,646,898	1,224,467 R	49.1%	48.1%	50.5%	49.5%

Notes: Does not include special elections. The Republicans did not run a candidate in Vermont. The following states allow cross-endorsement, that is, where third parties could endorse candidates of the major parties, and all such votes are credited to the major party with which the candidates identified: Connecticut, Delaware, Idaho, Mississippi, New York, Oregon, South Carolina, and Vermont. Louisiana has a unique election system for many offices, including the U.S. House of Representatives. All candidates, regardless of party, appeared together on the November ballot. The vote totals for all Republicans and all Democrats are included in the state total for each party. If the highest vote recipient does not win a majority of the votes, there is a runoff between the top two vote recipients in December. In the 3rd and 4th districts in Louisiana, there were runoffs held on December 10, 2016. The general election is included in the state vote totals, not the runoff. California and Washington hold jungle primaries, and the top two vote recipients, regardless of party, advance to the November general election. Where two candidates of the same party ran against each other, the vote totals for all Republicans and Democrats are included in the state total for each party.

UNITED STATES
SUMMARY OF HOUSE SPECIAL ELECTIONS, 2015–2016

REPRESENTATIVES

District	Former Member	New Member	Date Elected	Winning Percentage	Total Vote
New York 11th	Michael Grimm (R)	Daniel Donovan (R)	May 5, 2015	58.3%	42,509
Mississippi 1st	Alan Nunnelee (R)	Trent Kelly (R)	June 2, 2015	70.0%	99,347
Illinois 18th	Aaron Schock (R)	Darin LaHood (R)	September 10, 2015	68.8%	51,319
Ohio 8th	John Boehner (R)	Warren Davidson (R)	June 7, 2016	76.8%	28,162
Hawaii 1st	Mark Takai (D)	Colleen Hanabusa (D)	November 8, 2016	65.1%	198,391
Kentucky 1st	Ed Whitfield (R)	James Comer (R)	November 8, 2016	72.2%	290,623
Pennsylvania 2nd	Chaka Fattah (D)	Dwight Evans (D)	November 8, 2016	90.4%	310,100

SPECIAL ELECTIONS AND POSTELECTIONS CHANGES TO THE 114TH CONGRESS

From the beginning of 2015 through the general election of 2016, 7 special elections were held in the House to fill unexpired terms in the 114th Congress. Two vacancies, left by the resignation of Rep. Janice Hahn (D-Calif. 44) on December 4, 2016, and Rep. Candice Miller (R-Mich. 10) on December 31, 2016, were not filled. There were no special elections in the Senate in this time frame, and there were no party switches.

REPRESENTATIVES

CALIFORNIA 44TH CD

Janice Hahn (D) resigned December 4, 2016, to become a member of the Los Angeles County Board of Supervisors. This vacancy was not filled.

HAWAII 1ST CD

Mark Takai (D) passed away July 20, 2016, following a battle with pancreatic cancer. All candidates ran on the same ballot in the special general election on November 8, 2016, and the highest vote recipient filled the remainder of the term of the 114th Congress. This special election was distinct from the November 8, 2016, general election to the 115th Congress, although the same candidate—Colleen Hanabusa (D)—won both.

November 8, 2016, Special General Election

129,083 Colleen Hanabusa (D); 44,090 Shirlene Ostrov (R); 5,885 Angela Kaaihue (D); 5,559 Alan Yim (Libertarian); 4,259 Howard Kim (D); 3,420 Peter Cross (D); 2,824 Calvin C. Griffin (Nonpartisan); 1,893 Javier Ocasio (D); 1,050 Yvonne Perry (Nonpartisan); 328 Peter H. Plotzeneder (Nonpartisan).

ILLINOIS 18TH CD

Aaron Schock (R) resigned March 31, 2015, following a congressional ethics investigation into his misuse of campaign and public funds. Each party chose a nominee for the September 10, 2015, special general election. Darin LaHood (R) was elected September 10, 2015, to fill the remainder of the term of the 114th Congress.

July 7, 2015 Special Democratic Primary

4,613 Robert Mellon; 3,008 Adam Lopez.

July 7, 2015 Special Republican Primary

31,635 Darin LaHood; 12,593 Michael J. Flynn; 1,246 Donald Ray Rients; 16 Robin Miller.

September 10, 2015 Special General Election

35,329 Darin LaHood (R); 15,979 Robert Mellon (D); 7 Constant Vlakancic (Write-in); 4 Roger Davis (Write-in).

UNITED STATES
SUMMARY OF HOUSE SPECIAL ELECTIONS, 2015–2016

KENTUCKY 1ST CD

Ed Whitfield (R) resigned September 6, 2016, following a congressional ethics investigation into special access granted to his lobbyist wife. This special election was distinct from the November 8, 2016, general election to the 115th Congress, although the same candidate—James Comer (R)—won both. Comer filled the remainder of the term of the 114th Congress.

November 8, 2016 Special General Election

209,810 James Comer (R); 80,813 Samuel Gaskins (D).

MICHIGAN 10TH CD

Candice Miller (R) resigned December 31, 2016, to become Michigan's public works commissioner. This vacancy was not filled.

MISSISSIPPI 1ST CD

Alan Nunnelee (R) passed away February 6, 2015, following a battle with brain cancer. No candidate received a majority of the vote in the May 12, 2015, special general election, and the two highest vote recipients advanced to a runoff on June 2, 2015. Trent Kelly (R) was elected June 2, 2015, to fill the remainder of the term of the 114th Congress.

May 12, 2015 Special General Election

15,385 Walter Zinn (D); 14,418 Trent Kelly (R); 11,231 Mike Tagert (R); 7,142 Greg Pirkle (R); 6,993 Starner Jones (R); 6,929 Michael Mills (R); 4,313 Henry Ross (R); 4,037 Boyce Adams (R); 4,006 Nancy Collins (R); 4,000 Sam Adcock (R); 3,958 Edward Holliday (R); 3,124 Quentin Whitwell (R); 2,828 Daniel Sparks (R).

June 2, 2015 Special Runoff Election

69,516 Trent Kelly (R); 29,831 Walter Zinn (D).

NEW YORK 11TH CD

Michael Grimm (R) resigned January 5, 2015, after pleading guilty to fraud and tax evasion. Daniel Donovan (R) was elected May 5, 2015, to fill the remainder of the term of the 114th Congress.

May 5, 2015 Special General Election

24,797 Daniel Donovan (R); 17,049 Vincent Gentile (D); 567 James Lane (Green); 96 Write-in.

OHIO 8TH CD

John Boehner (R) resigned October 31, 2015, following pressure from conservative activists in the Republican House. Each party chose a nominee for the June 7, 2016, special general election. Warren Davidson (R) was elected June 7, 2016, to fill the remainder of the term of the 114th Congress.

March 15, 2016 Special Democratic Primary

Corey Foister (Unopposed).

March 15, 2016 Special Republican Primary

43,602 Warren Davidson; 32,578 Timothy Derickson; 26,424 Bill Beagle; 9,253 Jim Spurlino; 5,316 J.D. Winteregg; 3,069 Scott George; 2,879 Terri King; 2,314 Kevin White; 1,995 Michael Smith; 1,490 Matthew Ashworth; 1,560 John Robbins; 1,345 Eric Haemmerle; 1,008 George Wooley; 609 Edward Meer; 566 Joseph Matvey.

June 7, 2016 Special General Election

21,618 Warren Davidson (R); 5,937 Corey Foister (D); 607 James Condit (Green).

UNITED STATES
SUMMARY OF HOUSE SPECIAL ELECTIONS, 2015–2016

PENNSYLVANIA 2ND CD

Chaka Fattah (D) resigned June 23, 2016, following a conviction for fraud, racketeering, money laundering, and other corruption charges. This special election was distinct from the November 8, 2016, general election to the 115th Congress, although the same candidate—Dwight Evans (D)—won both. Evans was elected November 8, 2016, to fill the remainder of the term of the 114th Congress.

November 8, 2016 Special General Election

280,439 Dwight Evans (D); 29,661 James Jones (R).

CHANGES FOLLOWING THE 2016 ELECTION

Following the 2016 general election, and through August 18, 2017, the following changes took place in the membership of the 115th Congress.

SENATOR

Alabama—Jeff Sessions (R) resigned February 8, 2017, to become the U.S. Attorney General. Luther Strange (R) was sworn in February 9, 2017, to replace Sessions. A special election was scheduled for December 12, 2017, to fill the final three years of Sessions's term.

REPRESENTATIVES

California 34th District—Xavier Becerra (D) resigned January 24, 2017, to become California's attorney general. Jimmy Gomez (D) won a special election June 6, 2017, to replace him.

Georgia 6th District—Tom Price (R) resigned February 10, 2017, to become Secretary of the U.S. Department of Health and Human Services. Karen C. Handel (R) won a special election June 20, 2017, to replace him.

Kansas 4th District—Mike Pompeo (R) resigned January 23, 2017, to become the Director of the Central Intelligence Agency. Ron Estes (R) won a special election April 11, 2017, to replace him.

Montana At Large—Ryan K. Zinke (R) resigned March 1, 2017, to become Secretary of the U.S. Department of the Interior. Greg Gianforte (R) won a special election May 25, 2017, to replace him.

South Carolina 5th District—Mick Mulvaney resigned February 16, 2017, to become Director of the U.S. Office of Management and Budget. Ralph Norman (R) won a special election June 20, 2017, to replace him.

Utah 3rd District—Jason Chaffetz (R) resigned June 30, 2017, to return to the private sector. A special election was scheduled for November 7, 2017.

UNITED STATES
PRESIDENT 2016

The candidates listed below include all who appeared on the ballot in at least one state. Write-in votes for independent and third-party candidates are credited to their total below. See the minor parties table on page 10 for details. There, the state totals for the top three vote-recipient independent and third-party candidates in the 2016 presidential election are listed.

In New York, the Democratic total includes Working Families and Women's Equality votes and the Republican figures include Conservative and Independence votes.

In Minnesota, the Democratic candidate appears on the ballot as Democratic-Farmer-Labor, in North Dakota as Democratic Nonpartisan League. In many states, various non-major party candidates appeared on the ballot with variations of the party designation (for instance, in Massachusetts, the Green Party affiliate is the Green-Rainbow Party), were accompanied with entirely different party labels, or were listed as "Independent."

65,853,510	Hillary Clinton and Tim Kaine	Democratic
62,984,824	Donald J. Trump and Mike Pence	Republican
4,489,341	Gary Johnson and William Weld	Libertarian
1,457,217	Jill Stein and Ajamu Baraka	Green
731,733	Evan McMullin and Mindy Finn	Independent
203,010	Darrell Castle and Scott Bradley	Constitution
74,392	Gloria La Riva and Dennis J. Banks/Eugene Puryear	Socialism and Liberation
33,136	Roque De La Fuente and Michael Steinberg	American Delta
24,307	Richard Duncan and Ricky Johnson	Independent
13,537	Dan Vacek and Mark Elworth Jr.	Legal Marijuana Now
12,467	Alyson Kennedy and Osborne Hart	Socialist Workers Party
9,338	Mike Smith and Daniel White	Independent
7,205	Chris Keniston and Deacon Taylor	Veterans Party of America
6,474	Michael Maturen and Juan Muñoz	American Solidarity
5,733	Lynn Kahn and Kathy Monahan	Independent
5,617	James Hedges and Bill Bayes	Prohibition
4,771	Thomas Hoefling and Steve Schulin	America's Party
4,317	Monica Moorehead and Lamont Lilly	Workers World
3,581	Laurence Kotlikoff and Ed Leamer	Independent
3,250	Peter Skewes and Michael Lacy	American
2,752	Rocky Giordani and Farley M. Anderson	Independent American
2,693	Emidio Soltysik and Angela Walker	Socialist Party USA
2,356	Scott Copeland and J.R. Myers	Constitution
1,096	Kyle Kopitke and Nathan Revo Sorenson	Independent American
962	Joseph Maldonado and Douglas K. Terranova	Independent
754	Ryan Scott and Bruce Kendall Barnard	Unaffiliated
751	Rod Silva and Richard Silva	Nutrition
749	Princess Jacob and Milton Fambro	Loyal Trustworthy Compassion
475	Jerry White and Niles Niemuth	Socialist Equality
382	Bradford Lyttle and Hannah Walsh	Pacifist
337	Frank Atwood and Blake Huber	Approval Voting

Note: In addition to the votes listed above, 697,458 scattered write-in votes were reported in various states, and 28,863 votes were cast for "None of These Candidates" in Nevada.

UNITED STATES
PRESIDENT 2016

State	Electoral Vote Rep.	Dem.	Other	Total Vote	Republican (Trump)	Democratic (Clinton)	Other	Rep.-Dem. Plurality	Total Vote Rep.	Dem.	Major Vote Rep.	Dem.
Alabama	9			2,123,372	1,318,255	729,547	75,570	588,708 R	62.1%	34.4%	64.4%	35.6%
Alaska	3			318,608	163,387	116,454	38,767	46,933 R	51.3%	36.6%	58.4%	41.6%
Arizona	11			2,573,165	1,252,401	1,161,167	159,597	91,234 R	48.7%	45.1%	51.9%	48.1%
Arkansas	6			1,130,676	684,872	380,494	65,310	304,378 R	60.6%	33.7%	64.3%	35.7%
California		55		14,181,595	4,483,810	8,753,788	943,997	4,269,978 D	31.6%	61.7%	33.9%	66.1%
Colorado		9		2,780,247	1,202,484	1,338,870	238,893	136,386 D	43.3%	48.2%	47.3%	52.7%
Connecticut		7		1,644,920	673,215	897,572	74,133	224,357 D	40.9%	54.6%	42.9%	57.1%
Delaware		3		443,814	185,127	235,603	23,084	50,476 D	41.7%	53.1%	44.0%	56.0%
Florida	29			9,420,039	4,617,886	4,504,975	297,178	112,911 R	49.0%	47.8%	50.6%	49.4%
Georgia	16			4,114,732	2,089,104	1,877,963	147,665	211,141 R	50.8%	45.6%	52.7%	47.3%
Hawaii		3	1	428,937	128,847	266,891	33,199	138,044 D	30.0%	62.2%	32.6%	67.4%
Idaho	4			690,255	409,055	189,765	91,435	219,290 R	59.3%	27.5%	68.3%	31.7%
Illinois		20		5,536,424	2,146,015	3,090,729	299,680	944,714 D	38.8%	55.8%	41.0%	59.0%
Indiana	11			2,734,958	1,557,286	1,033,126	144,546	524,160 R	56.9%	37.8%	60.1%	39.9%
Iowa	6			1,566,031	800,983	653,669	111,379	147,314 R	51.1%	41.7%	55.1%	44.9%
Kansas	6			1,184,402	671,018	427,005	86,379	244,013 R	56.7%	36.1%	61.1%	38.9%
Kentucky	8			1,924,149	1,202,971	628,854	92,324	574,117 R	62.5%	32.7%	65.7%	34.3%
Louisiana	8			2,029,032	1,178,638	780,154	70,240	398,484 R	58.1%	38.4%	60.2%	39.8%
Maine	1	3		747,927	335,593	357,735	54,599	22,142 D	44.9%	47.8%	48.4%	51.6%
Maryland		10		2,781,446	943,169	1,677,928	160,349	734,759 D	33.9%	60.3%	36.0%	64.0%
Massachusetts		11		3,325,046	1,090,893	1,995,196	238,957	904,303 D	32.8%	60.0%	35.4%	64.7%
Michigan	16			4,799,284	2,279,543	2,268,839	250,902	10,704 R	47.5%	47.3%	50.1%	49.9%
Minnesota		10		2,944,813	1,322,951	1,367,716	254,146	44,765 D	44.9%	46.4%	49.2%	50.8%
Mississippi	6			1,209,357	700,714	485,131	23,512	215,583 R	57.9%	40.1%	59.1%	40.9%
Missouri	10			2,808,605	1,594,511	1,071,068	143,026	523,443 R	56.8%	38.1%	59.8%	40.2%
Montana	3			497,147	279,240	177,709	40,198	101,531 R	56.2%	35.7%	61.1%	38.9%
Nebraska	5			844,227	495,961	284,494	63,772	211,467 R	58.7%	33.7%	63.6%	36.5%
Nevada		6		1,125,385	512,058	539,260	74,067	27,202 D	45.5%	47.9%	48.7%	51.3%
New Hampshire		4		744,296	345,790	348,526	49,980	2,736 D	46.5%	46.8%	49.8%	50.2%
New Jersey		14		3,874,046	1,601,933	2,148,278	123,835	546,345 D	41.4%	55.5%	42.7%	57.3%
New Mexico		5		798,319	319,667	385,234	93,418	65,567 D	40.0%	48.3%	45.4%	54.7%
New York		29		7,721,442	2,819,533	4,556,118	345,791	1,736,585 D	36.5%	59.0%	38.2%	61.8%
North Carolina	15			4,741,564	2,362,631	2,189,316	189,617	173,315 R	49.8%	46.2%	51.9%	48.1%
North Dakota	3			344,360	216,794	93,758	33,808	123,036 R	63.0%	27.2%	69.8%	30.2%
Ohio	18			5,496,487	2,841,005	2,394,164	261,318	446,841 R	51.7%	43.6%	54.3%	45.7%
Oklahoma	7			1,452,992	949,136	420,375	83,481	528,761 R	65.3%	28.9%	69.3%	30.7%
Oregon		7		2,001,336	782,403	1,002,106	216,827	219,703 D	39.1%	50.1%	43.8%	56.2%
Pennsylvania	20			6,165,478	2,970,733	2,926,441	268,304	44,292 R	48.2%	47.5%	50.4%	49.6%
Rhode Island		4		464,144	180,543	252,525	31,076	71,982 D	38.9%	54.4%	41.7%	58.3%
South Carolina	9			2,103,027	1,155,389	855,373	92,265	300,016 R	54.9%	40.7%	57.5%	42.5%
South Dakota	3			370,093	227,721	117,458	24,914	110,263 R	61.5%	31.7%	66.0%	34.0%
Tennessee	11			2,508,027	1,522,925	870,695	114,407	652,230 R	60.7%	34.7%	63.6%	36.4%
Texas	36		2	8,969,226	4,685,047	3,877,868	406,311	807,179 R	52.2%	43.2%	54.7%	45.3%
Utah	6			1,131,430	515,231	310,676	305,523	204,555 R	45.5%	27.5%	62.4%	37.6%
Vermont		3		315,067	95,369	178,573	41,125	83,204 D	30.3%	56.7%	34.8%	65.2%
Virginia		13		3,982,752	1,769,443	1,981,473	231,836	212,030 D	44.4%	49.8%	47.2%	52.8%
Washington		8	4	3,317,019	1,221,747	1,742,718	352,554	520,971 D	36.8%	52.5%	41.2%	58.8%
West Virginia	5			714,423	489,371	188,794	36,258	300,577 R	68.5%	26.4%	72.2%	27.8%
Wisconsin	10			2,976,150	1,405,284	1,382,536	188,330	22,748 R	47.2%	46.5%	50.4%	49.6%
Wyoming	3			255,849	174,419	55,973	25,457	118,446 R	68.2%	21.9%	75.7%	24.3%
District of Columbia		3		311,268	12,723	282,830	15,715	270,107 D	4.1%	90.9%	4.3%	95.7%
Total	304	227	7	136,667,388	62,984,824	65,853,510	7,829,054	2,868,686 D	46.1%	48.2%	48.9%	51.1%

Notes: Due to faithless electors, the following individuals received electoral votes: Colin Powell (3), Faith Spotted Eagle (1), John Kasich (1), Ron Paul (1), Bernard "Bernie" Sanders (1).

UNITED STATES
PRESIDENT 2016 MINOR PARTIES

State	Total	Other Vote Total	Johnson (Libertarian)	Stein (Green)	McMullin (Independent)	Additional Candidates and Write-ins	Johnson (Lib.)	Stein (Green)	McMullin (Ind.)
							Percentage		
Alabama	2,123,372	75,570	44,467	9,391		21,712	2.1%	0.4%	
Alaska	318,608	38,767	18,725	5,735		14,307	5.9%	1.8%	
Arizona	2,573,165	159,597	106,327	34,345	17,449*	1,476	4.1%	1.3%	0.7%
Arkansas	1,130,676	65,310	29,949	9,473	13,176	12,712	2.6%	0.8%	1.2%
California	14,181,595	943,997	478,500	278,657	39,596*	147,244	3.4%	2.0%	0.3%
Colorado	2,780,247	238,893	144,121	38,437	28,917	27,418	5.2%	1.4%	1.0%
Connecticut	1,644,920	74,133	48,676	22,841	2,108*	508	3.0%	1.4%	0.1%
Delaware	443,813	23,084	14,757	6,103	706*	1,518	3.3%	1.4%	
Florida	9,420,039	297,178	207,043	64,399		25,736	2.2%	0.7%	
Georgia	4,114,732	147,665	125,306	7,674*	13,017	1,668	3.0%	0.2%	0.3%
Hawaii	428,937	33,199	15,954	12,737		4,508	3.7%	3.0%	
Idaho	690,255	91,435	28,331	8,496	46,476	8,132	4.1%	1.2%	6.7%
Illinois	5,536,424	299,680	209,596	76,802	11,655*	1,627	3.8%	1.4%	0.2%
Indiana	2,734,958	144,546	133,993	7,841*		2,712	4.9%	0.3%	
Iowa	1,566,031	111,379	59,186	11,479	12,366	28,348	3.8%	0.7%	0.8%
Kansas	1,184,402	86,379	55,406	23,506	6,520*	947	4.7%	2.0%	0.6%
Kentucky	1,924,149	92,324	53,752	13,913	22,780	1,879	2.8%	0.7%	1.2%
Louisiana	2,029,032	70,240	37,978	14,031	8,547	9,684	1.9%	0.7%	0.4%
Maine	747,927	54,599	38,105	14,251	1,887*	356	5.1%	1.9%	0.3%
Maryland	2,781,446	160,349	79,605	35,945	9,630*	35,169	2.9%	1.3%	0.3%
Massachusetts	3,325,046	238,957	138,018	47,661	2,719*	50,559	4.2%	1.4%	0.1%
Michigan	4,799,284	250,902	172,136	51,463	8,177*	19,126	3.6%	1.1%	0.2%
Minnesota	2,944,813	254,146	112,972	36,985	53,076	51,113	3.8%	1.3%	1.8%
Mississippi	1,209,357	23,512	14,435	3,731		5,346	1.2%	0.3%	
Missouri	2,808,605	143,026	97,359	25,419	7,071*	13,177	3.5%	0.9%	0.3%
Montana	497,147	40,198	28,037	7,970	2,297*	1,894	5.7%	1.6%	0.5%
Nebraska	844,227	63,772	38,946	8,775		16,051	4.6%	1.0%	
Nevada	1,125,385	74,067	37,384			36,683	3.3%		
New Hampshire	744,296	49,980	30,777	6,496	1,064*	11,643	4.1%	0.9%	0.1%
New Jersey	3,874,046	123,835	72,477	37,772		13,586	1.9%	1.0%	0.0%
New Mexico	798,319	93,418	74,541	9,879	5,825	3,173	9.3%	1.2%	0.7%
New York	7,721,442	345,791	176,598	107,935	10,397*	50,861	2.3%	1.4%	0.1%
North Carolina	4,741,564	189,617	130,126	12,105*		47,386	2.7%	0.3%	
North Dakota	344,360	33,808	21,434	3,780		8,594	6.2%	1.1%	
Ohio	5,496,487	261,318	174,498	46,271	12,574*	27,975	3.2%	0.8%	0.2%
Oklahoma	1,452,992	83,481	83,481				5.7%		
Oregon	2,001,336	216,827	94,231	50,002		72,594	4.7%	2.5%	
Pennsylvania	6,165,478	268,304	146,715	49,941	6,472*	65,176	2.4%	0.8%	0.1%
Rhode Island	464,144	31,076	14,746	6,220	516*	9,594	3.2%	1.3%	0.1%
South Carolina	2,103,027	92,265	49,204	13,034	21,016	9,011	2.3%	0.6%	1.0%
South Dakota	370,093	24,914	20,850			4,064	5.6%		
Tennessee	2,508,027	114,407	70,397	15,993	11,991*	16,026	2.8%	0.6%	0.5%
Texas	8,969,226	406,311	283,492	71,558	42,366*	8,895	3.2%	0.8%	0.5%
Utah	1,131,430	305,523	39,608	9,438	243,690	12,787	3.5%	0.8%	21.5%
Vermont	315,067	41,125	10,078	6,758	639*	23,650	3.2%	2.1%	0.2%
Virginia	3,982,752	231,836	118,274	27,638	54,054	31,870	3.0%	0.7%	1.4%
Washington	3,317,019	352,554	160,879	58,417		133,258	4.9%	1.8%	
West Virginia	714,423	36,258	23,004	8,075	1,104*	4,075	3.2%	1.1%	0.2%
Wisconsin	2,976,150	188,330	106,674	31,072	11,855*	38,729	3.6%	1.0%	0.4%
Wyoming	255,849	25,457	13,287	2,515		9,655	5.2%	1.0%	
District of Columbia	311,268	15,715	4,906	4,258		6,551	1.6%	1.4%	
Total	136,667,388	7,829,054	4,489,341	1,457,217	731,733	1,150,763	3.3%	1.1%	0.5%

An asterisk (*) indicates write-in votes.

UNITED STATES

POPULAR VOTE FOR PRESIDENT 1920 TO 2016

Year	Total Vote	Republican Vote	Republican Candidate	Democratic Vote	Democratic Candidate	Other Vote	Rep.-Dem. Plurality	Total Vote Rep.	Total Vote Dem.	Major Vote Rep.	Major Vote Dem.
2016	136,667,388	62,984,824	Trump, Donald J.	65,853,510	Clinton, Hillary	7,829,054	2,868,686 D	46.1%	48.2%	48.9%	51.1%
2012	129,085,474	60,933,500	Romney, W. Mitt	65,915,796	Obama, Barack	2,236,178	4,982,296 D	47.2%	51.1%	48.0%	52.0%
2008	131,313,820	59,948,323	McCain, John S. III	69,498,516	Obama, Barack	1,866,981	9,550,193 D	45.7%	52.9%	46.3%	53.7%
2004	122,295,345	62,040,610	Bush, George W.	59,028,439	Kerry, John	1,226,296	3,012,171 R	50.7%	48.3%	51.2%	48.8%
2000	105,396,627	50,455,156	Bush, George W.	50,992,335	Gore, Albert Jr.	3,949,136	537,179 D	47.9%	48.4%	49.7%	50.3%
1996	96,277,872	39,198,755	Dole, Bob	47,402,357	Clinton, Bill	9,676,760	8,203,602 D	40.7%	49.2%	45.3%	54.7%
1992	104,425,014	39,103,882	Bush, George H.	44,909,326	Clinton, Bill	20,411,806	5,805,444 D	37.4%	43.0%	46.5%	53.5%
1988	91,597,809	48,886,097	Bush, George H.	41,812,075	Dukakis, Michael S.	899,637	7,074,022 R	53.4%	45.6%	53.9%	46.1%
1984	92,652,842	54,455,075	Reagan, Ronald	37,577,185	Mondale, Walter F.	620,582	16,877,890 R	58.8%	40.6%	59.2%	40.8%
1980	86,515,221	43,904,153	Reagan, Ronald	35,483,883	Carter, Jimmy	7,127,185	8,420,270 R	50.7%	41.0%	55.3%	44.7%
1976	81,554,989	39,141,091	Ford, Gerald R.	40,829,763	Carter, Jimmy	1,584,135	1,688,672 D	48.0%	50.1%	48.9%	51.1%
1972	77,718,554	47,169,911	Nixon, Richard M.	29,170,383	McGovern, George S.	1,378,260	17,999,528 R	60.7%	37.5%	61.8%	38.2%
1968	73,211,875	31,785,480	Nixon, Richard M.	31,275,166	Humphrey, Hubert H.	10,151,229	510,314 R	43.4%	42.7%	50.4%	49.6%
1964	70,644,592	27,178,188	Goldwater, Barry M.	43,129,566	Johnson, Lyndon B.	336,838	15,951,378 D	38.5%	61.1%	38.7%	61.3%
1960	68,838,219	34,108,157	Nixon, Richard M.	34,226,731	Kennedy, John F.	503,331	118,574 D	49.5%	49.7%	49.9%	50.1%
1956	62,026,908	35,590,472	Eisenhower, Dwight D.	26,022,752	Stevenson, Adlai E.	413,684	9,567,720 R	57.4%	42.0%	57.8%	42.2%
1952	61,550,918	33,936,234	Eisenhower, Dwight D.	27,314,992	Stevenson, Adlai E.	299,692	6,621,242 R	55.1%	44.4%	55.4%	44.6%
1948	48,793,826	21,991,291	Dewey, Thomas E.	24,179,345	Truman, Harry S.	2,623,190	2,188,054 D	45.1%	49.6%	47.6%	52.4%
1944	47,976,670	22,017,617	Dewey, Thomas E.	25,612,610	Roosevelt, Franklin D.	346,443	3,594,993 D	45.9%	53.4%	46.2%	53.8%
1940	49,900,774	22,348,836	Willkie, Wendell	27,313,041	Roosevelt, Franklin D.	238,897	4,964,205 D	44.8%	54.7%	45.0%	55.0%
1936	45,654,763	16,684,231	Landon, Alfred M.	27,757,333	Roosevelt, Franklin D.	1,213,199	11,073,102 D	36.5%	60.8%	37.5%	62.5%
1932	39,761,034	15,760,684	Hoover, Herbert C.	22,829,501	Roosevelt, Franklin D.	1,170,849	7,068,817 D	39.6%	57.4%	40.8%	59.2%
1928	36,805,951	21,437,277	Hoover, Herbert C.	15,007,698	Smith, Alfred E.	360,976	6,429,579 R	58.2%	40.8%	58.8%	41.2%
1924	29,095,023	15,719,921	Coolidge, Calvin	8,386,704	Davis, John W.	4,988,398	7,333,217 R	54.0%	28.8%	65.2%	34.8%
1920	26,768,150	16,153,115	Harding, Warren G.	9,133,092	Cox, James M.	1,481,943	7,020,023 R	60.3%	34.1%	63.9%	36.1%

Republican Donald J. Trump lost the popular vote in 2016 but won the electoral vote and was elected president. Republican George W. Bush lost the popular vote in 2000 but won the electoral vote and was elected president. In past elections, the Other vote included: 2016—4,489,325 Libertarian (Gary Johnson); 2000—2,882,738 Green (Ralph Nader); 1996—8,085,402 Reform (Ross Perot); 1992—19,741,657 Independent (Ross Perot); 1980—5,720,060 Independent (John Anderson); 1968—9,906,473 American Independent (George Wallace); 1948—1,176,125 States' Rights (Strom Thurmond); 1948—1,157,326 Progressive (Henry Wallace); 1924—4,832,532 Progressive (Robert LaFollette).

ELECTORAL COLLEGE VOTE 1920 TO 2016

Year	Total	Republican	Democratic	Other	Other Candidate	Other Party
2016	538	304	227	7	See Note*	See Note
2012	538	206	332	0		
2008	538	173	365	0		
2004	538	286	251	1	John Edwards*	Democrat
2000	538	271	266	1	Abstained*	
1996	538	159	379	0		
1992	538	168	370	0		
1988	538	426	111	1	Lloyd Bentsen*	Democrat
1984	538	525	13	0		
1980	538	489	49	0		
1976	538	240	297	1	Ronald Reagan*	Republican
1972	538	520	17	1	John Hospers*	Libertarian
1968	538	301	191	46	George Wallace	American Independent
1964	538	52	486	0		
1960	537	219	303	15	Harry Byrd	Democrat
1956	531	457	73	1	Walter Jones*	Democrat
1952	531	442	89	0		
1948	531	189	303	39	Strom Thurmond	States' Rights
1944	531	99	432	0		
1940	531	82	449	0		
1936	531	8	523	0		
1932	531	59	472	0		
1928	531	444	87	0		
1924	531	382	136	13	Robert M. La Follette	Progressive
1920	531	404	127	0		

Note: An asterisk (*) indicates faithless electors, who did not vote for the presidential candidates to which they were pledged. One of the electoral votes for Strom Thurmond in 1948, Harry Byrd in 1960, and George Wallace in 1968 was cast by a faithless elector. The rest of Byrd's support in 1960 came from unpledged electors. Due to faithless electors in the 2016 election, the following individuals received electoral votes: Colin Powell (3), Faith Spotted Eagle (1), John Kasich (1), Ron Paul (1), Bernard "Bernie" Sanders (1).

UNITED STATES
PRESIDENT 2012

The candidates listed below include all who appeared on the ballot in at least one state. Write-in votes for independent and third-party candidates are credited to their total below. See the minor parties table on page 14 for details. There, the state totals for all independent and third-party candidates who received at least 100,000 votes in the 2012 presidential election are listed.

In New York the Democratic total includes Working Families votes and the Republican figures include Conservative and Independence votes.

In Minnesota the Democratic candidate appears on the ballot as Democratic-Farmer-Labor, in North Dakota as Democratic-Nonpartisan League. In many states various non-major party candidates appeared on the ballot with variations of the party designations (for instance, in Massachusetts, the Green Party affiliate is the Green-Rainbow Party), were carried with entirely different party labels, or were listed as "Independent."

65,915,796	Barack Obama and Joseph R. Biden Jr.	Democratic
60,933,500	W. Mitt Romney and Paul Ryan	Republican
1,275,970	Gary Johnson and James P. Gray	Libertarian
469,034	Jill Stein and Cheri Honkala/Ben Manski	Green
122,375	Virgil H. Goode Jr. and Jim Clymer	Constitution
67,037	Roseanne Barr and Cindy Sheehan	Peace and Freedom
39,997	Thomas Hoefling and J.D. Ellis/Robert Ornelas	American Independent
40,257	Ross C. "Rocky" Anderson and Luis J. Rodriguez	Justice
13,090	Randall Terry and Missy Smith	Independent
12,502	Richard Duncan and Rickey Johnson Sr.	Independent
7,791	Peta Lindsay and Yari Osorio	Socialism and Liberation
5,017	Chuck Baldwin and Joseph Martin	Reform
4,432	Will Christensen and Kenneth Gibbs	Constitution
4,091	Thomas Robert Stevens and Alden Link	Objectivist
4,051	Stewart Alexander and Alejandro "Alex" Mendoza	Socialist
3,992	James Harris and Alyson Kennedy/Maura DeLuca	Socialist Workers Party
3,149	Jim Carlson and George McMahon	Grassroots
2,669	Merlin Miller and Harry V. Bertram/Virginia Abernethy	American Third Position
2,589	Jill Reed and Tom Cary	Unaffiliated
2,559	Sheila Tittle and Matthew A. Turner	We the People
1,608	Gloria La Riva and Filberto Ramirez/Stefanie Beacham	Socialism and Liberation
1,097	Jerry White and Phyllis Scherrer	Socialist Equality
1,092	Dean Morstad and Josh Franke-Hyland	Constitutional Government
1,027	Jerry Litzel and Jim Litzel	Nominated by Petition
1,016	Barbara Dale Washer and Cathy L. Toole	Reform
1,007	Jeff Boss and Bob Pasternak	NSA Did 911
820	Andre Barnett and Ken Cross	Reform
518	Jack Fellure and Toby Davis	Prohibition

Note: In addition to the votes listed above, 116,751 scattered write-in votes were reported from various states, and 5,770 votes were cast for "None of These Candidates" in Nevada. Scattered write-ins may include some votes for the candidates listed above in states in which they were not on the ballot; however, all write-in votes for Gary Johnson, Jill Stein, and Virgil H. Goode Jr. should be included in their totals. The scattered write-in total does not include the votes received by Republican Ron Paul; Paul received 24,870 votes as a write-in candidate in California and Maine, although he did not appear on the ballot in either state.

UNITED STATES
PRESIDENT 2012

State	Electoral Vote Rep.	Electoral Vote Dem.	Total Vote	Republican	Democratic	Other	Rep.-Dem. Plurality	Total Vote Rep.	Total Vote Dem.	Major Vote Rep.	Major Vote Dem.
Alabama	9		2,074,338	1,255,925	795,696	22,717	460,229 R	60.5%	38.4%	61.2%	38.8%
Alaska	3		300,495	164,676	122,640	13,179	42,036 R	54.8%	40.8%	57.3%	42.7%
Arizona	11		2,299,254	1,233,654	1,025,232	40,368	208,422 R	53.7%	44.6%	54.6%	45.4%
Arkansas	6		1,069,468	647,744	394,409	27,315	253,335 R	60.6%	36.9%	62.2%	37.8%
California		55	13,038,547	4,839,958	7,854,285	344,304	3,014,327 D	37.1%	60.2%	38.1%	61.9%
Colorado		9	2,569,522	1,185,243	1,323,102	61,177	137,859 D	46.1%	51.5%	47.3%	52.7%
Connecticut		7	1,558,960	634,892	905,083	18,985	270,191 D	40.7%	58.1%	41.2%	58.8%
Delaware		3	413,921	165,484	242,584	5,853	77,100 D	40.0%	58.6%	40.6%	59.4%
Florida		29	8,474,179	4,163,447	4,237,756	72,976	74,309 D	49.1%	50.0%	49.6%	50.4%
Georgia	16		3,900,050	2,078,688	1,773,827	47,535	304,861 R	53.3%	45.5%	54.0%	46.0%
Hawaii		4	434,697	121,015	306,658	7,024	185,643 D	27.8%	70.5%	28.3%	71.7%
Idaho	4		652,346	420,911	212,787	18,648	208,124 R	64.5%	32.6%	66.4%	33.6%
Illinois		20	5,242,014	2,135,216	3,019,512	87,286	884,296 D	40.7%	57.6%	41.4%	58.6%
Indiana	11		2,624,534	1,420,543	1,152,887	51,104	267,656 R	54.1%	43.9%	55.2%	44.8%
Iowa		6	1,582,180	730,617	822,544	29,019	91,927 D	46.2%	52.0%	47.0%	53.0%
Kansas	6		1,159,971	692,634	440,726	26,611	251,908 R	59.7%	38.0%	61.1%	38.9%
Kentucky	8		1,797,212	1,087,190	679,370	30,652	407,820 R	60.5%	37.8%	61.5%	38.5%
Louisiana	8		1,994,065	1,152,262	809,141	32,662	343,121 R	57.8%	40.6%	58.7%	41.3%
Maine		4	713,180	292,276	401,306	19,598	109,030 D	41.0%	56.3%	42.1%	57.9%
Maryland		10	2,707,327	971,869	1,677,844	57,614	705,975 D	35.9%	62.0%	36.7%	63.3%
Massachusetts		11	3,167,767	1,188,314	1,921,290	58,163	732,976 D	37.5%	60.7%	38.2%	61.8%
Michigan		16	4,730,961	2,115,256	2,564,569	51,136	449,313 D	44.7%	54.2%	45.2%	54.8%
Minnesota		10	2,936,561	1,320,225	1,546,167	70,169	225,942 D	45.0%	52.7%	46.1%	53.9%
Mississippi	6		1,285,584	710,746	562,949	11,889	147,797 R	55.3%	43.8%	55.8%	44.2%
Missouri	10		2,757,323	1,482,440	1,223,796	51,087	258,644 R	53.8%	44.4%	54.8%	45.2%
Montana	3		484,048	267,928	201,839	14,281	66,089 R	55.4%	41.7%	57.0%	43.0%
Nebraska	5		794,379	475,064	302,081	17,234	172,983 R	59.8%	38.0%	61.1%	38.9%
Nevada		6	1,014,918	463,567	531,373	19,978	67,806 D	45.7%	52.4%	46.6%	53.4%
New Hampshire		4	710,972	329,918	369,561	11,493	39,643 D	46.4%	52.0%	47.2%	52.8%
New Jersey		14	3,640,292	1,477,568	2,125,101	37,623	647,533 D	40.6%	58.4%	41.0%	59.0%
New Mexico		5	783,757	335,788	415,335	32,634	79,547 D	42.8%	53.0%	44.7%	55.3%
New York		29	7,081,159	2,490,431	4,485,741	104,987	1,995,310 D	35.2%	63.3%	35.7%	64.3%
North Carolina	15		4,505,372	2,270,395	2,178,391	56,586	92,004 R	50.4%	48.4%	51.0%	49.0%
North Dakota	3		322,627	188,163	124,827	9,637	63,336 R	58.3%	38.7%	60.1%	39.9%
Ohio		18	5,580,840	2,661,433	2,827,710	91,697	166,277 D	47.7%	50.7%	48.5%	51.5%
Oklahoma	7		1,334,872	891,325	443,547		447,778 R	66.8%	33.2%	66.8%	33.2%
Oregon		7	1,789,270	754,175	970,488	64,607	216,313 D	42.1%	54.2%	43.7%	56.3%
Pennsylvania		20	5,753,670	2,680,434	2,990,274	82,962	309,840 D	46.6%	52.0%	47.3%	52.7%
Rhode Island		4	446,049	157,204	279,677	9,168	122,473 D	35.2%	62.7%	36.0%	64.0%
South Carolina	9		1,964,118	1,071,645	865,941	26,532	205,704 R	54.6%	44.1%	55.3%	44.7%
South Dakota	3		363,815	210,610	145,039	8,166	65,571 R	57.9%	39.9%	59.2%	40.8%
Tennessee	11		2,458,577	1,462,330	960,709	35,538	501,621 R	59.5%	39.1%	60.4%	39.6%
Texas	38		7,993,851	4,569,843	3,308,124	115,884	1,261,719 R	57.2%	41.4%	58.0%	42.0%
Utah	6		1,017,440	740,600	251,813	25,027	488,787 R	72.8%	24.7%	74.6%	25.4%
Vermont		3	299,290	92,698	199,239	7,353	106,541 D	31.0%	66.6%	31.8%	68.2%
Virginia		13	3,854,489	1,822,522	1,971,820	60,147	149,298 D	47.3%	51.2%	48.0%	52.0%
Washington		12	3,125,516	1,290,670	1,755,396	79,450	464,726 D	41.3%	56.2%	42.4%	57.6%
West Virginia	5		670,438	417,655	238,269	14,514	179,386 R	62.3%	35.5%	63.7%	36.3%
Wisconsin		10	3,068,434	1,407,966	1,620,985	39,483	213,019 D	45.9%	52.8%	46.5%	53.5%
Wyoming	3		249,061	170,962	69,286	8,813	101,676 R	68.6%	27.8%	71.2%	28.8%
District of Columbia		3	293,764	21,381	267,070	5,313	245,689 D	7.3%	90.9%	7.4%	92.6%
Total	206	332	129,085,474	60,933,500	65,915,796	2,236,178	4,982,296 D	47.2%	51.1%	48.0%	52.0%

UNITED STATES
PRESIDENT 2012 MINOR PARTIES

State	Total	Other Vote Total	Johnson (Libertarian)	Stein (Green)	Goode (Constitution)	Additional Candidates and Write-ins	Percentage Johnson (Lib.)	Stein (Green)	Goode (Con.)
Alabama	2,074,338	22,717	12,328	3,397	2,981	4,011	0.6%	0.2%	0.1%
Alaska	300,495	13,179	7,392	2,917		2,870	2.5%	1.0%	0.0%
Arizona	2,299,254	40,368	32,100	7,816	289*	163	1.4%	0.3%	0.0%
Arkansas	1,069,468	27,315	16,276	9,305		1,734	1.5%	0.9%	0.0%
California	13,038,547	344,304	143,221	85,638	503*	114,942	1.1%	0.7%	0.0%
Colorado	2,569,522	61,177	35,545	7,508	6,234	11,890	1.4%	0.3%	0.2%
Connecticut	1,558,960	18,985	12,580	863*		5,542	0.8%	0.0%	0.0%
Delaware	413,921	5,853	3,882	1,940	23*	8	0.9%	0.5%	0.0%
Florida	8,474,179	72,976	44,726	8,947	2,607	16,696	0.5%	0.1%	0.0%
Georgia	3,900,050	47,535	45,324	1,516*	432*	263	1.2%	0.0%	0.0%
Hawaii	434,697	7,024	3,840	3,184			0.9%	0.7%	0.0%
Idaho	652,346	18,648	9,453	4,402	2,222	2,571	1.4%	0.7%	0.3%
Illinois	5,242,014	87,286	56,229	30,222	415*	420	1.1%	0.6%	0.0%
Indiana	2,624,534	51,104	50,111	625*	290*	78	1.9%	0.0%	0.0%
Iowa	1,582,180	29,019	12,926	3,769	3,038	9,286	0.8%	0.2%	0.2%
Kansas	1,159,971	26,611	20,456	714*	187*	5,254	1.8%	0.1%	0.0%
Kentucky	1,797,212	30,652	17,063	6,337	245*	7,007	0.9%	0.4%	0.0%
Louisiana	1,994,065	32,662	18,157	6,978	2,508	5,019	0.9%	0.3%	0.1%
Maine	713,180	19,598	9,352	8,119		2,127	1.3%	1.1%	0.0%
Maryland	2,707,327	57,614	30,195	17,110	418*	9,891	1.1%	0.6%	0.0%
Massachusetts	3,167,767	58,163	30,920	20,691		6,552	1.0%	0.7%	0.0%
Michigan	4,730,961	51,136	7,774*	21,897	16,119	5,346	0.2%	0.5%	0.3%
Minnesota	2,936,561	70,169	35,098	13,023	3,722	18,326	1.2%	0.4%	0.1%
Mississippi	1,285,584	11,889	6,676	1,588	2,609	1,016	0.5%	0.1%	0.2%
Missouri	2,757,323	51,087	43,151		7,936		1.6%	0.0%	0.3%
Montana	484,048	14,281	14,165		39*	77	2.9%	0.0%	0.0%
Nebraska	794,379	17,234	11,109			6,125	1.4%	0.0%	0.0%
Nevada	1,014,918	19,978	10,968		3,240	5,770	1.1%	0.0%	0.3%
New Hampshire	710,972	11,493	8,212	324*	708	2,249	1.2%	0.0%	0.1%
New Jersey	3,640,292	37,623	21,045	9,888	2,064	4,626	0.6%	0.3%	0.1%
New Mexico	783,757	32,634	27,787	2,691	982	1,174	3.5%	0.3%	0.1%
New York	7,081,159	104,987	47,256	39,982	6,274	11,475	0.7%	0.6%	0.1%
North Carolina	4,505,372	56,586	44,515		534*	11,537	1.0%	0.0%	0.0%
North Dakota	322,627	9,637	5,231	1,361	1,185	1,860	1.6%	0.4%	0.4%
Ohio	5,580,840	91,697	49,493	18,574	8,151	15,479	0.9%	0.3%	0.1%
Oklahoma	1,334,872						0.0%	0.0%	0.0%
Oregon	1,789,270	64,607	24,089	19,427		21,091	1.3%	1.1%	0.0%
Pennsylvania	5,753,670	82,962	49,991	21,341	383*	11,247	0.9%	0.4%	0.0%
Rhode Island	446,049	9,168	4,388	2,421	430	1,929	1.0%	0.5%	0.1%
South Carolina	1,964,118	26,532	16,321	5,446	4,765		0.8%	0.3%	0.2%
South Dakota	363,815	8,166	5,795		2,371		1.6%	0.0%	0.7%
Tennessee	2,458,577	35,538	18,623	6,515	6,022	4,378	0.8%	0.3%	0.2%
Texas	7,993,851	115,884	88,580	24,657	1,287*	1,360	1.1%	0.3%	0.0%
Utah	1,017,440	25,027	12,572	3,817	2,871	5,767	1.2%	0.4%	0.3%
Vermont	299,290	7,353	3,487			3,866	1.2%	0.0%	0.0%
Virginia	3,854,489	60,147	31,216	8,627	13,058	7,246	0.8%	0.2%	0.3%
Washington	3,125,516	79,450	42,202	20,928	8,851	7,469	1.4%	0.7%	0.3%
West Virginia	670,438	14,514	6,302	4,406		3,806	0.9%	0.7%	0.0%
Wisconsin	3,068,434	39,483	20,439	7,665	4,930	6,449	0.7%	0.2%	0.2%
Wyoming	249,061	8,813	5,326		1,452	2,035	2.1%	0.0%	0.6%
District of Columbia	293,764	5,313	2,083	2,458		772	0.7%	0.8%	0.0%
Total	129,085,474	2,236,178	1,275,970	469,034	122,375	368,799	1.0%	0.4%	0.1%

Note: An asterisk (*) indicates write-in votes.

UNITED STATES
VOTER TURNOUT 2012

State	2012 Voting Age Population	Registration: 2012 General Election	Percentage Voting Age Registered	Presidential Vote	Presidential Vote as Percentage of		House Vote	Senate Vote	Governor Vote
					Voting Age Population	Registered Voters			
Alabama	3,600,000	3,162,135	87.8%	2,074,338	57.6%	65.6%	1,933,630	—	—
Alaska	517,000	506,434	98.0%	300,495	58.1%	59.3%	289,804	—	—
Arizona	4,472,000	3,725,362	83.3%	2,299,254	51.4%	61.7%	2,173,317	2,243,422	—
Arkansas	2,160,000	1,618,548	74.9%	1,069,468	49.5%	66.1%	1,038,054	—	—
California	23,572,000	18,245,970	77.4%	13,038,547	55.3%	71.5%	12,204,357	12,578,511	—
Colorado	3,635,000	3,645,274	100.3%	2,569,522	70.7%	70.5%	2,450,839	—	—
Connecticut	2,547,000	2,218,662	87.1%	1,558,960	61.2%	70.3%	1,466,511	1,511,764	—
Delaware	678,000	626,349	92.4%	413,921	61.1%	66.1%	388,059	399,607	398,033
Florida	13,542,000	11,934,446	88.1%	8,474,179	62.6%	71.0%	7,513,539	8,189,946	—
Georgia	6,865,000	5,428,980	79.1%	3,900,050	56.8%	71.8%	3,553,587	—	—
Hawaii	986,000	705,668	71.6%	434,697	44.1%	61.6%	422,539	430,483	—
Idaho	1,133,000	895,834	79.1%	652,346	57.6%	72.8%	635,218	—	—
Illinois	8,887,000	8,586,521	96.6%	5,242,014	59.0%	61.0%	5,058,133	—	—
Indiana	4,775,000	4,555,257	95.4%	2,624,534	55.0%	57.6%	2,553,746	2,560,102	2,577,329
Iowa	2,264,000	2,166,539	95.7%	1,582,180	69.9%	73.0%	1,536,849	—	—
Kansas	2,038,000	1,771,252	86.9%	1,159,971	56.9%	65.5%	1,057,739	—	—
Kentucky	3,286,000	3,037,153	92.4%	1,797,212	54.7%	59.2%	1,745,377	—	833,139
Louisiana	3,343,000	2,962,999	88.6%	1,994,065	59.6%	67.3%	1,705,617	—	1,023,163
Maine	1,054,000	963,152	91.4%	713,180	67.7%	74.0%	693,801	700,599	—
Maryland	4,096,000	3,694,527	90.2%	2,707,327	66.1%	73.3%	2,585,514	2,633,234	—
Massachussetts	4,700,000	4,342,841	92.4%	3,167,767	67.4%	72.9%	2,891,434	3,156,553	—
Michigan	7,317,000	7,454,553	101.9%	4,730,961	64.7%	63.5%	4,574,632	4,652,918	—
Minnesota	3,915,000	3,084,344	78.8%	2,936,561	75.0%	95.2%	2,813,383	2,843,207	—
Mississippi	2,203,000	1,905,605	86.5%	1,285,584	58.4%	67.5%	1,208,175	1,241,568	893,468
Missouri	4,525,000	4,180,659	92.4%	2,757,323	60.9%	66.0%	2,675,900	2,725,793	2,727,883
Montana	779,000	681,608	87.5%	484,048	62.1%	71.0%	479,740	486,066	483,489
Nebraska	1,330,000	1,163,871	87.5%	794,379	59.7%	68.3%	772,515	788,572	—
Nevada	1,869,000	1,257,621	67.3%	1,014,918	54.3%	80.7%	973,742	997,805	—
New Hampshire	1,022,000	791,434	77.4%	710,972	69.6%	89.8%	682,416	—	693,877
New Jersey	5,944,000	5,497,322	92.5%	3,640,292	61.2%	66.2%	3,281,954	3,374,668	—
New Mexico	1,463,000	1,255,273	85.8%	783,757	53.6%	62.4%	766,090	775,792	—
New York	13,302,000	11,969,192	90.0%	7,081,159	53.2%	59.2%	6,469,725	6,679,678	—
North Carolina	7,030,000	6,706,592	95.4%	4,505,372	64.1%	67.2%	4,384,112	—	4,468,295
North Dakota	523,000	See Notes	See Notes	322,627	See Notes	See Notes	316,071	320,851	317,812
Ohio	8,658,000	7,987,697	92.3%	5,580,840	64.5%	69.9%	5,140,574	5,449,114	—
Oklahoma	2,748,000	2,114,713	77.0%	1,334,872	48.6%	63.1%	1,325,935	—	—
Oregon	2,832,000	2,212,592	78.1%	1,789,270	63.2%	80.9%	1,708,168	—	—
Pennsylvania	9,677,000	8,503,377	87.9%	5,753,670	59.5%	67.7%	5,556,330	5,629,491	—
Rhode Island	768,000	725,309	94.4%	446,049	58.1%	61.5%	427,775	418,189	—
South Carolina	3,512,000	2,820,774	80.3%	1,964,118	55.9%	69.6%	1,802,734	—	—
South Dakota	613,000	531,664	86.7%	363,815	59.3%	68.4%	361,429	—	—
Tennessee	4,787,000	3,905,974	81.6%	2,458,577	51.4%	62.9%	2,283,727	2,321,477	—
Texas	16,302,000	13,646,226	83.7%	7,993,851	49.0%	58.6%	7,664,208	7,864,822	—
Utah	1,840,000	1,513,241	82.2%	1,017,440	55.3%	67.2%	998,897	1,006,901	1,006,524
Vermont	496,000	461,237	93.0%	299,290	60.3%	64.9%	289,931	294,267	295,261
Virginia	5,844,000	5,428,833	92.9%	3,854,489	66.0%	71.0%	3,740,455	3,802,196	—
Washington	4,861,000	4,335,775	89.2%	3,125,516	64.3%	72.1%	3,006,266	3,069,417	3,071,047
West Virginia	1,467,000	1,234,367	84.1%	670,438	45.7%	54.3%	641,354	660,212	664,455
Wisconsin	4,283,000	3,501,045	81.7%	3,068,434	71.6%	87.6%	2,866,050	3,009,411	—
Wyoming	435,000	240,438	55.3%	249,061	57.3%	103.6%	241,621	244,862	—
District of Columbia	464,000	501,535	108.1%	293,764	63.3%	58.6%	See Notes	—	—
Total	218,959,000	190,406,774	87.2%	129,085,474	58.9%	67.6%	121,351,573	93,061,498	19,453,775

Source: Registration and voting age population (VAP) figures were provided by the Center for the Study of the American Electorate. VAP figures are based on estimated numbers of citizens of voting age in each state (and nationally) at the time of the November 2012 general election. Figures do not account for felony or other forms of disenfranchisement. They also do not account for those living outside of the United States and those naturalized in 2012, both of which are enfranchised but not counted in the Census enumeration of age-eligible citizens. Registration figures must be viewed with significant caution. Some states give only "active" registration figures, while others include inactive voters as well, and both types of states include invalid registrations. These inaccuracies as well as estimations mean that some states have a registration number that is more than 100% of the VAP. North Dakota does not require voter registration. For more details on registration, consult the Election Assistance Commission's Election Administration and Voting Survey.

Notes: Does not include special elections or elections for non-voting delegates (such as the 278,563 votes for House delegate in the District of Columbia). The gubernatorial vote includes 2011 elections in Kentucky, Louisiana, and Mississippi. Includes vote totals for general election House races in Louisiana; does not include runoff votes in 3rd district. Because North Dakota does not conduct voter registration, the percentage of voting-age population registered and the presidential vote as percentage of registered voters exclude North Dakota.

UNITED STATES
PRESIDENT 2008

The candidates listed below include all who appeared on the ballot in at least one state. Write-in votes for independent and third-party candidates are credited to their total below. See the minor parties table on page 18 for details. There, the state totals for all independent and third-party candidates who received at least 100,000 votes in the 2008 presidential election are listed.

In New York the Democratic total includes Working Families votes and the Republican figures include Conservative and Independence votes.

In Minnesota the Democratic candidate appears on the ballot as Democratic-Farmer-Labor, in North Dakota as Democratic-Nonpartisan League. In many states various non-major party candidates appeared on the ballot with variations of the party designations, were carried with entirely different party labels, or were listed as "Independent."

69,498,516	Barack Obama and Joseph R. Biden Jr.	Democratic
59,948,323	John S. McCain III and Sarah Palin	Republican
739,034	Ralph Nader and Matt Gonzalez	Independent
523,715	Bob Barr and Wayne A. Root	Libertarian
199,750	Chuck Baldwin and Darrell L. Castle	Constitution
161,797	Cynthia A. McKinney and Rosa A. Clemente	Green
47,746	Alan Keyes and Brian Rohrbough	America's Independent
42,426	Ron Paul and Barry Goldwater Jr./Michael Peroutka	Constitution/Louisiana Taxpayers
6,818	Gloria La Riva and Eugene Puryear/Robert Moses	Socialism and Liberation
6,538	Brian Moore and Stewart A. Alexander	Socialist
5,151	Roger Calero and Alyson Kennedy	Socialist Workers
3,905	Richard Duncan and Ricky Johnson	Independent
2,424	James Harris and Alyson Kennedy	Socialist Workers
2,422	Charles Jay and Dan Sallis Jr.	Boston Tea
1,149	John Polachek and "no candidate"	New
829	Frank McEnulty and David Mangan	New American Independent
764	Jeffrey Wamboldt and David J. Klimisch	Independent
755	Thomas Stevens and Alden Link	Objectivist
653	Gene Amondson and Leroy J. Pletten	Prohibition
639	Jeffrey Boss and Andrea Marie Psoras	Vote Here
531	George Phillies and Christopher Bennett	Libertarian
481	Ted Weill and Frank McEnulty	Reform
480	Jonathan Allen and Jeffrey D. Stath	HeartQuake '08
110	Bradford Lyttle and Abraham Bassford	U.S. Pacifist

Notes: In addition to the votes listed above, 112,597 scattered write-in votes were reported from various states, and 6,267 votes were cast for "None of These Candidates" in Nevada. In addition to Ron Paul and Gloria La Riva, Chuck Baldwin, Charles Jay, and Alan Keyes had a different vice-presidential candidate in at least one state.

UNITED STATES
PRESIDENT 2008

State	Electoral Vote Rep.	Electoral Vote Dem.	Total Vote	Republican	Democratic	Other	Rep.-Dem. Plurality	Total Vote Rep.	Total Vote Dem.	Major Vote Rep.	Major Vote Dem.
Alabama	9		2,099,819	1,266,546	813,479	19,794	453,067 R	60.3%	38.7%	60.9%	39.1%
Alaska	3		326,197	193,841	123,594	8,762	70,247 R	59.4%	37.9%	61.1%	38.9%
Arizona	10		2,293,475	1,230,111	1,034,707	28,657	195,404 R	53.6%	45.1%	54.3%	45.7%
Arkansas	6		1,086,617	638,017	422,310	26,290	215,707 R	58.7%	38.9%	60.2%	39.8%
California		55	13,561,900	5,011,781	8,274,473	275,646	3,262,692 D	37.0%	61.0%	37.7%	62.3%
Colorado		9	2,401,462	1,073,629	1,288,633	39,200	215,004 D	44.7%	53.7%	45.4%	54.6%
Connecticut		7	1,646,797	629,428	997,772	19,597	368,344 D	38.2%	60.6%	38.7%	61.3%
Delaware		3	412,412	152,374	255,459	4,579	103,085 D	36.9%	61.9%	37.4%	62.6%
Florida		27	8,390,744	4,045,624	4,282,074	63,046	236,450 D	48.2%	51.0%	48.6%	51.4%
Georgia	15		3,924,486	2,048,759	1,844,123	31,604	204,636 R	52.2%	47.0%	52.6%	47.4%
Hawaii		4	453,568	120,566	325,871	7,131	205,305 D	26.6%	71.8%	27.0%	73.0%
Idaho	4		655,122	403,012	236,440	15,670	166,572 R	61.5%	36.1%	63.0%	37.0%
Illinois		21	5,522,371	2,031,179	3,419,348	71,844	1,388,169 D	36.8%	61.9%	37.3%	62.7%
Indiana		11	2,751,054	1,345,648	1,374,039	31,367	28,391 D	48.9%	49.9%	49.5%	50.5%
Iowa		7	1,537,123	682,379	828,940	25,804	146,561 D	44.4%	53.9%	45.2%	54.8%
Kansas	6		1,235,872	699,655	514,765	21,452	184,890 R	56.6%	41.7%	57.6%	42.4%
Kentucky	8		1,826,620	1,048,462	751,985	26,173	296,477 R	57.4%	41.2%	58.2%	41.8%
Louisiana	9		1,960,761	1,148,275	782,989	29,497	365,286 R	58.6%	39.9%	59.5%	40.5%
Maine		4	731,163	295,273	421,923	13,967	126,650 D	40.4%	57.7%	41.2%	58.8%
Maryland		10	2,631,596	959,862	1,629,467	42,267	669,605 D	36.5%	61.9%	37.1%	62.9%
Massachusetts		12	3,080,985	1,108,854	1,904,097	68,034	795,243 D	36.0%	61.8%	36.8%	63.2%
Michigan		17	5,001,766	2,048,639	2,872,579	80,548	823,940 D	41.0%	57.4%	41.6%	58.4%
Minnesota		10	2,910,369	1,275,409	1,573,354	61,606	297,945 D	43.8%	54.1%	44.8%	55.2%
Mississippi	6		1,289,865	724,597	554,662	10,606	169,935 R	56.2%	43.0%	56.6%	43.4%
Missouri	11		2,925,205	1,445,814	1,441,911	37,480	3,903 R	49.4%	49.3%	50.1%	49.9%
Montana	3		490,302	242,763	231,667	15,872	11,096 R	49.5%	47.2%	51.2%	48.8%
Nebraska	4	1	801,281	452,979	333,319	14,983	119,660 R	56.5%	41.6%	57.6%	42.4%
Nevada		5	967,848	412,827	533,736	21,285	120,909 D	42.7%	55.1%	43.6%	56.4%
New Hampshire		4	710,970	316,534	384,826	9,610	68,292 D	44.5%	54.1%	45.1%	54.9%
New Jersey		15	3,868,237	1,613,207	2,215,422	39,608	602,215 D	41.7%	57.3%	42.1%	57.9%
New Mexico		5	830,158	346,832	472,422	10,904	125,590 D	41.8%	56.9%	42.3%	57.7%
New York		31	7,640,931	2,752,771	4,804,945	83,215	2,052,174 D	36.0%	62.9%	36.4%	63.6%
North Carolina		15	4,310,789	2,128,474	2,142,651	39,664	14,177 D	49.4%	49.7%	49.8%	50.2%
North Dakota	3		316,621	168,601	141,278	6,742	27,323 R	53.3%	44.6%	54.4%	45.6%
Ohio		20	5,708,350	2,677,820	2,940,044	90,486	262,224 D	46.9%	51.5%	47.7%	52.3%
Oklahoma	7		1,462,661	960,165	502,496		457,669 R	65.6%	34.4%	65.6%	34.4%
Oregon		7	1,827,864	738,475	1,037,291	52,098	298,816 D	40.4%	56.7%	41.6%	58.4%
Pennsylvania		21	6,013,272	2,655,885	3,276,363	81,024	620,478 D	44.2%	54.5%	44.8%	55.2%
Rhode Island		4	471,766	165,391	296,571	9,804	131,180 D	35.1%	62.9%	35.8%	64.2%
South Carolina	8		1,920,969	1,034,896	862,449	23,624	172,447 R	53.9%	44.9%	54.5%	45.5%
South Dakota	3		381,975	203,054	170,924	7,997	32,130 R	53.2%	44.7%	54.3%	45.7%
Tennessee	11		2,599,749	1,479,178	1,087,437	33,134	391,741 R	56.9%	41.8%	57.6%	42.4%
Texas	34		8,077,795	4,479,328	3,528,633	69,834	950,695 R	55.5%	43.7%	55.9%	44.1%
Utah	5		952,370	596,030	327,670	28,670	268,360 R	62.6%	34.4%	64.5%	35.5%
Vermont		3	325,046	98,974	219,262	6,810	120,288 D	30.4%	67.5%	31.1%	68.9%
Virginia		13	3,723,260	1,725,005	1,959,532	38,723	234,527 D	46.3%	52.6%	46.8%	53.2%
Washington		11	3,036,878	1,229,216	1,750,848	56,814	521,632 D	40.5%	57.7%	41.2%	58.8%
West Virginia	5		713,451	397,466	303,857	12,128	93,609 R	55.7%	42.6%	56.7%	43.3%
Wisconsin		10	2,983,417	1,262,393	1,677,211	43,813	414,818 D	42.3%	56.2%	42.9%	57.1%
Wyoming	3		254,658	164,958	82,868	6,832	82,090 R	64.8%	32.5%	66.6%	33.4%
District of Columbia		3	265,853	17,367	245,800	2,686	228,433 D	6.5%	92.5%	6.6%	93.4%
Total	173	365	131,313,820	59,948,323	69,498,516	1,866,981	9,550,193 D	45.7%	52.9%	46.3%	53.7%

UNITED STATES
PRESIDENT 2008 MINOR PARTIES

State	Total	Nader (Independent)	Barr (Libertarian)	Baldwin (Constitution)	McKinney (Green)	Other Candidates and Scattered Write-ins	Nader (Ind.)	Barr (Libert.)	Baldwin (Const.)	McKinney (Green)
							Percentage			
Alabama	19,794	6,788	4,991	4,310		3,705	0.3%	0.2%	0.2%	
Alaska	8,762	3,783	1,589	1,660		1,730	1.2%	0.5%	0.5%	
Arizona	28,657	11,301	12,555	1,371*	3,406	24	0.5%	0.5%	0.1%	0.1%
Arkansas	26,290	12,882	4,776	4,023	3,470	1,139	1.2%	0.4%	0.4%	0.3%
California	275,646	108,381	67,582	3,145*	38,774	57,764	0.8%	0.5%		0.3%
Colorado	39,200	13,352	10,898	6,233	2,822	5,895	0.6%	0.5%	0.3%	0.1%
Connecticut	19,597	19,162		311*	90*	34	1.2%			
Delaware	4,579	2,401	1,109	626	385	58	0.6%	0.3%	0.2%	0.1%
Florida	63,046	28,124	17,218	7,915	2,887	6,902	0.3%	0.2%	0.1%	0.0%
Georgia	31,604	1,158*	28,731	1,402*	250*	63	0.0%	0.7%		
Hawaii	7,131	3,825	1,314	1,013	979		0.8%	0.3%	0.2%	0.2%
Idaho	15,670	7,175	3,658	4,747	39*	51	1.1%	0.6%	0.7%	
Illinois	71,844	30,948	19,642	8,256	11,838	1,160	0.6%	0.4%	0.1%	0.2%
Indiana	31,367	909*	29,257	1,024*	87*	90		1.1%		
Iowa	25,804	8,014	4,590	4,445	1,423	7,332	0.5%	0.3%	0.3%	0.1%
Kansas	21,452	10,527	6,706	4,148	35*	36	0.9%	0.5%	0.3%	
Kentucky	26,173	15,378	5,989	4,694		112	0.8%	0.3%	0.3%	
Louisiana	29,497	6,997		2,581	9,187	10,732	0.4%		0.1%	0.5%
Maine	13,967	10,636	251*	177*	2,900	3	1.5%			0.4%
Maryland	42,267	14,713	9,842	3,760	4,747	9,205	0.6%	0.4%	0.1%	0.2%
Massachusetts	68,034	28,841	13,189	4,971	6,550	14,483	0.9%	0.4%	0.2%	0.2%
Michigan	80,548	33,085	23,716	14,685	8,892	170	0.7%	0.5%	0.3%	0.2%
Minnesota	61,606	30,152	9,174	6,787	5,174	10,319	1.0%	0.3%	0.2%	0.2%
Mississippi	10,606	4,011	2,529	2,551	1,034	481	0.3%	0.2%	0.2%	0.1%
Missouri	37,480	17,813	11,386	8,201	80*		0.6%	0.4%	0.3%	
Montana	15,872	3,686	1,355	143*	23*	10,665	0.8%	0.3%		
Nebraska	14,983	5,406	2,740	2,972	1,028	2,837	0.7%	0.3%	0.4%	0.1%
Nevada	21,285	6,150	4,263	3,194	1,411	6,267	0.6%	0.4%	0.3%	0.1%
New Hampshire	9,610	3,503	2,217	226*	40*	3,624	0.5%	0.3%		
New Jersey	39,608	21,298	8,441	3,956	3,636	2,277	0.6%	0.2%	0.1%	0.1%
New Mexico	10,904	5,327	2,428	1,597	1,552		0.6%	0.3%	0.2%	0.2%
New York	83,215	41,249	19,596	634*	12,801	8,935	0.5%	0.3%		0.2%
North Carolina	39,664	1,448*	25,722		158*	12,336		0.6%		
North Dakota	6,742	4,189	1,354	1,199			1.3%	0.4%	0.4%	
Ohio	90,486	42,337	19,917	12,565	8,518	7,149	0.7%	0.3%	0.2%	0.1%
Oklahoma										
Oregon	52,098	18,614	7,635	7,693	4,543	13,613	1.0%	0.4%	0.4%	0.2%
Pennsylvania	81,024	42,977	19,912	1,092*		17,043	0.7%	0.3%		
Rhode Island	9,804	4,829	1,382	675	797	2,121	1.0%	0.3%	0.1%	0.2%
South Carolina	23,624	5,053	7,283	6,827	4,461		0.3%	0.4%	0.4%	0.2%
South Dakota	7,997	4,267	1,835	1,895			1.1%	0.5%	0.5%	
Tennessee	33,134	11,560	8,547	8,191	2,499	2,337	0.4%	0.3%	0.3%	0.1%
Texas	69,834	5,751*	56,116	5,708*	909*	1,350	0.1%	0.7%	0.1%	
Utah	28,670	8,416	6,966	12,012	982	294	0.9%	0.7%	1.3%	0.1%
Vermont	6,810	3,339	1,067	500	66*	1,838	1.0%	0.3%	0.2%	
Virginia	38,723	11,483	11,067	7,474	2,344	6,355	0.3%	0.3%	0.2%	0.1%
Washington	56,814	29,489	12,728	9,432	3,819	1,346	1.0%	0.4%	0.3%	0.1%
West Virginia	12,128	7,219		2,465	2,355	89	1.0%		0.3%	0.3%
Wisconsin	43,813	17,605	8,858	5,072	4,216	8,062	0.6%	0.3%	0.2%	0.1%
Wyoming	6,832	2,525	1,594	1,192		1,521	1.0%	0.6%	0.5%	
District of Columbia	2,686	958			590	1,138	0.4%			0.2%
Total	1,866,981	739,034	523,715	199,750	161,797	242,685	0.6%	0.4%	0.2%	0.1%

Note: An asterisk (*) indicates write-in votes.

UNITED STATES
PRESIDENT 2004

The candidates listed below include all who appeared on the ballot in at least one state. Write-in votes for third-party candidates are credited to their total below. See the minor parties table on page 21 for details.

In New York the Republican total includes votes for their candidate on the Conservative line and the Democratic total includes votes for their candidate on the Working Families line.

In Minnesota the Democratic candidate appears on the ballot as Democratic-Farmer-Labor, in North Dakota as Democratic-Nonpartisan League. In many states various third-party candidates appeared on the ballot with variations of the party designations, were carried with entirely different party labels, or were listed as "Independent."

62,040,610	George W. Bush and Richard B. Cheney	Republican
59,028,439	John Kerry and John Edwards	Democratic
465,650	Ralph Nader and Peter Miguel Camejo	Independent
397,265	Michael Badnarik and Richard V. Campagna	Libertarian
143,630	Michael Peroutka and Chuck Baldwin	Constitution
119,859	David Cobb and Patricia LaMarche	Green
27,607	Leonard Peltier and Janice Jordan	Peace and Freedom
10,837	Walter F. Brown and Mary Alice Herbert	Socialist
7,102	James Harris and Margaret Trowe	Socialist Workers
3,689	Roger Calero and Arrin Hawkins	Socialist Workers
2,387	Thomas J. Harens and Jennifer A. Ryan	Christian Freedom
1,944	Gene Amondson and Leroy Pletten	Concerns of People
1,861	Bill Van Auken and Jim Lawrence	Socialist Equality
1,646	John Parker and Teresa Gutierrez	Workers World
946	Charles Jay and Marilyn Chambers Taylor	Personal Choice
804	Stanford E. "Andy" Andress and Irene M. Deasy	Unaffiliated
140	Earl F. Dodge and Howard F. Lydick	Prohibition

Notes: In addition to the votes listed above, 37,241 scattered write-in votes were reported from various states, and 3,688 votes were cast for "None of These Candidates" in Nevada.

UNITED STATES
PRESIDENT 2004

State	Electoral Vote Rep.	Electoral Vote Dem.	Electoral Vote Other	Total Vote	Republican	Democratic	Other	Rep.-Dem. Plurality	Percentage Total Vote Rep.	Percentage Total Vote Dem.	Percentage Major Vote Rep.	Percentage Major Vote Dem.
Alabama	9			1,883,449	1,176,394	693,933	13,122	482,461 R	62.5%	36.8%	62.9%	37.1%
Alaska	3			312,598	190,889	111,025	10,684	79,864 R	61.1%	35.5%	63.2%	36.8%
Arizona	10			2,012,585	1,104,294	893,524	14,767	210,770 R	54.9%	44.4%	55.3%	44.7%
Arkansas	6			1,054,945	572,898	469,953	12,094	102,945 R	54.3%	44.5%	54.9%	45.1%
California		55		12,421,852	5,509,826	6,745,485	166,541	1,235,659 D	44.4%	54.3%	45.0%	55.0%
Colorado	9			2,130,330	1,101,255	1,001,732	27,343	99,523 R	51.7%	47.0%	52.4%	47.6%
Connecticut		7		1,578,769	693,826	857,488	27,455	163,662 D	43.9%	54.3%	44.7%	55.3%
Delaware		3		375,190	171,660	200,152	3,378	28,492 D	45.8%	53.3%	46.2%	53.8%
Florida	27			7,609,810	3,964,522	3,583,544	61,744	380,978 R	52.1%	47.1%	52.5%	47.5%
Georgia	15			3,301,875	1,914,254	1,366,149	21,472	548,105 R	58.0%	41.4%	58.4%	41.6%
Hawaii		4		429,013	194,191	231,708	3,114	37,517 D	45.3%	54.0%	45.6%	54.4%
Idaho	4			598,447	409,235	181,098	8,114	228,137 R	68.4%	30.3%	69.3%	30.7%
Illinois		21		5,274,322	2,345,946	2,891,550	36,826	545,604 D	44.5%	54.8%	44.8%	55.2%
Indiana	11			2,468,002	1,479,438	969,011	19,553	510,427 R	59.9%	39.3%	60.4%	39.6%
Iowa	7			1,506,908	751,957	741,898	13,053	10,059 R	49.9%	49.2%	50.3%	49.7%
Kansas	6			1,187,756	736,456	434,993	16,307	301,463 R	62.0%	36.6%	62.9%	37.1%
Kentucky	8			1,795,882	1,069,439	712,733	13,710	356,706 R	59.5%	39.7%	60.0%	40.0%
Louisiana	9			1,943,106	1,102,169	820,299	20,638	281,870 R	56.7%	42.2%	57.3%	42.7%
Maine		4		740,752	330,201	396,842	13,709	66,641 D	44.6%	53.6%	45.4%	54.6%
Maryland		10		2,386,678	1,024,703	1,334,493	27,482	309,790 D	42.9%	55.9%	43.4%	56.6%
Massachusetts		12		2,912,388	1,071,109	1,803,800	37,479	732,691 D	36.8%	61.9%	37.3%	62.7%
Michigan		17		4,839,252	2,313,746	2,479,183	46,323	165,437 D	47.8%	51.2%	48.3%	51.7%
Minnesota		9	1	2,828,387	1,346,695	1,445,014	36,678	98,319 D	47.6%	51.1%	48.2%	51.8%
Mississippi	6			1,152,145	684,981	458,094	9,070	226,887 R	59.5%	39.8%	59.9%	40.1%
Missouri	11			2,731,364	1,455,713	1,259,171	16,480	196,542 R	53.3%	46.1%	53.6%	46.4%
Montana	3			450,445	266,063	173,710	10,672	92,353 R	59.1%	38.6%	60.5%	39.5%
Nebraska	5			778,186	512,814	254,328	11,044	258,486 R	65.9%	32.7%	66.8%	33.2%
Nevada	5			829,587	418,690	397,190	13,707	21,500 R	50.5%	47.9%	51.3%	48.7%
New Hampshire		4		677,738	331,237	340,511	5,990	9,274 D	48.9%	50.2%	49.3%	50.7%
New Jersey		15		3,611,691	1,670,003	1,911,430	30,258	241,427 D	46.2%	52.9%	46.6%	53.4%
New Mexico	5			756,304	376,930	370,942	8,432	5,988 R	49.8%	49.0%	50.4%	49.6%
New York		31		7,391,036	2,962,567	4,314,280	114,189	1,351,713 D	40.1%	58.4%	40.7%	59.3%
North Carolina	15			3,501,007	1,961,166	1,525,849	13,992	435,317 R	56.0%	43.6%	56.2%	43.8%
North Dakota	3			312,833	196,651	111,052	5,130	85,599 R	62.9%	35.5%	63.9%	36.1%
Ohio	20			5,627,908	2,859,768	2,741,167	26,973	118,601 R	50.8%	48.7%	51.1%	48.9%
Oklahoma	7			1,463,758	959,792	503,966		455,826 R	65.6%	34.4%	65.6%	34.4%
Oregon		7		1,836,782	866,831	943,163	26,788	76,332 D	47.2%	51.3%	47.9%	52.1%
Pennsylvania		21		5,769,590	2,793,847	2,938,095	37,648	144,248 D	48.4%	50.9%	48.7%	51.3%
Rhode Island		4		437,134	169,046	259,760	8,328	90,714 D	38.7%	59.4%	39.4%	60.6%
South Carolina	8			1,617,730	937,974	661,699	18,057	276,275 R	58.0%	40.9%	58.6%	41.4%
South Dakota	3			388,215	232,584	149,244	6,387	83,340 R	59.9%	38.4%	60.9%	39.1%
Tennessee	11			2,437,319	1,384,375	1,036,477	16,467	347,898 R	56.8%	42.5%	57.2%	42.8%
Texas	34			7,410,765	4,526,917	2,832,704	51,144	1,694,213 R	61.1%	38.2%	61.5%	38.5%
Utah	5			927,844	663,742	241,199	22,903	422,543 R	71.5%	26.0%	73.3%	26.7%
Vermont		3		312,309	121,180	184,067	7,062	62,887 D	38.8%	58.9%	39.7%	60.3%
Virginia	13			3,198,367	1,716,959	1,454,742	26,666	262,217 R	53.7%	45.5%	54.1%	45.9%
Washington		11		2,859,084	1,304,894	1,510,201	43,989	205,307 D	45.6%	52.8%	46.4%	53.6%
West Virginia	5			755,887	423,778	326,541	5,568	97,237 R	56.1%	43.2%	56.5%	43.5%
Wisconsin		10		2,997,007	1,478,120	1,489,504	29,383	11,384 D	49.3%	49.7%	49.8%	50.2%
Wyoming	3			243,428	167,629	70,776	5,023	96,853 R	68.9%	29.1%	70.3%	29.7%
District of Columbia		3		227,586	21,256	202,970	3,360	181,714 D	9.3%	89.2%	9.5%	90.5%
Total	286	251	1	122,295,345	62,040,610	59,028,439	1,226,296	3,012,171 R	50.7%	48.3%	51.2%	48.8%

Note: A Democratic elector in Minnesota cast a vote for Edwards rather than Kerry.

UNITED STATES
PRESIDENT 2004 MINOR PARTIES

State	Total	Nader (Ind.)	Badnarik (Libert.)	Peroutka (Const.)	Cobb (Green)	Other Candidates and Scattered Write-ins
Alabama	13,122	6,701	3,529	1,994		898
Alaska	10,684	5,069	1,675	2,092	1,058	790
Arizona	14,767	2,773*	11,856		138*	
Arkansas	12,094	6,171	2,352	2,083	1,488	
California	166,541	21,213*	50,165	26,645	40,771	27,747
Colorado	27,343	12,718	7,664	2,562	1,591	2,808
Connecticut	27,455	12,969	3,367	1,543	9,564	12
Delaware	3,378	2,153	586	289	250	100
Florida	61,744	32,971	11,996	6,626	3,917	6,234
Georgia	21,472	2,231*	18,387	580*	228*	46
Hawaii	3,114		1,377		1,737	
Idaho	8,114	1,115*	3,844	3,084	58*	13
Illinois	36,826	3,571*	32,442	440*	241*	132
Indiana	19,553	1,328*	18,058		102*	65
Iowa	13,053	5,973	2,992	1,304	1,141	1,643
Kansas	16,307	9,348	4,013	2,899	33*	14
Kentucky	13,710	8,856	2,619	2,213		22
Louisiana	20,638	7,032	2,781	5,203	1,276	4,346
Maine	13,709	8,069	1,965	735	2,936	4
Maryland	27,482	11,854	6,094	3,421	3,632	2,481
Massachusetts	37,479	4,806*	15,022		10,623	7,028
Michigan	46,323	24,035	10,552	4,980	5,325	1,431
Minnesota	36,678	18,683	4,639	3,074	4,408	5,874
Mississippi	9,070	3,177	1,793	1,759	1,073	1,268
Missouri	16,480	1,294*	9,831	5,355		
Montana	10,672	6,168	1,733	1,764	996	11
Nebraska	11,044	5,698	2,041	1,314	978	1,013
Nevada	13,707	4,838	3,176	1,152	853	3,688
New Hampshire	5,990	4,479	372*	161*		978
New Jersey	30,258	19,418	4,514	2,750	1,807	1,769
New Mexico	8,432	4,053	2,382	771	1,226	
New York	114,189	99,873	11,607	207*	87*	2,415
North Carolina	13,992	1,805*	11,731		108*	348
North Dakota	5,130	3,756	851	514		9
Ohio	26,973		14,676	11,939	192*	166
Oklahoma						
Oregon	26,788		7,260	5,257	5,315	8,956
Pennsylvania	37,648	2,656*	21,185	6,318	6,319	1,170
Rhode Island	8,328	4,651	907	339	1,333	1,098
South Carolina	18,057	5,520	3,608	5,317	1,488	2,124
South Dakota	6,387	4,320	964	1,103		
Tennessee	16,467	8,992	4,866	2,570	33*	6
Texas	51,144	9,159*	38,787	1,636*	1,014*	548
Utah	22,903	11,305	3,375	6,841	39*	1,343
Vermont	7,062	4,494	1,102			1,466
Virginia	26,666	2,393*	11,032	10,161	104*	2,976
Washington	43,989	23,283	11,955	3,922	2,974	1,855
West Virginia	5,568	4,063	1,405	82*	5*	13
Wisconsin	29,383	16,390	6,464		2,661	3,868
Wyoming	5,023	2,741	1,171	631		480
District of Columbia	3,360	1,485	502		737	636
Total	*1,226,296*	*465,650*	*397,265*	*143,630*	*119,859*	*99,892*

Note: An asterisk (*) indicates write-in votes.

UNITED STATES
VOTER TURNOUT 2004

State	2004 Voting Age Population	Registration: 2004 General Election	Percent Voting Age Registered	Presidential Vote	Presidential Vote as Percentage of Voting Age Population	Presidential Vote as Percentage of Registered Voters	House Vote	Senate Vote	Governor Vote
Alabama	3,419,000	2,842,985	83.2%	1,883,449	55.1%	66.2%	1,792,759	1,839,066	—
Alaska	447,000	473,927	106.0%	312,598	69.9%	66.0%	299,996	308,315	—
Arizona	3,768,000	2,643,331	70.2%	2,012,585	53.4%	76.1%	1,871,445	1,961,677	—
Arkansas	2,057,000	1,684,684	81.9%	1,054,945	51.3%	62.6%	791,240	1,039,349	—
California	20,754,000	16,557,273	79.8%	12,421,852	59.9%	75.0%	11,623,753	12,053,295	8,657,915
Colorado	3,275,000	3,114,566	95.1%	2,130,330	65.0%	68.4%	2,039,011	2,107,554	—
Connecticut	2,390,000	2,044,181	85.5%	1,578,769	66.1%	77.2%	1,428,738	1,424,726	—
Delaware	601,000	553,885	92.2%	375,190	62.4%	67.7%	356,045	—	365,008
Florida	11,904,000	10,301,290	86.5%	7,609,810	63.9%	73.9%	5,627,494	7,429,894	—
Georgia	6,135,000	4,951,955	80.7%	3,301,875	53.8%	66.7%	2,960,763	3,220,981	—
Hawaii	877,000	647,238	73.8%	429,013	48.9%	66.3%	416,570	415,347	—
Idaho	985,000	798,015	81.0%	598,447	60.8%	75.0%	572,426	503,932	—
Illinois	8,544,000	7,499,488	87.8%	5,274,322	61.7%	70.3%	4,988,665	5,141,520	—
Indiana	4,572,000	4,296,602	94.0%	2,468,002	54.0%	57.4%	2,416,251	2,428,233	2,448,498
Iowa	2,190,000	2,106,658	96.2%	1,506,908	68.8%	71.5%	1,458,161	1,479,228	—
Kansas	1,954,000	1,591,428	81.4%	1,187,756	60.8%	74.6%	1,156,383	1,129,022	—
Kentucky	3,134,000	2,794,286	89.2%	1,795,882	57.3%	64.3%	1,635,243	1,724,362	1,083,443
Louisiana	3,310,000	2,923,395	88.3%	1,943,106	58.7%	66.5%	1,545,982	1,848,056	1,407,842
Maine	984,000	1,023,956	104.1%	740,752	75.3%	72.3%	710,176	—	—
Maryland	3,804,000	3,074,889	80.8%	2,386,678	62.7%	77.6%	2,255,955	2,323,183	—
Massachusetts	4,501,000	4,098,634	91.1%	2,912,388	64.7%	71.1%	2,580,955	—	—
Michigan	7,289,000	7,164,047	98.3%	4,839,252	66.4%	67.5%	4,631,058	—	—
Minnesota	3,658,000	3,559,400	97.3%	2,828,387	77.3%	79.5%	2,721,681	—	—
Mississippi	2,155,000	1,791,666	83.1%	1,152,145	53.5%	64.3%	1,116,203	—	894,487
Missouri	4,242,000	4,194,146	98.9%	2,731,364	64.4%	65.1%	2,667,023	2,706,402	2,719,599
Montana	709,000	638,474	90.1%	450,445	63.5%	70.6%	444,230	—	446,146
Nebraska	1,256,000	1,160,199	92.4%	778,186	62.0%	67.1%	764,972	—	—
Nevada	1,528,000	1,071,101	70.1%	829,587	54.3%	77.5%	791,433	810,068	—
New Hampshire	942,000	855,861	90.9%	677,738	71.9%	79.2%	651,566	657,086	667,020
New Jersey	5,702,000	5,005,959	87.8%	3,611,691	63.3%	72.1%	3,284,595	—	—
New Mexico	1,322,000	1,105,372	83.6%	756,304	57.2%	68.4%	742,899	—	—
New York	12,496,000	11,837,068	94.7%	7,391,036	59.1%	62.4%	6,222,418	6,702,875	—
North Carolina	6,208,000	5,519,992	88.9%	3,501,007	56.4%	63.4%	3,413,071	3,472,082	3,486,688
North Dakota	483,000	—		312,833	64.8%	—	310,814	310,696	309,873
Ohio	8,486,000	7,972,826	94.0%	5,627,908	66.3%	70.6%	5,183,508	5,426,196	—
Oklahoma	2,581,000	2,143,978	83.1%	1,463,758	56.7%	68.3%	1,374,610	1,446,846	—
Oregon	2,581,000	2,141,243	83.0%	1,836,782	71.2%	85.8%	1,772,306	1,780,550	—
Pennsylvania	9,230,000	8,366,663	90.6%	5,769,590	62.5%	69.0%	5,152,274	5,559,105	—
Rhode Island	752,000	651,950	86.7%	437,134	58.1%	67.1%	402,175	—	—
South Carolina	3,120,000	2,315,462	74.2%	1,617,730	51.9%	69.9%	1,439,118	1,597,221	—
South Dakota	569,000	552,441	97.1%	388,215	68.2%	70.3%	389,468	391,188	—
Tennessee	4,462,000	3,742,829	83.9%	2,437,319	54.6%	65.1%	2,218,738	—	—
Texas	14,197,000	13,098,329	92.3%	7,410,765	52.2%	56.6%	6,958,603	—	—
Utah	1,587,000	1,278,251	80.5%	927,844	58.5%	72.6%	908,857	911,726	919,960
Vermont	470,000	444,077	94.5%	312,309	66.4%	70.3%	305,000	307,208	309,285
Virginia	5,290,000	4,517,980	85.4%	3,198,367	60.5%	70.8%	3,004,007	—	—
Washington	4,370,000	3,508,208	80.3%	2,859,084	65.4%	81.5%	2,729,995	2,818,651	2,810,058
West Virginia	1,423,000	1,168,694	82.1%	755,887	53.1%	64.7%	721,656	—	744,433
Wisconsin	4,057,000	—		2,997,007	73.9%	—	2,821,613	2,949,743	—
Wyoming	380,000	232,396	61.2%	243,428	64.1%	104.7%	239,034	—	—
District of Columbia	391,000	383,919	98.2%	227,586	58.2%	59.3%	—	—	—
Total	201,541,000	172,445,197	85.6%	122,295,345	60.7%	70.9%	111,910,944	86,225,383	27,270,255

Sources: Voting age population figures were compiled by the Committee for the Study of the American Electorate (CSAE) and represent the estimated citizen voting age population in each state (and nationally) at the time of the November 2004 general election. CSAE employs a more conservative methodology than does the Census Bureau, which no longer provides election-year voting age population estimates. Registration figures are as of the November 2004 general election and were obtained from state election officials. In some cases, the registration totals are suspect as a number of states include inactive voters in their totals. In Alaska and Wyoming, for instance, the number of registered voters was more than 100 percent of the voting age population. The Minnesota total includes election-day registrations. The Mississippi total was as of April 2004. North Dakota and Wisconsin did not compile statewide registration figures.

Notes: Votes are from the November 2004 general election, with the exception of gubernatorial elections in California, Kentucky, Louisiana, and Mississippi, which were held in 2003. The California gubernatorial contest was a special recall election.

UNITED STATES
PRESIDENT 2000

The candidates listed below include all who appeared on the ballot in at least one state. Write-in votes for minor party candidates are credited to their total below. See the minor parties table on page 25 for details.

In New York the Republican figures include Conservative votes and the Democratic figures include Liberal and Working Families votes.

In Minnesota the Democratic candidate appears on the ballot as Democratic-Farmer-Labor. In many states various non-major party candidates appeared on the ballot with variations of the party designations, were carried with entirely different party labels, or were listed as "Independent."

50,455,156	George W. Bush and Richard B. Cheney	Republican
50,992,335	Al Gore and Joseph I. Lieberman	Democratic
2,882,738	Ralph Nader and Winona LaDuke	Green
449,077	Pat Buchanan and Ezola Foster	Reform
384,429	Harry Browne and Art Olivier	Libertarian
98,020	Howard Phillips and J. Curtis Frazier	Constitution
83,525	John Hagelin and Nat Goldhaber	Natural Law
7,378	James E. Harris Jr. and Margaret Trowe	Socialist Worker
5,775	L. Neil Smith and Vin Suprynowicz	Arizona Libertarian
5,602	David McReynolds and Mary Cal Hollis	Socialist
4,795	Monica Moorehead and Gloria La Riva	Workers World
1,606	Cathy Gordon Brown and Sabrina R. Allen	Independent
1,044	Denny Lane and Dale Wilkinson	Vermont Grassroots
535	Randall Venson and Gene Kelly	Independent
208	Earl F. Dodge and W. Dean Watkins	Prohibition
161	Louie G. Youngkeit and Robert Leo Beck	Unaffiliated

Notes: In addition to the votes listed above, 20,928 scattered write-in votes were reported from various states, and 3,315 votes were cast for "None of These Candidates" in Nevada.

UNITED STATES
PRESIDENT 2000

State	Electoral Vote Rep.	Electoral Vote Dem.	Electoral Vote Other	Total Vote	Republican	Democratic	Green (Nader)	Other	Rep.-Dem. Plurality	Percentage Rep.	Percentage Dem.	Percentage Green
Alabama	9			1,666,272	941,173	692,611	18,323	14,165	248,562 R	56.5%	41.6%	1.1%
Alaska	3			285,560	167,398	79,004	28,747	10,411	88,394 R	58.6%	27.7%	10.1%
Arizona	8			1,532,016	781,652	685,341	45,645	19,378	96,311 R	51.0%	44.7%	3.0%
Arkansas	6			921,781	472,940	422,768	13,421	12,652	50,172 R	51.3%	45.9%	1.5%
California		54		10,965,856	4,567,429	5,861,203	418,707	118,517	1,293,774 D	41.7%	53.4%	3.8%
Colorado	8			1,741,368	883,748	738,227	91,434	27,959	145,521 R	50.8%	42.4%	5.3%
Connecticut		8		1,459,525	561,094	816,015	64,452	17,964	254,921 D	38.4%	55.9%	4.4%
Delaware		3		327,622	137,288	180,068	8,307	1,959	42,780 D	41.9%	55.0%	2.5%
Florida	25			5,963,110	2,912,790	2,912,253	97,488	40,579	537 R	48.8%	48.8%	1.6%
Georgia	13			2,596,645	1,419,720	1,116,230	13,273	47,422	303,490 R	54.7%	43.0%	0.5%
Hawaii		4		367,951	137,845	205,286	21,623	3,197	67,441 D	37.5%	55.8%	5.9%
Idaho	4			501,621	336,937	138,637	12,292	13,755	198,300 R	67.2%	27.6%	2.5%
Illinois		22		4,742,123	2,019,421	2,589,026	103,759	29,917	569,605 D	42.6%	54.6%	2.2%
Indiana	12			2,199,302	1,245,836	901,980	18,531	32,955	343,856 R	56.6%	41.0%	0.8%
Iowa		7		1,315,563	634,373	638,517	29,374	13,299	4,144 D	48.2%	48.5%	2.2%
Kansas	6			1,072,218	622,332	399,276	36,086	14,524	223,056 R	58.0%	37.2%	3.4%
Kentucky	8			1,544,187	872,492	638,898	23,192	9,605	233,594 R	56.5%	41.4%	1.5%
Louisiana	9			1,765,656	927,871	792,344	20,473	24,968	135,527 R	52.6%	44.9%	1.2%
Maine		4		651,817	286,616	319,951	37,127	8,123	33,335 D	44.0%	49.1%	5.7%
Maryland		10		2,020,480	813,797	1,140,782	53,768	12,133	326,985 D	40.3%	56.5%	2.7%
Massachusetts		12		2,702,984	878,502	1,616,487	173,564	34,431	737,985 D	32.5%	59.8%	6.4%
Michigan		18		4,232,711	1,953,139	2,170,418	84,165	24,989	217,279 D	46.1%	51.3%	2.0%
Minnesota		10		2,438,685	1,109,659	1,168,266	126,696	34,064	58,607 D	45.5%	47.9%	5.2%
Mississippi	7			994,184	572,844	404,614	8,122	8,604	168,230 R	57.6%	40.7%	0.8%
Missouri	11			2,359,892	1,189,924	1,111,138	38,515	20,315	78,786 R	50.4%	47.1%	1.6%
Montana	3			410,997	240,178	137,126	24,437	9,256	103,052 R	58.4%	33.4%	5.9%
Nebraska	5			697,019	433,862	231,780	24,540	6,837	202,082 R	62.2%	33.3%	3.5%
Nevada	4			608,970	301,575	279,978	15,008	12,409	21,597 R	49.5%	46.0%	2.5%
New Hampshire	4			569,081	273,559	266,348	22,198	6,976	7,211 R	48.1%	46.8%	3.9%
New Jersey		15		3,187,226	1,284,173	1,788,850	94,554	19,649	504,677 D	40.3%	56.1%	3.0%
New Mexico		5		598,605	286,417	286,783	21,251	4,154	366 D	47.8%	47.9%	3.6%
New York		33		6,821,999	2,403,374	4,107,697	244,030	66,898	1,704,323 D	35.2%	60.2%	3.6%
North Carolina	14			2,911,262	1,631,163	1,257,692	—	22,407	373,471 R	56.0%	43.2%	—
North Dakota	3			288,256	174,852	95,284	9,486	8,634	79,568 R	60.7%	33.1%	3.3%
Ohio	21			4,701,998	2,350,363	2,183,628	117,799	50,208	166,735 R	50.0%	46.4%	2.5%
Oklahoma	8			1,234,229	744,337	474,276		15,616	270,061 R	60.3%	38.4%	—
Oregon		7		1,533,968	713,577	720,342	77,357	22,692	6,765 D	46.5%	47.0%	5.0%
Pennsylvania		23		4,913,119	2,281,127	2,485,967	103,392	42,633	204,840 D	46.4%	50.6%	2.1%
Rhode Island		4		409,047	130,555	249,508	25,052	3,932	118,953 D	31.9%	61.0%	6.1%
South Carolina	8			1,382,717	785,937	565,561	20,200	11,019	220,376 R	56.8%	40.9%	1.5%
South Dakota	3			316,269	190,700	118,804	—	6,765	71,896 R	60.3%	37.6%	—
Tennessee	11			2,076,181	1,061,949	981,720	19,781	12,731	80,229 R	51.1%	47.3%	1.0%
Texas	32			6,407,637	3,799,639	2,433,746	137,994	36,258	1,365,893 R	59.3%	38.0%	2.2%
Utah	5			770,754	515,096	203,053	35,850	16,755	312,043 R	66.8%	26.3%	4.7%
Vermont		3		294,308	119,775	149,022	20,374	5,137	29,247 D	40.7%	50.6%	6.9%
Virginia	13			2,739,447	1,437,490	1,217,290	59,398	25,269	220,200 R	52.5%	44.4%	2.2%
Washington		11		2,487,433	1,108,864	1,247,652	103,002	27,915	138,788 D	44.6%	50.2%	4.1%
West Virginia	5			648,124	336,475	295,497	10,680	5,472	40,978 R	51.9%	45.6%	1.6%
Wisconsin		11		2,598,607	1,237,279	1,242,987	94,070	24,271	5,708 D	47.6%	47.8%	3.6%
Wyoming	3			218,351	147,947	60,481	4,625	5,298	87,466 R	67.8%	27.7%	2.1%
District of Columbia		2	1	201,894	18,073	171,923	10,576	1,322	153,850 D	9.0%	85.2%	5.2%
Total	271	266	1	105,396,627	50,455,156	50,992,335	2,882,738	1,066,398	537,179 D	47.9%	48.4%	2.7%

UNITED STATES
PRESIDENT 2000 MINOR PARTIES

State	Total	Buchanan (Reform)	Browne (Libert.)	Phillips (Const.)	Hagelin (Nat. Law)	Other Candidates and Scattered Write-ins
Alabama	14,165	6,351	5,893	775	447	699
Alaska	10,411	5,192	2,636	596	919	1,068
Arizona	19,378	12,373		110	1,120	5,775
Arkansas	12,652	7,358	2,781	1,415	1,098	—
California	118,517	44,987	45,520	17,042	10,934	34
Colorado	27,959	10,465	12,799	1,319	2,240	1,136
Connecticut	17,964	4,731	3,484	9,695	40	14
Delaware	1,959	777	774	208	107	93
Florida	40,579	17,484	16,415	1,371	2,281	3,028
Georgia	47,422	10,926	36,332	140		24
Hawaii	3,197	1,071	1,477	343	306	—
Idaho	13,755	7,615	3,488	1,469	1,177	6
Illinois	29,917	16,106	11,623	57	2,127	4
Indiana	32,955	16,959	15,530	200	167	99
Iowa	13,299	5,731	3,209	613	2,281	1,465
Kansas	14,524	7,370	4,525	1,254	1,375	—
Kentucky	9,605	4,173	2,896	923	1,533	80
Louisiana	24,968	14,356	2,951	5,483	1,075	1,103
Maine	8,123	4,443	3,074	579		27
Maryland	12,133	4,248	5,310	919	176	1,480
Massachusetts	34,431	11,149	16,366		2,884	4,032
Michigan	24,989	2061	16,711	3,791	2,426	—
Minnesota	34,064	22,166	5,282	3,272	2,294	1,050
Mississippi	8,604	2,265	2,009	3,267	450	613
Missouri	20,315	9,818	7,436	1,957	1,104	—
Montana	9,256	5,697	1,718	1,155	675	11
Nebraska	6,837	3,646	2,245	468	478	—
Nevada	12,409	4,747	3,311	621	415	3,315
New Hampshire	6,976	2,615	2,757	328		1,276
New Jersey	19,649	6,989	6,312	1,409	2,215	2,724
New Mexico	4,154	1,392	2,058	343	361	—
New York	66,898	31,599	7,649	1,498	24,361	1,791
North Carolina	22,407	8,874	12,307			1,226
North Dakota	8,634	7,288	660	373	313	—
Ohio	50,208	26,721	13,473	3,823	6,181	10
Oklahoma	15,616	9,014	6,602			—
Oregon	22,692	7,063	7,447	2,189	2,574	3,419
Pennsylvania	42,633	16,023	11,248	14,428		934
Rhode Island	3,932	2,273	742	97	271	549
South Carolina	11,019	3,519	4,876	1,682	942	—
South Dakota	6,765	3,322	1,662	1,781		—
Tennessee	12,731	4,250	4,284	1,015	613	2,569
Texas	36,258	12,394	23,160	567		137
Utah	16,755	9,319	3,616	2,709	763	348
Vermont	5,137	2,192	784	153	219	1,789
Virginia	25,269	5,455	15,198	1,809		2,807
Washington	27,915	7,171	13,135	1,989	2,927	2,693
West Virginia	5,472	3,169	1,912	23	367	1
Wisconsin	24,271	11,446	6,640	2,042	878	3,265
Wyoming	5,298	2,724	1,443	720	411	—
District of Columbia	1,322		669			653
Total	1,066,398	449,077	384,429	98,020	83,525	51,347

UNITED STATES
VOTER TURNOUT 2000

State	2000 Voting Age Population Est.	November 2000 Registration	Percentage Voting Age Registered	Presidential Vote	Presidential Vote as Percentage of		House Vote	Senate Vote	Governor Vote
					Voting Age Population	Registered Voters			
Alabama	3,333,000	2,528,963	75.9%	1,666,272	50.0%	65.9%	1,438,994		
Alaska	430,000	473,648	110.2%	285,560	66.4%	60.3%	274,393		
Arizona	3,625,000	2,654,700	73.2%	1,532,016	42.3%	57.7%	1,465,656	1,397,076	
Arkansas	1,929,000	1,555,809	80.7%	921,781	47.8%	59.2%	632,765		
California	24,873,000	15,707,307	63.2%	10,965,856	44.1%	69.8%	10,437,665	10,623,614	
Colorado	3,067,000	2,858,239	93.2%	1,741,368	56.8%	60.9%	1,623,882		
Connecticut	2,499,000	2,031,626	81.3%	1,459,525	58.4%	71.8%	1,313,490	1,311,261	
Delaware	582,000	503,672	86.5%	327,622	56.3%	65.0%	313,171	327,017	323,688
Florida	11,774,000	8,752,717	74.3%	5,963,110	50.6%	68.1%	5,011,372	5,856,731	
Georgia	5,893,000	4,648,205	78.9%	2,596,645	44.1%	55.9%	2,416,622	2,428,510	
Hawaii	909,000	637,349	70.1%	367,951	40.5%	57.7%	340,424	345,623	
Idaho	921,000	728,085	79.1%	501,621	54.5%	68.9%	492,835		
Illinois	8,983,000	7,117,449	79.2%	4,742,123	52.8%	66.6%	4,393,352		
Indiana	4,448,000	4,000,809	89.9%	2,199,302	49.4%	55.0%	2,156,744	2,145,209	2,179,413
Iowa	2,165,000	1,969,199	91.0%	1,315,563	60.8%	66.8%	1,275,934		
Kansas	1,983,000	1,623,623	81.9%	1,072,218	54.1%	66.0%	1,038,379		
Kentucky	2,993,000	2,556,815	85.4%	1,544,187	51.6%	60.4%	1,435,409		580,074
Louisiana	3,255,000	2,782,929	85.5%	1,765,656	54.2%	63.4%	1,202,171		1,295,205
Maine	968,000	947,189	97.9%	651,817	67.3%	68.8%	638,399	634,872	
Maryland	3,925,000	2,715,366	69.2%	2,020,480	51.5%	74.4%	1,926,764	1,946,898	
Massachusetts	4,749,000	4,000,218	84.2%	2,702,984	56.9%	67.6%	2,347,375	2,599,420	
Michigan	7,358,000	6,861,342	93.3%	4,232,711	56.6%	60.7%	4,069,736	4,167,685	
Minnesota	3,547,000	2,801,077	79.0%	2,438,685	68.8%	87.1%	2,363,738	2,419,520	
Mississippi	2,047,000			994,184	48.6%		986,139	994,144	763,938
Missouri	4,105,000	3,676,664	89.6%	2,359,892	57.5%	64.2%	2,325,788	2,361,586	2,346,830
Montana	668,000	698,260	104.5%	410,997	61.5%	58.9%	410,523	411,601	410,192
Nebraska	1,234,000	1,085,272	87.9%	697,019	56.5%	64.2%	683,071	692,344	
Nevada	1,390,000	878,970	63.2%	608,970	43.8%	69.3%	585,204	600,250	
New Hampshire	911,000	856,519	94.0%	569,081	62.5%	66.4%	556,417		564,953
New Jersey	6,245,000	4,710,768	75.4%	3,187,226	51.0%	67.7%	2,988,233	3,015,662	
New Mexico	1,263,000	928,931	73.5%	598,605	47.4%	64.4%	587,514	589,526	
New York	13,805,000	11,262,816	81.6%	6,821,999	49.4%	60.6%	5,823,850	6,779,839	
North Carolina	5,797,000	5,186,094	89.5%	2,911,262	50.2%	56.1%	2,779,800		2,942,062
North Dakota	477,000			288,256	60.4%		285,658	287,539	289,412
Ohio	8,433,000	7,537,822	89.4%	4,701,998	55.8%	62.4%	4,517,838	4,448,801	
Oklahoma	2,531,000	2,233,602	88.2%	1,234,229	48.8%	55.3%	1,087,515		
Oregon	2,530,000	1,950,902	77.1%	1,533,968	60.6%	78.6%	1,440,002		
Pennsylvania	9,155,000	7,781,997	85.0%	4,913,119	53.7%	63.1%	4,554,347	4,735,504	
Rhode Island	753,000	655,107	87.0%	409,047	54.3%	62.4%	384,127	391,537	
South Carolina	2,977,000	2,266,200	76.1%	1,382,717	46.4%	61.0%	1,321,312		
South Dakota	542,000	520,881	96.1%	316,269	58.4%	60.7%	314,761		
Tennessee	4,221,000	3,400,487	80.6%	2,076,181	49.2%	61.1%	1,854,378	1,928,613	
Texas	14,850,000	12,365,235	83.3%	6,407,637	43.1%	51.8%	5,985,763	6,276,652	
Utah	1,465,000	1,120,129	76.5%	770,754	52.6%	68.8%	758,754	769,704	761,806
Vermont	460,000	427,354	92.9%	294,308	64.0%	68.9%	283,366	288,500	293,473
Virginia	5,263,000	4,071,471	77.4%	2,739,447	52.1%	67.3%	2,421,729	2,718,301	
Washington	4,368,000	3,335,714	76.4%	2,487,433	56.9%	74.6%	2,382,411	2,461,379	2,469,852
West Virginia	1,416,000	1,067,822	75.4%	648,124	45.8%	60.7%	579,872	603,477	648,047
Wisconsin	3,930,000			2,598,607	66.1%		2,506,314	2,540,083	
Wyoming	358,000	220,012	61.5%	218,351	61.0%	99.2%	212,312	213,659	
District of Columbia	411,000	354,410		201,894	49.1%	57.0%			
Total	205,814,000	159,049,775	77.3%	105,396,627	51.2%	66.3%	97,226,268	79,312,137	15,868,945

Sources: Registration figures—Committee for the Study of the American Electorate; voting age population—U.S. Census Bureau.

Notes: Voting age population excluding states without registration: 199,360,000. Wisconsin and North Dakota do not maintain registration systems. Figures for Mississippi were unavailable. Excluding these states, the percentage of the voting age population that was registered was 79.8 percent. The presidential vote as a percentage of the voting age population was 50.9 percent and as a percentage of registered voters was 63.8 percent.

UNITED STATES
PRESIDENT 1996

The candidates listed below include all who appeared on the ballot in at least one state. Write-in votes for minor party candidates are credited to their total below. See the minor parties table on page 29 for details.

In New York the Republican figures include Conservative, Freedom, and Right to Life votes and the Democratic figures include Liberal votes.

In Minnesota the Democratic candidate appears on the ballot as Democratic-Farmer-Labor. In many states various non-major party candidates appeared on the ballot with variations of the party designations, were carried with entirely different party labels, or were listed as "Independent."

47,402,357	Bill Clinton and Al Gore	Democratic
39,198,755	Bob Dole and Jack Kemp	Republican
8,085,402	Ross Perot and Pat Choate	Reform
685,040	Ralph Nader and Winona LaDuke	Green
485,798	Harry Browne and Jo Jorgensen	Libertarian
184,658	Howard Phillips and Herbert W. Titus	U.S. Taxpayers
113,668	John Hagelin and Mike Tompkins	Natural Law
29,083	Monica Moorehead and Gloria La Riva	Workers World
25,332	Marsha Feinland and Kate McClatchy	Peace and Freedom
8,930	Charles Collins and Rosemary Giumarra	Independent
8,476	James Harris and Laura Garza	Socialist Workers
5,378	Dennis Peron and Arlin D. Troutt Jr.	Grassroots
4,706	Mary Cal Hollis and Eric Chester	Socialist
2,438	Jerome White and Fred Mazelis	Socialist Equality
1,847	Diane Beall Templin and Gary Van Horn	American
1,298	Earl F. Dodge and Rachel B. Kelly	Prohibition
1,101	A. Peter Crane and Connie Chandler	Independent
932	Ralph Forbes and "Pro-Life" Anderson	America First
787	John Birrenbach and George McMahon	Independent Grassroots
752	Isabell Masters and Shirley Jean Masters	Looking Back
408	Steve Michael and Ann Northrop	Independent

Notes: In addition to the votes listed above, 25,118 scattered write-in votes were reported from various states, and 5,608 votes were cast for "None of These Candidates" in Nevada.

UNITED STATES
PRESIDENT 1996

State	Electoral Vote Rep.	Electoral Vote Dem.	Total Vote	Republican	Democratic	Reform	Other	Plurality		Percentage Rep.	Percentage Dem.	Percentage Reform
Alabama	9		1,534,349	769,044	662,165	92,149	10,991	106,879	R	50.1%	43.2%	6.0%
Alaska	3		241,620	122,746	80,380	26,333	12,161	42,366	R	50.8%	33.3%	10.9%
Arizona		8	1,404,405	622,073	653,288	112,072	16,972	31,215	D	44.3%	46.5%	8.0%
Arkansas		6	884,262	325,416	475,171	69,884	13,791	149,755	D	36.8%	53.7%	7.9%
California		54	10,019,484	3,828,380	5,119,835	697,847	373,422	1,291,455	D	38.2%	51.1%	7.0%
Colorado	8		1,510,704	691,848	671,152	99,629	48,075	20,696	R	45.8%	44.4%	6.6%
Connecticut		8	1,392,614	483,109	735,740	139,523	34,242	252,631	D	34.7%	52.8%	10.0%
Delaware		3	271,084	99,062	140,355	28,719	2,948	41,293	D	36.5%	51.8%	10.6%
Florida		25	5,303,794	2,244,536	2,546,870	483,870	28,518	302,334	D	42.3%	48.0%	9.1%
Georgia	13		2,299,071	1,080,843	1,053,849	146,337	18,042	26,994	R	47.0%	45.8%	6.4%
Hawaii		4	360,120	113,943	205,012	27,358	13,807	91,069	D	31.6%	56.9%	7.6%
Idaho	4		491,719	256,595	165,443	62,518	7,163	91,152	R	52.2%	33.6%	12.7%
Illinois		22	4,311,391	1,587,021	2,341,744	346,408	36,218	754,723	D	36.8%	54.3%	8.0%
Indiana	12		2,135,842	1,006,693	887,424	224,299	17,426	119,269	R	47.1%	41.5%	10.5%
Iowa		7	1,234,075	492,644	620,258	105,159	16,014	127,614	D	39.9%	50.3%	8.5%
Kansas	6		1,074,300	583,245	387,659	92,639	10,757	195,586	R	54.3%	36.1%	8.6%
Kentucky		8	1,388,708	623,283	636,614	120,396	8,415	13,331	D	44.9%	45.8%	8.7%
Louisiana		9	1,783,959	712,586	927,837	123,293	20,243	215,251	D	39.9%	52.0%	6.9%
Maine		4	605,897	186,378	312,788	85,970	20,761	126,410	D	30.8%	51.6%	14.2%
Maryland		10	1,780,870	681,530	966,207	115,812	17,321	284,677	D	38.3%	54.3%	6.5%
Massachusetts		12	2,556,785	718,107	1,571,763	227,217	39,698	853,656	D	28.1%	61.5%	8.9%
Michigan		18	3,848,844	1,481,212	1,989,653	336,670	41,309	508,441	D	38.5%	51.7%	8.7%
Minnesota		10	2,192,640	766,476	1,120,438	257,704	48,022	353,962	D	35.0%	51.1%	11.8%
Mississippi	7		893,857	439,838	394,022	52,222	7,775	45,816	R	49.2%	44.1%	5.8%
Missouri		11	2,158,065	890,016	1,025,935	217,188	24,926	135,919	D	41.2%	47.5%	10.1%
Montana	3		407,261	179,652	167,922	55,229	4,458	11,730	R	44.1%	41.2%	13.6%
Nebraska	5		677,415	363,467	236,761	71,278	5,909	126,706	R	53.7%	35.0%	10.5%
Nevada		4	464,279	199,244	203,974	43,986	17,075	4,730	D	42.9%	43.9%	9.5%
New Hampshire		4	499,175	196,532	246,214	48,390	8,039	49,682	D	39.4%	49.3%	9.7%
New Jersey		15	3,075,807	1,103,078	1,652,329	262,134	58,266	549,251	D	35.9%	53.7%	8.5%
New Mexico		5	556,074	232,751	273,495	32,257	17,571	40,744	D	41.9%	49.2%	5.8%
New York		33	6,316,129	1,933,492	3,756,177	503,458	123,002	1,822,685	D	30.6%	59.5%	8.0%
North Carolina	14		2,515,807	1,225,938	1,107,849	168,059	13,961	118,089	R	48.7%	44.0%	6.7%
North Dakota	3		266,411	125,050	106,905	32,515	1,941	18,145	R	46.9%	40.1%	12.2%
Ohio		21	4,534,434	1,859,883	2,148,222	483,207	43,122	288,339	D	41.0%	47.4%	10.7%
Oklahoma	8		1,206,713	582,315	488,105	130,788	5,505	94,210	R	48.3%	40.4%	10.8%
Oregon		7	1,377,760	538,152	649,641	121,221	68,746	111,489	D	39.1%	47.2%	8.8%
Pennsylvania		23	4,506,118	1,801,169	2,215,819	430,984	58,146	414,650	D	40.0%	49.2%	9.6%
Rhode Island		4	390,284	104,683	233,050	43,723	8,828	128,367	D	26.8%	59.7%	11.2%
South Carolina	8		1,151,689	573,458	506,283	64,386	7,562	67,175	R	49.8%	44.0%	5.6%
South Dakota	3		323,826	150,543	139,333	31,250	2,700	11,210	R	46.5%	43.0%	9.7%
Tennessee		11	1,894,105	863,530	909,146	105,918	15,511	45,616	D	45.6%	48.0%	5.6%
Texas	32		5,611,644	2,736,167	2,459,683	378,537	37,257	276,484	R	48.8%	43.8%	6.7%
Utah	5		665,629	361,911	221,633	66,461	15,624	140,278	R	54.4%	33.3%	10.0%
Vermont		3	258,449	80,352	137,894	31,024	9,179	57,542	D	31.1%	53.4%	12.0%
Virginia	13		2,416,642	1,138,350	1,091,060	159,861	27,371	47,290	R	47.1%	45.1%	6.6%
Washington		11	2,253,837	840,712	1,123,323	201,003	88,799	282,611	D	37.3%	49.8%	8.9%
West Virginia		5	636,459	233,946	327,812	71,639	3,062	93,866	D	36.8%	51.5%	11.3%
Wisconsin		11	2,196,169	845,029	1,071,971	227,339	51,830	226,942	D	38.5%	48.8%	10.4%
Wyoming	3		211,571	105,388	77,934	25,928	2,321	27,454	R	49.8%	36.8%	12.3%
District of Columbia		3	185,726	17,339	158,220	3,611	6,556	140,881	D	9.3%	85.2%	1.9%
Total	159	379	96,277,872	39,198,755	47,402,357	8,085,402	1,591,358	8,203,602	D	40.7%	49.2%	8.4%

UNITED STATES
PRESIDENT 1996 MINOR PARTIES

State	Total	Nader (Green)	Browne (Libert.)	Phillips (US Txpyrs)	Hagelin (Nat. Law)	Moorehead (Wkrs. World)	Feinland (P&F)	Other Candidates and Scattered Write-ins
Alabama	10,991		5,290	2,365	1,697			1,639
Alaska	12,161	7,597	2,276	925	729			634
Arizona	16,972	2,062*	14,358	347*	153*			52
Arkansas	13,791	3,649	3,076	2,065	729	747		3,525
California	373,422	237,016	73,600	21,202	15,403		25,332	869
Colorado	48,075	25,070	12,392	2,813	2,547	599		4,654
Connecticut	34,242	24,321	5,788	2,425	1,703			5
Delaware	2,948	156*	2,052	348	274			118
Florida	28,518	4,101*	23,965		418*			34
Georgia	18,042		17,870	145*				27
Hawaii	13,807	10,386	2,493	358	570			
Idaho	7,163		3,325	2,230	1,600			8
Illinois	36,218	1,447*	22,548	7,606	4,606			11
Indiana	17,426	895*	15,632	291*	118*			490
Iowa	16,014	6,550	2,315	2,229	3,349			1,571
Kansas	10,757	914*	4,557	3,519	1,655			112
Kentucky	8,415	701*	4,009	2,204	1,493			8
Louisiana	20,243	4,719	7,499	3,366	2,981	1,678		
Maine	20,761	15,279	2,996	1,517	825			144
Maryland	17,321	2,606*	8,765	3,402	2,517			31
Massachusetts	39,698	4,565*	20,426		5,184	3,277		6,246
Michigan	41,309	2,322*	27,670	539*	4,254	3,153		3,371
Minnesota	48,022	24,908	8,271	3,416	1,808			9,619
Mississippi	7,775		2,809	2,314	1,447			1,205
Missouri	24,926	534*	10,522	11,521	2,287			62
Montana	4,458		2,526	152*	1,754			26
Nebraska	5,909		2,792	1,928	1,189			
Nevada	17,075	4,730	4,460	1,732	545			5,608
New Hampshire	8,039		4,237	1,346				2,456
New Jersey	58,266	32,465	14,763	3,440	3,887	1,337		2,374
New Mexico	17,571	13,218	2,996	713	644			
New York	123,002	75,956	12,220	23,580	5,011	3,473		2,762
North Carolina	13,961	2,108*	8,740	258*	2,771			84
North Dakota	1,941		847	745	349			
Ohio	43,122	2,962*	12,851	7,361	9,120	10,813		15
Oklahoma	5,505		5,505					
Oregon	68,746	49,415	8,903	3,379	2,798			4,251
Pennsylvania	58,146	3,086*	28,000	19,552	5,783			1,725
Rhode Island	8,828	6,040	1,109	1,021	435	186		37
South Carolina	7,562		4,271	2,043	1,248			
South Dakota	2,700		1,472	912	316			
Tennessee	15,511	6,427	5,020	1,818	636			1,610
Texas	37,257	4,810*	20,256	7,472	4,422			297
Utah	15,624	4,615	4,129	2,601	1,085	298		2,896
Vermont	9,179	5,585	1,183	382	498			1,531
Virginia	27,371		9,174	13,687	4,510			
Washington	88,799	60,322	12,522	4,578	6,076	2,189		3,112
West Virginia	3,062		3,062					
Wisconsin	51,830	28,723	7,929	8,811	1,379	1,333		3,655
Wyoming	2,321		1,739		582			
District of Columbia	6,556	4,780	588		283			905
Total	1,591,358	685,040	485,798	184,658	113,668	29,083	25,332	67,779

Notes: An asterisk (*) indicates write-in votes. The vote, including write-ins, for other minor party candidates who were listed on the ballot in at least one state: 8,930 Collins (Arizona, Arkansas, California, Colorado, Georgia, Idaho, Kansas, Maryland, Mississippi, Missouri, Montana, Tennessee, Utah, Washington); 8,476 Harris (Alabama, California, Colorado, Connecticut, Florida, Georgia, Iowa, Minnesota, New Jersey, New York, North Carolina, Utah, Vermont, Washington, Wisconsin, District of Columbia); 5,378 Peron (Minnesota, Vermont); 4,706 Holllis (Arkansas, Colorado, Florida, Maryland, Massachusetts, Montana, Oregon, Texas, Utah, Vermont, Wisconsin); 2,438 White (Michigan, Minnesota, New Jersey); 1,847 Templin (Colorado, Utah); 1,298 Dodge (Arkansas, Colorado, Illinois, Massachusetts, Tennessee, Utah); 1,101 Crane (Utah); 932 Forbes (Arkansas); 787 Birrenbach (Minnesota); 752 Masters (Arkansas, California, Maryland); 408 Michael (Tennessee). The Other Candidates and Scattered Write-ins column includes 5,608 votes cast in Nevada for "None of These Candidates" and 25,118 scattered write-ins.

UNITED STATES
VOTER TURNOUT 1996

State	1996 Census Voting Age Pop. Est.	November 1996 Registration	Percentage Voting Age Registered	Total Valid Vote President	Percentage Voting Age Voted	Percentage Registered Voted
Alabama	3,218,000	2,470,766	76.8%	1,534,349	47.7%	62.1%
Alaska	425,000	414,817	97.6%	241,620	56.9%	58.2%
Arizona	3,094,000	2,244,672	72.5%	1,404,405	45.4%	62.6%
Arkansas	1,860,000	1,396,459	75.1%	884,262	47.5%	63.3%
California	23,133,000	15,662,075	67.7%	10,019,484	43.3%	64.0%
Colorado	2,843,000	2,285,503	80.4%	1,510,704	53.1%	66.1%
Connecticut	2,468,000	1,975,000	80.0%	1,392,614	56.4%	70.5%
Delaware	547,000	419,695	76.7%	271,084	49.6%	64.6%
Florida	11,043,000	8,077,877	73.1%	5,303,794	48.0%	65.7%
Georgia	5,396,000	3,811,284	70.6%	2,299,071	42.6%	60.3%
Hawaii	882,000	544,916	61.8%	360,120	40.8%	66.1%
Idaho	845,000	700,430	82.9%	491,719	58.2%	70.2%
Illinois	8,764,000	6,663,301	76.0%	4,311,391	49.2%	64.7%
Indiana	4,369,000	3,484,033	79.7%	2,135,842	48.9%	61.3%
Iowa	2,138,000	1,776,433	83.1%	1,234,075	57.7%	69.5%
Kansas	1,898,000	1,436,418	75.7%	1,074,300	56.6%	74.8%
Kentucky	2,924,000	2,396,086	81.9%	1,388,708	47.5%	58.0%
Louisiana	3,137,000	2,539,240	80.9%	1,783,959	56.9%	70.3%
Maine	939,000	1,001,292	106.6%	605,897	64.5%	60.5%
Maryland	3,811,000	2,587,977	67.9%	1,780,870	46.7%	68.8%
Massachusetts	4,623,000	3,459,193	74.8%	2,556,785	55.3%	73.9%
Michigan	7,067,000	6,688,893	94.6%	3,848,844	54.5%	57.5%
Minnesota	3,412,000	2,730,505	80.0%	2,192,640	64.3%	80.3%
Mississippi	1,961,000			893,857	45.6%	
Missouri	3,980,000	3,339,852	83.9%	2,158,065	54.2%	64.6%
Montana	647,000	590,749	91.3%	407,261	62.9%	68.9%
Nebraska	1,208,000	1,015,056	84.0%	677,415	56.1%	66.7%
Nevada	1,180,000	778,298	66.0%	464,279	39.3%	59.7%
New Hampshire	860,000	713,236	82.9%	499,175	58.0%	70.0%
New Jersey	6,005,000	4,320,866	72.0%	3,075,807	51.2%	71.2%
New Mexico	1,210,000	837,794	69.2%	556,074	46.0%	66.4%
New York	13,579,000	10,162,156	74.8%	6,316,129	46.5%	62.2%
North Carolina	5,499,000	4,315,723	78.5%	2,515,807	45.8%	58.3%
North Dakota	473,000			266,411	56.3%	
Ohio	8,358,000	6,879,687	82.3%	4,534,434	54.3%	65.9%
Oklahoma	2,419,000	1,979,017	81.8%	1,206,713	49.9%	61.0%
Oregon	2,396,000	1,962,155	81.9%	1,377,760	57.5%	70.2%
Pennsylvania	9,196,000	6,799,637	73.9%	4,506,118	49.0%	66.3%
Rhode Island	750,000	602,692	80.4%	390,284	52.0%	64.8%
South Carolina	2,777,000	1,814,777	65.4%	1,151,689	41.5%	63.5%
South Dakota	530,000	476,422	89.9%	323,826	61.1%	68.0%
Tennessee	4,021,000	3,097,336	77.0%	1,894,105	47.1%	61.2%
Texas	13,622,000	10,520,379	77.2%	5,611,644	41.2%	53.3%
Utah	1,323,000	1,050,452	79.4%	665,629	50.3%	63.4%
Vermont	441,000	385,328	87.4%	258,449	58.6%	67.1%
Virginia	5,089,000	3,322,740	65.3%	2,416,642	47.5%	72.7%
Washington	4,122,000	3,081,971	74.8%	2,253,837	54.7%	73.1%
West Virginia	1,414,000	970,745	68.7%	636,459	45.0%	65.6%
Wisconsin	3,824,000			2,196,169	57.4%	
Wyoming	352,000			211,571	60.1%	
District of Columbia	435,000	361,419	83.1%	185,726	42.7%	51.4%
Total	*196,507,000*	*144,145,352*	*73.4%*	*96,277,872*	*49.0%*	*66.8%*

Source: Registration figures—Committee for the Study of the American Electorate.

Notes: Mississippi, North Dakota, Wisconsin, and Wyoming do not maintain formal voter registration systems or had no figures readily available. Excluding these four states, the percentage of the voting age population registered in the remaining states was 75.9 percent, and the percentage of registered that voted was 64.3 percent.

UNITED STATES
PRESIDENT 1992

The candidates listed below include all who appeared on the ballot in at least one state. Write-in votes for minor party candidates are credited to their total below.

In New York the Republican figures include Conservative and Right to Life votes and the Democratic figures include Liberal votes.

In Minnesota the Republican candidates appear on the ballot as Independent-Republican, the Democratic as Democratic-Farmer-Labor. In many states various non-major party candidates appeared on the ballot with variations of the party designations, were carried with entirely different party labels, or were listed as "Independent." In several states minor party vice-presidential candidates were different from those listed below.

44,909,326	Bill Clinton and Al Gore	Democratic
39,103,882	George Bush and J. Danforth Quayle	Republican
19,741,657	Ross Perot and James Stockdale	Independent
291,627	Andre V. Marrou and Nancy Lord	Libertarian
107,014	James Gritz and Cyril Minett	America First
73,714	Lenora B. Fulani and Maria E. Munoz	New Alliance
43,434	Howard Phillips and Albion W. Knight	Taxpayers
39,179	John Hagelin and Mike Tompkins	Natural Law
27,961	Ron Daniels and Asiba Tupahache	Peace and Freedom
26,333	Lyndon H. LaRouche Jr. and James L. Bevel	Economic Recovery
23,096	James Warren and Willie Mae Reid	Socialist Workers
4,749	Drew Bradford and no vice-presidential candidate	Independent
3,875	Jack Herer and Derrick P. Grimmer	Grassroots
3,057	J. Quinn Brisben and Barbara Garson	Socialist
3,050	Helen Halyard and Fred Mazelis	Workers League
2,199	John Yiamouyiannis and Allen C. McCone	Take Back America
1,149	Delbert L. Ehlers and Rick Wendt	Independent
961	Earl F. Dodge and George Ormsby	Prohibition
956	Jim Boren and Will Weidman	Apathy
405	Eugene A. Hem and Joanne Roland	Third Party
339	Isabell Masters and Walter Masters	Looking Back
292	Robert J. Smith and Doris Feimer	American
181	Gloria La Riva and Larry Holmes	Workers World

Notes: In addition to the votes listed above, 14,041 scattered write-in votes were reported from various states, and 2,537 votes were cast for "None of These Candidates" in Nevada.

UNITED STATES
PRESIDENT 1992

State	Electoral Vote Rep.	Electoral Vote Dem.	Total Vote	Republican	Democratic	Independent	Other	Plurality		Percentage Rep.	Percentage Dem.	Percentage Ind.
Alabama	9		1,688,060	804,283	690,080	183,109	10,588	114,203	R	47.6%	40.9%	10.8%
Alaska	3		258,506	102,000	78,294	73,481	4,731	23,706	R	39.5%	30.3%	28.4%
Arizona	8		1,486,975	572,086	543,050	353,741	18,098	29,036	R	38.5%	36.5%	23.8%
Arkansas		6	950,653	337,324	505,823	99,132	8,374	168,499	D	35.5%	53.2%	10.4%
California		54	11,131,721	3,630,574	5,121,325	2,296,006	83,816	1,490,751	D	32.6%	46.0%	20.6%
Colorado		8	1,569,180	562,850	629,681	366,010	10,639	66,831	D	35.9%	40.1%	23.3%
Connecticut		8	1,616,332	578,313	682,318	348,771	6,930	104,005	D	35.8%	42.2%	21.6%
Delaware		3	289,735	102,313	126,054	59,213	2,155	23,741	D	35.3%	43.5%	20.4%
Florida	25		5,314,392	2,173,310	2,072,698	1,053,067	15,317	100,612	R	40.9%	39.0%	19.8%
Georgia		13	2,321,125	995,252	1,008,966	309,657	7,250	13,714	D	42.9%	43.5%	13.3%
Hawaii		4	372,842	136,822	179,310	53,003	3,707	42,488	D	36.7%	48.1%	14.2%
Idaho	4		482,142	202,645	137,013	130,395	12,089	65,632	R	42.0%	28.4%	27.0%
Illinois		22	5,050,157	1,734,096	2,453,350	840,515	22,196	719,254	D	34.3%	48.6%	16.6%
Indiana	12		2,305,871	989,375	848,420	455,934	12,142	140,955	R	42.9%	36.8%	19.8%
Iowa		7	1,354,607	504,891	586,353	253,468	9,895	81,462	D	37.3%	43.3%	18.7%
Kansas	6		1,157,335	449,951	390,434	312,358	4,592	59,517	R	38.9%	33.7%	27.0%
Kentucky		8	1,492,900	617,178	665,104	203,944	6,674	47,926	D	41.3%	44.6%	13.7%
Louisiana		9	1,790,017	733,386	815,971	211,478	29,182	82,585	D	41.0%	45.6%	11.8%
Maine		4	679,499	206,504	263,420	206,820	2,755	56,600	D	30.4%	38.8%	30.4%
Maryland		10	1,985,046	707,094	988,571	281,414	7,967	281,477	D	35.6%	49.8%	14.2%
Massachusetts		12	2,773,700	805,049	1,318,662	630,731	19,258	513,613	D	29.0%	47.5%	22.7%
Michigan		18	4,274,673	1,554,940	1,871,182	824,813	23,738	316,242	D	36.4%	43.8%	19.3%
Minnesota		10	2,347,948	747,841	1,020,997	562,506	16,604	273,156	D	31.9%	43.5%	24.0%
Mississippi	7		981,793	487,793	400,258	85,626	8,116	87,535	R	49.7%	40.8%	8.7%
Missouri		11	2,391,565	811,159	1,053,873	518,741	7,792	242,714	D	33.9%	44.1%	21.7%
Montana		3	410,611	144,207	154,507	107,225	4,672	10,300	D	35.1%	37.6%	26.1%
Nebraska	5		737,546	343,678	216,864	174,104	2,900	126,814	R	46.6%	29.4%	23.6%
Nevada		4	506,318	175,828	189,148	132,580	8,762	13,320	D	34.7%	37.4%	26.2%
New Hampshire		4	537,943	202,484	209,040	121,337	5,082	6,556	D	37.6%	38.9%	22.6%
New Jersey		15	3,343,594	1,356,865	1,436,206	521,829	28,694	79,341	D	40.6%	43.0%	15.6%
New Mexico		5	569,986	212,824	261,617	91,895	3,650	48,793	D	37.3%	45.9%	16.1%
New York		33	6,926,925	2,346,649	3,444,450	1,090,721	45,105	1,097,801	D	33.9%	49.7%	15.7%
North Carolina	14		2,611,850	1,134,661	1,114,042	357,864	5,283	20,619	R	43.4%	42.7%	13.7%
North Dakota	3		308,133	136,244	99,168	71,084	1,637	37,076	R	44.2%	32.2%	23.1%
Ohio		21	4,939,967	1,894,310	1,984,942	1,036,426	24,289	90,632	D	38.3%	40.2%	21.0%
Oklahoma	8		1,390,359	592,929	473,066	319,878	4,486	119,863	R	42.6%	34.0%	23.0%
Oregon		7	1,462,643	475,757	621,314	354,091	11,481	145,557	D	32.5%	42.5%	24.2%
Pennsylvania		23	4,959,810	1,791,841	2,239,164	902,667	26,138	447,323	D	36.1%	45.1%	18.2%
Rhode Island		4	453,477	131,601	213,299	105,045	3,532	81,698	D	29.0%	47.0%	23.2%
South Carolina	8		1,202,527	577,507	479,514	138,872	6,634	97,993	R	48.0%	39.9%	11.5%
South Dakota	3		336,254	136,718	124,888	73,295	1,353	11,830	R	40.7%	37.1%	21.8%
Tennessee		11	1,982,638	841,300	933,521	199,968	7,849	92,221	D	42.4%	47.1%	10.1%
Texas	32		6,154,018	2,496,071	2,281,815	1,354,781	21,351	214,256	R	40.6%	37.1%	22.0%
Utah	5		743,999	322,632	183,429	203,400	34,538	119,232	R	43.4%	24.7%	27.3%
Vermont		3	289,701	88,122	133,592	65,991	1,996	45,470	D	30.4%	46.1%	22.8%
Virginia	13		2,558,665	1,150,517	1,038,650	348,639	20,859	111,867	R	45.0%	40.6%	13.6%
Washington		11	2,288,230	731,234	993,037	541,780	22,179	261,803	D	32.0%	43.4%	23.7%
West Virginia		5	683,762	241,974	331,001	108,829	1,958	89,027	D	35.4%	48.4%	15.9%
Wisconsin		11	2,531,114	930,855	1,041,066	544,479	14,714	110,211	D	36.8%	41.1%	21.5%
Wyoming	3		200,598	79,347	68,160	51,263	1,828	11,187	R	39.6%	34.0%	25.6%
District of Columbia		3	227,572	20,698	192,619	9,681	4,574	171,921	D	9.1%	84.6%	4.3%
Total	168	370	104,425,014	39,103,882	44,909,326	19,741,657	670,149	5,805,444	D	37.4%	43.0%	18.9%

UNITED STATES
PRESIDENT 1988

In West Virginia one Democratic elector voted for Lloyd Bentsen for president and Michael S. Dukakis for vice president.

In New York the Republican figures include Conservative votes and the Democratic figures include Liberal votes.

In Minnesota the Republican candidates appear on the ballot as Independent-Republican, the Democratic as Democratic-Farmer-Labor. In many states various non-major party candidates appeared on the ballot with variations of the party designations, were listed as "Independent," or were carried with entirely different party labels.

In several states minor party vice-presidential candidates were different from those listed below. The full list of candidates for president and vice president was:

48,886,097	George Bush and J. Danforth Quayle	Republican
41,809,074	Michael S. Dukakis and Lloyd Bentsen	Democratic
432,179	Ron Paul and Andre V. Marrou	Libertarian
217,219	Lenora B. Fulani and Joyce Dattner	New Alliance
47,047	David E. Duke and Floyd C. Parker	Populist
30,905	Eugene J. McCarthy and Florence Rice	Consumer
27,818	James C. Griffin and Charles J. Morsa	American Independent
25,562	Lyndon H. LaRouche and Debra H. Freeman	National Economic Recovery
20,504	William A. Matra and Joan Andrews	Right to Life
18,693	Ed Winn and Barry Porster	Workers League
15,604	James Warren and Kathleen Mickells	Socialist Workers
10,370	Herbert Lewin and Vikki Murdock	Peace and Freedom
8,002	Earl F. Dodge and George Ormsby	Prohibition
7,846	Larry Holmes and Gloria LaRiva	Workers World
3,882	Willa Kenoyer and Ron Ehrenreich	Socialist
3,475	Delmar Dennis and Earl Jeppson	American
1,949	Jack Herer and Dana Beal	Grassroots
372	Louie G. Youngkeit and no vice-presidential candidate	Independent
236	John G. Martin and Cleveland Sparrow	Third World Assembly

Notes: The candidates listed above are those who appeared on the ballot in at least one state. Republican, Democratic, and New Alliance candidates appeared on the ballot in all 51 jurisdictions. The Libertarian nominees were on the ballot in 47 jurisdictions. Where identified by state authorities, write-in votes for minor party candidates were credited to their total above. In addition to the votes listed, 21,041 scattered write-in votes were reported from various states, and 6,934 votes were cast for "None of These Candidates" in Nevada.

UNITED STATES
PRESIDENT 1988

State	Electoral Vote Rep.	Electoral Vote Dem.	Electoral Vote Other	Total Vote	Republican	Democratic	Other	Plurality		Percentage Total Vote Rep.	Percentage Total Vote Dem.	Percentage Major Vote Rep.	Percentage Major Vote Dem.
Alabama	9			1,378,476	815,576	549,506	13,394	266,070	R	59.2%	39.9%	59.7%	40.3%
Alaska	3			200,116	119,251	72,584	8,281	46,667	R	59.6%	36.3%	62.2%	37.8%
Arizona	7			1,171,873	702,541	454,029	15,303	248,512	R	60.0%	38.7%	60.7%	39.3%
Arkansas	6			827,738	466,578	349,237	11,923	117,341	R	56.4%	42.2%	57.2%	42.8%
California	47			9,887,065	5,054,917	4,702,233	129,915	352,684	R	51.1%	47.6%	51.8%	48.2%
Colorado	8			1,372,394	728,177	621,453	22,764	106,724	R	53.1%	45.3%	54.0%	46.0%
Connecticut	8			1,443,394	750,241	676,584	16,569	73,657	R	52.0%	46.9%	52.6%	47.4%
Delaware	3			249,891	139,639	108,647	1,605	30,992	R	55.9%	43.5%	56.2%	43.8%
Florida	21			4,302,313	2,618,885	1,656,701	26,727	962,184	R	60.9%	38.5%	61.3%	38.7%
Georgia	12			1,809,672	1,081,331	714,792	13,549	366,539	R	59.8%	39.5%	60.2%	39.8%
Hawaii		4		354,461	158,625	192,364	3,472	33,739	D	44.8%	54.3%	45.2%	54.8%
Idaho	4			408,968	253,881	147,272	7,815	106,609	R	62.1%	36.0%	63.3%	36.7%
Illinois	24			4,559,120	2,310,939	2,215,940	32,241	94,999	R	50.7%	48.6%	51.0%	49.0%
Indiana	12			2,168,621	1,297,763	860,643	10,215	437,120	R	59.8%	39.7%	60.1%	39.9%
Iowa		8		1,225,614	545,355	670,557	9,702	125,202	D	44.5%	54.7%	44.9%	55.1%
Kansas	7			993,044	554,049	422,636	16,359	131,413	R	55.8%	42.6%	56.7%	43.3%
Kentucky	9			1,322,517	734,281	580,368	7,868	153,913	R	55.5%	43.9%	55.9%	44.1%
Louisiana	10			1,628,202	883,702	717,460	27,040	166,242	R	54.3%	44.1%	55.2%	44.8%
Maine	4			555,035	307,131	243,569	4,335	63,562	R	55.3%	43.9%	55.8%	44.2%
Maryland	10			1,714,358	876,167	826,304	11,887	49,863	R	51.1%	48.2%	51.5%	48.5%
Massachusetts		13		2,632,805	1,194,635	1,401,415	36,755	206,780	D	45.4%	53.2%	46.0%	54.0%
Michigan	20			3,669,163	1,965,486	1,675,783	27,894	289,703	R	53.6%	45.7%	54.0%	46.0%
Minnesota		10		2,096,790	962,337	1,109,471	24,982	147,134	D	45.9%	52.9%	46.4%	53.6%
Mississippi	7			931,527	557,890	363,921	9,716	193,969	R	59.9%	39.1%	60.5%	39.5%
Missouri	11			2,093,713	1,084,953	1,001,619	7,141	83,334	R	51.8%	47.8%	52.0%	48.0%
Montana	4			365,674	190,412	168,936	6,326	21,476	R	52.1%	46.2%	53.0%	47.0%
Nebraska	5			661,465	397,956	259,235	4,274	138,721	R	60.2%	39.2%	60.6%	39.4%
Nevada	4			350,067	206,040	132,738	11,289	73,302	R	58.9%	37.9%	60.8%	39.2%
New Hampshire	4			451,074	281,537	163,696	5,841	117,841	R	62.4%	36.3%	63.2%	36.8%
New Jersey	16			3,099,553	1,743,192	1,320,352	36,009	422,840	R	56.2%	42.6%	56.9%	43.1%
New Mexico	5			521,287	270,341	244,497	6,449	25,844	R	51.9%	46.9%	52.5%	47.5%
New York		36		6,485,683	3,081,871	3,347,882	55,930	266,011	D	47.5%	51.6%	47.9%	52.1%
North Carolina	13			2,134,370	1,237,258	890,167	6,945	347,091	R	58.0%	41.7%	58.2%	41.8%
North Dakota	3			297,261	166,559	127,739	2,963	38,820	R	56.0%	43.0%	56.6%	43.4%
Ohio	23			4,393,699	2,416,549	1,939,629	37,521	476,920	R	55.0%	44.1%	55.5%	44.5%
Oklahoma	8			1,171,036	678,367	483,423	9,246	194,944	R	57.9%	41.3%	58.4%	41.6%
Oregon		7		1,201,694	560,126	616,206	25,362	56,080	D	46.6%	51.3%	47.6%	52.4%
Pennsylvania	25			4,536,251	2,300,087	2,194,944	41,220	105,143	R	50.7%	48.4%	51.2%	48.8%
Rhode Island		4		404,620	177,761	225,123	1,736	47,362	D	43.9%	55.6%	44.1%	55.9%
South Carolina	8			986,009	606,443	370,554	9,012	235,889	R	61.5%	37.6%	62.1%	37.9%
South Dakota	3			312,991	165,415	145,560	2,016	19,855	R	52.8%	46.5%	53.2%	46.8%
Tennessee	11			1,636,250	947,233	679,794	9,223	267,439	R	57.9%	41.5%	58.2%	41.8%
Texas	29			5,427,410	3,036,829	2,352,748	37,833	684,081	R	56.0%	43.3%	56.3%	43.7%
Utah	5			647,008	428,442	207,343	11,223	221,099	R	66.2%	32.0%	67.4%	32.6%
Vermont	3			243,328	124,331	115,775	3,222	8,556	R	51.1%	47.6%	51.8%	48.2%
Virginia	12			2,191,609	1,309,162	859,799	22,648	449,363	R	59.7%	39.2%	60.4%	39.6%
Washington		10		1,865,253	903,835	933,516	27,902	29,681	D	48.5%	50.0%	49.2%	50.8%
West Virginia		5	1	653,311	310,065	341,016	2,230	30,951	D	47.5%	52.2%	47.6%	52.4%
Wisconsin		11		2,191,608	1,047,499	1,126,794	17,315	79,295	D	47.8%	51.4%	48.2%	51.8%
Wyoming	3			176,551	106,867	67,113	2,571	39,754	R	60.5%	38.0%	61.4%	38.6%
District of Columbia		3		192,877	27,590	159,407	5,880	131,817	D	14.3%	82.6%	14.8%	85.2%
Total	426	111	1	91,594,809	48,886,097	41,809,074	899,638	7,077,023	R	53.4%	45.6%	53.9%	46.1%

Note: Due to a faithless elector, Dukakis's running mate, Lloyd Bentsen, received one (1) electoral vote.

UNITED STATES
PRESIDENT 1984

In New York the Republican figures include Conservative votes and the Democratic figures include Liberal votes.

In Minnesota the Republican candidates appear on the ballot as Independent-Republican, the Democratic as Democratic-Farmer-Labor. In many states various non-major party candidates appeared on the ballot with variations of the party designations, were listed as "Independent" or "Non-Party," or were carried with entirely different party labels.

The Workers World candidate for president was Gavrielle Holmes in Ohio and Rhode Island; in several states minor party vice-presidential candidates were different from those listed below.

The full list of candidates for president and vice president was:

54,455,075	Ronald Reagan and George Bush	Republican
37,577,185	Walter F. Mondale and Geraldine A. Ferraro	Democratic
228,314	David Bergland and James A. Lewis	Libertarian
78,807	Lyndon H. LaRouche Jr. and Billy M. Davis	Independent
72,200	Sonia Johnson and Richard Walton	Citizens
66,336	Bob Richards and Maureen Salaman	Populist
46,868	Dennis L. Serrette and Nancy Ross	Alliance
36,386	Gus Hall and Angela Davis	Communist
24,706	Mel Mason and Matilde Zimmermann	Socialist Workers
17,985	Larry Holmes and Gloria La Riva	Workers World
13,161	Delmar Dennis and Traves Brownlee	American
10,801	Ed Winn and Helen Halyard	Workers League
4,242	Earl F. Dodge and Warren C. Martin	Prohibition
1,486	John B. Anderson and Grace Pierce	National Unity
892	Gerald Baker and Ferris Alger	Big Deal
825	Arthur J. Lowery and Raymond L. Garland	United Sovereign Citizens

Notes: The candidates listed above are those who appeared on the ballot in at least one state. Where identified by state authorities, write-in votes for minor party candidates are credited to their total above. In addition to the votes listed above, 13,623 scattered write-in votes were reported from various states, and 3,950 votes were cast for "None of These Candidates" in Nevada.

UNITED STATES
PRESIDENT 1984

State	Electoral Vote Rep.	Electoral Vote Dem.	Total Vote	Republican	Democratic	Other	Plurality		Percentage Total Vote Rep.	Total Vote Dem.	Major Vote Rep.	Major Vote Dem.
Alabama	9		1,441,713	872,849	551,899	16,965	320,950	R	60.5%	38.3%	61.3%	38.7%
Alaska	3		207,605	138,377	62,007	7,221	76,370	R	66.7%	29.9%	69.1%	30.9%
Arizona	7		1,025,897	681,416	333,854	10,627	347,562	R	66.4%	32.5%	67.1%	32.9%
Arkansas	6		884,406	534,774	338,646	10,986	196,128	R	60.5%	38.3%	61.2%	38.8%
California	47		9,505,423	5,467,009	3,922,519	115,895	1,544,490	R	57.5%	41.3%	58.2%	41.8%
Colorado	8		1,295,380	821,817	454,975	18,588	366,842	R	63.4%	35.1%	64.4%	35.6%
Connecticut	8		1,466,900	890,877	569,597	6,426	321,280	R	60.7%	38.8%	61.0%	39.0%
Delaware	3		254,572	152,190	101,656	726	50,534	R	59.8%	39.9%	60.0%	40.0%
Florida	21		4,180,051	2,730,350	1,448,816	885	1,281,534	R	65.3%	34.7%	65.3%	34.7%
Georgia	12		1,776,120	1,068,722	706,628	770	362,094	R	60.2%	39.8%	60.2%	39.8%
Hawaii	4		335,846	185,050	147,154	3,642	37,896	R	55.1%	43.8%	55.7%	44.3%
Idaho	4		411,144	297,523	108,510	5,111	189,013	R	72.4%	26.4%	73.3%	26.7%
Illinois	24		4,819,088	2,707,103	2,086,499	25,486	620,604	R	56.2%	43.3%	56.5%	43.5%
Indiana	12		2,233,069	1,377,230	841,481	14,358	535,749	R	61.7%	37.7%	62.1%	37.9%
Iowa	8		1,319,805	703,088	605,620	11,097	97,468	R	53.3%	45.9%	53.7%	46.3%
Kansas	7		1,021,991	677,296	333,149	11,546	344,147	R	66.3%	32.6%	67.0%	33.0%
Kentucky	9		1,369,345	821,702	539,539	8,104	282,163	R	60.0%	39.4%	60.4%	39.6%
Louisiana	10		1,706,822	1,037,299	651,586	17,937	385,713	R	60.8%	38.2%	61.4%	38.6%
Maine	4		553,144	336,500	214,515	2,129	121,985	R	60.8%	38.8%	61.1%	38.9%
Maryland	10		1,675,873	879,918	787,935	8,020	91,983	R	52.5%	47.0%	52.8%	47.2%
Massachusetts	13		2,559,453	1,310,936	1,239,606	8,911	71,330	R	51.2%	48.4%	51.4%	48.6%
Michigan	20		3,801,658	2,251,571	1,529,638	20,449	721,933	R	59.2%	40.2%	59.5%	40.5%
Minnesota		10	2,084,449	1,032,603	1,036,364	15,482	3,761	D	49.5%	49.7%	49.9%	50.1%
Mississippi	7		941,104	582,377	352,192	6,535	230,185	R	61.9%	37.4%	62.3%	37.7%
Missouri	11		2,122,783	1,274,188	848,583	12	425,605	R	60.0%	40.0%	60.0%	40.0%
Montana	4		384,377	232,450	146,742	5,185	85,708	R	60.5%	38.2%	61.3%	38.7%
Nebraska	5		652,090	460,054	187,866	4,170	272,188	R	70.6%	28.8%	71.0%	29.0%
Nevada	4		286,667	188,770	91,655	6,242	97,115	R	65.8%	32.0%	67.3%	32.7%
New Hampshire	4		389,066	267,051	120,395	1,620	146,656	R	68.6%	30.9%	68.9%	31.1%
New Jersey	16		3,217,862	1,933,630	1,261,323	22,909	672,307	R	60.1%	39.2%	60.5%	3 9.5%
New Mexico	5		514,370	307,101	201,769	5,500	105,332	R	59.7%	39.2%	60.3%	39.7%
New York	36		6,806,810	3,664,763	3,119,609	22,438	545,154	R	53.8%	45.8%	54.0%	46.0%
North Carolina	13		2,175,361	1,346,481	824,287	4,593	522,194	R	61.9%	37.9%	62.0%	38.0%
North Dakota	3		308,971	200,336	104,429	4,206	95,907	R	64.8%	33.8%	65.7%	34.3%
Ohio	23		4,547,619	2,678,560	1,825,440	43,619	853,120	R	58.9%	40.1%	59.5%	40.5%
Oklahoma	8		1,255,676	861,530	385,080	9,066	476,450	R	68.6%	30.7%	69.1%	30.9%
Oregon	7		1,226,527	685,700	536,479	4,348	149,221	R	55.9%	43.7%	56.1%	43.9%
Pennsylvania	25		4,844,903	2,584,323	2,228,131	32,449	356,192	R	53.3%	46.0%	53.7%	46.3%
Rhode Island	4		410,492	212,080	197,106	1,306	14,974	R	51.7%	48.0%	51.8%	48.2%
South Carolina	8		968,529	615,539	344,459	8,531	271,080	R	63.6%	35.6%	64.1%	35.9%
South Dakota	3		317,867	200,267	116,113	1,487	84,154	R	63.0%	36.5%	63.3%	36.7%
Tennessee	11		1,711,994	990,212	711,714	10,068	278,498	R	57.8%	41.6%	58.2%	41.8%
Texas	29		5,397,571	3,433,428	1,949,276	14,867	1,484,152	R	63.6%	36.1%	63.8%	36.2%
Utah	5		629,656	469,105	155,369	5,182	313,736	R	74.5%	24.7%	75.1%	24.9%
Vermont	3		234,561	135,865	95,730	2,966	40,135	R	57.9%	40.8%	58.7%	41.3%
Virginia	12		2,146,635	1,337,078	796,250	13,307	540,828	R	62.3%	37.1%	62.7%	37.3%
Washington	10		1,883,910	1,051,670	807,352	24,888	244,318	R	55.8%	42.9%	56.6%	43.4%
West Virginia	6		735,742	405,483	328,125	2,134	77,358	R	55.1%	44.6%	55.3%	44.7%
Wisconsin	11		2,211,689	1,198,584	995,740	17,365	202,844	R	54.2%	45.0%	54.6%	45.4%
Wyoming	3		188,968	133,241	53,370	2,357	79,871	R	70.5%	28.2%	71.4%	28.6%
District of Columbia		3	211,288	29,009	180,408	1,871	151,399	D	13.7%	85.4%	13.9%	86.1%
Total	525	13	92,652,842	54,455,075	37,577,185	620,582	16,877,890	R	58.8%	40.6%	59.2%	40.8%

UNITED STATES
PRESIDENT 1980

In New York the Republican figures include Conservative votes. In many states various non-major party candidates appeared on the ballot with variations of the party designations, without any party designation, or with entirely different party names.

In several cases vice-presidential nominees were different from those listed for most states. The Socialist Workers Party nominee for president varied from state to state.

43,904,153	Ronald Reagan and George Bush	Republican
35,483,883	Jimmy Carter and Walter F. Mondale	Democratic
5,720,060	John B. Anderson and Patrick J. Lucey	Independent
921,299	Edward E. Clark and David Koch	Libertarian
234,294	Barry Commoner and LaDonna Harris	Citizens
45,023	Gus Hall and Angela Davis	Communist
41,268	John R. Rarick and Eileen M. Shearer	American Independent
38,737	Clifton DeBerry and Matilde Zimmermann	Socialist Workers
32,327	Ellen McCormack and Carroll Driscoll	Right to Life
18,116	Maureen Smith and Elizabeth Barron	Peace and Freedom
13,300	Deirdre Griswold and Larry Holmes	Workers World
7,212	Benjamin C. Bubar and Earl F. Dodge	Statesman
6,898	David McReynolds and Diane Drufenbrock	Socialist
6,647	Percy L. Greaves and Frank L. Varnum	American
6,272	Andrew Pulley and Matilde Zimmermann	Socialist Workers
4,029	Richard Congress and Matilde Zimmermann	Socialist Workers
3,694	Kurt Lynen and Harry Kieve	Middle Class
1,718	Bill Gahres and J. F. Loughlin	Down With Lawyers
1,555	Frank W. Shelton and George E. Jackson	American
923	Martin E. Wendelken and no vice-presidential candidate	Independent
296	Harley McLain and Jewelie Goeller	Natural Peoples

Notes: In addition to the votes listed above, 13,185 scattered write-in votes were reported from various states, 6,139 votes were cast in Minnesota for American Party electors without designated national nominees, and 4,193 votes were cast for "None of These Candidates" in Nevada.

UNITED STATES
PRESIDENT 1980

State	Electoral Vote Rep.	Electoral Vote Dem.	Total Vote	Republican	Democratic	Other	Plurality		Percentage Total Vote Rep.	Percentage Total Vote Dem.	Percentage Major Vote Rep.	Percentage Major Vote Dem.
Alabama	9		1,341,929	654,192	636,730	51,007	17,462	R	48.8%	47.4%	50.7%	49.3%
Alaska	3		158,445	86,112	41,842	30,491	44,270	R	54.3%	26.4%	67.3%	32.7%
Arizona	6		873,945	529,688	246,843	97,414	282,845	R	60.6%	28.2%	68.2%	31.8%
Arkansas	6		837,582	403,164	398,041	36,377	5,123	R	48.1%	47.5%	50.3%	49.7%
California	45		8,587,063	4,524,858	3,083,661	978,544	1,441,197	R	52.7%	35.9%	59.5%	40.5%
Colorado	7		1,184,415	652,264	367,973	164,178	284,291	R	55.1%	31.1%	63.9%	36.1%
Connecticut	8		1,406,285	677,210	541,732	187,343	135,478	R	48.2%	38.5%	55.6%	44.4%
Delaware	3		235,900	111,252	105,754	18,894	5,498	R	47.2%	44.8%	51.3%	48.7%
Florida	17		3,686,930	2,046,951	1,419,475	220,504	627,476	R	55.5%	38.5%	59.1%	40.9%
Georgia		12	1,596,695	654,168	890,733	51,794	236,565	D	41.0%	55.8%	42.3%	57.7%
Hawaii		4	303,287	130,112	135,879	37,296	5,767	D	42.9%	44.8%	48.9%	51.1%
Idaho	4		437,431	290,699	110,192	36,540	180,507	R	66.5%	25.2%	72.5%	27.5%
Illinois	26		4,749,721	2,358,049	1,981,413	410,259	376,636	R	49.6%	41.7%	54.3%	45.7%
Indiana	13		2,242,033	1,255,656	844,197	142,180	411,459	R	56.0%	37.7%	59.8%	40.2%
Iowa	8		1,317,661	676,026	508,672	132,963	167,354	R	51.3%	38.6%	57.1%	42.9%
Kansas	7		979,795	566,812	326,150	86,833	240,662	R	57.9%	33.3%	63.5%	36.5%
Kentucky	9		1,294,627	635,274	616,417	42,936	18,857	R	49.1%	47.6%	50.8%	49.2%
Louisiana	10		1,548,591	792,853	708,453	47,285	84,400	R	51.2%	45.7%	52.8%	47.2%
Maine	4		523,011	238,522	220,974	63,515	17,548	R	45.6%	42.3%	51.9%	48.1%
Maryland		10	1,540,496	680,606	726,161	133,729	45,555	D	44.2%	47.1%	48.4%	51.6%
Massachusetts	14		2,524,298	1,057,631	1,053,802	412,865	3,829	R	41.9%	41.7%	50.1%	49.9%
Michigan	21		3,909,725	1,915,225	1,661,532	332,968	253,693	R	49.0%	42.5%	53.5%	46.5%
Minnesota		10	2,051,980	873,268	954,174	224,538	80,906	D	42.6%	46.5%	47.8%	52.2%
Mississippi	7		892,620	441,089	429,281	22,250	11,808	R	49.4%	48.1%	50.7%	49.3%
Missouri	12		2,099,824	1,074,181	931,182	94,461	142,999	R	51.2%	44.3%	53.6%	46.4%
Montana	4		363,952	206,814	118,032	39,106	88,782	R	56.8%	32.4%	63.7%	36.3%
Nebraska	5		640,854	419,937	166,851	54,066	253,086	R	65.5%	26.0%	71.6%	28.4%
Nevada	3		247,885	155,017	66,666	26,202	88,351	R	62.5%	26.9%	69.9%	30.1%
New Hampshire	4		383,990	221,705	108,864	53,421	112,841	R	57.7%	28.4%	67.1%	32.9%
New Jersey	17		2,975,684	1,546,557	1,147,364	281,763	399,193	R	52.0%	38.6%	57.4%	42.6%
New Mexico	4		456,971	250,779	167,826	38,366	82,953	R	54.9%	36.7%	59.9%	40.1%
New York	41		6,201,959	2,893,831	2,728,372	579,756	165,459	R	46.7%	44.0%	51.5%	48.5%
North Carolina	13		1,855,833	915,018	875,635	65,180	39,383	R	49.3%	47.2%	51.1%	48.9%
North Dakota	3		301,545	193,695	79,189	28,661	114,506	R	64.2%	26.3%	71.0%	29.0%
Ohio	25		4,283,603	2,206,545	1,752,414	324,644	454,131	R	51.5%	40.9%	55.7%	44.3%
Oklahoma	8		1,149,708	695,570	402,026	52,112	293,544	R	60.5%	35.0%	63.4%	36.6%
Oregon	6		1,181,516	571,044	456,890	153,582	114,154	R	48.3%	38.7%	55.6%	44.4%
Pennsylvania	27		4,561,501	2,261,872	1,937,540	362,089	324,332	R	49.6%	42.5%	53.9%	46.1%
Rhode Island		4	416,072	154,793	198,342	62,937	43,549	D	37.2%	47.7%	43.8%	56.2%
South Carolina	8		894,071	441,841	430,385	21,845	11,456	R	49.4%	48.1%	50.7%	49.3%
South Dakota	4		327,703	198,343	103,855	25,505	94,488	R	60.5%	31.7%	65.6%	34.4%
Tennessee	10		1,617,616	787,761	783,051	46,804	4,710	R	48.7%	48.4%	50.1%	49.9%
Texas	26		4,541,636	2,510,705	1,881,147	149,784	629,558	R	55.3%	41.4%	57.2%	42.8%
Utah	4		604,222	439,687	124,266	40,269	315,421	R	72.8%	20.6%	78.0%	22.0%
Vermont	3		213,299	94,628	81,952	36,719	12,676	R	44.4%	38.4%	53.6%	46.4%
Virginia	12		1,866,032	989,609	752,174	124,249	237,435	R	53.0%	40.3%	56.8%	43.2%
Washington	9		1,742,394	865,244	650,193	226,957	215,051	R	49.7%	37.3%	57.1%	42.9%
West Virginia		6	737,715	334,206	367,462	36,047	33,256	D	45.3%	49.8%	47.6%	52.4%
Wisconsin	11		2,273,221	1,088,845	981,584	202,792	107,261	R	47.9%	43.2%	52.6%	47.4%
Wyoming	3		176,713	110,700	49,427	16,586	61,273	R	62.6%	28.0%	69.1%	30.9%
District of Columbia		3	175,237	23,545	131,113	20,579	107,568	D	13.4%	74.8%	15.2%	84.8%
Total	489	49	86,515,221	43,904,153	35,483,883	7,127,185	8,420,270	R	50.7%	41.0%	55.3%	44.7%

UNITED STATES
PRESIDENT 1976

In Washington one Republican elector voted for Ronald Reagan for president and Robert Dole for vice president.

In New York the Republican figures include Conservative votes, and the Democratic figures include Liberal votes; in Vermont the Democratic figures include votes cast on the Independent Vermonters Party ticket.

In many states various non-major party candidates appeared on the ballot with variations of the party designations and in several states with entirely different party names.

The ballot designations for electors for Eugene J. McCarthy for president varied from state to state, as did the names of vice-presidential candidates running with him. In New Jersey the Maddox vice-presidential candidate was Edmund O. Matzal.

The full list of candidates for president and vice president was:

40,830,763	Jimmy Carter and Walter F. Mondale	Democratic
39,147,793	Gerald R. Ford and Robert Dole	Republican
756,691	Eugene J. McCarthy and various vice-presidential candidates	Independent
173,011	Roger L. MacBride and David D. Bergland	Libertarian
170,531	Lester G. Maddox and William D. Dyke	American Independent
160,773	Thomas J. Anderson and Rufus Shackelford	American
91,314	Peter Camejo and Willie Mae Reid	Socialist Workers
58,992	Gus Hall and Jarvis Tyner	Communist
49,024	Margaret Wright and Benjamin Spock	People's
40,043	Lyndon H. LaRouche Jr. and R. W. Evans	United States Labor
15,934	Benjamin C. Bubar and Earl F. Dodge	Prohibition
9,616	Julius Levin and Constance Blomen	Socialist Labor
6,038	Frank P. Zeidler and J. Q. Brisben	Socialist
361	Ernest L. Miller and Roy N. Eddy	Restoration
36	Frank Taylor and Henry Swan	United American

Notes: In addition to the votes listed above, 39,861 scattered write-in votes were reported from various states, and 5,108 votes were cast for "None of These Candidates" in Nevada.

UNITED STATES
PRESIDENT 1976

State	Electoral Vote Rep.	Dem.	Other	Total Vote	Republican	Democratic	Other	Plurality		Percentage Total Vote Rep.	Dem.	Major Vote Rep.	Dem.
Alabama		9		1,182,850	504,070	659,170	19,610	155,100	D	42.6%	55.7%	43.3%	56.7%
Alaska	3			123,574	71,555	44,058	7,961	27,497	R	57.9%	35.7%	61.9%	38.1%
Arizona	6			742,719	418,642	295,602	28,475	123,040	R	56.4%	39.8%	58.6%	41.4%
Arkansas		6		767,535	267,903	498,604	1,028	230,701	D	34.9%	65.0%	35.0%	65.0%
California	45			7,867,117	3,882,244	3,742,284	242,589	139,960	R	49.3%	47.6%	50.9%	49.1%
Colorado	7			1,081,554	584,367	460,353	36,834	124,014	R	54.0%	42.6%	55.9%	44.1%
Connecticut	8			1,381,526	719,261	647,895	14,370	71,366	R	52.1%	46.9%	52.6%	47.4%
Delaware		3		235,834	109,831	122,596	3,407	12,765	D	46.6%	52.0%	47.3%	52.7%
Florida		17		3,150,631	1,469,531	1,636,000	45,100	166,469	D	46.6%	51.9%	47.3%	52.7%
Georgia		12		1,467,458	483,743	979,409	4,306	495,666	D	33.0%	66.7%	33.1%	66.9%
Hawaii		4		291,301	140,003	147,375	3,923	7,372	D	48.1%	50.6%	48.7%	51.3%
Idaho	4			344,071	204,151	126,549	13,371	77,602	R	59.3%	36.8%	61.7%	38.3%
Illinois	26			4,718,914	2,364,269	2,271,295	83,350	92,974	R	50.1%	48.1%	51.0%	49.0%
Indiana	13			2,220,362	1,183,958	1,014,714	21,690	169,244	R	53.3%	45.7%	53.8%	46.2%
Iowa	8			1,279,306	632,863	619,931	26,512	12,932	R	49.5%	48.5%	50.5%	49.5%
Kansas	7			957,845	502,752	430,421	24,672	72,331	R	52.5%	44.9%	53.9%	46.1%
Kentucky		9		1,167,142	531,852	615,717	19,573	83,865	D	45.6%	52.8%	46.3%	53.7%
Louisiana		10		1,278,439	587,446	661,365	29,628	73,919	D	46.0%	51.7%	47.0%	53.0%
Maine	4			483,216	236,320	232,279	14,617	4,041	R	48.9%	48.1%	50.4%	49.6%
Maryland		10		1,439,897	672,661	759,612	7,624	86,951	D	46.7%	52.8%	47.0%	53.0%
Massachusetts		14		2,547,558	1,030,276	1,429,475	87,807	399,199	D	40.4%	56.1%	41.9%	58.1%
Michigan	21			3,653,749	1,893,742	1,696,714	63,293	197,028	R	51.8%	46.4%	52.7%	47.3%
Minnesota		10		1,949,931	819,395	1,070,440	60,096	251,045	D	42.0%	54.9%	43.4%	56.6%
Mississippi		7		769,361	366,846	381,309	21,206	14,463	D	47.7%	49.6%	49.0%	51.0%
Missouri		12		1,953,600	927,443	998,387	27,770	70,944	D	47.5%	51.1%	48.2%	51.8%
Montana	4			328,734	173,703	149,259	5,772	24,444	R	52.8%	45.4%	53.8%	46.2%
Nebraska	5			607,668	359,705	233,692	14,271	126,013	R	59.2%	38.5%	60.6%	39.4%
Nevada	3			201,876	101,273	92,479	8,124	8,794	R	50.2%	45.8%	52.3%	47.7%
New Hampshire	4			339,618	185,935	147,635	6,048	38,300	R	54.7%	43.5%	55.7%	44.3%
New Jersey	17			3,014,472	1,509,688	1,444,653	60,131	65,035	R	50.1%	47.9%	51.1%	48.9%
New Mexico	4			418,409	211,419	201,148	5,842	10,271	R	50.5%	48.1%	51.2%	48.8%
New York		41		6,534,170	3,100,791	3,389,558	43,821	288,767	D	47.5%	51.9%	47.8%	52.2%
North Carolina		13		1,678,914	741,960	927,365	9,589	185,405	D	44.2%	55.2%	44.4%	55.6%
North Dakota	3			297,188	153,470	136,078	7,640	17,392	R	51.6%	45.8%	53.0%	47.0%
Ohio		25		4,111,873	2,000,505	2,011,621	99,747	11,116	D	48.7%	48.9%	49.9%	50.1%
Oklahoma	8			1,092,251	545,708	532,442	14,101	13,266	R	50.0%	48.7%	50.6%	49.4%
Oregon	6			1,029,876	492,120	490,407	47,349	1,713	R	47.8%	47.6%	50.1%	49.9%
Pennsylvania		27		4,620,787	2,205,604	2,328,677	86,506	123,073	D	47.7%	50.4%	48.6%	51.4%
Rhode Island		4		411,170	181,249	227,636	2,285	46,387	D	44.1%	55.4%	44.3%	55.7%
South Carolina		8		802,583	346,149	450,807	5,627	104,658	D	43.1%	56.2%	43.4%	56.6%
South Dakota	4			300,678	151,505	147,068	2,105	4,437	R	50.4%	48.9%	50.7%	49.3%
Tennessee		10		1,476,345	633,969	825,879	16,497	191,910	D	42.9%	55.9%	43.4%	56.6%
Texas		26		4,071,884	1,953,300	2,082,319	36,265	129,019	D	48.0%	51.1%	48.4%	51.6%
Utah	4			541,198	337,908	182,110	21,180	155,798	R	62.4%	33.6%	65.0%	35.0%
Vermont	3			187,765	102,085	80,954	4,726	21,131	R	54.4%	43.1%	55.8%	44.2%
Virginia	12			1,697,094	836,554	813,896	46,644	22,658	R	49.3%	48.0%	50.7%	49.3%
Washington	8		1	1,555,534	777,732	717,323	60,479	60,409	R	50.0%	46.1%	52.0%	48.0%
West Virginia		6		750,964	314,760	435,914	290	121,154	D	41.9%	58.0%	41.9%	58.1%
Wisconsin		11		2,104,175	1,004,987	1,040,232	58,956	35,245	D	47.8%	49.4%	49.1%	50.9%
Wyoming	3			156,343	92,717	62,239	1,387	30,478	R	59.3%	39.8%	59.8%	40.2%
District of Columbia		3		168,830	27,873	137,818	3,139	109,945	D	16.5%	81.6%	16.8%	83.2%
Total	240	297	1	81,555,889	39,147,793	40,830,763	1,577,333	1,682,970	D	48.0%	50.1%	48.9%	51.1%

Note: Due to a faithless elector, Ronald Reagan received one (1) electoral vote.

UNITED STATES
PRESIDENT 1972

In Virginia one Republican elector voted for the Libertarian candidates for president and vice president.

In New York the Republican figures include Conservative votes and the Democratic figures include Liberal votes. In Alabama the Democratic figures include votes cast on the National Democratic Party of Alabama ticket, and in South Carolina they include United Citizens Party votes.

In many states various non-major party candidates appeared on the ballot under party names other than those used below; for the Socialist Workers Party the votes listed for Jenness and Pulley were actually cast for substitute candidates (Reed and DeBerry) or without named candidates in several states.

The Democratic vice-presidential candidate originally was Sen. Thomas F. Eagleton; upon his withdrawal shortly after the party convention, R. Sargent Shriver was named by the Democratic National Committee as the candidate.

The full list of candidates for president and vice president was:

47,169,911	Richard M. Nixon and Spiro T. Agnew	Republican
29,170,383	George S. McGovern and R. Sargent Shriver	Democratic
1,099,482	John G. Schmitz and Thomas J. Anderson	American
78,756	Benjamin Spock and Julius Hobson	People's
66,677	Linda Jenness and Andrew Pulley	Socialist Workers
53,814	Louis Fisher and Genevieve Gunderson	Socialist Labor
25,595	Gus Hail and Jarvis Tyner	Communist
13,505	E. Harold Munn and Marshall E. Uncapher	Prohibition
3,673	John Hospers and Theodora Nathan	Libertarian
1,743	John V. Mahalchik and Irving Homer	America First
220	Gabriel Green and Daniel Fry	Universal

Notes: In addition to the votes listed above, 34,795 scattered write-in votes were reported from various states. Vice President Agnew resigned in October 1973 and Rep. Gerald R. Ford of Michigan was nominated by President Nixon to fill the vacancy. In November (Senate) and December (House of Representatives) this action was approved by Congress. In August 1974 President Nixon resigned and was succeeded by Vice President Ford. In the same month Nelson A. Rockefeller, former governor of New York, was nominated to be vice president and was confirmed by Congress in December 1974.

UNITED STATES
PRESIDENT 1972

State	Electoral Vote Rep.	Electoral Vote Dem.	Electoral Vote Other	Total Vote	Republican	Democratic	Other	Plurality		Percentage Total Vote Rep.	Percentage Total Vote Dem.	Percentage Major Vote Rep.	Percentage Major Vote Dem.
Alabama	9			1,006,111	728,701	256,923	20,487	471,778	R	72.4%	25.5%	73.9%	26.1%
Alaska	3			95,219	55,349	32,967	6,903	22,382	R	58.1%	34.6%	62.7%	37.3%
Arizona	6			622,926	402,812	198,540	21,574	204,272	R	64.7%	31.9%	67.0%	33.0%
Arkansas	6			651,320	448,541	199,892	2,887	248,649	R	68.9%	30.7%	69.2%	30.8%
California	45			8,367,862	4,602,096	3,475,847	289,919	1,126,249	R	55.0%	41.5%	57.0%	43.0%
Colorado	7			953,884	597,189	329,980	26,715	267,209	R	62.6%	34.6%	64.4%	35.6%
Connecticut	8			1,384,277	810,763	555,498	18,016	255,265	R	58.6%	40.1%	59.3%	40.7%
Delaware	3			235,516	140,357	92,283	2,876	48,074	R	59.6%	39.2%	60.3%	39.7%
Florida	17			2,583,283	1,857,759	718,117	7,407	1,139,642	R	71.9%	27.8%	72.1%	27.9%
Georgia	12			1,174,772	881,496	289,529	3,747	591,967	R	75.0%	24.6%	75.3%	24.7%
Hawaii	4			270,274	168,865	101,409		67,456	R	62.5%	37.5%	62.5%	37.5%
Idaho	4			310,379	199,384	80,826	30,169	118,558	R	64.2%	26.0%	71.2%	28.8%
Illinois	26			4,723,236	2,788,179	1,913,472	21,585	874,707	R	59.0%	40.5%	59.3%	40.7%
Indiana	13			2,125,529	1,405,154	708,568	11,807	696,586	R	66.1%	33.3%	66.5%	33.5%
Iowa	8			1,225,944	706,207	496,206	23,531	210,001	R	57.6%	40.5%	58.7%	41.3%
Kansas	7			916,095	619,812	270,287	25,996	349,525	R	67.7%	29.5%	69.6%	30.4%
Kentucky	9			1,067,499	676,446	371,159	19,894	305,287	R	63.4%	34.8%	64.6%	35.4%
Louisiana	10			1,051,491	686,852	298,142	66,497	388,710	R	65.3%	28.4%	69.7%	30.3%
Maine	4			417,042	256,458	160,584		95,874	R	61.5%	38.5%	61.5%	38.5%
Maryland	10			1,353,812	829,305	505,781	18,726	323,524	R	61.3%	37.4%	62.1%	37.9%
Massachusetts		14		2,458,756	1,112,078	1,332,540	14,138	220,462	D	45.2%	54.2%	45.5%	54.5%
Michigan	21			3,489,727	1,961,721	1,459,435	68,571	502,286	R	56.2%	41.8%	57.3%	42.7%
Minnesota	10			1,741,652	898,269	802,346	41,037	95,923	R	51.6%	46.1%	52.8%	47.2%
Mississippi	7			645,963	505,125	126,782	14,056	378,343	R	78.2%	19.6%	79.9%	20.1%
Missouri	12			1,855,803	1,153,852	697,147	4,804	456,705	R	62.2%	37.6%	62.3%	37.7%
Montana	4			317,603	183,976	120,197	13,430	63,779	R	57.9%	37.8%	60.5%	39.5%
Nebraska	5			576,289	406,298	169,991		236,307	R	70.5%	29.5%	70.5%	29.5%
Nevada	3			181,766	115,750	66,016		49,734	R	63.7%	36.3%	63.7%	36.3%
New Hampshire	4			334,055	213,724	116,435	3,896	97,289	R	64.0%	34.9%	64.7%	35.3%
New Jersey	17			2,997,229	1,845,502	1,102,211	49,516	743,291	R	61.6%	36.8%	62.6%	37.4%
New Mexico	4			386,241	235,606	141,084	9,551	94,522	R	61.0%	36.5%	62.5%	37.5%
New York	41			7,165,919	4,192,778	2,951,084	22,057	1,241,694	R	58.5%	41.2%	58.7%	41.3%
North Carolina	13			1,518,612	1,054,889	438,705	25,018	616,184	R	69.5%	28.9%	70.6%	29.4%
North Dakota	3			280,514	174,109	100,384	6,021	73,725	R	62.1%	35.8%	63.4%	36.6%
Ohio	25			4,094,787	2,441,827	1,558,889	94,071	882,938	R	59.6%	38.1%	61.0%	39.0%
Oklahoma	8			1,029,900	759,025	247,147	23,728	511,878	R	73.7%	24.0%	75.4%	24.6%
Oregon	6			927,946	486,686	392,760	48,500	93,926	R	52.4%	42.3%	55.3%	44.7%
Pennsylvania	27			4,592,106	2,714,521	1,796,951	80,634	917,570	R	59.1%	39.1%	60.2%	39.8%
Rhode Island	4			415,808	220,383	194,645	780	25,738	R	53.0%	46.8%	53.1%	46.9%
South Carolina	8			673,960	477,044	186,824	10,092	290,220	R	70.8%	27.7%	71.9%	28.1%
South Dakota	4			307,415	166,476	139,945	994	26,531	R	54.2%	45.5%	54.3%	45.7%
Tennessee	10			1,201,182	813,147	357,293	30,742	455,854	R	67.7%	29.7%	69.5%	30.5%
Texas	26			3,471,281	2,298,896	1,154,289	18,096	1,144,607	R	66.2%	33.3%	66.6%	33.4%
Utah	4			478,476	323,643	126,284	28,549	197,359	R	67.6%	26.4%	71.9%	28.1%
Vermont	3			186,947	117,149	68,174	1,624	48,975	R	62.7%	36.5%	63.2%	36.8%
Virginia	11		1	1,457,019	988,493	438,887	29,639	549,606	R	67.8%	30.1%	69.3%	30.7%
Washington	9			1,470,847	837,135	568,334	65,378	268,801	R	56.9%	38.6%	59.6%	40.4%
West Virginia	6			762,399	484,964	277,435		207,529	R	63.6%	36.4%	63.6%	36.4%
Wisconsin	11			1,852,890	989,430	810,174	53,286	179,256	R	53.4%	43.7%	55.0%	45.0%
Wyoming	3			145,570	100,464	44,358	748	56,106	R	69.0%	30.5%	69.4%	30.6%
District of Columbia		3		163,421	35,226	127,627	568	92,401	D	21.6%	78.1%	21.6%	78.4%
Total	520	17	1	77,718,554	47,169,911	29,170,383	1,378,260	17,999,528	R	60.7%	37.5%	61.8%	38.2%

Note: Due to a faithless elector, John Hospers (Libertarian) received one (1) electoral vote.

UNITED STATES
PRESIDENT 1968

In North Carolina one Republican elector voted for the American Independent candidates for president and vice president.

In New York the Democratic figure includes Liberal votes, and in Alabama the Democratic vote is the total of the Alabama Independent Democratic and National Democratic Party of Alabama vote. In many states various non-major party candidates appeared on the ballot with variations of the party designations, and in most states the vice-presidential candidate of the American Independent party was listed as Marvin Griffin rather than Curtis E. LeMay.

The full list of candidates for president and vice president was:

31,785,480	Richard M. Nixon and Spiro T. Agnew	Republican
31,275,166	Hubert H. Humphrey and Edmund S. Muskie	Democratic
9,906,473	George C. Wallace and Curtis E. LeMay	American Independent
52,588	Henning A. Blomen and George S. Taylor	Socialist Labor
47,133	Dick Gregory and various vice-presidential candidates	Peace and Freedom
41,388	Fred Halstead and Paul Boutelle	Socialist Workers
36,563	Eldridge Cleaver and various vice-presidential candidates	Peace and Freedom
25,552	Eugene J. McCarthy but without indication of vice-presidential candidates	Under various titles and written in
15,123	E. Harold Munn and Rolland E. Fisher	Prohibition
1,519	Ventura Chavez and Adelicio Moya	People's Constitutional
1,075	Charlene Mitchell and Michael Zagarell	Communist
142	James Hensley and Roscoe B. MacKenna	Universal
34	Richard K. Troxell and Merle Thayer	Constitution
7	Kent M. Soeters and James P. Powers	Berkeley Defense Group

Notes: In addition to the votes listed above, 11,192 scattered write-in votes were reported from various states, and 12,430 were cast for elector tickets for which there were no formal presidential or vice-presidential candidates. In the vote listed above for Eldridge Cleaver, two states are included (California and Utah) in which only the party vice-presidential candidate appeared on the ballot.

UNITED STATES
PRESIDENT 1968

State	Electoral Vote Rep.	Dem.	Other	Total Vote	Republican	Democratic	American Independent	Other	Plurality		Percentage Rep.	Dem.	Amer. Ind.
Alabama			10	1,049,922	146,923	196,579	691,425	14,995	494,846	A	14.0%	18.7%	65.9%
Alaska	3			83,035	37,600	35,411	10,024		2,189	R	45.3%	42.6%	12.1%
Arizona	5			486,936	266,721	170,514	46,573	3,128	96,207	R	54.8%	35.0%	9.6%
Arkansas			6	619,969	190,759	188,228	240,982		50,223	A	30.8%	30.4%	38.9%
California	40			7,251,587	3,467,664	3,244,318	487,270	52,335	223,346	R	47.8%	44.7%	6.7%
Colorado	6			811,199	409,345	335,174	60,813	5,867	74,171	R	50.5%	41.3%	7.5%
Connecticut		8		1,256,232	556,721	621,561	76,650	1,300	64,840	D	44.3%	49.5%	6.1%
Delaware	3			214,367	96,714	89,194	28,459		7,520	R	45.1%	41.6%	13.3%
Florida	14			2,187,805	886,804	676,794	624,207		210,010	R	40.5%	30.9%	28.5%
Georgia			12	1,250,266	380,111	334,440	535,550	165	155,439	A	30.4%	26.7%	42.8%
Hawaii				236,218	91,425	141,324	3,469		49,899	D	38.7%	59.8%	1.5%
Idaho	4	4		291,183	165,369	89,273	36,541		76,096	R	56.8%	30.7%	12.5%
Illinois	26			4,619,749	2,174,774	2,039,814	390,958	14,203	134,960	R	47.1%	44.2%	8.5%
Indiana	13			2,123,597	1,067,885	806,659	243,108	5,945	261,226	R	50.3%	38.0%	11.4%
Iowa	9			1,167,931	619,106	476,699	66,422	5,704	142,407	R	53.0%	40.8%	5.7%
Kansas	7			872,783	478,674	302,996	88,921	2,192	175,678	R	54.8%	34.7%	10.2%
Kentucky	9			1,055,893	462,411	397,541	193,098	2,843	64,870	R	43.8%	37.6%	18.3%
Louisiana			10	1,097,450	257,535	309,615	530,300		220,685	A	23.5%	28.2%	48.3%
Maine		4		392,936	169,254	217,312	6,370		48,058	D	43.1%	55.3%	1.6%
Maryland		10		1,235,039	517,995	538,310	178,734		20,315	D	41.9%	43.6%	14.5%
Massachusetts		14		2,331,752	766,844	1,469,218	87,088	8,602	702,374	D	32.9%	63.0%	3.7%
Michigan		21		3,306,250	1,370,665	1,593,082	331,968	10,535	222,417	D	41.5%	48.2%	10.0%
Minnesota		10		1,588,506	658,643	857,738	68,931	3,194	199,095	D	41.5%	54.0%	4.3%
Mississippi			7	654,509	88,516	150,644	415,349		264,705	A	13.5%	23.0%	63.5%
Missouri	12			1,809,502	811,932	791,444	206,126		20,488	R	44.9%	43.7%	11.4%
Montana	4			274,404	138,835	114,117	20,015	1,437	24,718	R	50.6%	41.6%	7.3%
Nebraska	5			536,851	321,163	170,784	44,904		150,379	R	59.8%	31.8%	8.4%
Nevada	3			154,218	73,188	60,598	20,432		12,590	R	47.5%	39.3%	13.2%
New Hampshire	4			297,298	154,903	130,589	11,173	633	24,314	R	52.1%	43.9%	3.8%
New Jersey	17			2,875,395	1,325,467	1,264,206	262,187	23,535	61,261	R	46.1%	44.0%	9.1%
New Mexico	4			327,350	169,692	130,081	25,737	1,840	39,611	R	51.8%	39.7%	7.9%
New York		43		6,791,688	3,007,932	3,378,470	358,864	46,422	370,538	D	44.3%	49.7%	5.3%
North Carolina	12		1	1,587,493	627,192	464,113	496,188		131,004	R	39.5%	29.2%	31.3%
North Dakota	4			247,882	138,669	94,769	14,244	200	43,900	R	55.9%	38.2%	5.7%
Ohio	26			3,959,698	1,791,014	1,700,586	467,495	603	90,428	R	45.2%	42.9%	11.8%
Oklahoma	8			943,086	449,697	301,658	191,731		148,039	R	47.7%	32.0%	20.3%
Oregon	6			819,622	408,433	358,866	49,683	2,640	49,567	R	49.8%	43.8%	6.1%
Pennsylvania		29		4,747,928	2,090,017	2,259,405	378,582	19,924	169,388	D	44.0%	47.6%	8.0%
Rhode Island		4		385,000	122,359	246,518	15,678	445	124,159	D	31.8%	64.0%	4.1%
South Carolina	8			666,978	254,062	197,486	215,430		38,632	R	38.1%	29.6%	32.3%
South Dakota	4			281,264	149,841	118,023	13,400		31,818	R	53.3%	42.0%	4.8%
Tennessee	11			1,248,617	472,592	351,233	424,792		47,800	R	37.8%	28.1%	34.0%
Texas		25		3,079,216	1,227,844	1,266,804	584,269	299	38,960	D	39.9%	41.1%	19.0%
Utah	4			422,568	238,728	156,665	26,906	269	82,063	R	56.5%	37.1%	6.4%
Vermont	3			161,404	85,142	70,255	5,104	903	14,887	R	52.8%	43.5%	3.2%
Virginia	12			1,361,491	590,319	442,387	321,833	6,952	147,932	R	43.4%	32.5%	23.6%
Washington		9		1,304,281	588,510	616,037	96,990	2,744	27,527	D	45.1%	47.2%	7.4%
West Virginia		7		754,206	307,555	374,091	72,560		66,536	D	40.8%	49.6%	9.6%
Wisconsin	12			1,691,538	809,997	748,804	127,835	4,902	61,193	R	47.9%	44.3%	7.6%
Wyoming	3			127,205	70,927	45,173	11,105		25,754	R	55.8%	35.5%	8.7%
District of Columbia		3		170,578	31,012	139,566			108,554	D	18.2%	81.8%	
Total	*301*	*191*	*46*	*73,211,875*	*31,785,480*	*31,275,166*	*9,906,473*	*244,756*	*510,314*	*R*	*43.4%*	*42.7%*	*13.5%*

UNITED STATES
PRESIDENT 1964

In New York the Democratic figure includes Liberal votes.

The full list of candidates for president and vice president was:

43,129,566	Lyndon B. Johnson and Hubert H. Humphrey	Democratic
27,178,188	Barry M. Goldwater and William E. Miller	Republican
45,219	Eric Hass and Henning A. Blomen	Socialist Labor
32,720	Clifton DeBerry and Edward Shaw	Socialist Workers
23,267	E. Harold Munn and Mark R. Shaw	Prohibition
6,953	John Kasper and J. B. Stoner	National States Rights
5,060	Joseph B. Lightburn and T. C. Billings	Constitution
19	James Hensley and John O. Hopkins	Universal

Notes: In addition to the votes listed above, 12,868 scattered write-in votes were reported from various states, and 210,732 votes were cast in Alabama for an unpledged Democratic elector ticket.

UNITED STATES
PRESIDENT 1964

State	Electoral Vote Rep.	Electoral Vote Dem.	Total Vote	Republican	Democratic	Other	Plurality		Percentage Total Vote Rep.	Dem.	Major Vote Rep.	Dem.
Alabama	10		689,818	479,085		210,733	479,085	R	69.5%		100.0%	
Alaska		3	67,259	22,930	44,329		21,399	D	34.1%	65.9%	34.1%	65.9%
Arizona	5		480,770	242,535	237,753	482	4,782	R	50.4%	49.5%	50.5%	49.5%
Arkansas		6	560,426	243,264	314,197	2,965	70,933	D	43.4%	56.1%	43.6%	56.4%
California		40	7,057,586	2,879,108	4,171,877	6,601	1,292,769	D	40.8%	59.1%	40.8%	59.2%
Colorado		6	776,986	296,767	476,024	4,195	179,257	D	38.2%	61.3%	38.4%	61.6%
Connecticut		8	1,218,578	390,996	826,269	1,313	435,273	D	32.1%	67.8%	32.1%	67.9%
Delaware		3	201,320	78,078	122,704	538	44,626	D	38.8%	60.9%	38.9%	61.1%
Florida		14	1,854,481	905,941	948,540		42,599	D	48.9%	51.1%	48.9%	51.1%
Georgia	12		1,139,335	616,584	522,556	195	94,028	R	54.1%	45.9%	54.1%	45.9%
Hawaii		4	207,271	44,022	163,249		119,227	D	21.2%	78.8%	21.2%	78.8%
Idaho		4	292,477	143,557	148,920		5,363	D	49.1%	50.9%	49.1%	50.9%
Illinois		26	4,702,841	1,905,946	2,796,833	62	890,887	D	40.5%	59.5%	40.5%	59.5%
Indiana		13	2,091,606	911,118	1,170,848	9,640	259,730	D	43.6%	56.0%	43.8%	56.2%
Iowa		9	1,184,539	449,148	733,030	2,361	283,882	D	37.9%	61.9%	38.0%	62.0%
Kansas		7	857,901	386,579	464,028	7,294	77,449	D	45.1%	54.1%	45.4%	54.6%
Kentucky		9	1,046,105	372,977	669,659	3,469	296,682	D	35.7%	64.0%	35.8%	64.2%
Louisiana	10		896,293	509,225	387,068		122,157	R	56.8%	43.2%	56.8%	43.2%
Maine		4	380,965	118,701	262,264		143,563	D	31.2%	68.8%	31.2%	68.8%
Maryland		10	1,116,457	385,495	730,912	50	345,417	D	34.5%	65.5%	34.5%	65.5%
Massachusetts		14	2,344,798	549,727	1,786,422	8,649	1,236,695	D	23.4%	76.2%	23.5%	76.5%
Michigan		21	3,203,102	1,060,152	2,136,615	6,335	1,076,463	D	33.1%	66.7%	33.2%	66.8%
Minnesota		10	1,554,462	559,624	991,117	3,721	431,493	D	36.0%	63.8%	36.1%	63.9%
Mississippi	7		409,146	356,528	52,618		303,910	R	87.1%	12.9%	87.1%	12.9%
Missouri		12	1,817,879	653,535	1,164,344		510,809	D	36.0%	64.0%	36.0%	64.0%
Montana		4	278,628	113,032	164,246	1,350	51,214	D	40.6%	58.9%	40.8%	59.2%
Nebraska		5	584,154	276,847	307,307		30,460	D	47.4%	52.6%	47.4%	52.6%
Nevada		3	135,433	56,094	79,339		23,245	D	41.4%	58.6%	41.4%	58.6%
New Hampshire		4	288,093	104,029	184,064		80,035	D	36.1%	63.9%	36.1%	63.9%
New Jersey		17	2,847,663	964,174	1,868,231	15,258	904,057	D	33.9%	65.6%	34.0%	66.0%
New Mexico		4	328,645	132,838	194,015	1,792	61,177	D	40.4%	59.0%	40.6%	59.4%
New York		43	7,166,275	2,243,559	4,913,102	9,614	2,669,543	D	31.3%	68.6%	31.3%	68.7%
North Carolina		13	1,424,983	624,844	800,139		175,295	D	43.8%	56.2%	43.8%	56.2%
North Dakota		4	258,389	108,207	149,784	398	41,577	D	41.9%	58.0%	41.9%	58.1%
Ohio		26	3,969,196	1,470,865	2,498,331		1,027,466	D	37.1%	62.9%	37.1%	62.9%
Oklahoma		8	932,499	412,665	519,834		107,169	D	44.3%	55.7%	44.3%	55.7%
Oregon		6	786,305	282,779	501,017	2,509	218,238	D	36.0%	63.7%	36.1%	63.9%
Pennsylvania		29	4,822,690	1,673,657	3,130,954	18,079	1,457,297	D	34.7%	64.9%	34.8%	65.2%
Rhode Island		4	390,091	74,615	315,463	13	240,848	D	19.1%	80.9%	19.1%	80.9%
South Carolina	8		524,779	309,048	215,723	8	93,325	R	58.9%	41.1%	58.9%	41.1%
South Dakota		4	293,118	130,108	163,010		32,902	D	44.4%	55.6%	44.4%	55.6%
Tennessee		11	1,143,946	508,965	634,947	34	125,982	D	44.5%	55.5%	44.5%	55.5%
Texas		25	2,626,811	958,566	1,663,185	5,060	704,619	D	36.5%	63.3%	36.6%	63.4%
Utah		4	401,413	181,785	219,628		37,843	D	45.3%	54.7%	45.3%	54.7%
Vermont		3	163,089	54,942	108,127	20	53,185	D	33.7%	66.3%	33.7%	66.3%
Virginia		12	1,042,267	481,334	558,038	2,895	76,704	D	46.2%	53.5%	46.3%	53.7%
Washington		9	1,258,556	470,366	779,881	8,309	309,515	D	37.4%	62.0%	37.6%	62.4%
West Virginia		7	792,040	253,953	538,087		284,134	D	32.1%	67.9%	32.1%	67.9%
Wisconsin		12	1,691,815	638,495	1,050,424	2,896	411,929	D	37.7%	62.1%	37.8%	62.2%
Wyoming		3	142,716	61,998	80,718		18,720	D	43.4%	56.6%	43.4%	56.6%
District of Columbia		3	198,597	28,801	169,796		140,995	D	14.5%	85.5%	14.5%	85.5%
Total	52	486	70,644,592	27,178,188	43,129,566	336,838	15,951,378	D	38.5%	61.1%	38.7%	61.3%

UNITED STATES
PRESIDENT 1960

Sen. Harry Flood Byrd received 15 votes for president in the Electoral College; these were the votes of 6 of the 11 Democratic electors in Alabama, all 8 unpledged Democratic electors in Mississippi, and 1 of the 8 Republican electors in Oklahoma. The Alabama and Mississippi electors also cast 14 votes for Sen. Strom Thurmond for vice president; the single Oklahoma elector voted for Sen. Barry M. Goldwater for vice president.

In New York the Democratic figure includes Liberal votes.

The full list of candidates for president and vice president was:

34,226,731	John F. Kennedy and Lyndon B. Johnson	Democratic
34,108,157	Richard M. Nixon and Henry Cabot Lodge	Republican
47,522	Eric Hass and Georgia Cozzini	Socialist Labor
46,203	Rutherford L. Decker and E. Harold Munn	Prohibition
44,977	Orval E. Faubus and John G. Crommelin	National States Rights
40,165	Farrell Dobbs and Myra Tanner Weiss	Socialist Workers
18,162	Charles L. Sullivan and Merritt B. Curtis	Constitution
8,708	J. Bracken Lee and Kent H. Courtney	Conservative
4,204	C. Benton Coiner and Edward J. Silverman	Conservative
1,767	Lar Daly and B. M. Miller	Tax Cut
1,485	Clennon King and Reginald Carter	Independent Afro-American
1,401	Merritt B. Curtis and B. M. Miller	Constitution

Notes: In addition to the votes listed above, 2,378 scattered write-in votes were reported from various states, 169,572 votes were cast in Louisiana for Independent electors, and 116,248 votes were cast in Mississippi for an unpledged Democratic elector ticket. Another 539 votes were cast in Michigan for an Independent American ticket.

UNITED STATES
PRESIDENT 1960

State	Electoral Vote Rep.	Electoral Vote Dem.	Electoral Vote Other	Total Vote	Republican	Democratic	Other	Plurality		Percentage Total Vote Rep.	Percentage Total Vote Dem.	Percentage Major Vote Rep.	Percentage Major Vote Dem.
Alabama		5	6	570,225	237,981	324,050	8,194	86,069	D	41.7%	56.8%	42.3%	57.7%
Alaska	3			60,762	30,953	29,809		1,144	R	50.9%	49.1%	50.9%	49.1%
Arizona	4			398,491	221,241	176,781	469	44,460	R	55.5%	44.4%	55.6%	44.4%
Arkansas		8		428,509	184,508	215,049	28,952	30,541	D	43.1%	50.2%	46.2%	53.8%
California	32			6,506,578	3,259,722	3,224,099	22,757	35,623	R	50.1%	49.6%	50.3%	49.7%
Colorado	6			736,236	402,242	330,629	3,365	71,613	R	54.6%	44.9%	54.9%	45.1%
Connecticut		8		1,222,883	565,813	657,055	15	91,242	D	46.3%	53.7%	46.3%	53.7%
Delaware		3		196,683	96,373	99,590	720	3,217	D	49.0%	50.6%	49.2%	50.8%
Florida	10			1,544,176	795,476	748,700		46,776	R	51.5%	48.5%	51.5%	48.5%
Georgia		12		733,349	274,472	458,638	239	184,166	D	37.4%	62.5%	37.4%	62.6%
Hawaii		3		184,705	92,295	92,410		115	D	50.0%	50.0%	50.0%	50.0%
Idaho	4			300,450	161,597	138,853		22,744	R	53.8%	46.2%	53.8%	46.2%
Illinois		27		4,757,409	2,368,988	2,377,846	10,575	8,858	D	49.8%	50.0%	49.9%	50.1%
Indiana	13			2,135,360	1,175,120	952,358	7,882	222,762	R	55.0%	44.6%	55.2%	44.8%
Iowa	10			1,273,810	722,381	550,565	864	171,816	R	56.7%	43.2%	56.7%	43.3%
Kansas	8			928,825	561,474	363,213	4,138	198,261	R	60.4%	39.1%	60.7%	39.3%
Kentucky	10			1,124,462	602,607	521,855		80,752	R	53.6%	46.4%	53.6%	46.4%
Louisiana		10		807,891	230,980	407,339	169,572	176,359	D	28.6%	50.4%	36.2%	63.8%
Maine	5			421,767	240,608	181,159		59,449	R	57.0%	43.0%	57.0%	43.0%
Maryland		9		1,055,349	489,538	565,808	3	76,270	D	46.4%	53.6%	46.4%	53.6%
Massachusetts		16		2,469,480	976,750	1,487,174	5,556	510,424	D	39.6%	60.2%	39.6%	60.4%
Michigan		20		3,318,097	1,620,428	1,687,269	10,400	66,841	D	48.8%	50.9%	49.0%	51.0%
Minnesota		11		1,541,887	757,915	779,933	4,039	22,018	D	49.2%	50.6%	49.3%	50.7%
Mississippi			8	298,171	73,561	108,362	116,248	34,801	D	24.7%	36.3%	40.4%	59.6%
Missouri		13		1,934,422	962,221	972,201		9,980	D	49.7%	50.3%	49.7%	50.3%
Montana	4			277,579	141,841	134,891	847	6,950	R	51.1%	48.6%	51.3%	48.7%
Nebraska	6			613,095	380,553	232,542		148,011	R	62.1%	37.9%	62.1%	37.9%
Nevada		3		107,267	52,387	54,880		2,493	D	48.8%	51.2%	48.8%	51.2%
New Hampshire	4			295,761	157,989	137,772		20,217	R	53.4%	46.6%	53.4%	46.6%
New Jersey		16		2,773,111	1,363,324	1,385,415	24,372	22,091	D	49.2%	50.0%	49.6%	50.4%
New Mexico		4		311,107	153,733	156,027	1,347	2,294	D	49.4%	50.2%	49.6%	50.4%
New York		45		7,291,079	3,446,419	3,830,085	14,575	383,666	D	47.3%	52.5%	47.4%	52.6%
North Carolina		14		1,368,556	655,420	713,136		57,716	D	47.9%	52.1%	47.9%	52.1%
North Dakota	4			278,431	154,310	123,963	158	30,347	R	55.4%	44.5%	55.5%	44.5%
Ohio	25			4,161,859	2,217,611	1,944,248		273,363	R	53.3%	46.7%	53.3%	46.7%
Oklahoma	7		1	903,150	533,039	370,111		162,928	R	59.0%	41.0%	59.0%	41.0%
Oregon	6			776,421	408,060	367,402	959	40,658	R	52.6%	47.3%	52.6%	47.4%
Pennsylvania		32		5,006,541	2,439,956	2,556,282	10,303	116,326	D	48.7%	51.1%	48.8%	51.2%
Rhode Island		4		405,535	147,502	258,032	1	110,530	D	36.4%	63.6%	36.4%	63.6%
South Carolina		8		386,688	188,558	198,129	1	9,571	D	48.8%	51.2%	48.8%	51.2%
South Dakota	4			306,487	178,417	128,070		50,347	R	58.2%	41.8%	58.2%	41.8%
Tennessee	11			1,051,792	556,577	481,453	13,762	75,124	R	52.9%	45.8%	53.6%	46.4%
Texas		24		2,311,084	1,121,310	1,167,567	22,207	46,257	D	48.5%	50.5%	49.0%	51.0%
Utah	4			374,709	205,361	169,248	100	36,113	R	54.8%	45.2%	54.8%	45.2%
Vermont	3			167,324	98,131	69,186	7	28,945	R	58.6%	41.3%	58.6%	41.4%
Virginia	12			771,449	404,521	362,327	4,601	42,194	R	52.4%	47.0%	52.8%	47.2%
Washington	9			1,241,572	629,273	599,298	13,001	29,975	R	50.7%	48.3%	51.2%	48.8%
West Virginia		8		837,781	395,995	441,786		45,791	D	47.3%	52.7%	47.3%	52.7%
Wisconsin	12			1,729,082	895,175	830,805	3,102	64,370	R	51.8%	48.0%	51.9%	48.1%
Wyoming	3			140,782	77,451	63,331		14,120	R	55.0%	45.0%	55.0%	45.0%
Total	219	303	15	68,838,219	34,108,157	34,226,731	503,331	118,574	D	49.5%	49.7%	49.9%	50.1%

Note: The District of Columbia is not included because it did not receive the right to vote in presidential elections until 1961.

PRESIDENTIAL PRIMARIES 2016

In 2016, 39 states and the District of Columbia held presidential primaries, in which at least one of the parties held contests where voters balloted directly for candidates or for a statewide slate of delegates that was pledged to a candidate. States not listed in this listing held a caucus (with participation usually drawing a smaller number of voters than a primary). Jurisdictions without electoral votes are not included in this listing.

The list below, alphabetical by state, gives primary vote totals for all candidates who were listed on the ballot or received write-in votes that were counted. The subsequent tables give a chronological summary of the primary votes for those candidates in the Democratic and Republican parties who received at least 200,000 votes nationwide, with the vote totals for minor candidates in the footnotes.

Republican candidates on the ballot in at least one primary were: James Alexander-Pace, Joann Breivogel, Jeb Bush, Ben Carson, Chris Christie, Timothy Cook, Ted Cruz, John Dowell, Carly Fiorina, James Germalio, James S. Gilmore, Donald J. Gonzalez, Lindsey Graham, Elizabeth Gray, Mike Huckabee, Bobby Jindal, John R. Kasich, James P. Lynch, Peter Messina, James Orlando Ogle, George E. Pataki, Rand Paul, Marco Rubio, Rick Santorum, Troy Hugh Southern, David P. Thomson, Donald J. Trump, Frederic Vidal, Victor Williams.

Democratic candidates on the ballot in at least one primary were: Jon Adams, Andrew D. Basiago, Steve Burke, Willie F. Carter, Hillary Rodham Clinton, Lawrence Cohen, Roque De La Fuente, Eric Elbot, Paul T. Farrell, David Formhals, William D. French, Mark Stewart Greenstein, Henry Hewes, Brock C. Hutton, Keith Judd, Lloyd Thomas Kelso, Steven Roy Lipscomb, Star Locke, Robert Lovitt, Bill McGaughey, Raymond Michael Moroz, Ignacio Leon Nunez, Edward T. O'Donnell, Martin O'Malley, Brian O'Neill, Bernard "Bernie" Sanders, Graham Schwass, Sam Sloan, Edward Sonnino, Michael Alan Steinberg, Vermin Supreme, Doug Terry, David John Thistle, James Valentine, Richard Lyons Weil, Willie Wilson, John Wolfe.

ALABAMA   March 1

Republican   373,721 Trump; 181,479 Cruz; 160,606 Rubio; 88,094 Carson; 38,119 Kasich; 7,953 Uncommitted; 3,974 Bush; 2,539 Huckabee; 1,895 Paul; 858 Christie; 617 Santorum; 544 Fiorina; 253 Graham

Democrat   311,141 Clinton; 76,878 Sanders; 9,553 Uncommitted; 1,499 O'Malley; 818 De La Fuente

ARIZONA   March 22

Republican   286,743 Trump; 172,294 Cruz; 72,304 Rubio; 65,965 Kasich; 14,940 Carson; 4,393 Bush; 2,269 Paul; 1,300 Huckabee; 1,270 Fiorina; 988 Christie; 523 Santorum; 498 Graham; 309 Pataki; 243 Cook

Democrat   262,459 Clinton; 192,962 Sanders; 3,877 O'Malley; 2,797 De La Fuente; 2,295 Steinberg; 1,845 Hewes

ARKANSAS   March 1

Republican   134,744 Trump; 125,340 Cruz; 101,910 Rubio; 23,521 Carson; 15,305 Kasich; 4,792 Huckabee; 2,402 Bush; 1,151 Paul; 631 Christie; 411 Fiorina; 292 Santorum; 252 Graham; 169 Jindal

Democrat   146,057 Clinton; 66,236 Sanders; 2,785 O'Malley; 2,556 Wolfe; 1,702 Valentine; 1,684 De La Fuente

CALIFORNIA   June 27

Republican   1,665,135 Trump; 252,544 Kasich; 211,576 Cruz; 82,259 Carson; 15,691 Gilmore; 35 Thomson; 15 Breivogel; 14 Dowell; 10 Gonzalez; 7 Alexander-Pace; 6 Vidal; 5 Williams; 4 Southern; 3 Ogle; 2 Germalio

Democrat   2,745,302 Clinton; 2,381,722 Sanders; 12,014 Wilson; 10,880 Steinberg; 8,453 De La Fuente; 7,743 Hewes; 7,201 Judd; 13 Basiago; 6 Nunez; 3 Carter; 1 Terry

CONNECTICUT   April 26

Republican   123,523 Trump; 60,522 Kasich; 24,987 Cruz; 2,728 Uncommitted; 1,733 Carson

Democrat   170,045 Clinton; 152,379 Sanders; 4,871 Sanders; 960 De La Fuente

PRESIDENTIAL PRIMARIES 2016

DELAWARE April 26

Republican   42,472 Trump; 14,225 Kasich; 11,110 Cruz; 885 Carson; 622 Rubio; 578 Bush

Democrat   55,954 Clinton; 36,662 Sanders; 1,024 De La Fuente

DISTRICT OF COLUMBIA June 14

Democrat   76,704 Clinton; 20,361 Sanders; 485 Write-In; 213 De La Fuente

FLORIDA March 15

Republican   1,079,870 Trump; 638,661 Rubio; 404,891 Cruz; 159,976 Kasich; 43,511 Bush; 21,207 Carson; 4,450 Paul; 2,624 Huckabee; 2,493 Christie; 1,899 Fiorina; 1,211 Santorum; 693 Graham; 319 Gilmore

Democrat   1,101,414 Clinton; 568,839 Sanders; 38,930 O'Malley

GEORGIA March 1

Republican   502,994 Trump; 316,836 Rubio; 305,847 Cruz; 80,723 Carson; 72,508 Kasich; 7,686 Bush; 2,910 Paul; 2,625 Huckabee; 1,486 Christie; 1,146 Fiorina; 539 Santorum; 428 Graham; 236 Pataki

Democrat   545,674 Clinton; 215,797 Sanders; 2,129 O'Malley; 1,766 Steinberg

IDAHO March 8

Republican   100,889 Cruz; 62,413 Trump; 35,290 Rubio; 16,514 Kasich; 3,853 Carson; 939 Bush; 834 Paul; 358 Huckabee; 353 Christie; 242 Fiorina; 211 Santorum; 80 Graham; 28 Messina

ILLINOIS March 15

Republican   562,464 Trump; 438,235 Cruz; 286,118 Kasich; 126,681 Rubio; 11,469 Carson; 11,188 Bush; 4,718 Paul; 3,428 Christie; 2,737 Huckabee; 1,540 Fiorina; 1,154 Santorum; 16 Breivogel

Democrat   1,039,555 Clinton; 999,494 Sanders; 6,565 Wilson; 6,197 O'Malley; 2,407 Cohen; 1,802 De La Fuente; 25 Formhals; 2 O'Neill

INDIANA May 3

Republican   591,514 Trump; 406,783 Cruz; 84,111 Kasich; 8,914 Carson; 6,508 Bush; 5,175 Rubio; 4,306 Paul; 1,738 Christie; 1,494 Fiorina

Democrat   335,074 Sanders; 303,705 Clinton

KENTUCKY May 17

Democrat   212,534 Clinton; 210,623 Sanders; 24,101 Uncommitted; 5,713 O'Malley; 1,594 De La Fuente

LOUISIANA March 5

Republican   124,854 Trump; 113,968 Cruz; 33,813 Rubio; 19,359 Kasich; 4,544 Carson; 2,145 Bush; 670 Paul; 645 Huckabee; 401 Christie; 243 Fiorina; 219 Cook; 180 Santorum; 152 Graham; 48 Messina

Democrat   221,733 Clinton; 72,276 Sanders; 4,785 Burke; 4,512 Wolfe; 2,550 O'Malley; 1,423 Wilson; 1,357 Judd; 1,341 De La Fuente; 993 Steinberg; 806 Hewes

PRESIDENTIAL PRIMARIES 2016

MARYLAND   April 26

Republican
248,343 Trump; 106,614 Kasich; 87,093 Cruz; 5,946 Carson; 3,201 Rubio; 2,770 Bush; 1,533 Paul; 1,239 Christie; 1,012 Fiorina; 837 Huckabee; 478 Santorum

Democrat
573,242 Clinton; 309,990 Sanders; 29,949 Uncommitted; 3,582 De La Fuente

MASSACHUSETTS   March 1

Republican
312,425 Trump; 114,434 Kasich; 113,170 Rubio; 60,592 Cruz; 16,360 Carson; 6,559 Bush; 3,220 No Preference; 2,325 Write-In; 1,906 Christie; 1,864 Paul; 1,153 Fiorina; 753 Gilmore; 709 Huckabee; 500 Pataki; 293 Santorum

Democrat
606,822 Clinton; 589,803 Sanders; 8,090 No Preference; 4,927 Write-In; 4,783 O'Malley; 1,545 De La Fuente

MICHIGAN   March 8

Republican
483,753 Trump; 326,617 Cruz; 321,115 Kasich; 123,587 Rubio; 22,824 Uncommitted; 21,349 Carson; 10,685 Bush; 3,774 Paul; 3,116 Christie; 2,603 Huckabee; 1,722 Santorum; 1,415 Fiorina; 591 Pataki; 438 Graham

Democrat
598,943 Sanders; 581,775 Clinton; 21,601 Uncommitted; 2,363 O'Malley; 870 De La Fuente

MISSISSIPPI   March 8

Republican
196,659 Trump; 150,364 Cruz; 36,795 Kasich; 21,885 Rubio; 5,626 Carson; 1,697 Bush; 1,067 Huckabee; 643 Paul; 510 Santorum; 493 Christie; 224 Fiorina; 172 Graham; 135 Pataki

Democrat
187,334 Clinton; 37,748 Sanders; 919 Wilson; 672 O'Malley; 481 De La Fuente; 10 Write-In

MISSOURI   March 15

Republican
383,631 Trump; 381,666 Cruz; 94,857 Kasich; 57,244 Rubio; 8,233 Carson; 3,361 Bush; 3,225 Uncommitted; 2,148 Huckabee; 1,777 Paul; 1,681 Christie; 732 Santorum; 615 Fiorina; 100 Lynch

Democrat
312,285 Clinton; 310,711 Sanders; 3,717 Uncommitted; 650 Hewes; 442 O'Malley; 433 Adams; 345 De La Fuente; 307 Wilson; 288 Judd; 247 Wolfe

MONTANA   June 7

Republican
115,594 Trump; 14,682 Cruz; 10,777 Kasich; 7,369 No Preference; 5,192 Rubio; 3,274 Bush

Democrat
65,156 Sanders; 55,805 Clinton; 5,415 Preference

NEBRASKA   May 10

Republican
122,327 Trump; 36,703 Cruz; 22,709 Kasich; 10,016 Carson; 7,233 Rubio

Democrat
42,692 Clinton; 37,744 Sanders

NEW HAMPSHIRE   February 9

Republican
100,735 Trump; 44,932 Kasich; 33,244 Cruz; 30,071 Rubio; 21,089 Christie; 11,774 Fiorina; 6,527 Carson; 2,943 Write-In; 1,930 Paul; 216 Huckabee; 202 Martin; 160 Santorum; 134 Gilmore; 104 Witz; 79 Pataki; 73 Graham; 56 Cullison 55 Cook; 56 Cullison; 53 Jindal; 47 Lynch; 44 Robinson; 32 Comley; 16 Prag; 15 Dyas; 12 McCarthy; 9 Iwachiw; 8 Huey; 6 Drozd; 5 Messina; 5 Mann

Democrat
151,193 Sanders; 95,355 Clinton; 3,475 Write-In; 667 O'Malley; 268 Supreme; 226 Thistle; 143 Schwass; 108 Burke; 96 De La Fuente; 54 Wolfe; 53 Adams; 46 Kelso; 44 Judd; 36 Elbot; 33 Locke; 29 French; 29 Greenstein; 26 O'Donnell; 24 Valentine; 22 Lovitt; 21 Steinberg; 19 McGaughey; 18 Hewes; 17 Sonnino; 15 Sloan; 15 Lipscomb; 14 Hutton; 8 Moroz; 8 Weil

PRESIDENTIAL PRIMARIES 2016

NEW JERSEY   June 7

Republican   360,212 Trump; 59,866 Kasich; 27,874 Cruz

Democrat   566,247 Clinton; 328,058 Sanders

NEW MEXICO   June 7

Republican   73,908 Trump; 13,925 Cruz; 7,925 Kasich; 3,830 Carson; 3,531 Bush; 1,508 Fiorina

Democrat   111,334 Clinton; 104,741 Sanders

NEW YORK   April 19

Republican   554,522 Trump; 231,166 Kasich; 136,083 Cruz

Democrat   1,133,980 Clinton; 820,256 Sanders

NORTH CAROLINA   March 15

Republican   462,413 Trump; 422,621 Cruz; 145,659 Kasich; 88,907 Rubio; 11,019 Carson; 6,081 No Preference; 3,893 Bush; 3,071 Huckabee; 2,753 Paul; 1,256 Christie; 929 Fiorina; 663 Santorum; 265 Gilmore

Democrat   622,915 Clinton; 467,018 Sanders; 37,485 No Preference; 12,122 O'Malley; 3,376 De La Fuente

OHIO   March 15

Republican   933,886 Kasich; 713,404 Trump; 264,640 Cruz; 46,478 Rubio; 14,351 Carson; 5,398 Bush; 4,941 Huckabee; 2,430 Christie; 2,112 Fiorina; 1,320 Santorum

Democrat   696,681 Clinton; 535,395 Sanders; 9,402 De La Fuente

OKLAHOMA   March 1

Republican   158,078 Cruz; 130,267 Trump; 119,633 Rubio; 28,601 Carson; 16,524 Kasich; 2,091 Bush; 1,666 Paul; 1,308 Huckabee; 610 Fiorina; 545 Christie; 375 Santorum; 224 Graham

Democrat   174,228 Sanders; 139,443 Clinton; 7,672 O'Malley; 4,386 Judd; 4,171 Steinberg; 3,458 Locke; 2,485 De La Fuente

OREGON   May 17

Republican   252,748 Trump; 65,513 Cruz; 62,248 Kasich; 13,411 Write-In

Democrat   360,829 Sanders; 269,846 Clinton; 10,920 Write-In

PENNSYLVANIA   April 26

Republican   902,593 Trump; 345,506 Cruz; 310,003 Kasich; 14,842 Carson; 11,954 Rubio; 9,577 Bush

Democrat   935,107 Clinton; 731,881 Sanders; 14,439 De La Fuente

RHODE ISLAND   April 26

Republican   39,221 Trump; 14,963 Kasich; 6,416 Cruz; 417 Uncommitted; 382 Rubio; 215 Write-In

Democrat   66,993 Sanders; 52,749 Clinton; 1,662 Uncommitted; 673 Write-In; 236 Stewart; 145 De La Fuente

PRESIDENTIAL PRIMARIES 2016

SOUTH CAROLINA   February 20

Republican   240,882 Trump; 166,565 Rubio; 165,417 Cruz; 58,056 Bush; 56,410 Kasich; 53,551 Carson

Democrat   272,379 Clinton; 96,498 Sanders; 1,314 Wilson; 713 O'Malley

SOUTH DAKOTA   June 7

Republican   44,867 Trump; 11,352 Cruz; 10,660 Kasich

Democrat   27,047 Clinton; 25,959 Sanders

TENNESSEE   March 1

Republican   333,180 Trump; 211,471 Cruz; 181,274 Rubio; 64,951 Carson; 45,301 Kasich; 9,551 Bush; 2,415 Huckabee; 2,350 Paul; 1,849 Uncommitted; 1,256 Christie; 715 Fiorina; 710 Santorum; 267 Gilmore; 253 Graham; 186 Pataki

Democrat   245,930 Clinton; 120,800 Sanders; 3,467 Uncommitted; 2,025 O'Malley

TEXAS   March 1

Republican   1,241,118 Cruz; 758,762 Trump; 503,055 Rubio; 120,473 Kasich; 117,969 Carson; 35,420 Bush; 29,609 Uncommitted; 8,000 Paul; 6,226 Huckabee; 5,449 Gray; 3,448 Christie; 3,247 Fiorina; 2,006 Santorum; 1,706 Graham

Democrat   936,004 Clinton; 476,547 Sanders; 8,429 De La Fuente; 5,364 O'Malley; 3,254 Wilson; 2,569 Judd; 2,017 Hawes; 1,711 Locke

VERMONT   March 1

Republican   19,974 Trump; 18,534 Kasich; 11,781 Rubio; 5,932 Cruz; 2,551 Carson; 1,106 Bush; 423 Paul; 390 Write-In; 361 Christie; 212 Fiorina; 164 Santorum

Democrat   115,900 Sanders; 18,338 Clinton; 282 O'Malley; 238 Write-In; 80 De La Fuente

VIRGINIA   March 1

Republican   356,896 Trump; 327,936 Rubio; 171,162 Cruz; 97,791 Kasich; 60,237 Carson; 3,645 Bush; 2,920 Paul; 1,459 Huckabee; 1,102 Christie; 914 Fiorina; 653 Gilmore; 444 Graham; 399 Santorum; 59 Write-In

Democrat   504,791 Clinton; 276,387 Sanders; 3,930 O'Malley; 82 Write-In

WASHINGTON   May 24

Republican   455,023 Trump; 65,172 Cruz; 58,954 Kasich; 23,849 Carson

Democrat   420,461 Clinton; 382,293 Sanders

WEST VIRGINIA   May 10

Republican   157,238 Trump; 18,301 Cruz; 13,721 Kasich; 4,421 Carson; 2,908 Rubio; 2,305 Bush; 1,798 Paul; 1,780 Huckabee; 727 Christie; 659 Fiorina; 203 Hall

Democrat   124,700 Sanders; 86,914 Clinton; 21,694 Farrell; 4,460 Judd; 3,796 O'Malley; 975 De La Fuente

WISCONSIN   April 5

Republican   533,079 Cruz; 387,295 Trump; 155,902 Kasich; 10,591 Rubio; 5,660 Carson; 3,054 Bush; 2,519 Paul; 2,281 Uninstructed Delegation; 1,424 Huckabee; 1,381 Write-In; 1,191 Christie; 772 Fiorina; 511 Santorum; 245 Gilmore; 39 Williams

Democrat   570,192 Sanders; 433,739 Clinton; 1,732 O'Malley; 1,488 Uninstructed Delegation; 431 Write-In; 18 De La Fuente

DEMOCRATIC PRESIDENTIAL PRIMARIES 2016

Date	State	Total vote	Clinton	Sanders	Uncommitted	Other
February 9	New Hampshire	253,062	95,355 **37.7%**	152,193 **60.1%**		5,514 **2.2%**
February 27	South Carolina	370,904	272,379 **73.4%**	96,498 **26.0%**		2,027 **0.5%**
March 1	Alabama	399,889	311,141 **77.8%**	76,878 **19.2%**	9,553 **2.4%**	2,317 **0.6%**
March 1	Arkansas	221,020	146,057 **66.1%**	66,236 **30.0%**		8,727 **3.9%**
March 1	Georgia	765,366	545,674 **71.3%**	215,797 **28.2%**		3,895 **0.5%**
March 1	Massachusetts	1,215,970	606,822 **49.9%**	589,803 **48.5%**	8,090 **0.7%**	11,255 **0.9%**
March 1	Oklahoma	335,843	139,443 **41.5%**	174,228 **51.9%**		22,172 **6.6%**
March 1	Tennessee	372,222	245,930 **66.1%**	120,800 **32.5%**	3,467 **0.9%**	2,025 **0.5%**
March 1	Texas	1,435,895	936,004 **65.2%**	476,547 **33.2%**		23,344 **1.6%**
March 1	Vermont	134,838	18,338 **13.6%**	115,900 **86.0%**		600 **0.4%**
March 1	Virginia	785,190	504,791 **64.3%**	276,387 **35.2%**		4,012 **0.5%**
March 5	Louisiana	311,776	221,733 **71.1%**	72,276 **23.2%**		17,767 **5.7%**
March 8	Michigan	1,205,552	581,775 **48.3%**	598,943 **49.7%**	21,601 **1.8%**	3,233 **0.3%**
March 8	Mississippi	227,164	187,334 **82.5%**	37,748 **16.6%**		2,082 **0.9%**
March 15	Florida	1,709,183	1,101,414 **64.4%**	568,839 **33.3%**		38,930 **2.3%**
March 15	Illinois	2,056,047	1,039,555 **50.6%**	999,494 **48.6%**		16,998 **0.8%**
March 15	Missouri	629,425	312,285 **49.6%**	310,711 **49.4%**	3,717 **0.6%**	2,712 **0.4%**
March 15	North Carolina	1,142,916	622,915 **54.5%**	467,018 **40.9%**	37,485 **3.3%**	15,498 **1.4%**
March 15	Ohio	1,241,478	696,681 **56.1%**	535,395 **43.1%**		9,402 **0.8%**
March 22	Arizona	466,235	262,459 **56.3%**	192,962 **41.4%**		10,814 **2.3%**
March 26	Washington	802,754	420,461 **52.4%**	382,293 **47.6%**		
April 5	Wisconsin	1,007,600	433,739 **43.0%**	570,192 **56.6%**	1,488 **0.1%**	2,181 **0.2%**
April 19	New York	1,954,236	1,133,980 **58.0%**	820,256 **42.0%**		
April 26	Connecticut	328,255	170,045 **51.8%**	152,379 **46.4%**	4,871 **1.5%**	960 **0.3%**
April 26	Delaware	93,640	55,954 **59.8%**	36,662 **39.2%**		1,024 **1.1%**
April 26	Maryland	916,763	573,242 **62.5%**	309,990 **33.8%**	29,949 **3.3%**	3,582 **0.4%**
April 26	Pennsylvania	1,681,427	935,107 **55.6%**	731,881 **43.5%**		14,439 **0.9%**
April 26	Rhode Island	122,458	52,749 **43.1%**	66,993 **54.7%**	1,662 **1.4%**	1,054 **0.9%**
May 3	Indiana	638,779	303,705 **47.5%**	335,074 **52.5%**		
May 10	Nebraska	80,436	42,692 **53.1%**	37,744 **46.9%**		
May 10	West Virginia	242,539	86,914 **35.8%**	124,700 **51.4%**		30,925 **12.8%**
May 17	Kentucky	454,565	212,534 **46.8%**	210,623 **46.3%**	24,101 **5.3%**	7,307 **1.6%**

DEMOCRATIC PRESIDENTIAL PRIMARIES 2016

Date	State	Total vote	Clinton	Sanders	Uncommitted	Other
May 17	Oregon	641,595	269,846 **42.1%**	360,829 **56.2%**		10,920 **1.7%**
June 7	California	5,173,338	2,745,302 **53.1%**	2,381,722 **46.0%**		46,314 **0.9%**
June 7	Montana	126,376	55,805 **44.2%**	65,156 **51.6%**	5,415 **4.3%**	
June 7	New Jersey	894,305	566,247 **63.3%**	328,058 **36.7%**		
June 7	New Mexico	216,075	111,334 **51.5%**	104,741 **48.5%**		
June 7	South Dakota	53,006	27,047 **51.0%**	25,959 **49.0%**		
June 14	District of Columbia	97,763	76,704 **78.5%**	20,361 **20.8%**		698 **0.7%**
	Total	*30,805,885*	*17,121,492* **55.6%**	*13,210,266* **42.9%**	*151,399* **0.5%**	*322,728* **1.0%**

Notes: Table is limited to jurisdictions that vote for president in November—namely, the 50 states and District of Columbia. States not listed in the primary table held caucuses (Alaska, Colorado, Hawaii, Idaho, Iowa, Kansas, Maine, Minnesota, Nevada, North Dakota, Utah, Wyoming). The Democratic primaries in Nebraska and Washington were non-binding, and pledged delegates were bound to reflect the results of caucuses on March 5 and March 26, respectively.

Candidates who received at least 200,000 votes in the Democratic primaries are included in the table above. Other votes for names on the ballot in at least one primary: 110,243 Martin O'Malley; 66,954 Roque "Rocky" de la Fuente; 25,796 Willie Wilson; 21,694 Paul T. Farrell; 20,305 Keith Judd; 20,126 Michael Alan Steinberg; 11,062 Henry Hewes; 7,369 John Wolfe; 5,202 Star Locke; 4,893 Steve Burke; 2,407 Lawrence Cohen; 2,017 Calvis L. Hawes; 1,726 James Valentine; 486 Jon Adams; 268 Vermin Supreme; 265 Mark Stewart Greenstein; 226 David John Thistle; 143 Graham Schwass; 46 Lloyd Thomas Kelso; 36 Eric Elbot; 29 William D. French; 26 Edward T. O'Donnell; 25 David Formhals; 22 Robert Lovitt; 19 Bill McGaughey; 17 Edward Sonnino; 15 Steven Roy Lipscomb; 15 Sam Sloan; 14 Brock C. Hutton; 13 Andrew D. Basiago; 8 Raymond Michael Moroz; 8 Richard Lyons Weil; 6 Ignacio Leon Nunez; 3 Willie F. Carter; 2 Brian O'Neill; 1 Doug Terry; and 21,241 write-in votes. The Uncommitted column includes votes cast for an Uncommitted line or for a variation such as "No Preference" and "Uninstructed Delegation."

REPUBLICAN PRESIDENTIAL PRIMARIES 2016

Date	State	Total Vote	Trump	Cruz	Kasich	Rubio	Carson	Bush	Uncommitted	Other
February 9	New Hampshire	285,917	100,735 35.2%	33,244 11.6%	44,932 15.7%	30,071 10.5%	6,527 2.3%	31,341 11.0%		39,067 13.7%
February 20	South Carolina	740,881	240,882 32.5%	165,417 22.3%	56,410 7.6%	166,565 22.5%	53,551 7.2%	58,056 7.8%		
March 1	Alabama	860,652	373,721 43.4%	181,479 21.1%	38,119 4.4%	160,606 18.7%	88,094 10.2%	3,974 0.5%	7,953 0.9%	6,706 0.8%
March 1	Arkansas	410,920	134,744 32.8%	125,340 30.5%	15,305 3.7%	101,910 24.8%	23,521 5.7%	2,402 0.6%		7,698 1.9%
March 1	Georgia	1,295,964	502,994 38.8%	305,847 23.6%	72,508 5.6%	316,836 24.4%	80,723 6.2%	7,686 0.6%		9,370 0.7%
March 1	Massachusetts	636,263	312,425 49.1%	60,592 9.5%	114,434 18.0%	113,170 17.8%	16,360 2.6%	6,559 1.0%	3,220 0.5%	9,503 1.5%
March 1	Oklahoma	459,922	130,267 28.3%	158,078 34.4%	16,524 3.6%	119,633 26.0%	28,601 6.2%	2,091 0.5%		4,728 1.0%
March 1	Tennessee	855,729	333,180 38.9%	211,471 24.7%	45,301 5.3%	181,274 21.2%	64,951 7.6%	9,551 1.1%	1,849 0.2%	8,152 1.0%
March 1	Texas	2,836,488	758,762 26.8%	1,241,118 43.8%	120,473 4.2%	503,055 17.7%	117,969 4.2%	35,420 1.2%	29,609 1.0%	30,082 1.1%
March 1	Vermont	61,428	19,974 32.5%	5,932 9.7%	18,534 30.2%	11,781 19.2%	2,551 4.2%	1,106 1.8%		1,550 2.5%
March 1	Virginia	1,025,617	356,896 34.8%	171,162 16.7%	97,791 9.5%	327,936 32.0%	60,237 5.9%	3,645 0.4%		7,950 0.8%
March 5	Louisiana	301,241	124,854 41.4%	113,968 37.8%	19,359 6.4%	33,813 11.2%	4,544 1.5%	2,145 0.7%		2,558 0.8%
March 8	Idaho	222,004	62,413 28.1%	100,889 45.4%	16,514 7.4%	35,290 15.9%	3,853 1.7%	939 0.4%		2,106 0.9%
March 8	Michigan	1,323,589	483,753 36.5%	326,617 24.7%	321,115 24.3%	123,587 9.3%	21,349 1.6%	10,685 0.8%	22,824 1.7%	13,659 1.0%
March 8	Mississippi	416,270	196,659 47.2%	150,364 36.1%	36,795 8.8%	21,885 5.3%	5,626 1.4%	1,697 0.4%		3,244 0.8%
March 15	Florida	2,361,805	1,079,870 45.7%	404,891 17.1%	159,976 6.8%	638,661 27.0%	21,207 0.9%	43,511 1.8%		13,689 0.6%
March 15	Illinois	1,449,748	562,464 38.8%	438,235 30.2%	286,118 19.7%	126,681 8.7%	11,469 0.8%	11,188 0.8%		13,593 0.9%
March 15	Missouri	939,270	383,631 40.8%	381,666 40.6%	94,857 10.1%	57,244 6.1%	8,233 0.9%	3,361 0.4%	3,225 0.3%	7,053 0.8%
March 15	North Carolina	1,149,530	462,413 40.2%	422,621 36.8%	145,659 12.7%	88,907 7.7%	11,019 1.0%	3,893 0.3%	6,081 0.5%	8,937 0.8%
March 15	Ohio	1,988,960	713,404 35.9%	264,640 13.3%	933,886 47.0%	46,478 2.3%	14,351 0.7%	5,398 0.3%		10,803 0.5%
March 22	Arizona	624,039	286,743 45.9%	172,294 27.6%	65,965 10.6%	72,304 11.6%	14,940 2.4%	4,393 0.7%		7,400 1.2%
April 5	Wisconsin	1,105,944	387,295 35.0%	533,079 48.2%	155,902 14.1%	10,591 1.0%	5,660 0.5%	3,054 0.3%	2,281 0.2%	8,082 0.7%
April 19	New York	921,771	554,522 60.2%	136,083 14.8%	231,166 25.1%					
April 26	Connecticut	213,493	123,523 57.9%	24,987 11.7%	60,522 28.3%		1,733 0.8%		2,728 1.3%	
April 26	Delaware	69,892	42,472 60.8%	11,110 15.9%	14,225 20.4%	622 0.9%	885 1.3%	578 0.8%		
April 26	Maryland	459,066	248,343 54.1%	87,093 19.0%	106,614 23.2%	3,201 0.7%	5,946 1.3%	2,770 0.6%		5,099 1.1%
April 26	Pennsylvania	1,594,475	902,593 56.6%	345,506 21.7%	310,003 19.4%	11,954 0.7%	14,842 0.9%	9,577 0.6%		
April 26	Rhode Island	61,614	39,221 63.7%	6,416 10.4%	14,963 24.3%	382 0.6%			417 0.7%	215 0.3%
May 3	Indiana	1,110,543	591,514 53.3%	406,783 36.6%	84,111 7.6%	5,175 0.5%	8,914 0.8%	6,508 0.6%		7,538 0.7%
May 10	Nebraska	198,988	122,327 61.5%	36,703 18.4%	22,709 11.4%	7,233 3.6%	10,016 5.0%			
May 10	West Virginia	204,061	157,238 77.1%	18,301 9.0%	13,721 6.7%	2,908 1.4%	4,421 2.2%	2,305 1.1%		5,167 2.5%

REPUBLICAN PRESIDENTIAL PRIMARIES 2016

Date	State	Total Vote	Trump	Cruz	Kasich	Rubio	Carson	Bush	Uncommitted	Other
May 17	Oregon	393,920	252,748 64.2%	65,513 16.6%	62,248 15.8%					13,411 3.4%
May 24	Washington	602,998	455,023 75.5%	65,172 10.8%	58,954 9.8%		23,849 4.0%			
June 7	California	2,227,306	1,665,135 74.8%	211,576 9.5%	252,544 11.3%		82,259 3.7%			15,792 0.7%
June 7	Montana	156,888	115,594 73.7%	14,682 9.4%	10,777 6.9%	5,192 3.3%		3,274 2.1%	7,369 4.7%	
June 7	New Jersey	447,952	360,212 80.4%	27,874 6.2%	59,866 13.4%					
June 7	New Mexico	104,627	73,908 70.6%	13,925 13.3%	7,925 7.6%		3,830 3.7%	3,531 3.4%		1,508 1.4%
June 7	South Dakota	66,879	44,867 67.1%	11,352 17.0%	10,660 15.9%					
	Total	30,186,654	13,757,319 45.5%	7,452,020 24.7%	4,197,485 13.9%	3,324,945 11.0%	822,031 2.7%	280,638 0.9%	87,556 0.3%	264,660 0.9%

Notes: Table is limited to jurisdictions that vote for president in November—namely, the 50 states and District of Columbia. States not listed in the primary table held caucuses (Alaska, Colorado, District of Columbia, Hawaii, Iowa, Kansas, Kentucky, Maine, Minnesota, Nevada, North Dakota, Utah, Wyoming).

Candidates who recieved at least 200,000 votes in the Republican primaries are included in the table above. Other votes for names on the ballot in at least one primary: 57,153 Rand Paul; 54,216 Chris Christie; 47,824 Mike Huckabee; 36,660 Carly Fiorina; 18,327 James S. Gilmore; 14,770 Rick Santorum; 5,666 Lindsey Graham; 5,449 Elizabeth Gray; 2,036 George E. Pataki; 517 Timothy Cook; 222 Bobby Jindal; 203 David E. Hall; 202 Andy Martin; 104 Richard P.H. Witz; 100 James P. Lynch; 81 Peter Messina; 56 Brooks Cullison; 47 Frank Lynch; 44 Joe Robinson; 44 Victor Williams; 35 David P. Thompson; 32 Stephen Bradley Comley; 31 Joann Breivogel; 16 Chopmi Prag; 15 J. Daniel Dyas; 14 John Dowell; 12 Stephen John McCarthy; 10 Donald J. Gonzalez; 9 Walter N. Iwachiw; 8 Kevin Glenn Huey; 7 James Alexander-Pace; 6 Frederic Vidal; 6 Matt Drozd; 5 Troy Hugh Southern; 3 James Orlando Ogle; 2 James Germalio; and 20,724 write-ins. The Uncommitted column includes votes cast for an Uncommitted line or for a variation such as "No Preference" and "Uninstructed Delegation."

ALABAMA

Congressional districts first established for elections held in 2012

7 members

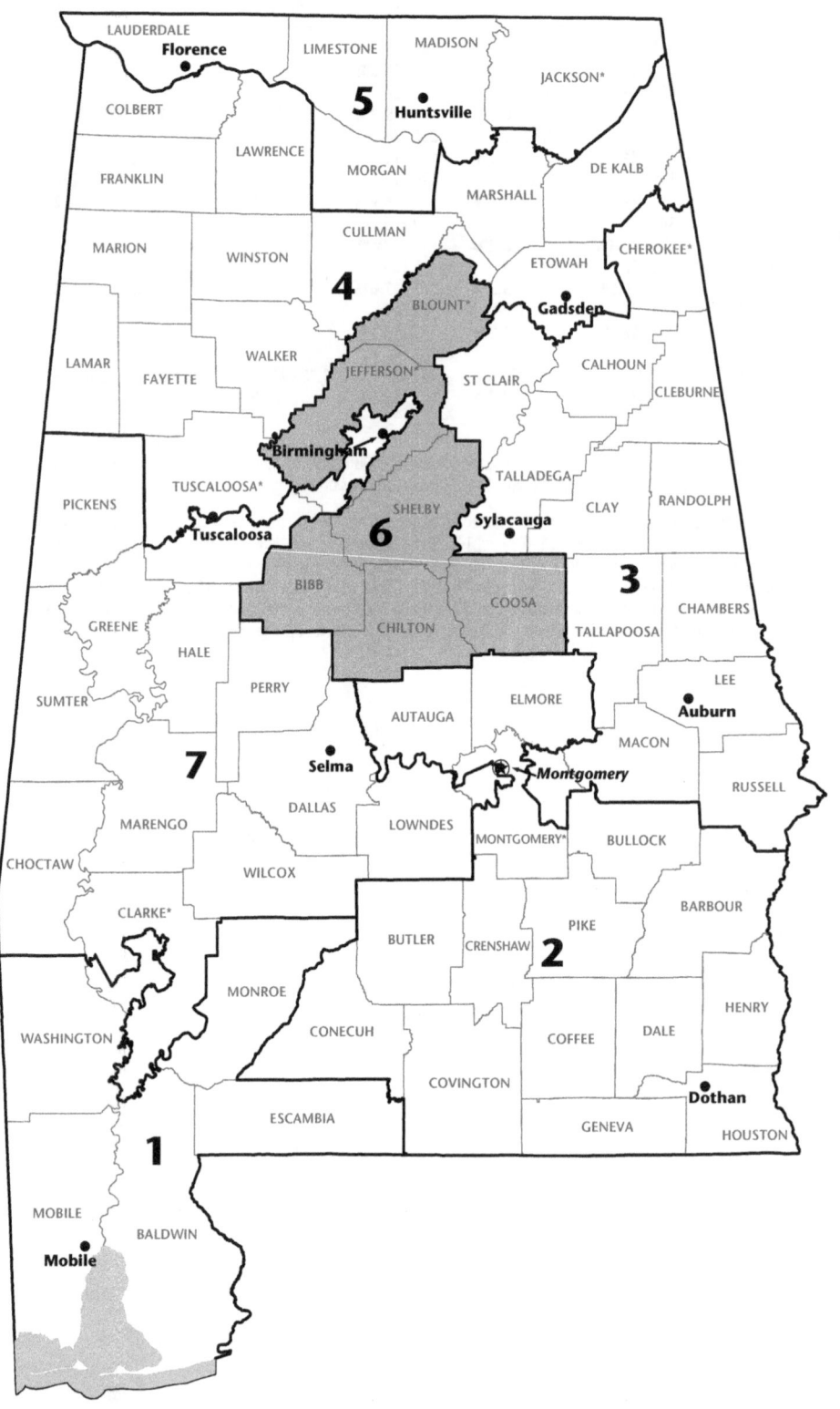

* Asterisk indicates a county whose boundaries include parts of two or more congressional districts.

ALABAMA

GOVERNOR

Kay Ivey (R). Sworn in April 10, 2017, to complete the remainder of the term vacated by the resignation of Robert Bentley (R). who left office under threat of impeachment. He pleaded guilty to two misdemeanors for using public resources to cover up an affair with a top adviser.

SENATORS (2 Republicans)

Luther Strange (R). Sworn in February 9, 2017, to fill temporarily the seat vacated by the resignation of Jeff Sessions to become U.S. attorney general, until the special election scheduled for December 12, 2017.

Richard C. Shelby (R). Re-elected 2016 to a six-year term. Previously elected 2010, 2004, 1998, 1992, 1986. Changed party affiliation from Democratic to Republican in November 1994.

REPRESENTATIVES (6 Republicans, 1 Democrat)

1. Bradley Byrne (R)
2. Martha Roby (R)
3. Mike Rogers (R)
4. Robert B. Aderholt (R)
5. Mo Brooks (R)
6. Gary J. Palmer (R)
7. Terri A. Sewell (D)

POSTWAR VOTE FOR PRESIDENT

Year	Total Vote	Republican Vote	Republican Candidate	Democratic Vote	Democratic Candidate	Other Vote	Rep.-Dem. Plurality	Total Vote Rep.	Total Vote Dem.	Major Vote Rep.	Major Vote Dem.
2016**	2,123,372	1,318,255	Trump, Donald J.	729,547	Clinton, Hillary Rodham	75,570	588,708 R	62.1%	34.4%	64.4%	35.6%
2012	2,074,338	1,255,925	Romney, W. Mitt	795,696	Obama, Barack H.*	22,717	460,229 R	60.5%	38.4%	61.2%	38.8%
2008	2,099,819	1,266,546	McCain, John S. III	813,479	Obama, Barack H.	19,794	453,067 R	60.3%	38.7%	60.9%	39.1%
2004	1,883,449	1,176,394	Bush, George W.*	693,933	Kerry, John F.	13,122	482,461 R	62.5%	36.8%	62.9%	37.1%
2000**	1,666,272	941,173	Bush, George W.	692,611	Gore, Albert Jr.	32,488	248,562 R	56.5%	41.6%	57.6%	42.4%
1996**	1,534,349	769,044	Dole, Robert "Bob"	662,165	Clinton, Bill*	103,140	106,879 R	50.1%	43.2%	53.7%	46.3%
1992**	1,688,060	804,283	Bush, George H.*	690,080	Clinton, Bill	193,697	114,203 R	47.6%	40.9%	53.8%	46.2%
1988	1,378,476	815,576	Bush, George H.	549,506	Dukakis, Michael S.	13,394	266,070 R	59.2%	39.9%	59.7%	40.3%
1984	1,441,713	872,849	Reagan, Ronald*	551,899	Mondale, Walter F.	16,965	320,950 R	60.5%	38.3%	61.3%	38.7%
1980**	1,341,929	654,192	Reagan, Ronald	636,730	Carter, Jimmy*	51,007	17,462 R	48.8%	47.4%	50.7%	49.3%
1976	1,182,850	504,070	Ford, Gerald R.*	659,170	Carter, Jimmy	19,610	155,100 D	42.6%	55.7%	43.3%	56.7%
1972	1,006,111	728,701	Nixon, Richard M.*	256,923	McGovern, George S.	20,487	471,778 R	72.4%	25.5%	73.9%	26.1%
1968**	1,049,922	146,923	Nixon, Richard M.	196,579	Humphrey, Hubert Horatio Jr.	706,420	49,656 D	14.0%	18.7%	42.8%	57.2%
1964**	689,818	479,085	Goldwater, Barry M. Sr.		Johnson, Lyndon B.*	210,733		69.5%		100.0%	
1960	570,225	237,981	Nixon, Richard M.	324,050	Kennedy, John F.	8,194	86,069 D	41.7%	56.8%	42.3%	57.7%
1956	496,861	195,694	Eisenhower, Dwight D.*	280,844	Stevenson, Adlai E. II	20,323	85,150 D	39.4%	56.5%	41.1%	58.9%
1952	426,120	149,231	Eisenhower, Dwight D.	275,075	Stevenson, Adlai E. II	1,814	125,844 D	35.0%	64.6%	35.2%	64.8%
1948**	214,980	40,930	Dewey, Thomas E.		Truman, Harry S.*	174,050		19.0%		100.0%	

Note: An asterisk (*) denotes incumbent. **In past elections, the other vote included: 2016 - 44,467 Independent (Gary Johnson); 2000 - 18,323 Green (Ralph Nader); 1996 - 92,149 Reform (Ross Perot); 1992 - 183,109 Independent (Perot); 1980 - 16,481 Independent (John Anderson); 1968 - 691,425 American Independent (George Wallace); 1964 - 210,732 Unpledged Democratic; 1948 - 171,443 States' Rights (Strom Thurmond). In 1964 and 1948, the Democratic presidential candidates were not listed on the ballot. Wallace carried Alabama in 1968 with 65.9 percent of the total vote. Thurmond won the state in 1948 with 79.7 percent.

ALABAMA

POSTWAR VOTE FOR GOVERNOR

Year	Total Vote	Republican Vote	Republican Candidate	Democratic Vote	Democratic Candidate	Other Vote	Rep.-Dem. Plurality	Total Vote Rep.	Total Vote Dem.	Major Vote Rep.	Major Vote Dem.
2014	1,180,413	750,231	Bentley, Robert*	427,787	Griffith, Parker	2,395	322,444 R	63.6%	36.2%	63.7%	36.3%
2010	1,494,273	860,472	Bentley, Robert	625,710	Sparks, Ron	8,091	234,762 R	57.6%	41.9%	57.9%	42.1%
2006	1,250,401	718,327	Riley, Robert*	519,827	Baxley, Lucy	12,247	198,500 R	57.4%	41.6%	58.0%	42.0%
2002	1,367,053	672,225	Riley, Robert	669,105	Siegelman, Don*	25,723	3,120 R	49.2%	48.9%	50.1%	49.9%
1998	1,317,842	554,746	James, Forrest H. "Fob" Jr.*	760,155	Siegelman, Don	2,941	205,409 D	42.1%	57.7%	42.2%	57.8%
1994	1,201,969	604,926	James, Forrest H. "Fob" Jr.	594,169	Folsom, James E. Jr.*	2,874	10,757 R	50.3%	49.4%	50.4%	49.6%
1990	1,216,250	633,519	Hunt, Guy*	582,106	Hubbert, Paul R.	625	51,413 R	52.1%	47.9%	52.1%	47.9%
1986	1,236,230	696,203	Hunt, Guy	537,163	Baxley, Bill	2,864	159,040 R	56.3%	43.5%	56.4%	43.6%
1982	1,128,725	440,815	Folmar, Emory	650,538	Wallace, George C.	37,372	209,723 D	39.1%	57.6%	40.4%	59.6%
1978	760,474	196,963	Hunt, Guy	551,886	James, Forrest H. "Fob" Jr.	11,625	354,923 D	25.9%	72.6%	26.3%	73.7%
1974	598,305	88,381	McCary, Elvin	497,574	Wallace, George C.*	12,350	409,193 D	14.8%	83.2%	15.1%	84.9%
1970**	854,952			637,046	Wallace, George C.	217,906	637,046 D		74.5%		100.0%
1966	848,101	262,943	Martin, James D.	537,505	Wallace, Lurleen B.	47,653	274,562 D	31.0%	63.4%	32.8%	67.2%
1962	315,776			303,987	Wallace, George C.	11,789	303,987 D		96.3%		100.0%
1958	270,952	30,415	Longshore, William L. Jr.	239,633	Patterson, John	904	209,218 D	11.2%	88.4%	11.3%	88.7%
1954	333,090	88,688	Abernethy, Tom	244,401	Folsom, James E.	1	155,713 D	26.6%	73.4%	26.6%	73.4%
1950	170,591	15,177	Crowder, John S.	155,414	Persons, Gordon		140,237 D	8.9%	91.1%	8.9%	91.1%
1946	197,321	22,362	Ward, Lyman	174,959	Folsom, James E.		152,597 D	11.3%	88.7%	11.3%	88.7%

Note: An asterisk (*) denotes incumbent. **In past elections, the other vote included: 1970 - 125,491 National Democratic Party of Alabama (John Logan Cashin, who finished second). The Republican Party did not run a candidate in the 1962 and 1970 gubernatorial elections.

POSTWAR VOTE FOR SENATOR

Year	Total Vote	Republican Vote	Republican Candidate	Democratic Vote	Democratic Candidate	Other Vote	Rep.-Dem. Plurality	Total Vote Rep.	Total Vote Dem.	Major Vote Rep.	Major Vote Dem.
2016	2,087,444	1,335,104	Shelby, Richard C.*	748,709	Crumpton, Ron	3,631	586,395 R	64.0%	35.9%	64.1%	35.9%
2014	818,090	795,606	Sessions, Jeff*			22,484	795,606 R	97.3%		100.0%	
2010	1,485,499	968,181	Shelby, Richard C.*	515,619	Barnes, William G.	1,699	452,562 R	65.2%	34.7%	65.3%	34.7%
2008	2,060,191	1,305,383	Sessions, Jeff*	752,391	Figures, Vivian Davis	2,417	552,992 R	63.4%	36.5%	63.4%	36.6%
2004	1,839,066	1,242,200	Shelby, Richard C.*	595,018	Sowell, Wayne	1,848	647,182 R	67.5%	32.4%	67.6%	32.4%
2002	1,353,023	792,561	Sessions, Jeff*	538,878	Parker, Susan	21,584	253,683 R	58.6%	39.8%	59.5%	40.5%
1998	1,293,405	817,973	Shelby, Richard C.*	474,568	Suddith, Clayton	864	343,405 R	63.2%	36.7%	63.3%	36.7%
1996	1,499,393	786,436	Sessions, Jeff	681,651	Bedford, Roger	31,306	104,785 R	52.5%	45.5%	53.6%	46.4%
1992	1,577,899	522,015	Sellers, Richard	1,022,698	Shelby, Richard C.	33,186	500,683 D	33.1%	64.8%	33.8%	66.2%
1990	1,185,563	467,190	Cabaniss, Bill	717,814	Heflin, Howell*	559	250,624 D	39.4%	60.5%	39.4%	60.6%
1986	1,211,953	602,537	Denton, Jeremiah*	609,360	Shelby, Richard C.	56	6,823 D	49.7%	50.3%	49.7%	50.3%
1984	1,371,238	498,508	Smith, Albert Lee Jr.	860,535	Heflin, Howell*	12,195	362,027 D	36.4%	62.8%	36.7%	63.3%
1980	1,296,757	650,362	Denton, Jeremiah	610,175	Folsom, James E. Jr.	36,220	40,187 R	50.2%	47.1%	51.6%	48.4%
1978	582,025			547,054	Heflin, Howell	34,971	547,054 D		94.0%		100.0%
1978S**	731,610	316,170	Martin, James D.	401,852	Stewart, Donald W.	13,588	85,682 D	43.2%	54.9%	44.0%	56.0%
1974	523,290			501,541	Allen, James B.*	21,749	501,541 D		95.8%		100.0%
1972	1,051,099	347,523	Blount, Winton M.	654,491	Sparkman, Richard D.*	49,085	306,968 D	33.1%	62.3%	34.7%	65.3%
1968	912,708	201,227	Hooper, Perry	638,774	Allen, James B.	72,707	437,547 D	22.0%	70.0%	24.0%	76.0%
1966	802,608	313,018	Grenier, John	482,138	Sparkman, John J.*	7,452	169,120 D	39.0%	60.1%	39.4%	60.6%
1962	397,079	195,134	Martin, James D.	201,937	Hill, Lister*	8	6,803 D	49.1%	50.9%	49.1%	50.9%
1960	554,081	164,868	Elgin, Julian	389,196	Sparkman, John J.*	17	224,328 D	29.8%	70.2%	29.8%	70.2%
1956	330,191			330,182	Hill, Lister*	9	330,182 D		100%		100.0%
1954	314,459	55,110	Guin, J. Foy Jr.	259,348	Sparkman, John J.*	1	204,238 D	17.5%	82.5%	17.5%	82.5%
1950	164,011			125,534	Hill, Lister*	38,477	125,534 D		76.5%		100.0%
1948	220,875	35,341	Parsons, Paul G.	185,534	Sparkman, John J.*		150,193 D	16.0%	84.0%	16.0%	84.0%
1946S**	163,217			163,217	Sparkman, John J.*		163,217 D		100%		100.0%

Note: An asterisk (*) denotes incumbent. **The 1946 election and one of the 1978 elections were for short terms to fill vacancies. The Republican Party did not run a candidate in Senate elections in 1946, 1950, 1956, 1974, and 1978.

ALABAMA

PRESIDENT 2016

2010 Census Population	County	Total Vote	Republican (Trump)	Democratic (Clinton)	Other	Rep.-Dem. Plurality	Percentage			
							Total Vote		Major Vote	
							Rep.	Dem.	Rep.	Dem.
54,571	AUTAUGA	24,973	18,172	5,936	865	12,236 R	72.8%	23.8%	75.4%	24.6%
182,265	BALDWIN	95,215	72,883	18,458	3,874	54,425 R	76.5%	19.4%	79.8%	20.2%
27,457	BARBOUR	10,469	5,454	4,871	144	583 R	52.1%	46.5%	52.8%	47.2%
22,915	BIBB	8,819	6,738	1,874	207	4,864 R	76.4%	21.2%	78.2%	21.8%
57,322	BLOUNT	25,588	22,859	2,156	573	20,703 R	89.3%	8.4%	91.4%	8.6%
10,914	BULLOCK	4,710	1,140	3,530	40	2,390 D	24.2%	74.9%	24.4%	75.6%
20,947	BUTLER	8,732	4,901	3,726	105	1,175 R	56.1%	42.7%	56.8%	43.2%
118,572	CALHOUN	47,864	32,865	13,242	1,757	19,623 R	68.7%	27.7%	71.3%	28.7%
34,215	CHAMBERS	13,900	7,843	5,784	273	2,059 R	56.4%	41.6%	57.6%	42.4%
25,989	CHEROKEE	10,733	8,953	1,547	233	7,406 R	83.4%	14.4%	85.3%	14.7%
43,643	CHILTON	18,369	15,081	2,911	377	12,170 R	82.1%	15.8%	83.8%	16.2%
13,859	CHOCTAW	7,292	4,106	3,109	77	997 R	56.3%	42.6%	56.9%	43.1%
25,833	CLARKE	13,031	7,140	5,749	142	1,391 R	54.8%	44.1%	55.4%	44.6%
13,932	CLAY	6,624	5,245	1,237	142	4,008 R	79.2%	18.7%	80.9%	19.1%
14,972	CLEBURNE	6,593	5,764	684	145	5,080 R	87.4%	10.4%	89.4%	10.6%
49,948	COFFEE	20,767	15,875	4,221	671	11,654 R	76.4%	20.3%	79.0%	21.0%
54,428	COLBERT	24,915	16,746	7,312	857	9,434 R	67.2%	29.3%	69.6%	30.4%
13,228	CONECUH	6,585	3,420	3,080	85	340 R	51.9%	46.8%	52.6%	47.4%
11,539	COOSA	5,252	3,381	1,782	89	1,599 R	64.4%	33.9%	65.5%	34.5%
37,765	COVINGTON	15,940	13,267	2,387	286	10,880 R	83.2%	15.0%	84.8%	15.2%
13,906	CRENSHAW	6,267	4,513	1,664	90	2,849 R	72.0%	26.6%	73.1%	26.9%
80,406	CULLMAN	37,873	32,989	3,798	1,086	29,191 R	87.1%	10.0%	89.7%	10.3%
50,251	DALE	18,749	13,808	4,413	528	9,395 R	73.6%	23.5%	75.8%	24.2%
43,820	DALLAS	18,792	5,789	12,836	167	7,047 D	30.8%	68.3%	31.1%	68.9%
71,109	DEKALB	25,826	21,405	3,622	799	17,783 R	82.9%	14.0%	85.5%	14.5%
79,303	ELMORE	37,260	27,634	8,443	1,183	19,191 R	74.2%	22.7%	76.6%	23.4%
38,319	ESCAMBIA	14,845	9,935	4,605	305	5,330 R	66.9%	31.0%	68.3%	31.7%
104,430	ETOWAH	44,164	32,353	10,442	1,369	21,911 R	73.3%	23.6%	75.6%	24.4%
17,241	FAYETTE	8,249	6,712	1,362	175	5,350 R	81.4%	16.5%	83.1%	16.9%
31,704	FRANKLIN	12,040	9,466	2,197	377	7,269 R	78.6%	18.2%	81.2%	18.8%
26,790	GENEVA	11,758	9,994	1,525	239	8,469 R	85.0%	13.0%	86.8%	13.2%
9,045	GREENE	4,880	838	4,013	29	3,175 D	17.2%	82.2%	17.3%	82.7%
15,760	HALE	8,040	3,173	4,775	92	1,602 D	39.5%	59.4%	39.9%	60.1%
17,302	HENRY	8,072	5,632	2,292	148	3,340 R	69.8%	28.4%	71.1%	28.9%
101,547	HOUSTON	42,639	30,728	10,664	1,247	20,064 R	72.1%	25.0%	74.2%	25.8%
53,227	JACKSON	20,984	16,672	3,673	639	12,999 R	79.5%	17.5%	81.9%	18.1%
658,466	JEFFERSON	304,191	134,768	156,873	12,550	22,105 D	44.3%	51.6%	46.2%	53.8%
14,564	LAMAR	6,966	5,823	1,036	107	4,787 R	83.6%	14.9%	84.9%	15.1%
92,709	LAUDERDALE	39,525	27,899	9,952	1,674	17,947 R	70.6%	25.2%	73.7%	26.3%
34,339	LAWRENCE	14,829	10,833	3,627	369	7,206 R	73.1%	24.5%	74.9%	25.1%
140,247	LEE	59,191	34,617	21,230	3,344	13,387 R	58.5%	35.9%	62.0%	38.0%
82,782	LIMESTONE	40,294	29,067	9,468	1,759	19,599 R	72.1%	23.5%	75.4%	24.6%
11,299	LOWNDES	6,684	1,751	4,883	50	3,132 D	26.2%	73.1%	26.4%	73.6%
21,452	MACON	9,140	1,431	7,566	143	6,135 D	15.7%	82.8%	15.9%	84.1%
334,811	MADISON	163,389	89,520	62,822	11,047	26,698 R	54.8%	38.4%	58.8%	41.2%
21,027	MARENGO	10,994	5,233	5,615	146	382 D	47.6%	51.1%	48.2%	51.8%
30,776	MARION	12,984	11,274	1,432	278	9,842 R	86.8%	11.0%	88.7%	11.3%
93,019	MARSHALL	35,316	29,233	4,917	1,166	24,316 R	82.8%	13.9%	85.6%	14.4%
412,992	MOBILE	172,737	95,116	72,186	5,435	22,930 R	55.1%	41.8%	56.9%	43.1%
23,068	MONROE	10,271	5,795	4,332	144	1,463 R	56.4%	42.2%	57.2%	42.8%
229,363	MONTGOMERY	95,878	34,003	58,916	2,959	24,913 D	35.5%	61.4%	36.6%	63.4%
119,490	MORGAN	50,644	37,486	11,254	1,904	26,232 R	74.0%	22.2%	76.9%	23.1%
10,591	PERRY	5,278	1,407	3,824	47	2,417 D	26.7%	72.5%	26.9%	73.1%
19,746	PICKENS	9,542	5,456	3,972	114	1,484 R	57.2%	41.6%	57.9%	42.1%
32,899	PIKE	13,168	7,693	5,056	419	2,637 R	58.4%	38.4%	60.3%	39.7%
22,913	RANDOLPH	10,187	7,705	2,291	191	5,414 R	75.6%	22.5%	77.1%	22.9%
52,947	RUSSELL	19,256	9,210	9,579	467	369 D	47.8%	49.7%	49.0%	51.0%
195,085	SHELBY	101,254	73,020	22,977	5,257	50,043 R	72.1%	22.7%	76.1%	23.9%
83,593	ST. CLAIR	38,400	31,651	5,589	1,160	26,062 R	82.4%	14.6%	85.0%	15.0%
13,763	SUMTER	6,411	1,581	4,746	84	3,165 D	24.7%	74.0%	25.0%	75.0%

ALABAMA
PRESIDENT 2016

2010 Census Population	County	Total Vote	Republican (Trump)	Democratic (Clinton)	Other	Rep.-Dem. Plurality	Percentage			
							Total Vote		Major Vote	
							Rep.	Dem.	Rep.	Dem.
82,291	TALLADEGA	33,407	20,614	12,121	672	8,493 R	61.7%	36.3%	63.0%	37.0%
41,616	TALLAPOOSA	19,486	13,594	5,519	373	8,075 R	69.8%	28.3%	71.1%	28.9%
194,656	TUSCALOOSA	82,700	47,723	31,762	3,215	15,961 R	57.7%	38.4%	60.0%	40.0%
67,023	WALKER	29,472	24,266	4,497	709	19,769 R	82.3%	15.3%	84.4%	15.6%
17,581	WASHINGTON	8,533	6,042	2,374	117	3,668 R	70.8%	27.8%	71.8%	28.2%
11,670	WILCOX	6,123	1,742	4,339	42	2,597 D	28.5%	70.9%	28.6%	71.4%
24,484	WINSTON	10,313	9,228	872	213	8,356 R	89.5%	8.5%	91.4%	8.6%
4,779,736	TOTAL	2,123,372	1,318,255	729,547	75,570	588,708 R	62.1%	34.4%	64.4%	35.6%

ALABAMA
SENATOR 2016

2010 Census Population	County	Total Vote	Republican (Shelby)	Democratic (Crumpton)	Other	Rep.-Dem. Plurality	Percentage			
							Total Vote		Major Vote	
							Rep.	Dem.	Rep.	Dem.
54,571	AUTAUGA	24,613	18,220	6,331	62	11,889 R	74.0%	25.7%	74.2%	25.8%
182,265	BALDWIN	93,414	74,021	19,145	248	54,876 R	79.2%	20.5%	79.5%	20.5%
27,457	BARBOUR	10,229	5,436	4,777	16	659 R	53.1%	46.7%	53.2%	46.8%
22,915	BIBB	8,711	6,612	2,082	17	4,530 R	75.9%	23.9%	76.1%	23.9%
57,322	BLOUNT	25,197	22,169	2,980	48	19,189 R	88.0%	11.8%	88.2%	11.8%
10,914	BULLOCK	4,537	1,167	3,364	6	2,197 D	25.7%	74.1%	25.8%	74.2%
20,947	BUTLER	8,510	4,840	3,663	7	1,177 R	56.9%	43.0%	56.9%	43.1%
118,572	CALHOUN	47,197	32,976	14,152	69	18,824 R	69.9%	30.0%	70.0%	30.0%
34,215	CHAMBERS	13,728	7,865	5,845	18	2,020 R	57.3%	42.6%	57.4%	42.6%
25,989	CHEROKEE	10,558	8,636	1,915	7	6,721 R	81.8%	18.1%	81.9%	18.1%
43,643	CHILTON	17,934	14,582	3,327	25	11,255 R	81.3%	18.6%	81.4%	18.6%
13,859	CHOCTAW	7,035	4,035	2,992	8	1,043 R	57.4%	42.5%	57.4%	42.6%
25,833	CLARKE	12,730	7,158	5,558	14	1,600 R	56.2%	43.7%	56.3%	43.7%
13,932	CLAY	6,528	5,147	1,377	4	3,770 R	78.8%	21.1%	78.9%	21.1%
14,972	CLEBURNE	6,407	5,554	847	6	4,707 R	86.7%	13.2%	86.8%	13.2%
49,948	COFFEE	20,292	15,745	4,498	49	11,247 R	77.6%	22.2%	77.8%	22.2%
54,428	COLBERT	24,337	15,866	8,443	28	7,423 R	65.2%	34.7%	65.3%	34.7%
13,228	CONECUH	6,311	3,298	3,006	7	292 R	52.3%	47.6%	52.3%	47.7%
11,539	COOSA	5,174	3,378	1,788	8	1,590 R	65.3%	34.6%	65.4%	34.6%
37,765	COVINGTON	15,466	12,690	2,740	36	9,950 R	82.1%	17.7%	82.2%	17.8%
13,906	CRENSHAW	6,137	4,392	1,734	11	2,658 R	71.6%	28.3%	71.7%	28.3%
80,406	CULLMAN	37,265	32,001	5,207	57	26,794 R	85.9%	14.0%	86.0%	14.0%
50,251	DALE	18,335	13,652	4,625	58	9,027 R	74.5%	25.2%	74.7%	25.3%
43,820	DALLAS	18,462	6,060	12,388	14	6,328 D	32.8%	67.1%	32.8%	67.2%
71,109	DEKALB	25,123	20,347	4,749	27	15,598 R	81.0%	18.9%	81.1%	18.9%
79,303	ELMORE	36,526	27,591	8,833	102	18,758 R	75.5%	24.2%	75.7%	24.3%
38,319	ESCAMBIA	14,197	9,555	4,625	17	4,930 R	67.3%	32.6%	67.4%	32.6%
104,430	ETOWAH	43,506	31,441	11,981	84	19,460 R	72.3%	27.5%	72.4%	27.6%
17,241	FAYETTE	8,065	6,555	1,497	13	5,058 R	81.3%	18.6%	81.4%	18.6%
31,704	FRANKLIN	11,534	8,670	2,850	14	5,820 R	75.2%	24.7%	75.3%	24.7%
26,790	GENEVA	11,437	9,606	1,803	28	7,803 R	84.0%	15.8%	84.2%	15.8%
9,045	GREENE	4,755	918	3,834	3	2,916 D	19.3%	80.6%	19.3%	80.7%
15,760	HALE	7,863	3,208	4,650	5	1,442 D	40.8%	59.1%	40.8%	59.2%
17,302	HENRY	7,895	5,506	2,366	23	3,140 R	69.7%	30.0%	69.9%	30.1%
101,547	HOUSTON	41,833	30,494	11,219	120	19,275 R	72.9%	26.8%	73.1%	26.9%

ALABAMA

SENATOR 2016

2010 Census Population	County	Total Vote	Republican (Shelby)	Democratic (Crumpton)	Other	Rep.-Dem. Plurality	Total Vote Rep.	Total Vote Dem.	Major Vote Rep.	Major Vote Dem.
53,227	JACKSON	20,301	15,742	4,538	21	11,204 R	77.5%	22.4%	77.6%	22.4%
658,466	JEFFERSON	301,163	144,136	156,574	453	12,438 D	47.9%	52.0%	47.9%	52.1%
14,564	LAMAR	6,763	5,634	1,125	4	4,509 R	83.3%	16.6%	83.4%	16.6%
92,709	LAUDERDALE	38,787	27,092	11,652	43	15,440 R	69.8%	30.0%	69.9%	30.1%
34,339	LAWRENCE	14,441	10,254	4,171	16	6,083 R	71.0%	28.9%	71.1%	28.9%
140,247	LEE	58,294	36,684	21,475	135	15,209 R	62.9%	36.8%	63.1%	36.9%
82,782	LIMESTONE	39,493	29,203	10,233	57	18,970 R	73.9%	25.9%	74.1%	25.9%
11,299	LOWNDES	6,426	1,839	4,580	7	2,741 D	28.6%	71.3%	28.6%	71.4%
21,452	MACON	9,004	1,553	7,442	9	5,889 D	17.2%	82.7%	17.3%	82.7%
334,811	MADISON	160,990	97,796	62,870	324	34,926 R	60.7%	39.1%	60.9%	39.1%
21,027	MARENGO	10,718	5,294	5,419	5	125 D	49.4%	50.6%	49.4%	50.6%
30,776	MARION	12,741	10,753	1,961	27	8,792 R	84.4%	15.4%	84.6%	15.4%
93,019	MARSHALL	34,485	28,532	5,898	55	22,634 R	82.7%	17.1%	82.9%	17.1%
412,992	MOBILE	169,892	97,911	71,602	379	26,309 R	57.6%	42.1%	57.8%	42.2%
23,068	MONROE	10,122	5,854	4,255	13	1,599 R	57.8%	42.0%	57.9%	42.1%
229,363	MONTGOMERY	94,611	36,477	57,972	162	21,495 D	38.6%	61.3%	38.6%	61.4%
119,490	MORGAN	49,830	37,448	12,325	57	25,123 R	75.2%	24.7%	75.2%	24.8%
10,591	PERRY	5,154	1,496	3,656	2	2,160 D	29.0%	70.9%	29.0%	71.0%
19,746	PICKENS	9,298	5,384	3,908	6	1,476 R	57.9%	42.0%	57.9%	42.1%
32,899	PIKE	12,899	7,835	5,037	27	2,798 R	60.7%	39.0%	60.9%	39.1%
22,913	RANDOLPH	9,887	7,454	2,424	9	5,030 R	75.4%	24.5%	75.5%	24.5%
52,947	RUSSELL	18,921	9,408	9,487	26	79 D	49.7%	50.1%	49.8%	50.2%
195,085	SHELBY	100,032	75,344	24,483	205	50,861 R	75.3%	24.5%	75.5%	24.5%
83,593	ST. CLAIR	37,994	31,279	6,635	80	24,644 R	82.3%	17.5%	82.5%	17.5%
13,763	SUMTER	6,271	1,656	4,611	4	2,955 D	26.4%	73.5%	26.4%	73.6%
82,291	TALLADEGA	33,107	20,446	12,632	29	7,814 R	61.8%	38.2%	61.8%	38.2%
41,616	TALLAPOOSA	19,222	13,401	5,804	17	7,597 R	69.7%	30.2%	69.8%	30.2%
194,656	TUSCALOOSA	81,655	49,923	31,602	130	18,321 R	61.1%	38.7%	61.2%	38.8%
67,023	WALKER	29,026	23,419	5,558	49	17,861 R	80.7%	19.1%	80.8%	19.2%
17,581	WASHINGTON	8,298	5,830	2,463	5	3,367 R	70.3%	29.7%	70.3%	29.7%
11,670	WILCOX	5,680	1,819	3,857	4	2,038 D	32.0%	67.9%	32.0%	68.0%
24,484	WINSTON	10,098	8,817	1,269	12	7,548 R	87.3%	12.6%	87.4%	12.6%
4,779,736	TOTAL	2,087,444	1,335,104	748,709	3,631	586,395 R	64.0%	35.9%	64.1%	35.9%

ALABAMA

HOUSE OF REPRESENTATIVES

CD	Year	Total Vote	Republican Vote	Republican Candidate	Democratic Vote	Democratic Candidate	Other Vote	Rep.-Dem. Plurality	Total Vote Rep.	Total Vote Dem.	Major Vote Rep.	Major Vote Dem.
1	2016	215,893	208,083	BYRNE, BRADLEY*			7,810	208,083 R	96.4%		100.0%	
1	2014	152,234	103,758	BYRNE, BRADLEY*	48,278	LEFLORE, BURTON R.	198	55,480 R	68.2%	31.7%	68.2%	31.8%
1	2012	200,676	196,374	BONNER, JOSIAH ROBBINS "JO" JR.*			4,302	196,374 R	97.9%		100.0%	
2	2016	276,584	134,886	ROBY, MARTHA*	112,089	MATHIS, NATHAN	29,609	22,797 R	48.8%	40.5%	54.6%	45.4%
2	2014	167,952	113,103	ROBY, MARTHA*	54,692	WRIGHT, ERICK	157	58,411 R	67.3%	32.6%	67.4%	32.6%
2	2012	283,953	180,591	ROBY, MARTHA*	103,092	FORD, THERESE	270	77,499 R	63.6%	36.3%	63.7%	36.3%
3	2016	287,104	192,164	ROGERS, MIKE D.*	94,549	SMITH, JESSE TREMAIN	391	97,615 R	66.9%	32.9%	67.0%	33.0%
3	2014	156,620	103,558	ROGERS, MIKE D.*	52,816	SMITH, JESSE TREMAIN	246	50,742 R	66.1%	33.7%	66.2%	33.8%
3	2012	273,930	175,306	ROGERS, MIKE D.*	98,141	HARRIS, JOHN ANDREW	483	77,165 R	64.0%	35.8%	64.1%	35.9%

ALABAMA

HOUSE OF REPRESENTATIVES

			Republican		Democratic				Total Vote		Major Vote	
CD	Year	Total Vote	Vote	Candidate	Vote	Candidate	Other Vote	Rep.-Dem. Plurality	Rep.	Dem.	Rep.	Dem.
4	2016	239,444	235,925	ADERHOLT, ROBERT*			3,519	235,925 R	98.5%		100.0%	
4	2014	134,752	132,831	ADERHOLT, ROBERT*			1,921	132,831 R	98.6%		100.0%	
4	2012	269,118	199,071	ADERHOLT, ROBERT*	69,706	BOMAN, DANIEL H.	341	129,365 R	74.0%	25.9%	74.1%	25.9%
5	2016	308,326	205,647	BROOKS, MO*	102,234	BOYD, WILL	445	103,413 R	66.7%	33.2%	66.8%	33.2%
5	2014	154,974	115,338	BROOKS, MO*			39,636	115,338 R	74.4%		100.0%	
5	2012	291,293	189,185	BROOKS, MO*	101,772	HOLLEY, CHARLIE L.	336	87,413 R	64.9%	34.9%	65.0%	35.0%
6	2016	329,306	245,313	PALMER, GARY*	83,709	PUTMAN, DAVID	284	161,604 R	74.5%	25.4%	74.6%	25.4%
6	2014	178,449	135,945	PALMER, GARY	42,291	LESTER, MARK	213	93,654 R	76.2%	23.7%	76.3%	23.7%
6	2012	308,102	219,262	BACHUS, SPENCER*	88,267	BAILEY, PENNY "COLONEL"	573	130,995 R	71.2%	28.6%	71.3%	28.7%
7	2016	233,028			229,330	SEWELL, TERRI A.*	3,698	229,330 D		98.4%		100.0%
7	2014	135,899			133,687	SEWELL, TERRI A.*	2,212	133,687 D		98.4%		100.0%
7	2012	306,558	73,835	CHAMBERLAIN, DON	232,520	SEWELL, TERRI A.*	203	158,685 D	24.1%	75.8%	24.1%	75.9%
TOTAL	2016	1,889,685	1,222,018		621,911		45,756	600,107 R	64.7%	32.9%	66.3%	33.7%
TOTAL	2014	1,080,880	704,533		331,764		44,583	372,769 R	65.2%	30.7%	68.0%	32.0%
TOTAL	2012	1,933,630	1,233,624		693,498		6,508	540,126 R	63.8%	35.9%	64.0%	36.0%

Note: An asterisk (*) denotes incumbent.

ALABAMA

GENERAL AND PRIMARY ELECTIONS

2016 GENERAL ELECTIONS: OTHER VOTES

President   Other vote was 44,467 Independent (Gary Johnson), 21,712 Write-in (Scattered Write-in), 9,391 Independent (Jill Stein)

Senate   Other vote was 3,631 Write-in (Scattered Write-in)

House   Other vote was:

CD 1   7,810 Write-in (Scattered Write-in)
CD 2   29,609 Write-in (Scattered Write-in)
CD 3   391 Write-in (Scattered Write-in)
CD 4   3,519 Write-in (Scattered Write-in)
CD 5   445 Write-in (Scattered Write-in)
CD 6   284 Write-in (Scattered Write-in)
CD 7   3,698 Write-in (Scattered Write-in)

2016 PRIMARY ELECTIONS: SUPPLEMENTARY INFORMATION

Primary   March 1, 2016   **Registration** (as of January 12, 2016 — includes 155,740 inactive registrants)   3,012,313   No Party Registration

Primary Runoff   April 12, 2016

Primary Type   Open—Any registered voter could vote in either the Democratic or the Republican primary. Democratic primary voters could participate in a Republican runoff. However, Republican primary voters could not cast a ballot in a Democratic runoff.

ALABAMA

GENERAL AND PRIMARY ELECTIONS

	REPUBLICAN PRIMARIES			DEMOCRATIC PRIMARIES		
President	Trump, Donald J.	373,721	43.4%	Clinton, Hillary Rodham	311,141	77.8%
	Cruz, Ted	181,479	21.1%	Sanders, Bernard	76,878	19.2%
	Rubio, Marco	160,606	18.7%	Uncommitted	9,553	2.4%
	Carson, Ben	88,094	10.2%	O'Malley, Martin	1,499	0.4%
	Kasich, John R.	38,119	4.4%	De La Fuente, Roque "Rocky"	818	0.2%
	Uncommitted	7,953	0.9%			
	Bush, Jeb	3,974	0.5%			
	Huckabee, Mike	2,539	0.3%			
	Paul, Rand	1,895	0.2%			
	Christie, Chris	858	0.1%			
	Santorum, Rick	617	0.1%			
	Fiorina, Carly	544	0.1%			
	Graham, Lindsey	253				
	TOTAL	*860,652*		*TOTAL*	*399,889*	
Senator	Shelby, Richard C.*	505,586	64.9%	Crumpton, Ron	153,897	56.1%
	McConnell, Jonathan Edward	214,770	27.6%	Nana, Charles	120,526	43.9%
	Martin, John W.	23,558	3.0%			
	Bowman, Marcus	19,707	2.5%			
	McGill, Shadrack	15,230	2.0%			
	TOTAL	*778,851*		*TOTAL*	*274,423*	
Congressional District 1	Byrne, Bradley*	71,310	60.1%			
	Young, Dean	47,319	39.9%			
	TOTAL	*118,629*				
Congressional District 2	Roby, Martha*	78,689	66.4%	Mathis, Nathan	Unopposed	
	Gerritson, Rebecca "Becky"	33,015	27.8%			
	Rogers, Robert L. "Bob"	6,856	5.8%			
	TOTAL	*118,560*				
Congressional District 3	Rogers, Mike D.*	77,432	76.0%	Smith, Jesse Tremain	Unopposed	
	DiChiara, Larry	24,474	24.0%			
	TOTAL	*101,906*				
Congressional District 4	Aderholt, Robert*	86,660	81.2%			
	Norris, Phillip	20,096	18.8%			
	TOTAL	*106,756*				
Congressional District 5	Brooks, Mo*	Unopposed		Boyd, Will	Unopposed	
Congressional District 6	Palmer, Gary*	Unopposed		Putman, David	Unopposed	
Congressional District 7				Sewell, Terri A.*	Unopposed	

Note: An asterisk (*) denotes incumbent.

ALASKA

One member At Large

Alaska reports election results by legislative district. The districts indicated were first effective for the 2014 elections.

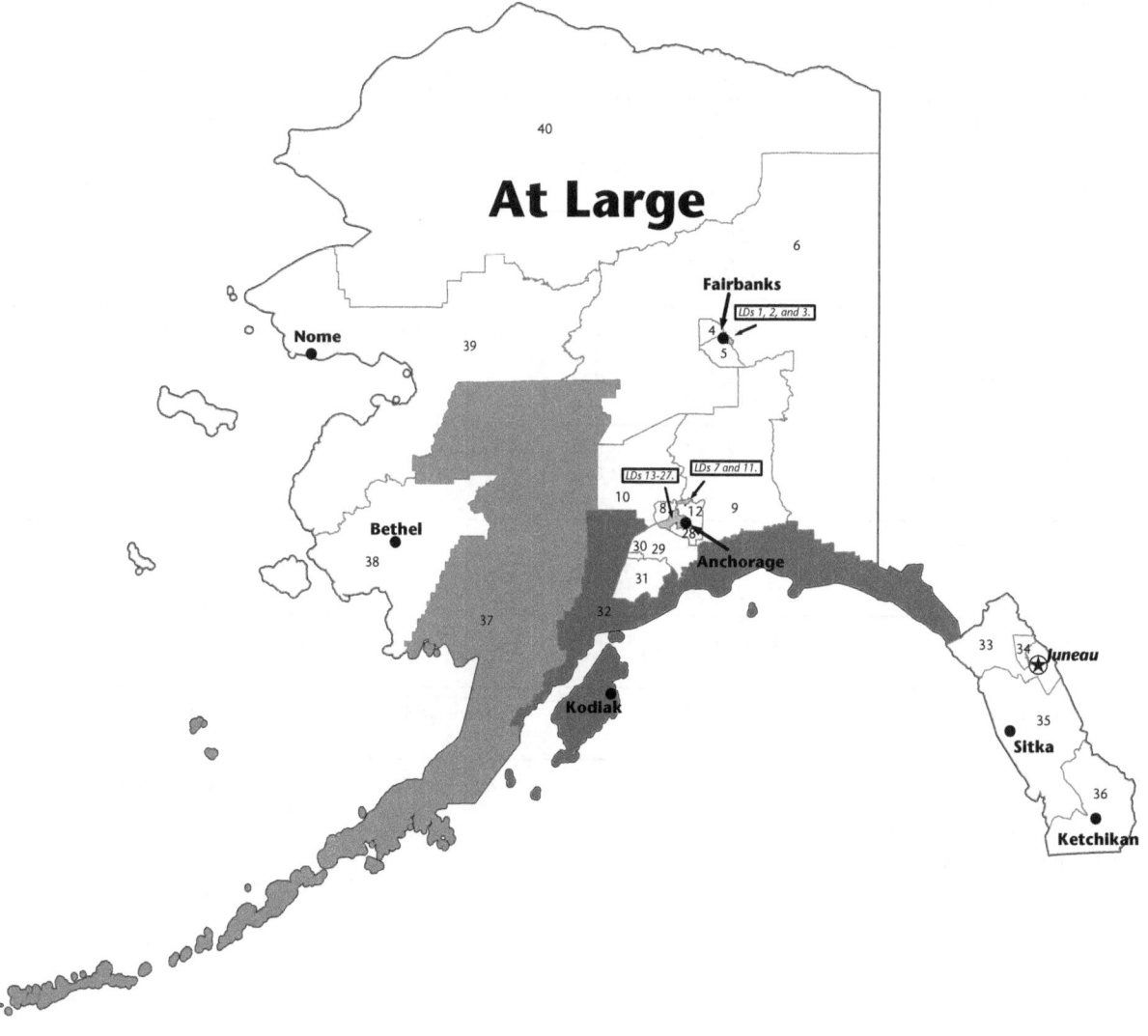

Alaska includes more islands to the west of those that are illustrated on this map.

ALASKA

GOVERNOR

Bill Walker (I). Elected 2014 to a four-year term.

SENATORS (2 Republicans)

Lisa Murkowski (R). Re-elected 2010 to a six-year term as a write-in candidate. Previously elected 2004. Had been appointed December 20, 2002, to fill the vacancy created by the resignation of her father, Frank H. Murkowski (R), to become governor of Alaska.

Daniel Sullivan (R). Elected 2014 to a six-year term.

REPRESENTATIVE (1 Republican)

At Large. Don Young (R)

POSTWAR VOTE FOR PRESIDENT

		Republican		Democratic		Other Vote	Rep.-Dem. Plurality	Percentage			
								Total Vote		Major Vote	
Year	Total Vote	Vote	Candidate	Vote	Candidate			Rep.	Dem.	Rep.	Dem.
2016**	318,608	163,387	Trump, Donald J.	116,454	Clinton, Hillary Rodham	38,767	46,933 R	51.3%	36.6%	58.4%	41.6%
2012	300,495	164,676	Romney, W. Mitt	122,640	Obama, Barack H.*	13,179	42,036 R	54.8%	40.8%	57.3%	42.7%
2008	326,197	193,841	McCain, John S. III	123,594	Obama, Barack H.	8,762	70,247 R	59.4%	37.9%	61.1%	38.9%
2004	312,598	190,889	Bush, George W.*	111,025	Kerry, John F.	10,684	79,864 R	61.1%	35.5%	63.2%	36.8%
2000**	285,560	167,398	Bush, George W.	79,004	Gore, Albert Jr.	39,158	88,394 R	58.6%	27.7%	67.9%	32.1%
1996**	241,620	122,746	Dole, Robert "Bob"	80,380	Clinton, Bill*	38,494	42,366 R	50.8%	33.3%	60.4%	39.6%
1992**	258,506	102,000	Bush, George H.*	78,294	Clinton, Bill	78,212	23,706 R	39.5%	30.3%	56.6%	43.4%
1988	200,116	119,251	Bush, George H.	72,584	Dukakis, Michael S.	8,281	46,667 R	59.6%	36.3%	62.2%	37.8%
1984	207,605	138,377	Reagan, Ronald*	62,007	Mondale, Walter F.	7,221	76,370 R	66.7%	29.9%	69.1%	30.9%
1980**	158,445	86,112	Reagan, Ronald	41,842	Carter, Jimmy*	30,491	44,270 R	54.3%	26.4%	67.3%	32.7%
1976	123,574	71,555	Ford, Gerald R.*	44,058	Carter, Jimmy	7,961	27,497 R	57.9%	35.7%	61.9%	38.1%
1972	95,219	55,349	Nixon, Richard M.*	32,967	McGovern, George S.	6,903	22,382 R	58.1%	34.6%	62.7%	37.3%
1968**	83,035	37,600	Nixon, Richard M.	35,411	Humphrey, Hubert Horatio Jr.	10,024	2,189 R	45.3%	42.6%	51.5%	48.5%
1964	67,259	22,930	Goldwater, Barry M. Sr.	44,329	Johnson, Lyndon B.*		21,399 D	34.1%	65.9%	34.1%	65.9%
1960	60,762	30,953	Nixon, Richard M.	29,809	Kennedy, John F.		1,144 R	50.9%	49.1%	50.9%	49.1%

Note: An asterisk (*) denotes incumbent. **In past elections, the other vote included: 2016 - 18,725 Libertarian (Gary Johnson); 2000 - 28,747 Green (Ralph Nader); 1996 - 26,333 Reform (Ross Perot); 1992 - 73,481 Independent (Perot); 1980 - 18,479 Libertarian (Ed Clark) and 11,155 Independent (John Anderson); 1968 - 10,024 American Independent (George Wallace). Alaska was formally admitted as a state in January 1959.

ALASKA

POSTWAR VOTE FOR GOVERNOR

Year	Total Vote	Republican Vote	Republican Candidate	Democratic Vote	Democratic Candidate	Other Vote	Rep.-Dem. Plurality	Percentage Total Vote Rep.	Percentage Total Vote Dem.	Percentage Major Vote Rep.	Percentage Major Vote Dem.
2014**	279,958	128,435	Parnell, Sean R.*			151,523	128,435 R#	45.9%		100.0%	
2010	256,192	151,318	Parnell, Sean R.*	96,519	Berkowitz, Ethan A.	8,355	54,799 R	59.1%	37.7%	61.1%	38.9%
2006	237,322	114,697	Palin, Sarah H.	97,238	Knowles, Tony	25,387	17,459 R	48.3%	41.0%	54.1%	45.9%
2002	231,484	129,279	Murkowski, Frank H.	94,216	Ulmer, Fran	7,989	35,063 R	55.8%	40.7%	57.8%	42.2%
1998**	220,177	39,331	Lindauer, John	112,879	Knowles, Tony*	67,967	73,548 D	17.9%	51.3%	25.8%	74.2%
1994**	213,435	87,157	Campbell, James O.	87,693	Knowles, Tony*	38,585	536 D	40.8%	41.1%	49.8%	50.2%
1990**	194,750	50,991	Sturgulewski, Arliss	60,201	Knowles, Tony	83,558	9,210 D#	26.2%	30.9%	45.9%	54.1%
1986	179,555	76,515	Sturgulewski, Arliss	84,943	Cowper, Steve	18,097	8,428 D	42.6%	47.3%	47.4%	52.6%
1982**	194,885	72,291	Fink, Tom	89,918	Sheffield, Bill	32,676	17,627 D	37.1%	46.1%	44.6%	55.4%
1978**	126,910	49,580	Hammond, Jay S.*	25,656	Croft, Chancy	51,674	23,924 R	39.1%	20.2%	65.9%	34.1%
1974	96,163	45,840	Hammond, Jay S.	45,553	Egan, William A.*	4,770	287 R	47.7%	47.4%	50.2%	49.8%
1970	80,779	37,264	Miller, Keith	42,309	Egan, William A.	1,206	5,045 D	46.1%	52.4%	46.8%	53.2%
1966	66,294	33,145	Hickel, Walter J.	32,065	Egan, William A.*	1,084	1,080 R	50.0%	48.4%	50.8%	49.2%
1962	56,681	27,054	Stepovich, Mike	29,627	Egan, William A.*		2,573 D	47.7%	52.3%	47.7%	52.3%
1958	48,968	19,299	Butrovich, John Jr.	29,189	Egan, William A.	480	9,890 D	39.4%	59.6%	39.8%	60.2%

Note: An asterisk (*) denotes incumbent. A pound sign (#) in the plurality column indicates that the winners in 1990 and 2014 were independents. **In past elections, the other vote included: 2014 - 134,658 Independent (Bill Walker); 1998 - 40,209 write-in (Robin Taylor, who finished second); 1994 - 27,838 Alaskan Independence (John B. "Jack" Coghill); 1990 - 75,721 Alaskan Independence (Walter J. Hickel); 1982 - 29,067 Libertarian (Richard L. Randolph); 1978 - 33,555 write-in (Hickel) and 15,656 Alaskans for Kelly (Tom Kelly). Walker won the 2014 election with 48.1 percent of the total vote and a plurality over the runner-up of 6,223 votes. Hickel won the 1990 election with 38.9 percent of the total vote and a plurality of 15,520 votes over the runner-up.

POSTWAR VOTE FOR SENATOR

Year	Total Vote	Republican Vote	Republican Candidate	Democratic Vote	Democratic Candidate	Other Vote	Rep.-Dem. Plurality	Percentage Total Vote Rep.	Percentage Total Vote Dem.	Percentage Major Vote Rep.	Percentage Major Vote Dem.
2016	311,441	138,149	Murkowski, Lisa A.*	36,200	Metcalfe, Ray	137,092	101,949 R	44.4%	11.6%	79.2%	20.8%
2014	282,400	135,445	Sullivan, Dan S.	129,431	Begich, Mark*	17,524	6,014 R	48.0%	45.8%	51.1%	48.9%
2010**	259,126	91,490	Miller, Joe	60,701	McAdams, Scott T.	106,935	30,789 R#	35.3%	23.4%	60.1%	39.9%
2008	317,723	147,814	Stevens, Ted*	151,767	Begich, Mark	18,142	3,953 D	46.5%	47.8%	49.3%	50.7%
2004	308,315	149,773	Murkowski, Lisa A.*	140,424	Knowles, Tony	18,118	9,349 R	48.6%	45.5%	51.6%	48.4%
2002	229,548	179,438	Stevens, Ted*	24,133	Vondersaar, Frank	25,977	155,305 R	78.2%	10.5%	88.1%	11.9%
1998	221,807	165,227	Murkowski, Frank H.*	43,743	Sonneman, Joseph	12,837	121,484 R	74.5%	19.7%	79.1%	20.9%
1996**	231,916	177,893	Stevens, Ted*	23,977	Obermeyer, Theresa N.	30,046	153,916 R	76.7%	10.3%	88.1%	11.9%
1992	239,714	127,163	Murkowski, Frank H.	92,065	Smith, Tony	20,486	35,098 R	53.0%	38.4%	58.0%	42.0%
1990	189,957	125,806	Stevens, Ted	61,152	Beasley, Michael	2,999	64,654 R	66.2%	32.2%	67.3%	32.7%
1986	180,801	97,674	Murkowski, Frank H.*	79,727	Olds, Glenn	3,400	17,947 R	54.0%	44.1%	55.1%	44.9%
1984	206,438	146,919	Stevens, Ted*	58,804	Havelock, John E.	715	88,115 R	71.2%	28.5%	71.4%	28.6%
1980	156,762	84,159	Murkowski, Frank H.	72,007	Gruening, Clark S.	596	12,152 R	53.7%	45.9%	53.9%	46.1%
1978	122,741	92,783	Stevens, Ted*	29,574	Hobbs, Donald W.	384	63,209 R	75.6%	24.1%	75.8%	24.2%
1974	93,275	38,914	Lewis, C. R.	54,361	Gravel, Mike		15,447 D	41.7%	58.3%	41.7%	58.3%
1972	96,007	74,216	Stevens, Ted*	21,791	Guess, Gene		52,425 R	77.3%	22.7%	77.3%	22.7%
1970S**	80,364	47,908	Stevens, Ted*	32,456	Kay, Wendell P.		15,452 R	59.6%	40.4%	59.6%	40.4%
1968	80,931	30,286	Rasmuson, Elmer	36,527	Gravel, Mike	14,118	6,241 D	37.4%	45.1%	45.3%	54.7%
1966	65,250	15,961	McKinley, Lee L.	49,289	Bartlett, E. L.*		33,328 D	24.5%	75.5%	24.5%	75.5%
1962	58,181	24,354	Stevens, Ted	33,827	Gruening, Ernest		9,473 D	41.9%	58.1%	41.9%	58.1%
1960	59,978	21,937	McKinley, Lee L.	38,041	Bartlett, E. L.*		16,104 D	36.6%	63.4%	36.6%	63.4%
1958**	48,837	7,299	Robertson, R. E.	40,939	Bartlett, E. L.	599	33,640 D	14.9%	83.8%	15.1%	84.9%
1958**	49,525	23,462	Stepovich, Mike	26,063	Gruening, Ernest		2,601 D	47.4%	52.6%	47.4%	52.6%

Note: An asterisk (*) denotes incumbent. A pound sign (#) in the plurality column indicates that the winner in 2010 was Republican Senator Lisa A. Murkowski, who ran as a write-in candidate. **In past elections, the other vote included: 2016 - 90,825 Libertarian (Joe Miller), who finished second, 47,324 votes behind Murkowski, and 41,194 Non-Affiliated (Margaret Stock), who finished third; 2010 - 101,091 Republican write-in (Lisa Murkowski), who won re-election with 39.6 percent of the total vote and a plurality of 10,252 votes over the runner-up; 1996 - 29,037 Green (Jed Whittaker, who finished second). The 1970 election was for a short term to fill a vacancy. The two 1958 elections were held to indeterminate terms and the Senate later determined by lot that Senator Gruening would serve four years, Senator Bartlett two. The plurality for 2010 shows the difference between the official Republican and Democratic candidates.

ALASKA

PRESIDENT 2016

2010 Census Population	Absentee Election District	Total Vote	Republican (Trump)	Democratic (Clinton)	Other	Rep.-Dem. Plurality	Percentage			
							Total Vote		Major Vote	
							Rep.	Dem.	Rep.	Dem.
17,726	Election District 1	6,638	3,180	2,573	885	607 R	47.9%	38.8%	55.3%	44.7%
17,738	Election District 2	5,492	3,188	1,585	719	1,603 R	58.0%	28.9%	66.8%	33.2%
17,673	Election District 3	7,613	5,403	1,241	969	4,162 R	71.0%	16.3%	81.3%	18.7%
17,786	Election District 4	9,521	4,070	4,162	1,289	92 D	42.7%	43.7%	49.4%	50.6%
17,837	Election District 5	7,906	3,683	3,187	1,036	496 R	46.6%	40.3%	53.6%	46.4%
17,807	Election District 6	8,460	4,929	2,536	995	2,393 R	58.3%	30.0%	66.0%	34.0%
17,703	Election District 7	8,294	5,935	1,510	849	4,425 R	71.6%	18.2%	79.7%	20.3%
17,830	Election District 8	8,073	6,126	1,218	729	4,908 R	75.9%	15.1%	83.4%	16.6%
17,739	Election District 9	8,954	6,100	1,843	1,011	4,257 R	68.1%	20.6%	76.8%	23.2%
17,827	Election District 10	9,040	6,255	1,808	977	4,447 R	69.2%	20.0%	77.6%	22.4%
17,716	Election District 11	9,689	6,444	2,142	1,103	4,302 R	66.5%	22.1%	75.1%	24.9%
17,671	Election District 12	9,543	6,629	1,928	986	4,701 R	69.5%	20.2%	77.5%	22.5%
17,678	Election District 13	6,533	4,028	1,684	821	2,344 R	61.7%	25.8%	70.5%	29.5%
17,818	Election District 14	10,420	5,978	3,043	1,399	2,935 R	57.4%	29.2%	66.3%	33.7%
17,672	Election District 15	4,982	2,525	1,828	629	697 R	50.7%	36.7%	58.0%	42.0%
17,806	Election District 16	7,436	3,203	3,294	939	91 D	43.1%	44.3%	49.3%	50.7%
17,797	Election District 17	6,788	2,618	3,290	880	672 D	38.6%	48.5%	44.3%	55.7%
17,925	Election District 18	7,402	2,684	3,909	809	1,225 D	36.3%	52.8%	40.7%	59.3%
17,692	Election District 19	4,792	1,636	2,669	487	1,033 D	34.1%	55.7%	38.0%	62.0%
17,718	Election District 20	7,140	2,187	4,151	802	1,964 D	30.6%	58.1%	34.5%	65.5%
17,642	Election District 21	8,647	3,479	4,224	944	745 D	40.2%	48.8%	45.2%	54.8%
17,755	Election District 22	8,372	4,203	3,270	899	933 R	50.2%	39.1%	56.2%	43.8%
17,809	Election District 23	6,924	3,246	2,894	784	352 R	46.9%	41.8%	52.9%	47.1%
17,702	Election District 24	9,290	4,709	3,578	1,003	1,131 R	50.7%	38.5%	56.8%	43.2%
17,924	Election District 25	8,127	3,816	3,378	933	438 R	47.0%	41.6%	53.0%	47.0%
17,693	Election District 26	8,905	4,548	3,374	983	1,174 R	51.1%	37.9%	57.4%	42.6%
17,678	Election District 27	8,783	4,085	3,729	969	356 R	46.5%	42.5%	52.3%	47.7%
17,778	Election District 28	11,427	5,423	4,749	1,255	674 R	47.5%	41.6%	53.3%	46.7%
18,026	Election District 29	9,394	6,347	2,101	946	4,246 R	67.6%	22.4%	75.1%	24.9%
18,021	Election District 30	8,950	6,194	1,816	940	4,378 R	69.2%	20.3%	77.3%	22.7%
17,971	Election District 31	10,182	5,617	3,466	1,099	2,151 R	55.2%	34.0%	61.8%	38.2%
18,077	Election District 32	7,472	3,764	2,701	1,007	1,063 R	50.4%	36.1%	58.2%	41.8%
17,635	Election District 33	9,934	2,732	5,978	1,224	3,246 D	27.5%	60.2%	31.4%	68.6%
17,668	Election District 34	9,431	3,955	4,220	1,256	265 D	41.9%	44.7%	48.4%	51.6%
17,825	Election District 35	9,042	4,105	3,749	1,188	356 R	45.4%	41.5%	52.3%	47.7%
17,874	Election District 36	8,264	4,460	2,693	1,111	1,767 R	54.0%	32.6%	62.4%	37.6%
17,448	Election District 37	5,062	1,938	2,421	703	483 D	38.3%	47.8%	44.5%	55.5%
17,546	Election District 38	5,095	1,143	2,758	1,194	1,615 D	22.4%	54.1%	29.3%	70.7%
17,677	Election District 39	5,639	1,405	3,142	1,092	1,737 D	24.9%	55.7%	30.9%	69.1%
17,323	Election District 40	4,610	1,377	2,338	895	961 D	29.9%	50.7%	37.1%	62.9%
	Federal Absentee	342	40	274	28	234 D	11.7%	80.1%	12.7%	87.3%
710,231	TOTAL	318,608	163,387	116,454	38,767	46,933 R	51.3%	36.6%	58.4%	41.6%

ALASKA

SENATOR 2016

2010 Census Population	County	Total Vote	Republican (Murkowsi)	Democratic (Metcalf)	Libertarian (Miller)	Independent (Stock)	Other Vote	Plurality	Rep.	Total Vote Percentage Dem.	Rep.	Dem.
17,726	Election District 1	6,413	2,950	802	1,830	722	109	1,120 R	46.0%	12.5%	28.5%	11.3%
17,738	Election District 2	5,005	2,368	615	1,552	340	130	816 R	47.3%	12.3%	31.0%	6.8%
17,673	Election District 3	7,452	3,360	423	3,124	389	156	236 R	45.1%	5.7%	41.9%	5.2%
17,786	Election District 4	9,408	3,924	1,142	2,444	1,778	120	1,480 R	41.7%	12.1%	26.0%	18.9%
17,837	Election District 5	7,769	3,487	965	2,080	1,118	119	1,407 R	44.9%	12.4%	26.8%	14.4%
17,807	Election District 6	8,195	3,606	791	2,760	877	161	846 R	44.0%	9.7%	33.7%	10.7%
17,703	Election District 7	8,093	3,262	564	3,469	625	173	207 L	40.3%	7.0%	42.9%	7.7%
17,830	Election District 8	7,833	2,880	472	3,785	524	172	905 L	36.8%	6.0%	48.3%	6.7%
17,739	Election District 9	8,723	3,558	727	3,554	723	161	4 R	40.8%	8.3%	40.7%	8.3%
17,827	Election District 10	8,837	3,325	671	3,856	796	189	531 L	37.6%	7.6%	43.6%	9.0%
17,716	Election District 11	9,546	3,967	679	3,768	941	191	199 R	41.6%	7.1%	39.5%	9.9%
17,671	Election District 12	9,394	3,930	650	3,879	790	145	51 R	41.8%	6.9%	41.3%	8.4%
17,678	Election District 13	6,190	2,848	629	2,072	526	115	776 R	46.0%	10.2%	33.5%	8.5%
17,818	Election District 14	10,231	4,969	914	3,156	1,048	144	1,813 R	48.6%	8.9%	30.8%	10.2%
17,672	Election District 15	4,737	2,075	816	1,328	421	97	747 R	43.8%	17.2%	28.0%	8.9%
17,806	Election District 16	7,260	3,014	1,203	1,915	998	130	1,099 R	41.5%	16.6%	26.4%	13.7%
17,797	Election District 17	6,575	2,834	1,092	1,385	1,164	100	1,449 R	43.1%	16.6%	21.1%	17.7%
17,925	Election District 18	7,236	2,845	1,206	1,470	1,601	114	1,244 R	39.3%	16.7%	20.3%	22.1%
17,692	Election District 19	4,664	1,724	996	1,028	794	122	696 R	37.0%	21.4%	22.0%	17.0%
17,718	Election District 20	6,959	2,773	1,298	1,124	1,648	116	1,125 R	39.8%	18.7%	16.2%	23.7%
17,642	Election District 21	8,523	3,780	1,212	1,743	1,677	111	2,037 R	44.4%	14.2%	20.5%	19.7%
17,755	Election District 22	8,280	4,080	917	2,057	1,118	108	2,023 R	49.3%	11.1%	24.8%	13.5%
17,809	Election District 23	6,768	2,941	933	1,753	1,000	141	1,188 R	43.5%	13.8%	25.9%	14.8%
17,702	Election District 24	9,206	4,631	944	2,309	1,201	121	2,322 R	50.3%	10.3%	25.1%	13.0%
17,924	Election District 25	7,962	3,556	1,014	2,086	1,189	117	1,470 R	44.7%	12.7%	26.2%	14.9%
17,693	Election District 26	8,782	4,259	952	2,275	1,182	114	1,984 R	48.5%	10.8%	25.9%	13.5%
17,678	Election District 27	8,650	3,695	1,305	2,246	1,286	118	1,449 R	42.7%	15.1%	26.0%	14.9%
17,778	Election District 28	11,350	5,585	1,039	2,535	2,097	94	3,050 R	49.2%	9.2%	22.3%	18.5%
18,026	Election District 29	9,202	3,479	729	3,819	1,014	161	340 L	37.8%	7.9%	41.5%	11.0%
18,021	Election District 30	8,774	3,512	545	3,554	1,012	151	42 L	40.0%	6.2%	40.5%	11.5%
17,971	Election District 31	9,939	3,362	970	3,352	2,125	130	10 R	33.8%	9.8%	33.7%	21.4%
18,077	Election District 32	7,237	3,422	737	1,821	1,124	133	1,601 R	47.3%	10.2%	25.2%	15.5%
17,635	Election District 33	9,749	3,756	2,160	1,429	2,316	88	1,440 R	38.5%	22.2%	14.7%	23.8%
17,668	Election District 34	9,276	4,245	1,495	2,060	1,373	103	2,185 R	45.8%	16.1%	22.2%	14.8%
17,825	Election District 35	8,874	4,253	1,402	1,947	1,112	160	2,306 R	47.9%	15.8%	21.9%	12.5%
17,874	Election District 36	8,039	4,341	801	1,881	880	136	2,460 R	54.0%	10.0%	23.4%	10.9%
17,448	Election District 37	4,953	2,927	592	963	389	82	1,964 R	59.1%	12.0%	19.4%	7.9%
17,546	Election District 38	5,009	2,663	630	1,147	481	88	1,516 R	53.2%	12.6%	22.9%	9.6%
17,677	Election District 39	5,538	3,309	509	1,259	386	75	2,050 R	59.8%	9.2%	22.7%	7.0%
17,323	Election District 40	4,512	2,583	466	996	392	75	1,587 R	57.2%	10.3%	22.1%	8.7%
	Federal Absentee	298	71	193	14	17	3	122 D	23.8%	64.8%	4.7%	5.7%
710,231	TOTAL	311,441	138,149	36,200	90,825	41,194	5,073	47,324 R	44.4%	11.6%	29.2%	13.2%

Note: The plurality measures the difference in the vote between the top candidates in each jurisdiction, regardless of party. In most cases that was the Republican (R) and Libertarian (L) candidates.

ALASKA
HOUSE OF REPRESENTATIVES

CD	Year	Total Vote	Republican		Democratic		Other Vote	Rep.-Dem. Plurality	Percentage			
									Total Vote		Major Vote	
			Vote	Candidate	Vote	Candidate			Rep.	Dem.	Rep.	Dem.
At Large	2016	308,198	155,088	YOUNG, DON*	111,019	LINDBECK, STEVE	42,091	44,069 R	50.3%	36.0%	58.3%	41.7%
At Large	2014	279,741	142,572	YOUNG, DON*	114,602	DUNBAR, FORREST	22,567	27,970 R	51.0%	41.0%	55.4%	44.6%
At Large	2012	289,804	185,296	YOUNG, DON*	82,927	CISSNA, SHARON M.	21,581	102,369 R	63.9%	28.6%	69.1%	30.9%
At Large	2010	254,335	175,384	YOUNG, DON*	77,606	CRAWFORD, HARRY T.	1,345	97,778 R	69.0%	30.5%	69.3%	30.7%
At Large	2008	316,978	158,939	YOUNG, DON*	142,560	BERKOWITZ, ETHAN A.	15,479	16,379 R	50.1%	45.0%	52.7%	47.3%
At Large	2006	234,645	132,743	YOUNG, DON*	93,879	BENSON, DIANE E.	8,023	38,864 R	56.6%	40.0%	58.6%	41.4%
At Large	2004	299,996	213,216	YOUNG, DON*	67,074	HIGGINS, THOMAS M.	19,706	146,142 R	71.1%	22.4%	76.1%	23.9%
At Large	2002	227,725	169,685	YOUNG, DON*	39,357	GREENE, CLIFFORD	18,683	130,328 R	74.5%	17.3%	81.2%	18.8%
At Large	2000	274,393	190,862	YOUNG, DON*	45,372	GREENE, CLIFFORD	38,159	145,490 R	69.6%	16.5%	80.8%	19.2%
At Large	1998	223,300	139,676	YOUNG, DON*	77,232	DUNCAN, JIM	6,392	62,444 R	62.6%	34.6%	64.4%	35.6%
At Large	1996	233,700	138,834	YOUNG, DON*	85,114	LINCOLN, GEORGIANNA	9,752	53,720 R	59.4%	36.4%	62.0%	38.0%
At Large	1994	208,240	118,537	YOUNG, DON*	68,172	SMITH, TONY	21,531	50,365 R	56.9%	32.7%	63.5%	36.5%
At Large	1992	239,116	111,849	YOUNG, DON*	102,378	DEVENS, JOHN S.	24,889	9,471 R	46.8%	42.8%	52.2%	47.8%
At Large	1990	191,647	99,003	YOUNG, DON*	91,677	DEVENS, JOHN S.	967	7,326 R	51.7%	47.8%	51.9%	48.1%
At Large	1988	192,955	120,595	YOUNG, DON*	71,881	GRUENSTEIN, PETER	479	48,714 R	62.5%	37.3%	62.7%	37.3%
At Large	1986	180,277	101,799	YOUNG, DON*	74,053	BEGICH, PEGGE	4,425	27,746 R	56.5%	41.1%	57.9%	42.1%
At Large	1984	206,437	113,582	YOUNG, DON*	86,052	BEGICH, PEGGE	6,803	27,530 R	55.0%	41.7%	56.9%	43.1%
At Large	1982	181,084	128,274	YOUNG, DON*	52,011	CARLSON, DAVE	799	76,263 R	70.8%	28.7%	71.2%	28.8%
At Large	1980	154,618	114,089	YOUNG, DON*	39,922	PARNELL, KEVIN	607	74,167 R	73.8%	25.8%	74.1%	25.9%
At Large	1978	124,187	68,811	YOUNG, DON*	55,176	RODEY, PATRICK	200	13,635 R	55.4%	44.4%	55.5%	44.5%
At Large	1976	118,208	83,722	YOUNG, DON*	34,194	HOPSON, EBEN	292	49,528 R	70.8%	28.9%	71.0%	29.0%
At Large	1974	95,921	51,641	YOUNG, DON*	44,280	HENSLEY, WILLIAM L.		7,361 R	53.8%	46.2%	53.8%	46.2%
At Large	1972	95,401	41,750	YOUNG, DON	53,651	BEGICH, NICHOLAS J.*		11,901 D	43.8%	56.2%	43.8%	56.2%
At Large	1970	80,084	35,947	MURKOWSKI, FRANK H.	44,137	BEGICH, NICHOLAS J.		8,190 D	44.9%	55.1%	44.9%	55.1%
At Large	1968	80,362	43,577	POLLOCK, HOWARD W.*	36,785	BEGICH, NICHOLAS J.		6,792 R	54.2%	45.8%	54.2%	45.8%
At Large	1966	65,907	34,040	POLLOCK, HOWARD W.	31,867	RIVERS, RALPH J.*		2,173 R	51.6%	48.4%	51.6%	48.4%
At Large	1964	67,156	32,566	THOMAS, LOWELL	34,590	RIVERS, RALPH J.*		2,024 D	48.5%	51.5%	48.5%	51.5%
At Large	1962	58,591	26,638	THOMAS, LOWELL	31,953	RIVERS, RALPH J.*		5,315 D	45.5%	54.5%	45.5%	54.5%
At Large	1960	59,063	25,517	RETTIG, R. L.	33,546	RIVERS, RALPH J.*		8,029 D	43.2%	56.8%	43.2%	56.8%
At Large	1958	48,644	20,699	BENSON, HENRY A.	27,945	RIVERS, RALPH J.		7,246 D	42.6%	57.4%	42.6%	57.4%

Note: An asterisk (*) denotes incumbent.

ALASKA
GENERAL AND PRIMARY ELECTIONS

2016 GENERAL ELECTIONS: OTHER VOTES

President   Other vote was 18,725 Libertarian (Gary Johnson), 9,201 Write-in (Scattered Write-in), 5,735 Green (Jill Stein), 3,866 Constitution (Darrell Castle), 1,240 Non-Affiliated (Roque De La Fuente)

Senate   Other vote was 90,825 Libertarian (Joe Miller), 41,194 Non-Affiliated (Margaret Stock), 2,609 Non-Affiliated (Breck Craig), 1,758 Non-Affiliated (Ted Gianoutsos), 706 Write-in (Scattered Write-in)

House   Other vote was:

At Large   31,770 Libertarian (Jim McDermott), 9,093 Non-Affiliated (Bernie Souphanavong), 1,228 Write-in (Scattered Write-in)

ALASKA

GENERAL AND PRIMARY ELECTIONS

2016 PRIMARY ELECTIONS: SUPPLEMENTARY INFORMATION

Presidential Caucus	March 1, 2016 (Republican) March 26, 2016 (Democratic)	**Registration** (as of August 3, 2016)	515,912	Republican Democratic Alaskan Independence Libertarian Green Veterans Constitution Nonpartisan Undeclared Other	140,287 77,126 16,770 7,064 1,558 1,107 303 85,472 186,207 18
Primary	August 16, 2016 (Congress)				

Primary Type Semi-closed—Both the Republican and Democratic caucuses for president were closed. Any registered voter could participate in the Democratic primary for Congress. The Republican primary was restricted to registered Republican, undeclared, and nonpartisan voters. Democratic candidates were listed on the primary ballot together with candidates of the Alaskan Independence and Libertarian parties. The highest vote-getter of each party went on to the general election ballot. Republican candidates were listed on a primary ballot of their own.

	REPUBLICAN PRIMARIES			DEMOCRATIC PRIMARIES		
Senator	Murkowski, Lisa A.*	39,545	71.5%	Metcalfe, Ray	15,228	60.1%
	Lochner, Bob	8,480	15.3%	Blatchford, Edgar	10,090	39.9%
	Kendall, Paul	4,272	7.7%			
	Lamb, Thomas	2,996	5.4%			
	TOTAL	55,293		TOTAL	25,318	
Congressional At Large	Young, Don*	38,998	71.5%	Lindbeck, Steve	17,009	67.9%
	Wright, Stephen T.	10,189	18.7%	Hinz, Lynette "Moreno"	5,130	20.5%
	Heikes, Gerald L. "Tap"	2,817	5.2%	Hibler, William D. "Bill"	2,918	11.6%
	Tingley, Jesse J. "Messy"	2,524	4.6%			
	TOTAL	54,528		TOTAL	25,057	

Note: An asterisk (*) denotes incumbent.

ARIZONA

Congressional districts first established for elections held in 2012

9 members

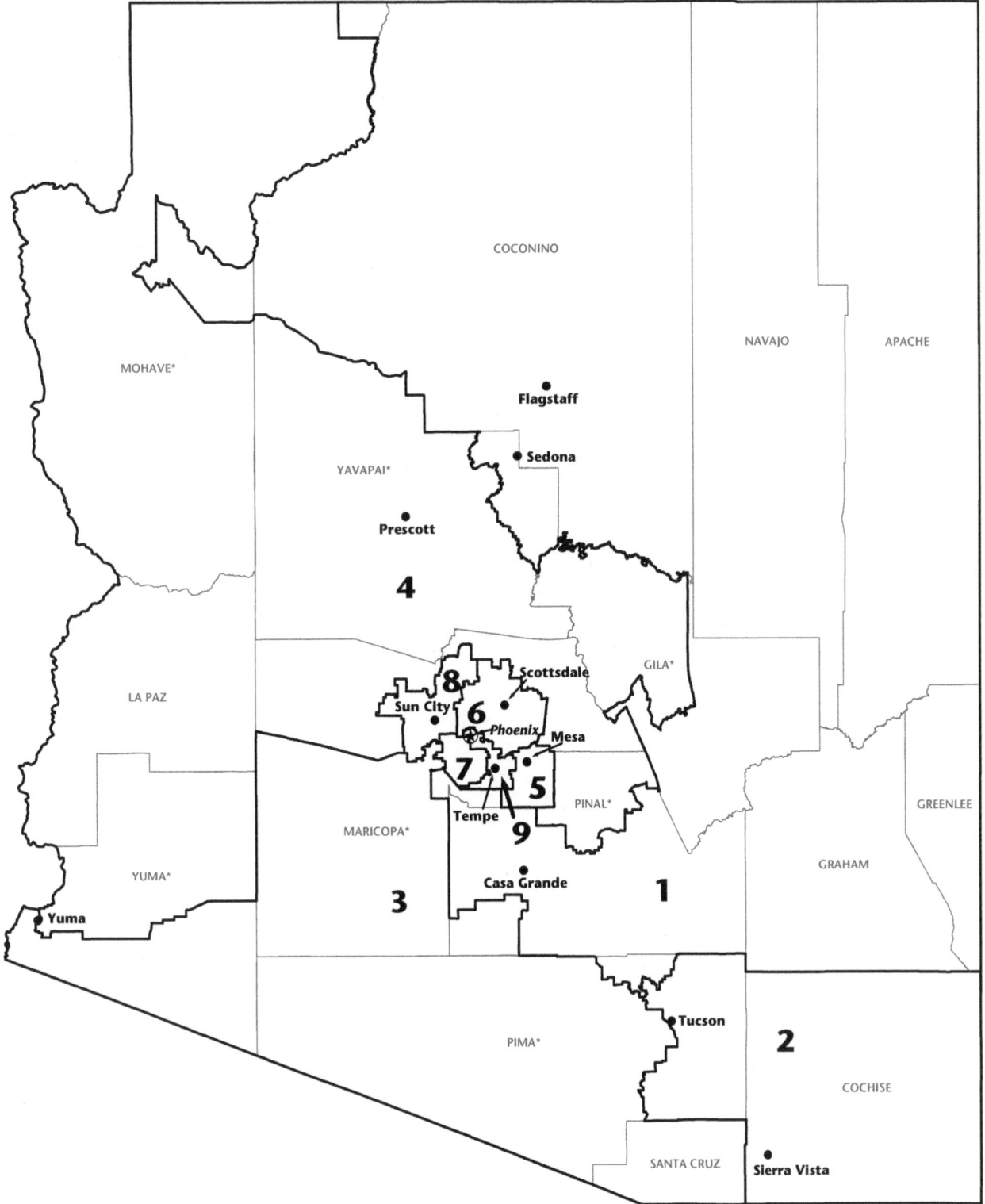

COCONINO

NAVAJO

APACHE

MOHAVE*

● Flagstaff

YAVAPAI*

● Sedona

● Prescott

4

LA PAZ

GILA*

8

Scottsdale

Sun City ●

6

Phoenix ● Mesa

GREENLEE

7

5

PINAL*

Tempe

9

GRAHAM

MARICOPA*

YUMA*

CASA GRANDE ●

3

1

● Yuma

Casa Grande

COCHISE

● Tucson

2

PIMA*

SANTA CRUZ

● Sierra Vista

* Asterisk indicates a county whose boundaries include parts of two or more congressional districts.

ARIZONA
Greater Phoenix Area

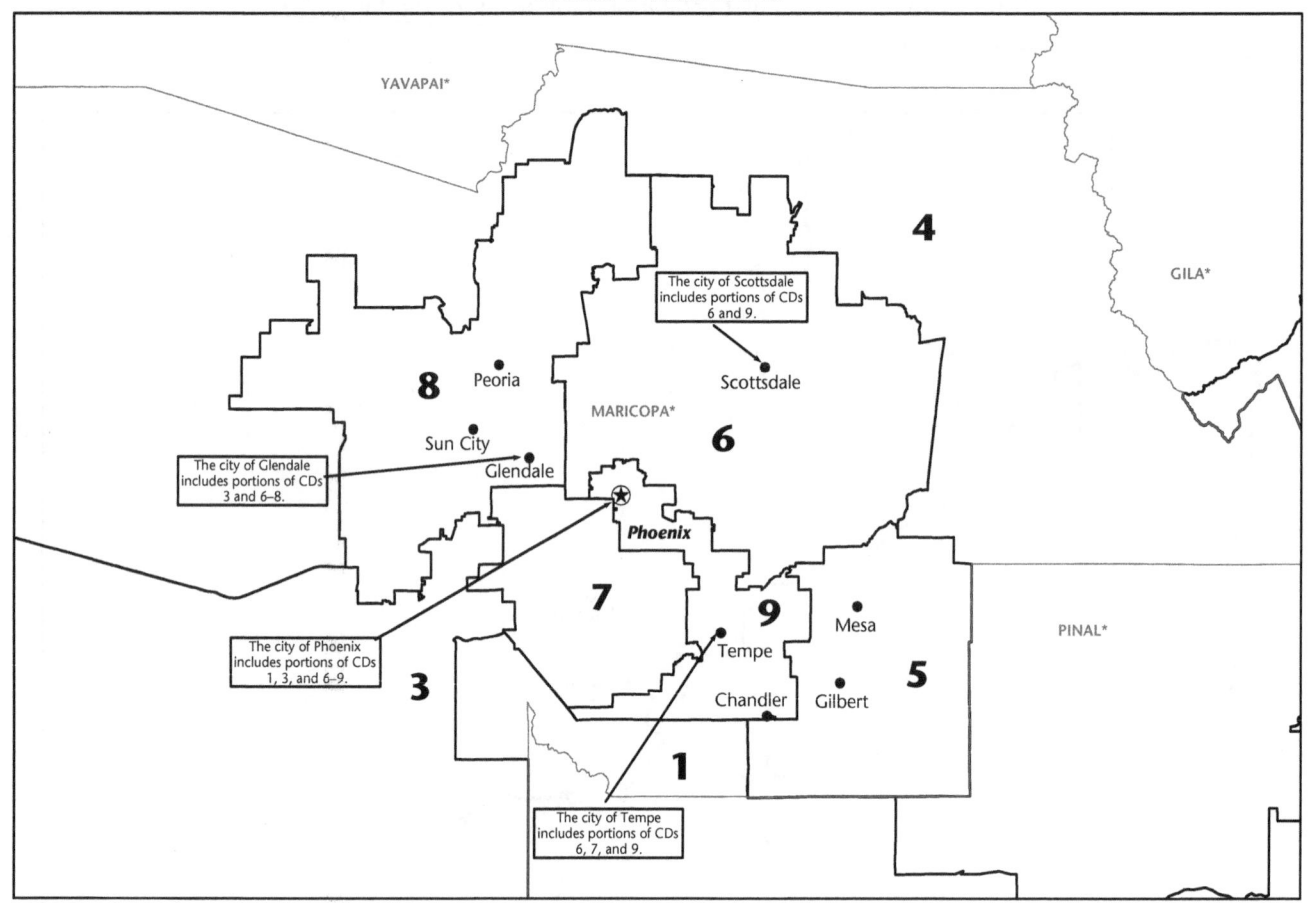

ARIZONA

GOVERNOR
Doug Ducey (R). Elected 2014 to a four-year term.

SENATORS (2 Republicans)
Jeff Flake (R). Elected 2012 to a six-year term.

John McCain (R). Re-elected 2016 to a six-year term. Previously elected 2010, 2004, 1998, 1992, 1986.

REPRESENTATIVES (5 Republicans, 4 Democrats)

1. Tom O'Halleran (D)
2. Martha McSally (R)
3. Raúl M. Grijalva (D)
4. Paul A. Gosar (R)
5. Andy Biggs (R)
6. David Schweikert (R)
7. Ruben Gallego (D)
8. Trent Franks (R)
9. Kyrsten Sinema (D)

POSTWAR VOTE FOR PRESIDENT

| Year | Total Vote | Republican | | Democratic | | Other Vote | Rep.-Dem. Plurality | Percentage | | | |
| | | | | | | | | Total Vote | | Major Vote | |
		Vote	Candidate	Vote	Candidate			Rep.	Dem.	Rep.	Dem.
2016**	2,573,165	1,252,401	Trump, Donald J.	1,161,167	Clinton, Hillary Rodham	159,597	91,234 R	48.7%	45.1%	51.9%	48.1%
2012	2,299,254	1,233,654	Romney, W. Mitt	1,025,232	Obama, Barack H.*	40,368	208,422 R	53.7%	44.6%	54.6%	45.4%
2008	2,293,475	1,230,111	McCain, John S. III	1,034,707	Obama, Barack H.	28,657	195,404 R	53.6%	45.1%	54.3%	45.7%
2004	2,012,585	1,104,294	Bush, George W.*	893,524	Kerry, John F.	14,767	210,770 R	54.9%	44.4%	55.3%	44.7%
2000**	1,532,016	781,652	Bush, George W.	685,341	Gore, Albert Jr.	65,023	96,311 R	51.0%	44.7%	53.3%	46.7%
1996**	1,404,405	622,073	Dole, Robert "Bob"	653,288	Clinton, Bill*	129,044	31,215 D	44.3%	46.5%	48.8%	51.2%
1992**	1,486,975	572,086	Bush, George H.*	543,050	Clinton, Bill	371,839	29,036 R	38.5%	36.5%	51.3%	48.7%
1988	1,171,873	702,541	Bush, George H.	454,029	Dukakis, Michael S.	15,303	248,512 R	60.0%	38.7%	60.7%	39.3%
1984	1,025,897	681,416	Reagan, Ronald*	333,854	Mondale, Walter F.	10,627	347,562 R	66.4%	32.5%	67.1%	32.9%
1980**	873,945	529,688	Reagan, Ronald	246,843	Carter, Jimmy*	97,414	282,845 R	60.6%	28.2%	68.2%	31.8%
1976	742,719	418,642	Ford, Gerald R.*	295,602	Carter, Jimmy	28,475	123,040 R	56.4%	39.8%	58.6%	41.4%
1972	622,926	402,812	Nixon, Richard M.*	198,540	McGovern, George S.	21,574	204,272 R	64.7%	31.9%	67.0%	33.0%
1968**	486,936	266,721	Nixon, Richard M.	170,514	Humphrey, Hubert Horatio Jr.	49,701	96,207 R	54.8%	35.0%	61.0%	39.0%
1964	480,770	242,535	Goldwater, Barry M. Sr.	237,753	Johnson, Lyndon B.*	482	4,782 R	50.4%	49.5%	50.5%	49.5%
1960	398,491	221,241	Nixon, Richard M.	176,781	Kennedy, John F.	469	44,460 R	55.5%	44.4%	55.6%	44.4%
1956	290,173	176,990	Eisenhower, Dwight D.*	112,880	Stevenson, Adlai E. II	303	64,110 R	61.0%	38.9%	61.1%	38.9%
1952	260,570	152,042	Eisenhower, Dwight D.	108,528	Stevenson, Adlai E. II		43,514 R	58.3%	41.7%	58.3%	41.7%
1948	177,065	77,597	Dewey, Thomas E.	95,251	Truman, Harry S.*	4,217	17,654 D	43.8%	53.8%	44.9%	55.1%

Note: An asterisk (*) denotes incumbent. **In past elections, the other vote included: 2016 - Libertarian 106,327 (Gary Johnson); 2000 - 45,645 Green (Ralph Nader); 1996 - 112,072 Reform (Ross Perot); 1992 - 353,741 Independent (Perot); 1980 - 76,952 Independent (John Anderson); 1968 - 46,573 American Independent (George Wallace).

ARIZONA

POSTWAR VOTE FOR GOVERNOR

Year	Total Vote	Republican		Democratic		Other Vote	Rep.-Dem. Plurality	Percentage			
								Total Vote		Major Vote	
		Vote	Candidate	Vote	Candidate			Rep.	Dem.	Rep.	Dem.
2014	1,506,416	805,062	Ducey, Doug	626,921	Duval, Fred	74,433	178,141 R	53.4%	41.6%	56.2%	43.8%
2010	1,728,081	938,934	Brewer, Jan*	733,935	Goddard, Terry	55,212	204,999 R	54.3%	42.5%	56.1%	43.9%
2006	1,533,645	543,528	Munsil, Len	959,830	Napolitano, Janet*	30,287	416,302 D	35.4%	62.6%	36.2%	63.8%
2002	1,226,111	554,465	Salmon, Matt	566,284	Napolitano, Janet	105,362	11,819 D	45.2%	46.2%	49.5%	50.5%
1998	1,017,616	620,188	Hull, Jane Dee*	361,552	Johnson, Paul	35,876	258,636 R	60.9%	35.5%	63.2%	36.8%
1994	1,129,607	593,492	Symington, Fife*	500,702	Basha, Eddie	35,413	92,790 R	52.5%	44.3%	54.2%	45.8%
1991S**	940,737	492,569	Symington, Fife	448,168	Goddard, Terry		44,401 R	52.4%	47.6%	52.4%	47.6%
1986**	866,984	343,913	Mecham, Evan	298,986	Warner, Carolyn	224,085	44,927 R	39.7%	34.5%	53.5%	46.5%
1982	726,364	235,877	Corbet, Leo	453,795	Babbitt, Bruce*	36,692	217,918 D	32.5%	62.5%	34.2%	65.8%
1978	538,556	241,093	Mecham, Evan	282,605	Babbitt, Bruce*	14,858	41,512 D	44.8%	52.5%	46.0%	54.0%
1974	552,202	273,674	Williams, Jack R.*	278,375	Castro, Raul H.	153	4,701 D	49.6%	50.4%	49.6%	50.4%
1970**	411,409	209,522	Williams, Jack R.*	201,887	Castro, Raul H.		7,635 R	50.9%	49.1%	50.9%	49.1%
1968	483,998	279,923	Williams, Jack R.*	204,075	Goddard, Sam		75,848 R	57.8%	42.2%	57.8%	42.2%
1966	378,342	203,438	Williams, Jack R.	174,904	Goddard, Sam*		28,534 R	53.8%	46.2%	53.8%	46.2%
1964	473,502	221,404	Kleindienst, Richard	252,098	Goddard, Sam		30,694 D	46.8%	53.2%	46.8%	53.2%
1962	365,841	200,578	Fannin, Paul*	165,263	Goddard, Sam		35,315 R	54.8%	45.2%	54.8%	45.2%
1960	397,107	235,502	Fannin, Paul*	161,605	Ackerman, Lee		73,897 R	59.3%	40.7%	59.3%	40.7%
1958	290,465	160,136	Fannin, Paul	130,329	Morrison, Robert		29,807 R	55.1%	44.9%	55.1%	44.9%
1956	288,592	116,744	Griffen, Horace B.	171,848	McFarland, Ernest W.*		55,104 D	40.5%	59.5%	40.5%	59.5%
1954	243,970	115,866	Pyle, Howard*	128,104	McFarland, Ernest W.		12,238 D	47.5%	52.5%	47.5%	52.5%
1952	260,285	156,592	Pyle, Howard*	103,693	Haldiman, Joe C.		52,899 R	60.2%	39.8%	60.2%	39.8%
1950	195,227	99,109	Pyle, Howard	96,118	Frohmiller, Ana		2,991 R	50.8%	49.2%	50.8%	49.2%
1948	175,767	70,419	Brockett, Bruce D.	104,008	Garvey, Dan E.	1,340	33,589 D	40.1%	59.2%	40.4%	59.6%
1946	122,462	48,867	Brockett, Bruce D.	73,595	Osborn, Sidney P.*		24,728 D	39.9%	60.1%	39.9%	60.1%

Note: An asterisk (*) denotes incumbent. **In past elections, the other vote included: 1986 - 224,085 Independent (Bill Schulz). In 1990 neither major party candidate won an absolute majority, therefore a runoff election was held February 26, 1991; the vote above is for the February runoff. In the November 1990 election, a total of 1,055,406 votes were cast as follows: 523,984 (49.6%) Republican (Fife Symington); 519,691 (49.2%) Democratic (Terry Goddard); 11,731 (1.1%) Other. The term of office for Arizona's governor was increased from two to four years effective with the 1970 election.

POSTWAR VOTE FOR SENATOR

Year	Total Vote	Republican		Democratic		Other Vote	Rep.-Dem. Plurality	Percentage			
								Total Vote		Major Vote	
		Vote	Candidate	Vote	Candidate			Rep.	Dem.	Rep.	Dem.
2016	2,530,730	1,359,267	McCain, John S. III*	1,031,245	Kirkpatrick, Ann	140,218	328,022 R	53.7%	40.7%	56.9%	43.1%
2012	2,243,422	1,104,457	Flake, Jeff	1,036,542	Carmona, Richard	102,423	67,915 R	49.2%	46.2%	51.6%	48.4%
2010	1,708,484	1,005,615	McCain, John S. III*	592,011	Glassman, Rodney	110,858	413,604 R	58.9%	34.7%	62.9%	37.1%
2006	1,526,782	814,398	Kyl, Jon*	664,141	Pederson, Jim	48,243	150,257 R	53.3%	43.5%	55.1%	44.9%
2004	1,961,677	1,505,372	McCain, John S. III*	404,507	Starky, Stuart Marc	51,798	1,100,865 R	76.7%	20.6%	78.8%	21.2%
2000	1,397,076	1,108,196	Kyl, Jon*			288,880	1,108,196 R	79.3%		100.0%	
1998	1,013,280	696,577	McCain, John S. III*	275,224	Ranger, Ed	41,479	421,353 R	68.7%	27.2%	71.7%	28.3%
1994	1,119,060	600,999	Kyl, Jon	442,510	Coppersmith, Sam G.	75,551	158,489 R	53.7%	39.5%	57.6%	42.4%
1992**	1,382,051	771,395	McCain, John S. III*	436,321	Sargent, Claire	174,335	335,074 R	55.8%	31.6%	63.9%	36.1%
1988	1,164,539	478,060	DeGreen, Keith	660,403	DeConcini, Dennis*	26,076	182,343 D	41.1%	56.7%	42.0%	58.0%
1986	862,921	521,850	McCain, John S. III	340,965	Kimball, Richard	106	180,885 R	60.5%	39.5%	60.5%	39.5%
1982	723,885	291,749	Dunn, Pete	411,970	DeConcini, Dennis*	20,166	120,221 D	40.3%	56.9%	41.5%	58.5%
1980	874,178	432,371	Goldwater, Barry M. Sr.*	422,972	Schulz, Bill	18,835	9,399 R	49.5%	48.4%	50.5%	49.5%
1976	741,210	321,236	Steiger, Sam	400,334	DeConcini, Dennis	19,640	79,098 D	43.3%	54.0%	44.5%	55.5%
1974	549,919	320,396	Goldwater, Barry M. Sr.*	229,523	Marshall, Jonathan		90,873 R	58.3%	41.7%	58.3%	41.7%
1970	407,796	228,284	Fannin, Paul*	179,512	Grossman, Sam		48,772 R	56.0%	44.0%	56.0%	44.0%
1968	479,945	274,607	Goldwater, Barry M. Sr.	205,338	Elson, Roy L.		69,269 R	57.2%	42.8%	57.2%	42.8%
1964	468,788	241,084	Fannin, Paul	227,704	Elson, Roy L.		13,380 R	51.4%	48.6%	51.4%	48.6%
1962	362,605	163,388	Mecham, Evan	199,217	Hayden, Carl*		35,829 D	45.1%	54.9%	45.1%	54.9%
1958	293,623	164,593	Goldwater, Barry M. Sr.*	129,030	McFarland, Ernest W.		35,563 R	56.1%	43.9%	56.1%	43.9%
1956	278,263	107,447	Jones, Ross F.	170,816	Hayden, Carl*		63,369 D	38.6%	61.4%	38.6%	61.4%
1952	257,401	132,063	Goldwater, Barry M. Sr.	125,338	McFarland, Ernest W.*		6,725 R	51.3%	48.7%	51.3%	48.7%
1950	185,092	68,846	Brockett, Bruce	116,246	Hayden, Carl*		47,400 D	37.2%	62.8%	37.2%	62.8%
1946	116,239	35,022	Powers, Ward S.	80,415	McFarland, Ernest W.*	802	45,393 D	30.1%	69.2%	30.3%	69.7%

Note: An asterisk (*) denotes incumbent. **In past elections, the other vote included: 1992 - 145,361 Independent (Evan Mecham). The Democratic Party did not run a candidate in the 2000 Senate election.

ARIZONA

PRESIDENT 2016

2010 Census Population	County	Total Vote	Republican (Trump)	Democratic (Clinton)	Other	Rep.-Dem. Plurality		Percentage			
								Total Vote		Major Vote	
								Rep.	Dem.	Rep.	Dem.
71,518	APACHE	27,119	8,240	17,083	1,796	8,843	D	30.4%	63.0%	32.5%	67.5%
131,346	COCHISE	49,384	28,092	17,450	3,842	10,642	R	56.9%	35.3%	61.7%	38.3%
134,421	COCONINO	58,440	21,108	32,404	4,928	11,296	D	36.1%	55.4%	39.4%	60.6%
53,597	GILA	22,312	14,182	7,003	1,127	7,179	R	63.6%	31.4%	66.9%	33.1%
37,220	GRAHAM	12,134	8,025	3,301	808	4,724	R	66.1%	27.2%	70.9%	29.1%
8,437	GREENLEE	3,270	1,892	1,092	286	800	R	57.9%	33.4%	63.4%	36.6%
20,489	LA PAZ	5,877	4,003	1,575	299	2,428	R	68.1%	26.8%	71.8%	28.2%
3,817,117	MARICOPA	1,549,098	747,361	702,907	98,830	44,454	R	48.2%	45.4%	51.5%	48.5%
200,186	MOHAVE	79,346	58,282	17,455	3,609	40,827	R	73.5%	22.0%	77.0%	23.0%
107,449	NAVAJO	39,654	20,577	16,459	2,618	4,118	R	51.9%	41.5%	55.6%	44.4%
980,263	PIMA	416,418	167,428	224,661	24,329	57,233	D	40.2%	54.0%	42.7%	57.3%
375,770	PINAL	128,254	72,819	47,892	7,543	24,927	R	56.8%	37.3%	60.3%	39.7%
47,420	SANTA CRUZ	16,287	3,897	11,690	700	7,793	D	23.9%	71.8%	25.0%	75.0%
211,033	YAVAPAI	113,156	71,330	35,590	6,236	35,740	R	63.0%	31.5%	66.7%	33.3%
195,751	YUMA	52,416	25,165	24,605	2,646	560	R	48.0%	46.9%	50.6%	49.4%
6,392,017	TOTAL	2,573,165	1,252,401	1,161,167	159,597	91,234	R	48.7%	45.1%	51.9%	48.1%

ARIZONA

SENATOR 2016

2010 Census Population	County	Total Vote	Republican (McCain)	Democratic (Kirkpatrick)	Other	Rep.-Dem. Plurality		Percentage			
								Total Vote		Major Vote	
								Rep.	Dem.	Rep.	Dem.
71,518	APACHE	27,736	7,944	18,446	1,346	10,502	D	28.6%	66.5%	30.1%	69.9%
131,346	COCHISE	48,488	27,636	17,642	3,210	9,994	R	57.0%	36.4%	61.0%	39.0%
134,421	COCONINO	58,898	24,031	31,695	3,172	7,664	D	40.8%	53.8%	43.1%	56.9%
53,597	GILA	21,495	13,157	6,701	1,637	6,456	R	61.2%	31.2%	66.3%	33.7%
37,220	GRAHAM	11,893	7,728	3,280	885	4,448	R	65.0%	27.6%	70.2%	29.8%
8,437	GREENLEE	3,241	1,784	1,189	268	595	R	55.0%	36.7%	60.0%	40.0%
20,489	LA PAZ	5,741	3,662	1,629	450	2,033	R	63.8%	28.4%	69.2%	30.8%
3,817,117	MARICOPA	1,525,746	842,425	602,635	80,686	239,790	R	55.2%	39.5%	58.3%	41.7%
200,186	MOHAVE	76,162	50,486	19,045	6,631	31,441	R	66.3%	25.0%	72.6%	27.4%
107,449	NAVAJO	39,150	18,760	17,645	2,745	1,115	R	47.9%	45.1%	51.5%	48.5%
980,263	PIMA	409,737	187,910	202,213	19,614	14,303	D	45.9%	49.4%	48.2%	51.8%
375,770	PINAL	126,682	72,787	45,402	8,493	27,385	R	57.5%	35.8%	61.6%	38.4%
47,420	SANTA CRUZ	15,989	5,635	9,745	609	4,110	D	35.2%	60.9%	36.6%	63.4%
211,033	YAVAPAI	110,267	68,032	34,527	7,708	33,505	R	61.7%	31.3%	66.3%	33.7%
195,751	YUMA	49,505	27,290	19,451	2,764	7,839	R	55.1%	39.3%	58.4%	41.6%
6,392,017	TOTAL	2,530,730	1,359,267	1,031,245	140,218	328,022	R	53.7%	40.7%	56.9%	43.1%

ARIZONA

HOUSE OF REPRESENTATIVES

CD	Year	Total Vote	Republican Vote	Republican Candidate	Democratic Vote	Democratic Candidate	Other Vote	Rep.-Dem. Plurality	Total Vote Rep.	Total Vote Dem.	Major Vote Rep.	Major Vote Dem.
1	2016	280,710	121,745	BABEU, PAUL	142,219	O'HALLERAN, TOM	16,746	20,474 D	43.4%	50.7%	46.1%	53.9%
1	2014	185,114	87,723	TOBIN, ANDY	97,391	KIRKPATRICK, ANN*		9,668 D	47.4%	52.6%	47.4%	52.6%
1	2012	251,595	113,594	PATON, JONATHAN	122,774	KIRKPATRICK, ANN	15,227	9,180 D	45.1%	48.8%	48.1%	51.9%
2	2016	315,679	179,806	MCSALLY, MARTHA*	135,873	HEINZ, MATT		43,933 R	57.0%	43.0%	57.0%	43.0%
2	2014	219,351	109,704	MCSALLY, MARTHA	109,543	BARBER, RON*	104	161 R	50.0%	49.9%	50.0%	50.0%
2	2012	292,279	144,884	MCSALLY, MARTHA	147,338	BARBER, RON*	57	2,454 D	49.6%	50.4%	49.6%	50.4%
3	2016	151,035			148,973	GRIJALVA, RAÚL M.*	2,062	148,973 D		98.6%		100.0%
3	2014	104,428	46,185	SAUCEDO MERCER, GABRIELLA	58,192	GRIJALVA, RAÚL M.*	51	12,007 D	44.2%	55.7%	44.2%	55.8%
3	2012	168,698	62,663	SAUCEDO MERCER, GABRIELLA	98,468	GRIJALVA, RAUL M.*	7,567	35,805 D	37.1%	58.4%	38.9%	61.1%
4	2016	284,783	203,487	GOSAR, PAUL*	81,296	WEISSER, MIKEL		122,191 R	71.5%	28.5%	71.5%	28.5%
4	2014	175,179	122,560	GOSAR, PAUL*	45,179	WEISSER, MIKEL	7,440	77,381 R	70.0%	25.8%	73.1%	26.9%
4	2012	243,760	162,907	GOSAR, PAUL*	69,154	ROBINSON, JOHNNIE	11,699	93,753 R	66.8%	28.4%	70.2%	29.8%
5	2016	320,124	205,184	BIGGS, ANDY	114,940	FUENTES, TALIA		90,244 R	64.1%	35.9%	64.1%	35.9%
5	2014	179,463	124,867	SALMON, MATT*	54,596	WOODS, JAMES ISSAC		70,271 R	69.6%	30.4%	69.6%	30.4%
5	2012	273,059	183,470	SALMON, MATT	89,589	MORGAN, SPENCER		93,881 R	67.2%	32.8%	67.2%	32.8%
6	2016	324,444	201,578	SCHWEIKERT, DAVID*	122,866	WILLIAMSON, W. JOHN		78,712 R	62.1%	37.9%	62.1%	37.9%
6	2014	199,776	129,578	SCHWEIKERT, DAVID*	70,198	WILLIAMSON, W. JOHN		59,380 R	64.9%	35.1%	64.9%	35.1%
6	2012	293,177	179,706	SCHWEIKERT, DAVID*	97,666	JETTE, MATTHEW	15,805	82,040 R	61.3%	33.3%	64.8%	35.2%
7	2016	158,811	39,286	NUNEZ, EVE	119,465	GALLEGO, RUBEN*	60	80,179 D	24.7%	75.2%	24.7%	75.3%
7	2014	72,452			54,235	GALLEGO, RUBEN	18,217	54,235 D		74.9%		100.0%
7	2012	127,827			104,489	PASTOR, ED*	23,338	104,489 D		81.7%		100.0%
8	2016	298,971	204,942	FRANKS, TRENT*			94,029	204,942 R	68.5%		100.0%	
8	2014	169,776	128,710	FRANKS, TRENT*			41,066	128,710 R	75.8%		100.0%	
8	2012	272,791	172,809	FRANKS, TRENT*	95,635	SCHARER, GENE	4,347	77,174 R	63.3%	35.1%	64.4%	35.6%
9	2016	277,507	108,350	GILES, DAVE	169,055	SINEMA, KYRSTEN*	102	60,705 D	39.0%	60.9%	39.1%	60.9%
9	2014	162,062	67,841	ROGERS, WENDY	88,609	SINEMA, KYRSTEN*	5,612	20,768 D	41.9%	54.7%	43.4%	56.6%
9	2012	250,131	111,630	PARKER, VERNON B.	121,881	SINEMA, KYRSTEN	16,620	10,251 D	44.6%	48.7%	47.8%	52.2%
TOTAL	2016	2,412,064	1,264,378		1,034,687		112,999	229,691 R	52.4%	42.9%	55.0%	45.0%
TOTAL	2014	1,467,601	817,168		577,943		72,490	239,225 R	55.7%	39.4%	58.6%	41.4%
TOTAL	2012	2,173,317	1,131,663		946,994		94,660	184,669 R	52.1%	43.6%	54.4%	45.6%

Note: An asterisk (*) denotes incumbent.

ARIZONA

GENERAL AND PRIMARY ELECTIONS

2016 GENERAL ELECTIONS: OTHER VOTES

President Other vote was Libertarian 106,327 (Gary Johnson), 34,345 Green (Jill Stein), 17,449 Write-in (Evan McMullin), 1,058 Write-in (Darrell Castle), 271 Write-in (Scattered Write-in), 85 Write-in (Thomas Hoefling), 62 Write-in (Mike Smith), 29 Write-in (Roque De La Fuente)

Senate Other vote was 138,634 Green (Gary Swing), 694 Write-in (Pat Quinn), 494 Write-in (Sydney Dudikoff), 223 Write-in (Selena Lopez), 83 Write-in (Leonard Clark), 45 Write-in (Anthony Camboni), 34 Write-in (Shelia Bilyeu), 7 Write-in (Gene Scott), 4 Write-in (Santos Chavez)

House Other vote was:

CD 1 16,746 Green (Ray Parrish)

CD 3 1,303 Write-in (Bill Abatecola), 332 Write-in (Jaime Vasquez), 283 Write-in (Harvey Martin), 144 Write-in (F. Sanchez)

CD 7 60 Write-in (Neil Westbrooks)

CD 8 93,954 Green (Mark Salazar), 75 Write-in (Hayden Keener)

CD 9 56 Write-in (Cary Dolego), 46 Write-in (Axel Bello)

ARIZONA

GENERAL AND PRIMARY ELECTIONS

2016 PRIMARY ELECTIONS: SUPPLEMENTARY INFORMATION

| Primary | March 22, 2016 (President) August 30, 2016 (Congress) | **Registration** (as of August 22, 2016 — includes 541,299 inactive registrants) | 3,941,910 | Republican Democratic Libertarian Green Other | 1,322,003 1,163,111 32,704 6,941 1,417,151 |

Primary Type Semi-open—Registered Democrats and Republicans could vote only in their party's primary. But voters not registered with any political party could participate in either the Democratic or Republican primary.

	REPUBLICAN PRIMARIES			DEMOCRATIC PRIMARIES		
President	Trump, Donald J.	286,743	45.9%	Clinton, Hillary Rodham	262,459	56.3%
	Cruz, Ted	172,294	27.6%	Sanders, Bernard	192,962	41.4%
	Rubio, Marco	72,304	11.6%	O'Malley, Martin	3,877	0.8%
	Kasich, John R.	65,965	10.6%	De La Fuente, Roque "Rocky"	2,797	0.6%
	Carson, Ben	14,940	2.4%	Steinberg, Michael Alan	2,295	0.5%
	Bush, Jeb	4,393	0.7%	Hewes, Henry	1,845	0.4%
	Paul, Rand	2,269	0.4%			
	Huckabee, Mike	1,300	0.2%			
	Fiorina, Carly	1,270	0.2%			
	Christie, Chris	988	0.2%			
	Santorum, Rick	523	0.1%			
	Graham, Lindsey	498	0.1%			
	Pataki, George E.	309				
	Cook, Timothy	243				
	TOTAL	*624,039*		*TOTAL*	*466,235*	
Senator	McCain, John S. III*	302,532	51.2%	Kirkpatrick, Ann	333,586	99.8%
	Ward, Kelli	235,988	39.9%	Bello, Axel (write-in)	508	0.2%
	Meluskey, Alex	31,159	5.3%			
	Van Steenwyk, Clair (write-in)	21,476	3.6%			
	Webster, Sean (write-in)	175				
	TOTAL	*591,330*		*TOTAL*	*334,094*	
Congressional District 1	Babeu, Paul	19,533	30.8%	O'Halleran, Tom	30,833	58.8%
	Kiehne, Gary	14,854	23.4%	Olivas, Miguel	21,632	41.2%
	Rogers, Wendy	14,222	22.4%			
	Bennett, Ken	10,578	16.7%			
	Redd, Shawn	2,098	3.3%			
	Gowan, David	2,091	3.3%			
	TOTAL	*63,376*		*TOTAL*	*52,465*	
Congressional District 2	McSally, Martha*	69,378	100.0%	Heinz, Matt	32,017	52.8%
				Steele, Victoria	28,658	47.2%
	TOTAL	*69,378*		*TOTAL*	*60,675*	
Congressional District 3				Grijalva, Raúl M.*	35,844	100.0%
				TOTAL	*35,844*	
Congressional District 4	Gosar, Paul*	64,947	71.4%	Weisser, Mikel	24,097	99.8%
	Strauss, Ray	25,991	28.6%	Hixon, Robert (write-in)	49	0.2%
	TOTAL	*90,938*		*TOTAL*	*24,146*	
Congressional District 5	Biggs, Andy	25,240	29.5%	Fuentes, Talia	16,408	65.4%
	Jones, Christine	25,224	29.5%	Remaklus, Kinsey	8,663	34.6%
	Stapley, Don	17,745	20.7%			
	Olson, Justin	17,386	20.3%			
	TOTAL	*85,595*		*TOTAL*	*25,071*	

ARIZONA

GENERAL AND PRIMARY ELECTIONS

	REPUBLICAN PRIMARIES			DEMOCRATIC PRIMARIES		
Congressional District 6	Schweikert, David*	63,378	80.3%	Williamson, W. John	17,561	58.8%
	Wittenberg, Russ	15,535	19.7%	Sinuk, Brian	12,293	41.2%
	TOTAL	78,913		TOTAL	29,854	
Congressional District 7	Nunez, Eve	10,912	100.0%	Gallego, Ruben*	29,705	100.0%
	TOTAL	10,912		TOTAL	29,705	
Congressional District 8	Franks, Trent*	59,042	71.1%	DeVivo, Joe (write-in)	640	100.0%
	Van Steenwyk, Clair	24,042	28.9%			
	TOTAL	83,084		TOTAL	640	
Congressional District 9	Giles, Dave	25,963	60.7%	Sinema, Kyrsten*	38,948	100.0%
	Agra, John	16,817	39.3%			
	TOTAL	42,780		TOTAL	38,948	

Note: An asterisk (*) denotes incumbent.

ARKANSAS

Congressional districts first established for elections held in 2012

4 members

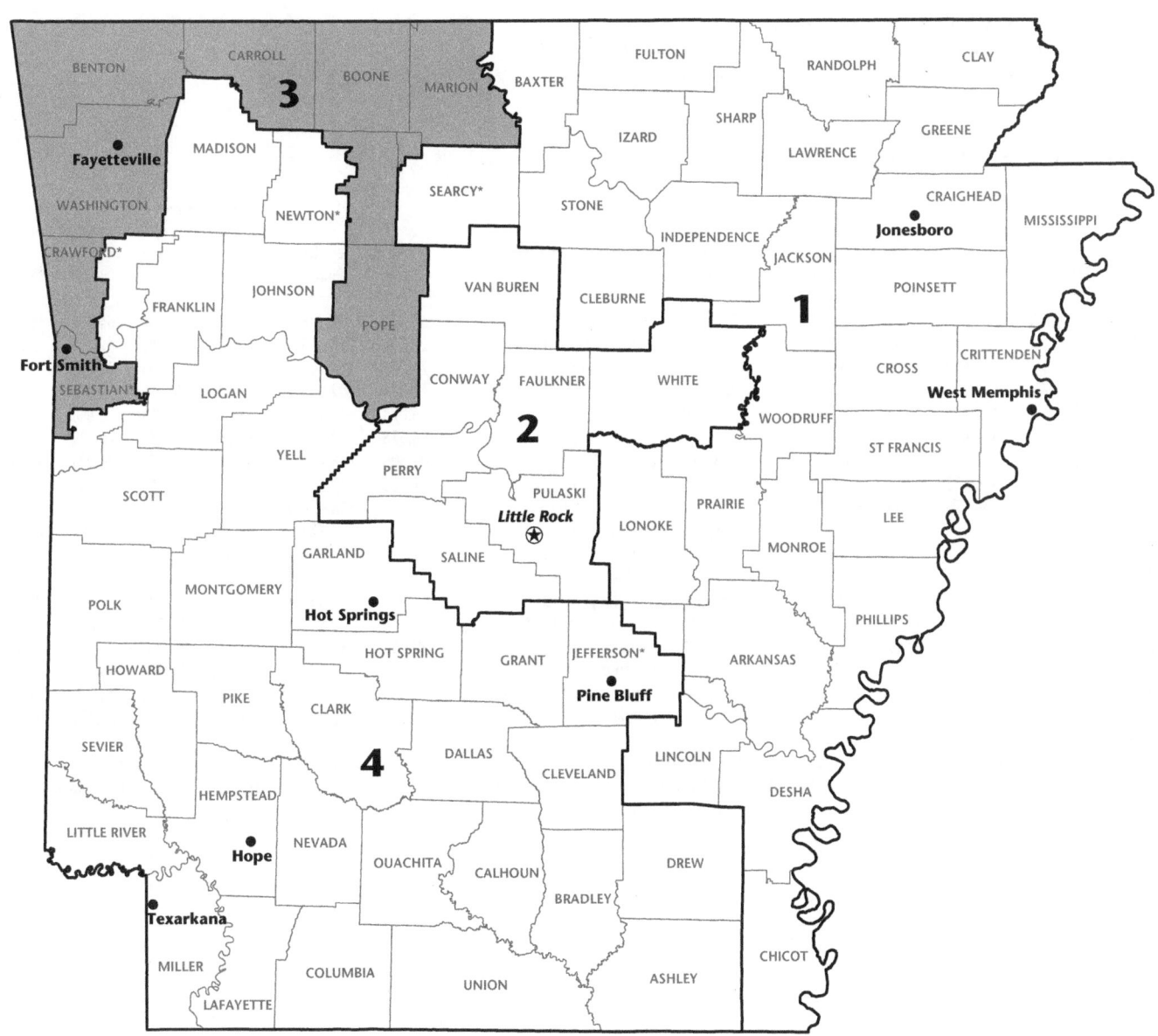

* Asterisk indicates a county whose boundaries include parts of two or more congressional districts.

ARKANSAS

GOVERNOR
Asa Hutchinson (R). Elected 2014 to a four-year term.

SENATORS (2 Republicans)
John Boozman (R). Re-elected 2016 to a six-year term. Previously elected 2010.

Tom Cotton (R). Elected 2014 to a six-year term.

REPRESENTATIVES (4 Republicans)
1. Rick Crawford (R)
2. French Hill (R)
3. Steve Womack (R)
4. Bruce Westerman (R)

POSTWAR VOTE FOR PRESIDENT

Year	Total Vote	Republican		Democratic		Other Vote	Rep.-Dem. Plurality	Percentage			
		Vote	Candidate	Vote	Candidate			Total Vote		Major Vote	
								Rep.	Dem.	Rep.	Dem.
2016**	1,130,676	684,872	Trump, Donald J.	380,494	Clinton, Hillary Rodham	65,310	304,378 R	60.6%	33.7%	64.3%	35.7%
2012	1,069,468	647,744	Romney, W. Mitt	394,409	Obama, Barack H.*	27,315	253,335 R	60.6%	36.9%	62.2%	37.8%
2008	1,086,617	638,017	McCain, John S. III	422,310	Obama, Barack H.	26,290	215,707 R	58.7%	38.9%	60.2%	39.8%
2004	1,054,945	572,898	Bush, George W.*	469,953	Kerry, John F.	12,094	102,945 R	54.3%	44.5%	54.9%	45.1%
2000**	921,781	472,940	Bush, George W.	422,768	Gore, Albert Jr.	26,073	50,172 R	51.3%	45.9%	52.8%	47.2%
1996**	884,262	325,416	Dole, Robert "Bob"	475,171	Clinton, Bill*	83,675	149,755 D	36.8%	53.7%	40.6%	59.4%
1992**	950,653	337,324	Bush, George H.*	505,823	Clinton, Bill	107,506	168,499 D	35.5%	53.2%	40.0%	60.0%
1988	827,738	466,578	Bush, George H.	349,237	Dukakis, Michael S.	11,923	117,341 R	56.4%	42.2%	57.2%	42.8%
1984	884,406	534,774	Reagan, Ronald*	338,646	Mondale, Walter F.	10,986	196,128 R	60.5%	38.3%	61.2%	38.8%
1980**	837,582	403,164	Reagan, Ronald	398,041	Carter, Jimmy*	36,377	5,123 R	48.1%	47.5%	50.3%	49.7%
1976	767,535	267,903	Ford, Gerald R.*	498,604	Carter, Jimmy	1,028	230,701 D	34.9%	65.0%	35.0%	65.0%
1972	651,320	448,541	Nixon, Richard M.*	199,892	McGovern, George S.	2,887	248,649 R	68.9%	30.7%	69.2%	30.8%
1968**	619,969	190,759	Nixon, Richard M.	188,228	Humphrey, Hubert Horatio Jr.	240,982	2,531 R	30.8%	30.4%	50.3%	49.7%
1964	560,426	243,264	Goldwater, Barry M. Sr.	314,197	Johnson, Lyndon B.*	2,965	70,933 D	43.4%	56.1%	43.6%	56.4%
1960	428,509	184,508	Nixon, Richard M.	215,049	Kennedy, John F.	28,952	30,541 D	43.1%	50.2%	46.2%	53.8%
1956	406,572	186,287	Eisenhower, Dwight D.*	213,277	Stevenson, Adlai E. II	7,008	26,990 D	45.8%	52.5%	46.6%	53.4%
1952	404,800	177,155	Eisenhower, Dwight D.	226,300	Stevenson, Adlai E. II	1,345	49,145 D	43.8%	55.9%	43.9%	56.1%
1948**	242,475	50,959	Dewey, Thomas E.	149,659	Truman, Harry S.*	41,857	98,700 D	21.0%	61.7%	25.4%	74.6%

Note: An asterisk (*) denotes incumbent. **In past elections, the other vote included: 2016 - 29,949 Libertarian (Gary Johnson); 2000 - 13,421 Green (Ralph Nader); 1996 - 69,884 Reform (Ross Perot); 1992 - 99,132 Independent (Perot); 1980 - 22,468 Independent (John Anderson); 1968 - 240,982 American Independent (Wallace); 1948 - 40,068 States' Rights (Strom Thurmond). Wallace carried Arkansas in 1968 with 38.9 percent of the vote.

ARKANSAS

POSTWAR VOTE FOR GOVERNOR

Year	Total Vote	Republican Vote	Republican Candidate	Democratic Vote	Democratic Candidate	Other Vote	Rep.-Dem. Plurality	Total Vote Rep.	Total Vote Dem.	Major Vote Rep.	Major Vote Dem.
2014	848,592	470,429	Hutchinson, Asa	352,115	Ross, Mike	26,048	118,314 R	55.4%	41.5%	57.2%	42.8%
2010	781,333	262,784	Keet, Jim	503,336	Beebe, Mike D.*	15,213	240,552 D	33.6%	64.4%	34.3%	65.7%
2006	774,680	315,040	Hutchinson, Asa	430,765	Beebe, Mike D.	28,875	115,725 D	40.7%	55.6%	42.2%	57.8%
2002	805,696	427,082	Huckabee, Mike*	378,250	Fisher, Jimmie Lou	364	48,832 R	53.0%	46.9%	53.0%	47.0%
1998	728,619	430,919	Huckabee, Mike*	278,155	King, James	19,545	152,764 R	59.1%	38.2%	60.8%	39.2%
1994	716,840	287,904	Nelson, Sheffield	428,936	Tucker, Jim Guy*		141,032 D	40.2%	59.8%	40.2%	59.8%
1990	696,412	295,925	Nelson, Sheffield	400,386	Clinton, Bill*	101	104,461 D	42.5%	57.5%	42.5%	57.5%
1986**	688,551	248,427	White, Frank D.	439,882	Clinton, Bill*	242	191,455 D	36.1%	63.9%	36.1%	63.9%
1984	886,548	331,987	Freeman, Woody	554,561	Clinton, Bill*		222,574 D	37.4%	62.6%	37.4%	62.6%
1982	789,351	357,496	White, Frank D.*	431,855	Clinton, Bill		74,359 D	45.3%	54.7%	45.3%	54.7%
1980	838,925	435,684	White, Frank D.	403,241	Clinton, Bill*		32,443 R	51.9%	48.1%	51.9%	48.1%
1978	528,912	193,746	Lowe, A. Lynn	335,101	Clinton, Bill	65	141,355 D	36.6%	63.4%	36.6%	63.4%
1976	726,949	121,716	Griffith, Leon	605,083	Pryor, David H.*	150	483,367 D	16.7%	83.2%	16.7%	83.3%
1974	545,974	187,872	Coon, Ken	358,018	Pryor, David H.	84	170,146 D	34.4%	65.6%	34.4%	65.6%
1972	648,069	159,177	Blaylock, Len E.	488,892	Bumpers, Dale*		329,715 D	24.6%	75.4%	24.6%	75.4%
1970	608,198	196,418	Rockefeller, Winthrop*	375,648	Bumpers, Dale	36,132	179,230 D	32.3%	61.8%	34.3%	65.7%
1968	615,590	322,777	Rockefeller, Winthrop*	292,813	Crank, Marion		29,964 R	52.4%	47.6%	52.4%	47.6%
1966	563,527	306,324	Rockefeller, Winthrop	257,203	Johnson, James Douglas		49,121 R	54.4%	45.6%	54.4%	45.6%
1964	592,113	254,561	Rockefeller, Winthrop	337,489	Faubus, Orval E.*	63	82,928 D	43.0%	57.0%	43.0%	57.0%
1962	308,092	82,349	Ricketts, Willis	225,743	Faubus, Orval E.*		143,394 D	26.7%	73.3%	26.7%	73.3%
1960	421,985	129,921	Britt, Henry M.	292,064	Faubus, Orval E.*		162,143 D	30.8%	69.2%	30.8%	69.2%
1958	286,886	50,288	Johnson, George W.	236,598	Faubus, Orval E.*		186,310 D	17.5%	82.5%	17.5%	82.5%
1956	399,012	77,215	Mitchell, Roy	321,797	Faubus, Orval E.*		244,582 D	19.4%	80.6%	19.4%	80.6%
1954	335,176	127,004	Remmel, Pratt C.	208,121	Faubus, Orval E.	51	81,117 D	37.9%	62.1%	37.9%	62.1%
1952	391,592	49,292	Speck, Jefferson W.	342,292	Cherry, Francis	8	293,000 D	12.6%	87.4%	12.6%	87.4%
1950	317,081	50,303	Speck, Jefferson W.	266,778	McMath, Sidney S.*		216,475 D	15.9%	84.1%	15.9%	84.1%
1948	244,271	26,500	Black, Charles R.	217,771	McMath, Sidney S.		191,271 D	10.8%	89.2%	10.8%	89.2%
1946	152,162	24,133	Mills, W. T.	128,029	Laney, Ben*		103,896 D	15.9%	84.1%	15.9%	84.1%

Note: An asterisk (*) denotes incumbent. **The term of office for Arkansas governor was increased from two to four years effective with the 1986 election.

POSTWAR VOTE FOR SENATOR

Year	Total Vote	Republican Vote	Republican Candidate	Democratic Vote	Democratic Candidate	Other Vote	Rep.-Dem. Plurality	Total Vote Rep.	Total Vote Dem.	Major Vote Rep.	Major Vote Dem.
2016	1,107,522	661,984	Boozman, John*	400,602	Eldridge, Conner	44,936	261,382 R	59.8%	36.2%	62.3%	37.7%
2014	847,505	478,819	Cotton, Tom	334,174	Pryor, Mark*	34,512	144,645 R	56.5%	39.4%	58.9%	41.1%
2010	779,957	451,618	Boozman, John	288,156	Lincoln, Blanche L.*	40,183	163,462 R	57.9%	36.9%	61.0%	39.0%
2008**	1,011,754			804,678	Pryor, Mark*	207,076	804,678 D		79.5%		100.0%
2004	1,039,349	458,036	Holt, Jim L.	580,973	Lincoln, Blanche L.	340	122,937 D	44.1%	55.9%	44.1%	55.9%
2002	803,959	370,653	Hutchinson, Tim*	433,306	Pryor, Mark		62,653 D	46.1%	53.9%	46.1%	53.9%
1998	700,644	295,870	Boozman, Fay	385,878	Lincoln, Blanche L.	18,896	90,008 D	42.2%	55.1%	43.4%	56.6%
1996	846,183	445,942	Hutchinson, Tim	400,241	Bryant, Winston		45,701 R	52.7%	47.3%	52.7%	47.3%
1992	920,008	366,373	Huckabee, Mike	553,635	Bumpers, Dale*		187,262 D	39.8%	60.2%	39.8%	60.2%
1990**	494,735			493,910	Pryor, David H.*	825	493,910 D		99.8%		100.0%
1986	695,487	262,313	Hutchinson, Asa	433,122	Bumpers, Dale*	52	170,809 D	37.7%	62.3%	37.7%	62.3%
1984	875,956	373,615	Bethune, Ed	502,341	Pryor, David H.*		128,726 D	42.7%	57.3%	42.7%	57.3%
1980	808,812	330,576	Clark, Bill	477,905	Bumpers, Dale*	331	147,329 D	40.9%	59.1%	40.9%	59.1%
1978	522,239	84,722	Kelly, Tom	399,916	Pryor, David H.	37,601	315,194 D	16.2%	76.6%	17.5%	82.5%
1974	543,082	82,026	Jones, John Harris	461,056	Bumpers, Dale		379,030 D	15.1%	84.9%	15.1%	84.9%
1972	634,636	248,238	Babbitt, Wayne H.	386,398	McClellan, John L.*		138,160 D	39.1%	60.9%	39.1%	60.9%
1968	591,704	241,739	Bernard, Charles T.	349,965	Fulbright, J. William*		108,226 D	40.9%	59.1%	40.9%	59.1%
1966**					McClellan, John L.*		D				
1962	312,880	98,013	Jones, Kenneth	214,867	Fulbright, J. William*		116,854 D	31.3%	68.7%	31.3%	68.7%
1960**					McClellan, John L.*		D				
1956	399,695	68,016	Henley, Ben C.	331,679	Fulbright, J. William*		263,663 D	17.0%	83.0%	17.0%	83.0%
1954	291,058			291,058	McClellan, John L.*		291,058 D		100.0%		100.0%
1950	302,582			302,582	Fulbright, J. William*		302,582 D		100.0%		100.0%
1948	231,922			216,401	McClellan, John L.*	15,521	216,401 D		93.3%		100.0%

Note: An asterisk (*) denotes incumbent. **In past elections, the other vote included: 2008 - 207,076 Green (Rebekah Kennedy, who finished second). In 1990 the vote for Senator David H. Pryor was not canvassed in seven counties because he was unopposed. Senator John L. McClellan was re-elected in 1960 and in 1966, but his vote was not canvassed in many counties. The Republican Party did not run a candidate in the 1948, 1950, 1954, 1960, 1966, 1990, and 2008 Senate elections.

ARKANSAS

PRESIDENT 2016

2010 Census Population	County	Total Vote	Republican (Trump)	Democratic (Clinton)	Other	Rep.-Dem. Plurality		Total Vote		Major Vote	
								Rep.	Dem.	Rep.	Dem.
19,019	ARKANSAS	6,212	3,826	1,939	447	1,887	R	61.6%	31.2%	66.4%	33.6%
21,853	ASHLEY	8,083	5,338	2,408	337	2,930	R	66.0%	29.8%	68.9%	31.1%
41,513	BAXTER	19,766	14,682	4,169	915	10,513	R	74.3%	21.1%	77.9%	22.1%
221,339	BENTON	96,824	60,871	28,005	7,948	32,866	R	62.9%	28.9%	68.5%	31.5%
36,903	BOONE	16,111	12,235	2,926	950	9,309	R	75.9%	18.2%	80.7%	19.3%
11,508	BRADLEY	3,653	2,164	1,317	172	847	R	59.2%	36.1%	62.2%	37.8%
5,368	CALHOUN	2,269	1,556	639	74	917	R	68.6%	28.2%	70.9%	29.1%
27,446	CARROLL	10,758	6,786	3,342	630	3,444	R	63.1%	31.1%	67.0%	33.0%
11,800	CHICOT	4,176	1,716	2,350	110	634	D	41.1%	56.3%	42.2%	57.8%
22,995	CLARK	8,526	4,404	3,620	502	784	R	51.7%	42.5%	54.9%	45.1%
16,083	CLAY	5,200	3,781	1,199	220	2,582	R	72.7%	23.1%	75.9%	24.1%
25,970	CLEBURNE	12,085	9,458	2,101	526	7,357	R	78.3%	17.4%	81.8%	18.2%
8,689	CLEVELAND	3,354	2,462	723	169	1,739	R	73.4%	21.6%	77.3%	22.7%
24,552	COLUMBIA	8,887	5,456	3,140	291	2,316	R	61.4%	35.3%	63.5%	36.5%
21,273	CONWAY	7,927	4,849	2,656	422	2,193	R	61.2%	33.5%	64.6%	35.4%
96,443	CRAIGHEAD	35,573	22,892	10,538	2,143	12,354	R	64.4%	29.6%	68.5%	31.5%
61,948	CRAWFORD	22,450	16,686	4,488	1,276	12,198	R	74.3%	20.0%	78.8%	21.2%
50,902	CRITTENDEN	15,952	6,964	8,410	578	1,446	D	43.7%	52.7%	45.3%	54.7%
17,870	CROSS	6,874	4,584	1,999	291	2,585	R	66.7%	29.1%	69.6%	30.4%
8,116	DALLAS	2,771	1,509	1,165	97	344	R	54.5%	42.0%	56.4%	43.6%
13,008	DESHA	4,257	1,919	2,228	110	309	D	45.1%	52.3%	46.3%	53.7%
18,509	DREW	6,595	3,968	2,365	262	1,603	R	60.2%	35.9%	62.7%	37.3%
113,237	FAULKNER	47,527	29,346	14,629	3,552	14,717	R	61.7%	30.8%	66.7%	33.3%
18,125	FRANKLIN	6,770	5,039	1,376	355	3,663	R	74.4%	20.3%	78.6%	21.4%
12,245	FULTON	4,772	3,471	1,067	234	2,404	R	72.7%	22.4%	76.5%	23.5%
96,024	GARLAND	40,805	26,087	12,311	2,407	13,776	R	63.9%	30.2%	67.9%	32.1%
17,853	GRANT	7,445	5,725	1,373	347	4,352	R	76.9%	18.4%	80.7%	19.3%
42,090	GREENE	14,600	10,720	3,071	809	7,649	R	73.4%	21.0%	77.7%	22.3%
22,609	HEMPSTEAD	7,049	4,401	2,377	271	2,024	R	62.4%	33.7%	64.9%	35.1%
32,923	HOT SPRING	11,944	8,172	3,149	623	5,023	R	68.4%	26.4%	72.2%	27.8%
13,789	HOWARD	4,674	3,157	1,351	166	1,806	R	67.5%	28.9%	70.0%	30.0%
36,647	INDEPENDENCE	13,614	9,936	2,881	797	7,055	R	73.0%	21.2%	77.5%	22.5%
13,696	IZARD	5,448	4,042	1,113	293	2,929	R	74.2%	20.4%	78.4%	21.6%
17,997	JACKSON	5,156	3,267	1,583	306	1,684	R	63.4%	30.7%	67.4%	32.6%
77,435	JEFFERSON	25,894	9,250	15,772	872	6,522	D	35.7%	60.9%	37.0%	63.0%
25,540	JOHNSON	9,112	6,091	2,427	594	3,664	R	66.8%	26.6%	71.5%	28.5%
7,645	LAFAYETTE	2,860	1,758	1,032	70	726	R	61.5%	36.1%	63.0%	37.0%
17,415	LAWRENCE	5,685	4,064	1,263	358	2,801	R	71.5%	22.2%	76.3%	23.7%
10,424	LEE	3,026	1,229	1,735	62	506	D	40.6%	57.3%	41.5%	58.5%
14,134	LINCOLN	3,826	2,455	1,252	119	1,203	R	64.2%	32.7%	66.2%	33.8%
13,171	LITTLE RIVER	5,227	3,605	1,397	225	2,208	R	69.0%	26.7%	72.1%	27.9%
22,353	LOGAN	7,921	5,746	1,715	460	4,031	R	72.5%	21.7%	77.0%	23.0%
68,356	LONOKE	27,100	19,958	5,664	1,478	14,294	R	73.6%	20.9%	77.9%	22.1%
15,717	MADISON	6,841	4,928	1,588	325	3,340	R	72.0%	23.2%	75.6%	24.4%
16,653	MARION	7,107	5,336	1,434	337	3,902	R	75.1%	20.2%	78.8%	21.2%
43,462	MILLER	16,091	11,294	4,273	524	7,021	R	70.2%	26.6%	72.6%	27.4%
46,480	MISSISSIPPI	13,204	7,061	5,670	473	1,391	R	53.5%	42.9%	55.5%	44.5%
8,149	MONROE	2,884	1,489	1,312	83	177	R	51.6%	45.5%	53.2%	46.8%
9,487	MONTGOMERY	3,559	2,643	748	168	1,895	R	74.3%	21.0%	77.9%	22.1%
8,997	NEVADA	3,246	2,000	1,157	89	843	R	61.6%	35.6%	63.4%	36.6%
8,330	NEWTON	3,753	2,875	699	179	2,176	R	76.6%	18.6%	80.4%	19.6%
26,120	OUACHITA	9,935	5,351	4,321	263	1,030	R	53.9%	43.5%	55.3%	44.7%
10,445	PERRY	4,306	3,008	1,049	249	1,959	R	69.9%	24.4%	74.1%	25.9%
21,757	PHILLIPS	6,953	2,446	4,310	197	1,864	D	35.2%	62.0%	36.2%	63.8%
11,291	PIKE	3,981	3,150	685	146	2,465	R	79.1%	17.2%	82.1%	17.9%
24,583	POINSETT	7,722	5,502	1,880	340	3,622	R	71.3%	24.3%	74.5%	25.5%
20,662	POLK	8,231	6,618	1,212	401	5,406	R	80.4%	14.7%	84.5%	15.5%
61,754	POPE	22,569	16,256	5,000	1,313	11,256	R	72.0%	22.2%	76.5%	23.5%
8,715	PRAIRIE	3,444	2,505	814	125	1,691	R	72.7%	23.6%	75.5%	24.5%
382,748	PULASKI	159,776	61,257	89,574	8,945	28,317	D	38.3%	56.1%	40.6%	59.4%

ARKANSAS

PRESIDENT 2016

2010 Census Population	County	Total Vote	Republican (Trump)	Democratic (Clinton)	Other	Rep.-Dem. Plurality	Percentage Total Vote Rep.	Dem.	Major Vote Rep.	Dem.
17,969	RANDOLPH	6,379	4,509	1,425	445	3,084 R	70.7%	22.3%	76.0%	24.0%
107,118	SALINE	52,100	35,863	13,256	2,981	22,607 R	68.8%	25.4%	73.0%	27.0%
11,233	SCOTT	3,510	2,731	602	177	2,129 R	77.8%	17.2%	81.9%	18.1%
8,195	SEARCY	3,728	2,955	601	172	2,354 R	79.3%	16.1%	83.1%	16.9%
125,744	SEBASTIAN	44,637	29,127	12,300	3,210	16,827 R	65.3%	27.6%	70.3%	29.7%
17,058	SEVIER	4,562	3,282	1,075	205	2,207 R	71.9%	23.6%	75.3%	24.7%
17,264	SHARP	7,249	5,407	1,472	370	3,935 R	74.6%	20.3%	78.6%	21.4%
28,258	ST. FRANCIS	7,430	3,195	4,031	204	836 D	43.0%	54.3%	44.2%	55.8%
12,394	STONE	5,618	4,113	1,203	302	2,910 R	73.2%	21.4%	77.4%	22.6%
41,639	UNION	16,894	10,456	5,855	583	4,601 R	61.9%	34.7%	64.1%	35.9%
17,295	VAN BUREN	7,339	5,382	1,549	408	3,833 R	73.3%	21.1%	77.7%	22.3%
203,065	WASHINGTON	81,861	41,476	33,366	7,019	8,110 R	50.7%	40.8%	55.4%	44.6%
77,076	WHITE	27,999	21,077	5,170	1,752	15,907 R	75.3%	18.5%	80.3%	19.7%
7,260	WOODRUFF	2,571	1,347	1,118	106	229 R	52.4%	43.5%	54.6%	45.4%
22,185	YELL	6,439	4,608	1,480	351	3,128 R	71.6%	23.0%	75.7%	24.3%
2,915,918	TOTAL	1,130,676	684,872	380,494	65,310	304,378 R	60.6%	33.7%	64.3%	35.7%

ARKANSAS

SENATOR 2016

2010 Census Population	County	Total Vote	Republican (Boozman)	Democratic (Eldridge)	Other	Rep.-Dem. Plurality	Percentage Total Vote Rep.	Dem.	Major Vote Rep.	Dem.
19,019	ARKANSAS	6,150	3,684	2,341	125	1,343 R	59.9%	38.1%	61.1%	38.9%
21,853	ASHLEY	7,737	5,106	2,346	285	2,760 R	66.0%	30.3%	68.5%	31.5%
41,513	BAXTER	19,255	14,074	4,231	950	9,843 R	73.1%	22.0%	76.9%	23.1%
221,339	BENTON	95,499	63,503	27,434	4,562	36,069 R	66.5%	28.7%	69.8%	30.2%
36,903	BOONE	15,839	12,490	2,620	729	9,870 R	78.9%	16.5%	82.7%	17.3%
11,508	BRADLEY	3,483	2,019	1,343	121	676 R	58.0%	38.6%	60.1%	39.9%
5,368	CALHOUN	2,193	1,336	773	84	563 R	60.9%	35.2%	63.3%	36.7%
27,446	CARROLL	10,511	6,771	3,318	422	3,453 R	64.4%	31.6%	67.1%	32.9%
11,800	CHICOT	4,202	1,824	2,288	90	464 D	43.4%	54.5%	44.4%	55.6%
22,995	CLARK	8,276	3,947	4,087	242	140 D	47.7%	49.4%	49.1%	50.9%
16,083	CLAY	5,049	3,286	1,527	236	1,759 R	65.1%	30.2%	68.3%	31.7%
25,970	CLEBURNE	11,780	8,382	2,902	496	5,480 R	71.2%	24.6%	74.3%	25.7%
8,689	CLEVELAND	3,302	2,164	1,034	104	1,130 R	65.5%	31.3%	67.7%	32.3%
24,552	COLUMBIA	8,461	5,440	2,757	264	2,683 R	64.3%	32.6%	66.4%	33.6%
21,273	CONWAY	7,728	4,403	3,023	302	1,380 R	57.0%	39.1%	59.3%	40.7%
96,443	CRAIGHEAD	34,933	23,218	10,241	1,474	12,977 R	66.5%	29.3%	69.4%	30.6%
61,948	CRAWFORD	22,006	16,008	5,042	956	10,966 R	72.7%	22.9%	76.0%	24.0%
50,902	CRITTENDEN	14,765	6,779	7,412	574	633 D	45.9%	50.2%	47.8%	52.2%
17,870	CROSS	6,671	4,456	1,997	218	2,459 R	66.8%	29.9%	69.1%	30.9%
8,116	DALLAS	2,689	1,429	1,171	89	258 R	53.1%	43.5%	55.0%	45.0%
13,008	DESHA	4,079	1,727	2,256	96	529 D	42.3%	55.3%	43.4%	56.6%
18,509	DREW	6,327	3,701	2,413	213	1,288 R	58.5%	38.1%	60.5%	39.5%
113,237	FAULKNER	46,753	27,632	16,770	2,351	10,862 R	59.1%	35.9%	62.2%	37.8%
18,125	FRANKLIN	6,719	4,749	1,690	280	3,059 R	70.7%	25.2%	73.8%	26.2%
12,245	FULTON	4,545	3,254	1,059	232	2,195 R	71.6%	23.3%	75.4%	24.6%
96,024	GARLAND	40,380	24,262	14,385	1,733	9,877 R	60.1%	35.6%	62.8%	37.2%
17,853	GRANT	7,256	5,015	1,877	364	3,138 R	69.1%	25.9%	72.8%	27.2%
42,090	GREENE	14,042	9,842	3,405	795	6,437 R	70.1%	24.2%	74.3%	25.7%
22,609	HEMPSTEAD	6,711	4,168	2,352	191	1,816 R	62.1%	35.0%	63.9%	36.1%
32,923	HOT SPRING	11,655	7,259	4,006	390	3,253 R	62.3%	34.4%	64.4%	35.6%

ARKANSAS

SENATOR 2016

2010 Census Population	County	Total Vote	Republican (Boozman)	Democratic (Eldridge)	Other	Rep.-Dem. Plurality	Percentage Total Vote Rep.	Dem.	Major Vote Rep.	Dem.
13,789	HOWARD	4,481	2,969	1,377	135	1,592 R	66.3%	30.7%	68.3%	31.7%
36,647	INDEPENDENCE	13,268	9,020	3,747	501	5,273 R	68.0%	28.2%	70.7%	29.3%
13,696	IZARD	5,224	3,593	1,404	227	2,189 R	68.8%	26.9%	71.9%	28.1%
17,997	JACKSON	5,078	2,958	1,951	169	1,007 R	58.3%	38.4%	60.3%	39.7%
77,435	JEFFERSON	24,930	8,805	15,342	783	6,537 D	35.3%	61.5%	36.5%	63.5%
25,540	JOHNSON	8,880	5,680	2,882	318	2,798 R	64.0%	32.5%	66.3%	33.7%
7,645	LAFAYETTE	2,739	1,713	954	72	759 R	62.5%	34.8%	64.2%	35.8%
17,415	LAWRENCE	5,528	3,912	1,380	236	2,532 R	70.8%	25.0%	73.9%	26.1%
10,424	LEE	2,994	1,271	1,636	87	365 D	42.5%	54.6%	43.7%	56.3%
14,134	LINCOLN	3,720	2,190	1,440	90	750 R	58.9%	38.7%	60.3%	39.7%
13,171	LITTLE RIVER	4,999	3,368	1,443	188	1,925 R	67.4%	28.9%	70.0%	30.0%
22,353	LOGAN	7,849	5,209	2,342	298	2,867 R	66.4%	29.8%	69.0%	31.0%
68,356	LONOKE	26,453	17,483	7,666	1,304	9,817 R	66.1%	29.0%	69.5%	30.5%
15,717	MADISON	6,828	4,520	2,045	263	2,475 R	66.2%	30.0%	68.8%	31.2%
16,653	MARION	6,967	5,265	1,320	382	3,945 R	75.6%	18.9%	80.0%	20.0%
43,462	MILLER	15,567	10,974	4,099	494	6,875 R	70.5%	26.3%	72.8%	27.2%
46,480	MISSISSIPPI	12,310	6,835	5,023	452	1,812 R	55.5%	40.8%	57.6%	42.4%
8,149	MONROE	2,783	1,363	1,361	59	2 R	49.0%	48.9%	50.0%	50.0%
9,487	MONTGOMERY	3,473	2,366	985	122	1,381 R	68.1%	28.4%	70.6%	29.4%
8,997	NEVADA	3,121	1,881	1,115	125	766 R	60.3%	35.7%	62.8%	37.2%
8,330	NEWTON	3,727	2,833	754	140	2,079 R	76.0%	20.2%	79.0%	21.0%
26,120	OUACHITA	9,564	5,277	4,052	235	1,225 R	55.2%	42.4%	56.6%	43.4%
10,445	PERRY	4,199	2,588	1,394	217	1,194 R	61.6%	33.2%	65.0%	35.0%
21,757	PHILLIPS	6,368	2,400	3,777	191	1,377 D	37.7%	59.3%	38.9%	61.1%
11,291	PIKE	3,911	2,819	955	137	1,864 R	72.1%	24.4%	74.7%	25.3%
24,583	POINSETT	7,628	5,357	2,026	245	3,331 R	70.2%	26.6%	72.6%	27.4%
20,662	POLK	8,026	6,062	1,654	310	4,408 R	75.5%	20.6%	78.6%	21.4%
61,754	POPE	22,241	15,344	5,819	1,078	9,525 R	69.0%	26.2%	72.5%	27.5%
8,715	PRAIRIE	3,316	2,130	1,093	93	1,037 R	64.2%	33.0%	66.1%	33.9%
382,748	PULASKI	158,339	64,378	88,892	5,069	24,514 D	40.7%	56.1%	42.0%	58.0%
17,969	RANDOLPH	6,255	4,266	1,659	330	2,607 R	68.2%	26.5%	72.0%	28.0%
107,118	SALINE	51,640	33,125	16,140	2,375	16,985 R	64.1%	31.3%	67.2%	32.8%
11,233	SCOTT	3,444	2,461	867	116	1,594 R	71.5%	25.2%	73.9%	26.1%
8,195	SEARCY	3,624	2,704	725	195	1,979 R	74.6%	20.0%	78.9%	21.1%
125,744	SEBASTIAN	44,560	29,405	13,060	2,095	16,345 R	66.0%	29.3%	69.2%	30.8%
17,058	SEVIER	4,321	3,036	1,076	209	1,960 R	70.3%	24.9%	73.8%	26.2%
17,264	SHARP	7,053	5,127	1,609	317	3,518 R	72.7%	22.8%	76.1%	23.9%
28,258	ST. FRANCIS	6,966	3,153	3,643	170	490 D	45.3%	52.3%	46.4%	53.6%
12,394	STONE	5,486	3,690	1,530	266	2,160 R	67.3%	27.9%	70.7%	29.3%
41,639	UNION	15,753	10,168	4,902	683	5,266 R	64.5%	31.1%	67.5%	32.5%
17,295	VAN BUREN	7,133	4,670	2,145	318	2,525 R	65.5%	30.1%	68.5%	31.5%
203,065	WASHINGTON	81,107	43,137	34,475	3,495	8,662 R	53.2%	42.5%	55.6%	44.4%
77,076	WHITE	27,830	19,413	7,341	1,076	12,072 R	69.8%	26.4%	72.6%	27.4%
7,260	WOODRUFF	2,487	917	1,521	49	604 D	36.9%	61.2%	37.6%	62.4%
22,185	YELL	6,356	4,221	1,881	254	2,340 R	66.4%	29.6%	69.2%	30.8%
2,915,918	TOTAL	1,107,522	661,984	400,602	44,936	261,382 R	59.8%	36.2%	62.3%	37.7%

ARKANSAS

HOUSE OF REPRESENTATIVES

CD	Year	Total Vote	Republican		Democratic		Other Vote	Rep.-Dem. Plurality	Percentage			
									Total Vote		Major Vote	
			Vote	Candidate	Vote	Candidate			Rep.	Dem.	Rep.	Dem.
1	2016	241,047	183,866	CRAWFORD, RICK*			57,181	183,866 R	76.3%		100.0%	
1	2014	196,256	124,139	CRAWFORD, RICK*	63,555	MCPHERSON, JACKIE	8,562	60,584 R	63.3%	32.4%	66.1%	33.9%
1	2012	246,843	138,800	CRAWFORD, RICK*	96,601	ELLINGTON, SCOTT	11,442	42,199 R	56.2%	39.1%	59.0%	41.0%
2	2016	302,464	176,472	HILL, FRENCH*	111,347	CURRY, DIANNE	14,645	65,125 R	58.3%	36.8%	61.3%	38.7%
2	2014	237,330	123,073	HILL, FRENCH	103,477	HAYS, PATRICK	10,780	19,596 R	51.9%	43.6%	54.3%	45.7%
2	2012	286,598	158,175	GRIFFIN, TIM*	113,156	RULE, HERB	15,267	45,019 R	55.2%	39.5%	58.3%	41.7%
3	2016	280,907	217,192	WOMACK, STEVE*			63,715	217,192 R	77.3%		100.0%	
3	2014	190,935	151,630	WOMACK, STEVE*			39,305	151,630 R	79.4%		100.0%	
3	2012	245,660	186,467	WOMACK, STEVE*			59,193	186,467 R	75.9%		100.0%	
4	2016	244,159	182,885	WESTERMAN, BRUCE*			61,274	182,885 R	74.9%		100.0%	
4	2014	206,131	110,789	WESTERMAN, BRUCE	87,742	WITT, JAMES LEE	7,600	23,047 R	53.7%	42.6%	55.8%	44.2%
4	2012	258,953	154,149	COTTON, TOM	95,013	JEFFRESS, GENE	9,791	59,136 R	59.5%	36.7%	61.9%	38.1%
TOTAL	2016	1,068,577	760,415		111,347		196,815	649,068 R	71.2%	10.4%	87.2%	12.8%
TOTAL	2014	830,652	509,631		254,774		66,247	254,857 R	61.4%	30.7%	66.7%	33.3%
TOTAL	2012	1,038,054	637,591		304,770		95,693	332,821 R	61.4%	29.4%	67.7%	32.3%

Note: An asterisk (*) denotes incumbent.

ARKANSAS

GENERAL AND PRIMARY ELECTIONS

2016 GENERAL ELECTIONS: OTHER VOTES

President   Other vote was 29,949 Libertarian (Gary Johnson), 13,176 Better for America (Evan McMullin), 9,473 Green (Jill Stein), 4,709 Independent (James Hedges), 4,613 Constitution (Darrell Castle), 3,390 Independent (Lynn Kahn)

Senate   Other vote was 43,866 Libertarian (Frank Gilbert), 1,070 Write-in (Scattered Write-in)

House   Other vote was:

CD 1   57,181 Libertarian (Mark West)
CD 2   14,342 Libertarian (Chris Hayes), 303 Write-in (Scattered Write-in)
CD 3   63,715 Libertarian (Steve Isaacson)
CD 4   61,274 Libertarian (Kerry Hicks)

2016 PRIMARY ELECTIONS: SUPPLEMENTARY INFORMATION

Primary   March 1, 2016   **Registration** (as of June 1, 2016)   1,703,609   No Party Registration

Primary Runoff   March 22, 2016

Primary Type   Open—Any registered voter could participate in either the Democratic or the Republican primary. However, if they participated in one party's primary they could not vote in the runoff of the other party.

ARKANSAS

GENERAL AND PRIMARY ELECTIONS

	REPUBLICAN PRIMARIES			DEMOCRATIC PRIMARIES		
President	Trump, Donald J.	134,744	32.8%	Clinton, Hillary Rodham	146,057	66.1%
	Cruz, Ted	125,340	30.5%	Sanders, Bernard	66,236	30.0%
	Rubio, Marco	101,910	24.8%	O'Malley, Martin	2,785	1.3%
	Carson, Ben	23,521	5.7%	Wolfe, John	2,556	1.2%
	Kasich, John R.	15,305	3.7%	Valentine, James	1,702	0.8%
	Huckabee, Mike	4,792	1.2%	De La Fuente, Roque "Rocky"	1,684	0.8%
	Bush, Jeb	2,402	0.6%			
	Paul, Rand	1,151	0.3%			
	Christie, Chris	631	0.2%			
	Fiorina, Carly	411	0.1%			
	Santorum, Rick	292	0.1%			
	Graham, Lindsey	252	0.1%			
	Jindal, Bobby	169				
	TOTAL	*410,920*		*TOTAL*	*221,020*	
Senator	Boozman, John*	298,039	76.5%	Eldridge, Conner	Unopposed	
	Coleman, Curtis	91,795	23.5%			
	TOTAL	*389,834*				
Congressional District 1	Crawford, Rick*	Unopposed				
Congressional District 2	Hill, French*	86,474	84.5%	Curry, Dianne	Unopposed	
	Olree, Brock	15,811	15.5%			
	TOTAL	*102,285*				
Congressional District 3	Womack, Steve*	Unopposed				
Congressional District 4	Westerman, Bruce*	Unopposed				

Note: An asterisk (*) denotes incumbent.

CALIFORNIA

Congressional districts first established for elections held in 2012

53 members

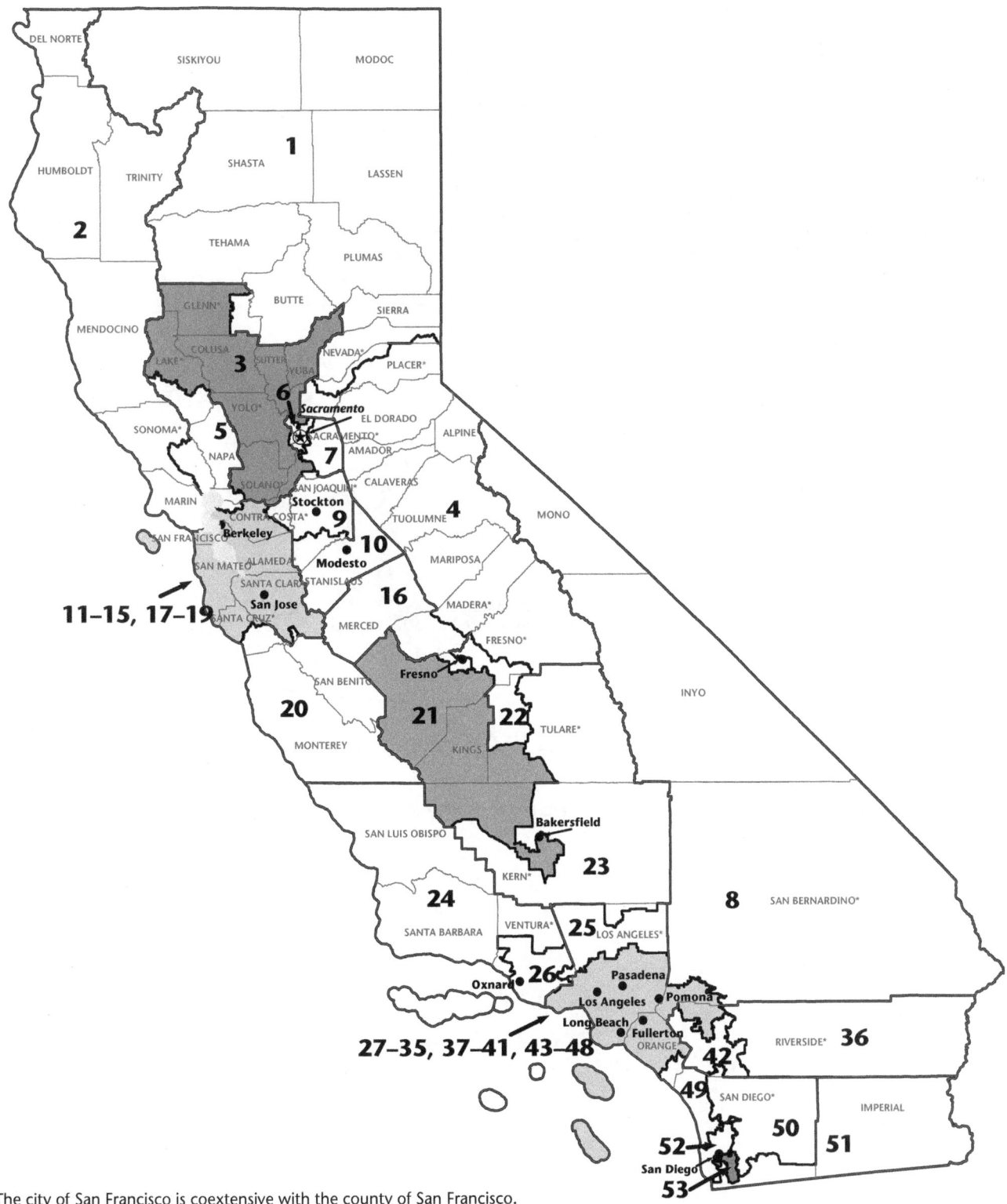

The city of San Francisco is coextensive with the county of San Francisco.

* Asterisk indicates a county whose boundaries include parts of two or more congressional districts.

CALIFORNIA

Greater Los Angeles, San Diego Areas

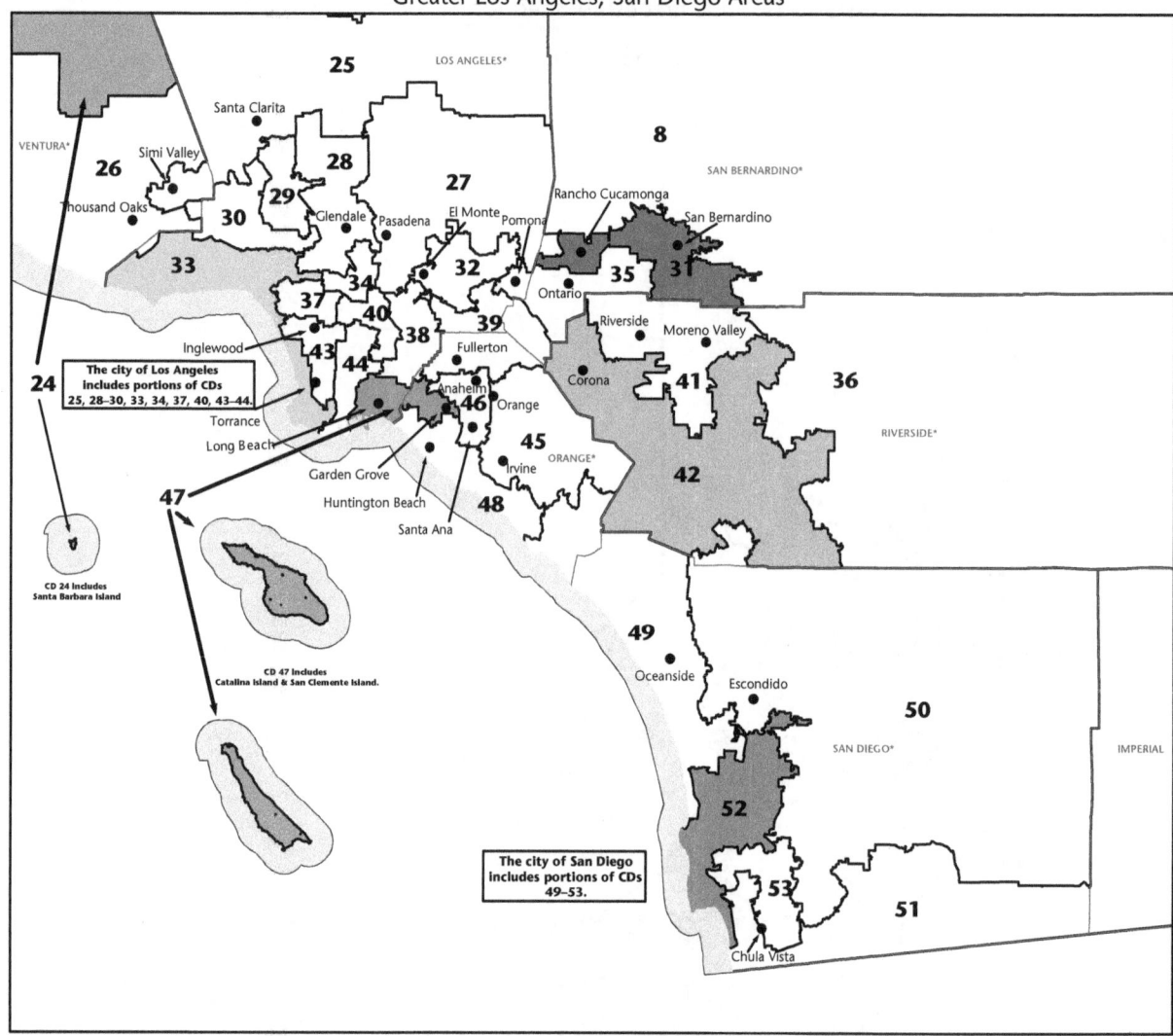

The city of Los Angeles includes portions of CDs 25, 28–30, 33, 34, 37, 40, 43–44.

CD 24 includes Santa Barbara Island

CD 47 includes Catalina Island & San Clemente Island.

The city of San Diego includes portions of CDs 49–53.

* Asterisk indicates a county whose boundaries include parts of two or more congressional districts.

CALIFORNIA

Greater San Francisco Bay Area

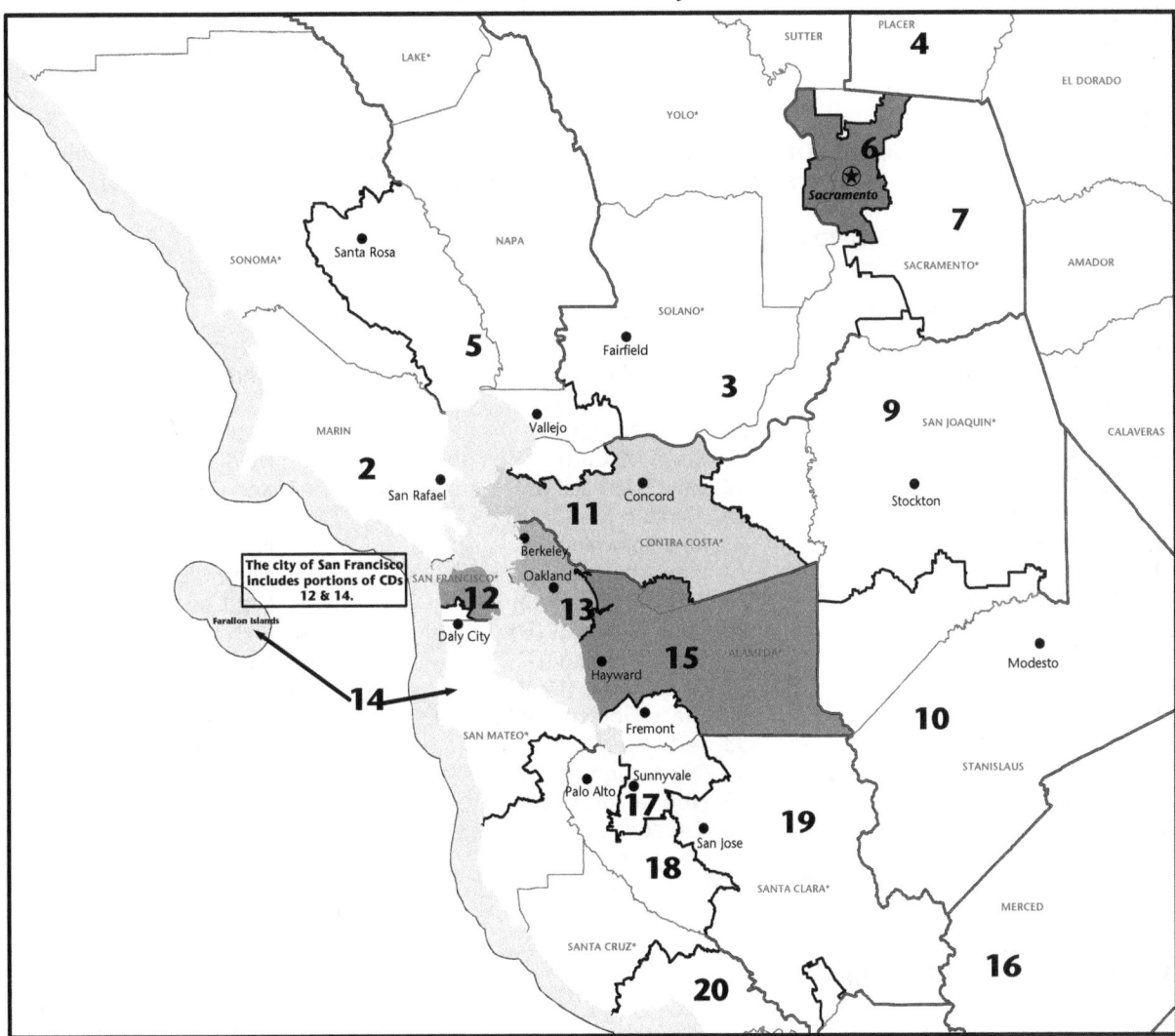

* Asterisk indicates a county whose boundaries include parts of two or more congressional districts.

CALIFORNIA

GOVERNOR
Edmund G. "Jerry" Brown Jr. (D). Re-elected 2014 to a four-year term. Previously elected 2010, 1978, 1974.

SENATORS (2 Democrats)
Dianne Feinstein (D). Re-elected 2012 to a six-year term. Previously elected 2006, 2000, 1994, and 1992 to fill the remaining two years of the term vacated when Senator Pete Wilson (R) was elected governor in November 1990.

Kamala Harris (D). Elected 2016 to a six-year term.

REPRESENTATIVES (14 Republicans, 39 Democrats)

1. Doug LaMalfa (R)
2. Jared Huffman (D)
3. John Garamendi (D)
4. Tom McClintock (R)
5. Mike Thompson (D)
6. Doris Matsui (D)
7. Ami Bera (D)
8. Paul Cook (R)
9. Jerry McNerney (D)
10. Jeff Denham (R)
11. Mark DeSaulnier (D)
12. Nancy Pelosi (D)
13. Barbara Lee (D)
14. Jackie Speier (D)
15. Eric Swalwell (D)
16. Jim Costa (D)
17. Ro Khanna (D)
18. Anna G. Eshoo (D)
19. Zoe Lofgren (D)
20. Jimmy Panetta (D)
21. David Valadao (R)
22. Devin Nunes (R)
23. Kevin McCarthy (R)
24. Salud Carbajal (D)
25. Stephen Knight (R)
26. Julia Brownley (D)
27. Judy Chu (D)
28. Adam B. Schiff (D)
29. Tony Cárdenas (D)
30. Brad Sherman (D)
31. Pete Aguilar (D)
32. Grace Flores Napolitano (D)
33. Ted Lieu (D)
34. Jimmy Gomez (D)
35. Norma Torres (D)
36. Raul Ruiz (D)
37. Karen Bass (D)
38. Linda Sánchez (D)
39. Ed Royce (R)
40. Lucille Roybal-Allard (D)
41. Mark A. Takano (D)
42. Ken Calvert (R)
43. Maxine Waters (D)
44. Nanette Diaz Barragan (D)
45. Mimi Walters (R)
46. Lou Correa (D)
47. Alan Lowenthal (D)
48. Dana Rohrabacher (R)
49. Darrell Issa (R)
50. Duncan D. Hunter (R)
51. Juan Vargas (D)
52. Scott Peters (D)
53. Susan A. Davis (D)

Note: In CD 34, Jimmy Gomez (D) won a special election on June 6, 2017, to fill the vacancy created by the resignation of Xavier Becerra (D), who had been re-elected in 2016.

POSTWAR VOTE FOR PRESIDENT

Year	Total Vote	Republican		Democratic		Other Vote	Rep.-Dem. Plurality	Total Vote		Major Vote	
		Vote	Candidate	Vote	Candidate			Rep.	Dem.	Rep.	Dem.
2016**	14,181,595	4,483,810	Trump, Donald J.	8,753,788	Clinton, Hillary Rodham	943,997	4,269,978 D	31.6%	61.7%	33.9%	66.1%
2012	13,038,547	4,839,958	Romney, W. Mitt	7,854,285	Obama, Barack H.*	344,304	3,014,327 D	37.1%	60.2%	38.1%	61.9%
2008	13,561,900	5,011,781	McCain, John S. III	8,274,473	Obama, Barack H.	275,646	3,262,692 D	37.0%	61.0%	37.7%	62.3%
2004	12,421,852	5,509,826	Bush, George W.*	6,745,485	Kerry, John F.	166,541	1,235,659 D	44.4%	54.3%	45.0%	55.0%
2000**	10,965,856	4,567,429	Bush, George W.	5,861,203	Gore, Albert Jr.	537,224	1,293,774 D	41.7%	53.4%	43.8%	56.2%
1996**	10,019,484	3,828,380	Dole, Robert "Bob"	5,119,835	Clinton, Bill*	1,071,269	1,291,455 D	38.2%	51.1%	42.8%	57.2%
1992**	11,131,721	3,630,574	Bush, George H.*	5,121,325	Clinton, Bill	2,379,822	1,490,751 D	32.6%	46.0%	41.5%	58.5%
1988	9,887,065	5,054,917	Bush, George H.	4,702,233	Dukakis, Michael S.	129,915	352,684 R	51.1%	47.6%	51.8%	48.2%
1984	9,505,423	5,467,009	Reagan, Ronald*	3,922,519	Mondale, Walter F.	115,895	1,544,490 R	57.5%	41.3%	58.2%	41.8%
1980**	8,587,063	4,524,858	Reagan, Ronald	3,083,661	Carter, Jimmy*	978,544	1,441,197 R	52.7%	35.9%	59.5%	40.5%
1976	7,867,117	3,882,244	Ford, Gerald R.*	3,742,284	Carter, Jimmy	242,589	139,960 R	49.3%	47.6%	50.9%	49.1%
1972	8,367,862	4,602,096	Nixon, Richard M.*	3,475,847	McGovern, George S.	289,919	1,126,249 R	55.0%	41.5%	57.0%	43.0%
1968**	7,251,587	3,467,664	Nixon, Richard M.	3,244,318	Humphrey, Hubert Horatio Jr.	539,605	223,346 R	47.8%	44.7%	51.7%	48.3%
1964	7,057,586	2,879,108	Goldwater, Barry M. Sr.	4,171,877	Johnson, Lyndon B.*	6,601	1,292,769 D	40.8%	59.1%	40.8%	59.2%
1960	6,506,578	3,259,722	Nixon, Richard M.	3,224,099	Kennedy, John F.	22,757	35,623 R	50.1%	49.6%	50.3%	49.7%
1956	5,466,355	3,027,668	Eisenhower, Dwight D.*	2,420,135	Stevenson, Adlai E. II	18,552	607,533 R	55.4%	44.3%	55.6%	44.4%
1952	5,141,849	2,897,310	Eisenhower, Dwight D.	2,197,548	Stevenson, Adlai E. II	46,991	699,762 R	56.3%	42.7%	56.9%	43.1%
1948	4,021,538	1,895,269	Dewey, Thomas E.	1,913,134	Truman, Harry S.*	213,135	17,865 D	47.1%	47.6%	49.8%	50.2%

Note: An asterisk (*) denotes incumbent. **In past elections, the other vote included: 2016 - 478,500 Libertarian (Gary Johnson); 2000 - 418,707 Green (Ralph Nader); 1996 - 697,847 Reform (Ross Perot); 1992 - 2,296,006 Independent (Perot); 1980 - 739,833 Independent (John Anderson); 1968 - 487,270 American Independent (George Wallace).

CALIFORNIA

POSTWAR VOTE FOR GOVERNOR

Year	Total Vote	Republican		Democratic		Other Vote	Rep.-Dem. Plurality	Percentage			
		Vote	Candidate	Vote	Candidate			Total Vote		Major Vote	
								Rep.	Dem.	Rep.	Dem.
2014	7,317,581	2,929,213	Kashkari, Neel	4,388,368	Brown, Edmund G. Jr.*		1,459,155 D	40.0%	60.0%	40.0%	60.0%
2010	10,095,185	4,127,391	Whitman, Meg	5,428,149	Brown, Edmund G. Jr.	539,645	1,300,758 D	40.9%	53.8%	43.2%	56.8%
2006	8,679,416	4,850,157	Schwarzenegger, Arnold*	3,376,732	Angelides, Phil	452,527	1,473,425 R	55.9%	38.9%	59.0%	41.0%
2003S**	8,657,915	4,206,284	Schwarzenegger, Arnold	2,724,874	Bustamante, Cruz	1,726,757	1,481,410 R	48.6%	31.5%	60.7%	39.3%
2002	7,476,311	3,169,801	Simon, Bill	3,533,490	Davis, Gray*	773,020	363,689 D	42.4%	47.3%	47.3%	52.7%
1998	8,385,196	3,218,030	Lungren, Dan	4,860,702	Davis, Gray	306,464	1,642,672 D	38.4%	58.0%	39.8%	60.2%
1994	8,665,375	4,781,766	Wilson, Pete*	3,519,799	Brown, Kathleen	363,810	1,261,967 R	55.2%	40.6%	57.6%	42.4%
1990	7,699,467	3,791,904	Wilson, Pete	3,525,197	Feinstein, Dianne	382,366	266,707 R	49.2%	45.8%	51.8%	48.2%
1986	7,443,551	4,506,601	Deukmejian, George*	2,781,714	Bradley, Tom	155,236	1,724,887 R	60.5%	37.4%	61.8%	38.2%
1982	7,876,698	3,881,014	Deukmejian, George	3,787,669	Bradley, Tom	208,015	93,345 R	49.3%	48.1%	50.6%	49.4%
1978	6,922,378	2,526,534	Younger, Evelle J.	3,878,812	Brown, Edmund G. Jr.*	517,032	1,352,278 D	36.5%	56.0%	39.4%	60.6%
1974	6,248,070	2,952,954	Flournoy, Houston I.	3,131,648	Brown, Edmund G. Jr.	163,468	178,694 D	47.3%	50.1%	48.5%	51.5%
1970	6,510,272	3,439,664	Reagan, Ronald*	2,938,807	Unruh, Jess	131,801	500,857 R	52.8%	45.1%	53.9%	46.1%
1966	6,503,445	3,742,913	Reagan, Ronald	2,749,174	Brown, Edmund G.	11,358	993,739 R	57.6%	42.3%	57.7%	42.3%
1962	5,853,270	2,740,351	Nixon, Richard M.	3,037,109	Brown, Edmund G.*	75,810	296,758 D	46.8%	51.9%	47.4%	52.6%
1958	5,255,777	2,110,911	Knowland, William F.	3,140,076	Brown, Edmund G.	4,790	1,029,165 D	40.2%	59.7%	40.2%	59.8%
1954	4,030,368	2,290,519	Knight, Goodwin J.*	1,739,368	Graves, Richard Perrin	481	551,151 R	56.8%	43.2%	56.8%	43.2%
1950	3,796,090	2,461,754	Warren, Earl*	1,333,856	Roosevelt, James	480	1,127,898 R	64.8%	35.1%	64.9%	35.1%
1946**	2,738,978	2,344,542	Warren, Earl*			394,436	2,344,542 R	85.6%		100.0%	

Note: An asterisk (*) denotes incumbent. **The 2003 election was for a short term to fill a vacancy created by voter approval of a measure to remove Governor Gray Davis (D) from office. The measure passed by a vote of 4,976,274 votes (55.4 percent) for recall to 4,007,783 (44.6 percent) against recall. In the same election, more than 100 candidates ran for the right to succeed Davis. No primary election was held to cull the field. All candidates, regardless of party, ran together on the same ballot. The winner, Arnold Schwarzenegger, is listed as the Republican candidate. The leading Democratic vote-getter, Cruz Bustamante, is listed as the Democratic candidate. The percentages given are for Schwarzenegger and Bustamante. The leading other candidate was Republican Tom McClintock, who received 1,161,287 votes (13.4 percent of the total). The percentage columns are for Schwarzenegger and Bustamante and do not include additional candidates. In 1946 the Republican candidate won both major party nominations.

POSTWAR VOTE FOR SENATOR

Year	Total Vote	Republican		Democratic		Other Vote	Rep.-Dem. Plurality	Percentage			
		Vote	Candidate	Vote	Candidate			Total Vote		Major Vote	
								Rep.	Dem.	Rep.	Dem.
2016**	12,244,170			12,244,170	Harris, Kamala D.		12,244,170 D		100.0%		100.0%
2012	12,578,511	4,713,887	Emken, Elizabeth	7,864,624	Feinstein, Dianne*		3,150,737 D	37.5%	62.5%	37.5%	62.5%
2010	9,999,860	4,217,386	Fiorina, Carly	5,218,137	Boxer, Barbara*	564,337	1,000,751 D	42.2%	52.2%	44.7%	55.3%
2006	8,541,476	2,990,822	Mountjoy, Dick	5,076,289	Feinstein, Dianne*	474,365	2,085,467 D	35.0%	59.4%	37.1%	62.9%
2004	12,053,295	4,555,922	Jones, Bill	6,955,728	Boxer, Barbara*	541,645	2,399,806 D	37.8%	57.7%	39.6%	60.4%
2000	10,623,614	3,886,853	Campbell, Tom	5,932,522	Feinstein, Dianne*	804,239	2,045,669 D	36.6%	55.8%	39.6%	60.4%
1998	8,314,953	3,576,351	Fong, Matt	4,411,705	Boxer, Barbara*	326,897	835,354 D	43.0%	53.1%	44.8%	55.2%
1994	8,514,089	3,817,025	Huffington, Michael	3,979,152	Feinstein, Dianne*	717,912	162,127 D	44.8%	46.7%	49.0%	51.0%
1992	10,799,703	4,644,182	Sargent, Claire	5,173,467	Boxer, Barbara	982,054	529,285 D	43.0%	47.9%	47.3%	52.7%
1992S**	10,782,743	4,093,501	Seymour, John*	5,853,651	Feinstein, Dianne	835,591	1,760,150 D	38.0%	54.3%	41.2%	58.8%
1988	9,743,598	5,143,409	Wilson, Pete*	4,287,253	McCarthy, Leo T.	312,936	856,156 R	52.8%	44.0%	54.5%	45.5%
1986	7,398,522	3,541,804	Zschau, Ed	3,646,672	Cranston, Alan*	210,046	104,868 D	47.9%	49.3%	49.3%	50.7%
1982	7,805,538	4,022,565	Wilson, Pete	3,494,968	Brown, Edmund G. Jr.	288,005	527,597 R	51.5%	44.8%	53.5%	46.5%
1980	8,327,481	3,093,426	Gann, Paul	4,705,399	Cranston, Alan*	528,656	1,611,973 D	37.1%	56.5%	39.7%	60.3%
1976	7,472,268	3,748,973	Hayakawa, S. I.	3,502,862	Tunney, John V.*	220,433	246,111 R	50.2%	46.9%	51.7%	48.3%
1974	6,102,432	2,210,267	Richardson, H. L.	3,693,160	Cranston, Alan*	199,005	1,482,893 D	36.2%	60.5%	37.4%	62.6%
1970	6,492,157	2,877,617	Murphy, George*	3,496,558	Tunney, John V.	117,982	618,941 D	44.3%	53.9%	45.1%	54.9%
1968	7,102,465	3,329,148	Rafferty, Max	3,680,352	Cranston, Alan	92,965	351,204 D	46.9%	51.8%	47.5%	52.5%
1964	7,041,821	3,628,555	Murphy, George	3,411,912	Salinger, Pierre*	1,354	216,643 R	51.5%	48.5%	51.5%	48.5%
1962	5,647,952	3,180,483	Kuchel, Thomas H.*	2,452,839	Richards, Richard	14,630	727,644 R	56.3%	43.4%	56.5%	43.5%
1958	5,135,221	2,204,337	Knight, Goodwin J.	2,927,693	Engle, Clair	3,191	723,356 D	42.9%	57.0%	43.0%	57.0%
1956	5,361,467	2,892,918	Kuchel, Thomas H.*	2,445,816	Richards, Richard	22,733	447,102 R	54.0%	45.6%	54.2%	45.8%
1954S**	3,929,668	2,090,836	Kuchel, Thomas H.*	1,788,071	Yorty, Samuel W.	50,761	302,765 R	53.2%	45.5%	53.9%	46.1%
1952**	4,542,548	3,982,448	Knowland, William F.*			560,100	3,982,448 R	87.7%		100.0%	
1950	3,686,315	2,183,454	Nixon, Richard M.	1,502,507	Douglas, Helen Gahagan	354	680,947 R	59.2%	40.8%	59.2%	40.8%
1946	2,639,465	1,428,067	Knowland, William F.*	1,167,161	Rogers, Will Jr.	44,237	260,906 R	54.1%	44.2%	55.0%	45.0%

Note: An asterisk (*) denotes incumbent. **In 2016, California's jungle primary sent two Democrats to the general election, with the results as follows: 7,542,753 Kamala D. Harris (61.6 percent); 4,701,417 Loretta Sanchez (38.4 percent). Harris won by a plurality of 2,841,336 votes. In past elections, the other vote included: 1952 - 542,270 Progressive (Reuben W. Borough, who finished second). The Republican candidate that year (William F. Knowland) won both major party nominations. The 1954 election was for a short term to fill a vacancy, as was one of the 1992 elections.

CALIFORNIA

PRESIDENT 2016

2010 Census Population	County	Total Vote	Republican (Trump)	Democratic (Clinton)	Other	Rep.-Dem. Plurality	Percentage Total Vote Rep.	Total Vote Dem.	Major Vote Rep.	Major Vote Dem.
1,510,271	ALAMEDA	654,266	95,922	514,842	43,502	418,920 D	14.7%	78.7%	15.7%	84.3%
1,175	ALPINE	602	217	334	51	117 D	36.0%	55.5%	39.4%	60.6%
38,091	AMADOR	17,734	10,485	6,004	1,245	4,481 R	59.1%	33.9%	63.6%	36.4%
220,000	BUTTE	95,564	45,144	41,567	8,853	3,577 R	47.2%	43.5%	52.1%	47.9%
45,578	CALAVERAS	23,136	13,511	7,944	1,681	5,567 R	58.4%	34.3%	63.0%	37.0%
21,419	COLUSA	6,632	3,551	2,661	420	890 R	53.5%	40.1%	57.2%	42.8%
1,049,025	CONTRA COSTA	466,175	115,956	319,287	30,932	203,331 D	24.9%	68.5%	26.6%	73.4%
28,610	DEL NORTE	9,558	5,134	3,485	939	1,649 R	53.7%	36.5%	59.6%	40.4%
181,058	EL DORADO	93,591	49,247	36,404	7,940	12,843 R	52.6%	38.9%	57.5%	42.5%
930,450	FRESNO	282,319	124,049	141,341	16,929	17,292 D	43.9%	50.1%	46.7%	53.3%
28,122	GLENN	9,470	5,788	3,065	617	2,723 R	61.1%	32.4%	65.4%	34.6%
134,623	HUMBOLDT	59,246	18,373	33,200	7,673	14,827 D	31.0%	56.0%	35.6%	64.4%
174,528	IMPERIAL	48,091	12,704	32,667	2,720	19,963 D	26.4%	67.9%	28.0%	72.0%
18,546	INYO	8,086	4,248	3,155	683	1,093 R	52.5%	39.0%	57.4%	42.6%
839,631	KERN	244,163	129,584	98,689	15,890	30,895 R	53.1%	40.4%	56.8%	43.2%
152,982	KINGS	33,915	18,093	13,617	2,205	4,476 R	53.3%	40.2%	57.1%	42.9%
64,665	LAKE	24,496	10,599	11,496	2,401	897 D	43.3%	46.9%	48.0%	52.0%
34,895	LASSEN	10,524	7,574	2,224	726	5,350 R	72.0%	21.1%	77.3%	22.7%
9,818,605	LOS ANGELES	3,434,308	769,743	2,464,364	200,201	1,694,621 D	22.4%	71.8%	23.8%	76.2%
150,865	MADERA	43,112	23,357	17,029	2,726	6,328 R	54.2%	39.5%	57.8%	42.2%
252,409	MARIN	139,273	21,771	108,707	8,795	86,936 D	15.6%	78.1%	16.7%	83.3%
18,251	MARIPOSA	8,877	5,185	3,122	570	2,063 R	58.4%	35.2%	62.4%	37.6%
87,841	MENDOCINO	37,477	10,888	22,079	4,510	11,191 D	29.1%	58.9%	33.0%	67.0%
255,793	MERCED	70,789	28,725	37,317	4,747	8,592 D	40.6%	52.7%	43.5%	56.5%
9,686	MODOC	3,788	2,696	877	215	1,819 R	71.2%	23.2%	75.5%	24.5%
14,202	MONO	5,276	2,111	2,773	392	662 D	40.0%	52.6%	43.2%	56.8%
415,057	MONTEREY	133,408	34,895	89,088	9,425	54,193 D	26.2%	66.8%	28.1%	71.9%
136,484	NAPA	61,372	17,411	39,199	4,762	21,788 D	28.4%	63.9%	30.8%	69.2%
98,764	NEVADA	54,935	23,365	26,053	5,517	2,688 D	42.5%	47.4%	47.3%	52.7%
3,010,232	ORANGE	1,197,521	507,148	609,961	80,412	102,813 D	42.3%	50.9%	45.4%	54.6%
348,432	PLACER	182,839	95,138	73,509	14,192	21,629 R	52.0%	40.2%	56.4%	43.6%
20,007	PLUMAS	9,676	5,420	3,459	797	1,961 R	56.0%	35.7%	61.0%	39.0%
2,189,641	RIVERSIDE	751,391	333,243	373,695	44,453	40,452 D	44.4%	49.7%	47.1%	52.9%
1,418,788	SACRAMENTO	559,330	189,789	326,023	43,518	136,234 D	33.9%	58.3%	36.8%	63.2%
55,269	SAN BENITO	21,924	7,841	12,521	1,562	4,680 D	35.8%	57.1%	38.5%	61.5%
2,035,210	SAN BERNARDINO	653,983	271,240	340,833	41,910	69,593 D	41.5%	52.1%	44.3%	55.7%
3,095,313	SAN DIEGO	1,306,400	477,766	735,476	93,158	257,710 D	36.6%	56.3%	39.4%	60.6%
805,235	SAN FRANCISCO	405,792	37,688	345,084	23,020	307,396 D	9.3%	85.0%	9.8%	90.2%
685,306	SAN JOAQUIN	224,166	88,936	121,124	14,106	32,188 D	39.7%	54.0%	42.3%	57.7%
269,637	SAN LUIS OBISPO	135,009	56,164	67,107	11,738	10,943 D	41.6%	49.7%	45.6%	54.4%
718,451	SAN MATEO	314,384	57,929	237,882	18,573	179,953 D	18.4%	75.7%	19.6%	80.4%
423,895	SANTA BARBARA	176,786	56,365	107,142	13,279	50,777 D	31.9%	60.6%	34.5%	65.5%
1,781,642	SANTA CLARA	703,709	144,826	511,684	47,199	366,858 D	20.6%	72.7%	22.1%	77.9%
262,382	SANTA CRUZ	128,821	22,438	95,249	11,134	72,811 D	17.4%	73.9%	19.1%	80.9%
177,223	SHASTA	80,053	51,778	22,301	5,974	29,477 R	64.7%	27.9%	69.9%	30.1%
3,240	SIERRA	1,830	1,048	601	181	447 R	57.3%	32.8%	63.6%	36.4%
44,900	SISKIYOU	20,492	11,341	7,234	1,917	4,107 R	55.3%	35.3%	61.1%	38.9%
413,344	SOLANO	166,113	51,920	102,360	11,833	50,440 D	31.3%	61.6%	33.7%	66.3%
483,878	SONOMA	231,253	51,408	160,435	19,410	109,027 D	22.2%	69.4%	24.3%	75.7%
514,453	STANISLAUS	172,146	78,494	81,647	12,005	3,153 D	45.6%	47.4%	49.0%	51.0%
94,737	SUTTER	33,523	18,176	13,076	2,271	5,100 R	54.2%	39.0%	58.2%	41.8%
63,463	TEHAMA	23,908	15,494	6,809	1,605	8,685 R	64.8%	28.5%	69.5%	30.5%
13,786	TRINITY	5,686	2,812	2,214	660	598 R	49.5%	38.9%	55.9%	44.1%
442,179	TULARE	112,334	58,299	47,585	6,450	10,714 R	51.9%	42.4%	55.1%	44.9%
55,365	TUOLUMNE	25,529	14,551	9,123	1,855	5,428 R	57.0%	35.7%	61.5%	38.5%
823,318	VENTURA	351,726	132,323	194,402	25,001	62,079 D	37.6%	55.3%	40.5%	59.5%
200,849	YOLO	82,090	20,739	54,752	6,599	34,013 D	25.3%	66.7%	27.5%	72.5%
72,155	YUBA	22,998	13,170	7,910	1,918	5,260 R	57.3%	34.4%	62.5%	37.5%
37,253,956	TOTAL	14,181,595	4,483,810	8,753,788	943,997	4,269,978 D	31.6%	61.7%	33.9%	66.1%

CALIFORNIA

SENATOR 2016

2010 Census Population	County	Total Vote	Democratic (Harris)	Democratic (Sanchez)	Plurality	Percentage	
						Harris	Sanchez
1,510,271	ALAMEDA	587,670	443,536	144,134	299,402 H	75.5%	24.5%
1,175	ALPINE	475	342	133	209 H	72.0%	28.0%
38,091	AMADOR	13,562	8,690	4,872	3,818 H	64.1%	35.9%
220,000	BUTTE	74,171	43,491	30,680	12,811 H	58.6%	41.4%
45,578	CALAVERAS	17,561	11,259	6,302	4,957 H	64.1%	35.9%
21,419	COLUSA	5,141	2,639	2,502	137 H	51.3%	48.7%
1,049,025	CONTRA COSTA	407,318	282,587	124,731	157,856 H	69.4%	30.6%
28,610	DEL NORTE	7,542	4,603	2,939	1,664 H	61.0%	39.0%
181,058	EL DORADO	72,079	45,671	26,408	19,263 H	63.4%	36.6%
930,450	FRESNO	236,104	117,956	118,148	192 S	50.0%	50.0%
28,122	GLENN	7,216	3,423	3,793	370 S	47.4%	52.6%
134,623	HUMBOLDT	49,006	32,729	16,277	16,452 H	66.8%	33.2%
174,528	IMPERIAL	42,847	13,975	28,872	14,897 S	32.6%	67.4%
18,546	INYO	6,121	3,863	2,258	1,605 H	63.1%	36.9%
839,631	KERN	196,215	98,526	97,689	837 H	50.2%	49.8%
152,982	KINGS	27,813	14,655	13,158	1,497 H	52.7%	47.3%
64,665	LAKE	20,191	13,188	7,003	6,185 H	65.3%	34.7%
34,895	LASSEN	7,377	4,151	3,226	925 H	56.3%	43.7%
9,818,605	LOS ANGELES	3,113,911	1,895,675	1,218,236	677,439 H	60.9%	39.1%
150,865	MADERA	34,331	16,769	17,562	793 S	48.8%	51.2%
252,409	MARIN	125,297	98,196	27,101	71,095 H	78.4%	21.6%
18,251	MARIPOSA	6,653	4,134	2,519	1,615 H	62.1%	37.9%
87,841	MENDOCINO	31,899	22,335	9,564	12,771 H	70.0%	30.0%
255,793	MERCED	60,007	30,172	29,835	337 H	50.3%	49.7%
9,686	MODOC	2,575	1,531	1,044	487 H	59.5%	40.5%
14,202	MONO	4,202	2,611	1,591	1,020 H	62.1%	37.9%
415,057	MONTEREY	120,719	77,659	43,060	34,599 H	64.3%	35.7%
136,484	NAPA	53,703	35,925	17,778	18,147 H	66.9%	33.1%
98,764	NEVADA	42,968	29,639	13,329	16,310 H	69.0%	31.0%
3,010,232	ORANGE	1,042,242	555,459	486,783	68,676 H	53.3%	46.7%
348,432	PLACER	141,879	89,687	52,192	37,495 H	63.2%	36.8%
20,007	PLUMAS	7,024	4,606	2,418	2,188 H	65.6%	34.4%
2,189,641	RIVERSIDE	620,934	339,497	281,437	58,060 H	54.7%	45.3%
1,418,788	SACRAMENTO	473,711	312,038	161,673	150,365 H	65.9%	34.1%
55,269	SAN BENITO	18,719	11,151	7,568	3,583 H	59.6%	40.4%
2,035,210	SAN BERNARDINO	551,984	300,738	251,246	49,492 H	54.5%	45.5%
3,095,313	SAN DIEGO	1,071,906	625,843	446,063	179,780 H	58.4%	41.6%
805,235	SAN FRANCISCO	367,708	286,723	80,985	205,738 H	78.0%	22.0%
685,306	SAN JOAQUIN	192,858	111,563	81,295	30,268 H	57.8%	42.2%
269,637	SAN LUIS OBISPO	106,645	69,190	37,455	31,735 H	64.9%	35.1%
718,451	SAN MATEO	281,046	199,956	81,090	118,866 H	71.1%	28.9%
423,895	SANTA BARBARA	149,856	88,861	60,995	27,866 H	59.3%	40.7%
1,781,642	SANTA CLARA	619,145	411,765	207,380	204,385 H	66.5%	33.5%
262,382	SANTA CRUZ	114,163	81,443	32,720	48,723 H	71.3%	28.7%
177,223	SHASTA	56,246	31,877	24,369	7,508 H	56.7%	43.3%
3,240	SIERRA	1,268	826	442	384 H	65.1%	34.9%
44,900	SISKIYOU	15,201	8,744	6,457	2,287 H	57.5%	42.5%
413,344	SOLANO	146,639	97,410	49,229	48,181 H	66.4%	33.6%
483,878	SONOMA	202,132	147,532	54,600	92,932 H	73.0%	27.0%
514,453	STANISLAUS	141,721	80,502	61,219	19,283 H	56.8%	43.2%
94,737	SUTTER	26,891	15,191	11,700	3,491 H	56.5%	43.5%
63,463	TEHAMA	17,447	9,456	7,991	1,465 H	54.2%	45.8%
13,786	TRINITY	4,491	2,696	1,795	901 H	60.0%	40.0%
442,179	TULARE	91,189	47,145	44,044	3,101 H	51.7%	48.3%
55,365	TUOLUMNE	18,584	12,239	6,345	5,894 H	65.9%	34.1%
823,318	VENTURA	297,749	181,785	115,964	65,821 H	61.1%	38.9%
200,849	YOLO	72,330	48,901	23,429	25,472 H	67.6%	32.4%
72,155	YUBA	17,788	9,999	7,789	2,210 H	56.2%	43.8%
37,253,956	TOTAL	12,244,170	7,542,753	4,701,417	2,841,336 H	61.6%	38.4%

Note: In California's jungle primary, the top two vote recipients, Kamala Harris and Loretta Sanchez, were both Democrats.

96

CALIFORNIA

HOUSE OF REPRESENTATIVES

			Republican		Democratic		Other	Rep.-Dem.	Total Vote		Major Vote	
CD	Year	Total Vote	Vote	Candidate	Vote	Candidate	Vote	Plurality	Rep.	Dem.	Rep.	Dem.
1	2016	314,036	185,448	LAMALFA, DOUG*	128,588	REED, JIM		56,860 R	59.1%	40.9%	59.1%	40.9%
1	2014	216,372	132,052	LAMALFA, DOUG*	84,320	HALL, HEIDI		47,732 R	61.0%	39.0%	61.0%	39.0%
1	2012	294,213	168,827	LAMALFA, DOUG	125,386	REED, JIM		43,441 R	57.4%	42.6%	57.4%	42.6%
2	2016	330,766	76,572	MENSING, DALE	254,194	HUFFMAN, JARED*		177,622 D	23.1%	76.9%	23.1%	76.9%
2	2014	217,524	54,400	MENSING, DALE	163,124	HUFFMAN, JARED*		108,724 D	25.0%	75.0%	25.0%	75.0%
2	2012	317,526	91,310	ROBERTS, DANIEL W.	226,216	HUFFMAN, JARED		134,906 D	28.8%	71.2%	28.8%	71.2%
3	2016	256,966	104,453	CLEEK, N. EUGENE	152,513	GARAMENDI, JOHN*		48,060 D	40.6%	59.4%	40.6%	59.4%
3	2014	150,260	71,036	LOGUE, DAN	79,224	GARAMENDI, JOHN*		8,188 D	47.3%	52.7%	47.3%	52.7%
3	2012	233,968	107,086	VANN, KIM	126,882	GARAMENDI, JOHN*		19,796 D	45.8%	54.2%	45.8%	54.2%
4	2016	350,978	220,133	MCCLINTOCK, TOM*	130,845	DERLET, ROBERT W.		89,288 R	62.7%	37.3%	62.7%	37.3%
4	2014	211,134	126,784	MCCLINTOCK, TOM*			84,350	126,784 R	60.0%		100.0%	
4	2012	323,688	197,803	MCCLINTOCK, TOM*	125,885	UPPAL, JACK		71,918 R	61.1%	38.9%	61.1%	38.9%
5	2016	292,091	67,565	SANTAMARIA, CARLOS	224,526	THOMPSON, MIKE*		156,961 D	23.1%	76.9%	23.1%	76.9%
5	2014	171,148			129,613	THOMPSON, MIKE*	41,535	129,613 D		75.7%		100.0%
5	2012	272,417	69,545	LOFTIN, RANDY	202,872	THOMPSON, MIKE*		133,327 D	25.5%	74.5%	25.5%	74.5%
6	2016	235,413	57,848	EVANS, ROBERT H. JR.	177,565	MATSUI, DORIS*		119,717 D	24.6%	75.4%	24.6%	75.4%
6	2014	133,456	36,448	MCCRAY, JOSEPH SR.	97,008	MATSUI, DORIS*		60,560 D	27.3%	72.7%	27.3%	72.7%
6	2012	214,073	53,406	MCCRAY, JOSEPH SR.	160,667	MATSUI, DORIS*		107,261 D	24.9%	75.1%	24.9%	75.1%
7	2016	297,301	145,168	JONES, SCOTT R.	152,133	BERA, AMI*		6,965 D	48.8%	51.2%	48.8%	51.2%
7	2014	183,587	91,066	OSE, DOUG	92,521	BERA, AMI*		1,455 D	49.6%	50.4%	49.6%	50.4%
7	2012	273,291	132,050	LUNGREN, DAN*	141,241	BERA, AMI		9,191 D	48.3%	51.7%	48.3%	51.7%
8	2016	220,007	136,972	COOK, PAUL*	83,035	RAMIREZ, RITA		53,937 R	62.3%	37.7%	62.3%	37.7%
8	2014	114,536	77,480	COOK, PAUL*	37,056	CONAWAY, ROBERT DEAN "BOB"		40,424 R	67.6%	32.4%	67.6%	32.4%
8	2012	179,644	103,093	COOK, PAUL			76,551	103,093 R	57.4%		100.0%	
9	2016	232,155	98,992	AMADOR, ANTONIO C. "TONY"	133,163	MCNERNEY, JERRY*		34,171 D	42.6%	57.4%	42.6%	57.4%
9	2014	121,204	57,729	AMADOR, ANTONIO C. "TONY"	63,475	MCNERNEY, JERRY*		5,746 D	47.6%	52.4%	47.6%	52.4%
9	2012	213,077	94,704	GILL, RICKY	118,373	MCNERNEY, JERRY*		23,669 D	44.4%	55.6%	44.4%	55.6%
10	2016	241,141	124,671	DENHAM, JEFF*	116,470	EGGMAN, MICHAEL		8,201 R	51.7%	48.3%	51.7%	48.3%
10	2014	125,705	70,582	DENHAM, JEFF*	55,123	EGGMAN, MICHAEL		15,459 R	56.1%	43.9%	56.1%	43.9%
10	2012	209,199	110,265	DENHAM, JEFF*	98,934	HERNANDEZ, JOSE		11,331 R	52.7%	47.3%	52.7%	47.3%
11	2016	298,209	83,341	PETERSEN, ROGER ALLEN	214,868	DESAULNIER, MARK*		131,527 D	27.9%	72.1%	27.9%	72.1%
11	2014	174,662	57,160	PHAN-QUANG, TUE	117,502	DESAULNIER, MARK		60,342 D	32.7%	67.3%	32.7%	67.3%
11	2012	287,879	87,136	FULLER, VIRGINIA	200,743	MILLER, GEORGE*		113,607 D	30.3%	69.7%	30.3%	69.7%
12	2016	338,845			274,035	PELOSI, NANCY*	64,810	274,035 D		80.9%		100.0%
12	2014	192,264	32,197	DENNIS, JOHN	160,067	PELOSI, NANCY*		127,870 D	16.7%	83.3%	16.7%	83.3%
12	2012	298,187	44,478	DENNIS, JOHN	253,709	PELOSI, NANCY*		209,231 D	14.9%	85.1%	14.9%	85.1%
13	2016	322,871	29,754	CARO, SUE	293,117	LEE, BARBARA*		263,363 D	9.2%	90.8%	9.2%	90.8%
13	2014	190,431	21,940	SUNDEEN, DAKIN	168,491	LEE, BARBARA*		146,551 D	11.5%	88.5%	11.5%	88.5%
13	2012	288,582			250,436	LEE, BARBARA*	38,146	250,436 D		86.8%		100.0%
14	2016	286,447	54,817	CARDENAS, ANGEL	231,630	SPEIER, JACKIE*		176,813 D	19.1%	80.9%	19.1%	80.9%
14	2014	149,146	34,757	CHEW, ROBIN	114,389	SPEIER, JACKIE*		79,632 D	23.3%	76.7%	23.3%	76.7%
14	2012	258,283	54,455	BACIGALUPI, DEBORAH "DEBBIE"	203,828	SPEIER, JACKIE*		149,373 D	21.1%	78.9%	21.1%	78.9%
15	2016	269,197	70,619	TURNER, DANNY R.	198,578	SWALWELL, ERIC*		127,959 D	26.2%	73.8%	26.2%	73.8%
15	2014	142,906	43,150	BUSSELL, HUGH	99,756	SWALWELL, ERIC*		56,606 D	30.2%	69.8%	30.2%	69.8%
15	2012	231,034			120,388	SWALWELL, ERIC	110,646	120,388 D		52.1%		100.0%
16	2016	167,956	70,483	TACHERRA, JOHNNY M.	97,473	COSTA, JIM*		26,990 D	42.0%	58.0%	42.0%	58.0%
16	2014	91,220	44,943	TACHERRA, JOHNNY M.	46,277	COSTA, JIM*		1,334 D	49.3%	50.7%	49.3%	50.7%
16	2012	147,450	62,801	WHELAN, BRIAN DANIEL	84,649	COSTA, JIM*		21,848 D	42.6%	57.4%	42.6%	57.4%
17	2016	233,192			142,268	KHANNA, RO*	90,924	142,268 D		61.0%		100.0%
17	2014	134,408			69,561	HONDA, MIKE M.*	64,847	69,561 D		51.8%		100.0%
17	2012	216,728	57,336	LI, EVELYN	159,392	HONDA, MIKE M.*		102,056 D	26.5%	73.5%	26.5%	73.5%
18	2016	323,930	93,470	FOX, RICHARD B.	230,460	ESHOO, ANNA G.*		136,990 D	28.9%	71.1%	28.9%	71.1%
18	2014	196,386	63,326	FOX, RICHARD B.	133,060	ESHOO, ANNA G.*		69,734 D	32.2%	67.8%	32.2%	67.8%
18	2012	301,934	89,103	CHAPMAN, DAVE	212,831	ESHOO, ANNA G.*		123,728 D	29.5%	70.5%	29.5%	70.5%
19	2016	245,863	64,061	LANCASTER, G. BURT	181,802	LOFGREN, ZOE*		117,741 D	26.1%	73.9%	26.1%	73.9%
19	2014	127,788			85,888	LOFGREN, ZOE*	41,900	85,888 D		67.2%		100.0%
19	2012	221,613	59,313	MURRAY, ROBERT	162,300	LOFGREN, ZOE*		102,987 D	26.8%	73.2%	26.8%	73.2%

CALIFORNIA

HOUSE OF REPRESENTATIVES

CD	Year	Total Vote	Republican		Democratic		Other Vote	Rep.-Dem. Plurality	Percentage			
			Vote	Candidate	Vote	Candidate			Total Vote		Major Vote	
									Rep.	Dem.	Rep.	Dem.
20	2016	255,791	74,811	LUCIUS, CASEY	180,980	PANETTA, JIMMY		106,169 D	29.2%	70.8%	29.2%	70.8%
20	2014	141,044			106,034	FARR, SAM*	35,010	106,034 D		75.2%		100.0%
20	2012	233,562	60,566	TAYLOR, JEFF	172,996	FARR, SAM*		112,430 D	25.9%	74.1%	25.9%	74.1%
21	2016	132,408	75,126	VALADAO, DAVID*	57,282	HUERTA, EMILIO JESUS		17,844 R	56.7%	43.3%	56.7%	43.3%
21	2014	79,377	45,907	VALADAO, DAVID*	33,470	RENTERIA, AMANDA		12,437 R	57.8%	42.2%	57.8%	42.2%
21	2012	116,283	67,164	VALADAO, DAVID	49,119	HERNANDEZ, JOHN		18,045 R	57.8%	42.2%	57.8%	42.2%
22	2016	234,966	158,755	NUNES, DEVIN*	76,211	CAMPOS, LOUIE J.		82,544 R	67.6%	32.4%	67.6%	32.4%
22	2014	133,342	96,053	NUNES, DEVIN*	37,289	AGUILERA-MARRERO, SUZANNA "SAM"		58,764 R	72.0%	28.0%	72.0%	28.0%
22	2012	213,941	132,386	NUNES, DEVIN*	81,555	LEE, OTTO		50,831 R	61.9%	38.1%	61.9%	38.1%
23	2016	241,584	167,116	MCCARTHY, KEVIN*	74,468	REED, WENDY		92,648 R	69.2%	30.8%	69.2%	30.8%
23	2014	134,043	100,317	MCCARTHY, KEVIN*	33,726	GARCIA, RAUL		66,591 R	74.8%	25.2%	74.8%	25.2%
23	2012	216,003	158,161	MCCARTHY, KEVIN*			57,842	158,161 R	73.2%		100.0%	
24	2016	310,814	144,780	FAREED, JUSTIN	166,034	CARBAJAL, SALUD		21,254 D	46.6%	53.4%	46.6%	53.4%
24	2014	198,794	95,566	MITCHUM, CHRIS	103,228	CAPPS, LOIS*		7,662 D	48.1%	51.9%	48.1%	51.9%
24	2012	284,495	127,746	MALDONADO, ABEL	156,749	CAPPS, LOIS*		29,003 D	44.9%	55.1%	44.9%	55.1%
25	2016	261,161	138,755	KNIGHT, STEVE*	122,406	CAFORIO, BRYAN		16,349 R	53.1%	46.9%	53.1%	46.9%
25	2014	114,072	60,847	KNIGHT, STEVE			53,225	60,847 R	53.3%		100.0%	
25	2012	236,575	129,593	MCKEON, HOWARD P. "BUCK"*	106,982	ROGERS, LEE C.		22,611 R	54.8%	45.2%	54.8%	45.2%
26	2016	280,307	111,059	DAGNESSES, RAFAEL	169,248	BROWNLEY, JULIA*		58,189 D	39.6%	60.4%	39.6%	60.4%
26	2014	169,829	82,653	GORELL, JEFF	87,176	BROWNLEY, JULIA*		4,523 D	48.7%	51.3%	48.7%	51.3%
26	2012	263,935	124,863	STRICKLAND, TONY	139,072	BROWNLEY, JULIA		14,209 D	47.3%	52.7%	47.3%	52.7%
27	2016	250,632	81,655	ORSWELL, JACK	168,977	CHU, JUDY*		87,322 D	32.6%	67.4%	32.6%	67.4%
27	2014	127,580	51,852	ORSWELL, JACK	75,728	CHU, JUDY*		23,876 D	40.6%	59.4%	40.6%	59.4%
27	2012	241,008	86,817	ORSWELL, JACK	154,191	CHU, JUDY*		67,374 D	36.0%	64.0%	36.0%	64.0%
28	2016	270,409	59,526	SOLIS, LENORE	210,883	SCHIFF, ADAM B.*		151,357 D	22.0%	78.0%	22.0%	78.0%
28	2014	120,264			91,996	SCHIFF, ADAM B.*	28,268	91,996 D		76.5%		100.0%
28	2012	246,711	58,008	JENNERJAHN, PHIL	188,703	SCHIFF, ADAM B.*		130,695 D	23.5%	76.5%	23.5%	76.5%
29	2016	171,824			128,407	CARDENAS, TONY*	43,417	128,407 D		74.7%		100.0%
29	2014	67,141	17,045	LEADER, WILLIAM O'CALLAGHAN	50,096	CARDENAS, TONY*		33,051 D	25.4%	74.6%	25.4%	74.6%
29	2012	150,281			111,287	CARDENAS, TONY	38,994	111,287 D		74.1%		100.0%
30	2016	282,604	77,325	REED, MARK	205,279	SHERMAN, BRAD*		127,954 D	27.4%	72.6%	27.4%	72.6%
30	2014	131,883	45,315	REED, MARK	86,568	SHERMAN, BRAD*		41,253 D	34.4%	65.6%	34.4%	65.6%
30	2012	247,851			149,456	SHERMAN, BRAD	98,395	149,456 D		60.3%		100.0%
31	2016	215,936	94,866	CHABOT, PAUL	121,070	AGUILAR, PETE*		26,204 D	43.9%	56.1%	43.9%	56.1%
31	2014	99,784	48,162	CHABOT, PAUL	51,622	AGUILAR, PETE		3,460 D	48.3%	51.7%	48.3%	51.7%
31	2012	161,219	88,964	MILLER, GARY G.*			72,255	88,964 R	55.2%		100.0%	
32	2016	186,646			114,926	NAPOLITANO, GRACE FLORES*	71,720	114,926 D		61.6%		100.0%
32	2014	84,406	34,053	ALAS, ARTURO "ART"	50,353	NAPOLITANO, GRACE FLORES*		16,300 D	40.3%	59.7%	40.3%	59.7%
32	2012	190,111	65,208	MILLER, DAVID L	124,903	NAPOLITANO, GRACE FLORES*		59,695 D	34.3%	65.7%	34.3%	65.7%
33	2016	330,219	110,822	WRIGHT, KENNETH W.	219,397	LIEU, TED*		108,575 D	33.6%	66.4%	33.6%	66.4%
33	2014	183,031	74,700	CARR, ELAN S.	108,331	LIEU, TED		33,631 D	40.8%	59.2%	40.8%	59.2%
33	2012	318,520			171,860	WAXMAN, HENRY A.*	146,660	171,860 D		54.0%		100.0%
34	2016	159,156			122,842	BECERRA, XAVIER*	36,314	122,842 D		77.2%		100.0%
34	2014	61,621			44,697	BECERRA, XAVIER*	16,924	44,697 D		72.5%		100.0%
34	2012	140,590	20,223	SMITH, STEPHEN	120,367	BECERRA, XAVIER*		100,144 D	14.4%	85.6%	14.4%	85.6%
35	2016	171,353	47,309	FISCHELLA, TYLER	124,044	TORRES, NORMA*		76,735 D	27.6%	72.4%	27.6%	72.4%
35	2014	62,475			39,502	TORRES, NORMA	22,973	39,502 D		63.2%		100.0%
35	2012	142,680			79,698	MCLEOD, GLORIA NEGRETE	62,982	79,698 D		55.9%		100.0%
36	2016	232,617	88,269	STONE, JEFF	144,348	RUIZ, RAUL*		56,079 D	37.9%	62.1%	37.9%	62.1%
36	2014	134,139	61,457	NESTANDE, BRIAN	72,682	RUIZ, RAUL*		11,225 D	45.8%	54.2%	45.8%	54.2%
36	2012	208,142	97,953	BONO MACK, MARY*	110,189	RUIZ, RAUL		12,236 D	47.1%	52.9%	47.1%	52.9%
37	2016	237,272			192,490	BASS, KAREN*	44,782	192,490 D		81.1%		100.0%
37	2014	114,838	18,051	KING, R. ADAM	96,787	BASS, KAREN*		78,736 D	15.7%	84.3%	15.7%	84.3%
37	2012	239,580	32,541	OSBORNE, MORGAN	207,039	BASS, KAREN*		174,498 D	13.6%	86.4%	13.6%	86.4%
38	2016	232,114	68,524	DOWNING, RYAN	163,590	SANCHEZ, LINDA*		95,066 D	29.5%	70.5%	29.5%	70.5%
38	2014	98,480	40,288	CAMPOS, BENJAMIN	58,192	SANCHEZ, LINDA*		17,904 D	40.9%	59.1%	40.9%	59.1%
38	2012	215,087	69,807	CAMPOS, BENJAMIN	145,280	SÁNCHEZ, LINDA*		75,473 D	32.5%	67.5%	32.5%	67.5%

CALIFORNIA

HOUSE OF REPRESENTATIVES

			Republican		Democratic				Total Vote		Major Vote	
CD	Year	Total Vote	Vote	Candidate	Vote	Candidate	Other Vote	Rep.-Dem. Plurality	Rep.	Dem.	Rep.	Dem.
39	2016	263,456	150,777	ROYCE, ED*	112,679	MURDOCK, BRETT		38,098 R	57.2%	42.8%	57.2%	42.8%
39	2014	133,225	91,319	ROYCE, ED*	41,906	ANDERSON, PETER		49,413 R	68.5%	31.5%	68.5%	31.5%
39	2012	251,967	145,607	ROYCE, ED*	106,360	CHEN, JAY		39,247 R	57.8%	42.2%	57.8%	42.2%
40	2016	149,297			106,554	ROYBAL-ALLARD, LUCILLE*	42,743	106,554 D		71.4%		100.0%
40	2014	49,379			30,208	ROYBAL-ALLARD, LUCILLE*	19,171	30,208 D		61.2%		100.0%
40	2012	125,553			73,940	ROYBAL-ALLARD, LUCILLE*	51,613	73,940 D		58.9%		100.0%
41	2016	197,323	69,159	SHEPHERD, DOUG	128,164	TAKANO, MARK A.*		59,005 D	35.0%	65.0%	35.0%	65.0%
41	2014	82,884	35,936	ADAMS, STEVE	46,948	TAKANO, MARK A.*		11,012 D	43.4%	56.6%	43.4%	56.6%
41	2012	175,652	72,074	TAVAGLIONE, JOHN	103,578	TAKANO, MARK A.		31,504 D	41.0%	59.0%	41.0%	59.0%
42	2016	254,236	149,547	CALVERT, KEN*	104,689	SHERIDAN, TIM		44,858 R	58.8%	41.2%	58.8%	41.2%
42	2014	113,390	74,540	CALVERT, KEN*	38,850	SHERIDAN, TIM		35,690 R	65.7%	34.3%	65.7%	34.3%
42	2012	214,947	130,245	CALVERT, KEN*	84,702	WILLIAMSON, MICHAEL		45,543 R	60.6%	39.4%	60.6%	39.4%
43	2016	219,516	52,499	NAVARRO, OMAR	167,017	WATERS, MAXINE*		114,518 D	23.9%	76.1%	23.9%	76.1%
43	2014	98,202	28,521	WOOD JR., JOHN	69,681	WATERS, MAXINE*		41,160 D	29.0%	71.0%	29.0%	71.0%
43	2012	200,894			143,123	WATERS, MAXINE*	57,771	143,123 D		71.2%		100.0%
44	2016	178,413			93,124	BARRAGAN, NANETTE DIAZ	85,289	93,124 D		52.2%		100.0%
44	2014	68,862			59,670	HAHN, JANICE*	9,192	59,670 D		86.7%		100.0%
44	2012	165,898			99,909	HAHN, JANICE	65,989	99,909 D		60.2%		100.0%
45	2016	311,849	182,618	WALTERS, MIMI*	129,231	VARASTEH, RON		53,387 R	58.6%	41.4%	58.6%	41.4%
45	2014	162,902	106,083	WALTERS, MIMI	56,819	LEAVENS, DREW		49,264 R	65.1%	34.9%	65.1%	34.9%
45	2012	293,231	171,417	CAMPBELL, JOHN*	121,814	KANG, SUKHEE		49,603 R	58.5%	41.5%	58.5%	41.5%
46	2016	164,593			115,248	CORREA, LOU	49,345	115,248 D		70.0%		100.0%
46	2014	83,315	33,577	NICK, ADAM	49,738	SANCHEZ, LORETTA*		16,161 D	40.3%	59.7%	40.3%	59.7%
46	2012	149,815	54,121	HAYDEN, JERRY	95,694	SANCHEZ, LORETTA*		41,573 D	36.1%	63.9%	36.1%	63.9%
47	2016	242,868	88,109	WHALLON, ANDY	154,759	LOWENTHAL, ALAN*		66,650 D	36.3%	63.7%	36.3%	63.7%
47	2014	123,400	54,309	WHALLON, ANDY	69,091	LOWENTHAL, ALAN*		14,782 D	44.0%	56.0%	44.0%	56.0%
47	2012	230,012	99,919	DELONG, GARY	130,093	LOWENTHAL, ALAN		30,174 D	43.4%	56.6%	43.4%	56.6%
48	2016	306,416	178,701	ROHRABACHER, DANA*	127,715	SAVARY, SUE		50,986 R	58.3%	41.7%	58.3%	41.7%
48	2014	174,795	112,082	ROHRABACHER, DANA*	62,713	SAVARY, SUE		49,369 R	64.1%	35.9%	64.1%	35.9%
48	2012	290,502	177,144	ROHRABACHER, DANA*	113,358	VARASTEH, RON		63,786 R	61.0%	39.0%	61.0%	39.0%
49	2016	310,155	155,888	ISSA, DARRELL*	154,267	APPLEGATE, DOUG		1,621 R	50.3%	49.7%	50.3%	49.7%
49	2014	163,142	98,161	ISSA, DARRELL*	64,981	PEISER, DAVE		33,180 R	60.2%	39.8%	60.2%	39.8%
49	2012	274,618	159,725	ISSA, DARRELL*	114,893	TETALMAN, JERRY		44,832 R	58.2%	41.8%	58.2%	41.8%
50	2016	283,583	179,937	HUNTER, DUNCAN D.*	103,646	MALLOY, PATRICK		76,291 R	63.5%	36.5%	63.5%	36.5%
50	2014	157,299	111,997	HUNTER, DUNCAN D.*	45,302	KIMBER, JAMES H.		66,695 R	71.2%	28.8%	71.2%	28.8%
50	2012	258,293	174,838	HUNTER, DUNCAN D.*	83,455	SECOR, DAVID B.		91,383 R	67.7%	32.3%	67.7%	32.3%
51	2016	199,524	54,362	HIDALGO, JUAN M. JR.	145,162	VARGAS, JUAN*		90,800 D	27.2%	72.8%	27.2%	72.8%
51	2014	81,950	25,577	MEADE, STEPHEN	56,373	VARGAS, JUAN*		30,796 D	31.2%	68.8%	31.2%	68.8%
51	2012	159,398	45,464	CRIMMINS, MICHAEL	113,934	VARGAS, JUAN		68,470 D	28.5%	71.5%	28.5%	71.5%
52	2016	320,656	139,403	GITSHAM, DENISE	181,253	PETERS, SCOTT*		41,850 D	43.5%	56.5%	43.5%	56.5%
52	2014	191,572	92,746	DEMAIO, CARL	98,826	PETERS, SCOTT*		6,080 D	48.4%	51.6%	48.4%	51.6%
52	2012	295,910	144,459	BILBRAY, BRIAN P.*	151,451	PETERS, SCOTT		6,992 D	48.8%	51.2%	48.8%	51.2%
53	2016	296,956	97,968	VELTMEYER, JAMES	198,988	DAVIS, SUSAN A.*		101,020 D	33.0%	67.0%	33.0%	67.0%
53	2014	148,044	60,940	WILSKE, LARRY	87,104	DAVIS, SUSAN A.*		26,164 D	41.2%	58.8%	41.2%	58.8%
53	2012	268,307	103,482	POPADITCH, NICK	164,825	DAVIS, SUSAN A.*		61,343 D	38.6%	61.4%	38.6%	61.4%
TOTAL	2016	13,414,018	4,682,033		8,202,641		529,344	3,520,608 D	34.9%	61.1%	36.3%	63.7%
TOTAL	2014	7,132,641	2,813,104		3,855,865		463,672	1,042,761 D	39.4%	54.1%	42.2%	57.8%
TOTAL	2012	12,204,357	4,381,206		6,945,307		877,844	2,564,101 D	35.9%	56.9%	38.7%	61.3%

Note: An asterisk (*) denotes incumbent. Due to California's all-party primary, which qualifies the top two vote recipients for the general election, the general election in seven districts pitted two Democrats: 17th district, second place was incumbent Mike Honda, who received 90,924 votes (39.0 percent); 29th district, second place was Richard Alarcon, who received 43,417 votes (25.3 percent); 32nd district, second place was Roger Hernandez, who received 71,720 votes (38.4 percent); 34th district, second place was Adrienne Edwards, who received 36,314 votes (22.8 percent); 37th district, second place was Chris Wiggins, who received 44,782 votes (18.9 percent); 44th district, second place was Isadore Hall, who received 85,289 votes (47.8 percent); 46th district, second place was Bao Nguyen, who received 49,345 votes (30.0 percent). When this happened, the second-place same-party candidate is included in the other vote in the table above; only the top vote recipient from the party is used to calculate the plurality, total vote, and major vote. Because there are two candidates only in the general election, the other vote is exactly the total of the second place finisher. For notes on the 2012 and 2014 elections with candidates of the same party running on the general election ballot, consult America Votes 30 and 31, respectively.

CALIFORNIA

GENERAL AND PRIMARY ELECTIONS

2016 GENERAL ELECTIONS: OTHER VOTES

President Other vote was 478,500 Libertarian (Gary Johnson), 278,657 Green (Jill Stein), 79,341 Write-in (Bernard Sanders), 66,101 Peace and Freedom (Gloria La Riva), 39,596 Write-in (Evan McMullin), 1,316 Write-in (Michael Maturen), 402 Write-in (Laurence Kotlikoff), 84 Write-in (Jerry White)

House Other vote was:

CD 12	64,810 No Party (Preston Picus)
CD 17	90,924 Democrat (Mike Honda)
CD 29	43,417 Democrat (Richard Alarcon)
CD 32	71,720 Democrat (Roger Hernandez)
CD 34	36,314 Democrat (Adrienne Edwards)
CD 37	44,782 Democrat (Chris Wiggins)
CD 40	42,743 No Party (Roman Gonzalez)
CD 44	85,289 Democrat (Isadore Hall)
CD 46	49,345 Democrat (Bao Nguyen)

2016 PRIMARY ELECTIONS: SUPPLEMENTARY INFORMATION

Primary June 7, 2016 **Registration** (as of May 23, 2016) 17,915,053

Democratic	8,029,130
Republican	4,888,771
Other	819,504
No Party Preference	4,177,648

Primary Type Open—Registered Republicans and Democrats could vote only their presidential primary, although those claiming no party preference could request a Democratic ballot. For all other offices, any registered voter could participate in the "top two" primary, in which candidates of all parties (and independents) run together on the same ballot and the top two finishers in each primary race advanced to the general election.

	REPUBLICAN PRIMARIES			DEMOCRATIC PRIMARIES		
President	Trump, Donald J.	1,665,135	74.8%	Clinton, Hillary Rodham	2,745,302	53.1%
	Kasich, John R.	252,544	11.3%	Sanders, Bernard	2,381,722	46.0%
	Cruz, Ted	211,576	9.5%	Wilson, Willie	12,014	0.2%
	Carson, Ben	82,259	3.7%	Steinberg, Michael Alan	10,880	0.2%
	Gilmore, James S. III	15,691	0.7%	De La Fuente, Roque "Rocky"	8,453	0.2%
	Thomson, David P. (Write-in)	35		Hewes, Henry	7,743	0.1%
	Breivogel, Joann (Write-in)	15		Judd, Keith	7,201	0.1%
	Dowell, John (Write-in)	14		Basiago, Andrew D. (Write-in)	13	
	Gonzalez, Donald J. (Write-in)	10		Nunez, Ignacio Leon (Write-in)	6	
	Alexander-Pace, James (Write-in)	7		Carter, Willie F. (Write-in)	3	
	Vidal, Frederic (Write-in)	6		Terry, Doug (Write-in)	1	
	Williams, Victor (Write-in)	5				
	Southern, Troy Hugh (Write-in)	4				
	Ogle, James Orlando III (Write-in)	3				
	Germalio, James (Write-in)	2				
	TOTAL	*2,227,306*		*TOTAL*	*5,173,338*	

CALIFORNIA

GENERAL AND PRIMARY ELECTIONS

ALL-PARTY PRIMARIES

Senator	Harris, Kamala D. (Democrat)#	3,000,689	39.9%
	Sanchez, Loretta (Democrat)#	1,416,203	18.9%
	Sundheim, George "Duf" (Republican)	584,251	7.8%
	Wyman, Phil (Republican)	352,821	4.7%
	Del Beccaro, Thomas G. (Republican)	323,614	4.3%
	Conlon, Greg (Republican)	230,944	3.1%
	Stokes, Steve (Democrat)	168,805	2.2%
	Yang, George C. (Republican)	112,055	1.5%
	Roseberry, Karen (Republican)	110,557	1.5%
	Lightfoot, Gail K. (Libertarian)	99,761	1.3%
	Munroe, Massie (Democrat)	98,150	1.3%
	Elizondo, Pamela (Green)	95,677	1.3%
	Palzer, Tom (Republican)	93,263	1.2%
	Unz, Ron K. (Republican)	92,325	1.2%
	Krampe, Donald (Republican)	69,635	0.9%
	Garcia, Eleanor (No Party)	65,084	0.9%
	Williamson, Jarrell (Republican)	64,120	0.9%
	Hougo, Von (Republican)	63,609	0.8%
	Grappo, President Cristina (Democrat)	63,330	0.8%
	Laws, Jerry J. (Republican)	53,023	0.7%
	Herd, Mark Matthew (Libertarian)	41,344	0.6%
	Parker, John Thompson (Peace and Freedom)	35,998	0.5%
	Shi, Ling Ling (No Party)	35,196	0.5%
	Peters, Herb (Democrat)	32,638	0.4%
	Rodgers, Emory (Democrat)	31,485	0.4%
	Beitiks, Mike (Independent)	31,450	0.4%
	Grey, Clive (Independent)	29,418	0.4%
	Hanania, Jason (No Party)	27,715	0.4%
	Merritt, Paul (No Party)	24,031	0.3%
	Kraus, Jason (No Party)	19,318	0.3%
	Grundmann, Don J. (No Party)	15,317	0.2%
	Vineberg, Scott A. (No Party)	11,843	0.2%
	Gildersleeve, Tim (No Party)	9,798	0.1%
	Myers, Gar (No Party)	8,726	0.1%
	Falling, Billy (Write-in)	87	
	Llewellyn, Ric M. (Write-in)	32	
	Stuart, Alexis (Write-in)	10	
	TOTAL	7,512,322	
Congressional District 1	LaMalfa, Doug* (Republican)#	86,136	40.8%
	Reed, Jim (Democrat)#	59,665	28.3%
	Montes, Joe (Republican)	35,875	17.0%
	Peterson, David (Democrat)	13,430	6.4%
	Oxley, Gary Allen (Republican)	6,885	3.3%
	Gerlach, Jeffrey D. (No Party)	4,958	2.3%
	Cheadle, Gregory (Republican)	4,217	2.0%
	TOTAL	211,166	
Congressional District 2	Huffman, Jared* (Democrat)#	157,897	68.3%
	Mensing, Dale K. (Republican)#	36,187	15.7%
	Schrode, Erin A. (Democrat)	20,998	9.1%
	Wookey, Matthew Robert (No Party)	16,092	7.0%
	Caffrey, Andrew Augustine (Write-in)	6	
	TOTAL	231,180	
Congressional District 3	Garamendi, John* (Democrat)#	98,430	63.1%
	Cleek, N. Eugene (Republican)#	37,843	24.3%
	Detert, Ryan (Republican)	19,699	12.6%
	TOTAL	155,972	
Congressional District 4	McClintock, Tom* (Republican)#	135,626	61.5%
	Derlet, Robert W. (Democrat)#	60,574	27.5%
	White, Sean (Democrat)	24,460	11.1%
	TOTAL	220,660	

CALIFORNIA

GENERAL AND PRIMARY ELECTIONS

ALL-PARTY PRIMARIES

Congressional District 5	Thompson, Mike* (Democrat)#	124,634	65.7%
	Santamaria, Carlos (Republican)#	36,430	19.2%
	Palsson, Nils (Democrat)	23,639	12.5%
	Poling, Alex (Democrat)	4,998	2.6%
	TOTAL	189,701	
Congressional District 6	Matsui, Doris* (Democrat)#	99,599	70.4%
	Evans, Robert H. Jr. (Republican)#	26,000	18.4%
	Jefferson, Jrmar (Democrat)	7,631	5.4%
	Galvan, Mario (No Party)	6,354	4.5%
	Seretskiy, Yuriy (No Party)	1,930	1.4%
	TOTAL	141,514	
Congressional District 7	Bera, Ami* (Democrat)#	93,506	54.0%
	Jones, Scott R. (Republican)#	79,640	46.0%
	TOTAL	173,146	
Congressional District 8	Cook, Paul* (Republican)#	50,425	42.0%
	Ramirez, Rita (Democrat)#	26,325	21.9%
	Donnelly, Tim (Republican)	24,886	20.7%
	Pinkerton, John (Democrat)	11,780	9.8%
	La Plante, Roger (Democrat)	6,661	5.5%
	TOTAL	120,077	
Congressional District 9	McNerney, Jerry* (Democrat)#	71,634	55.3%
	Amador, Antonio C. "Tony" (Republican)#	28,161	21.7%
	Nance, Kathryn (Republican)	24,783	19.1%
	Appleby, Alex (Libertarian)	5,029	3.9%
	TOTAL	129,607	
Congressional District 10	Denham, Jeff* (Republican)#	61,290	47.7%
	Eggman, Michael (Democrat)#	35,413	27.6%
	Barkley, Michael "Mike" (Democrat)	18,576	14.5%
	Hodges, Robert (Republican)	13,130	10.2%
	TOTAL	128,409	
Congressional District 11	DeSaulnier, Mark* (Democrat)#	133,317	75.3%
	Petersen, Roger Allen (Republican)#	43,654	24.7%
	TOTAL	176,971	
Congressional District 12	Pelosi, Nancy* (Democrat)#	169,537	78.1%
	Picus, Preston (No Party)#	16,633	7.7%
	Miller, Bob (Republican)	16,583	7.6%
	Hermanson, Barry (Green)	14,289	6.6%
	TOTAL	217,042	
Congressional District 13	Lee, Barbara* (Democrat)#	192,227	92.0%
	Caro, Sue (Republican)#	16,818	8.0%
	TOTAL	209,045	
Congressional District 14	Speier, Jackie* (Democrat)#	144,719	99.0%
	Cardenas, Angel (Write-in)#	1,400	1.0%
	TOTAL	146,119	
Congressional District 15	Swalwell, Eric* (Democrat)#	110,803	76.5%
	Turner, Danny R. (Republican)#	34,032	23.5%
	TOTAL	144,835	
Congressional District 16	Costa, Jim* (Democrat)#	52,822	55.9%
	Tacherra, Johnny M. (Republican)#	31,028	32.8%
	Rogers, David (Republican)	10,606	11.2%
	Gomez, Richard (Write-in)	13	
	TOTAL	94,469	

CALIFORNIA

GENERAL AND PRIMARY ELECTIONS

ALL-PARTY PRIMARIES

Congressional District 17			
	Khanna, Ro (Democrat)#	52,059	39.1%
	Honda, Mike M.* (Democrat)#	49,823	37.4%
	Kuo, Peter (Republican)	12,224	9.2%
	Cohen, Ron (Republican)	10,448	7.8%
	Oliverio, Pierluigi C. (Democrat)	5,533	4.2%
	Watson, Kennita (Libertarian)	3,125	2.3%
	TOTAL	133,212	

Congressional District 18			
	Eshoo, Anna G.* (Democrat)#	132,726	68.2%
	Fox, Richard B. (Republican)#	47,484	24.4%
	Harlow, Bob (Democrat)	14,411	7.4%
	TOTAL	194,621	

Congressional District 19			
	Lofgren, Zoe* (Democrat)#	107,773	76.1%
	Lancaster, G. Burt (Republican)#	33,889	23.9%
	TOTAL	141,662	

Congressional District 20			
	Panetta, Jimmy (Democrat)#	116,826	70.8%
	Lucius, Casey (Republican)#	32,726	19.8%
	Williams, Joe (Peace and Freedom)	6,400	3.9%
	Honegger, Barbara (No Party)	6,054	3.7%
	Digby, Jack (No Party)	2,932	1.8%
	TOTAL	164,938	

Congressional District 21			
	Valadao, David* (Republican)#	37,367	54.0%
	Huerta, Emilio Jesus (Democrat)#	16,743	24.2%
	Parra, Daniel (Democrat)	15,056	21.8%
	TOTAL	69,166	

Congressional District 22			
	Nunes, Devin* (Republican)#	86,479	63.8%
	Campos, Louie J. (Democrat)#	40,247	29.7%
	Andres, Teresita "Tess" (Republican)	8,808	6.5%
	TOTAL	135,534	

Congressional District 23			
	McCarthy, Kevin* (Republican)#	76,166	55.5%
	Reed, Wendy (Democrat)#	37,696	27.4%
	Mettler, Ken (Republican)	17,738	12.9%
	Morris, Gerald (Republican)	5,734	4.2%
	TOTAL	137,334	

Congressional District 24			
	Carbajal, Salud (Democrat)#	66,402	31.9%
	Fareed, Justin (Republican)#	42,521	20.5%
	Achadjian, K.H. Katcho (Republican)	37,716	18.1%
	Schneider, Helene (Democrat)	31,046	14.9%
	Ostrander, William "Bill" (Democrat)	12,657	6.1%
	Kokkonen, Matt T. (Republican)	11,636	5.6%
	Uebersax, John (No Party)	2,188	1.1%
	Isakson, Steve (No Party)	2,172	1.0%
	Lucas, Benjamin (Democrat)	1,568	0.8%
	TOTAL	207,906	

Congressional District 25			
	Knight, Steve* (Republican)#	63,769	48.3%
	Caforio, Bryan (Democrat)#	38,382	29.0%
	Vince, Lou (Democrat)	20,327	15.4%
	Moffatt, Jeffrey (Republican)	9,620	7.3%
	Bomberger, Jeff (Write-in)	44	
	TOTAL	132,142	

Congressional District 26			
	Brownley, Julia* (Democrat)#	108,937	64.0%
	Dagnesses, Rafael (Republican)#	61,219	36.0%
	TOTAL	170,156	

CALIFORNIA

GENERAL AND PRIMARY ELECTIONS

ALL-PARTY PRIMARIES

Congressional District 27	Chu, Judy* (Democrat)#	93,204	66.2%
	Orswell, Jack (Republican)#	39,574	28.1%
	Sweeney, Tim (No Party)	8,063	5.7%
	TOTAL	*140,841*	
Congressional District 28	Schiff, Adam B.* (Democrat)#	111,766	70.2%
	Solis, Lenore (Republican)#	29,336	18.4%
	Genovese, Sal (Democrat)	18,026	11.3%
	TOTAL	*159,128*	
Congressional District 29	Cardenas, Tony* (Democrat)#	58,616	61.4%
	Alarcon, Richard (Democrat)#	12,397	13.0%
	Shammas, Joseph "Joe" (Democrat)	10,847	11.4%
	Bernal, Benny "Benito" (Democrat)	10,006	10.5%
	Guzman, David Z. (Democrat)	3,654	3.8%
	TOTAL	*95,520*	
Congressional District 30	Sherman, Brad* (Democrat)#	92,448	60.1%
	Reed, Mark (Republican)#	21,458	14.0%
	Patrick, Patrea (Democrat)	14,628	9.5%
	Rab, A. "Raji" (Democrat)	8,847	5.8%
	Singh, Navraj (Republican)	6,517	4.2%
	Davis, Luke (Democrat)	5,150	3.3%
	Townsend, Christopher David (Republican)	4,741	3.1%
	TOTAL	*153,789*	
Congressional District 31	Aguilar, Pete* (Democrat)#	48,518	43.1%
	Chabot, Paul (Republican)#	25,534	22.7%
	Baca, Joe (Republican)	14,020	12.4%
	Ahmed, Kaisar (Democrat)	12,418	11.0%
	Flynn, Sean (Republican)	12,130	10.8%
	TOTAL	*112,620*	
Congressional District 32	Napolitano, Grace Flores* (Democrat)#	54,987	51.4%
	Hernandez, Roger (Democrat)#	26,386	24.7%
	Fisher, Gordon E. (Republican)	25,594	23.9%
	TOTAL	*106,967*	
Congressional District 33	Lieu, Ted* (Democrat)#	127,733	69.2%
	Wright, Kenneth W. (Republican)#	56,976	30.8%
	TOTAL	*184,709*	
Congressional District 34	Becerra, Xavier* (Democrat)#	71,982	77.6%
	Edwards, Adrienne Nicole (Democrat)#	19,624	21.2%
	Mejia, Kenneth (Write-in)	1,177	1.3%
	TOTAL	*92,783*	
Congressional District 35	Torres, Norma* (Democrat)#	65,226	75.6%
	Fischella, Tyler (Republican)#	21,089	24.4%
	TOTAL	*86,315*	
Congressional District 36	Ruiz, Raul* (Democrat)#	76,213	58.5%
	Stone, Jeff (Republican)#	41,190	31.6%
	Wolkowicz, Stephan "Steven" (Republican)	12,923	9.9%
	TOTAL	*130,326*	
Congressional District 37	Bass, Karen* (Democrat)#	115,597	80.2%
	Wiggins, Chris Blake (Democrat)#	15,362	10.7%
	Hasan, Shariff A. (Republican)	13,158	9.1%
	TOTAL	*144,117*	

CALIFORNIA

GENERAL AND PRIMARY ELECTIONS

ALL-PARTY PRIMARIES

Congressional District 38	Sanchez, Linda* (Democrat)#	86,396	70.0%
	Downing, Ryan (Republican)#	25,801	20.9%
	Adams, Scott Michael (No Party)	11,189	9.1%
	TOTAL	123,386	
Congressional District 39	Royce, Ed* (Republican)#	85,035	60.5%
	Murdock, Brett (Democrat)#	55,520	39.5%
	TOTAL	140,555	
Congressional District 40	Roybal-Allard, Lucille* (Democrat)#	60,691	76.3%
	Gonzalez, Roman Gabriel (No Party)#	18,844	23.7%
	Flores, J. Cesar (Write-in)	6	
	TOTAL	79,541	
Congressional District 41	Takano, Mark A.* (Democrat)#	63,706	64.5%
	Shepherd, Doug (Republican)#	17,255	17.5%
	Fox, Randy (Republican)	14,844	15.0%
	Ryan, Cody (Republican)	2,893	2.9%
	TOTAL	98,698	
Congressional District 42	Calvert, Ken* (Republican)#	66,418	54.9%
	Sheridan, Tim (Democrat)#	45,389	37.5%
	Condley, Kerri (No Party)	9,076	7.5%
	TOTAL	120,883	
Congressional District 43	Waters, Maxine* (Democrat)#	92,909	76.1%
	Navarro, Omar (Republican)#	29,152	23.9%
	TOTAL	122,061	
Congressional District 44	Hall, Isadore III (Democrat)#	40,200	40.1%
	Barragan, Nanette Diaz (Democrat)#	22,031	22.0%
	Sotomayor, Armando (Democrat)	10,087	10.1%
	Ortiz, Sylvia (Democrat)	6,062	6.0%
	Delgadillo, Martha C. (Democrat)	5,771	5.8%
	Siegel, Ronald (Republican)	5,565	5.5%
	Castillo, Christopher (Republican)	3,651	3.6%
	Griffin, Morris F. (Democrat)	3,624	3.6%
	Musante, Marcus C. (Democrat)	2,366	2.4%
	De Mauricio, Michael (No Party)	919	0.9%
	TOTAL	100,276	
Congressional District 45	Walters, Mimi* (Republican)#	65,773	40.9%
	Varasteh, Ron (Democrat)#	44,449	27.6%
	Raths, Greg G. (Republican)	30,961	19.2%
	Gouron, Max (Democrat)	19,716	12.3%
	TOTAL	160,899	
Congressional District 46	Correa, Lou (Democrat)#	40,880	43.7%
	Nguyen, Bao (Democrat)#	13,625	14.6%
	Peterson, Bob (Republican)	11,781	12.6%
	Dunn, Joe (Democrat)	11,596	12.4%
	Schott, Lynn (Republican)	7,373	7.9%
	Contreras, Louie A. (Republican)	3,441	3.7%
	Marin, Nancy Trinidad (No Party)	3,306	3.5%
	Gaona, Rodolfo "Rudy" (Republican)	1,567	1.7%
	TOTAL	93,569	
Congressional District 47	Lowenthal, Alan* (Democrat)#	90,595	66.1%
	Whallon, Andy (Republican)#	30,054	21.9%
	Kahn, Sanford W. (Republican)	16,364	11.9%
	Camp, Rich (Write-in)	9	
	TOTAL	137,022	

CALIFORNIA

GENERAL AND PRIMARY ELECTIONS

ALL-PARTY PRIMARIES

Congressional District 48	Rohrabacher, Dana* (Republican)#	92,815	56.6%
	Savary, Suzanne (Democrat)#	47,395	28.9%
	Banuelos, Robert J. (Democrat)	23,867	14.5%
	TOTAL	*164,077*	
Congressional District 49	Issa, Darrell* (Republican)#	84,626	50.8%
	Applegate, Doug (Democrat)#	75,808	45.5%
	Wingo, Ryan Glenn (No Party)	6,087	3.7%
	TOTAL	*166,521*	
Congressional District 50	Hunter, Duncan D.* (Republican)#	86,534	56.5%
	Malloy, Patrick (Democrat)#	33,348	21.8%
	Secor, David B. (Democrat)	17,590	11.5%
	Meisterlin, Scott C. (Republican)	10,458	6.8%
	Shioura, Hilaire Fuji (No Party)	5,359	3.5%
	TOTAL	*153,289*	
Congressional District 51	Vargas, Juan* (Democrat)#	69,522	66.8%
	Hidalgo, Juan M. Jr. (Republican)#	16,053	15.4%
	Mercado-Flores, Juan "Charly" (Democrat)	9,781	9.4%
	Sanchez, Carlos J. (Republican)	8,681	8.3%
	TOTAL	*104,037*	
Congressional District 52	Peters, Scott* (Democrat)#	108,020	58.9%
	Gitsham, Denise (Republican)#	29,658	16.2%
	Atkinson, Jacquie (Republican)	23,927	13.0%
	Canada, Kenneth "Mike" (Republican)	8,268	4.5%
	Allvord, Terry Reagan (Republican)	8,194	4.5%
	Horst, John (Republican)	5,435	3.0%
	TOTAL	*183,502*	
Congressional District 53	Davis, Susan A.* (Democrat)#	110,831	65.5%
	Veltmeyer, James (Republican)#	25,656	15.2%
	Ash, Jim (Republican)	25,410	15.0%
	Walpert, Nicholas "Nick" (Democrat)	7,363	4.4%
	TOTAL	*169,260*	

Note: An asterisk (*) denotes incumbent. A pound sign (#) next to the top two candidates in each primary indicates that they qualified for the general election.

COLORADO

Congressional districts first established for elections held in 2012

7 members

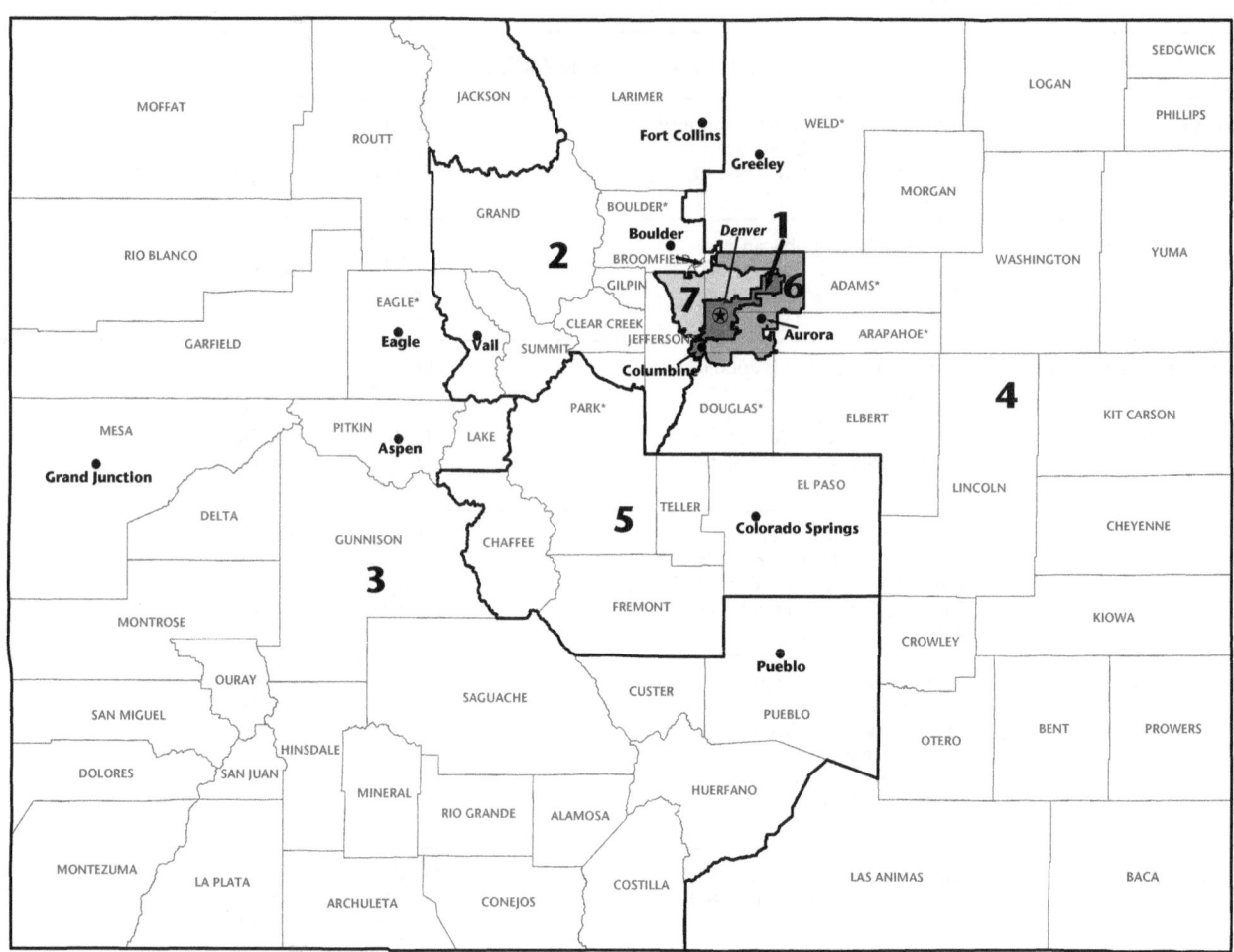

* Asterisk indicates a county whose boundaries include parts of two or more congressional districts.

COLORADO
Denver Area

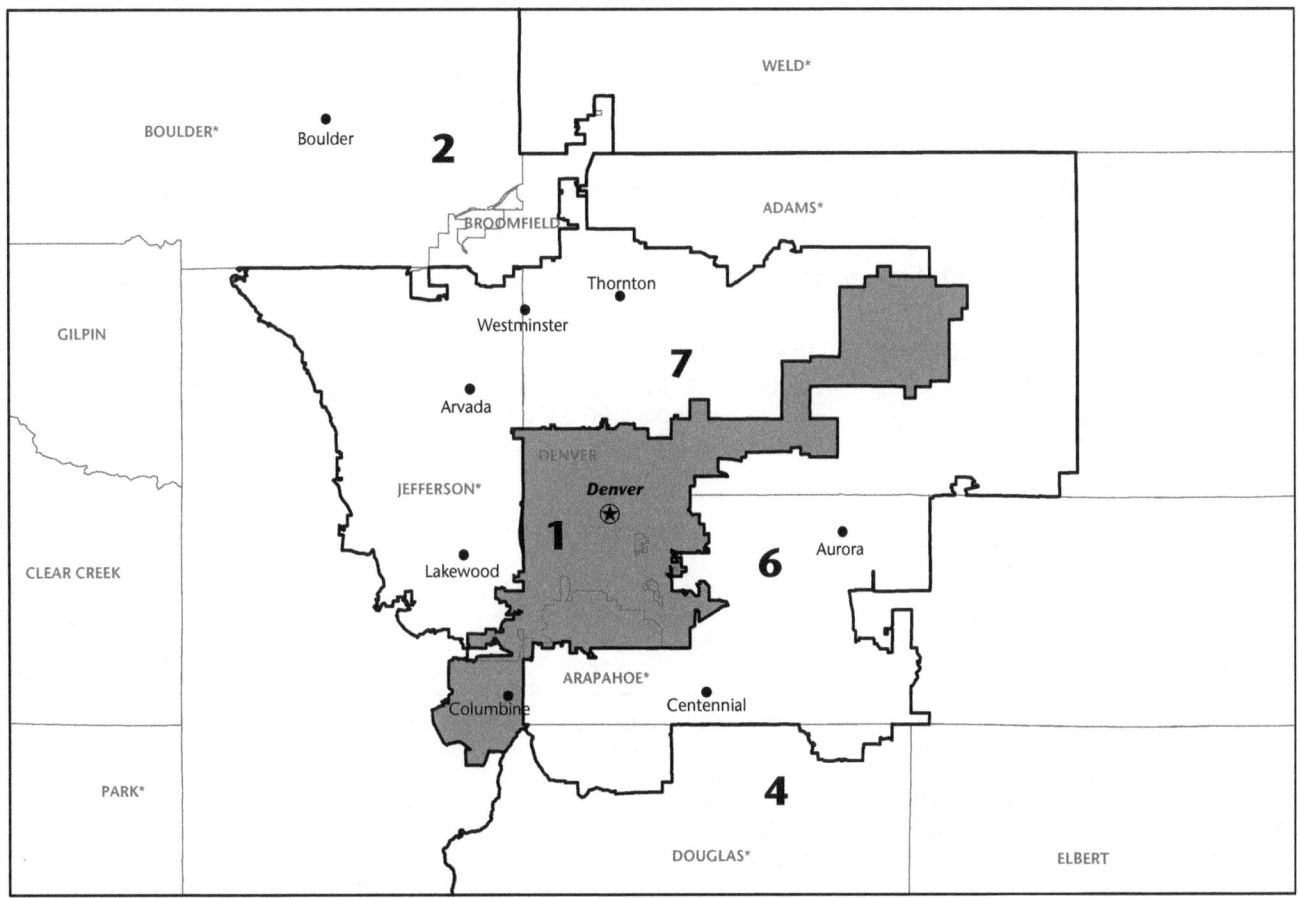

* Asterisk indicates a county whose boundaries include parts of two or more congressional districts.

COLORADO

GOVERNOR
John Hickenlooper (D). Re-elected 2014 to a four-year term. Previously elected 2010.

SENATORS (1 Democrat, 1 Republican)
Michael F. Bennet (D). Re-elected 2016 to a six-year term. Sworn in as senator January 22, 2009, to fill the vacancy created by the resignation of Ken Salazar (D) to become U.S. secretary of interior, and elected 2010.

Cory Gardner (R). Elected 2014 to a six-year term.

REPRESENTATIVES (4 Republicans, 3 Democrats)
1. Diana L. DeGette (D)
2. Jared Polis (D)
3. Scott Tipton (R)
4. Ken Buck (R)
5. Doug Lamborn (R)
6. Mike Coffman (R)
7. Ed Perlmutter (D)

POSTWAR VOTE FOR PRESIDENT

Year	Total Vote	Republican Vote	Republican Candidate	Democratic Vote	Democratic Candidate	Other Vote	Rep.-Dem. Plurality	Total Vote Rep.	Total Vote Dem.	Major Vote Rep.	Major Vote Dem.
2016**	2,780,247	1,202,484	Trump, Donald J.	1,338,870	Clinton, Hillary Rodham	238,893	136,386 D	43.3%	48.2%	47.3%	52.7%
2012	2,569,522	1,185,243	Romney, W. Mitt	1,323,102	Obama, Barack H.*	61,177	137,859 D	46.1%	51.5%	47.3%	52.7%
2008	2,401,462	1,073,629	McCain, John S. III	1,288,633	Obama, Barack H.	39,200	215,004 D	44.7%	53.7%	45.4%	54.6%
2004	2,130,330	1,101,255	Bush, George W.*	1,001,732	Kerry, John F.	27,343	99,523 R	51.7%	47.0%	52.4%	47.6%
2000**	1,741,368	883,748	Bush, George W.	738,227	Gore, Albert Jr.	119,393	145,521 R	50.8%	42.4%	54.5%	45.5%
1996**	1,510,704	691,848	Dole, Robert "Bob"	671,152	Clinton, Bill*	147,704	20,696 R	45.8%	44.4%	50.8%	49.2%
1992**	1,569,180	562,850	Bush, George H.*	629,681	Clinton, Bill	376,649	66,831 D	35.9%	40.1%	47.2%	52.8%
1988	1,372,394	728,177	Bush, George H.	621,453	Dukakis, Michael S.	22,764	106,724 R	53.1%	45.3%	54.0%	46.0%
1984	1,295,380	821,817	Reagan, Ronald*	454,975	Mondale, Walter F.	18,588	366,842 R	63.4%	35.1%	64.4%	35.6%
1980**	1,184,415	652,264	Reagan, Ronald	367,973	Carter, Jimmy*	164,178	284,291 R	55.1%	31.1%	63.9%	36.1%
1976	1,081,554	584,367	Ford, Gerald R.*	460,353	Carter, Jimmy	36,834	124,014 R	54.0%	42.6%	55.9%	44.1%
1972	953,884	597,189	Nixon, Richard M.*	329,980	McGovern, George S.	26,715	267,209 R	62.6%	34.6%	64.4%	35.6%
1968**	811,199	409,345	Nixon, Richard M.	335,174	Humphrey, Hubert Horatio Jr.	66,680	74,171 R	50.5%	41.3%	55.0%	45.0%
1964	776,986	296,767	Goldwater, Barry M. Sr.	476,024	Johnson, Lyndon B.*	4,195	179,257 D	38.2%	61.3%	38.4%	61.6%
1960	736,236	402,242	Nixon, Richard M.	330,629	Kennedy, John F.	3,365	71,613 R	54.6%	44.9%	54.9%	45.1%
1956	657,074	394,479	Eisenhower, Dwight D.*	257,997	Stevenson, Adlai E. II	4,598	136,482 R	60.0%	39.3%	60.5%	39.5%
1952	630,103	379,782	Eisenhower, Dwight D.	245,504	Stevenson, Adlai E. II	4,817	134,278 R	60.3%	39.0%	60.7%	39.3%
1948	515,237	239,714	Dewey, Thomas E.	267,288	Truman, Harry S.*	8,235	27,574 D	46.5%	51.9%	47.3%	52.7%

Note: An asterisk (*) denotes incumbent. **In past elections, the other vote included: 2016 - 144,121 Libertarian (Gary Johnson); 2000 - 91,434 Green (Ralph Nader); 1996 - 99,629 Reform (Ross Perot); 1992 - 366,010 Independent (Perot); 1980 - 130,633 Independent (John Anderson); 1968 - 60,813 American Independent (George Wallace).

COLORADO

POSTWAR VOTE FOR GOVERNOR

Year	Total Vote	Republican		Democratic		Other Vote	Rep.-Dem. Plurality	Percentage			
								Total Vote		Major Vote	
		Vote	Candidate	Vote	Candidate			Rep.	Dem.	Rep.	Dem.
2014	2,041,607	938,195	Beauprez, Bob	1,006,433	Hickenlooper, John*	96,979	68,238 D	46.0%	49.3%	48.2%	51.8%
2010**	1,788,001	199,062	Maes, Dan	912,189	Hickenlooper, John	676,750	713,127 D	11.1%	51.0%	17.9%	82.1%
2006	1,558,387	625,886	Beauprez, Bob	888,096	Ritter, Bill Jr.	44,405	262,210 D	40.2%	57.0%	41.3%	58.7%
2002	1,412,602	884,583	Owens, Bill*	475,373	Heath, Rollie	52,646	409,210 R	62.6%	33.7%	65.0%	35.0%
1998	1,323,530	649,688	Owens, Bill	639,358	Schoettler, Gail	34,484	10,330 R	49.1%	48.3%	50.4%	49.6%
1994	1,116,307	432,042	Benson, Bruce	619,205	Romer, Roy*	65,060	187,163 D	38.7%	55.5%	41.1%	58.9%
1990	1,011,272	358,403	Andrews, John	626,032	Romer, Roy*	26,837	267,629 D	35.4%	61.9%	36.4%	63.6%
1986	1,058,928	434,420	Strickland, Ted	616,325	Romer, Roy	8,183	181,905 D	41.0%	58.2%	41.3%	58.7%
1982	956,021	302,740	Fuhr, John D.	627,960	Lamm, Richard D.*	25,321	325,220 D	31.7%	65.7%	32.5%	67.5%
1978	823,807	317,292	Strickland, Ted	483,985	Lamm, Richard D.*	22,530	166,693 D	38.5%	58.7%	39.6%	60.4%
1974	828,968	378,907	Vanderhoof, John D.*	441,199	Lamm, Richard D.	8,862	62,292 D	45.7%	53.2%	46.2%	53.8%
1970	668,496	350,690	Love, John A.*	302,432	Hogan, Mark	15,374	48,258 R	52.5%	45.2%	53.7%	46.3%
1966	660,063	356,730	Love, John A.*	287,132	Knous, Robert L.	16,201	69,598 R	54.0%	43.5%	55.4%	44.6%
1962	616,481	349,342	Love, John A.	262,890	McNichols, Stephen L.R.*	4,249	86,452 R	56.7%	42.6%	57.1%	42.9%
1958**	549,808	228,643	Burch, Palmer L.	321,165	McNichols, Stephen L.R.*		92,522 D	41.6%	58.4%	41.6%	58.4%
1956	645,233	313,950	Brotzman, Donald G.	331,283	McNichols, Stephen L.R.		17,333 D	48.7%	51.3%	48.7%	51.3%
1954	489,540	227,335	Brotzman, Donald G.	262,205	Johnson, Edwin C.		34,870 D	46.4%	53.6%	46.4%	53.6%
1952	613,034	349,924	Thornton, Dan*	260,044	Metzger, John W.	3,066	89,880 R	57.1%	42.4%	57.4%	42.6%
1950	450,994	236,472	Thornton, Dan	212,976	Johnson, Walter W.	1,546	23,496 R	52.4%	47.2%	52.6%	47.4%
1948	501,680	168,928	Hamil, David A.	332,752	Knous, William Lee*		163,824 D	33.7%	66.3%	33.7%	66.3%
1946	335,087	160,483	Lavington, Leon E.	174,604	Knous, William Lee		14,121 D	47.9%	52.1%	47.9%	52.1%

Note: An asterisk (*) denotes incumbent. **In past elections, the other vote included: 2010 - 651,232 American Constitution (Tom Tancredo, who finished second). The term of office of Colorado's Governor was increased from two to four years effective with the 1958 election.

POSTWAR VOTE FOR SENATOR

Year	Total Vote	Republican		Democratic		Other Vote	Rep.-Dem. Plurality	Percentage			
								Total Vote		Major Vote	
		Vote	Candidate	Vote	Candidate			Rep.	Dem.	Rep.	Dem.
2016	2,743,029	1,215,318	Glenn, Darryl	1,370,710	Bennet, Michael F.*	157,001	155,392 D	44.3%	50.0%	47.0%	53.0%
2014	2,041,058	983,891	Gardner, Cory	944,203	Udall, Mark*	112,964	39,688 R	48.2%	46.3%	51.0%	49.0%
2010	1,777,464	824,789	Buck, Ken	854,685	Bennet, Michael F.*	97,990	29,896 D	46.4%	48.1%	49.1%	50.9%
2008	2,331,712	990,784	Schaffer, Bob	1,231,049	Udall, Mark	109,879	240,265 D	42.5%	52.8%	44.6%	55.4%
2004	2,107,554	980,668	Coors, Pete	1,081,188	Salazar, Ken	45,698	100,520 D	46.5%	51.3%	47.6%	52.4%
2002	1,416,082	717,893	Allard, Wayne*	648,130	Strickland, Tom	50,059	69,763 R	50.7%	45.8%	52.6%	47.4%
1998	1,327,235	829,370	Campbell, Ben Nighthorse*	464,754	Lamm, Dottie	33,111	364,616 R	62.5%	35.0%	64.1%	35.9%
1996	1,469,611	750,325	Allard, Wayne	677,600	Strickland, Tom	41,686	72,725 R	51.1%	46.1%	52.5%	47.5%
1992	1,552,289	662,893	Considine, Terry	803,725	Campbell, Ben Nighthorse	85,671	140,832 D	42.7%	51.8%	45.2%	54.8%
1990	1,022,027	569,048	Brown, Hank	425,746	Heath, Josie	27,233	143,302 R	55.7%	41.7%	57.2%	42.8%
1986	1,060,765	512,994	Kramer, Ken	529,449	Wirth, Timothy E.	18,322	16,455 D	48.4%	49.9%	49.2%	50.8%
1984	1,297,809	833,821	Armstrong, William L.*	449,327	Dick, Nancy	14,661	384,494 R	64.2%	34.6%	65.0%	35.0%
1980	1,173,646	571,295	Buchanan, Mary E.	590,501	Hart, Gary W.*	11,850	19,206 D	48.7%	50.3%	49.2%	50.8%
1978	819,150	480,596	Armstrong, William L.	330,247	Haskell, Floyd K.*	8,307	150,349 R	58.7%	40.3%	59.3%	40.7%
1974	824,166	325,508	Dominick, Peter H.*	471,691	Hart, Gary W.	26,967	146,183 D	39.5%	57.2%	40.8%	59.2%
1972	926,093	447,957	Alott, Gordon Llewellyn*	457,545	Haskell, Floyd K.	20,591	9,588 D	48.4%	49.4%	49.5%	50.5%
1968	785,536	459,952	Dominick, Peter H.*	325,584	McNichols, Stephen L.R.		134,368 R	58.6%	41.4%	58.6%	41.4%
1966	634,837	368,307	Alott, Gordon Llewellyn*	266,198	Romer, Roy	332	102,109 R	58.0%	41.9%	58.0%	42.0%
1962	613,444	328,655	Dominick, Peter H.	279,586	Carroll, John Albert*	5,203	49,069 R	53.6%	45.6%	54.0%	46.0%
1960	727,633	389,428	Alott, Gordon Llewellyn*	334,854	Knous, Robert L.	3,351	54,574 R	53.5%	46.0%	53.8%	46.2%
1956	636,974	317,102	Thornton, Dan	319,872	Carroll, John Albert		2,770 D	49.8%	50.2%	49.8%	50.2%
1954	484,188	248,502	Alott, Gordon Llewellyn	235,686	Carroll, John Albert		12,816 R	51.3%	48.7%	51.3%	48.7%
1950	450,176	239,734	Millikin, Eugene D.*	210,442	Carroll, John Albert		29,292 R	53.3%	46.7%	53.3%	46.7%
1948	510,121	165,069	Nicholson, Will F.	340,719	Johnson, Edwin C.*	4,333	175,650 D	32.4%	66.8%	32.6%	67.4%

Note: An asterisk (*) denotes incumbent.

COLORADO

PRESIDENT 2016

2010 Census Population	County	Total Vote	Republican (Trump)	Democratic (Clinton)	Other	Rep.-Dem. Plurality	Percentage Total Vote Rep.	Dem.	Major Vote Rep.	Dem.
441,603	ADAMS	193,677	80,082	96,558	17,037	16,476 D	41.3%	49.9%	45.3%	54.7%
15,445	ALAMOSA	6,939	3,046	3,189	704	143 D	43.9%	46.0%	48.9%	51.1%
572,003	ARAPAHOE	303,048	117,053	159,885	26,110	42,832 D	38.6%	52.8%	42.3%	57.7%
12,084	ARCHULETA	7,339	4,264	2,500	575	1,764 R	58.1%	34.1%	63.0%	37.0%
3,788	BACA	2,153	1,753	283	117	1,470 R	81.4%	13.1%	86.1%	13.9%
6,499	BENT	1,927	1,188	590	149	598 R	61.7%	30.6%	66.8%	33.2%
294,567	BOULDER	188,145	41,396	132,334	14,415	90,938 D	22.0%	70.3%	23.8%	76.2%
55,889	BROOMFIELD	37,690	14,367	19,731	3,592	5,364 D	38.1%	52.4%	42.1%	57.9%
17,809	CHAFFEE	11,250	5,391	4,888	971	503 R	47.9%	43.4%	52.4%	47.6%
1,836	CHEYENNE	1,102	925	132	45	793 R	83.9%	12.0%	87.5%	12.5%
9,088	CLEAR CREEK	5,866	2,575	2,729	562	154 D	43.9%	46.5%	48.5%	51.5%
8,256	CONEJOS	4,022	1,914	1,771	337	143 R	47.6%	44.0%	51.9%	48.1%
3,524	COSTILLA	1,848	588	1,125	135	537 D	31.8%	60.9%	34.3%	65.7%
5,823	CROWLEY	1,527	1,079	339	109	740 R	70.7%	22.2%	76.1%	23.9%
4,255	CUSTER	3,066	2,061	797	208	1,264 R	67.2%	26.0%	72.1%	27.9%
30,952	DELTA	16,790	11,655	4,087	1,048	7,568 R	69.4%	24.3%	74.0%	26.0%
600,158	DENVER	331,852	62,690	244,551	24,611	181,861 D	18.9%	73.7%	20.4%	79.6%
2,064	DOLORES	1,255	944	242	69	702 R	75.2%	19.3%	79.6%	20.4%
285,465	DOUGLAS	187,500	102,573	68,657	16,270	33,916 R	54.7%	36.6%	59.9%	40.1%
52,197	EAGLE	25,223	8,990	14,099	2,134	5,109 D	35.6%	55.9%	38.9%	61.1%
622,263	EL PASO	318,968	179,228	108,010	31,730	71,218 R	56.2%	33.9%	62.4%	37.6%
23,086	ELBERT	15,980	11,705	3,134	1,141	8,571 R	73.2%	19.6%	78.9%	21.1%
46,824	FREMONT	21,973	15,122	5,297	1,554	9,825 R	68.8%	24.1%	74.1%	25.9%
56,389	GARFIELD	26,470	13,132	11,271	2,067	1,861 R	49.6%	42.6%	53.8%	46.2%
5,441	GILPIN	3,576	1,566	1,634	376	68 D	43.8%	45.7%	48.9%	51.1%
14,843	GRAND	8,588	4,494	3,358	736	1,136 R	52.3%	39.1%	57.2%	42.8%
15,324	GUNNISON	9,412	3,289	5,128	995	1,839 D	34.9%	54.5%	39.1%	60.9%
843	HINSDALE	589	339	197	53	142 R	57.6%	33.4%	63.2%	36.8%
6,711	HUERFANO	3,783	1,883	1,633	267	250 R	49.8%	43.2%	53.6%	46.4%
1,394	JACKSON	861	629	171	61	458 R	73.1%	19.9%	78.6%	21.4%
534,543	JEFFERSON	328,883	138,177	160,776	29,930	22,599 D	42.0%	48.9%	46.2%	53.8%
1,398	KIOWA	855	728	91	36	637 R	85.1%	10.6%	88.9%	11.1%
8,270	KIT CARSON	3,702	2,967	536	199	2,431 R	80.1%	14.5%	84.7%	15.3%
51,334	LA PLATA	31,150	12,587	15,525	3,038	2,938 D	40.4%	49.8%	44.8%	55.2%
7,310	LAKE	3,199	1,270	1,616	313	346 D	39.7%	50.5%	44.0%	56.0%
299,630	LARIMER	195,981	83,430	93,113	19,438	9,683 D	42.6%	47.5%	47.3%	52.7%
15,507	LAS ANIMAS	6,793	3,710	2,650	433	1,060 R	54.6%	39.0%	58.3%	41.7%
5,467	LINCOLN	2,436	1,892	409	135	1,483 R	77.7%	16.8%	82.2%	17.8%
22,709	LOGAN	9,722	7,282	1,851	589	5,431 R	74.9%	19.0%	79.7%	20.3%
146,723	MESA	77,654	49,779	21,729	6,146	28,050 R	64.1%	28.0%	69.6%	30.4%
712	MINERAL	652	344	237	71	107 R	52.8%	36.3%	59.2%	40.8%
13,795	MOFFAT	6,525	5,305	874	346	4,431 R	81.3%	13.4%	85.9%	14.1%
25,535	MONTEZUMA	12,858	7,853	3,973	1,032	3,880 R	61.1%	30.9%	66.4%	33.6%
41,276	MONTROSE	21,186	14,382	5,466	1,338	8,916 R	67.9%	25.8%	72.5%	27.5%
28,159	MORGAN	11,960	8,145	3,151	664	4,994 R	68.1%	26.3%	72.1%	27.9%
18,831	OTERO	8,452	4,928	2,943	581	1,985 R	58.3%	34.8%	62.6%	37.4%
4,436	OURAY	3,310	1,351	1,697	262	346 D	40.8%	51.3%	44.3%	55.7%
16,206	PARK	10,417	6,135	3,421	861	2,714 R	58.9%	32.8%	64.2%	35.8%
4,442	PHILLIPS	2,332	1,791	436	105	1,355 R	76.8%	18.7%	80.4%	19.6%
17,148	PITKIN	10,523	2,550	7,333	640	4,783 D	24.2%	69.7%	25.8%	74.2%
12,551	PROWERS	5,016	3,531	1,186	299	2,345 R	70.4%	23.6%	74.9%	25.1%
159,063	PUEBLO	78,646	36,265	35,875	6,506	390 R	46.1%	45.6%	50.3%	49.7%
6,666	RIO BLANCO	3,450	2,791	436	223	2,355 R	80.9%	12.6%	86.5%	13.5%
11,982	RIO GRANDE	5,534	3,085	2,001	448	1,084 R	55.7%	36.2%	60.7%	39.3%
23,509	ROUTT	13,986	5,230	7,600	1,156	2,370 D	37.4%	54.3%	40.8%	59.2%
6,108	SAGUACHE	2,835	1,147	1,417	271	270 D	40.5%	50.0%	44.7%	55.3%
699	SAN JUAN	506	215	265	26	50 D	42.5%	52.4%	44.8%	55.2%
7,359	SAN MIGUEL	4,329	1,033	2,975	321	1,942 D	23.9%	68.7%	25.8%	74.2%
2,379	SEDGWICK	1,364	1,015	267	82	748 R	74.4%	19.6%	79.2%	20.8%
27,994	SUMMIT	16,174	5,100	9,557	1,517	4,457 D	31.5%	59.1%	34.8%	65.2%

COLORADO

PRESIDENT 2016

2010 Census Population	County	Total Vote	Republican (Trump)	Democratic (Clinton)	Other	Rep.-Dem. Plurality	Total Vote Rep.	Total Vote Dem.	Major Vote Rep.	Major Vote Dem.
23,350	TELLER	14,444	9,745	3,603	1,096	6,142 R	67.5%	24.9%	73.0%	27.0%
4,814	WASHINGTON	2,733	2,299	296	138	2,003 R	84.1%	10.8%	88.6%	11.4%
252,825	WELD	135,430	76,651	46,519	12,260	30,132 R	56.6%	34.3%	62.2%	37.8%
10,043	YUMA	4,791	3,850	726	215	3,124 R	80.4%	15.2%	84.1%	15.9%
5,029,196	TOTAL	2,780,247	1,202,484	1,338,870	238,893	136,386 D	43.3%	48.2%	47.3%	52.7%

COLORADO

SENATOR 2016

2010 Census Population	County	Total Vote	Republican (Glenn)	Democratic (Bennet)	Other	Rep.-Dem. Plurality	Total Vote Rep.	Total Vote Dem.	Major Vote Rep.	Major Vote Dem.
441,603	ADAMS	184,996	76,285	97,402	11,309	21,117 D	41.2%	52.7%	43.9%	56.1%
15,445	ALAMOSA	6,972	2,894	3,695	383	801 D	41.5%	53.0%	43.9%	56.1%
572,003	ARAPAHOE	301,361	123,509	162,747	15,105	39,238 D	41.0%	54.0%	43.1%	56.9%
12,084	ARCHULETA	7,252	4,072	2,750	430	1,322 R	56.2%	37.9%	59.7%	40.3%
3,788	BACA	2,138	1,469	577	92	892 R	68.7%	27.0%	71.8%	28.2%
6,499	BENT	1,918	1,034	810	74	224 R	53.9%	42.2%	56.1%	43.9%
294,567	BOULDER	185,820	45,755	126,334	13,731	80,579 D	24.6%	68.0%	26.6%	73.4%
55,889	BROOMFIELD	36,617	15,077	19,431	2,109	4,354 D	41.2%	53.1%	43.7%	56.3%
17,809	CHAFFEE	11,261	5,384	5,259	618	125 R	47.8%	46.7%	50.6%	49.4%
1,836	CHEYENNE	1,090	828	220	42	608 R	76.0%	20.2%	79.0%	21.0%
9,088	CLEAR CREEK	5,875	2,541	2,883	451	342 D	43.3%	49.1%	46.8%	53.2%
8,256	CONEJOS	4,056	1,878	2,073	105	195 D	46.3%	51.1%	47.5%	52.5%
3,524	COSTILLA	1,823	547	1,186	90	639 D	30.0%	65.1%	31.6%	68.4%
5,823	CROWLEY	1,518	936	504	78	432 R	61.7%	33.2%	65.0%	35.0%
4,255	CUSTER	3,060	1,984	944	132	1,040 R	64.8%	30.8%	67.8%	32.2%
30,952	DELTA	16,761	10,970	4,916	875	6,054 R	65.4%	29.3%	69.1%	30.9%
600,158	DENVER	327,293	71,078	238,774	17,441	167,696 D	21.7%	73.0%	22.9%	77.1%
2,064	DOLORES	1,205	808	338	59	470 R	67.1%	28.0%	70.5%	29.5%
285,465	DOUGLAS	186,384	107,920	70,005	8,459	37,915 R	57.9%	37.6%	60.7%	39.3%
52,197	EAGLE	24,819	8,772	13,707	2,340	4,935 D	35.3%	55.2%	39.0%	61.0%
622,263	EL PASO	316,719	183,709	113,726	19,284	69,983 R	58.0%	35.9%	61.8%	38.2%
23,086	ELBERT	15,913	11,558	3,684	671	7,874 R	72.6%	23.2%	75.8%	24.2%
46,824	FREMONT	21,954	14,154	6,671	1,129	7,483 R	64.5%	30.4%	68.0%	32.0%
56,389	GARFIELD	26,201	12,596	12,039	1,566	557 R	48.1%	45.9%	51.1%	48.9%
5,441	GILPIN	3,581	1,503	1,729	349	226 D	42.0%	48.3%	46.5%	53.5%
14,843	GRAND	8,566	4,402	3,623	541	779 R	51.4%	42.3%	54.9%	45.1%
15,324	GUNNISON	9,392	3,216	5,517	659	2,301 D	34.2%	58.7%	36.8%	63.2%
843	HINSDALE	586	316	246	24	70 R	53.9%	42.0%	56.2%	43.8%
6,711	HUERFANO	3,789	1,694	1,942	153	248 D	44.7%	51.3%	46.6%	53.4%
1,394	JACKSON	854	583	235	36	348 R	68.3%	27.5%	71.3%	28.7%
534,543	JEFFERSON	321,371	139,237	163,172	18,962	23,935 D	43.3%	50.8%	46.0%	54.0%
1,398	KIOWA	838	621	196	21	425 R	74.1%	23.4%	76.0%	24.0%
8,270	KIT CARSON	3,631	2,607	894	130	1,713 R	71.8%	24.6%	74.5%	25.5%
51,334	LA PLATA	30,638	12,678	15,903	2,057	3,225 D	41.4%	51.9%	44.4%	55.6%
7,310	LAKE	3,145	1,174	1,704	267	530 D	37.3%	54.2%	40.8%	59.2%
299,630	LARIMER	193,866	86,101	95,789	11,976	9,688 D	44.4%	49.4%	47.3%	52.7%
15,507	LAS ANIMAS	6,774	3,174	3,305	295	131 D	46.9%	48.8%	49.0%	51.0%
5,467	LINCOLN	2,413	1,742	588	83	1,154 R	72.2%	24.4%	74.8%	25.2%
22,709	LOGAN	9,666	6,534	2,768	364	3,766 R	67.6%	28.6%	70.2%	29.8%
146,723	MESA	77,268	48,559	24,109	4,600	24,450 R	62.8%	31.2%	66.8%	33.2%

COLORADO

SENATOR 2016

2010 Census Population	County	Total Vote	Republican (Glenn)	Democratic (Bennet)	Other	Rep.-Dem. Plurality		Percentage Total Vote Rep.	Dem.	Major Vote Rep.	Dem.
712	MINERAL	658	326	301	31	25	R	49.5%	45.7%	52.0%	48.0%
13,795	MOFFAT	6,395	4,786	1,338	271	3,448	R	74.8%	20.9%	78.2%	21.8%
25,535	MONTEZUMA	12,599	7,484	4,305	810	3,179	R	59.4%	34.2%	63.5%	36.5%
41,276	MONTROSE	20,986	13,946	6,055	985	7,891	R	66.5%	28.9%	69.7%	30.3%
28,159	MORGAN	11,874	7,516	3,910	448	3,606	R	63.3%	32.9%	65.8%	34.2%
18,831	OTERO	8,533	4,561	3,651	321	910	R	53.5%	42.8%	55.5%	44.5%
4,436	OURAY	3,309	1,397	1,735	177	338	D	42.2%	52.4%	44.6%	55.4%
16,206	PARK	10,377	5,937	3,722	718	2,215	R	57.2%	35.9%	61.5%	38.5%
4,442	PHILLIPS	2,316	1,570	695	51	875	R	67.8%	30.0%	69.3%	30.7%
17,148	PITKIN	10,020	2,656	6,847	517	4,191	D	26.5%	68.3%	27.9%	72.1%
12,551	PROWERS	4,945	3,110	1,648	187	1,462	R	62.9%	33.3%	65.4%	34.6%
159,063	PUEBLO	77,819	33,051	40,475	4,293	7,424	D	42.5%	52.0%	45.0%	55.0%
6,666	RIO BLANCO	3,375	2,641	600	134	2,041	R	78.3%	17.8%	81.5%	18.5%
11,982	RIO GRANDE	5,573	2,974	2,372	227	602	R	53.4%	42.6%	55.6%	44.4%
23,509	ROUTT	13,780	5,265	7,793	722	2,528	D	38.2%	56.6%	40.3%	59.7%
6,108	SAGUACHE	2,849	1,042	1,570	237	528	D	36.6%	55.1%	39.9%	60.1%
699	SAN JUAN	498	193	279	26	86	D	38.8%	56.0%	40.9%	59.1%
7,359	SAN MIGUEL	4,308	1,055	2,951	302	1,896	D	24.5%	68.5%	26.3%	73.7%
2,379	SEDGWICK	1,340	863	426	51	437	R	64.4%	31.8%	67.0%	33.0%
27,994	SUMMIT	15,914	5,178	9,536	1,200	4,358	D	32.5%	59.9%	35.2%	64.8%
23,350	TELLER	14,330	9,547	4,064	719	5,483	R	66.6%	28.4%	70.1%	29.9%
4,814	WASHINGTON	2,702	2,092	527	83	1,565	R	77.4%	19.5%	79.9%	20.1%
252,825	WELD	134,383	74,843	52,263	7,277	22,580	R	55.7%	38.9%	58.9%	41.1%
10,043	YUMA	4,762	3,386	1,252	124	2,134	R	71.1%	26.3%	73.0%	27.0%
5,029,196	TOTAL	2,743,029	1,215,318	1,370,710	157,001	155,392	D	44.3%	50.0%	47.0%	53.0%

COLORADO

HOUSE OF REPRESENTATIVES

CD	Year	Total Vote	Republican Vote	Candidate	Democratic Vote	Candidate	Other Vote	Rep.-Dem. Plurality		Percentage Total Vote Rep.	Dem.	Major Vote Rep.	Dem.
1	2016	379,036	105,030	STOCKHAM , CHARLES "CASPER"	257,254	DEGETTE, DIANA L.*	16,752	152,224	D	27.7%	67.9%	29.0%	71.0%
1	2014	278,494	80,682	WALSH, MARTIN H.	183,281	DEGETTE, DIANA L.*	14,531	102,599	D	29.0%	65.8%	30.6%	69.4%
1	2012	348,228	93,217	STROUD, DANNY	237,579	DEGETTE, DIANA L.*	17,432	144,362	D	26.8%	68.2%	28.2%	71.8%
2	2016	457,312	170,001	MORSE, NICHOLAS	260,175	POLIS, JARED*	27,136	90,174	D	37.2%	56.9%	39.5%	60.5%
2	2014	345,945	149,645	LEING, GEORGE	196,300	POLIS, JARED*		46,655	D	43.3%	56.7%	43.3%	56.7%
2	2012	421,580	162,639	LUNDBERG, KEVIN	234,758	POLIS, JARED*	24,183	72,119	D	38.6%	55.7%	40.9%	59.1%
3	2016	374,037	204,220	TIPTON, SCOTT*	150,914	SCHWARTZ, GAIL	18,903	53,306	R	54.6%	40.3%	57.5%	42.5%
3	2014	281,141	163,011	TIPTON, SCOTT*	100,364	TAPIA, ABEL	17,766	62,647	R	58.0%	35.7%	61.9%	38.1%
3	2012	347,574	185,291	TIPTON, SCOTT*	142,920	PACE, SAL	19,363	42,371	R	53.3%	41.1%	56.5%	43.5%
4	2016	390,635	248,230	BUCK, KEN*	123,642	SEAY, BOB	18,763	124,588	R	63.5%	31.7%	66.8%	33.2%
4	2014	286,507	185,292	BUCK, KEN	83,727	MEYERS, VIC	17,488	101,565	R	64.7%	29.2%	68.9%	31.1%
4	2012	342,336	200,006	GARDNER, CORY*	125,800	SHAFFER, BRANDON	16,530	74,206	R	58.4%	36.7%	61.4%	38.6%
5	2016	362,114	225,445	LAMBORN, DOUG*	111,676	PLOWRIGHT, MISTY	24,993	113,769	R	62.3%	30.8%	66.9%	33.1%
5	2014	262,855	157,182	LAMBORN, DOUG*	105,673	HALTER JR., IRVING LESLIE "IRV"		51,509	R	59.8%	40.2%	59.8%	40.2%
5	2012	307,237	199,639	LAMBORN, DOUG*			107,598			65.0%		100%	
6	2016	376,417	191,626	COFFMAN, MIKE*	160,372	CARROLL, MORGAN	24,419	31,254	R	50.9%	42.6%	54.4%	45.6%
6	2014	276,440	143,467	COFFMAN, MIKE*	118,847	ROMANOFF, ANDREW	14,126	24,620	R	51.9%	43.0%	54.7%	45.3%
6	2012	342,914	163,938	COFFMAN, MIKE*	156,937	MIKLOSI, JOE	22,039	7,001	R	47.8%	45.8%	51.1%	48.9%

COLORADO

HOUSE OF REPRESENTATIVES

			Republican		Democratic		Other	Rep.-Dem.	Percentage			
									Total Vote		Major Vote	
CD	Year	Total Vote	Vote	Candidate	Vote	Candidate	Vote	Plurality	Rep.	Dem.	Rep.	Dem.
7	2016	362,010	144,066	ATHANASOPOULOS, GEORGE	199,758	PERLMUTTER, ED*	18,186	55,692 D	39.8%	55.2%	41.9%	58.1%
7	2014	269,143	120,918	YTTERBERG, DON	148,225	PERLMUTTER, ED*		27,307 D	44.9%	55.1%	44.9%	55.1%
7	2012	340,970	139,066	COORS, JOE	182,460	PERLMUTTER, ED*	19,444	43,394 D	40.8%	53.5%	43.3%	56.7%
TOTAL	2016	2,701,561	1,288,618		1,263,791		149,152	24,827 R	47.7%	46.8%	50.5%	49.5%
TOTAL	2014	2,000,525	1,000,197		936,417		63,911	63,780 R	50.0%	46.8%	51.6%	48.4%
TOTAL	2012	2,450,839	1,143,796		1,080,454		226,589	63,342 R	46.7%	44.1%	51.4%	48.6%

Note: An asterisk (*) denotes incumbent.

COLORADO

GENERAL AND PRIMARY ELECTIONS

2016 GENERAL ELECTIONS: OTHER VOTES

President Other vote was 144,121 Libertarian (Gary Johnson), 38,437 Green (Jill Stein), 28,917 Unaffiliated (Evan McMullin), 11,699 Constitution (Darrell Castle), 5,028 Veterans (Chris Keniston), 1,819 Unaffiliated (Mike Smith), 1,255 American Delta (Roque De La Fuente), 1,096 Independent American (Kyle Kopitke), 872 Independent People of Colorado (Joseph Maldonado), 862 American Solidarity (Michael Maturen), 751 Nutrition (Rod Silva), 749 Unaffiliated (Ryan Scott), 710 America's (Tom Hoefling), 531 Socialism and Liberation (Gloria La Riva), 452 Socialist Workers (Alyson Kennedy), 392 Kotlikoff for President (Laurence Kotlikoff), 382 Nonviolent Resistance/Pacifist (Bradford Lyttle), 337 Approval Voting (Frank Atwood), 271 Socialist Party USA (Emidio Soltysik), 185 Prohibition (Jim Hedges), 11 Write-in (David Perry), 6 Write-in (Corey Sterner), 4 Write-in (Brian Perry), 3 Write-in (Bruch Lohmiller), 2 Write-in (Cherunda Fox), 1 Write-in (Thomas Nieman).

Senate Other vote was 99,277 Libertarian (Lily Williams), 36,805 Green (Arnold Menconi), 9,336 Unity Party of Colorado (Bill Hammons), 8,361 Unaffiliated (Dan Chapin), 3,216 Unaffiliated (Paul Fiorino), 6 Write-in (Don Willoughby).

House Other vote was:

CD 1 16,752 Libertarian (Darrell Dinges)
CD 2 27,136 Libertarian (Richard Longstreth)
CD 3 18,903 Libertarian (Gaylon Kent)
CD 4 18,761 Libertarian (Bruce Griffith), 2 Write-in (Donald Howbert)
CD 5 24,872 Libertarian (Mike McRedmond), 121 Write-in (Curtis Imrie)
CD 6 18,778 Libertarian (Norm Olsen), 5,641 Green (Robert Worthey)
CD 7 18,186 Libertarian (Martin Buchanan)

2016 PRIMARY ELECTIONS: SUPPLEMENTARY INFORMATION

Primary March 1, 2016 (Presidential Caucus) June 28, 2016 (Congress) **Registration** (as of June 1, 2016 — includes 615,530 inactive registrants) 3,606,458

Republican	1,127,709
Democratic	1,131,853
Libertarian	33,583
Green	10,028
American Constitution	9,435
Unity	308
Unaffiliated	1,299,542

Primary Type Semi-open—Registered Democrats and Republicans could vote only in their party's primary. Any other registered voter could participate in either the Democratic or Republican primary but in the process had to declare his or her affiliation with that party.

COLORADO

GENERAL AND PRIMARY ELECTIONS

	REPUBLICAN PRIMARIES			DEMOCRATIC PRIMARIES		
Senator	Glenn, Darryl	131,125	37.7%	Bennet, Michael F.*	262,344	100.0%
	Graham, Jack	85,400	24.6%			
	Blaha, Robert	57,196	16.5%			
	Keyser, Jon	43,509	12.5%			
	Frazier, Ryan	30,241	8.7%			
	Eller, Jerry	68				
	TOTAL	347,539		TOTAL	262,344	
Congressional District 1	Stockham, Charles "Casper"	15,616	100.0%	DeGette, Diana L.*	55,925	86.4%
				Norris, Chuck	8,770	13.6%
	TOTAL	15,616		TOTAL	64,695	
Congressional District 2	Morse, Nicholas	36,417	100.0%	Polis, Jared*	43,660	97.0%
				Todd, Steven	1,357	3.0%
	TOTAL	36,417		TOTAL	45,017	
Congressional District 3	Tipton, Scott*	43,992	78.9%	Schwartz, Gail	35,823	100.0%
	Beinstein, Alexander	11,790	21.1%			
	TOTAL	55,782		TOTAL	35,823	
Congressional District 4	Buck, Ken*	58,848	100.0%	Seay, Bob	22,520	100.0%
	TOTAL	58,848		TOTAL	22,520	
Congressional District 5	Lamborn, Doug*	51,018	68.0%	Plowright, Misty	13,419	58.1%
	Vargas, Calandra	23,968	32.0%	Martinez, Donald E.	9,658	41.9%
	TOTAL	74,986		TOTAL	23,077	
Congressional District 6	Coffman, Mike*	41,288	100.0%	Carroll, Morgan	30,704	100.0%
	TOTAL	41,288		TOTAL	30,704	
Congressional District 7	Athanasopoulos, George	29,614	100.0%	Perlmutter, Ed*	35,196	100.0%
	TOTAL	29,614		TOTAL	35,196	

Note: An asterisk (*) denotes incumbent.

CONNECTICUT

Congressional districts first established for elections held in 2012

5 members

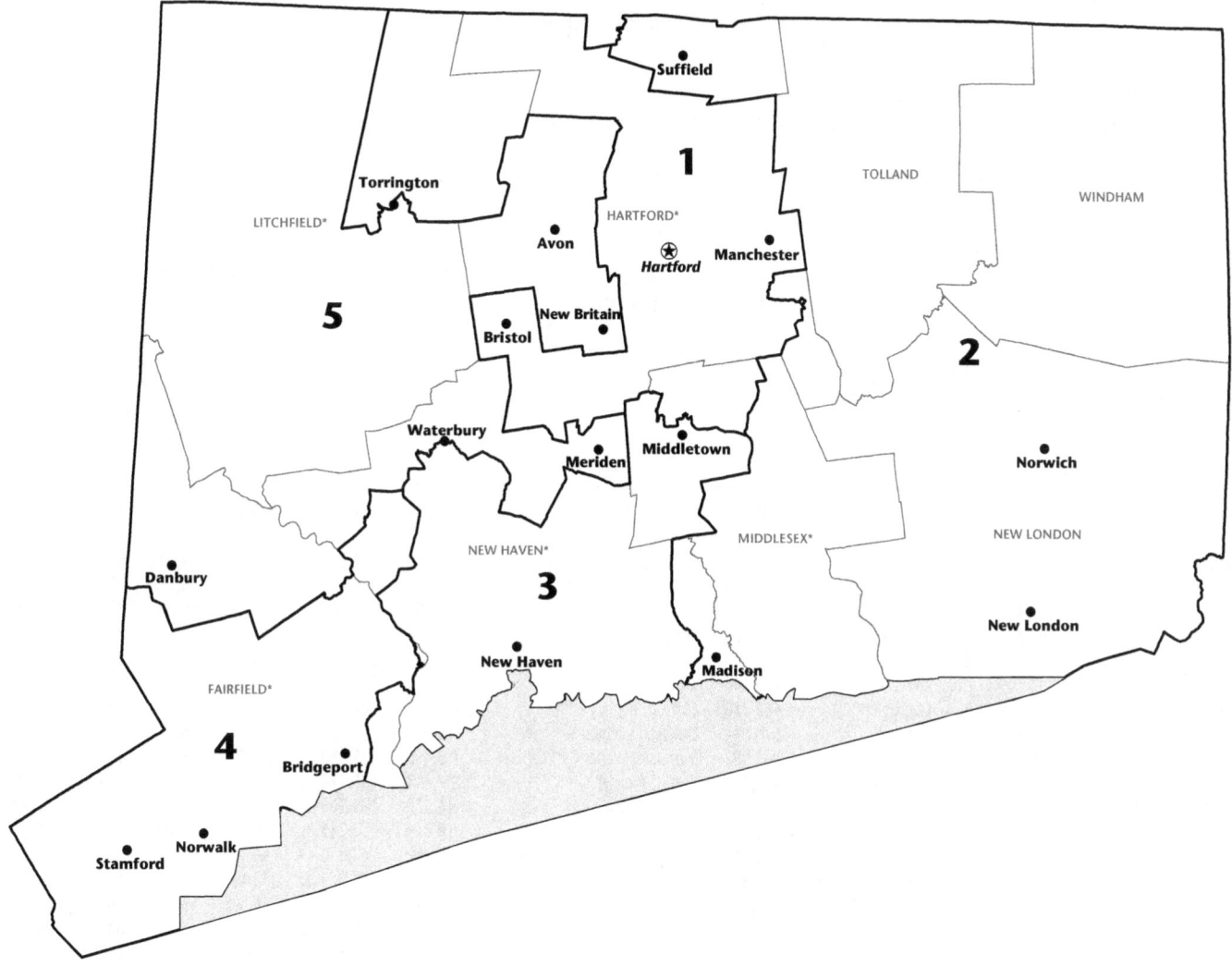

* Asterisk indicates a county whose boundaries include parts of two or more congressional districts.

CONNECTICUT

GOVERNOR

Dan Malloy (D). Re-elected 2014 to a four-year term. Previously elected 2010.

SENATORS (2 Democrats)

Richard Blumenthal (D). Re-elected 2016 to a six-year term. Previously elected 2010.

Christopher Murphy (D). Elected 2012 to a six-year term.

REPRESENTATIVES (5 Democrats)

1. John B. Larson (D)
2. Joe Courtney (D)
3. Rosa L. DeLauro (D)
4. Jim Himes (D)
5. Elizabeth Esty (D)

POSTWAR VOTE FOR PRESIDENT

Year	Total Vote	Republican		Democratic		Other Vote	Rep.-Dem. Plurality	Percentage			
								Total Vote		Major Vote	
		Vote	Candidate	Vote	Candidate			Rep.	Dem.	Rep.	Dem.
2016**	1,644,920	673,215	Trump, Donald J.	897,572	Clinton, Hillary Rodham	74,133	224,357 D	40.9%	54.6%	42.9%	57.1%
2012	1,558,960	634,892	Romney, W. Mitt	905,083	Obama, Barack H.*	18,985	270,191 D	40.7%	58.1%	41.2%	58.8%
2008	1,646,792	629,428	McCain, John S. III	997,772	Obama, Barack H.	19,592	368,344 D	38.2%	60.6%	38.7%	61.3%
2004	1,578,769	693,826	Bush, George W.*	857,488	Kerry, John F.	27,455	163,662 D	43.9%	54.3%	44.7%	55.3%
2000**	1,459,525	561,094	Bush, George W.	816,015	Gore, Albert Jr.	82,416	254,921 D	38.4%	55.9%	40.7%	59.3%
1996**	1,392,614	483,109	Dole, Robert "Bob"	735,740	Clinton, Bill*	173,765	252,631 D	34.7%	52.8%	39.6%	60.4%
1992**	1,616,332	578,313	Bush, George H.*	682,318	Clinton, Bill	355,701	104,005 D	35.8%	42.2%	45.9%	54.1%
1988	1,443,394	750,241	Bush, George H.	676,584	Dukakis, Michael S.	16,569	73,657 R	52.0%	46.9%	52.6%	47.4%
1984	1,466,900	890,877	Reagan, Ronald*	569,597	Mondale, Walter F.	6,426	321,280 R	60.7%	38.8%	61.0%	39.0%
1980**	1,406,285	677,210	Reagan, Ronald	541,732	Carter, Jimmy*	187,343	135,478 R	48.2%	38.5%	55.6%	44.4%
1976	1,381,526	719,261	Ford, Gerald R.*	647,895	Carter, Jimmy	14,370	71,366 R	52.1%	46.9%	52.6%	47.4%
1972	1,384,277	810,763	Nixon, Richard M.*	555,498	McGovern, George S.	18,016	255,265 R	58.6%	40.1%	59.3%	40.7%
1968**	1,256,232	556,721	Nixon, Richard M.	621,561	Humphrey, Hubert Horatio Jr.	77,950	64,840 D	44.3%	49.5%	47.2%	52.8%
1964	1,218,578	390,996	Goldwater, Barry M. Sr.	826,269	Johnson, Lyndon B.*	1,313	435,273 D	32.1%	67.8%	32.1%	67.9%
1960	1,222,883	565,813	Nixon, Richard M.	657,055	Kennedy, John F.	15	91,242 D	46.3%	53.7%	46.3%	53.7%
1956	1,117,121	711,837	Eisenhower, Dwight D.*	405,079	Stevenson, Adlai E. II	205	306,758 R	63.7%	36.3%	63.7%	36.3%
1952	1,096,911	611,012	Eisenhower, Dwight D.	481,649	Stevenson, Adlai E. II	4,250	129,363 R	55.7%	43.9%	55.9%	44.1%
1948	883,518	437,754	Dewey, Thomas E.	423,297	Truman, Harry S.*	22,467	14,457 R	49.5%	47.9%	50.8%	49.2%

Note: An asterisk (*) denotes incumbent. **In past elections, the other vote included: 2016 - 48,676 Libertarian (Gary Johnson); 2000 - 64,452 Green (Ralph Nader); 1996 - 139,523 Reform (Ross Perot); 1992 - 348,771 Independent (Perot); 1980 - 171,807 Independent (John Anderson); 1968 - 76,650 American Independent (George Wallace).

CONNECTICUT

POSTWAR VOTE FOR GOVERNOR

		Republican		Democratic		Other Vote	Rep.-Dem. Plurality	Percentage			
								Total Vote		Major Vote	
Year	Total Vote	Vote	Candidate	Vote	Candidate			Rep.	Dem.	Rep.	Dem.
2014	1,092,773	526,295	Foley, Tom C.	554,314	Malloy, Dan*	12,164	28,019 D	48.2%	50.7%	48.7%	51.3%
2010	1,145,799	560,874	Foley, Tom C.	567,278	Malloy, Dan	17,647	6,404 D	49.0%	49.5%	49.7%	50.3%
2006	1,123,466	710,048	Rell, M. Jodi*	398,220	DeStefano, John Jr.	15,198	311,828 R	63.2%	35.4%	64.1%	35.9%
2002	1,022,998	573,958	Rowland, John G.*	448,984	Curry, Bill	56	124,974 R	56.1%	43.9%	56.1%	43.9%
1998	999,537	628,707	Rowland, John G.*	354,187	Kennelly, Barbara B.	16,643	274,520 R	62.9%	35.4%	64.0%	36.0%
1994**	1,147,084	415,201	Rowland, John G.	375,133	Curry, Bill	356,750	40,068 R	36.2%	32.7%	52.5%	47.5%
1990**	1,142,101	427,840	Rowland, John G.	237,641	Morrison, Bruce A.	476,620	190,199 R#	37.5%	20.8%	64.3%	35.7%
1986	993,692	408,489	Belaga, Julie D.	575,638	O'Neill, William A.*	9,565	167,149 D	41.1%	57.9%	41.5%	58.5%
1982	1,083,876	497,773	Rome, Lewis B.	578,264	O'Neill, William A.*	7,839	80,491 D	45.9%	53.4%	46.3%	53.7%
1978	1,036,608	422,316	Sarasin, Ronald A.	613,109	Grasso, Ella T.*	1,183	190,793 D	40.7%	59.1%	40.8%	59.2%
1974	1,102,773	440,169	Steele, Robert H.	643,490	Grasso, Ella T.	19,114	203,321 D	39.9%	58.4%	40.6%	59.4%
1970	1,082,797	582,160	Meskill, Thomas J.	500,561	Daddario, Emilio Q.	76	81,599 R	53.8%	46.2%	53.8%	46.2%
1966	1,008,557	446,536	Gengras, E. Clayton	561,599	Dempsey, John N.*	422	115,063 D	44.3%	55.7%	44.3%	55.7%
1962	1,031,902	482,852	Alsop, John	549,027	Dempsey, John N.*	23	66,175 D	46.8%	53.2%	46.8%	53.2%
1958	974,509	360,644	Zeller, Fred R.	607,012	Ribicoff, Abraham A.*	6,853	246,368 D	37.0%	62.3%	37.3%	62.7%
1954	936,753	460,528	Lodge, John D.	463,643	Ribicoff, Abraham A.	12,582	3,115 D	49.2%	49.5%	49.8%	50.2%
1950**	878,735	436,418	Lodge, John D.	419,404	Bowles, Chester*	22,913	17,014 R	49.7%	47.7%	51.0%	49.0%
1948	875,620	429,071	Shannon, James C.*	431,746	Bowles, Chester	14,803	2,675 D	49.0%	49.3%	49.8%	50.2%
1946	683,831	371,852	McConaughy, James L.	276,335	Snow, Wilbert*	35,644	95,517 R	54.4%	40.4%	57.4%	42.6%

Note: An asterisk (*) denotes incumbent. A pound sign (#) in the plurality column indicates that the winner in 1990 did not run under the banner of either major party. **In past elections, the other vote included: 1994 - 216,585 A Connecticut Party (Elaine Strong Groark), 130,128 Independent (Tom Scott); 1990 - 460,576 A Connecticut Party (Lowell P. Weicker Jr.). Weicker won the 1990 election with 40.4 percent of the total vote and a plurality of 32,736 votes. The term of office for Connecticut's governor was increased from two to four years effective with the 1950 election.

POSTWAR VOTE FOR SENATOR

		Republican		Democratic		Other Vote	Rep.-Dem. Plurality	Percentage			
								Total Vote		Major Vote	
Year	Total Vote	Vote	Candidate	Vote	Candidate			Rep.	Dem.	Rep.	Dem.
2016	1,596,276	552,621	Carter, Dan	1,008,714	Blumenthal, Richard*	34,941	456,093 D	34.6%	63.2%	35.4%	64.6%
2012	1,511,764	651,089	McMahon, Linda E.	828,761	Murphy, Christopher S.	31,914	177,672 D	43.1%	54.8%	44.0%	56.0%
2010	1,153,115	498,341	McMahon, Linda E.	636,040	Blumenthal, Richard	18,734	137,699 D	43.2%	55.2%	43.9%	56.1%
2006**	1,134,780	109,198	Achlesinger, Alan	450,844	Lamont, Ned	574,738	341,646 D#	9.6%	39.7%	19.5%	80.5%
2004	1,424,726	457,749	Orchulli, Jack	945,347	Dodd, Christopher J.*	21,630	487,598 D	32.1%	66.4%	32.6%	67.4%
2000	1,311,261	448,077	Giordano, Phil	828,902	Lieberman, Joseph I.*	34,282	380,825 D	34.2%	63.2%	35.1%	64.9%
1998	964,457	312,177	Franks, Gary A.	628,306	Dodd, Christopher J.*	23,974	316,129 D	32.4%	65.1%	33.2%	66.8%
1994	1,079,767	334,833	Labriola, Jerry Jr.	723,842	Lieberman, Joseph I.*	21,092	389,009 D	31.0%	67.0%	31.6%	68.4%
1992	1,500,709	572,036	Johnson, Brook	882,569	Dodd, Christopher J.*	46,104	310,533 D	38.1%	58.8%	39.3%	60.7%
1988	1,383,526	678,454	Weicker, Lowell P. Jr.*	688,499	Lieberman, Joseph I.	16,573	10,045 D	49.0%	49.8%	49.6%	50.4%
1986	976,933	340,438	Eddy, Roger W.	632,695	Dodd, Christopher J.*	3,800	292,257 D	34.8%	64.8%	35.0%	65.0%
1982	1,083,613	545,987	Weicker, Lowell P. Jr.*	499,146	Moffett, Anthony T.	38,480	46,841 R	50.4%	46.1%	52.2%	47.8%
1980	1,356,075	581,884	Buckley, James L.	763,969	Dodd, Christopher J.	10,222	182,085 D	42.9%	56.3%	43.2%	56.8%
1976	1,361,666	785,683	Weicker, Lowell P. Jr.*	561,018	Schaffer, Gloria	14,965	224,665 R	57.7%	41.2%	58.3%	41.7%
1974	1,084,918	372,055	Brannen, James H.	690,820	Ribicoff, Abraham A.*	22,043	318,765 D	34.3%	63.7%	35.0%	65.0%
1970**	1,089,353	454,721	Weicker, Lowell P. Jr.	368,111	Duffey, Joseph D.	266,521	86,610 R	41.7%	33.8%	55.3%	44.7%
1968	1,206,537	551,455	May, Edwin H. Jr.	655,043	Ribicoff, Abraham A.*	39	103,588 D	45.7%	54.3%	45.7%	54.3%
1964	1,208,163	426,939	Lodge, Henry Cabot Jr.	781,008	Dodd, Thomas J.*	216	354,069 D	35.3%	64.6%	35.3%	64.7%
1962	1,029,301	501,694	Seely-Brown, Horace Jr.	527,522	Ribicoff, Abraham A.	85	25,828 D	48.7%	51.3%	48.7%	51.3%
1958	965,463	410,622	Purtell, William A.*	554,841	Dodd, Thomas J.		144,219 D	42.5%	57.5%	42.5%	57.5%
1956	1,113,819	610,829	Bush, Prescott S.*	479,460	Dodd, Thomas J.	23,530	131,369 R	54.8%	43.0%	56.0%	44.0%
1952	1,093,467	573,854	Purtell, William A.	485,066	Benton, William*	34,547	88,788 R	52.5%	44.4%	54.2%	45.8%
1952S**	1,093,268	559,465	Bush, Prescott S.	530,505	Ribicoff, Abraham A.	3,298	28,960 R	51.2%	48.5%	51.3%	48.7%
1950	877,827	409,053	Talbot, Joseph E.	453,646	McMahon, Brien*	15,128	44,593 D	46.6%	51.7%	47.4%	52.6%
1950S**	877,135	430,311	Bush, Prescott S.	431,413	Benton, William	15,411	1,102 D	49.1%	49.2%	49.9%	50.1%
1946	682,921	381,328	Baldwin, Raymond E.*	276,424	Tone, Joseph M.	25,169	104,904 R	55.8%	40.5%	58.0%	42.0%

Note: An asterisk (*) denotes incumbent. A pound sign (#) in the plurality column indicates that the winner in 2006 did not run under the banner of either major party. **In past elections, the other vote included: 2006 - 564,095 Connecticut For Lieberman (Joseph I. Lieberman); 1970 - 266,497 Independent (Thomas J. Dodd). Lieberman won the 2006 election with 49.7 percent of the vote and a plurality of 113,251 votes. One each of the 1950 and 1952 elections were for short terms to fill a vacancy.

CONNECTICUT

PRESIDENT 2016

2010 Census Population	County	Total Vote	Republican (Trump)	Democratic (Clinton)	Other	Rep.-Dem. Plurality		Percentage Total Vote Rep.	Dem.	Major Vote Rep.	Dem.
916,829	FAIRFIELD	420,486	160,077	243,852	16,557	83,775	D	38.1%	58.0%	39.6%	60.4%
894,014	HARTFORD	406,253	148,173	240,403	17,677	92,230	D	36.5%	59.2%	38.1%	61.9%
189,927	LITCHFIELD	97,271	53,051	39,775	4,445	13,276	R	54.5%	40.9%	57.2%	42.8%
165,676	MIDDLESEX	88,481	38,867	45,357	4,257	6,490	D	43.9%	51.3%	46.1%	53.9%
862,477	NEW HAVEN	378,533	159,048	205,609	13,876	46,561	D	42.0%	54.3%	43.6%	56.4%
274,055	NEW LONDON	123,300	54,058	62,278	6,964	8,220	D	43.8%	50.5%	46.5%	53.5%
152,691	TOLLAND	77,251	34,194	38,506	4,551	4,312	D	44.3%	49.8%	47.0%	53.0%
118,428	WINDHAM	50,729	25,747	21,792	3,190	3,955	R	50.8%	43.0%	54.2%	45.8%
	Votes Not Reported by County	2,616			2,616						
3,574,097	TOTAL	1,644,920	673,215	897,572	74,133	224,357	D	40.9%	54.6%	42.9%	57.1%

2010 Census Population	City/Town	Total Vote	Republican (Trump)	Democratic (Clinton)	Other	Rep.-Dem. Plurality		Percentage Total Vote Rep.	Dem.	Major Vote Rep.	Dem.
19,249	ANSONIA	7,474	3,621	3,532	321	89	R	48.4%	47.3%	50.6%	49.4%
20,486	BLOOMFIELD	11,627	1,683	9,637	307	7,954	D	14.5%	82.9%	14.9%	85.1%
28,026	BRANFORD	15,583	6,585	8,453	545	1,868	D	42.3%	54.2%	43.8%	56.2%
144,229	BRIDGEPORT	39,549	6,596	32,035	918	25,439	D	16.7%	81.0%	17.1%	82.9%
60,477	BRISTOL	26,421	12,752	12,499	1,170	253	R	48.3%	47.3%	50.5%	49.5%
29,261	CHESHIRE	15,404	7,105	7,572	727	467	D	46.1%	49.2%	48.4%	51.6%
80,893	DANBURY	28,838	11,626	16,084	1,128	4,458	D	40.3%	55.8%	42.0%	58.0%
20,732	DARIEN	11,233	4,625	5,942	666	1,317	D	41.2%	52.9%	43.8%	56.2%
51,252	EAST HARTFORD	19,032	5,213	13,180	639	7,967	D	27.4%	69.3%	28.3%	71.7%
29,257	EAST HAVEN	12,657	6,867	5,425	365	1,442	R	54.3%	42.9%	55.9%	44.1%
44,654	ENFIELD	18,933	9,233	8,646	1,054	587	R	48.8%	45.7%	51.6%	48.4%
59,404	FAIRFIELD	31,486	12,112	18,041	1,333	5,929	D	38.5%	57.3%	40.2%	59.8%
25,340	FARMINGTON	14,273	5,977	7,634	662	1,657	D	41.9%	53.5%	43.9%	56.1%
34,427	GLASTONBURY	19,580	7,533	11,074	973	3,541	D	38.5%	56.6%	40.5%	59.5%
61,171	GREENWICH	31,166	12,215	17,630	1,321	5,415	D	39.2%	56.6%	40.9%	59.1%
40,115	GROTON	15,323	5,936	8,453	934	2,517	D	38.7%	55.2%	41.3%	58.7%
22,375	GUILFORD	13,290	4,929	7,864	497	2,935	D	37.1%	59.2%	38.5%	61.5%
60,960	HAMDEN	27,649	7,790	18,962	897	11,172	D	28.2%	68.6%	29.1%	70.9%
124,775	HARTFORD	33,663	2,531	30,375	757	27,844	D	7.5%	90.2%	7.7%	92.3%
58,241	MANCHESTER	24,800	8,358	15,109	1,333	6,751	D	33.7%	60.9%	35.6%	64.4%
26,543	MANSFIELD	11,451	2,433	8,309	709	5,876	D	21.2%	72.6%	22.6%	77.4%
60,868	MERIDEN	22,431	8,660	12,788	983	4,128	D	38.6%	57.0%	40.4%	59.6%
47,648	MIDDLETOWN	21,209	7,126	12,959	1,124	5,833	D	33.6%	61.1%	35.5%	64.5%
52,759	MILFORD	28,121	13,383	13,598	1,140	215	D	47.6%	48.4%	49.6%	50.4%
31,862	NAUGATUCK	13,168	7,310	5,219	639	2,091	R	55.5%	39.6%	58.3%	41.7%
73,206	NEW BRITAIN	22,310	6,055	15,468	787	9,413	D	27.1%	69.3%	28.1%	71.9%
129,779	NEW HAVEN	41,584	4,540	35,933	1,111	31,393	D	10.9%	86.4%	11.2%	88.8%
27,620	NEW LONDON	8,683	1,924	6,305	454	4,381	D	22.2%	72.6%	23.4%	76.6%
28,142	NEW MILFORD	13,648	6,865	6,136	647	729	R	50.3%	45.0%	52.8%	47.2%
30,562	NEWINGTON	15,674	6,557	8,425	692	1,868	D	41.8%	53.8%	43.8%	56.2%
27,560	NEWTOWN	15,311	7,154	7,448	709	294	D	46.7%	48.6%	49.0%	51.0%
24,093	NORTH HAVEN	13,574	7,268	5,837	469	1,431	R	53.5%	43.0%	55.5%	44.5%
85,603	NORWALK	38,196	12,324	24,414	1,458	12,090	D	32.3%	63.9%	33.5%	66.5%
40,493	NORWICH	13,463	5,217	7,453	793	2,236	D	38.8%	55.4%	41.2%	58.8%
24,638	RIDGEFIELD	14,249	5,680	7,907	662	2,227	D	39.9%	55.5%	41.8%	58.2%
39,559	SHELTON	20,836	12,051	8,001	784	4,050	R	57.8%	38.4%	60.1%	39.9%
23,511	SIMSBURY	13,941	5,357	7,825	759	2,468	D	38.4%	56.1%	40.6%	59.4%
25,709	SOUTH WINDSOR	13,942	5,557	7,721	664	2,164	D	39.9%	55.4%	41.9%	58.1%
43,069	SOUTHINGTON	23,291	12,383	9,890	1,018	2,493	R	53.2%	42.5%	55.6%	44.4%
122,643	STAMFORD	52,181	16,222	34,148	1,811	17,926	D	31.1%	65.4%	32.2%	67.8%

CONNECTICUT

PRESIDENT 2016

2010 Census Population	City/Town	Total Vote	Republican (Trump)	Democratic (Clinton)	Other	Rep.-Dem. Plurality	Percentage			
							Total Vote		Major Vote	
							Rep.	Dem.	Rep.	Dem.
51,384	STRATFORD	25,201	10,534	13,729	938	3,195 D	41.8%	54.5%	43.4%	56.6%
36,383	TORRINGTON	15,115	8,673	5,713	729	2,960 R	57.4%	37.8%	60.3%	39.7%
36,018	TRUMBULL	19,771	9,753	9,299	719	454 R	49.3%	47.0%	51.2%	48.8%
29,179	VERNON	13,540	5,666	7,084	790	1,418 D	41.8%	52.3%	44.4%	55.6%
45,135	WALLINGFORD	22,608	10,940	10,651	1,017	289 R	48.4%	47.1%	50.7%	49.3%
110,366	WATERBURY	33,710	12,837	19,870	1,003	7,033 D	38.1%	58.9%	39.2%	60.8%
22,514	WATERTOWN	11,884	7,730	3,732	422	3,998 R	65.0%	31.4%	67.4%	32.6%
63,268	WEST HARTFORD	33,274	8,055	23,781	1,438	15,726 D	24.2%	71.5%	25.3%	74.7%
55,564	WEST HAVEN	20,960	7,774	12,477	709	4,703 D	37.1%	59.5%	38.4%	61.6%
26,391	WESTPORT	15,395	4,169	10,655	571	6,486 D	27.1%	69.2%	28.1%	71.9%
26,668	WETHERSFIELD	14,169	5,794	7,734	641	1,940 D	40.9%	54.6%	42.8%	57.2%
25,268	WINDHAM	8,393	2,564	5,375	454	2,811 D	30.5%	64.0%	32.3%	67.7%
29,044	WINDSOR	15,999	4,013	11,370	616	7,357 D	25.1%	71.1%	26.1%	73.9%

CONNECTICUT

SENATOR 2016

2010 Census Population	County	Total Vote	Republican (Carter)	Democratic (Blumenthal)	Other	Rep.-Dem. Plurality	Percentage			
							Total Vote		Major Vote	
							Rep.	Dem.	Rep.	Dem.
916,829	FAIRFIELD	406,694	148,935	249,887	7,872	100,952 D	36.6%	61.4%	37.3%	62.7%
894,014	HARTFORD	396,069	122,624	265,018	8,427	142,394 D	31.0%	66.9%	31.6%	68.4%
189,927	LITCHFIELD	95,527	43,519	49,872	2,136	6,353 D	45.6%	52.2%	46.6%	53.4%
165,676	MIDDLESEX	86,913	30,996	53,960	1,957	22,964 D	35.7%	62.1%	36.5%	63.5%
862,477	NEW HAVEN	367,045	119,774	239,991	7,280	120,217 D	32.6%	65.4%	33.3%	66.7%
274,055	NEW LONDON	118,840	40,238	75,188	3,414	34,950 D	33.9%	63.3%	34.9%	65.1%
152,691	TOLLAND	76,099	27,989	45,949	2,161	17,960 D	36.8%	60.4%	37.9%	62.1%
118,428	WINDHAM	49,051	18,546	28,849	1,656	10,303 D	37.8%	58.8%	39.1%	60.9%
	Votes Not Reported by County	38			38					
3,574,097	*TOTAL*	*1,596,276*	*552,621*	*1,008,714*	*34,941*	*456,093 D*	*34.6%*	*63.2%*	*35.4%*	*64.6%*

Note: Candidates in Connecticut can appear on the ballot line of more than one party. In the 2016 Senate election, Richard Blumenthal received the following votes per party: 920,766 (Democrat), 87,948 (Working Families).

2010 Census Population	City/Town	Total Vote	Republican (Carter)	Democratic (Blumenthal)	Other	Rep.-Dem. Plurality	Percentage			
							Total Vote		Major Vote	
							Rep.	Dem.	Rep.	Dem.
19,249	ANSONIA	9,301	2,414	6,737	150	4,323 D	26.0%	72.4%	26.4%	73.6%
20,486	BLOOMFIELD	11,389	1,566	9,637	186	8,071 D	13.8%	84.6%	14.0%	86.0%
28,026	BRANFORD	15,350	4,884	10,196	270	5,312 D	31.8%	66.4%	32.4%	67.6%
144,229	BRIDGEPORT	36,849	4,727	31,447	675	26,720 D	12.8%	85.3%	13.1%	86.9%
60,477	BRISTOL	25,700	9,185	15,929	586	6,744 D	35.7%	62.0%	36.6%	63.4%
29,261	CHESHIRE	15,299	6,252	8,783	264	2,531 D	40.9%	57.4%	41.6%	58.4%
80,893	DANBURY	26,753	9,536	16,576	641	7,040 D	35.6%	62.0%	36.5%	63.5%
20,732	DARIEN	11,175	6,092	4,926	157	1,166 R	54.5%	44.1%	55.3%	44.7%
51,252	EAST HARTFORD	18,274	3,784	14,097	393	10,313 D	20.7%	77.1%	21.2%	78.8%
29,257	EAST HAVEN	12,022	4,226	7,566	230	3,340 D	35.2%	62.9%	35.8%	64.2%

CONNECTICUT

SENATOR 2016

2010 Census Population	City/Town	Total Vote	Republican (Carter)	Democratic (Blumenthal)	Other	Rep.-Dem. Plurality	Percentage			
							Total Vote		Major Vote	
							Rep.	Dem.	Rep.	Dem.
44,654	ENFIELD	18,309	6,639	11,168	502	4,529 D	36.3%	61.0%	37.3%	62.7%
59,404	FAIRFIELD	31,078	12,133	18,448	497	6,315 D	39.0%	59.4%	39.7%	60.3%
25,340	FARMINGTON	14,163	5,627	8,264	272	2,637 D	39.7%	58.3%	40.5%	59.5%
34,427	GLASTONBURY	19,542	7,270	11,906	366	4,636 D	37.2%	60.9%	37.9%	62.1%
61,171	GREENWICH	31,098	13,649	16,933	516	3,284 D	43.9%	54.5%	44.6%	55.4%
40,115	GROTON	14,786	4,595	9,763	428	5,168 D	31.1%	66.0%	32.0%	68.0%
22,375	GUILFORD	13,115	4,168	8,720	227	4,552 D	31.8%	66.5%	32.3%	67.7%
60,960	HAMDEN	27,001	5,987	20,487	527	14,500 D	22.2%	75.9%	22.6%	77.4%
124,775	HARTFORD	31,121	2,089	28,462	570	26,373 D	6.7%	91.5%	6.8%	93.2%
58,241	MANCHESTER	24,088	6,822	16,603	663	9,781 D	28.3%	68.9%	29.1%	70.9%
26,543	MANSFIELD	11,087	2,292	8,391	404	6,099 D	20.7%	75.7%	21.5%	78.5%
60,868	MERIDEN	21,443	6,358	14,565	520	8,207 D	29.7%	67.9%	30.4%	69.6%
47,648	MIDDLETOWN	20,587	5,521	14,470	596	8,949 D	26.8%	70.3%	27.6%	72.4%
52,759	MILFORD	27,535	9,766	17,231	538	7,465 D	35.5%	62.6%	36.2%	63.8%
31,862	NAUGATUCK	12,722	5,367	6,996	359	1,629 D	42.2%	55.0%	43.4%	56.6%
73,206	NEW BRITAIN	20,785	4,232	16,004	549	11,772 D	20.4%	77.0%	20.9%	79.1%
129,779	NEW HAVEN	37,575	3,492	33,246	837	29,754 D	9.3%	88.5%	9.5%	90.5%
27,620	NEW LONDON	8,138	1,314	6,459	365	5,145 D	16.1%	79.4%	16.9%	83.1%
28,142	NEW MILFORD	13,535	5,690	7,531	314	1,841 D	42.0%	55.6%	43.0%	57.0%
30,562	NEWINGTON	15,374	5,011	10,057	306	5,046 D	32.6%	65.4%	33.3%	66.7%
27,560	NEWTOWN	15,033	6,442	8,304	287	1,862 D	42.9%	55.2%	43.7%	56.3%
24,093	NORTH HAVEN	13,264	5,049	8,004	211	2,955 D	38.1%	60.3%	38.7%	61.3%
85,603	NORWALK	36,554	10,597	25,168	789	14,571 D	29.0%	68.9%	29.6%	70.4%
40,493	NORWICH	11,927	3,535	7,967	425	4,432 D	29.6%	66.8%	30.7%	69.3%
24,638	RIDGEFIELD	14,146	6,271	7,644	231	1,373 D	44.3%	54.0%	45.1%	54.9%
39,559	SHELTON	20,260	9,126	10,821	313	1,695 D	45.0%	53.4%	45.8%	54.2%
23,511	SIMSBURY	13,858	5,428	8,122	308	2,694 D	39.2%	58.6%	40.1%	59.9%
25,709	SOUTH WINDSOR	13,913	4,023	9,609	281	5,586 D	28.9%	69.1%	29.5%	70.5%
43,069	SOUTHINGTON	22,932	9,660	12,878	394	3,218 D	42.1%	56.2%	42.9%	57.1%
122,643	STAMFORD	48,152	14,433	32,678	1,041	18,245 D	30.0%	67.9%	30.6%	69.4%
51,384	STRATFORD	24,455	7,080	16,560	815	9,480 D	29.0%	67.7%	29.9%	70.1%
36,383	TORRINGTON	14,705	6,607	7,730	368	1,123 D	44.9%	52.6%	46.1%	53.9%
36,018	TRUMBULL	19,533	8,263	10,987	283	2,724 D	42.3%	56.2%	42.9%	57.1%
29,179	VERNON	13,501	4,526	8,618	357	4,092 D	33.5%	63.8%	34.4%	65.6%
45,135	WALLINGFORD	22,154	7,993	13,685	476	5,692 D	36.1%	61.8%	36.9%	63.1%
110,366	WATERBURY	31,707	9,368	21,607	732	12,239 D	29.5%	68.1%	30.2%	69.8%
22,514	WATERTOWN	11,513	6,037	5,265	211	772 R	52.4%	45.7%	53.4%	46.6%
63,268	WEST HARTFORD	32,935	8,489	23,715	731	15,226 D	25.8%	72.0%	26.4%	73.6%
55,564	WEST HAVEN	20,021	4,950	14,630	441	9,680 D	24.7%	73.1%	25.3%	74.7%
26,391	WESTPORT	15,320	5,177	9,918	225	4,741 D	33.8%	64.7%	34.3%	65.7%
26,668	WETHERSFIELD	14,239	5,015	8,926	298	3,911 D	35.2%	62.7%	36.0%	64.0%
25,268	WINDHAM	7,851	1,658	5,925	268	4,267 D	21.1%	75.5%	21.9%	78.1%
29,044	WINDSOR	15,761	3,489	11,975	297	8,486 D	22.1%	76.0%	22.6%	77.4%

CONNECTICUT

HOUSE OF REPRESENTATIVES

CD	Year	Total Vote	Republican		Democratic		Other Vote	Rep.-Dem. Plurality	Percentage			
			Vote	Candidate	Vote	Candidate			Total Vote		Major Vote	
									Rep.	Dem.	Rep.	Dem.
1	2016	312,925	105,674	COREY, MATTHEW M.	200,686	LARSON, JOHN B.*	6,565	95,012 D	33.8%	64.1%	34.5%	65.5%
1	2014	217,881	78,609	COREY, MATTHEW M.	135,825	LARSON, JOHN B.*	3,447	57,216 D	36.1%	62.3%	36.7%	63.3%
1	2012	297,061	82,321	DECKER, JOHN HENRY	206,973	LARSON, JOHN B.*	7,767	124,652 D	27.7%	69.7%	28.5%	71.5%

CONNECTICUT

HOUSE OF REPRESENTATIVES

CD	Year	Total Vote	Republican		Democratic		Other Vote	Rep.-Dem. Plurality	Percentage			
			Vote	Candidate	Vote	Candidate			Total Vote		Major Vote	
									Rep.	Dem.	Rep.	Dem.
2	2016	330,257	111,149	NOVAK, DARIA	208,818	COURTNEY, JOE*	10,290	97,669 D	33.7%	63.2%	34.7%	65.3%
2	2014	227,936	80,837	HOPKINS-CAVANAGH, LORI	141,948	COURTNEY, JOE*	5,151	61,111 D	35.5%	62.3%	36.3%	63.7%
2	2012	299,960	88,103	FORMICA, PAUL	204,708	COURTNEY, JOE*	7,149	116,605 D	29.4%	68.2%	30.1%	69.9%
3	2016	309,379	95,786	CADENA, ANGEL LUIS JR.	213,572	DELAURO, ROSA L.*	21	117,786 D	31.0%	69.0%	31.0%	69.0%
3	2014	209,939	69,454	BROWN, JAMES E.	140,485	DELAURO, ROSA L.*		71,031 D	33.1%	66.9%	33.1%	66.9%
3	2012	291,301	73,726	WINSLEY, WAYNE	217,573	DELAURO, ROSA L.*	2	143,847 D	25.3%	74.7%	25.3%	74.7%
4	2016	313,540	125,724	SHABAN, JOHN	187,811	HIMES, JIM*	5	62,087 D	40.1%	59.9%	40.1%	59.9%
4	2014	198,800	91,922	DEBICELLA, DAN	106,873	HIMES, JIM*	5	14,951 D	46.2%	53.8%	46.2%	53.8%
4	2012	293,432	117,503	OBSITNIK, STEVE	175,929	HIMES, JIM*		58,426 D	40.0%	60.0%	40.0%	60.0%
5	2016	309,082	129,801	COPE, CLAY	179,252	ESTY, ELIZABETH*	29	49,451 D	42.0%	58.0%	42.0%	58.0%
5	2014	213,301	97,767	GREENBERG, MARK	113,564	ESTY, ELIZABETH*	1,970	15,797 D	45.8%	53.2%	46.3%	53.7%
5	2012	284,757	138,637	RORABACK, ANDREW	146,098	ESTY, ELIZABETH	22	7,461 D	48.7%	51.3%	48.7%	51.3%
TOTAL	2016	1,575,183	568,134		990,139		16,910	422,005 D	36.1%	62.9%	36.5%	63.5%
TOTAL	2014	1,067,857	418,589		638,695		10,573	220,106 D	39.2%	59.8%	39.6%	60.4%
TOTAL	2012	1,466,511	500,290		951,281		14,940	450,991 D	34.1%	64.9%	34.5%	65.5%

Note: An asterisk (*) denotes incumbent. Votes received by each Democratic and Republican candidate on the ballot lines of other parties are included in their totals above. All Democratic Party candidates except Jim Himes received Working Families Party votes in 2016. Republicans John Shaban (4th district) and Clay Cope (5th district) received Independent Party votes.

CONNECTICUT

GENERAL AND PRIMARY ELECTIONS

2016 GENERAL ELECTIONS: OTHER VOTES

President Other vote was 48,676 Libertarian (Gary Johnson), 22,841 Green (Jill Stein), 2,108 Write-in (Evan McMullin), 147 Write-in (Darrell Castle), 361 Write-in (Scattered Write-in)

Senate Other vote was 18,190 Libertarian (Richard Lion), 16,713 Green (Jeffery Russell), 26 Write-in (Andrew Rule), 12 Write-in (John Traceski)

House Other vote was:

CD 1 6,563 Green (S. DeRosa), 1 Write-in (Charles Jackson), 1 Write-in (Mark Stewart)
CD 2 5,332 Green (Jonathan Pelto), 4,949 Libertarian (Daniel Reale), 9 Write-in (Elizabeth Traceski)
CD 3 18 Write-in (Christopher Schaefer), 3 Write-in (Andrew Rule)
CD 4 5 Write-in (Carl Vassar)
CD 5 28 Write-in (John Pistone), 1 Write-in (Ann-Marie Adams)

2016 PRIMARY ELECTIONS: SUPPLEMENTARY INFORMATION

Primary	April 26, 2016 (President) August 9, 2016 (Congress)	**Registration** (as of October 27, 2015 — includes 206,276 inactive registrants)	2,129,379	Democratic 776,886 Republican 429,301 Other 22,493 Unaffiliated 900,699

Primary Type Closed—Only registered Democrats and Republicans could vote in their party's primary.

CONNECTICUT

GENERAL AND PRIMARY ELECTIONS

	REPUBLICAN PRIMARIES			DEMOCRATIC PRIMARIES		
President	Trump, Donald J.	123,523	57.9%	Clinton, Hillary Rodham	170,045	51.8%
	Kasich, John R.	60,522	28.3%	Sanders, Bernard	152,379	46.4%
	Cruz, Ted	24,987	11.7%	Uncommitted	4,871	1.5%
	Uncommitted	2,728	1.3%	De La Fuente, Roque "Rocky"	960	0.3%
	Carson, Ben	1,733	0.8%			
	TOTAL	*213,493*		*TOTAL*	*328,255*	
Senator	Carter, Dan	Unopposed		Blumenthal, Richard*	Unopposed	
Congressional District 1	Corey, Matthew M.	Unopposed		Larson, John B.*	Unopposed	
Congressional District 2	Novak, Daria	Unopposed		Courtney, Joe*	Unopposed	
Congressional District 3	Cadena, Angel Luis Jr.	Unopposed		DeLauro, Rosa L.*	Unopposed	
Congressional District 4	Shaban, John	Unopposed		Himes, Jim*	Unopposed	
Congressional District 5	Cope, Clay	Unopposed		Esty, Elizabeth*	Unopposed	

Note: An asterisk (*) denotes incumbent.

DELAWARE

One member At Large

DELAWARE

GOVERNOR
John C. Carney Jr. (D). Elected 2016 to a four-year term.

SENATORS (2 Democrats)
Thomas R. Carper (D). Re-elected 2012 to a six-year term. Previously elected 2006, 2000.

Christopher A. Coons (D). Re-elected 2014 to a six-year term. Previously elected 2010 in a special election.

REPRESENTATIVE (1 Democrat)
At Large. Lisa Blunt Rochester (D)

POSTWAR VOTE FOR PRESIDENT

| Year | Total Vote | Republican | | Democratic | | Other Vote | Rep.-Dem. Plurality | Percentage | | | |
| | | Vote | Candidate | Vote | Candidate | | | Total Vote | | Major Vote | |
								Rep.	Dem.	Rep.	Dem.
2016**	443,814	185,127	Trump, Donald J.	235,603	Clinton, Hillary Rodham	23,084	50,476 D	41.7%	53.1%	44.0%	56.0%
2012	413,921	165,484	Romney, W. Mitt	242,584	Obama, Barack H.*	5,853	77,100 D	40.0%	58.6%	40.6%	59.4%
2008	412,412	152,374	McCain, John S. III	255,459	Obama, Barack H.	4,579	103,085 D	36.9%	61.9%	37.4%	62.6%
2004	375,190	171,660	Bush, George W.*	200,152	Kerry, John F.	3,378	28,492 D	45.8%	53.3%	46.2%	53.8%
2000**	327,622	137,288	Bush, George W.	180,068	Gore, Albert Jr.	10,266	42,780 D	41.9%	55.0%	43.3%	56.7%
1996**	271,084	99,062	Dole, Robert "Bob"	140,355	Clinton, Bill*	31,667	41,293 D	36.5%	51.8%	41.4%	58.6%
1992**	289,735	102,313	Bush, George H.*	126,054	Clinton, Bill	61,368	23,741 D	35.3%	43.5%	44.8%	55.2%
1988	249,891	139,639	Bush, George H.	108,647	Dukakis, Michael S.	1,605	30,992 R	55.9%	43.5%	56.2%	43.8%
1984	254,572	152,190	Reagan, Ronald*	101,656	Mondale, Walter F.	726	50,534 R	59.8%	39.9%	60.0%	40.0%
1980**	235,900	111,252	Reagan, Ronald	105,754	Carter, Jimmy*	18,894	5,498 R	47.2%	44.8%	51.3%	48.7%
1976	235,834	109,831	Ford, Gerald R.*	122,596	Carter, Jimmy	3,407	12,765 D	46.6%	52.0%	47.3%	52.7%
1972	235,516	140,357	Nixon, Richard M.*	92,283	McGovern, George S.	2,876	48,074 R	59.6%	39.2%	60.3%	39.7%
1968**	214,367	96,714	Nixon, Richard M.	89,194	Humphrey, Hubert Horatio Jr.	28,459	7,520 R	45.1%	41.6%	52.0%	48.0%
1964	201,320	78,078	Goldwater, Barry M. Sr.	122,704	Johnson, Lyndon B.*	538	44,626 D	38.8%	60.9%	38.9%	61.1%
1960	196,683	96,373	Nixon, Richard M.	99,590	Kennedy, John F.	720	3,217 D	49.0%	50.6%	49.2%	50.8%
1956	177,988	98,057	Eisenhower, Dwight D.*	79,421	Stevenson, Adlai E. II	510	18,636 R	55.1%	44.6%	55.3%	44.7%
1952	174,025	90,059	Eisenhower, Dwight D.	83,315	Stevenson, Adlai E. II	651	6,744 R	51.8%	47.9%	51.9%	48.1%
1948	139,073	69,588	Dewey, Thomas E.	67,813	Truman, Harry S.*	1,672	1,775 R	50.0%	48.8%	50.6%	49.4%

Note: An asterisk (*) denotes incumbent. **In past elections, the other vote included: 2016 - 14,757 Libertarian (Gary Johnson); 2000 - 8,307 Green (Ralph Nader); 1996 - 28,719 Reform (Ross Perot); 1992 - 59,213 Independent (Perot); 1980 - 16,288 Independent (John Anderson); 1968 - 28,459 American Independent (George Wallace).

DELAWARE

POSTWAR VOTE FOR GOVERNOR

| Year | Total Vote | Republican | | Democratic | | Other Vote | Rep.-Dem. Plurality | Percentage | | | |
| | | Vote | Candidate | Vote | Candidate | | | Total Vote | | Major Vote | |
								Rep.	Dem.	Rep.	Dem.
2016	425,812	166,852	Bonini, Colin	248,404	Carney, John C. Jr.	10,556	81,552 D	39.2%	58.3%	40.2%	59.8%
2012	398,033	113,793	Cragg, Jeffrey	275,993	Markell, Jack*	8,247	162,200 D	28.6%	69.3%	29.2%	70.8%
2008	395,204	126,662	Lee, William Swain	266,861	Markell, Jack	1,681	140,199 D	32.0%	67.5%	32.2%	67.8%
2004	365,008	167,115	Lee, William Swain	185,687	Minner, Ruth Ann*	12,206	18,572 D	45.8%	50.9%	47.4%	52.6%
2000	323,688	128,603	Burris, John M.	191,695	Minner, Ruth Ann	3,390	63,092 D	39.7%	59.2%	40.2%	59.8%
1996	271,122	82,654	Rzewnicki, Janet C.	188,300	Carper, Thomas R.*	168	105,646 D	30.5%	69.5%	30.5%	69.5%
1992	277,058	90,725	Scott, B. Gary	179,365	Carper, Thomas R.	6,968	88,640 D	32.7%	64.7%	33.6%	66.4%
1988	239,969	169,733	Castle, Michael N.*	70,236	Kreshtoll, Jacob		99,497 R	70.7%	29.3%	70.7%	29.3%
1984	243,565	135,250	Castle, Michael N.	108,315	Quillen, William T.		26,935 R	55.5%	44.5%	55.5%	44.5%
1980	225,081	159,004	du Pont, Pierre S. IV*	64,217	Gordy, William J.	1,860	94,787 R	70.6%	28.5%	71.2%	28.8%
1976	229,563	130,531	du Pont, Pierre S. IV	97,480	Tribbitt, Sherman W.*	1,552	33,051 R	56.9%	42.5%	57.2%	42.8%
1972	228,722	109,583	Peterson, Russell W.*	117,274	Tribbitt, Sherman W.	1,865	7,691 D	47.9%	51.3%	48.3%	51.7%
1968	206,834	104,474	Peterson, Russell W.	102,360	Terry, Charles L. Jr.*		2,114 R	50.5%	49.5%	50.5%	49.5%
1964	200,171	97,374	Buckson, David P.	102,797	Terry, Charles L. Jr.		5,423 D	48.6%	51.4%	48.6%	51.4%
1960	194,835	94,043	Rollins, John W.	100,792	Carvel, Elbert N.		6,749 D	48.3%	51.7%	48.3%	51.7%
1956	177,012	91,965	Boggs, James Caleb*	85,047	McConnell, J. H. Tyler		6,918 R	52.0%	48.0%	52.0%	48.0%
1952	170,749	88,977	Boggs, James Caleb	81,772	Carvel, Elbert N.*		7,205 R	52.1%	47.9%	52.1%	47.9%
1948	140,335	64,996	George, Hyland P.	75,339	Carvel, Elbert N.		10,343 D	46.3%	53.7%	46.3%	53.7%

Note: An asterisk (*) denotes incumbent.

POSTWAR VOTE FOR SENATOR

| Year | Total Vote | Republican | | Democratic | | Other Vote | Rep.-Dem. Plurality | Percentage | | | |
| | | Vote | Candidate | Vote | Candidate | | | Total Vote | | Major Vote | |
								Rep.	Dem.	Rep.	Dem.
2014	234,038	98,823	Wade, Kevin	130,655	Coons, Christopher A.*	4,560	31,832 D	42.2%	55.8%	43.1%	56.9%
2012	399,607	115,700	Wade, Kevin	265,415	Carper, Thomas R.*	18,492	149,715 D	29.0%	66.4%	30.4%	69.6%
2010S**	307,402	123,053	O'Donnell, Christine	174,012	Coons, Christopher A.	10,337	50,959 D	40.0%	56.6%	41.4%	58.6%
2008	398,134	140,595	O'Donnell, Christine	257,539	Biden, Joseph R. Jr.*		116,944 D	35.3%	64.7%	35.3%	64.7%
2006	254,099	69,734	Ting, Jan	170,567	Carper, Thomas R.*	13,798	100,833 D	27.4%	67.1%	29.0%	71.0%
2002	232,314	94,793	Clatworthy, Raymond J.	135,253	Biden, Joseph R. Jr.*	2,268	40,460 D	40.8%	58.2%	41.2%	58.8%
2000	327,017	142,891	Roth, William V.*	181,566	Carper, Thomas R.	2,560	38,675 D	43.7%	55.5%	44.0%	56.0%
1996	275,591	105,088	Clatworthy, Raymond J.	165,465	Biden, Joseph R. Jr.*	5,038	60,377 D	38.1%	60.0%	38.8%	61.2%
1994	199,029	111,088	Roth, William V.*	84,554	Oberly, Charles M.	3,387	26,534 R	55.8%	42.5%	56.8%	43.2%
1990	180,152	64,554	Brady, M. Jane	112,918	Biden, Joseph R. Jr.*	2,680	48,364 D	35.8%	62.7%	36.4%	63.6%
1988	243,493	151,115	Roth, William V.*	92,378	Woo, S. B.		58,737 R	62.1%	37.9%	62.1%	37.9%
1984	245,932	98,101	Burris, John M.	147,831	Biden, Joseph R. Jr.*		49,730 D	39.9%	60.1%	39.9%	60.1%
1982	190,960	105,357	Roth, William V.*	84,413	Levinson, David N.	1,190	20,944 R	55.2%	44.2%	55.5%	44.5%
1978	162,072	66,479	Baxter, James H.	93,930	Biden, Joseph R. Jr.*	1,663	27,451 D	41.0%	58.0%	41.4%	58.6%
1976	224,859	125,502	Roth, William V.*	98,055	Maloney, Thomas C.	1,302	27,447 R	55.8%	43.6%	56.1%	43.9%
1972	229,828	112,844	Boggs, James Caleb*	116,006	Biden, Joseph R. Jr.	978	3,162 D	49.1%	50.5%	49.3%	50.7%
1970	161,439	94,979	Roth, William V.	64,740	Zimmerman, Jacob	1,720	30,239 R	58.8%	40.1%	59.5%	40.5%
1966	164,531	97,268	Boggs, James Caleb*	67,263	Tunnell, James M. Jr.		30,005 R	59.1%	40.9%	59.1%	40.9%
1964	200,703	103,782	Williams, John J.*	96,850	Carvel, Elbert N.	71	6,932 R	51.7%	48.3%	51.7%	48.3%
1960	194,964	98,874	Boggs, James Caleb	96,090	Frear, J. Allen Jr.*		2,784 R	50.7%	49.3%	50.7%	49.3%
1958	154,432	82,280	Williams, John J.*	72,152	Carvel, Elbert N.		10,128 R	53.3%	46.7%	53.3%	46.7%
1954	144,900	62,389	Warburton, Herbert B.	82,511	Frear, J. Allen Jr.*		20,122 D	43.1%	56.9%	43.1%	56.9%
1952	170,705	93,020	Williams, John J.*	77,685	du Pont Bayard, Alexis I.		15,335 R	54.5%	45.5%	54.5%	45.5%
1948	141,362	68,246	Buck, Clayton Douglass*	71,888	Frear, J. Allen Jr.	1,228	3,642 D	48.3%	50.9%	48.7%	51.3%
1946	113,513	62,603	Williams, John J.	50,910	Tunnell, James M.*		11,693 R	55.2%	44.8%	55.2%	44.8%

Note: An asterisk (*) denotes incumbent. **The 2010 election was for a short term to fill a vacancy.

DELAWARE

PRESIDENT 2016 2017

2010 Census Population	County	Total Vote	Republican (Trump)	Democratic (Clinton)	Other	Rep.-Dem. Plurality	Total Vote Rep.	Dem.	Major Vote Rep.	Dem.
162,310	KENT	74,729	36,991	33,351	4,387	3,640 R	49.5%	44.6%	52.6%	47.4%
538,479	NEW CASTLE	262,979	85,525	162,919	14,535	77,394 D	32.5%	62.0%	34.4%	65.6%
197,145	SUSSEX	106,106	62,611	39,333	4,162	23,278 R	59.0%	37.1%	61.4%	38.6%
897,934	TOTAL	443,814	185,127	235,603	23,084	50,476 D	41.7%	53.1%	44.0%	56.0%

DELAWARE

GOVERNOR 2016

2010 Census Population	County	Total Vote	Republican (Bonini)	Democratic (Carney)	Other	Rep.-Dem. Plurality	Total Vote Rep.	Dem.	Major Vote Rep.	Dem.
162,310	KENT	72,378	34,777	35,955	1,646	1,178 D	48.0%	49.7%	49.2%	50.8%
538,479	NEW CASTLE	250,691	77,839	165,973	6,879	88,134 D	31.0%	66.2%	31.9%	68.1%
197,145	SUSSEX	102,743	54,236	46,476	2,031	7,760 R	52.8%	45.2%	53.9%	46.1%
897,934	TOTAL	425,812	166,852	248,404	10,556	81,552 D	39.2%	58.3%	40.2%	59.8%

DELAWARE

HOUSE OF REPRESENTATIVES

CD	Year	Total Vote	Rep. Vote	Republican Candidate	Dem. Vote	Democratic Candidate	Other Vote	Rep.-Dem. Plurality	Total Vote Rep.	Dem.	Major Vote Rep.	Dem.
At Large	2016	420,682	172,301	REIGLE, HANS	233,554	ROCHESTER, LISA BLUNT	14,827	61,253 D	41.0%	55.5%	42.5%	57.5%
At Large	2014	231,617	85,146	IZZO, ROSE	137,251	CARNEY, JOHN C. JR.*	9,220	52,105 D	36.8%	59.3%	38.3%	61.7%
At Large	2012	388,059	129,757	KOVACH, THOMAS H.	249,933	CARNEY, JOHN C. JR.*	8,369	120,176 D	33.4%	64.4%	34.2%	65.8%
At Large	2010	305,636	125,442	URQUHART, GLEN	173,543	CARNEY, JOHN C. JR.	6,651	48,101 D	41.0%	56.8%	42.0%	58.0%
At Large	2008	385,457	235,437	CASTLE, MICHAEL N.*	146,434	HARTLEY-NAGLE, KAREN	3,586	89,003 R	61.1%	38.0%	61.7%	38.3%
At Large	2006	251,694	143,897	CASTLE, MICHAEL N.*	97,565	SPIVACK, DENNIS	10,232	46,332 R	57.2%	38.8%	59.6%	40.4%
At Large	2004	356,045	245,978	CASTLE, MICHAEL N.*	105,716	DONNELLY, PAUL	4,351	140,262 R	69.1%	29.7%	69.9%	30.1%
At Large	2002	228,405	164,605	CASTLE, MICHAEL N.*	61,011	MILLER, MICHAEL C.	2,789	103,594 R	72.1%	26.7%	73.0%	27.0%
At Large	2000	313,171	211,797	CASTLE, MICHAEL N.*	96,488	MILLER, MICHAEL C.	4,886	115,309 R	67.6%	30.8%	68.7%	31.3%
At Large	1998	180,527	119,811	CASTLE, MICHAEL N.*	57,446	WILLIAMS, DENNIS E.	3,270	62,365 R	66.4%	31.8%	67.6%	32.4%
At Large	1996	266,836	185,576	CASTLE, MICHAEL N.*	73,253	WILLIAMS, DENNIS E.	8,007	112,323 R	69.5%	27.5%	71.7%	28.3%
At Large	1994	195,037	137,960	CASTLE, MICHAEL N.*	51,803	DESANTIS, CAROL ANN	5,274	86,157 R	70.7%	26.6%	72.7%	27.3%
At Large	1992	276,157	153,037	CASTLE, MICHAEL N.	117,426	WOO, S. B.	5,694	35,611 R	55.4%	42.5%	56.6%	43.4%
At Large	1990	177,432	58,037	WILLIAMS, RALPH O.	116,274	CARPER, THOMAS R.*	3,121	58,237 D	32.7%	65.5%	33.3%	66.7%
At Large	1988	234,517	76,179	KRAPF, JAMES P.	158,338	CARPER, THOMAS R.*		82,159 D	32.5%	67.5%	32.5%	67.5%
At Large	1986	160,757	53,767	NEUBERGER, THOMAS S.	106,351	CARPER, THOMAS R.*	639	52,584 D	33.4%	66.2%	33.6%	66.4%
At Large	1984	243,014	100,650	DUPONT, ELISE	142,070	CARPER, THOMAS R.*	294	41,420 D	41.4%	58.5%	41.5%	58.5%
At Large	1982	188,064	87,153	EVANS, THOMAS B.*	98,533	CARPER, THOMAS R.	2,378	11,380 D	46.3%	52.4%	46.9%	53.1%
At Large	1980	216,629	133,842	EVANS, THOMAS B.*	81,227	MAXWELL, ROBERT L.	1,560	52,615 R	61.8%	37.5%	62.2%	37.8%
At Large	1978	157,566	91,689	EVANS, THOMAS B.*	64,863	HINDES, GARY E.	1,014	26,826 R	58.2%	41.2%	58.6%	41.4%
At Large	1976	214,799	110,677	EVANS, THOMAS B.	102,431	SHIPLEY, SAMUEL L.	1,691	8,246 R	51.5%	47.7%	51.9%	48.1%
At Large	1974	160,328	93,826	DU PONT, PIERRE S. IV*	63,490	SOLES, JAMES	3,012	30,336 R	58.5%	39.6%	59.6%	40.4%
At Large	1972	225,851	141,237	DU PONT, PIERRE S. IV*	83,230	HANDLOFF, NORMA	1,384	58,007 R	62.5%	36.9%	62.9%	37.1%
At Large	1970	160,313	86,125	DU PONT, PIERRE S. IV	71,429	DANIELLO, JOHN D.	2,759	14,696 R	53.7%	44.6%	54.7%	45.3%
At Large	1968	200,820	117,827	ROTH, WILLIAM V.*	82,993	MCDOWELL, HARRIS B. JR.		34,834 R	58.7%	41.3%	58.7%	41.3%
At Large	1966	163,093	90,961	ROTH, WILLIAM V.	72,132	MCDOWELL, HARRIS B. JR.*		18,829 R	55.8%	44.2%	55.8%	44.2%
At Large	1964	198,691	86,254	SNOWDEN, JAMES H.	112,361	MCDOWELL, HARRIS B. JR.*	76	26,107 D	43.4%	56.6%	43.4%	56.6%
At Large	1962	153,356	71,934	WILLIAMS, WILMER F.	81,166	MCDOWELL, HARRIS B. JR.*	256	9,232 D	46.9%	52.9%	47.0%	53.0%
At Large	1960	194,564	96,337	MCKINSTRY, JAMES T.	98,227	MCDOWELL, HARRIS B. JR.*		1,890 D	49.5%	50.5%	49.5%	50.5%
At Large	1958	152,896	76,099	HASKELL, HARRY G. JR.*	76,797	MCDOWELL, HARRIS B. JR.*		698 D	49.8%	50.2%	49.8%	50.2%

DELAWARE

HOUSE OF REPRESENTATIVES

| | | | Republican | | Democratic | | Other Vote | Rep.-Dem. Plurality | Percentage | | | |
| | | | | | | | | | Total Vote | | Major Vote | |
CD	Year	Total Vote	Vote	Candidate	Vote	Candidate			Rep.	Dem.	Rep.	Dem.
At Large	1956	176,182	91,538	HASKELL, HARRY G. JR.	84,644	MCDOWELL, HARRIS B. JR.*		6,894 R	52.0%	48.0%	52.0%	48.0%
At Large	1954	144,236	65,035	MARTIN, LILLIAN I.	79,201	MCDOWELL, HARRIS B. JR.		14,166 D	45.1%	54.9%	45.1%	54.9%
At Large	1952	170,015	88,285	WARBURTON, H. B.	81,730	SCANNELL, JOSEPH S.		6,555 R	51.9%	48.1%	51.9%	48.1%
At Large	1950	129,404	73,313	BOGGS, JAMES CALEB*	56,091	WINCHESTER, H. M.		17,222 R	56.7%	43.3%	56.7%	43.3%
At Large	1948	140,535	71,127	BOGGS, JAMES CALEB*	68,909	MCGUIGAN, J. CARL	499	2,218 R	50.6%	49.0%	50.8%	49.2%
At Large	1946	112,621	63,516	BOGGS, JAMES CALEB	49,105	TRAYNOR, PHILIP A.*		14,411 R	56.4%	43.6%	56.4%	43.6%

Note: An asterisk (*) denotes incumbent.

DELAWARE

GENERAL AND PRIMARY ELECTIONS

2016 GENERAL ELECTIONS: OTHER VOTES

President Other vote was 14,757 Libertarian (Gary Johnson), 6,103 Green (Jill Stein), 1,444 Write-in (Scattered Write-in), 706 Write-in (Evan McMullin), 74 Write-in (Darrell Castle)

Governor Other vote was 5,951 Green (Andrew Groff), 4,577 Libertarian (Sean Goward), 28 Write-in (Scattered Write-in)

House Other vote was:

At Large 8,326 Green (Mark Perri), 6,436 Libertarian (Scott Gesty), 42 Write-in (Scattered Write-in), 14 Write-in (Scott Walker), 4 Write-in (Robert Nelson Franz III), 4 Write-in (Campbell Smith), 1 Write-in (Rachelle Lee Linney)

2016 PRIMARY ELECTIONS: SUPPLEMENTARY INFORMATION

Primary	April 26, 2016 (President) September 13, 2016 (Congress)	**Registration** (as of April 1, 2016)	690,625	Democratic Republican Independent Libertarian Green Other Nonpartisan Unaffiliated	305,191 193,688 5,626 1,604 838 3,635 789 158,031	

Primary Type Closed—Only registered Democrats and Republicans could vote in their party's primary.

DELAWARE

GENERAL AND PRIMARY ELECTIONS

	REPUBLICAN PRIMARIES			DEMOCRATIC PRIMARIES		
President	Trump, Donald J.	42,472	60.8%	Clinton, Hillary Rodham	55,954	59.8%
	Kasich, John R.	14,225	20.4%	Sanders, Bernard	36,662	39.2%
	Cruz, Ted	11,110	15.9%	De La Fuente, Roque "Rocky"	1,024	1.1%
	Carson, Ben	885	1.3%			
	Rubio, Marco	622	0.9%			
	Bush, Jeb	578	0.8%			
	TOTAL	69,892		TOTAL	93,640	
Governor	Bonini, Colin	21,150	69.9%	Carney, John C. Jr.	Unopposed	
	Lafferty, Lacey	9,115	30.1%			
	TOTAL	30,265				
Congressional At Large	Reigle, Hans	Unopposed		Rochester, Lisa Blunt	27,920	43.8%
				Townsend, Bryan	15,847	24.8%
				Barney, Sean	12,891	20.2%
				Miller, Michael C. Sr.	3,500	5.5%
				Walker, Scott	3,156	4.9%
				Weir, Elias J.	480	0.8%
				TOTAL	63,794	

Note: An asterisk (*) denotes incumbent.

FLORIDA

Congressional districts first established for elections held in 2016

27 members

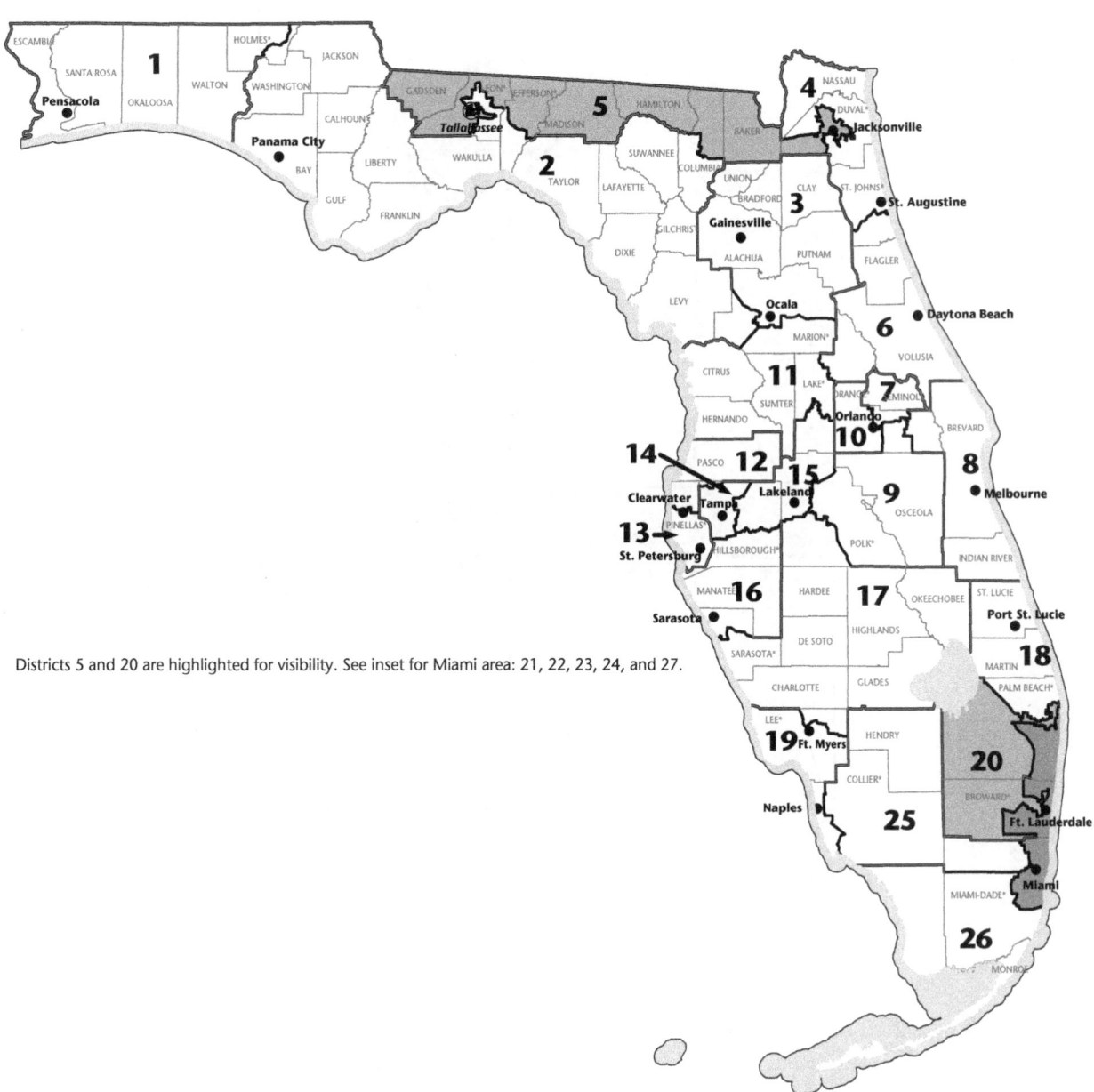

Districts 5 and 20 are highlighted for visibility. See inset for Miami area: 21, 22, 23, 24, and 27.

* Asterisk indicates a county whose boundaries include parts of two or more congressional districts.

FLORIDA

Greater Miami, Fort Lauderdale Areas

OSCEOLA **9**

8 INDIAN RIVER

ST. LUCIE

OKEECHOBEE

HIGHLANDS

Port St. Lucie

17

MARTIN

GLADES

18

PALM BEACH*

West Palm Beach

20

21

HENDRY

Boca Raton

Coral Springs **22**

BROWARD*

Pompano Beach

Sunrise

Fort Lauderdale

Plantation

COLLIER*

23

Pembroke Pines

Hollywood

24

25

Hialeah

Miami Beach

Miami

MIAMI-DADE*

27

MONROE

26

* Asterisk indicates a county whose boundaries include parts of two or more conressional districts.

FLORIDA

GOVERNOR

Rick Scott (R). Elected 2014 to a four-year term. Previously elected 2010.

SENATORS (1 Republican, 1 Democrat)

Bill Nelson (D). Re-elected 2012 to a six-year term. Previously elected 2006, 2000.

Marco Rubio (R). Re-elected 2016 to a six-year term. Previously elected 2010.

REPRESENTATIVES (16 Republicans, 11 Democrats)

1. Matt Gaetz (R)
2. Neal Dunn (R)
3. Ted Yoho (R)
4. John Rutherford (R)
5. Al Lawson (D)
6. Ron DeSantis (R)
7. Stephanie Murphy (D)
8. Bill Posey (R)
9. Darren Soto (D)
10. Val B. Demings (D)
11. Daniel A. Webster (R)
12. Gus Michael Bilirakis (R)
13. Charlie Crist (D)
14. Kathy Castor (D)
15. Dennis A. Ross (R)
16. Vern Buchanan (R)
17. Tom Rooney (R)
18. Brian Mast (R)
19. Francis Rooney (R)
20. Alcee L. Hastings (D)
21. Lois Frankel (D)
22. Ted Deutch (D)
23. Debbie Wasserman-Schultz (D)
24. Frederica S. Wilson (D)
25. Mario Diaz-Balart (R)
26. Carlos Curbelo (R)
27. Ileana Ros-Lehtinen (R)

POSTWAR VOTE FOR PRESIDENT

| Year | Total Vote | Republican | | Democratic | | Other Vote | Rep.-Dem. Plurality | Percentage | | | |
| | | Vote | Candidate | Vote | Candidate | | | Total Vote | | Major Vote | |
								Rep.	Dem.	Rep.	Dem.
2016**	9,420,039	4,617,886	Trump, Donald J.	4,504,975	Clinton, Hillary Rodham	297,178	112,911 R	49.0%	47.8%	50.6%	49.4%
2012	8,474,179	4,163,447	Romney, W. Mitt	4,237,756	Obama, Barack H.*	72,976	74,309 D	49.1%	50.0%	49.6%	50.4%
2008	8,390,744	4,045,624	McCain, John S. III	4,282,074	Obama, Barack H.	63,046	236,450 D	48.2%	51.0%	48.6%	51.4%
2004	7,609,810	3,964,522	Bush, George W.*	3,583,544	Kerry, John F.	61,744	380,978 R	52.1%	47.1%	52.5%	47.5%
2000**	5,963,110	2,912,790	Bush, George W.	2,912,253	Gore, Albert Jr.	138,067	537 R	48.8%	48.8%	50.0%	50.0%
1996**	5,303,794	2,244,536	Dole, Robert "Bob"	2,546,870	Clinton, Bill*	512,388	302,334 D	42.3%	48.0%	46.8%	53.2%
1992**	5,314,392	2,173,310	Bush, George H.*	2,072,698	Clinton, Bill	1,068,384	100,612 R	40.9%	39.0%	51.2%	48.8%
1988	4,302,313	2,618,885	Bush, George H.	1,656,701	Dukakis, Michael S.	26,727	962,184 R	60.9%	38.5%	61.3%	38.7%
1984	4,180,051	2,730,350	Reagan, Ronald*	1,448,816	Mondale, Walter F.	885	1,281,534 R	65.3%	34.7%	65.3%	34.7%
1980**	3,686,930	2,046,951	Reagan, Ronald	1,419,475	Carter, Jimmy*	220,504	627,476 R	55.5%	38.5%	59.1%	40.9%
1976	3,150,631	1,469,531	Ford, Gerald R.*	1,636,000	Carter, Jimmy	45,100	166,469 D	46.6%	51.9%	47.3%	52.7%
1972	2,583,283	1,857,759	Nixon, Richard M.*	718,117	McGovern, George S.	7,407	1,139,642 R	71.9%	27.8%	72.1%	27.9%
1968**	2,187,805	886,804	Nixon, Richard M.	676,794	Humphrey, Hubert Horatio Jr.	624,207	210,010 R	40.5%	30.9%	56.7%	43.3%
1964	1,854,481	905,941	Goldwater, Barry M. Sr.	948,540	Johnson, Lyndon B.*		42,599 D	48.9%	51.1%	48.9%	51.1%
1960	1,544,176	795,476	Nixon, Richard M.	748,700	Kennedy, John F.		46,776 R	51.5%	48.5%	51.5%	48.5%
1956	1,125,762	643,849	Eisenhower, Dwight D.*	480,371	Stevenson, Adlai E. II	1,542	163,478 R	57.2%	42.7%	57.3%	42.7%
1952	989,337	544,036	Eisenhower, Dwight D.	444,950	Stevenson, Adlai E. II	351	99,086 R	55.0%	45.0%	55.0%	45.0%
1948**	577,643	194,280	Dewey, Thomas E.	281,988	Truman, Harry S.*	101,375	87,708 D	33.6%	48.8%	40.8%	59.2%

Note: An asterisk (*) denotes incumbent. **In past elections, the other vote included: 2016 - 207,043 (Gary Johnson); 2000 - 97,488 Green (Ralph Nader); 1996 - 483,870 Reform (Ross Perot); 1992 - 1,053,067 Independent (Perot); 1980 - 189,692 Independent (John Anderson); 1968 - 624,207 American Independent (George Wallace); 1948 - 89,755 States' Rights (Strom Thurmond).

FLORIDA

POSTWAR VOTE FOR GOVERNOR

Year	Total Vote	Republican Vote	Republican Candidate	Democratic Vote	Democratic Candidate	Other Vote	Rep.-Dem. Plurality	Total Vote Rep.	Total Vote Dem.	Major Vote Rep.	Major Vote Dem.
2014	5,951,561	2,865,343	Scott, Rick*	2,801,198	Crist, Charlie	285,020	64,145 R	48.1%	47.1%	50.6%	49.4%
2010	5,359,735	2,619,335	Scott, Rick	2,557,785	Sink, Alex	182,615	61,550 R	48.9%	47.7%	50.6%	49.4%
2006	4,829,270	2,519,845	Crist, Charlie	2,178,289	Davis, Jim	131,136	341,556 R	52.2%	45.1%	53.6%	46.4%
2002	5,100,581	2,856,845	Bush, Jeb*	2,201,427	McBride, Bill	42,309	655,418 R	56.0%	43.2%	56.5%	43.5%
1998	3,964,441	2,191,105	Bush, Jeb	1,773,054	MacKay, Kenneth H. "Buddy"*	282	418,051 R	55.3%	44.7%	55.3%	44.7%
1994	4,206,659	2,071,068	Bush, Jeb	2,135,008	Chiles, Lawton*	583	63,940 D	49.2%	50.8%	49.2%	50.8%
1990	3,530,871	1,535,068	Martinez, Bob*	1,995,206	Chiles, Lawton	597	460,138 D	43.5%	56.5%	43.5%	56.5%
1986	3,386,171	1,847,525	Martinez, Bob	1,538,620	Pajcic, Steve	26	308,905 R	54.6%	45.4%	54.6%	45.4%
1982	2,688,566	949,013	Bafalis, L. A.	1,739,553	Graham, Bob*		790,540 D	35.3%	64.7%	35.3%	64.7%
1978	2,530,468	1,123,888	Eckerd, Jack M.	1,406,580	Graham, Bob		282,692 D	44.4%	55.6%	44.4%	55.6%
1974	1,828,392	709,438	Thomas, Jerry	1,118,954	Askew, Reubin*		409,516 D	38.8%	61.2%	38.8%	61.2%
1970	1,730,813	746,243	Kirk, Claude R. Jr.*	984,305	Askew, Reubin	265	238,062 D	43.1%	56.9%	43.1%	56.9%
1966	1,489,661	821,190	Kirk, Claude R. Jr.	668,233	High, Robert King	238	152,957 R	55.1%	44.9%	55.1%	44.9%
1964**	1,663,481	686,297	Holley, Charles R.	933,554	Burns, Haydon	43,630	247,257 D	41.3%	56.1%	42.4%	57.6%
1960	1,419,343	569,936	Petersen, George C.	849,407	Bryant, Farris		279,471 D	40.2%	59.8%	40.2%	59.8%
1956	1,014,733	266,980	Washburn, William A. Jr.	747,753	Collins, Leroy*		480,773 D	26.3%	73.7%	26.3%	73.7%
1954S**	357,783	69,852	Watson, J. Tom	287,769	Collins, Leroy	162	217,917 D	19.5%	80.4%	19.5%	80.5%
1952	834,518	210,009	Swan, Harry S.	624,463	McCarty, Daniel T.	46	414,454 D	25.2%	74.8%	25.2%	74.8%
1948	457,638	76,153	Acker, Bert L.	381,459	Warren, Fuller	26	305,306 D	16.6%	83.4%	16.6%	83.4%

Note: An asterisk (*) denotes incumbent. **The 1964 election was for a two-year term to permit shifting the vote for governor to non-presidential years. The 1954 election was for a short term to fill a vacancy.

POSTWAR VOTE FOR SENATOR

Year	Total Vote	Republican Vote	Republican Candidate	Democratic Vote	Democratic Candidate	Other Vote	Rep.-Dem. Plurality	Total Vote Rep.	Total Vote Dem.	Major Vote Rep.	Major Vote Dem.
2016	9,301,820	4,835,191	Rubio, Marco*	4,122,088	Murphy, Patrick	344,541	713,103 R	52.0%	44.3%	54.0%	46.0%
2012	8,189,946	3,458,267	Mack, Connie IV	4,523,451	Nelson, Bill*	208,228	1,065,184 D	42.2%	55.2%	43.3%	56.7%
2010**	5,411,106	2,645,743	Rubio, Marco	1,092,936	Meek, Kendrick B.	1,672,427	1,552,807 R	48.9%	20.2%	70.8%	29.2%
2006	4,793,534	1,826,127	Harris, Katherine	2,890,548	Nelson, C. W. "Bill"*	76,859	1,064,421 D	38.1%	60.3%	38.7%	61.3%
2004	7,429,894	3,672,864	Martinez, Mel	3,590,201	Castor, Betty	166,829	82,663 R	49.4%	48.3%	50.6%	49.4%
2000	5,856,731	2,705,348	McCollum, Bill	2,989,487	Nelson, C. W. "Bill"	161,896	284,139 D	46.2%	51.0%	47.5%	52.5%
1998	3,900,162	1,463,755	Crist, Charlie	2,436,407	Graham, Bob*		972,652 D	37.5%	62.5%	37.5%	62.5%
1994	4,106,176	2,894,726	Mack, Connie III*	1,210,412	Rodham, Hugh E.	1,038	1,684,314 R	70.5%	29.5%	70.5%	29.5%
1992	4,962,290	1,716,505	Grant, Bill	3,245,565	Graham, Bob*	220	1,529,060 D	34.6%	65.4%	34.6%	65.4%
1988	4,068,209	2,051,071	Mack, Connie III	2,016,553	MacKay, Buddy	585	34,518 R	50.4%	49.6%	50.4%	49.6%
1986	3,429,996	1,552,376	Hawkins, Paula*	1,877,543	Graham, Bob	77	325,167 D	45.3%	54.7%	45.3%	54.7%
1982	2,653,419	1,015,330	Poole, Van B.	1,637,667	Chiles, Lawton*	422	622,337 D	38.3%	61.7%	38.3%	61.7%
1980	3,528,028	1,822,460	Hawkins, Paula	1,705,409	Gunter, Bill	159	117,051 R	51.7%	48.3%	51.7%	48.3%
1976	2,857,534	1,057,886	Grady, John	1,799,518	Chiles, Lawton*	130	741,632 D	37.0%	63.0%	37.0%	63.0%
1974**	1,800,539	736,674	Eckerd, Jack M.	781,031	Stone, Richard	282,834	44,357 D	40.9%	43.4%	48.5%	51.5%
1970	1,675,378	772,817	Cramer, William C.	902,438	Chiles, Lawton	123	129,621 D	46.1%	53.9%	46.1%	53.9%
1968	2,024,136	1,131,499	Gurney, Edward J.	892,637	Collins, Leroy		238,862 R	55.9%	44.1%	55.9%	44.1%
1964	1,560,337	562,212	Kirk, Claude R. Jr.	997,585	Holland, Spessard L.*	540	435,373 D	36.0%	63.9%	36.0%	64.0%
1962	939,207	281,381	Rupert, Emerson H.	657,633	Smathers, George A.*	193	376,252 D	30.0%	70.0%	30.0%	70.0%
1958	542,069	155,956	Hyzer, Leland	386,113	Holland, Spessard L.*		230,157 D	28.8%	71.2%	28.8%	71.2%
1956	655,418			655,418	Smathers, George A.*		655,418 D		100.0%		100.0%
1952	617,800			616,665	Holland, Spessard L.*	1,135	616,665 D		99.8%		100.0%
1950	313,487	74,228	Booth, John P.	238,987	Smathers, George A.	272	164,759 D	23.7%	76.2%	23.7%	76.3%
1946	198,645	42,413	Schad, J. Harry	156,232	Holland, Spessard L.		113,819 D	21.4%	78.6%	21.4%	78.6%

Note: An asterisk (*) denotes incumbent. **In past elections, the other vote included: 2010 - 1,607,549 Independent (Charlie Crist, who finished second); 1974 - 282,659 American (John Grady). The Republican Party did not run a candidate in the 1952 and 1956 Senate elections.

FLORIDA

PRESIDENT 2016

2010 Census Population	County	Total Vote	Republican (Trump)	Democratic (Clinton)	Other	Rep.-Dem. Plurality	Percentage Total Vote Rep.	Dem.	Major Vote Rep.	Dem.
247,336	ALACHUA	128,571	46,834	75,820	5,917	28,986 D	36.4%	59.0%	38.2%	61.8%
27,115	BAKER	12,637	10,294	2,112	231	8,182 R	81.5%	16.7%	83.0%	17.0%
168,852	BAY	87,450	62,194	21,797	3,459	40,397 R	71.1%	24.9%	74.0%	26.0%
28,520	BRADFORD	12,098	8,913	2,924	261	5,989 R	73.7%	24.2%	75.3%	24.7%
543,376	BREVARD	314,752	181,848	119,679	13,225	62,169 R	57.8%	38.0%	60.3%	39.7%
1,748,066	BROWARD	831,951	260,951	553,320	17,680	292,369 D	31.4%	66.5%	32.0%	68.0%
14,625	CALHOUN	6,081	4,655	1,241	185	3,414 R	76.5%	20.4%	79.0%	21.0%
159,978	CHARLOTTE	96,374	60,218	33,445	2,711	26,773 R	62.5%	34.7%	64.3%	35.7%
141,236	CITRUS	79,700	54,456	22,789	2,455	31,667 R	68.3%	28.6%	70.5%	29.5%
190,865	CLAY	106,483	74,963	27,822	3,698	47,141 R	70.4%	26.1%	72.9%	27.1%
321,520	COLLIER	170,789	105,423	61,085	4,281	44,338 R	61.7%	35.8%	63.3%	36.7%
67,531	COLUMBIA	28,707	20,368	7,601	738	12,767 R	71.0%	26.5%	72.8%	27.2%
34,862	DESOTO	10,818	6,778	3,781	259	2,997 R	62.7%	35.0%	64.2%	35.8%
16,422	DIXIE	7,202	5,822	1,270	110	4,552 R	80.8%	17.6%	82.1%	17.9%
864,263	DUVAL	432,695	211,672	205,704	15,319	5,968 R	48.9%	47.5%	50.7%	49.3%
297,619	ESCAMBIA	152,469	88,808	57,461	6,200	31,347 R	58.2%	37.7%	60.7%	39.3%
95,696	FLAGLER	57,503	33,850	22,026	1,627	11,824 R	58.9%	38.3%	60.6%	39.4%
11,549	FRANKLIN	6,015	4,125	1,744	146	2,381 R	68.6%	29.0%	70.3%	29.7%
46,389	GADSDEN	22,113	6,728	15,020	365	8,292 D	30.4%	67.9%	30.9%	69.1%
16,939	GILCHRIST	8,420	6,740	1,458	222	5,282 R	80.0%	17.3%	82.2%	17.8%
12,884	GLADES	4,353	2,996	1,271	86	1,725 R	68.8%	29.2%	70.2%	29.8%
15,863	GULF	7,293	5,329	1,720	244	3,609 R	73.1%	23.6%	75.6%	24.4%
14,799	HAMILTON	5,460	3,443	1,904	113	1,539 R	63.1%	34.9%	64.4%	35.6%
27,731	HARDEE	7,583	5,242	2,149	192	3,093 R	69.1%	28.3%	70.9%	29.1%
39,140	HENDRY	11,115	6,195	4,615	305	1,580 R	55.7%	41.5%	57.3%	42.7%
172,778	HERNANDO	93,796	58,970	31,795	3,031	27,175 R	62.9%	33.9%	65.0%	35.0%
98,786	HIGHLANDS	45,686	29,565	14,937	1,184	14,628 R	64.7%	32.7%	66.4%	33.6%
1,229,226	HILLSBOROUGH	597,660	266,870	307,896	22,894	41,026 D	44.7%	51.5%	46.4%	53.6%
19,927	HOLMES	8,514	7,483	853	178	6,630 R	87.9%	10.0%	89.8%	10.2%
138,028	INDIAN RIVER	80,009	48,620	29,043	2,346	19,577 R	60.8%	36.3%	62.6%	37.4%
49,746	JACKSON	21,041	14,257	6,397	387	7,860 R	67.8%	30.4%	69.0%	31.0%
14,761	JEFFERSON	7,645	3,930	3,541	174	389 R	51.4%	46.3%	52.6%	47.4%
8,870	LAFAYETTE	3,392	2,809	518	65	2,291 R	82.8%	15.3%	84.4%	15.6%
297,052	LAKE	170,462	102,188	62,838	5,436	39,350 R	59.9%	36.9%	61.9%	38.1%
618,754	LEE	326,420	191,551	124,908	9,961	66,643 R	58.7%	38.3%	60.5%	39.5%
275,487	LEON	152,132	53,821	92,068	6,243	38,247 D	35.4%	60.5%	36.9%	63.1%
40,801	LEVY	19,395	13,775	5,101	519	8,674 R	71.0%	26.3%	73.0%	27.0%
8,365	LIBERTY	3,296	2,543	651	102	1,892 R	77.2%	19.8%	79.6%	20.4%
19,224	MADISON	8,505	4,851	3,526	128	1,325 R	57.0%	41.5%	57.9%	42.1%
322,833	MANATEE	178,958	101,944	71,224	5,790	30,720 R	57.0%	39.8%	58.9%	41.1%
331,298	MARION	174,700	107,833	62,041	4,826	45,792 R	61.7%	35.5%	63.5%	36.5%
146,318	MARTIN	85,792	53,204	30,185	2,403	23,019 R	62.0%	35.2%	63.8%	36.2%
2,496,435	MIAMI-DADE	980,204	333,999	624,146	22,059	290,147 D	34.1%	63.7%	34.9%	65.1%
73,090	MONROE	42,478	21,904	18,971	1,603	2,933 R	51.6%	44.7%	53.6%	46.4%
73,314	NASSAU	46,607	34,266	10,869	1,472	23,397 R	73.5%	23.3%	75.9%	24.1%
180,822	OKALOOSA	100,855	71,893	23,780	5,182	48,113 R	71.3%	23.6%	75.1%	24.9%
39,996	OKEECHOBEE	13,653	9,356	3,959	338	5,397 R	68.5%	29.0%	70.3%	29.7%
1,145,956	ORANGE	546,275	195,216	329,894	21,165	134,678 D	35.7%	60.4%	37.2%	62.8%
268,685	OSCEOLA	140,206	50,301	85,458	4,447	35,157 D	35.9%	61.0%	37.1%	62.9%
1,320,134	PALM BEACH	662,332	272,402	374,673	15,257	102,271 D	41.1%	56.6%	42.1%	57.9%
464,697	PASCO	241,139	142,101	90,142	8,896	51,959 R	58.9%	37.4%	61.2%	38.8%
916,542	PINELLAS	492,403	239,201	233,701	19,501	5,500 R	48.6%	47.5%	50.6%	49.4%
602,095	POLK	284,314	157,430	117,433	9,451	39,997 R	55.4%	41.3%	57.3%	42.7%
74,364	PUTNAM	33,117	22,138	10,094	885	12,044 R	66.8%	30.5%	68.7%	31.3%
151,372	SANTA ROSA	87,745	65,339	18,464	3,942	46,875 R	74.5%	21.0%	78.0%	22.0%
379,448	SARASOTA	229,063	124,438	97,870	6,755	26,568 R	54.3%	42.7%	56.0%	44.0%
422,718	SEMINOLE	224,896	109,443	105,914	9,539	3,529 R	48.7%	47.1%	50.8%	49.2%
190,039	ST. JOHNS	136,514	88,684	43,099	4,731	45,585 R	65.0%	31.6%	67.3%	32.7%
277,789	ST. LUCIE	140,847	70,289	66,881	3,677	3,408 R	49.9%	47.5%	51.2%	48.8%
93,420	SUMTER	76,665	52,730	22,638	1,297	30,092 R	68.8%	29.5%	70.0%	30.0%

FLORIDA

PRESIDENT 2016

2010 Census Population	County	Total Vote	Republican (Trump)	Democratic (Clinton)	Other	Rep.-Dem. Plurality	Percentage Total Vote Rep.	Dem.	Major Vote Rep.	Dem.
41,551	SUWANNEE	18,694	14,287	3,964	443	10,323 R	76.4%	21.2%	78.3%	21.7%
22,570	TAYLOR	9,290	6,930	2,152	208	4,778 R	74.6%	23.2%	76.3%	23.7%
15,535	UNION	5,694	4,568	1,014	112	3,554 R	80.2%	17.8%	81.8%	18.2%
494,593	VOLUSIA	260,869	143,007	109,091	8,771	33,916 R	54.8%	41.8%	56.7%	43.3%
30,776	WAKULLA	15,351	10,512	4,348	491	6,164 R	68.5%	28.3%	70.7%	29.3%
55,043	WALTON	33,637	25,756	6,876	1,005	18,880 R	76.6%	20.4%	78.9%	21.1%
24,896	WASHINGTON	11,156	8,637	2,264	255	6,373 R	77.4%	20.3%	79.2%	20.8%
18,801,310	TOTAL	9,420,039	4,617,886	4,504,975	297,178	112,911 R	49.0%	47.8%	50.6%	49.4%

FLORIDA

SENATOR 2016

2010 Census Population	County	Total Vote	Republican (Rubio)	Democratic (Murphy)	Other	Rep.-Dem. Plurality	Percentage Total Vote Rep.	Dem.	Major Vote Rep.	Dem.
247,336	ALACHUA	127,334	54,203	69,399	3,732	15,196 D	42.6%	54.5%	43.9%	56.1%
27,115	BAKER	12,458	9,901	2,135	422	7,766 R	79.5%	17.1%	82.3%	17.7%
168,852	BAY	86,713	62,906	19,971	3,836	42,935 R	72.5%	23.0%	75.9%	24.1%
28,520	BRADFORD	11,867	8,720	2,694	453	6,026 R	73.5%	22.7%	76.4%	23.6%
543,376	BREVARD	311,397	181,496	112,914	16,987	68,582 R	58.3%	36.3%	61.6%	38.4%
1,748,066	BROWARD	819,082	278,766	522,932	17,384	244,166 D	34.0%	63.8%	34.8%	65.2%
14,625	CALHOUN	6,005	4,331	1,275	399	3,056 R	72.1%	21.2%	77.3%	22.7%
159,978	CHARLOTTE	95,074	60,194	30,207	4,673	29,987 R	63.3%	31.8%	66.6%	33.4%
141,236	CITRUS	78,262	48,798	24,038	5,426	24,760 R	62.4%	30.7%	67.0%	33.0%
190,865	CLAY	105,312	77,965	23,251	4,096	54,714 R	74.0%	22.1%	77.0%	23.0%
321,520	COLLIER	169,364	115,719	49,470	4,175	66,249 R	68.3%	29.2%	70.1%	29.9%
67,531	COLUMBIA	28,301	19,924	7,361	1,016	12,563 R	70.4%	26.0%	73.0%	27.0%
34,862	DESOTO	10,639	6,844	3,346	449	3,498 R	64.3%	31.5%	67.2%	32.8%
16,422	DIXIE	6,979	5,040	1,582	357	3,458 R	72.2%	22.7%	76.1%	23.9%
864,263	DUVAL	427,814	241,000	171,598	15,216	69,402 R	56.3%	40.1%	58.4%	41.6%
297,619	ESCAMBIA	151,415	94,200	51,316	5,899	42,884 R	62.2%	33.9%	64.7%	35.3%
95,696	FLAGLER	56,625	32,914	21,260	2,451	11,654 R	58.1%	37.5%	60.8%	39.2%
11,549	FRANKLIN	5,908	3,861	1,826	221	2,035 R	65.4%	30.9%	67.9%	32.1%
46,389	GADSDEN	21,953	6,887	14,573	493	7,686 D	31.4%	66.4%	32.1%	67.9%
16,939	GILCHRIST	8,324	6,303	1,675	346	4,628 R	75.7%	20.1%	79.0%	21.0%
12,884	GLADES	4,295	2,927	1,196	172	1,731 R	68.1%	27.8%	71.0%	29.0%
15,863	GULF	7,206	5,191	1,750	265	3,441 R	72.0%	24.3%	74.8%	25.2%
14,799	HAMILTON	5,358	3,050	2,106	202	944 R	56.9%	39.3%	59.2%	40.8%
27,731	HARDEE	7,494	5,151	2,025	318	3,126 R	68.7%	27.0%	71.8%	28.2%
39,140	HENDRY	10,926	6,683	3,892	351	2,791 R	61.2%	35.6%	63.2%	36.8%
172,778	HERNANDO	92,304	53,708	32,766	5,830	20,942 R	58.2%	35.5%	62.1%	37.9%
98,786	HIGHLANDS	44,975	28,123	14,498	2,354	13,625 R	62.5%	32.2%	66.0%	34.0%
1,229,226	HILLSBOROUGH	590,553	283,871	281,122	25,560	2,749 R	48.1%	47.6%	50.2%	49.8%
19,927	HOLMES	8,414	7,039	976	399	6,063 R	83.7%	11.6%	87.8%	12.2%
138,028	INDIAN RIVER	78,988	48,181	28,288	2,519	19,893 R	61.0%	35.8%	63.0%	37.0%
49,746	JACKSON	20,862	13,820	6,362	680	7,458 R	66.2%	30.5%	68.5%	31.5%
14,761	JEFFERSON	7,596	3,751	3,623	222	128 R	49.4%	47.7%	50.9%	49.1%
8,870	LAFAYETTE	3,361	2,572	669	120	1,903 R	76.5%	19.9%	79.4%	20.6%
297,052	LAKE	167,960	100,664	59,151	8,145	41,513 R	59.9%	35.2%	63.0%	37.0%
618,754	LEE	321,840	204,778	104,591	12,471	100,187 R	63.6%	32.5%	66.2%	33.8%
275,487	LEON	151,071	59,958	86,641	4,472	26,683 D	39.7%	57.4%	40.9%	59.1%
40,801	LEVY	19,067	12,914	5,294	859	7,620 R	67.7%	27.8%	70.9%	29.1%
8,365	LIBERTY	3,209	2,290	748	171	1,542 R	71.4%	23.3%	75.4%	24.6%
19,224	MADISON	8,401	4,584	3,564	253	1,020 R	54.6%	42.4%	56.3%	43.7%
322,833	MANATEE	177,197	102,717	66,545	7,935	36,172 R	58.0%	37.6%	60.7%	39.3%

FLORIDA

SENATOR 2016

2010 Census Population	County	Total Vote	Republican (Rubio)	Democratic (Murphy)	Other	Rep.-Dem. Plurality	Percentage			
							Total Vote		Major Vote	
							Rep.	Dem.	Rep.	Dem.
331,298	MARION	172,323	104,400	59,537	8,386	44,863 R	60.6%	34.5%	63.7%	36.3%
146,318	MARTIN	85,520	49,806	33,685	2,029	16,121 R	58.2%	39.4%	59.7%	40.3%
2,496,435	MIAMI-DADE	969,997	420,063	529,445	20,489	109,382 D	43.3%	54.6%	44.2%	55.8%
73,090	MONROE	41,813	21,629	18,738	1,446	2,891 R	51.7%	44.8%	53.6%	46.4%
73,314	NASSAU	46,110	34,974	9,544	1,592	25,430 R	75.8%	20.7%	78.6%	21.4%
180,822	OKALOOSA	99,992	74,749	20,813	4,430	53,936 R	74.8%	20.8%	78.2%	21.8%
39,996	OKEECHOBEE	13,491	8,647	4,287	557	4,360 R	64.1%	31.8%	66.9%	33.1%
1,145,956	ORANGE	539,825	224,853	293,696	21,276	68,843 D	41.7%	54.4%	43.4%	56.6%
268,685	OSCEOLA	138,523	57,103	75,646	5,774	18,543 D	41.2%	54.6%	43.0%	57.0%
1,320,134	PALM BEACH	652,813	287,899	350,625	14,289	62,726 D	44.1%	53.7%	45.1%	54.9%
464,697	PASCO	237,602	134,779	88,665	14,158	46,114 R	56.7%	37.3%	60.3%	39.7%
916,542	PINELLAS	484,314	236,421	222,928	24,965	13,493 R	48.8%	46.0%	51.5%	48.5%
602,095	POLK	280,287	156,196	110,363	13,728	45,833 R	55.7%	39.4%	58.6%	41.4%
74,364	PUTNAM	32,701	21,474	9,910	1,317	11,564 R	65.7%	30.3%	68.4%	31.6%
151,372	SANTA ROSA	87,023	66,921	16,284	3,818	50,637 R	76.9%	18.7%	80.4%	19.6%
379,448	SARASOTA	225,556	124,163	92,332	9,061	31,831 R	55.0%	40.9%	57.4%	42.6%
422,718	SEMINOLE	221,412	117,734	94,449	9,229	23,285 R	53.2%	42.7%	55.5%	44.5%
190,039	ST. JOHNS	135,585	95,753	35,580	4,252	60,173 R	70.6%	26.2%	72.9%	27.1%
277,789	ST. LUCIE	139,581	66,222	69,590	3,769	3,368 D	47.4%	49.9%	48.8%	51.2%
93,420	SUMTER	75,895	51,846	21,187	2,862	30,659 R	68.3%	27.9%	71.0%	29.0%
41,551	SUWANNEE	18,503	13,335	4,483	685	8,852 R	72.1%	24.2%	74.8%	25.2%
22,570	TAYLOR	9,232	6,216	2,658	358	3,558 R	67.3%	28.8%	70.0%	30.0%
15,535	UNION	5,575	4,313	1,064	198	3,249 R	77.4%	19.1%	80.2%	19.8%
494,593	VOLUSIA	256,677	139,933	104,531	12,213	35,402 R	54.5%	40.7%	57.2%	42.8%
30,776	WAKULLA	15,199	9,773	4,852	574	4,921 R	64.3%	31.9%	66.8%	33.2%
55,043	WALTON	33,338	25,722	6,334	1,282	19,388 R	77.2%	19.0%	80.2%	19.8%
24,896	WASHINGTON	11,030	8,323	2,232	475	6,091 R	75.5%	20.2%	78.9%	21.1%
18,801,310	TOTAL	9,301,820	4,835,191	4,122,088	344,541	713,103 R	52.0%	44.3%	54.0%	46.0%

FLORIDA

HOUSE OF REPRESENTATIVES

CD	Year	Total Vote	Republican		Democratic		Other Vote	Rep.-Dem. Plurality	Percentage			
			Vote	Candidate	Vote	Candidate			Total Vote		Major Vote	
									Rep.	Dem.	Rep.	Dem.
1	2016**	369,186	255,107	GAETZ, MATT	114,079	SPECHT, STEVEN		141,028 R	69.1%	30.9%	69.1%	30.9%
1	2014	235,343	165,086	MILLER, JEFF*	54,976	BRYAN, JAMES "JIM"	15,281	110,110 R	70.1%	23.4%	75.0%	25.0%
1	2012	342,594	238,440	MILLER, JEFF*	92,961	BRYAN, JAMES "JIM"	11,193	145,479 R	69.6%	27.1%	71.9%	28.1%
2	2016	343,362	231,163	DUNN, NEAL	102,801	DARTLAND, WALTER	9,398	128,362 R	67.3%	29.9%	69.2%	30.8%
2	2014	249,780	123,262	SOUTHERLAND, STEVE*	126,096	GRAHAM, GWEN	422	2,834 D	49.3%	50.5%	49.4%	50.6%
2	2012	333,718	175,856	SOUTHERLAND, STEVE*	157,634	LAWSON, AL	228	18,222 R	52.7%	47.2%	52.7%	47.3%
3	2016	342,700	193,843	YOHO, TED*	136,338	MCGURN, KENNETH "KEN"	12,519	57,505 R	56.6%	39.8%	58.7%	41.3%
3	2014	228,809	148,691	YOHO, TED*	73,910	WHEELER, MARIHELEN HADDOCK	6,208	74,781 R	65.0%	32.3%	66.8%	33.2%
3	2012	315,669	204,331	YOHO, TED	102,468	GAILLOT, J.R.	8,870	101,863 R	64.7%	32.5%	66.6%	33.4%
4	2016	409,662	287,509	RUTHERFORD, JOHN	113,088	BRUDERLY, DAVID E.	9,065	174,421 R	70.2%	27.6%	71.8%	28.2%
4	2014	227,253	177,887	CRENSHAW, ANDER*			49,366	177,887 R	78.3%		100.0%	
4	2012	315,470	239,988	CRENSHAW, ANDER*			75,482	239,988 R	76.1%		100.0%	
5	2016	302,874	108,325	SCURRY-SMITH, GLOREATHA "GLO"	194,549	LAWSON, AL		86,224 D	35.8%	64.2%	35.8%	64.2%
5	2014	171,577	59,237	SCURRY-SMITH, GLOREATHA "GLO"	112,340	BROWN, CORRINE*		53,103 D	34.5%	65.5%	34.5%	65.5%
5	2012	269,153	70,700	KOLB, LEANNE	190,472	BROWN, CORRINE*	7,981	119,772 D	26.3%	70.8%	27.1%	72.9%
6	2016	364,570	213,519	DESANTIS, RON*	151,051	MCCULLOUGH, WILLIAM "BILL"		62,468 R	58.6%	41.4%	58.6%	41.4%
6	2014	265,817	166,254	DESANTIS, RON*	99,563	COX, DAVID		66,691 R	62.5%	37.5%	62.5%	37.5%
6	2012	342,451	195,962	DESANTIS, RON	146,489	BEAVEN, HEATHER		49,473 R	57.2%	42.8%	57.2%	42.8%

FLORIDA

HOUSE OF REPRESENTATIVES

CD	Year	Total Vote	Republican Vote	Republican Candidate	Democratic Vote	Democratic Candidate	Other Vote	Rep.-Dem. Plurality	Total Vote Rep.	Total Vote Dem.	Major Vote Rep.	Major Vote Dem.
7	2016	353,655	171,583	MICA, JOHN L.*	182,039	MURPHY, STEPHANIE	33	10,456 D	48.5%	51.5%	48.5%	51.5%
7	2014	227,164	144,474	MICA, JOHN L.*	73,011	NEUMAN, WESLEY RYAN "WES"	9,679	71,463 R	63.6%	32.1%	66.4%	33.6%
7	2012	316,010	185,518	MICA, JOHN L.*	130,479	KENDALL, JASON H.	13	55,039 R	58.7%	41.3%	58.7%	41.3%
8	2016**	390,561	246,483	POSEY, BILL*	127,127	WESTBROOK, CORRY	16,951	119,356 R	63.1%	32.5%	66.0%	34.0%
8	2014	274,513	180,728	POSEY, BILL*	93,724	ROTHBLATT, GABRIEL	61	87,004 R	65.8%	34.1%	65.9%	34.1%
8	2012	348,909	205,432	POSEY, BILL*	130,870	ROBERTS, SHANNON	12,607	74,562 R	58.9%	37.5%	61.1%	38.9%
9	2016	339,761	144,450	LIEBNITZKY, WAYNE	195,311	SOTO, DARREN		50,861 D	42.5%	57.5%	42.5%	57.5%
9	2014	173,878	74,963	PLATT, CAROL	93,850	GRAYSON, ALAN*	5,065	18,887 D	43.1%	54.0%	44.4%	55.6%
9	2012	263,747	98,856	LONG, TODD	164,891	GRAYSON, ALAN		66,035 D	37.5%	62.5%	37.5%	62.5%
10	2016	305,989	107,498	LOWE, THUY "TWEE"	198,491	DEMINGS, VAL B.		90,993 D	35.1%	64.9%	35.1%	64.9%
10	2014	232,574	143,128	WEBSTER, DANIEL A.*	89,426	MCKENNA, MICHAEL PATRICK	20	53,702 R	61.5%	38.5%	61.5%	38.5%
10	2012	318,269	164,649	WEBSTER, DANIEL A.*	153,574	DEMINGS, VAL B.	46	11,075 R	51.7%	48.3%	51.7%	48.3%
11	2016	394,719	258,016	WEBSTER, DANIEL A.	124,713	KOLLER, DAVID C.	11,990	133,303 R	65.4%	31.6%	67.4%	32.6%
11	2014	272,294	181,508	NUGENT, RICHARD B.*	90,786	KOLLER, DAVID C.		90,722 R	66.7%	33.3%	66.7%	33.3%
11	2012	338,663	218,360	NUGENT, RICHARD B.*	120,303	WERDER, H. DAVID		98,057 R	64.5%	35.5%	64.5%	35.5%
12	2016	369,669	253,559	BILIRAKIS, GUS MICHAEL*	116,110	TAGER, ROBERT MATTHEW		137,449 R	68.6%	31.4%	68.6%	31.4%
12	2014		Unopposed	BILIRAKIS, GUS MICHAEL*				R				
12	2012	330,167	209,604	BILIRAKIS, GUS MICHAEL*	108,770	SNOW, JONATHAN MICHAEL	11,793	100,834 R	63.5%	32.9%	65.8%	34.2%
13	2016	355,842	171,149	JOLLY, DAVID W.*	184,693	CRIST, CHARLIE		13,544 D	48.1%	51.9%	48.1%	51.9%
13	2014	223,576	168,172	JOLLY, DAVID W.*			55,404	168,172 R	75.2%		100.0%	
13	2012	329,347	189,605	YOUNG, C.W. BILL*	139,742	EHRLICH, JESSICA		49,863 R	57.6%	42.4%	57.6%	42.4%
14	2016	316,877	121,088	QUINN, CHRISTINE	195,789	CASTOR, KATHY*		74,701 D	38.2%	61.8%	38.2%	61.8%
14	2014				Unopposed	CASTOR, KATHY*		D				
14	2012	280,601	83,480	OTERO, EVELIO "EJ"	197,121	CASTOR, KATHY*		113,641 D	29.8%	70.2%	29.8%	70.2%
15	2016	318,474	182,999	ROSS, DENNIS A.*	135,475	LANGE, JIM		47,524 R	57.5%	42.5%	57.5%	42.5%
15	2014	213,582	128,750	ROSS, DENNIS A.*	84,832	COHN, ALAN MICHAEL		43,918 R	60.3%	39.7%	60.3%	39.7%
15	2012		Unopposed	ROSS, DENNIS A.				R				
16	2016	385,916	230,654	BUCHANAN, VERN*	155,262	SCHNEIDER, JAN		75,392 R	59.8%	40.2%	59.8%	40.2%
16	2014	274,829	169,126	BUCHANAN, VERN*	105,483	LAWRENCE, HENRY	220	63,643 R	61.5%	38.4%	61.6%	38.4%
16	2012	349,076	187,147	BUCHANAN, VERN*	161,929	FITZGERALD, KEITH		25,218 R	53.6%	46.4%	53.6%	46.4%
17	2016	338,675	209,348	ROONEY, TOM*	115,974	FREEMAN, APRIL	13,353	93,374 R	61.8%	34.2%	64.4%	35.6%
17	2014	223,756	141,493	ROONEY, TOM*	82,263	BRONSON, WILLIAM		59,230 R	63.2%	36.8%	63.2%	36.8%
17	2012	282,271	165,488	ROONEY, TOM*	116,766	BRONSON, WILLIAM	17	48,722 R	58.6%	41.4%	58.6%	41.4%
18	2016	375,918	201,488	MAST, BRIAN	161,918	PERKINS, RANDY	12,512	39,570 R	53.6%	43.1%	55.4%	44.6%
18	2014	253,374	101,896	DOMINO, CARL J.	151,478	MURPHY, PATRICK*		49,582 D	40.2%	59.8%	40.2%	59.8%
18	2012	330,665	164,353	WEST, ALLEN*	166,257	MURPHY, PATRICK	55	1,904 D	49.7%	50.3%	49.7%	50.3%
19	2016**	363,166	239,225	ROONEY, FRANCIS	123,812	NEELD, ROBERT M.	129	115,413 R	65.9%	34.1%	65.9%	34.1%
19	2014	246,861	159,354	CLAWSON, CURT J.*	80,824	FREEMAN, APRIL	6,683	78,530 R	64.6%	32.7%	66.3%	33.7%
19	2012	306,216	189,833	RADEL, TREY	109,746	ROACH, JIM	6,637	80,087 R	62.0%	35.8%	63.4%	36.6%
20	2016	277,560	54,646	STEIN, GARY	222,914	HASTINGS, ALCEE L.*		168,268 D	19.7%	80.3%	19.7%	80.3%
20	2014	157,466	28,968	BONNER, JAY	128,498	HASTINGS, ALCEE L.*		99,530 D	18.4%	81.6%	18.4%	81.6%
20	2012	244,285			214,727	HASTINGS, ALCEE L.*	29,558	214,727 D		87.9%		100.0%
21	2016	335,861	118,038	SPAIN, PAUL DOUGLAS	210,606	FRANKEL, LOIS	7,217	92,568 D	35.1%	62.7%	35.9%	64.1%
21	2014	153,970			153,395	DEUTCH, TED*	575	153,395 D		99.6%		100.0%
21	2012	284,400			221,263	DEUTCH, TED*	63,137	221,263 D		77.8%		100.0%
22	2016	337,850	138,737	MCGEE, ANDREA LEIGH	199,113	DEUTCH, TED		60,376 D	41.1%	58.9%	41.1%	58.9%
22	2014	216,096	90,685	SPAIN, PAUL DOUGLAS	125,404	FRANKEL, LOIS*	7	34,719 D	42.0%	58.0%	42.0%	58.0%
22	2012	313,071	142,050	HASNER, ADAM	171,021	FRANKEL, LOIS		28,971 D	45.4%	54.6%	45.4%	54.6%
23	2016	323,120	130,818	KAUFMAN, JOSEPH "JOE"	183,225	WASSERMAN-SCHULTZ, DEBBIE*	9,077	52,407 D	40.5%	56.7%	41.7%	58.3%
23	2014	164,788	61,519	KAUFMAN, JOSEPH "JOE"	103,269	WASSERMAN-SCHULTZ, DEBBIE*		41,750 D	37.3%	62.7%	37.3%	62.7%
23	2012	275,430	98,096	HARRINGTON, KAREN	174,205	WASSERMAN-SCHULTZ, DEBBIE*	3,129	76,109 D	35.6%	63.2%	36.0%	64.0%
24	2016				Unopposed	WILSON, FREDERICA S.*		D				
24	2014	149,918	15,239	NEREE, DUFIRSTSON	129,192	WILSON, FREDERICA S.*	5,487	113,953 D	10.2%	86.2%	10.6%	89.4%
24	2012				Unopposed	WILSON, FREDERICA S.		D				

FLORIDA

HOUSE OF REPRESENTATIVES

CD	Year	Total Vote	Republican Vote	Republican Candidate	Democratic Vote	Democratic Candidate	Other Vote	Rep.-Dem. Plurality	Total Vote Rep.	Total Vote Dem.	Major Vote Rep.	Major Vote Dem.
25	2016	253,240	157,921	DIAZ-BALART, MARIO*	95,319	VALDES, ALINA		62,602 R	62.4%	37.6%	62.4%	37.6%
25	2014		Unopposed	DIAZ-BALART, MARIO*				R				
25	2012	200,229	151,466	DIAZ-BALART, MARIO*			48,763	151,466 R	75.6%		100.0%	
26	2016	280,542	148,547	CURBELO, CARLOS*	115,493	GARCIA, JOE	16,502	33,054 R	53.0%	41.2%	56.3%	43.7%
26	2014	161,337	83,031	CURBELO, CARLOS	78,306	GARCIA, JOE*		4,725 R	51.5%	48.5%	51.5%	48.5%
26	2012	252,957	108,820	RIVERA, DAVID*	135,694	GARCIA, JOE	8,443	26,874 D	43.0%	53.6%	44.5%	55.5%
27	2016	287,677	157,917	ROS-LEHTINEN, ILEANA*	129,760	FUHRMAN, SCOTT		28,157 R	54.9%	45.1%	54.9%	45.1%
27	2014		Unopposed	ROS-LEHTINEN, ILEANA*				R				
27	2012	230,171	138,488	ROS-LEHTINEN, ILEANA*	85,020	YEVANCEY, MANNY	6,663	53,468 R	60.2%	36.9%	62.0%	38.0%
TOTAL	2016	8,837,426	4,733,630		3,985,050		118,746	748,580 R	53.6%	45.1%	54.3%	45.7%
TOTAL	2014	4,998,555	2,713,451		2,130,626		154,478	582,825 R	54.3%	42.6%	56.0%	44.0%
TOTAL	2012	7,513,539	3,826,522		3,392,402		294,615	434,120 R	50.9%	45.2%	53.0%	47.0%

Note: An asterisk (*) denotes incumbent. **Due to mid-decade redistricting, boundaries for all districts except CD 1, 8, and 19 are not comparable to those used in the 2012 and 2014 races.

FLORIDA

GENERAL AND PRIMARY ELECTIONS

2016 GENERAL ELECTIONS: OTHER VOTES

President Other vote was 207,043 (Gary Johnson), 64,399 Green (Jill Stein), 16,475 Constitution (Darrell Castle), 9,108 Reform (Roque De La Fuente), 74 Write-in (Laurence Kotlikoff), 25 Write-in (Richard Duncan), 24 Write-in (Andrew D. Basiago), 19 Write-in (Zoltan Gyurko), 9 Write-in (Anthony Valdivia), 2 Write-in (Cherunda Fox).

Senate Other vote was 196,956 Libertarian (Paul Stanton), 52,451 No Party Affiliation (Bruce Nathan), 45,820 No Party Affiliation (Tony Khoury), 26,918 No Party Affiliation (Steven Machat), 22,236 No Party Affiliation (Basil Dalack), 56 Write-in (Charles Tolbert), 50 Write-in (Howard Knepper), 37 Write-in (Angela Walls-Windhauser), 10 Write-in (Robert Kaplan), 7 Write-in (Bradley Patrick).

House Other vote was:

CD 2 9,395 Libertarian (Robert Lapham), 3 Write-in (Antoine Roberts)
CD 3 12,519 No Party Affiliation (Tom Wells)
CD 4 9,054 No Party Affiliation (Gary Koniz), 11 Write-in (Daniel Murphy)
CD 7 33 Write-in (Mike Plaskon)
CD 8 16,951 No Party Affiliation (Bill Stinson)
CD 11 11,990 No Party Affiliation (Bruce Riggs)
CD 17 13,353 No Party Affiliation (John Sawyer)
CD 18 12,503 No Party Affiliation (Carla Spalding), 9 Write-in (Marilyn Holloman)
CD 19 109 Write-in (David Byron), 20 Write-in (Timothy Rossano)
CD 21 7,217 No Party Affiliation (W. Trout)
CD 23 5,180 No Party Affiliation (Don Endriss), 3,897 No Party Affiliation (Lyle Milstein)
CD 26 16,502 No Party Affiliation (Jose Peixoto)

FLORIDA

GENERAL AND PRIMARY ELECTIONS

2016 PRIMARY ELECTIONS: SUPPLEMENTARY INFORMATION

Primary	February 16, 2016 (President) August 30, 2016 (Congress)	**Registration** (as of February 16, 2016)	11,993,496	Democratic Republican Other Parties No Party Affiliation	4,534,845 4,209,039 343,423 2,906,189

Primary Type Closed—Only registered Democrats and Republicans could vote in their party's primary, with the exception of races where there were to be no other candidates (including write-ins) on the general election ballot. Then, the contested primary would be open to all voters.

	REPUBLICAN PRIMARIES			DEMOCRATIC PRIMARIES		
President	Trump, Donald J.	1,079,870	45.7%	Clinton, Hillary Rodham	1,101,414	64.4%
	Rubio, Marco	638,661	27.0%	Sanders, Bernard	568,839	33.3%
	Cruz, Ted	404,891	17.1%	O'Malley, Martin	38,930	2.3%
	Kasich, John R.	159,976	6.8%			
	Bush, Jeb	43,511	1.8%			
	Carson, Ben	21,207	0.9%			
	Paul, Rand	4,450	0.2%			
	Huckabee, Mike	2,624	0.1%			
	Christie, Chris	2,493	0.1%			
	Fiorina, Carly	1,899	0.1%			
	Santorum, Rick	1,211	0.1%			
	Graham, Lindsey	693				
	Gilmore, James S. III	319				
	TOTAL	*2,361,805*		*TOTAL*	*1,709,183*	
Senator	Rubio, Marco*	1,029,830	72.0%	Murphy, Patrick	665,985	58.9%
	Beruff, Carlos	264,427	18.5%	Grayson, Alan	199,929	17.7%
	Young, Dwight Mark Anthony	91,082	6.4%	Keith, Pamela "Pam"	173,919	15.4%
	Rivera, Ernesto "Ernie"	45,153	3.2%	De La Fuente, Roque "Rocky"	60,810	5.4%
				Luster, Reginald	29,138	2.6%
	TOTAL	*1,430,492*		*TOTAL*	*1,129,781*	
Congressional District 1	Gaetz, Matt	35,689	36.1%	Specht, Steven	Unopposed	
	Evers, Greg	21,540	21.8%			
	Dosev, Cris	20,610	20.9%			
	Bydlak, Rebekah Johansen	7,689	7.8%			
	Zumwalt, James	7,660	7.8%			
	Frazier, Brian	3,817	3.9%			
	Wichern, Mark	1,798	1.8%			
	TOTAL	*98,803*				
Congressional District 2	Dunn, Neal	33,886	41.4%	Dartland, Walter	30,115	50.1%
	Thomas, Mary	32,178	39.3%	Crapps, Steve	29,982	49.9%
	Sukhia, Ken	15,826	19.3%			
	TOTAL	*81,890*		*TOTAL*	*60,097*	
Congressional District 3	Yoho, Ted*	Unopposed		McGurn, Kenneth "Ken"	Unopposed	
Congressional District 4	Rutherford, John	38,784	38.7%	Bruderly, David E.	Unopposed	
	Ray, Lake	20,164	20.1%			
	Tanzler, Hans III	19,051	19.0%			
	McClure, Bill	9,867	9.8%			
	Malin, Edward "Ed"	7,895	7.9%			
	Kaufman, Stephen J.	2,419	2.4%			
	Pueschel, Deborah Katz	2,145	2.1%			
	TOTAL	*100,325*				

FLORIDA

GENERAL AND PRIMARY ELECTIONS

	REPUBLICAN PRIMARIES			DEMOCRATIC PRIMARIES		
Congressional District 5	Scurry-Smith, Gloreatha "Glo"	Unopposed		Lawson, Al	39,306	47.6%
				Brown, Corrine*	32,235	39.0%
				Holloway, LaShonda "L.J."	11,048	13.4%
				TOTAL	*82,589*	
Congressional District 6	DeSantis, Ron*	41,311	61.0%	McCullough, William "Bill"	16,043	36.6%
	Costello, Fred	16,690	24.7%	Taylor, Dwayne L.	12,625	28.8%
	Galloway, G.G.	9,683	14.3%	McGovern, Jay	8,388	19.1%
				Pappas, George	6,762	15.4%
	TOTAL	*67,684*		*TOTAL*	*43,818*	
Congressional District 7	Mica, John L.*	38,528	77.2%	Murphy, Stephanie	Unopposed	
	Busch, Mark	11,407	22.8%			
	TOTAL	*49,935*				
Congressional District 8	Posey, Bill*	Unopposed		Westbrook, Corry	Unopposed	
Congressional District 9	Liebnitzky, Wayne	22,725	67.6%	Soto, Darren	14,496	36.3%
	Rentas, Wanda	10,911	32.4%	Randolph, Susannah	11,267	28.2%
				Grayson, Dena	11,122	27.8%
				Crabtree, Valleri	3,093	7.7%
	TOTAL	*33,636*		*TOTAL*	*39,978*	
Congressional District 10	Lowe, Thuy "Twee"	Unopposed		Demings, Val B.	23,260	57.1%
				Thompson, Geraldine F.	8,192	20.1%
				Poe, Bob	6,918	17.0%
				Fahmy, Fatima Rita	2,349	5.8%
				TOTAL	*40,719*	
Congressional District 11	Webster, Daniel A.	52,876	59.8%	Koller, David C.	Unopposed	
	Grabelle, Justin	35,525	40.2%			
	TOTAL	*88,401*				
Congressional District 12	Bilirakis, Gus Michael*	Unopposed		Tager, Robert Matthew	Unopposed	
Congressional District 13	Jolly, David W.*	41,005	75.1%	Crist, Charlie	Unopposed	
	Bircher, Mark	13,592	24.9%			
	TOTAL	*54,597*				
Congressional District 14	Quinn, Christine	Unopposed		Castor, Kathy*	Unopposed	
Congressional District 15	Ross, Dennis A.*	Unopposed		Lange, Jim	Unopposed	
Congressional District 16	Buchanan, Vern	53,706	80.6%	Schneider, Jan	31,387	76.2%
	Satcher, James	12,900	19.4%	King, Brent	9,782	23.8%
	TOTAL	*66,606*		*TOTAL*	*41,169*	
Congressional District 17	Rooney, Tom*	Unopposed		Freeman, April	Unopposed	
Congressional District 18	Mast, Brian	24,099	38.0%	Perkins, Randy	27,861	60.4%
	Negron, Rebecca	16,242	25.6%	Chane, Jonathan	14,897	32.3%
	Freeman, Mark	10,000	15.8%	Xuna, John "Juan"	3,394	7.4%
	Domino, Carl J.	7,942	12.5%			
	Kozell, Rick	4,334	6.8%			
	Nikpour, Noelle	835	1.3%			
	TOTAL	*63,452*		*TOTAL*	*46,152*	

FLORIDA

GENERAL AND PRIMARY ELECTIONS

	REPUBLICAN PRIMARIES			DEMOCRATIC PRIMARIES		
Congressional District 19	Rooney, Francis	46,821	52.7%	Neeld, Robert M.	Unopposed	
	Goss, Chauncey Porter	26,537	29.9%			
	Bongino, Dan	15,439	17.4%			
	TOTAL	88,797				
Congressional District 20	Stein, Gary	Unopposed		Hastings, Alcee L.*	Unopposed	
Congressional District 21	Spain, Paul Douglas	Unopposed		Frankel, Lois*	Unopposed	
Congressional District 22	McGee, Andrea Leigh	Unopposed		Deutch, Ted*	Unopposed	
Congressional District 23	Kaufman, Joseph "Joe"	13,412	73.1%	Wasserman-Schultz, Debbie*	28,809	56.8%
	Feigenbaum, Martin "Marty"	4,948	26.9%	Canova, Tim	21,907	43.2%
	TOTAL	18,360		TOTAL	50,716	
Congressional District 24				Wilson, Frederica S.*	50,822	78.4%
				Hill, Randal	14,023	21.6%
				TOTAL	64,845	
Congressional District 25	Diaz-Balart, Mario*	Unopposed		Valdes, Alina	Unopposed	
Congressional District 26	Curbelo, Carlos*	Unopposed		Garcia, Joe	14,834	51.3%
				Taddeo, Annette	14,108	48.7%
				TOTAL	28,942	
Congressional District 27	Ros-Lehtinen, Ileana*	30,485	80.5%	Fuhrman, Scott	17,068	58.9%
	Peiro, Maria	4,450	11.7%	Perez, Frank	7,087	24.5%
	Adams, David "Tubbs"	2,945	7.8%	Sackrin, Adam	4,808	16.6%
	TOTAL	37,880		TOTAL	28,963	

Note: An asterisk (*) denotes incumbent.

GEORGIA

Congressional districts first established for elections held in 2012

14 members

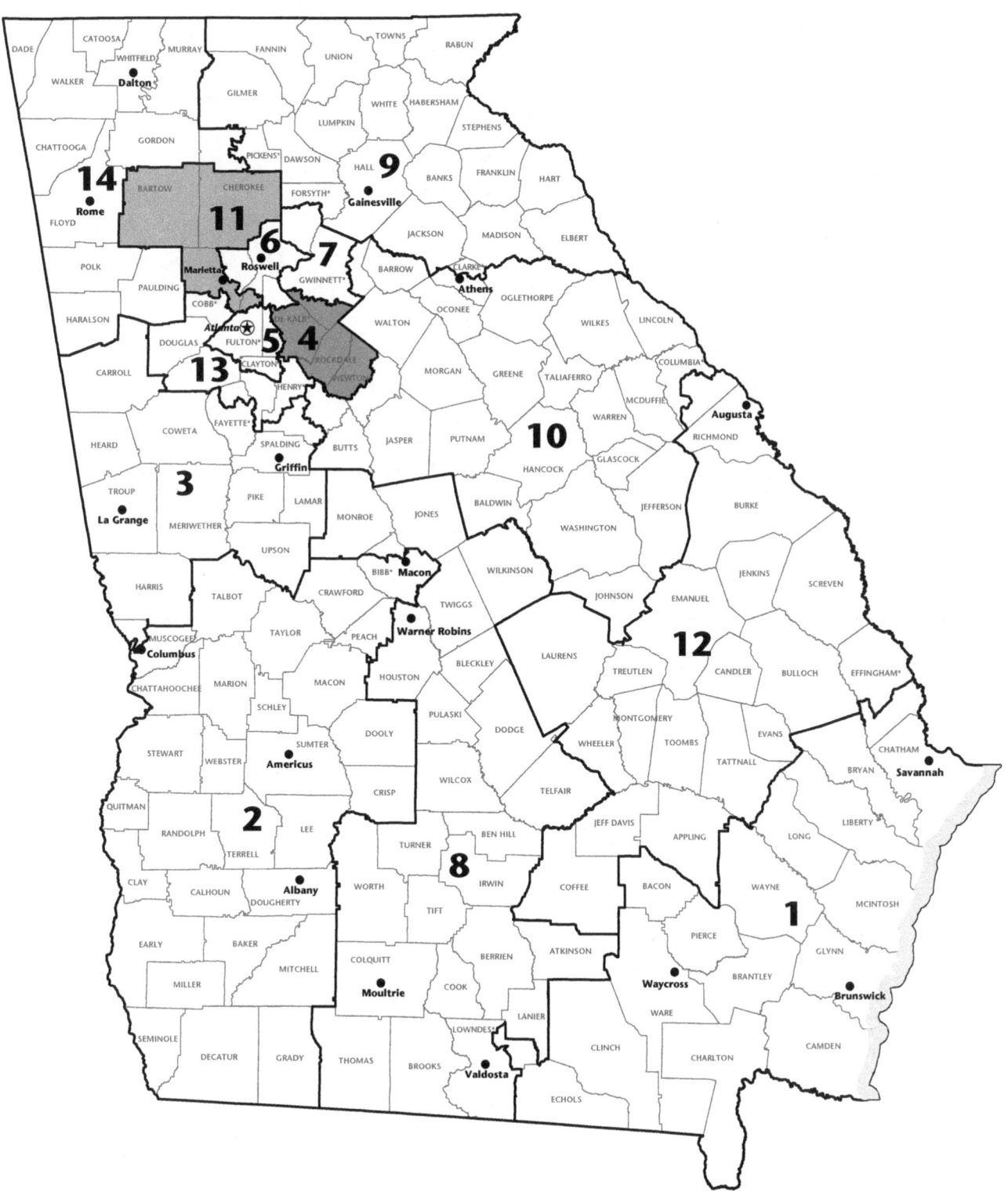

* Asterisk indicates a county whose boundaries include parts of two or more congressional districts.

GEORGIA
Atlanta Area

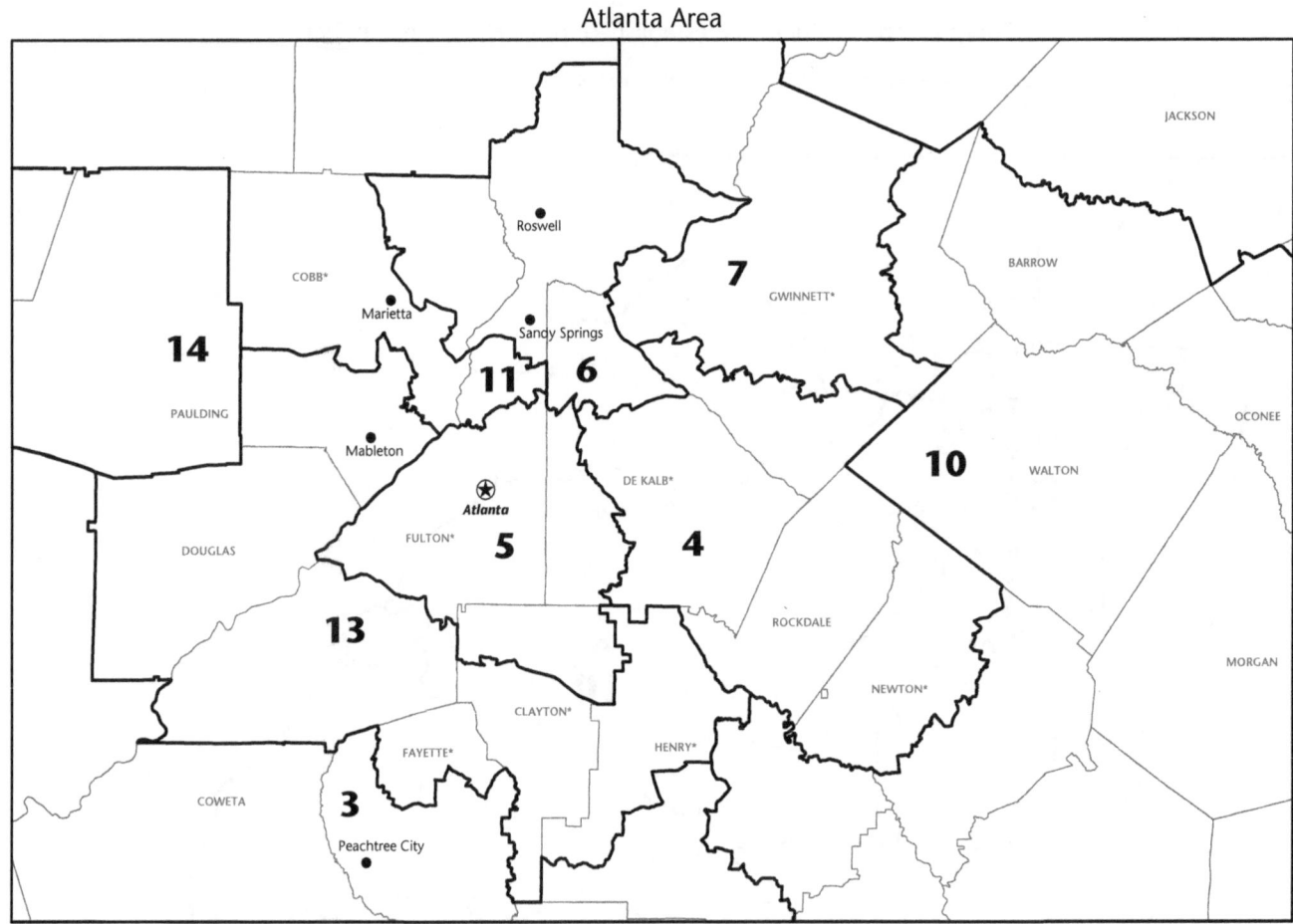

* Asterisk indicates a county whose boundaries include parts of two or more congressional districts.

GEORGIA

GOVERNOR
Nathan Deal (R). Re-elected 2014 to a four-year term. Previously elected 2010.

SENATORS (2 Republicans)
Johnny Isakson (R). Re-elected 2016 to a six-year term. Previously elected 2010, 2004.

David A. Perdue (R). Elected 2014 to a six-year term.

REPRESENTATIVES (10 Republicans, 4 Democrats)

1. Earl Leroy "Buddy" Carter (R)	6. Karen Handel (R)	11. Barry Loudermilk (R)
2. Sanford Bishop (D)	7. Rob Woodall (R)	12. Rick W. Allen (R)
3. Drew Ferguson (R)	8. Austin Scott (R)	13. David Scott (D)
4. Henry C. "Hank" Johnson (D)	9. Doug Collins (R)	14. Tom Graves (R)
5. John Lewis (D)	10. Jody Hice (R)	

Note: Thomas E. Price·(R) had won re-election in the 6th District in 2016, but resigned to become secretary of health and human services in the Trump administration. Karen Handel (R) won a special election on June 20, 2017, to fill the vacancy created by Price's departure.

POSTWAR VOTE FOR PRESIDENT

Year	Total Vote	Republican		Democratic		Other Vote	Rep.-Dem. Plurality	Percentage			
		Vote	Candidate	Vote	Candidate			Total Vote		Major Vote	
								Rep.	Dem.	Rep.	Dem.
2016**	4,114,732	2,089,104	Trump, Donald J.	1,877,963	Clinton, Hillary Rodham	147,665	211,141 R	50.8%	45.6%	52.7%	47.3%
2012	3,900,050	2,078,688	Romney, W. Mitt	1,773,827	Obama, Barack H.	47,535	304,861 R	53.3%	45.5%	54.0%	46.0%
2008	3,924,486	2,048,759	McCain, John S. III	1,844,123	Obama, Barack H.	31,604	204,636 R	52.2%	47.0%	52.6%	47.4%
2004	3,301,875	1,914,254	Bush, George W.*	1,366,149	Kerry, John F.	21,472	548,105 R	58.0%	41.4%	58.4%	41.6%
2000**	2,596,645	1,419,720	Bush, George W.	1,116,230	Gore, Albert Jr.	60,695	303,490 R	54.7%	43.0%	56.0%	44.0%
1996**	2,299,071	1,080,843	Dole, Robert "Bob"	1,053,849	Clinton, Bill*	164,379	26,994 R	47.0%	45.8%	50.6%	49.4%
1992**	2,321,125	995,252	Bush, George H.*	1,008,966	Clinton, Bill	316,907	13,714 D	42.9%	43.5%	49.7%	50.3%
1988	1,812,672	1,081,331	Bush, George H.	717,792	Dukakis, Michael S.	13,549	363,539 R	59.7%	39.6%	60.1%	39.9%
1984	1,776,120	1,068,722	Reagan, Ronald*	706,628	Mondale, Walter F.	770	362,094 R	60.2%	39.8%	60.2%	39.8%
1980**	1,596,695	654,168	Reagan, Ronald	890,733	Carter, Jimmy*	51,794	236,565 D	41.0%	55.8%	42.3%	57.7%
1976	1,467,458	483,743	Ford, Gerald R.*	979,409	Carter, Jimmy	4,306	495,666 D	33.0%	66.7%	33.1%	66.9%
1972	1,174,772	881,496	Nixon, Richard M.*	289,529	McGovern, George S.	3,747	591,967 R	75.0%	24.6%	75.3%	24.7%
1968**	1,250,266	380,111	Nixon, Richard M.	334,440	Humphrey, Hubert Horatio Jr.	535,715	45,671 R	30.4%	26.7%	53.2%	46.8%
1964	1,139,335	616,584	Goldwater, Barry M. Sr.	522,556	Johnson, Lyndon B.*	195	94,028 R	54.1%	45.9%	54.1%	45.9%
1960	733,349	274,472	Nixon, Richard M.	458,638	Kennedy, John F.	239	184,166 D	37.4%	62.5%	37.4%	62.6%
1956	669,655	222,778	Eisenhower, Dwight D.*	444,688	Stevenson, Adlai E. II	2,189	221,910 D	33.3%	66.4%	33.4%	66.6%
1952	655,785	198,961	Eisenhower, Dwight D.	456,823	Stevenson, Adlai E. II	1	257,862 D	30.3%	69.7%	30.3%	69.7%
1948**	418,844	76,691	Dewey, Thomas E.	254,646	Truman, Harry S.*	87,507	177,955 D	18.3%	60.8%	23.1%	76.9%

Note: An asterisk (*) denotes incumbent. **In past elections, the other vote included: 2016 - 125,306 Libertarian (Gary Johnson); 2000 - 13,273 Green (Ralph Nader); 1996 - 146,337 Reform (Ross Perot); 1992 - 309,657 Independent (Perot); 1980 - 36,055 Independent (John Anderson); 1968 - 535,550 American Independent (George Wallace); 1948 - 85,135 States' Rights (Strom Thurmond, who finished second statewide). Wallace carried Georgia in 1968 with 42.8 percent of the vote.

GEORGIA

POSTWAR VOTE FOR GOVERNOR

Year	Total Vote	Republican Vote	Republican Candidate	Democratic Vote	Democratic Candidate	Other Vote	Rep.-Dem. Plurality	Total Vote Rep.	Total Vote Dem.	Major Vote Rep.	Major Vote Dem.
2014	2,550,648	1,345,237	Deal, Nathan*	1,144,794	Carter, Jason J.	60,617	200,443 R	52.7%	44.9%	54.0%	46.0%
2010	2,576,161	1,365,832	Deal, Nathan	1,107,011	Barnes, Roy E.	103,318	258,821 R	53.0%	43.0%	55.2%	44.8%
2006	2,122,258	1,229,724	Perdue, Sonny*	811,049	Taylor, Mark	81,485	418,675 R	57.9%	38.2%	60.3%	39.7%
2002	2,027,177	1,041,700	Perdue, Sonny	937,070	Barnes, Roy E.*	48,407	104,630 R	51.4%	46.2%	52.6%	47.4%
1998	1,792,808	790,201	Millner, Guy	941,076	Barnes, Roy E.	61,531	150,875 D	44.1%	52.5%	45.6%	54.4%
1994	1,545,328	756,371	Millner, Guy	788,926	Miller, Zell*	31	32,555 D	48.9%	51.1%	48.9%	51.1%
1990	1,449,682	645,625	Isakson, Johnny	766,662	Miller, Zell	37,395	121,037 D	44.5%	52.9%	45.7%	54.3%
1986	1,175,114	346,512	Davis, Guy	828,465	Harris, Joe Frank*	137	481,953 D	29.5%	70.5%	29.5%	70.5%
1982	1,169,043	434,496	Bell, Robert H.	734,092	Harris, Joe Frank	455	299,596 D	37.2%	62.8%	37.2%	62.8%
1978	662,862	128,139	Cook, Rodney M.	534,572	Busbee, George*	151	406,433 D	19.3%	80.6%	19.3%	80.7%
1974	936,438	289,113	Thompson, Ronnie	646,777	Busbee, George	548	357,664 D	30.9%	69.1%	30.9%	69.1%
1970	1,046,663	424,983	Suit, Hal	620,419	Carter, Jimmy	1,261	195,436 D	40.6%	59.3%	40.7%	59.3%
1966**	975,019	453,665	Callaway, Howard H.	450,626	Maddox, Lester	70,728	3,039 R	46.5%	46.2%	50.2%	49.8%
1962	311,691			311,524	Sanders, Carl E.	167	311,524 D		99.9%		100.0%
1958	168,497			168,414	Vandiver, S. Ernest	83	168,414 D		100.0%		100.0%
1954	331,966			331,899	Griffin, S. Marvin	67	331,899 D		100.0%		100.0%
1950	234,430			230,771	Talmadge, Herman E.*	3,659	230,771 D		98.4%		100.0%
1948S**	363,764			354,712	Talmadge, Herman E.	9,052	354,712 D		97.5%		100.0%
1946	146,191			144,067	Talmadge, Eugene	2,124	144,067 D		98.5%		100.0%

Note: An asterisk (*) denotes incumbent. **In 1966 in the absence of a majority for any candidate, the State Legislature elected Democrat Lester Maddox to a four-year term. The 1948 election was for a short term to fill a vacancy. The Republican Party did not run a candidate in the 1946, 1948, 1950, 1954, 1958, and 1962 gubernatorial elections.

POSTWAR VOTE FOR SENATOR

Year	Total Vote	Republican Vote	Republican Candidate	Democratic Vote	Democratic Candidate	Other Vote	Rep.-Dem. Plurality	Total Vote Rep.	Total Vote Dem.	Major Vote Rep.	Major Vote Dem.
2016	3,898,605	2,135,806	Isakson, Johnny*	1,599,726	Barksdale, Jim	163,073	536,080 R	54.8%	41.0%	57.2%	42.8%
2014	2,567,805	1,358,088	Perdue, David A.	1,160,811	Nunn, Michelle	48,906	197,277 R	52.9%	45.2%	53.9%	46.1%
2010	2,555,258	1,489,904	Isakson, Johnny*	996,516	Thurmond, Michael	68,838	493,388 R	58.3%	39.0%	59.9%	40.1%
2008**	3,752,485	1,867,097	Chambliss, Saxby*	1,757,393	Martin, Jim	127,995	109,704 R	49.8%	46.8%	51.5%	48.5%
2008**	2,137,956	1,228,033	Chambliss, Saxby*	909,923	Martin, Jim		318,110 R	57.4%	42.6%	57.4%	42.6%
2004	3,220,981	1,864,202	Isakson, Johnny	1,287,690	Majette, Denise L.	69,089	576,512 R	57.9%	40.0%	59.1%	40.9%
2002	2,030,608	1,071,464	Chambliss, Saxby	932,156	Cleland, Max*	26,988	139,308 R	52.8%	45.9%	53.5%	46.5%
2000S**	2,428,510	920,478	Mattingly, Mack F.	1,413,224	Miller, Zell*	94,808	492,746 D	37.9%	58.2%	39.4%	60.6%
1998	1,753,911	918,540	Coverdell, Paul*	791,904	Coles, Michael	43,467	126,636 R	52.4%	45.2%	53.7%	46.3%
1996	2,259,232	1,073,969	Millner, Guy	1,103,993	Cleland, Max	81,270	30,024 D	47.5%	48.9%	49.3%	50.7%
1992**	2,251,587	1,073,282	Coverdell, Paul	1,108,416	Fowler, Wyche Jr.*	69,889	35,134 D	47.7%	49.2%	49.2%	50.8%
1992**	1,253,991	635,114	Coverdell, Paul	618,877	Fowler, Wyche Jr.*		16,237 R	50.6%	49.4%	50.6%	49.4%
1990	1,033,517			1,033,439	Nunn, Sam*	78			100.0%		100.0%
1986	1,225,008	601,241	Mattingly, Mack F.*	623,707	Fowler, Wyche Jr.	60	22,466 D	49.1%	50.9%	49.1%	50.9%
1984	1,681,344	337,196	Hicks, John Michael	1,344,104	Nunn, Sam*	44	1,006,908 D	20.1%	79.9%	20.1%	79.9%
1980	1,580,340	803,686	Mattingly, Mack F.	776,143	Talmadge, Herman E.*	511	27,543 R	50.9%	49.1%	50.9%	49.1%
1978	645,164	108,808	Stokes, John W.	536,320	Nunn, Sam*	36	427,512 D	16.9%	83.1%	16.9%	83.1%
1974	874,555	246,866	Johnson, Jerry R.	627,376	Talmadge, Herman E.*	313	380,510 D	28.2%	71.7%	28.2%	71.8%
1972	1,178,708	542,331	Thompson, S. Fletcher	635,970	Nunn, Sam	407	93,639 D	46.0%	54.0%	46.0%	54.0%
1968	1,141,889	256,796	Patton, E. Earl	885,093	Talmadge, Herman E.*		628,297 D	22.5%	77.5%	22.5%	77.5%
1966	631,330			631,002	Russell, Richard Brevard Jr.*	328	631,002 D		99.9%		100.0%
1962	306,250			306,250	Talmadge, Herman E.*		306,250 D		100.0%		100.0%
1960	576,495			576,140	Russell, Richard Brevard Jr.*	355	576,140 D		99.9%		100.0%
1956	541,267			541,094	Talmadge, Herman E.	173	541,094 D		100.0%		100.0%
1954	333,936			333,917	Russell, Richard Brevard Jr.*	19	333,917 D		100.0%		100.0%
1950	261,293			261,290	George, Walter F.*	3	261,290 D		100.0%		100.0%
1948	362,504			362,104	Russell, Richard Brevard Jr.*	400	362,104 D		99.9%		100.0%

Note: An asterisk (*) denotes incumbent. **The 2000 election was for a short term to fill a vacancy. In 1992 and 2008, no candidate drew a majority of the general election vote required by state law, forcing runoff elections. In each case, the general election vote is presented first and the runoff vote second. The 2008 runoff was held December 2; the 1992 runoff took place on November 24. The Republican Party did not run a candidate in the 1948, 1950, 1954, 1956, 1960, 1962, 1966, and 1990 Senate elections.

GEORGIA
PRESIDENT 2016

2010 Census Population	County	Total Vote	Republican (Trump)	Democratic (Clinton)	Other	Rep.-Dem. Plurality		Percentage Total Vote Rep.	Dem.	Major Vote Rep.	Dem.
18,236	APPLING	7,012	5,494	1,434	84	4,060	R	78.4%	20.5%	79.3%	20.7%
8,375	ATKINSON	2,610	1,878	697	35	1,181	R	72.0%	26.7%	72.9%	27.1%
11,096	BACON	4,020	3,364	608	48	2,756	R	83.7%	15.1%	84.7%	15.3%
3,451	BAKER	1,440	775	650	15	125	R	53.8%	45.1%	54.4%	45.6%
45,720	BALDWIN	16,116	7,697	7,970	449	273	D	47.8%	49.5%	49.1%	50.9%
18,395	BANKS	6,975	6,134	684	157	5,450	R	87.9%	9.8%	90.0%	10.0%
69,367	BARROW	29,061	21,108	6,580	1,373	14,528	R	72.6%	22.6%	76.2%	23.8%
100,157	BARTOW	39,550	29,911	8,212	1,427	21,699	R	75.6%	20.8%	78.5%	21.5%
17,634	BEN HILL	5,936	3,739	2,101	96	1,638	R	63.0%	35.4%	64.0%	36.0%
19,286	BERRIEN	6,590	5,422	1,047	121	4,375	R	82.3%	15.9%	83.8%	16.2%
155,547	BIBB	62,596	24,043	36,787	1,766	12,744	D	38.4%	58.8%	39.5%	60.5%
13,063	BLECKLEY	4,974	3,719	1,101	154	2,618	R	74.8%	22.1%	77.2%	22.8%
18,411	BRANTLEY	6,301	5,567	619	115	4,948	R	88.4%	9.8%	90.0%	10.0%
16,243	BROOKS	6,336	3,701	2,528	107	1,173	R	58.4%	39.9%	59.4%	40.6%
30,233	BRYAN	15,173	10,529	4,014	630	6,515	R	69.4%	26.5%	72.4%	27.6%
70,217	BULLOCH	25,316	15,097	9,261	958	5,836	R	59.6%	36.6%	62.0%	38.0%
23,316	BURKE	9,351	4,491	4,731	129	240	D	48.0%	50.6%	48.7%	51.3%
23,655	BUTTS	9,514	6,717	2,566	231	4,151	R	70.6%	27.0%	72.4%	27.6%
6,694	CALHOUN	2,025	830	1,179	16	349	D	41.0%	58.2%	41.3%	58.7%
50,513	CAMDEN	18,901	12,310	5,930	661	6,380	R	65.1%	31.4%	67.5%	32.5%
10,998	CANDLER	3,763	2,664	1,026	73	1,638	R	70.8%	27.3%	72.2%	27.8%
110,527	CARROLL	44,121	30,029	12,464	1,628	17,565	R	68.1%	28.2%	70.7%	29.3%
63,942	CATOOSA	26,757	20,876	4,771	1,110	16,105	R	78.0%	17.8%	81.4%	18.6%
12,171	CHARLTON	4,016	2,951	1,004	61	1,947	R	73.5%	25.0%	74.6%	25.4%
265,128	CHATHAM	112,142	45,688	62,290	4,164	16,602	D	40.7%	55.5%	42.3%	57.7%
11,267	CHATTAHOOCHEE	1,390	751	594	45	157	R	54.0%	42.7%	55.8%	44.2%
26,015	CHATTOOGA	8,252	6,462	1,613	177	4,849	R	78.3%	19.5%	80.0%	20.0%
214,346	CHEROKEE	112,043	80,649	25,231	6,163	55,418	R	72.0%	22.5%	76.2%	23.8%
116,714	CLARKE	44,976	12,717	29,603	2,656	16,886	D	28.3%	65.8%	30.0%	70.0%
3,183	CLAY	1,273	566	697	10	131	D	44.5%	54.8%	44.8%	55.2%
259,424	CLAYTON	92,859	12,645	78,220	1,994	65,575	D	13.6%	84.2%	13.9%	86.1%
6,798	CLINCH	2,455	1,727	686	42	1,041	R	70.3%	27.9%	71.6%	28.4%
688,078	COBB	330,819	152,912	160,121	17,786	7,209	D	46.2%	48.4%	48.8%	51.2%
42,356	COFFEE	13,915	9,588	4,094	233	5,494	R	68.9%	29.4%	70.1%	29.9%
45,498	COLQUITT	13,624	9,898	3,463	263	6,435	R	72.7%	25.4%	74.1%	25.9%
124,053	COLUMBIA	64,743	43,085	18,887	2,771	24,198	R	66.5%	29.2%	69.5%	30.5%
17,212	COOK	6,057	4,176	1,753	128	2,423	R	68.9%	28.9%	70.4%	29.6%
127,317	COWETA	61,745	42,533	16,583	2,629	25,950	R	68.9%	26.9%	71.9%	28.1%
12,630	CRAWFORD	5,176	3,635	1,421	120	2,214	R	70.2%	27.5%	71.9%	28.1%
23,439	CRISP	7,512	4,549	2,837	126	1,712	R	60.6%	37.8%	61.6%	38.4%
16,633	DADE	6,242	5,051	965	226	4,086	R	80.9%	15.5%	84.0%	16.0%
22,330	DAWSON	11,765	9,900	1,448	417	8,452	R	84.1%	12.3%	87.2%	12.8%
27,842	DECATUR	10,286	6,020	4,124	142	1,896	R	58.5%	40.1%	59.3%	40.7%
691,893	DEKALB	314,757	51,468	251,370	11,919	199,902	D	16.4%	79.9%	17.0%	83.0%
21,796	DODGE	7,009	5,021	1,839	149	3,182	R	71.6%	26.2%	73.2%	26.8%
14,918	DOOLY	3,859	1,951	1,872	36	79	R	50.6%	48.5%	51.0%	49.0%
94,565	DOUGHERTY	34,087	10,232	23,311	544	13,079	D	30.0%	68.4%	30.5%	69.5%
132,403	DOUGLAS	57,738	24,817	31,005	1,916	6,188	D	43.0%	53.7%	44.5%	55.5%
11,008	EARLY	4,785	2,552	2,168	65	384	R	53.3%	45.3%	54.1%	45.9%
4,034	ECHOLS	1,182	1,007	156	19	851	R	85.2%	13.2%	86.6%	13.4%
52,250	EFFINGHAM	23,458	17,874	4,853	731	13,021	R	76.2%	20.7%	78.6%	21.4%
20,166	ELBERT	7,987	5,292	2,539	156	2,753	R	66.3%	31.8%	67.6%	32.4%
22,598	EMANUEL	7,860	5,335	2,435	90	2,900	R	67.9%	31.0%	68.7%	31.3%
11,000	EVANS	3,613	2,404	1,130	79	1,274	R	66.5%	31.3%	68.0%	32.0%
23,682	FANNIN	11,812	9,632	1,923	257	7,709	R	81.5%	16.3%	83.4%	16.6%
106,567	FAYETTE	60,913	35,048	23,284	2,581	11,764	R	57.5%	38.2%	60.1%	39.9%
96,317	FLOYD	34,608	24,114	9,159	1,335	14,955	R	69.7%	26.5%	72.5%	27.5%
175,511	FORSYTH	98,221	69,851	23,462	4,908	46,389	R	71.1%	23.9%	74.9%	25.1%
22,084	FRANKLIN	8,502	7,054	1,243	205	5,811	R	83.0%	14.6%	85.0%	15.0%
920,581	FULTON	431,391	117,783	297,051	16,557	179,268	D	27.3%	68.9%	28.4%	71.6%

GEORGIA
PRESIDENT 2016

2010 Census Population	County	Total Vote	Republican (Trump)	Democratic (Clinton)	Other	Rep.-Dem. Plurality		Total Vote Rep.	Total Vote Dem.	Major Vote Rep.	Major Vote Dem.
28,292	GILMER	12,773	10,477	1,965	331	8,512	R	82.0%	15.4%	84.2%	15.8%
3,082	GLASCOCK	1,390	1,235	138	17	1,097	R	88.8%	9.9%	89.9%	10.1%
79,626	GLYNN	34,263	21,512	11,775	976	9,737	R	62.8%	34.4%	64.6%	35.4%
55,186	GORDON	18,959	15,191	3,181	587	12,010	R	80.1%	16.8%	82.7%	17.3%
25,011	GRADY	9,213	6,053	3,013	147	3,040	R	65.7%	32.7%	66.8%	33.2%
15,994	GREENE	8,852	5,490	3,199	163	2,291	R	62.0%	36.1%	63.2%	36.8%
805,321	GWINNETT	328,331	146,989	166,153	15,189	19,164	D	44.8%	50.6%	46.9%	53.1%
43,041	HABERSHAM	16,243	13,190	2,483	570	10,707	R	81.2%	15.3%	84.2%	15.8%
179,684	HALL	70,694	51,733	16,180	2,781	35,553	R	73.2%	22.9%	76.2%	23.8%
9,429	HANCOCK	3,580	843	2,701	36	1,858	D	23.5%	75.4%	23.8%	76.2%
28,780	HARALSON	11,357	9,585	1,475	297	8,110	R	84.4%	13.0%	86.7%	13.3%
32,024	HARRIS	16,502	11,936	4,086	480	7,850	R	72.3%	24.8%	74.5%	25.5%
25,213	HART	10,117	7,286	2,585	246	4,701	R	72.0%	25.6%	73.8%	26.2%
11,834	HEARD	4,223	3,370	743	110	2,627	R	79.8%	17.6%	81.9%	18.1%
203,922	HENRY	98,766	45,724	50,057	2,985	4,333	D	46.3%	50.7%	47.7%	52.3%
139,900	HOUSTON	60,079	35,430	22,553	2,096	12,877	R	59.0%	37.5%	61.1%	38.9%
9,538	IRWIN	3,670	2,716	891	63	1,825	R	74.0%	24.3%	75.3%	24.7%
60,485	JACKSON	27,190	21,784	4,491	915	17,293	R	80.1%	16.5%	82.9%	17.1%
13,900	JASPER	6,045	4,360	1,544	141	2,816	R	72.1%	25.5%	73.8%	26.2%
15,068	JEFF DAVIS	5,096	4,104	901	91	3,203	R	80.5%	17.7%	82.0%	18.0%
16,930	JEFFERSON	6,968	3,063	3,821	84	758	D	44.0%	54.8%	44.5%	55.5%
8,340	JENKINS	3,056	1,895	1,123	38	772	R	62.0%	36.7%	62.8%	37.2%
9,980	JOHNSON	3,686	2,519	1,136	31	1,383	R	68.3%	30.8%	68.9%	31.1%
28,669	JONES	12,551	8,305	3,961	285	4,344	R	66.2%	31.6%	67.7%	32.3%
18,317	LAMAR	7,612	5,190	2,270	152	2,920	R	68.2%	29.8%	69.6%	30.4%
10,078	LANIER	2,871	1,984	806	81	1,178	R	69.1%	28.1%	71.1%	28.9%
48,434	LAURENS	19,530	12,411	6,752	367	5,659	R	63.5%	34.6%	64.8%	35.2%
28,298	LEE	14,143	10,646	3,170	327	7,476	R	75.3%	22.4%	77.1%	22.9%
63,453	LIBERTY	16,143	6,134	9,556	453	3,422	D	38.0%	59.2%	39.1%	60.9%
7,996	LINCOLN	4,102	2,759	1,273	70	1,486	R	67.3%	31.0%	68.4%	31.6%
14,464	LONG	4,117	2,626	1,360	131	1,266	R	63.8%	33.0%	65.9%	34.1%
109,233	LOWNDES	37,805	21,635	15,064	1,106	6,571	R	57.2%	39.8%	59.0%	41.0%
29,966	LUMPKIN	12,425	9,619	2,220	586	7,399	R	77.4%	17.9%	81.2%	18.8%
14,740	MACON	4,287	1,540	2,705	42	1,165	D	35.9%	63.1%	36.3%	63.7%
28,120	MADISON	11,998	9,201	2,425	372	6,776	R	76.7%	20.2%	79.1%	20.9%
8,742	MARION	3,190	1,921	1,213	56	708	R	60.2%	38.0%	61.3%	38.7%
21,875	MCDUFFIE	9,268	5,432	3,699	137	1,733	R	58.6%	39.9%	59.5%	40.5%
14,333	MCINTOSH	5,903	3,487	2,303	113	1,184	R	59.1%	39.0%	60.2%	39.8%
21,992	MERIWETHER	9,217	5,222	3,804	191	1,418	R	56.7%	41.3%	57.9%	42.1%
6,125	MILLER	2,544	1,891	623	30	1,268	R	74.3%	24.5%	75.2%	24.8%
23,498	MITCHELL	7,880	4,279	3,493	108	786	R	54.3%	44.3%	55.1%	44.9%
26,424	MONROE	12,687	8,832	3,571	284	5,261	R	69.6%	28.1%	71.2%	28.8%
9,123	MONTGOMERY	3,576	2,670	847	59	1,823	R	74.7%	23.7%	75.9%	24.1%
17,868	MORGAN	9,475	6,559	2,663	253	3,896	R	69.2%	28.1%	71.1%	28.9%
39,628	MURRAY	12,458	10,341	1,800	317	8,541	R	83.0%	14.4%	85.2%	14.8%
189,885	MUSCOGEE	69,032	26,976	39,851	2,205	12,875	D	39.1%	57.7%	40.4%	59.6%
99,958	NEWTON	43,987	20,913	21,943	1,131	1,030	D	47.5%	49.9%	48.8%	51.2%
32,808	OCONEE	20,149	13,425	5,581	1,143	7,844	R	66.6%	27.7%	70.6%	29.4%
14,899	OGLETHORPE	6,674	4,625	1,831	218	2,794	R	69.3%	27.4%	71.6%	28.4%
142,324	PAULDING	64,890	44,662	18,025	2,203	26,637	R	68.8%	27.8%	71.2%	28.8%
27,695	PEACH	10,752	5,413	5,100	239	313	R	50.3%	47.4%	51.5%	48.5%
29,431	PICKENS	14,058	11,651	1,979	428	9,672	R	82.9%	14.1%	85.5%	14.5%
18,758	PIERCE	7,311	6,302	903	106	5,399	R	86.2%	12.4%	87.5%	12.5%
17,869	PIKE	8,725	7,278	1,240	207	6,038	R	83.4%	14.2%	85.4%	14.6%
41,475	POLK	14,215	11,014	2,867	334	8,147	R	77.5%	20.2%	79.3%	20.7%
12,010	PULASKI	3,605	2,437	1,104	64	1,333	R	67.6%	30.6%	68.8%	31.2%
21,218	PUTNAM	9,488	6,544	2,758	186	3,786	R	69.0%	29.1%	70.4%	29.6%
2,513	QUITMAN	1,044	575	461	8	114	R	55.1%	44.2%	55.5%	44.5%
16,276	RABUN	7,992	6,287	1,444	261	4,843	R	78.7%	18.1%	81.3%	18.7%
7,719	RANDOLPH	2,899	1,271	1,598	30	327	D	43.8%	55.1%	44.3%	55.7%

GEORGIA

PRESIDENT 2016

2010 Census Population	County	Total Vote	Republican (Trump)	Democratic (Clinton)	Other	Rep.-Dem. Plurality		Total Vote Rep.	Dem.	Major Vote Rep.	Dem.
200,549	RICHMOND	75,515	24,461	48,814	2,240	24,353	D	32.4%	64.6%	33.4%	66.6%
85,215	ROCKDALE	37,869	13,478	23,255	1,136	9,777	D	35.6%	61.4%	36.7%	63.3%
5,010	SCHLEY	1,909	1,472	401	36	1,071	R	77.1%	21.0%	78.6%	21.4%
14,593	SCREVEN	5,715	3,305	2,300	110	1,005	R	57.8%	40.2%	59.0%	41.0%
8,729	SEMINOLE	3,588	2,345	1,189	54	1,156	R	65.4%	33.1%	66.4%	33.6%
64,073	SPALDING	25,704	15,646	9,357	701	6,289	R	60.9%	36.4%	62.6%	37.4%
26,175	STEPHENS	9,815	7,686	1,837	292	5,849	R	78.3%	18.7%	80.7%	19.3%
6,058	STEWART	2,058	805	1,222	31	417	D	39.1%	59.4%	39.7%	60.3%
32,819	SUMTER	10,974	5,276	5,520	178	244	D	48.1%	50.3%	48.9%	51.1%
6,865	TALBOT	3,246	1,196	2,002	48	806	D	36.8%	61.7%	37.4%	62.6%
1,717	TALIAFERRO	897	349	545	3	196	D	38.9%	60.8%	39.0%	61.0%
25,520	TATTNALL	6,903	5,096	1,681	126	3,415	R	73.8%	24.4%	75.2%	24.8%
8,906	TAYLOR	3,408	2,064	1,296	48	768	R	60.6%	38.0%	61.4%	38.6%
16,500	TELFAIR	3,796	2,450	1,313	33	1,137	R	64.5%	34.6%	65.1%	34.9%
9,315	TERRELL	4,189	1,874	2,267	48	393	D	44.7%	54.1%	45.3%	54.7%
44,720	THOMAS	18,802	11,228	7,142	432	4,086	R	59.7%	38.0%	61.1%	38.9%
40,118	TIFT	14,219	9,584	4,347	288	5,237	R	67.4%	30.6%	68.8%	31.2%
27,223	TOOMBS	9,138	6,615	2,338	185	4,277	R	72.4%	25.6%	73.9%	26.1%
10,471	TOWNS	6,764	5,383	1,210	171	4,173	R	79.6%	17.9%	81.6%	18.4%
6,885	TREUTLEN	2,703	1,809	862	32	947	R	66.9%	31.9%	67.7%	32.3%
67,044	TROUP	26,111	15,750	9,713	648	6,037	R	60.3%	37.2%	61.9%	38.1%
8,930	TURNER	3,398	2,095	1,246	57	849	R	61.7%	36.7%	62.7%	37.3%
9,023	TWIGGS	4,059	2,035	1,971	53	64	R	50.1%	48.6%	50.8%	49.2%
21,356	UNION	12,063	9,852	1,963	248	7,889	R	81.7%	16.3%	83.4%	16.6%
27,153	UPSON	10,934	7,292	3,475	167	3,817	R	66.7%	31.8%	67.7%	32.3%
68,756	WALKER	23,956	18,950	4,215	791	14,735	R	79.1%	17.6%	81.8%	18.2%
83,768	WALTON	40,698	31,125	8,292	1,281	22,833	R	76.5%	20.4%	79.0%	21.0%
36,312	WARE	12,184	8,513	3,440	231	5,073	R	69.9%	28.2%	71.2%	28.8%
5,834	WARREN	2,334	991	1,314	29	323	D	42.5%	56.3%	43.0%	57.0%
21,187	WASHINGTON	8,461	4,149	4,200	112	51	D	49.0%	49.6%	49.7%	50.3%
30,099	WAYNE	10,413	8,153	2,041	219	6,112	R	78.3%	19.6%	80.0%	20.0%
2,799	WEBSTER	1,116	630	473	13	157	R	56.5%	42.4%	57.1%	42.9%
7,421	WHEELER	2,102	1,421	646	35	775	R	67.6%	30.7%	68.7%	31.3%
27,144	WHITE	11,823	9,761	1,674	388	8,087	R	82.6%	14.2%	85.4%	14.6%
102,599	WHITFIELD	30,658	21,537	7,937	1,184	13,600	R	70.2%	25.9%	73.1%	26.9%
9,255	WILCOX	2,976	2,096	852	28	1,244	R	70.4%	28.6%	71.1%	28.9%
10,593	WILKES	4,486	2,572	1,848	66	724	R	57.3%	41.2%	58.2%	41.8%
9,563	WILKINSON	4,287	2,333	1,894	60	439	R	54.4%	44.2%	55.2%	44.8%
21,679	WORTH	8,295	6,152	2,020	123	4,132	R	74.2%	24.4%	75.3%	24.7%
9,687,653	TOTAL	4,114,732	2,089,104	1,877,963	147,665	211,141	R	50.8%	45.6%	52.7%	47.3%

GEORGIA

SENATOR 2016

2010 Census Population	County	Total Vote	Republican (Isakson)	Democratic (Barksdale)	Other	Rep.-Dem. Plurality		Total Vote Rep.	Dem.	Major Vote Rep.	Dem.
18,236	APPLING	6,512	5,170	1,187	155	3,983	R	79.4%	18.2%	81.3%	18.7%
8,375	ATKINSON	2,339	1,678	596	65	1,082	R	71.7%	25.5%	73.8%	26.2%
11,096	BACON	3,615	3,046	474	95	2,572	R	84.3%	13.1%	86.5%	13.5%
3,451	BAKER	1,323	763	531	29	232	R	57.7%	40.1%	59.0%	41.0%
45,720	BALDWIN	15,048	7,796	6,787	465	1,009	R	51.8%	45.1%	53.5%	46.5%

GEORGIA
SENATOR 2016

2010 Census Population	County	Total Vote	Republican (Isakson)	Democratic (Barksdale)	Other	Rep.-Dem. Plurality	Percentage Total Vote Rep.	Dem.	Major Vote Rep.	Dem.
18,395	BANKS	6,683	5,705	673	305	5,032 R	85.4%	10.1%	89.4%	10.6%
69,367	BARROW	27,580	20,281	5,691	1,608	14,590 R	73.5%	20.6%	78.1%	21.9%
100,157	BARTOW	37,381	28,073	7,291	2,017	20,782 R	75.1%	19.5%	79.4%	20.6%
17,634	BEN HILL	5,463	3,589	1,739	135	1,850 R	65.7%	31.8%	67.4%	32.6%
19,286	BERRIEN	6,182	5,061	895	226	4,166 R	81.9%	14.5%	85.0%	15.0%
155,547	BIBB	58,836	25,601	31,533	1,702	5,932 D	43.5%	53.6%	44.8%	55.2%
13,063	BLECKLEY	4,768	3,698	923	147	2,775 R	77.6%	19.4%	80.0%	20.0%
18,411	BRANTLEY	5,703	4,844	611	248	4,233 R	84.9%	10.7%	88.8%	11.2%
16,243	BROOKS	5,745	3,465	2,092	188	1,373 R	60.3%	36.4%	62.4%	37.6%
30,233	BRYAN	14,360	10,488	3,216	656	7,272 R	73.0%	22.4%	76.5%	23.5%
70,217	BULLOCH	24,287	15,530	7,738	1,019	7,792 R	63.9%	31.9%	66.7%	33.3%
23,316	BURKE	8,716	4,448	4,068	200	380 R	51.0%	46.7%	52.2%	47.8%
23,655	BUTTS	8,835	6,320	2,167	348	4,153 R	71.5%	24.5%	74.5%	25.5%
6,694	CALHOUN	1,899	862	1,007	30	145 D	45.4%	53.0%	46.1%	53.9%
50,513	CAMDEN	17,557	11,454	5,097	1,006	6,357 R	65.2%	29.0%	69.2%	30.8%
10,998	CANDLER	3,548	2,588	855	105	1,733 R	72.9%	24.1%	75.2%	24.8%
110,527	CARROLL	41,911	29,043	10,867	2,001	18,176 R	69.3%	25.9%	72.8%	27.2%
63,942	CATOOSA	24,296	18,888	4,121	1,287	14,767 R	77.7%	17.0%	82.1%	17.9%
12,171	CHARLTON	3,504	2,489	873	142	1,616 R	71.0%	24.9%	74.0%	26.0%
265,128	CHATHAM	105,977	49,740	52,146	4,091	2,406 D	46.9%	49.2%	48.8%	51.2%
11,267	CHATTAHOOCHEE	1,270	700	508	62	192 R	55.1%	40.0%	57.9%	42.1%
26,015	CHATTOOGA	7,744	5,827	1,622	295	4,205 R	75.2%	20.9%	78.2%	21.8%
214,346	CHEROKEE	107,347	80,166	20,717	6,464	59,449 R	74.7%	19.3%	79.5%	20.5%
116,714	CLARKE	43,223	15,529	25,474	2,220	9,945 D	35.9%	58.9%	37.9%	62.1%
3,183	CLAY	1,157	560	574	23	14 D	48.4%	49.6%	49.4%	50.6%
259,424	CLAYTON	86,776	14,918	69,400	2,458	54,482 D	17.2%	80.0%	17.7%	82.3%
6,798	CLINCH	2,118	1,549	493	76	1,056 R	73.1%	23.3%	75.9%	24.1%
688,078	COBB	320,184	169,269	133,871	17,044	35,398 R	52.9%	41.8%	55.8%	44.2%
42,356	COFFEE	12,738	8,883	3,494	361	5,389 R	69.7%	27.4%	71.8%	28.2%
45,498	COLQUITT	12,682	9,618	2,726	338	6,892 R	75.8%	21.5%	77.9%	22.1%
124,053	COLUMBIA	61,137	42,891	15,800	2,446	27,091 R	70.2%	25.8%	73.1%	26.9%
17,212	COOK	5,694	4,045	1,462	187	2,583 R	71.0%	25.7%	73.5%	26.5%
127,317	COWETA	58,885	41,972	14,088	2,825	27,884 R	71.3%	23.9%	74.9%	25.1%
12,630	CRAWFORD	4,849	3,494	1,193	162	2,301 R	72.1%	24.6%	74.5%	25.5%
23,439	CRISP	6,962	4,546	2,245	171	2,301 R	65.3%	32.2%	66.9%	33.1%
16,633	DADE	5,675	4,448	880	347	3,568 R	78.4%	15.5%	83.5%	16.5%
22,330	DAWSON	11,208	9,314	1,233	661	8,081 R	83.1%	11.0%	88.3%	11.7%
27,842	DECATUR	9,412	5,593	3,529	290	2,064 R	59.4%	37.5%	61.3%	38.7%
691,893	DEKALB	301,198	70,994	218,383	11,821	147,389 D	23.6%	72.5%	24.5%	75.5%
21,796	DODGE	6,379	4,766	1,441	172	3,325 R	74.7%	22.6%	76.8%	23.2%
14,918	DOOLY	3,533	2,022	1,441	70	581 R	57.2%	40.8%	58.4%	41.6%
94,565	DOUGHERTY	31,969	11,048	20,354	567	9,306 D	34.6%	63.7%	35.2%	64.8%
132,403	DOUGLAS	55,364	25,102	28,166	2,096	3,064 D	45.3%	50.9%	47.1%	52.9%
11,008	EARLY	4,504	2,515	1,877	112	638 R	55.8%	41.7%	57.3%	42.7%
4,034	ECHOLS	1,065	874	146	45	728 R	82.1%	13.7%	85.7%	14.3%
52,250	EFFINGHAM	22,303	17,389	4,049	865	13,340 R	78.0%	18.2%	81.1%	18.9%
20,166	ELBERT	7,345	4,960	2,154	231	2,806 R	67.5%	29.3%	69.7%	30.3%
22,598	EMANUEL	7,222	5,062	1,974	186	3,088 R	70.1%	27.3%	71.9%	28.1%
11,000	EVANS	3,327	2,395	852	80	1,543 R	72.0%	25.6%	73.8%	26.2%
23,682	FANNIN	11,084	8,841	1,778	465	7,063 R	79.8%	16.0%	83.3%	16.7%
106,567	FAYETTE	58,517	36,356	19,602	2,559	16,754 R	62.1%	33.5%	65.0%	35.0%
96,317	FLOYD	32,616	23,480	7,812	1,324	15,668 R	72.0%	24.0%	75.0%	25.0%
175,511	FORSYTH	94,290	70,833	18,169	5,288	52,664 R	75.1%	19.3%	79.6%	20.4%
22,084	FRANKLIN	7,928	6,488	1,113	327	5,375 R	81.8%	14.0%	85.4%	14.6%
920,581	FULTON	415,531	151,689	246,397	17,445	94,708 D	36.5%	59.3%	38.1%	61.9%
28,292	GILMER	11,921	9,508	1,795	618	7,713 R	79.8%	15.1%	84.1%	15.9%
3,082	GLASCOCK	1,280	1,101	142	37	959 R	86.0%	11.1%	88.6%	11.4%
79,626	GLYNN	31,503	20,887	9,439	1,177	11,448 R	66.3%	30.0%	68.9%	31.1%
55,186	GORDON	17,762	14,092	2,854	816	11,238 R	79.3%	16.1%	83.2%	16.8%
25,011	GRADY	8,466	5,534	2,671	261	2,863 R	65.4%	31.5%	67.4%	32.6%

GEORGIA

SENATOR 2016

2010 Census Population	County	Total Vote	Republican (Isakson)	Democratic (Barksdale)	Other	Rep.-Dem. Plurality		Total Vote		Major Vote	
								Rep.	Dem.	Rep.	Dem.
15,994	GREENE	8,514	5,735	2,625	154	3,110	R	67.4%	30.8%	68.6%	31.4%
805,321	GWINNETT	311,194	154,572	141,141	15,481	13,431	R	49.7%	45.4%	52.3%	47.7%
43,041	HABERSHAM	15,407	12,493	2,173	741	10,320	R	81.1%	14.1%	85.2%	14.8%
179,684	HALL	67,297	50,124	13,602	3,571	36,522	R	74.5%	20.2%	78.7%	21.3%
9,429	HANCOCK	3,297	946	2,295	56	1,349	D	28.7%	69.6%	29.2%	70.8%
28,780	HARALSON	10,758	8,833	1,444	481	7,389	R	82.1%	13.4%	85.9%	14.1%
32,024	HARRIS	15,588	11,608	3,395	585	8,213	R	74.5%	21.8%	77.4%	22.6%
25,213	HART	9,228	6,703	2,180	345	4,523	R	72.6%	23.6%	75.5%	24.5%
11,834	HEARD	3,951	3,099	679	173	2,420	R	78.4%	17.2%	82.0%	18.0%
203,922	HENRY	92,810	45,234	44,108	3,468	1,126	R	48.7%	47.5%	50.6%	49.4%
139,900	HOUSTON	56,560	35,289	19,191	2,080	16,098	R	62.4%	33.9%	64.8%	35.2%
9,538	IRWIN	3,431	2,581	762	88	1,819	R	75.2%	22.2%	77.2%	22.8%
60,485	JACKSON	26,095	20,965	3,906	1,224	17,059	R	80.3%	15.0%	84.3%	15.7%
13,900	JASPER	5,772	4,180	1,362	230	2,818	R	72.4%	23.6%	75.4%	24.6%
15,068	JEFF DAVIS	4,635	3,716	775	144	2,941	R	80.2%	16.7%	82.7%	17.3%
16,930	JEFFERSON	6,245	3,040	3,091	114	51	D	48.7%	49.5%	49.6%	50.4%
8,340	JENKINS	2,822	1,826	934	62	892	R	64.7%	33.1%	66.2%	33.8%
9,980	JOHNSON	3,338	2,373	888	77	1,485	R	71.1%	26.6%	72.8%	27.2%
28,669	JONES	11,952	8,125	3,482	345	4,643	R	68.0%	29.1%	70.0%	30.0%
18,317	LAMAR	7,182	4,929	2,003	250	2,926	R	68.6%	27.9%	71.1%	28.9%
10,078	LANIER	2,574	1,792	661	121	1,131	R	69.6%	25.7%	73.1%	26.9%
48,434	LAURENS	18,442	12,449	5,563	430	6,886	R	67.5%	30.2%	69.1%	30.9%
28,298	LEE	13,510	10,305	2,876	329	7,429	R	76.3%	21.3%	78.2%	21.8%
63,453	LIBERTY	15,256	6,497	8,147	612	1,650	D	42.6%	53.4%	44.4%	55.6%
7,996	LINCOLN	3,864	2,671	1,098	95	1,573	R	69.1%	28.4%	70.9%	29.1%
14,464	LONG	3,845	2,524	1,152	169	1,372	R	65.6%	30.0%	68.7%	31.3%
109,233	LOWNDES	35,227	20,802	13,087	1,338	7,715	R	59.1%	37.2%	61.4%	38.6%
29,966	LUMPKIN	11,924	9,197	1,955	772	7,242	R	77.1%	16.4%	82.5%	17.5%
14,740	MACON	3,885	1,678	2,129	78	451	D	43.2%	54.8%	44.1%	55.9%
28,120	MADISON	11,436	8,828	2,164	444	6,664	R	77.2%	18.9%	80.3%	19.7%
8,742	MARION	2,955	1,845	1,033	77	812	R	62.4%	35.0%	64.1%	35.9%
21,875	MCDUFFIE	8,509	5,253	3,045	211	2,208	R	61.7%	35.8%	63.3%	36.7%
14,333	MCINTOSH	5,514	3,420	1,905	189	1,515	R	62.0%	34.5%	64.2%	35.8%
21,992	MERIWETHER	8,625	5,158	3,194	273	1,964	R	59.8%	37.0%	61.8%	38.2%
6,125	MILLER	2,272	1,709	503	60	1,206	R	75.2%	22.1%	77.3%	22.7%
23,498	MITCHELL	7,347	4,243	2,977	127	1,266	R	57.8%	40.5%	58.8%	41.2%
26,424	MONROE	12,069	8,719	2,965	385	5,754	R	72.2%	24.6%	74.6%	25.4%
9,123	MONTGOMERY	3,303	2,532	676	95	1,856	R	76.7%	20.5%	78.9%	21.1%
17,868	MORGAN	9,069	6,533	2,216	320	4,317	R	72.0%	24.4%	74.7%	25.3%
39,628	MURRAY	11,116	8,922	1,741	453	7,181	R	80.3%	15.7%	83.7%	16.3%
189,885	MUSCOGEE	63,814	27,940	33,620	2,254	5,680	D	43.8%	52.7%	45.4%	54.6%
99,958	NEWTON	41,842	20,584	19,851	1,407	733	R	49.2%	47.4%	50.9%	49.1%
32,808	OCONEE	19,645	14,344	4,423	878	9,921	R	73.0%	22.5%	76.4%	23.6%
14,899	OGLETHORPE	6,390	4,502	1,629	259	2,873	R	70.5%	25.5%	73.4%	26.6%
142,324	PAULDING	61,862	42,974	15,732	3,156	27,242	R	69.5%	25.4%	73.2%	26.8%
27,695	PEACH	10,196	5,419	4,454	323	965	R	53.1%	43.7%	54.9%	45.1%
29,431	PICKENS	13,419	11,001	1,739	679	9,262	R	82.0%	13.0%	86.4%	13.6%
18,758	PIERCE	6,751	5,817	751	183	5,066	R	86.2%	11.1%	88.6%	11.4%
17,869	PIKE	8,327	6,913	1,101	313	5,812	R	83.0%	13.2%	86.3%	13.7%
41,475	POLK	13,353	10,219	2,613	521	7,606	R	76.5%	19.6%	79.6%	20.4%
12,010	PULASKI	3,374	2,415	871	88	1,544	R	71.6%	25.8%	73.5%	26.5%
21,218	PUTNAM	9,046	6,435	2,334	277	4,101	R	71.1%	25.8%	73.4%	26.6%
2,513	QUITMAN	912	501	382	29	119	R	54.9%	41.9%	56.7%	43.3%
16,276	RABUN	7,564	5,977	1,256	331	4,721	R	79.0%	16.6%	82.6%	17.4%
7,719	RANDOLPH	2,609	1,293	1,275	41	18	R	49.6%	48.9%	50.4%	49.6%
200,549	RICHMOND	70,341	25,908	42,229	2,204	16,321	D	36.8%	60.0%	38.0%	62.0%
85,215	ROCKDALE	36,294	13,893	21,223	1,178	7,330	D	38.3%	58.5%	39.6%	60.4%
5,010	SCHLEY	1,828	1,445	345	38	1,100	R	79.0%	18.9%	80.7%	19.3%
14,593	SCREVEN	5,341	3,289	1,942	110	1,347	R	61.6%	36.4%	62.9%	37.1%
8,729	SEMINOLE	3,172	2,070	1,012	90	1,058	R	65.3%	31.9%	67.2%	32.8%

GEORGIA

SENATOR 2016

2010 Census Population	County	Total Vote	Republican (Isakson)	Democratic (Barksdale)	Other	Rep.-Dem. Plurality	Total Vote Rep.	Total Vote Dem.	Major Vote Rep.	Major Vote Dem.
64,073	SPALDING	23,966	15,172	7,879	915	7,293 R	63.3%	32.9%	65.8%	34.2%
26,175	STEPHENS	9,178	7,284	1,548	346	5,736 R	79.4%	16.9%	82.5%	17.5%
6,058	STEWART	1,750	807	900	43	93 D	46.1%	51.4%	47.3%	52.7%
32,819	SUMTER	10,491	5,418	4,876	197	542 R	51.6%	46.5%	52.6%	47.4%
6,865	TALBOT	2,965	1,228	1,639	98	411 D	41.4%	55.3%	42.8%	57.2%
1,717	TALIAFERRO	798	341	443	14	102 D	42.7%	55.5%	43.5%	56.5%
25,520	TATTNALL	6,461	4,960	1,354	147	3,606 R	76.8%	21.0%	78.6%	21.4%
8,906	TAYLOR	3,146	1,974	1,091	81	883 R	62.7%	34.7%	64.4%	35.6%
16,500	TELFAIR	3,506	2,327	1,120	59	1,207 R	66.4%	31.9%	67.5%	32.5%
9,315	TERRELL	3,932	1,997	1,857	78	140 R	50.8%	47.2%	51.8%	48.2%
44,720	THOMAS	17,365	10,823	6,002	540	4,821 R	62.3%	34.6%	64.3%	35.7%
40,118	TIFT	13,301	9,510	3,432	359	6,078 R	71.5%	25.8%	73.5%	26.5%
27,223	TOOMBS	8,568	6,367	1,953	248	4,414 R	74.3%	22.8%	76.5%	23.5%
10,471	TOWNS	6,354	4,964	1,164	226	3,800 R	78.1%	18.3%	81.0%	19.0%
6,885	TREUTLEN	2,390	1,700	626	64	1,074 R	71.1%	26.2%	73.1%	26.9%
67,044	TROUP	24,436	15,293	8,312	831	6,981 R	62.6%	34.0%	64.8%	35.2%
8,930	TURNER	3,145	2,039	1,031	75	1,008 R	64.8%	32.8%	66.4%	33.6%
9,023	TWIGGS	3,725	1,975	1,655	95	320 R	53.0%	44.4%	54.4%	45.6%
21,356	UNION	11,434	9,181	1,820	433	7,361 R	80.3%	15.9%	83.5%	16.5%
27,153	UPSON	10,283	7,063	2,911	309	4,152 R	68.7%	28.3%	70.8%	29.2%
68,756	WALKER	21,952	17,086	3,750	1,116	13,336 R	77.8%	17.1%	82.0%	18.0%
83,768	WALTON	38,546	29,723	7,183	1,640	22,540 R	77.1%	18.6%	80.5%	19.5%
36,312	WARE	11,140	7,872	2,871	397	5,001 R	70.7%	25.8%	73.3%	26.7%
5,834	WARREN	2,148	993	1,110	45	117 D	46.2%	51.7%	47.2%	52.8%
21,187	WASHINGTON	7,811	4,092	3,608	111	484 R	52.4%	46.2%	53.1%	46.9%
30,099	WAYNE	9,683	7,686	1,705	292	5,981 R	79.4%	17.6%	81.8%	18.2%
2,799	WEBSTER	1,051	649	387	15	262 R	61.8%	36.8%	62.6%	37.4%
7,421	WHEELER	1,904	1,304	545	55	759 R	68.5%	28.6%	70.5%	29.5%
27,144	WHITE	11,339	9,212	1,541	586	7,671 R	81.2%	13.6%	85.7%	14.3%
102,599	WHITFIELD	27,952	19,808	6,763	1,381	13,045 R	70.9%	24.2%	74.5%	25.5%
9,255	WILCOX	2,775	2,036	669	70	1,367 R	73.4%	24.1%	75.3%	24.7%
10,593	WILKES	4,131	2,507	1,525	99	982 R	60.7%	36.9%	62.2%	37.8%
9,563	WILKINSON	3,961	2,266	1,616	79	650 R	57.2%	40.8%	58.4%	41.6%
21,679	WORTH	7,884	5,884	1,839	161	4,045 R	74.6%	23.3%	76.2%	23.8%
9,687,653	TOTAL	3,898,605	2,135,806	1,599,726	163,073	536,080 R	54.8%	41.0%	57.2%	42.8%

GEORGIA

HOUSE OF REPRESENTATIVES

CD	Year	Total Vote	Republican Vote	Republican Candidate	Democratic Vote	Democratic Candidate	Other Vote	Rep.-Dem. Plurality	Total Vote Rep.	Total Vote Dem.	Major Vote Rep.	Major Vote Dem.
1	2016	211,112	210,243	CARTER, EARL LEROY "BUDDY"*			869	210,243 R	99.6%		100.0%	
1	2014	156,512	95,337	CARTER, EARL LEROY "BUDDY"	61,175	REESE, BRIAN CORWIN		34,162 R	60.9%	39.1%	60.9%	39.1%
1	2012	249,580	157,181	KINGSTON, JACK*	92,399	MESSINGER, LESLI		64,782 R	63.0%	37.0%	63.0%	37.0%
2	2016	242,599	94,056	DUKE, GREG	148,543	BISHOP, SANFORD*		54,487 D	38.8%	61.2%	38.8%	61.2%
2	2014	162,900	66,537	DUKE, GREG	96,363	BISHOP, SANFORD*		29,826 D	40.8%	59.2%	40.8%	59.2%
2	2012	255,161	92,410	HOUSE, JOHN	162,751	BISHOP, SANFORD*		70,341 D	36.2%	63.8%	36.2%	63.8%
3	2016	303,187	207,218	FERGUSON, DREW	95,969	PENDLEY, ANGELA		111,249 R	68.3%	31.7%	68.3%	31.7%
3	2014	156,277	156,277	WESTMORELAND, LYNN A.*				156,277 R	100.0%		100.0%	
3	2012	232,485	232,380	WESTMORELAND, LYNN A.*			105	232,380 R	100.0%		100.0%	

GEORGIA

HOUSE OF REPRESENTATIVES

CD	Year	Total Vote	Republican		Democratic		Other Vote	Rep.-Dem. Plurality	Percentage			
									Total Vote		Major Vote	
			Vote	Candidate	Vote	Candidate			Rep.	Dem.	Rep.	Dem.
4	2016	290,739	70,593	ARMENDARIZ, VICTOR	220,146	JOHNSON, HENRY C. "HANK"*		149,553 D	24.3%	75.7%	24.3%	75.7%
4	2014	161,320			161,211	JOHNSON, HENRY C. "HANK"*	109	161,211 D		99.9%		100.0%
4	2012	283,962	75,041	VAUGHN, J. CHRIS	208,861	JOHNSON, HENRY C. "HANK"*	60	133,820 D	26.4%	73.6%	26.4%	73.6%
5	2016	300,549	46,768	BELL, DOUGLAS	253,781	LEWIS, JOHN*		207,013 D	15.6%	84.4%	15.6%	84.4%
5	2014	170,326			170,326	LEWIS, JOHN*		170,326 D		100.0%		100.0%
5	2012	277,689	43,335	STOPECK, HOWARD	234,330	LEWIS, JOHN*	24	190,995 D	15.6%	84.4%	15.6%	84.4%
6	2016	326,005	201,088	PRICE, THOMAS E.*	124,917	STOOKSBURY, RODNEY		76,171 R	61.7%	38.3%	61.7%	38.3%
6	2014	210,504	139,018	PRICE, THOMAS E.*	71,486	MONTIGEL, ROBERT		67,532 R	66.0%	34.0%	66.0%	34.0%
6	2012	294,034	189,669	PRICE, THOMAS E.*	104,365	KAZANOW, JEFF		85,304 R	64.5%	35.5%	64.5%	35.5%
7	2016	288,301	174,081	WOODALL, ROB*	114,220	MALIK, RASHID		59,861 R	60.4%	39.6%	60.4%	39.6%
7	2014	173,669	113,557	WOODALL, ROB*	60,112	WIGHT, THOMAS D.		53,445 R	65.4%	34.6%	65.4%	34.6%
7	2012	252,066	156,689	WOODALL, ROB*	95,377	REILLY, STEVE		61,312 R	62.2%	37.8%	62.2%	37.8%
8	2016	257,208	173,983	SCOTT, AUSTIN*	83,225	HARRIS, JAMES NEAL		90,758 R	67.6%	32.4%	67.6%	32.4%
8	2014	130,057	129,938	SCOTT, AUSTIN*			119	129,938 R	99.9%		100.0%	
8	2012	197,789	197,789	SCOTT, AUSTIN*				197,789 R	100.0%		100.0%	
9	2016	256,535	256,535	COLLINS, DOUG*				256,535 R	100.0%		100.0%	
9	2014	181,047	146,059	COLLINS, DOUG*	34,988	VOGEL, DAVID D.		111,071 R	80.7%	19.3%	80.7%	19.3%
9	2012	252,153	192,101	COLLINS, DOUG	60,052	COOLEY, JODY		132,049 R	76.2%	23.8%	76.2%	23.8%
10	2016	244,821	243,725	HICE, JODY*			1,096	243,725 R	99.6%		100.0%	
10	2014	196,480	130,703	HICE, JODY	65,777	DIOUS, IVORY KENNETH "KEN"		64,926 R	66.5%	33.5%	66.5%	33.5%
10	2012	211,466	211,065	BROUN, PAUL*			401	211,065 R	99.8%		100.0%	
11	2016	323,318	217,935	LOUDERMILK, BARRY*	105,383	WILSON, DON		112,552 R	67.4%	32.6%	67.4%	32.6%
11	2014	161,532	161,532	LOUDERMILK, BARRY				161,532 R	100.0%		100.0%	
11	2012	287,351	196,968	GINGREY, PHIL*	90,353	THOMPSON, PATRICK	30	106,615 R	68.5%	31.4%	68.6%	31.4%
12	2016	258,912	159,492	ALLEN, RICK W.*	99,420	MCCRACKEN, PATRICIA CARPENTER "TRICIA"		60,072 R	61.6%	38.4%	61.6%	38.4%
12	2014	166,814	91,336	ALLEN, RICK W.	75,478	BARROW, JOHN*		15,858 R	54.8%	45.2%	54.8%	45.2%
12	2012	259,121	119,973	ANDERSON, LEE	139,148	BARROW, JOHN*		19,175 D	46.3%	53.7%	46.3%	53.7%
13	2016	252,833			252,833	SCOTT, DAVID*		252,833 D		100.0%		100.0%
13	2014	159,445			159,445	SCOTT, DAVID*		159,445 D		100.0%		100.0%
13	2012	281,538	79,550	MALIK, S.	201,988	SCOTT, DAVID*		122,438 D	28.3%	71.7%	28.3%	71.7%
14	2016	216,743	216,743	GRAVES, TOM*				216,743 R	100.0%		100.0%	
14	2014	118,782	118,782	GRAVES, TOM*				118,782 R	100.0%		100.0%	
14	2012	219,192	159,947	GRAVES, TOM*	59,245	GRANT, DANIEL "DANNY"		100,702 R	73.0%	27.0%	73.0%	27.0%
TOTAL	2016	3,772,862	2,272,460		1,498,437		1,965	774,023 R	60.2%	39.7%	60.3%	39.7%
TOTAL	2014	2,305,665	1,349,076		956,361		228	392,715 R	58.5%	41.5%	58.5%	41.5%
TOTAL	2012	3,553,587	2,104,098		1,448,869		620	655,229 R	59.2%	40.8%	59.2%	40.8%

Note: An asterisk (*) denotes incumbent.

GEORGIA

GENERAL AND PRIMARY ELECTIONS

2016 GENERAL ELECTIONS: OTHER VOTES

President Other vote was 125,306 Libertarian (Gary Johnson), 13,017 Write-in (Evan McMullin), 7,674 Write-in (Jill Stein), 1,110 Write-in (Darrell Castle), 151 Write-in (Michael Maturen), 407 Write-in (Scattered Write-in)

Senate Other vote was 162,260 Libertarian (Allen Buckley), 813 Write-in (Michelle Gates)

House Other vote was:

CD 1 869 Write-in (Nathan Russo)

CD 10 886 Write-in (Leonard Ware), 210 Write-in (Patrick Boggs)

GEORGIA

GENERAL AND PRIMARY ELECTIONS

2016 PRIMARY ELECTIONS: SUPPLEMENTARY INFORMATION

Primary	March 1, 2016 (President) May 24, 2016 (Congress)	**Registration** (as of May 24, 2016)	5,819,471	No Party Registration
Primary Runoff	July 26, 2016			

Primary Type   Open—Any registered voter could participate in either the Democratic or the Republican primary, although if voters cast a ballot in one party's primary they could not participate in a primary runoff of the other party. Voters who did not participate in the primary could vote in either party's runoff.

	REPUBLICAN PRIMARIES			DEMOCRATIC PRIMARIES		
President	Trump, Donald J.	502,994	38.8%	Clinton, Hillary Rodham	545,674	71.3%
	Rubio, Marco	316,836	24.4%	Sanders, Bernard	215,797	28.2%
	Cruz, Ted	305,847	23.6%	O'Malley, Martin	2,129	0.3%
	Carson, Ben	80,723	6.2%	Steinberg, Michael Alan	1,766	0.2%
	Kasich, John R.	72,508	5.6%			
	Bush, Jeb	7,686	0.6%			
	Paul, Rand	2,910	0.2%			
	Huckabee, Mike	2,625	0.2%			
	Christie, Chris	1,486	0.1%			
	Fiorina, Carly	1,146	0.1%			
	Santorum, Rick	539				
	Graham, Lindsey	428				
	Pataki, George E.	236				
	TOTAL	*1,295,964*		*TOTAL*	*765,366*	
Senator	Isakson, Johnny*	447,661	77.5%	Barksdale, Jim	166,627	53.7%
	Grayson, Derrick E.	69,101	12.0%	Copeland, Cheryl	130,822	42.2%
	Bacallao, Mary Kay	60,898	10.5%	Coyne, John	12,604	4.1%
	TOTAL	*577,660*		*TOTAL*	*310,053*	
Congressional District 1	Carter, Earl Leroy "Buddy"*	37,758	100.0%			
	TOTAL	*37,758*				
Congressional District 2	Duke, Greg	12,959	79.0%	Bishop, Sanford*	55,880	100.0%
	Vann, Diane	3,446	21.0%			
	TOTAL	*16,405*		*TOTAL*	*55,880*	
Congressional District 3	Crane, Mike	15,584	26.9%	Pendley, Angela	6,495	50.2%
	Ferguson, Drew	15,491	26.8%	Cook, Tamarkus	6,444	49.8%
	Pace, Jim	13,312	23.0%			
	Flanegan, "Chip"	5,728	9.9%			
	Mix, Richard	5,285	9.1%			
	Anders, Samuel	1,657	2.9%			
	Thomas, Arnall "Rod"	812	1.4%			
	TOTAL	*57,869*		*TOTAL*	*12,939*	
	PRIMARY RUNOFF					
	Ferguson, Drew	22,836	53.9%			
	Crane, Mike	19,498	46.1%			
	TOTAL	*42,334*				
Congressional District 4	Armendariz, Victor	10,260	100.0%	Johnson, Henry C. "Hank"*	44,509	100.0%
	TOTAL	*10,260*		*TOTAL*	*44,509*	
Congressional District 5	Bell, Douglas	3,635	100.0%	Lewis, John*	47,313	100.0%
	TOTAL	*3,635*		*TOTAL*	*47,313*	

GEORGIA

GENERAL AND PRIMARY ELECTIONS

	REPUBLICAN PRIMARIES			DEMOCRATIC PRIMARIES		
Congressional District 6	Price, Thomas E.*	32,021	100.0%	Stooksbury, Rodney	11,050	100.0%
	TOTAL	*32,021*		*TOTAL*	*11,050*	
Congressional District 7	Woodall, Rob*	24,201	100.0%	Malik, Rashid	5,593	100.0%
	TOTAL	*24,201*		*TOTAL*	*5,593*	
Congressional District 8	Scott, Austin*	34,919	77.8%	Harris, James Neal	18,647	100.0%
	Hicks, Angela	9,988	22.2%			
	TOTAL	*44,907*		*TOTAL*	*18,647*	
Congressional District 9	Collins, Doug*	52,080	61.3%			
	Broun, Paul	18,772	22.1%			
	Fitzpatrick, Roger D.	8,945	10.5%			
	Scupin, Mike	2,856	3.4%			
	Fontaine, Bernard "Bernie"	2,342	2.8%			
	TOTAL	*84,995*				
Congressional District 10	Hice, Jody*	49,062	100.0%			
	TOTAL	*49,062*				
Congressional District 11	Loudermilk, Barry*	29,903	60.3%	Wilson, Don	6,861	100.0%
	Cowan, Daniel	9,169	18.5%			
	Llop, William	4,857	9.8%			
	Collins, Hayden	3,247	6.5%			
	Davis, Billy	2,435	4.9%			
	TOTAL	*49,611*		*TOTAL*	*6,861*	
Congressional District 12	Allen, Rick W.*	46,686	79.0%	McCracken, Patricia "Tricia" Carpenter	16,138	62.2%
	Yu, Eugene	12,441	21.0%	Nolin, Joyce	9,787	37.8%
	TOTAL	*59,127*		*TOTAL*	*25,925*	
Congressional District 13				Scott, David*	36,214	100.0%
				TOTAL	*36,214*	
Congressional District 14	Graves, Tom*	44,260	75.6%			
	Tuck, Mickey	7,493	12.8%			
	Levene, Allan	6,755	11.5%			
	TOTAL	*58,508*				

Note: An asterisk (*) denotes incumbent.

HAWAII

Congressional districts first established for elections held in 2012

2 members

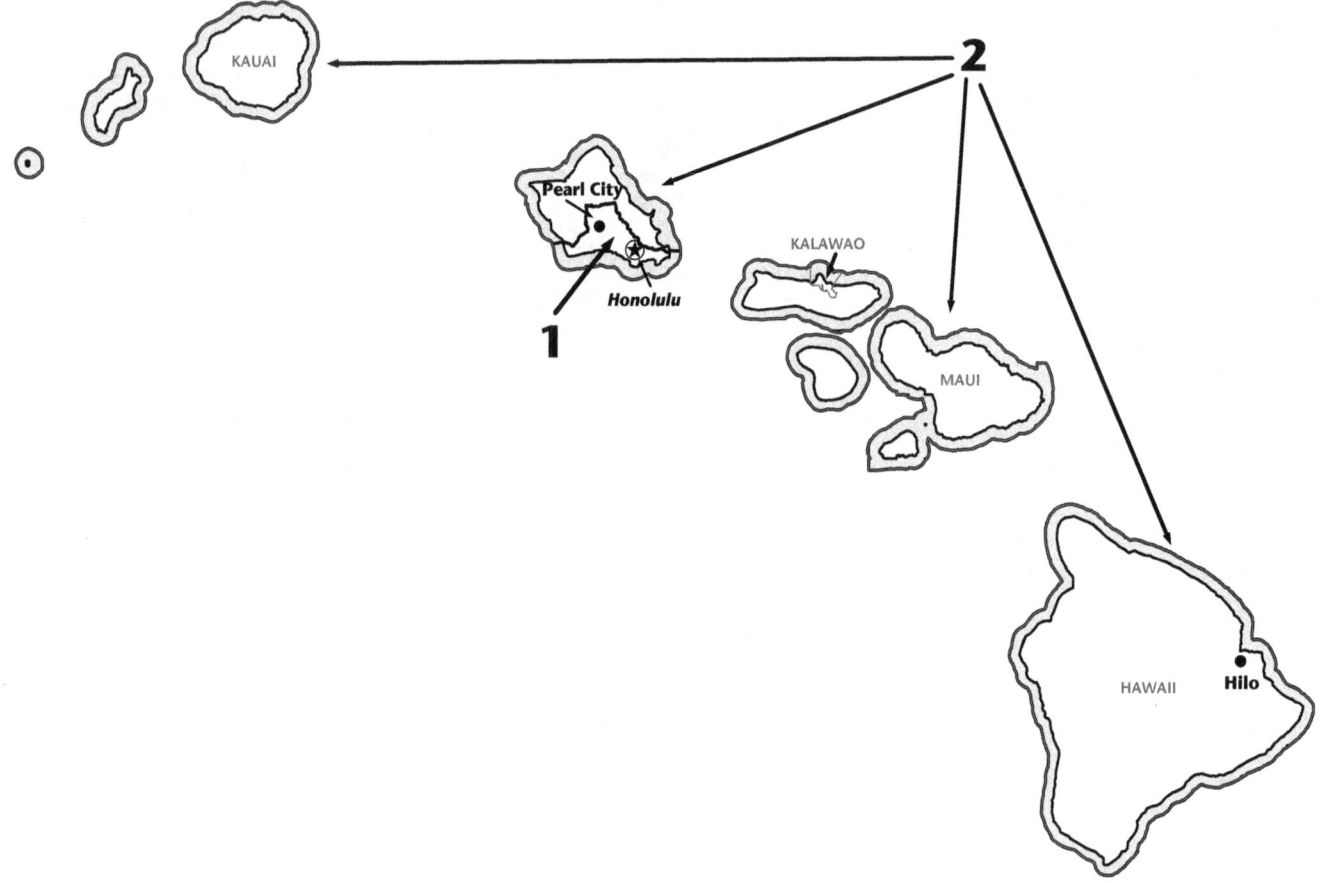

Hawaii includes more islands to the west of those that are illustrated on this map.

HAWAII

GOVERNOR
David Ige (D). Elected 2014 to a four-year term.

SENATORS (2 Democrats)
Mazie K. Hirono (D). Elected 2012 to a six-year term.

Brian Schatz (D). Re-elected 2016 to a six-year term. Elected November 4, 2014, in a special election following the death of Senator Daniel K. Inouye. Schatz was initially appointed December 27, 2012, to fill the vacancy.

REPRESENTATIVES (2 Democrats)
1. Colleen Hanabusa (D)   2. Tulsi Gabbard (D)

POSTWAR VOTE FOR PRESIDENT

| | | Republican | | Democratic | | Other Vote | Rep.-Dem. Plurality | Percentage | | | |
| | | | | | | | | Total Vote | | Major Vote | |
Year	Total Vote	Vote	Candidate	Vote	Candidate			Rep.	Dem.	Rep.	Dem.
2016**	428,937	128,847	Trump, Donald J.	266,891	Clinton, Hillary Rodham	33,199	138,044 D	30.0%	62.2%	32.6%	67.4%
2012	434,697	121,015	Romney, W. Mitt	306,658	Obama, Barack H.*	7,024	185,643 D	27.8%	70.5%	28.3%	71.7%
2008	453,568	120,566	McCain, John S. III	325,871	Obama, Barack H.	7,131	205,305 D	26.6%	71.8%	27.0%	73.0%
2004	429,013	194,191	Bush, George W.*	231,708	Kerry, John F.	3,114	37,517 D	45.3%	54.0%	45.6%	54.4%
2000**	367,951	137,845	Bush, George W.	205,286	Gore, Albert Jr.	24,820	67,441 D	37.5%	55.8%	40.2%	59.8%
1996**	360,120	113,943	Dole, Robert "Bob"	205,012	Clinton, Bill*	41,165	91,069 D	31.6%	56.9%	35.7%	64.3%
1992**	372,842	136,822	Bush, George H.*	179,310	Clinton, Bill	56,710	42,488 D	36.7%	48.1%	43.3%	56.7%
1988	354,461	158,625	Bush, George H.	192,364	Dukakis, Michael S.	3,472	33,739 D	44.8%	54.3%	45.2%	54.8%
1984	335,846	185,050	Reagan, Ronald*	147,154	Mondale, Walter F.	3,642	37,896 R	55.1%	43.8%	55.7%	44.3%
1980**	303,287	130,112	Reagan, Ronald	135,879	Carter, Jimmy*	37,296	5,767 D	42.9%	44.8%	48.9%	51.1%
1976	291,301	140,003	Ford, Gerald R.*	147,375	Carter, Jimmy	3,923	7,372 D	48.1%	50.6%	48.7%	51.3%
1972	270,274	168,865	Nixon, Richard M.*	101,409	McGovern, George S.		67,456 R	62.5%	37.5%	62.5%	37.5%
1968**	236,218	91,425	Nixon, Richard M.	141,324	Humphrey, Hubert Horatio Jr.	3,469	49,899 D	38.7%	59.8%	39.3%	60.7%
1964	207,271	44,022	Goldwater, Barry M. Sr.	163,249	Johnson, Lyndon B.*		119,227 D	21.2%	78.8%	21.2%	78.8%
1960	184,705	92,295	Nixon, Richard M.	92,410	Kennedy, John F.		115 D	50.0%	50.0%	50.0%	50.0%

Note: An asterisk (*) denotes incumbent. **In past elections, the other vote included: 2016 - 15,954 Libertarian (Gary Johnson); 2000 - 21,623 Green (Ralph Nader); 1996 - 27,358 Reform (Ross Perot); 1992 - 53,003 Independent (Perot); 1980 - 32,021 Independent (John Anderson); 1968 - 3,469 American Independent (George Wallace). Hawaii was formally admitted as a state in August 1959.

HAWAII

POSTWAR VOTE FOR GOVERNOR

Year	Total Vote	Republican		Democratic		Other Vote	Rep.-Dem. Plurality	Percentage			
								Total Vote		Major Vote	
		Vote	Candidate	Vote	Candidate			Rep.	Dem.	Rep.	Dem.
2014	366,210	135,775	Aiona, Duke	181,106	Ige, David Yutaka	49,329	45,331 D	37.1%	49.5%	42.8%	57.2%
2010	382,563	157,311	Aiona, Duke	222,724	Abercrombie, Neil	2,528	65,413 D	41.1%	58.2%	41.4%	58.6%
2006	344,315	215,313	Lingle, Linda*	121,717	Iwase, Randy	7,285	93,596 R	62.5%	35.4%	63.9%	36.1%
2002	382,110	197,009	Lingle, Linda	179,647	Hirono, Mazie K.	5,454	17,362 R	51.6%	47.0%	52.3%	47.7%
1998	407,556	198,952	Lingle, Linda	204,206	Cayetano, Benjamin J.*	4,398	5,254 D	48.8%	50.1%	49.3%	50.7%
1994**	369,013	107,908	Saiki, Patricia	134,978	Cayetano, Benjamin J.	126,127	27,070 D	29.2%	36.6%	44.4%	55.6%
1990	340,132	131,310	Hemmings, Fred	203,491	Waihee, John*	5,331	72,181 D	38.6%	59.8%	39.2%	60.8%
1986	334,115	160,460	Anderson, D. G.	173,655	Waihee, John		13,195 D	48.0%	52.0%	48.0%	52.0%
1982**	311,853	81,507	Anderson, D. G.	141,043	Ariyoshi, George R.*	89,303	59,536 D	26.1%	45.2%	36.6%	63.4%
1978	281,587	124,610	Leopold, John	153,394	Ariyoshi, George R.*	3,583	28,784 D	44.3%	54.5%	44.8%	55.2%
1974	249,650	113,388	Crossley, Randolph	136,262	Ariyoshi, George R.		22,874 D	45.4%	54.6%	45.4%	54.6%
1970	239,061	101,249	King, Samuel P.	137,812	Burns, John A.*		36,563 D	42.4%	57.6%	42.4%	57.6%
1966	213,164	104,324	Crossley, Randolph	108,840	Burns, John A.*		4,516 D	48.9%	51.1%	48.9%	51.1%
1962	196,015	81,707	Quinn, Willam F.*	114,308	Burns, John A.		32,601 D	41.7%	58.3%	41.7%	58.3%
1959**	168,662	86,213	Quinn, Willam F.	82,074	Burns, John A.	375	4,139 R	51.1%	48.7%	51.2%	48.8%

Note: An asterisk (*) denotes incumbent. **In past elections, the other vote included: 1994 - 113,158 Best Party (Frank F. Fasi); 1982 - 89,303 Independent Democrat (Fasi). In both 1982 and 1994, Fasi finished second. The 1959 election was for a short term pending the regular vote in 1962.

POSTWAR VOTE FOR SENATOR

Year	Total Vote	Republican		Democratic		Other Vote	Rep.-Dem. Plurality	Percentage			
								Total Vote		Major Vote	
		Vote	Candidate	Vote	Candidate			Rep.	Dem.	Rep.	Dem.
2016	416,562	92,653	Carroll, John S.	306,604	Schatz, Brian*	17,305	213,951 D	22.2%	73.6%	23.2%	76.8%
2014S**	353,774	98,006	Cavasso, Cam	246,827	Schatz, Brian*	8,941	148,821 D	27.7%	69.8%	28.4%	71.6%
2012	430,910	161,091	Lingle, Linda	269,819	Hirono, Mazie K.		108,728 D	37.4%	62.6%	37.4%	62.6%
2010	370,660	79,954	Cavasso, Cam	277,289	Inouye, Daniel K.*	13,417	197,335 D	21.6%	74.8%	22.4%	77.6%
2006	342,842	126,097	Thielen, Cynthia	210,330	Akaka, Daniel K.*	6,415	84,233 D	36.8%	61.3%	37.5%	62.5%
2004	415,347	87,172	Cavasso, Cam	313,629	Inouye, Daniel K.*	14,546	226,457 D	21.0%	75.5%	21.7%	78.3%
2000	345,623	84,701	Carroll, John	251,215	Akaka, Daniel K.*	9,707	166,514 D	24.5%	72.7%	25.2%	74.8%
1998	398,124	70,964	Young, Crystal	315,252	Inouye, Daniel K.*	11,908	244,288 D	17.8%	79.2%	18.4%	81.6%
1994	356,902	86,320	Hustace, Maria M.	256,189	Akaka, Daniel K.*	14,393	169,869 D	24.2%	71.8%	25.2%	74.8%
1992**	363,662	97,928	Reed, Rick	208,266	Inouye, Daniel K.*	57,468	110,338 D	26.9%	57.3%	32.0%	68.0%
1990S**	349,666	155,978	Saiki, Patricia	188,901	Akaka, Daniel K.	4,787	32,923 D	44.6%	54.0%	45.2%	54.8%
1988	323,876	66,987	Hustace, Maria M.	247,941	Matsunaga, Spark M.*	8,948	180,954 D	20.7%	76.6%	21.3%	78.7%
1986	328,797	86,910	Hutchinson, Frank	241,887	Inouye, Daniel K.*		154,977 D	26.4%	73.6%	26.4%	73.6%
1982	306,410	52,071	Brown, Clarence J.	245,386	Matsunaga, Spark M.*	8,953	193,315 D	17.0%	80.1%	17.5%	82.5%
1980	288,006	53,068	Brown, Cooper	224,485	Inouye, Daniel K.*	10,453	171,417 D	18.4%	77.9%	19.1%	80.9%
1976	302,092	122,724	Quinn, Willam F.	162,305	Matsunaga, Spark M.	17,063	39,581 D	40.6%	53.7%	43.1%	56.9%
1974**	250,221			207,454	Inouye, Daniel K.*	42,767	207,454 D		82.9%		100.0%
1970	240,760	124,163	Fong, Hiram L.*	116,597	Heftel, Cecil		7,566 R	51.6%	48.4%	51.6%	48.4%
1968	226,927	34,008	Thiessen, Wayne C.	189,248	Inouye, Daniel K.*	3,671	155,240 D	15.0%	83.4%	15.2%	84.8%
1964	208,814	110,747	Fong, Hiram L.*	96,789	Gill, Thomas P.	1,278	13,958 R	53.0%	46.4%	53.4%	46.6%
1962	196,361	60,067	Dillingham, Ben	136,294	Inouye, Daniel K.		76,227 D	30.6%	69.4%	30.6%	69.4%
1959**	163,875	79,123	Tsukiyama, Wilfred C.	83,700	Long, Oren E.	1,052	4,577 D	48.3%	51.1%	48.6%	51.4%
1959	164,808	87,161	Fong, Hiram L.	77,647	Fasi, Frank F.		9,514 R	52.9%	47.1%	52.9%	47.1%

Note: An asterisk (*) denotes incumbent. **In past elections, the other vote was: 1992 - 49,921 Green (Linda B. Martin); 1974 - 42,767 Peoples (James D. Kimmel, who finished second). The 1990 and 2014 elections were for a short term to fill a vacancy. The two 1959 elections were held to indeterminate terms and the Senate later determined by lot that Senator Long would serve a short term, Senator Fong a long term. The Republican Party did not run a Senate candidate in the 1974 election.

HAWAII

PRESIDENT 2016

2010 Census Population	County	Total Vote	Republican (Trump)	Democratic (Clinton)	Other	Rep.-Dem. Plurality	Percentage			
							Total Vote		Major Vote	
							Rep.	Dem.	Rep.	Dem.
185,079	HAWAII	64,867	17,501	41,259	6,107	23,758 D	27.0%	63.6%	29.8%	70.2%
953,207	HONOLULU	285,790	90,326	175,696	19,768	85,370 D	31.6%	61.5%	34.0%	66.0%
67,091	KAUAI	26,335	7,574	16,456	2,305	8,882 D	28.8%	62.5%	31.5%	68.5%
154,834	MAUI	51,945	13,446	33,480	5,019	20,034 D	25.9%	64.5%	28.7%	71.3%
1,360,211	TOTAL	428,937	128,847	266,891	33,199	138,044 D	30.0%	62.2%	32.6%	67.4%

HAWAII

SENATOR 2016

2010 Census Population	County	Total Vote	Republican (Carroll)	Democratic (Schatz)	Other	Rep.-Dem. Plurality	Percentage			
							Total Vote		Major Vote	
							Rep.	Dem.	Rep.	Dem.
185,079	HAWAII	63,015	12,766	47,003	3,246	34,237 D	20.3%	74.6%	21.4%	78.6%
953,207	HONOLULU	278,656	64,939	203,372	10,345	138,433 D	23.3%	73.0%	24.2%	75.8%
67,091	KAUAI	24,976	4,745	19,015	1,216	14,270 D	19.0%	76.1%	20.0%	80.0%
154,834	MAUI	49,915	10,203	37,214	2,498	27,011 D	20.4%	74.6%	21.5%	78.5%
1,360,211	TOTAL	416,562	92,653	306,604	17,305	213,951 D	22.2%	73.6%	23.2%	76.8%

HAWAII

HOUSE OF REPRESENTATIVES

CD	Year	Total Vote	Republican		Democratic		Other Vote	Rep.-Dem. Plurality	Percentage			
			Vote	Candidate	Vote	Candidate			Total Vote		Major Vote	
									Rep.	Dem.	Rep.	Dem.
1	2016	202,357	45,958	OSTROV, SHIRLENE D. "SHIRL"	145,417	HANABUSA, COLLEEN	10,982	99,459 D	22.7%	71.9%	24.0%	76.0%
1	2014	179,844	86,454	DJOU, CHARLES	93,390	TAKAI, MARK		6,936 D	48.1%	51.9%	48.1%	51.9%
1	2012	213,329	96,824	DJOU, CHARLES	116,505	HANABUSA, COLLEEN*		19,681 D	45.4%	54.6%	45.4%	54.6%
2	2016	210,516	39,668	KAAIHUE, ANGELA AULANI	170,848	GABBARD, TULSI *		131,180 D	18.8%	81.2%	18.8%	81.2%
2	2014	180,333	33,630	CROWLEY, KAWIKA	142,010	GABBARD, TULSI *	4,693	108,380 D	18.6%	78.7%	19.1%	80.9%
2	2012	209,210	40,707	CROWLEY, KAWIKA	168,503	GABBARD, TULSI		127,796 D	19.5%	80.5%	19.5%	80.5%
TOTAL	2016	412,873	85,626		316,265		10,982	230,639 D	20.7%	76.6%	21.3%	78.7%
TOTAL	2014	360,177	120,084		235,400		4,693	115,316 D	33.3%	65.4%	33.8%	66.2%
TOTAL	2012	422,539	137,531		285,008			147,477 D	32.5%	67.5%	32.5%	67.5%

Note: An asterisk (*) denotes incumbent.

HAWAII

GENERAL AND PRIMARY ELECTIONS

2016 GENERAL ELECTIONS: OTHER VOTES

President	Other vote was 15,954 Libertarian (Gary Johnson), 12,737 Green (Jill Stein), 4,508 Constitution (Darrell Castle)
Senate	Other vote was 9,103 Constitution (Joy Allison), 6,809 Libertarian (Michael Kokoski), 1,393 American Shopping Party (John Giuffre)
House	Other vote was:
CD 1	6,601 Libertarian (Alan Yim), 4,381 No Party Affiliation (Calvin Griffin)

2016 PRIMARY ELECTIONS: SUPPLEMENTARY INFORMATION

Primary	August 13, 2016	**Registration** (as of August 9, 2016)	726,940	No Party Registration

Primary Type Open—Any registered voter could participate in the party primary of his or her choice.

	REPUBLICAN PRIMARIES			DEMOCRATIC PRIMARIES		
Senator	Carroll, John S.	26,749	74.6%	Schatz, Brian*	162,905	86.2%
	Roco, John	3,956	11.0%	Christensen, Makani	11,899	6.3%
	Gottschalk, Karla "Bart"	3,045	8.5%	Shiratori, Miles	8,620	4.6%
	Pirkowski, Eddie	2,115	5.9%	Reyes, Arturo P. "Art"	3,820	2.0%
				Honeychurch, Tutz	1,815	1.0%
	TOTAL	*35,865*		*TOTAL*	*189,059*	
Congressional District 1	Ostrov, Shirlene D. "Shirl"	13,645	100%	Hanabusa, Colleen	74,022	80.4%
				Ahu Isa, Lei "Leinaala"	11,518	12.5%
				Kim, Howard	2,750	3.0%
				Ocasio, Javier	1,117	1.2%
				Puletasi, Sam	1,036	1.1%
				Sharsh-Davis, Lei	915	1.0%
				Tataii, Steve	737	0.8%
	TOTAL	*13,645*		*TOTAL*	*92,095*	
Congressional District 2	Kaaihue, Angela Aulani	7,449	55.9%	Gabbard, Tulsi*	80,026	84.5%
	Hafner, Eric	5,876	44.1%	Chan Hodges, Shay	14,643	15.5%
	TOTAL	*13,325*		*TOTAL*	*94,669*	

Note: An asterisk (*) denotes incumbent.

IDAHO

Congressional districts first established for elections held in 2012

2 members

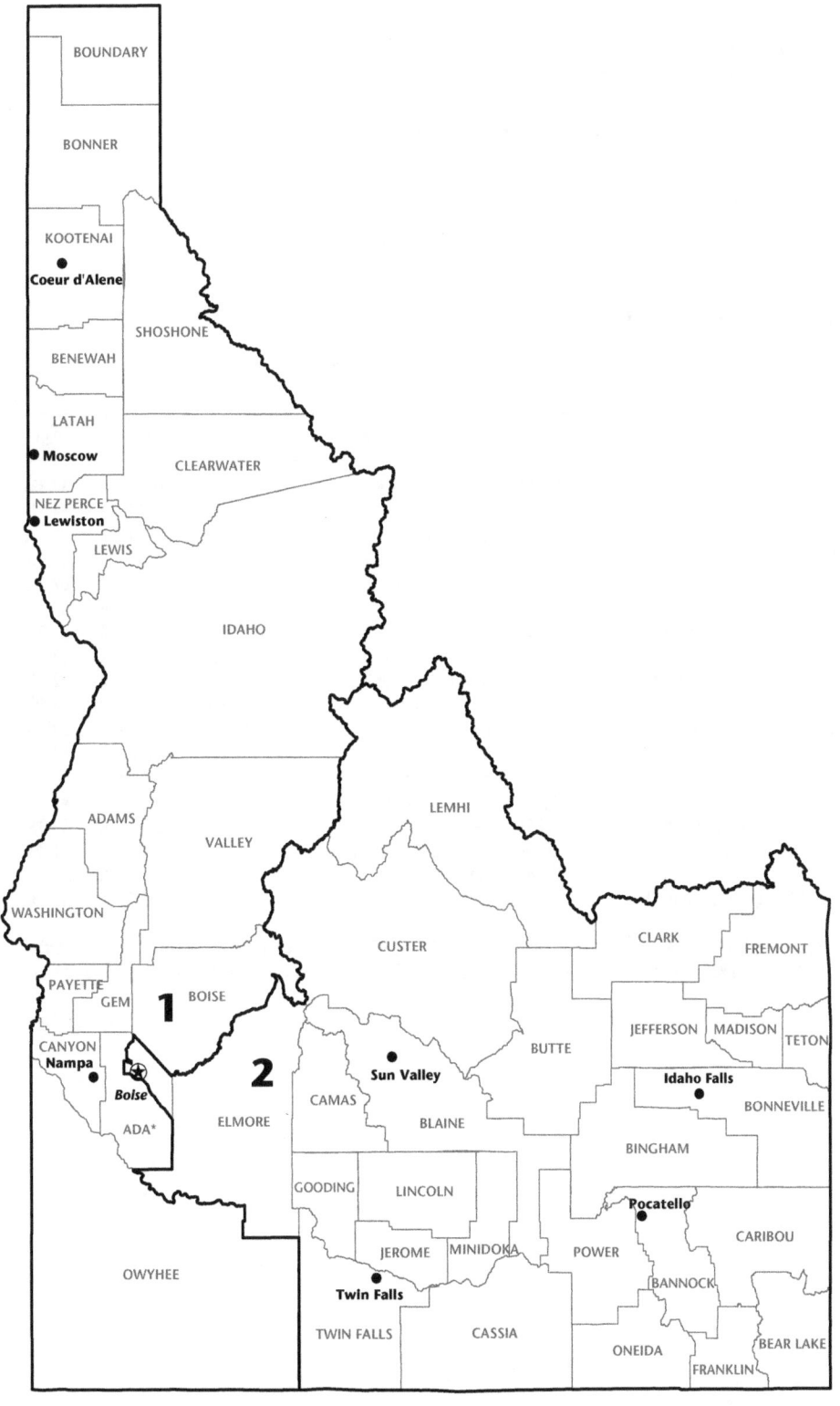

* Asterisk indicates a county whose boundaries include parts of two or more congressional districts.

IDAHO

GOVERNOR

C. L. "Butch" Otter (R). Re-elected 2014 to a four-year term. Previously elected 2010, 2006.

SENATORS (2 Republicans)

Michael D. Crapo (R). Re-elected 2016 to a six-year term. Previously elected 2010, 2004, 1998.

Jim Risch (R). Re-elected 2014 to a six-year term. Previously elected 2008.

REPRESENTATIVES (2 Republicans)

1. Raúl R. Labrador (R)   2. Michael K. Simpson (R)

POSTWAR VOTE FOR PRESIDENT

| | | Republican | | Democratic | | Other | Rep.-Dem. | Percentage | | | |
| | | | | | | | | Total Vote | | Major Vote | |
Year	Total Vote	Vote	Candidate	Vote	Candidate	Vote	Plurality	Rep.	Dem.	Rep.	Dem.
2016**	690,255	409,055	Trump, Donald J.	189,765	Clinton, Hillary Rodham	91,435	219,290 R	59.3%	27.5%	68.3%	31.7%
2012	652,346	420,911	Romney, W. Mitt	212,787	Obama, Barack H.*	18,648	208,124 R	64.5%	32.6%	66.4%	33.6%
2008	655,122	403,012	McCain, John S. III	236,440	Obama, Barack H.	15,670	166,572 R	61.5%	36.1%	63.0%	37.0%
2004	598,447	409,235	Bush, George W.*	181,098	Kerry, John F.	8,114	228,137 R	68.4%	30.3%	69.3%	30.7%
2000**	501,621	336,937	Bush, George W.	138,637	Gore, Albert Jr.	26,047	198,300 R	67.2%	27.6%	70.8%	29.2%
1996**	491,719	256,595	Dole, Robert "Bob"	165,443	Clinton, Bill*	69,681	91,152 R	52.2%	33.6%	60.8%	39.2%
1992**	482,142	202,645	Bush, George H.*	137,013	Clinton, Bill	142,484	65,632 R	42.0%	28.4%	59.7%	40.3%
1988	408,968	253,881	Bush, George H.	147,272	Dukakis, Michael S.	7,815	106,609 R	62.1%	36.0%	63.3%	36.7%
1984	411,144	297,523	Reagan, Ronald*	108,510	Mondale, Walter F.	5,111	189,013 R	72.4%	26.4%	73.3%	26.7%
1980**	437,431	290,699	Reagan, Ronald	110,192	Carter, Jimmy*	36,540	180,507 R	66.5%	25.2%	72.5%	27.5%
1976	344,071	204,151	Ford, Gerald R.*	126,549	Carter, Jimmy	13,371	77,602 R	59.3%	36.8%	61.7%	38.3%
1972	310,379	199,384	Nixon, Richard M.*	80,826	McGovern, George S.	30,169	118,558 R	64.2%	26.0%	71.2%	28.8%
1968**	291,183	165,369	Nixon, Richard M.	89,273	Humphrey, Hubert Horatio Jr.	36,541	76,096 R	56.8%	30.7%	64.9%	35.1%
1964	292,477	143,557	Goldwater, Barry M. Sr.	148,920	Johnson, Lyndon B.*		5,363 D	49.1%	50.9%	49.1%	50.9%
1960	300,450	161,597	Nixon, Richard M.	138,853	Kennedy, John F.		22,744 R	53.8%	46.2%	53.8%	46.2%
1956	272,989	166,979	Eisenhower, Dwight D.*	105,868	Stevenson, Adlai E. II	142	61,111 R	61.2%	38.8%	61.2%	38.8%
1952	276,254	180,707	Eisenhower, Dwight D.	95,081	Stevenson, Adlai E. II	466	85,626 R	65.4%	34.4%	65.5%	34.5%
1948	214,816	101,514	Dewey, Thomas E.	107,370	Truman, Harry S.*	5,932	5,856 D	47.3%	50.0%	48.6%	51.4%

Note: An asterisk (*) denotes incumbent. **In past elections, the other vote included: 2016 - 46,476 Independent (Evan McMullin), 28,331 Libertarian (Johnson); 2000 - 12,292 Green (Ralph Nader); 1996 - 62,518 Reform (Ross Perot); 1992 - 130,395 Independent (Perot); 1980 - 27,058 Independent (John Anderson); 1968 - 36,541 American Independent (George Wallace).

IDAHO

POSTWAR VOTE FOR GOVERNOR

Year	Total Vote	Republican Vote	Republican Candidate	Democratic Vote	Democratic Candidate	Other Vote	Rep.-Dem. Plurality	Total Vote Rep.	Total Vote Dem.	Major Vote Rep.	Major Vote Dem.
2014	439,830	235,405	Otter, C. L. "Butch"*	169,556	Balukoff, A. J.	34,869	65,849 R	53.5%	38.6%	58.1%	41.9%
2010	452,535	267,483	Otter, C. L. "Butch"*	148,680	Allred, Keith	36,372	118,803 R	59.1%	32.9%	64.3%	35.7%
2006	450,850	237,437	Otter, C. L. "Butch"	198,845	Brady, Jerry M.	14,568	38,592 R	52.7%	44.1%	54.4%	45.6%
2002	411,477	231,566	Kempthorne, Dirk*	171,711	Brady, Jerry M.	8,200	59,855 R	56.3%	41.7%	57.4%	42.6%
1998	381,248	258,095	Kempthorne, Dirk	110,815	Huntley, Robert C.	12,338	147,280 R	67.7%	29.1%	70.0%	30.0%
1994	413,346	216,123	Batt, Phil	181,363	Echohawk, Larry	15,860	34,760 R	52.3%	43.9%	54.4%	45.6%
1990	320,610	101,937	Fairchild, Roger	218,673	Andrus, Cecil D.*		116,736 D	31.8%	68.2%	31.8%	68.2%
1986	387,426	189,794	Leroy, David H.	193,429	Andrus, Cecil D.	4,203	3,635 D	49.0%	49.9%	49.5%	50.5%
1982	326,522	161,157	Batt, Phil	165,365	Evans, John V.*		4,208 D	49.4%	50.6%	49.4%	50.6%
1978	288,566	114,149	Larsen, Allan	169,540	Evans, John V.*	4,877	55,391 D	39.6%	58.8%	40.2%	59.8%
1974	259,632	68,731	Murphy, Jack M.	184,142	Andrus, Cecil D.*	6,759	115,411 D	26.5%	70.9%	27.2%	72.8%
1970	245,112	117,108	Samuelson, Don*	128,004	Andrus, Cecil D.		10,896 D	47.8%	52.2%	47.8%	52.2%
1966**	252,593	104,586	Samuelson, Don	93,744	Andrus, Cecil D.	54,263	10,842 R	41.4%	37.1%	52.7%	47.3%
1962	255,454	139,578	Smylie, Robert E.*	115,876	Smith, Vernon K.		23,702 R	54.6%	45.4%	54.6%	45.4%
1958	239,046	121,810	Smylie, Robert E.*	117,236	Derr, A. M.		4,574 R	51.0%	49.0%	51.0%	49.0%
1954	228,685	124,038	Smylie, Robert E.	104,647	Hamilton, Clark		19,391 R	54.2%	45.8%	54.2%	45.8%
1950	204,792	107,642	Jordan, Len B.	97,150	Wright, Calvin E.		10,492 R	52.6%	47.4%	52.6%	47.4%
1946	181,364	102,233	Robins, Charles A.	79,131	Williams, Arnold*		23,102 R	56.4%	43.6%	56.4%	43.6%

Note: An asterisk (*) denotes incumbent. **In past elections, the other vote included: 1966 - 30,913 Independent (Perry Swisher).

POSTWAR VOTE FOR SENATOR

Year	Total Vote	Republican Vote	Republican Candidate	Democratic Vote	Democratic Candidate	Other Vote	Rep.-Dem. Plurality	Total Vote Rep.	Total Vote Dem.	Major Vote Rep.	Major Vote Dem.
2016	678,943	449,017	Crapo, Michael D.*	188,249	Sturgill, Jerry	41,677	260,768 R	66.1%	27.7%	70.5%	29.5%
2014	437,170	285,596	Risch, Jim*	151,574	Mitchell, Nels		134,022 R	65.3%	34.7%	65.3%	34.7%
2010	449,530	319,953	Crapo, Michael D.*	112,057	Sullivan, P. Tom	17,520	207,896 R	71.2%	24.9%	74.1%	25.9%
2008	644,780	371,744	Risch, Jim	219,903	Larocco, Larry	53,133	151,841 R	57.7%	34.1%	62.8%	37.2%
2004**	503,932	499,796	Crapo, Michael D.*			4,136	499,796 R	99.2%		100.0%	
2002	408,544	266,215	Craig, Larry E.*	132,975	Blinken, Alan	9,354	133,240 R	65.2%	32.5%	66.7%	33.3%
1998	378,174	262,966	Crapo, Michael D.	107,375	Mauk, Bill	7,833	155,591 R	69.5%	28.4%	71.0%	29.0%
1996	497,233	283,532	Craig, Larry E.*	198,422	Minnick, Walt	15,279	85,110 R	57.0%	39.9%	58.8%	41.2%
1992	478,504	270,468	Kempthorne, Dirk	208,036	Stallings, Richard		62,432 R	56.5%	43.5%	56.5%	43.5%
1990	315,936	193,641	Craig, Larry E.	122,295	Twilegar, Ron J.		71,346 R	61.3%	38.7%	61.3%	38.7%
1986	382,024	196,958	Symms, Steven D.*	185,066	Evans, John V.		11,892 R	51.6%	48.4%	51.6%	48.4%
1984	406,168	293,193	McClure, James A.*	105,591	Busch, Peter M.	7,384	187,602 R	72.2%	26.0%	73.5%	26.5%
1980	439,647	218,701	Symms, Steven D.	214,439	Church, Frank*	6,507	4,262 R	49.7%	48.8%	50.5%	49.5%
1978	284,047	194,412	McClure, James A.*	89,635	Jensen, Dwight		104,777 R	68.4%	31.6%	68.4%	31.6%
1974	258,847	109,072	Smith, Robert L.	145,140	Church, Frank*	4,635	36,068 D	42.1%	56.1%	42.9%	57.1%
1972	309,602	161,804	McClure, James A.	140,913	Davis, William E. Bud	6,885	20,891 R	52.3%	45.5%	53.5%	46.5%
1968	287,876	114,394	Hansen, George V.	173,482	Church, Frank*		59,088 D	39.7%	60.3%	39.7%	60.3%
1966	252,456	139,819	Jordan, Len B.*	112,637	Harding, Ralph R.		27,182 R	55.4%	44.6%	55.4%	44.6%
1962	258,786	117,129	Hawley, Jack	141,657	Church, Frank*		24,528 D	45.3%	54.7%	45.3%	54.7%
1962S**	257,677	131,279	Jordan, Len B.*	126,398	Pfost, Gracie B.		4,881 R	50.9%	49.1%	50.9%	49.1%
1960	292,096	152,648	Dworshak, Henry C.*	139,448	McLaughlin, R. F.		13,200 R	52.3%	47.7%	52.3%	47.7%
1956	265,292	102,781	Welker, Herman*	149,096	Church, Frank	13,415	46,315 D	38.7%	56.2%	40.8%	59.2%
1954	226,408	142,269	Dworshak, Henry C.*	84,139	Taylor, Glen H.		58,130 R	62.8%	37.2%	62.8%	37.2%
1950	201,417	124,237	Welker, Herman	77,180	Clark, D. Worth		47,057 R	61.7%	38.3%	61.7%	38.3%
1950S**	201,700	104,608	Dworshak, Henry C.	97,092	Burtenshaw, Claude		7,516 R	51.9%	48.1%	51.9%	48.1%
1948	214,188	103,868	Dworshak, Henry C.*	107,000	Miller, Bert H.	3,320	3,132 D	48.5%	50.0%	49.3%	50.7%
1946S**	180,152	105,523	Dworshak, Henry C.	74,629	Donart, George E.		30,894 R	58.6%	41.4%	58.6%	41.4%

Note: An asterisk (*) denotes incumbent. **In 2004 there was no candidate on the Democratic line. A write-in candidate, who was a Democrat, received 4,136 votes, which are listed in the Other Vote column. The 1946 election and one each of the 1950 and 1962 elections were for short terms to fill vacancies.

IDAHO

PRESIDENT 2016

2010 Census Population	County	Total Vote	Republican (Trump)	Democratic (Clinton)	Other	Rep.-Dem. Plurality		Percentage Total Vote Rep.	Dem.	Major Vote Rep.	Dem.
392,365	ADA	195,626	93,752	75,677	26,197	18,075	R	47.9%	38.7%	55.3%	44.7%
3,976	ADAMS	2,183	1,556	415	212	1,141	R	71.3%	19.0%	78.9%	21.1%
82,839	BANNOCK	33,405	17,180	10,342	5,883	6,838	R	51.4%	31.0%	62.4%	37.6%
5,986	BEAR LAKE	2,928	2,203	255	470	1,948	R	75.2%	8.7%	89.6%	10.4%
9,285	BENEWAH	4,184	3,103	770	311	2,333	R	74.2%	18.4%	80.1%	19.9%
45,607	BINGHAM	16,625	10,907	2,924	2,794	7,983	R	65.6%	17.6%	78.9%	21.1%
21,376	BLAINE	10,723	3,340	6,416	967	3,076	D	31.1%	59.8%	34.2%	65.8%
7,028	BOISE	3,812	2,673	777	362	1,896	R	70.1%	20.4%	77.5%	22.5%
40,877	BONNER	20,925	13,343	5,819	1,763	7,524	R	63.8%	27.8%	69.6%	30.4%
104,234	BONNEVILLE	44,212	26,699	8,930	8,583	17,769	R	60.4%	20.2%	74.9%	25.1%
10,972	BOUNDARY	5,162	3,789	933	440	2,856	R	73.4%	18.1%	80.2%	19.8%
2,891	BUTTE	1,230	914	160	156	754	R	74.3%	13.0%	85.1%	14.9%
1,117	CAMAS	590	410	110	70	300	R	69.5%	18.6%	78.8%	21.2%
188,923	CANYON	72,765	47,222	16,883	8,660	30,339	R	64.9%	23.2%	73.7%	26.3%
6,963	CARIBOU	3,035	2,275	271	489	2,004	R	75.0%	8.9%	89.4%	10.6%
22,952	CASSIA	8,178	5,949	1,036	1,193	4,913	R	72.7%	12.7%	85.2%	14.8%
982	CLARK	283	203	44	36	159	R	71.7%	15.5%	82.2%	17.8%
8,761	CLEARWATER	3,801	2,852	704	245	2,148	R	75.0%	18.5%	80.2%	19.8%
4,368	CUSTER	2,413	1,777	427	209	1,350	R	73.6%	17.7%	80.6%	19.4%
27,038	ELMORE	8,519	5,816	1,814	889	4,002	R	68.3%	21.3%	76.2%	23.8%
12,786	FRANKLIN	5,499	3,901	385	1,213	3,516	R	70.9%	7.0%	91.0%	9.0%
13,242	FREMONT	5,713	4,090	651	972	3,439	R	71.6%	11.4%	86.3%	13.7%
16,719	GEM	7,952	5,980	1,229	743	4,751	R	75.2%	15.5%	83.0%	17.0%
15,464	GOODING	5,191	3,743	930	518	2,813	R	72.1%	17.9%	80.1%	19.9%
16,267	IDAHO	8,226	6,441	1,196	589	5,245	R	78.3%	14.5%	84.3%	15.7%
26,140	JEFFERSON	11,471	8,436	976	2,059	7,460	R	73.5%	8.5%	89.6%	10.4%
22,374	JEROME	6,751	4,644	1,329	778	3,315	R	68.8%	19.7%	77.7%	22.3%
138,494	KOOTENAI	66,286	44,449	16,264	5,573	28,185	R	67.1%	24.5%	73.2%	26.8%
37,244	LATAH	18,156	7,265	8,093	2,798	828	D	40.0%	44.6%	47.3%	52.7%
7,936	LEMHI	4,096	3,011	733	352	2,278	R	73.5%	17.9%	80.4%	19.6%
3,821	LEWIS	1,590	1,202	270	118	932	R	75.6%	17.0%	81.7%	18.3%
5,208	LINCOLN	1,748	1,184	360	204	824	R	67.7%	20.6%	76.7%	23.3%
37,536	MADISON	15,687	8,941	1,201	5,545	7,740	R	57.0%	7.7%	88.2%	11.8%
20,069	MINIDOKA	6,870	4,887	1,167	816	3,720	R	71.1%	17.0%	80.7%	19.3%
39,265	NEZ PERCE	17,195	10,699	4,828	1,668	5,871	R	62.2%	28.1%	68.9%	31.1%
4,286	ONEIDA	2,068	1,531	184	353	1,347	R	74.0%	8.9%	89.3%	10.7%
11,526	OWYHEE	3,924	3,052	591	281	2,461	R	77.8%	15.1%	83.8%	16.2%
22,623	PAYETTE	8,704	6,489	1,507	708	4,982	R	74.6%	17.3%	81.2%	18.8%
7,817	POWER	2,758	1,666	699	393	967	R	60.4%	25.3%	70.4%	29.6%
12,765	SHOSHONE	5,120	3,297	1,384	439	1,913	R	64.4%	27.0%	70.4%	29.6%
10,170	TETON	4,975	2,167	2,159	649	8	R	43.6%	43.4%	50.1%	49.9%
77,230	TWIN FALLS	29,873	19,828	6,233	3,812	13,595	R	66.4%	20.9%	76.1%	23.9%
9,862	VALLEY	5,349	2,906	1,913	530	993	R	54.3%	35.8%	60.3%	39.7%
10,198	WASHINGTON	4,454	3,283	776	395	2,507	R	73.7%	17.4%	80.9%	19.1%
1,567,582	TOTAL	690,255	409,055	189,765	91,435	219,290	R	59.3%	27.5%	68.3%	31.7%

IDAHO

SENATOR 2016

2010 Census Population	County	Total Vote	Republican (Crapo)	Democratic (Sturgill)	Other	Rep.-Dem. Plurality	Percentage Total Vote Rep.	Dem.	Major Vote Rep.	Dem.
392,365	ADA	187,143	104,650	72,847	9,646	31,803 R	55.9%	38.9%	59.0%	41.0%
3,976	ADAMS	2,124	1,463	459	202	1,004 R	68.9%	21.6%	76.1%	23.9%
82,839	BANNOCK	33,649	19,883	11,585	2,181	8,298 R	59.1%	34.4%	63.2%	36.8%
5,986	BEAR LAKE	2,914	2,415	291	208	2,124 R	82.9%	10.0%	89.2%	10.8%
9,285	BENEWAH	4,142	3,103	746	293	2,357 R	74.9%	18.0%	80.6%	19.4%
45,607	BINGHAM	16,512	12,114	2,997	1,401	9,117 R	73.4%	18.2%	80.2%	19.8%
21,376	BLAINE	10,749	4,562	5,961	226	1,399 D	42.4%	55.5%	43.4%	56.6%
7,028	BOISE	3,748	2,497	860	391	1,637 R	66.6%	22.9%	74.4%	25.6%
40,877	BONNER	20,704	13,908	5,767	1,029	8,141 R	67.2%	27.9%	70.7%	29.3%
104,234	BONNEVILLE	43,480	31,093	9,158	3,229	21,935 R	71.5%	21.1%	77.2%	22.8%
10,972	BOUNDARY	5,155	3,961	920	274	3,041 R	76.8%	17.8%	81.2%	18.8%
2,891	BUTTE	1,233	948	185	100	763 R	76.9%	15.0%	83.7%	16.3%
1,117	CAMAS	576	414	126	36	288 R	71.9%	21.9%	76.7%	23.3%
188,923	CANYON	72,255	50,006	17,007	5,242	32,999 R	69.2%	23.5%	74.6%	25.4%
6,963	CARIBOU	3,034	2,450	350	234	2,100 R	80.8%	11.5%	87.5%	12.5%
22,952	CASSIA	8,150	6,418	1,011	721	5,407 R	78.7%	12.4%	86.4%	13.6%
982	CLARK	280	225	32	23	193 R	80.4%	11.4%	87.5%	12.5%
8,761	CLEARWATER	3,734	2,865	711	158	2,154 R	76.7%	19.0%	80.1%	19.9%
4,368	CUSTER	2,375	1,693	429	253	1,264 R	71.3%	18.1%	79.8%	20.2%
27,038	ELMORE	8,421	6,059	1,752	610	4,307 R	72.0%	20.8%	77.6%	22.4%
12,786	FRANKLIN	5,488	4,682	441	365	4,241 R	85.3%	8.0%	91.4%	8.6%
13,242	FREMONT	5,711	4,521	692	498	3,829 R	79.2%	12.1%	86.7%	13.3%
16,719	GEM	7,851	5,779	1,378	694	4,401 R	73.6%	17.6%	80.7%	19.3%
15,464	GOODING	5,191	3,834	958	399	2,876 R	73.9%	18.5%	80.0%	20.0%
16,267	IDAHO	8,113	6,272	1,247	594	5,025 R	77.3%	15.4%	83.4%	16.6%
26,140	JEFFERSON	11,383	9,120	1,196	1,067	7,924 R	80.1%	10.5%	88.4%	11.6%
22,374	JEROME	6,758	4,931	1,253	574	3,678 R	73.0%	18.5%	79.7%	20.3%
138,494	KOOTENAI	65,946	47,636	15,365	2,945	32,271 R	72.2%	23.3%	75.6%	24.4%
37,244	LATAH	18,321	9,626	8,050	645	1,576 R	52.5%	43.9%	54.5%	45.5%
7,936	LEMHI	4,045	3,013	723	309	2,290 R	74.5%	17.9%	80.6%	19.4%
3,821	LEWIS	1,598	1,239	257	102	982 R	77.5%	16.1%	82.8%	17.2%
5,208	LINCOLN	1,740	1,263	354	123	909 R	72.6%	20.3%	78.1%	21.9%
37,536	MADISON	15,416	12,826	1,473	1,117	11,353 R	83.2%	9.6%	89.7%	10.3%
20,069	MINIDOKA	6,766	5,067	1,108	591	3,959 R	74.9%	16.4%	82.1%	17.9%
39,265	NEZ PERCE	17,369	12,188	4,621	560	7,567 R	70.2%	26.6%	72.5%	27.5%
4,286	ONEIDA	2,058	1,719	206	133	1,513 R	83.5%	10.0%	89.3%	10.7%
11,526	OWYHEE	3,834	2,909	581	344	2,328 R	75.9%	15.2%	83.4%	16.6%
22,623	PAYETTE	8,629	6,480	1,549	600	4,931 R	75.1%	18.0%	80.7%	19.3%
7,817	POWER	2,790	1,942	686	162	1,256 R	69.6%	24.6%	73.9%	26.1%
12,765	SHOSHONE	5,145	3,463	1,477	205	1,986 R	67.3%	28.7%	70.1%	29.9%
10,170	TETON	4,985	2,659	2,156	170	503 R	53.3%	43.2%	55.2%	44.8%
77,230	TWIN FALLS	29,712	20,701	6,559	2,452	14,142 R	69.7%	22.1%	75.9%	24.1%
9,862	VALLEY	5,325	3,202	1,883	240	1,319 R	60.1%	35.4%	63.0%	37.0%
10,198	WASHINGTON	4,391	3,218	842	331	2,376 R	73.3%	19.2%	79.3%	20.7%
1,567,582	TOTAL	678,943	449,017	188,249	41,677	260,768 R	66.1%	27.7%	70.5%	29.5%

IDAHO

HOUSE OF REPRESENTATIVES

| CD | Year | Total Vote | Republican | | Democratic | | Other Vote | Rep.-Dem. Plurality | Percentage | | | |
| | | | Vote | Candidate | Vote | Candidate | | | Total Vote | | Major Vote | |
									Rep.	Dem.	Rep.	Dem.
1	2016	355,357	242,252	LABRADOR, RAUL R.*	113,052	PIOTROWSKI, JAMES	53	129,200 R	68.2%	31.8%	68.2%	31.8%
1	2014	220,864	143,580	LABRADOR, RAUL R.*	77,277	RINGO, SHIRLEY G.	7	66,303 R	65.0%	35.0%	65.0%	35.0%
1	2012	316,724	199,402	LABRADOR, RAUL R.*	97,450	FARRIS, JIMMY	19,872	101,952 R	63.0%	30.8%	67.2%	32.8%
2	2016	326,237	205,292	SIMPSON, MICHAEL K.*	95,940	MARTINEZ, JENNIFER	25,005	109,352 R	62.9%	29.4%	68.2%	31.8%
2	2014	214,293	131,492	SIMPSON, MICHAEL K.*	82,801	STALLINGS, RICHARD		48,691 R	61.4%	38.6%	61.4%	38.6%
2	2012	318,494	207,412	SIMPSON, MICHAEL K.*	110,847	LEFAVOUR, NICOLE	235	96,565 R	65.1%	34.8%	65.2%	34.8%
TOTAL	2016	681,594	447,544		208,992		25,058	238,552 R	65.7%	30.7%	68.2%	31.8%
TOTAL	2014	435,157	275,072		160,078		7	114,994 R	63.2%	36.8%	63.2%	36.8%
TOTAL	2012	635,218	406,814		208,297		20,107	198,517 R	64.0%	32.8%	66.1%	33.9%

Note: An asterisk (*) denotes incumbent.

IDAHO

GENERAL AND PRIMARY ELECTIONS

2016 GENERAL ELECTIONS: OTHER VOTES

President   Other vote was 46,476 Independent (Evan McMullin), 28,331 Libertarian (Gary Johnson), 8,496 Independent (Jill Stein), 4,403 Independent (Darrell Castle), 2,356 Constitution (Scott Copeland), 1,373 Independent (Roque De La Fuente)

Senate   Other vote was 41,677 Constitution (Ray Writz)

House   Other vote was:

CD 1   53 Write-in (Scattered Write-in)
CD 2   25,005 Constitution (Anthony Tomkins)

2016 PRIMARY ELECTIONS: SUPPLEMENTARY INFORMATION

Primary	March 8, 2016 (Republican President) March 22, 2016 (Democratic Presidential Caucus) May 17, 2016 (Congress)	**Registration** (as of May 2, 2016)	763,932	Republican	365,741
				Democratic	72,993
				Libertarian	4,190
				Constitution	2,307
				Unaffiliated	318,701

Primary Type   Semi-Open—Registered Democrats and unaffiliated voters could participate in the Democratic primary. Only registered Republicans could vote in the Republican primary.

IDAHO

GENERAL AND PRIMARY ELECTIONS

	REPUBLICAN PRIMARIES			DEMOCRATIC PRIMARIES		
President	Cruz, Ted	100,889	45.4%			
	Trump, Donald J.	62,413	28.1%			
	Rubio, Marco	35,290	15.9%			
	Kasich, John R.	16,514	7.4%			
	Carson, Ben	3,853	1.7%			
	Bush, Jeb	939	0.4%			
	Paul, Rand	834	0.4%			
	Huckabee, Mike	358	0.2%			
	Christie, Chris	353	0.2%			
	Fiorina, Carly	242	0.1%			
	Santorum, Rick	211	0.1%			
	Graham, Lindsey	80				
	Messina, Peter	28				
	TOTAL	222,004				
Senator	Crapo, Michael D.*	119,633	100.0%	Sturgill, Jerry	26,471	100.0%
	TOTAL	119,633		TOTAL	26,471	
Congressional District 1	Labrador, Raul R.*	51,568	81.0%	Piotrowski, James	6,954	56.2%
	Counsil, Gordon	6,510	10.2%	Fox, Shizandra	3,428	27.7%
	Haugen, Isaac M.	5,605	8.8%	Nikolova, Staniela	2,002	16.2%
	TOTAL	63,683		TOTAL	12,384	
Congressional District 2	Simpson, Michael K.*	47,116	73.0%	Martinez, Jennifer	13,816	100.0%
	Marie, Lisa	17,442	27.0%			
	TOTAL	64,558		TOTAL	13,816	

Note: An asterisk (*) denotes incumbent.

ILLINOIS

Congressional districts first established for elections held in 2012

18 members

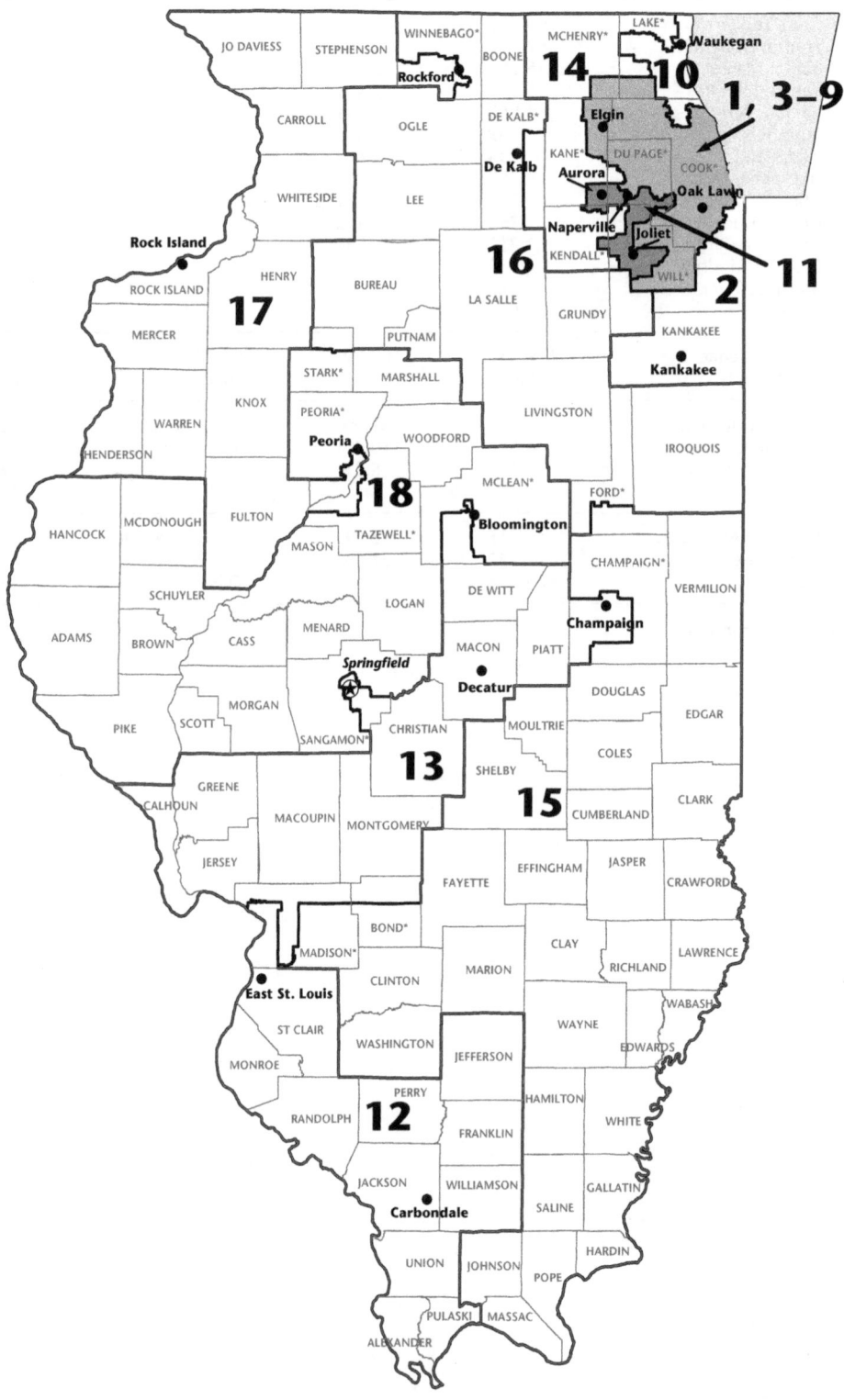

* Asterisk indicates a county whose boundaries include parts of two or more congressional districts.

ILLINOIS
Chicago Area

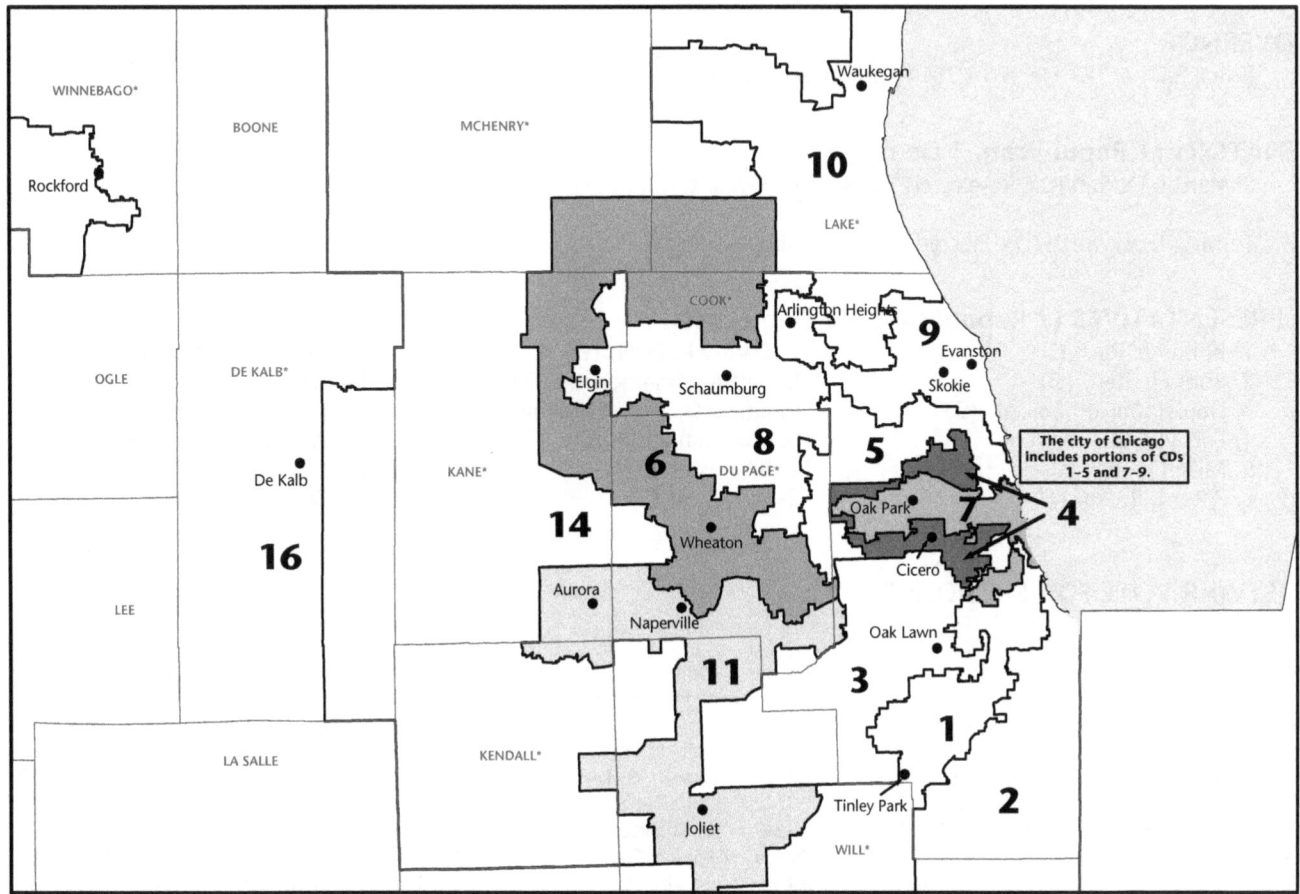

* Asterisk indicates a county whose boundaries include parts of two or more congressional districts.

ILLINOIS

GOVERNOR
Bruce Rauner (R). Elected 2014 to a four-year term.

SENATORS (1 Republican, 1 Democrat)
Richard J. Durbin (D). Re-elected 2014 to a six-year term. Previously elected 2008, 2002, 1996.

Tammy Duckworth (D). Elected 2016 to a six-year term.

REPRESENTATIVES (7 Republicans, 11 Democrats)
1. Bobby L. Rush (D)
2. Robin L. Kelly (D)
3. Daniel William Lipinski (D)
4. Luis V. Gutiérrez (D)
5. Mike Quigley (D)
6. Peter J. Roskam (R)
7. Danny K. Davis (D)
8. Raja Krishnamoorthi (D)
9. Janice D. "Jan" Schakowsky (D)
10. Brad Schneider (D)
11. Bill Foster (D)
12. Mike Bost (R)
13. Rodney L. Davis (R)
14. Randy M. Hultgren (R)
15. John M. Shimkus (R)
16. Adam Kinzinger (R)
17. Cheri Bustos (D)
18. Darin LaHood (R)

POSTWAR VOTE FOR PRESIDENT

		Republican		Democratic		Other Vote	Rep.-Dem. Plurality	Total Vote		Major Vote	
Year	Total Vote	Vote	Candidate	Vote	Candidate			Rep.	Dem.	Rep.	Dem.
2016**	5,536,424	2,146,015	Trump, Donald J.	3,090,729	Clinton, Hillary Rodham	299,680	944,714 D	38.8%	55.8%	41.0%	59.0%
2012	5,242,014	2,135,216	Romney, W. Mitt	3,019,512	Obama, Barack H.*	87,286	884,296 D	40.7%	57.6%	41.4%	58.6%
2008	5,522,371	2,031,179	McCain, John S. III	3,419,348	Obama, Barack H.	71,844	1,388,169 D	36.8%	61.9%	37.3%	62.7%
2004	5,274,322	2,345,946	Bush, George W.*	2,891,550	Kerry, John F.	36,826	545,604 D	44.5%	54.8%	44.8%	55.2%
2000**	4,742,123	2,019,421	Bush, George W.	2,589,026	Gore, Albert Jr.	133,676	569,605 D	42.6%	54.6%	43.8%	56.2%
1996**	4,311,391	1,587,021	Dole, Robert "Bob"	2,341,744	Clinton, Bill*	382,626	754,723 D	36.8%	54.3%	40.4%	59.6%
1992**	5,050,157	1,734,096	Bush, George H.*	2,453,350	Clinton, Bill	862,711	719,254 D	34.3%	48.6%	41.4%	58.6%
1988	4,559,120	2,310,939	Bush, George H.	2,215,940	Dukakis, Michael S.	32,241	94,999 R	50.7%	48.6%	51.0%	49.0%
1984	4,819,088	2,707,103	Reagan, Ronald*	2,086,499	Mondale, Walter F.	25,486	620,604 R	56.2%	43.3%	56.5%	43.5%
1980**	4,749,721	2,358,049	Reagan, Ronald	1,981,413	Carter, Jimmy*	410,259	376,636 R	49.6%	41.7%	54.3%	45.7%
1976	4,718,914	2,364,269	Ford, Gerald R.*	2,271,295	Carter, Jimmy	83,350	92,974 R	50.1%	48.1%	51.0%	49.0%
1972	4,723,236	2,788,179	Nixon, Richard M.*	1,913,472	McGovern, George S.	21,585	874,707 R	59.0%	40.5%	59.3%	40.7%
1968**	4,619,749	2,174,774	Nixon, Richard M.	2,039,814	Humphrey, Hubert Horatio Jr.	405,161	134,960 R	47.1%	44.2%	51.6%	48.4%
1964	4,702,841	1,905,946	Goldwater, Barry M. Sr.	2,796,833	Johnson, Lyndon B.*	62	890,887 D	40.5%	59.5%	40.5%	59.5%
1960	4,757,409	2,368,988	Nixon, Richard M.	2,377,846	Kennedy, John F.	10,575	8,858 D	49.8%	50.0%	49.9%	50.1%
1956	4,407,407	2,623,327	Eisenhower, Dwight D.*	1,775,682	Stevenson, Adlai E. II	8,398	847,645 R	59.5%	40.3%	59.6%	40.4%
1952	4,481,058	2,457,327	Eisenhower, Dwight D.	2,013,920	Stevenson, Adlai E. II	9,811	443,407 R	54.8%	44.9%	55.0%	45.0%
1948	3,984,046	1,961,103	Dewey, Thomas E.	1,994,715	Truman, Harry S.*	28,228	33,612 D	49.2%	50.1%	49.6%	50.4%

Note: An asterisk (*) denotes incumbent. **In past elections, the other vote included: 2016 - 209,596 Libertarian (Gary Johnson); 2000 - 103,759 Green (Ralph Nader); 1996 - 346,408 Reform (Ross Perot); 1992 - 840,515 Independent (Perot); 1980 - 346,754 Independent (John Anderson); 1968 - 390,958 American Independent (George Wallace).

ILLINOIS

POSTWAR VOTE FOR GOVERNOR

Year	Total Vote	Republican Vote	Republican Candidate	Democratic Vote	Democratic Candidate	Other Vote	Rep.-Dem. Plurality	Total Vote Rep.	Total Vote Dem.	Major Vote Rep.	Major Vote Dem.
2014	3,627,690	1,823,627	Rauner, Bruce	1,681,343	Quinn, Pat*	122,720	142,284 R	50.3%	46.3%	52.0%	48.0%
2010	3,729,989	1,713,385	Brady, Bill	1,745,219	Quinn, Pat*	271,385	31,834 D	45.9%	46.8%	49.5%	50.5%
2006**	3,487,989	1,369,315	Topinka, Judy Baar	1,736,731	Blagojevich, Rod R.*	381,943	367,416 D	39.3%	49.8%	44.1%	55.9%
2002	3,538,891	1,594,960	Ryan, Jim	1,847,040	Blagojevich, Rod R.	96,891	252,080 D	45.1%	52.2%	46.3%	53.7%
1998	3,358,705	1,714,094	Ryan, George H.	1,594,191	Poshard, Glenn	50,420	119,903 R	51.0%	47.5%	51.8%	48.2%
1994	3,106,566	1,984,318	Edgar, Jim*	1,069,850	Netsch, Dawn C.	52,398	914,468 R	63.9%	34.4%	65.0%	35.0%
1990	3,257,410	1,653,126	Edgar, Jim	1,569,217	Hartigan, Neil F.	35,067	83,909 R	50.7%	48.2%	51.3%	48.7%
1986**	3,143,978	1,655,849	Thompson, James R.*	208,830	(See note)	1,279,299	1,447,019 R	52.7%	6.6%	88.8%	11.2%
1982	3,673,681	1,816,101	Thompson, James R.*	1,811,027	Stevenson, Adlai E. II	46,553	5,074 R	49.4%	49.3%	50.1%	49.9%
1978	3,150,095	1,859,684	Thompson, James R.*	1,263,134	Bakalis, Michael	27,277	596,550 R	59.0%	40.1%	59.6%	40.4%
1976**	4,635,728	3,000,395	Thompson, James R.	1,606,989	Howlett, Michael J.	28,344	1,393,406 R	64.7%	34.7%	65.1%	34.9%
1972	4,678,802	2,293,809	Ogilvie, Richard B.*	2,371,301	Walker, Daniel	13,692	77,492 D	49.0%	50.7%	49.2%	50.8%
1968	4,506,000	2,307,295	Ogilvie, Richard B.	2,179,501	Shapiro, Samuel H.	19,204	127,794 R	51.2%	48.4%	51.4%	48.6%
1964	4,657,500	2,239,095	Percy, Charles H.	2,418,394	Kerner, Otto*	11	179,299 D	48.1%	51.9%	48.1%	51.9%
1960	4,674,187	2,070,479	Stratton, William G.*	2,594,731	Kerner, Otto	8,977	524,252 D	44.3%	55.5%	44.4%	55.6%
1956	4,314,611	2,171,786	Stratton, William G.*	2,134,909	Austin, Richard B.	7,916	36,877 R	50.3%	49.5%	50.4%	49.6%
1952	4,415,864	2,317,363	Stratton, William G.	2,089,721	Dixon, Sherwood	8,780	227,642 R	52.5%	47.3%	52.6%	47.4%
1948	3,940,257	1,678,007	Green, Dwight H.*	2,250,074	Stevenson, Adlai E. II	12,176	572,067 D	42.6%	57.1%	42.7%	57.3%

Note: An asterisk (*) denotes incumbent. **In past elections, the other vote included: 2006 - 361,336 Green (Rich Whitney); 1986 - 1,256,626 Illinois Solidarity (Adlai E. Stevenson III). In 1986 there was no Democratic candidate for Governor on the ballot. Mark Fairchild, a supporter of Lyndon H. LaRouche Jr., was the "paired" Democratic candidate for Lt. Governor and the Democratic vote was cast for this ticket of "no name" and Fairchild. Running on the Illinois Solidarity line, Stevenson finished second with 40.0 percent of the vote. The 1976 vote was for a two-year term to permit shifting the election for governor to non-presidential years.

POSTWAR VOTE FOR SENATOR

Year	Total Vote	Republican Vote	Republican Candidate	Democratic Vote	Democratic Candidate	Other Vote	Rep.-Dem. Plurality	Total Vote Rep.	Total Vote Dem.	Major Vote Rep.	Major Vote Dem.
2016	5,491,878	2,184,692	Kirk, Mark Steven*	3,012,940	Duckworth, Tammy	294,246	828,248 D	39.8%	54.9%	42.0%	58.0%
2014	3,603,519	1,538,522	Oberweis, James D.	1,929,637	Durbin, Richard J.*	135,360	391,115 D	42.7%	53.5%	44.4%	55.6%
2010	3,704,473	1,778,698	Kirk, Mark Steven	1,719,478	Giannoulias, Alexander	206,297	59,220 R	48.0%	46.4%	50.8%	49.2%
2008	5,329,884	1,520,621	Sauerberg, Steve	3,615,844	Durbin, Richard J.*	193,419	2,095,223 D	28.5%	67.8%	29.6%	70.4%
2004	5,141,520	1,390,690	Keyes, Alan	3,597,456	Obama, Barack H.	153,374	2,206,766 D	27.0%	70.0%	27.9%	72.1%
2002	3,486,851	1,325,703	Durkin, Jim	2,103,766	Durbin, Richard J.*	57,382	778,063 D	38.0%	60.3%	38.7%	61.3%
1998	3,395,033	1,709,041	Fitzgerald, Peter G.	1,610,496	Moseley-Braun, Carol*	75,496	98,545 R	50.3%	47.4%	51.5%	48.5%
1996	4,250,722	1,728,824	Salvi, Al	2,384,028	Durbin, Richard J.	137,870	655,204 D	40.7%	56.1%	42.0%	58.0%
1992	4,939,558	2,126,833	Williamson, Richard S.	2,631,229	Moseley-Braun, Carol	181,496	504,396 D	43.1%	53.3%	44.7%	55.3%
1990	3,251,005	1,135,628	Martin, Lynn	2,115,377	Simon, Paul*		979,749 D	34.9%	65.1%	34.9%	65.1%
1986	3,122,883	1,053,734	Koehler, Judy	2,033,783	Dixon, Alan J.*	35,366	980,049 D	33.7%	65.1%	34.1%	65.9%
1984	4,787,473	2,308,039	Percy, Charles H.*	2,397,303	Simon, Paul	82,131	89,264 D	48.2%	50.1%	49.1%	50.9%
1980	4,580,029	1,946,296	O'Neal, David C.	2,565,302	Dixon, Alan J.	68,431	619,006 D	42.5%	56.0%	43.1%	56.9%
1978	3,184,764	1,698,711	Percy, Charles H.*	1,448,187	Seith, Alex	37,866	250,524 R	53.3%	45.5%	54.0%	46.0%
1974	2,914,666	1,084,884	Burditt, George M.	1,811,496	Stevenson, Adlai E. II*	18,286	726,612 D	37.2%	62.2%	37.5%	62.5%
1972	4,608,380	2,867,078	Percy, Charles H.*	1,721,031	Pucinski, Roman C.	20,271	1,146,047 R	62.2%	37.3%	62.5%	37.5%
1970S	3,599,272	1,519,718	Smith, Ralph T.*	2,065,054	Stevenson, Adlai E. II	14,500	545,336 D	42.2%	57.4%	42.4%	57.6%
1968	4,449,757	2,358,947	Dirksen, Everett Mckinley*	2,073,242	Clark, William G.	17,568	285,705 R	53.0%	46.6%	53.2%	46.8%
1966	3,822,725	2,100,449	Percy, Charles H.	1,678,147	Douglas, Paul H.*	44,129	422,302 R	54.9%	43.9%	55.6%	44.4%
1962	3,709,216	1,961,202	Dirksen, Everett Mckinley*	1,748,007	Yates, Sidney R.	7	213,195 R	52.9%	47.1%	52.9%	47.1%
1960	4,632,796	2,093,846	Witwer, Samuel W.	2,530,943	Douglas, Paul H.*	8,007	437,097 D	45.2%	54.6%	45.3%	54.7%
1956	4,264,830	2,307,352	Dirksen, Everett Mckinley*	1,949,883	Stengel, Richard	7,595	357,469 R	54.1%	45.7%	54.2%	45.8%
1954	3,368,025	1,563,683	Meek, Joseph T.	1,804,338	Douglas, Paul H.*	4	240,655 D	46.4%	53.6%	46.4%	53.6%
1950	3,622,673	1,951,984	Dirksen, Everett Mckinley	1,657,630	Lucas, Scott W.*	13,059	294,354 R	53.9%	45.8%	54.1%	45.9%
1948	3,900,285	1,740,026	Brooks, C. Wayland*	2,147,754	Douglas, Paul H.	12,505	407,728 D	44.6%	55.1%	44.8%	55.2%

Note: An asterisk (*) denotes incumbent. The 1970 election was for a short term to fill a vacancy.

ILLINOIS

PRESIDENT 2016

2010 Census Population	County	Total Vote	Republican (Trump)	Democratic (Clinton)	Other	Rep.-Dem. Plurality	Percentage Total Vote Rep.	Dem.	Major Vote Rep.	Dem.
67,103	ADAMS	31,947	22,790	7,676	1,481	15,114 R	71.3%	24.0%	74.8%	25.2%
8,238	ALEXANDER	2,820	1,496	1,262	62	234 R	53.0%	44.8%	54.2%	45.8%
17,768	BOND	7,510	4,888	2,068	554	2,820 R	65.1%	27.5%	70.3%	29.7%
54,165	BOONE	22,729	12,282	8,986	1,461	3,296 R	54.0%	39.5%	57.7%	42.3%
6,937	BROWN	2,359	1,796	476	87	1,320 R	76.1%	20.2%	79.0%	21.0%
34,978	BUREAU	16,389	9,281	6,029	1,079	3,252 R	56.6%	36.8%	60.6%	39.4%
5,089	CALHOUN	2,561	1,721	739	101	982 R	67.2%	28.9%	70.0%	30.0%
15,387	CARROLL	7,393	4,434	2,447	512	1,987 R	60.0%	33.1%	64.4%	35.6%
13,642	CASS	5,075	3,216	1,621	238	1,595 R	63.4%	31.9%	66.5%	33.5%
201,081	CHAMPAIGN	90,569	33,368	50,137	7,064	16,769 D	36.8%	55.4%	40.0%	60.0%
34,800	CHRISTIAN	15,364	10,543	3,992	829	6,551 R	68.6%	26.0%	72.5%	27.5%
16,335	CLARK	7,841	5,622	1,877	342	3,745 R	71.7%	23.9%	75.0%	25.0%
13,815	CLAY	6,314	5,021	1,020	273	4,001 R	79.5%	16.2%	83.1%	16.9%
37,762	CLINTON	17,327	12,412	3,945	970	8,467 R	71.6%	22.8%	75.9%	24.1%
53,873	COLES	21,679	13,003	7,309	1,367	5,694 R	60.0%	33.7%	64.0%	36.0%
5,194,675	COOK	2,158,615	453,287	1,611,946	93,382	1,158,659 D	21.0%	74.7%	21.9%	78.1%
19,817	CRAWFORD	8,672	6,277	1,992	403	4,285 R	72.4%	23.0%	75.9%	24.1%
11,048	CUMBERLAND	5,526	4,206	1,031	289	3,175 R	76.1%	18.7%	80.3%	19.7%
16,561	DE WITT	7,492	5,077	1,910	505	3,167 R	67.8%	25.5%	72.7%	27.3%
105,160	DEKALB	43,003	19,091	20,466	3,446	1,375 D	44.4%	47.6%	48.3%	51.7%
19,980	DOUGLAS	8,125	5,698	1,949	478	3,749 R	70.1%	24.0%	74.5%	25.5%
916,924	DU PAGE	423,666	166,415	228,622	28,629	62,207 D	39.3%	54.0%	42.1%	57.9%
18,576	EDGAR	7,841	5,645	1,793	403	3,852 R	72.0%	22.9%	75.9%	24.1%
6,721	EDWARDS	3,324	2,778	434	112	2,344 R	83.6%	13.1%	86.5%	13.5%
34,242	EFFINGHAM	17,514	13,635	3,083	796	10,552 R	77.9%	17.6%	81.6%	18.4%
22,140	FAYETTE	9,552	7,372	1,819	361	5,553 R	77.2%	19.0%	80.2%	19.8%
14,081	FORD	6,338	4,480	1,414	444	3,066 R	70.7%	22.3%	76.0%	24.0%
39,561	FRANKLIN	18,567	13,116	4,727	724	8,389 R	70.6%	25.5%	73.5%	26.5%
37,069	FULTON	15,651	8,492	6,133	1,026	2,359 R	54.3%	39.2%	58.1%	41.9%
5,589	GALLATIN	2,699	1,942	657	100	1,285 R	72.0%	24.3%	74.7%	25.3%
13,886	GREENE	5,559	4,145	1,205	209	2,940 R	74.6%	21.7%	77.5%	22.5%
50,063	GRUNDY	23,022	13,454	8,065	1,503	5,389 R	58.4%	35.0%	62.5%	37.5%
8,457	HAMILTON	4,156	3,206	802	148	2,404 R	77.1%	19.3%	80.0%	20.0%
19,104	HANCOCK	9,049	6,430	2,139	480	4,291 R	71.1%	23.6%	75.0%	25.0%
4,320	HARDIN	2,137	1,653	420	64	1,233 R	77.4%	19.7%	79.7%	20.3%
7,331	HENDERSON	3,489	2,155	1,155	179	1,000 R	61.8%	33.1%	65.1%	34.9%
50,486	HENRY	24,365	13,985	8,871	1,509	5,114 R	57.4%	36.4%	61.2%	38.8%
29,718	IROQUOIS	12,996	9,750	2,504	742	7,246 R	75.0%	19.3%	79.6%	20.4%
60,218	JACKSON	24,268	10,843	11,634	1,791	791 D	44.7%	47.9%	48.2%	51.8%
9,698	JASPER	5,112	3,975	924	213	3,051 R	77.8%	18.1%	81.1%	18.9%
38,827	JEFFERSON	16,876	11,695	4,425	756	7,270 R	69.3%	26.2%	72.5%	27.5%
22,985	JERSEY	10,938	7,748	2,679	511	5,069 R	70.8%	24.5%	74.3%	25.7%
22,678	JO DAVIESS	11,225	6,121	4,462	642	1,659 R	54.5%	39.8%	57.8%	42.2%
12,582	JOHNSON	6,043	4,649	1,142	252	3,507 R	76.9%	18.9%	80.3%	19.7%
515,269	KANE	199,314	82,734	103,665	12,915	20,931 D	41.5%	52.0%	44.4%	55.6%
113,449	KANKAKEE	46,783	25,129	18,971	2,683	6,158 R	53.7%	40.6%	57.0%	43.0%
114,736	KENDALL	53,447	24,961	24,884	3,602	77 R	46.7%	46.6%	50.1%	49.9%
52,919	KNOX	22,243	10,737	10,083	1,423	654 R	48.3%	45.3%	51.6%	48.4%
113,924	LA SALLE	49,251	26,689	19,543	3,019	7,146 R	54.2%	39.7%	57.7%	42.3%
703,462	LAKE	299,040	109,767	171,095	18,178	61,328 D	36.7%	57.2%	39.1%	60.9%
16,833	LAWRENCE	6,058	4,521	1,290	247	3,231 R	74.6%	21.3%	77.8%	22.2%
36,031	LEE	15,304	8,612	5,528	1,164	3,084 R	56.3%	36.1%	60.9%	39.1%
38,950	LIVINGSTON	15,206	10,208	4,023	975	6,185 R	67.1%	26.5%	71.7%	28.3%
30,305	LOGAN	12,257	8,181	3,313	763	4,868 R	66.7%	27.0%	71.2%	28.8%
110,768	MACON	47,608	26,866	18,343	2,399	8,523 R	56.4%	38.5%	59.4%	40.6%
47,765	MACOUPIN	22,223	14,322	6,689	1,212	7,633 R	64.4%	30.1%	68.2%	31.8%
269,282	MADISON	128,759	70,490	50,587	7,682	19,903 R	54.7%	39.3%	58.2%	41.8%
39,437	MARION	16,964	11,859	4,369	736	7,490 R	69.9%	25.8%	73.1%	26.9%
12,640	MARSHALL	5,939	3,785	1,789	365	1,996 R	63.7%	30.1%	67.9%	32.1%
14,666	MASON	6,454	4,058	2,014	382	2,044 R	62.9%	31.2%	66.8%	33.2%

ILLINOIS

PRESIDENT 2016

2010 Census Population	County	Total Vote	Republican (Trump)	Democratic (Clinton)	Other	Rep.-Dem. Plurality	Percentage — Total Vote Rep.	Dem.	Major Vote Rep.	Dem.
15,429	MASSAC	6,654	4,846	1,558	250	3,288 R	72.8%	23.4%	75.7%	24.3%
32,612	MCDONOUGH	12,980	6,795	5,288	897	1,507 R	52.3%	40.7%	56.2%	43.8%
308,760	MCHENRY	142,290	71,612	60,803	9,875	10,809 R	50.3%	42.7%	54.1%	45.9%
169,572	MCLEAN	79,835	37,237	36,196	6,402	1,041 R	46.6%	45.3%	50.7%	49.3%
12,705	MENARD	6,464	4,231	1,817	416	2,414 R	65.5%	28.1%	70.0%	30.0%
16,434	MERCER	8,447	4,807	3,071	569	1,736 R	56.9%	36.4%	61.0%	39.0%
32,957	MONROE	19,106	12,629	5,535	942	7,094 R	66.1%	29.0%	69.5%	30.5%
30,104	MONTGOMERY	12,878	8,630	3,504	744	5,126 R	67.0%	27.2%	71.1%	28.9%
35,547	MORGAN	14,645	9,076	4,696	873	4,380 R	62.0%	32.1%	65.9%	34.1%
14,846	MOULTRIE	6,231	4,455	1,481	295	2,974 R	71.5%	23.8%	75.1%	24.9%
53,497	OGLE	23,869	14,352	8,050	1,467	6,302 R	60.1%	33.7%	64.1%	35.9%
186,494	PEORIA	79,102	35,633	38,060	5,409	2,427 D	45.0%	48.1%	48.4%	51.6%
22,350	PERRY	9,798	6,855	2,462	481	4,393 R	70.0%	25.1%	73.6%	26.4%
16,729	PIATT	8,972	5,634	2,645	693	2,989 R	62.8%	29.5%	68.1%	31.9%
16,430	PIKE	7,480	5,754	1,413	313	4,341 R	76.9%	18.9%	80.3%	19.7%
4,470	POPE	2,136	1,678	375	83	1,303 R	78.6%	17.6%	81.7%	18.3%
6,161	PULASKI	2,712	1,675	962	75	713 R	61.8%	35.5%	63.5%	36.5%
6,006	PUTNAM	3,086	1,767	1,147	172	620 R	57.3%	37.2%	60.6%	39.4%
33,476	RANDOLPH	14,099	10,023	3,439	637	6,584 R	71.1%	24.4%	74.5%	25.5%
16,233	RICHLAND	7,649	5,739	1,584	326	4,155 R	75.0%	20.7%	78.4%	21.6%
147,546	ROCK ISLAND	63,171	26,998	32,298	3,875	5,300 D	42.7%	51.1%	45.5%	54.5%
24,913	SALINE	11,296	8,276	2,572	448	5,704 R	73.3%	22.8%	76.3%	23.7%
197,465	SANGAMON	97,234	49,944	40,907	6,383	9,037 R	51.4%	42.1%	55.0%	45.0%
7,544	SCHUYLER	3,800	2,524	1,075	201	1,449 R	66.4%	28.3%	70.1%	29.9%
5,355	SCOTT	2,597	1,966	535	96	1,431 R	75.7%	20.6%	78.6%	21.4%
22,363	SHELBY	10,983	8,229	2,288	466	5,941 R	74.9%	20.8%	78.2%	21.8%
270,056	ST. CLAIR	120,580	53,857	60,756	5,967	6,899 D	44.7%	50.4%	47.0%	53.0%
5,994	STARK	2,717	1,778	751	188	1,027 R	65.4%	27.6%	70.3%	29.7%
47,711	STEPHENSON	20,086	11,083	7,768	1,235	3,315 R	55.2%	38.7%	58.8%	41.2%
135,394	TAZEWELL	63,931	38,707	20,685	4,539	18,022 R	60.5%	32.4%	65.2%	34.8%
17,808	UNION	8,551	5,790	2,402	359	3,388 R	67.7%	28.1%	70.7%	29.3%
81,625	VERMILION	30,570	19,087	10,039	1,444	9,048 R	62.4%	32.8%	65.5%	34.5%
11,947	WABASH	5,428	4,047	1,151	230	2,896 R	74.6%	21.2%	77.9%	22.1%
17,707	WARREN	7,730	4,275	2,987	468	1,288 R	55.3%	38.6%	58.9%	41.1%
14,716	WASHINGTON	7,394	5,571	1,448	375	4,123 R	75.3%	19.6%	79.4%	20.6%
16,760	WAYNE	8,265	6,967	1,048	250	5,919 R	84.3%	12.7%	86.9%	13.1%
14,665	WHITE	7,296	5,640	1,412	244	4,228 R	77.3%	19.4%	80.0%	20.0%
58,498	WHITESIDE	25,280	12,615	11,035	1,630	1,580 R	49.9%	43.7%	53.3%	46.7%
677,560	WILL	300,904	132,720	151,927	16,257	19,207 D	44.1%	50.5%	46.6%	53.4%
66,357	WILLIAMSON	31,623	21,570	8,581	1,472	12,989 R	68.2%	27.1%	71.5%	28.5%
295,266	WINNEBAGO	118,376	55,624	55,713	7,039	89 D	47.0%	47.1%	50.0%	50.0%
38,664	WOODFORD	19,632	13,207	5,092	1,333	8,115 R	67.3%	25.9%	72.2%	27.8%
12,830,632	TOTAL	5,536,424	2,146,015	3,090,729	299,680	944,714 D	38.8%	55.8%	41.0%	59.0%

ILLINOIS

SENATOR 2016

2010 Census Population	County	Total Vote	Republican (Kirk)	Democratic (Duckworth)	Other	Rep.-Dem. Plurality	Percentage Total Vote Rep.	Dem.	Major Vote Rep.	Dem.
67,103	ADAMS	31,732	18,094	12,391	1,247	5,703 R	57.0%	39.0%	59.4%	40.6%
8,238	ALEXANDER	2,723	1,121	1,511	91	390 D	41.2%	55.5%	42.6%	57.4%
17,768	BOND	7,449	3,841	3,203	405	638 R	51.6%	43.0%	54.5%	45.5%
54,165	BOONE	22,579	12,520	8,509	1,550	4,011 R	55.4%	37.7%	59.5%	40.5%
6,937	BROWN	2,272	1,380	794	98	586 R	60.7%	34.9%	63.5%	36.5%
34,978	BUREAU	16,224	8,434	6,842	948	1,592 R	52.0%	42.2%	55.2%	44.8%
5,089	CALHOUN	2,476	1,131	1,272	73	141 D	45.7%	51.4%	47.1%	52.9%
15,387	CARROLL	7,326	4,354	2,577	395	1,777 R	59.4%	35.2%	62.8%	37.2%
13,642	CASS	5,021	2,917	1,799	305	1,118 R	58.1%	35.8%	61.9%	38.1%
201,081	CHAMPAIGN	89,719	38,731	45,760	5,228	7,029 D	43.2%	51.0%	45.8%	54.2%
34,800	CHRISTIAN	15,182	9,316	4,876	990	4,440 R	61.4%	32.1%	65.6%	34.4%
16,335	CLARK	7,737	4,953	2,394	390	2,559 R	64.0%	30.9%	67.4%	32.6%
13,815	CLAY	6,103	3,905	1,917	281	1,988 R	64.0%	31.4%	67.1%	32.9%
37,762	CLINTON	17,166	10,049	6,419	698	3,630 R	58.5%	37.4%	61.0%	39.0%
53,873	COLES	21,447	12,555	7,516	1,376	5,039 R	58.5%	35.0%	62.6%	37.4%
5,194,675	COOK	2,130,558	529,781	1,499,900	100,877	970,119 D	24.9%	70.4%	26.1%	73.9%
19,817	CRAWFORD	8,540	5,455	2,648	437	2,807 R	63.9%	31.0%	67.3%	32.7%
11,048	CUMBERLAND	5,501	3,797	1,329	375	2,468 R	69.0%	24.2%	74.1%	25.9%
16,561	DE WITT	7,466	5,009	1,943	514	3,066 R	67.1%	26.0%	72.1%	27.9%
105,160	DEKALB	42,784	19,355	20,025	3,404	670 D	45.2%	46.8%	49.1%	50.9%
19,980	DOUGLAS	8,072	5,599	1,972	501	3,627 R	69.4%	24.4%	74.0%	26.0%
916,924	DU PAGE	424,880	193,069	208,669	23,142	15,600 D	45.4%	49.1%	48.1%	51.9%
18,576	EDGAR	7,739	5,290	2,027	422	3,263 R	68.4%	26.2%	72.3%	27.7%
6,721	EDWARDS	3,184	2,322	727	135	1,595 R	72.9%	22.8%	76.2%	23.8%
34,242	EFFINGHAM	17,273	12,520	3,810	943	8,710 R	72.5%	22.1%	76.7%	23.3%
22,140	FAYETTE	9,383	5,751	3,201	431	2,550 R	61.3%	34.1%	64.2%	35.8%
14,081	FORD	6,328	4,507	1,421	400	3,086 R	71.2%	22.5%	76.0%	24.0%
39,561	FRANKLIN	18,324	8,894	8,537	893	357 R	48.5%	46.6%	51.0%	49.0%
37,069	FULTON	15,595	7,702	6,726	1,167	976 R	49.4%	43.1%	53.4%	46.6%
5,589	GALLATIN	2,557	1,209	1,263	85	54 D	47.3%	49.4%	48.9%	51.1%
13,886	GREENE	5,407	3,064	2,023	320	1,041 R	56.7%	37.4%	60.2%	39.8%
50,063	GRUNDY	22,820	11,624	9,475	1,721	2,149 R	50.9%	41.5%	55.1%	44.9%
8,457	HAMILTON	3,962	2,171	1,628	163	543 R	54.8%	41.1%	57.1%	42.9%
19,104	HANCOCK	8,926	5,127	3,394	405	1,733 R	57.4%	38.0%	60.2%	39.8%
4,320	HARDIN	2,069	1,137	865	67	272 R	55.0%	41.8%	56.8%	43.2%
7,331	HENDERSON	3,426	1,820	1,407	199	413 R	53.1%	41.1%	56.4%	43.6%
50,486	HENRY	24,028	13,214	9,488	1,326	3,726 R	55.0%	39.5%	58.2%	41.8%
29,718	IROQUOIS	12,896	9,379	2,755	762	6,624 R	72.7%	21.4%	77.3%	22.7%
60,218	JACKSON	24,138	8,938	13,739	1,461	4,801 D	37.0%	56.9%	39.4%	60.6%
9,698	JASPER	4,946	3,312	1,420	214	1,892 R	67.0%	28.7%	70.0%	30.0%
38,827	JEFFERSON	16,586	8,790	6,903	893	1,887 R	53.0%	41.6%	56.0%	44.0%
22,985	JERSEY	10,638	5,840	4,233	565	1,607 R	54.9%	39.8%	58.0%	42.0%
22,678	JO DAVIESS	11,103	5,988	4,525	590	1,463 R	53.9%	40.8%	57.0%	43.0%
12,582	JOHNSON	5,937	3,572	2,056	309	1,516 R	60.2%	34.6%	63.5%	36.5%
515,269	KANE	197,681	87,886	97,088	12,707	9,202 D	44.5%	49.1%	47.5%	52.5%
113,449	KANKAKEE	46,530	22,850	20,901	2,779	1,949 R	49.1%	44.9%	52.2%	47.8%
114,736	KENDALL	53,077	25,202	24,035	3,840	1,167 R	47.5%	45.3%	51.2%	48.8%
52,919	KNOX	22,204	10,350	10,651	1,203	301 D	46.6%	48.0%	49.3%	50.7%
113,924	LA SALLE	48,559	23,471	22,073	3,015	1,398 R	48.3%	45.5%	51.5%	48.5%
703,462	LAKE	300,054	135,334	150,351	14,369	15,017 D	45.1%	50.1%	47.4%	52.6%
16,833	LAWRENCE	5,886	3,701	1,938	247	1,763 R	62.9%	32.9%	65.6%	34.4%
36,031	LEE	15,258	8,640	5,587	1,031	3,053 R	56.6%	36.6%	60.7%	39.3%
38,950	LIVINGSTON	15,142	10,169	4,019	954	6,150 R	67.2%	26.5%	71.7%	28.3%
30,305	LOGAN	12,231	8,236	3,272	723	4,964 R	67.3%	26.8%	71.6%	28.4%
110,768	MACON	47,348	26,114	18,600	2,634	7,514 R	55.2%	39.3%	58.4%	41.6%
47,765	MACOUPIN	21,897	10,550	10,264	1,083	286 R	48.2%	46.9%	50.7%	49.3%
269,282	MADISON	127,529	56,665	64,240	6,624	7,575 D	44.4%	50.4%	46.9%	53.1%
39,437	MARION	16,711	9,162	6,827	722	2,335 R	54.8%	40.9%	57.3%	42.7%
12,640	MARSHALL	5,894	3,588	1,921	385	1,667 R	60.9%	32.6%	65.1%	34.9%
14,666	MASON	6,391	3,708	2,301	382	1,407 R	58.0%	36.0%	61.7%	38.3%

ILLINOIS
SENATOR 2016

2010 Census Population	County	Total Vote	Republican (Kirk)	Democratic (Duckworth)	Other	Rep.-Dem. Plurality	Total Vote Rep.	Dem.	Major Vote Rep.	Dem.
15,429	MASSAC	6,531	3,739	2,461	331	1,278 R	57.3%	37.7%	60.3%	39.7%
32,612	MCDONOUGH	12,900	5,917	6,254	729	337 D	45.9%	48.5%	48.6%	51.4%
308,760	MCHENRY	141,603	72,296	58,815	10,492	13,481 R	51.1%	41.5%	55.1%	44.9%
169,572	MCLEAN	80,141	41,579	33,204	5,358	8,375 R	51.9%	41.4%	55.6%	44.4%
12,705	MENARD	6,405	4,278	1,773	354	2,505 R	66.8%	27.7%	70.7%	29.3%
16,434	MERCER	8,337	4,465	3,391	481	1,074 R	53.6%	40.7%	56.8%	43.2%
32,957	MONROE	19,062	10,885	7,458	719	3,427 R	57.1%	39.1%	59.3%	40.7%
30,104	MONTGOMERY	12,680	6,662	5,367	651	1,295 R	52.5%	42.3%	55.4%	44.6%
35,547	MORGAN	14,634	9,112	4,733	789	4,379 R	62.3%	32.3%	65.8%	34.2%
14,846	MOULTRIE	6,196	4,264	1,574	358	2,690 R	68.8%	25.4%	73.0%	27.0%
53,497	OGLE	23,890	14,768	7,645	1,477	7,123 R	61.8%	32.0%	65.9%	34.1%
186,494	PEORIA	79,323	38,169	36,548	4,606	1,621 R	48.1%	46.1%	51.1%	48.9%
22,350	PERRY	9,652	4,925	4,279	448	646 R	51.0%	44.3%	53.5%	46.5%
16,729	PIATT	8,988	5,954	2,563	471	3,391 R	66.2%	28.5%	69.9%	30.1%
16,430	PIKE	7,368	4,377	2,654	337	1,723 R	59.4%	36.0%	62.3%	37.7%
4,470	POPE	2,066	1,279	703	84	576 R	61.9%	34.0%	64.5%	35.5%
6,161	PULASKI	2,675	1,206	1,394	75	188 D	45.1%	52.1%	46.4%	53.6%
6,006	PUTNAM	3,011	1,587	1,255	169	332 R	52.7%	41.7%	55.8%	44.2%
33,476	RANDOLPH	13,987	7,364	6,119	504	1,245 R	52.6%	43.7%	54.6%	45.4%
16,233	RICHLAND	7,460	4,900	2,208	352	2,692 R	65.7%	29.6%	68.9%	31.1%
147,546	ROCK ISLAND	62,903	26,767	32,952	3,184	6,185 D	42.6%	52.4%	44.8%	55.2%
24,913	SALINE	10,848	5,612	4,797	439	815 R	51.7%	44.2%	53.9%	46.1%
197,465	SANGAMON	97,193	51,849	39,928	5,416	11,921 R	53.3%	41.1%	56.5%	43.5%
7,544	SCHUYLER	3,748	1,943	1,612	193	331 R	51.8%	43.0%	54.7%	45.3%
5,355	SCOTT	2,561	1,606	848	107	758 R	62.7%	33.1%	65.4%	34.6%
22,363	SHELBY	10,855	7,418	2,733	704	4,685 R	68.3%	25.2%	73.1%	26.9%
270,056	ST. CLAIR	120,021	45,998	68,709	5,314	22,711 D	38.3%	57.2%	40.1%	59.9%
5,994	STARK	2,703	1,760	782	161	978 R	65.1%	28.9%	69.2%	30.8%
47,711	STEPHENSON	20,104	11,453	7,411	1,240	4,042 R	57.0%	36.9%	60.7%	39.3%
135,394	TAZEWELL	64,075	38,386	21,215	4,474	17,171 R	59.9%	33.1%	64.4%	35.6%
17,808	UNION	8,435	4,231	3,843	361	388 R	50.2%	45.6%	52.4%	47.6%
81,625	VERMILION	30,413	18,076	10,511	1,826	7,565 R	59.4%	34.6%	63.2%	36.8%
11,947	WABASH	5,270	3,500	1,541	229	1,959 R	66.4%	29.2%	69.4%	30.6%
17,707	WARREN	7,714	4,184	3,025	505	1,159 R	54.2%	39.2%	58.0%	42.0%
14,716	WASHINGTON	7,261	4,417	2,553	291	1,864 R	60.8%	35.2%	63.4%	36.6%
16,760	WAYNE	7,944	5,616	1,924	404	3,692 R	70.7%	24.2%	74.5%	25.5%
14,665	WHITE	7,087	4,356	2,408	323	1,948 R	61.5%	34.0%	64.4%	35.6%
58,498	WHITESIDE	25,193	12,149	11,672	1,372	477 R	48.2%	46.3%	51.0%	49.0%
677,560	WILL	299,133	127,473	152,790	18,870	25,317 D	42.6%	51.1%	45.5%	54.5%
66,357	WILLIAMSON	31,136	16,075	13,518	1,543	2,557 R	51.6%	43.4%	54.3%	45.7%
295,266	WINNEBAGO	118,170	57,643	52,730	7,797	4,913 R	48.8%	44.6%	52.2%	47.8%
38,664	WOODFORD	19,588	13,291	5,083	1,214	8,208 R	67.9%	25.9%	72.3%	27.7%
12,830,632	TOTAL	5,491,878	2,184,692	3,012,940	294,246	828,248 D	39.8%	54.9%	42.0%	58.0%

ILLINOIS

HOUSE OF REPRESENTATIVES

CD	Year	Total Vote	Republican Vote	Republican Candidate	Democratic Vote	Democratic Candidate	Other Vote	Rep.-Dem. Plurality	Total Vote Rep.	Total Vote Dem.	Major Vote Rep.	Major Vote Dem.
1	2016	315,862	81,817	DEUSER, AUGUST (O'NEILL)	234,037	RUSH, BOBBY L.*	8	152,220 D	25.9%	74.1%	25.9%	74.1%
1	2014	222,017	59,749	TILLMAN, JIMMY LEE II	162,268	RUSH, BOBBY L.*		102,519 D	26.9%	73.1%	26.9%	73.1%
1	2012	320,844	83,989	PELOQUIN, DONALD E.	236,854	RUSH, BOBBY L.*	1	152,865 D	26.2%	73.8%	26.2%	73.8%
2	2016	294,522	59,471	MORROW, JOHN F.	235,051	KELLY, ROBIN L.*		175,580 D	20.2%	79.8%	20.2%	79.8%
2	2014	204,266	43,799	WALLACE, ERIC M.	160,337	KELLY, ROBIN L.*	130	116,538 D	21.4%	78.5%	21.5%	78.5%
2	2012	297,712	69,115	WOODWORTH, BRIAN	188,303	JACKSON, JESSE L. JR.*	40,294	119,188 D	23.2%	63.3%	26.8%	73.2%
3	2016	225,411			225,320	LIPINSKI, DANIEL WILLIAM*	91	225,320 D		100.0%		100.0%
3	2014	180,855	64,091	BRANNIGAN, SHARON M.	116,764	LIPINSKI, DANIEL WILLIAM*		52,673 D	35.4%	64.6%	35.4%	64.6%
3	2012	246,398	77,653	GRABOWSKI, RICHARD	168,738	LIPINSKI, DANIEL WILLIAM*	7	91,085 D	31.5%	68.5%	31.5%	68.5%
4	2016	171,297			171,297	GUTIERREZ, LUIS V.*		171,297 D		100.0%		100.0%
4	2014	101,944	22,278	CONCEPCION, HECTOR	79,666	GUTIERREZ, LUIS V.*		57,388 D	21.9%	78.1%	21.9%	78.1%
4	2012	160,509	27,279	CONCEPCION, HECTOR	133,226	GUTIERREZ, LUIS V.*	4	105,947 D	17.0%	83.0%	17.0%	83.0%
5	2016	313,724	86,222	KOLBER, VINCENT A. "VINCE"	212,842	QUIGLEY, MIKE*	14,660	126,620 D	27.5%	67.8%	28.8%	71.2%
5	2014	184,019	56,350	KOLBER, VINCENT A. "VINCE"	116,364	QUIGLEY, MIKE*	11,305	60,014 D	30.6%	63.2%	32.6%	67.4%
5	2012	270,377	77,289	SCHMITT, DAN	177,729	QUIGLEY, MIKE*	15,359	100,440 D	28.6%	65.7%	30.3%	69.7%
6	2016	352,146	208,555	ROSKAM, PETER J.*	143,591	HOWLAND, AMANDA		64,964 R	59.2%	40.8%	59.2%	40.8%
6	2014	238,752	160,287	ROSKAM, PETER J.*	78,465	MASON, MICHAEL		81,822 R	67.1%	32.9%	67.1%	32.9%
6	2012	326,129	193,138	ROSKAM, PETER J.*	132,991	COOLIDGE, LESLIE		60,147 R	59.2%	40.8%	59.2%	40.8%
7	2016	297,466	46,882	LEEF, JEFFREY A	250,584	DAVIS, DANNY K.*		203,702 D	15.8%	84.2%	15.8%	84.2%
7	2014	182,278	27,168	BUMPERS, ROBERT L.	155,110	DAVIS, DANNY K.*		127,942 D	14.9%	85.1%	14.9%	85.1%
7	2012	286,435	31,466	ZAK, RITA	242,439	DAVIS, DANNY K.*	12,530	210,973 D	11.0%	84.6%	11.5%	88.5%
8	2016	248,571	103,617	DICIANNI, PETER "PETE"	144,954	KRISHNAMOORTHI, RAJA		41,337 D	41.7%	58.3%	41.7%	58.3%
8	2014	151,056	66,878	KAIFESH, LAWRENCE JOSEPH "LARRY"	84,178	DUCKWORTH, TAMMY*		17,300 D	44.3%	55.7%	44.3%	55.7%
8	2012	225,066	101,860	WALSH, JOE*	123,206	DUCKWORTH, TAMMY		21,346 D	45.3%	54.7%	45.3%	54.7%
9	2016	326,948	109,550	LASONDE, JOAN MCCARTHY	217,306	SCHAKOWSKY, JANICE D. "JAN"*	92	107,756 D	33.5%	66.5%	33.5%	66.5%
9	2014	213,450	72,384	ATANUS, SUSANNE	141,000	SCHAKOWSKY, JANICE D. "JAN"*	66	68,616 D	33.9%	66.1%	33.9%	66.1%
9	2012	293,807	98,924	WOLFE, TIMOTHY	194,869	SCHAKOWSKY, JANICE D. "JAN"*	14	95,945 D	33.7%	66.3%	33.7%	66.3%
10	2016	285,996	135,535	DOLD, ROBERT*	150,435	SCHNEIDER, BRAD	26	14,900 D	47.4%	52.6%	47.4%	52.6%
10	2014	187,128	95,992	DOLD, ROBERT	91,136	SCHNEIDER, BRAD*		4,856 R	51.3%	48.7%	51.3%	48.7%
10	2012	264,454	130,564	DOLD, ROBERT*	133,890	SCHNEIDER, BRAD		3,326 D	49.4%	50.6%	49.4%	50.6%
11	2016	275,573	108,995	KHOURI, TONIA	166,578	FOSTER, BILL*		57,583 D	39.6%	60.4%	39.6%	60.4%
11	2014	174,772	81,335	SENGER, DARLENE	93,436	FOSTER, BILL*	1	12,101 D	46.5%	53.5%	46.5%	53.5%
11	2012	254,295	105,348	BIGGERT, JUDY*	148,928	FOSTER, BILL	19	43,580 D	41.4%	58.6%	41.4%	58.6%
12	2016	313,002	169,976	BOST, MIKE*	124,246	BARICEVIC, CHARLES "C.J."	18,780	45,730 R	54.3%	39.7%	57.8%	42.2%
12	2014	209,738	110,038	BOST, MIKE	87,860	ENYART, WILLIAM*	11,840	22,178 R	52.5%	41.9%	55.6%	44.4%
12	2012	303,949	129,902	PLUMMER, JASON	157,000	ENYART, WILLIAM	17,047	27,098 D	42.7%	51.7%	45.3%	54.7%
13	2016	314,394	187,583	DAVIS, RODNEY L.*	126,811	WICKLUND, MARK D.		60,772 R	59.7%	40.3%	59.7%	40.3%
13	2014	210,272	123,337	DAVIS, RODNEY L.*	86,935	CALLIS, ANN E.		36,402 R	58.7%	41.3%	58.7%	41.3%
13	2012	294,385	137,034	DAVIS, RODNEY L.	136,032	GILL, DAVID M.	21,319	1,002 R	46.5%	46.2%	50.2%	49.8%
14	2016	338,097	200,508	HULTGREN, RANDY M.*	137,589	WALZ, JIM		62,919 R	59.3%	40.7%	59.3%	40.7%
14	2014	222,230	145,369	HULTGREN, RANDY M.*	76,861	ANDERSON, DENNIS		68,508 R	65.4%	34.6%	65.4%	34.6%
14	2012	301,954	177,603	HULTGREN, RANDY M.*	124,351	ANDERSON, DENNIS		53,252 R	58.8%	41.2%	58.8%	41.2%
15	2016	274,554	274,554	SHIMKUS, JOHN M.*				274,554 R	100.0%		100.0%	
15	2014	221,926	166,274	SHIMKUS, JOHN M.*	55,652	THORSLAND, ERIC		110,622 R	74.9%	25.1%	74.9%	25.1%
15	2012	299,937	205,775	SHIMKUS, JOHN M.*	94,162	MICHAEL, ANGELA		111,613 R	68.6%	31.4%	68.6%	31.4%
16	2016	259,853	259,722	KINZINGER, ADAM*			131	259,722 R	99.9%		100.0%	
16	2014	217,198	153,388	KINZINGER, ADAM*	63,810	OLSEN, RANDALL WAYNE		89,578 R	70.6%	29.4%	70.6%	29.4%
16	2012	294,090	181,789	KINZINGER, ADAM*	112,301	ROHL, WANDA		69,488 R	61.8%	38.2%	61.8%	38.2%

ILLINOIS

HOUSE OF REPRESENTATIVES

CD	Year	Total Vote	Republican		Democratic		Other Vote	Rep.-Dem. Plurality	Percentage			
			Vote	Candidate	Vote	Candidate			Total Vote		Major Vote	
									Rep.	Dem.	Rep.	Dem.
17	2016	287,068	113,943	HARLAN, PATRICK	173,125	BUSTOS, CHERI*		59,182 D	39.7%	60.3%	39.7%	60.3%
17	2014	199,361	88,785	SCHILLING, BOBBY	110,560	BUSTOS, CHERI*	16	21,775 D	44.5%	55.5%	44.5%	55.5%
17	2012	288,161	134,623	SCHILLING, BOBBY*	153,519	BUSTOS, CHERI	19	18,896 D	46.7%	53.3%	46.7%	53.3%
18	2016	347,283	250,506	LAHOOD, DARIN*	96,770	RODRIGUEZ, JUNIUS	7	153,736 R	72.1%	27.9%	72.1%	27.9%
18	2014	246,740	184,363	SCHOCK, AARON*	62,377	MILLER, DARREL ERVIN		121,986 R	74.7%	25.3%	74.7%	25.3%
18	2012	329,631	244,467	SCHOCK, AARON*	85,164	WATERWORTH, STEVE		159,303 R	74.2%	25.8%	74.2%	25.8%
TOTAL	2016	5,241,767	2,397,436		2,810,536		33,795	413,100 D	45.7%	53.6%	46.0%	54.0%
TOTAL	2014	3,568,002	1,721,865		1,822,779		23,358	100,914 D	48.3%	51.1%	48.6%	51.4%
TOTAL	2012	5,058,133	2,207,818		2,743,702		106,613	535,884 D	43.6%	54.2%	44.6%	55.4%

Note: An asterisk (*) denotes incumbent.

ILLINOIS

GENERAL AND PRIMARY ELECTIONS

2016 GENERAL ELECTIONS: OTHER VOTES

President Other vote was 209,596 Libertarian (Gary Johnson), 76,802 Green (Jill Stein), 11,655 Write-in (Evan McMullin), 1,138 Write-in (Darrell Castle), 314 Write-in (Scattered Write-in), 175 Write-in (Thomas Hoefling)

Senate Other vote was 175,988 Libertarian (Kenton McMillen), 117,619 Green (Scott Summers), 408 Write-in (Chad Koppie), 106 Write-in (Jim Brown), 77 Write-in (Chris Aguayo), 42 Write-in (Susana Sandoval), 5 Write-in (Eric Stewart), 1 Write-in (Patricia Beard)

House Other vote was:

CD 1 8 Write-in (Tabitha Carson)
CD 3 91 Write-in (Diane Harris)
CD 5 14,657 Green (Rob Sherman), 3 Write-in (Michael Krynski)
CD 9 79 Write-in (David Williams III), 13 Write-in (Susanne Atanus)
CD 10 26 Write-in (Joseph Kopsick)
CD 12 18,780 Green (Paula Bradshaw)
CD 16 131 Write-in (John Burchardt)
CD 18 7 Write-in (Don Vance)

2016 PRIMARY ELECTIONS: SUPPLEMENTARY INFORMATION

Primary March 15, 2016 **Registration** (as of March 15, 2016) 7,666,763 No Party Registration

Primary Type Open—Any registered voter could participate in the primary of either party.

ILLINOIS

GENERAL AND PRIMARY ELECTIONS

	REPUBLICAN PRIMARIES			DEMOCRATIC PRIMARIES		
President	Trump, Donald J.	562,464	38.8%	Clinton, Hillary Rodham	1,039,555	50.6%
	Cruz, Ted	438,235	30.2%	Sanders, Bernard	999,494	48.6%
	Kasich, John R.	286,118	19.7%	Wilson, Willie	6,565	0.3%
	Rubio, Marco	126,681	8.7%	O'Malley, Martin	6,197	0.3%
	Carson, Ben	11,469	0.8%	Cohen, Lawrence "Larry"	2,407	0.1%
	Bush, Jeb	11,188	0.8%	De La Fuente, Roque "Rocky"	1,802	0.1%
	Paul, Rand	4,718	0.3%	Formhals, David (Write-in)	25	
	Christie, Chris	3,428	0.2%	O'Neill, Brian (Write-in)	2	
	Huckabee, Mike	2,737	0.2%			
	Fiorina, Carly	1,540	0.1%			
	Santorum, Rick	1,154	0.1%			
	Breivogel, Joann (Write-in)	16				
	TOTAL	*1,449,748*		*TOTAL*	*2,056,047*	
Senator	Kirk, Mark Steven*	931,619	70.6%	Duckworth, Tammy	1,220,128	64.4%
	Marter, James T.	388,571	29.4%	Zopp, Andrea	455,729	24.0%
				Harris, Napoleon	219,286	11.6%
				Beard, Patricia Elaine (Write-in)	1	
	TOTAL	*1,320,190*		*TOTAL*	*1,895,144*	
Congressional District 1	Deuser, August (O'Neill)	24,584	73.8%	Rush, Bobby L.*	128,402	71.4%
	Tillman, Jimmy Lee II	8,737	26.2%	Brookins, Howard B. Jr.	34,645	19.3%
				Brutus, O. Patrick	16,696	9.3%
	TOTAL	*33,321*		*TOTAL*	*179,743*	
Congressional District 2	Morrow, John F.	27,303	100.0%	Kelly, Robin L.*	115,752	73.9%
				Lewis, Marcus	25,280	16.1%
				Rayburn, Charles	9,559	6.1%
				Myrickes, Dorian C.L.	6,002	3.8%
	TOTAL	*27,303*		*TOTAL*	*156,593*	
Congressional District 3				Lipinski, Daniel William*	107,620	100.0%
				TOTAL	*107,620*	
Congressional District 4				Gutierrez, Luis V.*	92,779	75.2%
				Salas, Javier	30,640	24.8%
				TOTAL	*123,419*	
Congressional District 5				Quigley, Mike*	127,679	100.0%
				TOTAL	*127,679*	
Congressional District 6	Roskam, Peter J.*	83,344	68.8%	Howland, Amanda	51,101	67.1%
	Kinzler, Gordon "Jay"	37,834	31.2%	Marshall, Robert	25,027	32.9%
	TOTAL	*121,178*		*TOTAL*	*76,128*	
Congressional District 7				Davis, Danny K.*	139,378	81.2%
				Day, Thomas	32,261	18.8%
				Collins, Frederick (Write-in)	25	
				TOTAL	*171,664*	
Congressional District 8	DiCianni, Peter "Pete"	51,047	100.0%	Krishnamoorthi, Raja	44,950	57.0%
	Straw, Andrew (Write-in)	13		Noland, Michael	22,925	29.1%
				Bullwinkel, Deborah M.	11,005	14.0%
	TOTAL	*51,060*		*TOTAL*	*78,880*	
Congressional District 9	Lasonde, Joan McCarthy	47,948	100.0%	Schakowsky, Janice D. "Jan"*	134,961	100.0%
	TOTAL	*47,948*		*TOTAL*	*134,961*	
Congressional District 10	Dold, Robert*	61,968	100.0%	Schneider, Brad	50,916	53.7%
				Rotering, Nancy	43,842	46.3%
	TOTAL	*61,968*		*TOTAL*	*94,758*	

ILLINOIS

GENERAL AND PRIMARY ELECTIONS

	REPUBLICAN PRIMARIES			DEMOCRATIC PRIMARIES		
Congressional District 11	Khouri, Tonia	22,859	36.9%	Foster, Bill*	82,984	100.0%
	Stella, Dominick J. "Nick"	22,489	36.3%			
	White, Herman B.	16,536	26.7%			
	TOTAL	61,884		TOTAL	82,984	
Congressional District 12	Bost, Mike*	74,454	100.0%	Baricevic, Charles "C.J."	70,580	100.0%
	TOTAL	74,454		TOTAL	70,580	
Congressional District 13	Davis, Rodney L.*	71,447	77.0%	Wicklund, Mark D.	71,430	100.0%
	Vandersand, Ethan	21,401	23.0%			
	TOTAL	92,848		TOTAL	71,430	
Congressional District 14	Hultgren, Randy M.*	101,299	100.0%	Walz, Jim	27,706	42.7%
				Hosta, John J.	24,866	38.3%
				Maggitt, Jesse	12,311	19.0%
	TOTAL	101,299		TOTAL	64,883	
Congressional District 15	Shimkus, John M.*	76,547	60.4%			
	McCarter, Kyle	50,245	39.6%			
	TOTAL	126,792				
Congressional District 16	Kinzinger, Adam*	101,421	100.0%			
	McGroarty, Colin M. (Write-in)	2				
	TOTAL	101,423				
Congressional District 17	Harlan, Patrick	52,405	75.7%	Bustos, Cheri*	70,319	100.0%
	Boccarossa, Jack	16,805	24.3%			
	TOTAL	69,210		TOTAL	70,319	
Congressional District 18	LaHood, Darin*	130,419	100.0%	Miller, Darrel Ervin (Write-in)	148	100.0%
	TOTAL	130,419		TOTAL	148	

Note: An asterisk (*) denotes incumbent.

INDIANA

Congressional districts first established for elections held in 2012

9 members

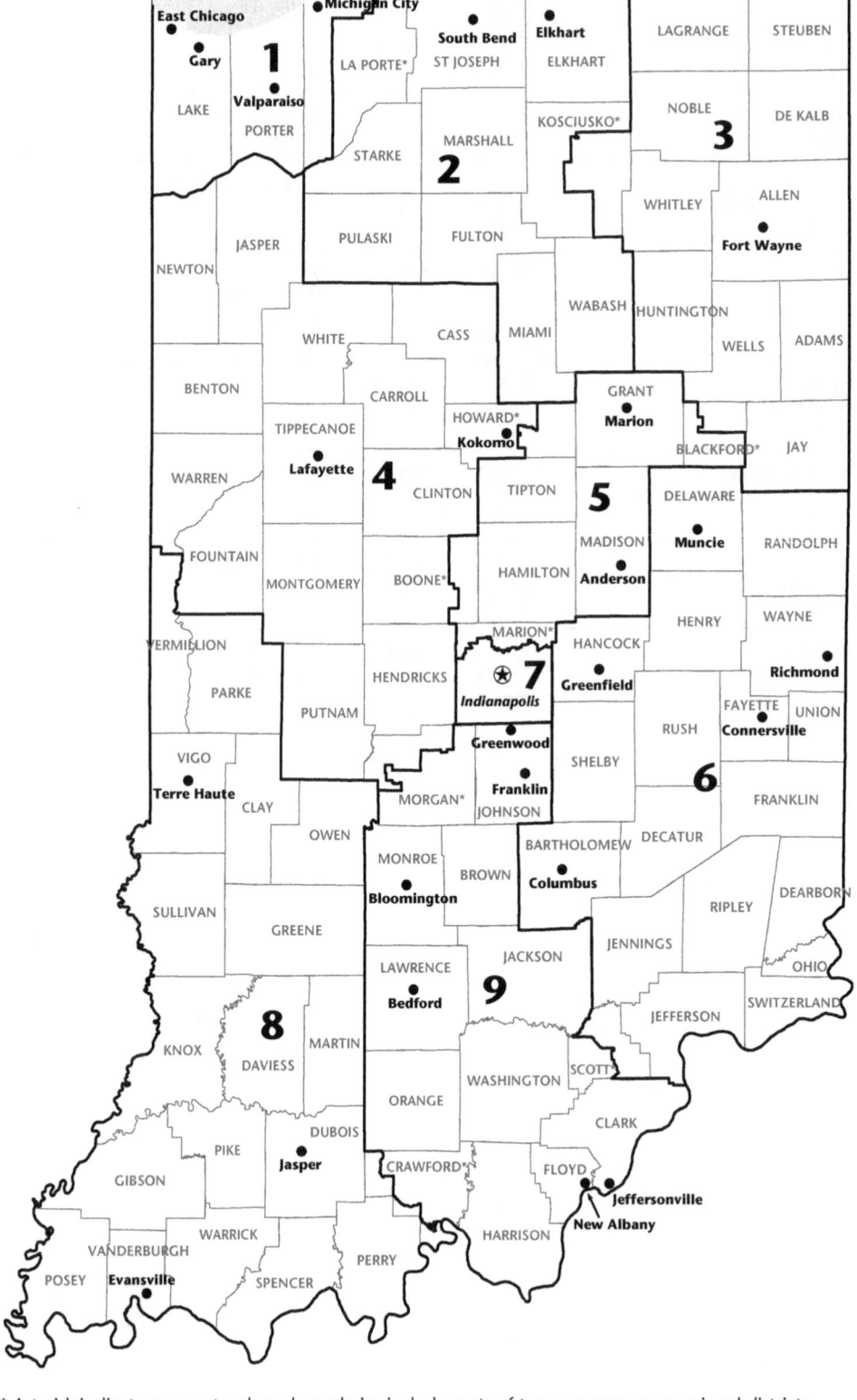

* Asterisk indicates a county whose boundaries include parts of two or more congressional districts.

INDIANA

GOVERNOR

Eric Holcomb (R). Elected 2016 to a four-year term.

SENATORS (1 Republican, 1 Democrat)

Joe Donnelly (D). Elected 2012 to a six-year term.

Todd C. Young (R). Elected 2016 to a six-year term.

REPRESENTATIVES (7 Republicans, 2 Democrats)

1. Peter J. Visclosky (D)
2. Jackie Walorski (R)
3. James "Jim" Banks (R)
4. Todd Rokita (R)
5. Susan Brooks (R)
6. Luke Messer (R)
7. Andre Carson (D)
8. Larry D. Bucshon (R)
9. Trey Hollingsworth (R)

POSTWAR VOTE FOR PRESIDENT

| | | Republican | | Democratic | | Other Vote | Rep.-Dem. Plurality | Percentage | | | |
| | | | | | | | | Total Vote | | Major Vote | |
Year	Total Vote	Vote	Candidate	Vote	Candidate			Rep.	Dem.	Rep.	Dem.
2016**	2,734,958	1,557,286	Trump, Donald J.	1,033,126	Clinton, Hillary Rodham	144,546	524,160 R	56.9%	37.8%	60.1%	39.9%
2012	2,624,534	1,420,543	Romney, W. Mitt	1,152,887	Obama, Barack H.*	51,104	267,656 R	54.1%	43.9%	55.2%	44.8%
2008	2,751,054	1,345,648	McCain, John S. III	1,374,039	Obama, Barack H.	31,367	28,391 D	48.9%	49.9%	49.5%	50.5%
2004	2,468,002	1,479,438	Bush, George W.*	969,011	Kerry, John F.	19,553	510,427 R	59.9%	39.3%	60.4%	39.6%
2000**	2,199,305	1,245,836	Bush, George W.	901,980	Gore, Albert Jr.	51,489	343,856 R	56.6%	41.0%	58.0%	42.0%
1996**	2,135,842	1,006,693	Dole, Robert "Bob"	887,424	Clinton, Bill*	241,725	119,269 R	47.1%	41.5%	53.1%	46.9%
1992**	2,305,871	989,375	Bush, George H.*	848,420	Clinton, Bill	468,076	140,955 R	42.9%	36.8%	53.8%	46.2%
1988	2,168,621	1,297,763	Bush, George H.	860,643	Dukakis, Michael S.	10,215	437,120 R	59.8%	39.7%	60.1%	39.9%
1984	2,233,069	1,377,230	Reagan, Ronald*	841,481	Mondale, Walter F.	14,358	535,749 R	61.7%	37.7%	62.1%	37.9%
1980**	2,242,033	1,255,656	Reagan, Ronald	844,197	Carter, Jimmy*	142,180	411,459 R	56.0%	37.7%	59.8%	40.2%
1976	2,220,362	1,183,958	Ford, Gerald R.*	1,014,714	Carter, Jimmy	21,690	169,244 R	53.3%	45.7%	53.8%	46.2%
1972	2,125,529	1,405,154	Nixon, Richard M.*	708,568	McGovern, George S.	11,807	696,586 R	66.1%	33.3%	66.5%	33.5%
1968**	2,123,597	1,067,885	Nixon, Richard M.	806,659	Humphrey, Hubert Horatio Jr.	249,053	261,226 R	50.3%	38.0%	57.0%	43.0%
1964	2,091,606	911,118	Goldwater, Barry M. Sr.	1,170,848	Johnson, Lyndon B.*	9,640	259,730 D	43.6%	56.0%	43.8%	56.2%
1960	2,135,360	1,175,120	Nixon, Richard M.	952,358	Kennedy, John F.	7,882	222,762 R	55.0%	44.6%	55.2%	44.8%
1956	1,974,607	1,182,811	Eisenhower, Dwight D.*	783,908	Stevenson, Adlai E. II	7,888	398,903 R	59.9%	39.7%	60.1%	39.9%
1952	1,955,049	1,136,259	Eisenhower, Dwight D.	801,530	Stevenson, Adlai E. II	17,260	334,729 R	58.1%	41.0%	58.6%	41.4%
1948	1,656,212	821,079	Dewey, Thomas E.	807,831	Truman, Harry S.*	27,302	13,248 R	49.6%	48.8%	50.4%	49.6%

Note: An asterisk (*) denotes incumbent. **In past elections, the other vote included: 2016 - 133,993 Libertarian (Gary Johnson); 2000 - 18,531 Green (Ralph Nader); 1996 - 224,299 Reform (Ross Perot); 1992 - 455,934 Independent (Perot); 1980 - 111,639 Independent (John Anderson); 1968 - 243,108 American Independent (George Wallace).

INDIANA

POSTWAR VOTE FOR GOVERNOR

		Republican		Democratic		Other	Rep.-Dem.	Percentage			
								Total Vote		Major Vote	
Year	Total Vote	Vote	Candidate	Vote	Candidate	Vote	Plurality	Rep.	Dem.	Rep.	Dem.
2016	2,719,968	1,397,396	Holcomb, Eric	1,235,503	Gregg, John R.	87,069	161,893 R	51.4%	45.4%	53.1%	46.9%
2012	2,577,329	1,275,424	Pence, Mike	1,200,016	Gregg, John R.	101,889	75,408 R	49.5%	46.6%	51.5%	48.5%
2008	2,703,752	1,563,885	Daniels, Mitch*	1,082,463	Thompson, Jill Long	57,404	481,422 R	57.8%	40.0%	59.1%	40.9%
2004	2,448,498	1,302,912	Daniels, Mitch	1,113,900	Kernan, Joseph E.	31,686	189,012 R	53.2%	45.5%	53.9%	46.1%
2000	2,179,413	908,285	McIntosh, David M.	1,232,525	O'Bannon, Frank*	38,603	324,240 D	41.7%	56.6%	42.4%	57.6%
1996	2,110,047	986,982	Goldsmith, Stephen	1,087,128	O'Bannon, Frank	35,937	100,146 D	46.8%	51.5%	47.6%	52.4%
1992	2,229,116	822,533	Pearson, Linley E.	1,382,151	Bayh, Evan*	24,432	559,618 D	36.9%	62.0%	37.3%	62.7%
1988	2,140,781	1,002,207	Mutz, John M.	1,138,574	Bayh, Evan		136,367 D	46.8%	53.2%	46.8%	53.2%
1984	2,197,988	1,146,497	Orr, Robert D.*	1,036,922	Townsend, W. Wayne	14,569	109,575 R	52.2%	47.2%	52.5%	47.5%
1980	2,178,403	1,257,383	Orr, Robert D.	913,116	Hillenbrand, John A.	7,904	344,267 R	57.7%	41.9%	57.9%	42.1%
1976	2,175,324	1,236,555	Bowen, Otis R.*	927,243	Conrad, Larry A.	11,526	309,312 R	56.8%	42.6%	57.1%	42.9%
1972	2,120,847	1,203,903	Bowen, Otis R.	900,489	Welsh, Matthew E.	16,455	303,414 R	56.8%	42.5%	57.2%	42.8%
1968	2,049,063	1,080,262	Whitcomb, Edgar D.	965,816	Rock, Robert L.	2,985	114,446 R	52.7%	47.1%	52.8%	47.2%
1964	2,073,058	901,342	Ristine, Richard O.	1,164,763	Branigin, Roger D.	6,953	263,421 D	43.5%	56.2%	43.6%	56.4%
1960	2,128,965	1,049,540	Parker, Crawford F.	1,072,717	Welsh, Matthew E.	6,708	23,177 D	49.3%	50.4%	49.5%	50.5%
1956	1,954,290	1,086,868	Handley, Harold W.	859,393	Tucker, Ralph	8,029	227,475 R	55.6%	44.0%	55.8%	44.2%
1952	1,931,869	1,075,685	Craig, George N.	841,984	Watkins, John A.	14,200	233,701 R	55.7%	43.6%	56.1%	43.9%
1948	1,652,321	745,892	Creighton, Hobart	884,995	Schricker, Henry F.	21,434	139,103 D	45.1%	53.6%	45.7%	54.3%

Note: An asterisk (*) denotes incumbent.

POSTWAR VOTE FOR SENATOR

		Republican		Democratic		Other	Rep.-Dem.	Percentage			
								Total Vote		Major Vote	
Year	Total Vote	Vote	Candidate	Vote	Candidate	Vote	Plurality	Rep.	Dem.	Rep.	Dem.
2016	2,732,546	1,423,991	Young, Todd C.	1,158,947	Bayh, Evan	149,608	265,044 R	52.1%	42.4%	55.1%	44.9%
2012	2,560,102	1,133,621	Mourdock, Richard E.	1,281,181	Donnelly, Joseph S.	145,300	147,560 D	44.3%	50.0%	46.9%	53.1%
2010	1,744,481	952,116	Coats, Daniel R.	697,775	Ellsworth, Brad	94,590	254,341 R	54.6%	40.0%	57.7%	42.3%
2006**	1,341,111	1,171,553	Lugar, Richard G.*			169,558	1,171,553 R	87.4%		100.0%	
2004	2,428,233	903,913	Scott, Marvin B.	1,496,976	Bayh, Evan*	27,344	593,063 D	37.2%	61.6%	37.6%	62.4%
2000	2,145,209	1,427,944	Lugar, Richard G.*	683,273	Johnson, David L.	33,992	744,671 R	66.6%	31.9%	67.6%	32.4%
1998	1,588,617	552,732	Helmke, Paul	1,012,244	Bayh, Evan	23,641	459,512 D	34.8%	63.7%	35.3%	64.7%
1994	1,543,568	1,039,625	Lugar, Richard G.*	470,799	Jontz, Jim	33,144	568,826 R	67.4%	30.5%	68.8%	31.2%
1992	2,211,426	1,267,972	Coats, Daniel R.*	900,148	Hogsett, Joseph H.	43,306	367,824 R	57.3%	40.7%	58.5%	41.5%
1990S**	1,504,302	806,048	Coats, Daniel R.	696,639	Hill, Baron P.	1,615	109,409 R	53.6%	46.3%	53.6%	46.4%
1988	2,099,303	1,430,525	Lugar, Richard G.*	668,778	Wickes, Jack		761,747 R	68.1%	31.9%	68.1%	31.9%
1986	1,545,563	936,143	Quayle, John Danforth*	595,192	Long, Jill Lynette	14,228	340,951 R	60.6%	38.5%	61.1%	38.9%
1982	1,817,287	978,301	Lugar, Richard G.*	828,400	Fithian, Floyd	10,586	149,901 R	53.8%	45.6%	54.1%	45.9%
1980	2,198,376	1,182,414	Quayle, John Danforth	1,015,962	Bayh, Birch Evan*		166,452 R	53.8%	46.2%	53.8%	46.2%
1976	2,171,187	1,275,833	Lugar, Richard G.	878,522	Hartke, R. Vance*	16,832	397,311 R	58.8%	40.5%	59.2%	40.8%
1974	1,752,978	814,117	Lugar, Richard G.	889,269	Bayh, Birch Evan*	49,592	75,152 D	46.4%	50.7%	47.8%	52.2%
1970	1,737,697	866,707	Roudebush, Richard	870,990	Hartke, R. Vance*		4,283 D	49.9%	50.1%	49.9%	50.1%
1968	2,053,118	988,571	Ruckelshaus, William	1,060,456	Bayh, Birch Evan*	4,091	71,885 D	48.1%	51.7%	48.2%	51.8%
1964	2,076,963	941,519	Bontrager, D. Russell	1,128,505	Hartke, R. Vance*	6,939	186,986 D	45.3%	54.3%	45.5%	54.5%
1962	1,800,038	894,547	Capehart, Homer E.*	905,491	Bayh, Birch Evan		10,944 D	49.7%	50.3%	49.7%	50.3%
1958	1,724,598	731,635	Handley, Harold W.	973,636	Hartke, R. Vance	19,327	242,001 D	42.4%	56.5%	42.9%	57.1%
1956	1,963,986	1,084,262	Capehart, Homer E.*	871,781	Wickard, Claude R.	7,943	212,481 R	55.2%	44.4%	55.4%	44.6%
1952	1,946,118	1,020,605	Jenner, William E.*	911,169	Schricker, Henry F.	14,344	109,436 R	52.4%	46.8%	52.8%	47.2%
1950	1,598,724	844,303	Capehart, Homer E.*	741,025	Campbell, Alex M.	13,396	103,278 R	52.8%	46.4%	53.3%	46.7%
1946	1,347,434	739,809	Jenner, William E.	584,288	Townsend, M. Clifford	23,337	155,521 R	54.9%	43.4%	55.9%	44.1%

Note: An asterisk (*) denotes incumbent. **In past elections, the other vote included: 2006 - 168,820 Libertarian (Steve Osborn, who finished second). The 1990 election was for a short term to fill a vacancy. The Democratic Party did not run a candidate in the 2006 Senate election.

INDIANA

PRESIDENT 2016

2010 Census Population	County	Total Vote	Republican (Trump)	Democratic (Clinton)	Other	Rep.-Dem. Plurality		Percentage			
								Total Vote		Major Vote	
								Rep.	Dem.	Rep.	Dem.
34,387	ADAMS	13,090	9,648	2,805	637	6,843	R	73.7%	21.4%	77.5%	22.5%
355,329	ALLEN	147,137	83,930	55,382	7,825	28,548	R	57.0%	37.6%	60.2%	39.8%
76,794	BARTHOLOMEW	32,490	20,640	9,841	2,009	10,799	R	63.5%	30.3%	67.7%	32.3%
8,854	BENTON	3,666	2,579	860	227	1,719	R	70.3%	23.5%	75.0%	25.0%
12,766	BLACKFORD	4,839	3,350	1,243	246	2,107	R	69.2%	25.7%	72.9%	27.1%
56,640	BOONE	32,178	19,654	10,181	2,343	9,473	R	61.1%	31.6%	65.9%	34.1%
15,242	BROWN	7,945	5,016	2,518	411	2,498	R	63.1%	31.7%	66.6%	33.4%
20,155	CARROLL	8,643	6,273	1,892	478	4,381	R	72.6%	21.9%	76.8%	23.2%
38,966	CASS	14,209	9,701	3,759	749	5,942	R	68.3%	26.5%	72.1%	27.9%
110,232	CLARK	51,147	30,035	18,808	2,304	11,227	R	58.7%	36.8%	61.5%	38.5%
26,890	CLAY	11,282	8,531	2,306	445	6,225	R	75.6%	20.4%	78.7%	21.3%
33,224	CLINTON	11,936	8,531	2,819	586	5,712	R	71.5%	23.6%	75.2%	24.8%
10,713	CRAWFORD	4,593	3,015	1,323	255	1,692	R	65.6%	28.8%	69.5%	30.5%
31,648	DAVIESS	10,768	8,545	1,800	423	6,745	R	79.4%	16.7%	82.6%	17.4%
50,047	DEARBORN	23,987	18,113	4,883	991	13,230	R	75.5%	20.4%	78.8%	21.2%
25,740	DECATUR	11,127	8,490	2,121	516	6,369	R	76.3%	19.1%	80.0%	20.0%
42,223	DEKALB	16,902	12,054	3,942	906	8,112	R	71.3%	23.3%	75.4%	24.6%
117,671	DELAWARE	45,123	24,263	18,153	2,707	6,110	R	53.8%	40.2%	57.2%	42.8%
41,889	DUBOIS	19,984	13,365	5,389	1,230	7,976	R	66.9%	27.0%	71.3%	28.7%
197,559	ELKHART	65,630	41,867	20,740	3,023	21,127	R	63.8%	31.6%	66.9%	33.1%
24,277	FAYETTE	9,530	6,839	2,252	439	4,587	R	71.8%	23.6%	75.2%	24.8%
74,578	FLOYD	37,425	21,432	13,945	2,048	7,487	R	57.3%	37.3%	60.6%	39.4%
17,240	FOUNTAIN	7,492	5,662	1,476	354	4,186	R	75.6%	19.7%	79.3%	20.7%
23,087	FRANKLIN	11,013	8,669	1,969	375	6,700	R	78.7%	17.9%	81.5%	18.5%
20,836	FULTON	8,374	6,010	1,960	404	4,050	R	71.8%	23.4%	75.4%	24.6%
33,503	GIBSON	15,484	11,081	3,721	682	7,360	R	71.6%	24.0%	74.9%	25.1%
70,061	GRANT	25,312	17,008	7,010	1,294	9,998	R	67.2%	27.7%	70.8%	29.2%
33,165	GREENE	13,801	10,277	2,929	595	7,348	R	74.5%	21.2%	77.8%	22.2%
274,569	HAMILTON	154,256	87,404	57,263	9,589	30,141	R	56.7%	37.1%	60.4%	39.6%
70,002	HANCOCK	36,181	25,074	8,904	2,203	16,170	R	69.3%	24.6%	73.8%	26.2%
39,364	HARRISON	18,558	12,943	4,783	832	8,160	R	69.7%	25.8%	73.0%	27.0%
145,448	HENDRICKS	75,559	48,337	22,600	4,622	25,737	R	64.0%	29.9%	68.1%	31.9%
49,462	HENRY	20,155	13,895	5,124	1,136	8,771	R	68.9%	25.4%	73.1%	26.9%
82,752	HOWARD	36,844	23,675	11,215	1,954	12,460	R	64.3%	30.4%	67.9%	32.1%
37,124	HUNTINGTON	16,043	11,649	3,506	888	8,143	R	72.6%	21.9%	76.9%	23.1%
42,376	JACKSON	17,572	12,859	3,843	870	9,016	R	73.2%	21.9%	77.0%	23.0%
33,478	JASPER	13,378	9,382	3,329	667	6,053	R	70.1%	24.9%	73.8%	26.2%
21,253	JAY	7,986	5,697	1,889	400	3,808	R	71.3%	23.7%	75.1%	24.9%
32,428	JEFFERSON	13,544	8,546	4,326	672	4,220	R	63.1%	31.9%	66.4%	33.6%
28,525	JENNINGS	11,150	8,224	2,364	562	5,860	R	73.8%	21.2%	77.7%	22.3%
139,654	JOHNSON	66,500	45,456	17,318	3,726	28,138	R	68.4%	26.0%	72.4%	27.6%
38,440	KNOX	15,516	11,077	3,772	667	7,305	R	71.4%	24.3%	74.6%	25.4%
77,358	KOSCIUSKO	32,084	23,935	6,313	1,836	17,622	R	74.6%	19.7%	79.1%	20.9%
111,467	LA PORTE	45,203	22,687	19,798	2,718	2,889	R	50.2%	43.8%	53.4%	46.6%
37,128	LAGRANGE	9,566	7,025	2,080	461	4,945	R	73.4%	21.7%	77.2%	22.8%
496,005	LAKE	201,205	75,625	116,935	8,645	41,310	D	37.6%	58.1%	39.3%	60.7%
46,134	LAWRENCE	19,152	14,035	4,210	907	9,825	R	73.3%	22.0%	76.9%	23.1%
131,636	MADISON	53,909	32,376	18,595	2,938	13,781	R	60.1%	34.5%	63.5%	36.5%
903,393	MARION	362,372	130,360	212,899	19,113	82,539	D	36.0%	58.8%	38.0%	62.0%
47,051	MARSHALL	18,082	12,288	4,798	996	7,490	R	68.0%	26.5%	71.9%	28.1%
10,334	MARTIN	4,809	3,697	881	231	2,816	R	76.9%	18.3%	80.8%	19.2%
36,903	MIAMI	13,482	9,975	2,766	741	7,209	R	74.0%	20.5%	78.3%	21.7%
137,974	MONROE	58,454	20,592	34,216	3,646	13,624	D	35.2%	58.5%	37.6%	62.4%
38,124	MONTGOMERY	15,156	11,059	3,362	735	7,697	R	73.0%	22.2%	76.7%	23.3%
68,894	MORGAN	31,280	23,674	6,040	1,566	17,634	R	75.7%	19.3%	79.7%	20.3%
14,244	NEWTON	5,795	4,077	1,404	314	2,673	R	70.4%	24.2%	74.4%	25.6%
47,536	NOBLE	16,890	12,198	3,904	788	8,294	R	72.2%	23.1%	75.8%	24.2%
6,128	OHIO	2,921	2,118	686	117	1,432	R	72.5%	23.5%	75.5%	24.5%
19,840	ORANGE	8,192	5,803	2,048	341	3,755	R	70.8%	25.0%	73.9%	26.1%
21,575	OWEN	8,557	6,153	1,946	458	4,207	R	71.9%	22.7%	76.0%	24.0%

INDIANA

PRESIDENT 2016

2010 Census Population	County	Total Vote	Republican (Trump)	Democratic (Clinton)	Other	Rep.-Dem. Plurality		Percentage			
								Total Vote		Major Vote	
								Rep.	Dem.	Rep.	Dem.
17,339	PARKE	6,582	4,863	1,441	278	3,422	R	73.9%	21.9%	77.1%	22.9%
19,338	PERRY	8,055	4,556	3,062	437	1,494	R	56.6%	38.0%	59.8%	40.2%
12,845	PIKE	5,977	4,398	1,297	282	3,101	R	73.6%	21.7%	77.2%	22.8%
164,343	PORTER	77,190	38,832	33,676	4,682	5,156	R	50.3%	43.6%	53.6%	46.4%
25,910	POSEY	12,467	8,404	3,521	542	4,883	R	67.4%	28.2%	70.5%	29.5%
13,402	PULASKI	5,459	3,854	1,327	278	2,527	R	70.6%	24.3%	74.4%	25.6%
37,963	PUTNAM	14,715	10,637	3,356	722	7,281	R	72.3%	22.8%	76.0%	24.0%
26,171	RANDOLPH	10,458	7,517	2,446	495	5,071	R	71.9%	23.4%	75.4%	24.6%
28,818	RIPLEY	12,810	9,806	2,471	533	7,335	R	76.5%	19.3%	79.9%	20.1%
17,392	RUSH	7,214	5,292	1,525	397	3,767	R	73.4%	21.1%	77.6%	22.4%
24,181	SCOTT	9,101	6,074	2,642	385	3,432	R	66.7%	29.0%	69.7%	30.3%
44,436	SHELBY	17,994	12,718	4,247	1,029	8,471	R	70.7%	23.6%	75.0%	25.0%
20,952	SPENCER	9,979	6,572	2,861	546	3,711	R	65.9%	28.7%	69.7%	30.3%
266,931	ST. JOSEPH	110,060	52,021	52,252	5,787	231	D	47.3%	47.5%	49.9%	50.1%
23,363	STARKE	9,226	6,367	2,489	370	3,878	R	69.0%	27.0%	71.9%	28.1%
34,185	STEUBEN	14,566	10,133	3,744	689	6,389	R	69.6%	25.7%	73.0%	27.0%
21,475	SULLIVAN	8,559	6,138	2,113	308	4,025	R	71.7%	24.7%	74.4%	25.6%
10,613	SWITZERLAND	3,699	2,558	930	211	1,628	R	69.2%	25.1%	73.3%	26.7%
172,780	TIPPECANOE	62,515	30,768	27,282	4,465	3,486	R	49.2%	43.6%	53.0%	47.0%
15,936	TIPTON	7,510	5,589	1,587	334	4,002	R	74.4%	21.1%	77.9%	22.1%
7,516	UNION	3,291	2,445	715	131	1,730	R	74.3%	21.7%	77.4%	22.6%
179,703	VANDERBURGH	72,507	40,496	28,530	3,481	11,966	R	55.9%	39.3%	58.7%	41.3%
16,212	VERMILLION	6,939	4,513	2,081	345	2,432	R	65.0%	30.0%	68.4%	31.6%
107,848	VIGO	39,818	21,937	15,931	1,950	6,006	R	55.1%	40.0%	57.9%	42.1%
32,888	WABASH	13,468	9,821	3,018	629	6,803	R	72.9%	22.4%	76.5%	23.5%
8,508	WARREN	3,930	2,898	839	193	2,059	R	73.7%	21.3%	77.5%	22.5%
59,689	WARRICK	29,589	19,113	9,086	1,390	10,027	R	64.6%	30.7%	67.8%	32.2%
28,262	WASHINGTON	11,382	8,209	2,636	537	5,573	R	72.1%	23.2%	75.7%	24.3%
68,917	WAYNE	25,579	16,028	8,322	1,229	7,706	R	62.7%	32.5%	65.8%	34.2%
27,636	WELLS	13,185	10,005	2,586	594	7,419	R	75.9%	19.6%	79.5%	20.5%
24,643	WHITE	10,053	6,893	2,590	570	4,303	R	68.6%	25.8%	72.7%	27.3%
33,292	WHITLEY	15,623	11,358	3,379	886	7,979	R	72.7%	21.6%	77.1%	22.9%
6,483,802	TOTAL	2,734,958	1,557,286	1,033,126	144,546	524,160	R	56.9%	37.8%	60.1%	39.9%

INDIANA

GOVERNOR 2016

2010 Census Population	County	Total Vote	Republican (Holcomb)	Democratic (Gregg)	Other	Rep.-Dem. Plurality		Percentage			
								Total Vote		Major Vote	
								Rep.	Dem.	Rep.	Dem.
34,387	ADAMS	13,051	8,408	4,272	371	4,136	R	64.4%	32.7%	66.3%	33.7%
355,329	ALLEN	146,819	80,458	61,879	4,482	18,579	R	54.8%	42.1%	56.5%	43.5%
76,794	BARTHOLOMEW	32,054	19,063	11,869	1,122	7,194	R	59.5%	37.0%	61.6%	38.4%
8,854	BENTON	3,669	2,318	1,201	150	1,117	R	63.2%	32.7%	65.9%	34.1%
12,766	BLACKFORD	4,789	2,719	1,857	213	862	R	56.8%	38.8%	59.4%	40.6%
56,640	BOONE	32,146	19,269	11,868	1,009	7,401	R	59.9%	36.9%	61.9%	38.1%
15,242	BROWN	7,961	4,488	3,201	272	1,287	R	56.4%	40.2%	58.4%	41.6%
20,155	CARROLL	8,657	5,381	2,923	353	2,458	R	62.2%	33.8%	64.8%	35.2%
38,966	CASS	14,232	8,059	5,662	511	2,397	R	56.6%	39.8%	58.7%	41.3%
110,232	CLARK	50,330	28,440	20,293	1,597	8,147	R	56.5%	40.3%	58.4%	41.6%

INDIANA
GOVERNOR 2016

2010 Census Population	County	Total Vote	Republican (Holcomb)	Democratic (Gregg)	Other	Rep.-Dem. Plurality	Percentage Total Vote Rep.	Dem.	Major Vote Rep.	Dem.
26,890	CLAY	11,056	6,457	4,260	339	2,197 R	58.4%	38.5%	60.3%	39.7%
33,224	CLINTON	11,669	7,126	4,120	423	3,006 R	61.1%	35.3%	63.4%	36.6%
10,713	CRAWFORD	4,461	2,381	1,924	156	457 R	53.4%	43.1%	55.3%	44.7%
31,648	DAVIESS	10,726	6,460	4,049	217	2,411 R	60.2%	37.7%	61.5%	38.5%
50,047	DEARBORN	23,212	16,606	5,936	670	10,670 R	71.5%	25.6%	73.7%	26.3%
25,740	DECATUR	10,832	7,231	3,291	310	3,940 R	66.8%	30.4%	68.7%	31.3%
42,223	DEKALB	16,559	10,501	5,340	718	5,161 R	63.4%	32.2%	66.3%	33.7%
117,671	DELAWARE	44,625	20,777	22,195	1,653	1,418 D	46.6%	49.7%	48.4%	51.6%
41,889	DUBOIS	19,954	10,821	8,171	962	2,650 R	54.2%	40.9%	57.0%	43.0%
197,559	ELKHART	65,845	40,161	23,749	1,935	16,412 R	61.0%	36.1%	62.8%	37.2%
24,277	FAYETTE	9,295	5,485	3,369	441	2,116 R	59.0%	36.2%	61.9%	38.1%
74,578	FLOYD	37,001	20,783	15,176	1,042	5,607 R	56.2%	41.0%	57.8%	42.2%
17,240	FOUNTAIN	7,473	4,792	2,404	277	2,388 R	64.1%	32.2%	66.6%	33.4%
23,087	FRANKLIN	10,746	7,795	2,697	254	5,098 R	72.5%	25.1%	74.3%	25.7%
20,836	FULTON	8,410	5,142	2,977	291	2,165 R	61.1%	35.4%	63.3%	36.7%
33,503	GIBSON	15,516	9,203	5,969	344	3,234 R	59.3%	38.5%	60.7%	39.3%
70,061	GRANT	25,061	14,928	9,257	876	5,671 R	59.6%	36.9%	61.7%	38.3%
33,165	GREENE	13,754	6,834	6,610	310	224 R	49.7%	48.1%	50.8%	49.2%
274,569	HAMILTON	154,705	90,381	60,176	4,148	30,205 R	58.4%	38.9%	60.0%	40.0%
70,002	HANCOCK	36,302	22,681	12,350	1,271	10,331 R	62.5%	34.0%	64.7%	35.3%
39,364	HARRISON	18,411	11,690	6,303	418	5,387 R	63.5%	34.2%	65.0%	35.0%
145,448	HENDRICKS	74,615	45,207	27,180	2,228	18,027 R	60.6%	36.4%	62.5%	37.5%
49,462	HENRY	20,106	10,769	7,551	1,786	3,218 R	53.6%	37.6%	58.8%	41.2%
82,752	HOWARD	37,005	19,903	15,812	1,290	4,091 R	53.8%	42.7%	55.7%	44.3%
37,124	HUNTINGTON	15,712	10,092	4,941	679	5,151 R	64.2%	31.4%	67.1%	32.9%
42,376	JACKSON	17,399	11,320	5,613	466	5,707 R	65.1%	32.3%	66.9%	33.1%
33,478	JASPER	13,194	8,086	4,730	378	3,356 R	61.3%	35.8%	63.1%	36.9%
21,253	JAY	7,814	4,603	2,935	276	1,668 R	58.9%	37.6%	61.1%	38.9%
32,428	JEFFERSON	13,222	7,505	5,373	344	2,132 R	56.8%	40.6%	58.3%	41.7%
28,525	JENNINGS	11,039	7,089	3,609	341	3,480 R	64.2%	32.7%	66.3%	33.7%
139,654	JOHNSON	66,722	42,465	22,263	1,994	20,202 R	63.6%	33.4%	65.6%	34.4%
38,440	KNOX	15,400	6,511	8,597	292	2,086 D	42.3%	55.8%	43.1%	56.9%
77,358	KOSCIUSKO	32,017	22,296	8,454	1,267	13,842 R	69.6%	26.4%	72.5%	27.5%
111,467	LA PORTE	44,272	18,465	24,139	1,668	5,674 D	41.7%	54.5%	43.3%	56.7%
37,128	LAGRANGE	9,612	6,316	2,951	345	3,365 R	65.7%	30.7%	68.2%	31.8%
496,005	LAKE	197,128	64,997	127,491	4,640	62,494 D	33.0%	64.7%	33.8%	66.2%
46,134	LAWRENCE	18,661	11,683	6,402	576	5,281 R	62.6%	34.3%	64.6%	35.4%
131,636	MADISON	53,683	27,579	24,041	2,063	3,538 R	51.4%	44.8%	53.4%	46.6%
903,393	MARION	364,296	127,462	226,116	10,718	98,654 D	35.0%	62.1%	36.0%	64.0%
47,051	MARSHALL	17,830	10,481	6,772	577	3,709 R	58.8%	38.0%	60.7%	39.3%
10,334	MARTIN	4,772	2,829	1,823	120	1,006 R	59.3%	38.2%	60.8%	39.2%
36,903	MIAMI	13,239	8,094	4,596	549	3,498 R	61.1%	34.7%	63.8%	36.2%
137,974	MONROE	58,138	19,915	36,304	1,919	16,389 D	34.3%	62.4%	35.4%	64.6%
38,124	MONTGOMERY	15,164	9,412	5,201	551	4,211 R	62.1%	34.3%	64.4%	35.6%
68,894	MORGAN	30,914	20,430	9,356	1,128	11,074 R	66.1%	30.3%	68.6%	31.4%
14,244	NEWTON	5,755	3,484	2,066	205	1,418 R	60.5%	35.9%	62.8%	37.2%
47,536	NOBLE	16,624	10,475	5,512	637	4,963 R	63.0%	33.2%	65.5%	34.5%
6,128	OHIO	2,861	1,805	996	60	809 R	63.1%	34.8%	64.4%	35.6%
19,840	ORANGE	8,027	4,827	2,971	229	1,856 R	60.1%	37.0%	61.9%	38.1%
21,575	OWEN	8,492	5,085	3,073	334	2,012 R	59.9%	36.2%	62.3%	37.7%
17,339	PARKE	6,639	3,824	2,608	207	1,216 R	57.6%	39.3%	59.5%	40.5%
19,338	PERRY	7,935	3,520	4,222	193	702 D	44.4%	53.2%	45.5%	54.5%
12,845	PIKE	5,915	3,114	2,671	130	443 R	52.6%	45.2%	53.8%	46.2%
164,343	PORTER	76,868	32,913	41,563	2,392	8,650 D	42.8%	54.1%	44.2%	55.8%
25,910	POSEY	12,480	7,202	5,028	250	2,174 R	57.7%	40.3%	58.9%	41.1%
13,402	PULASKI	5,255	3,001	2,069	185	932 R	57.1%	39.4%	59.2%	40.8%
37,963	PUTNAM	14,633	9,094	5,049	490	4,045 R	62.1%	34.5%	64.3%	35.7%
26,171	RANDOLPH	10,197	6,094	3,621	482	2,473 R	59.8%	35.5%	62.7%	37.3%
28,818	RIPLEY	12,779	8,948	3,540	291	5,408 R	70.0%	27.7%	71.7%	28.3%
17,392	RUSH	7,139	4,393	2,440	306	1,953 R	61.5%	34.2%	64.3%	35.7%

INDIANA

GOVERNOR 2016

2010 Census Population	County	Total Vote	Republican (Holcomb)	Democratic (Gregg)	Other	Rep.-Dem. Plurality		Percentage			
								Total Vote		Major Vote	
								Rep.	Dem.	Rep.	Dem.
24,181	SCOTT	8,944	4,869	3,830	245	1,039	R	54.4%	42.8%	56.0%	44.0%
44,436	SHELBY	17,851	10,998	6,162	691	4,836	R	61.6%	34.5%	64.1%	35.9%
20,952	SPENCER	9,774	5,511	4,030	233	1,481	R	56.4%	41.2%	57.8%	42.2%
266,931	ST. JOSEPH	110,095	48,839	57,835	3,421	8,996	D	44.4%	52.5%	45.8%	54.2%
23,363	STARKE	8,965	4,694	3,903	368	791	R	52.4%	43.5%	54.6%	45.4%
34,185	STEUBEN	14,604	9,180	4,917	507	4,263	R	62.9%	33.7%	65.1%	34.9%
21,475	SULLIVAN	8,519	3,623	4,720	176	1,097	D	42.5%	55.4%	43.4%	56.6%
10,613	SWITZERLAND	3,595	2,116	1,379	100	737	R	58.9%	38.4%	60.5%	39.5%
172,780	TIPPECANOE	62,677	30,141	30,234	2,302	93	D	48.1%	48.2%	49.9%	50.1%
15,936	TIPTON	7,463	4,712	2,492	259	2,220	R	63.1%	33.4%	65.4%	34.6%
7,516	UNION	3,262	2,179	936	147	1,243	R	66.8%	28.7%	70.0%	30.0%
179,703	VANDERBURGH	72,461	38,188	32,370	1,903	5,818	R	52.7%	44.7%	54.1%	45.9%
16,212	VERMILLION	6,875	3,279	3,339	257	60	D	47.7%	48.6%	49.5%	50.5%
107,848	VIGO	39,709	16,772	21,841	1,096	5,069	D	42.2%	55.0%	43.4%	56.6%
32,888	WABASH	13,314	8,636	4,262	416	4,374	R	64.9%	32.0%	67.0%	33.0%
8,508	WARREN	3,924	2,538	1,260	126	1,278	R	64.7%	32.1%	66.8%	33.2%
59,689	WARRICK	29,479	17,418	11,434	627	5,984	R	59.1%	38.8%	60.4%	39.6%
28,262	WASHINGTON	11,227	7,293	3,593	341	3,700	R	65.0%	32.0%	67.0%	33.0%
68,917	WAYNE	25,694	13,472	9,518	2,704	3,954	R	52.4%	37.0%	58.6%	41.4%
27,636	WELLS	13,096	8,766	3,902	428	4,864	R	66.9%	29.8%	69.2%	30.8%
24,643	WHITE	10,045	6,074	3,586	385	2,488	R	60.5%	35.7%	62.9%	37.1%
33,292	WHITLEY	15,521	9,972	4,933	616	5,039	R	64.2%	31.8%	66.9%	33.1%
6,483,802	TOTAL	2,719,968	1,397,396	1,235,503	87,069	161,893	R	51.4%	45.4%	53.1%	46.9%

INDIANA

SENATOR 2016

2010 Census Population	County	Total Vote	Republican (Young)	Democratic (Bayh)	Other	Rep.-Dem. Plurality		Percentage			
								Total Vote		Major Vote	
								Rep.	Dem.	Rep.	Dem.
34,387	ADAMS	13,136	8,430	3,840	866	4,590	R	64.2%	29.2%	68.7%	31.3%
355,329	ALLEN	147,744	79,370	59,868	8,506	19,502	R	53.7%	40.5%	57.0%	43.0%
76,794	BARTHOLOMEW	32,244	19,050	11,355	1,839	7,695	R	59.1%	35.2%	62.7%	37.3%
8,854	BENTON	3,694	2,316	1,132	246	1,184	R	62.7%	30.6%	67.2%	32.8%
12,766	BLACKFORD	4,820	2,748	1,707	365	1,041	R	57.0%	35.4%	61.7%	38.3%
56,640	BOONE	32,264	19,966	10,583	1,715	9,383	R	61.9%	32.8%	65.4%	34.6%
15,242	BROWN	7,985	4,616	2,907	462	1,709	R	57.8%	36.4%	61.4%	38.6%
20,155	CARROLL	8,682	5,512	2,522	648	2,990	R	63.5%	29.0%	68.6%	31.4%
38,966	CASS	14,246	8,306	4,927	1,013	3,379	R	58.3%	34.6%	62.8%	37.2%
110,232	CLARK	51,093	27,684	21,414	1,995	6,270	R	54.2%	41.9%	56.4%	43.6%
26,890	CLAY	11,115	6,439	3,979	697	2,460	R	57.9%	35.8%	61.8%	38.2%
33,224	CLINTON	11,724	7,291	3,693	740	3,598	R	62.2%	31.5%	66.4%	33.6%
10,713	CRAWFORD	4,559	2,500	1,890	169	610	R	54.8%	41.5%	56.9%	43.1%
31,648	DAVIESS	10,677	7,096	3,131	450	3,965	R	66.5%	29.3%	69.4%	30.6%
50,047	DEARBORN	23,492	17,288	5,251	953	12,037	R	73.6%	22.4%	76.7%	23.3%
25,740	DECATUR	10,926	7,301	3,022	603	4,279	R	66.8%	27.7%	70.7%	29.3%
42,223	DEKALB	16,671	10,229	5,029	1,413	5,200	R	61.4%	30.2%	67.0%	33.0%
117,671	DELAWARE	44,883	21,557	20,578	2,748	979	R	48.0%	45.8%	51.2%	48.8%
41,889	DUBOIS	19,683	11,029	7,692	962	3,337	R	56.0%	39.1%	58.9%	41.1%
197,559	ELKHART	66,106	39,291	23,416	3,399	15,875	R	59.4%	35.4%	62.7%	37.3%

INDIANA

SENATOR 2016

2010 Census Population	County	Total Vote	Republican (Young)	Democratic (Bayh)	Other	Rep.-Dem. Plurality	Percentage Total Vote Rep.	Total Vote Dem.	Major Vote Rep.	Major Vote Dem.
24,277	FAYETTE	9,381	5,602	3,170	609	2,432 R	59.7%	33.8%	63.9%	36.1%
74,578	FLOYD	37,588	20,735	15,504	1,349	5,231 R	55.2%	41.2%	57.2%	42.8%
17,240	FOUNTAIN	7,502	4,982	2,071	449	2,911 R	66.4%	27.6%	70.6%	29.4%
23,087	FRANKLIN	10,910	7,926	2,625	359	5,301 R	72.6%	24.1%	75.1%	24.9%
20,836	FULTON	8,421	5,076	2,793	552	2,283 R	60.3%	33.2%	64.5%	35.5%
33,503	GIBSON	15,515	9,220	5,519	776	3,701 R	59.4%	35.6%	62.6%	37.4%
70,061	GRANT	25,266	15,280	8,345	1,641	6,935 R	60.5%	33.0%	64.7%	35.3%
33,165	GREENE	13,627	7,866	5,062	699	2,804 R	57.7%	37.1%	60.8%	39.2%
274,569	HAMILTON	155,282	92,773	55,708	6,801	37,065 R	59.7%	35.9%	62.5%	37.5%
70,002	HANCOCK	36,373	23,196	10,775	2,402	12,421 R	63.8%	29.6%	68.3%	31.7%
39,364	HARRISON	18,603	11,442	6,580	581	4,862 R	61.5%	35.4%	63.5%	36.5%
145,448	HENDRICKS	75,038	46,722	24,427	3,889	22,295 R	62.3%	32.6%	65.7%	34.3%
49,462	HENRY	20,136	11,664	6,915	1,557	4,749 R	57.9%	34.3%	62.8%	37.2%
82,752	HOWARD	37,121	20,402	14,311	2,408	6,091 R	55.0%	38.6%	58.8%	41.2%
37,124	HUNTINGTON	15,766	9,941	4,545	1,280	5,396 R	63.1%	28.8%	68.6%	31.4%
42,376	JACKSON	17,616	11,269	5,626	721	5,643 R	64.0%	31.9%	66.7%	33.3%
33,478	JASPER	13,240	8,556	4,106	578	4,450 R	64.6%	31.0%	67.6%	32.4%
21,253	JAY	7,846	4,529	2,721	596	1,808 R	57.7%	34.7%	62.5%	37.5%
32,428	JEFFERSON	13,428	7,541	5,424	463	2,117 R	56.2%	40.4%	58.2%	41.8%
28,525	JENNINGS	11,166	6,949	3,702	515	3,247 R	62.2%	33.2%	65.2%	34.8%
139,654	JOHNSON	66,982	43,317	19,897	3,768	23,420 R	64.7%	29.7%	68.5%	31.5%
38,440	KNOX	15,129	7,816	6,503	810	1,313 R	51.7%	43.0%	54.6%	45.4%
77,358	KOSCIUSKO	32,194	22,188	8,025	1,981	14,163 R	68.9%	24.9%	73.4%	26.6%
111,467	LA PORTE	44,900	19,733	22,401	2,766	2,668 D	43.9%	49.9%	46.8%	53.2%
37,128	LAGRANGE	9,622	6,222	2,782	618	3,440 R	64.7%	28.9%	69.1%	30.9%
496,005	LAKE	197,232	67,657	122,036	7,539	54,379 D	34.3%	61.9%	35.7%	64.3%
46,134	LAWRENCE	18,827	12,327	5,493	1,007	6,834 R	65.5%	29.2%	69.2%	30.8%
131,636	MADISON	53,934	28,057	22,188	3,689	5,869 R	52.0%	41.1%	55.8%	44.2%
903,393	MARION	365,206	131,576	213,483	20,147	81,907 D	36.0%	58.5%	38.1%	61.9%
47,051	MARSHALL	17,941	10,659	6,223	1,059	4,436 R	59.4%	34.7%	63.1%	36.9%
10,334	MARTIN	4,790	2,934	1,595	261	1,339 R	61.3%	33.3%	64.8%	35.2%
36,903	MIAMI	13,296	8,453	3,836	1,007	4,617 R	63.6%	28.9%	68.8%	31.2%
137,974	MONROE	58,768	21,049	34,241	3,478	13,192 D	35.8%	58.3%	38.1%	61.9%
38,124	MONTGOMERY	15,177	9,808	4,393	976	5,415 R	64.6%	28.9%	69.1%	30.9%
68,894	MORGAN	31,037	21,193	7,821	2,023	13,372 R	68.3%	25.2%	73.0%	27.0%
14,244	NEWTON	5,771	3,670	1,788	313	1,882 R	63.6%	31.0%	67.2%	32.8%
47,536	NOBLE	16,722	10,509	4,996	1,217	5,513 R	62.8%	29.9%	67.8%	32.2%
6,128	OHIO	2,896	1,948	853	95	1,095 R	67.3%	29.5%	69.5%	30.5%
19,840	ORANGE	8,220	5,134	2,795	291	2,339 R	62.5%	34.0%	64.7%	35.3%
21,575	OWEN	8,532	5,333	2,642	557	2,691 R	62.5%	31.0%	66.9%	33.1%
17,339	PARKE	6,633	3,859	2,339	435	1,520 R	58.2%	35.3%	62.3%	37.7%
19,338	PERRY	7,990	3,612	3,990	388	378 D	45.2%	49.9%	47.5%	52.5%
12,845	PIKE	5,946	3,404	2,228	314	1,176 R	57.2%	37.5%	60.4%	39.6%
164,343	PORTER	76,723	35,629	36,828	4,266	1,199 D	46.4%	48.0%	49.2%	50.8%
25,910	POSEY	12,512	7,058	4,857	597	2,201 R	56.4%	38.8%	59.2%	40.8%
13,402	PULASKI	5,340	3,109	1,859	372	1,250 R	58.2%	34.8%	62.6%	37.4%
37,963	PUTNAM	14,690	9,510	4,319	861	5,191 R	64.7%	29.4%	68.8%	31.2%
26,171	RANDOLPH	10,255	6,411	3,230	614	3,181 R	62.5%	31.5%	66.5%	33.5%
28,818	RIPLEY	12,873	9,227	3,182	464	6,045 R	71.7%	24.7%	74.4%	25.6%
17,392	RUSH	7,151	4,472	2,238	441	2,234 R	62.5%	31.3%	66.6%	33.4%
24,181	SCOTT	9,097	5,046	3,763	288	1,283 R	55.5%	41.4%	57.3%	42.7%
44,436	SHELBY	17,929	11,267	5,549	1,113	5,718 R	62.8%	30.9%	67.0%	33.0%
20,952	SPENCER	9,883	5,465	3,960	458	1,505 R	55.3%	40.1%	58.0%	42.0%
266,931	ST. JOSEPH	110,884	47,353	56,749	6,782	9,396 D	42.7%	51.2%	45.5%	54.5%
23,363	STARKE	9,037	4,895	3,443	699	1,452 R	54.2%	38.1%	58.7%	41.3%
34,185	STEUBEN	14,641	9,078	4,546	1,017	4,532 R	62.0%	31.0%	66.6%	33.4%
21,475	SULLIVAN	8,449	4,164	3,856	429	308 R	49.3%	45.6%	51.9%	48.1%
10,613	SWITZERLAND	3,641	2,260	1,242	139	1,018 R	62.1%	34.1%	64.5%	35.5%
172,780	TIPPECANOE	63,016	30,081	28,921	4,014	1,160 R	47.7%	45.9%	51.0%	49.0%
15,936	TIPTON	7,519	4,760	2,260	499	2,500 R	63.3%	30.1%	67.8%	32.2%

INDIANA

SENATOR 2016

2010 Census Population	County	Total Vote	Republican (Young)	Democratic (Bayh)	Other	Rep.-Dem. Plurality	Total Vote Rep.	Total Vote Dem.	Major Vote Rep.	Major Vote Dem.
7,516	UNION	3,289	2,252	901	136	1,351 R	68.5%	27.4%	71.4%	28.6%
179,703	VANDERBURGH	72,699	36,835	32,077	3,787	4,758 R	50.7%	44.1%	53.5%	46.5%
16,212	VERMILLION	6,899	3,247	3,197	455	50 R	47.1%	46.3%	50.4%	49.6%
107,848	VIGO	39,838	16,581	21,028	2,229	4,447 D	41.6%	52.8%	44.1%	55.9%
32,888	WABASH	13,368	8,595	3,925	848	4,670 R	64.3%	29.4%	68.7%	31.3%
8,508	WARREN	3,959	2,589	1,159	211	1,430 R	65.4%	29.3%	69.1%	30.9%
59,689	WARRICK	29,656	17,255	11,092	1,309	6,163 R	58.2%	37.4%	60.9%	39.1%
28,262	WASHINGTON	11,375	7,197	3,773	405	3,424 R	63.3%	33.2%	65.6%	34.4%
68,917	WAYNE	25,690	14,703	9,309	1,678	5,394 R	57.2%	36.2%	61.2%	38.8%
27,636	WELLS	13,163	8,811	3,516	836	5,295 R	66.9%	26.7%	71.5%	28.5%
24,643	WHITE	10,083	6,128	3,255	700	2,873 R	60.8%	32.3%	65.3%	34.7%
33,292	WHITLEY	15,573	9,865	4,500	1,208	5,365 R	63.3%	28.9%	68.7%	31.3%
6,483,802	TOTAL	2,732,546	1,423,991	1,158,947	149,608	265,044 R	52.1%	42.4%	55.1%	44.9%

INDIANA

HOUSE OF REPRESENTATIVES

CD	Year	Total Vote	Republican Vote	Republican Candidate	Democratic Vote	Democratic Candidate	Other Vote	Rep.-Dem. Plurality	Total Vote Rep.	Total Vote Dem.	Major Vote Rep.	Major Vote Dem.
1	2016	254,583			207,515	VISCLOSKY, PETER J.*	47,068	207,515 D		81.5%		100.0%
1	2014	142,293	51,000	LEYVA, MARK J.	86,579	VISCLOSKY, PETER J.*	4,714	35,579 D	35.8%	60.8%	37.1%	62.9%
1	2012	279,034	91,291	PHELPS, JOEL	187,743	VISCLOSKY, PETER J.*		96,452 D	32.7%	67.3%	32.7%	67.3%
2	2016	277,357	164,355	WALORSKI, JACKIE*	102,401	COLEMAN, LYNN C.	10,601	61,954 R	59.3%	36.9%	61.6%	38.4%
2	2014	145,200	85,583	WALORSKI, JACKIE*	55,590	BOCK, JOE	4,027	29,993 R	58.9%	38.3%	60.6%	39.4%
2	2012	273,475	134,033	WALORSKI, JACKIE	130,113	MULLEN, BRENDAN	9,329	3,920 R	49.0%	47.6%	50.7%	49.3%
3	2016	287,247	201,396	BANKS, JAMES "JIM"	66,023	SCHRADER, THOMAS ALLEN	19,828	135,373 R	70.1%	23.0%	75.3%	24.7%
3	2014	148,793	102,889	STUTZMAN, MARLIN A.*	39,771	KUHNLE, JUSTIN	6,133	63,118 R	69.1%	26.7%	72.1%	27.9%
3	2012	280,235	187,872	STUTZMAN, MARLIN A.*	92,363	BOYD, KEVIN		95,509 R	67.0%	33.0%	67.0%	33.0%
4	2016	299,434	193,412	ROKITA, TODD*	91,256	DALE, JOHN	14,766	102,156 R	64.6%	30.5%	67.9%	32.1%
4	2014	142,054	94,998	ROKITA, TODD*	47,056	DALE, JOHN		47,942 R	66.9%	33.1%	66.9%	33.1%
4	2012	272,268	168,688	ROKITA, TODD*	93,015	NELSON, TARA E.	10,565	75,673 R	62.0%	34.2%	64.5%	35.5%
5	2016	361,135	221,957	BROOKS, SUSAN*	123,849	DEMAREE, ANGELA	15,329	98,108 R	61.5%	34.3%	64.2%	35.8%
5	2014	161,440	105,277	BROOKS, SUSAN*	49,756	DENNEY, SHAWN A.	6,407	55,521 R	65.2%	30.8%	67.9%	32.1%
5	2012	333,359	194,570	BROOKS, SUSAN	125,347	RESKE, SCOTT	13,442	69,223 R	58.4%	37.6%	60.8%	39.2%
6	2016	296,385	204,920	MESSER, LUKE*	79,135	WELSH, BARRY A.	12,330	125,785 R	69.1%	26.7%	72.1%	27.9%
6	2014	155,071	102,187	MESSER, LUKE*	45,509	HEITZMAN, SUSAN HALL	7,375	56,678 R	65.9%	29.3%	69.2%	30.8%
6	2012	275,253	162,613	MESSER, LUKE	96,678	BOOKOUT, BRAD	15,962	65,935 R	59.1%	35.1%	62.7%	37.3%
7	2016	264,670	94,456	PING, CATHERINE "CAT"	158,739	CARSON, ANDRE D.*	11,475	64,283 D	35.7%	60.0%	37.3%	62.7%
7	2014	112,261	46,887	PING, CATHERINE "CAT"	61,443	CARSON, ANDRE D.*	3,931	14,556 D	41.8%	54.7%	43.3%	56.7%
7	2012	257,950	95,828	MAY, CARLOS	162,122	CARSON, ANDRE D.*		66,294 D	37.1%	62.9%	37.1%	62.9%
8	2016	294,713	187,702	BUCSHON, LARRY D.*	93,356	DRAKE, RON	13,655	94,346 R	63.7%	31.7%	66.8%	33.2%
8	2014	171,315	103,344	BUCSHON, LARRY D.	61,384	SPANGLER, TOM	6,587	41,960 R	60.3%	35.8%	62.7%	37.3%
8	2012	283,992	151,533	BUCSHON, LARRY D.*	122,325	CROOKS, DAVE	10,134	29,208 R	53.4%	43.1%	55.3%	44.7%
9	2016	322,843	174,791	HOLLINGSWORTH, TREY	130,627	YODER, SHELLI	17,425	44,164 R	54.1%	40.5%	57.2%	42.8%
9	2014	162,387	101,594	YOUNG, TODD C.*	55,016	BAILEY, BILL	5,777	46,578 R	62.6%	33.9%	64.9%	35.1%
9	2012	298,180	165,332	YOUNG, TODD C.*	132,848	YODER, SHELLI		32,484 R	55.4%	44.6%	55.4%	44.6%
TOTAL	2016	2,658,367	1,442,989		1,052,901		162,477	390,088 R	54.3%	39.6%	57.8%	42.2%
TOTAL	2014	1,340,814	793,759		502,104		44,951	291,655 R	59.2%	37.4%	61.3%	38.7%
TOTAL	2012	2,553,746	1,351,760		1,142,554		59,432	209,206 R	52.9%	44.7%	54.2%	45.8%

Note: An asterisk (*) denotes incumbent.

INDIANA

GENERAL AND PRIMARY ELECTIONS

2016 GENERAL ELECTIONS: OTHER VOTES

President   Other vote was 133,993 Libertarian (Gary Johnson), 7,841 Write-in (Jill Stein), 1,937 Write-in (Darrell Castle), 775 Write-in (Scattered Write-in)

Governor   Other vote was 87,025 Libertarian (Rex Bell), 41 Write-in (Jack Adkins), 3 Write-in (Christopher Stried)

Senate   Other vote was 149,481 Libertarian (Lucy Brenton), 127 Write-in (James Johnson)

House   Other vote was:

CD 1	47,051 Libertarian (Donna Dunn), 17 Write-in (John Meyer)
CD 2	10,601 Libertarian (Ron Cenkush)
CD 3	19,828 Libertarian (Pepper Snyder)
CD 4	14,766 Libertarian (Steven Mayoras)
CD 5	15,329 Libertarian (Matther Wittlief)
CD 6	12,330 Libertarian (Rich Turvey)
CD 7	11,475 Libertarian (Drew Thompson)
CD 8	13,655 Libertarian (Andrew Horning)
CD 9	17,425 Libertarian (Russell Brooksbank)

2016 PRIMARY ELECTIONS: SUPPLEMENTARY INFORMATION

Primary   May 3, 2016   **Registration**   4,715,292   No Party Registration
(as of May 3, 2016)

Primary Type   Open—Any registered voter could participate in the primary of either party, although he or she could be challenged based on party affiliation. When a voter is challenged, they must execute a statement saying that they voted for a majority of the party's candidates in the previous general election. If they did not vote in the previous general election, they must indicate that they will vote for a majority of the party's candidates in the next general election.

	REPUBLICAN PRIMARIES			DEMOCRATIC PRIMARIES		
President	Trump, Donald J.	591,514	53.3%	Sanders, Bernard	335,074	52.5%
	Cruz, Ted	406,783	36.6%	Clinton, Hillary Rodham	303,705	47.5%
	Kasich, John R.	84,111	7.6%			
	Carson, Ben	8,914	0.8%			
	Bush, Jeb	6,508	0.6%			
	Rubio, Marco	5,175	0.5%			
	Paul, Rand	4,306	0.4%			
	Christie, Chris	1,738	0.2%			
	Fiorina, Carly	1,494	0.1%			
	TOTAL	*1,110,543*		*TOTAL*	*638,779*	
Senator	Young, Todd C.	661,136	67.1%	Hill, Baron P. (see note)	516,183	100.0%
	Stutzman, Marlin A.	324,429	32.9%			
	TOTAL	*985,565*		*TOTAL*	*516,183*	
Governor	Pence, Mike* (see note)	815,699	100.0%	Gregg, John R.	547,375	100.0%
	TOTAL	*815,699*		*TOTAL*	*547,375*	
Congressional District 1				Visclosky, Peter J.*	77,095	80.0%
				Brown, Willie "Faithful and True"	19,315	20.0%
				TOTAL	*96,410*	

INDIANA

GENERAL AND PRIMARY ELECTIONS

	REPUBLICAN PRIMARIES			DEMOCRATIC PRIMARIES		
Congressional District 2	Walorski, Jackie*	77,400	69.8%	Coleman, Lynn C.	39,372	73.8%
	Petermann, Jeff	33,523	30.2%	Carpenter, Douglas M.	14,013	26.2%
	TOTAL	110,923		TOTAL	53,385	
Congressional District 3	Banks, James "Jim"	46,533	34.3%	Schrader, Thomas Allen	15,267	37.5%
	Tom, Kip	42,732	31.5%	Nightenhelser, Todd	12,956	31.8%
	Brown, Elizabeth "Liz"	33,654	24.8%	Roberson, John Forrest	12,487	30.7%
	Galloway, Pamela Gail "Pam"	9,543	7.0%			
	Howell, Kevin	1,970	1.5%			
	Baringer, Mark William	1,266	0.9%			
	TOTAL	135,698		TOTAL	40,710	
Congressional District 4	Rokita, Todd*	86,051	69.3%	Dale, John	43,401	100.0%
	Grant, Kevin Jay	38,200	30.7%			
	TOTAL	124,251		TOTAL	43,401	
Congressional District 5	Brooks, Susan*	95,209	69.5%	Demaree, Angela	52,530	74.9%
	MacKenzie, Stephen M.	21,575	15.7%	Davidson, Allen Ray	17,587	25.1%
	Campbell, Mike	20,202	14.7%			
	TOTAL	136,986		TOTAL	70,117	
Congressional District 6	Messer, Luke*	91,828	77.7%	Welsh, Barry A.	15,258	35.6%
	Smith, Jeff	14,963	12.7%	Basham, Danny	10,474	24.4%
	Johnson, Charles "Chuck" Jr.	11,447	9.7%	Holland, George Thomas	8,851	20.6%
				Peavler, Bruce W.	4,897	11.4%
				Spelbring, Ralph	3,385	7.9%
	TOTAL	118,238		TOTAL	42,865	
Congressional District 7	Ping, Catherine "Cat"	30,514	53.1%	Carson, Andre D.*	70,006	85.6%
	Harmon, Wayne E.	16,955	29.5%	Godfrey, Curtis	8,306	10.2%
	Miniear, JD	10,031	17.4%	Pullins, Pierre Quincy	3,435	4.2%
	TOTAL	57,500		TOTAL	81,747	
Congressional District 8	Bucshon, Larry D.*	72,889	65.0%	Drake, Ron	29,270	50.1%
	Moss, Richard	39,168	35.0%	Orentlicher, David	29,206	49.9%
	TOTAL	112,057		TOTAL	58,476	
Congressional District 9	Hollingsworth, Trey	40,767	33.5%	Yoder, Shelli	44,253	70.1%
	Houchin, Erin	30,396	25.0%	Kern, Bob	7,298	11.6%
	Zoeller, Greg	26,554	21.9%	McClure, James R. Jr.	6,574	10.4%
	Waltz, Brent	15,759	13.0%	Thomas, William Joseph "Bill"	4,990	7.9%
	Hall, Robert	8,036	6.6%			
	TOTAL	121,512		TOTAL	63,115	

Note: An asterisk (*) denotes incumbent. After the primary, Baron P. Hill withdrew from the Senate race in favor of Evan Bayh. Gubernatorial candidate Mike Pence was selected by Donald Trump as his vice presidential runningmate. Eric Holcomb replaced Pence as the Republican gubernatorial candidate.

IOWA

Congressional districts first established for elections held in 2012

4 members

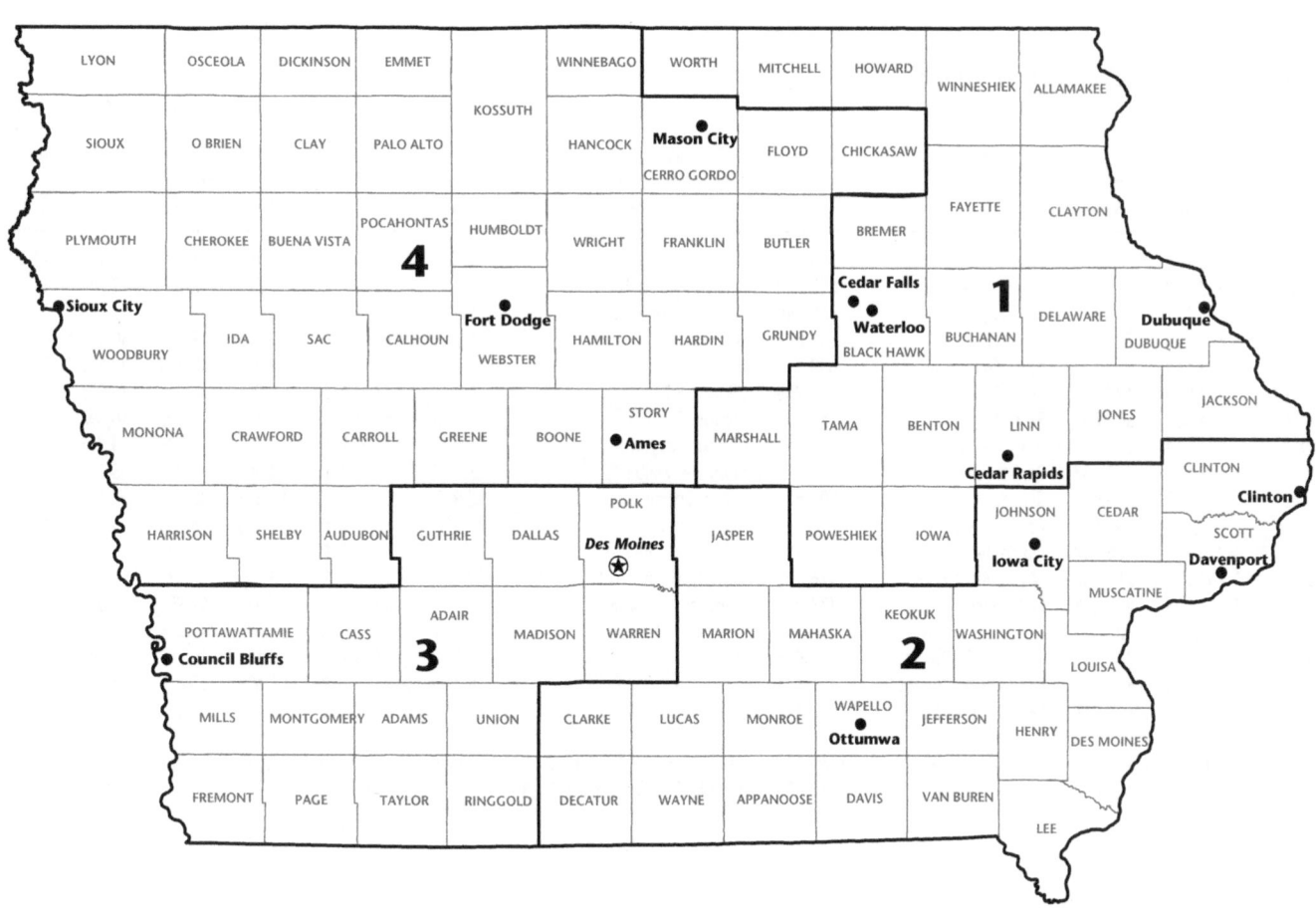

IOWA

GOVERNOR

Kim Reynolds (R). Appointed May 24, 2017, to serve the remainder of the term vacated by the resignation of Terry E. Branstad to become the U.S. ambassador to China.

SENATORS (2 Republicans)

Joni Ernst (R). Elected 2014 to a six-year term.

Chuck E. Grassley (R). Re-elected 2016 to a six-year term. Previously elected 2010, 2004, 1998, 1992, 1986, 1980.

REPRESENTATIVES (3 Republicans, 1 Democrat)

1. Rod Blum (R)
2. David Loebsack (D)
3. David Young (R)
4. Steve King (R)

POSTWAR VOTE FOR PRESIDENT

Year	Total Vote	Republican Vote	Republican Candidate	Democratic Vote	Democratic Candidate	Other Vote	Rep.-Dem. Plurality	Total Vote Rep.	Total Vote Dem.	Major Vote Rep.	Major Vote Dem.
2016**	1,566,031	800,983	Trump, Donald J.	653,669	Clinton, Hillary Rodham	111,379	147,314 R	51.1%	41.7%	55.1%	44.9%
2012	1,582,180	730,617	Romney, W. Mitt	822,544	Obama, Barack H.*	29,019	91,927 D	46.2%	52.0%	47.0%	53.0%
2008	1,537,123	682,379	McCain, John S. III	828,940	Obama, Barack H.	25,804	146,561 D	44.4%	53.9%	45.2%	54.8%
2004	1,506,908	751,957	Bush, George W.*	741,898	Kerry, John F.	13,053	10,059 R	49.9%	49.2%	50.3%	49.7%
2000**	1,315,563	634,373	Bush, George W.	638,517	Gore, Albert Jr.	42,673	4,144 D	48.2%	48.5%	49.8%	50.2%
1996**	1,234,075	492,644	Dole, Robert "Bob"	620,258	Clinton, Bill*	121,173	127,614 D	39.9%	50.3%	44.3%	55.7%
1992**	1,354,607	504,891	Bush, George H.*	586,353	Clinton, Bill	263,363	81,462 D	37.3%	43.3%	46.3%	53.7%
1988	1,225,614	545,355	Bush, George H.	670,557	Dukakis, Michael S.	9,702	125,202 D	44.5%	54.7%	44.9%	55.1%
1984	1,319,805	703,088	Reagan, Ronald*	605,620	Mondale, Walter F.	11,097	97,468 R	53.3%	45.9%	53.7%	46.3%
1980**	1,317,661	676,026	Reagan, Ronald	508,672	Carter, Jimmy*	132,963	167,354 R	51.3%	38.6%	57.1%	42.9%
1976	1,279,306	632,863	Ford, Gerald R.*	619,931	Carter, Jimmy	26,512	12,932 R	49.5%	48.5%	50.5%	49.5%
1972	1,225,944	706,207	Nixon, Richard M.*	496,206	McGovern, George S.	23,531	210,001 R	57.6%	40.5%	58.7%	41.3%
1968**	1,167,931	619,106	Nixon, Richard M.	476,699	Humphrey, Hubert Horatio Jr.	72,126	142,407 R	53.0%	40.8%	56.5%	43.5%
1964	1,184,539	449,148	Goldwater, Barry M. Sr.	733,030	Johnson, Lyndon B.*	2,361	283,882 D	37.9%	61.9%	38.0%	62.0%
1960	1,273,810	722,381	Nixon, Richard M.	550,565	Kennedy, John F.	864	171,816 R	56.7%	43.2%	56.7%	43.3%
1956	1,234,564	729,187	Eisenhower, Dwight D.*	501,858	Stevenson, Adlai E. II	3,519	227,329 R	59.1%	40.7%	59.2%	40.8%
1952	1,268,773	808,906	Eisenhower, Dwight D.	451,513	Stevenson, Adlai E. II	8,354	357,393 R	63.8%	35.6%	64.2%	35.8%
1948	1,038,264	494,018	Dewey, Thomas E.	522,380	Truman, Harry S.*	21,866	28,362 D	47.6%	50.3%	48.6%	51.4%

Note: An asterisk (*) denotes incumbent. **In past elections, the other vote included: 2016 - 59,186 Libertarian (Gary Johnson); 2000 - 29,374 Green (Ralph Nader); 1996 - 105,159 Reform (Ross Perot); 1992 - 253,468 Independent (Perot); 1980 - 115,633 Independent (John Anderson); 1968 - 66,422 American Independent (George Wallace).

IOWA

POSTWAR VOTE FOR GOVERNOR

Year	Total Vote	Republican Vote	Republican Candidate	Democratic Vote	Democratic Candidate	Other Vote	Rep.-Dem. Plurality	Total Vote Rep.	Total Vote Dem.	Major Vote Rep.	Major Vote Dem.
2014	1,129,057	666,032	Branstad, Terry E.*	420,787	Hatch, Jack	42,238	245,245 R	59.0%	37.3%	61.3%	38.7%
2010	1,122,013	592,494	Branstad, Terry E.	484,798	Culver, Chet*	44,721	107,696 R	52.8%	43.2%	55.0%	45.0%
2006	1,053,255	467,425	Nussle, Jim	569,021	Culver, Chet	16,809	101,596 D	44.4%	54.0%	45.1%	54.9%
2002	1,025,802	456,612	Gross, Doug	540,449	Vilsack, Tom*	28,741	83,837 D	44.5%	52.7%	45.8%	54.2%
1998	956,418	444,787	Lightfoot, Jim Ross	500,231	Vilsack, Tom	11,400	55,444 D	46.5%	52.3%	47.1%	52.9%
1994	997,248	566,395	Branstad, Terry E.*	414,453	Campbell, Bonnie J.	16,400	151,942 R	56.8%	41.6%	57.7%	42.3%
1990	976,483	591,852	Branstad, Terry E.*	379,372	Avenson, Donald D.	5,259	212,480 R	60.6%	38.9%	60.9%	39.1%
1986	910,623	472,712	Branstad, Terry E.*	436,987	Junkins, Lowell L.	924	35,725 R	51.9%	48.0%	52.0%	48.0%
1982	1,038,229	548,313	Branstad, Terry E.	483,291	Conlin, Roxanne	6,625	65,022 R	52.8%	46.5%	53.2%	46.8%
1978	843,190	491,713	Ray, Robert E.*	345,519	Fitzgerald, Jerome D.	5,958	146,194 R	58.3%	41.0%	58.7%	41.3%
1974**	920,458	534,518	Ray, Robert E.*	377,553	Schaben, James F.	8,387	156,965 R	58.1%	41.0%	58.6%	41.4%
1972	1,210,222	707,177	Ray, Robert E.*	487,282	Franzenburg, Paul	15,763	219,895 R	58.4%	40.3%	59.2%	40.8%
1970	791,241	403,394	Ray, Robert E.*	368,911	Fulton, Robert	18,936	34,483 R	51.0%	46.6%	52.2%	47.8%
1968	1,135,988	613,827	Ray, Robert E.	521,216	Franzenburg, Paul	945	92,611 R	54.0%	45.9%	54.1%	45.9%
1966	893,175	394,518	Murray, William G.	494,259	Hughes, Harold E.*	4,398	99,741 D	44.2%	55.3%	44.4%	55.6%
1964	1,167,734	365,131	Hultman, Evan	794,610	Hughes, Harold E.*	7,993	429,479 D	31.3%	68.0%	31.5%	68.5%
1962	819,854	388,955	Erbe, Norman A.*	430,899	Hughes, Harold E.		41,944 D	47.4%	52.6%	47.4%	52.6%
1960	1,237,089	645,026	Erbe, Norman A.	592,063	McManus, E. J.		52,963 R	52.1%	47.9%	52.1%	47.9%
1958	859,095	394,071	Murray, William G.	465,024	Loveless, Herschel C.*		70,953 D	45.9%	54.1%	45.9%	54.1%
1956	1,204,235	587,383	Hoegh, Leo A.*	616,852	Loveless, Herschel C.		29,469 D	48.8%	51.2%	48.8%	51.2%
1954	848,592	435,944	Hoegh, Leo A.	410,255	Herring, Clyde E.	2,393	25,689 R	51.4%	48.3%	51.5%	48.5%
1952	1,230,045	638,388	Beardsley, William*	587,671	Loveless, Herschel C.	3,986	50,717 R	51.9%	47.8%	52.1%	47.9%
1950	857,213	506,642	Beardsley, William*	347,176	Gillette, Lester S.	3,395	159,466 R	59.1%	40.5%	59.3%	40.7%
1948	994,833	553,900	Beardsley, William	434,432	Switzer, Carroll O.	6,501	119,468 R	55.7%	43.7%	56.0%	44.0%
1946	631,681	362,592	Blue, Robert D.	266,190	Miles, Frank	2,899	96,402 R	57.4%	42.1%	57.7%	42.3%

Note: An asterisk (*) denotes incumbent. **The term of office of Iowa's governor was increased from two to four years effective with the 1974 election.

POSTWAR VOTE FOR SENATOR

Year	Total Vote	Republican Vote	Republican Candidate	Democratic Vote	Democratic Candidate	Other Vote	Rep.-Dem. Plurality	Total Vote Rep.	Total Vote Dem.	Major Vote Rep.	Major Vote Dem.
2016	1,541,036	926,007	Grassley, Charles E.*	549,460	Judge, Patty	65,569	376,547 R	60.1%	35.7%	62.8%	37.2%
2014	1,129,700	588,575	Ernst, Joni	494,370	Braley, Bruce	46,755	94,205 R	52.1%	43.8%	54.3%	45.7%
2010	1,116,063	718,215	Grassley, Charles E.*	371,686	Conlin, Roxanne	26,162	346,529 R	64.4%	33.3%	65.9%	34.1%
2008	1,502,918	560,006	Reed, Christopher	941,665	Harkin, Tom*	1,247	381,659 D	37.3%	62.7%	37.3%	62.7%
2004	1,479,228	1,038,175	Grassley, Charles E.*	412,365	Small, Arthur A.	28,688	625,810 R	70.2%	27.9%	71.6%	28.4%
2002	1,023,075	447,892	Ganske, Greg	554,278	Harkin, Tom*	20,905	106,386 D	43.8%	54.2%	44.7%	55.3%
1998	947,907	648,480	Grassley, Charles E.*	289,049	Osterberg, David	10,378	359,431 R	68.4%	30.5%	69.2%	30.8%
1996	1,224,054	571,807	Lightfoot, Jim Ross	634,166	Harkin, Tom*	18,081	62,359 D	46.7%	51.8%	47.4%	52.6%
1992	1,292,494	899,761	Grassley, Charles E.*	351,561	Lloyd-Jones, Jean	41,172	548,200 R	69.6%	27.2%	71.9%	28.1%
1990	983,933	446,869	Tauke, Tom	535,975	Harkin, Tom*	1,089	89,106 D	45.4%	54.5%	45.5%	54.5%
1986	891,762	588,880	Grassley, Charles E.*	299,406	Roehrick, John P.	3,476	289,474 R	66.0%	33.6%	66.3%	33.7%
1984	1,292,700	564,381	Jepsen, Roger W.*	716,883	Harkin, Tom	11,436	152,502 D	43.7%	55.5%	44.0%	56.0%
1980	1,277,034	683,014	Grassley, Charles E.	581,545	Culver, John C.*	12,475	101,469 R	53.5%	45.5%	54.0%	46.0%
1978	824,654	421,598	Jepsen, Roger W.	395,066	Clark, Richard*	7,990	26,532 R	51.1%	47.9%	51.6%	48.4%
1974	889,561	420,546	Stanley, David M.	462,947	Culver, John C.	6,068	42,401 D	47.3%	52.0%	47.6%	52.4%
1972	1,203,333	530,525	Miller, Jack*	662,637	Clark, Richard	10,171	132,112 D	44.1%	55.1%	44.5%	55.5%
1968	1,144,086	568,469	Stanley, David M.	574,884	Hughes, Harold E.	733	6,415 D	49.7%	50.2%	49.7%	50.3%
1966	857,496	522,339	Miller, Jack*	324,114	Smith, E. B.	11,043	198,225 R	60.9%	37.8%	61.7%	38.3%
1962	807,972	431,364	Hickenlooper, Bourke B.*	376,602	Smith, E. B.	6	54,762 R	53.4%	46.6%	53.4%	46.6%
1960	1,237,582	642,463	Miller, Jack	595,119	Loveless, Herschel C.		47,344 R	51.9%	48.1%	51.9%	48.1%
1956	1,178,655	635,499	Hickenlooper, Bourke B.*	543,156	Evans, R. M.		92,343 R	53.9%	46.1%	53.9%	46.1%
1954	847,355	442,409	Martin, Thomas E.	402,712	Gillette, Guy M.*	2,234	39,697 R	52.2%	47.5%	52.3%	47.7%
1950	858,523	470,613	Hickenlooper, Bourke B.*	383,766	Loveland, Albert J.	4,144	86,847 R	54.8%	44.7%	55.1%	44.9%
1948	1,000,412	415,778	Wilson, George*	578,226	Gillette, Guy M.	6,408	162,448 D	41.6%	57.8%	41.8%	58.2%

Note: An asterisk (*) denotes incumbent.

IOWA

PRESIDENT 2016

2010 Census Population	County	Total Vote	Republican (Trump)	Democratic (Clinton)	Other	Rep.-Dem. Plurality	Percentage			
							Total Vote		Major Vote	
							Rep.	Dem.	Rep.	Dem.
7,682	ADAIR	3,811	2,461	1,133	217	1,328 R	64.6%	29.7%	68.5%	31.5%
4,029	ADAMS	2,106	1,395	565	146	830 R	66.2%	26.8%	71.2%	28.8%
14,330	ALLAMAKEE	6,923	4,093	2,421	409	1,672 R	59.1%	35.0%	62.8%	37.2%
12,887	APPANOOSE	6,136	4,033	1,814	289	2,219 R	65.7%	29.6%	69.0%	31.0%
6,119	AUDUBON	3,412	2,136	1,080	196	1,056 R	62.6%	31.7%	66.4%	33.6%
26,076	BENTON	13,844	8,232	4,678	934	3,554 R	59.5%	33.8%	63.8%	36.2%
131,090	BLACK HAWK	64,405	27,476	32,233	4,696	4,757 D	42.7%	50.0%	46.0%	54.0%
26,306	BOONE	14,196	7,484	5,541	1,171	1,943 R	52.7%	39.0%	57.5%	42.5%
24,276	BREMER	13,538	7,208	5,356	974	1,852 R	53.2%	39.6%	57.4%	42.6%
20,958	BUCHANAN	10,252	5,510	3,970	772	1,540 R	53.7%	38.7%	58.1%	41.9%
20,260	BUENA VISTA	8,278	4,903	2,856	519	2,047 R	59.2%	34.5%	63.2%	36.8%
14,867	BUTLER	7,513	4,921	2,157	435	2,764 R	65.5%	28.7%	69.5%	30.5%
9,670	CALHOUN	5,159	3,468	1,398	293	2,070 R	67.2%	27.1%	71.3%	28.7%
20,816	CARROLL	10,544	6,638	3,309	597	3,329 R	63.0%	31.4%	66.7%	33.3%
13,956	CASS	7,125	4,761	1,951	413	2,810 R	66.8%	27.4%	70.9%	29.1%
18,499	CEDAR	9,541	5,295	3,599	647	1,696 R	55.5%	37.7%	59.5%	40.5%
44,151	CERRO GORDO	22,965	11,621	9,862	1,482	1,759 R	50.6%	42.9%	54.1%	45.9%
12,072	CHEROKEE	6,258	4,192	1,679	387	2,513 R	67.0%	26.8%	71.4%	28.6%
12,439	CHICKASAW	6,435	3,742	2,266	427	1,476 R	58.2%	35.2%	62.3%	37.7%
9,286	CLARKE	4,454	2,713	1,465	276	1,248 R	60.9%	32.9%	64.9%	35.1%
16,667	CLAY	8,617	5,877	2,249	491	3,628 R	68.2%	26.1%	72.3%	27.7%
18,129	CLAYTON	9,129	5,317	3,237	575	2,080 R	58.2%	35.5%	62.2%	37.8%
49,116	CLINTON	23,067	11,276	10,095	1,696	1,181 R	48.9%	43.8%	52.8%	47.2%
17,096	CRAWFORD	6,935	4,617	1,991	327	2,626 R	66.6%	28.7%	69.9%	30.1%
66,135	DALLAS	38,252	19,339	15,701	3,212	3,638 R	50.6%	41.0%	55.2%	44.8%
8,753	DAVIS	3,882	2,723	977	182	1,746 R	70.1%	25.2%	73.6%	26.4%
8,457	DECATUR	3,734	2,296	1,201	237	1,095 R	61.5%	32.2%	65.7%	34.3%
17,764	DELAWARE	9,241	5,694	2,957	590	2,737 R	61.6%	32.0%	65.8%	34.2%
40,325	DES MOINES	19,103	9,529	8,212	1,362	1,317 R	49.9%	43.0%	53.7%	46.3%
16,667	DICKINSON	10,354	6,753	3,056	545	3,697 R	65.2%	29.5%	68.8%	31.2%
93,653	DUBUQUE	49,721	23,460	22,850	3,411	610 R	47.2%	46.0%	50.7%	49.3%
10,302	EMMET	4,753	3,124	1,357	272	1,767 R	65.7%	28.6%	69.7%	30.3%
20,880	FAYETTE	9,975	5,620	3,689	666	1,931 R	56.3%	37.0%	60.4%	39.6%
16,303	FLOYD	8,060	4,375	3,179	506	1,196 R	54.3%	39.4%	57.9%	42.1%
10,680	FRANKLIN	4,968	3,163	1,493	312	1,670 R	63.7%	30.1%	67.9%	32.1%
7,441	FREMONT	3,595	2,407	963	225	1,444 R	67.0%	26.8%	71.4%	28.6%
9,336	GREENE	4,821	2,820	1,691	310	1,129 R	58.5%	35.1%	62.5%	37.5%
12,453	GRUNDY	6,872	4,527	1,856	489	2,671 R	65.9%	27.0%	70.9%	29.1%
10,954	GUTHRIE	5,750	3,628	1,732	390	1,896 R	63.1%	30.1%	67.7%	32.3%
15,673	HAMILTON	7,694	4,463	2,726	505	1,737 R	58.0%	35.4%	62.1%	37.9%
11,341	HANCOCK	5,871	3,977	1,587	307	2,390 R	67.7%	27.0%	71.5%	28.5%
17,534	HARDIN	8,533	5,254	2,787	492	2,467 R	61.6%	32.7%	65.3%	34.7%
14,928	HARRISON	7,465	4,902	2,131	432	2,771 R	65.7%	28.5%	69.7%	30.3%
20,145	HENRY	9,404	5,779	2,904	721	2,875 R	61.5%	30.9%	66.6%	33.4%
9,566	HOWARD	4,559	2,611	1,677	271	934 R	57.3%	36.8%	60.9%	39.1%
9,815	HUMBOLDT	5,087	3,568	1,252	267	2,316 R	70.1%	24.6%	74.0%	26.0%
7,089	IDA	3,612	2,655	792	165	1,863 R	73.5%	21.9%	77.0%	23.0%
16,355	IOWA	8,904	5,205	3,084	615	2,121 R	58.5%	34.6%	62.8%	37.2%
19,848	JACKSON	10,310	5,824	3,837	649	1,987 R	56.5%	37.2%	60.3%	39.7%
36,842	JASPER	19,034	10,560	7,109	1,365	3,451 R	55.5%	37.3%	59.8%	40.2%
16,843	JEFFERSON	8,156	3,748	3,710	698	38 R	46.0%	45.5%	50.3%	49.7%
130,882	JOHNSON	76,940	21,044	50,200	5,696	29,156 D	27.4%	65.2%	29.5%	70.5%
20,638	JONES	10,133	5,720	3,787	626	1,933 R	56.4%	37.4%	60.2%	39.8%
10,511	KEOKUK	4,985	3,390	1,342	253	2,048 R	68.0%	26.9%	71.6%	28.4%
15,543	KOSSUTH	8,607	5,653	2,543	411	3,110 R	65.7%	29.5%	69.0%	31.0%
35,862	LEE	16,151	8,803	6,215	1,133	2,588 R	54.5%	38.5%	58.6%	41.4%
211,226	LINN	117,098	48,390	58,935	9,773	10,545 D	41.3%	50.3%	45.1%	54.9%
11,387	LOUISA	5,008	3,069	1,648	291	1,421 R	61.3%	32.9%	65.1%	34.9%
8,898	LUCAS	4,354	2,877	1,239	238	1,638 R	66.1%	28.5%	69.9%	30.1%
11,581	LYON	6,377	5,192	920	265	4,272 R	81.4%	14.4%	84.9%	15.1%

IOWA

PRESIDENT 2016

2010 Census Population	County	Total Vote	Republican (Trump)	Democratic (Clinton)	Other	Rep.-Dem. Plurality		Percentage			
								Total Vote		Major Vote	
								Rep.	Dem.	Rep.	Dem.
15,679	MADISON	8,636	5,360	2,678	598	2,682	R	62.1%	31.0%	66.7%	33.3%
22,381	MAHASKA	10,632	7,432	2,619	581	4,813	R	69.9%	24.6%	73.9%	26.1%
33,309	MARION	17,816	10,962	5,482	1,372	5,480	R	61.5%	30.8%	66.7%	33.3%
40,648	MARSHALL	17,980	9,146	7,652	1,182	1,494	R	50.9%	42.6%	54.4%	45.6%
15,059	MILLS	7,698	5,067	2,090	541	2,977	R	65.8%	27.1%	70.8%	29.2%
10,776	MITCHELL	5,417	3,190	1,888	339	1,302	R	58.9%	34.9%	62.8%	37.2%
9,243	MONONA	4,572	3,120	1,247	205	1,873	R	68.2%	27.3%	71.4%	28.6%
7,970	MONROE	3,865	2,638	1,056	171	1,582	R	68.3%	27.3%	71.4%	28.6%
10,740	MONTGOMERY	5,044	3,436	1,314	294	2,122	R	68.1%	26.1%	72.3%	27.7%
42,745	MUSCATINE	19,434	9,584	8,368	1,482	1,216	R	49.3%	43.1%	53.4%	46.6%
14,398	O'BRIEN	7,406	5,752	1,315	339	4,437	R	77.7%	17.8%	81.4%	18.6%
6,462	OSCEOLA	3,213	2,531	552	130	1,979	R	78.8%	17.2%	82.1%	17.9%
15,932	PAGE	7,044	4,893	1,807	344	3,086	R	69.5%	25.7%	73.0%	27.0%
9,421	PALO ALTO	4,703	3,081	1,398	224	1,683	R	65.5%	29.7%	68.8%	31.2%
24,986	PLYMOUTH	13,190	9,680	2,885	625	6,795	R	73.4%	21.9%	77.0%	23.0%
7,310	POCAHONTAS	3,865	2,702	963	200	1,739	R	69.9%	24.9%	73.7%	26.3%
430,640	POLK	231,555	93,492	119,804	18,259	26,312	D	40.4%	51.7%	43.8%	56.2%
93,158	POTTAWATTAMIE	42,680	24,447	15,355	2,878	9,092	R	57.3%	36.0%	61.4%	38.6%
18,914	POWESHIEK	9,833	4,946	4,304	583	642	R	50.3%	43.8%	53.5%	46.5%
5,131	RINGGOLD	2,707	1,824	753	130	1,071	R	67.4%	27.8%	70.8%	29.2%
10,350	SAC	5,212	3,703	1,270	239	2,433	R	71.0%	24.4%	74.5%	25.5%
165,224	SCOTT	86,220	39,149	40,440	6,631	1,291	D	45.4%	46.9%	49.2%	50.8%
12,167	SHELBY	6,370	4,362	1,662	346	2,700	R	68.5%	26.1%	72.4%	27.6%
33,704	SIOUX	18,194	14,785	2,300	1,109	12,485	R	81.3%	12.6%	86.5%	13.5%
89,542	STORY	50,667	19,458	25,709	5,500	6,251	D	38.4%	50.7%	43.1%	56.9%
17,767	TAMA	8,752	4,971	3,196	585	1,775	R	56.8%	36.5%	60.9%	39.1%
6,317	TAYLOR	3,029	2,111	758	160	1,353	R	69.7%	25.0%	73.6%	26.4%
12,534	UNION	5,832	3,525	1,922	385	1,603	R	60.4%	33.0%	64.7%	35.3%
7,570	VAN BUREN	3,561	2,527	845	189	1,682	R	71.0%	23.7%	74.9%	25.1%
35,625	WAPELLO	15,149	8,715	5,594	840	3,121	R	57.5%	36.9%	60.9%	39.1%
46,225	WARREN	27,300	14,814	10,411	2,075	4,403	R	54.3%	38.1%	58.7%	41.3%
21,704	WASHINGTON	10,929	6,173	3,943	813	2,230	R	56.5%	36.1%	61.0%	39.0%
6,403	WAYNE	2,940	2,069	719	152	1,350	R	70.4%	24.5%	74.2%	25.8%
38,013	WEBSTER	17,430	10,056	6,305	1,069	3,751	R	57.7%	36.2%	61.5%	38.5%
10,866	WINNEBAGO	5,787	3,447	1,931	409	1,516	R	59.6%	33.4%	64.1%	35.9%
21,056	WINNESHIEK	11,362	5,344	5,254	764	90	R	47.0%	46.2%	50.4%	49.6%
102,172	WOODBURY	43,718	24,727	16,210	2,781	8,517	R	56.6%	37.1%	60.4%	39.6%
7,598	WORTH	4,257	2,453	1,530	274	923	R	57.6%	35.9%	61.6%	38.4%
13,229	WRIGHT	6,026	3,800	1,896	330	1,904	R	63.1%	31.5%	66.7%	33.3%
3,046,355	TOTAL	1,566,031	800,983	653,669	111,379	147,314	R	51.1%	41.7%	55.1%	44.9%

IOWA

SENATOR 2016

2010 Census Population	County	Total Vote	Republican (Grassley)	Democratic (Judge)	Other	Rep.-Dem. Plurality		Percentage			
								Total Vote		Major Vote	
								Rep.	Dem.	Rep.	Dem.
7,682	ADAIR	3,772	2,708	894	170	1,814	R	71.8%	23.7%	75.2%	24.8%
4,029	ADAMS	2,062	1,515	454	93	1,061	R	73.5%	22.0%	76.9%	23.1%
14,330	ALLAMAKEE	6,827	4,473	2,099	255	2,374	R	65.5%	30.7%	68.1%	31.9%
12,887	APPANOOSE	6,013	4,122	1,690	201	2,432	R	68.6%	28.1%	70.9%	29.1%
6,119	AUDUBON	3,282	2,323	847	112	1,476	R	70.8%	25.8%	73.3%	26.7%

IOWA
SENATOR 2016

2010 Census Population	County	Total Vote	Republican (Grassley)	Democratic (Judge)	Other	Rep.-Dem. Plurality	Percentage Total Vote Rep.	Total Vote Dem.	Major Vote Rep.	Major Vote Dem.
26,076	BENTON	13,685	9,351	3,811	523	5,540 R	68.3%	27.8%	71.0%	29.0%
131,090	BLACK HAWK	63,527	33,884	27,245	2,398	6,639 R	53.3%	42.9%	55.4%	44.6%
26,306	BOONE	14,056	8,593	4,820	643	3,773 R	61.1%	34.3%	64.1%	35.9%
24,276	BREMER	13,415	8,583	4,357	475	4,226 R	64.0%	32.5%	66.3%	33.7%
20,958	BUCHANAN	10,149	6,382	3,313	454	3,069 R	62.9%	32.6%	65.8%	34.2%
20,260	BUENA VISTA	8,050	5,369	2,382	299	2,987 R	66.7%	29.6%	69.3%	30.7%
14,867	BUTLER	7,464	5,433	1,782	249	3,651 R	72.8%	23.9%	75.3%	24.7%
9,670	CALHOUN	5,118	3,798	1,154	166	2,644 R	74.2%	22.5%	76.7%	23.3%
20,816	CARROLL	10,344	7,259	2,714	371	4,545 R	70.2%	26.2%	72.8%	27.2%
13,956	CASS	6,929	5,081	1,558	290	3,523 R	73.3%	22.5%	76.5%	23.5%
18,499	CEDAR	9,410	6,103	2,908	399	3,195 R	64.9%	30.9%	67.7%	32.3%
44,151	CERRO GORDO	22,633	13,417	8,173	1,043	5,244 R	59.3%	36.1%	62.1%	37.9%
12,072	CHEROKEE	6,193	4,670	1,331	192	3,339 R	75.4%	21.5%	77.8%	22.2%
12,439	CHICKASAW	6,382	4,177	1,956	249	2,221 R	65.4%	30.6%	68.1%	31.9%
9,286	CLARKE	4,385	2,903	1,273	209	1,630 R	66.2%	29.0%	69.5%	30.5%
16,667	CLAY	8,472	6,260	1,894	318	4,366 R	73.9%	22.4%	76.8%	23.2%
18,129	CLAYTON	9,012	5,851	2,779	382	3,072 R	64.9%	30.8%	67.8%	32.2%
49,116	CLINTON	22,754	12,821	8,852	1,081	3,969 R	56.3%	38.9%	59.2%	40.8%
17,096	CRAWFORD	6,721	4,674	1,771	276	2,903 R	69.5%	26.4%	72.5%	27.5%
66,135	DALLAS	37,775	24,374	11,876	1,525	12,498 R	64.5%	31.4%	67.2%	32.8%
8,753	DAVIS	3,843	2,750	972	121	1,778 R	71.6%	25.3%	73.9%	26.1%
8,457	DECATUR	3,681	2,488	1,037	156	1,451 R	67.6%	28.2%	70.6%	29.4%
17,764	DELAWARE	9,180	6,445	2,369	366	4,076 R	70.2%	25.8%	73.1%	26.9%
40,325	DES MOINES	18,669	10,353	7,589	727	2,764 R	55.5%	40.7%	57.7%	42.3%
16,667	DICKINSON	10,235	7,489	2,421	325	5,068 R	73.2%	23.7%	75.6%	24.4%
93,653	DUBUQUE	48,500	27,348	19,291	1,861	8,057 R	56.4%	39.8%	58.6%	41.4%
10,302	EMMET	4,711	3,341	1,171	199	2,170 R	70.9%	24.9%	74.0%	26.0%
20,880	FAYETTE	9,947	6,412	3,069	466	3,343 R	64.5%	30.9%	67.6%	32.4%
16,303	FLOYD	7,978	4,947	2,725	306	2,222 R	62.0%	34.2%	64.5%	35.5%
10,680	FRANKLIN	4,940	3,550	1,172	218	2,378 R	71.9%	23.7%	75.2%	24.8%
7,441	FREMONT	3,505	2,582	735	188	1,847 R	73.7%	21.0%	77.8%	22.2%
9,336	GREENE	4,743	3,197	1,344	202	1,853 R	67.4%	28.3%	70.4%	29.6%
12,453	GRUNDY	6,868	5,261	1,370	237	3,891 R	76.6%	19.9%	79.3%	20.7%
10,954	GUTHRIE	5,724	4,004	1,413	307	2,591 R	70.0%	24.7%	73.9%	26.1%
15,673	HAMILTON	7,619	5,142	2,170	307	2,972 R	67.5%	28.5%	70.3%	29.7%
11,341	HANCOCK	5,819	4,232	1,324	263	2,908 R	72.7%	22.8%	76.2%	23.8%
17,534	HARDIN	8,464	5,841	2,284	339	3,557 R	69.0%	27.0%	71.9%	28.1%
14,928	HARRISON	7,298	5,108	1,788	402	3,320 R	70.0%	24.5%	74.1%	25.9%
20,145	HENRY	9,225	6,294	2,535	396	3,759 R	68.2%	27.5%	71.3%	28.7%
9,566	HOWARD	4,510	2,859	1,459	192	1,400 R	63.4%	32.4%	66.2%	33.8%
9,815	HUMBOLDT	5,039	3,860	999	180	2,861 R	76.6%	19.8%	79.4%	20.6%
7,089	IDA	3,571	2,868	590	113	2,278 R	80.3%	16.5%	82.9%	17.1%
16,355	IOWA	8,824	6,062	2,443	319	3,619 R	68.7%	27.7%	71.3%	28.7%
19,848	JACKSON	10,057	6,283	3,450	324	2,833 R	62.5%	34.3%	64.6%	35.4%
36,842	JASPER	18,855	11,688	6,170	997	5,518 R	62.0%	32.7%	65.4%	34.6%
16,843	JEFFERSON	7,936	4,094	3,447	395	647 R	51.6%	43.4%	54.3%	45.7%
130,882	JOHNSON	74,833	28,914	42,699	3,220	13,785 D	38.6%	57.1%	40.4%	59.6%
20,638	JONES	10,071	6,551	3,063	457	3,488 R	65.0%	30.4%	68.1%	31.9%
10,511	KEOKUK	4,915	3,697	1,045	173	2,652 R	75.2%	21.3%	78.0%	22.0%
15,543	KOSSUTH	8,574	6,027	2,247	300	3,780 R	70.3%	26.2%	72.8%	27.2%
35,862	LEE	15,846	8,441	6,382	1,023	2,059 R	53.3%	40.3%	56.9%	43.1%
211,226	LINN	115,614	62,737	47,635	5,242	15,102 R	54.3%	41.2%	56.8%	43.2%
11,387	LOUISA	4,939	3,303	1,429	207	1,874 R	66.9%	28.9%	69.8%	30.2%
8,898	LUCAS	4,277	3,064	1,068	145	1,996 R	71.6%	25.0%	74.2%	25.8%
11,581	LYON	6,254	5,328	761	165	4,567 R	85.2%	12.2%	87.5%	12.5%
15,679	MADISON	8,520	5,921	2,205	394	3,716 R	69.5%	25.9%	72.9%	27.1%
22,381	MAHASKA	10,482	7,812	2,302	368	5,510 R	74.5%	22.0%	77.2%	22.8%
33,309	MARION	17,621	12,407	4,562	652	7,845 R	70.4%	25.9%	73.1%	26.9%
40,648	MARSHALL	17,739	10,432	6,585	722	3,847 R	58.8%	37.1%	61.3%	38.7%
15,059	MILLS	7,422	5,290	1,740	392	3,550 R	71.3%	23.4%	75.2%	24.8%

IOWA

SENATOR 2016

2010 Census Population	County	Total Vote	Republican (Grassley)	Democratic (Judge)	Other	Rep.-Dem. Plurality	Total Vote Rep.	Total Vote Dem.	Major Vote Rep.	Major Vote Dem.
10,776	MITCHELL	5,379	3,680	1,536	163	2,144 R	68.4%	28.6%	70.6%	29.4%
9,243	MONONA	4,530	3,315	1,049	166	2,266 R	73.2%	23.2%	76.0%	24.0%
7,970	MONROE	3,837	2,458	1,280	99	1,178 R	64.1%	33.4%	65.8%	34.2%
10,740	MONTGOMERY	4,949	3,646	1,067	236	2,579 R	73.7%	21.6%	77.4%	22.6%
42,745	MUSCATINE	19,095	11,157	6,963	975	4,194 R	58.4%	36.5%	61.6%	38.4%
14,398	O'BRIEN	7,304	6,076	1,060	168	5,016 R	83.2%	14.5%	85.1%	14.9%
6,462	OSCEOLA	3,143	2,601	455	87	2,146 R	82.8%	14.5%	85.1%	14.9%
15,932	PAGE	6,921	5,208	1,461	252	3,747 R	75.2%	21.1%	78.1%	21.9%
9,421	PALO ALTO	4,653	3,377	1,109	167	2,268 R	72.6%	23.8%	75.3%	24.7%
24,986	PLYMOUTH	12,970	10,338	2,300	332	8,038 R	79.7%	17.7%	81.8%	18.2%
7,310	POCAHONTAS	3,824	2,891	784	149	2,107 R	75.6%	20.5%	78.7%	21.3%
430,640	POLK	228,391	118,164	100,317	9,910	17,847 R	51.7%	43.9%	54.1%	45.9%
93,158	POTTAWATTAMIE	41,466	25,721	12,943	2,802	12,778 R	62.0%	31.2%	66.5%	33.5%
18,914	POWESHIEK	9,731	5,617	3,748	366	1,869 R	57.7%	38.5%	60.0%	40.0%
5,131	RINGGOLD	2,686	1,989	617	80	1,372 R	74.1%	23.0%	76.3%	23.7%
10,350	SAC	5,131	3,965	1,015	151	2,950 R	77.3%	19.8%	79.6%	20.4%
165,224	SCOTT	84,692	46,415	34,503	3,774	11,912 R	54.8%	40.7%	57.4%	42.6%
12,167	SHELBY	6,110	4,480	1,409	221	3,071 R	73.3%	23.1%	76.1%	23.9%
33,704	SIOUX	17,932	15,902	1,709	321	14,193 R	88.7%	9.5%	90.3%	9.7%
89,542	STORY	49,316	25,475	21,472	2,369	4,003 R	51.7%	43.5%	54.3%	45.7%
17,767	TAMA	8,722	5,536	2,769	417	2,767 R	63.5%	31.7%	66.7%	33.3%
6,317	TAYLOR	2,941	2,220	613	108	1,607 R	75.5%	20.8%	78.4%	21.6%
12,534	UNION	5,775	3,913	1,625	237	2,288 R	67.8%	28.1%	70.7%	29.3%
7,570	VAN BUREN	3,531	2,618	764	149	1,854 R	74.1%	21.6%	77.4%	22.6%
35,625	WAPELLO	14,790	8,692	5,365	733	3,327 R	58.8%	36.3%	61.8%	38.2%
46,225	WARREN	26,879	17,081	8,700	1,098	8,381 R	63.5%	32.4%	66.3%	33.7%
21,704	WASHINGTON	10,777	7,251	3,062	464	4,189 R	67.3%	28.4%	70.3%	29.7%
6,403	WAYNE	2,929	2,195	645	89	1,550 R	74.9%	22.0%	77.3%	22.7%
38,013	WEBSTER	17,159	11,045	5,396	718	5,649 R	64.4%	31.4%	67.2%	32.8%
10,866	WINNEBAGO	5,761	3,938	1,590	233	2,348 R	68.4%	27.6%	71.2%	28.8%
21,056	WINNESHIEK	11,219	6,349	4,436	434	1,913 R	56.6%	39.5%	58.9%	41.1%
102,172	WOODBURY	43,012	27,166	13,909	1,937	13,257 R	63.2%	32.3%	66.1%	33.9%
7,598	WORTH	4,222	2,774	1,246	202	1,528 R	65.7%	29.5%	69.0%	31.0%
13,229	WRIGHT	5,981	4,208	1,550	223	2,658 R	70.4%	25.9%	73.1%	26.9%
3,046,355	TOTAL	1,541,036	926,007	549,460	65,569	376,547 R	60.1%	35.7%	62.8%	37.2%

IOWA

HOUSE OF REPRESENTATIVES

CD	Year	Total Vote	Republican Vote	Republican Candidate	Democratic Vote	Democratic Candidate	Other Vote	Rep.-Dem. Plurality	Total Vote Rep.	Total Vote Dem.	Major Vote Rep.	Major Vote Dem.
1	2016	384,977	206,903	BLUM, ROD*	177,403	VERNON, MONICA	671	29,500 R	53.7%	46.1%	53.8%	46.2%
1	2014	289,306	147,762	BLUM, ROD	141,145	MURPHY, PAT	399	6,617 R	51.1%	48.8%	51.1%	48.9%
1	2012	390,849	162,465	LANGE, BENJAMIN M.	222,422	BRALEY, BRUCE*	5,962	59,957 D	41.6%	56.9%	42.2%	57.8%
2	2016	370,032	170,933	PETERS, CHRISTOPHER	198,571	LOEBSACK, DAVID*	528	27,638 D	46.2%	53.7%	46.3%	53.7%
2	2014	273,329	129,455	MILLER-MEEKS, MARIANNETTE	143,431	LOEBSACK, DAVID*	443	13,976 D	47.4%	52.5%	47.4%	52.6%
2	2012	381,275	161,977	ARCHER, JOHN	211,863	LOEBSACK, DAVID*	7,435	49,886 D	42.5%	55.6%	43.3%	56.7%
3	2016	390,287	208,598	YOUNG, DAVID*	155,002	MOWRER, JIM	26,687	53,596 R	53.4%	39.7%	57.4%	42.6%
3	2014	282,066	148,814	YOUNG, DAVID	119,109	APPEL, STACI	14,143	29,705 R	52.8%	42.2%	55.5%	44.5%
3	2012	386,842	202,000	LATHAM, TOM*	168,632	BOSWELL, LEONARD L.	16,210	33,368 R	52.2%	43.6%	54.5%	45.5%

IOWA

HOUSE OF REPRESENTATIVES

			Republican		Democratic		Other Vote	Rep.-Dem. Plurality	Percentage			
									Total Vote		Major Vote	
CD	Year	Total Vote	Vote	Candidate	Vote	Candidate			Rep.	Dem.	Rep.	Dem.
4	2016	370,259	226,719	KING, STEVE*	142,993	WEAVER, KIM	547	83,726 R	61.2%	38.6%	61.3%	38.7%
4	2014	275,633	169,834	KING, STEVE*	105,504	MOWRER, JIM	295	64,330 R	61.6%	38.3%	61.7%	38.3%
4	2012	377,883	200,063	KING, STEVE*	169,470	VILSACK, CHRISTIE	8,350	30,593 R	52.9%	44.8%	54.1%	45.9%
TOTAL	2016	1,515,555	813,153		673,969		28,433	139,184 R	53.7%	44.5%	54.7%	45.3%
TOTAL	2014	1,120,334	595,865		509,189		15,280	86,676 R	53.2%	45.4%	53.9%	46.1%
TOTAL	2012	1,536,849	726,505		772,387		37,957	45,882 D	47.3%	50.3%	48.5%	51.5%

Note: An asterisk (*) denotes incumbent.

IOWA

GENERAL AND PRIMARY ELECTIONS

2016 GENERAL ELECTIONS: OTHER VOTES

President   Other vote was 59,186 Libertarian (Gary Johnson), 17,746 Write-in (Scattered Write-in), 12,366 Nominated by Petition (Evan McMullin), 11,479 Iowa Green Party (Jill Stein), 5,335 Constitution (Darrell Castle), 2,247 Independent Party Iowa (Lynn Kahn), 2,246 Legal Marijuana Now (Dan Vacek), 451 Nominated by Petition (Roque De La Fuente), 323 Socialism and Liberation (Gloria La Riva)

Senate   Other vote was 41,794 Libertarian (Charles Aldrich), 17,649 New Independent (Jim Hennager), 4,441 Nominated by Petition (Michael Luick-Thrams), 1,685 Write-in (Scattered Write-in)

House   Other vote was:

CD 1   671 Write-in (Scattered Write-in)

CD 2   528 Write-in (Scattered Write-in)

CD 3   15,372 Libertarian (Bryan Holder), 6,348 Independent (Claudia Addy), 4,518 Independent (Joe Grandanette), 449 Write-in (Scattered Write-in)

CD 4   547 Write-in (Scattered Write-in)

2016 PRIMARY ELECTIONS: SUPPLEMENTARY INFORMATION

Primary	February 1, 2016 (Presidential caucus) June 7, 2016 (Congress)	**Registration** (as of June 1, 2016 — includes 186,257 inactive registrants)	2,113,230	Republican Democratic No Party Other	639,476 610,608 670,068 6,821

Primary Type   Semi-open—Registered Democrats and Republicans could vote only in their party's primary, although any registered voter (including those not affiliated with either party) could participate in either party's primary by changing his or her registration to that party on primary day.

	REPUBLICAN PRIMARIES			DEMOCRATIC PRIMARIES		
Senator	Grassley, Charles E.*	90,089	98.4%	Judge, Patty	46,322	47.6%
	Write-In	1,500	1.6%	Hogg, Robert M.	37,801	38.9%
				Fiegen, Thomas L.	6,573	6.8%
				Krause, Bob	6,425	6.6%
				Write-In	154	0.2%
	TOTAL	91,589		TOTAL	97,275	

IOWA

GENERAL AND PRIMARY ELECTIONS

	REPUBLICAN PRIMARIES			DEMOCRATIC PRIMARIES		
Congressional District 1	Blum, Rod*	13,411	99.3%	Vernon, Monica	21,032	67.5%
	Write-In	88	0.7%	Murphy, Pat	10,090	32.4%
				Write-In	38	0.1%
	TOTAL	*13,499*		*TOTAL*	*31,160*	
Congressional District 2	Peters, Christopher	14,987	99.3%	Loebsack, David*	23,738	99.0%
	Write-In	107	0.7%	Write-In	238	1.0%
	TOTAL	*15,094*		*TOTAL*	*23,976*	
Congressional District 3	Young, David*	17,977	84.8%	Mowrer, Jim	13,024	49.5%
	Grandanette, Joe	3,143	14.8%	Sherzan, Mike	9,573	36.4%
	Write-In	85	0.4%	Adams, Desmund	3,650	13.9%
				Write-In	38	0.1%
	TOTAL	*21,205*		*TOTAL*	*26,285*	
Congressional District 4	King, Steve*	29,098	64.6%	Weaver, Kim	12,738	99.5%
	Bertrand, Rick	15,872	35.3%	Write-In	62	0.5%
	Write-In	49	0.1%			
	TOTAL	*45,019*		*TOTAL*	*12,800*	

Note: An asterisk (*) denotes incumbent. At the presidential level, Iowa held both a Republican and a Democratic precinct caucus on February 1, 2016, which is not a primary, but is highly reported and influential. On the Republican side, Ted Cruz won with 27.6% of the vote, followed by Donald Trump (24.3%), Marco Rubio (23.1%), and Ben Carson (9.3%). All other candidates together received a total of 15.6% of the vote. On the Democratic side, Hillary Rodham Clinton prevailed over Bernard Sanders, 49.8% to 49.6%, with 0.6% for others. The vote was measured by a method unique to the Iowa Democratic Party known as "state delegate equivalents."

KANSAS

Congressional districts first established for elections held in 2012
4 members

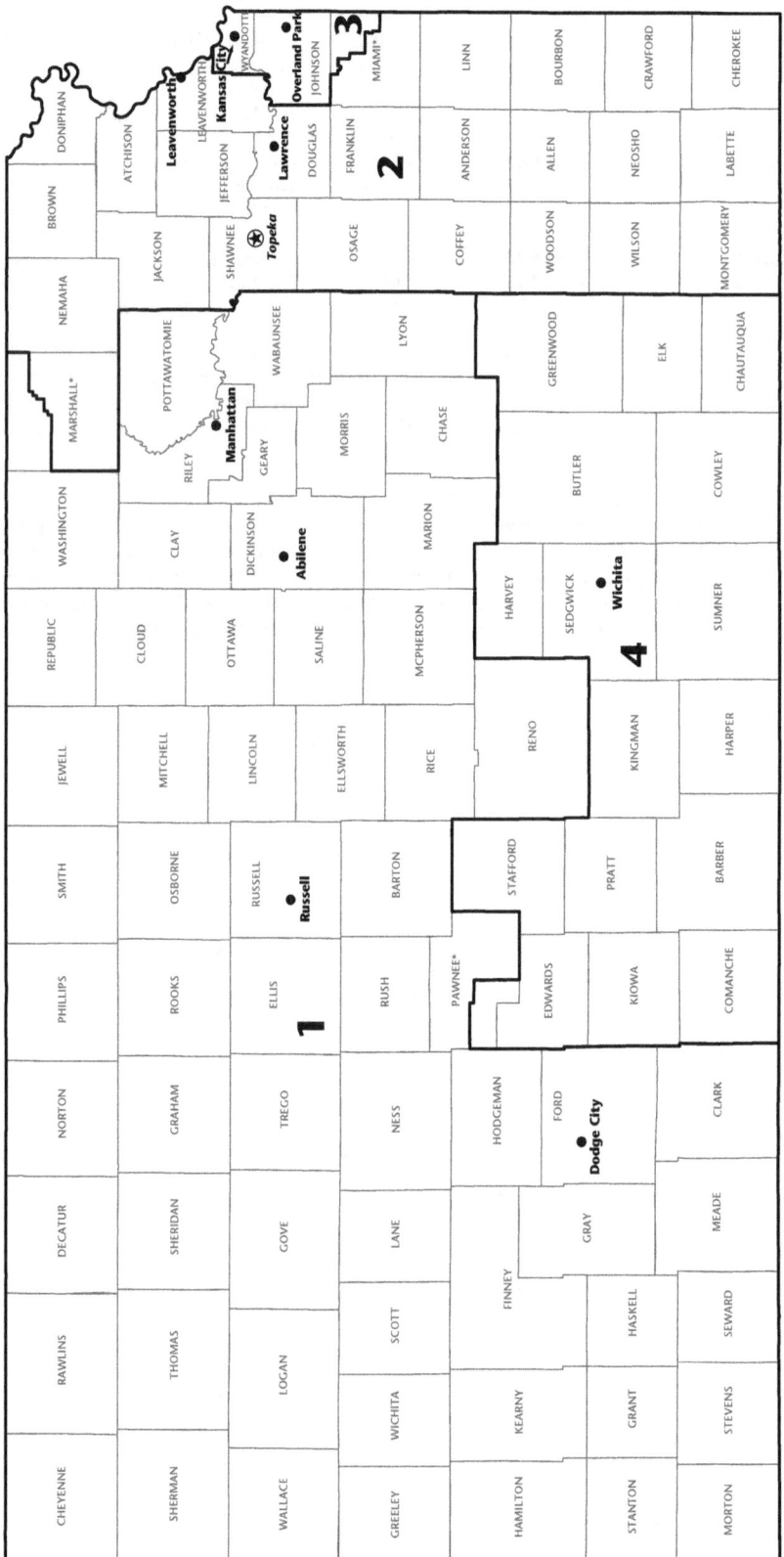

* Asterisk indicates a county whose boundaries include parts of two or more congressional districts.

KANSAS

GOVERNOR

Sam Brownback (R). Re-elected 2014 to a four-year term. Previously elected 2010.

SENATORS (2 Republicans)

Jerry Moran (R). Re-elected 2016 to a six-year term. Previously elected 2010.

Pat Roberts (R). Re-elected 2014 to a six-year term. Previously elected 2008, 2002, 1996.

REPRESENTATIVES (4 Republicans)

1. Roger Marshall (R)
2. Lynn Jenkins (R)
3. Kevin Yoder (R)
4. Ron Estes (R)

Note: In CD 4, Mike Pompeo (R) won re-election in 2016, but resigned his seat after the election to become director of the CIA Ron Estes (R) won a special election April 11, 2017, to fill the vacancy.

POSTWAR VOTE FOR PRESIDENT

| Year | Total Vote | Republican | | Democratic | | Other Vote | Rep.-Dem. Plurality | Percentage | | | |
| | | Vote | Candidate | Vote | Candidate | | | Total Vote | | Major Vote | |
								Rep.	Dem.	Rep.	Dem.
2016**	1,184,402	671,018	Trump, Donald J.	427,005	Clinton, Hillary Rodham	86,379	244,013 R	56.7%	36.1%	61.1%	38.9%
2012	1,159,971	692,634	Romney, W. Mitt	440,726	Obama, Barack H.*	26,611	251,908 R	59.7%	38.0%	61.1%	38.9%
2008	1,235,872	699,655	McCain, John S. III	514,765	Obama, Barack H.	21,452	184,890 R	56.6%	41.7%	57.6%	42.4%
2004	1,187,756	736,456	Bush, George W.*	434,993	Kerry, John F.	16,307	301,463 R	62.0%	36.6%	62.9%	37.1%
2000**	1,072,218	622,332	Bush, George W.	399,276	Gore, Albert Jr.	50,610	223,056 R	58.0%	37.2%	60.9%	39.1%
1996**	1,074,300	583,245	Dole, Robert "Bob"	387,659	Clinton, Bill*	103,396	195,586 R	54.3%	36.1%	60.1%	39.9%
1992**	1,157,335	449,951	Bush, George H.*	390,434	Clinton, Bill	316,950	59,517 R	38.9%	33.7%	53.5%	46.5%
1988	993,044	554,049	Bush, George H.	422,636	Dukakis, Michael S.	16,359	131,413 R	55.8%	42.6%	56.7%	43.3%
1984	1,021,991	677,296	Reagan, Ronald*	333,149	Mondale, Walter F.	11,546	344,147 R	66.3%	32.6%	67.0%	33.0%
1980**	979,795	566,812	Reagan, Ronald	326,150	Carter, Jimmy*	86,833	240,662 R	57.9%	33.3%	63.5%	36.5%
1976	957,845	502,752	Ford, Gerald R.*	430,421	Carter, Jimmy	24,672	72,331 R	52.5%	44.9%	53.9%	46.1%
1972	916,095	619,812	Nixon, Richard M.*	270,287	McGovern, George S.	25,996	349,525 R	67.7%	29.5%	69.6%	30.4%
1968**	872,783	478,674	Nixon, Richard M.	302,996	Humphrey, Hubert Horatio Jr.	91,113	175,678 R	54.8%	34.7%	61.2%	38.8%
1964	857,901	386,579	Goldwater, Barry M. Sr.	464,028	Johnson, Lyndon B.*	7,294	77,449 D	45.1%	54.1%	45.4%	54.6%
1960	928,825	561,474	Nixon, Richard M.	363,213	Kennedy, John F.	4,138	198,261 R	60.4%	39.1%	60.7%	39.3%
1956	866,243	566,878	Eisenhower, Dwight D.*	296,317	Stevenson, Adlai E. II	3,048	270,561 R	65.4%	34.2%	65.7%	34.3%
1952	896,166	616,302	Eisenhower, Dwight D.	273,296	Stevenson, Adlai E. II	6,568	343,006 R	68.8%	30.5%	69.3%	30.7%
1948	788,819	423,039	Dewey, Thomas E.	351,902	Truman, Harry S.*	13,878	71,137 R	53.6%	44.6%	54.6%	45.4%

Note: An asterisk (*) denotes incumbent. **In past elections, the other vote included: 2016 - 55,406 Libertarian (Gary Johnson); 2000 - 36,086 Green (Ralph Nader); 1996 - 92,639 Reform (Ross Perot); 1992 - 312,358 Independent (Perot); 1980 - 68,231 Independent (John Anderson); 1968 - 88,921 American Independent (George Wallace).

KANSAS

POSTWAR VOTE FOR GOVERNOR

Year	Total Vote	Republican		Democratic		Other Vote	Rep.-Dem. Plurality	Percentage			
		Vote	Candidate	Vote	Candidate			Total Vote		Major Vote	
								Rep.	Dem.	Rep.	Dem.
2014	869,502	433,196	Brownback, Sam*	401,100	Davis, Paul	35,206	32,096 R	49.8%	46.1%	51.9%	48.1%
2010	838,790	530,760	Brownback, Sam	270,166	Holland, Tom	37,864	260,594 R	63.3%	32.2%	66.3%	33.7%
2006	849,700	343,586	Barnett, Jim	491,993	Sebelius, Kathleen*	14,121	148,407 D	40.4%	57.9%	41.1%	58.9%
2002	835,692	376,830	Shallenburger, Tim	441,858	Sebelius, Kathleen	17,004	65,028 D	45.1%	52.9%	46.0%	54.0%
1998	742,665	544,882	Graves, Bill*	168,243	Sawyer, Tom	29,540	376,639 R	73.4%	22.7%	76.4%	23.6%
1994	821,030	526,113	Graves, Bill	294,733	Slattery, Jim	184	231,380 R	64.1%	35.9%	64.1%	35.9%
1990	783,325	333,589	Hayden, Mike*	380,609	Finney, Joan	69,127	47,020 D	42.6%	48.6%	46.7%	53.3%
1986	840,605	436,267	Hayden, Mike	404,338	Docking, Thomas R.		31,929 R	51.9%	48.1%	51.9%	48.1%
1982	763,263	339,356	Hardage, Sam	405,772	Carlin, John*	18,135	66,416 D	44.5%	53.2%	45.5%	54.5%
1978	736,246	348,015	Bennett, Robert F.*	363,835	Carlin, John	24,396	15,820 D	47.3%	49.4%	48.9%	51.1%
1974**	783,875	387,792	Bennett, Robert F.	384,115	Miller, Vern	11,968	3,677 R	49.5%	49.0%	50.2%	49.8%
1972	921,550	341,438	Kay, Morris	571,256	Docking, Robert*	8,856	229,818 D	37.1%	62.0%	37.4%	62.6%
1970	745,196	333,227	Frizzell, Kent	404,611	Docking, Robert*	7,358	71,384 D	44.7%	54.3%	45.2%	54.8%
1968	862,473	410,673	Harman, Rick	447,269	Docking, Robert*	4,531	36,596 D	47.6%	51.9%	47.9%	52.1%
1966	692,955	304,325	Avery, William H.*	380,030	Docking, Robert	8,600	75,705 D	43.9%	54.8%	44.5%	55.5%
1964	850,414	432,667	Avery, William H.	400,264	Wiles, Harry G.	17,483	32,403 R	50.9%	47.1%	51.9%	48.1%
1962	638,798	341,257	Anderson, John Jr.*	291,285	Saffels, Dale E.	6,256	49,972 R	53.4%	45.6%	54.0%	46.0%
1960	922,522	511,534	Anderson, John Jr.	402,261	Docking, George*	8,727	109,273 R	55.4%	43.6%	56.0%	44.0%
1958	735,939	313,036	Reed, Clyde M.	415,506	Docking, George*	7,397	102,470 D	42.5%	56.5%	43.0%	57.0%
1956	864,935	364,340	Shaw, Warren W.	479,701	Docking, George	20,894	115,361 D	42.1%	55.5%	43.2%	56.8%
1954	622,633	329,868	Hall, Fred	286,218	Docking, George	6,547	43,650 R	53.0%	46.0%	53.5%	46.5%
1952	872,139	491,338	Arn, Edward F.*	363,482	Rooney, Charles	17,319	127,856 R	56.3%	41.7%	57.5%	42.5%
1950	619,310	333,001	Arn, Edward F.	275,494	Anderson, Kenneth T.	10,815	57,507 R	53.8%	44.5%	54.7%	45.3%
1948	760,407	433,396	Carlson, Frank*	307,485	Carpenter, Randolph	19,526	125,911 R	57.0%	40.4%	58.5%	41.5%
1946	577,694	309,064	Carlson, Frank	254,283	Woodring, Harry H.	14,347	54,781 R	53.5%	44.0%	54.9%	45.1%

Note: An asterisk (*) denotes incumbent. **The term of office of Kansas's governor was increased from two to four years effective with the 1974 election.

POSTWAR VOTE FOR SENATOR

Year	Total Vote	Republican		Democratic		Other Vote	Rep.-Dem. Plurality	Percentage			
		Vote	Candidate	Vote	Candidate			Total Vote		Major Vote	
								Rep.	Dem.	Rep.	Dem.
2016	1,177,922	732,376	Moran, Jerry*	379,740	Wiesner, Patrick	65,806	352,636 R	62.2%	32.2%	65.9%	34.1%
2014**	866,191	460,350	Roberts, Pat*			405,841	460,350 R	53.1%		100.0%	
2010	837,692	587,175	Moran, Jerry	220,971	Johnston, Lisa	29,546	366,204 R	70.1%	26.4%	72.7%	27.3%
2008	1,210,690	727,121	Roberts, Pat*	441,399	Slattery, Jim	42,170	285,722 R	60.1%	36.5%	62.2%	37.8%
2004	1,129,022	780,863	Brownback, Sam*	310,337	Jones, Lee	37,822	470,526 R	69.2%	27.5%	71.6%	28.4%
2002	776,850	641,075	Roberts, Pat*			135,775	641,075 R	82.5%		100.0%	
1998	727,236	474,639	Brownback, Sam*	229,718	Feleciano, Paul Jr.	22,879	244,921 R	65.3%	31.6%	67.4%	32.6%
1996	1,052,300	652,677	Roberts, Pat	362,380	Thompson, Sally	37,243	290,297 R	62.0%	34.4%	64.3%	35.7%
1996S**	1,064,716	574,021	Brownback, Sam	461,344	Docking, Jill	29,351	112,677 R	53.9%	43.3%	55.4%	44.6%
1992	1,126,447	706,246	Dole, Robert "Bob"*	349,525	O'Dell, Gloria	70,676	356,721 R	62.7%	31.0%	66.9%	33.1%
1990	786,235	578,605	Kassebaum, Nancy Landon*	207,491	Williams, Dick	139	371,114 R	73.6%	26.4%	73.6%	26.4%
1986	823,566	576,902	Dole, Robert "Bob"*	246,664	MacDonald, Guy		330,238 R	70.0%	30.0%	70.0%	30.0%
1984	996,729	757,402	Kassebaum, Nancy Landon*	211,664	Maher, James R.	27,663	545,738 R	76.0%	21.2%	78.2%	21.8%
1980	938,957	598,686	Dole, Robert "Bob"*	340,271	Simpson, John		258,415 R	63.8%	36.2%	63.8%	36.2%
1978	748,839	403,354	Kassebaum, Nancy Landon	317,602	Roy, William R.	27,883	85,752 R	53.9%	42.4%	55.9%	44.1%
1974	794,437	403,983	Dole, Robert "Bob"*	390,451	Roy, William R.	3	13,532 R	50.9%	49.1%	50.9%	49.1%
1972	871,702	622,591	Pearson, James B.*	200,764	Tetzlaff, Arch O.	48,347	421,827 R	71.4%	23.0%	75.6%	24.4%
1968	817,096	490,911	Dole, Robert "Bob"	315,911	Robinson, William I.	10,274	175,000 R	60.1%	38.7%	60.8%	39.2%
1966	671,345	350,077	Pearson, James B.*	303,223	Breeding, J. Floyd	18,045	46,854 R	52.1%	45.2%	53.6%	46.4%
1962	622,232	388,500	Carlson, Frank*	223,630	Smith, K. L.	10,102	164,870 R	62.4%	35.9%	63.5%	36.5%
1962S**	613,250	344,689	Pearson, James B.*	260,756	Aylward, Paul L.	7,805	83,933 R	56.2%	42.5%	56.9%	43.1%
1960	888,592	485,499	Schoeppel, Andrew F.*	388,895	Theis, Frank	14,198	96,604 R	54.6%	43.8%	55.5%	44.5%
1956	825,280	477,822	Carlson, Frank*	333,939	Hart, George	13,519	143,883 R	57.9%	40.5%	58.9%	41.1%
1954	618,063	348,144	Schoeppel, Andrew F.*	258,575	McGill, George	11,344	89,569 R	56.3%	41.8%	57.4%	42.6%
1950	619,104	335,880	Carlson, Frank*	271,365	Aiken, Paul	11,859	64,515 R	54.3%	43.8%	55.3%	44.7%
1948	716,342	393,412	Schoeppel, Andrew F.	305,987	McGill, George	16,943	87,425 R	54.9%	42.7%	56.3%	43.7%

Note: An asterisk (*) denotes incumbent. **In past elections, the other vote included: 2014 - 368,372 Independent (Greg Orman). One of the 1996 and 1962 elections was for a short term to fill a vacancy. The Democratic Party did not run a candidate in the 2002 and 2014 Senate elections.

KANSAS

PRESIDENT 2016

2010 Census Population	County	Total Vote	Republican (Trump)	Democratic (Clinton)	Other	Rep.-Dem. Plurality	Percentage Total Vote Rep.	Percentage Total Vote Dem.	Percentage Major Vote Rep.	Percentage Major Vote Dem.
13,371	ALLEN	5,454	3,651	1,433	370	2,218 R	66.9%	26.3%	71.8%	28.2%
8,102	ANDERSON	3,350	2,435	672	243	1,763 R	72.7%	20.1%	78.4%	21.6%
16,924	ATCHISON	6,575	4,049	1,989	537	2,060 R	61.6%	30.3%	67.1%	32.9%
4,861	BARBER	2,252	1,850	286	116	1,564 R	82.1%	12.7%	86.6%	13.4%
27,674	BARTON	10,268	7,888	1,839	541	6,049 R	76.8%	17.9%	81.1%	18.9%
15,173	BOURBON	6,093	4,424	1,336	333	3,088 R	72.6%	21.9%	76.8%	23.2%
9,984	BROWN	4,036	2,906	863	267	2,043 R	72.0%	21.4%	77.1%	22.9%
65,880	BUTLER	27,657	19,073	6,573	2,011	12,500 R	69.0%	23.8%	74.4%	25.6%
2,790	CHASE	1,369	969	316	84	653 R	70.8%	23.1%	75.4%	24.6%
3,669	CHAUTAUQUA	1,481	1,236	197	48	1,039 R	83.5%	13.3%	86.3%	13.7%
21,603	CHEROKEE	8,620	6,182	2,005	433	4,177 R	71.7%	23.3%	75.5%	24.5%
2,726	CHEYENNE	1,407	1,173	181	53	992 R	83.4%	12.9%	86.6%	13.4%
2,215	CLARK	1,005	825	120	60	705 R	82.1%	11.9%	87.3%	12.7%
8,535	CLAY	3,820	2,891	677	252	2,214 R	75.7%	17.7%	81.0%	19.0%
9,533	CLOUD	3,930	2,919	761	250	2,158 R	74.3%	19.4%	79.3%	20.7%
8,601	COFFEY	4,068	3,050	727	291	2,323 R	75.0%	17.9%	80.8%	19.2%
1,891	COMANCHE	867	715	102	50	613 R	82.5%	11.8%	87.5%	12.5%
36,311	COWLEY	12,621	8,270	3,551	800	4,719 R	65.5%	28.1%	70.0%	30.0%
39,134	CRAWFORD	14,891	8,624	5,199	1,068	3,425 R	57.9%	34.9%	62.4%	37.6%
2,961	DECATUR	1,452	1,210	178	64	1,032 R	83.3%	12.3%	87.2%	12.8%
19,754	DICKINSON	8,210	6,029	1,609	572	4,420 R	73.4%	19.6%	78.9%	21.1%
7,945	DONIPHAN	3,378	2,606	587	185	2,019 R	77.1%	17.4%	81.6%	18.4%
110,826	DOUGLAS	50,087	14,688	31,195	4,204	16,507 D	29.3%	62.3%	32.0%	68.0%
3,037	EDWARDS	1,319	1,037	212	70	825 R	78.6%	16.1%	83.0%	17.0%
2,882	ELK	1,259	1,048	160	51	888 R	83.2%	12.7%	86.8%	13.2%
28,452	ELLIS	11,947	8,466	2,742	739	5,724 R	70.9%	23.0%	75.5%	24.5%
6,497	ELLSWORTH	2,679	1,969	521	189	1,448 R	73.5%	19.4%	79.1%	20.9%
36,776	FINNEY	10,159	6,350	3,195	614	3,155 R	62.5%	31.4%	66.5%	33.5%
33,848	FORD	7,718	5,114	2,149	455	2,965 R	66.3%	27.8%	70.4%	29.6%
25,992	FRANKLIN	10,965	7,185	2,892	888	4,293 R	65.5%	26.4%	71.3%	28.7%
34,362	GEARY	7,504	4,274	2,722	508	1,552 R	57.0%	36.3%	61.1%	38.9%
2,695	GOVE	1,343	1,140	149	54	991 R	84.9%	11.1%	88.4%	11.6%
2,597	GRAHAM	1,284	1,025	188	71	837 R	79.8%	14.6%	84.5%	15.5%
7,829	GRANT	2,389	1,804	441	144	1,363 R	75.5%	18.5%	80.4%	19.6%
6,006	GRAY	2,066	1,698	263	105	1,435 R	82.2%	12.7%	86.6%	13.4%
1,247	GREELEY	650	534	83	33	451 R	82.2%	12.8%	86.5%	13.5%
6,689	GREENWOOD	2,840	2,160	485	195	1,675 R	76.1%	17.1%	81.7%	18.3%
2,690	HAMILTON	876	705	121	50	584 R	80.5%	13.8%	85.4%	14.6%
6,034	HARPER	2,578	1,996	393	189	1,603 R	77.4%	15.2%	83.5%	16.5%
34,684	HARVEY	14,916	8,668	5,068	1,180	3,600 R	58.1%	34.0%	63.1%	36.9%
4,256	HASKELL	1,354	1,040	245	69	795 R	76.8%	18.1%	80.9%	19.1%
1,916	HODGEMAN	1,017	855	124	38	731 R	84.1%	12.2%	87.3%	12.7%
13,462	JACKSON	5,818	3,939	1,512	367	2,427 R	67.7%	26.0%	72.3%	27.7%
19,126	JEFFERSON	8,337	5,213	2,518	606	2,695 R	62.5%	30.2%	67.4%	32.6%
3,077	JEWELL	1,494	1,223	180	91	1,043 R	81.9%	12.0%	87.2%	12.8%
544,179	JOHNSON	290,090	137,490	129,852	22,748	7,638 R	47.4%	44.8%	51.4%	48.6%
3,977	KEARNY	1,316	1,075	174	67	901 R	81.7%	13.2%	86.1%	13.9%
7,858	KINGMAN	3,334	2,530	599	205	1,931 R	75.9%	18.0%	80.9%	19.1%
2,553	KIOWA	1,079	900	114	65	786 R	83.4%	10.6%	88.8%	11.2%
21,607	LABETTE	8,107	5,335	2,291	481	3,044 R	65.8%	28.3%	70.0%	30.0%
1,750	LANE	871	718	106	47	612 R	82.4%	12.2%	87.1%	12.9%
76,227	LEAVENWORTH	30,301	17,638	10,209	2,454	7,429 R	58.2%	33.7%	63.3%	36.7%
3,241	LINCOLN	1,464	1,179	215	70	964 R	80.5%	14.7%	84.6%	15.4%
9,656	LINN	4,427	3,484	736	207	2,748 R	78.7%	16.6%	82.6%	17.4%
2,756	LOGAN	1,357	1,132	149	76	983 R	83.4%	11.0%	88.4%	11.6%
33,690	LYON	12,288	6,552	4,649	1,087	1,903 R	53.3%	37.8%	58.5%	41.5%
12,660	MARION	5,624	4,003	1,204	417	2,799 R	71.2%	21.4%	76.9%	23.1%
10,117	MARSHALL	4,673	3,307	1,072	294	2,235 R	70.8%	22.9%	75.5%	24.5%
29,180	MCPHERSON	12,742	8,549	3,226	967	5,323 R	67.1%	25.3%	72.6%	27.4%
4,575	MEADE	1,720	1,415	210	95	1,205 R	82.3%	12.2%	87.1%	12.9%

KANSAS

PRESIDENT 2016

2010 Census Population	County	Total Vote	Republican (Trump)	Democratic (Clinton)	Other	Rep.-Dem. Plurality	Percentage Total Vote Rep.	Dem.	Major Vote Rep.	Dem.
32,787	MIAMI	15,022	10,003	3,991	1,028	6,012 R	66.6%	26.6%	71.5%	28.5%
6,373	MITCHELL	2,942	2,308	477	157	1,831 R	78.5%	16.2%	82.9%	17.1%
35,471	MONTGOMERY	12,004	8,679	2,637	688	6,042 R	72.3%	22.0%	76.7%	23.3%
5,923	MORRIS	2,624	1,820	601	203	1,219 R	69.4%	22.9%	75.2%	24.8%
3,233	MORTON	1,192	995	147	50	848 R	83.5%	12.3%	87.1%	12.9%
10,178	NEMAHA	5,122	4,124	725	273	3,399 R	80.5%	14.2%	85.0%	15.0%
16,512	NEOSHO	6,314	4,431	1,501	382	2,930 R	70.2%	23.8%	74.7%	25.3%
3,107	NESS	1,454	1,228	162	64	1,066 R	84.5%	11.1%	88.3%	11.7%
5,671	NORTON	2,234	1,840	281	113	1,559 R	82.4%	12.6%	86.8%	13.2%
16,295	OSAGE	7,046	4,826	1,753	467	3,073 R	68.5%	24.9%	73.4%	26.6%
3,858	OSBORNE	1,788	1,460	233	95	1,227 R	81.7%	13.0%	86.2%	13.8%
6,091	OTTAWA	2,903	2,283	424	196	1,859 R	78.6%	14.6%	84.3%	15.7%
6,973	PAWNEE	2,661	1,904	579	178	1,325 R	71.6%	21.8%	76.7%	23.3%
5,642	PHILLIPS	2,664	2,233	300	131	1,933 R	83.8%	11.3%	88.2%	11.8%
21,604	POTTAWATOMIE	10,693	7,612	2,225	856	5,387 R	71.2%	20.8%	77.4%	22.6%
9,656	PRATT	3,842	2,838	771	233	2,067 R	73.9%	20.1%	78.6%	21.4%
2,519	RAWLINS	1,472	1,220	163	89	1,057 R	82.9%	11.1%	88.2%	11.8%
64,511	RENO	24,210	15,513	6,837	1,860	8,676 R	64.1%	28.2%	69.4%	30.6%
4,980	REPUBLIC	2,529	2,024	375	130	1,649 R	80.0%	14.8%	84.4%	15.6%
10,083	RICE	3,804	2,837	695	272	2,142 R	74.6%	18.3%	80.3%	19.7%
71,115	RILEY	21,532	10,107	9,341	2,084	766 R	46.9%	43.4%	52.0%	48.0%
5,181	ROOKS	2,419	2,031	275	113	1,756 R	84.0%	11.4%	88.1%	11.9%
3,307	RUSH	1,503	1,197	233	73	964 R	79.6%	15.5%	83.7%	16.3%
6,970	RUSSELL	3,193	2,574	461	158	2,113 R	80.6%	14.4%	84.8%	15.2%
55,606	SALINE	22,064	13,828	6,317	1,919	7,511 R	62.7%	28.6%	68.6%	31.4%
4,936	SCOTT	2,202	1,865	236	101	1,629 R	84.7%	10.7%	88.8%	11.2%
498,365	SEDGWICK	188,783	104,353	69,627	14,803	34,726 R	55.3%	36.9%	60.0%	40.0%
22,952	SEWARD	5,038	3,159	1,628	251	1,531 R	62.7%	32.3%	66.0%	34.0%
177,934	SHAWNEE	75,406	35,934	33,926	5,546	2,008 R	47.7%	45.0%	51.4%	48.6%
2,556	SHERIDAN	1,374	1,197	127	50	1,070 R	87.1%	9.2%	90.4%	9.6%
6,010	SHERMAN	2,612	2,089	347	176	1,742 R	80.0%	13.3%	85.8%	14.2%
3,853	SMITH	2,042	1,661	297	84	1,364 R	81.3%	14.5%	84.8%	15.2%
4,437	STAFFORD	1,896	1,490	304	102	1,186 R	78.6%	16.0%	83.1%	16.9%
2,235	STANTON	637	492	115	30	377 R	77.2%	18.1%	81.1%	18.9%
5,724	STEVENS	1,891	1,599	220	72	1,379 R	84.6%	11.6%	87.9%	12.1%
24,132	SUMNER	9,722	6,984	2,076	662	4,908 R	71.8%	21.4%	77.1%	22.9%
7,900	THOMAS	3,576	2,908	473	195	2,435 R	81.3%	13.2%	86.0%	14.0%
3,001	TREGO	1,482	1,227	198	57	1,029 R	82.8%	13.4%	86.1%	13.9%
7,053	WABAUNSEE	3,380	2,372	776	232	1,596 R	70.2%	23.0%	75.3%	24.7%
1,485	WALLACE	798	721	46	31	675 R	90.4%	5.8%	94.0%	6.0%
5,799	WASHINGTON	2,765	2,194	387	184	1,807 R	79.3%	14.0%	85.0%	15.0%
2,234	WICHITA	956	769	140	47	629 R	80.4%	14.6%	84.6%	15.4%
9,409	WILSON	3,591	2,788	594	209	2,194 R	77.6%	16.5%	82.4%	17.6%
3,309	WOODSON	1,443	1,082	273	88	809 R	75.0%	18.9%	79.9%	20.1%
157,505	WYANDOTTE	48,781	15,806	30,146	2,829	14,340 D	32.4%	61.8%	34.4%	65.6%
2,853,118	TOTAL	1,184,402	671,018	427,005	86,379	244,013 R	56.7%	36.1%	61.1%	38.9%

KANSAS
SENATOR 2016

2010 Census Population	County	Total Vote	Republican (Moran)	Democratic (Wiesner)	Other	Rep.-Dem. Plurality	Percentage Total Vote Rep.	Dem.	Major Vote Rep.	Dem.
13,371	ALLEN	5,402	3,889	1,192	321	2,697 R	72.0%	22.1%	76.5%	23.5%
8,102	ANDERSON	3,304	2,426	717	161	1,709 R	73.4%	21.7%	77.2%	22.8%
16,924	ATCHISON	6,513	4,295	1,917	301	2,378 R	65.9%	29.4%	69.1%	30.9%
4,861	BARBER	2,225	1,836	275	114	1,561 R	82.5%	12.4%	87.0%	13.0%
27,674	BARTON	10,172	8,321	1,308	543	7,013 R	81.8%	12.9%	86.4%	13.6%
15,173	BOURBON	6,082	4,427	1,308	347	3,119 R	72.8%	21.5%	77.2%	22.8%
9,984	BROWN	4,047	3,105	751	191	2,354 R	76.7%	18.6%	80.5%	19.5%
65,880	BUTLER	27,528	19,705	5,915	1,908	13,790 R	71.6%	21.5%	76.9%	23.1%
2,790	CHASE	1,375	1,021	271	83	750 R	74.3%	19.7%	79.0%	21.0%
3,669	CHAUTAUQUA	1,463	1,186	198	79	988 R	81.1%	13.5%	85.7%	14.3%
21,603	CHEROKEE	8,552	5,938	2,165	449	3,773 R	69.4%	25.3%	73.3%	26.7%
2,726	CHEYENNE	1,400	1,227	125	48	1,102 R	87.6%	8.9%	90.8%	9.2%
2,215	CLARK	994	840	103	51	737 R	84.5%	10.4%	89.1%	10.9%
8,535	CLAY	3,831	3,250	419	162	2,831 R	84.8%	10.9%	88.6%	11.4%
9,533	CLOUD	3,905	3,089	597	219	2,492 R	79.1%	15.3%	83.8%	16.2%
8,601	COFFEY	4,025	3,146	604	275	2,542 R	78.2%	15.0%	83.9%	16.1%
1,891	COMANCHE	866	732	98	36	634 R	84.5%	11.3%	88.2%	11.8%
36,311	COWLEY	12,571	8,530	3,286	755	5,244 R	67.9%	26.1%	72.2%	27.8%
39,134	CRAWFORD	14,802	8,957	5,065	780	3,892 R	60.5%	34.2%	63.9%	36.1%
2,961	DECATUR	1,418	1,237	127	54	1,110 R	87.2%	9.0%	90.7%	9.3%
19,754	DICKINSON	8,173	6,368	1,273	532	5,095 R	77.9%	15.6%	83.3%	16.7%
7,945	DONIPHAN	3,296	2,538	602	156	1,936 R	77.0%	18.3%	80.8%	19.2%
110,826	DOUGLAS	50,329	17,563	30,436	2,330	12,873 D	34.9%	60.5%	36.6%	63.4%
3,037	EDWARDS	1,322	1,078	166	78	912 R	81.5%	12.6%	86.7%	13.3%
2,882	ELK	1,249	1,012	154	83	858 R	81.0%	12.3%	86.8%	13.2%
28,452	ELLIS	11,988	9,319	2,211	458	7,108 R	77.7%	18.4%	80.8%	19.2%
6,497	ELLSWORTH	2,695	2,199	384	112	1,815 R	81.6%	14.2%	85.1%	14.9%
36,776	FINNEY	10,053	7,165	2,348	540	4,817 R	71.3%	23.4%	75.3%	24.7%
33,848	FORD	7,590	5,530	1,655	405	3,875 R	72.9%	21.8%	77.0%	23.0%
25,992	FRANKLIN	10,863	7,394	2,735	734	4,659 R	68.1%	25.2%	73.0%	27.0%
34,362	GEARY	7,443	4,918	2,187	338	2,731 R	66.1%	29.4%	69.2%	30.8%
2,695	GOVE	1,356	1,200	117	39	1,083 R	88.5%	8.6%	91.1%	8.9%
2,597	GRAHAM	1,284	1,095	135	54	960 R	85.3%	10.5%	89.0%	11.0%
7,829	GRANT	2,344	1,897	316	131	1,581 R	80.9%	13.5%	85.7%	14.3%
6,006	GRAY	2,060	1,756	222	82	1,534 R	85.2%	10.8%	88.8%	11.2%
1,247	GREELEY	641	570	48	23	522 R	88.9%	7.5%	92.2%	7.8%
6,689	GREENWOOD	2,802	2,164	460	178	1,704 R	77.2%	16.4%	82.5%	17.5%
2,690	HAMILTON	863	729	87	47	642 R	84.5%	10.1%	89.3%	10.7%
6,034	HARPER	2,518	2,021	371	126	1,650 R	80.3%	14.7%	84.5%	15.5%
34,684	HARVEY	14,877	9,815	4,237	825	5,578 R	66.0%	28.5%	69.8%	30.2%
4,256	HASKELL	1,344	1,137	158	49	979 R	84.6%	11.8%	87.8%	12.2%
1,916	HODGEMAN	1,012	889	83	40	806 R	87.8%	8.2%	91.5%	8.5%
13,462	JACKSON	5,831	4,115	1,425	291	2,690 R	70.6%	24.4%	74.3%	25.7%
19,126	JEFFERSON	8,364	5,456	2,504	404	2,952 R	65.2%	29.9%	68.5%	31.5%
3,077	JEWELL	1,467	1,263	127	77	1,136 R	86.1%	8.7%	90.9%	9.1%
544,179	JOHNSON	288,702	160,074	112,283	16,345	47,791 R	55.4%	38.9%	58.8%	41.2%
3,977	KEARNY	1,344	1,132	161	51	971 R	84.2%	12.0%	87.5%	12.5%
7,858	KINGMAN	3,337	2,661	490	186	2,171 R	79.7%	14.7%	84.4%	15.6%
2,553	KIOWA	1,080	950	83	47	867 R	88.0%	7.7%	92.0%	8.0%
21,607	LABETTE	8,039	5,212	2,319	508	2,893 R	64.8%	28.8%	69.2%	30.8%
1,750	LANE	881	763	79	39	684 R	86.6%	9.0%	90.6%	9.4%
76,227	LEAVENWORTH	30,267	18,287	10,171	1,809	8,116 R	60.4%	33.6%	64.3%	35.7%
3,241	LINCOLN	1,470	1,234	167	69	1,067 R	83.9%	11.4%	88.1%	11.9%
9,656	LINN	4,341	3,261	796	284	2,465 R	75.1%	18.3%	80.4%	19.6%
2,756	LOGAN	1,346	1,197	106	43	1,091 R	88.9%	7.9%	91.9%	8.1%
33,690	LYON	12,303	7,925	3,760	618	4,165 R	64.4%	30.6%	67.8%	32.2%
12,660	MARION	5,652	4,490	913	249	3,577 R	79.4%	16.2%	83.1%	16.9%
10,117	MARSHALL	4,649	3,591	867	191	2,724 R	77.2%	18.6%	80.6%	19.4%
29,180	MCPHERSON	12,777	9,637	2,527	613	7,110 R	75.4%	19.8%	79.2%	20.8%
4,575	MEADE	1,712	1,491	158	63	1,333 R	87.1%	9.2%	90.4%	9.6%

KANSAS

SENATOR 2016

2010 Census Population	County	Total Vote	Republican (Moran)	Democratic (Wiesner)	Other	Rep.-Dem. Plurality	Percentage			
							Total Vote		Major Vote	
							Rep.	Dem.	Rep.	Dem.
32,787	MIAMI	14,937	10,448	3,773	716	6,675 R	69.9%	25.3%	73.5%	26.5%
6,373	MITCHELL	2,913	2,463	336	114	2,127 R	84.6%	11.5%	88.0%	12.0%
35,471	MONTGOMERY	11,853	8,232	2,702	919	5,530 R	69.5%	22.8%	75.3%	24.7%
5,923	MORRIS	2,636	2,087	420	129	1,667 R	79.2%	15.9%	83.2%	16.8%
3,233	MORTON	1,186	1,010	108	68	902 R	85.2%	9.1%	90.3%	9.7%
10,178	NEMAHA	5,126	4,294	667	165	3,627 R	83.8%	13.0%	86.6%	13.4%
16,512	NEOSHO	6,251	4,378	1,427	446	2,951 R	70.0%	22.8%	75.4%	24.6%
3,107	NESS	1,442	1,290	109	43	1,181 R	89.5%	7.6%	92.2%	7.8%
5,671	NORTON	2,243	1,895	238	110	1,657 R	84.5%	10.6%	88.8%	11.2%
16,295	OSAGE	7,107	4,977	1,636	494	3,341 R	70.0%	23.0%	75.3%	24.7%
3,858	OSBORNE	1,794	1,521	188	85	1,333 R	84.8%	10.5%	89.0%	11.0%
6,091	OTTAWA	2,887	2,316	354	217	1,962 R	80.2%	12.3%	86.7%	13.3%
6,973	PAWNEE	2,677	2,108	432	137	1,676 R	78.7%	16.1%	83.0%	17.0%
5,642	PHILLIPS	2,641	2,316	211	114	2,105 R	87.7%	8.0%	91.7%	8.3%
21,604	POTTAWATOMIE	10,726	8,407	1,829	490	6,578 R	78.4%	17.1%	82.1%	17.9%
9,656	PRATT	3,837	3,019	602	216	2,417 R	78.7%	15.7%	83.4%	16.6%
2,519	RAWLINS	1,470	1,263	126	81	1,137 R	85.9%	8.6%	90.9%	9.1%
64,511	RENO	24,297	17,218	5,532	1,547	11,686 R	70.9%	22.8%	75.7%	24.3%
4,980	REPUBLIC	2,501	2,117	274	110	1,843 R	84.6%	11.0%	88.5%	11.5%
10,083	RICE	3,820	2,979	611	230	2,368 R	78.0%	16.0%	83.0%	17.0%
71,115	RILEY	21,635	13,438	7,170	1,027	6,268 R	62.1%	33.1%	65.2%	34.8%
5,181	ROOKS	2,410	2,104	192	114	1,912 R	87.3%	8.0%	91.6%	8.4%
3,307	RUSH	1,509	1,281	169	59	1,112 R	84.9%	11.2%	88.3%	11.7%
6,970	RUSSELL	3,174	2,635	380	159	2,255 R	83.0%	12.0%	87.4%	12.6%
55,606	SALINE	21,915	15,123	5,117	1,675	10,006 R	69.0%	23.3%	74.7%	25.3%
4,936	SCOTT	2,183	1,902	187	94	1,715 R	87.1%	8.6%	91.0%	9.0%
498,365	SEDGWICK	186,810	112,455	62,816	11,539	49,639 R	60.2%	33.6%	64.2%	35.8%
22,952	SEWARD	4,716	3,168	1,213	335	1,955 R	67.2%	25.7%	72.3%	27.7%
177,934	SHAWNEE	76,036	41,689	30,925	3,422	10,764 R	54.8%	40.7%	57.4%	42.6%
2,556	SHERIDAN	1,358	1,201	119	38	1,082 R	88.4%	8.8%	91.0%	9.0%
6,010	SHERMAN	2,577	2,158	296	123	1,862 R	83.7%	11.5%	87.9%	12.1%
3,853	SMITH	2,049	1,744	219	86	1,525 R	85.1%	10.7%	88.8%	11.2%
4,437	STAFFORD	1,873	1,563	230	80	1,333 R	83.4%	12.3%	87.2%	12.8%
2,235	STANTON	620	506	78	36	428 R	81.6%	12.6%	86.6%	13.4%
5,724	STEVENS	1,844	1,600	169	75	1,431 R	86.8%	9.2%	90.4%	9.6%
24,132	SUMNER	9,619	6,825	2,124	670	4,701 R	71.0%	22.1%	76.3%	23.7%
7,900	THOMAS	3,576	3,012	417	147	2,595 R	84.2%	11.7%	87.8%	12.2%
3,001	TREGO	1,467	1,202	203	62	999 R	81.9%	13.8%	85.6%	14.4%
7,053	WABAUNSEE	3,398	2,580	619	199	1,961 R	75.9%	18.2%	80.7%	19.3%
1,485	WALLACE	794	733	35	26	698 R	92.3%	4.4%	95.4%	4.6%
5,799	WASHINGTON	2,736	2,341	285	110	2,056 R	85.6%	10.4%	89.1%	10.9%
2,234	WICHITA	947	793	114	40	679 R	83.7%	12.0%	87.4%	12.6%
9,409	WILSON	3,562	2,806	544	212	2,262 R	78.8%	15.3%	83.8%	16.2%
3,309	WOODSON	1,412	1,063	257	92	806 R	75.3%	18.2%	80.5%	19.5%
157,505	WYANDOTTE	47,219	15,863	28,525	2,831	12,662 D	33.6%	60.4%	35.7%	64.3%
2,853,118	TOTAL	1,177,922	732,376	379,740	65,806	352,636 R	62.2%	32.2%	65.9%	34.1%

KANSAS

HOUSE OF REPRESENTATIVES

CD	Year	Total Vote	Republican Vote	Republican Candidate	Democratic Vote	Democratic Candidate	Other Vote	Rep.-Dem. Plurality	Total Vote Rep.	Total Vote Dem.	Major Vote Rep.	Major Vote Dem.
1	2016	257,971	169,992	MARSHALL, ROGER			87,979	169,992 R	65.9%		100.0%	
1	2014	204,161	138,764	HUELSKAMP, TIM*	65,397	SHEROW, JAMES E.		73,367 R	68.0%	32.0%	68.0%	32.0%
1	2012	211,337	211,337	HUELSKAMP, TIM*				211,337 R	100.0%		100.0%	
2	2016	297,401	181,228	JENKINS, LYNN*	96,840	POTTER, BRITANI	19,333	84,388 R	60.9%	32.6%	65.2%	34.8%
2	2014	225,686	128,742	JENKINS, LYNN*	87,153	WAKEFIELD, MARGIE	9,791	41,589 R	57.0%	38.6%	59.6%	40.4%
2	2012	293,718	167,463	JENKINS, LYNN*	113,735	SCHLINGENSIEPEN, TOBIAS	12,520	53,728 R	57.0%	38.7%	59.6%	40.4%
3	2016	343,113	176,022	YODER, KEVIN*	139,300	SIDIE, JAY	27,791	36,722 R	51.3%	40.6%	55.8%	44.2%
3	2014	224,077	134,493	YODER, KEVIN*	89,584	KULTALA, KELLY		44,909 R	60.0%	40.0%	60.0%	40.0%
3	2012	293,762	201,087	YODER, KEVIN*			92,675	201,087 R	68.5%		100.0%	
4	2016	275,251	166,998	POMPEO, MIKE*	81,495	GIROUX, DANIEL B.	26,758	85,503 R	60.7%	29.6%	67.2%	32.8%
4	2014	208,153	138,757	POMPEO, MIKE*	69,396	SCHUCKMAN, PERRY		69,361 R	66.7%	33.3%	66.7%	33.3%
4	2012	258,922	161,094	POMPEO, MIKE*	81,770	TILLMAN, ROBERT	16,058	79,324 R	62.2%	31.6%	66.3%	33.7%
TOTAL	2016	1,173,736	694,240		317,635		161,861	376,605 R	59.1%	27.1%	68.6%	31.4%
TOTAL	2014	862,077	540,756		311,530		9,791	229,226 R	62.7%	36.1%	63.4%	36.6%
TOTAL	2012	1,057,739	740,981		195,505		121,253	545,476 R	70.1%	18.5%	79.1%	20.9%

Note: An asterisk (*) denotes incumbent.

KANSAS

GENERAL AND PRIMARY ELECTIONS

2016 GENERAL ELECTIONS: OTHER VOTES

President   Other vote was 55,406 Libertarian (Gary Johnson), 23,506 Independent (Jill Stein), 6,520 Write-in (Evan McMullin), 947 Write-in (Scattered Write-in)

Senate   Other vote was 65,760 Libertarian (Robert Garrard), 46 Write-in (Della Smith)

House   Other vote was:

CD 1   67,739 Independent (Alan LaPolice), 19,366 Libertarian (Kerry Burt), 874 Write-in (Tim Huelskamp)
CD 2   19,333 Libertarian (James Bales)
CD 3   27,791 Libertarian (Steven Hohe)
CD 4   19,021 Independent (Miranda Allen), 7,737 Libertarian (Gordon Bakken)

2016 PRIMARY ELECTIONS: SUPPLEMENTARY INFORMATION

Primary	March 5, 2016 (Presidential caucus) August 2, 2016 (Congress)	**Registration** (as of May 5, 2016)	1,705,537	Republican Democratic Libertarian Unaffiliated	760,159 408,601 13,181 523,596

Primary Type   Semi-open—Registered Democrats and Republicans could vote only in their party's primary. "Unaffiliated" voters could participate in either primary, although they had to change their registration to that party on primary day.

KANSAS

GENERAL AND PRIMARY ELECTIONS

	REPUBLICAN PRIMARIES			DEMOCRATIC PRIMARIES		
Senator	Moran, Jerry*	230,907	79.1%	Wiesner, Patrick	59,522	62.9%
	Smith, Della Jean "D.J."	61,056	20.9%	Singh, Monique	35,042	37.1%
	TOTAL	291,963		TOTAL	94,564	
Congressional District 1	Marshall, Roger	59,889	56.6%			
	Huelskamp, Tim*	45,997	43.4%			
	TOTAL	105,886				
Congressional District 2	Jenkins, Lynn*	54,958	100.0%	Potter, Britani	24,383	100.0%
	TOTAL	54,958		TOTAL	24,383	
Congressional District 3	Yoder, Kevin*	37,681	63.6%	Sidie, Jay	13,879	41.5%
	Goode, Greg	21,563	36.4%	McLaughlin, Nathaniel W.	12,105	36.2%
				Marselus, Reginald "Reggie"	7,435	22.2%
	TOTAL	59,244		TOTAL	33,419	
Congressional District 4	Pompeo, Mike*	56,808	100.0%	Giroux, Daniel B.	9,489	51.5%
				Tillman, Robert	8,936	48.5%
	TOTAL	56,808		TOTAL	18,425	

Note: An asterisk (*) denotes incumbent.

KENTUCKY

Congressional districts first established for elections held in 2012

6 members

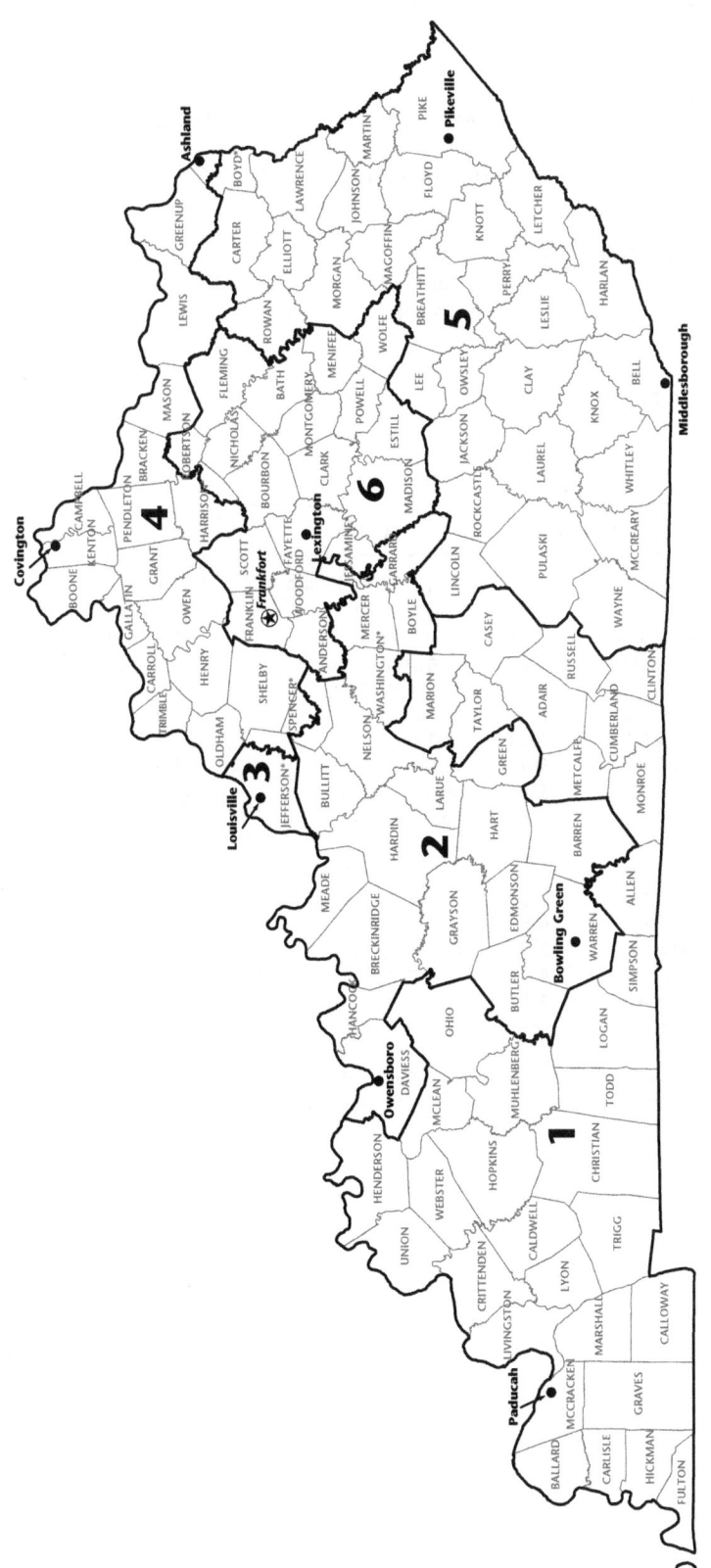

KENTUCKY

GOVERNOR
Matt Bevin (R). Elected 2015 to a four-year term.

SENATORS (2 Republicans)
Mitch McConnell (R). Re-elected 2014 to a six-year term. Previously elected 2008, 2002, 1996, 1990, 1984.

Rand Paul (R). Re-elected 2016 to a six-year term. Previously elected 2010.

REPRESENTATIVES (5 Republicans, 1 Democrat)
1. James R. Comer (R)
2. Brett Guthrie (R)
3. John Yarmuth (D)
4. Thomas Massie (R)
5. Harold Rogers (R)
6. Garland "Andy" Barr (R)

POSTWAR VOTE FOR PRESIDENT

Year	Total Vote	Republican Vote	Republican Candidate	Democratic Vote	Democratic Candidate	Other Vote	Rep.-Dem. Plurality	Total Vote Rep.	Total Vote Dem.	Major Vote Rep.	Major Vote Dem.
2016**	1,924,149	1,202,971	Trump, Donald J.	628,854	Clinton, Hillary Rodham	92,324	574,117 R	62.5%	32.7%	65.7%	34.3%
2012	1,797,212	1,087,190	Romney, W. Mitt	679,370	Obama, Barack H.*	30,652	407,820 R	60.5%	37.8%	61.5%	38.5%
2008	1,826,620	1,048,462	McCain, John S. III	751,985	Obama, Barack H.	26,173	296,477 R	57.4%	41.2%	58.2%	41.8%
2004	1,795,882	1,069,439	Bush, George W.*	712,733	Kerry, John F.	13,710	356,706 R	59.5%	39.7%	60.0%	40.0%
2000**	1,544,187	872,492	Bush, George W.	638,898	Gore, Albert Jr.	32,797	233,594 R	56.5%	41.4%	57.7%	42.3%
1996**	1,388,708	623,283	Dole, Robert "Bob"	636,614	Clinton, Bill*	128,811	13,331 D	44.9%	45.8%	49.5%	50.5%
1992**	1,492,900	617,178	Bush, George H.*	665,104	Clinton, Bill	210,618	47,926 D	41.3%	44.6%	48.1%	51.9%
1988	1,322,517	734,281	Bush, George H.	580,368	Dukakis, Michael S.	7,868	153,913 R	55.5%	43.9%	55.9%	44.1%
1984	1,369,345	821,702	Reagan, Ronald*	539,539	Mondale, Walter F.	8,104	282,163 R	60.0%	39.4%	60.4%	39.6%
1980**	1,294,627	635,274	Reagan, Ronald	616,417	Carter, Jimmy*	42,936	18,857 R	49.1%	47.6%	50.8%	49.2%
1976	1,167,142	531,852	Ford, Gerald R.*	615,717	Carter, Jimmy	19,573	83,865 D	45.6%	52.8%	46.3%	53.7%
1972	1,067,499	676,446	Nixon, Richard M.*	371,159	McGovern, George S.	19,894	305,287 R	63.4%	34.8%	64.6%	35.4%
1968**	1,055,893	462,411	Nixon, Richard M.	397,541	Humphrey, Hubert Horatio Jr.	195,941	64,870 R	43.8%	37.6%	53.8%	46.2%
1964	1,046,105	372,977	Goldwater, Barry M. Sr.	669,659	Johnson, Lyndon B.*	3,469	296,682 D	35.7%	64.0%	35.8%	64.2%
1960	1,124,462	602,607	Nixon, Richard M.	521,855	Kennedy, John F.		80,752 R	53.6%	46.4%	53.6%	46.4%
1956	1,053,805	572,192	Eisenhower, Dwight D.*	476,453	Stevenson, Adlai E. II	5,160	95,739 R	54.3%	45.2%	54.6%	45.4%
1952	993,148	495,029	Eisenhower, Dwight D.	495,729	Stevenson, Adlai E. II	2,390	700 D	49.8%	49.9%	50.0%	50.0%
1948	822,658	341,210	Dewey, Thomas E.	466,756	Truman, Harry S.*	14,692	125,546 D	41.5%	56.7%	42.2%	57.8%

Note: An asterisk (*) denotes incumbent. **In past elections, the other vote included: 2016 - 53,752 Independent (Gary Johnson); 2000 - 23,192 Green (Ralph Nader); 1996 - 120,396 Reform (Ross Perot); 1992 - 203,944 Independent (Perot); 1980 - 31,127 Independent (John Anderson); 1968 - 193,098 American Independent (George Wallace).

KENTUCKY

POSTWAR VOTE FOR GOVERNOR

Year	Total Vote	Republican		Democratic		Other Vote	Rep.-Dem. Plurality	Percentage			
								Total Vote		Major Vote	
		Vote	Candidate	Vote	Candidate			Rep.	Dem.	Rep.	Dem.
2015	973,692	511,374	Bevin, Matt G.	426,620	Conway, Jack	35,698	84,754 R	52.5%	43.8%	54.5%	45.5%
2011	833,139	294,034	Williams, David Lynn	464,245	Beshear, Steven L.*	74,860	170,211 D	35.3%	55.7%	38.8%	61.2%
2007	1,055,325	435,773	Fletcher, Ernest*	619,552	Beshear, Steven L.		183,779 D	41.3%	58.7%	41.3%	58.7%
2003	1,083,443	596,284	Fletcher, Ernest	487,159	Chandler, Ben		109,125 R	55.0%	45.0%	55.0%	45.0%
1999**	580,074	128,788	Martin, Peppy	352,099	Patton, Paul E.*	99,187	223,311 D	22.2%	60.7%	26.8%	73.2%
1995	983,979	479,227	Forgy, Larry	500,787	Patton, Paul E.	3,965	21,560 D	48.7%	50.9%	48.9%	51.1%
1991	834,920	294,452	Harper, John	540,468	Jones, Brereton C.		246,016 D	35.3%	64.7%	35.3%	64.7%
1987	777,815	273,141	Harper, John	504,674	Wilkinson, Wallace G.		231,533 D	35.1%	64.9%	35.1%	64.9%
1983	1,030,628	454,650	Bunning, Jim	561,674	Collins, Martha Layne	14,304	107,024 D	44.1%	54.5%	44.7%	55.3%
1979	939,366	381,278	Nunn, Louie B.	558,088	Brown, J. Y. Jr.		176,810 D	40.6%	59.4%	40.6%	59.4%
1975	748,157	277,998	Gable, Robert E.	470,159	Carroll, Julian*		192,161 D	37.2%	62.8%	37.2%	62.8%
1971	930,792	412,653	Emberton, Thomas	470,722	Ford, Wendell H.	47,417	58,069 D	44.3%	50.6%	46.7%	53.3%
1967	886,146	453,323	Nunn, Louie B.	425,674	Ward, Henry	7,149	27,649 R	51.2%	48.0%	51.6%	48.4%
1963	886,047	436,496	Nunn, Louie B.	449,551	Breathitt, Edward T.		13,055 D	49.3%	50.7%	49.3%	50.7%
1959	853,005	336,456	Robsion, John M. Jr.	516,549	Combs, Bert T.		180,093 D	39.4%	60.6%	39.4%	60.6%
1955	778,488	322,671	Denney, Edwin R.	451,647	Chandler, Happy	4,170	128,976 D	41.4%	58.0%	41.7%	58.3%
1951	634,359	288,014	Siler, Eugene	346,345	Wetherby, Lawrence W.		58,331 D	45.4%	54.6%	45.4%	54.6%
1947	675,551	287,756	Dummit, Eldon S.	387,795	Clements, Earle C.		100,039 D	42.6%	57.4%	42.6%	57.4%

Note: An asterisk (*) denotes incumbent. **In past elections, the other vote included: 1999 - 88,930 Reform (Gatewood Galbraith).

POSTWAR VOTE FOR SENATOR

Year	Total Vote	Republican		Democratic		Other Vote	Rep.-Dem. Plurality	Percentage			
								Total Vote		Major Vote	
		Vote	Candidate	Vote	Candidate			Rep.	Dem.	Rep.	Dem.
2016	1,903,465	1,090,177	Paul, Rand*	813,246	Gray, Jim	42	276,931 R	57.3%	42.7%	57.3%	42.7%
2014	1,435,868	806,787	McConnell, Mitch*	584,698	Grimes, Alison Lundergan	44,383	222,089 R	56.2%	40.7%	58.0%	42.0%
2010	1,356,468	755,411	Paul, Rand	599,843	Conway, Jack	1,214	155,568 R	55.7%	44.2%	55.7%	44.3%
2008	1,800,821	953,816	McConnell, Mitch*	847,005	Lunsford, Bruce		106,811 R	53.0%	47.0%	53.0%	47.0%
2004	1,724,362	873,507	Bunning, Jim*	850,855	Mongiardo, Frank Daniel		22,652 R	50.7%	49.3%	50.7%	49.3%
2002	1,131,475	731,679	McConnell, Mitch*	399,634	Weinberg, Lois Combs	162	332,045 R	64.7%	35.3%	64.7%	35.3%
1998	1,145,414	569,817	Bunning, Jim	563,051	Baesler, Scott	12,546	6,766 R	49.7%	49.2%	50.3%	49.7%
1996	1,307,046	724,794	McConnell, Mitch*	560,012	Beshear, Steven L.	22,240	164,782 R	55.5%	42.8%	56.4%	43.6%
1992	1,330,858	476,604	Williams, David Lynn	836,888	Ford, Wendell H.*	17,366	360,284 D	35.8%	62.9%	36.3%	63.7%
1990	916,010	478,034	McConnell, Mitch*	437,976	Sloane, Harvey		40,058 R	52.2%	47.8%	52.2%	47.8%
1986	677,280	173,330	Andrews, Jackson M.	503,775	Ford, Wendell H.*	175	330,445 D	25.6%	74.4%	25.6%	74.4%
1984	1,292,407	644,990	McConnell, Mitch	639,721	Huddleston, Walter*	7,696	5,269 R	49.9%	49.5%	50.2%	49.8%
1980	1,106,890	386,029	Foust, Mary Louise	720,861	Ford, Wendell H.*		334,832 D	34.9%	65.1%	34.9%	65.1%
1978	476,783	175,766	Guenthner, Louie	290,730	Huddleston, Walter*	10,287	114,964 D	36.9%	61.0%	37.7%	62.3%
1974	745,994	328,982	Cook, Marlow W.*	399,406	Ford, Wendell H.	17,606	70,424 D	44.1%	53.5%	45.2%	54.8%
1972	1,037,861	494,337	Nunn, Louie B.	528,550	Huddleston, Walter	14,974	34,213 D	47.6%	50.9%	48.3%	51.7%
1968	942,865	484,260	Cook, Marlow W.	448,960	Peden, Katherine	9,645	35,300 R	51.4%	47.6%	51.9%	48.1%
1966	749,884	483,805	Cooper, John Sherman*	266,079	Brown, John Young		217,726 R	64.5%	35.5%	64.5%	35.5%
1962	820,088	432,648	Morton, Thruston B.*	387,440	Wyatt, Wilson W.		45,208 R	52.8%	47.2%	52.8%	47.2%
1960	1,088,377	644,087	Cooper, John Sherman*	444,290	Johnson, Keen		199,797 R	59.2%	40.8%	59.2%	40.8%
1956	1,006,825	506,903	Morton, Thruston B.	499,922	Clements, Earle C.*		6,981 R	50.3%	49.7%	50.3%	49.7%
1956S**	1,011,645	538,505	Cooper, John Sherman	473,140	Wetherby, Lawrence W.		65,365 R	53.2%	46.8%	53.2%	46.8%
1954	797,057	362,948	Cooper, John Sherman*	434,109	Barkley, Alben W.		71,161 D	45.5%	54.5%	45.5%	54.5%
1952S**	960,228	494,576	Cooper, John Sherman	465,652	Underwood, Thomas R.		28,924 R	51.5%	48.5%	51.5%	48.5%
1950	612,617	278,368	Dawson, Charles I.	334,249	Clements, Earle C.*		55,881 D	45.4%	54.6%	45.4%	54.6%
1948	794,469	383,776	Cooper, John Sherman	408,256	Chapman, Virgil	2,437	24,480 D	48.3%	51.4%	48.5%	51.5%
1946S**	615,119	327,652	Cooper, John Sherman	285,829	Brown, John Young	1,638	41,823 R	53.3%	46.5%	53.4%	46.6%

Note: An asterisk (*) denotes incumbent. **The elections in 1946 and 1952 as well as one in 1956 were for short terms to fill vacancies.

KENTUCKY

PRESIDENT 2016

2010 Census Population	County	Total Vote	Republican (Trump)	Democratic (Clinton)	Other	Rep.-Dem. Plurality		Percentage			
								Total Vote		Major Vote	
								Rep.	Dem.	Rep.	Dem.
18,656	ADAIR	8,233	6,637	1,323	273	5,314	R	80.6%	16.1%	83.4%	16.6%
19,956	ALLEN	8,096	6,466	1,349	281	5,117	R	79.9%	16.7%	82.7%	17.3%
21,421	ANDERSON	11,422	8,242	2,634	546	5,608	R	72.2%	23.1%	75.8%	24.2%
8,249	BALLARD	4,101	3,161	816	124	2,345	R	77.1%	19.9%	79.5%	20.5%
42,173	BARREN	18,488	13,483	4,275	730	9,208	R	72.9%	23.1%	75.9%	24.1%
11,591	BATH	4,587	3,082	1,361	144	1,721	R	67.2%	29.7%	69.4%	30.6%
28,691	BELL	9,718	7,764	1,720	234	6,044	R	79.9%	17.7%	81.9%	18.1%
118,811	BOONE	57,618	39,082	15,026	3,510	24,056	R	67.8%	26.1%	72.2%	27.8%
19,985	BOURBON	8,803	5,569	2,791	443	2,778	R	63.3%	31.7%	66.6%	33.4%
49,542	BOYD	20,454	13,591	6,021	842	7,570	R	66.4%	29.4%	69.3%	30.7%
28,432	BOYLE	12,946	8,040	4,281	625	3,759	R	62.1%	33.1%	65.3%	34.7%
8,488	BRACKEN	3,527	2,711	705	111	2,006	R	76.9%	20.0%	79.4%	20.6%
13,878	BREATHITT	5,738	3,991	1,537	210	2,454	R	69.6%	26.8%	72.2%	27.8%
20,059	BRECKINRIDGE	8,774	6,484	1,960	330	4,524	R	73.9%	22.3%	76.8%	23.2%
74,319	BULLITT	36,069	26,210	8,255	1,604	17,955	R	72.7%	22.9%	76.0%	24.0%
12,690	BUTLER	5,576	4,428	947	201	3,481	R	79.4%	17.0%	82.4%	17.6%
12,984	CALDWELL	5,975	4,507	1,260	208	3,247	R	75.4%	21.1%	78.2%	21.8%
37,191	CALLOWAY	16,049	10,367	4,749	933	5,618	R	64.6%	29.6%	68.6%	31.4%
90,336	CAMPBELL	42,510	25,050	14,658	2,802	10,392	R	58.9%	34.5%	63.1%	36.9%
5,104	CARLISLE	2,601	2,094	432	75	1,662	R	80.5%	16.6%	82.9%	17.1%
10,811	CARROLL	3,855	2,588	1,106	161	1,482	R	67.1%	28.7%	70.1%	29.9%
27,720	CARTER	10,278	7,587	2,276	415	5,311	R	73.8%	22.1%	76.9%	23.1%
15,955	CASEY	6,439	5,482	767	190	4,715	R	85.1%	11.9%	87.7%	12.3%
73,955	CHRISTIAN	22,083	14,108	7,188	787	6,920	R	63.9%	32.5%	66.2%	33.8%
35,613	CLARK	16,205	10,710	4,706	789	6,004	R	66.1%	29.0%	69.5%	30.5%
21,730	CLAY	6,767	5,861	752	154	5,109	R	86.6%	11.1%	88.6%	11.4%
10,272	CLINTON	4,462	3,809	547	106	3,262	R	85.4%	12.3%	87.4%	12.6%
9,315	CRITTENDEN	4,037	3,290	617	130	2,673	R	81.5%	15.3%	84.2%	15.8%
6,856	CUMBERLAND	3,066	2,502	459	105	2,043	R	81.6%	15.0%	84.5%	15.5%
96,656	DAVIESS	45,807	28,907	14,163	2,737	14,744	R	63.1%	30.9%	67.1%	32.9%
12,161	EDMONSON	5,244	4,135	979	130	3,156	R	78.9%	18.7%	80.9%	19.1%
7,852	ELLIOTT	2,855	2,000	740	115	1,260	R	70.1%	25.9%	73.0%	27.0%
14,672	ESTILL	5,545	4,236	1,108	201	3,128	R	76.4%	20.0%	79.3%	20.7%
295,803	FAYETTE	136,315	56,894	69,778	9,643	12,884	D	41.7%	51.2%	44.9%	55.1%
14,348	FLEMING	6,260	4,722	1,348	190	3,374	R	75.4%	21.5%	77.8%	22.2%
39,451	FLOYD	16,540	11,993	4,015	532	7,978	R	72.5%	24.3%	74.9%	25.1%
49,285	FRANKLIN	23,865	11,819	10,717	1,329	1,102	R	49.5%	44.9%	52.4%	47.6%
6,813	FULTON	2,382	1,549	774	59	775	R	65.0%	32.5%	66.7%	33.3%
8,589	GALLATIN	3,338	2,443	749	146	1,694	R	73.2%	22.4%	76.5%	23.5%
16,912	GARRARD	7,623	5,904	1,453	266	4,451	R	77.4%	19.1%	80.3%	19.7%
24,662	GRANT	9,559	7,268	1,910	381	5,358	R	76.0%	20.0%	79.2%	20.8%
37,121	GRAVES	16,606	12,671	3,308	627	9,363	R	76.3%	19.9%	79.3%	20.7%
25,746	GRAYSON	10,576	8,219	1,959	398	6,260	R	77.7%	18.5%	80.8%	19.2%
11,258	GREEN	5,333	4,372	832	129	3,540	R	82.0%	15.6%	84.0%	16.0%
36,910	GREENUP	16,277	11,546	4,146	585	7,400	R	70.9%	25.5%	73.6%	26.4%
8,565	HANCOCK	4,295	2,788	1,244	263	1,544	R	64.9%	29.0%	69.1%	30.9%
105,543	HARDIN	43,156	26,971	13,944	2,241	13,027	R	62.5%	32.3%	65.9%	34.1%
29,278	HARLAN	10,757	9,129	1,372	256	7,757	R	84.9%	12.8%	86.9%	13.1%
18,846	HARRISON	7,781	5,435	2,031	315	3,404	R	69.8%	26.1%	72.8%	27.2%
18,199	HART	7,264	5,320	1,730	214	3,590	R	73.2%	23.8%	75.5%	24.5%
46,250	HENDERSON	19,710	12,159	6,707	844	5,452	R	61.7%	34.0%	64.4%	35.6%
15,416	HENRY	7,149	4,944	1,828	377	3,116	R	69.2%	25.6%	73.0%	27.0%
4,902	HICKMAN	2,157	1,657	449	51	1,208	R	76.8%	20.8%	78.7%	21.3%
46,920	HOPKINS	20,345	15,277	4,310	758	10,967	R	75.1%	21.2%	78.0%	22.0%
13,494	JACKSON	5,501	4,889	482	130	4,407	R	88.9%	8.8%	91.0%	9.0%
741,096	JEFFERSON	353,099	143,768	190,836	18,495	47,068	D	40.7%	54.0%	43.0%	57.0%
48,586	JESSAMINE	23,326	15,474	6,144	1,708	9,330	R	66.3%	26.3%	71.6%	28.4%
23,356	JOHNSON	9,572	8,043	1,250	279	6,793	R	84.0%	13.1%	86.5%	13.5%
159,720	KENTON	71,998	42,958	24,214	4,826	18,744	R	59.7%	33.6%	64.0%	36.0%
16,346	KNOTT	5,763	4,357	1,245	161	3,112	R	75.6%	21.6%	77.8%	22.2%

KENTUCKY

PRESIDENT 2016

2010 Census Population	County	Total Vote	Republican (Trump)	Democratic (Clinton)	Other	Rep.-Dem. Plurality	Percentage Total Vote Rep.	Dem.	Major Vote Rep.	Dem.
31,883	KNOX	12,012	9,885	1,761	366	8,124 R	82.3%	14.7%	84.9%	15.1%
14,193	LARUE	6,367	4,799	1,278	290	3,521 R	75.4%	20.1%	79.0%	21.0%
58,849	LAUREL	24,833	20,592	3,440	801	17,152 R	82.9%	13.9%	85.7%	14.3%
15,860	LAWRENCE	6,042	4,816	1,045	181	3,771 R	79.7%	17.3%	82.2%	17.8%
7,887	LEE	2,667	2,151	444	72	1,707 R	80.7%	16.6%	82.9%	17.1%
11,310	LESLIE	4,492	4,015	400	77	3,615 R	89.4%	8.9%	90.9%	9.1%
24,519	LETCHER	9,134	7,293	1,542	299	5,751 R	79.8%	16.9%	82.5%	17.5%
13,870	LEWIS	5,298	4,363	785	150	3,578 R	82.4%	14.8%	84.8%	15.2%
24,742	LINCOLN	9,561	7,338	1,865	358	5,473 R	76.7%	19.5%	79.7%	20.3%
9,519	LIVINGSTON	4,645	3,570	887	188	2,683 R	76.9%	19.1%	80.1%	19.9%
26,835	LOGAN	10,899	7,778	2,755	366	5,023 R	71.4%	25.3%	73.8%	26.2%
8,314	LYON	3,962	2,789	1,045	128	1,744 R	70.4%	26.4%	72.7%	27.3%
82,916	MADISON	37,371	23,431	11,793	2,147	11,638 R	62.7%	31.6%	66.5%	33.5%
13,333	MAGOFFIN	5,116	3,824	1,172	120	2,652 R	74.7%	22.9%	76.5%	23.5%
19,820	MARION	8,111	5,122	2,679	310	2,443 R	63.1%	33.0%	65.7%	34.3%
31,448	MARSHALL	16,698	12,322	3,672	704	8,650 R	73.8%	22.0%	77.0%	23.0%
12,929	MARTIN	3,953	3,503	363	87	3,140 R	88.6%	9.2%	90.6%	9.4%
17,490	MASON	7,219	4,944	1,970	305	2,974 R	68.5%	27.3%	71.5%	28.5%
65,565	MCCRACKEN	31,307	20,774	9,134	1,399	11,640 R	66.4%	29.2%	69.5%	30.5%
18,306	MCCREARY	5,776	5,012	664	100	4,348 R	86.8%	11.5%	88.3%	11.7%
9,531	MCLEAN	4,566	3,381	988	197	2,393 R	74.0%	21.6%	77.4%	22.6%
28,602	MEADE	12,231	8,660	3,026	545	5,634 R	70.8%	24.7%	74.1%	25.9%
6,306	MENIFEE	2,779	2,010	700	69	1,310 R	72.3%	25.2%	74.2%	25.8%
21,331	MERCER	10,585	7,740	2,395	450	5,345 R	73.1%	22.6%	76.4%	23.6%
10,099	METCALFE	4,620	3,491	976	153	2,515 R	75.6%	21.1%	78.2%	21.8%
10,963	MONROE	4,991	4,278	601	112	3,677 R	85.7%	12.0%	87.7%	12.3%
26,499	MONTGOMERY	11,452	7,856	3,158	438	4,698 R	68.6%	27.6%	71.3%	28.7%
13,923	MORGAN	4,775	3,628	1,006	141	2,622 R	76.0%	21.1%	78.3%	21.7%
31,499	MUHLENBERG	13,060	9,393	3,272	395	6,121 R	71.9%	25.1%	74.2%	25.8%
43,437	NELSON	20,802	13,431	6,434	937	6,997 R	64.6%	30.9%	67.6%	32.4%
7,135	NICHOLAS	2,841	1,957	787	97	1,170 R	68.9%	27.7%	71.3%	28.7%
23,842	OHIO	10,398	7,942	2,080	376	5,862 R	76.4%	20.0%	79.2%	20.8%
60,316	OLDHAM	32,853	20,469	10,268	2,116	10,201 R	62.3%	31.3%	66.6%	33.4%
10,841	OWEN	5,001	3,745	1,062	194	2,683 R	74.9%	21.2%	77.9%	22.1%
4,755	OWSLEY	1,759	1,474	256	29	1,218 R	83.8%	14.6%	85.2%	14.8%
14,877	PENDLETON	6,007	4,604	1,164	239	3,440 R	76.6%	19.4%	79.8%	20.2%
28,712	PERRY	10,572	8,158	2,136	278	6,022 R	77.2%	20.2%	79.3%	20.7%
65,024	PIKE	24,665	19,747	4,280	638	15,467 R	80.1%	17.4%	82.2%	17.8%
12,613	POWELL	4,957	3,513	1,272	172	2,241 R	70.9%	25.7%	73.4%	26.6%
63,063	PULASKI	28,041	22,902	4,208	931	18,694 R	81.7%	15.0%	84.5%	15.5%
2,282	ROBERTSON	1,013	759	222	32	537 R	74.9%	21.9%	77.4%	22.6%
17,056	ROCKCASTLE	6,691	5,609	915	167	4,694 R	83.8%	13.7%	86.0%	14.0%
23,333	ROWAN	8,848	5,174	3,295	379	1,879 R	58.5%	37.2%	61.1%	38.9%
17,565	RUSSELL	8,174	6,863	1,093	218	5,770 R	84.0%	13.4%	86.3%	13.7%
47,173	SCOTT	24,200	15,052	7,715	1,433	7,337 R	62.2%	31.9%	66.1%	33.9%
42,074	SHELBY	20,580	13,196	6,276	1,108	6,920 R	64.1%	30.5%	67.8%	32.2%
17,327	SIMPSON	7,531	5,077	2,144	310	2,933 R	67.4%	28.5%	70.3%	29.7%
17,061	SPENCER	9,515	7,196	1,921	398	5,275 R	75.6%	20.2%	78.9%	21.1%
24,512	TAYLOR	11,306	8,320	2,553	433	5,767 R	73.6%	22.6%	76.5%	23.5%
12,460	TODD	4,779	3,612	1,042	125	2,570 R	75.6%	21.8%	77.6%	22.4%
14,339	TRIGG	6,751	4,931	1,587	233	3,344 R	73.0%	23.5%	75.7%	24.3%
8,809	TRIMBLE	3,798	2,771	879	148	1,892 R	73.0%	23.1%	75.9%	24.1%
15,007	UNION	6,211	4,701	1,331	179	3,370 R	75.7%	21.4%	77.9%	22.1%
113,792	WARREN	48,454	28,673	16,966	2,815	11,707 R	59.2%	35.0%	62.8%	37.2%
11,717	WASHINGTON	5,636	4,013	1,420	203	2,593 R	71.2%	25.2%	73.9%	26.1%
20,813	WAYNE	7,992	6,371	1,431	190	4,940 R	79.7%	17.9%	81.7%	18.3%
13,621	WEBSTER	5,805	4,397	1,240	168	3,157 R	75.7%	21.4%	78.0%	22.0%
35,637	WHITLEY	13,774	11,312	2,067	395	9,245 R	82.1%	15.0%	84.6%	15.4%
7,355	WOLFE	2,635	1,804	753	78	1,051 R	68.5%	28.6%	70.6%	29.4%
24,939	WOODFORD	13,563	7,697	4,958	908	2,739 R	56.7%	36.6%	60.8%	39.2%
4,339,367	TOTAL	1,924,149	1,202,971	628,854	92,324	574,117 R	62.5%	32.7%	65.7%	34.3%

KENTUCKY

GOVERNOR 2015

2010 Census Population	County	Total Vote	Republican (Bevin)	Democratic (Conway)	Other	Rep.-Dem. Plurality	Percentage Total Vote Rep.	Dem.	Major Vote Rep.	Dem.
18,656	ADAIR	4,111	2,727	1,268	116	1,459 R	66.3%	30.8%	68.3%	31.7%
19,956	ALLEN	3,397	2,344	977	76	1,367 R	69.0%	28.8%	70.6%	29.4%
21,421	ANDERSON	6,729	3,724	2,635	370	1,089 R	55.3%	39.2%	58.6%	41.4%
8,249	BALLARD	2,377	1,312	990	75	322 R	55.2%	41.6%	57.0%	43.0%
42,173	BARREN	9,217	5,289	3,568	360	1,721 R	57.4%	38.7%	59.7%	40.3%
11,591	BATH	2,240	1,045	1,117	78	72 D	46.7%	49.9%	48.3%	51.7%
28,691	BELL	4,138	2,425	1,556	157	869 R	58.6%	37.6%	60.9%	39.1%
118,811	BOONE	24,082	15,842	7,418	822	8,424 R	65.8%	30.8%	68.1%	31.9%
19,985	BOURBON	4,857	2,202	2,510	145	308 D	45.3%	51.7%	46.7%	53.3%
49,542	BOYD	9,182	4,747	4,154	281	593 R	51.7%	45.2%	53.3%	46.7%
28,432	BOYLE	7,252	3,968	2,948	336	1,020 R	54.7%	40.7%	57.4%	42.6%
8,488	BRACKEN	1,588	854	680	54	174 R	53.8%	42.8%	55.7%	44.3%
13,878	BREATHITT	2,636	1,313	1,208	115	105 R	49.8%	45.8%	52.1%	47.9%
20,059	BRECKINRIDGE	4,664	2,648	1,858	158	790 R	56.8%	39.8%	58.8%	41.2%
74,319	BULLITT	17,038	9,856	6,492	690	3,364 R	57.8%	38.1%	60.3%	39.7%
12,690	BUTLER	2,656	1,786	807	63	979 R	67.2%	30.4%	68.9%	31.1%
12,984	CALDWELL	3,117	1,838	1,180	99	658 R	59.0%	37.9%	60.9%	39.1%
37,191	CALLOWAY	8,554	4,742	3,558	254	1,184 R	55.4%	41.6%	57.1%	42.9%
90,336	CAMPBELL	19,709	10,671	8,258	780	2,413 R	54.1%	41.9%	56.4%	43.6%
5,104	CARLISLE	1,482	899	561	22	338 R	60.7%	37.9%	61.6%	38.4%
10,811	CARROLL	1,860	867	923	70	56 D	46.6%	49.6%	48.4%	51.6%
27,720	CARTER	4,485	2,405	1,954	126	451 R	53.6%	43.6%	55.2%	44.8%
15,955	CASEY	3,578	2,836	649	93	2,187 R	79.3%	18.1%	81.4%	18.6%
73,955	CHRISTIAN	8,487	4,830	3,446	211	1,384 R	56.9%	40.6%	58.4%	41.6%
35,613	CLARK	8,346	4,551	3,448	347	1,103 R	54.5%	41.3%	56.9%	43.1%
21,730	CLAY	3,251	2,311	866	74	1,445 R	71.1%	26.6%	72.7%	27.3%
10,272	CLINTON	2,005	1,531	444	30	1,087 R	76.4%	22.1%	77.5%	22.5%
9,315	CRITTENDEN	2,213	1,450	705	58	745 R	65.5%	31.9%	67.3%	32.7%
6,856	CUMBERLAND	1,307	927	342	38	585 R	70.9%	26.2%	73.0%	27.0%
96,656	DAVIESS	24,461	13,483	10,366	612	3,117 R	55.1%	42.4%	56.5%	43.5%
12,161	EDMONSON	2,385	1,503	805	77	698 R	63.0%	33.8%	65.1%	34.9%
7,852	ELLIOTT	1,231	495	706	30	211 D	40.2%	57.4%	41.2%	58.8%
14,672	ESTILL	2,811	1,770	890	151	880 R	63.0%	31.7%	66.5%	33.5%
295,803	FAYETTE	69,960	27,788	38,220	3,952	10,432 D	39.7%	54.6%	42.1%	57.9%
14,348	FLEMING	3,308	1,907	1,284	117	623 R	57.6%	38.8%	59.8%	40.2%
39,451	FLOYD	8,064	3,390	4,392	282	1,002 D	42.0%	54.5%	43.6%	56.4%
49,285	FRANKLIN	16,882	5,942	9,839	1,101	3,897 D	35.2%	58.3%	37.7%	62.3%
6,813	FULTON	1,104	568	504	32	64 R	51.4%	45.7%	53.0%	47.0%
8,589	GALLATIN	1,316	739	525	52	214 R	56.2%	39.9%	58.5%	41.5%
16,912	GARRARD	3,871	2,542	1,158	171	1,384 R	65.7%	29.9%	68.7%	31.3%
24,662	GRANT	3,892	2,433	1,326	133	1,107 R	62.5%	34.1%	64.7%	35.3%
37,121	GRAVES	8,828	5,370	3,189	269	2,181 R	60.8%	36.1%	62.7%	37.3%
25,746	GRAYSON	5,164	3,246	1,732	186	1,514 R	62.9%	33.5%	65.2%	34.8%
11,258	GREEN	2,897	2,018	806	73	1,212 R	69.7%	27.8%	71.5%	28.5%
36,910	GREENUP	7,759	4,432	3,109	218	1,323 R	57.1%	40.1%	58.8%	41.2%
8,565	HANCOCK	2,231	1,114	1,064	53	50 R	49.9%	47.7%	51.1%	48.9%
105,543	HARDIN	20,430	11,586	8,029	815	3,557 R	56.7%	39.3%	59.1%	40.9%
29,278	HARLAN	4,971	3,099	1,671	201	1,428 R	62.3%	33.6%	65.0%	35.0%
18,846	HARRISON	4,092	2,093	1,778	221	315 R	51.1%	43.5%	54.1%	45.9%
18,199	HART	3,554	2,043	1,379	132	664 R	57.5%	38.8%	59.7%	40.3%
46,250	HENDERSON	10,251	4,837	5,117	297	280 D	47.2%	49.9%	48.6%	51.4%
15,416	HENRY	4,030	2,126	1,720	184	406 R	52.8%	42.7%	55.3%	44.7%
4,902	HICKMAN	1,255	771	458	26	313 R	61.4%	36.5%	62.7%	37.3%
46,920	HOPKINS	9,594	5,802	3,524	268	2,278 R	60.5%	36.7%	62.2%	37.8%
13,494	JACKSON	2,774	2,310	393	71	1,917 R	83.3%	14.2%	85.5%	14.5%
741,096	JEFFERSON	192,972	74,427	112,232	6,313	37,805 D	38.6%	58.2%	39.9%	60.1%
48,586	JESSAMINE	12,242	7,581	4,134	527	3,447 R	61.9%	33.8%	64.7%	35.3%
23,356	JOHNSON	4,649	3,040	1,432	177	1,608 R	65.4%	30.8%	68.0%	32.0%
159,720	KENTON	31,457	18,007	12,301	1,149	5,706 R	57.2%	39.1%	59.4%	40.6%
16,346	KNOTT	2,885	1,612	1,141	132	471 R	55.9%	39.5%	58.6%	41.4%

KENTUCKY

GOVERNOR 2015

2010 Census Population	County	Total Vote	Republican (Bevin)	Democratic (Conway)	Other	Rep.-Dem. Plurality	Percentage			
							Total Vote		Major Vote	
							Rep.	Dem.	Rep.	Dem.
31,883	KNOX	5,505	3,706	1,634	165	2,072 R	67.3%	29.7%	69.4%	30.6%
14,193	LARUE	3,363	2,009	1,214	140	795 R	59.7%	36.1%	62.3%	37.7%
58,849	LAUREL	11,791	8,781	2,663	347	6,118 R	74.5%	22.6%	76.7%	23.3%
15,860	LAWRENCE	2,656	1,616	973	67	643 R	60.8%	36.6%	62.4%	37.6%
7,887	LEE	1,536	1,042	422	72	620 R	67.8%	27.5%	71.2%	28.8%
11,310	LESLIE	2,136	1,654	431	51	1,223 R	77.4%	20.2%	79.3%	20.7%
24,519	LETCHER	4,318	2,360	1,775	183	585 R	54.7%	41.1%	57.1%	42.9%
13,870	LEWIS	2,492	1,833	584	75	1,249 R	73.6%	23.4%	75.8%	24.2%
24,742	LINCOLN	5,110	3,289	1,626	195	1,663 R	64.4%	31.8%	66.9%	33.1%
9,519	LIVINGSTON	2,331	1,340	927	64	413 R	57.5%	39.8%	59.1%	40.9%
26,835	LOGAN	4,009	2,345	1,565	99	780 R	58.5%	39.0%	60.0%	40.0%
8,314	LYON	2,309	1,208	1,043	58	165 R	52.3%	45.2%	53.7%	46.3%
82,916	MADISON	18,394	10,268	7,348	778	2,920 R	55.8%	39.9%	58.3%	41.7%
13,333	MAGOFFIN	2,282	1,229	987	66	242 R	53.9%	43.3%	55.5%	44.5%
19,820	MARION	3,863	1,591	2,132	140	541 D	41.2%	55.2%	42.7%	57.3%
31,448	MARSHALL	11,210	5,969	4,830	411	1,139 R	53.2%	43.1%	55.3%	44.7%
12,929	MARTIN	1,731	1,268	419	44	849 R	73.3%	24.2%	75.2%	24.8%
17,490	MASON	3,418	1,792	1,531	95	261 R	52.4%	44.8%	53.9%	46.1%
65,565	MCCRACKEN	15,453	9,028	6,031	394	2,997 R	58.4%	39.0%	60.0%	40.0%
18,306	MCCREARY	2,083	1,362	648	73	714 R	65.4%	31.1%	67.8%	32.2%
9,531	MCLEAN	2,411	1,364	984	63	380 R	56.6%	40.8%	58.1%	41.9%
28,602	MEADE	6,444	3,310	2,838	296	472 R	51.4%	44.0%	53.8%	46.2%
6,306	MENIFEE	2,164	1,160	897	107	263 R	53.6%	41.5%	56.4%	43.6%
21,331	MERCER	5,840	3,517	2,054	269	1,463 R	60.2%	35.2%	63.1%	36.9%
10,099	METCALFE	2,327	1,344	888	95	456 R	57.8%	38.2%	60.2%	39.8%
10,963	MONROE	2,439	1,642	721	76	921 R	67.3%	29.6%	69.5%	30.5%
26,499	MONTGOMERY	5,990	3,271	2,479	240	792 R	54.6%	41.4%	56.9%	43.1%
13,923	MORGAN	2,467	1,355	1,009	103	346 R	54.9%	40.9%	57.3%	42.7%
31,499	MUHLENBERG	7,328	3,613	3,453	262	160 R	49.3%	47.1%	51.1%	48.9%
43,437	NELSON	10,142	4,902	4,880	360	22 R	48.3%	48.1%	50.1%	49.9%
7,135	NICHOLAS	1,474	563	857	54	294 D	38.2%	58.1%	39.6%	60.4%
23,842	OHIO	5,244	3,115	2,000	129	1,115 R	59.4%	38.1%	60.9%	39.1%
60,316	OLDHAM	17,998	10,896	6,403	699	4,493 R	60.5%	35.6%	63.0%	37.0%
10,841	OWEN	2,574	1,444	1,000	130	444 R	56.1%	38.9%	59.1%	40.9%
4,755	OWSLEY	825	580	220	25	360 R	70.3%	26.7%	72.5%	27.5%
14,877	PENDLETON	2,615	1,567	936	112	631 R	59.9%	35.8%	62.6%	37.4%
28,712	PERRY	5,284	3,276	1,857	151	1,419 R	62.0%	35.1%	63.8%	36.2%
65,024	PIKE	11,224	6,146	4,741	337	1,405 R	54.8%	42.2%	56.5%	43.5%
12,613	POWELL	2,544	1,335	1,110	99	225 R	52.5%	43.6%	54.6%	45.4%
63,063	PULASKI	14,763	10,623	3,664	476	6,959 R	72.0%	24.8%	74.4%	25.6%
2,282	ROBERTSON	465	247	202	16	45 R	53.1%	43.4%	55.0%	45.0%
17,056	ROCKCASTLE	3,415	2,536	744	135	1,792 R	74.3%	21.8%	77.3%	22.7%
23,333	ROWAN	4,669	2,179	2,321	169	142 D	46.7%	49.7%	48.4%	51.6%
17,565	RUSSELL	4,595	3,312	1,144	139	2,168 R	72.1%	24.9%	74.3%	25.7%
47,173	SCOTT	12,014	6,165	5,232	617	933 R	51.3%	43.5%	54.1%	45.9%
42,074	SHELBY	11,586	6,573	4,575	438	1,998 R	56.7%	39.5%	59.0%	41.0%
17,327	SIMPSON	2,773	1,652	1,059	62	593 R	59.6%	38.2%	60.9%	39.1%
17,061	SPENCER	5,043	3,169	1,705	169	1,464 R	62.8%	33.8%	65.0%	35.0%
24,512	TAYLOR	6,286	3,852	2,260	174	1,592 R	61.3%	36.0%	63.0%	37.0%
12,460	TODD	1,451	903	503	45	400 R	62.2%	34.7%	64.2%	35.8%
14,339	TRIGG	3,174	1,746	1,342	86	404 R	55.0%	42.3%	56.5%	43.5%
8,809	TRIMBLE	1,896	1,033	797	66	236 R	54.5%	42.0%	56.4%	43.6%
15,007	UNION	3,848	1,829	1,928	91	99 D	47.5%	50.1%	48.7%	51.3%
113,792	WARREN	22,496	12,411	9,354	731	3,057 R	55.2%	41.6%	57.0%	43.0%
11,717	WASHINGTON	3,130	1,796	1,205	129	591 R	57.4%	38.5%	59.8%	40.2%
20,813	WAYNE	3,738	2,412	1,239	87	1,173 R	64.5%	33.1%	66.1%	33.9%
13,621	WEBSTER	2,807	1,567	1,168	72	399 R	55.8%	41.6%	57.3%	42.7%
35,637	WHITLEY	6,844	4,772	1,857	215	2,915 R	69.7%	27.1%	72.0%	28.0%
7,355	WOLFE	1,493	689	763	41	74 D	46.1%	51.1%	47.5%	52.5%
24,939	WOODFORD	8,004	3,804	3,704	496	100 R	47.5%	46.3%	50.7%	49.3%
4,339,367	TOTAL	973,692	511,374	426,620	35,698	84,754 R	52.5%	43.8%	54.5%	45.5%

KENTUCKY

SENATOR 2016

2010 Census Population	County	Total Vote	Republican (Paul)	Democratic (Gray)	Other	Rep.-Dem. Plurality	Percentage			
							Total Vote		Major Vote	
							Rep.	Dem.	Rep.	Dem.
18,656	ADAIR	7,969	5,897	2,072		3,825 R	74.0%	26.0%	74.0%	26.0%
19,956	ALLEN	7,919	5,979	1,940		4,039 R	75.5%	24.5%	75.5%	24.5%
21,421	ANDERSON	11,385	6,910	4,475		2,435 R	60.7%	39.3%	60.7%	39.3%
8,249	BALLARD	4,092	2,725	1,367		1,358 R	66.6%	33.4%	66.6%	33.4%
42,173	BARREN	18,336	10,876	7,460		3,416 R	59.3%	40.7%	59.3%	40.7%
11,591	BATH	4,478	2,324	2,154		170 R	51.9%	48.1%	51.9%	48.1%
28,691	BELL	9,275	6,637	2,638		3,999 R	71.6%	28.4%	71.6%	28.4%
118,811	BOONE	57,335	42,032	15,303		26,729 R	73.3%	26.7%	73.3%	26.7%
19,985	BOURBON	8,761	4,411	4,350		61 R	50.3%	49.7%	50.3%	49.7%
49,542	BOYD	20,266	10,730	9,536		1,194 R	52.9%	47.1%	52.9%	47.1%
28,432	BOYLE	12,919	6,982	5,937		1,045 R	54.0%	46.0%	54.0%	46.0%
8,488	BRACKEN	3,452	2,488	964		1,524 R	72.1%	27.9%	72.1%	27.9%
13,878	BREATHITT	5,528	2,854	2,673	1	181 R	51.6%	48.4%	51.6%	48.4%
20,059	BRECKINRIDGE	8,646	5,413	3,233		2,180 R	62.6%	37.4%	62.6%	37.4%
74,319	BULLITT	35,643	23,022	12,619	2	10,403 R	64.6%	35.4%	64.6%	35.4%
12,690	BUTLER	5,500	4,055	1,444	1	2,611 R	73.7%	26.3%	73.7%	26.3%
12,984	CALDWELL	5,924	3,887	2,037		1,850 R	65.6%	34.4%	65.6%	34.4%
37,191	CALLOWAY	16,005	9,848	6,154	3	3,694 R	61.5%	38.5%	61.5%	38.5%
90,336	CAMPBELL	42,346	27,418	14,926	2	12,492 R	64.7%	35.2%	64.8%	35.2%
5,104	CARLISLE	2,582	1,813	769		1,044 R	70.2%	29.8%	70.2%	29.8%
10,811	CARROLL	3,818	2,193	1,625		568 R	57.4%	42.6%	57.4%	42.6%
27,720	CARTER	10,068	5,640	4,428		1,212 R	56.0%	44.0%	56.0%	44.0%
15,955	CASEY	6,307	4,789	1,518		3,271 R	75.9%	24.1%	75.9%	24.1%
73,955	CHRISTIAN	21,749	14,074	7,675		6,399 R	64.7%	35.3%	64.7%	35.3%
35,613	CLARK	16,143	9,023	7,120		1,903 R	55.9%	44.1%	55.9%	44.1%
21,730	CLAY	6,423	4,917	1,506		3,411 R	76.6%	23.4%	76.6%	23.4%
10,272	CLINTON	4,192	3,513	679		2,834 R	83.8%	16.2%	83.8%	16.2%
9,315	CRITTENDEN	3,968	2,877	1,090	1	1,787 R	72.5%	27.5%	72.5%	27.5%
6,856	CUMBERLAND	2,892	2,261	631		1,630 R	78.2%	21.8%	78.2%	21.8%
96,656	DAVIESS	45,420	26,652	18,768		7,884 R	58.7%	41.3%	58.7%	41.3%
12,161	EDMONSON	5,201	3,553	1,648		1,905 R	68.3%	31.7%	68.3%	31.7%
7,852	ELLIOTT	2,634	1,157	1,477		320 D	43.9%	56.1%	43.9%	56.1%
14,672	ESTILL	5,448	3,528	1,920		1,608 R	64.8%	35.2%	64.8%	35.2%
295,803	FAYETTE	136,483	54,068	82,403	12	28,335 D	39.6%	60.4%	39.6%	60.4%
14,348	FLEMING	6,152	3,597	2,555		1,042 R	58.5%	41.5%	58.5%	41.5%
39,451	FLOYD	15,697	8,082	7,615		467 R	51.5%	48.5%	51.5%	48.5%
49,285	FRANKLIN	23,860	10,000	13,860		3,860 D	41.9%	58.1%	41.9%	58.1%
6,813	FULTON	2,351	1,322	1,029		293 R	56.2%	43.8%	56.2%	43.8%
8,589	GALLATIN	3,297	2,358	939		1,419 R	71.5%	28.5%	71.5%	28.5%
16,912	GARRARD	7,549	5,034	2,515		2,519 R	66.7%	33.3%	66.7%	33.3%
24,662	GRANT	9,459	7,125	2,334		4,791 R	75.3%	24.7%	75.3%	24.7%
37,121	GRAVES	16,390	10,996	5,394		5,602 R	67.1%	32.9%	67.1%	32.9%
25,746	GRAYSON	10,405	7,097	3,307	1	3,790 R	68.2%	31.8%	68.2%	31.8%
11,258	GREEN	5,147	3,688	1,459		2,229 R	71.7%	28.3%	71.7%	28.3%
36,910	GREENUP	16,074	8,946	7,128		1,818 R	55.7%	44.3%	55.7%	44.3%
8,565	HANCOCK	4,226	2,383	1,842	1	541 R	56.4%	43.6%	56.4%	43.6%
105,543	HARDIN	42,938	24,892	18,046		6,846 R	58.0%	42.0%	58.0%	42.0%
29,278	HARLAN	10,110	7,455	2,655		4,800 R	73.7%	26.3%	73.7%	26.3%
18,846	HARRISON	7,697	4,225	3,472		753 R	54.9%	45.1%	54.9%	45.1%
18,199	HART	7,151	4,504	2,647		1,857 R	63.0%	37.0%	63.0%	37.0%
46,250	HENDERSON	19,542	10,659	8,882	1	1,777 R	54.5%	45.5%	54.5%	45.5%
15,416	HENRY	7,094	4,300	2,794		1,506 R	60.6%	39.4%	60.6%	39.4%
4,902	HICKMAN	2,131	1,409	722		687 R	66.1%	33.9%	66.1%	33.9%
46,920	HOPKINS	20,082	13,625	6,457		7,168 R	67.8%	32.2%	67.8%	32.2%
13,494	JACKSON	5,233	4,264	969		3,295 R	81.5%	18.5%	81.5%	18.5%
741,096	JEFFERSON	352,238	144,628	207,610		62,982 D	41.1%	58.9%	41.1%	58.9%
48,586	JESSAMINE	23,283	13,821	9,462		4,359 R	59.4%	40.6%	59.4%	40.6%
23,356	JOHNSON	9,155	6,187	2,968		3,219 R	67.6%	32.4%	67.6%	32.4%
159,720	KENTON	71,749	47,376	24,370	3	23,006 R	66.0%	34.0%	66.0%	34.0%
16,346	KNOTT	5,454	3,085	2,369		716 R	56.6%	43.4%	56.6%	43.4%

KENTUCKY

SENATOR 2016

2010 Census Population	County	Total Vote	Republican (Paul)	Democratic (Gray)	Other	Rep.-Dem. Plurality	Percentage Total Vote Rep.	Dem.	Percentage Major Vote Rep.	Dem.
31,883	KNOX	11,484	8,162	3,322		4,840 R	71.1%	28.9%	71.1%	28.9%
14,193	LARUE	6,296	4,111	2,185		1,926 R	65.3%	34.7%	65.3%	34.7%
58,849	LAUREL	24,284	18,216	6,065	3	12,151 R	75.0%	25.0%	75.0%	25.0%
15,860	LAWRENCE	5,870	3,652	2,218		1,434 R	62.2%	37.8%	62.2%	37.8%
7,887	LEE	2,586	1,688	898		790 R	65.3%	34.7%	65.3%	34.7%
11,310	LESLIE	4,254	3,575	679		2,896 R	84.0%	16.0%	84.0%	16.0%
24,519	LETCHER	8,539	5,364	3,175		2,189 R	62.8%	37.2%	62.8%	37.2%
13,870	LEWIS	5,003	3,569	1,434		2,135 R	71.3%	28.7%	71.3%	28.7%
24,742	LINCOLN	9,408	6,144	3,264		2,880 R	65.3%	34.7%	65.3%	34.7%
9,519	LIVINGSTON	4,577	3,063	1,514		1,549 R	66.9%	33.1%	66.9%	33.1%
26,835	LOGAN	10,769	7,555	3,214		4,341 R	70.2%	29.8%	70.2%	29.8%
8,314	LYON	3,939	2,431	1,508		923 R	61.7%	38.3%	61.7%	38.3%
82,916	MADISON	37,256	20,817	16,439		4,378 R	55.9%	44.1%	55.9%	44.1%
13,333	MAGOFFIN	4,927	2,756	2,171		585 R	55.9%	44.1%	55.9%	44.1%
19,820	MARION	7,973	3,887	4,086		199 D	48.8%	51.2%	48.8%	51.2%
31,448	MARSHALL	16,666	10,635	6,031		4,604 R	63.8%	36.2%	63.8%	36.2%
12,929	MARTIN	3,723	2,814	909		1,905 R	75.6%	24.4%	75.6%	24.4%
17,490	MASON	7,092	4,452	2,640		1,812 R	62.8%	37.2%	62.8%	37.2%
65,565	MCCRACKEN	31,251	19,699	11,552		8,147 R	63.0%	37.0%	63.0%	37.0%
18,306	MCCREARY	5,541	4,303	1,238		3,065 R	77.7%	22.3%	77.7%	22.3%
9,531	MCLEAN	4,501	2,820	1,681		1,139 R	62.7%	37.3%	62.7%	37.3%
28,602	MEADE	12,113	7,043	5,069	1	1,974 R	58.1%	41.8%	58.1%	41.9%
6,306	MENIFEE	2,715	1,514	1,201		313 R	55.8%	44.2%	55.8%	44.2%
21,331	MERCER	10,478	6,365	4,113		2,252 R	60.7%	39.3%	60.7%	39.3%
10,099	METCALFE	4,505	2,845	1,660		1,185 R	63.2%	36.8%	63.2%	36.8%
10,963	MONROE	4,723	3,842	881		2,961 R	81.3%	18.7%	81.3%	18.7%
26,499	MONTGOMERY	11,332	6,220	5,112		1,108 R	54.9%	45.1%	54.9%	45.1%
13,923	MORGAN	4,612	2,602	2,010		592 R	56.4%	43.6%	56.4%	43.6%
31,499	MUHLENBERG	12,843	7,354	5,489		1,865 R	57.3%	42.7%	57.3%	42.7%
43,437	NELSON	20,579	11,747	8,832		2,915 R	57.1%	42.9%	57.1%	42.9%
7,135	NICHOLAS	2,799	1,365	1,434		69 D	48.8%	51.2%	48.8%	51.2%
23,842	OHIO	10,247	6,742	3,505		3,237 R	65.8%	34.2%	65.8%	34.2%
60,316	OLDHAM	32,969	21,250	11,718	1	9,532 R	64.5%	35.5%	64.5%	35.5%
10,841	OWEN	4,915	3,388	1,527		1,861 R	68.9%	31.1%	68.9%	31.1%
4,755	OWSLEY	1,641	1,160	481		679 R	70.7%	29.3%	70.7%	29.3%
14,877	PENDLETON	5,869	4,376	1,493		2,883 R	74.6%	25.4%	74.6%	25.4%
28,712	PERRY	10,190	6,310	3,880		2,430 R	61.9%	38.1%	61.9%	38.1%
65,024	PIKE	23,726	14,427	9,299		5,128 R	60.8%	39.2%	60.8%	39.2%
12,613	POWELL	4,889	2,664	2,225		439 R	54.5%	45.5%	54.5%	45.5%
63,063	PULASKI	27,622	19,972	7,648	2	12,324 R	72.3%	27.7%	72.3%	27.7%
2,282	ROBERTSON	994	650	344		306 R	65.4%	34.6%	65.4%	34.6%
17,056	ROCKCASTLE	6,506	4,889	1,614	3	3,275 R	75.1%	24.8%	75.2%	24.8%
23,333	ROWAN	8,750	4,123	4,625	2	502 D	47.1%	52.9%	47.1%	52.9%
17,565	RUSSELL	7,965	5,904	2,061		3,843 R	74.1%	25.9%	74.1%	25.9%
47,173	SCOTT	24,175	13,340	10,835		2,505 R	55.2%	44.8%	55.2%	44.8%
42,074	SHELBY	20,488	12,477	8,011		4,466 R	60.9%	39.1%	60.9%	39.1%
17,327	SIMPSON	7,437	4,819	2,618		2,201 R	64.8%	35.2%	64.8%	35.2%
17,061	SPENCER	9,437	6,447	2,989	1	3,458 R	68.3%	31.7%	68.3%	31.7%
24,512	TAYLOR	11,137	7,276	3,861		3,415 R	65.3%	34.7%	65.3%	34.7%
12,460	TODD	4,684	3,514	1,170		2,344 R	75.0%	25.0%	75.0%	25.0%
14,339	TRIGG	6,664	4,752	1,912		2,840 R	71.3%	28.7%	71.3%	28.7%
8,809	TRIMBLE	3,760	2,326	1,434		892 R	61.9%	38.1%	61.9%	38.1%
15,007	UNION	6,142	3,840	2,302		1,538 R	62.5%	37.5%	62.5%	37.5%
113,792	WARREN	48,380	29,188	19,191	1	9,997 R	60.3%	39.7%	60.3%	39.7%
11,717	WASHINGTON	5,556	3,365	2,191		1,174 R	60.6%	39.4%	60.6%	39.4%
20,813	WAYNE	7,693	5,159	2,534		2,625 R	67.1%	32.9%	67.1%	32.9%
13,621	WEBSTER	5,708	3,712	1,996		1,716 R	65.0%	35.0%	65.0%	35.0%
35,637	WHITLEY	13,543	9,748	3,795		5,953 R	72.0%	28.0%	72.0%	28.0%
7,355	WOLFE	2,575	1,307	1,268		39 R	50.8%	49.2%	50.8%	49.2%
24,939	WOODFORD	13,594	6,838	6,756		82 R	50.3%	49.7%	50.3%	49.7%
4,339,367	TOTAL	1,903,465	1,090,177	813,246	42	276,931 R	57.3%	42.7%	57.3%	42.7%

KENTUCKY

HOUSE OF REPRESENTATIVES

CD	Year	Total Vote	Republican		Democratic		Other Vote	Rep.-Dem. Plurality	Percentage			
									Total Vote		Major Vote	
			Vote	Candidate	Vote	Candidate			Rep.	Dem.	Rep.	Dem.
1	2016	299,001	216,959	COMER, JAMES R.	81,710	GASKINS, SAM	332	135,249 R	72.6%	27.3%	72.6%	27.4%
1	2014	236,618	173,022	WHITFIELD, EDWARD*	63,596	HATCHETT, CHARLES KENDALL		109,426 R	73.1%	26.9%	73.1%	26.9%
1	2012	287,155	199,956	WHITFIELD, EDWARD*	87,199	HATCHETT, CHARLES KENDALL		112,757 R	69.6%	30.4%	69.6%	30.4%
2	2016	251,825	251,825	GUTHRIE, BRETT*				251,825 R	100.0%		100.0%	
2	2014	226,834	156,936	GUTHRIE, BRETT*	69,898	LEACH, RON		87,038 R	69.2%	30.8%	69.2%	30.8%
2	2012	282,267	181,508	GUTHRIE, BRETT*	89,541	WILLIAMS, DAVID LYNN	11,218	91,967 R	64.3%	31.7%	67.0%	33.0%
3	2016	334,494	122,093	BRATCHER, HAROLD	212,401	YARMUTH, JOHN*		90,308 D	36.5%	63.5%	36.5%	63.5%
3	2014	247,355	87,981	MACFARLANE, MICHAEL	157,056	YARMUTH, JOHN*	2,318	69,075 D	35.6%	63.5%	35.9%	64.1%
3	2012	322,656	111,452	WICKER, BROOKS	206,385	YARMUTH, JOHN*	4,819	94,933 D	34.5%	64.0%	35.1%	64.9%
4	2016	327,987	233,922	MASSIE, THOMAS*	94,065	SIDLE, CALVIN		139,857 R	71.3%	28.7%	71.3%	28.7%
4	2014	222,158	150,464	MASSIE, THOMAS*	71,694	NEWBERRY, PETER		78,770 R	67.7%	32.3%	67.7%	32.3%
4	2012	299,444	186,036	MASSIE, THOMAS*	104,734	ADKINS, WILLIAM R. "BILL"	8,674	81,302 R	62.1%	35.0%	64.0%	36.0%
5	2016	221,242	221,242	ROGERS, HAROLD*				221,242 R	100.0%		100.0%	
5	2014	218,967	171,350	ROGERS, HAROLD*	47,617	STEPP, KENNETH		123,733 R	78.3%	21.7%	78.3%	21.7%
5	2012	250,855	195,408	ROGERS, HAROLD*	55,447	STEPP, KENNETH		139,961 R	77.9%	22.1%	77.9%	22.1%
6	2016	330,827	202,099	BARR, GARLAND "ANDY"*	128,728	KEMPER, NANCY JO		73,371 R	61.1%	38.9%	61.1%	38.9%
6	2014	245,694	147,404	BARR, GARLAND "ANDY"*	98,290	JENSEN, ELISABETH		49,114 R	60.0%	40.0%	60.0%	40.0%
6	2012	303,000	153,222	BARR, GARLAND "ANDY"	141,438	CHANDLER, BEN*	8,340	11,784 R	50.6%	46.7%	52.0%	48.0%
TOTAL	2016	1,765,376	1,248,140		516,904		332	731,236 R	70.7%	29.3%	70.7%	29.3%
TOTAL	2014	1,397,626	887,157		508,151		2,318	379,006 R	63.5%	36.4%	63.6%	36.4%
TOTAL	2012	1,745,377	1,027,582		684,744		33,051	342,838 R	58.9%	39.2%	60.0%	40.0%

Note: An asterisk (*) denotes incumbent.

KENTUCKY

GENERAL AND PRIMARY ELECTIONS

2016 GENERAL ELECTIONS: OTHER VOTES

President   Other vote was 53,752 Independent (Gary Johnson), 22,780 Independent (Evan McMullin), 13,913 Independent (Jill Stein), 1,128 Independent (Roque De La Fuente), 438 Write-in (Darrell Castle), 313 Write-in (Scattered Write-in).

Governor (2015)   Other vote was 35,597 Independent (Drew Curtis), 71 Write-in (Blackii Whyte), 30 Write-in (Gatewood Galbraith)

Senate   Other vote was 36 Write-in (Billy Wilson), 6 Write-in (Angel Doss)

House   Other vote was:

CD 1   332 Write-in (Terry McIntosh)

2016 PRIMARY ELECTIONS: SUPPLEMENTARY INFORMATION

Primary   March 5, 2016 (Republican Presidential caucus) May 17, 2016   **Registration** (as of May 17, 2016)   3,243,078

Primary Type   Closed—Only registered Democrats and Republicans could vote in their party's primary.

KENTUCKY

GENERAL AND PRIMARY ELECTIONS

	REPUBLICAN PRIMARIES			DEMOCRATIC PRIMARIES		
President				Clinton, Hillary Rodham	212,534	46.8%
				Sanders, Bernard	210,623	46.3%
				Uncommitted	24,101	5.3%
				O'Malley, Martin	5,713	1.3%
				De La Fuente, Roque "Rocky"	1,594	0.4%
				TOTAL	454,565	
Senator	Paul, Rand*	169,180	84.8%	Gray, Jim	240,598	58.7%
	Gould, James R.	16,611	8.3%	Wilder, Sellus	52,729	12.9%
	Slaughter, Stephen Howard	13,728	6.9%	Leach, Ron	39,026	9.5%
				Recktenwald, Tom	21,910	5.3%
				Short, Grant T.	21,558	5.3%
				Kender, Jeff	20,237	4.9%
				Houlihan, Rory	13,585	3.3%
	TOTAL	199,519		TOTAL	409,643	
Governor (2015)	Bevin, Matt G.	70,480	32.9%	Conway, Jack	140,645	78.8%
	Comer, James R.	70,397	32.9%	Young, Geoff M.	37,896	21.2%
	Heiner, Hal	57,951	27.1%			
	Scott, Will T.	15,365	7.2%			
	TOTAL	214,193		TOTAL	178,541	
Congressional District 1	Comer, James R.	24,342	60.6%	Gaskins, Sam	Unopposed	
	Pape, Mike	9,357	23.3%			
	Batts, Jason	5,578	13.9%			
	Caughey, Miles A. Jr.	896	2.2%			
	TOTAL	40,173				
Congressional District 2	Guthrie, Brett*	Unopposed				
Congressional District 3	Bratcher, Harold	9,578	44.5%	Yarmuth, John*	Unopposed	
	Corley, Everett	7,857	36.5%			
	DeVore, Bob Jr.	4,075	18.9%			
	TOTAL	21,510				
Congressional District 4	Massie, Thomas*	Unopposed		Sidle, Calvin	Unopposed	
Congressional District 5	Rogers, Harold*	35,984	82.4%			
	Burk, John Jr.	7,669	17.6%			
	TOTAL	43,653				
Congressional District 6	Barr, Garland "Andy"*	25,212	84.5%	Kemper, Nancy Jo	63,440	80.1%
	Brill, Roger Q.	4,608	15.5%	Young, Geoff M.	15,772	19.9%
	TOTAL	29,820		TOTAL	79,212	

Note: An asterisk (*) denotes incumbent.

LOUISIANA

Congressional districts first established for elections held in 2012

6 members

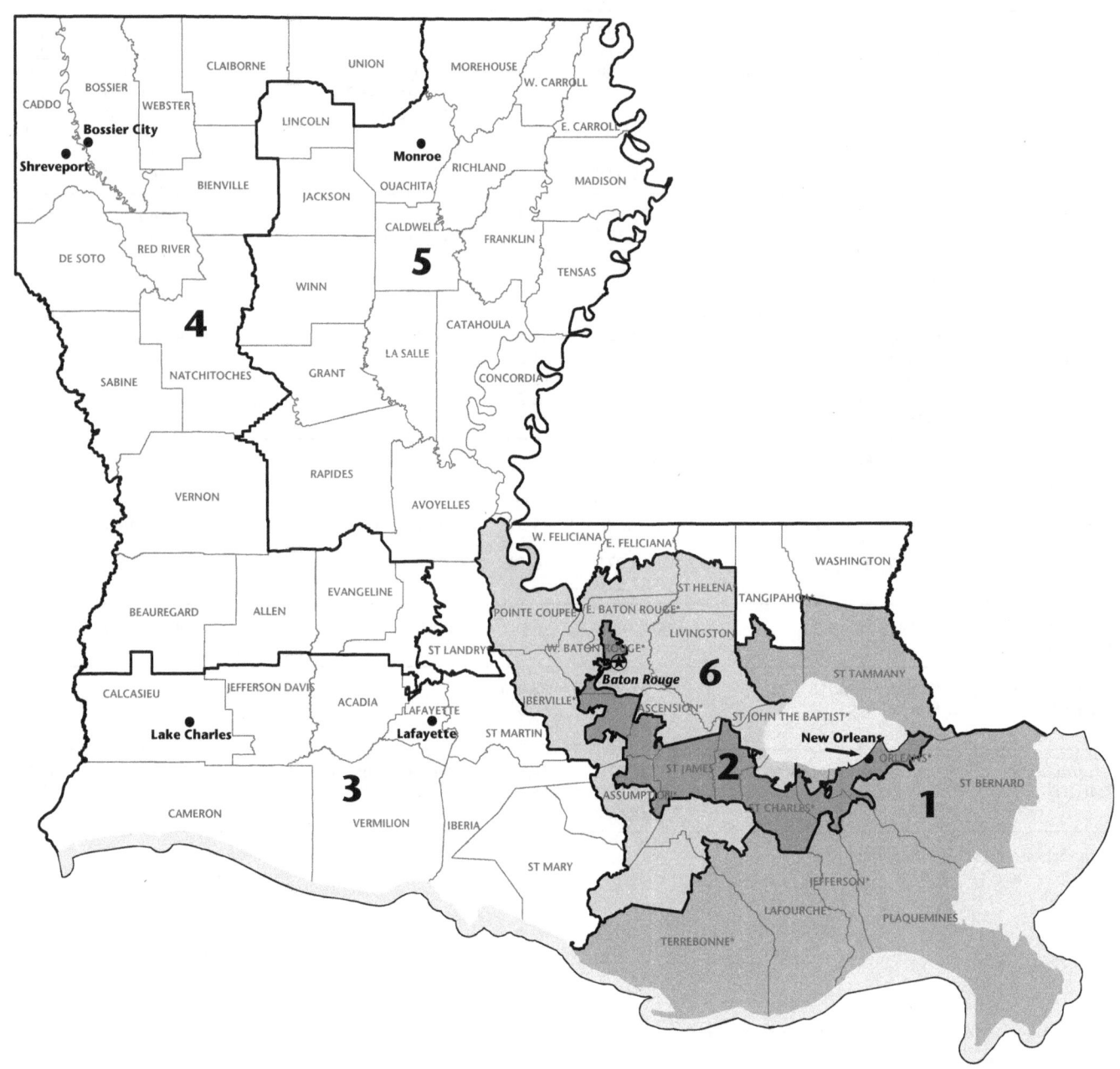

* Asterisk indicates a county whose boundaries include parts of two or more congressional districts.

LOUISIANA

GOVERNOR

John Bel Edwards (D). Elected 2015 to a four-year term.

SENATORS (2 Republicans)

Bill Cassidy (R). Elected 2014 to a six-year term.

John Neely Kennedy (R). Elected 2016 to a six-year term.

REPRESENTATIVES (5 Republicans, 1 Democrat)

1. Steve Scalise (R)
2. Cedric L. Richmond (D)
3. Clay Higgins (R)
4. Mike Johnson (R)
5. Ralph Lee Abraham (R)
6. Garret Graves (R)

POSTWAR VOTE FOR PRESIDENT

| Year | Total Vote | Republican | | Democratic | | Other Vote | Rep.-Dem. Plurality | Percentage | | | |
| | | Vote | Candidate | Vote | Candidate | | | Total Vote | | Major Vote | |
								Rep.	Dem.	Rep.	Dem.
2016**	2,029,032	1,178,638	Trump, Donald J.	780,154	Clinton, Hillary Rodham	70,240	398,484 R	58.1%	38.4%	60.2%	39.8%
2012	1,994,065	1,152,262	Romney, W. Mitt	809,141	Obama, Barack H.*	32,662	343,121 R	57.8%	40.6%	58.7%	41.3%
2008	1,960,761	1,148,275	McCain, John S. III	782,989	Obama, Barack H.	29,497	365,286 R	58.6%	39.9%	59.5%	40.5%
2004	1,943,106	1,102,169	Bush, George W.*	820,299	Kerry, John F.	20,638	281,870 R	56.7%	42.2%	57.3%	42.7%
2000**	1,765,656	927,871	Bush, George W.	792,344	Gore, Albert Jr.	45,441	135,527 R	52.6%	44.9%	53.9%	46.1%
1996**	1,783,959	712,586	Dole, Robert "Bob"	927,837	Clinton, Bill*	143,536	215,251 D	39.9%	52.0%	43.4%	56.6%
1992**	1,790,017	733,386	Bush, George H.*	815,971	Clinton, Bill	240,660	82,585 D	41.0%	45.6%	47.3%	52.7%
1988	1,628,202	883,702	Bush, George H.	717,460	Dukakis, Michael S.	27,040	166,242 R	54.3%	44.1%	55.2%	44.8%
1984	1,706,822	1,037,299	Reagan, Ronald*	651,586	Mondale, Walter F.	17,937	385,713 R	60.8%	38.2%	61.4%	38.6%
1980**	1,548,591	792,853	Reagan, Ronald	708,453	Carter, Jimmy*	47,285	84,400 R	51.2%	45.7%	52.8%	47.2%
1976	1,278,539	587,446	Ford, Gerald R.*	661,365	Carter, Jimmy	29,728	73,919 D	45.9%	51.7%	47.0%	53.0%
1972	1,051,491	686,852	Nixon, Richard M.*	298,142	McGovern, George S.	66,497	388,710 R	65.3%	28.4%	69.7%	30.3%
1968**	1,097,450	257,535	Nixon, Richard M.	309,615	Humphrey, Hubert Horatio Jr.	530,300	52,080 D	23.5%	28.2%	45.4%	54.6%
1964	896,293	509,225	Goldwater, Barry M. Sr.	387,068	Johnson, Lyndon B.*		122,157 R	56.8%	43.2%	56.8%	43.2%
1960**	807,891	230,980	Nixon, Richard M.	407,339	Kennedy, John F.	169,572	176,359 D	28.6%	50.4%	36.2%	63.8%
1956	617,544	329,047	Eisenhower, Dwight D.*	243,977	Stevenson, Adlai E. II	44,520	85,070 R	53.3%	39.5%	57.4%	42.6%
1952	651,952	306,925	Eisenhower, Dwight D.	345,027	Stevenson, Adlai E. II		38,102 D	47.1%	52.9%	47.1%	52.9%
1948**	416,336	72,657	Dewey, Thomas E.	136,344	Truman, Harry S.*	207,335	63,687 D	17.5%	32.7%	34.8%	65.2%

Note: An asterisk (*) denotes incumbent. **In past elections, the other vote included: 2016 - 37,978 Libertarian (Gary Johnson); 2000 - 20,473 Green (Ralph Nader); 1996 - 123,293 Reform (Ross Perot); 1992 - 211,478 Independent (Perot); 1980 - 26,345 Independent (John Anderson); 1968 - 530,300 American Independent (George Wallace); 1960 - 169,572 Unpledged Independent Electors; 1948 - 204,290 States' Rights (Strom Thurmond). Wallace carried Louisiana in 1968 with 48.3 percent of the vote. Thurmond won the state in 1948 with 49.1 percent.

LOUISIANA

POSTWAR VOTE FOR GOVERNOR

Year	Total Vote	Republican		Democratic		Other Vote	Rep.-Dem. Plurality	Percentage			
								Total Vote		Major Vote	
		Vote	Candidate	Vote	Candidate			Rep.	Dem.	Rep.	Dem.
2015**	1,152,864	505,940	Vitter, David B.	646,924	Edwards, John Bel		140,984 D	43.9%	56.1%	43.9%	56.1%
2011	1,023,163	673,239	Jindal, Bobby*	182,925	Hollis, Tara	166,999	490,314 R	65.8%	17.9%	78.6%	21.4%
2007**	1,297,840	699,275	Jindal, Bobby	226,476	Boasso, Walter J.	372,089	472,799 R	53.9%	17.5%	75.5%	24.5%
2003**	1,407,842	676,484	Jindal, Bobby	731,358	Kathleen, Babineaux		54,874 D	48.1%	51.9%	48.1%	51.9%
1999	1,295,205	805,203	Foster, Mike*	382,445	Jefferson, William J.	107,557	422,758 R	62.2%	29.5%	67.8%	32.2%
1995**	1,550,360	984,499	Foster, Mike	565,861	Fields, Cleo		418,638 R	63.5%	36.5%	63.5%	36.5%
1991**	1,728,040	671,009	Duke, David E.	1,057,031	Edwards, Edwin W.		386,022 D	38.8%	61.2%	38.8%	61.2%
1987**	1,558,730	287,780	Livingston, Bob	516,078	Roemer, Charles	754,872	228,298 D	18.5%	33.1%	35.8%	64.2%
1983	1,615,905	588,508	Treen, David Conner*	1,006,561	Edwards, Edwin W.	20,836	418,053 D	36.4%	62.3%	36.9%	63.1%
1979**	1,371,825	690,691	Treen, David Conner	681,134	Lambert, Louis		9,557 R	50.3%	49.7%	50.3%	49.7%
1975	430,095			430,095	Edwards, Edwin W.*		430,095		100.0%		100.0%
1972	1,121,570	480,424	Treen, David Conner	641,146	Edwards, Edwin W.		160,722 D	42.8%	57.2%	42.8%	57.2%
1968	372,762			372,762	McKeithen, John J.*		372,762		100.0%		100.0%
1964	773,390	297,753	Lyons, Charlton H. Sr.	469,589	McKeithen, John J.	6,048	171,836 D	38.5%	60.7%	38.8%	61.2%
1960	506,562	86,135	Grevemberg, F. C.	407,907	Davis, Jimmie H.	12,520	321,772 D	17.0%	80.5%	17.4%	82.6%
1956	172,291			172,291	Long, Earl K.		172,291 D		100.0%		100.0%
1952	118,723			118,723	Kennon, Robert F.		118,723 D		100.0%		100.0%
1948	76,566			76,566	Long, Earl K.		76,566 D		100.0%		100.0%

Note: An asterisk (*) denotes incumbent. **Since the 1970s, Louisiana has had a two-tier election system for governor in which all candidates, regardless of party, run together in an open election. A candidate who wins a majority of the vote is elected. If no candidate receives 50 percent, a runoff is held between the top two finishers. The results of the runoff are listed in this chart for 1979, 1991, 1995, 2003, and 2015. In elections that did not require a runoff, the leading Democratic and Republican candidates are listed with their votes from the first-round, open election. The votes for other candidates are listed in the "Other Vote" column, regardless of whether they were Democratic, Republican, or independent. In past elections, the other vote included: 2007 - 186,682 No Party (John Georges), 161,665 Democrat (Foster Campbell); 1987 - 437,801 Democrat (Edwin W. Edwards). In 1987, Edwards withdrew after finishing second in the initial round of voting. Democrat Charles Roemer finished first with 33.1 percent, and with Edwards's withdrawal, no runoff was held. The major party vote percentages are calculated for the top vote-getter for each party only; it does not include additional members of the same party. The Republican Party did not run a candidate in the 1948, 1952, 1956, 1968, and 1975 gubernatorial elections.

LOUISIANA

POSTWAR VOTE FOR SENATOR

Year	Total Vote	Republican Vote	Republican Candidate	Democratic Vote	Democratic Candidate	Other Vote	Rep.-Dem. Plurality	Total Vote Rep.	Total Vote Dem.	Major Vote Rep.	Major Vote Dem.
2016**	884,007	536,191	Kennedy, John Neely	347,816	Campbell, Foster		188,375 R	60.7%	39.3%	60.7%	39.3%
2014**	1,273,589	712,379	Cassidy, Bill	561,210	Landrieu, Mary L.*		151,169 R	55.9%	44.1%	55.9%	44.1%
2010**	1,264,994	715,415	Vitter, David B.*	476,572	Melancon, Charlie R.	73,007	238,843 R	56.6%	37.7%	60.0%	40.0%
2008**	1,896,574	867,177	Kennedy, John	988,298	Landrieu, Mary L.*	41,099	121,121 D	45.7%	52.1%	46.7%	53.3%
2004**	1,848,056	943,014	Vitter, David B.	542,150	John, Chris	362,892	400,864 R	51.0%	29.3%	63.5%	36.5%
2002**	1,235,296	596,642	Terrell, Suzanne Haik	638,654	Landrieu, Mary L.*		42,012 D	48.3%	51.7%	48.3%	51.7%
1998	969,165	306,616	Donelon, Jim	620,502	Breaux, John B.*	42,047	313,886 D	31.6%	64.0%	33.1%	66.9%
1996**	1,700,102	847,157	Jenkins, Louis E. "Woody" Jr.	852,945	Landrieu, Mary L.		5,788 D	49.8%	50.2%	49.8%	50.2%
1992	843,037	69,986	Stockstill, Lyle	616,021	Breaux, John B.*	157,030	546,035 D	8.3%	73.1%	10.2%	89.8%
1990	1,396,113	607,391	Duke, David E.	752,902	Johnston, J. Bennett*	35,820	145,511 D	43.5%	53.9%	44.7%	55.3%
1986**	1,369,897	646,311	Moore, W. Henson	723,586	Breaux, John B.		77,275 D	47.2%	52.8%	47.2%	52.8%
1984	977,473	86,546	Ross, Robert M.	838,181	Johnston, J. Bennett*	52,746	751,635 D	8.9%	85.7%	9.4%	90.6%
1980**	843,362	13,739	Bardwell, Jerry C.	484,770	Long, Russell B.*	342,504	471,031 D	1.6%	57.6%		100.0%
1978**	839,669			498,773	Johnston, J. Bennett*	340,896	498,773 D		59.4%		100.0%
1974	434,643			434,643	Long, Russell B.*		434,643 D		100.0%		100.0%
1972**	1,084,904	206,846	Toledano, Ben C.	598,987	Johnston, J. Bennett	279,071	392,141 D	19.1%	55.2%	25.7%	74.3%
1968	518,586			518,586	Long, Russell B.*		518,586 D		100.0%		100.0%
1966	437,695			437,695	Ellender, Allen J.*		437,695 D		100.0%		100.0%
1962	421,904	103,066	O'Hearn, Taylor Walters	318,838	Long, Russell B.*		215,772 D	24.4%	75.6%	24.4%	75.6%
1960	541,928	109,698	Reese, George W. Jr.	432,228	Ellender, Allen J.*	2	322,530 D	20.2%	79.8%	20.2%	79.8%
1956	335,564			335,564	Long, Russell B.*		335,564 D		100.0%		100.0%
1954	207,115			207,115	Ellender, Allen J.*		207,115 D		100.0%		100.0%
1950	251,838	30,931	Gerth, Charles S.	220,907	Long, Russell B.*		189,976 D	12.3%	87.7%	12.3%	87.7%
1948	330,324			330,315	Ellender, Allen J.	9	330,315 D		100.0%		100.0%
1948S**	407,685	102,339	Clarke, Clem S.	305,346	Long, Russell B.		203,007 D	25.1%	74.9%	25.1%	74.9%

Note: An asterisk (*) denotes incumbent. **In 2008 and 2010, Louisiana used the more typical system of party primaries followed by a general election to fill seats in Congress. Since 1978, all other Senate seats were decided in open elections in which candidates of all parties ran together on the same ballot. If no candidate won a majority of the vote in the first round, a runoff was held between the top two vote-getters, regardless of party. The Senate elections in 1986, 1996, 2002, 2014, and 2016 were decided by a runoff, with the results of the runoff listed in this chart. In elections that did not require a runoff, the leading Democratic and Republican candidates are listed with their votes in the first-round, open election. The votes for other candidates are listed in the "Other Vote" column, regardless of whether they were Democratic, Republican, or independent. In past elections, the other vote included: 2004 - 275,821 Democrat (John Kennedy); 1980 - 325,922 Democrat (Louis Jenkins, who finished second); 1978 - 340,896 Democrat (Louis Jenkins, who finished second); 1972 - 250,161 Independent (John J. McKeithen, who finished second). One of the 1948 elections was for a short term to fill a vacancy. The major party vote percentages are calculated for the top vote-getter for each party only; it does not include additional members of the same party. The Republican Party did not run a candidate in Senate elections in 1948, 1954, 1956, 1966, 1968, 1974, and 1978.

LOUISIANA

PRESIDENT 2016

2010 Census Population	Parish	Total Vote	Republican (Trump)	Democratic (Clinton)	Other	Rep.-Dem. Plurality	Total Vote Rep.	Total Vote Dem.	Major Vote Rep.	Major Vote Dem.
61,773	ACADIA	27,389	21,162	5,638	589	15,524 R	77.3%	20.6%	79.0%	21.0%
25,764	ALLEN	9,245	6,867	2,106	272	4,761 R	74.3%	22.8%	76.5%	23.5%
107,215	ASCENSION	54,678	36,143	16,476	2,059	19,667 R	66.1%	30.1%	68.7%	31.3%
23,421	ASSUMPTION	10,904	6,714	3,931	259	2,783 R	61.6%	36.1%	63.1%	36.9%
42,073	AVOYELLES	16,586	11,165	5,035	386	6,130 R	67.3%	30.4%	68.9%	31.1%
35,654	BEAUREGARD	15,078	12,238	2,393	447	9,845 R	81.2%	15.9%	83.6%	16.4%
14,353	BIENVILLE	7,005	3,756	3,129	120	627 R	53.6%	44.7%	54.6%	45.4%
116,979	BOSSIER	49,848	35,474	12,641	1,733	22,833 R	71.2%	25.4%	73.7%	26.3%
254,969	CADDO	105,804	49,006	53,483	3,315	4,477 D	46.3%	50.5%	47.8%	52.2%
192,768	CALCASIEU	83,785	54,191	26,296	3,298	27,895 R	64.7%	31.4%	67.3%	32.7%

LOUISIANA

PRESIDENT 2016

2010 Census Population	Parish	Total Vote	Republican (Trump)	Democratic (Clinton)	Other	Rep.-Dem. Plurality	Percentage			
							Total Vote		Major Vote	
							Rep.	Dem.	Rep.	Dem.
10,132	CALDWELL	4,692	3,822	788	82	3,034 R	81.5%	16.8%	82.9%	17.1%
6,839	CAMERON	3,692	3,256	323	113	2,933 R	88.2%	8.7%	91.0%	9.0%
10,407	CATAHOULA	4,856	3,479	1,322	55	2,157 R	71.6%	27.2%	72.5%	27.5%
17,195	CLAIBORNE	6,421	3,585	2,717	119	868 R	55.8%	42.3%	56.9%	43.1%
20,822	CONCORDIA	8,872	5,477	3,272	123	2,205 R	61.7%	36.9%	62.6%	37.4%
26,656	DE SOTO	13,500	8,068	5,165	267	2,903 R	59.8%	38.3%	61.0%	39.0%
440,171	EAST BATON ROUGE	196,491	84,660	102,828	9,003	18,168 D	43.1%	52.3%	45.2%	54.8%
7,759	EAST CARROLL	2,939	1,059	1,838	42	779 D	36.0%	62.5%	36.6%	63.4%
20,267	EAST FELICIANA	10,042	5,569	4,235	238	1,334 R	55.5%	42.2%	56.8%	43.2%
33,984	EVANGELINE	14,882	10,360	4,208	314	6,152 R	69.6%	28.3%	71.1%	28.9%
20,767	FRANKLIN	9,162	6,514	2,506	142	4,008 R	71.1%	27.4%	72.2%	27.8%
22,309	GRANT	8,821	7,408	1,181	232	6,227 R	84.0%	13.4%	86.2%	13.8%
73,240	IBERIA	32,454	20,903	10,698	853	10,205 R	64.4%	33.0%	66.1%	33.9%
33,387	IBERVILLE	16,043	7,320	8,324	399	1,004 D	45.6%	51.9%	46.8%	53.2%
16,274	JACKSON	7,464	5,169	2,139	156	3,030 R	69.3%	28.7%	70.7%	29.3%
432,552	JEFFERSON	181,639	100,398	73,670	7,571	26,728 R	55.3%	40.6%	57.7%	42.3%
31,594	JEFFERSON DAVIS	14,277	10,775	3,080	422	7,695 R	75.5%	21.6%	77.8%	22.2%
14,890	LA SALLE	6,569	5,836	605	128	5,231 R	88.8%	9.2%	90.6%	9.4%
221,578	LAFAYETTE	105,603	68,195	32,726	4,682	35,469 R	64.6%	31.0%	67.6%	32.4%
96,318	LAFOURCHE	41,645	31,959	8,423	1,263	23,536 R	76.7%	20.2%	79.1%	20.9%
46,735	LINCOLN	18,669	10,761	7,107	801	3,654 R	57.6%	38.1%	60.2%	39.8%
128,026	LIVINGSTON	57,730	48,824	6,950	1,956	41,874 R	84.6%	12.0%	87.5%	12.5%
12,093	MADISON	4,732	1,927	2,744	61	817 D	40.7%	58.0%	41.3%	58.7%
27,979	MOREHOUSE	11,852	6,502	5,155	195	1,347 R	54.9%	43.5%	55.8%	44.2%
39,566	NATCHITOCHES	16,621	8,968	7,144	509	1,824 R	54.0%	43.0%	55.7%	44.3%
343,829	ORLEANS	165,812	24,292	133,996	7,524	109,704 D	14.7%	80.8%	15.3%	84.7%
153,720	OUACHITA	68,017	41,734	24,428	1,855	17,306 R	61.4%	35.9%	63.1%	36.9%
23,042	PLAQUEMINES	10,573	6,900	3,347	326	3,553 R	65.3%	31.7%	67.3%	32.7%
22,802	POINTE COUPEE	11,761	6,789	4,764	208	2,025 R	57.7%	40.5%	58.8%	41.2%
131,613	RAPIDES	56,844	36,816	18,322	1,706	18,494 R	64.8%	32.2%	66.8%	33.2%
9,091	RED RIVER	4,422	2,391	1,938	93	453 R	54.1%	43.8%	55.2%	44.8%
20,725	RICHLAND	9,597	6,287	3,157	153	3,130 R	65.5%	32.9%	66.6%	33.4%
24,233	SABINE	9,787	7,879	1,703	205	6,176 R	80.5%	17.4%	82.2%	17.8%
35,897	ST. BERNARD	15,815	10,237	4,960	618	5,277 R	64.7%	31.4%	67.4%	32.6%
52,780	ST. CHARLES	26,192	16,621	8,559	1,012	8,062 R	63.5%	32.7%	66.0%	34.0%
11,203	ST. HELENA	5,964	2,497	3,353	114	856 D	41.9%	56.2%	42.7%	57.3%
22,102	ST. JAMES	12,085	5,456	6,418	211	962 D	45.1%	53.1%	45.9%	54.1%
45,924	ST. JOHN THE BAPTIST	20,743	7,569	12,661	513	5,092 D	36.5%	61.0%	37.4%	62.6%
83,384	ST. LANDRY	39,977	21,971	17,209	797	4,762 R	55.0%	43.0%	56.1%	43.9%
52,160	ST. MARTIN	25,750	16,873	8,266	611	8,607 R	65.5%	32.1%	67.1%	32.9%
54,650	ST. MARY	22,877	14,359	8,050	468	6,309 R	62.8%	35.2%	64.1%	35.9%
233,740	ST. TAMMANY	124,392	90,915	27,717	5,760	63,198 R	73.1%	22.3%	76.6%	23.4%
121,097	TANGIPAHOA	52,416	33,959	16,878	1,579	17,081 R	64.8%	32.2%	66.8%	33.2%
5,252	TENSAS	2,548	1,182	1,332	34	150 D	46.4%	52.3%	47.0%	53.0%
111,860	TERREBONNE	43,896	31,902	10,665	1,329	21,237 R	72.7%	24.3%	74.9%	25.1%
22,721	UNION	10,894	7,972	2,691	231	5,281 R	73.2%	24.7%	74.8%	25.2%
57,999	VERMILION	25,632	20,063	4,857	712	15,206 R	78.3%	18.9%	80.5%	19.5%
52,334	VERNON	16,633	13,471	2,665	497	10,806 R	81.0%	16.0%	83.5%	16.5%
47,168	WASHINGTON	18,628	12,556	5,692	380	6,864 R	67.4%	30.6%	68.8%	31.2%
41,207	WEBSTER	18,145	11,542	6,260	343	5,282 R	63.6%	34.5%	64.8%	35.2%
23,788	WEST BATON ROUGE	12,712	6,927	5,383	402	1,544 R	54.5%	42.3%	56.3%	43.7%
11,604	WEST CARROLL	4,759	3,970	715	74	3,255 R	83.4%	15.0%	84.7%	15.3%
15,625	WEST FELICIANA	5,799	3,390	2,248	161	1,142 R	58.5%	38.8%	60.1%	39.9%
15,313	WINN	6,372	4,608	1,644	120	2,964 R	72.3%	25.8%	73.7%	26.3%
4,533,372	TOTAL	2,029,032	1,178,638	780,154	70,240	398,484 R	58.1%	38.4%	60.2%	39.8%

LOUISIANA
GOVERNOR RUNOFF 2015

2010 Census Population	Parish	Total Vote	Republican (Vitter)	Democrat (Edwards)	Rep.-Dem. Plurality	Total Vote Rep.	Total Vote Dem.	Major Vote Rep.	Major Vote Dem.
61,773	ACADIA	14,990	8,595	6,395	2,200 R	57.3%	42.7%	57.3%	42.7%
25,764	ALLEN	5,307	2,392	2,915	523 D	45.1%	54.9%	45.1%	54.9%
107,215	ASCENSION	30,607	14,618	15,989	1,371 D	47.8%	52.2%	47.8%	52.2%
23,421	ASSUMPTION	6,464	2,332	4,132	1,800 D	36.1%	63.9%	36.1%	63.9%
42,073	AVOYELLES	8,802	3,176	5,626	2,450 D	36.1%	63.9%	36.1%	63.9%
35,654	BEAUREGARD	9,581	5,344	4,237	1,107 R	55.8%	44.2%	55.8%	44.2%
14,353	BIENVILLE	4,711	1,933	2,778	845 D	41.0%	59.0%	41.0%	59.0%
116,979	BOSSIER	24,776	15,518	9,258	6,260 R	62.6%	37.4%	62.6%	37.4%
254,969	CADDO	62,302	23,896	38,406	14,510 D	38.4%	61.6%	38.4%	61.6%
192,768	CALCASIEU	43,689	18,103	25,586	7,483 D	41.4%	58.6%	41.4%	58.6%
10,132	CALDWELL	4,119	2,530	1,589	941 R	61.4%	38.6%	61.4%	38.6%
6,839	CAMERON	2,328	1,184	1,144	40 R	50.9%	49.1%	50.9%	49.1%
10,407	CATAHOULA	2,814	1,563	1,251	312 R	55.5%	44.5%	55.5%	44.5%
17,195	CLAIBORNE	3,655	1,690	1,965	275 D	46.2%	53.8%	46.2%	53.8%
20,822	CONCORDIA	4,293	1,996	2,297	301 D	46.5%	53.5%	46.5%	53.5%
26,656	DE SOTO	7,911	3,653	4,258	605 D	46.2%	53.8%	46.2%	53.8%
440,171	EAST BATON ROUGE	119,225	38,623	80,602	41,979 D	32.4%	67.6%	32.4%	67.6%
7,759	EAST CARROLL	1,936	648	1,288	640 D	33.5%	66.5%	33.5%	66.5%
20,267	EAST FELICIANA	6,566	2,197	4,369	2,172 D	33.5%	66.5%	33.5%	66.5%
33,984	EVANGELINE	8,296	3,576	4,720	1,144 D	43.1%	56.9%	43.1%	56.9%
20,767	FRANKLIN	4,906	2,780	2,126	654 R	56.7%	43.3%	56.7%	43.3%
22,309	GRANT	4,543	2,841	1,702	1,139 R	62.5%	37.5%	62.5%	37.5%
73,240	IBERIA	20,252	10,545	9,707	838 R	52.1%	47.9%	52.1%	47.9%
33,387	IBERVILLE	11,144	3,030	8,114	5,084 D	27.2%	72.8%	27.2%	72.8%
16,274	JACKSON	4,752	2,496	2,256	240 R	52.5%	47.5%	52.5%	47.5%
432,552	JEFFERSON	98,535	48,633	49,902	1,269 D	49.4%	50.6%	49.4%	50.6%
31,594	JEFFERSON DAVIS	7,082	3,225	3,857	632 D	45.5%	54.5%	45.5%	54.5%
14,890	LA SALLE	3,591	2,537	1,054	1,483 R	70.6%	29.4%	70.6%	29.4%
221,578	LAFAYETTE	59,217	31,291	27,926	3,365 R	52.8%	47.2%	52.8%	47.2%
96,318	LAFOURCHE	22,496	12,520	9,976	2,544 R	55.7%	44.3%	55.7%	44.3%
46,735	LINCOLN	9,387	4,402	4,985	583 D	46.9%	53.1%	46.9%	53.1%
128,026	LIVINGSTON	28,118	16,950	11,168	5,782 R	60.3%	39.7%	60.3%	39.7%
12,093	MADISON	2,821	932	1,889	957 D	33.0%	67.0%	33.0%	67.0%
27,979	MOREHOUSE	6,707	2,951	3,756	805 D	44.0%	56.0%	44.0%	56.0%
39,566	NATCHITOCHES	9,282	3,860	5,422	1,562 D	41.6%	58.4%	41.6%	58.4%
343,829	ORLEANS	94,650	12,748	81,902	69,154 D	13.5%	86.5%	13.5%	86.5%
153,720	OUACHITA	35,758	18,181	17,577	604 R	50.8%	49.2%	50.8%	49.2%
23,042	PLAQUEMINES	6,002	3,048	2,954	94 R	50.8%	49.2%	50.8%	49.2%
22,802	POINTE COUPEE	7,635	2,289	5,346	3,057 D	30.0%	70.0%	30.0%	70.0%
131,613	RAPIDES	28,362	13,496	14,866	1,370 D	47.6%	52.4%	47.6%	52.4%
9,091	RED RIVER	2,438	1,063	1,375	312 D	43.6%	56.4%	43.6%	56.4%
20,725	RICHLAND	7,912	3,984	3,928	56 R	50.4%	49.6%	50.4%	49.6%
24,233	SABINE	5,175	3,552	1,623	1,929 R	68.6%	31.4%	68.6%	31.4%
35,897	ST. BERNARD	11,494	5,106	6,388	1,282 D	44.4%	55.6%	44.4%	55.6%
52,780	ST. CHARLES	15,773	7,792	7,981	189 D	49.4%	50.6%	49.4%	50.6%
11,203	ST. HELENA	4,694	898	3,796	2,898 D	19.1%	80.9%	19.1%	80.9%
22,102	ST. JAMES	9,270	2,789	6,481	3,692 D	30.1%	69.9%	30.1%	69.9%
45,924	ST. JOHN THE BAPTIST	16,262	4,700	11,562	6,862 D	28.9%	71.1%	28.9%	71.1%
83,384	ST. LANDRY	22,604	8,279	14,325	6,046 D	36.6%	63.4%	36.6%	63.4%
52,160	ST. MARTIN	14,570	6,758	7,812	1,054 D	46.4%	53.6%	46.4%	53.6%
54,650	ST. MARY	12,346	6,050	6,296	246 D	49.0%	51.0%	49.0%	51.0%
233,740	ST. TAMMANY	70,545	42,801	27,744	15,057 R	60.7%	39.3%	60.7%	39.3%
121,097	TANGIPAHOA	33,034	13,098	19,936	6,838 D	39.7%	60.3%	39.7%	60.3%
5,252	TENSAS	1,671	611	1,060	449 D	36.6%	63.4%	36.6%	63.4%
111,860	TERREBONNE	21,703	12,603	9,100	3,503 R	58.1%	41.9%	58.1%	41.9%
22,721	UNION	5,844	3,574	2,270	1,304 R	61.2%	38.8%	61.2%	38.8%
57,999	VERMILION	12,710	7,594	5,116	2,478 R	59.7%	40.3%	59.7%	40.3%
52,334	VERNON	8,126	4,941	3,185	1,756 R	60.8%	39.2%	60.8%	39.2%
47,168	WASHINGTON	11,065	4,998	6,067	1,069 D	45.2%	54.8%	45.2%	54.8%
41,207	WEBSTER	10,057	4,768	5,289	521 D	47.4%	52.6%	47.4%	52.6%

LOUISIANA

GOVERNOR RUNOFF 2015

2010 Census Population	Parish	Total Vote	Republican (Vitter)	Democrat (Edwards)	Rep.-Dem. Plurality	Percentage			
						Total Vote		Major Vote	
						Rep.	Dem.	Rep.	Dem.
23,788	WEST BATON ROUGE	7,886	2,671	5,215	2,544 D	33.9%	66.1%	33.9%	66.1%
11,604	WEST CARROLL	2,327	1,506	821	685 R	64.7%	35.3%	64.7%	35.3%
15,625	WEST FELICIANA	4,016	1,321	2,695	1,374 D	32.9%	67.1%	32.9%	67.1%
15,313	WINN	3,730	2,161	1,569	592 R	57.9%	42.1%	57.9%	42.1%
4,533,372	TOTAL	1,152,864	505,940	646,924	140,984 D	43.9%	56.1%	43.9%	56.1%

LOUISIANA

SENATE RUNOFF 2016

2010 Census Population	Parish	Total Vote	Republican (Kennedy)	Democrat (Campbell)	Rep.-Dem. Plurality	Percentage			
						Total Vote		Major Vote	
						Rep.	Dem.	Rep.	Dem.
61,773	ACADIA	12,640	9,887	2,753	7,134 R	78.2%	21.8%	78.2%	21.8%
25,764	ALLEN	3,355	2,424	931	1,493 R	72.3%	27.7%	72.3%	27.7%
107,215	ASCENSION	20,736	13,950	6,786	7,164 R	67.3%	32.7%	67.3%	32.7%
23,421	ASSUMPTION	4,224	2,616	1,608	1,008 R	61.9%	38.1%	61.9%	38.1%
42,073	AVOYELLES	6,992	4,529	2,463	2,066 R	64.8%	35.2%	64.8%	35.2%
35,654	BEAUREGARD	5,453	4,339	1,114	3,225 R	79.6%	20.4%	79.6%	20.4%
14,353	BIENVILLE	3,540	1,856	1,684	172 R	52.4%	47.6%	52.4%	47.6%
116,979	BOSSIER	22,345	16,634	5,711	10,923 R	74.4%	25.6%	74.4%	25.6%
254,969	CADDO	49,407	24,732	24,675	57 R	50.1%	49.9%	50.1%	49.9%
192,768	CALCASIEU	29,628	19,365	10,263	9,102 R	65.4%	34.6%	65.4%	34.6%
10,132	CALDWELL	2,138	1,723	415	1,308 R	80.6%	19.4%	80.6%	19.4%
6,839	CAMERON	1,442	1,169	273	896 R	81.1%	18.9%	81.1%	18.9%
10,407	CATAHOULA	1,977	1,404	573	831 R	71.0%	29.0%	71.0%	29.0%
17,195	CLAIBORNE	2,966	1,807	1,159	648 R	60.9%	39.1%	60.9%	39.1%
20,822	CONCORDIA	3,363	2,045	1,318	727 R	60.8%	39.2%	60.8%	39.2%
26,656	DE SOTO	6,479	3,913	2,566	1,347 R	60.4%	39.6%	60.4%	39.6%
440,171	EAST BATON ROUGE	114,666	55,039	59,627	4,588 D	48.0%	52.0%	48.0%	52.0%
7,759	EAST CARROLL	1,213	496	717	221 D	40.9%	59.1%	40.9%	59.1%
20,267	EAST FELICIANA	5,406	3,052	2,354	698 R	56.5%	43.5%	56.5%	43.5%
33,984	EVANGELINE	4,945	3,460	1,485	1,975 R	70.0%	30.0%	70.0%	30.0%
20,767	FRANKLIN	4,150	3,155	995	2,160 R	76.0%	24.0%	76.0%	24.0%
22,309	GRANT	3,313	2,823	490	2,333 R	85.2%	14.8%	85.2%	14.8%
73,240	IBERIA	13,840	10,247	3,593	6,654 R	74.0%	26.0%	74.0%	26.0%
33,387	IBERVILLE	6,851	3,272	3,579	307 D	47.8%	52.2%	47.8%	52.2%
16,274	JACKSON	3,190	2,157	1,033	1,124 R	67.6%	32.4%	67.6%	32.4%
432,552	JEFFERSON	77,992	49,812	28,180	21,632 R	63.9%	36.1%	63.9%	36.1%
31,594	JEFFERSON DAVIS	5,771	4,338	1,433	2,905 R	75.2%	24.8%	75.2%	24.8%
14,890	LA SALLE	2,722	2,456	266	2,190 R	90.2%	9.8%	90.2%	9.8%
221,578	LAFAYETTE	44,886	31,784	13,102	18,682 R	70.8%	29.2%	70.8%	29.2%
96,318	LAFOURCHE	16,768	13,670	3,098	10,572 R	81.5%	18.5%	81.5%	18.5%
46,735	LINCOLN	7,365	4,523	2,842	1,681 R	61.4%	38.6%	61.4%	38.6%
128,026	LIVINGSTON	20,123	17,471	2,652	14,819 R	86.8%	13.2%	86.8%	13.2%
12,093	MADISON	1,729	762	967	205 D	44.1%	55.9%	44.1%	55.9%
27,979	MOREHOUSE	4,782	2,766	2,016	750 R	57.8%	42.2%	57.8%	42.2%
39,566	NATCHITOCHES	6,979	4,203	2,776	1,427 R	60.2%	39.8%	60.2%	39.8%
343,829	ORLEANS	77,994	13,798	64,196	50,398 D	17.7%	82.3%	17.7%	82.3%
153,720	OUACHITA	25,378	15,995	9,383	6,612 R	63.0%	37.0%	63.0%	37.0%
23,042	PLAQUEMINES	6,222	4,482	1,740	2,742 R	72.0%	28.0%	72.0%	28.0%
22,802	POINTE COUPEE	5,170	3,032	2,138	894 R	58.6%	41.4%	58.6%	41.4%
131,613	RAPIDES	21,476	13,966	7,510	6,456 R	65.0%	35.0%	65.0%	35.0%

LOUISIANA

SENATE RUNOFF 2016

2010 Census Population	Parish	Total Vote	Republican (Kennedy)	Democrat (Campbell)	Rep.-Dem. Plurality	Total Vote Rep.	Total Vote Dem.	Major Vote Rep.	Major Vote Dem.
9,091	RED RIVER	2,194	1,145	1,049	96 R	52.2%	47.8%	52.2%	47.8%
20,725	RICHLAND	4,226	2,929	1,297	1,632 R	69.3%	30.7%	69.3%	30.7%
24,233	SABINE	4,277	3,623	654	2,969 R	84.7%	15.3%	84.7%	15.3%
35,897	ST. BERNARD	5,012	3,388	1,624	1,764 R	67.6%	32.4%	67.6%	32.4%
52,780	ST. CHARLES	10,237	6,934	3,303	3,631 R	67.7%	32.3%	67.7%	32.3%
11,203	ST. HELENA	2,855	1,242	1,613	371 D	43.5%	56.5%	43.5%	56.5%
22,102	ST. JAMES	5,582	2,631	2,951	320 D	47.1%	52.9%	47.1%	52.9%
45,924	ST. JOHN THE BAPTIST	9,666	4,087	5,579	1,492 D	42.3%	57.7%	42.3%	57.7%
83,384	ST. LANDRY	14,751	7,897	6,854	1,043 R	53.5%	46.5%	53.5%	46.5%
52,160	ST. MARTIN	13,088	9,531	3,557	5,974 R	72.8%	27.2%	72.8%	27.2%
54,650	ST. MARY	9,104	6,546	2,558	3,988 R	71.9%	28.1%	71.9%	28.1%
233,740	ST. TAMMANY	53,770	42,408	11,362	31,046 R	78.9%	21.1%	78.9%	21.1%
121,097	TANGIPAHOA	18,934	13,079	5,855	7,224 R	69.1%	30.9%	69.1%	30.9%
5,252	TENSAS	1,517	655	862	207 D	43.2%	56.8%	43.2%	56.8%
111,860	TERREBONNE	16,095	12,780	3,315	9,465 R	79.4%	20.6%	79.4%	20.6%
22,721	UNION	4,933	3,619	1,314	2,305 R	73.4%	26.6%	73.4%	26.6%
57,999	VERMILION	11,383	9,279	2,104	7,175 R	81.5%	18.5%	81.5%	18.5%
52,334	VERNON	5,795	4,835	960	3,875 R	83.4%	16.6%	83.4%	16.6%
47,168	WASHINGTON	7,055	5,096	1,959	3,137 R	72.2%	27.8%	72.2%	27.8%
41,207	WEBSTER	8,372	5,220	3,152	2,068 R	62.4%	37.6%	62.4%	37.6%
23,788	WEST BATON ROUGE	7,156	4,102	3,054	1,048 R	57.3%	42.7%	57.3%	42.7%
11,604	WEST CARROLL	2,393	2,011	382	1,629 R	84.0%	16.0%	84.0%	16.0%
15,625	WEST FELICIANA	3,322	2,050	1,272	778 R	61.7%	38.3%	61.7%	38.3%
15,313	WINN	2,674	1,952	722	1,230 R	73.0%	27.0%	73.0%	27.0%
4,533,372	TOTAL	884,007	536,191	347,816	188,375 R	60.7%	39.3%	60.7%	39.3%

LOUISIANA

HOUSE OF REPRESENTATIVES

CD	Year	Total Vote	Republican Vote	Republican Candidate	Democratic Vote	Democratic Candidate	Other Vote	Rep.-Dem. Plurality	Total Vote Rep.	Total Vote Dem.	Major Vote Rep.	Major Vote Dem.
1	2016	326,788	243,645	SCALISE, STEVE*	41,840	LEE, DUGAS A.	41,303	201,805 R	74.6%	12.8%	85.3%	14.7%
1	2014	244,004	189,250	SCALISE, STEVE*	24,761	MENDOZA, M.V. VINNY	29,993	164,489 R	77.6%	10.1%	88.4%	11.6%
1	2012	290,410	193,496	SCALISE, STEVE*	61,703	MENDOZA, M.V. VINNY	35,211	131,793 R	66.6%	21.2%	75.8%	24.2%
2	2016	284,269			198,289	RICHMOND, CEDRIC L.*	85,980	198,289 D		69.8%		100.0%
2	2014	221,570			152,201	RICHMOND, CEDRIC L.*	69,369	152,201 D		68.7%		100.0%
2	2012	287,354	38,801	BAILEY, DWAYNE	158,501	RICHMOND, CEDRIC L.*	90,052	119,700 D	13.5%	55.2%	19.7%	80.3%
3**	2016	138,433	77,671	HIGGINS, CLAY			60,762	77,671 R	56.1%		100.0%	
3	2014	236,268	185,867	BOUSTANY, CHARLES W. JR.*			50,401	185,867 R	78.7%		100.0%	
3	2012	311,393	139,123	BOUSTANY, CHARLES W. JR.*	67,070	RICHARD, RON	105,200	72,053 R	44.7%	21.5%	67.5%	32.5%
4**	2016	133,949	87,370	JOHNSON, MIKE	46,579	JONES, MARSHALL		40,791 R	65.2%	34.8%	65.2%	34.8%
4	2014	207,919	152,683	FLEMING, JOHN*			55,236	152,683 R	73.4%		100.0%	
4	2012	249,531	187,894	FLEMING, JOHN*			61,637	187,894 R	75.3%		100.0%	
5	2016	255,662	208,545	ABRAHAM, RALPH LEE*			47,117	208,545 R	81.6%		100.0%	
5**	2014	209,622	134,616	ABRAHAM, RALPH LEE	75,006	MAYO, JAMIE		59,610 R	64.2%	35.8%	64.2%	35.8%
5	2012	260,216	202,536	ALEXANDER, RODNEY*			57,680	202,536 R	77.8%		100.0%	

LOUISIANA

HOUSE OF REPRESENTATIVES

CD	Year	Total Vote	Republican		Democratic		Other Vote	Rep.-Dem. Plurality	Percentage			
									Total Vote		Major Vote	
			Vote	Candidate	Vote	Candidate			Rep.	Dem.	Rep.	Dem.
6	2016	331,098	207,483	GRAVES, GARRET*	49,380	LIEBERMAN, RICHARD	74,235	158,103 R	62.7%	9.0%	80.8%	19.2%
6**	2014	222,990	139,209	GRAVES, GARRET	83,781	EDWARDS, EDWIN W.		55,428 R	62.4%	37.6%	62.4%	37.6%
6	2012	306,713	243,553	CASSIDY, BILL*			63,160	243,553 R	79.4%		100.0%	
TOTAL	2016	1,362,091	756,440		370,489		309,397	385,951 R	55.5%	27.2%	67.1%	32.9%
TOTAL	2014	1,342,373	823,684		394,840		123,849	428,844 R	61.4%	29.4%	67.6%	32.4%
TOTAL	2012	1,705,617	1,005,403		287,274		412,940	718,129 R	58.9%	16.8%	77.8%	22.2%

Note: An asterisk (*) denotes incumbent. **Indicates results of a runoff. Louisiana has a unique two-tier electoral system for House seats, with a first round of voting that featured candidates from all parties running together on the same ballot. A candidate who won a majority of the vote in the first round was elected. Otherwise, the top two finishers participated in a runoff. In the 2016 election, the 3rd and 4th districts required a runoff on December 10, 2016, with results in the table above. See the First-Round Vote table (Nov. 8, 2016) for the opening round results in these districts. In elections that did not require a runoff, the leading Democratic and Republican candidates are listed with their votes in the first-round, open election. The votes for other candidates are listed in the "Other Vote" column regardless of whether they were Democratic, Republican, or unaffiliated with either major party. The major vote and total vote percentages are calculated only for the top candidate for each party in the district.

LOUISIANA

GENERAL AND PRIMARY ELECTIONS

2016 GENERAL ELECTIONS: OTHER VOTES (NOVEMBER 8, 2016)

President Other vote was 37,978 Libertarian (Gary Johnson), 14,031 Green (Jill Stein), 8,547 Other (Evan McMullin), 3,129 Constitution (Darrell Castle), 1,881 Veterans (Chris Keniston), 1,581 Other (Thomas Hoefling), 1,048 Other (Laurence Kotlikoff), 749 Other (Princess Jacob), 480 Socialist Workers (Alyson Kennedy), 446 Socialism and Liberation (Gloria La Riva), 370 Socialist Equality (Jerry White)

Governor (2015) See "First-Round Vote" table.

Senate See "First-Round Vote" table.

House Other vote was:

CD 1 12,708 Democrat (Danil Faust), 9,405 Libertarian (Howard Kearney), 9,237 Democrat (Joseph Swider), 6,717 Green (Eliot Barron), 3,236 No Party (Chuemai Yang)

CD 2 57,125 Democrat (Melvin Holden), 28,855 Democrat (Kenneth Cutno)

CD 3 See "First-Round Vote" table.

CD 4 See "First-Round Vote" table.

CD 5 47,117 Republican (Billy Burkette)

CD 6 33,592 Republican (Robert Bell), 29,822 Democrat (Jermaine Sampson), 7,603 Libertarian (Richard Fontanesi), 3,218 Other (Devin Graham)

2016 PRIMARY ELECTIONS: SUPPLEMENTARY INFORMATION

Primary March 5, 2016 (President)
November 8, 2016
(Congress First-Round Vote)

Registration (as of November 1, 2016) 3,022,075

Democratic	1,344,703
Republican	898,254
Other Parties	779,118

Runoff December 10, 2016

Primary Type For governor and other federal offices, Louisiana has a two-tier electoral system open to all voters, with a first round of voting (sometimes called an open or "jungle" primary) that features candidates from all parties running together on the same ballot. A candidate who wins a majority of the vote in the first round is elected. Otherwise, there is a runoff held several weeks later between the top two finishers.

Primary Data See "First-Round Vote" table.

LOUISIANA

GENERAL AND PRIMARY ELECTIONS

REPUBLICAN PRIMARIES				DEMOCRATIC PRIMARIES		
President	Trump, Donald J.	124,854	41.4%	Clinton, Hillary Rodham	221,733	71.1%
	Cruz, Ted	113,968	37.8%	Sanders, Bernard	72,276	23.2%
	Rubio, Marco	33,813	11.2%	Burke, Steve	4,785	1.5%
	Kasich, John R.	19,359	6.4%	Wolfe, John	4,512	1.4%
	Carson, Ben	4,544	1.5%	O'Malley, Martin	2,550	0.8%
	Bush, Jeb	2,145	0.7%	Wilson, Willie	1,423	0.5%
	Paul, Rand	670	0.2%	Judd, Keith	1,357	0.4%
	Huckabee, Mike	645	0.2%	De La Fuente, Roque "Rocky"	1,341	0.4%
	Christie, Chris	401	0.1%	Steinberg, Michael Alan	993	0.3%
	Fiorina, Carly	243	0.1%	Hewes, Henry	806	0.3%
	Cook, Timothy	219	0.1%			
	Santorum, Rick	180	0.1%			
	Graham, Lindsey	152	0.1%			
	Messina, Peter	48				
	TOTAL	*301,241*		*TOTAL*	*311,776*	

FIRST-ROUND VOTE (NOV. 8, 2016)

Governor (2015)	Edwards, John Bel (D)#	444,517	40.0%
	Vitter, David (R)#	256,300	23.0%
	Angelle, Scott (R)	214,982	19.3%
	Dardenne, Jay (R)	166,656	15.0%
	Deaton, Cary (D)	11,763	1.1%
	Simpson, S. (D)	7,420	0.7%
	Billiot, Beryl (No Party)	5,694	0.5%
	Odom, Jeremy (No Party)	4,756	0.4%
	Ogeron, Eric (Other)	2,248	0.2%
	TOTAL	*1,114,336*	
Senator	Kennedy, John (R)#	482,591	25.0%
	Campbell, Foster (D)#	337,833	17.5%
	Boustany, Charles W. Jr. (R)	298,008	15.4%
	Fayard, Caroline (D)	240,917	12.5%
	Fleming, John (R)	204,026	10.6%
	Maness, Robert (R)	90,856	5.7%
	Duke, David (R)	58,606	3.0%
	Edwards, Derrick (D)	51,774	2.7%
	Landrieu, Gary (D)	45,587	2.4%
	Crawford, Donald (R)	25,523	1.3%
	Cao, Anh (R)	21,019	1.1%
	Billiot, Beryl (No Party)	19,352	1.0%
	Clements, Thomas (Libertarian)	11,370	0.6%
	Hebert, Troy (No Party)	9,503	0.5%
	Pellerin, Joshua (D)	7,395	0.4%
	Williams, Peter (D)	6,855	0.4%
	Mendoza, M.V. (D)	4,927	0.3%
	Marone, Kaitlin (No Party)	4,108	0.2%
	Gillam, Le Roy (Libertarian)	4,067	0.2%
	Marsala, Charles (R)	3,684	0.2%
	Patel, Abhay (R)	1,576	0.1%
	Wells, Arden (No Party)	1,483	0.1%
	Lang, William (No Party)	1,427	0.1%
	Taylor, Gregory (Other)	1,151	
	TOTAL	*1,933,635*	

LOUISIANA

GENERAL AND PRIMARY ELECTIONS

FIRST-ROUND VOTE (NOV. 8, 2016)

Congressional District 3	Scott Angelle (R)#	91,532	28.6%
	Clay Higgins (R)#	84,912	26.5%
	Jacob Hebert (D)	28,385	8.9%
	Larry Rader (D)	27,830	8.7%
	Gus Rantz (R)	25,662	8.0%
	Greg Ellison (R)	24,882	7.8%
	Brett Geymann (R)	21,607	6.7%
	Bryan Barrilleaux (R)	6,223	1.9%
	Guy McLendon (Libertarian)	2,937	0.9%
	Kenny Scelfo (No Party)	2,670	0.8%
	Grover Rees (R)	2,457	0.8%
	Herman Vidrine (R)	1,357	0.4%
	TOTAL	*320,454*	
Congressional District 4	Marshall Jones (D)#	80,593	28.2%
	Mike Johnson (R)#	70,580	24.7%
	Ralph Baucum (R)	50,412	17.6%
	Oliver Jenkins (R)	44,521	15.6%
	Elbert Guillory (R)	21,017	7.3%
	Rick John (R)	13,220	4.6%
	Mark Halverson (No Party)	3,149	1.1%
	Kenneth Krefft (No Party)	2,493	0.9%
	TOTAL	*285,985*	

Note: The table above lists the first-round results for races that were decided in a December 10, 2016, runoff. A pound sign (#) indicates the candidates in each race who qualified for the runoff.

MAINE

Congressional districts first established for elections held in 2012

2 members

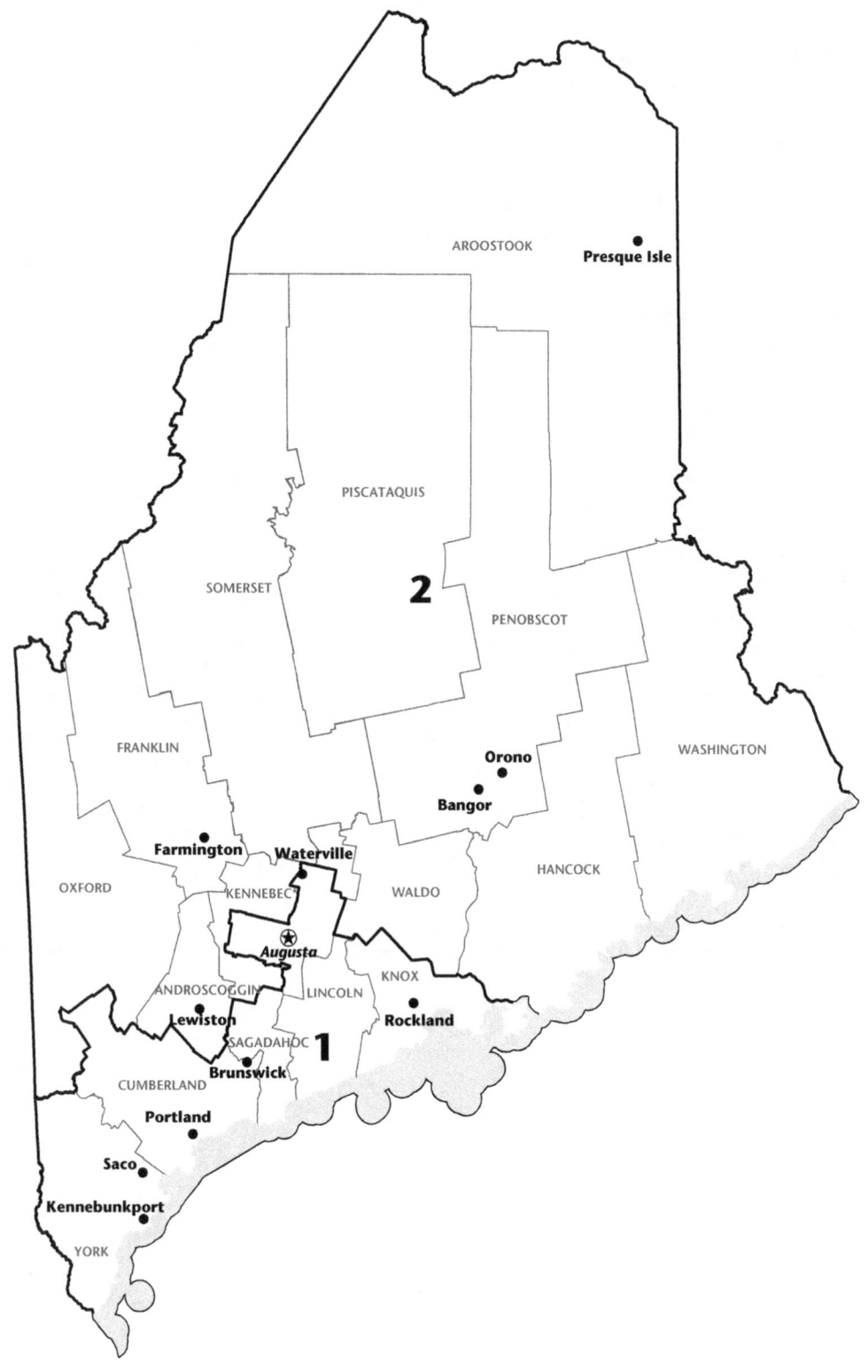

* Asterisk indicates a county whose boundaries include parts of two or more congressional districts.

MAINE

GOVERNOR
Paul R. LePage (R). Re-elected 2014 to a four-year term. Previously elected 2010.

SENATORS (1 Republican, 1 Independent)
Susan M. Collins (R). Re-elected 2014 to a six-year term. Previously elected 2008, 2002, 1996.

Angus S. King Jr. (Ind.). Elected 2012 to a six-year term.

REPRESENTATIVES (1 Democrat, 1 Republican)
1. Chellie Pingree (D)   2. Bruce L. Poliquin (R)

POSTWAR VOTE FOR PRESIDENT

| | | Republican | | Democratic | | | | Percentage | | | |
| | | | | | | | | Total Vote | | Major Vote | |
Year	Total Vote	Vote	Candidate	Vote	Candidate	Other Vote	Rep.-Dem. Plurality	Rep.	Dem.	Rep.	Dem.
2016**	747,927	335,593	Trump, Donald J.	357,735	Clinton, Hillary Rodham	54,599	22,142 D	44.9%	47.8%	48.4%	51.6%
2012	713,180	292,276	Romney, W. Mitt	401,306	Obama, Barack H.*	19,598	109,030 D	41.0%	56.3%	42.1%	57.9%
2008	731,163	295,273	McCain, John S. III	421,923	Obama, Barack H.	13,967	126,650 D	40.4%	57.7%	41.2%	58.8%
2004	740,752	330,201	Bush, George W.*	396,842	Kerry, John F.	13,709	66,641 D	44.6%	53.6%	45.4%	54.6%
2000**	651,817	286,616	Bush, George W.	319,951	Gore, Albert Jr.	45,250	33,335 D	44.0%	49.1%	47.3%	52.7%
1996**	605,897	186,378	Dole, Robert "Bob"	312,788	Clinton, Bill*	106,731	126,410 D	30.8%	51.6%	37.3%	62.7%
1992**	679,499	206,504	Bush, George H.*	263,420	Clinton, Bill	209,575	56,916 D	30.4%	38.8%	43.9%	56.1%
1988	555,035	307,131	Bush, George H.	243,569	Dukakis, Michael S.	4,335	63,562 R	55.3%	43.9%	55.8%	44.2%
1984	553,144	336,500	Reagan, Ronald*	214,515	Mondale, Walter F.	2,129	121,985 R	60.8%	38.8%	61.1%	38.9%
1980**	523,011	238,522	Reagan, Ronald	220,974	Carter, Jimmy*	63,515	17,548 R	45.6%	42.3%	51.9%	48.1%
1976	483,216	236,320	Ford, Gerald R.*	232,279	Carter, Jimmy	14,617	4,041 R	48.9%	48.1%	50.4%	49.6%
1972	417,042	256,458	Nixon, Richard M.*	160,584	McGovern, George S.		95,874 R	61.5%	38.5%	61.5%	38.5%
1968**	392,936	169,254	Nixon, Richard M.	217,312	Humphrey, Hubert Horatio Jr.	6,370	48,058 D	43.1%	55.3%	43.8%	56.2%
1964	380,965	118,701	Goldwater, Barry M. Sr.	262,264	Johnson, Lyndon B.*		143,563 D	31.2%	68.8%	31.2%	68.8%
1960	421,767	240,608	Nixon, Richard M.	181,159	Kennedy, John F.		59,449 R	57.0%	43.0%	57.0%	43.0%
1956	351,706	249,238	Eisenhower, Dwight D.*	102,468	Stevenson, Adlai E. II		146,770 R	70.9%	29.1%	70.9%	29.1%
1952	351,786	232,353	Eisenhower, Dwight D.	118,806	Stevenson, Adlai E. II	627	113,547 R	66.0%	33.8%	66.2%	33.8%
1948	264,787	150,234	Dewey, Thomas E.	111,916	Truman, Harry S.*	2,637	38,318 R	56.7%	42.3%	57.3%	42.7%

Note: An asterisk (*) denotes incumbent. **In past elections, the other vote included: 2016 - 38,105 Libertarian (Gary Johnson); 2000 - 37,127 Green (Ralph Nader); 1996 - 85,970 Reform (Ross Perot); 1992 - 206,820 Independent (Perot, who finished second); 1980 - 53,327 Independent (John Anderson); 1968 - 6,370 American Independent (George Wallace).

MAINE

POSTWAR VOTE FOR GOVERNOR

Year	Total Vote	Republican Vote	Republican Candidate	Democratic Vote	Democratic Candidate	Other Vote	Rep.-Dem. Plurality	Total Vote Rep.	Total Vote Dem.	Major Vote Rep.	Major Vote Dem.
2014	611,227	294,519	LePage, Paul R.*	265,114	Michaud, Michael H.	51,594	29,405 R	48.2%	43.4%	52.6%	47.4%
2010**	572,766	218,065	LePage, Paul R.	109,387	Mitchell, Elizabeth H. "Libby"	245,314	108,678 R	38.1%	19.1%	66.6%	33.4%
2006**	550,865	166,425	Woodcock, Chandler E.	209,927	Baldacci, John*	174,513	43,502 D	30.2%	38.1%	44.2%	55.8%
2002	505,190	209,496	Cianchette, Peter E.	238,179	Baldacci, John	57,515	28,683 D#	41.5%	47.1%	46.8%	53.2%
1998**	421,009	79,716	Longley, James B. Jr.	50,506	Connolly, Thomas J.	290,787	29,210 R	18.9%	12.0%	61.2%	38.8%
1994**	511,308	117,990	Collins, Susan M.	172,951	Brennan, Joseph E.	220,367	54,961 D#	23.1%	33.8%	40.6%	59.4%
1990	522,492	243,766	McKernan, John R.*	230,038	Brennan, Joseph E.	48,688	13,728 R	46.7%	44.0%	51.4%	48.6%
1986**	426,861	170,312	McKernan, John R.	128,744	Tierney, James	127,805	41,568 R	39.9%	30.2%	56.9%	43.1%
1982	460,295	172,949	Cragin, Charles L.	281,066	Brennan, Joseph E.*	6,280	108,117 D	37.6%	61.1%	38.1%	61.9%
1978**	370,258	126,862	Palmer, Linwood E.	176,493	Brennan, Joseph E.	66,903	49,631 D	34.3%	47.7%	41.8%	58.2%
1974**	363,945	84,176	Erwin, James S.*	132,219	Mitchell, George J.	147,550	48,043 D#	23.1%	36.3%	38.9%	61.1%
1970	325,386	162,248	Erwin, James S.	163,138	Curtis, Kenneth M.*		890 D	49.9%	50.1%	49.9%	50.1%
1966	323,838	151,802	Reed, John H.*	172,036	Curtis, Kenneth M.		20,234 D	46.9%	53.1%	46.9%	53.1%
1962	292,725	146,604	Reed, John H.*	146,121	Dolloff, Maynard C.		483 R	50.1%	49.9%	50.1%	49.9%
1960S**	417,215	219,768	Reed, John H.	197,447	Coffin, Frank M.		22,321 R	52.7%	47.3%	52.7%	47.3%
1958**	280,245	134,572	Hildreth, Horace A.	145,673	Clauson, Clinton A.		11,101 D	48.0%	52.0%	48.0%	52.0%
1956	304,649	124,395	Trafton, Willis A. Jr.	180,254	Muskie, Edmund S.*		55,859 D	40.8%	59.2%	40.8%	59.2%
1954	248,971	113,298	Cross, Burton M.*	135,673	Muskie, Edmund S.		22,375 D	45.5%	54.5%	45.5%	54.5%
1952	248,441	128,532	Cross, Burton M.	82,538	Oliver, James C.	37,371	45,994 R	51.7%	33.2%	60.9%	39.1%
1950	241,177	145,823	Payne, Frederick G.*	94,304	Grant, Earle S.	1,050	51,519 R	60.5%	39.1%	60.7%	39.3%
1948	222,500	145,956	Payne, Frederick G.	76,544	Lausier, Louis B.		69,412 R	65.6%	34.4%	65.6%	34.4%
1946	179,951	110,327	Hildreth, Horace A.	69,624	Clark, F. Davis		40,703 R	61.3%	38.7%	61.3%	38.7%

Note: An asterisk (*) denotes incumbent. A pound sign (#) in the plurality column indicates that the winners in 1974, 1994, and 1998 were independents. **In past elections, the other vote included: 2010 - 208,270 Independent (Eliot R. Cutler, who finished second); 2006 - 118,715 Independent Maine Course (Barbara Merrill); 1998 - 246,772 Independent (Angus King, who was re-elected with 58.6 percent of the total vote); 1994 - 180,829 Independent (King, who was elected with 35.4 percent of the total vote); 1986 - 64,317 Independent (Sherry F. Huber), 63,474 Independent (John E. Menario); 1978 - 65,889 Independent (Herman C. Frankland); 1974 - 142,464 Independent (James B. Longley, who was elected with 39.1 percent of the total vote). The 1960 election was for a short term to fill a vacancy. The term of office of Maine's governor was increased from two to four years effective with the 1958 election.

POSTWAR VOTE FOR SENATOR

Year	Total Vote	Republican Vote	Republican Candidate	Democratic Vote	Democratic Candidate	Other Vote	Rep.-Dem. Plurality	Total Vote Rep.	Total Vote Dem.	Major Vote Rep.	Major Vote Dem.
2014	604,008	413,495	Collins, Susan M.*	190,244	Bellows, Shenna	269	223,251 R	68.5%	31.5%	68.5%	31.5%
2012**	700,599	215,399	Summers, Charles E.	92,900	Dill, Cynthia Ann	392,300	122,499 R#	30.7%	13.3%	69.9%	30.1%
2008	724,430	444,300	Collins, Susan M.*	279,510	Allen, Tom	620	164,790 R	61.3%	38.6%	61.4%	38.6%
2006	543,981	402,598	Snowe, Olympia J.*	111,984	Bright, Jean Hay	29,399	290,614 R	74.0%	20.6%	78.2%	21.8%
2002	504,899	295,041	Collins, Susan M.*	209,858	Pingree, Chellie		85,183 R	58.4%	41.6%	58.4%	41.6%
2000	634,872	437,689	Snowe, Olympia J.*	197,183	Lawrence, Mark W.		240,506 R	68.9%	31.1%	68.9%	31.1%
1996	606,777	298,422	Collins, Susan M.	266,226	Brennan, Joseph E.	42,129	32,196 R	49.2%	43.9%	52.9%	47.1%
1994	511,733	308,244	Snowe, Olympia J.	186,042	Andrews, Thomas H.	17,447	122,202 R	60.2%	36.4%	62.4%	37.6%
1990	520,320	319,167	Cohen, William S.*	201,053	Rolde, Neil	100	118,114 R	61.3%	38.6%	61.4%	38.6%
1988	557,375	104,758	Wyman, Jasper S.	452,590	Mitchell, George J.*	27	347,832 D	18.8%	81.2%	18.8%	81.2%
1984	551,406	404,414	Cohen, William S.*	142,626	Mitchell, Elizabeth H. "Libby"	4,366	261,788 R	73.3%	25.9%	73.9%	26.1%
1982	459,715	179,882	Emery, David F.	279,819	Mitchell, George J.	14	99,937 D	39.1%	60.9%	39.1%	60.9%
1978	375,172	212,294	Cohen, William S.	127,327	Hathaway, William D.*	35,551	84,967 R	56.6%	33.9%	62.5%	37.5%
1976	486,254	193,489	Monks, Robert A.G.	292,704	Muskie, Edmund S.*	61	99,215 D	39.8%	60.2%	39.8%	60.2%
1972	421,310	197,040	Smith, Margaret Chase*	224,270	Hathaway, William D.		27,230 D	46.8%	53.2%	46.8%	53.2%
1970	323,860	123,906	Bishop, Neil S.	199,954	Muskie, Edmund S.*		76,048 D	38.3%	61.7%	38.3%	61.7%
1966	319,535	188,291	Smith, Margaret Chase*	131,136	Violette, Elmer H.	108	57,155 R	58.9%	41.0%	58.9%	41.1%
1964	380,551	127,040	McIntire, Clifford G.	253,511	Muskie, Edmund S.*		126,471 D	33.4%	66.6%	33.4%	66.6%
1960	416,699	256,890	Smith, Margaret Chase*	159,809	Cormier, Lucia M.		97,081 R	61.6%	38.4%	61.6%	38.4%
1958	284,364	111,522	Payne, Frederick G.*	172,842	Muskie, Edmund S.		61,320 D	39.2%	60.8%	39.2%	60.8%
1954	246,605	144,530	Smith, Margaret Chase*	102,075	Fullam, Paul A.		42,455 R	58.6%	41.4%	58.6%	41.4%
1952	237,164	139,205	Payne, Frederick G.	82,665	Dube, Roger P.	15,294	56,540 R	58.7%	34.9%	62.7%	37.3%
1948	223,256	159,182	Smith, Margaret Chase	64,074	Scolten, Adrian H.		95,108 R	71.3%	28.7%	71.3%	28.7%
1946	175,014	111,215	Brewster, Ralph O.*	63,799	MacDonald, Peter M.		47,416 R	63.5%	36.5%	63.5%	36.5%

Note: An asterisk (*) denotes incumbent. A pound sign (#) in the plurality column indicates that the winner in 2012 was an independent. **In past elections, the other vote included: 2012 - 370,580 Independent (Angus King, who received 52.9 percent of the total vote and was elected with a plurality of 155,181 votes).

MAINE

PRESIDENT 2016

2010 Census Population	County	Total Vote	Republican (Trump)	Democratic (Clinton)	Other	Rep.-Dem. Plurality		Percentage			
								Total Vote		Major Vote	
								Rep.	Dem.	Rep.	Dem.
107,702	ANDROSCOGGIN	55,601	28,227	23,009	4,365	5,218	R	50.8%	41.4%	55.1%	44.9%
71,870	AROOSTOOK	35,097	19,419	13,386	2,292	6,033	R	55.3%	38.1%	59.2%	40.8%
281,674	CUMBERLAND	171,818	57,709	102,981	11,128	45,272	D	33.6%	59.9%	35.9%	64.1%
30,768	FRANKLIN	16,488	7,918	7,016	1,554	902	R	48.0%	42.6%	53.0%	47.0%
54,418	HANCOCK	32,130	13,705	16,117	2,308	2,412	D	42.7%	50.2%	46.0%	54.0%
122,151	KENNEBEC	66,208	31,675	29,302	5,231	2,373	R	47.8%	44.3%	51.9%	48.1%
39,736	KNOX	23,147	9,148	12,443	1,556	3,295	D	39.5%	53.8%	42.4%	57.6%
34,457	LINCOLN	21,503	9,727	10,241	1,535	514	D	45.2%	47.6%	48.7%	51.3%
57,833	OXFORD	31,201	16,210	12,172	2,819	4,038	R	52.0%	39.0%	57.1%	42.9%
153,923	PENOBSCOT	80,540	41,622	32,838	6,080	8,784	R	51.7%	40.8%	55.9%	44.1%
17,535	PISCATAQUIS	9,182	5,406	3,098	678	2,308	R	58.9%	33.7%	63.6%	36.4%
35,293	SAGADAHOC	21,616	9,304	10,664	1,648	1,360	D	43.0%	49.3%	46.6%	53.4%
52,228	SOMERSET	26,064	15,001	9,092	1,971	5,909	R	57.6%	34.9%	62.3%	37.7%
38,786	WALDO	22,707	10,378	10,440	1,889	62	D	45.7%	46.0%	49.9%	50.1%
32,856	WASHINGTON	16,365	9,093	6,075	1,197	3,018	R	55.6%	37.1%	59.9%	40.1%
197,131	YORK	114,274	50,403	55,844	8,027	5,441	D	44.1%	48.9%	47.4%	52.6%
	Votes Not Reported by County	3,986	648	3,017	321	2,369	D	16.3%	75.7%	17.7%	82.3%
1,328,361	TOTAL	747,927	335,593	357,735	54,599	22,142	D	44.9%	47.8%	48.4%	51.6%

2010 Census Population	City/Town	Total Vote	Republican (Trump)	Democratic (Clinton)	Other	Rep.-Dem. Plurality		Percentage			
								Total Vote		Major Vote	
								Rep.	Dem.	Rep.	Dem.
23,055	AUBURN	11,608	5,325	5,296	987	29	R	45.9%	45.6%	50.1%	49.9%
19,136	AUGUSTA	8,909	3,805	4,396	708	591	D	42.7%	49.3%	46.4%	53.6%
33,039	BANGOR	15,424	6,001	8,155	1,268	2,154	D	38.9%	52.9%	42.4%	57.6%
8,514	BATH	4,660	1,571	2,717	372	1,146	D	33.7%	58.3%	36.6%	63.4%
6,668	BELFAST	3,876	1,241	2,351	284	1,110	D	32.0%	60.7%	34.5%	65.5%
7,246	BERWICK	3,901	2,086	1,539	276	547	R	53.5%	39.5%	57.5%	42.5%
21,277	BIDDEFORD	9,965	3,729	5,505	731	1,776	D	37.4%	55.2%	40.4%	59.6%
9,482	BREWER	5,144	2,585	2,165	394	420	R	50.3%	42.1%	54.4%	45.6%
20,278	BRUNSWICK	12,479	3,647	7,992	840	4,345	D	29.2%	64.0%	31.3%	68.7%
8,034	BUXTON	4,766	2,538	1,895	333	643	R	53.3%	39.8%	57.3%	42.7%
4,850	CAMDEN	3,380	802	2,430	148	1,628	D	23.7%	71.9%	24.8%	75.2%
9,015	CAPE ELIZABETH	6,379	1,593	4,480	306	2,887	D	25.0%	70.2%	26.2%	73.8%
8,189	CARIBOU	3,977	2,106	1,595	276	511	R	53.0%	40.1%	56.9%	43.1%
7,211	CUMBERLAND TOWN	5,305	1,755	3,184	366	1,429	D	33.1%	60.0%	35.5%	64.5%
6,204	ELIOT	4,224	1,704	2,257	263	553	D	40.3%	53.4%	43.0%	57.0%
7,741	ELLSWORTH	4,272	2,113	1,810	349	303	R	49.5%	42.4%	53.9%	46.1%
6,735	FAIRFIELD	3,269	1,745	1,250	274	495	R	53.4%	38.2%	58.3%	41.7%
11,185	FALMOUTH	7,943	2,633	4,877	433	2,244	D	33.1%	61.4%	35.1%	64.9%
7,760	FARMINGTON	3,844	1,483	1,979	382	496	D	38.6%	51.5%	42.8%	57.2%
7,879	FREEPORT	5,447	1,644	3,442	361	1,798	D	30.2%	63.2%	32.3%	67.7%
5,800	GARDINER	3,049	1,361	1,446	242	85	D	44.6%	47.4%	48.5%	51.5%
16,381	GORHAM	9,689	3,945	4,995	749	1,050	D	40.7%	51.6%	44.1%	55.9%
7,761	GRAY	4,782	2,397	2,021	364	376	R	50.1%	42.3%	54.3%	45.7%
7,257	HAMPDEN	4,401	2,103	1,929	369	174	R	47.8%	43.8%	52.2%	47.8%
4,740	HARPSWELL	3,386	1,316	1,881	189	565	D	38.9%	55.6%	41.2%	58.8%
6,123	HOULTON	2,692	1,573	940	179	633	R	58.4%	34.9%	62.6%	37.4%
4,851	JAY	2,502	1,184	1,143	175	41	R	47.3%	45.7%	50.9%	49.1%
10,798	KENNEBUNK	7,342	2,648	4,224	470	1,576	D	36.1%	57.5%	38.5%	61.5%
9,490	KITTERY	5,586	1,746	3,474	366	1,728	D	31.3%	62.2%	33.4%	66.6%
36,592	LEWISTON	16,792	7,336	8,222	1,234	886	D	43.7%	49.0%	47.2%	52.8%

MAINE

PRESIDENT 2016

2010 Census Population	City/Town	Total Vote	Republican (Trump)	Democratic (Clinton)	Other	Rep.-Dem. Plurality		Percentage			
								Total Vote		Major Vote	
								Rep.	Dem.	Rep.	Dem.
2,314	LIMESTONE	789	410	325	54	85 R		52.0%	41.2%	55.8%	44.2%
5,085	LINCOLN TOWN	2,444	1,574	704	166	870 R		64.4%	28.8%	69.1%	30.9%
9,009	LISBON	4,827	2,749	1,697	381	1,052 R		57.0%	35.2%	61.8%	38.2%
4,506	MILLINOCKET	2,207	1,161	913	133	248 R		52.6%	41.4%	56.0%	44.0%
6,240	OAKLAND	3,464	1,715	1,442	307	273 R		49.5%	41.6%	54.3%	45.7%
8,624	OLD ORCHARD BEACH	5,437	2,147	2,978	312	831 D		39.5%	54.8%	41.9%	58.1%
7,840	OLD TOWN	3,887	1,514	2,029	344	515 D		39.0%	52.2%	42.7%	57.3%
10,362	ORONO	5,365	1,445	3,420	500	1,975 D		26.9%	63.7%	29.7%	70.3%
66,194	PORTLAND	37,596	6,789	28,534	2,273	21,745 D		18.1%	75.9%	19.2%	80.8%
9,692	PRESQUE ISLE	4,267	2,102	1,779	386	323 R		49.3%	41.7%	54.2%	45.8%
7,297	ROCKLAND	3,501	1,209	2,024	268	815 D		34.5%	57.8%	37.4%	62.6%
5,841	RUMFORD	2,793	1,400	1,137	256	263 R		50.1%	40.7%	55.2%	44.8%
18,482	SACO	10,656	4,067	5,902	687	1,835 D		38.2%	55.4%	40.8%	59.2%
20,798	SANFORD	10,003	4,744	4,447	812	297 R		47.4%	44.5%	51.6%	48.4%
18,919	SCARBOROUGH	12,575	4,918	6,893	764	1,975 D		39.1%	54.8%	41.6%	58.4%
8,589	SKOWHEGAN	4,002	2,046	1,674	282	372 R		51.1%	41.8%	55.0%	45.0%
7,220	SOUTH BERWICK	4,148	1,616	2,227	305	611 D		39.0%	53.7%	42.1%	57.9%
25,002	SOUTH PORTLAND	14,708	3,950	9,919	839	5,969 D		26.9%	67.4%	28.5%	71.5%
9,874	STANDISH	5,392	2,873	2,144	375	729 R		53.3%	39.8%	57.3%	42.7%
8,784	TOPSHAM	5,889	2,328	3,109	452	781 D		39.5%	52.8%	42.8%	57.2%
15,722	WATERVILLE	7,186	2,424	4,171	591	1,747 D		33.7%	58.0%	36.8%	63.2%
9,589	WELLS	6,522	2,807	3,275	440	468 D		43.0%	50.2%	46.2%	53.8%
17,494	WESTBROOK	9,708	3,573	5,431	704	1,858 D		36.8%	55.9%	39.7%	60.3%
17,001	WINDHAM	9,881	4,860	4,308	713	552 R		49.2%	43.6%	53.0%	47.0%
7,794	WINSLOW	4,253	2,100	1,825	328	275 R		49.4%	42.9%	53.5%	46.5%
6,092	WINTHROP	3,591	1,602	1,683	306	81 D		44.6%	46.9%	48.8%	51.2%
8,349	YARMOUTH	5,520	1,503	3,705	312	2,202 D		27.2%	67.1%	28.9%	71.1%
12,529	YORK TOWN	8,691	3,260	4,929	502	1,669 D		37.5%	56.7%	39.8%	60.2%

MAINE

HOUSE OF REPRESENTATIVES

CD	Year	Total Vote	Republican		Democratic		Other Vote	Rep.-Dem. Plurality	Percentage			
			Vote	Candidate	Vote	Candidate			Total Vote		Major Vote	
									Rep.	Dem.	Rep.	Dem.
1	2016	392,391	164,569	HOLBROOK, MARK I.	227,546	PINGREE, CHELLIE*	276	62,977 D	41.9%	58.0%	42.0%	58.0%
1	2014	308,898	94,751	MISIUK, ISAAC J.	186,674	PINGREE, CHELLIE*	27,473	91,923 D	30.7%	60.4%	33.7%	66.3%
1	2012	364,803	128,440	COURTNEY, JONATHAN T.E.	236,363	PINGREE, CHELLIE*		107,923 D	35.2%	64.8%	35.2%	64.8%
2	2016	352,183	192,878	POLIQUIN, BRUCE L.*	159,081	CAIN, EMILY ANN	224	33,797 R	54.8%	45.2%	54.8%	45.2%
2	2014	283,448	133,308	POLIQUIN, BRUCE L.	118,556	CAIN, EMILY ANN	31,584	14,752 R	47.0%	41.8%	52.9%	47.1%
2	2012	328,998	137,542	RAYE, KEVIN L.	191,456	MICHAUD, MICHAEL H.*		53,914 D	41.8%	58.2%	41.8%	58.2%
TOTAL	2016	744,574	357,447		386,627		500	29,180 D	48.0%	51.9%	48.0%	52.0%
TOTAL	2014	592,346	228,059		305,230		59,057	77,171 D	38.5%	51.5%	42.8%	57.2%
TOTAL	2012	693,801	265,982		427,819			161,837 D	38.3%	61.7%	38.3%	61.7%

Note: An asterisk (*) denotes incumbent.

MAINE

GENERAL AND PRIMARY ELECTIONS

2016 GENERAL ELECTIONS: OTHER VOTES

President   Other vote was 38,105 Libertarian (Gary Johnson), 14,251 Green (Jill Stein), 1,887 Write-in (Evan McMullin), 333 Write-in (Darrell Castle), 16 Write-in (Laurence Kotlikoff), 7 Write-in (Cherunda Fox)

House   Other vote was:

CD 1   276 Write-in (James Bouchard)
CD 2   224 Write-in (Jay Dresser)

2016 PRIMARY ELECTIONS: SUPPLEMENTARY INFORMATION

Presidential Caucus   March 5, 2016 (Republican) March 6, 2016 (Democratic)   **Registration** (as of March 9, 2016 — includes 5,550 inactive registrants)   983,530

Primary   June 14, 2016 (Congress)

Primary Type   Semi-open—Registered voters in a political party could participate only in their party's primary. "Unenrolled" and new voters could vote in either party's primary by enrolling in that party on primary day.

	REPUBLICAN PRIMARIES			DEMOCRATIC PRIMARIES		
Congressional District 1	Holbrook, Mark I.	10,360	50.1%	Pingree, Chellie*	28,143	100%
	Smith, Ande Allen	10,303	49.9%			
	TOTAL	20,663		TOTAL	28,143	
Congressional District 2	Poliquin, Bruce L.*	19,252	100%	Cain, Emily Ann	19,003	100%
	TOTAL	19,252		TOTAL	19,003	

Note: An asterisk (*) denotes incumbent.

MARYLAND

Congressional districts first established for elections held in 2012
8 members

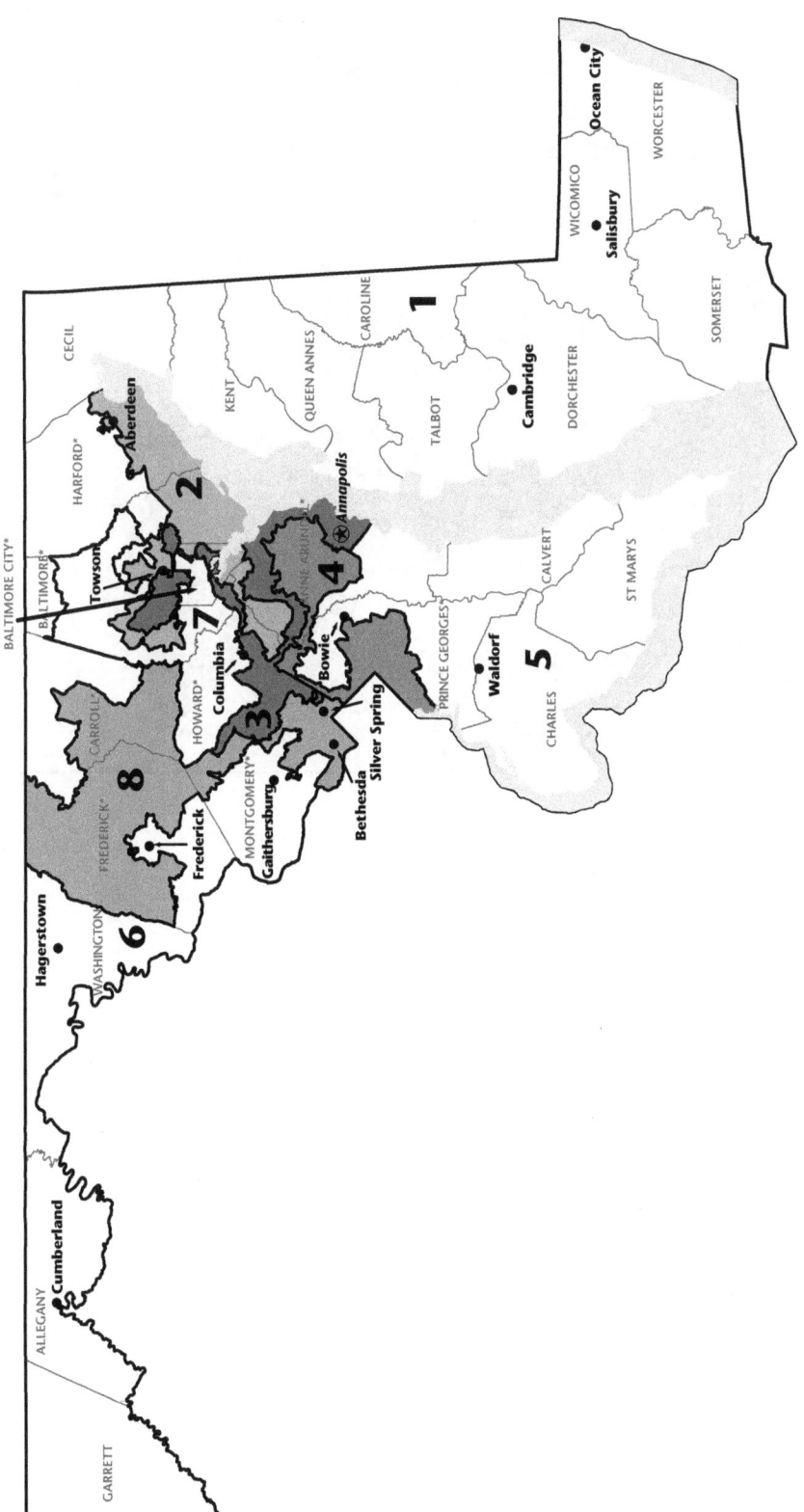

The city of Baltimore City is an independent city that is treated as a county equivalent.

* Asterisk indicates a county whose boundaries include parts of two or more congressional districts.

MARYLAND
Baltimore, Washington, D.C., Areas

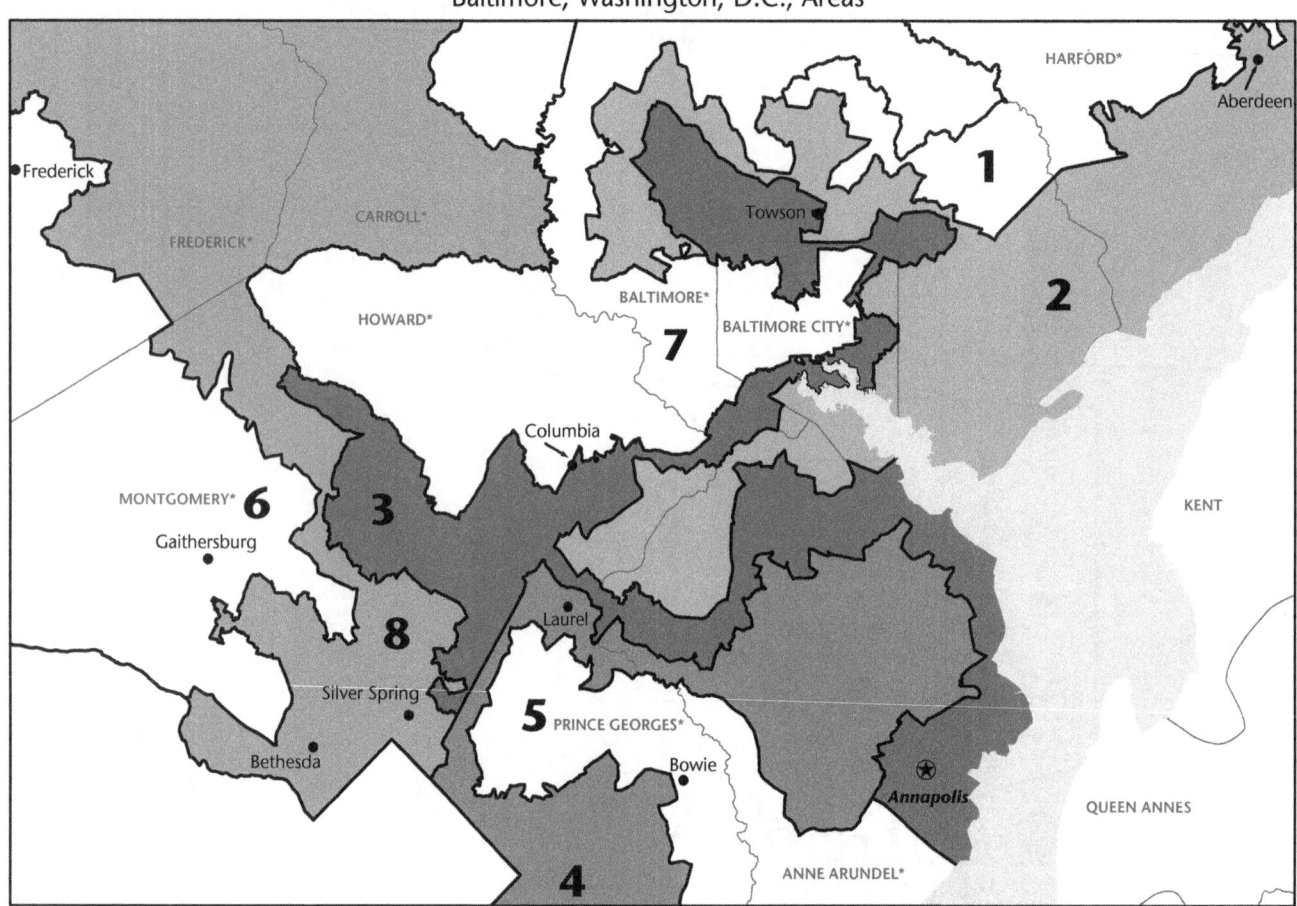

* Asterisk indicates a county whose boundaries include parts of two or more congressional districts.

MARYLAND

GOVERNOR
Larry Hogan (R). Elected 2014 to a four-year term.

SENATORS (2 Democrats)
Benjamin L. Cardin (D). Re-elected 2012 to a six-year term. Previously elected 2006.

Chris Van Hollen Jr. (D). Elected 2016 to a six-year term.

REPRESENTATIVES (1 Republican, 7 Democrats)
1. Andy Harris (R)
2. C. A. Dutch Ruppersberger (D)
3. John P. Sarbanes (D)
4. Anthony G. Brown (D)
5. Steny H. Hoyer (D)
6. John Delaney (D)
7. Elijah E. Cummings (D)
8. Jamie Raskin (D)

POSTWAR VOTE FOR PRESIDENT

| | | Republican | | Democratic | | | | Percentage | | | |
| | | | | | | | | Total Vote | | Major Vote | |
Year	Total Vote	Vote	Candidate	Vote	Candidate	Other Vote	Rep.-Dem. Plurality	Rep.	Dem.	Rep.	Dem.
2016**	2,781,446	943,169	Trump, Donald J.	1,677,928	Clinton, Hillary Rodham	160,349	734,759 D	33.9%	60.3%	36.0%	64.0%
2012	2,707,327	971,869	Romney, W. Mitt	1,677,844	Obama, Barack H.*	57,614	705,975 D	35.9%	62.0%	36.7%	63.3%
2008	2,631,596	959,862	McCain, John S. III	1,629,467	Obama, Barack H.	42,267	669,605 D	36.5%	61.9%	37.1%	62.9%
2004	2,386,678	1,024,703	Bush, George W.*	1,334,493	Kerry, John F.	27,482	309,790 D	42.9%	55.9%	43.4%	56.6%
2000**	2,020,480	813,797	Bush, George W.	1,140,782	Gore, Albert Jr.	65,901	326,985 D	40.3%	56.5%	41.6%	58.4%
1996**	1,780,870	681,530	Dole, Robert "Bob"	966,207	Clinton, Bill*	133,133	284,677 D	38.3%	54.3%	41.4%	58.6%
1992**	1,985,046	707,094	Bush, George H.*	988,571	Clinton, Bill	289,381	281,477 D	35.6%	49.8%	41.7%	58.3%
1988	1,714,358	876,167	Bush, George H.	826,304	Dukakis, Michael S.	11,887	49,863 R	51.1%	48.2%	51.5%	48.5%
1984	1,675,873	879,918	Reagan, Ronald*	787,935	Mondale, Walter F.	8,020	91,983 R	52.5%	47.0%	52.8%	47.2%
1980**	1,540,496	680,606	Reagan, Ronald	726,161	Carter, Jimmy*	133,729	45,555 D	44.2%	47.1%	48.4%	51.6%
1976	1,439,897	672,661	Ford, Gerald R.*	759,612	Carter, Jimmy	7,624	86,951 D	46.7%	52.8%	47.0%	53.0%
1972	1,353,812	829,305	Nixon, Richard M.*	505,781	McGovern, George S.	18,726	323,524 R	61.3%	37.4%	62.1%	37.9%
1968**	1,235,039	517,995	Nixon, Richard M.	538,310	Humphrey, Hubert Horatio Jr.	178,734	20,315 D	41.9%	43.6%	49.0%	51.0%
1964	1,116,457	385,495	Goldwater, Barry M. Sr.	730,912	Johnson, Lyndon B.*	50	345,417 D	34.5%	65.5%	34.5%	65.5%
1960	1,055,349	489,538	Nixon, Richard M.	565,808	Kennedy, John F.	3	76,270 D	46.4%	53.6%	46.4%	53.6%
1956	932,827	559,738	Eisenhower, Dwight D.*	372,613	Stevenson, Adlai E. II	476	187,125 R	60.0%	39.9%	60.0%	40.0%
1952	902,074	499,424	Eisenhower, Dwight D.	395,337	Stevenson, Adlai E. II	7,313	104,087 R	55.4%	43.8%	55.8%	44.2%
1948	596,748	294,814	Dewey, Thomas E.	286,521	Truman, Harry S.*	15,413	8,293 R	49.4%	48.0%	50.7%	49.3%

Note: An asterisk (*) denotes incumbent. **In past elections, the other vote included: 2016 - 79,605 Libertarian (Gary Johnson); 2000 - 53,768 Green (Ralph Nader); 1996 - 115,812 Reform (Ross Perot); 1992 - 281,414 Independent (Perot); 1980 - 119,537 Independent (John Anderson); 1968 - 178,734 American Independent (George Wallace).

MARYLAND

POSTWAR VOTE FOR GOVERNOR

Year	Total Vote	Republican		Democratic		Other Vote	Rep.-Dem. Plurality	Percentage			
								Total Vote		Major Vote	
		Vote	Candidate	Vote	Candidate			Rep.	Dem.	Rep.	Dem.
2014	1,733,177	884,400	Hogan, Larry	818,890	Brown, Anthony G.	29,887	65,510 R	51.0%	47.2%	51.9%	48.1%
2010	1,857,880	776,319	Ehrlich, Robert L. "Bob" Jr.	1,044,961	O'Malley, Martin*	36,600	268,642 D	41.8%	56.2%	42.6%	57.4%
2006	1,788,316	825,464	Ehrlich, Robert L. "Bob" Jr.*	942,279	O'Malley, Martin	20,573	116,815 D	46.2%	52.7%	46.7%	53.3%
2002	1,706,179	879,592	Ehrlich, Robert L. "Bob" Jr.	813,422	Townsend, Kathleen Kennedy	13,165	66,170 R	51.6%	47.7%	52.0%	48.0%
1998	1,535,978	688,357	Sauerbrey, Ellen R.	846,972	Glendening, Parris N.*	649	158,615 D	44.8%	55.1%	44.8%	55.2%
1994	1,410,300	702,101	Sauerbrey, Ellen R.	708,094	Glendening, Parris N.	105	5,993 D	49.8%	50.2%	49.8%	50.2%
1990	1,111,088	446,980	Shepard, William S.	664,015	Schaefer, William D.*	93	217,035 D	40.2%	59.8%	40.2%	59.8%
1986	1,101,476	194,185	Mooney, Thomas J.	907,291	Schaefer, William D.		713,106 D	17.6%	82.4%	17.6%	82.4%
1982	1,139,149	432,826	Pascal, Robert A.	705,910	Hughes, Harry R.*	413	273,084 D	38.0%	62.0%	38.0%	62.0%
1978	1,011,963	293,635	Beall, John Glenn Jr.	718,328	Hughes, Harry R.		424,693 D	29.0%	71.0%	29.0%	71.0%
1974	949,097	346,449	Gore, Louise	602,648	Mandel, Marvin*		256,199 D	36.5%	63.5%	36.5%	63.5%
1970	973,099	314,336	Blair, C. Stanley	639,579	Mandel, Marvin*	19,184	325,243 D	32.3%	65.7%	33.0%	67.0%
1966	919,760	455,318	Agnew, Spiro T.	373,543	Mahoney, George P.	90,899	81,775 R	49.5%	40.6%	54.9%	45.1%
1962	769,347	341,271	Small, Frank Jr.	428,071	Tawes, J. Millard*	5	86,800 D	44.4%	55.6%	44.4%	55.6%
1958	763,234	278,173	Devereux, James Patrick	485,061	Tawes, J. Millard		206,888 D	36.4%	63.6%	36.4%	63.6%
1954	700,484	381,451	McKeldin, Theodore R.*	319,033	Byrd, Harry Clifton		62,418 R	54.5%	45.5%	54.5%	45.5%
1950	645,631	369,807	McKeldin, Theodore R.	275,824	Lane, William Preston		93,983 R	57.3%	42.7%	57.3%	42.7%
1946	489,836	221,752	McKeldin, Theodore R.	268,084	Lane, William Preston		46,332 D	45.3%	54.7%	45.3%	54.7%

Note: An asterisk (*) denotes incumbent.

POSTWAR VOTE FOR SENATOR

Year	Total Vote	Republican		Democratic		Other Vote	Rep.-Dem. Plurality	Percentage			
								Total Vote		Major Vote	
		Vote	Candidate	Vote	Candidate			Rep.	Dem.	Rep.	Dem.
2016	2,726,170	972,557	Szeliga, Kathy	1,659,907	Van Hollen, Chris Jr.*	93,706	687,350 D	35.7%	60.9%	36.9%	63.1%
2012**	2,633,234	693,291	Bongino, Daniel John	1,474,028	Cardin, Benjamin L.*	465,915	780,737 D	26.3%	56.0%	32.0%	68.0%
2010	1,833,858	655,666	Wartotz, Eric	1,140,531	Mikulski, Barbara A.*	37,661	484,865 D	35.8%	62.2%	36.5%	63.5%
2006	1,781,139	787,182	Steele, Michael	965,477	Cardin, Benjamin L.	28,480	178,295 D	44.2%	54.2%	44.9%	55.1%
2004	2,323,183	783,055	Pipkin, Edward J.	1,504,691	Mikulski, Barbara A.*	35,437	721,636 D	33.7%	64.8%	34.2%	65.8%
2000	1,946,898	715,178	Rappaport, Paul H.	1,230,013	Sarbanes, Paul S.*	1,707	514,835 D	36.7%	63.2%	36.8%	63.2%
1998	1,507,447	444,637	Pierpont, Ross Z.	1,062,810	Mikulski, Barbara A.*		618,173 D	29.5%	70.5%	29.5%	70.5%
1994	1,369,104	559,908	Brock, William E.	809,125	Sarbanes, Paul S.*	71	249,217 D	40.9%	59.1%	40.9%	59.1%
1992	1,841,735	533,688	Keyes, Alan	1,307,610	Mikulski, Barbara A.*	437	773,922 D	29.0%	71.0%	29.0%	71.0%
1988	1,617,065	617,537	Keyes, Alan	999,166	Sarbanes, Paul S.*	362	381,629 D	38.2%	61.8%	38.2%	61.8%
1986	1,112,637	437,411	Chavez, Linda	675,225	Mikulski, Barbara A.	1	237,814 D	39.3%	60.7%	39.3%	60.7%
1982	1,114,690	407,334	Hogan, Lawrence J.	707,356	Sarbanes, Paul S.*		300,022 D	36.5%	63.5%	36.5%	63.5%
1980	1,286,088	850,970	Mathias, Charles McCurdy Jr.*	435,118	Conroy, Edward T.		415,852 R	66.2%	33.8%	66.2%	33.8%
1976	1,365,568	530,439	Beall, John Glenn Jr.*	772,101	Sarbanes, Paul S.	63,028	241,662 D	38.8%	56.5%	40.7%	59.3%
1974	877,786	503,223	Mathias, Charles McCurdy Jr.*	374,563	Mikulski, Barbara A.		128,660 R	57.3%	42.7%	57.3%	42.7%
1970	956,370	484,960	Beall, John Glenn Jr.	460,422	Tydings, Joseph D.*	10,988	24,538 R	50.7%	48.1%	51.3%	48.7%
1968**	1,133,727	541,893	Mathias, Charles McCurdy Jr.	443,367	Brewster, Daniel B.*	148,467	98,526 R	47.8%	39.1%	55.0%	45.0%
1964	1,081,049	402,393	Beall, James Glenn*	678,649	Tydings, Joseph D.	7	276,256 D	37.2%	62.8%	37.2%	62.8%
1962	708,855	269,131	Miller, Edward T.	439,723	Brewster, Daniel B.	1	170,592 D	38.0%	62.0%	38.0%	62.0%
1958	749,291	382,021	Beall, James Glenn*	367,270	D'Alesandro, Thomas Jr.		14,751 R	51.0%	49.0%	51.0%	49.0%
1956	892,167	473,059	Butler, John Marshall*	419,108	Mahoney, George P.		53,951 R	53.0%	47.0%	53.0%	47.0%
1952	856,193	449,823	Beall, James Glenn	406,370	Mahoney, George P.		43,453 R	52.5%	47.5%	52.5%	47.5%
1950	615,614	326,291	Butler, John Marshall	283,180	Tydings, Millard E.*	6,143	43,111 R	53.0%	46.0%	53.5%	46.5%
1946	472,232	235,000	Markey, David John	237,232	O'Conor, Herbert R.		2,232 D	49.8%	50.2%	49.8%	50.2%

Note: An asterisk (*) denotes incumbent. **In past elections, the other vote included: 2012 - 430,934 Independent (S. Rob Sobhani); 1968 - 148,467 Independent (George P. Mahoney).

MARYLAND

PRESIDENT 2016

2010 Census Population	County	Total Vote	Republican (Trump)	Democratic (Clinton)	Other	Rep.-Dem. Plurality		Percentage			
								Total Vote		Major Vote	
								Rep.	Dem.	Rep.	Dem.
75,087	ALLEGANY	30,654	21,270	7,875	1,509	13,395	R	69.4%	25.7%	73.0%	27.0%
537,656	ANNE ARUNDEL	270,081	122,403	128,419	19,259	6,016	D	45.3%	47.5%	48.8%	51.2%
805,029	BALTIMORE	390,682	149,477	218,412	22,793	68,935	D	38.3%	55.9%	40.6%	59.4%
620,961	BALTIMORE CITY	239,402	25,205	202,673	11,524	177,468	D	10.5%	84.7%	11.1%	88.9%
88,737	CALVERT	47,408	26,176	18,225	3,007	7,951	R	55.2%	38.4%	59.0%	41.0%
33,066	CAROLINE	14,113	9,368	4,009	736	5,359	R	66.4%	28.4%	70.0%	30.0%
167,134	CARROLL	91,847	58,215	26,567	7,065	31,648	R	63.4%	28.9%	68.7%	31.3%
101,108	CECIL	45,270	28,868	13,650	2,752	15,218	R	63.8%	30.2%	67.9%	32.1%
146,551	CHARLES	78,303	25,614	49,341	3,348	23,727	D	32.7%	63.0%	34.2%	65.8%
32,618	DORCHESTER	15,225	8,413	6,245	567	2,168	R	55.3%	41.0%	57.4%	42.6%
233,385	FREDERICK	125,677	59,522	56,522	9,633	3,000	R	47.4%	45.0%	51.3%	48.7%
30,097	GARRETT	14,011	10,776	2,567	668	8,209	R	76.9%	18.3%	80.8%	19.2%
244,826	HARFORD	133,672	77,860	47,077	8,735	30,783	R	58.2%	35.2%	62.3%	37.7%
287,085	HOWARD	162,193	47,484	102,597	12,112	55,113	D	29.3%	63.3%	31.6%	68.4%
20,197	KENT	10,021	4,876	4,575	570	301	R	48.7%	45.7%	51.6%	48.4%
971,777	MONTGOMERY	478,873	92,704	357,837	28,332	265,133	D	19.4%	74.7%	20.6%	79.4%
863,420	PRINCE GEORGES	390,385	32,811	344,049	13,525	311,238	D	8.4%	88.1%	8.7%	91.3%
47,798	QUEEN ANNES	26,524	16,993	7,973	1,558	9,020	R	64.1%	30.1%	68.1%	31.9%
26,470	SOMERSET	9,900	5,341	4,196	363	1,145	R	53.9%	42.4%	56.0%	44.0%
105,151	ST. MARYS	49,842	28,663	17,534	3,645	11,129	R	57.5%	35.2%	62.0%	38.0%
37,782	TALBOT	20,553	10,724	8,653	1,176	2,071	R	52.2%	42.1%	55.3%	44.7%
147,430	WASHINGTON	65,990	40,998	21,129	3,863	19,869	R	62.1%	32.0%	66.0%	34.0%
98,733	WICOMICO	42,547	22,198	18,050	2,299	4,148	R	52.2%	42.4%	55.2%	44.8%
51,454	WORCESTER	28,273	17,210	9,753	1,310	7,457	R	60.9%	34.5%	63.8%	36.2%
5,773,552	TOTAL	2,781,446	943,169	1,677,928	160,349	734,759	D	33.9%	60.3%	36.0%	64.0%

MARYLAND

SENATOR 2016

2010 Census Population	County	Total Vote	Republican (Szeliga)	Democratic (Van Hollen)	Other	Rep.-Dem. Plurality		Percentage			
								Total Vote		Major Vote	
								Rep.	Dem.	Rep.	Dem.
75,087	ALLEGANY	29,118	18,072	9,761	1,285	8,311	R	62.1%	33.5%	64.9%	35.1%
537,656	ANNE ARUNDEL	264,923	128,268	127,961	8,694	307	R	48.4%	48.3%	50.1%	49.9%
805,029	BALTIMORE	360,447	155,079	193,819	11,549	38,740	D	43.0%	53.8%	44.4%	55.6%
620,961	BALTIMORE CITY	259,185	29,306	217,151	12,728	187,845	D	11.3%	83.8%	11.9%	88.1%
88,737	CALVERT	45,897	25,431	18,534	1,932	6,897	R	55.4%	40.4%	57.8%	42.2%
33,066	CAROLINE	13,859	8,903	4,596	360	4,307	R	64.2%	33.2%	66.0%	34.0%
167,134	CARROLL	90,294	60,195	27,649	2,450	32,546	R	66.7%	30.6%	68.5%	31.5%
101,108	CECIL	43,930	27,372	14,846	1,712	12,526	R	62.3%	33.8%	64.8%	35.2%
146,551	CHARLES	76,968	25,507	48,994	2,467	23,487	D	33.1%	63.7%	34.2%	65.8%
32,618	DORCHESTER	14,835	7,763	6,697	375	1,066	R	52.3%	45.1%	53.7%	46.3%
233,385	FREDERICK	122,572	60,516	57,084	4,972	3,432	R	49.4%	46.6%	51.5%	48.5%
30,097	GARRETT	13,333	10,210	2,696	427	7,514	R	76.6%	20.2%	79.1%	20.9%
244,826	HARFORD	132,133	80,355	47,858	3,920	32,497	R	60.8%	36.2%	62.7%	37.3%
287,085	HOWARD	159,193	55,888	97,622	5,683	41,734	D	35.1%	61.3%	36.4%	63.6%
20,197	KENT	9,886	4,936	4,709	241	227	R	49.9%	47.6%	51.2%	48.8%
971,777	MONTGOMERY	471,389	103,401	354,149	13,839	250,748	D	21.9%	75.1%	22.6%	77.4%
863,420	PRINCE GEORGES	381,289	34,067	334,265	12,957	300,198	D	8.9%	87.7%	9.2%	90.8%
47,798	QUEEN ANNES	26,137	17,006	8,472	659	8,534	R	65.1%	32.4%	66.7%	33.3%
26,470	SOMERSET	11,457	5,178	4,277	2,002	901	R	45.2%	37.3%	54.8%	45.2%
105,151	ST. MARYS	46,393	28,207	17,980	206	10,227	R	60.8%	38.8%	61.1%	38.9%

MARYLAND

SENATOR 2016

2010 Census Population	County	Total Vote	Republican (Szeliga)	Democratic (Van Hollen)	Other	Rep.-Dem. Plurality	Percentage			
							Total Vote		Major Vote	
							Rep.	Dem.	Rep.	Dem.
37,782	TALBOT	20,281	10,861	8,967	453	1,894 R	53.6%	44.2%	54.8%	45.2%
147,430	WASHINGTON	63,223	37,278	23,313	2,632	13,965 R	59.0%	36.9%	61.5%	38.5%
98,733	WICOMICO	41,775	22,027	18,382	1,366	3,645 R	52.7%	44.0%	54.5%	45.5%
51,454	WORCESTER	27,653	16,731	10,125	797	6,606 R	60.5%	36.6%	62.3%	37.7%
5,773,552	TOTAL	2,726,170	972,557	1,659,907	93,706	687,350 D	35.7%	60.9%	36.9%	63.1%

MARYLAND

HOUSE OF REPRESENTATIVES

CD	Year	Total Vote	Republican		Democratic		Other Vote	Rep.-Dem. Plurality	Percentage			
			Vote	Candidate	Vote	Candidate			Total Vote		Major Vote	
									Rep.	Dem.	Rep.	Dem.
1	2016	362,097	242,574	HARRIS, ANDY *	103,622	WERNER, JOSEPH	15,901	138,952 R	67.0%	28.6%	70.1%	29.9%
1	2014	250,418	176,342	HARRIS, ANDY *	73,843	TILGHMAN, BILL	233	102,499 R	70.4%	29.5%	70.5%	29.5%
1	2012	337,760	214,204	HARRIS, ANDY *	92,812	ROSEN, WENDY	30,744	121,392 R	63.4%	27.5%	69.8%	30.2%
2	2016	309,480	102,577	MCDONOUGH, PATRICK L.	192,183	RUPPERSBERGER, C.A. DUTCH *	14,720	89,606 D	33.1%	62.1%	34.8%	65.2%
2	2014	196,354	70,411	BANACH, DAVID	120,412	RUPPERSBERGER, C.A. DUTCH *	5,531	50,001 D	35.9%	61.3%	36.9%	63.1%
2	2012	295,940	92,071	JACOBS, NANCY C.	194,088	RUPPERSBERGER, C.A. DUTCH *	9,781	102,017 D	31.1%	65.6%	32.2%	67.8%
3	2016	339,675	115,048	PLASTER, MARK	214,640	SARBANES, JOHN P. *	9,987	99,592 D	33.9%	63.2%	34.9%	65.1%
3	2014	215,946	87,029	LONG, CHARLES A.	128,594	SARBANES, JOHN P. *	323	41,565 D	40.3%	59.5%	40.4%	59.6%
3	2012	319,859	94,549	KNOWLES, ERIC DELANO	213,747	SARBANES, JOHN P. *	11,563	119,198 D	29.6%	66.8%	30.7%	69.3%
4	2016	320,650	68,670	MCDERMOTT, GEORGE E.	237,501	BROWN, ANTHONY G.	14,479	168,831 D	21.4%	74.1%	22.4%	77.6%
4	2014	191,837	54,217	HOYT, NANCY	134,628	EDWARDS, DONNA *	2,992	80,411 D	28.3%	70.2%	28.7%	71.3%
4	2012	311,512	64,560	LOUDON, FAITH M.	240,385	EDWARDS, DONNA *	6,567	175,825 D	20.7%	77.2%	21.2%	78.8%
5	2016	360,634	105,931	ARNESS, MARK KENNETH	242,989	HOYER, STENY H. *	11,714	137,058 D	29.4%	67.4%	30.4%	69.6%
5	2014	226,040	80,752	CHAFFEE, CHRIS	144,725	HOYER, STENY H. *	563	63,973 D	35.7%	64.0%	35.8%	64.2%
5	2012	343,820	95,271	O'DONNELL, TONY	238,618	HOYER, STENY H. *	9,931	143,347 D	27.7%	69.4%	28.5%	71.5%
6	2016	331,973	133,081	HOEBER, AMIE	185,770	DELANEY, JOHN *	13,122	52,689 D	40.1%	56.0%	41.7%	58.3%
6	2014	190,536	91,930	BONGINO, DANIEL JOHN	94,704	DELANEY, JOHN *	3,902	2,774 D	48.2%	49.7%	49.3%	50.7%
6	2012	309,549	117,313	BARTLETT, ROSCOE G. *	181,921	DELANEY, JOHN	10,315	64,608 D	37.9%	58.8%	39.2%	60.8%
7	2016	318,912	69,556	VAUGHN, CORROGAN R.	238,838	CUMMINGS, ELIJAH E. *	10,518	169,282 D	21.8%	74.9%	22.6%	77.4%
7	2014	206,809	55,860	VAUGHN, CORROGAN R.	144,639	CUMMINGS, ELIJAH E. *	6,310	88,779 D	27.0%	69.9%	27.9%	72.1%
7	2012	323,818	67,405	MIRABILE, FRANK C.	247,770	CUMMINGS, ELIJAH E. *	8,643	180,365 D	20.8%	76.5%	21.4%	78.6%
8	2016	364,324	124,651	COX, DAN	220,657	RASKIN, JAMIE	19,016	96,006 D	34.2%	60.6%	36.1%	63.9%
8	2014	225,097	87,859	WALLACE, DAVE	136,722	VAN HOLLEN, CHRIS JR.*	516	48,863 D	39.0%	60.7%	39.1%	60.9%
8	2012	343,256	113,033	TIMMERMAN, KENNETH R.	217,531	VAN HOLLEN, CHRIS JR.*	12,692	104,498 D	32.9%	63.4%	34.2%	65.8%
TOTAL	2016	2,707,745	962,088		1,636,200		109,457	674,112 D	35.5%	60.4%	37.0%	63.0%
TOTAL	2014	1,703,037	704,400		978,267		20,370	273,867 D	41.4%	57.4%	41.9%	58.1%
TOTAL	2012	2,585,514	858,406		1,626,872		100,236	768,466 D	33.2%	62.9%	34.5%	65.5%

Note: An asterisk (*) denotes incumbent.

MARYLAND
GENERAL AND PRIMARY ELECTIONS

2016 GENERAL ELECTIONS: OTHER VOTES

President Other vote was 79,605 Libertarian (Gary Johnson), 35,945 Green (Jill Stein), 34,603 Write-in (Scattered Write-in), 9,630 Write-in (Evan McMullin), 566 Write-in (Darrell Castle)

Senate Other vote was 89,970 Green (Margaret Flowers), 3,231 Write-in (Scattered Write-in), 242 Write-in (Greg Dorsey), 138 Write-in (Ed Tinus), 77 Write-in (Lih Young), 26 Write-in (Charles Smith), 15 Write-in (Bob Robinson), 7 Write-in (Jeffrey Binkins)

House Other vote was:

CD 1 15,370 Libertarian (Matt Beers), 531 Write-in (Scattered Write-in)

CD 2 14,128 Libertarian (Kristin Kasprzak), 592 Write-in (Scattered Write-in)

CD 3 9,461 Green (Nnabu Eze), 463 Write-in (Scattered Write-in), 63 Write-in (Ann Dalrymple)

CD 4 8,204 Green (Kamesha Clark), 5,744 Libertarian (Benjamin Krause), 513 Write-in (Scattered Write-in), 18 Write-in (Adrian Petrus)

CD 5 11,078 Libertarian (Jason Summers), 636 Write-in (Scattered Write-in)

CD 6 6,889 Libertarian (David Howser), 5,824 Green (George Gluck), 306 Write-in (Scattered Write-in), 103 Write-in (Ted Athey)

CD 7 9,715 Green (Myles Hoenig), 584 Write-in (Scattered Write-in), 202 Write-in (William Newton), 17 Write-in (Michael Pearson)

CD 8 11,201 Green (Nancy Wallace), 7,283 Libertarian (Jasen Wunder), 527 Write-in (Scattered Write-in), 5 Write-in (Kevin Little)

2016 PRIMARY ELECTIONS: SUPPLEMENTARY INFORMATION

Primary	April 26, 2016	**Registration** (as of April 10, 2016)	3,432,720	Democratic	2,093,657
				Republican	995,057
				Libertarian	6,906
				Green	3,081
				Other	11,669
				Unaffiliated	322,350

Primary Type Closed—Only registered Democrats and Republicans could vote in their party's primary.

	REPUBLICAN PRIMARIES			DEMOCRATIC PRIMARIES		
President	Trump, Donald J.	248,343	54.1%	Clinton, Hillary Rodham	573,242	62.5%
	Kasich, John R.	106,614	23.2%	Sanders, Bernard	309,990	33.8%
	Cruz, Ted	87,093	19.0%	Uncommitted	29,949	3.3%
	Carson, Ben	5,946	1.3%	De La Fuente, Roque "Rocky"	3,582	0.4%
	Rubio, Marco	3,201	0.7%			
	Bush, Jeb	2,770	0.6%			
	Paul, Rand	1,533	0.3%			
	Christie, Chris	1,239	0.3%			
	Fiorina, Carly	1,012	0.2%			
	Huckabee, Mike	837	0.2%			
	Santorum, Rick	478	0.1%			
	TOTAL	*459,066*		*TOTAL*	*916,763*	
Senator	Szeliga, Kathy	135,337	35.6%	Van Hollen, Chris Jr.	470,320	53.2%
	Chaffee, Chris	52,066	13.7%	Edwards, Donna	343,620	38.9%
	Kefalas, Chrysovalantis "Chrys"	36,340	9.6%	Dickson Jr., Fred Donald	14,856	1.7%
	Douglas, Richard J.	29,007	7.6%	Scaldaferri, Theresa C.	13,178	1.5%
	Wallace, Dave	23,226	6.1%	Staley, Violet	10,244	1.2%
	Connor, Sean	21,727	5.7%	Young, Lih	8,561	1.0%
	Richardson, Lynn	20,792	5.5%	Smith, Charles U.	7,912	0.9%
	Graziani, John R.	16,722	4.4%	Jaffe, Ralph	7,161	0.8%
	Holmes, Greg	16,148	4.3%	Taylor, Blaine	5,932	0.7%
	McNicholas, Mark	9,988	2.6%	Tinus, Ed	2,560	0.3%
	Hooe, Joseph David	8,282	2.2%			
	Seda, Anthony	3,873	1.0%			
	Shawver, Richard	3,155	0.8%			
	Yarrington, Garry Thomas	2,988	0.8%			
	TOTAL	*379,651*		*TOTAL*	*884,344*	

MARYLAND

GENERAL AND PRIMARY ELECTIONS

	REPUBLICAN PRIMARIES			DEMOCRATIC PRIMARIES		
Congressional District 1	Harris, Andy*	79,497	78.4%	Werner, Joseph	29,729	51.0%
	Smigiel, Michael D. Sr.	10,897	10.7%	Ireton, Jim	28,547	49.0%
	Goff, Jonathan	6,135	6.0%			
	Jackson, Sean M.	4,891	4.8%			
	TOTAL	101,420		TOTAL	58,276	
Congressional District 2	McDonough, Patrick L.	28,397	71.4%	Ruppersberger, C.A. Dutch*	89,820	100.0%
	Magee, Carl H. Jr.	4,195	10.6%			
	Heine, Bill	3,203	8.1%			
	Morgan, Yuripzy	2,257	5.7%			
	Shell, Mark Gerard	1,709	4.3%			
	TOTAL	39,761		TOTAL	89,820	
Congressional District 3	Plaster, Mark	25,455	63.6%	Sarbanes, John P.*	101,355	87.2%
	Harris, Thomas E. "Pinkston"	14,564	36.4%	Rea, John	14,917	12.8%
	TOTAL	40,019		TOTAL	116,272	
Congressional District 4	McDermott, George E.	10,882	45.8%	Brown, Anthony G.	47,678	41.6%
	Therrien, David	6,219	26.2%	Ivey, Glenn F.	38,966	34.0%
	Broadus, Robert	3,977	16.7%	Peña-Melnyk, Joseline	21,724	19.0%
	Buck, Rob	2,703	11.4%	Christopher, Warren	3,973	3.5%
				Fogg, Matthew	1,437	1.3%
				Strait, Terence	845	0.7%
	TOTAL	23,781		TOTAL	114,623	
Congressional District 5	Arness, Mark Kenneth	22,613	53.3%	Hoyer, Steny H.*	83,787	75.9%
	Faddis, Charles "Sam"	19,846	46.7%	Beck, Kristin	13,320	12.1%
				Wilson, Debbie F.	13,304	12.0%
	TOTAL	42,459		TOTAL	110,411	
Congressional District 6	Hoeber, Amie	17,967	29.3%	Delaney, John*	69,343	84.9%
	Baker, Terry L.	13,837	22.6%	Puca, Anthony P.	12,317	15.1%
	Howard, Frank	10,677	17.4%			
	Ficker, Robin	7,014	11.4%			
	Vogt, David E. III.	5,774	9.4%			
	Mason, Christopher James	2,590	4.2%			
	Cheng, Xiangfei "Scott"	2,303	3.8%			
	Painter, Harold W.	1,117	1.8%			
	TOTAL	61,279		TOTAL	81,660	
Congressional District 7	Vaughn, Corrogan R.	10,645	41.6%	Cummings, Elijah E.*	130,555	92.1%
	Newton, William Thomas	10,599	41.4%	Petrus, Adrian	11,272	7.9%
	Bly, Raymond J.	4,351	17.0%			
	TOTAL	25,595		TOTAL	141,827	
Congressional District 8	Cox, Dan	20,647	44.4%	Raskin, Jamie	43,776	33.6%
	Jones, Jeffrey W.	9,343	20.1%	Trone, David	35,400	27.1%
	Matory, Liz	7,295	15.7%	Matthews, Kathleen	31,186	23.9%
	Skolnick, Shelly	5,835	12.5%	Gutierrez, Ana Sol	7,185	5.5%
	Shudofsky, Aryeh	3,421	7.4%	Jawando, William	6,058	4.6%
				Barve, Kumar P.	3,149	2.4%
				Anderson, David M.	1,511	1.2%
				Rubin, Joel	1,426	1.1%
				Bolling, Dan	712	0.5%
	TOTAL	46,541		TOTAL	130,403	

Note: An asterisk (*) denotes incumbent.

MASSACHUSETTS

Congressional districts first established for elections held in 2012
9 members

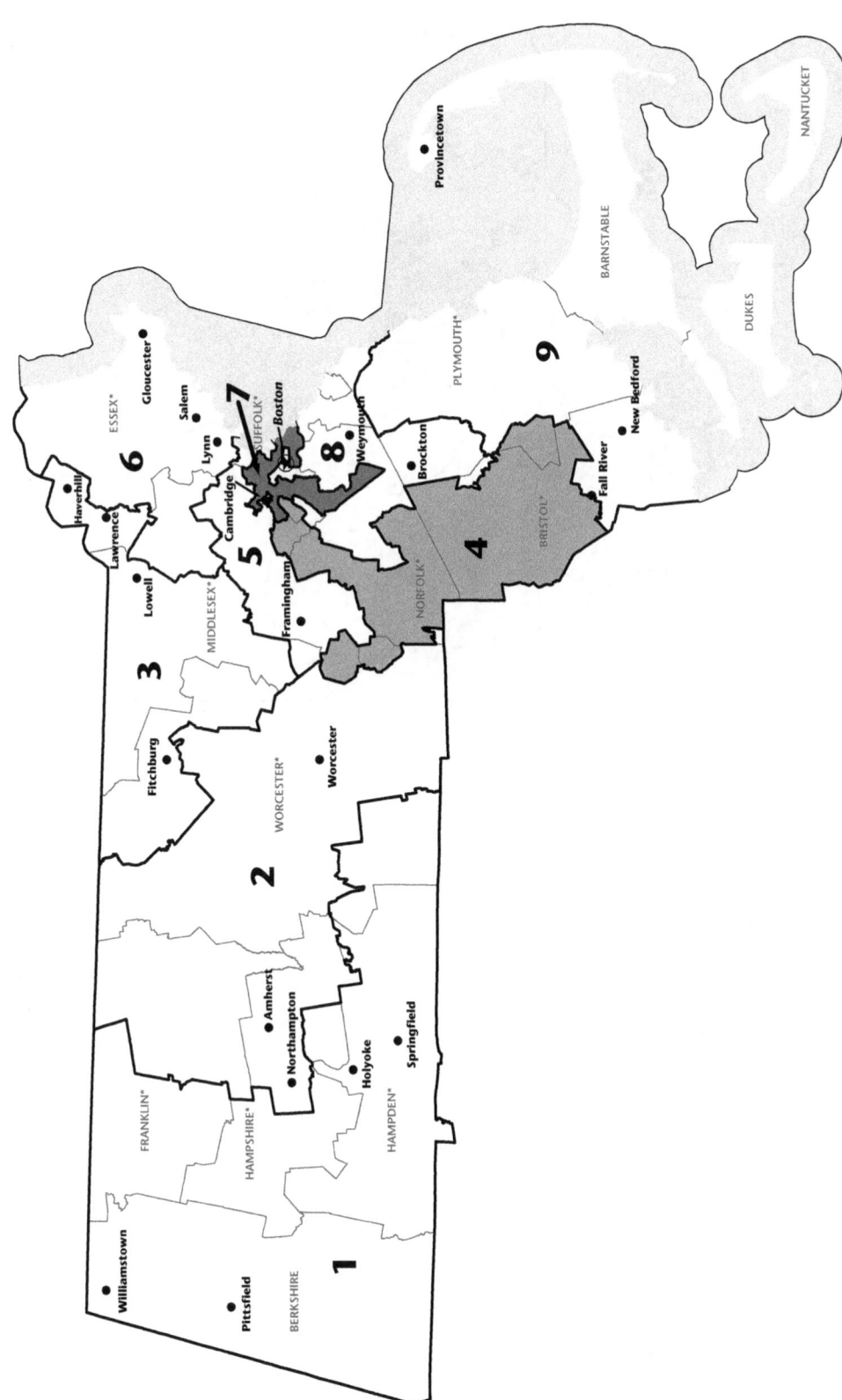

NANTUCKET

Provincetown

BARNSTABLE

DUKES*

PLYMOUTH*

9

New Bedford

Gloucester

Salem

7

SUFFOLK*

Boston

ESSEX*

Fall River

6

Lynn

8

Weymouth

BRISTOL*

Cambridge

Brockton

Haverhill

5

Lawrence

4

NORFOLK*

Lowell

MIDDLESEX*

Framingham

3

Worcester

Fitchburg

WORCESTER*

2

Amherst

FRANKLIN*

Northampton

Springfield

HAMPSHIRE*

Holyoke

HAMPDEN*

Williamstown

1

Pittsfield

BERKSHIRE

* Asterisk indicates a county whose boundaries include parts of two or more congressional districts.

MASSACHUSETTS

Boston Area

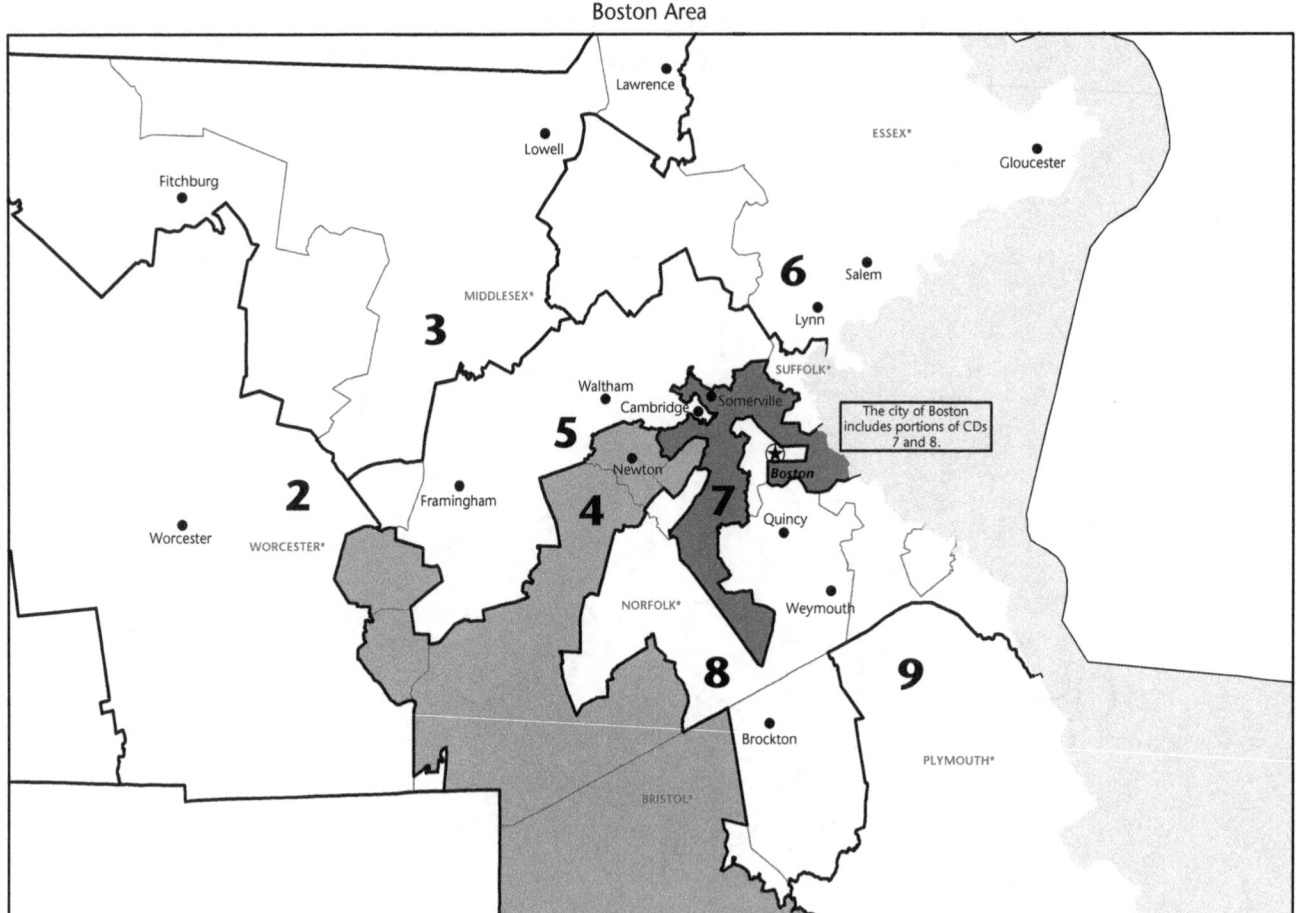

The city of Boston includes portions of CDs 7 and 8.

* Asterisk indicates a county whose boundaries include parts of two or more congressional districts.

MASSACHUSETTS

GOVERNOR
Charles D. Baker (R). Elected 2014 to a four-year term.

SENATORS (2 Democrats)
Edward J. Markey (D). Re-elected 2014 to a full six-year term. Previously elected June 25, 2013, to serve the remainder of the term vacated by the January 2013 resignation of John Kerry to become secretary of state. William "Mo" Cowan (D) had been appointed on January 30, 2013, to fill the vacant seat until the June 2013 special election.

Elizabeth Warren (D). Elected 2012 to a six-year term.

REPRESENTATIVES (9 Democrats)
1. Richard E. Neal (D)
2. James McGovern (D)
3. Nicola S. Tsongas (D)
4. Joseph Patrick Kennedy III (D)
5. Katherine M. Clark (D)
6. Seth Moulton (D)
7. Michael E. Capuano (D)
8. Stephen F. Lynch (D)
9. William R. Keating (D)

POSTWAR VOTE FOR PRESIDENT

		Republican		Democratic		Other Vote	Rep.-Dem. Plurality	Percentage			
								Total Vote		Major Vote	
Year	Total Vote	Vote	Candidate	Vote	Candidate			Rep.	Dem.	Rep.	Dem.
2016**	3,325,046	1,090,893	Trump, Donald J.	1,995,196	Clinton, Hillary Rodham	238,957	904,303 D	32.8%	60.0%	35.3%	64.7%
2012	3,167,767	1,188,314	Romney, W. Mitt	1,921,290	Obama, Barack H.*	58,163	732,976 D	37.5%	60.7%	38.2%	61.8%
2008	3,080,985	1,108,854	McCain, John S. III	1,904,097	Obama, Barack H.	68,034	795,243 D	36.0%	61.8%	36.8%	63.2%
2004	2,912,388	1,071,109	Bush, George W.*	1,803,800	Kerry, John F.	37,479	732,691 D	36.8%	61.9%	37.3%	62.7%
2000**	2,702,984	878,502	Bush, George W.	1,616,487	Gore, Albert Jr.	207,995	737,985 D	32.5%	59.8%	35.2%	64.8%
1996**	2,556,785	718,107	Dole, Robert "Bob"	1,571,763	Clinton, Bill*	266,915	853,656 D	28.1%	61.5%	31.4%	68.6%
1992**	2,773,700	805,049	Bush, George H.*	1,318,662	Clinton, Bill	649,989	513,613 D	29.0%	47.5%	37.9%	62.1%
1988	2,632,805	1,194,635	Bush, George H.	1,401,415	Dukakis, Michael S.	36,755	206,780 D	45.4%	53.2%	46.0%	54.0%
1984	2,559,453	1,310,936	Reagan, Ronald*	1,239,606	Mondale, Walter F.	8,911	71,330 R	51.2%	48.4%	51.4%	48.6%
1980**	2,524,298	1,057,631	Reagan, Ronald	1,053,802	Carter, Jimmy*	412,865	3,829 R	41.9%	41.7%	50.1%	49.9%
1976	2,547,558	1,030,276	Ford, Gerald R.*	1,429,475	Carter, Jimmy	87,807	399,199 D	40.4%	56.1%	41.9%	58.1%
1972	2,458,756	1,112,078	Nixon, Richard M.*	1,332,540	McGovern, George S.	14,138	220,462 D	45.2%	54.2%	45.5%	54.5%
1968**	2,331,752	766,844	Nixon, Richard M.	1,469,218	Humphrey, Hubert Horatio Jr.	95,690	702,374 D	32.9%	63.0%	34.3%	65.7%
1964	2,344,798	549,727	Goldwater, Barry M. Sr.	1,786,422	Johnson, Lyndon B.*	8,649	1,236,695 D	23.4%	76.2%	23.5%	76.5%
1960	2,469,480	976,750	Nixon, Richard M.	1,487,174	Kennedy, John F.	5,556	510,424 D	39.6%	60.2%	39.6%	60.4%
1956	2,348,506	1,393,197	Eisenhower, Dwight D.*	948,190	Stevenson, Adlai E. II	7,119	445,007 R	59.3%	40.4%	59.5%	40.5%
1952	2,383,398	1,292,325	Eisenhower, Dwight D.	1,083,525	Stevenson, Adlai E. II	7,548	208,800 R	54.2%	45.5%	54.4%	45.6%
1948	2,107,146	909,370	Dewey, Thomas E.	1,151,788	Truman, Harry S.*	45,988	242,418 D	43.2%	54.7%	44.1%	55.9%

Note: An asterisk (*) denotes incumbent. **In past elections, the other vote included: 2016 - 138,018 Libertarian (Gary Johnson); 2000 - 173,564 - Green (Ralph Nader); 1996 - 227,217 Reform (Ross Perot); 1992 - 630,731 Independent (Perot); 1980 - 382,539 Independent (John Anderson); 1968 - 87,088 American Independent (George Wallace).

MASSACHUSETTS

POSTWAR VOTE FOR GOVERNOR

Year	Total Vote	Republican		Democratic		Other Vote	Rep.-Dem. Plurality	Percentage			
								Total Vote		Major Vote	
		Vote	Candidate	Vote	Candidate			Rep.	Dem.	Rep.	Dem.
2014	2,158,326	1,044,573	Baker, Charles D.	1,004,408	Coakley, Martha	109,345	40,165 R	48.4%	46.5%	51.0%	49.0%
2010	2,297,039	964,866	Baker, Charles D.	1,112,283	Patrick, Deval*	219,890	147,417 D	42.0%	48.4%	46.5%	53.5%
2006	2,219,779	784,342	Healey, Kerry	1,234,984	Patrick, Deval	200,453	450,642 D	35.3%	55.6%	38.8%	61.2%
2002	2,194,179	1,091,988	Romney, W. Mitt	985,981	O'Brien, Shannon P.	116,210	106,007 R	49.8%	44.9%	52.6%	47.4%
1998	1,903,336	967,160	Cellucci, Argeo Paul*	901,843	Harshbarger, Scott	34,333	65,317 R	50.8%	47.4%	51.7%	48.3%
1994	2,255,150	1,599,141	Weld, William F.*	636,138	Roosevelt, Mark	19,871	963,003 R	70.9%	28.2%	71.5%	28.5%
1990	2,342,927	1,175,817	Weld, William F.	1,099,878	Silber, John	67,232	75,939 R	50.2%	46.9%	51.7%	48.3%
1986	1,684,079	525,364	Kariotis, George	1,157,786	Dukakis, Michael S.*	929	632,422 D	31.2%	68.7%	31.2%	68.8%
1982	2,050,254	749,679	Sears, John W.	1,219,109	Dukakis, Michael S.	81,466	469,430 D	36.6%	59.5%	38.1%	61.9%
1978	1,962,251	926,072	Hatch, Francis W.	1,030,294	King, Edward J.	5,885	104,222 D	47.2%	52.5%	47.3%	52.7%
1974	1,854,798	784,353	Sargent, Francis W.*	992,284	Dukakis, Michael S.	78,161	207,931 D	42.3%	53.5%	44.1%	55.9%
1970	1,867,906	1,058,623	Sargent, Francis W.*	799,269	White, Kevin H.	10,014	259,354 R	56.7%	42.8%	57.0%	43.0%
1966**	2,041,177	1,277,358	Volpe, John A.*	752,720	McCormack, Edward J.	11,099	524,638 R	62.6%	36.9%	62.9%	37.1%
1964	2,340,130	1,176,462	Volpe, John A.	1,153,416	Bellotti, Francis X.	10,252	23,046 R	50.3%	49.3%	50.5%	49.5%
1962	2,109,089	1,047,891	Volpe, John A.*	1,053,322	Peabody, Endicott	7,876	5,431 D	49.7%	49.9%	49.9%	50.1%
1960	2,417,133	1,269,295	Volpe, John A.	1,130,810	Ward, Joseph D.	17,028	138,485 R	52.5%	46.8%	52.9%	47.1%
1958	1,899,117	818,463	Gibbons, Charles	1,067,020	Furcolo, Foster*	13,634	248,557 D	43.1%	56.2%	43.4%	56.6%
1956	2,339,884	1,096,759	Whittier, Sumner G.	1,234,618	Furcolo, Foster	8,507	137,859 D	46.9%	52.8%	47.0%	53.0%
1954	1,903,774	985,339	Herter, Christian A.*	910,087	Murphy, Robert F.	8,348	75,252 R	51.8%	47.8%	52.0%	48.0%
1952	2,356,298	1,175,955	Herter, Christian A.	1,161,499	Dever, Paul A.*	18,844	14,456 R	49.9%	49.3%	50.3%	49.7%
1950	1,910,180	824,069	Coolidge, Arthur W.	1,074,570	Dever, Paul A.	11,541	250,501 D	43.1%	56.3%	43.4%	56.6%
1948	2,099,250	849,895	Bradford, Robert F.*	1,239,247	Dever, Paul A.	10,108	389,352 D	40.5%	59.0%	40.7%	59.3%
1946	1,683,452	911,152	Bradford, Robert F.	762,743	Tobin, Maurice J.*	9,557	148,409 R	54.1%	45.3%	54.4%	45.6%

Note: An asterisk (*) denotes incumbent. **The term of office of Massachusetts's governor was increased from two to four years effective with the 1966 election.

POSTWAR VOTE FOR SENATOR

Year	Total Vote	Republican		Democratic		Other Vote	Rep.-Dem. Plurality	Percentage			
								Total Vote		Major Vote	
		Vote	Candidate	Vote	Candidate			Rep.	Dem.	Rep.	Dem.
2014	2,084,972	791,950	Herr, Brian J.	1,289,944	Markey, Edward J.*	3,078	497,994 D	38.0%	61.9%	38.0%	62.0%
2013S**	1,177,790	525,307	Gomez, Gabriel E.	645,429	Markey, Edward J.	7,054	120,122 D	44.6%	54.8%	44.9%	55.1%
2012	3,156,553	1,458,048	Brown, Scott P.*	1,696,346	Warren, Elizabeth	2,159	238,298 D	46.2%	53.7%	46.2%	53.8%
2010S**	2,252,582	1,168,178	Brown, Scott P.	1,060,861	Coakley, Martha	23,543	107,317 R	51.9%	47.1%	52.4%	47.6%
2008	2,994,247	926,044	Beatty, Jeffrey K.	1,971,974	Kerry, John F.*	96,229	1,045,930 D	30.9%	65.9%	32.0%	68.0%
2006	2,165,490	661,532	Chase, Kenneth G.	1,500,738	Kennedy, Edward M.*	3,220	839,206 D	30.5%	69.3%	30.6%	69.4%
2002**	2,006,758			1,605,976	Kerry, John F.*	400,782	1,605,976 D		80.0%		100.0%
2000**	2,599,420	334,341	Robinson, Jack E. III	1,889,494	Kennedy, Edward M.*	375,585	1,555,153 D	12.9%	72.7%	15.0%	85.0%
1996	2,555,886	1,142,837	Weld, William F.	1,334,345	Kerry, John F.*	78,704	191,508 D	44.7%	52.2%	46.1%	53.9%
1994	2,179,964	894,005	Romney, W. Mitt	1,266,011	Kennedy, Edward M.*	19,948	372,006 D	41.0%	58.1%	41.4%	58.6%
1990	2,316,212	992,917	Rappaport, Jim	1,321,712	Kerry, John F.*	1,583	328,795 D	42.9%	57.1%	42.9%	57.1%
1988	2,606,225	884,267	Malone, Joseph D.	1,693,344	Kennedy, Edward M.*	28,614	809,077 D	33.9%	65.0%	34.3%	65.7%
1984	2,530,195	1,136,806	Shamie, Raymond	1,392,981	Kerry, John F.	408	256,175 D	44.9%	55.1%	44.9%	55.1%
1982	2,050,769	784,602	Shamie, Raymond	1,247,084	Kennedy, Edward M.*	19,083	462,482 D	38.3%	60.8%	38.6%	61.4%
1978	1,985,700	890,584	Brooke, Edward W. III*	1,093,283	Tsongas, Paul E.	1,833	202,699 D	44.8%	55.1%	44.9%	55.1%
1976	2,491,255	722,641	Robertson, Michael	1,726,657	Kennedy, Edward M.*	41,957	1,004,016 D	29.0%	69.3%	29.5%	70.5%
1972	2,370,676	1,505,932	Brooke, Edward W. III*	823,278	Droney, John J.	41,466	682,654 R	63.5%	34.7%	64.7%	35.3%
1970	1,935,607	715,978	Spaulding, Josiah A.	1,202,856	Kennedy, Edward M.*	16,773	486,878 D	37.0%	62.1%	37.3%	62.7%
1966	1,999,949	1,213,473	Brooke, Edward W. III	774,761	Peabody, Endicott	11,715	438,712 R	60.7%	38.7%	61.0%	39.0%
1964	2,312,028	587,663	Whitmore, Howard Jr.	1,716,907	Kennedy, Edward M.*	7,458	1,129,244 D	25.4%	74.3%	25.5%	74.5%
1962S**	2,097,085	877,669	Lodge, George C.	1,162,611	Kennedy, Edward M.	56,805	284,942 D	41.9%	55.4%	43.0%	57.0%
1960	2,417,813	1,358,556	Saltonstall, Leverett*	1,050,725	O'Connor, Thomas J. Jr.	8,532	307,831 R	56.2%	43.5%	56.4%	43.6%
1958	1,862,041	488,318	Celeste, Vincent J.	1,362,926	Kennedy, John F.*	10,797	874,608 D	26.2%	73.2%	26.4%	73.6%
1954	1,892,710	956,605	Saltonstall, Leverett*	927,899	Furcolo, Foster	8,206	28,706 R	50.5%	49.0%	50.8%	49.2%
1952	2,360,425	1,141,247	Lodge, Henry Cabot Jr.*	1,211,984	Kennedy, John F.	7,194	70,737 D	48.3%	51.3%	48.5%	51.5%
1948	2,055,798	1,088,475	Saltonstall, Leverett*	954,398	Fitzgerald, John I.	12,925	134,077 R	52.9%	46.4%	53.3%	46.7%
1946	1,662,063	989,736	Lodge, Henry Cabot Jr.	660,200	Walsh, David I.*	12,127	329,536 R	59.5%	39.7%	60.0%	40.0%

Note: An asterisk (*) denotes incumbent. **In past elections, the other vote included: 2002 - 369,807 Libertarian (Michael E. Cloud); 2000 - 308,748 Libertarian (Carla Howell). The Republican Party did not run a candidate in the 2002 Senate election. The 1962, 2010, and 2013 elections were for short terms to fill a vacancy; the 2010 election was held in January 2010.

MASSACHUSETTS

PRESIDENT 2016

2010 Census Population	County	Total Vote	Republican (Trump)	Democratic (Clinton)	Other	Rep.-Dem. Plurality	Total Vote Rep.	Total Vote Dem.	Major Vote Rep.	Major Vote Dem.
215,888	BARNSTABLE	135,781	54,099	72,430	9,252	18,331 D	39.8%	53.3%	42.8%	57.2%
131,219	BERKSHIRE	65,617	16,839	43,714	5,064	26,875 D	25.7%	66.6%	27.8%	72.2%
548,285	BRISTOL	252,140	105,443	129,540	17,157	24,097 D	41.8%	51.4%	44.9%	55.1%
16,535	DUKES	11,674	2,477	8,400	797	5,923 D	21.2%	72.0%	22.8%	77.2%
743,159	ESSEX	385,370	136,316	222,310	26,744	85,994 D	35.4%	57.7%	38.0%	62.0%
71,372	FRANKLIN	38,821	10,364	24,478	3,979	14,114 D	26.7%	63.1%	29.7%	70.3%
463,490	HAMPDEN	206,101	78,685	112,590	14,826	33,905 D	38.2%	54.6%	41.1%	58.9%
158,080	HAMPSHIRE	84,193	21,790	55,367	7,036	33,577 D	25.9%	65.8%	28.2%	71.8%
1,503,085	MIDDLESEX	796,735	219,793	520,360	56,582	300,567 D	27.6%	65.3%	29.7%	70.3%
10,172	NANTUCKET	6,508	1,892	4,146	470	2,254 D	29.1%	63.7%	31.3%	68.7%
670,850	NORFOLK	367,695	119,723	221,819	26,153	102,096 D	32.6%	60.3%	35.1%	64.9%
494,919	PLYMOUTH	271,177	115,369	135,513	20,295	20,144 D	42.5%	50.0%	46.0%	54.0%
722,023	SUFFOLK	313,283	50,421	245,751	17,111	195,330 D	16.1%	78.4%	17.0%	83.0%
798,552	WORCESTER	389,951	157,682	198,778	33,491	41,096 D	40.4%	51.0%	44.2%	55.8%
6,547,629	TOTAL	3,325,046	1,090,893	1,995,196	238,957	904,303 D	32.8%	60.0%	35.3%	64.7%

2010 Census Population	City/Town	Total Vote	Republican (Trump)	Democratic (Clinton)	Other	Rep.-Dem. Plurality	Total Vote Rep.	Total Vote Dem.	Major Vote Rep.	Major Vote Dem.
21,924	ACTON	12,783	2,555	9,198	1,030	6,643 D	20.0%	72.0%	78.3%	21.7%
28,438	AGAWAM	14,685	7,421	6,208	1,056	1,213 R	50.5%	42.3%	54.5%	45.5%
37,819	AMHERST	14,927	1,248	12,357	1,322	11,109 D	8.4%	82.8%	9.2%	90.8%
33,201	ANDOVER	19,219	6,522	11,222	1,475	4,700 D	33.9%	58.4%	36.8%	63.2%
42,844	ARLINGTON	26,861	4,652	20,539	1,670	15,887 D	17.3%	76.5%	18.5%	81.5%
43,593	ATTLEBORO	20,572	8,571	10,518	1,483	1,947 D	41.7%	51.1%	44.9%	55.1%
45,193	BARNSTABLE	26,029	11,195	13,005	1,829	1,810 D	43.0%	50.0%	46.3%	53.7%
24,729	BELMONT	14,475	3,106	10,252	1,117	7,146 D	21.5%	70.8%	23.3%	76.7%
39,502	BEVERLY	21,951	6,904	13,185	1,862	6,281 D	31.5%	60.1%	34.4%	65.6%
40,243	BILLERICA	22,082	10,319	10,100	1,663	219 R	46.7%	45.7%	50.5%	49.5%
617,594	BOSTON	274,429	38,087	221,093	15,249	183,006 D	13.9%	80.6%	14.7%	85.3%
35,744	BRAINTREE	20,265	8,427	10,469	1,369	2,042 D	41.6%	51.7%	44.6%	55.4%
93,810	BROCKTON	36,039	8,801	25,593	1,645	16,792 D	24.4%	71.0%	25.6%	74.4%
58,732	BROOKLINE	29,359	3,175	24,583	1,601	21,408 D	10.8%	83.7%	11.4%	88.6%
24,498	BURLINGTON	13,977	5,434	7,633	910	2,199 D	38.9%	54.6%	41.6%	58.4%
105,162	CAMBRIDGE	52,948	3,323	46,563	3,062	43,240 D	6.3%	87.9%	6.7%	93.3%
21,561	CANTON	12,885	4,731	7,308	846	2,577 D	36.7%	56.7%	39.3%	60.7%
33,802	CHELMSFORD	20,141	7,661	10,705	1,775	3,044 D	38.0%	53.2%	41.7%	58.3%
55,298	CHICOPEE	24,156	9,841	12,338	1,977	2,497 D	40.7%	51.1%	44.4%	55.6%
17,668	CONCORD	11,242	1,951	8,460	831	6,509 D	17.4%	75.3%	18.7%	81.3%
26,493	DANVERS	15,404	6,484	7,752	1,168	1,268 D	42.1%	50.3%	45.5%	54.5%
34,032	DARTMOUTH	16,424	6,738	8,586	1,100	1,848 D	41.0%	52.3%	44.0%	56.0%
24,729	DEDHAM	14,427	4,778	8,621	1,028	3,843 D	33.1%	59.8%	35.7%	64.3%
29,457	DRACUT	15,972	8,319	6,645	1,008	1,674 R	52.1%	41.6%	55.6%	44.4%
23,112	EASTON	12,684	5,231	6,556	897	1,325 D	41.2%	51.7%	44.4%	55.6%
41,667	EVERETT	14,060	3,940	9,461	659	5,521 D	28.0%	67.3%	29.4%	70.6%
88,857	FALL RIVER	29,998	10,850	17,467	1,681	6,617 D	36.2%	58.2%	38.3%	61.7%
31,531	FALMOUTH	19,946	7,165	11,467	1,314	4,302 D	35.9%	57.5%	38.5%	61.5%
40,318	FITCHBURG	15,411	5,587	8,590	1,234	3,003 D	36.3%	55.7%	39.4%	60.6%
68,318	FRAMINGHAM	29,705	7,063	20,520	2,122	13,457 D	23.8%	69.1%	25.6%	74.4%

MASSACHUSETTS

PRESIDENT 2016

2010 Census Population	City/Town	Total Vote	Republican (Trump)	Democratic (Clinton)	Other	Rep.-Dem. Plurality	Percentage Total Vote Rep.	Dem.	Major Vote Rep.	Dem.
31,635	FRANKLIN	18,149	6,996	9,527	1,626	2,531 D	38.5%	52.5%	42.3%	57.7%
28,789	GLOUCESTER	16,461	5,355	9,808	1,298	4,453 D	32.5%	59.6%	35.3%	64.7%
60,879	HAVERHILL	29,773	12,050	15,407	2,316	3,357 D	40.5%	51.7%	43.9%	56.1%
22,157	HINGHAM	14,561	4,810	8,510	1,241	3,700 D	33.0%	58.4%	36.1%	63.9%
39,880	HOLYOKE	16,728	4,022	11,656	1,050	7,634 D	24.0%	69.7%	25.7%	74.3%
76,377	LAWRENCE	24,271	3,535	19,852	884	16,317 D	14.6%	81.8%	15.1%	84.9%
40,759	LEOMINSTER	19,612	8,199	9,840	1,573	1,641 D	41.8%	50.2%	45.5%	54.5%
31,394	LEXINGTON	18,038	3,279	13,900	859	10,621 D	18.2%	77.1%	19.1%	80.9%
106,519	LOWELL	36,721	10,584	23,555	2,582	12,971 D	28.8%	64.1%	31.0%	69.0%
90,329	LYNN	33,295	9,311	22,164	1,820	12,853 D	28.0%	66.6%	29.6%	70.4%
59,450	MALDEN	22,706	5,538	15,845	1,323	10,307 D	24.4%	69.8%	25.9%	74.1%
19,808	MARBLEHEAD	12,901	3,759	8,111	1,031	4,352 D	29.1%	62.9%	31.7%	68.3%
38,499	MARLBOROUGH	17,999	5,959	10,577	1,463	4,618 D	33.1%	58.8%	36.0%	64.0%
25,132	MARSHFIELD	15,692	7,215	7,343	1,134	128 D	46.0%	46.8%	49.6%	50.4%
56,173	MEDFORD	30,187	7,671	20,690	1,826	13,019 D	25.4%	68.5%	27.0%	73.0%
26,983	MELROSE	16,695	4,832	10,687	1,176	5,855 D	28.9%	64.0%	31.1%	68.9%
47,255	METHUEN	23,190	10,235	11,662	1,293	1,427 D	44.1%	50.3%	46.7%	53.3%
27,999	MILFORD	13,594	5,237	7,370	987	2,133 D	38.5%	54.2%	41.5%	58.5%
27,003	MILTON	16,097	4,286	10,752	1,059	6,466 D	26.6%	66.8%	28.5%	71.5%
33,006	NATICK	19,831	4,870	13,420	1,541	8,550 D	24.6%	67.7%	26.6%	73.4%
28,886	NEEDHAM	18,182	4,019	12,797	1,366	8,778 D	22.1%	70.4%	23.9%	76.1%
95,072	NEW BEDFORD	33,165	10,327	20,812	2,026	10,485 D	31.1%	62.8%	33.2%	66.8%
85,146	NEWTON	46,968	7,764	36,463	2,741	28,699 D	16.5%	77.6%	17.6%	82.4%
28,352	NORTH ANDOVER	15,879	6,391	8,499	989	2,108 D	40.2%	53.5%	42.9%	57.1%
28,712	NORTH ATTLEBOROUGH	15,142	6,716	7,059	1,367	343 D	44.4%	46.6%	48.8%	51.2%
28,549	NORTHAMPTON	16,609	1,878	13,512	1,219	11,634 D	11.3%	81.4%	12.2%	87.8%
28,602	NORWOOD	15,856	5,692	9,000	1,164	3,308 D	35.9%	56.8%	38.7%	61.3%
51,251	PEABODY	28,159	12,036	14,395	1,728	2,359 D	42.7%	51.1%	45.5%	54.5%
44,737	PITTSFIELD	20,202	4,771	13,907	1,524	9,136 D	23.6%	68.8%	25.5%	74.5%
56,468	PLYMOUTH	32,582	14,309	15,602	2,671	1,293 D	43.9%	47.9%	47.8%	52.2%
92,271	QUINCY	40,821	13,321	25,477	2,023	12,156 D	32.6%	62.4%	34.3%	65.7%
32,112	RANDOLPH	15,264	3,098	11,509	657	8,411 D	20.3%	75.4%	21.2%	78.8%
24,747	READING	15,372	5,373	8,848	1,151	3,475 D	35.0%	57.6%	37.8%	62.2%
51,755	REVERE	19,790	6,895	11,964	931	5,069 D	34.8%	60.5%	36.6%	63.4%
41,340	SALEM	21,908	5,458	14,950	1,500	9,492 D	24.9%	68.2%	26.7%	73.3%
26,628	SAUGUS	14,356	7,305	6,385	666	920 R	50.9%	44.5%	53.4%	46.6%
18,133	SCITUATE	11,879	4,457	6,512	910	2,055 D	37.5%	54.8%	40.6%	59.4%
35,608	SHREWSBURY	18,923	6,808	10,620	1,495	3,812 D	36.0%	56.1%	39.1%	60.9%
75,754	SOMERVILLE	40,420	4,128	33,740	2,552	29,612 D	10.2%	83.5%	10.9%	89.1%
153,060	SPRINGFIELD	54,526	11,231	40,341	2,954	29,110 D	20.6%	74.0%	21.8%	78.2%
21,437	STONEHAM	12,840	5,243	6,962	635	1,719 D	40.8%	54.2%	43.0%	57.0%
26,962	STOUGHTON	14,194	4,920	8,451	823	3,531 D	34.7%	59.5%	36.8%	63.2%
55,874	TAUNTON	24,130	9,973	12,365	1,792	2,392 D	41.3%	51.2%	44.6%	55.4%
28,961	TEWKSBURY	17,385	8,432	7,602	1,351	830 R	48.5%	43.7%	52.6%	47.4%
24,932	WAKEFIELD	15,556	6,060	8,294	1,202	2,234 D	39.0%	53.3%	42.2%	57.8%
24,070	WALPOLE	14,535	6,046	7,270	1,219	1,224 D	41.6%	50.0%	45.4%	54.6%
60,632	WALTHAM	26,583	7,592	17,355	1,636	9,763 D	28.6%	65.3%	30.4%	69.6%
31,915	WATERTOWN	18,467	3,941	13,166	1,360	9,225 D	21.3%	71.3%	23.0%	77.0%
27,982	WELLESLEY	14,873	3,235	10,568	1,070	7,333 D	21.8%	71.1%	23.4%	76.6%
28,391	WEST SPRINGFIELD	12,220	5,537	5,711	972	174 D	45.3%	46.7%	49.2%	50.8%
41,094	WESTFIELD	18,944	9,021	8,225	1,698	796 R	47.6%	43.4%	52.3%	47.7%
53,743	WEYMOUTH	29,494	11,983	15,398	2,113	3,415 D	40.6%	52.2%	43.8%	56.2%
21,374	WINCHESTER	12,774	3,701	8,062	1,011	4,361 D	29.0%	63.1%	31.5%	68.5%
38,120	WOBURN	20,461	8,342	10,915	1,204	2,573 D	40.8%	53.3%	43.3%	56.7%
181,045	WORCESTER	65,393	17,732	43,084	4,577	25,352 D	27.1%	65.9%	29.2%	70.8%
23,793	YARMOUTH	14,056	5,848	7,304	904	1,456 D	41.6%	52.0%	44.5%	55.5%

MASSACHUSETTS

HOUSE OF REPRESENTATIVES

CD	Year	Total Vote	Republican Vote	Republican Candidate	Democratic Vote	Democratic Candidate	Other Vote	Rep.-Dem. Plurality	Total Vote Rep.	Total Vote Dem.	Major Vote Rep.	Major Vote Dem.
1	2016	321,539			235,803	NEAL, RICHARD E.*	85,736	235,803 D		73.3%		100.0%
1	2014	171,110			167,612	NEAL, RICHARD E.*	3,498	167,612 D		98.0%		100.0%
1	2012	266,133			261,936	NEAL, RICHARD E.*	4,197	261,936 D		98.4%		100.0%
2	2016	280,411			275,487	MCGOVERN, JAMES*	4,924	275,487 D		98.2%		100.0%
2	2014	172,745			169,640	MCGOVERN, JAMES*	3,105	169,640 D		98.2%		100.0%
2	2012	263,335			259,257	MCGOVERN, JAMES*	4,078	259,257 D		98.5%		100.0%
3	2016	344,592	107,519	WOFFORD, ROSEANN EHRHARD	236,713	TSONGAS, NICOLA S.*	360	129,194 D	31.2%	68.7%	31.2%	68.8%
3	2014	220,946	81,638	WOFFORD, ROSEANN EHRHARD	139,104	TSONGAS, NICOLA S.*	204	57,466 D	36.9%	63.0%	37.0%	63.0%
3	2012	321,753	109,372	GOLNIK, JONATHAN A.	212,119	TSONGAS, NICOLA S.*	262	102,747 D	34.0%	65.9%	34.0%	66.0%
4	2016	379,213	113,055	ROSA, DAVID A.	265,823	KENNEDY, JOSEPH PATRICK III*	335	152,768 D	29.8%	70.1%	29.8%	70.2%
4	2014	188,098			184,158	KENNEDY, JOSEPH PATRICK III*	3,940	184,158 D		97.9%		100.0%
4	2012	362,245	129,936	BIELAT, SEAN	221,303	KENNEDY, JOSEPH PATRICK III	11,006	91,367 D	35.9%	61.1%	37.0%	63.0%
5	2016	289,807			285,606	CLARK, KATHERINE M.*	4,201	285,606 D		98.6%		100.0%
5	2014	185,260			182,100	CLARK, KATHERINE M.*	3,160	182,100 D		98.3%		100.0%
5	2012	341,109	82,944	TIERNEY, TOM	257,490	MARKEY, EDWARD J.*	675	174,546 D	24.3%	75.5%	24.4%	75.6%
6	2016	314,055			308,923	MOULTON, SETH*	5,132	308,923 D		98.4%		100.0%
6	2014	272,219	111,989	TISEI, RICHARD	149,638	MOULTON, SETH	10,592	37,649 D	41.1%	55.0%	42.8%	57.2%
6	2012	374,807	176,612	TISEI, RICHARD	180,942	TIERNEY, JOHN F.*	17,253	4,330 D	47.1%	48.3%	49.4%	50.6%
7	2016	256,911			253,354	CAPUANO, MICHAEL E.*	3,557	253,354 D		98.6%		100.0%
7	2014	144,546			142,133	CAPUANO, MICHAEL E.*	2,413	142,133 D		98.3%		100.0%
7	2012	252,836			210,794	CAPUANO, MICHAEL E.*	42,042	210,794 D		83.4%		100.0%
8	2016	374,265	102,744	BURKE, WILLIAM	271,019	LYNCH, STEPHEN F.*	502	168,275 D	27.5%	72.4%	27.5%	72.5%
8	2014	203,351			200,644	LYNCH, STEPHEN F.*	2,707	200,644 D		98.7%		100.0%
8	2012	346,811	82,242	SELVAGGI, JOE	263,999	LYNCH, STEPHEN F.*	570	181,757 D	23.7%	76.1%	23.8%	76.2%
9	2016	379,895	127,803	ALLIEGRO, MARK C.	211,790	KEATING, WILLIAM R.*	40,302	83,987 D	33.6%	55.7%	37.6%	62.4%
9	2014	255,541	114,971	CHAPMAN, JOHN C.	140,413	KEATING, WILLIAM R.*	157	25,442 D	45.0%	54.9%	45.0%	55.0%
9	2012	362,405	116,531	SHELDON, CHRISTOPHER	212,754	KEATING, WILLIAM R.*	33,120	96,223 D	32.2%	58.7%	35.4%	64.6%
TOTAL	2016	2,940,688	451,121		2,344,518		145,049	1,893,397 D	15.3%	79.7%	16.1%	83.9%
TOTAL	2014	1,813,816	308,598		1,475,442		29,776	1,166,844 D	17.0%	81.3%	17.3%	82.7%
TOTAL	2012	2,891,434	697,637		2,080,594		113,203	1,382,957 D	24.1%	72.0%	25.1%	74.9%

Note: An asterisk (*) denotes incumbent.

MASSACHUSETTS

GENERAL AND PRIMARY ELECTIONS

2016 GENERAL ELECTIONS: OTHER VOTES

President Other vote was 138,018 Libertarian (Gary Johnson), 50,559 Write-in (Scattered Write-in), 47,661 Green (Jill Stein), 2,719 Write-in (Evan McMullin).

House Other vote was:

CD 1	57,504 Unenrolled (Frederick Mayock), 27,511 Libertarian (Thomas Simmons), 721 Write-in (All Others)
CD 2	4,924 Write-in (All Others)
CD 3	360 Write-in (All Others)
CD 4	335 Write-in (All Others)
CD 5	4,201 Write-in (All Others)
CD 6	5,132 Write-in (All Others)
CD 7	3,557 Write-in (All Others)
CD 8	502 Write-in (All Others)
CD 9	26,233 Unenrolled (Paul Harrington), 8,338 Unenrolled (Christopher Cataldo), 5,320 Unenrolled (Anna Raduc), 411 Write-in (All Others)

2016 PRIMARY ELECTIONS: SUPPLEMENTARY INFORMATION

Primary March 1, 2016 (President) September 8, 2016 (Congress)

Registration (as of August 19, 2016) 4,366,712

Democratic	1,509,113
Republican	473,220
United Independent	25,423
Green-Rainbow	5,413
Other	13,978
Unenrolled	2,339,565

Primary Type Semi-open—Registered Democrats and Republicans could vote only in their party's primary. "Unenrolled" voters could participate in either party's primary.

	REPUBLICAN PRIMARIES			DEMOCRATIC PRIMARIES		
President	Trump, Donald J.	312,425	49.1%	Clinton, Hillary Rodham	606,822	49.9%
	Kasich, John R.	114,434	18.0%	Sanders, Bernard	589,803	48.5%
	Rubio, Marco	113,170	17.8%	No Preference	8,090	0.7%
	Cruz, Ted	60,592	9.5%	All Others	4,927	0.4%
	Carson, Ben	16,360	2.6%	O'Malley, Martin	4,783	0.4%
	Bush, Jeb	6,559	1.0%	De La Fuente, Roque "Rocky"	1,545	0.1%
	No Preference	3,220	0.5%			
	All Others	2,325	0.4%			
	Christie, Chris	1,906	0.3%			
	Paul, Rand	1,864	0.3%			
	Fiorina, Carly	1,153	0.2%			
	Gilmore, James S. III	753	0.1%			
	Huckabee, Mike	709	0.1%			
	Pataki, George E.	500	0.1%			
	Santorum, Rick	293				
	TOTAL	*636,263*		*TOTAL*	*1,215,970*	
Congressional District 1				Neal, Richard E.*	44,857	98.5%
				Write-In	706	1.5%
				TOTAL	*45,563*	
Congressional District 2				McGovern, James*	21,562	99.2%
				Write-In	166	0.8%
				TOTAL	*21,728*	

MASSACHUSETTS

GENERAL AND PRIMARY ELECTIONS

	REPUBLICAN PRIMARIES			DEMOCRATIC PRIMARIES		
Congressional District 3	Wofford, Roseann Ehrhard Write-In TOTAL	5,774 54 5,828	99.1% 0.9%	Tsongas, Nicola S.* Write-In TOTAL	21,047 291 21,338	98.6% 1.4%
Congressional District 4	Rosa, David A. Write-In TOTAL	4,299 87 4,386	98.0% 2.0%	Kennedy, Joseph Patrick III* Write-In TOTAL	15,849 216 16,065	98.7% 1.3%
Congressional District 5				Clark, Katherine M.* Write-In TOTAL	30,066 455 30,521	98.5% 1.5%
Congressional District 6				Moulton, Seth* Write-In TOTAL	28,206 267 28,473	99.1% 0.9%
Congressional District 7				Capuano, Michael E.* Write-In TOTAL	37,547 666 38,213	98.3% 1.7%
Congressional District 8	Burke, William Write-In TOTAL	5,856 291 6,147	95.3% 4.7%	Lynch, Stephen F.* Write-In TOTAL	27,335 737 28,072	97.4% 2.6%
Congressional District 9	Alliegro, Mark C. O'Malley, Thomas Joseph Jr. Write-In TOTAL	12,467 7,632 55 20,154	61.9% 37.9% 0.3%	Keating, William R.* Write-In TOTAL	31,074 215 31,289	99.3% 0.7%

Note: An asterisk (*) denotes incumbent.

MICHIGAN

Congressional districts first established for elections held in 2012

14 members

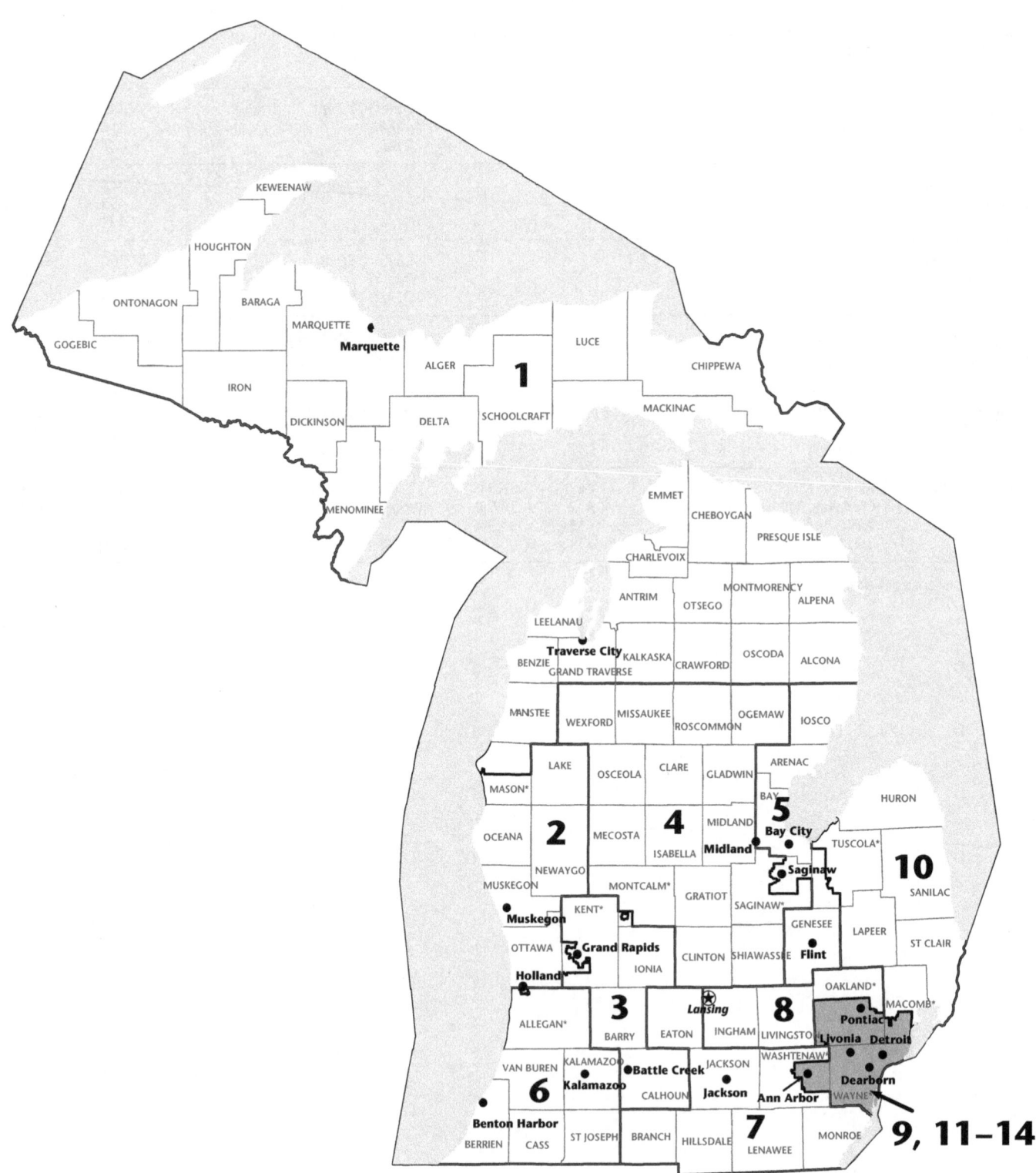

* Asterisk indicates a county whose boundaries include parts of two or more congressional districts.

MICHIGAN
Detroit Area

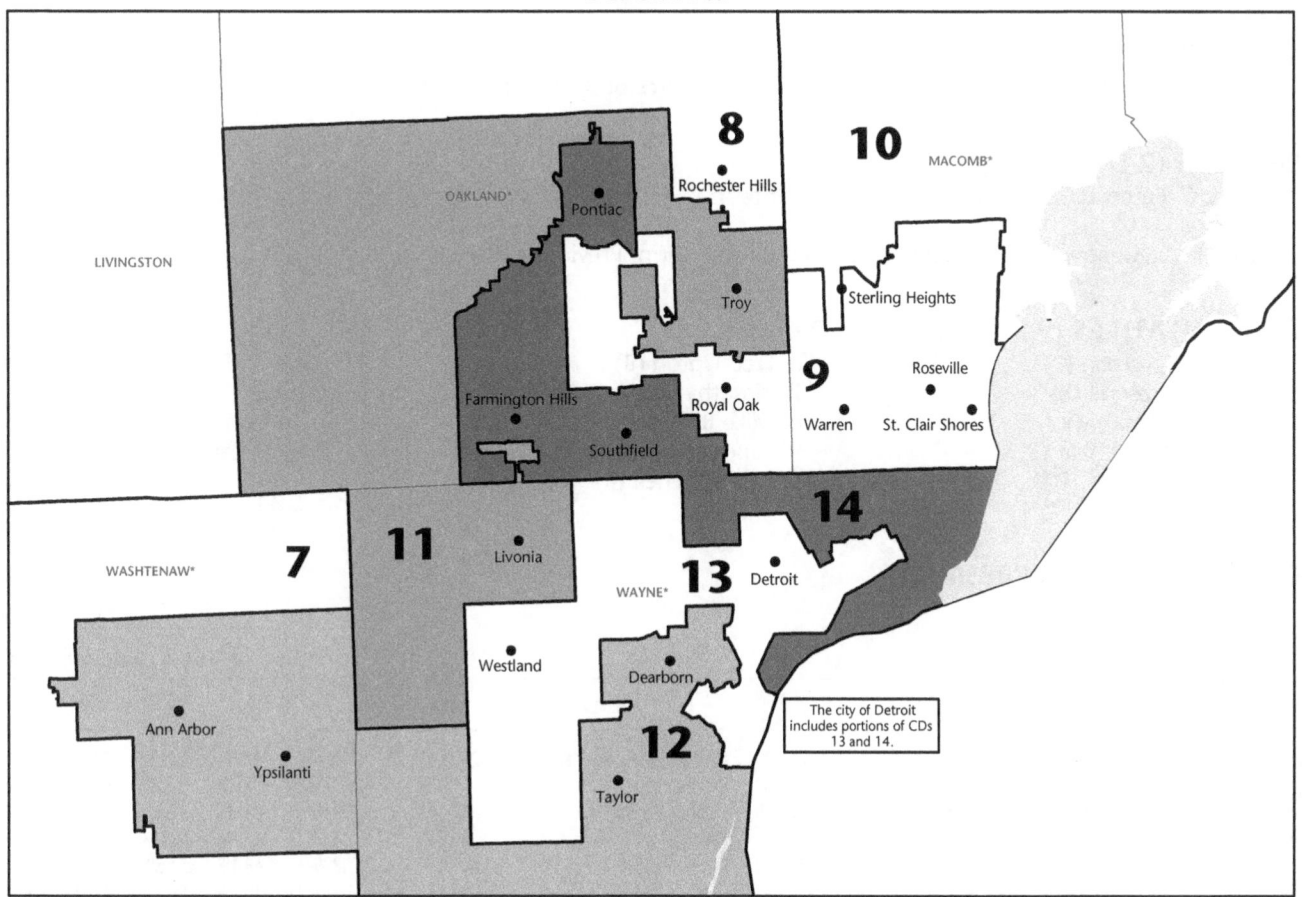

* Asterisk indicates a county whose boundaries include parts of two or more congressional districts.

MICHIGAN

GOVERNOR

Rick Snyder (R). Re-elected 2014 to a four-year term. Previously elected 2010.

SENATORS (2 Democrats)

Gary C. Peters (D). Elected 2014 to a six-year term.

Debbie Stabenow (D). Re-elected 2012 to a six-year term. Previously elected 2006, 2000.

REPRESENTATIVES (9 Republicans, 5 Democrats)

1. Jack Bergman (R)
2. Bill Huizenga (R)
3. Justin Amash (R)
4. John Moolenaar (R)
5. Daniel Kildee (D)
6. Fred Upton (R)
7. Timothy Walberg (R)
8. Mike Bishop (R)
9. Sander M. Levin (D)
10. Paul Mitchell (R)
11. Dave A. Trott (R)
12. Debbie Dingell (D)
13. John Conyers Jr. (D)
14. Brenda Lawrence (D)

POSTWAR VOTE FOR PRESIDENT

| | | Republican | | Democratic | | Other Vote | Rep.-Dem. Plurality | Percentage | | | |
| | | | | | | | | Total Vote | | Major Vote | |
Year	Total Vote	Vote	Candidate	Vote	Candidate			Rep.	Dem.	Rep.	Dem.
2016**	4,799,284	2,279,543	Trump, Donald J.	2,268,839	Clinton, Hillary Rodham	250,902	10,704 R	47.5%	47.3%	50.1%	49.9%
2012	4,730,961	2,115,256	Romney, W. Mitt	2,564,569	Obama, Barack H.*	51,136	449,313 D	44.7%	54.2%	45.2%	54.8%
2008	5,001,766	2,048,639	McCain, John S. III	2,872,579	Obama, Barack H.	80,548	823,940 D	41.0%	57.4%	41.6%	58.4%
2004	4,839,252	2,313,746	Bush, George W.*	2,479,183	Kerry, John F.	46,323	165,437 D	47.8%	51.2%	48.3%	51.7%
2000**	4,232,711	1,953,139	Bush, George W.	2,170,418	Gore, Albert Jr.	109,154	217,279 D	46.1%	51.3%	47.4%	52.6%
1996**	3,848,844	1,481,212	Dole, Robert "Bob"	1,989,653	Clinton, Bill*	377,979	508,441 D	38.5%	51.7%	42.7%	57.3%
1992**	4,274,673	1,554,940	Bush, George H.*	1,871,182	Clinton, Bill	848,551	316,242 D	36.4%	43.8%	45.4%	54.6%
1988	3,669,163	1,965,486	Bush, George H.	1,675,783	Dukakis, Michael S.	27,894	289,703 R	53.6%	45.7%	54.0%	46.0%
1984	3,801,658	2,251,571	Reagan, Ronald*	1,529,638	Mondale, Walter F.	20,449	721,933 R	59.2%	40.2%	59.5%	40.5%
1980**	3,909,725	1,915,225	Reagan, Ronald	1,661,532	Carter, Jimmy*	332,968	253,693 R	49.0%	42.5%	53.5%	46.5%
1976	3,653,749	1,893,742	Ford, Gerald R.*	1,696,714	Carter, Jimmy	63,293	197,028 R	51.8%	46.4%	52.7%	47.3%
1972	3,489,727	1,961,721	Nixon, Richard M.*	1,459,435	McGovern, George S.	68,571	502,286 R	56.2%	41.8%	57.3%	42.7%
1968**	3,306,250	1,370,665	Nixon, Richard M.	1,593,082	Humphrey, Hubert Horatio Jr.	342,503	222,417 D	41.5%	48.2%	46.2%	53.8%
1964	3,203,102	1,060,152	Goldwater, Barry M. Sr.	2,136,615	Johnson, Lyndon B.*	6,335	1,076,463 D	33.1%	66.7%	33.2%	66.8%
1960	3,318,097	1,620,428	Nixon, Richard M.	1,687,269	Kennedy, John F.	10,400	66,841 D	48.8%	50.9%	49.0%	51.0%
1956	3,080,468	1,713,647	Eisenhower, Dwight D.*	1,359,898	Stevenson, Adlai E. II	6,923	353,749 R	55.6%	44.1%	55.8%	44.2%
1952	2,798,592	1,551,529	Eisenhower, Dwight D.	1,230,657	Stevenson, Adlai E. II	16,406	320,872 R	55.4%	44.0%	55.8%	44.2%
1948	2,109,609	1,038,595	Dewey, Thomas E.	1,003,448	Truman, Harry S.*	67,566	35,147 R	49.2%	47.6%	50.9%	49.1%

Note: An asterisk (*) denotes incumbent. **In past elections, the other vote included: 2016 - 172,136 Libertarian (Gary Johnson); 2000 - 84,165 Green (Ralph Nader); 1996 - 336,670 Reform (Ross Perot); 1992 - 824,813 Independent (Perot); 1980 - 275,223 Independent (John Anderson); 1968 - 331,968 American Independent (George Wallace).

MICHIGAN

POSTWAR VOTE FOR GOVERNOR

Year	Total Vote	Republican		Democratic		Other Vote	Rep.-Dem. Plurality	Percentage			
								Total Vote		Major Vote	
		Vote	Candidate	Vote	Candidate			Rep.	Dem.	Rep.	Dem.
2014	3,156,531	1,607,399	Snyder, Rick*	1,479,057	Schauer, Mark H.	70,075	128,342 R	50.9%	46.9%	52.1%	47.9%
2010	3,226,088	1,874,834	Snyder, Rick	1,287,320	Bernero, Virg	63,934	587,514 R	58.1%	39.9%	59.3%	40.7%
2006	3,801,256	1,608,086	DeVos, Dick	2,142,513	Granholm, Jennifer M.*	50,657	534,427 D	42.3%	56.4%	42.9%	57.1%
2002	3,177,565	1,506,104	Posthumus, Dick	1,633,796	Granholm, Jennifer M.	37,665	127,692 D	47.4%	51.4%	48.0%	52.0%
1998	3,027,104	1,883,005	Engler, John*	1,143,574	Fieger, Geoffrey	525	739,431 R	62.2%	37.8%	62.2%	37.8%
1994	3,089,077	1,899,101	Engler, John*	1,188,438	Wolpe, Howard	1,538	710,663 R	61.5%	38.5%	61.5%	38.5%
1990	2,564,563	1,276,134	Engler, John	1,258,539	Blanchard, James J.*	29,890	17,595 R	49.8%	49.1%	50.3%	49.7%
1986	2,396,564	753,647	Lucas, William	1,632,138	Blanchard, James J.*	10,779	878,491 D	31.4%	68.1%	31.6%	68.4%
1982	3,040,008	1,369,582	Headlee, Richard H.	1,561,291	Blanchard, James J.	109,135	191,709 D	45.1%	51.4%	46.7%	53.3%
1978	2,867,212	1,628,485	Milliken, William G.*	1,237,256	Fitzgerald, William	1,471	391,229 R	56.8%	43.2%	56.8%	43.2%
1974	2,657,020	1,356,865	Milliken, William G.*	1,242,250	Levin, Sander M.	57,905	114,615 R	51.1%	46.8%	52.2%	47.8%
1970	2,656,093	1,338,711	Milliken, William G.*	1,294,600	Levin, Sander M.	22,782	44,111 R	50.4%	48.7%	50.8%	49.2%
1966**	2,461,909	1,490,430	Romney, George W.*	963,383	Ferency, Zoltan A.	8,096	527,047 R	60.5%	39.1%	60.7%	39.3%
1964	3,158,102	1,764,355	Romney, George W.*	1,381,442	Staebler, Neil	12,305	382,913 R	55.9%	43.7%	56.1%	43.9%
1962	2,764,839	1,420,086	Romney, George W.	1,339,513	Swainson, John B.*	5,240	80,573 R	51.4%	48.4%	51.5%	48.5%
1960	3,255,991	1,602,022	Bagwell, Paul D.	1,643,634	Swainson, John B.	10,335	41,612 D	49.2%	50.5%	49.4%	50.6%
1958	2,312,184	1,078,089	Bagwell, Paul D.	1,225,533	Williams, G. Mennen*	8,562	147,444 D	46.6%	53.0%	46.8%	53.2%
1956	3,049,651	1,376,376	Cobo, Albert E.	1,666,689	Williams, G. Mennen*	6,586	290,313 D	45.1%	54.7%	45.2%	54.8%
1954	2,187,027	963,300	Leonard, Donald S.	1,216,308	Williams, G. Mennen*	7,419	253,008 D	44.0%	55.6%	44.2%	55.8%
1952	2,865,980	1,423,275	Alger, Fred M. Jr.	1,431,893	Williams, G. Mennen*	10,812	8,618 D	49.7%	50.0%	49.8%	50.2%
1950	1,879,382	933,998	Kelly, Harry F.	935,152	Williams, G. Mennen	10,232	1,154 D	49.7%	49.8%	50.0%	50.0%
1948	2,113,122	964,810	Sigler, Kim*	1,128,664	Williams, G. Mennen	19,648	163,854 D	45.7%	53.4%	46.1%	53.9%
1946	1,665,475	1,003,878	Sigler, Kim	644,540	Van Wagoner, Murray D.	17,057	359,338 R	60.3%	38.7%	60.9%	39.1%

Note: An asterisk (*) denotes incumbent. **The term of office of Michigan's governor was increased from two to four years effective with the 1966 election.

POSTWAR VOTE FOR SENATOR

Year	Total Vote	Republican		Democratic		Other Vote	Rep.-Dem. Plurality	Percentage			
								Total Vote		Major Vote	
		Vote	Candidate	Vote	Candidate			Rep.	Dem.	Rep.	Dem.
2014	3,121,775	1,290,199	Land, Terri Lynn	1,704,936	Peters, Gary C.	126,640	414,737 D	41.3%	54.6%	43.1%	56.9%
2012	4,652,918	1,767,386	Hoekstra, Peter	2,735,826	Stabenow, Debbie*	149,706	968,440 D	38.0%	58.8%	39.2%	60.8%
2008	4,848,620	1,641,070	Hoogendyk, Jack Jr.	3,038,386	Levin, Carl*	169,164	1,397,316 D	33.8%	62.7%	35.1%	64.9%
2006	3,780,142	1,559,597	Bouchard, Michael	2,151,278	Stabenow, Debbie*	69,267	591,681 D	41.3%	56.9%	42.0%	58.0%
2002	3,129,287	1,185,545	Raczkowski, Andrew	1,896,614	Levin, Carl*	47,128	711,069 D	37.9%	60.6%	38.5%	61.5%
2000	4,167,685	1,994,693	Abraham, Spencer*	2,061,952	Stabenow, Debbie	111,040	67,259 D	47.9%	49.5%	49.2%	50.8%
1996	3,762,575	1,500,106	Romney, Ronna	2,195,738	Levin, Carl*	66,731	695,632 D	39.9%	58.4%	40.6%	59.4%
1994	3,043,385	1,578,770	Abraham, Spencer	1,300,960	Carr, M. Robert	163,655	277,810 R	51.9%	42.7%	54.8%	45.2%
1990	2,560,494	1,055,695	Schuette, Bill	1,471,753	Levin, Carl*	33,046	416,058 D	41.2%	57.5%	41.8%	58.2%
1988	3,505,985	1,348,219	Dunn, Jim	2,116,865	Riegle, Donald Wayne Jr.*	40,901	768,646 D	38.5%	60.4%	38.9%	61.1%
1984	3,700,938	1,745,302	Lousma, Jack	1,915,831	Levin, Carl*	39,805	170,529 D	47.2%	51.8%	47.7%	52.3%
1982	2,994,334	1,223,288	Ruppe, Philip E.	1,728,793	Riegle, Donald Wayne Jr.*	42,253	505,505 D	40.9%	57.7%	41.4%	58.6%
1978	2,846,630	1,362,165	Griffin, Robert P.*	1,484,193	Levin, Carl	272	122,028 D	47.9%	52.1%	47.9%	52.1%
1976	3,484,664	1,635,087	Esch, Marvin L.	1,831,031	Riegle, Donald Wayne Jr.	18,546	195,944 D	46.9%	52.5%	47.2%	52.8%
1972	3,406,906	1,781,065	Griffin, Robert P.*	1,577,178	Kelley, Frank J.	48,663	203,887 R	52.3%	46.3%	53.0%	47.0%
1970	2,610,763	858,438	Romney, Lenore	1,744,672	Hart, Philip A.*	7,653	886,234 D	32.9%	66.8%	33.0%	67.0%
1966	2,439,365	1,363,530	Griffin, Robert P.*	1,069,484	Williams, G. Mennen	6,351	294,046 R	55.9%	43.8%	56.0%	44.0%
1964	3,101,667	1,096,272	Peterson, Elly M.	1,996,912	Hart, Philip A.*	8,483	900,640 D	35.3%	64.4%	35.4%	64.6%
1960	3,226,647	1,548,873	Bentley, Alvin M.	1,669,179	McNamara, Patrick V.*	8,595	120,306 D	48.0%	51.7%	48.1%	51.9%
1958	2,271,644	1,046,963	Potter, Charles E.*	1,216,966	Hart, Philip A.	7,715	170,003 D	46.1%	53.6%	46.2%	53.8%
1954	2,144,840	1,049,420	Ferguson, Homer*	1,088,550	McNamara, Patrick V.	6,870	39,130 D	48.9%	50.8%	49.1%	50.9%
1952	2,821,133	1,428,352	Potter, Charles E.	1,383,416	Moody, Blair	9,365	44,936 R	50.6%	49.0%	50.8%	49.2%
1948	2,062,097	1,045,156	Ferguson, Homer*	1,000,329	Hook, Frank E.	16,612	44,827 R	50.7%	48.5%	51.1%	48.9%
1946	1,618,720	1,085,570	Vandenberg, Arthur H.*	517,923	Lee, James H.	15,227	567,647 R	67.1%	32.0%	67.7%	32.3%

Note: An asterisk (*) denotes incumbent.

MICHIGAN

PRESIDENT 2016

2010 Census Population	County	Total Vote	Republican (Trump)	Democratic (Clinton)	Other	Rep.-Dem. Plurality	Percentage			
							Total Vote		Major Vote	
							Rep.	Dem.	Rep.	Dem.
10,942	ALCONA	6,198	4,201	1,732	265	2,469 R	67.8%	27.9%	70.8%	29.2%
9,601	ALGER	4,518	2,585	1,663	270	922 R	57.2%	36.8%	60.9%	39.1%
111,408	ALLEGAN	55,786	34,183	18,050	3,553	16,133 R	61.3%	32.4%	65.4%	34.6%
29,598	ALPENA	14,698	9,090	4,877	731	4,213 R	61.8%	33.2%	65.1%	34.9%
23,580	ANTRIM	13,582	8,469	4,448	665	4,021 R	62.4%	32.7%	65.6%	34.4%
15,899	ARENAC	7,696	4,950	2,384	362	2,566 R	64.3%	31.0%	67.5%	32.5%
8,860	BARAGA	3,490	2,158	1,156	176	1,002 R	61.8%	33.1%	65.1%	34.9%
59,173	BARRY	30,329	19,202	9,114	2,013	10,088 R	63.3%	30.1%	67.8%	32.2%
107,771	BAY	52,977	28,328	21,642	3,007	6,686 R	53.5%	40.9%	56.7%	43.3%
17,525	BENZIE	10,228	5,539	4,108	581	1,431 R	54.2%	40.2%	57.4%	42.6%
156,813	BERRIEN	72,031	38,647	29,495	3,889	9,152 R	53.7%	40.9%	56.7%	43.3%
45,248	BRANCH	17,663	11,786	5,061	816	6,725 R	66.7%	28.7%	70.0%	30.0%
136,146	CALHOUN	58,902	31,494	24,157	3,251	7,337 R	53.5%	41.0%	56.6%	43.4%
52,293	CASS	22,595	14,243	7,270	1,082	6,973 R	63.0%	32.2%	66.2%	33.8%
25,949	CHARLEVOIX	14,589	8,674	5,137	778	3,537 R	59.5%	35.2%	62.8%	37.2%
26,152	CHEBOYGAN	13,672	8,683	4,302	687	4,381 R	63.5%	31.5%	66.9%	33.1%
38,520	CHIPPEWA	15,456	9,122	5,379	955	3,743 R	59.0%	34.8%	62.9%	37.1%
30,926	CLARE	13,389	8,505	4,249	635	4,256 R	63.5%	31.7%	66.7%	33.3%
75,382	CLINTON	40,655	21,636	16,492	2,527	5,144 R	53.2%	40.6%	56.7%	43.3%
14,074	CRAWFORD	6,844	4,354	2,110	380	2,244 R	63.6%	30.8%	67.4%	32.6%
37,069	DELTA	18,492	11,121	6,436	935	4,685 R	60.1%	34.8%	63.3%	36.7%
26,168	DICKINSON	13,165	8,580	3,923	662	4,657 R	65.2%	29.8%	68.6%	31.4%
107,759	EATON	56,221	27,609	24,938	3,674	2,671 R	49.1%	44.4%	52.5%	47.5%
32,694	EMMET	18,802	10,616	6,972	1,214	3,644 R	56.5%	37.1%	60.4%	39.6%
425,790	GENESEE	196,296	84,175	102,751	9,370	18,576 D	42.9%	52.3%	45.0%	55.0%
25,692	GLADWIN	12,472	8,124	3,794	554	4,330 R	65.1%	30.4%	68.2%	31.8%
16,427	GOGEBIC	7,329	4,018	2,925	386	1,093 R	54.8%	39.9%	57.9%	42.1%
86,986	GRAND TRAVERSE	51,589	27,413	20,965	3,211	6,448 R	53.1%	40.6%	56.7%	43.3%
42,476	GRATIOT	16,465	9,880	5,666	919	4,214 R	60.0%	34.4%	63.6%	36.4%
46,688	HILLSDALE	19,940	14,095	4,799	1,046	9,296 R	70.7%	24.1%	74.6%	25.4%
36,628	HOUGHTON	15,624	8,475	6,018	1,131	2,457 R	54.2%	38.5%	58.5%	41.5%
33,118	HURON	15,917	10,692	4,579	646	6,113 R	67.2%	28.8%	70.0%	30.0%
280,895	INGHAM	131,138	43,868	79,110	8,160	35,242 D	33.5%	60.3%	35.7%	64.3%
63,905	IONIA	26,854	16,635	8,352	1,867	8,283 R	61.9%	31.1%	66.6%	33.4%
25,887	IOSCO	13,361	8,345	4,345	671	4,000 R	62.5%	32.5%	65.8%	34.2%
11,817	IRON	5,910	3,675	2,004	231	1,671 R	62.2%	33.9%	64.7%	35.3%
70,311	ISABELLA	25,392	12,338	11,404	1,650	934 R	48.6%	44.9%	52.0%	48.0%
160,248	JACKSON	69,677	39,793	25,795	4,089	13,998 R	57.1%	37.0%	60.7%	39.3%
250,331	KALAMAZOO	126,299	51,034	67,148	8,117	16,114 D	40.4%	53.2%	43.2%	56.8%
17,153	KALKASKA	8,833	6,116	2,280	437	3,836 R	69.2%	25.8%	72.8%	27.2%
602,622	KENT	308,184	148,180	138,683	21,321	9,497 R	48.1%	45.0%	51.7%	48.3%
2,156	KEWEENAW	1,434	814	527	93	287 R	56.8%	36.8%	60.7%	39.3%
11,539	LAKE	5,328	3,159	1,939	230	1,220 R	59.3%	36.4%	62.0%	38.0%
88,319	LAPEER	45,183	30,037	12,734	2,412	17,303 R	66.5%	28.2%	70.2%	29.8%
21,708	LEELANAU	14,757	7,239	6,774	744	465 R	49.1%	45.9%	51.7%	48.3%
99,892	LENAWEE	45,939	26,430	16,750	2,759	9,680 R	57.5%	36.5%	61.2%	38.8%
180,967	LIVINGSTON	105,865	65,680	34,384	5,801	31,296 R	62.0%	32.5%	65.6%	34.4%
6,631	LUCE	2,579	1,756	681	142	1,075 R	68.1%	26.4%	72.1%	27.9%
11,113	MACKINAC	6,097	3,744	2,085	268	1,659 R	61.4%	34.2%	64.2%	35.8%
840,978	MACOMB	419,312	224,665	176,317	18,330	48,348 R	53.6%	42.0%	56.0%	44.0%
24,733	MANISTEE	12,599	6,915	4,979	705	1,936 R	54.9%	39.5%	58.1%	41.9%
67,077	MARQUETTE	32,976	14,646	16,042	2,288	1,396 D	44.4%	48.6%	47.7%	52.3%
28,705	MASON	14,685	8,505	5,281	899	3,224 R	57.9%	36.0%	61.7%	38.3%
42,798	MECOSTA	17,168	10,305	5,827	1,036	4,478 R	60.0%	33.9%	63.9%	36.1%
24,029	MENOMINEE	10,768	6,702	3,539	527	3,163 R	62.2%	32.9%	65.4%	34.6%
83,629	MIDLAND	42,506	23,846	15,635	3,025	8,211 R	56.1%	36.8%	60.4%	39.6%
14,849	MISSAUKEE	7,317	5,386	1,565	366	3,821 R	73.6%	21.4%	77.5%	22.5%
152,021	MONROE	74,218	43,261	26,863	4,094	16,398 R	58.3%	36.2%	61.7%	38.3%
63,342	MONTCALM	26,609	16,907	7,874	1,828	9,033 R	63.5%	29.6%	68.2%	31.8%
9,765	MONTMORENCY	5,009	3,498	1,287	224	2,211 R	69.8%	25.7%	73.1%	26.9%

MICHIGAN

PRESIDENT 2016

2010 Census Population	County	Total Vote	Republican (Trump)	Democratic (Clinton)	Other	Rep.-Dem. Plurality		Percentage Total Vote Rep.	Dem.	Major Vote Rep.	Dem.
172,188	MUSKEGON	78,089	36,127	37,304	4,658	1,177	D	46.3%	47.8%	49.2%	50.8%
48,460	NEWAYGO	22,640	15,173	6,212	1,255	8,961	R	67.0%	27.4%	71.0%	29.0%
1,202,362	OAKLAND	664,614	289,203	343,070	32,341	53,867	D	43.5%	51.6%	45.7%	54.3%
26,570	OCEANA	11,930	7,228	3,973	729	3,255	R	60.6%	33.3%	64.5%	35.5%
21,699	OGEMAW	10,387	6,827	3,030	530	3,797	R	65.7%	29.2%	69.3%	30.7%
6,780	ONTONAGON	3,426	2,066	1,176	184	890	R	60.3%	34.3%	63.7%	36.3%
23,528	OSCEOLA	10,609	7,336	2,705	568	4,631	R	69.1%	25.5%	73.1%	26.9%
8,640	OSCODA	4,073	2,843	1,044	186	1,799	R	69.8%	25.6%	73.1%	26.9%
24,164	OTSEGO	12,538	8,266	3,556	716	4,710	R	65.9%	28.4%	69.9%	30.1%
263,801	OTTAWA	142,734	88,467	44,973	9,294	43,494	R	62.0%	31.5%	66.3%	33.7%
13,376	PRESQUE ISLE	7,218	4,488	2,400	330	2,088	R	62.2%	33.3%	65.2%	34.8%
24,449	ROSCOMMON	13,041	8,141	4,287	613	3,854	R	62.4%	32.9%	65.5%	34.5%
200,169	SAGINAW	94,320	45,469	44,396	4,455	1,073	R	48.2%	47.1%	50.6%	49.4%
43,114	SANILAC	19,249	13,446	4,873	930	8,573	R	69.9%	25.3%	73.4%	26.6%
8,485	SCHOOLCRAFT	4,154	2,556	1,369	229	1,187	R	61.5%	33.0%	65.1%	34.9%
70,648	SHIAWASSEE	34,111	19,230	12,546	2,335	6,684	R	56.4%	36.8%	60.5%	39.5%
163,040	ST. CLAIR	78,003	49,051	24,553	4,399	24,498	R	62.9%	31.5%	66.6%	33.4%
61,295	ST. JOSEPH	23,757	14,884	7,526	1,347	7,358	R	62.7%	31.7%	66.4%	33.6%
55,729	TUSCOLA	25,796	17,102	7,429	1,265	9,673	R	66.3%	28.8%	69.7%	30.3%
76,258	VAN BUREN	33,274	17,890	13,258	2,126	4,632	R	53.8%	39.8%	57.4%	42.6%
344,791	WASHTENAW	188,578	50,631	128,483	9,464	77,852	D	26.8%	68.1%	28.3%	71.7%
1,820,584	WAYNE	777,838	228,993	519,444	29,401	290,451	D	29.4%	66.8%	30.6%	69.4%
32,735	WEXFORD	15,298	10,000	4,436	862	5,564	R	65.4%	29.0%	69.3%	30.7%
9,883,640	TOTAL	4,799,284	2,279,543	2,268,839	250,902	10,704	R	47.5%	47.3%	50.1%	49.9%

MICHIGAN

HOUSE OF REPRESENTATIVES

CD	Year	Total Vote	Republican Vote	Candidate	Democratic Vote	Candidate	Other Vote	Rep.-Dem. Plurality		Total Vote Rep.	Dem.	Major Vote Rep.	Dem.
1	2016	360,271	197,777	BERGMAN, JACK	144,334	JOHNSON, LONNIE BARTON "LON"	18,160	53,443	R	54.9%	40.1%	57.8%	42.2%
1	2014	250,131	130,414	BENISHEK, DAN*	113,263	CANNON, JERRY	6,454	17,151	R	52.1%	45.3%	53.5%	46.5%
1	2012	347,037	167,060	BENISHEK, DAN*	165,179	MCDOWELL, GARY	14,798	1,881	R	48.1%	47.6%	50.3%	49.7%
2	2016	339,328	212,508	HUIZENGA, BILL*	110,391	MURPHY, DENNIS B.	16,429	102,117	R	62.6%	32.5%	65.8%	34.2%
2	2014	213,072	135,568	HUIZENGA, BILL*	70,851	VANDERSTELT, DEAN	6,653	64,717	R	63.6%	33.3%	65.7%	34.3%
2	2012	318,267	194,653	HUIZENGA, BILL*	108,973	GERMAN, WILLIE JR.	14,641	85,680	R	61.2%	34.2%	64.1%	35.9%
3	2016	342,365	203,545	AMASH, JUSTIN*	128,400	SMITH, DOUGLAS	10,420	75,145	R	59.5%	37.5%	61.3%	38.7%
3	2014	217,165	125,754	AMASH, JUSTIN*	84,720	GOODRICH, BOB	6,691	41,034	R	57.9%	39.0%	59.7%	40.3%
3	2012	326,283	171,675	AMASH, JUSTIN*	144,108	PESTKA, STEVE	10,500	27,567	R	52.6%	44.2%	54.4%	45.6%
4	2016	315,751	194,572	MOOLENAAR, JOHN*	101,277	WIRTH, DEBRA FREIDELL	19,902	93,295	R	61.6%	32.1%	65.8%	34.2%
4	2014	219,423	123,962	MOOLENAAR, JOHN	85,777	HOLMES, JEFF	9,684	38,185	R	56.5%	39.1%	59.1%	40.9%
4	2012	312,949	197,386	CAMP, DAVE*	104,996	WIRTH, DEBRA FREIDELL	10,567	92,390	R	63.1%	33.6%	65.3%	34.7%
5	2016	319,291	112,102	HARDWICK, ALLEN	195,279	KILDEE, DANIEL*	11,910	83,177	D	35.1%	61.2%	36.5%	63.5%
5	2014	222,138	69,222	HARDWICK, ALLEN	148,182	KILDEE, DANIEL*	4,734	78,960	D	31.2%	66.7%	31.8%	68.2%
5	2012	330,146	103,931	SLEZAK, JIM	214,531	KILDEE, DANIEL	11,684	110,600	D	31.5%	65.0%	32.6%	67.4%
6	2016	329,565	193,259	UPTON, FRED*	119,980	CLEMENTS, PAUL C.	16,326	73,279	R	58.6%	36.4%	61.7%	38.3%
6	2014	208,976	116,801	UPTON, FRED*	84,391	CLEMENTS, PAUL C.	7,784	32,410	R	55.9%	40.4%	58.1%	41.9%
6	2012	320,475	174,955	UPTON, FRED*	136,563	O'BRIEN, MIKE	8,957	38,392	R	54.6%	42.6%	56.2%	43.8%
7	2016	334,807	184,321	WALBERG, TIMOTHY*	134,010	DRISKELL, GRETCHEN D.	16,476	50,311	R	55.1%	40.0%	57.9%	42.1%
7	2014	223,685	119,564	WALBERG, TIMOTHY*	92,083	BYRNES, PAM	12,038	27,481	R	53.5%	41.2%	56.5%	43.5%
7	2012	318,069	169,668	WALBERG, TIMOTHY*	136,849	HASKELL, KURT R.	11,552	32,819	R	53.3%	43.0%	55.4%	44.6%

MICHIGAN

HOUSE OF REPRESENTATIVES

CD	Year	Total Vote	Republican Vote	Candidate	Democratic Vote	Candidate	Other Vote	Rep.-Dem. Plurality	Total Vote Rep.	Total Vote Dem.	Major Vote Rep.	Major Vote Dem.
8	2016	366,968	205,629	BISHOP, MIKE*	143,791	SHKRELI, SUZANNA	17,548	61,838 R	56.0%	39.2%	58.8%	41.2%
8	2014	243,125	132,739	BISHOP, MIKE	102,269	SCHERTZING, ERIC	8,117	30,470 R	54.6%	42.1%	56.5%	43.5%
8	2012	345,054	202,217	ROGERS, MIKE*	128,657	ENDERLE, LANCE	14,180	73,560 R	58.6%	37.3%	61.1%	38.9%
9	2016	344,775	128,937	MORSE, CHRISTOPHER R.	199,661	LEVIN, SANDER M.*	16,177	70,724 D	37.4%	57.9%	39.2%	60.8%
9	2014	225,757	81,470	BRIKHO, GEORGE	136,342	LEVIN, SANDER M.*	7,945	54,872 D	36.1%	60.4%	37.4%	62.6%
9	2012	337,316	114,760	VOLARIC, DON	208,846	LEVIN, SANDER M.*	13,710	94,086 D	34.0%	61.9%	35.5%	64.5%
10	2016	340,983	215,132	MITCHELL, PAUL	110,112	ACCAVITTI, FRANK JR.	15,739	105,020 R	63.1%	32.3%	66.1%	33.9%
10	2014	228,692	157,069	MILLER, CANDICE S.*	67,143	STADLER, CHUCK	4,480	89,926 R	68.7%	29.4%	70.1%	29.9%
10	2012	328,612	226,075	MILLER, CANDICE S.*	97,734	STADLER, CHUCK	4,803	128,341 R	68.8%	29.7%	69.8%	30.2%
11	2016	379,488	200,872	TROTT, DAVE A.*	152,461	KUMAR, ANIL	26,155	48,411 R	52.9%	40.2%	56.9%	43.1%
11	2014	251,238	140,435	TROTT, DAVE A.	101,681	MCKENZIE, BOBBY	9,122	38,754 R	55.9%	40.5%	58.0%	42.0%
11	2012	358,139	181,788	BENTIVOLIO, KERRY	158,879	TAJ, SYED	17,472	22,909 R	50.8%	44.4%	53.4%	46.6%
12	2016	328,542	96,104	JONES, JEFF	211,378	DINGELL, DEBBIE*	21,060	115,274 D	29.3%	64.3%	31.3%	68.7%
12	2014	206,660	64,716	BOWMAN, TERRENCE "TERRY"	134,346	DINGELL, DEBBIE	7,598	69,630 D	31.3%	65.0%	32.5%	67.5%
12	2012	319,223	92,472	KALLGREN, CYNTHIA	216,884	DINGELL, JOHN D. JR.*	9,867	124,412 D	29.0%	67.9%	29.9%	70.1%
13	2016	257,797	40,541	GORMAN, JEFF	198,771	CONYERS, JOHN JR.*	18,485	158,230 D	15.7%	77.1%	16.9%	83.1%
13	2014	166,947	27,234	GORMAN, JEFF	132,710	CONYERS, JOHN JR.*	7,003	105,476 D	16.3%	79.5%	17.0%	83.0%
13	2012	284,270	38,769	SAWICKI, HARRY	235,336	CONYERS, JOHN JR.*	10,165	196,567 D	13.6%	82.8%	14.1%	85.9%
14	2016	310,974	58,103	KLAUSNER, HOWARD	244,135	LAWRENCE, BRENDA*	8,736	186,032 D	18.7%	78.5%	19.2%	80.8%
14	2014	212,468	41,801	BARR, CHRISTINA	165,272	LAWRENCE, BRENDA	5,395	123,471 D	19.7%	77.8%	20.2%	79.8%
14	2012	328,792	51,395	HAULER, JOHN	270,450	PETERS, GARY C.*	6,947	219,055 D	15.6%	82.3%	16.0%	84.0%
TOTAL	2016	4,670,905	2,243,402		2,193,980		233,523	49,422 R	48.0%	47.0%	50.6%	49.4%
TOTAL	2014	3,089,477	1,466,749		1,519,030		103,698	52,281 D	47.5%	49.2%	49.1%	50.9%
TOTAL	2012	4,574,632	2,086,804		2,327,985		159,843	241,181 D	45.6%	50.9%	47.3%	52.7%

Note: An asterisk (*) denotes incumbent.

MICHIGAN

GENERAL AND PRIMARY ELECTIONS

2016 GENERAL ELECTIONS: OTHER VOTES

President Other vote was 172,136 Libertarian (Gary Johnson), 51,463 Green (Jill Stein), 16,139 U.S. Taxpayers (Darrell Castle), 8,177 Write-in (Evan McMullin), 2,209 Natural Law (Emidio Soltysik), 778 Write-in (Scattered Write-in)

House Other vote was:

CD 1 13,386 Libertarian (Diane Bostow), 4,774 Green (Ellis Boal)

CD 2 8,154 Libertarian (Erwin Haas), 5,353 Green (Matthew Brady), 2,904 U.S. Taxpayers (Ronald Graeser), 18 Write-in (Joshua Arnold)

CD 3 10,420 U.S. Taxpayers (Ted Gerrard)

CD 4 8,516 Libertarian (Leonard Schwartz), 5,595 U.S. Taxpayers (George Zimmer), 3,953 Green (Jordan Salvi), 1,838 Natural Law (Keith Butkovich)

CD 5 7,006 Libertarian (Steve Sluka), 4,904 Green (Harley Mikkelson)

CD 6 16,248 Libertarian (Lorence Wenke), 78 Write-in (Richard Overton)

CD 7 16,476 Libertarian (Kenneth Proctor)

CD 8 9,619 Libertarian (Jeff Wood), 5,679 Green (Maria Green), 2,250 Natural Law (Jeremy Burgess)

CD 9 9,563 Libertarian (Matthew Orlando), 6,614 Green (John McDermott)

CD 10 10,612 Libertarian (Lisa Gioia), 5,127 Green (Benjamin Nofs)

CD 11 16,610 Independent (Kerry Bentivolio), 9,545 Libertarian (Jonathan Osment)

CD 12 9,183 Working Class (Gary Walkowicz)

CD 13 9,648 Libertarian (Tiffany Hayden), 8,835 Working Class (Sam Johnson), 2 Write-in (Clyde Lynch)

CD 14 4,893 Libertarian (Gregory Creswell), 3,843 Green (Marcia Squier)

MICHIGAN

GENERAL AND PRIMARY ELECTIONS

2016 PRIMARY ELECTIONS: SUPPLEMENTARY INFORMATION

Primary	March 8, 2016 (President) August 2, 2016 (Congress)	**Registration** (as of July 2016 – includes 765,937 inactive registrants)	7,360,506	No Party Registration

Primary Type Open—Any registered voter could participate in the primary of either party.

	REPUBLICAN PRIMARIES			DEMOCRATIC PRIMARIES		
President	Trump, Donald J.	483,753	36.5%	Sanders, Bernard	598,943	49.7%
	Cruz, Ted	326,617	24.7%	Clinton, Hillary Rodham	581,775	48.3%
	Kasich, John R.	321,115	24.3%	Uncommitted	21,601	1.8%
	Rubio, Marco	123,587	9.3%	O'Malley, Martin	2,363	0.2%
	Uncommitted	22,824	1.7%	De La Fuente, Roque "Rocky"	870	0.1%
	Carson, Ben	21,349	1.6%			
	Bush, Jeb	10,685	0.8%			
	Paul, Rand	3,774	0.3%			
	Christie, Chris	3,116	0.2%			
	Huckabee, Mike	2,603	0.2%			
	Santorum, Rick	1,722	0.1%			
	Fiorina, Carly	1,415	0.1%			
	Pataki, George E.	591				
	Graham, Lindsey	438				
	TOTAL	*1,323,589*		*TOTAL*	*1,205,552*	
Congressional District 1	Bergman, Jack	33,632	38.6%	Johnson, Lonnie Barton "Lon"	31,677	71.6%
	Casperson, Tom	27,813	31.9%	Cannon, Jerry	12,539	28.4%
	Allen, Jason	25,607	29.4%			
	TOTAL	*87,052*		*TOTAL*	*44,216*	
Congressional District 2	Huizenga, Bill*	60,844	100.0%	Murphy, Dennis B.	26,498	100.0%
	TOTAL	*60,844*		*TOTAL*	*26,498*	
Congressional District 3	Amash, Justin*	55,889	100.0%	Smith, Douglas	20,352	100.0%
	TOTAL	*55,889*		*TOTAL*	*20,352*	
Congressional District 4	Moolenaar, John*	57,886	100.0%	Wirth, Debra Freidell	2,013	100.0%
	TOTAL	*57,886*		*TOTAL*	*2,013*	
Congressional District 5	Hardwick, Allen	18,246	100.0%	Kildee, Daniel*	59,090	100.0%
	TOTAL	*18,246*		*TOTAL*	*59,090*	
Congressional District 6	Upton, Fred*	49,733	100.0%	Clements, Paul C.	21,622	100.0%
	TOTAL	*49,733*		*TOTAL*	*21,622*	
Congressional District 7	Walberg, Timothy*	43,120	75.2%	Driskell, Gretchen D.	25,611	100.0%
	North, Douglas Radcliffe	14,247	24.8%			
	TOTAL	*57,367*		*TOTAL*	*25,611*	
Congressional District 8	Bishop, Mike*	56,424	100.0%	Gilbert, Melissa	28,810	100.0%
	TOTAL	*56,424*		*TOTAL*	*28,810*	
Congressional District 9	Morse, Christopher R.	32,964	100.0%	Levin, Sander M.*	48,393	100.0%
	TOTAL	*32,964*		*TOTAL*	*48,393*	
Congressional District 10	Mitchell, Paul	30,114	38.0%	Accavitti, Frank Jr.	20,710	100.0%
	Pavlov, Phillip S.	22,018	27.7%			
	Sanborn, Alan	12,640	15.9%			
	Forlini, Anthony G. "Tony"	7,888	9.9%			
	VanAssche, David J.	6,690	8.4%			
	TOTAL	*79,350*		*TOTAL*	*20,710*	

MICHIGAN

GENERAL AND PRIMARY ELECTIONS

	REPUBLICAN PRIMARIES			DEMOCRATIC PRIMARIES		
Congressional District 11	Trott, Dave A.*	51,221	100.0%	Kumar, Anil	29,349	100.0%
	TOTAL	*51,221*		*TOTAL*	*29,349*	
Congressional District 12	Jones, Jeff	15,115	100.0%	Dingell, Debbie*	55,046	100.0%
	TOTAL	*15,115*		*TOTAL*	*55,046*	
Congressional District 13	Gorman, Jeff	4,894	100.0%	Conyers, John Jr.*	30,971	60.8%
				Winfrey, Janice	19,965	39.2%
	TOTAL	*4,894*		*TOTAL*	*50,936*	
Congressional District 14	Klausner, Howard	10,964	100.0%	Lawrence, Brenda*	55,544	87.4%
				Moss, Vanessa	5,253	8.3%
				Morrison, Terrance	2,770	4.4%
	TOTAL	*10,964*		*TOTAL*	*63,567*	

Note: An asterisk (*) denotes incumbent.

MINNESOTA

Congressional districts first established for elections held in 2012

8 members

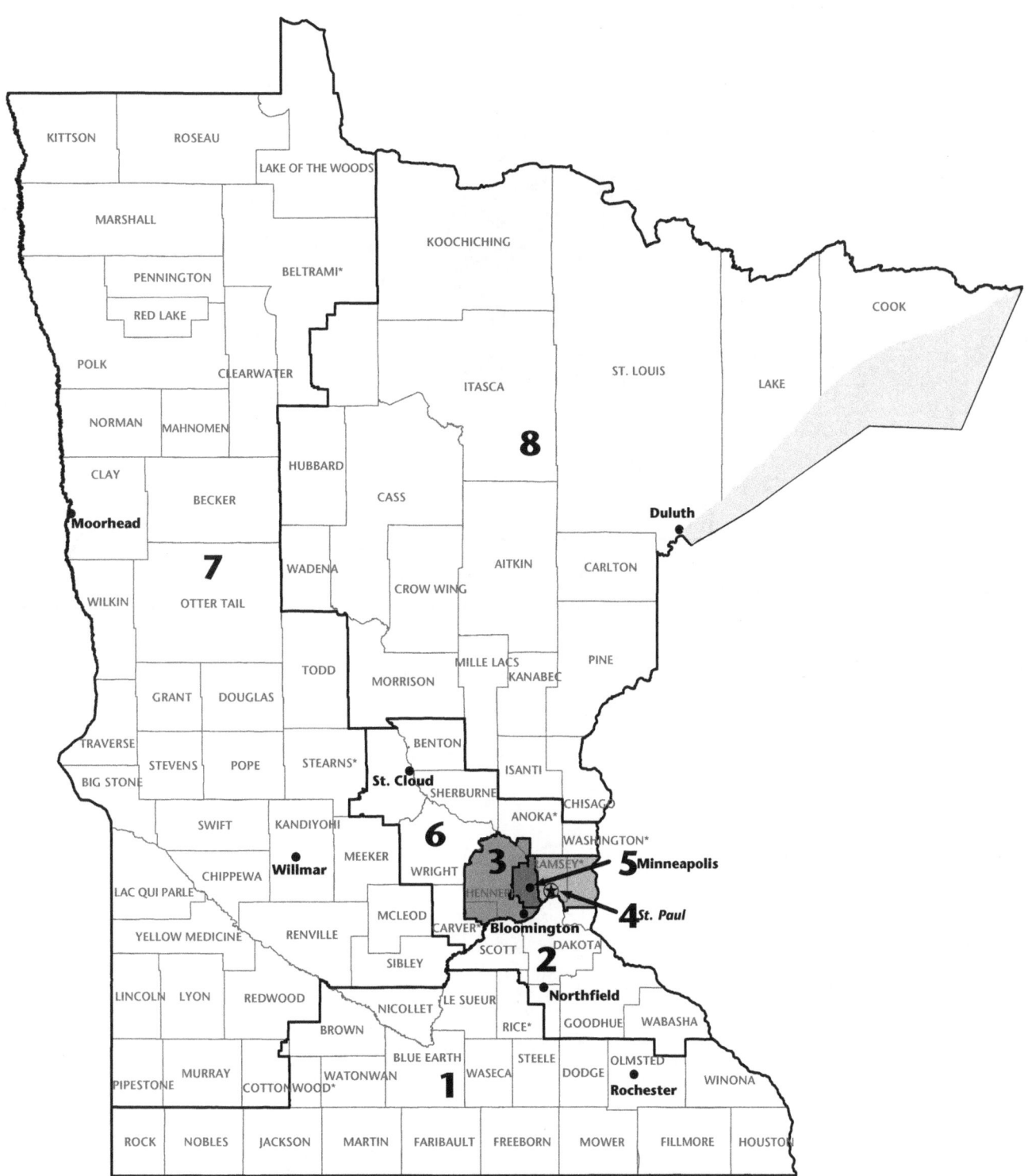

* Asterisk indicates a county whose boundaries include parts of two or more congressional districts.

MINNESOTA
Minneapolis–St. Paul Area

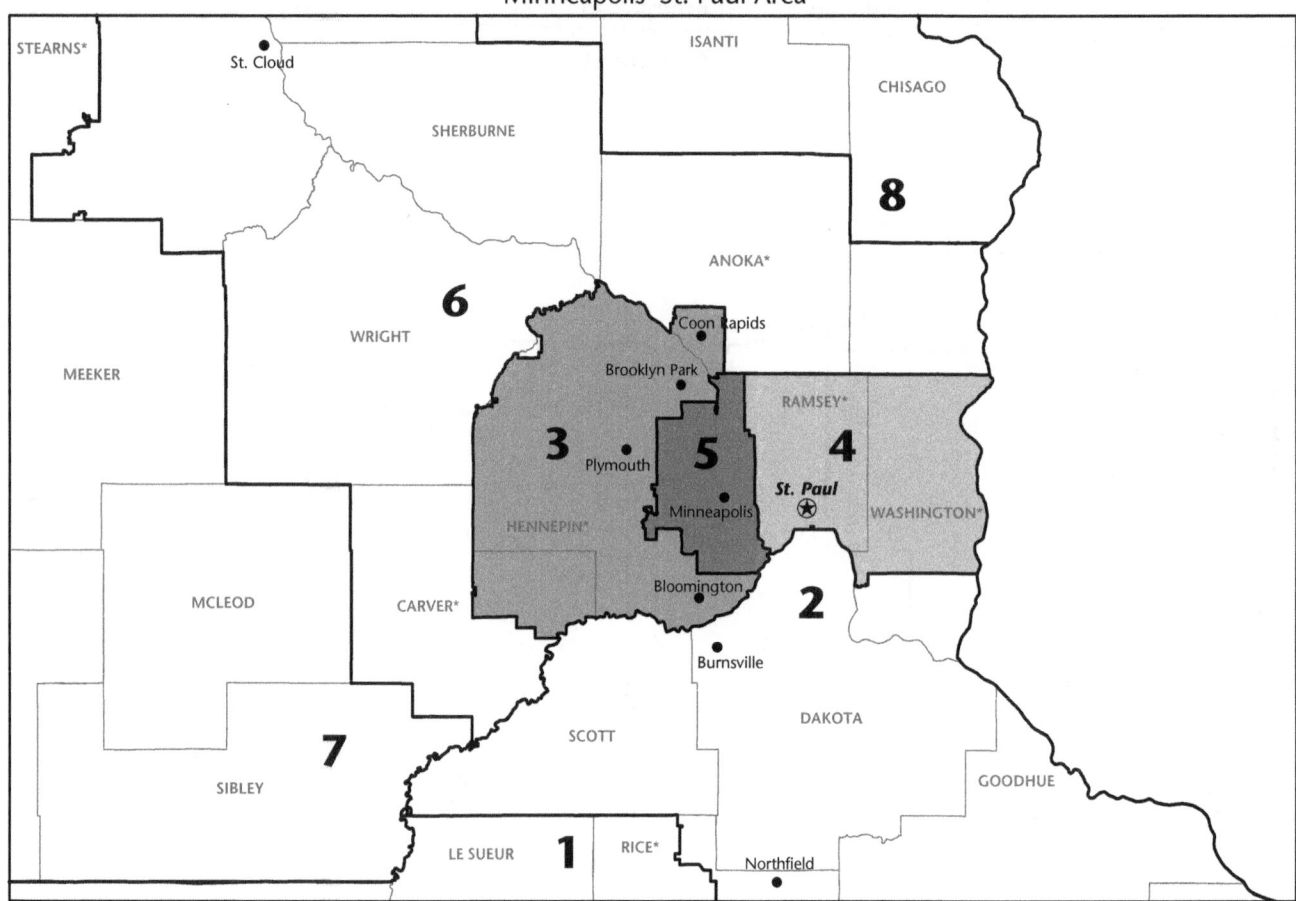

* Asterisk indicates a county whose boundaries include parts of two or more congressional districts.

MINNESOTA

GOVERNOR
Mark Dayton (D). Re-elected 2014 to a four-year term. Previously elected 2010.

SENATORS (2 Democrats)
Al Franken (D). Re-elected 2014 to a six-year term. Previously elected 2008.

Amy Klobuchar (D). Re-elected 2012 to a six-year term. Previously elected 2006.

REPRESENTATIVES (3 Republicans, 5 Democrats)
1. Timothy J. Walz (D)
2. Jason Mark Lewis (R)
3. Erik Paulsen (R)
4. Betty McCollum (D)
5. Keith Ellison (D)
6. Tom Emmer (R)
7. Collin C. Peterson (D)
8. Richard M. Nolan (D)

POSTWAR VOTE FOR PRESIDENT

| Year | Total Vote | Republican | | Democratic | | Other Vote | Rep.-Dem. Plurality | Percentage | | | |
| | | Vote | Candidate | Vote | Candidate | | | Total Vote | | Major Vote | |
								Rep.	Dem.	Rep.	Dem.
2016**	2,944,813	1,322,951	Trump, Donald J.	1,367,716	Clinton, Hillary Rodham	254,146	44,765 D	44.9%	46.4%	49.2%	50.8%
2012	2,936,561	1,320,225	Romney, W. Mitt	1,546,167	Obama, Barack H.*	70,169	225,942 D	45.0%	52.7%	46.1%	53.9%
2008	2,910,369	1,275,409	McCain, John S. III	1,573,354	Obama, Barack H.	61,606	297,945 D	43.8%	54.1%	44.8%	55.2%
2004	2,828,387	1,346,695	Bush, George W.*	1,445,014	Kerry, John F.	36,678	98,319 D	47.6%	51.1%	48.2%	51.8%
2000**	2,438,685	1,109,659	Bush, George W.	1,168,266	Gore, Albert Jr.	160,760	58,607 D	45.5%	47.9%	48.7%	51.3%
1996**	2,192,640	766,476	Dole, Robert "Bob"	1,120,438	Clinton, Bill*	305,726	353,962 D	35.0%	51.1%	40.6%	59.4%
1992**	2,347,948	747,841	Bush, George H.*	1,020,997	Clinton, Bill	579,110	273,156 D	31.9%	43.5%	42.3%	57.7%
1988	2,096,790	962,337	Bush, George H.	1,109,471	Dukakis, Michael S.	24,982	147,134 D	45.9%	52.9%	46.4%	53.6%
1984	2,084,449	1,032,603	Reagan, Ronald*	1,036,364	Mondale, Walter F.	15,482	3,761 D	49.5%	49.7%	49.9%	50.1%
1980**	2,051,980	873,268	Reagan, Ronald	954,174	Carter, Jimmy*	224,538	80,906 D	42.6%	46.5%	47.8%	52.2%
1976	1,949,931	819,395	Ford, Gerald R.*	1,070,440	Carter, Jimmy	60,096	251,045 D	42.0%	54.9%	43.4%	56.6%
1972	1,741,652	898,269	Nixon, Richard M.*	802,346	McGovern, George S.	41,037	95,923 R	51.6%	46.1%	52.8%	47.2%
1968**	1,588,506	658,643	Nixon, Richard M.	857,738	Humphrey, Hubert Horatio Jr.	72,125	199,095 D	41.5%	54.0%	43.4%	56.6%
1964	1,554,462	559,624	Goldwater, Barry M. Sr.	991,117	Johnson, Lyndon B.*	3,721	431,493 D	36.0%	63.8%	36.1%	63.9%
1960	1,541,887	757,915	Nixon, Richard M.	779,933	Kennedy, John F.	4,039	22,018 D	49.2%	50.6%	49.3%	50.7%
1956	1,340,005	719,302	Eisenhower, Dwight D.*	617,525	Stevenson, Adlai E. II	3,178	101,777 R	53.7%	46.1%	53.8%	46.2%
1952	1,379,483	763,211	Eisenhower, Dwight D.	608,458	Stevenson, Adlai E. II	7,814	154,753 R	55.3%	44.1%	55.6%	44.4%
1948	1,212,226	483,617	Dewey, Thomas E.	692,966	Truman, Harry S.*	35,643	209,349 D	39.9%	57.2%	41.1%	58.9%

Note: An asterisk (*) denotes incumbent. **In past elections, the other vote included: 2016 - 112,972 Libertarian (Gary Johnson); 2000 - 126,696 Green (Nader); 1996 - 257,704 Reform (Ross Perot); 1992 - 562,506 Independent (Perot); 1980 - 174,990 Independent (John Anderson); 1968 - 68,931 American Independent (George Wallace).

MINNESOTA

POSTWAR VOTE FOR GOVERNOR

Year	Total Vote	Republican Vote	Republican Candidate	Democratic Vote	Democratic Candidate	Other Vote	Rep.-Dem. Plurality	Total Vote Rep.	Total Vote Dem.	Major Vote Rep.	Major Vote Dem.
2014	1,975,406	879,257	Johnson, Jeff	989,113	Dayton, Mark*	107,036	109,856 D	44.5%	50.1%	47.1%	52.9%
2010**	2,107,021	910,462	Emmer, Tom	919,232	Dayton, Mark	277,327	8,770 D	43.2%	43.6%	49.8%	50.2%
2006	2,202,937	1,028,568	Pawlenty, Tim*	1,007,460	Hatch, Mike	166,909	21,108 R	46.7%	45.7%	50.5%	49.5%
2002**	2,252,473	999,473	Pawlenty, Tim	821,268	Moe, Roger D.	431,732	178,205 R	44.4%	36.5%	54.9%	45.1%
1998**	2,090,518	716,880	Coleman, Norm	587,060	Humphrey, Hubert Horatio "Skip" III	786,578	129,820 R#	34.3%	28.1%	55.0%	45.0%
1994	1,765,590	1,094,165	Carlson, Arne*	589,344	Marty, John	82,081	504,821 R	62.0%	33.4%	65.0%	35.0%
1990	1,806,777	895,988	Carlson, Arne	836,218	Perpich, Rudy*	74,571	59,770 R	49.6%	46.3%	51.7%	48.3%
1986	1,415,989	606,755	Ludeman, Cal R.	790,138	Perpich, Rudy*	19,096	183,383 D	42.9%	55.8%	43.4%	56.6%
1982	1,789,539	715,796	Whitney, Wheelock	1,049,104	Perpich, Rudy*	24,639	333,308 D	40.0%	58.6%	40.6%	59.4%
1978	1,585,702	830,019	Quie, Albert H.	718,244	Perpich, Rudy*	37,439	111,775 R	52.3%	45.3%	53.6%	46.4%
1974	1,252,898	367,722	Johnson, John W.	786,787	Anderson, Wendell R.*	98,389	419,065 D	29.3%	62.8%	31.9%	68.1%
1970	1,365,443	621,780	Head, Douglas M.	737,921	Anderson, Wendell R.	5,742	116,141 D	45.5%	54.0%	45.7%	54.3%
1966	1,295,058	680,593	Levander, Harold	607,943	Rolvaag, Karl F.*	6,522	72,650 R	52.6%	46.9%	52.8%	47.2%
1962**	1,246,904	619,751	Andersen, Elmer L.*	619,842	Rolvaag, Karl F.	7,311	91 D	49.7%	49.7%	50.0%	50.0%
1960	1,550,265	783,813	Andersen, Elmer L.	760,934	Freeman, Orville L.	5,518	22,879 R	50.6%	49.1%	50.7%	49.3%
1958	1,159,915	490,731	MacKinnon, George	658,326	Freeman, Orville L.*	10,858	167,595 D	42.3%	56.8%	42.7%	57.3%
1956	1,422,161	685,196	Nelsen, Ancher	731,180	Freeman, Orville L.*	5,785	45,984 D	48.2%	51.4%	48.4%	51.6%
1954	1,151,417	538,865	Anderson, C. Elmer*	607,099	Freeman, Orville L.	5,453	68,234 D	46.8%	52.7%	47.0%	53.0%
1952	1,418,869	785,125	Anderson, C. Elmer	624,480	Freeman, Orville L.	9,264	160,645 R	55.3%	44.0%	55.7%	44.3%
1950	1,046,632	635,800	Youngdahl, Luther W.*	400,637	Peterson, Harry H.	10,195	235,163 R	60.7%	38.3%	61.3%	38.7%
1948	1,210,874	643,572	Youngdahl, Luther W.*	545,746	Halsted, Charles L.	21,556	97,826 R	53.1%	45.1%	54.1%	45.9%
1946	880,348	519,067	Youngdahl, Luther W.	349,565	Barker, Harold H.	11,716	169,502 R	59.0%	39.7%	59.8%	40.2%

Note: An asterisk (*) denotes incumbent. A pound sign (#) in the plurality column indicates that the winner ran on the Reform Party line. **In past elections, the other vote included: 2010 - 251,487 Independence (Tom Horner); 2002 - 364,534 Independence (Timothy J. Penny); 1998 - 773,403 Reform (Jesse Ventura, who was elected with 37.0 percent of the total vote and a plurality of 56,523 votes). The term of office of Minnesota's governor was increased from two to four years effective with the 1962 election.

POSTWAR VOTE FOR SENATOR

Year	Total Vote	Republican Vote	Republican Candidate	Democratic Vote	Democratic Candidate	Other Vote	Rep.-Dem. Plurality	Total Vote Rep.	Total Vote Dem.	Major Vote Rep.	Major Vote Dem.
2014	1,981,528	850,227	McFadden, Mike	1,053,205	Franken, Al*	78,096	202,978 D	42.9%	53.2%	44.7%	55.3%
2012	2,843,207	867,974	Bills, Kurt	1,854,595	Klobuchar, Amy*	120,638	986,621 D	30.5%	65.2%	31.9%	68.1%
2008**	2,887,646	1,212,317	Coleman, Norm*	1,212,629	Franken, Al	462,700	312 D	42.0%	42.0%	50.0%	50.0%
2006	2,202,772	835,653	Kennedy, Mark	1,278,849	Klobuchar, Amy	88,270	443,196 D	37.9%	58.1%	39.5%	60.5%
2002**	2,254,639	1,116,697	Coleman, Norm	1,067,246	Mondale, Walter F.	70,696	49,451 R	49.5%	47.3%	51.1%	48.9%
2000	2,419,520	1,047,474	Grams, Rod*	1,181,553	Dayton, Mark	190,493	134,079 D	43.3%	48.8%	47.0%	53.0%
1996	2,183,062	901,282	Boschwitz, Rudy	1,098,493	Wellstone, Paul D.*	183,287	197,211 D	41.3%	50.3%	45.1%	54.9%
1994	1,772,929	869,653	Grams, Rod	781,860	Wynia, Ann	121,416	87,793 R	49.1%	44.1%	52.7%	47.3%
1990	1,808,045	864,375	Boschwitz, Rudy*	911,999	Wellstone, Paul D.	31,671	47,624 D	47.8%	50.4%	48.7%	51.3%
1988	2,093,953	1,176,210	Durenberger, David*	856,694	Humphrey, Hubert Horatio "Skip" III	61,049	319,516 R	56.2%	40.9%	57.9%	42.1%
1984	2,066,143	1,199,926	Boschwitz, Rudy*	852,844	Growe, Joan Anderson	13,373	347,082 R	58.1%	41.3%	58.5%	41.5%
1982	1,804,676	949,207	Durenberger, David*	840,401	Dayton, Mark	15,068	108,806 R	52.6%	46.6%	53.0%	47.0%
1978	1,580,778	894,092	Boschwitz, Rudy	638,375	Anderson, Wendell R.*	48,311	255,717 R	56.6%	40.4%	58.3%	41.7%
1978S**	1,560,724	957,908	Durenberger, David	538,675	Short, Robert E.	64,141	419,233 R	61.4%	34.5%	64.0%	36.0%
1976	1,912,068	478,611	Brekke, Gerald W.	1,290,736	Humphrey, Hubert Horatio Jr.*	142,721	812,125 D	25.0%	67.5%	27.1%	72.9%
1972	1,731,653	742,121	Hansen, Philip	981,340	Mondale, Walter F.*	8,192	239,219 D	42.9%	56.7%	43.1%	56.9%
1970	1,364,887	568,025	MacGregor, Clark	788,256	Humphrey, Hubert Horatio Jr.*	8,606	220,231 D	41.6%	57.8%	41.9%	58.1%
1966	1,271,426	574,868	Forsythe, Robert A.	685,840	Mondale, Walter F.	10,718	110,972 D	45.2%	53.9%	45.6%	54.4%
1964	1,543,600	605,933	Whitney, Wheelock	931,363	McCarthy, Eugene J.*	6,304	325,430 D	39.3%	60.3%	39.4%	60.6%
1960	1,536,839	648,586	Peterson, P. Kenneth	884,168	Humphrey, Hubert Horatio Jr.*	4,085	235,582 D	42.2%	57.5%	42.3%	57.7%
1958	1,150,883	536,629	Thye, Edward J.	608,847	McCarthy, Eugene J.	5,407	72,218 D	46.6%	52.9%	46.8%	53.2%
1954	1,138,952	479,619	Bjornson, Val	642,193	Humphrey, Hubert Horatio Jr.*	17,140	162,574 D	42.1%	56.4%	42.8%	57.2%
1952	1,387,419	785,649	Thye, Edward J.*	590,011	Carlson, William E.	11,759	195,638 R	56.6%	42.5%	57.1%	42.9%
1948	1,217,250	482,801	Ball, Joseph H.*	729,494	Humphrey, Hubert Horatio Jr.	4,955	246,693 D	39.7%	59.9%	39.8%	60.2%
1946	878,731	517,775	Thye, Edward J.	349,520	Jorgenson, Theodore	11,436	168,255 R	58.9%	39.8%	59.7%	40.3%

Note: An asterisk (*) denotes incumbent. **In past elections, the other vote included: 2008 - 437,505 Independence (Dean Barkley). In October 2002 the Democratic incumbent, Paul Wellstone, was killed in an airplane crash. Walter F. Mondale was named to replace him on the general election ballot. One of the 1978 elections was for a short term to fill a vacancy.

MINNESOTA

PRESIDENT 2016

2010 Census Population	County	Total Vote	Republican (Trump)	Democratic (Clinton)	Other	Rep.-Dem. Plurality	Percentage — Total Vote Rep.	Total Vote Dem.	Major Vote Rep.	Major Vote Dem.
16,202	AITKIN	9,231	5,516	3,134	581	2,382 R	59.8%	34.0%	63.8%	36.2%
330,844	ANOKA	185,758	93,339	75,500	16,919	17,839 R	50.2%	40.6%	55.3%	44.7%
32,504	BECKER	17,222	10,880	5,208	1,134	5,672 R	63.2%	30.2%	67.6%	32.4%
44,442	BELTRAMI	21,564	10,783	8,688	2,093	2,095 R	50.0%	40.3%	55.4%	44.6%
38,451	BENTON	20,058	12,872	5,640	1,546	7,232 R	64.2%	28.1%	69.5%	30.5%
5,269	BIG STONE	2,755	1,608	921	226	687 R	58.4%	33.4%	63.6%	36.4%
64,013	BLUE EARTH	33,593	15,667	14,428	3,498	1,239 R	46.6%	42.9%	52.1%	47.9%
25,893	BROWN	13,779	8,708	3,763	1,308	4,945 R	63.2%	27.3%	69.8%	30.2%
35,386	CARLTON	18,211	8,160	8,460	1,591	300 D	44.8%	46.5%	49.1%	50.9%
91,042	CARVER	55,696	29,056	21,508	5,132	7,548 R	52.2%	38.6%	57.5%	42.5%
28,567	CASS	15,999	9,982	4,949	1,068	5,033 R	62.4%	30.9%	66.9%	33.1%
12,441	CHIPPEWA	6,222	3,764	1,978	480	1,786 R	60.5%	31.8%	65.6%	34.4%
53,887	CHISAGO	30,228	18,441	9,278	2,509	9,163 R	61.0%	30.7%	66.5%	33.5%
58,999	CLAY	29,398	13,543	12,971	2,884	572 R	46.1%	44.1%	51.1%	48.9%
8,695	CLEARWATER	4,245	2,925	1,100	220	1,825 R	68.9%	25.9%	72.7%	27.3%
5,176	COOK	3,395	1,156	1,912	327	756 D	34.1%	56.3%	37.7%	62.3%
11,687	COTTONWOOD	5,721	3,679	1,678	364	2,001 R	64.3%	29.3%	68.7%	31.3%
62,500	CROW WING	35,842	22,287	10,982	2,573	11,305 R	62.2%	30.6%	67.0%	33.0%
398,552	DAKOTA	231,440	99,583	110,483	21,374	10,900 D	43.0%	47.7%	47.4%	52.6%
20,087	DODGE	10,654	6,527	3,102	1,025	3,425 R	61.3%	29.1%	67.8%	32.2%
36,009	DOUGLAS	21,785	13,966	6,227	1,592	7,739 R	64.1%	28.6%	69.2%	30.8%
14,553	FARIBAULT	7,412	4,659	2,153	600	2,506 R	62.9%	29.0%	68.4%	31.6%
20,866	FILLMORE	11,055	6,271	3,872	912	2,399 R	56.7%	35.0%	61.8%	38.2%
31,255	FREEBORN	16,051	8,808	6,041	1,202	2,767 R	54.9%	37.6%	59.3%	40.7%
46,183	GOODHUE	25,717	14,041	9,446	2,230	4,595 R	54.6%	36.7%	59.8%	40.2%
6,018	GRANT	3,473	2,063	1,105	305	958 R	59.4%	31.8%	65.1%	34.9%
1,152,425	HENNEPIN	679,977	191,770	429,288	58,919	237,518 D	28.2%	63.1%	30.9%	69.1%
19,027	HOUSTON	10,604	5,616	4,145	843	1,471 R	53.0%	39.1%	57.5%	42.5%
20,428	HUBBARD	11,505	7,261	3,423	821	3,838 R	63.1%	29.8%	68.0%	32.0%
37,816	ISANTI	21,016	13,635	5,657	1,724	7,978 R	64.9%	26.9%	70.7%	29.3%
45,058	ITASCA	23,880	12,920	9,015	1,945	3,905 R	54.1%	37.8%	58.9%	41.1%
10,266	JACKSON	5,484	3,609	1,492	383	2,117 R	65.8%	27.2%	70.8%	29.2%
16,239	KANABEC	8,177	5,230	2,327	620	2,903 R	64.0%	28.5%	69.2%	30.8%
42,239	KANDIYOHI	21,772	12,785	7,266	1,721	5,519 R	58.7%	33.4%	63.8%	36.2%
4,552	KITTSON	2,385	1,349	823	213	526 R	56.6%	34.5%	62.1%	37.9%
13,311	KOOCHICHING	6,363	3,569	2,306	488	1,263 R	56.1%	36.2%	60.7%	39.3%
7,259	LAC QUI PARLE	3,860	2,293	1,305	262	988 R	59.4%	33.8%	63.7%	36.3%
10,866	LAKE	6,521	2,932	3,077	512	145 D	45.0%	47.2%	48.8%	51.2%
4,045	LAKE OF THE WOODS	2,242	1,540	553	149	987 R	68.7%	24.7%	73.6%	26.4%
27,703	LE SUEUR	14,971	9,182	4,623	1,166	4,559 R	61.3%	30.9%	66.5%	33.5%
5,896	LINCOLN	3,019	1,931	860	228	1,071 R	64.0%	28.5%	69.2%	30.8%
25,857	LYON	12,215	7,256	3,825	1,134	3,431 R	59.4%	31.3%	65.5%	34.5%
5,413	MAHNOMEN	2,088	991	930	167	61 R	47.5%	44.5%	51.6%	48.4%
9,439	MARSHALL	4,817	3,208	1,225	384	1,983 R	66.6%	25.4%	72.4%	27.6%
20,840	MARTIN	10,531	7,062	2,733	736	4,329 R	67.1%	26.0%	72.1%	27.9%
36,651	MCLEOD	18,807	12,155	4,978	1,674	7,177 R	64.6%	26.5%	70.9%	29.1%
23,300	MEEKER	12,282	8,104	3,191	987	4,913 R	66.0%	26.0%	71.7%	28.3%
26,097	MILLE LACS	13,017	8,340	3,710	967	4,630 R	64.1%	28.5%	69.2%	30.8%
33,198	MORRISON	17,614	12,925	3,637	1,052	9,288 R	73.4%	20.6%	78.0%	22.0%
39,163	MOWER	17,715	8,823	7,437	1,455	1,386 R	49.8%	42.0%	54.3%	45.7%
8,725	MURRAY	4,668	2,974	1,295	399	1,679 R	63.7%	27.7%	69.7%	30.3%
32,727	NICOLLET	18,097	8,437	7,886	1,774	551 R	46.6%	43.6%	51.7%	48.3%
21,378	NOBLES	8,632	5,299	2,733	600	2,566 R	61.4%	31.7%	66.0%	34.0%
6,852	NORMAN	3,261	1,699	1,264	298	435 R	52.1%	38.8%	57.3%	42.7%
144,248	OLMSTED	80,129	35,668	36,268	8,193	600 D	44.5%	45.3%	49.6%	50.4%
57,303	OTTER TAIL	32,500	20,939	9,340	2,221	11,599 R	64.4%	28.7%	69.2%	30.8%
13,930	PENNINGTON	6,715	4,000	2,147	568	1,853 R	59.6%	32.0%	65.1%	34.9%
29,750	PINE	13,811	8,191	4,580	1,040	3,611 R	59.3%	33.2%	64.1%	35.9%
9,596	PIPESTONE	4,808	3,338	1,127	343	2,211 R	69.4%	23.4%	74.8%	25.2%
31,600	POLK	14,796	8,979	4,712	1,105	4,267 R	60.7%	31.8%	65.6%	34.4%

MINNESOTA

PRESIDENT 2016

2010 Census Population	County	Total Vote	Republican (Trump)	Democratic (Clinton)	Other	Rep.-Dem. Plurality		Total Vote		Major Vote	
								Rep.	Dem.	Rep.	Dem.
10,995	POPE	6,319	3,793	2,106	420	1,687	R	60.0%	33.3%	64.3%	35.7%
508,640	RAMSEY	273,143	70,894	177,738	24,511	106,844	D	26.0%	65.1%	28.5%	71.5%
4,089	RED LAKE	1,881	1,141	540	200	601	R	60.7%	28.7%	67.9%	32.1%
16,059	REDWOOD	7,611	5,137	1,887	587	3,250	R	67.5%	24.8%	73.1%	26.9%
15,730	RENVILLE	7,606	4,890	2,117	599	2,773	R	64.3%	27.8%	69.8%	30.2%
64,142	RICE	32,443	15,429	14,437	2,577	992	R	47.6%	44.5%	51.7%	48.3%
9,687	ROCK	4,839	3,091	1,373	375	1,718	R	63.9%	28.4%	69.2%	30.8%
15,629	ROSEAU	7,804	5,451	1,856	497	3,595	R	69.8%	23.8%	74.6%	25.4%
129,928	SCOTT	75,029	39,948	28,502	6,579	11,446	R	53.2%	38.0%	58.4%	41.6%
88,499	SHERBURNE	48,283	31,053	13,293	3,937	17,760	R	64.3%	27.5%	70.0%	30.0%
15,226	SIBLEY	7,774	5,193	1,954	627	3,239	R	66.8%	25.1%	72.7%	27.3%
200,226	ST. LOUIS	112,422	44,630	57,771	10,021	13,141	D	39.7%	51.4%	43.6%	56.4%
150,642	STEARNS	79,592	47,617	25,576	6,399	22,041	R	59.8%	32.1%	65.1%	34.9%
36,576	STEELE	19,179	11,198	6,241	1,740	4,957	R	58.4%	32.5%	64.2%	35.8%
9,726	STEVENS	5,398	2,799	2,116	483	683	R	51.9%	39.2%	56.9%	43.1%
9,783	SWIFT	4,994	2,963	1,686	345	1,277	R	59.3%	33.8%	63.7%	36.3%
24,895	TODD	11,993	8,485	2,783	725	5,702	R	70.7%	23.2%	75.3%	24.7%
3,558	TRAVERSE	1,798	1,049	630	119	419	R	58.3%	35.0%	62.5%	37.5%
21,676	WABASHA	11,832	6,989	3,866	977	3,123	R	59.1%	32.7%	64.4%	35.6%
13,843	WADENA	6,934	4,837	1,684	413	3,153	R	69.8%	24.3%	74.2%	25.8%
19,136	WASECA	9,653	5,967	2,838	848	3,129	R	61.8%	29.4%	67.8%	32.2%
238,136	WASHINGTON	144,235	64,428	67,086	12,721	2,658	D	44.7%	46.5%	49.0%	51.0%
11,211	WATONWAN	4,998	2,768	1,814	416	954	R	55.4%	36.3%	60.4%	39.6%
6,576	WILKIN	3,302	2,129	893	280	1,236	R	64.5%	27.0%	70.5%	29.5%
51,461	WINONA	26,074	12,122	11,366	2,586	756	R	46.5%	43.6%	51.6%	48.4%
124,700	WRIGHT	69,618	43,274	20,334	6,010	22,940	R	62.2%	29.2%	68.0%	32.0%
10,438	YELLOW MEDICINE	5,276	3,382	1,524	370	1,858	R	64.1%	28.9%	68.9%	31.1%
5,303,925	TOTAL	2,944,813	1,322,951	1,367,716	254,146	44,765	D	44.9%	46.4%	49.2%	50.8%

Note: Democratic candidates apear on the ballot in Minnesota for the Democratic-Farmer-Labor (DFL) Party.

MINNESOTA

HOUSE OF REPRESENTATIVES

CD	Year	Total Vote	Republican		Democratic		Other Vote	Rep.-Dem. Plurality		Total Vote		Major Vote	
			Vote	Candidate	Vote	Candidate				Rep.	Dem.	Rep.	Dem.
1	2016	335,877	166,526	HAGEDORN, JAMES "JIM"	169,074	WALZ, TIMOTHY J.*	277	2,548	D	49.6%	50.3%	49.6%	50.4%
1	2014	226,695	103,536	HAGEDORN, JAMES "JIM"	122,851	WALZ, TIMOTHY J.*	308	19,315	D	45.7%	54.2%	45.7%	54.3%
1	2012	335,880	142,164	QUIST, ALLEN	193,211	WALZ, TIMOTHY J.*	505	51,047	D	42.3%	57.5%	42.4%	57.6%
2	2016	370,514	173,970	LEWIS, JASON MARK	167,315	CRAIG, ANGELA "ANGIE"	29,229	6,655	R	47.0%	45.2%	51.0%	49.0%
2	2014	245,848	137,778	KLINE, JOHN*	95,565	OBERMUELLER, MIKE	12,505	42,213	R	56.0%	38.9%	59.0%	41.0%
2	2012	358,446	193,587	KLINE, JOHN*	164,338	OBERMUELLER, MIKE	521	29,249	R	54.0%	45.8%	54.1%	45.9%
3	2016	393,464	223,077	PAULSEN, ERIK*	169,243	BONOFF, TERRI E.	1,144	53,834	R	56.7%	43.0%	56.9%	43.1%
3	2014	269,585	167,515	PAULSEN, ERIK*	101,846	SUND, SHARON	224	65,669	R	62.1%	37.8%	62.2%	37.8%
3	2012	382,705	222,335	PAULSEN, ERIK*	159,937	BARNES, BRIAN	433	62,398	R	58.1%	41.8%	58.2%	41.8%
4	2016	351,944	121,032	RYAN, GREG	203,299	MCCOLLUM, BETTY*	27,613	82,267	D	34.4%	57.8%	37.3%	62.7%
4	2014	241,637	79,492	WAHLGREN, SHARNA	147,857	MCCOLLUM, BETTY*	14,288	68,365	D	32.9%	61.2%	35.0%	65.0%
4	2012	347,991	109,659	HERNANDEZ, TONY	216,685	MCCOLLUM, BETTY*	21,647	107,026	D	31.5%	62.3%	33.6%	66.4%
5	2016	361,882	80,660	DRAKE, FRANK NELSON	249,964	ELLISON, KEITH*	31,258	169,304	D	22.3%	69.1%	24.4%	75.6%
5	2014	236,010	56,577	DAGGETT, DOUG J.	167,079	ELLISON, KEITH*	12,354	110,502	D	24.0%	70.8%	25.3%	74.7%
5	2012	351,969	88,753	FIELDS, CHRIS	262,102	ELLISON, KEITH*	1,114	173,349	D	25.2%	74.5%	25.3%	74.7%

MINNESOTA

HOUSE OF REPRESENTATIVES

CD	Year	Total Vote	Republican		Democratic		Other Vote	Rep.-Dem. Plurality	Percentage			
									Total Vote		Major Vote	
			Vote	Candidate	Vote	Candidate			Rep.	Dem.	Rep.	Dem.
6	2016	358,924	235,380	EMMER, TOM*	123,008	SNYDER, DAVID	536	112,372 R	65.6%	34.3%	65.7%	34.3%
6	2014	236,846	133,328	EMMER, TOM	90,926	PERSKE, JOE	12,592	42,402 R	56.3%	38.4%	59.5%	40.5%
6	2012	355,153	179,240	BACHMANN, MICHELE*	174,944	GRAVES, JIM	969	4,296 R	50.5%	49.3%	50.6%	49.4%
7	2016	330,848	156,952	HUGHES, DAVE	173,589	PETERSON, COLLIN C.*	307	16,637 D	47.4%	52.5%	47.5%	52.5%
7	2014	240,835	109,955	WESTROM, TORREY NORMAN	130,546	PETERSON, COLLIN C.*	334	20,591 D	45.7%	54.2%	45.7%	54.3%
7	2012	327,576	114,151	BYBERG, LEE	197,791	PETERSON, COLLIN C.*	15,634	83,640 D	34.8%	60.4%	36.6%	63.4%
8	2016	356,979	177,089	MILLS, STEWART	179,098	NOLAN, RICHARD M.*	792	2,009 D	49.6%	50.2%	49.7%	50.3%
8	2014	266,083	125,358	MILLS, STEWART	129,090	NOLAN, RICHARD M.*	11,635	3,732 D	47.1%	48.5%	49.3%	50.7%
8	2012	353,663	160,520	CRAVAACK, CHIP*	191,976	NOLAN, RICHARD M.	1,167	31,456 D	45.4%	54.3%	45.5%	54.5%
TOTAL	2016	2,860,432	1,334,686		1,434,590		91,156	99,904 D	46.7%	50.2%	48.2%	51.8%
TOTAL	2014	1,963,539	913,539		985,760		64,240	72,221 D	46.5%	50.2%	48.1%	51.9%
TOTAL	2012	2,813,383	1,210,409		1,560,984		41,990	350,575 D	43.0%	55.5%	43.7%	56.3%

Note: An asterisk (*) denotes incumbent. Democratic candidates in Minnesota appear on the ballot for the Democratic-Farmer-Labor (DFL) party.

MINNESOTA

GENERAL AND PRIMARY ELECTIONS

2016 GENERAL ELECTIONS: OTHER VOTES

President Other vote was 112,972 Libertarian (Gary Johnson), 53,076 Independent (Evan McMullin), 36,985 Green (Jill Stein), 27,263 Write-in (Scattered Write-In), 11,291 Legal Marijuana Now (Dan Vacek), 9,456 Constitution (Darrell Castle), 1,672 Socialist Workers (Alyson Kennedy), 1,431 American Delta (Roque De La Fuente)

House Other vote was:

CD 1 277 Write-in (Scattered Write-in)
CD 2 28,869 Independence (Paula Overby), 360 Write-in (Scattered Write-in)
CD 3 1,144 Write-in (Scattered Write-in)
CD 4 27,152 Legalize Marijuana (Susan Sindt), 461 Write-in (Scattered Write-in)
CD 5 30,759 Legalize Marijuana (Dennis Schuller), 499 Write-in (Scattered Write-in)
CD 6 536 Write-in (Scattered Write-in)
CD 7 307 Write-in (Scattered Write-in)
CD 8 792 Write-in (Scattered Write-in)

2016 PRIMARY ELECTIONS: SUPPLEMENTARY INFORMATION

Presidential Caucus March 1, 2016 **Registration** (as of May 1, 2016) 3,123,453 No Party Registration

Primary August 9, 2016

Primary Type Open—Any registered voter could participate in the party primary of their choice.

MINNESOTA

GENERAL AND PRIMARY ELECTIONS

	REPUBLICAN PRIMARIES			DEMOCRATIC PRIMARIES		
Congressional District 1	Hagedorn, James "Jim"	10,851	76.5%	Walz, Timothy J.*	13,538	100.0%
	Williams, Steve	3,330	23.5%			
	TOTAL	*14,181*		*TOTAL*	*13,538*	
Congressional District 2	Lewis, Jason Mark	11,641	48.9%	Craig, Angela "Angie"	15,155	100.0%
	Miller, Darlene	7,305	30.7%			
	Howe, John	3,244	13.6%			
	Erickson, Matthew D.	1,612	6.8%			
	TOTAL	*23,802*		*TOTAL*	*15,155*	
Congressional District 3	Paulsen, Erik*	Unopposed		Bonoff, Terri E.	Unopposed	
Congressional District 4	Ryan, Greg	5,618	82.0%	McCollum, Betty*	33,336	94.0%
	Rechtzigel, Gene	845	12.3%	Carlson, Steve	2,128	6.0%
	Bey, Nikolay Nikolayevich	390	5.7%			
	TOTAL	*6,853*		*TOTAL*	*35,464*	
Congressional District 5	Drake, Frank Nelson	4,177	100.0%	Ellison, Keith*	40,380	91.7%
				Iverson, Gregg A.	1,887	4.3%
				Bauer, Lee	1,757	4.0%
	TOTAL	*4,177*		*TOTAL*	*44,024*	
Congressional District 6	Emmer, Tom*	13,590	68.7%	Snyder, David	4,402	46.0%
	Kern, Aliena Jeanene "A.J."	5,219	26.4%	Adams, Judy Evelyn	3,569	37.3%
	Munro, Patrick D.	962	4.9%	Helland, Bob	1,595	16.7%
	TOTAL	*19,771*		*TOTAL*	*9,566*	
Congressional District 7	Hughes, Dave	8,769	59.0%	Peterson, Collin C.*	16,253	100.0%
	Hinson, Amanda Lynn	6,104	41.0%			
	TOTAL	*14,873*		*TOTAL*	*16,253*	
Congressional District 8	Mills, Stewart	Unopposed		Nolan, Richard M.*	Unopposed	

Note: An asterisk (*) denotes incumbent.

MISSISSIPPI

Congressional districts first established for elections held in 2012

4 members

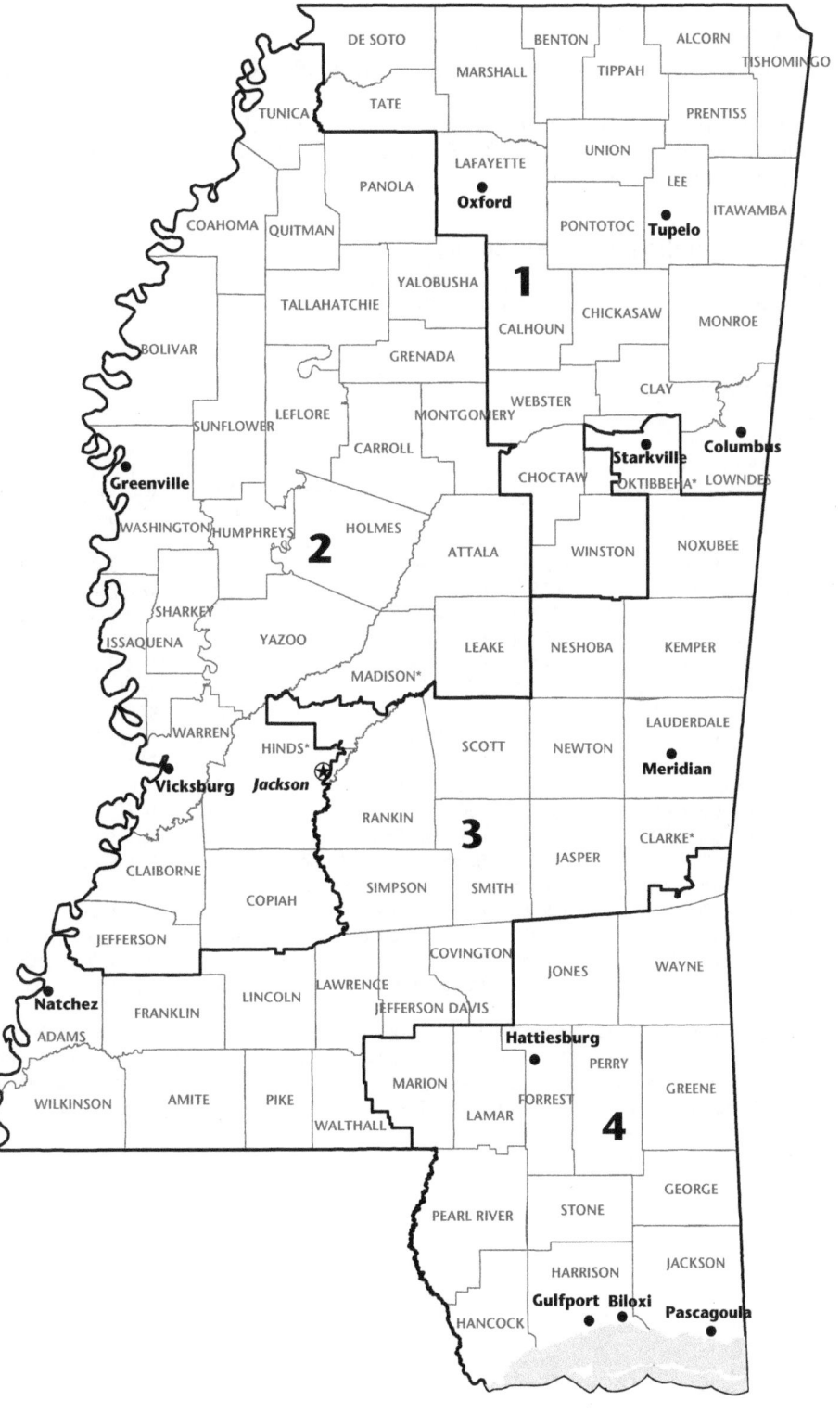

* Asterisk indicates a county whose boundaries include parts of two or more congressional districts.

MISSISSIPPI

GOVERNOR

Phil Bryant (R). Re-elected 2015 to a four-year term. Previously elected 2011.

SENATORS (2 Republicans)

W. Thad Cochran (R). Re-elected 2014 to a six-year term. Previously elected 2008, 2002, 1996, 1990, 1984, 1978.

Roger F. Wicker (R). Re-elected 2012 to a six-year term. Previously elected 2008 to fill the final four years of the term vacated by the December 2007 resignation of C. Trent Lott. Wicker had been appointed to fill the vacancy and was sworn in as senator on December 31, 2007.

REPRESENTATIVES (3 Republicans, 1 Democrat)

1. Trent Kelly (R)
2. Bennie Thompson (D)
3. Gregg Harper (R)
4. Steven Palazzo (R)

POSTWAR VOTE FOR PRESIDENT

Year	Total Vote	Republican		Democratic		Other Vote	Rep.-Dem. Plurality	Percentage			
								Total Vote		Major Vote	
		Vote	Candidate	Vote	Candidate			Rep.	Dem.	Rep.	Dem.
2016**	1,209,357	700,714	Trump, Donald J.	485,131	Clinton, Hillary Rodham	23,512	215,583 R	57.9%	40.1%	59.1%	40.9%
2012	1,285,584	710,746	Romney, W. Mitt	562,949	Obama, Barack H.*	11,889	147,797 R	55.3%	43.8%	55.8%	44.2%
2008	1,289,865	724,597	McCain, John S. III	554,662	Obama, Barack H.	10,606	169,935 R	56.2%	43.0%	56.6%	43.4%
2004	1,152,145	684,981	Bush, George W.*	458,094	Kerry, John F.	9,070	226,887 R	59.5%	39.8%	59.9%	40.1%
2000**	994,184	572,844	Bush, George W.	404,614	Gore, Albert Jr.	16,726	168,230 R	57.6%	40.7%	58.6%	41.4%
1996**	893,857	439,838	Dole, Robert "Bob"	394,022	Clinton, Bill*	59,997	45,816 R	49.2%	44.1%	52.7%	47.3%
1992**	981,793	487,793	Bush, George H.*	400,258	Clinton, Bill	93,742	87,535 R	49.7%	40.8%	54.9%	45.1%
1988	931,527	557,890	Bush, George H.	363,921	Dukakis, Michael S.	9,716	193,969 R	59.9%	39.1%	60.5%	39.5%
1984	941,104	582,377	Reagan, Ronald*	352,192	Mondale, Walter F.	6,535	230,185 R	61.9%	37.4%	62.3%	37.7%
1980**	892,620	441,089	Reagan, Ronald	429,281	Carter, Jimmy*	22,250	11,808 R	49.4%	48.1%	50.7%	49.3%
1976	769,361	366,846	Ford, Gerald R.*	381,309	Carter, Jimmy	21,206	14,463 D	47.7%	49.6%	49.0%	51.0%
1972	645,963	505,125	Nixon, Richard M.*	126,782	McGovern, George S.	14,056	378,343 R	78.2%	19.6%	79.9%	20.1%
1968**	654,509	88,516	Nixon, Richard M.	150,644	Humphrey, Hubert Horatio Jr.	415,349	62,128 D#	13.5%	23.0%	37.0%	63.0%
1964	409,146	356,528	Goldwater, Barry M. Sr.	52,618	Johnson, Lyndon B.*		303,910 R	87.1%	12.9%	87.1%	12.9%
1960**	298,171	73,561	Nixon, Richard M.	108,362	Kennedy, John F.	116,248	34,801 D#	24.7%	36.3%	40.4%	59.6%
1956	248,104	60,685	Eisenhower, Dwight D.*	144,453	Stevenson, Adlai E. II	42,966	83,768 D	24.5%	58.2%	29.6%	70.4%
1952	285,532	112,966	Eisenhower, Dwight D.	172,566	Stevenson, Adlai E. II		59,600 D	39.6%	60.4%	39.6%	60.4%
1948**	192,190	5,043	Dewey, Thomas E.	19,384	Truman, Harry S.*	167,763	14,341 D#	2.6%	10.1%	20.6%	79.4%

Note: An asterisk (*) denotes incumbent. A pound sign (#) indicates that the state was carried by a third party candidate or independent electoral state. **In past elections, the other vote included: 2016 - 14,435 Libertarian (Gary Johnson); 2000 - 8,122 Green (Ralph Nader); 1996 - 52,222 Reform (Ross Perot); 1992 - 85,626 Independent (Perot); 1980 - 12,036 Independent (John Anderson); 1968 - 415,349 American Independent (George Wallace); 1960 - 116,248 Unpledged Independent Democratic electors; 1948 - 167,538 States' Rights (Strom Thurmond). Thurmond won Mississippi in 1948 with 87.2 percent of the vote. The slate of Unpledged Independent Democratic electors carried the state in 1960 with 39.0 percent. Wallace won Mississippi in 1968 with 63.5 percent of the vote.

MISSISSIPPI

POSTWAR VOTE FOR GOVERNOR

| Year | Total Vote | Republican | | Democratic | | Other Vote | Rep.-Dem. Plurality | Percentage | | | |
| | | Vote | Candidate | Vote | Candidate | | | Total Vote | | Major Vote | |
								Rep.	Dem.	Rep.	Dem.
2015	725,207	480,399	Bryant, Phil*	234,858	Gray, Robert	9,950	245,541 R	66.2%	32.4%	67.2%	32.8%
2011	893,468	544,851	Bryant, Phil	348,617	DuPree, Johnny L.		196,234 R	61.0%	39.0%	61.0%	39.0%
2007	744,039	430,807	Barbour, Haley*	313,232	Eaves, John Arthur Jr.		117,575 R	57.9%	42.1%	57.9%	42.1%
2003	894,487	470,404	Barbour, Haley	409,787	Musgrove, Ronnie*	14,296	60,617 R	52.6%	45.8%	53.4%	46.6%
1999**	763,938	370,691	Parker, Mike	379,034	Musgrove, Ronnie	14,213	8,343 D	48.5%	49.6%	49.4%	50.6%
1995	819,471	455,261	Fordice, Kirk*	364,210	Molpus, Dick		91,051 R	55.6%	44.4%	55.6%	44.4%
1991	711,188	361,500	Fordice, Kirk	338,435	Mabus, Ray*	11,253	23,065 R	50.8%	47.6%	51.6%	48.4%
1987	721,695	336,006	Reed, Jack R.	385,689	Mabus, Ray		49,683 D	46.6%	53.4%	46.6%	53.4%
1983	742,737	288,764	Bramlett, Leon	409,209	Allain, William A.	44,764	120,445 D	38.9%	55.1%	41.4%	58.6%
1979	677,322	263,702	Carmichael, Gil	413,620	Winter, William		149,918 D	38.9%	61.1%	38.9%	61.1%
1975	708,033	319,632	Carmichael, Gil	369,568	Finch, Cliff	18,833	49,936 D	45.1%	52.2%	46.4%	53.6%
1971**	780,537			601,122	Waller, William L.	179,415	601,122 D		77.0%		100.0%
1967	448,696	133,378	Phillips, Rubel L.	315,318	Williams, John Bell		181,940 D	29.7%	70.3%	29.7%	70.3%
1963	363,971	138,515	Phillips, Rubel L.	225,456	Johnson, Paul B. Jr.		86,941 D	38.1%	61.9%	38.1%	61.9%
1959	57,671			57,671	Barnett, Ross R.		57,671 D		100.0%		100.0%
1955	40,707			40,707	Coleman, James P.		40,707 D		100.0%		100.0%
1951	43,422			43,422	White, Hugh L.		43,422 D		100.0%		100.0%
1947	166,095			161,993	Wright, Fielding L.	4,102	161,993 D		97.5%		100.0%

Note: An asterisk (*) denotes incumbent. **In past elections, the other vote included: 1971 - 172,762 Independent (Charles Evers), who finished second. In 1999 no candidate received a majority of the vote. Democrat Ronnie Musgrove was elected in January 2000 by the Mississippi House of Representatives. The Republican Party did not run a gubernatorial candidate in 1947, 1951, 1955, 1959, and 1971.

POSTWAR VOTE FOR SENATOR

| Year | Total Vote | Republican | | Democratic | | Other Vote | Rep.-Dem. Plurality | Percentage | | | |
| | | Vote | Candidate | Vote | Candidate | | | Total Vote | | Major Vote | |
								Rep.	Dem.	Rep.	Dem.
2014	631,858	378,481	Cochran, W. Thad*	239,439	Childers, Travis	13,938	139,042 R	59.9%	37.9%	61.3%	38.7%
2012	1,241,568	709,626	Wicker, Roger F.*	503,467	Gore, Albert N. Jr.	28,475	206,159 R	57.2%	40.6%	58.5%	41.5%
2008S	1,243,473	683,409	Wicker, Roger F.*	560,064	Musgrove, Ronnie		123,345 R	55.0%	45.0%	55.0%	45.0%
2008	1,247,026	766,111	Cochran, W. Thad*	480,915	Fleming, Erik R.		285,196 R	61.4%	38.6%	61.4%	38.6%
2006	610,921	388,399	Lott, C. Trent*	213,000	Fleming, Erik R.	9,522	175,399 R	63.6%	34.9%	64.6%	35.4%
2002**	630,495	533,269	Cochran, W. Thad*			97,226	533,269 R	84.6%		100.0%	
2000	994,144	654,941	Lott, C. Trent*	314,090	Brown, Troy	25,113	340,851 R	65.9%	31.6%	67.6%	32.4%
1996	878,662	624,154	Cochran, W. Thad*	240,647	Hunt, James W. "Bootie"	13,861	383,507 R	71.0%	27.4%	72.2%	27.8%
1994	608,085	418,333	Lott, C. Trent*	189,752	Harper, Ken		228,581 R	68.8%	31.2%	68.8%	31.2%
1990	274,244	274,244	Cochran, W. Thad*				274,244 R	100.0%		100.0%	
1988	946,719	510,380	Lott, C. Trent	436,339	Dowdy, Wayne		74,041 R	53.9%	46.1%	53.9%	46.1%
1984	952,240	580,314	Cochran, W. Thad*	371,926	Winter, William		208,388 R	60.9%	39.1%	60.9%	39.1%
1982	645,026	230,927	Barbour, Haley	414,099	Stennis, John*		183,172 D	35.8%	64.2%	35.8%	64.2%
1978**	583,936	263,089	Cochran, W. Thad	185,454	Dantin, Maurice	135,393	77,635 R	45.1%	31.8%	58.7%	41.3%
1976	554,433			554,433	Stennis, John*		554,433 D		100.0%		100.0%
1972	645,746	249,779	Carmichael, Gil	375,102	Eastland, James O.*	20,865	125,323 D	38.7%	58.1%	40.0%	60.0%
1970**	324,215			286,622	Stennis, John*	37,593	286,622 D		88.4%		100.0%
1966	394,541	105,652	Walker, Prentiss	258,248	Eastland, James O.*	30,641	152,596 D	26.8%	65.5%	29.0%	71.0%
1964	343,364			343,364	Stennis, John*		343,364 D		100.0%		100.0%
1960	266,148	21,807	Moore, Joe A.	244,341	Eastland, James O.*		222,534 D	8.2%	91.8%	8.2%	91.8%
1958	61,039			61,039	Stennis, John*		61,039 D		100.0%		100.0%
1954	105,526	4,678	White, James A.	100,848	Eastland, James O.*		96,170 D	4.4%	95.6%	4.4%	95.6%
1952	233,919			233,919	Stennis, John*		233,919 D		100.0%		100.0%
1948	151,478			151,478	Eastland, James O.*		151,478 D		100.0%		100.0%
1947S**	193,086					193,086	D				
1946	46,747			46,747	Bilbo, Theodore G.*		46,747 D		100.0%		100.0%

Note: An asterisk (*) denotes incumbent. **In past elections, the other vote included: 2002 - 97,226 Reform (Shawn O'Hara, who finished second); 1978 - 133,646 Independent (Charles Evers). The 1947 election and one of the 2008 elections were for short terms to fill a vacancy. Both special elections were held without party designation or nomination. In 1947 John Stennis received 52,068 votes (26.9 percent of the total vote) and won the election with a plurality of 6,343 votes. Other candidates that year included: 45,725 W. M. Colmer; 43,642 Forrest B. Jackson; 27,159 Paul B. Johnson; 24,492 John E. Rankin. The Republican Party did not run a candidate in Senate elections in 1946, 1948, 1952, 1958, 1964, 1970, and 1976. The Democratic Party did not run a candidate in Senate elections in 1990 and 2002.

MISSISSIPPI
PRESIDENT 2016

2010 Census Population	County	Total Vote	Republican (Trump)	Democratic (Clinton)	Other	Rep.-Dem. Plurality		Percentage			
								Total Vote		Major Vote	
								Rep.	Dem.	Rep.	Dem.
32,297	ADAMS	13,836	5,874	7,757	205	1,883	D	42.5%	56.1%	43.1%	56.9%
37,057	ALCORN	14,783	11,819	2,684	280	9,135	R	79.9%	18.2%	81.5%	18.5%
13,131	AMITE	7,050	4,289	2,697	64	1,592	R	60.8%	38.3%	61.4%	38.6%
19,564	ATTALA	8,256	4,897	3,242	117	1,655	R	59.3%	39.3%	60.2%	39.8%
8,729	BENTON	4,013	2,251	1,719	43	532	R	56.1%	42.8%	56.7%	43.3%
34,145	BOLIVAR	13,824	4,590	9,046	188	4,456	D	33.2%	65.4%	33.7%	66.3%
14,962	CALHOUN	6,396	4,390	1,910	96	2,480	R	68.6%	29.9%	69.7%	30.3%
10,597	CARROLL	5,528	3,799	1,680	49	2,119	R	68.7%	30.4%	69.3%	30.7%
17,392	CHICKASAW	7,890	4,127	3,649	114	478	R	52.3%	46.2%	53.1%	46.9%
8,547	CHOCTAW	4,065	2,788	1,218	59	1,570	R	68.6%	30.0%	69.6%	30.4%
9,604	CLAIBORNE	4,272	540	3,708	24	3,168	D	12.6%	86.8%	12.7%	87.3%
16,732	CLARKE	7,791	5,137	2,585	69	2,552	R	65.9%	33.2%	66.5%	33.5%
20,634	CLAY	10,003	4,150	5,722	131	1,572	D	41.5%	57.2%	42.0%	58.0%
26,151	COAHOMA	8,912	2,426	6,378	108	3,952	D	27.2%	71.6%	27.6%	72.4%
29,449	COPIAH	12,982	6,103	6,741	138	638	D	47.0%	51.9%	47.5%	52.5%
19,568	COVINGTON	8,811	5,435	3,276	100	2,159	R	61.7%	37.2%	62.4%	37.6%
161,252	DE SOTO	65,695	43,089	20,591	2,015	22,498	R	65.6%	31.3%	67.7%	32.3%
74,934	FORREST	28,064	15,461	11,716	887	3,745	R	55.1%	41.7%	56.9%	43.1%
8,118	FRANKLIN	4,290	2,721	1,502	67	1,219	R	63.4%	35.0%	64.4%	35.6%
22,578	GEORGE	9,891	8,696	1,027	168	7,669	R	87.9%	10.4%	89.4%	10.6%
14,400	GREENE	5,369	4,335	974	60	3,361	R	80.7%	18.1%	81.7%	18.3%
21,906	GRENADA	10,513	5,970	4,424	119	1,546	R	56.8%	42.1%	57.4%	42.6%
43,929	HANCOCK	17,637	13,811	3,344	482	10,467	R	78.3%	19.0%	80.5%	19.5%
187,105	HARRISON	63,313	40,354	21,169	1,790	19,185	R	63.7%	33.4%	65.6%	34.4%
245,285	HINDS	94,681	25,275	67,594	1,812	42,319	D	26.7%	71.4%	27.2%	72.8%
19,198	HOLMES	8,076	1,309	6,689	78	5,380	D	16.2%	82.8%	16.4%	83.6%
9,375	HUMPHREYS	4,253	1,151	3,071	31	1,920	D	27.1%	72.2%	27.3%	72.7%
1,406	ISSAQUENA	699	298	395	6	97	D	42.6%	56.5%	43.0%	57.0%
23,401	ITAWAMBA	9,737	8,470	1,117	150	7,353	R	87.0%	11.5%	88.3%	11.7%
139,668	JACKSON	49,567	33,629	14,657	1,281	18,972	R	67.8%	29.6%	69.6%	30.4%
17,062	JASPER	8,475	4,038	4,368	69	330	D	47.6%	51.5%	48.0%	52.0%
7,726	JEFFERSON	3,860	490	3,337	33	2,847	D	12.7%	86.5%	12.8%	87.2%
12,487	JEFFERSON DAVIS	6,237	2,466	3,720	51	1,254	D	39.5%	59.6%	39.9%	60.1%
67,761	JONES	28,352	20,133	7,791	428	12,342	R	71.0%	27.5%	72.1%	27.9%
10,456	KEMPER	4,639	1,778	2,827	34	1,049	D	38.3%	60.9%	38.6%	61.4%
47,351	LAFAYETTE	19,643	10,872	7,969	802	2,903	R	55.3%	40.6%	57.7%	42.3%
55,658	LAMAR	24,592	18,751	5,190	651	13,561	R	76.2%	21.1%	78.3%	21.7%
80,261	LAUDERDALE	29,506	17,741	11,269	496	6,472	R	60.1%	38.2%	61.2%	38.8%
12,929	LAWRENCE	6,364	4,091	2,195	78	1,896	R	64.3%	34.5%	65.1%	34.9%
23,805	LEAKE	8,449	4,782	3,584	83	1,198	R	56.6%	42.4%	57.2%	42.8%
82,910	LEE	32,913	22,220	10,029	664	12,191	R	67.5%	30.5%	68.9%	31.1%
32,317	LEFLORE	11,140	3,212	7,787	141	4,575	D	28.8%	69.9%	29.2%	70.8%
34,869	LINCOLN	15,193	10,550	4,458	185	6,092	R	69.4%	29.3%	70.3%	29.7%
59,779	LOWNDES	25,575	13,271	11,819	485	1,452	R	51.9%	46.2%	52.9%	47.1%
95,203	MADISON	49,802	28,265	20,343	1,194	7,922	R	56.8%	40.8%	58.1%	41.9%
27,088	MARION	11,693	7,836	3,677	180	4,159	R	67.0%	31.4%	68.1%	31.9%
37,144	MARSHALL	14,839	6,587	8,023	229	1,436	D	44.4%	54.1%	45.1%	54.9%
36,989	MONROE	15,884	10,167	5,524	193	4,643	R	64.0%	34.8%	64.8%	35.2%
10,925	MONTGOMERY	4,996	2,818	2,115	63	703	R	56.4%	42.3%	57.1%	42.9%
29,676	NESHOBA	10,553	7,679	2,715	159	4,964	R	72.8%	25.7%	73.9%	26.1%
21,720	NEWTON	9,438	6,548	2,756	134	3,792	R	69.4%	29.2%	70.4%	29.6%
11,545	NOXUBEE	5,574	1,200	4,347	27	3,147	D	21.5%	78.0%	21.6%	78.4%
47,671	OKTIBBEHA	18,124	8,576	8,859	689	283	D	47.3%	48.9%	49.2%	50.8%
34,707	PANOLA	15,064	7,449	7,431	184	18	R	49.4%	49.3%	50.1%	49.9%
55,834	PEARL RIVER	21,883	17,782	3,604	497	14,178	R	81.3%	16.5%	83.1%	16.9%
12,250	PERRY	5,432	4,135	1,220	77	2,915	R	76.1%	22.5%	77.2%	22.8%
40,404	PIKE	16,310	8,009	8,043	258	34	D	49.1%	49.3%	49.9%	50.1%
29,957	PONTOTOC	12,984	10,336	2,386	262	7,950	R	79.6%	18.4%	81.2%	18.8%
25,276	PRENTISS	9,872	7,648	2,067	157	5,581	R	77.5%	20.9%	78.7%	21.3%
8,223	QUITMAN	3,365	1,001	2,312	52	1,311	D	29.7%	68.7%	30.2%	69.8%

MISSISSIPPI

PRESIDENT 2016

2010 Census Population	County	Total Vote	Republican (Trump)	Democratic (Clinton)	Other	Rep.-Dem. Plurality	Percentage			
							Total Vote		Major Vote	
							Rep.	Dem.	Rep.	Dem.
141,617	RANKIN	62,768	47,178	14,110	1,480	33,068 R	75.2%	22.5%	77.0%	23.0%
28,264	SCOTT	10,522	6,122	4,268	132	1,854 R	58.2%	40.6%	58.9%	41.1%
4,916	SHARKEY	2,190	692	1,479	19	787 D	31.6%	67.5%	31.9%	68.1%
27,503	SIMPSON	11,419	7,393	3,874	152	3,519 R	64.7%	33.9%	65.6%	34.4%
16,491	SMITH	7,627	5,928	1,617	82	4,311 R	77.7%	21.2%	78.6%	21.4%
17,786	STONE	7,045	5,306	1,573	166	3,733 R	75.3%	22.3%	77.1%	22.9%
29,450	SUNFLOWER	9,598	2,794	6,725	79	3,931 D	29.1%	70.1%	29.4%	70.6%
15,378	TALLAHATCHIE	5,870	2,462	3,337	71	875 D	41.9%	56.8%	42.5%	57.5%
28,886	TATE	11,627	7,495	3,926	206	3,569 R	64.5%	33.8%	65.6%	34.4%
22,232	TIPPAH	9,235	7,240	1,842	153	5,398 R	78.4%	19.9%	79.7%	20.3%
19,593	TISHOMINGO	8,371	7,166	999	206	6,167 R	85.6%	11.9%	87.8%	12.2%
10,778	TUNICA	3,567	853	2,667	47	1,814 D	23.9%	74.8%	24.2%	75.8%
27,134	UNION	11,496	9,235	2,012	249	7,223 R	80.3%	17.5%	82.1%	17.9%
15,443	WALTHALL	6,919	4,056	2,790	73	1,266 R	58.6%	40.3%	59.2%	40.8%
48,773	WARREN	19,416	9,767	9,284	365	483 R	50.3%	47.8%	51.3%	48.7%
51,137	WASHINGTON	16,825	5,244	11,380	201	6,136 D	31.2%	67.6%	31.5%	68.5%
20,747	WAYNE	9,599	5,990	3,524	85	2,466 R	62.4%	36.7%	63.0%	37.0%
10,253	WEBSTER	5,069	3,976	1,019	74	2,957 R	78.4%	20.1%	79.6%	20.4%
9,878	WILKINSON	4,218	1,318	2,857	43	1,539 D	31.2%	67.7%	31.6%	68.4%
19,198	WINSTON	8,881	4,910	3,850	121	1,060 R	55.3%	43.4%	56.1%	43.9%
12,678	YALOBUSHA	6,077	3,376	2,582	119	794 R	55.6%	42.5%	56.7%	43.3%
28,065	YAZOO	10,070	4,598	5,369	103	771 D	45.7%	53.3%	46.1%	53.9%
2,967,297	TOTAL	1,209,357	700,714	485,131	23,512	215,583 R	57.9%	40.1%	59.1%	40.9%

MISSISSIPPI

GOVERNOR 2015

2010 Census Population	County	Total Vote	Republican (Bryant)	Democratic (Gray)	Other	Rep.-Dem. Plurality	Percentage			
							Total Vote		Major Vote	
							Rep.	Dem.	Rep.	Dem.
32,297	ADAMS	7,377	3,767	3,539	71	228 R	51.1%	48.0%	51.6%	48.4%
37,057	ALCORN	10,579	8,817	1,649	113	7,168 R	83.3%	15.6%	84.2%	15.8%
13,131	AMITE	5,126	3,176	1,874	76	1,302 R	62.0%	36.6%	62.9%	37.1%
19,564	ATTALA	5,075	3,449	1,577	49	1,872 R	68.0%	31.1%	68.6%	31.4%
8,729	BENTON	2,765	1,753	958	54	795 R	63.4%	34.6%	64.7%	35.3%
34,145	BOLIVAR	9,393	4,255	5,040	98	785 D	45.3%	53.7%	45.8%	54.2%
14,962	CALHOUN	5,152	3,957	1,144	51	2,813 R	76.8%	22.2%	77.6%	22.4%
10,597	CARROLL	4,061	2,934	1,096	31	1,838 R	72.2%	27.0%	72.8%	27.2%
17,392	CHICKASAW	5,740	3,545	2,141	54	1,404 R	61.8%	37.3%	62.3%	37.7%
8,547	CHOCTAW	2,816	2,215	570	31	1,645 R	78.7%	20.2%	79.5%	20.5%
9,604	CLAIBORNE	3,484	1,158	2,250	76	1,092 D	33.2%	64.6%	34.0%	66.0%
16,732	CLARKE	5,930	4,253	1,595	82	2,658 R	71.7%	26.9%	72.7%	27.3%
20,634	CLAY	7,224	3,601	3,547	76	54 R	49.8%	49.1%	50.4%	49.6%
26,151	COAHOMA	4,008	1,867	2,095	46	228 D	46.6%	52.3%	47.1%	52.9%
29,449	COPIAH	7,344	4,088	3,162	94	926 R	55.7%	43.1%	56.4%	43.6%
19,568	COVINGTON	6,385	4,471	1,838	76	2,633 R	70.0%	28.8%	70.9%	29.1%
161,252	DE SOTO	21,080	16,837	3,904	339	12,933 R	79.9%	18.5%	81.2%	18.8%
74,934	FORREST	17,236	11,998	4,968	270	7,030 R	69.6%	28.8%	70.7%	29.3%
8,118	FRANKLIN	3,089	2,053	996	40	1,057 R	66.5%	32.2%	67.3%	32.7%
22,578	GEORGE	6,111	5,348	634	129	4,714 R	87.5%	10.4%	89.4%	10.6%

MISSISSIPPI

GOVERNOR 2015

2010 Census Population	County	Total Vote	Republican (Bryant)	Democratic (Gray)	Other	Rep.-Dem. Plurality	Percentage			
							Total Vote		Major Vote	
							Rep.	Dem.	Rep.	Dem.
14,400	GREENE	3,882	3,097	697	88	2,400 R	79.8%	18.0%	81.6%	18.4%
21,906	GRENADA	6,853	4,462	2,324	67	2,138 R	65.1%	33.9%	65.8%	34.2%
43,929	HANCOCK	8,488	6,675	1,634	179	5,041 R	78.6%	19.3%	80.3%	19.7%
187,105	HARRISON	30,996	21,548	8,709	739	12,839 R	69.5%	28.1%	71.2%	28.8%
245,285	HINDS	56,963	22,403	33,548	1,012	11,145 D	39.3%	58.9%	40.0%	60.0%
19,198	HOLMES	4,961	1,610	3,272	79	1,662 D	32.5%	66.0%	33.0%	67.0%
9,375	HUMPHREYS	2,653	1,133	1,490	30	357 D	42.7%	56.2%	43.2%	56.8%
1,406	ISSAQUENA	564	346	211	7	135 R	61.3%	37.4%	62.1%	37.9%
23,401	ITAWAMBA	6,973	6,053	840	80	5,213 R	86.8%	12.0%	87.8%	12.2%
139,668	JACKSON	24,817	18,323	6,000	494	12,323 R	73.8%	24.2%	75.3%	24.7%
17,062	JASPER	6,409	3,644	2,654	111	990 R	56.9%	41.4%	57.9%	42.1%
7,726	JEFFERSON	2,732	713	1,971	48	1,258 D	26.1%	72.1%	26.6%	73.4%
12,487	JEFFERSON DAVIS	4,080	2,009	2,032	39	23 D	49.2%	49.8%	49.7%	50.3%
67,761	JONES	17,563	13,960	3,356	247	10,604 R	79.5%	19.1%	80.6%	19.4%
10,456	KEMPER	3,805	1,952	1,814	39	138 R	51.3%	47.7%	51.8%	48.2%
47,351	LAFAYETTE	10,964	6,881	3,898	185	2,983 R	62.8%	35.6%	63.8%	36.2%
55,658	LAMAR	13,654	11,555	1,941	158	9,614 R	84.6%	14.2%	85.6%	14.4%
80,261	LAUDERDALE	16,993	12,130	4,686	177	7,444 R	71.4%	27.6%	72.1%	27.9%
12,929	LAWRENCE	4,970	3,446	1,475	49	1,971 R	69.3%	29.7%	70.0%	30.0%
23,805	LEAKE	6,022	3,885	2,090	47	1,795 R	64.5%	34.7%	65.0%	35.0%
82,910	LEE	19,291	14,402	4,665	224	9,737 R	74.7%	24.2%	75.5%	24.5%
32,317	LEFLORE	7,122	3,177	3,868	77	691 D	44.6%	54.3%	45.1%	54.9%
34,869	LINCOLN	10,426	7,984	2,362	80	5,622 R	76.6%	22.7%	77.2%	22.8%
59,779	LOWNDES	17,575	10,287	7,137	151	3,150 R	58.5%	40.6%	59.0%	41.0%
95,203	MADISON	27,284	18,937	8,002	345	10,935 R	69.4%	29.3%	70.3%	29.7%
27,088	MARION	7,509	5,674	1,762	73	3,912 R	75.6%	23.5%	76.3%	23.7%
37,144	MARSHALL	6,585	3,412	3,105	68	307 R	51.8%	47.2%	52.4%	47.6%
36,989	MONROE	10,734	7,682	2,951	101	4,731 R	71.6%	27.5%	72.2%	27.8%
10,925	MONTGOMERY	3,916	2,497	1,385	34	1,112 R	63.8%	35.4%	64.3%	35.7%
29,676	NESHOBA	7,320	5,968	1,291	61	4,677 R	81.5%	17.6%	82.2%	17.8%
21,720	NEWTON	6,832	5,175	1,584	73	3,591 R	75.7%	23.2%	76.6%	23.4%
11,545	NOXUBEE	3,456	1,217	2,190	49	973 D	35.2%	63.4%	35.7%	64.3%
47,671	OKTIBBEHA	11,245	6,773	4,349	123	2,424 R	60.2%	38.7%	60.9%	39.1%
34,707	PANOLA	11,325	6,868	4,344	113	2,524 R	60.6%	38.4%	61.3%	38.7%
55,834	PEARL RIVER	9,195	7,501	1,501	193	6,000 R	81.6%	16.3%	83.3%	16.7%
12,250	PERRY	4,045	3,282	688	75	2,594 R	81.1%	17.0%	82.7%	17.3%
40,404	PIKE	11,955	6,682	5,126	147	1,556 R	55.9%	42.9%	56.6%	43.4%
29,957	PONTOTOC	8,410	7,008	1,315	87	5,693 R	83.3%	15.6%	84.2%	15.8%
25,276	PRENTISS	6,471	5,155	1,258	58	3,897 R	79.7%	19.4%	80.4%	19.6%
8,223	QUITMAN	2,866	1,449	1,359	58	90 R	50.6%	47.4%	51.6%	48.4%
141,617	RANKIN	33,822	27,584	5,811	427	21,773 R	81.6%	17.2%	82.6%	17.4%
28,264	SCOTT	7,122	4,688	2,365	69	2,323 R	65.8%	33.2%	66.5%	33.5%
4,916	SHARKEY	1,677	840	816	21	24 R	50.1%	48.7%	50.7%	49.3%
27,503	SIMPSON	7,820	5,656	2,077	87	3,579 R	72.3%	26.6%	73.1%	26.9%
16,491	SMITH	5,761	4,680	1,003	78	3,677 R	81.2%	17.4%	82.4%	17.6%
17,786	STONE	5,253	4,093	1,058	102	3,035 R	77.9%	20.1%	79.5%	20.5%
29,450	SUNFLOWER	5,766	2,771	2,903	92	132 D	48.1%	50.3%	48.8%	51.2%
15,378	TALLAHATCHIE	3,629	2,114	1,459	56	655 R	58.3%	40.2%	59.2%	40.8%
28,886	TATE	6,096	4,486	1,527	83	2,959 R	73.6%	25.0%	74.6%	25.4%
22,232	TIPPAH	6,509	5,329	1,109	71	4,220 R	81.9%	17.0%	82.8%	17.2%
19,593	TISHOMINGO	6,719	5,437	1,163	119	4,274 R	80.9%	17.3%	82.4%	17.6%
10,778	TUNICA	2,544	1,201	1,281	62	80 D	47.2%	50.4%	48.4%	51.6%
27,134	UNION	7,650	6,548	1,027	75	5,521 R	85.6%	13.4%	86.4%	13.6%
15,443	WALTHALL	4,858	3,312	1,470	76	1,842 R	68.2%	30.3%	69.3%	30.7%
48,773	WARREN	11,978	7,641	4,196	141	3,445 R	63.8%	35.0%	64.6%	35.4%

MISSISSIPPI

GOVERNOR 2015

2010 Census Population	County	Total Vote	Republican (Bryant)	Democratic (Gray)	Other	Rep.-Dem. Plurality	Total Vote Rep.	Total Vote Dem.	Major Vote Rep.	Major Vote Dem.
51,137	WASHINGTON	9,648	4,386	5,153	109	767 D	45.5%	53.4%	46.0%	54.0%
20,747	WAYNE	6,406	4,377	1,929	100	2,448 R	68.3%	30.1%	69.4%	30.6%
10,253	WEBSTER	3,507	2,898	582	27	2,316 R	82.6%	16.6%	83.3%	16.7%
9,878	WILKINSON	3,650	1,311	2,255	84	944 D	35.9%	61.8%	36.8%	63.2%
19,198	WINSTON	6,356	4,140	2,178	38	1,962 R	65.1%	34.3%	65.5%	34.5%
12,678	YALOBUSHA	3,822	2,433	1,341	48	1,092 R	63.7%	35.1%	64.5%	35.5%
28,065	YAZOO	6,735	3,977	2,694	64	1,283 R	59.0%	40.0%	59.6%	40.4%
2,967,297	TOTAL	725,207	480,399	234,858	9,950	245,541 R	66.2%	32.4%	67.2%	32.8%

MISSISSIPPI

HOUSE OF REPRESENTATIVES

CD	Year	Total Vote	Republican Vote	Republican Candidate	Democratic Vote	Democratic Candidate	Other Vote	Rep.-Dem. Plurality	Total Vote Rep.	Total Vote Dem.	Major Vote Rep.	Major Vote Dem.
1	2016	300,423	206,455	KELLY, TRENT*	83,947	OWENS, JACOB	10,021	122,508 R	68.7%	27.9%	71.1%	28.9%
1	2014	151,111	102,622	NUNNELEE, ALAN*	43,713	DICKEY, RON E.	4,776	58,909 R	67.9%	28.9%	70.1%	29.9%
1	2012	309,177	186,760	NUNNELEE, ALAN*	114,076	MORRIS, BRAD	8,341	72,684 R	60.4%	36.9%	62.1%	37.9%
2	2016	286,626	83,542	BOUIE, JOHN II	192,343	THOMPSON, BENNIE*	10,741	108,801 D	29.1%	67.1%	30.3%	69.7%
2	2014	148,646			100,688	THOMPSON, BENNIE*	47,958	100,688 D		67.7%		100.0%
2	2012	320,244	99,160	MARCY, BILL	214,978	THOMPSON, BENNIE*	6,106	115,818 D	31.0%	67.1%	31.6%	68.4%
3	2016	316,445	209,490	HARPER, GREGG*	96,101	QUINN, DENNIS C.	10,854	113,389 R	66.2%	30.4%	68.6%	31.4%
3	2014	170,946	117,771	HARPER, GREGG*	47,744	MAGEE, DOUGLAS MACARTHUR "DOUG"	5,431	70,027 R	68.9%	27.9%	71.2%	28.8%
3	2012	293,322	234,717	HARPER, GREGG*			58,605	234,717 R	80.0%		100.0%	
4	2016	278,779	181,323	PALAZZO, STEVEN*	77,505	GLADNEY, MARK	19,951	103,818 R	65.0%	27.8%	70.1%	29.9%
4	2014	155,576	108,776	PALAZZO, STEVEN*	37,869	MOORE, MATT	8,931	70,907 R	69.9%	24.3%	74.2%	25.8%
4	2012	285,432	182,998	PALAZZO, STEVEN*	82,344	MOORE, MATT	20,090	100,654 R	64.1%	28.8%	69.0%	31.0%
TOTAL	2016	1,182,273	680,810		449,896		51,567	230,914 R	57.6%	38.1%	60.2%	39.8%
TOTAL	2014	626,279	329,169		230,014		67,096	99,155 R	52.6%	36.7%	58.9%	41.1%
TOTAL	2012	1,208,175	703,635		411,398		93,142	292,237 R	58.2%	34.1%	63.1%	36.9%

Note: An asterisk (*) denotes incumbent.

MISSISSIPPI

GENERAL AND PRIMARY ELECTIONS

2016 GENERAL ELECTIONS: OTHER VOTES

President Other vote was 14,435 Libertarian (Gary Johnson), 3,987 Constitution (Darrell Castle), 3,731 Green (Jill Stein), 715 Prohibition (James Hedges), 644 American Delta (Roque De La Fuente)

Governor (2015) Other vote was 9,950 Reform (Shawn O'Hara)

House Other vote was:

CD 1 6,181 Libertarian (Chase Wilson), 3,840 Reform (Cathy Toole)
CD 2 6,918 Independent (Troy Ray), 3,823 Reform (Johnny McLeod)
CD 3 8,696 Veterans Party of America (Roger Gerrard), 2,158 Reform (Lajena Sheets)
CD 4 14,687 Libertarian (Richard McCluskey), 5,264 Reform (Shawn O'Hara)

MISSISSIPPI

GENERAL AND PRIMARY ELECTIONS

2016 PRIMARY ELECTIONS: SUPPLEMENTARY INFORMATION

Primary March 8, 2016 **Registration** 1,849,079 No Party Registration
(as of March 8, 2016)

Primary Type Open—Any registered voter could participate in the party primary of his or her choice. But any voter who cast a ballot in the primary of one party could not vote in the runoff of the other party.

	REPUBLICAN PRIMARIES			DEMOCRATIC PRIMARIES		
President	Trump, Donald J.	196,659	47.2%	Clinton, Hillary Rodham	187,334	82.5%
	Cruz, Ted	150,364	36.1%	Sanders, Bernard	37,748	16.6%
	Kasich, John R.	36,795	8.8%	Wilson, Willie	919	0.4%
	Rubio, Marco	21,885	5.3%	O'Malley, Martin	672	0.3%
	Carson, Ben	5,626	1.4%	De La Fuente, Roque "Rocky"	481	0.2%
	Bush, Jeb	1,697	0.4%	Write-In	10	
	Huckabee, Mike	1,067	0.3%			
	Paul, Rand	643	0.2%			
	Santorum, Rick	510	0.1%			
	Christie, Chris	493	0.1%			
	Fiorina, Carly	224	0.1%			
	Graham, Lindsey	172				
	Pataki, George E.	135				
	TOTAL	*416,270*		*TOTAL*	*227,164*	
Governor (2015)	Bryant, Phil	254,779	91.8%	Gray, Robert	152,087	50.8%
	Young, Mitch*	22,628	8.2%	Slater, Vicki	91,104	30.4%
				Short, Valerie Adream Smartt	56,177	18.1%
	TOTAL	*277,407*		*TOTAL*	*299,368*	
Congressional District 1	Kelly, Trent*	95,049	89.3%	Owens, Jacob	Unopposed	
	Clever, Paul	11,397	10.7%			
	TOTAL	*106,446*				
Congressional District 2	Bouie, John II	35,871	100.0%	Thompson, Bennie*	Unopposed	
	TOTAL	*35,871*				
Congressional District 3	Harper, Gregg*	87,997	89.1%	Quinn, Dennis C.	29,149	65.5%
	Giles, Jimmy	10,760	10.9%	Stewart, Nathan	15,384	34.5%
	TOTAL	*98,757*		*TOTAL*	*44,533*	
Congressional District 4	Palazzo, Steven*	103,558	100.0%	Gladney, Mark	Unopposed	
	TOTAL	*103,558*				

Note: An asterisk (*) denotes incumbent.

MISSOURI

Congressional districts first established for elections held in 2012

8 members

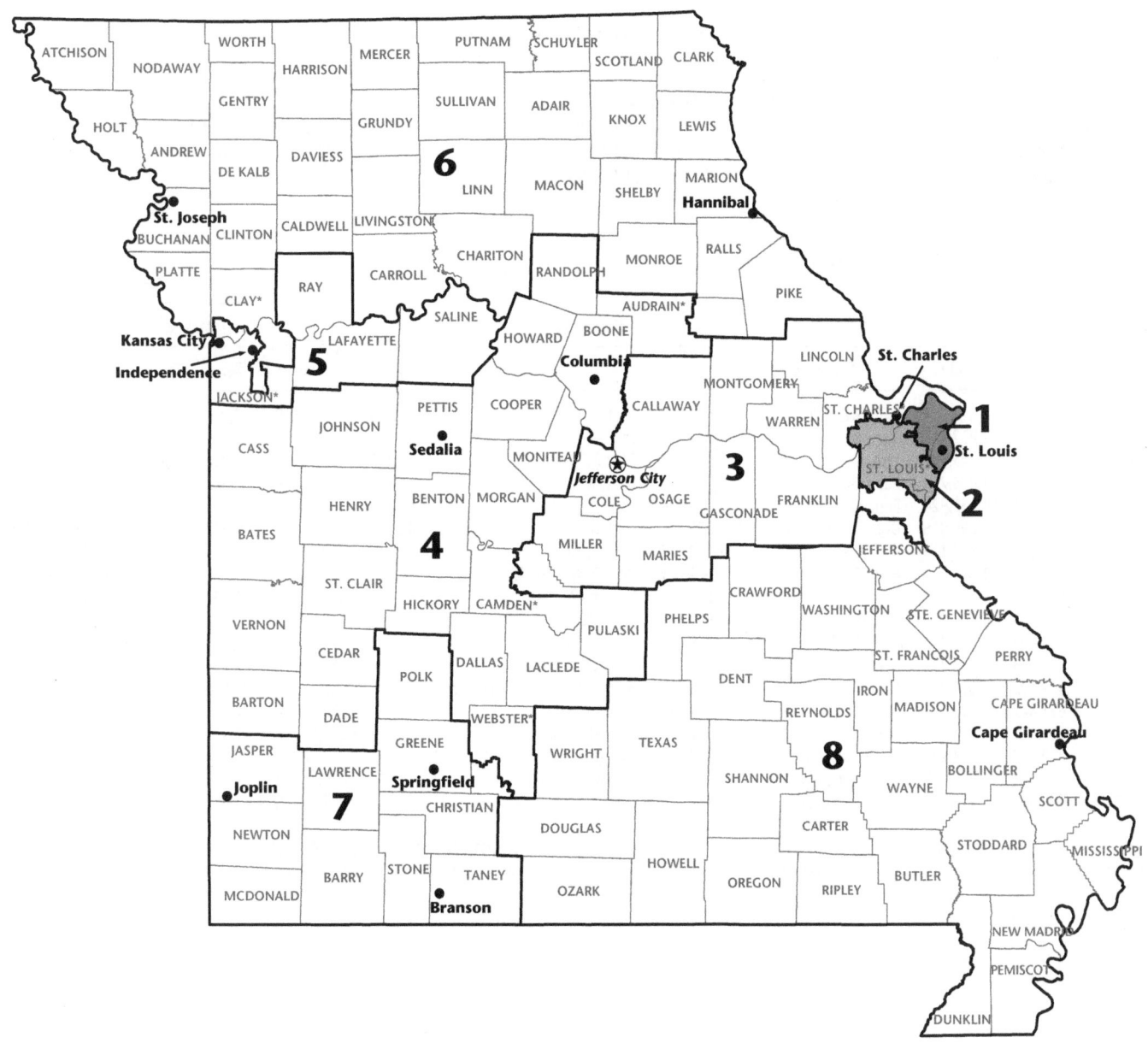

The city of St. Louis is an independent city that is treated as a county equivalent; as is Kansas City for voting purposes.

* Asterisk indicates a county whose boundaries include parts of two or more congressional districts.

MISSOURI

GOVERNOR
Eric Greitens (R). Elected 2016 to a four-year term.

SENATORS (1 Republican, 1 Democrat)
Roy Blunt (R). Re-elected 2016 to a six-year term. Previously elected 2010.

Claire McCaskill (D). Re-elected 2012 to a six-year term. Previously elected 2006.

REPRESENTATIVES (6 Republicans, 2 Democrats)
1. William Lacy Clay Jr. (D)
2. Ann Wagner (R)
3. Blaine Luetkemeyer (R)
4. Vicky Hartzler (R)
5. Emanuel Cleaver (D)
6. Samuel Graves Jr. (R)
7. Billy Long (R)
8. Jason Smith (R)

POSTWAR VOTE FOR PRESIDENT

| | | Republican | | Democratic | | | | Percentage | | | |
| | | | | | | | | Total Vote | | Major Vote | |
Year	Total Vote	Vote	Candidate	Vote	Candidate	Other Vote	Rep.-Dem. Plurality	Rep.	Dem.	Rep.	Dem.
2016**	2,808,605	1,594,511	Trump, Donald J.	1,071,068	Clinton, Hillary Rodham	143,026	523,443 R	56.8%	38.1%	59.8%	40.2%
2012	2,757,323	1,482,440	Romney, W. Mitt	1,223,796	Obama, Barack H.*	51,087	258,644 R	53.8%	44.4%	54.8%	45.2%
2008	2,925,205	1,445,814	McCain, John S. III	1,441,911	Obama, Barack H.	37,480	3,903 R	49.4%	49.3%	50.1%	49.9%
2004	2,731,364	1,455,713	Bush, George W.*	1,259,171	Kerry, John F.	16,480	196,542 R	53.3%	46.1%	53.6%	46.4%
2000**	2,359,892	1,189,924	Bush, George W.	1,111,138	Gore, Albert Jr.	58,830	78,786 R	50.4%	47.1%	51.7%	48.3%
1996**	2,158,065	890,016	Dole, Robert "Bob"	1,025,935	Clinton, Bill*	242,114	135,919 D	41.2%	47.5%	46.5%	53.5%
1992**	2,391,565	811,159	Bush, George H.*	1,053,873	Clinton, Bill	526,533	242,714 D	33.9%	44.1%	43.5%	56.5%
1988	2,093,713	1,084,953	Bush, George H.	1,001,619	Dukakis, Michael S.	7,141	83,334 R	51.8%	47.8%	52.0%	48.0%
1984	2,122,783	1,274,188	Reagan, Ronald*	848,583	Mondale, Walter F.	12	425,605 R	60.0%	40.0%	60.0%	40.0%
1980**	2,099,824	1,074,181	Reagan, Ronald	931,182	Carter, Jimmy*	94,461	142,999 R	51.2%	44.3%	53.6%	46.4%
1976	1,953,600	927,443	Ford, Gerald R.*	998,387	Carter, Jimmy	27,770	70,944 D	47.5%	51.1%	48.2%	51.8%
1972	1,855,803	1,153,852	Nixon, Richard M.*	697,147	McGovern, George S.	4,804	456,705 R	62.2%	37.6%	62.3%	37.7%
1968**	1,809,502	811,932	Nixon, Richard M.	791,444	Humphrey, Hubert Horatio Jr.	206,126	20,488 R	44.9%	43.7%	50.6%	49.4%
1964	1,817,879	653,535	Goldwater, Barry M. Sr.	1,164,344	Johnson, Lyndon B.*		510,809 D	36.0%	64.0%	36.0%	64.0%
1960	1,934,422	962,221	Nixon, Richard M.	972,201	Kennedy, John F.		9,980 D	49.7%	50.3%	49.7%	50.3%
1956	1,832,562	914,289	Eisenhower, Dwight D.*	918,273	Stevenson, Adlai E. II		3,984 D	49.9%	50.1%	49.9%	50.1%
1952	1,892,062	959,429	Eisenhower, Dwight D.	929,830	Stevenson, Adlai E. II	2,803	29,599 R	50.7%	49.1%	50.8%	49.2%
1948	1,578,628	655,039	Dewey, Thomas E.	917,315	Truman, Harry S.*	6,274	262,276 D	41.5%	58.1%	41.7%	58.3%

Note: An asterisk (*) denotes incumbent. **In past elections, the other vote included: 2016 - 97,359 Libertarian (Gary Johnson); 2000 - 38,515 Green (Ralph Nader); 1996 - 217,188 Reform (Ross Perot); 1992 - 518,741 Independent (Perot); 1980 - 77,920 Independent (John Anderson); 1968 - 206,126 American Independent (George Wallace).

MISSOURI

POSTWAR VOTE FOR GOVERNOR

| | | Republican | | Democratic | | Other Vote | Rep.-Dem. Plurality | Percentage | | | |
| | | | | | | | | Total Vote | | Major Vote | |
Year	Total Vote	Vote	Candidate	Vote	Candidate			Rep.	Dem.	Rep.	Dem.
2016	2,803,046	1,433,397	Greitens, Eric	1,277,360	Koster, Chris	92,289	156,037 R	51.1%	45.6%	52.9%	47.1%
2012	2,727,883	1,160,265	Spence, David "Dave"	1,494,056	Nixon, Jay W.*	73,562	333,791 D	42.5%	54.8%	43.7%	56.3%
2008	2,877,778	1,136,364	Hulshof, Kenny	1,680,611	Nixon, Jay W.	60,803	544,247 D	39.5%	58.4%	40.3%	59.7%
2004	2,719,599	1,382,419	Blunt, Matt	1,301,442	McCaskill, Claire	35,738	80,977 R	50.8%	47.9%	51.5%	48.5%
2000	2,346,830	1,131,307	Talent, James M.	1,152,752	Holden, Bob	62,771	21,445 D	48.2%	49.1%	49.5%	50.5%
1996	2,142,518	866,268	Kelly, Margaret	1,224,801	Carnahan, Mel*	51,449	358,533 D	40.4%	57.2%	41.4%	58.6%
1992	2,343,999	968,574	Webster, William L.	1,375,425	Carnahan, Mel		406,851 D	41.3%	58.7%	41.3%	58.7%
1988	2,085,928	1,339,531	Ashcroft, John*	724,919	Hearnes, Betty C.	21,478	614,612 R	64.2%	34.8%	64.9%	35.1%
1984	2,108,210	1,194,506	Ashcroft, John	913,700	Rothman, Kenneth J.	4	280,806 R	56.7%	43.3%	56.7%	43.3%
1980	2,088,028	1,098,950	Bond, Kit	981,884	Teasdale, Joseph P.*	7,194	117,066 R	52.6%	47.0%	52.8%	47.2%
1976	1,933,575	958,110	Bond, Kit*	971,184	Teasdale, Joseph P.	4,281	13,074 D	49.6%	50.2%	49.7%	50.3%
1972	1,865,683	1,029,451	Bond, Kit	832,751	Dowd, Edward L.	3,481	196,700 R	55.2%	44.6%	55.3%	44.7%
1968	1,764,602	691,797	Roos, Lawrence K.	1,072,805	Hearnes, Warren E.*		381,008 D	39.2%	60.8%	39.2%	60.8%
1964	1,789,600	678,949	Shepley, Ethan A.H.	1,110,651	Hearnes, Warren E.		431,702 D	37.9%	62.1%	37.9%	62.1%
1960	1,887,326	792,131	Farmer, Edward G.	1,095,195	Dalton, John M.		303,064 D	42.0%	58.0%	42.0%	58.0%
1956	1,808,338	866,810	Hocker, Lon	941,528	Blair, James T. Jr.		74,718 D	47.9%	52.1%	47.9%	52.1%
1952	1,870,998	886,270	Elliott, Howard	983,169	Donnelly, Phil M.	1,559	96,899 D	47.4%	52.5%	47.4%	52.6%
1948	1,567,338	670,064	Thompson, Murray E.	893,092	Smith, Forrest	4,182	223,028 D	42.8%	57.0%	42.9%	57.1%

Note: An asterisk (*) denotes incumbent.

POSTWAR VOTE FOR SENATOR

| | | Republican | | Democratic | | Other Vote | Rep.-Dem. Plurality | Percentage | | | |
| | | | | | | | | Total Vote | | Major Vote | |
Year	Total Vote	Vote	Candidate	Vote	Candidate			Rep.	Dem.	Rep.	Dem.
2016	2,802,641	1,378,458	Blunt, Roy*	1,300,200	Kander, Jason	123,983	78,258 R	49.2%	46.4%	51.5%	48.5%
2012	2,725,793	1,066,159	Akin, Todd	1,494,125	McCaskill, Claire*	165,509	427,966 D	39.1%	54.8%	41.6%	58.4%
2010	1,943,899	1,054,160	Blunt, Roy	789,736	Carnahan, Robin	100,003	264,424 R	54.2%	40.6%	57.2%	42.8%
2006	2,128,459	1,006,941	Talent, James M.*	1,055,255	McCaskill, Claire	66,263	48,314 D	47.3%	49.6%	48.8%	51.2%
2004	2,706,402	1,518,089	Bond, Kit*	1,158,261	Farmer, Nancy	30,052	359,828 R	56.1%	42.8%	56.7%	43.3%
2002S**	1,877,620	935,032	Talent, James M.	913,778	Carnahan, Jean*	28,810	21,254 R	49.8%	48.7%	50.6%	49.4%
2000**	2,361,586	1,142,852	Ashcroft, John*	1,191,812	Carnahan, Mel	26,922	48,960 D	48.4%	50.5%	49.0%	51.0%
1998	1,576,857	830,625	Bond, Kit*	690,208	Nixon, Jay W.	56,024	140,417 R	52.7%	43.8%	54.6%	45.4%
1994	1,775,116	1,060,149	Ashcroft, John	633,697	Wheat, Alan	81,270	426,452 R	59.7%	35.7%	62.6%	37.4%
1992	2,354,925	1,221,901	Bond, Kit*	1,057,967	Rothman-Serot, Geri	75,057	163,934 R	51.9%	44.9%	53.6%	46.4%
1988	2,078,875	1,407,416	Danforth, John C.*	660,045	Nixon, Jay W.	11,414	747,371 R	67.7%	31.8%	68.1%	31.9%
1986	1,477,327	777,612	Bond, Kit	699,624	Woods, Harriett	91	77,988 R	52.6%	47.4%	52.6%	47.4%
1982	1,543,521	784,876	Danforth, John C.*	758,629	Woods, Harriett	16	26,247 R	50.8%	49.1%	50.9%	49.1%
1980	2,066,965	985,399	McNary, Gene	1,074,859	Eagleton, Thomas F.*	6,707	89,460 D	47.7%	52.0%	47.8%	52.2%
1976	1,914,777	1,090,067	Danforth, John C.*	813,571	Hearnes, Warren E.	11,139	276,496 R	56.9%	42.5%	57.3%	42.7%
1974	1,224,303	480,900	Curtis, Thomas B.	735,433	Eagleton, Thomas F.*	7,970	254,533 D	39.3%	60.1%	39.5%	60.5%
1970	1,283,912	617,903	Danforth, John C.	655,431	Symington, Stuart*	10,578	37,528 D	48.1%	51.0%	48.5%	51.5%
1968	1,737,958	850,544	Curtis, Thomas B.	887,414	Eagleton, Thomas F.		36,870 D	48.9%	51.1%	48.9%	51.1%
1964	1,783,043	596,377	Bradshaw, Jean Paul	1,186,666	Symington, Stuart*		590,289 D	33.4%	66.6%	33.4%	66.6%
1962	1,222,259	555,330	Kemper, Crosby	666,929	Long, Edward V.*		111,599 D	45.4%	54.6%	45.4%	54.6%
1960S**	1,880,232	880,576	Hocker, Lon	999,656	Long, Edward V.		119,080 D	46.8%	53.2%	46.8%	53.2%
1958	1,173,930	393,847	Palmer, Hazel	780,083	Symington, Stuart*		386,236 D	33.5%	66.5%	33.5%	66.5%
1956	1,800,984	785,048	Douglas, Herbert	1,015,936	Hennings, Thomas Carey Jr.*		230,888 D	43.6%	56.4%	43.6%	56.4%
1952	1,868,083	858,170	Kem, James P.*	1,008,523	Symington, Stuart	1,390	150,353 D	45.9%	54.0%	46.0%	54.0%
1950	1,279,631	593,139	Donnell, Forrest C.*	685,732	Hennings, Thomas Carey Jr.	760	92,593 D	46.4%	53.6%	46.4%	53.6%
1946	1,084,100	572,556	Kem, James P.	511,544	Briggs, Frank		61,012 R	52.8%	47.2%	52.8%	47.2%

Note: An asterisk (*) denotes incumbent. **In 2000 the Democratic candidate, Mel Carnahan, was killed in an airplane crash in October but his name remained on the ballot and he won the election in November. Subsequently, his widow, Jean Carnahan, was appointed to fill the seat until an election could be held in 2002 for the remaining four years of the term. The 1960 and 2002 elections were for short terms to fill a vacancy.

MISSOURI
PRESIDENT 2016

2010 Census Population	County	Total Vote	Republican (Trump)	Democratic (Clinton)	Other	Rep.-Dem. Plurality	Total Vote Rep.	Total Vote Dem.	Major Vote Rep.	Major Vote Dem.
25,607	ADAIR	10,226	6,030	3,500	696	2,530 R	59.0%	34.2%	63.3%	36.7%
17,291	ANDREW	9,140	6,665	2,045	430	4,620 R	72.9%	22.4%	76.5%	23.5%
5,685	ATCHISON	2,730	2,060	541	129	1,519 R	75.5%	19.8%	79.2%	20.8%
25,529	AUDRAIN	10,061	6,981	2,570	510	4,411 R	69.4%	25.5%	73.1%	26.9%
35,597	BARRY	14,605	11,428	2,710	467	8,718 R	78.2%	18.6%	80.8%	19.2%
12,402	BARTON	5,939	4,959	795	185	4,164 R	83.5%	13.4%	86.2%	13.8%
17,049	BATES	8,031	6,001	1,618	412	4,383 R	74.7%	20.1%	78.8%	21.2%
19,056	BENTON	9,590	7,213	2,025	352	5,188 R	75.2%	21.1%	78.1%	21.9%
12,363	BOLLINGER	5,676	4,827	705	144	4,122 R	85.0%	12.4%	87.3%	12.7%
162,642	BOONE	83,868	36,200	41,125	6,543	4,925 D	43.2%	49.0%	46.8%	53.2%
89,201	BUCHANAN	35,659	21,320	12,013	2,326	9,307 R	59.8%	33.7%	64.0%	36.0%
42,794	BUTLER	17,259	13,650	3,036	573	10,614 R	79.1%	17.6%	81.8%	18.2%
9,424	CALDWELL	4,312	3,232	838	242	2,394 R	75.0%	19.4%	79.4%	20.6%
44,332	CALLAWAY	19,193	13,057	4,989	1,147	8,068 R	68.0%	26.0%	72.4%	27.6%
44,002	CAMDEN	22,514	16,944	4,768	802	12,176 R	75.3%	21.2%	78.0%	22.0%
75,674	CAPE GIRARDEAU	37,038	27,017	8,492	1,529	18,525 R	72.9%	22.9%	76.1%	23.9%
9,295	CARROLL	4,361	3,480	745	136	2,735 R	79.8%	17.1%	82.4%	17.6%
6,265	CARTER	2,850	2,324	436	90	1,888 R	81.5%	15.3%	84.2%	15.8%
99,478	CASS	50,990	33,098	14,846	3,046	18,252 R	64.9%	29.1%	69.0%	31.0%
13,982	CEDAR	6,288	5,021	1,011	256	4,010 R	79.9%	16.1%	83.2%	16.8%
7,831	CHARITON	3,969	2,950	888	131	2,062 R	74.3%	22.4%	76.9%	23.1%
77,422	CHRISTIAN	41,531	30,946	8,508	2,077	22,438 R	74.5%	20.5%	78.4%	21.6%
7,139	CLARK	3,316	2,458	724	134	1,734 R	74.1%	21.8%	77.2%	22.8%
221,939	CLAY	110,176	57,476	45,304	7,396	12,172 R	52.2%	41.1%	55.9%	44.1%
20,743	CLINTON	10,208	7,067	2,572	569	4,495 R	69.2%	25.2%	73.3%	26.7%
75,990	COLE	37,374	24,616	10,913	1,845	13,703 R	65.9%	29.2%	69.3%	30.7%
17,601	COOPER	7,986	5,624	1,932	430	3,692 R	70.4%	24.2%	74.4%	25.6%
24,696	CRAWFORD	9,920	7,724	1,824	372	5,900 R	77.9%	18.4%	80.9%	19.1%
7,883	DADE	3,951	3,184	637	130	2,547 R	80.6%	16.1%	83.3%	16.7%
16,777	DALLAS	7,453	5,895	1,272	286	4,623 R	79.1%	17.1%	82.3%	17.7%
8,433	DAVIESS	3,738	2,767	730	241	2,037 R	74.0%	19.5%	79.1%	20.9%
12,892	DEKALB	4,594	3,540	824	230	2,716 R	77.1%	17.9%	81.1%	18.9%
15,657	DENT	6,791	5,600	978	213	4,622 R	82.5%	14.4%	85.1%	14.9%
13,684	DOUGLAS	6,666	5,486	984	196	4,502 R	82.3%	14.8%	84.8%	15.2%
31,953	DUNKLIN	10,578	8,026	2,360	192	5,666 R	75.9%	22.3%	77.3%	22.7%
101,492	FRANKLIN	50,113	35,430	12,341	2,342	23,089 R	70.7%	24.6%	74.2%	25.8%
15,222	GASCONADE	7,451	5,670	1,520	261	4,150 R	76.1%	20.4%	78.9%	21.1%
6,738	GENTRY	3,043	2,304	605	134	1,699 R	75.7%	19.9%	79.2%	20.8%
275,174	GREENE	129,231	78,035	42,728	8,468	35,307 R	60.4%	33.1%	64.6%	35.4%
10,261	GRUNDY	4,428	3,462	780	186	2,682 R	78.2%	17.6%	81.6%	18.4%
8,957	HARRISON	3,689	2,965	574	150	2,391 R	80.4%	15.6%	83.8%	16.2%
22,272	HENRY	9,866	7,075	2,357	434	4,718 R	71.7%	23.9%	75.0%	25.0%
9,627	HICKORY	4,724	3,542	1,016	166	2,526 R	75.0%	21.5%	77.7%	22.3%
4,912	HOLT	2,355	1,926	347	82	1,579 R	81.8%	14.7%	84.7%	15.3%
10,144	HOWARD	4,868	3,277	1,283	308	1,994 R	67.3%	26.4%	71.9%	28.1%
40,400	HOWELL	17,455	13,893	2,881	681	11,012 R	79.6%	16.5%	82.8%	17.2%
10,630	IRON	4,269	3,173	933	163	2,240 R	74.3%	21.9%	77.3%	22.7%
674,158	JACKSON	173,275	91,557	71,237	10,481	20,320 R	52.8%	41.1%	56.2%	43.8%
117,404	JASPER	48,326	35,070	10,572	2,684	24,498 R	72.6%	21.9%	76.8%	23.2%
218,733	JEFFERSON	106,238	69,036	31,568	5,634	37,468 R	65.0%	29.7%	68.6%	31.4%
52,595	JOHNSON	21,132	13,719	5,930	1,483	7,789 R	64.9%	28.1%	69.8%	30.2%
	KANSAS CITY	128,601	24,654	97,735	6,212	73,081 D	19.2%	76.0%	20.1%	79.9%
4,131	KNOX	1,870	1,416	379	75	1,037 R	75.7%	20.3%	78.9%	21.1%
35,571	LACLEDE	16,051	12,881	2,553	617	10,328 R	80.3%	15.9%	83.5%	16.5%
33,381	LAFAYETTE	15,876	10,988	4,053	835	6,935 R	69.2%	25.5%	73.1%	26.9%
38,634	LAWRENCE	16,715	13,089	2,901	725	10,188 R	78.3%	17.4%	81.9%	18.1%
10,211	LEWIS	4,456	3,344	934	178	2,410 R	75.0%	21.0%	78.2%	21.8%
52,566	LINCOLN	24,962	18,159	5,575	1,228	12,584 R	72.7%	22.3%	76.5%	23.5%
12,761	LINN	5,587	4,088	1,240	259	2,848 R	73.2%	22.2%	76.7%	23.3%
15,195	LIVINGSTON	6,421	4,879	1,265	277	3,614 R	76.0%	19.7%	79.4%	20.6%

MISSOURI
PRESIDENT 2016

2010 Census Population	County	Total Vote	Republican (Trump)	Democratic (Clinton)	Other	Rep.-Dem. Plurality	Total Vote Rep.	Total Vote Dem.	Major Vote Rep.	Major Vote Dem.
15,566	MACON	7,631	5,798	1,548	285	4,250 R	76.0%	20.3%	78.9%	21.1%
12,226	MADISON	5,321	4,102	1,005	214	3,097 R	77.1%	18.9%	80.3%	19.7%
9,176	MARIES	4,500	3,561	794	145	2,767 R	79.1%	17.6%	81.8%	18.2%
28,781	MARION	12,938	9,419	2,994	525	6,425 R	72.8%	23.1%	75.9%	24.1%
23,083	MCDONALD	8,242	6,599	1,329	314	5,270 R	80.1%	16.1%	83.2%	16.8%
3,785	MERCER	1,745	1,486	216	43	1,270 R	85.2%	12.4%	87.3%	12.7%
24,748	MILLER	11,416	9,285	1,750	381	7,535 R	81.3%	15.3%	84.1%	15.9%
14,358	MISSISSIPPI	5,169	3,600	1,458	111	2,142 R	69.6%	28.2%	71.2%	28.8%
15,607	MONITEAU	6,830	5,347	1,237	246	4,110 R	78.3%	18.1%	81.2%	18.8%
8,840	MONROE	4,156	3,159	853	144	2,306 R	76.0%	20.5%	78.7%	21.3%
12,236	MONTGOMERY	5,429	4,127	1,119	183	3,008 R	76.0%	20.6%	78.7%	21.3%
20,565	MORGAN	8,821	6,760	1,768	293	4,992 R	76.6%	20.0%	79.3%	20.7%
18,956	NEW MADRID	7,357	5,270	1,933	154	3,337 R	71.6%	26.3%	73.2%	26.8%
58,114	NEWTON	26,606	20,553	4,990	1,063	15,563 R	77.2%	18.8%	80.5%	19.5%
23,370	NODAWAY	9,458	6,380	2,529	549	3,851 R	67.5%	26.7%	71.6%	28.4%
10,881	OREGON	4,668	3,671	865	132	2,806 R	78.6%	18.5%	80.9%	19.1%
13,878	OSAGE	7,090	5,856	998	236	4,858 R	82.6%	14.1%	85.4%	14.6%
9,723	OZARK	4,505	3,639	724	142	2,915 R	80.8%	16.1%	83.4%	16.6%
18,296	PEMISCOT	6,027	3,964	1,947	116	2,017 R	65.8%	32.3%	67.1%	32.9%
18,971	PERRY	8,740	6,908	1,520	312	5,388 R	79.0%	17.4%	82.0%	18.0%
42,201	PETTIS	18,111	12,810	4,324	977	8,486 R	70.7%	23.9%	74.8%	25.2%
45,156	PHELPS	18,553	12,709	4,766	1,078	7,943 R	68.5%	25.7%	72.7%	27.3%
18,516	PIKE	7,382	5,274	1,806	302	3,468 R	71.4%	24.5%	74.5%	25.5%
89,322	PLATTE	49,100	25,933	20,057	3,110	5,876 R	52.8%	40.8%	56.4%	43.6%
31,137	POLK	13,763	10,438	2,631	694	7,807 R	75.8%	19.1%	79.9%	20.1%
52,274	PULASKI	13,488	9,876	2,922	690	6,954 R	73.2%	21.7%	77.2%	22.8%
4,979	PUTNAM	2,346	1,936	353	57	1,583 R	82.5%	15.0%	84.6%	15.4%
10,167	RALLS	5,266	3,969	1,138	159	2,831 R	75.4%	21.6%	77.7%	22.3%
25,414	RANDOLPH	10,309	7,529	2,283	497	5,246 R	73.0%	22.1%	76.7%	23.3%
23,494	RAY	10,869	7,104	3,090	675	4,014 R	65.4%	28.4%	69.7%	30.3%
6,696	REYNOLDS	3,038	2,406	540	92	1,866 R	79.2%	17.8%	81.7%	18.3%
14,100	RIPLEY	5,524	4,522	830	172	3,692 R	81.9%	15.0%	84.5%	15.5%
23,370	SALINE	9,274	5,977	2,789	508	3,188 R	64.4%	30.1%	68.2%	31.8%
4,431	SCHUYLER	1,936	1,505	354	77	1,151 R	77.7%	18.3%	81.0%	19.0%
4,843	SCOTLAND	1,968	1,525	365	78	1,160 R	77.5%	18.5%	80.7%	19.3%
39,191	SCOTT	17,256	13,168	3,575	513	9,593 R	76.3%	20.7%	78.6%	21.4%
8,441	SHANNON	3,904	2,966	776	162	2,190 R	76.0%	19.9%	79.3%	20.7%
6,373	SHELBY	3,255	2,524	606	125	1,918 R	77.5%	18.6%	80.6%	19.4%
360,485	ST. CHARLES	201,005	121,650	68,626	10,729	53,024 R	60.5%	34.1%	63.9%	36.1%
9,805	ST. CLAIR	4,630	3,501	936	193	2,565 R	75.6%	20.2%	78.9%	21.1%
65,359	ST. FRANCOIS	24,728	17,468	6,250	1,010	11,218 R	70.6%	25.3%	73.6%	26.4%
998,954	ST. LOUIS	514,858	202,434	286,704	25,720	84,270 D	39.3%	55.7%	41.4%	58.6%
319,294	ST. LOUIS CITY	131,191	20,832	104,235	6,124	83,403 D	15.9%	79.5%	16.7%	83.3%
18,145	STE. GENEVIEVE	8,469	5,496	2,542	431	2,954 R	64.9%	30.0%	68.4%	31.6%
29,968	STODDARD	13,291	11,079	1,876	336	9,203 R	83.4%	14.1%	85.5%	14.5%
32,202	STONE	16,567	13,158	2,887	522	10,271 R	79.4%	17.4%	82.0%	18.0%
6,714	SULLIVAN	2,486	1,884	526	76	1,358 R	75.8%	21.2%	78.2%	21.8%
51,675	TANEY	23,515	18,276	4,373	866	13,903 R	77.7%	18.6%	80.7%	19.3%
26,008	TEXAS	10,956	8,875	1,728	353	7,147 R	81.0%	15.8%	83.7%	16.3%
21,159	VERNON	8,599	6,533	1,707	359	4,826 R	76.0%	19.9%	79.3%	20.7%
32,513	WARREN	15,784	11,111	3,915	758	7,196 R	70.4%	24.8%	73.9%	26.1%
25,195	WASHINGTON	9,282	7,048	1,926	308	5,122 R	75.9%	20.7%	78.5%	21.5%
13,521	WAYNE	5,762	4,658	948	156	3,710 R	80.8%	16.5%	83.1%	16.9%
36,202	WEBSTER	16,743	12,840	3,177	726	9,663 R	76.7%	19.0%	80.2%	19.8%
2,171	WORTH	1,046	808	195	43	613 R	77.2%	18.6%	80.6%	19.4%
18,815	WRIGHT	8,119	6,707	1,170	242	5,537 R	82.6%	14.4%	85.1%	14.9%
5,988,927	TOTAL	2,808,605	1,594,511	1,071,068	143,026	523,443 R	56.8%	38.1%	59.8%	40.2%

Note: Although Kansas City is part of Jackson County, its results are listed separately.

MISSOURI

GOVERNOR 2016

2010 Census Population	County	Total Vote	Republican (Greitens)	Democratic (Koster)	Other	Rep.-Dem. Plurality	Total Vote Rep.	Total Vote Dem.	Major Vote Rep.	Major Vote Dem.
25,607	ADAIR	10,199	5,762	4,145	292	1,617 R	56.5%	40.6%	58.2%	41.8%
17,291	ANDREW	9,128	5,771	3,176	181	2,595 R	63.2%	34.8%	64.5%	35.5%
5,685	ATCHISON	2,677	1,746	842	89	904 R	65.2%	31.5%	67.5%	32.5%
25,529	AUDRAIN	10,043	5,831	3,836	376	1,995 R	58.1%	38.2%	60.3%	39.7%
35,597	BARRY	14,602	9,943	4,161	498	5,782 R	68.1%	28.5%	70.5%	29.5%
12,402	BARTON	5,899	4,553	1,203	143	3,350 R	77.2%	20.4%	79.1%	20.9%
17,049	BATES	8,001	4,772	2,989	240	1,783 R	59.6%	37.4%	61.5%	38.5%
19,056	BENTON	9,536	6,047	3,199	290	2,848 R	63.4%	33.5%	65.4%	34.6%
12,363	BOLLINGER	5,609	4,051	1,416	142	2,635 R	72.2%	25.2%	74.1%	25.9%
162,642	BOONE	82,619	34,106	45,396	3,117	11,290 D	41.3%	54.9%	42.9%	57.1%
89,201	BUCHANAN	35,580	18,714	15,628	1,238	3,086 R	52.6%	43.9%	54.5%	45.5%
42,794	BUTLER	17,075	12,598	4,039	438	8,559 R	73.8%	23.7%	75.7%	24.3%
9,424	CALDWELL	4,320	2,726	1,443	151	1,283 R	63.1%	33.4%	65.4%	34.6%
44,332	CALLAWAY	19,238	11,149	7,340	749	3,809 R	58.0%	38.2%	60.3%	39.7%
44,002	CAMDEN	22,434	15,050	6,686	698	8,364 R	67.1%	29.8%	69.2%	30.8%
75,674	CAPE GIRARDEAU	36,849	24,209	11,539	1,101	12,670 R	65.7%	31.3%	67.7%	32.3%
9,295	CARROLL	4,344	2,837	1,392	115	1,445 R	65.3%	32.0%	67.1%	32.9%
6,265	CARTER	2,807	2,051	651	105	1,400 R	73.1%	23.2%	75.9%	24.1%
99,478	CASS	50,972	28,571	20,713	1,688	7,858 R	56.1%	40.6%	58.0%	42.0%
13,982	CEDAR	6,284	4,415	1,667	202	2,748 R	70.3%	26.5%	72.6%	27.4%
7,831	CHARITON	3,966	2,364	1,523	79	841 R	59.6%	38.4%	60.8%	39.2%
77,422	CHRISTIAN	41,496	28,618	11,593	1,285	17,025 R	69.0%	27.9%	71.2%	28.8%
7,139	CLARK	3,293	2,053	1,144	96	909 R	62.3%	34.7%	64.2%	35.8%
221,939	CLAY	110,024	53,883	52,429	3,712	1,454 R	49.0%	47.7%	50.7%	49.3%
20,743	CLINTON	10,225	6,030	3,861	334	2,169 R	59.0%	37.8%	61.0%	39.0%
75,990	COLE	37,555	20,872	15,806	877	5,066 R	55.6%	42.1%	56.9%	43.1%
17,601	COOPER	8,011	4,958	2,838	215	2,120 R	61.9%	35.4%	63.6%	36.4%
24,696	CRAWFORD	9,877	5,899	2,892	1,086	3,007 R	59.7%	29.3%	67.1%	32.9%
7,883	DADE	3,946	2,720	1,112	114	1,608 R	68.9%	28.2%	71.0%	29.0%
16,777	DALLAS	7,414	4,943	2,211	260	2,732 R	66.7%	29.8%	69.1%	30.9%
8,433	DAVIESS	3,731	2,300	1,301	130	999 R	61.6%	34.9%	63.9%	36.1%
12,892	DEKALB	4,594	3,061	1,413	120	1,648 R	66.6%	30.8%	68.4%	31.6%
15,657	DENT	6,799	4,967	1,635	197	3,332 R	73.1%	24.0%	75.2%	24.8%
13,684	DOUGLAS	6,660	4,818	1,607	235	3,211 R	72.3%	24.1%	75.0%	25.0%
31,953	DUNKLIN	10,445	7,253	3,014	178	4,239 R	69.4%	28.9%	70.6%	29.4%
101,492	FRANKLIN	50,131	28,069	18,756	3,306	9,313 R	56.0%	37.4%	59.9%	40.1%
15,222	GASCONADE	7,425	4,681	2,402	342	2,279 R	63.0%	32.4%	66.1%	33.9%
6,738	GENTRY	3,028	1,940	1,010	78	930 R	64.1%	33.4%	65.8%	34.2%
275,174	GREENE	129,643	73,601	51,201	4,841	22,400 R	56.8%	39.5%	59.0%	41.0%
10,261	GRUNDY	4,441	3,046	1,269	126	1,777 R	68.6%	28.6%	70.6%	29.4%
8,957	HARRISON	3,664	2,473	1,081	110	1,392 R	67.5%	29.5%	69.6%	30.4%
22,272	HENRY	9,851	5,852	3,695	304	2,157 R	59.4%	37.5%	61.3%	38.7%
9,627	HICKORY	4,713	2,936	1,608	169	1,328 R	62.3%	34.1%	64.6%	35.4%
4,912	HOLT	2,343	1,515	753	75	762 R	64.7%	32.1%	66.8%	33.2%
10,144	HOWARD	4,829	2,727	1,944	158	783 R	56.5%	40.3%	58.4%	41.6%
40,400	HOWELL	17,362	12,266	4,459	637	7,807 R	70.6%	25.7%	73.3%	26.7%
10,630	IRON	4,279	2,600	1,497	182	1,103 R	60.8%	35.0%	63.5%	36.5%
674,158	JACKSON	172,629	83,918	82,240	6,471	1,678 R	48.6%	47.6%	50.5%	49.5%
117,404	JASPER	48,382	33,436	13,236	1,710	20,200 R	69.1%	27.4%	71.6%	28.4%
218,733	JEFFERSON	105,837	56,755	45,234	3,848	11,521 R	53.6%	42.7%	55.6%	44.4%
52,595	JOHNSON	21,168	12,040	8,335	793	3,705 R	56.9%	39.4%	59.1%	40.9%
See Note	KANSAS CITY	128,078	25,284	98,336	4,458	73,052 D	19.7%	76.8%	20.5%	79.5%
4,131	KNOX	1,826	1,125	672	29	453 R	61.6%	36.8%	62.6%	37.4%
35,571	LACLEDE	16,012	11,362	4,122	528	7,240 R	71.0%	25.7%	73.4%	26.6%
33,381	LAFAYETTE	15,847	9,167	6,097	583	3,070 R	57.8%	38.5%	60.1%	39.9%
38,634	LAWRENCE	16,679	11,565	4,482	632	7,083 R	69.3%	26.9%	72.1%	27.9%
10,211	LEWIS	4,431	2,815	1,491	125	1,324 R	63.5%	33.6%	65.4%	34.6%
52,566	LINCOLN	24,822	14,536	9,352	934	5,184 R	58.6%	37.7%	60.9%	39.1%
12,761	LINN	5,562	3,414	1,986	162	1,428 R	61.4%	35.7%	63.2%	36.8%
15,195	LIVINGSTON	6,338	4,189	1,992	157	2,197 R	66.1%	31.4%	67.8%	32.2%

MISSOURI

GOVERNOR 2016

2010 Census Population	County	Total Vote	Republican (Greitens)	Democratic (Koster)	Other	Rep.-Dem. Plurality	Percentage Total Vote Rep.	Dem.	Major Vote Rep.	Dem.
15,566	MACON	7,564	5,065	2,315	184	2,750 R	67.0%	30.6%	68.6%	31.4%
12,226	MADISON	5,307	3,405	1,707	195	1,698 R	64.2%	32.2%	66.6%	33.4%
9,176	MARIES	4,511	2,827	1,510	174	1,317 R	62.7%	33.5%	65.2%	34.8%
28,781	MARION	12,886	8,484	4,105	297	4,379 R	65.8%	31.9%	67.4%	32.6%
23,083	MCDONALD	8,153	5,915	1,853	385	4,062 R	72.5%	22.7%	76.1%	23.9%
3,785	MERCER	1,710	1,224	455	31	769 R	71.6%	26.6%	72.9%	27.1%
24,748	MILLER	11,377	7,924	3,114	339	4,810 R	69.6%	27.4%	71.8%	28.2%
14,358	MISSISSIPPI	5,084	3,004	1,943	137	1,061 R	59.1%	38.2%	60.7%	39.3%
15,607	MONITEAU	6,792	4,351	2,256	185	2,095 R	64.1%	33.2%	65.9%	34.1%
8,840	MONROE	4,126	2,659	1,367	100	1,292 R	64.4%	33.1%	66.0%	34.0%
12,236	MONTGOMERY	5,407	3,261	1,956	190	1,305 R	60.3%	36.2%	62.5%	37.5%
20,565	MORGAN	8,771	5,820	2,689	262	3,131 R	66.4%	30.7%	68.4%	31.6%
18,956	NEW MADRID	7,285	4,392	2,754	139	1,638 R	60.3%	37.8%	61.5%	38.5%
58,114	NEWTON	26,590	19,123	6,607	860	12,516 R	71.9%	24.8%	74.3%	25.7%
23,370	NODAWAY	9,413	5,790	3,370	253	2,420 R	61.5%	35.8%	63.2%	36.8%
10,881	OREGON	4,611	3,081	1,385	145	1,696 R	66.8%	30.0%	69.0%	31.0%
13,878	OSAGE	7,084	4,579	2,321	184	2,258 R	64.6%	32.8%	66.4%	33.6%
9,723	OZARK	4,483	3,078	1,228	177	1,850 R	68.7%	27.4%	71.5%	28.5%
18,296	PEMISCOT	5,877	3,534	2,209	134	1,325 R	60.1%	37.6%	61.5%	38.5%
18,971	PERRY	8,618	5,725	2,664	229	3,061 R	66.4%	30.9%	68.2%	31.8%
42,201	PETTIS	17,997	11,150	6,281	566	4,869 R	62.0%	34.9%	64.0%	36.0%
45,156	PHELPS	18,610	11,633	6,168	809	5,465 R	62.5%	33.1%	65.4%	34.6%
18,516	PIKE	7,383	4,389	2,755	239	1,634 R	59.4%	37.3%	61.4%	38.6%
89,322	PLATTE	49,280	24,738	22,973	1,569	1,765 R	50.2%	46.6%	51.8%	48.2%
31,137	POLK	13,823	9,251	4,168	404	5,083 R	66.9%	30.2%	68.9%	31.1%
52,274	PULASKI	13,420	9,060	3,862	498	5,198 R	67.5%	28.8%	70.1%	29.9%
4,979	PUTNAM	2,290	1,691	547	52	1,144 R	73.8%	23.9%	75.6%	24.4%
10,167	RALLS	5,229	3,371	1,763	95	1,608 R	64.5%	33.7%	65.7%	34.3%
25,414	RANDOLPH	10,364	6,505	3,561	298	2,944 R	62.8%	34.4%	64.6%	35.4%
23,494	RAY	10,828	5,686	4,719	423	967 R	52.5%	43.6%	54.6%	45.4%
6,696	REYNOLDS	2,970	1,969	879	122	1,090 R	66.3%	29.6%	69.1%	30.9%
14,100	RIPLEY	5,411	3,959	1,311	141	2,648 R	73.2%	24.2%	75.1%	24.9%
23,370	SALINE	9,246	4,901	4,004	341	897 R	53.0%	43.3%	55.0%	45.0%
4,431	SCHUYLER	1,899	1,259	594	46	665 R	66.3%	31.3%	67.9%	32.1%
4,843	SCOTLAND	1,949	1,273	610	66	663 R	65.3%	31.3%	67.6%	32.4%
39,191	SCOTT	17,161	11,323	5,412	426	5,911 R	66.0%	31.5%	67.7%	32.3%
8,441	SHANNON	3,855	2,365	1,322	168	1,043 R	61.3%	34.3%	64.1%	35.9%
6,373	SHELBY	3,241	2,143	1,037	61	1,106 R	66.1%	32.0%	67.4%	32.6%
360,485	ST. CHARLES	201,281	109,741	85,704	5,836	24,037 R	54.5%	42.6%	56.1%	43.9%
9,805	ST. CLAIR	4,656	2,927	1,560	169	1,367 R	62.9%	33.5%	65.2%	34.8%
65,359	ST. FRANCOIS	24,668	14,433	9,424	811	5,009 R	58.5%	38.2%	60.5%	39.5%
998,954	ST. LOUIS	515,254	199,827	301,115	14,312	101,288 D	38.8%	58.4%	39.9%	60.1%
319,294	ST. LOUIS CITY	130,910	21,385	105,242	4,283	83,857 D	16.3%	80.4%	16.9%	83.1%
18,145	STE. GENEVIEVE	8,432	4,242	3,969	221	273 R	50.3%	47.1%	51.7%	48.3%
29,968	STODDARD	13,260	9,792	3,179	289	6,613 R	73.8%	24.0%	75.5%	24.5%
32,202	STONE	16,491	11,920	4,135	436	7,785 R	72.3%	25.1%	74.2%	25.8%
6,714	SULLIVAN	2,480	1,642	787	51	855 R	66.2%	31.7%	67.6%	32.4%
51,675	TANEY	23,341	16,579	5,992	770	10,587 R	71.0%	25.7%	73.5%	26.5%
26,008	TEXAS	10,964	7,659	2,918	387	4,741 R	69.9%	26.6%	72.4%	27.6%
21,159	VERNON	8,548	5,699	2,621	228	3,078 R	66.7%	30.7%	68.5%	31.5%
32,513	WARREN	15,729	9,056	6,055	618	3,001 R	57.6%	38.5%	59.9%	40.1%
25,195	WASHINGTON	9,262	5,681	3,141	440	2,540 R	61.3%	33.9%	64.4%	35.6%
13,521	WAYNE	5,689	4,098	1,425	166	2,673 R	72.0%	25.0%	74.2%	25.8%
36,202	WEBSTER	16,760	11,149	5,039	572	6,110 R	66.5%	30.1%	68.9%	31.1%
2,171	WORTH	1,038	714	293	31	421 R	68.8%	28.2%	70.9%	29.1%
18,815	WRIGHT	8,106	5,993	1,897	216	4,096 R	73.9%	23.4%	76.0%	24.0%
5,988,927	TOTAL	2,803,046	1,433,397	1,277,360	92,289	156,037 R	51.1%	45.6%	52.9%	47.1%

Note: Although Kansas City is part of Jackson County, its results are listed separately.

MISSOURI

SENATOR 2016

2010 Census Population	County	Total Vote	Republican (Blunt)	Democratic (Kander)	Other	Rep.-Dem. Plurality	Percentage Total Vote Rep.	Dem.	Major Vote Rep.	Dem.
25,607	ADAIR	10,201	5,603	4,198	400	1,405 R	54.9%	41.2%	57.2%	42.8%
17,291	ANDREW	9,102	5,610	3,122	370	2,488 R	61.6%	34.3%	64.2%	35.8%
5,685	ATCHISON	2,675	1,861	704	110	1,157 R	69.6%	26.3%	72.6%	27.4%
25,529	AUDRAIN	10,000	5,726	3,680	594	2,046 R	57.3%	36.8%	60.9%	39.1%
35,597	BARRY	14,645	10,059	3,864	722	6,195 R	68.7%	26.4%	72.2%	27.8%
12,402	BARTON	5,911	4,479	1,231	201	3,248 R	75.8%	20.8%	78.4%	21.6%
17,049	BATES	7,975	4,630	2,866	479	1,764 R	58.1%	35.9%	61.8%	38.2%
19,056	BENTON	9,522	5,891	3,097	534	2,794 R	61.9%	32.5%	65.5%	34.5%
12,363	BOLLINGER	5,608	4,016	1,379	213	2,637 R	71.6%	24.6%	74.4%	25.6%
162,642	BOONE	83,071	34,171	45,100	3,800	10,929 D	41.1%	54.3%	43.1%	56.9%
89,201	BUCHANAN	35,602	17,658	16,103	1,841	1,555 R	49.6%	45.2%	52.3%	47.7%
42,794	BUTLER	16,995	11,764	4,543	688	7,221 R	69.2%	26.7%	72.1%	27.9%
9,424	CALDWELL	4,314	2,513	1,517	284	996 R	58.3%	35.2%	62.4%	37.6%
44,332	CALLAWAY	19,187	10,983	7,084	1,120	3,899 R	57.2%	36.9%	60.8%	39.2%
44,002	CAMDEN	22,427	14,434	6,995	998	7,439 R	64.4%	31.2%	67.4%	32.6%
75,674	CAPE GIRARDEAU	36,815	24,173	11,219	1,423	12,954 R	65.7%	30.5%	68.3%	31.7%
9,295	CARROLL	4,343	2,875	1,290	178	1,585 R	66.2%	29.7%	69.0%	31.0%
6,265	CARTER	2,785	1,908	742	135	1,166 R	68.5%	26.6%	72.0%	28.0%
99,478	CASS	50,874	27,532	20,628	2,714	6,904 R	54.1%	40.5%	57.2%	42.8%
13,982	CEDAR	6,295	4,445	1,541	309	2,904 R	70.6%	24.5%	74.3%	25.7%
7,831	CHARITON	3,960	2,322	1,465	173	857 R	58.6%	37.0%	61.3%	38.7%
77,422	CHRISTIAN	41,556	27,812	11,857	1,887	15,955 R	66.9%	28.5%	70.1%	29.9%
7,139	CLARK	3,277	2,037	1,059	181	978 R	62.2%	32.3%	65.8%	34.2%
221,939	CLAY	110,098	49,173	55,322	5,603	6,149 D	44.7%	50.2%	47.1%	52.9%
20,743	CLINTON	10,223	5,614	3,990	619	1,624 R	54.9%	39.0%	58.5%	41.5%
75,990	COLE	37,476	21,940	14,216	1,320	7,724 R	58.5%	37.9%	60.7%	39.3%
17,601	COOPER	7,972	4,668	2,920	384	1,748 R	58.6%	36.6%	61.5%	38.5%
24,696	CRAWFORD	9,831	6,163	3,144	524	3,019 R	62.7%	32.0%	66.2%	33.8%
7,883	DADE	3,945	2,810	969	166	1,841 R	71.2%	24.6%	74.4%	25.6%
16,777	DALLAS	7,428	5,101	1,980	347	3,121 R	68.7%	26.7%	72.0%	28.0%
8,433	DAVIESS	3,731	2,213	1,266	252	947 R	59.3%	33.9%	63.6%	36.4%
12,892	DEKALB	4,571	2,826	1,478	267	1,348 R	61.8%	32.3%	65.7%	34.3%
15,657	DENT	6,767	4,653	1,795	319	2,858 R	68.8%	26.5%	72.2%	27.8%
13,684	DOUGLAS	6,665	4,753	1,556	356	3,197 R	71.3%	23.3%	75.3%	24.7%
31,953	DUNKLIN	10,371	6,536	3,433	402	3,103 R	63.0%	33.1%	65.6%	34.4%
101,492	FRANKLIN	49,952	28,258	19,102	2,592	9,156 R	56.6%	38.2%	59.7%	40.3%
15,222	GASCONADE	7,420	4,743	2,319	358	2,424 R	63.9%	31.3%	67.2%	32.8%
6,738	GENTRY	3,015	1,860	1,025	130	835 R	61.7%	34.0%	64.5%	35.5%
275,174	GREENE	129,827	72,993	50,967	5,867	22,026 R	56.2%	39.3%	58.9%	41.1%
10,261	GRUNDY	4,435	2,898	1,325	212	1,573 R	65.3%	29.9%	68.6%	31.4%
8,957	HARRISON	3,665	2,415	1,053	197	1,362 R	65.9%	28.7%	69.6%	30.4%
22,272	HENRY	9,853	5,500	3,785	568	1,715 R	55.8%	38.4%	59.2%	40.8%
9,627	HICKORY	4,702	2,959	1,490	253	1,469 R	62.9%	31.7%	66.5%	33.5%
4,912	HOLT	2,333	1,614	629	90	985 R	69.2%	27.0%	72.0%	28.0%
10,144	HOWARD	4,834	2,671	1,928	235	743 R	55.3%	39.9%	58.1%	41.9%
40,400	HOWELL	17,339	12,070	4,375	894	7,695 R	69.6%	25.2%	73.4%	26.6%
10,630	IRON	4,227	2,329	1,671	227	658 R	55.1%	39.5%	58.2%	41.8%
674,158	JACKSON	172,676	77,941	85,664	9,071	7,723 D	45.1%	49.6%	47.6%	52.4%
117,404	JASPER	48,414	32,123	13,799	2,492	18,324 R	66.4%	28.5%	70.0%	30.0%
218,733	JEFFERSON	105,710	53,218	46,975	5,517	6,243 R	50.3%	44.4%	53.1%	46.9%
52,595	JOHNSON	21,156	11,611	8,315	1,230	3,296 R	54.9%	39.3%	58.3%	41.7%
See Note	KANSAS CITY	128,699	24,048	100,102	4,549	76,054 D	18.7%	77.8%	19.4%	80.6%
4,131	KNOX	1,825	1,208	558	59	650 R	66.2%	30.6%	68.4%	31.6%
35,571	LACLEDE	16,044	11,316	3,965	763	7,351 R	70.5%	24.7%	74.1%	25.9%
33,381	LAFAYETTE	15,865	8,812	6,150	903	2,662 R	55.5%	38.8%	58.9%	41.1%
38,634	LAWRENCE	16,692	11,525	4,336	831	7,189 R	69.0%	26.0%	72.7%	27.3%
10,211	LEWIS	4,418	2,732	1,472	214	1,260 R	61.8%	33.3%	65.0%	35.0%
52,566	LINCOLN	24,800	14,061	9,264	1,475	4,797 R	56.7%	37.4%	60.3%	39.7%
12,761	LINN	5,565	3,245	2,058	262	1,187 R	58.3%	37.0%	61.2%	38.8%
15,195	LIVINGSTON	6,347	3,834	2,208	305	1,626 R	60.4%	34.8%	63.5%	36.5%

MISSOURI
SENATOR 2016

2010 Census Population	County	Total Vote	Republican (Blunt)	Democratic (Kander)	Other	Rep.-Dem. Plurality		Percentage			
								Total Vote		Major Vote	
								Rep.	Dem.	Rep.	Dem.
15,566	MACON	7,551	4,894	2,323	334	2,571 R		64.8%	30.8%	67.8%	32.2%
12,226	MADISON	5,289	3,203	1,766	320	1,437 R		60.6%	33.4%	64.5%	35.5%
9,176	MARIES	4,494	2,978	1,339	177	1,639 R		66.3%	29.8%	69.0%	31.0%
28,781	MARION	12,852	8,239	4,115	498	4,124 R		64.1%	32.0%	66.7%	33.3%
23,083	MCDONALD	8,176	5,812	1,793	571	4,019 R		71.1%	21.9%	76.4%	23.6%
3,785	MERCER	1,701	1,231	396	74	835 R		72.4%	23.3%	75.7%	24.3%
24,748	MILLER	11,333	7,760	3,032	541	4,728 R		68.5%	26.8%	71.9%	28.1%
14,358	MISSISSIPPI	5,068	2,826	2,063	179	763 R		55.8%	40.7%	57.8%	42.2%
15,607	MONITEAU	6,787	4,431	2,097	259	2,334 R		65.3%	30.9%	67.9%	32.1%
8,840	MONROE	4,109	2,584	1,330	195	1,254 R		62.9%	32.4%	66.0%	34.0%
12,236	MONTGOMERY	5,417	3,405	1,722	290	1,683 R		62.9%	31.8%	66.4%	33.6%
20,565	MORGAN	8,768	5,410	2,916	442	2,494 R		61.7%	33.3%	65.0%	35.0%
18,956	NEW MADRID	7,254	4,157	2,844	253	1,313 R		57.3%	39.2%	59.4%	40.6%
58,114	NEWTON	26,612	18,598	6,691	1,323	11,907 R		69.9%	25.1%	73.5%	26.5%
23,370	NODAWAY	9,405	5,516	3,466	423	2,050 R		58.6%	36.9%	61.4%	38.6%
10,881	OREGON	4,631	3,031	1,385	215	1,646 R		65.5%	29.9%	68.6%	31.4%
13,878	OSAGE	7,064	4,789	2,039	236	2,750 R		67.8%	28.9%	70.1%	29.9%
9,723	OZARK	4,470	3,085	1,113	272	1,972 R		69.0%	24.9%	73.5%	26.5%
18,296	PEMISCOT	5,854	3,476	2,203	175	1,273 R		59.4%	37.6%	61.2%	38.8%
18,971	PERRY	8,592	5,599	2,637	356	2,962 R		65.2%	30.7%	68.0%	32.0%
42,201	PETTIS	17,991	10,361	6,657	973	3,704 R		57.6%	37.0%	60.9%	39.1%
45,156	PHELPS	18,532	11,063	6,576	893	4,487 R		59.7%	35.5%	62.7%	37.3%
18,516	PIKE	7,352	4,084	2,872	396	1,212 R		55.5%	39.1%	58.7%	41.3%
89,322	PLATTE	49,039	22,929	23,795	2,315	866 D		46.8%	48.5%	49.1%	50.9%
31,137	POLK	13,861	9,693	3,605	563	6,088 R		69.9%	26.0%	72.9%	27.1%
52,274	PULASKI	13,429	8,663	4,065	701	4,598 R		64.5%	30.3%	68.1%	31.9%
4,979	PUTNAM	2,281	1,708	486	87	1,222 R		74.9%	21.3%	77.8%	22.2%
10,167	RALLS	5,201	3,220	1,763	218	1,457 R		61.9%	33.9%	64.6%	35.4%
25,414	RANDOLPH	10,358	6,135	3,656	567	2,479 R		59.2%	35.3%	62.7%	37.3%
23,494	RAY	10,809	5,415	4,725	669	690 R		50.1%	43.7%	53.4%	46.6%
6,696	REYNOLDS	2,939	1,780	1,009	150	771 R		60.6%	34.3%	63.8%	36.2%
14,100	RIPLEY	5,383	3,814	1,340	229	2,474 R		70.9%	24.9%	74.0%	26.0%
23,370	SALINE	9,241	4,613	4,061	567	552 R		49.9%	43.9%	53.2%	46.8%
4,431	SCHUYLER	1,903	1,259	547	97	712 R		66.2%	28.7%	69.7%	30.3%
4,843	SCOTLAND	1,940	1,283	570	87	713 R		66.1%	29.4%	69.2%	30.8%
39,191	SCOTT	17,132	11,040	5,439	653	5,601 R		64.4%	31.7%	67.0%	33.0%
8,441	SHANNON	3,876	2,436	1,234	206	1,202 R		62.8%	31.8%	66.4%	33.6%
6,373	SHELBY	3,218	2,129	989	100	1,140 R		66.2%	30.7%	68.3%	31.7%
360,485	ST. CHARLES	200,749	103,946	88,238	8,565	15,708 R		51.8%	44.0%	54.1%	45.9%
9,805	ST. CLAIR	4,654	2,941	1,460	253	1,481 R		63.2%	31.4%	66.8%	33.2%
65,359	ST. FRANCOIS	24,589	13,110	10,117	1,362	2,993 R		53.3%	41.1%	56.4%	43.6%
998,954	ST. LOUIS	515,813	189,726	308,925	17,162	119,199 D		36.8%	59.9%	38.0%	62.0%
319,294	ST. LOUIS CITY	130,972	19,586	107,070	4,316	87,484 D		15.0%	81.8%	15.5%	84.5%
18,145	STE. GENEVIEVE	8,390	4,096	3,929	365	167 R		48.8%	46.8%	51.0%	49.0%
29,968	STODDARD	13,229	9,318	3,426	485	5,892 R		70.4%	25.9%	73.1%	26.9%
32,202	STONE	16,522	11,620	4,162	740	7,458 R		70.3%	25.2%	73.6%	26.4%
6,714	SULLIVAN	2,472	1,662	735	75	927 R		67.2%	29.7%	69.3%	30.7%
51,675	TANEY	23,358	16,117	6,143	1,098	9,974 R		69.0%	26.3%	72.4%	27.6%
26,008	TEXAS	10,935	7,619	2,829	487	4,790 R		69.7%	25.9%	72.9%	27.1%
21,159	VERNON	8,551	5,448	2,700	403	2,748 R		63.7%	31.6%	66.9%	33.1%
32,513	WARREN	15,731	8,918	5,928	885	2,990 R		56.7%	37.7%	60.1%	39.9%
25,195	WASHINGTON	9,173	5,083	3,516	574	1,567 R		55.4%	38.3%	59.1%	40.9%
13,521	WAYNE	5,636	3,636	1,706	294	1,930 R		64.5%	30.3%	68.1%	31.9%
36,202	WEBSTER	16,799	11,450	4,612	737	6,838 R		68.2%	27.5%	71.3%	28.7%
2,171	WORTH	1,034	667	321	46	346 R		64.5%	31.0%	67.5%	32.5%
18,815	WRIGHT	8,091	5,930	1,836	325	4,094 R		73.3%	22.7%	76.4%	23.6%
5,988,927	TOTAL	2,802,641	1,378,458	1,300,200	123,983	78,258 R		49.2%	46.4%	51.5%	48.5%

Note: Although Kansas City is part of Jackson County, its results are listed separately.

MISSOURI

HOUSE OF REPRESENTATIVES

CD	Year	Total Vote	Republican		Democratic		Other Vote	Rep.-Dem. Plurality	Percentage			
									Total Vote		Major Vote	
			Vote	Candidate	Vote	Candidate			Rep.	Dem.	Rep.	Dem.
1	2016	314,024	62,714	BAILEY, STEVEN G.	236,993	CLAY, WILLIAM LACY JR.*	14,317	174,279 D	20.0%	75.5%	20.9%	79.1%
1	2014	163,494	35,273	ELDER, DANIEL J.	119,315	CLAY, WILLIAM LACY JR.*	8,906	84,042 D	21.6%	73.0%	22.8%	77.2%
1	2012	340,583	60,832	HAMLIN, ROBYN	267,927	CLAY, WILLIAM LACY JR.*	11,824	207,095 D	17.9%	78.7%	18.5%	81.5%
2	2016	413,296	241,954	WAGNER, ANN*	155,689	OTTO, BILL	15,653	86,265 R	58.5%	37.7%	60.8%	39.2%
2	2014	231,117	148,191	WAGNER, ANN*	75,384	LIEBER, ARTHUR	7,542	72,807 R	64.1%	32.6%	66.3%	33.7%
2	2012	394,448	236,971	WAGNER, ANN	146,272	KOENEN, GLENN	11,205	90,699 R	60.1%	37.1%	61.8%	38.2%
3	2016	368,333	249,865	LUETKEMEYER, BLAINE*	102,891	MILLER, KEVIN	15,577	146,974 R	67.8%	27.9%	70.8%	29.2%
3	2014	191,620	130,940	LUETKEMEYER, BLAINE*	52,021	DENTON, COURTNEY	8,659	78,919 R	68.3%	27.1%	71.6%	28.4%
3	2012	338,385	214,843	LUETKEMEYER, BLAINE*	111,189	MAYER, ERIC C.	12,353	103,654 R	63.5%	32.9%	65.9%	34.1%
4	2016	332,234	225,348	HARTZLER, VICKY*	92,510	CHRISTENSEN, GORDON	14,376	132,838 R	67.8%	27.8%	70.9%	29.1%
4	2014	176,286	120,014	HARTZLER, VICKY*	46,464	IRVIN, NATE A.	9,808	73,550 R	68.1%	26.4%	72.1%	27.9%
4	2012	318,723	192,237	HARTZLER, VICKY*	113,120	HENSLEY, TERESA	13,366	79,117 R	60.3%	35.5%	63.0%	37.0%
5	2016	324,270	123,771	TURK, JACOB	190,766	CLEAVER, EMANUEL*	9,733	66,995 D	38.2%	58.8%	39.4%	60.6%
5	2014	153,635	69,071	TURK, JACOB	79,256	CLEAVER, EMANUEL*	5,308	10,185 D	45.0%	51.6%	46.6%	53.4%
5	2012	330,942	122,149	TURK, JACOB	200,290	CLEAVER, EMANUEL*	8,503	78,141 D	36.9%	60.5%	37.9%	62.1%
6	2016	350,444	238,388	GRAVES, SAMUEL B. JR.*	99,692	BLACKWELL, DAVID M.	12,364	138,696 R	68.0%	28.4%	70.5%	29.5%
6	2014	186,970	124,616	GRAVES, SAMUEL B. JR.*	55,157	HEDGE, W.A. "BILL"	7,197	69,459 R	66.7%	29.5%	69.3%	30.7%
6	2012	333,688	216,906	GRAVES, SAMUEL B. JR.*	108,503	YARBER, KYLE	8,279	108,403 R	65.0%	32.5%	66.7%	33.3%
7	2016	338,607	228,692	LONG, BILLY*	92,756	WILLIAMS, GENEVIEVE	17,159	135,936 R	67.5%	27.4%	71.1%	28.9%
7	2014	163,957	104,054	LONG, BILLY*	47,282	EVANS, JIM	12,621	56,772 R	63.5%	28.8%	68.8%	31.2%
7	2012	318,740	203,565	LONG, BILLY*	98,498	EVANS, JIM	16,677	105,067 R	63.9%	30.9%	67.4%	32.6%
8	2016	308,871	229,792	SMITH, JASON*	70,009	COWELL, DAVE	9,070	159,783 R	74.4%	22.7%	76.6%	23.4%
8	2014	159,224	106,124	SMITH, JASON*	38,721	STOCKER, BARBARA HAMILL	14,379	67,403 R	66.7%	24.3%	73.3%	26.7%
8	2012	300,391	216,083	EMERSON, JO ANN*	73,755	RUSHIN, JACK	10,553	142,328 R	71.9%	24.6%	74.6%	25.4%
TOTAL	2016	2,750,079	1,600,524		1,041,306		108,249	559,218 R	58.2%	37.9%	60.6%	39.4%
TOTAL	2014	1,426,303	838,283		513,600		74,420	324,683 R	58.8%	36.0%	62.0%	38.0%
TOTAL	2012	2,675,900	1,463,586		1,119,554		92,760	344,032 R	54.7%	41.8%	56.7%	43.3%

Note: An asterisk (*) denotes incumbent.

MISSOURI

GENERAL AND PRIMARY ELECTIONS

2016 GENERAL ELECTIONS: OTHER VOTES

President Other vote was 97,359 Libertarian (Gary Johnson), 25,419 Green (Jill Stein), 13,092 Constitution (Darrell Castle), 7,071 Write-in (Evan McMullin), 85 Write-in (Scattered Write-in)

Governor 41,154 Libertarian (Cisse Spragins), 30,019 Independent (Lester Turilli), 21,088 Green (Don Fitz), 22 Write-in (Dave Altis), 3 Write-in (Theo Brown), 3 Write-in (Martin Lindstedt)

Senate Other vote was 67,738 Libertarian (Jonathan Dine), 30,743 Green (Johnathan McFarland), 25,407 Constitution (Fred Ryman), 53 Write-in (Patrick Lee), 21 Write-in (Gina Bufe), 12 Write-in (Nathaniel Malone), 4 Write-in (Jon Kelly), 4 Write-in (Thomas Morgan), 1 Write-in (Steven Wallace)

House Other vote was:

CD 1 14,317 Libertarian (Robb Cunningham)
CD 2 11,758 Libertarian (Jim Higgins), 3,895 Green (David Arnold)
CD 3 11,962 Libertarian (Dan Hogan), 3,605 Constitution (Doanita Simmons), 10 Write-in (Harold Davis)
CD 4 14,376 Libertarian (Mark Bliss)
CD 5 9,733 Libertarian (Roy Welborn)
CD 6 8,123 Libertarian (Russ Monchil), 4,241 Green (Mike Diel)
CD 7 17,153 Libertarian (Benjamin Brixey), 6 Write-in (Amber Thomsen)
CD 8 9,070 Libertarian (Jonathan Shell)

MISSOURI

GENERAL AND PRIMARY ELECTIONS

2016 PRIMARY ELECTIONS: SUPPLEMENTARY INFORMATION

Primary   March 15, 2016 (President)   **Registration**   4,098,134
August 2, 2016 (Congress)   (as of August 1, 2016)

Primary Type   Open—Any registered voter could participate in the party primary of his or her choice.

	REPUBLICAN PRIMARIES			DEMOCRATIC PRIMARIES		
President	Trump, Donald J.	383,631	40.8%	Clinton, Hillary Rodham	312,285	49.6%
	Cruz, Ted	381,666	40.6%	Sanders, Bernard	310,711	49.4%
	Kasich, John R.	94,857	10.1%	Uncommitted	3,717	0.6%
	Rubio, Marco	57,244	6.1%	Hewes, Henry	650	0.1%
	Carson, Ben	8,233	0.9%	O'Malley, Martin	442	0.1%
	Bush, Jeb	3,361	0.4%	Adams, Jon	433	0.1%
	Uncommitted	3,225	0.3%	De La Fuente, Roque "Rocky"	345	0.1%
	Huckabee, Mike	2,148	0.2%	Wilson, Willie	307	
	Paul, Rand	1,777	0.2%	Judd, Keith	288	
	Christie, Chris	1,681	0.2%	Wolfe, John	247	
	Santorum, Rick	732	0.1%			
	Fiorina, Carly	615	0.1%			
	Lynch, James P. "Jim" Sr.	100				
	TOTAL	*939,270*		*TOTAL*	*629,425*	
Senator	Blunt, Roy*	481,444	72.6%	Kander, Jason	223,492	69.9%
	Nichols, Kristi	134,025	20.2%	Bush, Cori	42,453	13.3%
	Luethy, Ryan D.	29,328	4.4%	Wana Dubie, Chief	30,432	9.5%
	Mowinski, Bernie	18,789	2.8%	Mack, Robert	23,509	7.3%
	TOTAL	*663,586*		*TOTAL*	*319,886*	
Governor	Greitens, Eric	236,481	34.6%	Koster, Chris	256,272	78.8%
	Brunner, John G.	169,620	24.8%	Morrison, Eric	31,474	9.7%
	Kinder, Peter D.	141,629	20.7%	Wheeler, Charles B.	25,756	7.9%
	Hanaway, Catherine	136,521	20.0%	Steinman, Leonard	11,911	3.7%
	TOTAL	*684,251*		*TOTAL*	*325,413*	
Congressional District 1	Bailey, Steven G.	12,450	67.2%	Clay, William Lacy Jr.*	56,139	62.6%
	Berry, Paul III	6,067	32.8%	Chappelle-Nadal, Maria N.	24,059	26.8%
				Haas, William C. "Bill"	9,422	10.5%
	TOTAL	*18,517*		*TOTAL*	*89,620*	
Congressional District 2	Wagner, Ann*	77,084	82.6%	Otto, Bill	40,379	100.0%
	Sears, Greg	16,263	17.4%			
	TOTAL	*93,347*		*TOTAL*	*40,379*	
Congressional District 3	Luetkemeyer, Blaine*	84,274	73.5%	Miller, Kevin	26,369	100.0%
	Davis, Cynthia Lynn	30,440	26.5%			
	TOTAL	*114,714*		*TOTAL*	*26,369*	
Congressional District 4	Hartzler, Vicky*	73,853	72.5%	Christensen, Gordon	17,160	62.7%
	Webb, John	28,037	27.5%	Truman, Jack	10,196	37.3%
	TOTAL	*101,890*		*TOTAL*	*27,356*	
Congressional District 5	Turk, Jacob	28,096	68.0%	Cleaver, Emanuel*	48,755	88.2%
	Burris, Michael Craig	6,898	16.7%	Gough, Roberta	6,519	11.8%
	Rucker, Austin	4,137	10.0%			
	Knox, Berton A.	2,166	5.2%			
	TOTAL	*41,297*		*TOTAL*	*55,274*	

MISSOURI

GENERAL AND PRIMARY ELECTIONS

	REPUBLICAN PRIMARIES			DEMOCRATIC PRIMARIES		
Congressional District 6	Graves, Samuel B. Jr.*	62,764	76.2%	Blackwell, David M.	7,983	28.0%
	Ryan, Christopher	11,686	14.2%	Yarber, Kyle	7,116	24.9%
	Reid, Kyle	7,910	9.6%	Gonzalez, Travis	6,623	23.2%
				Fields, Edward Dwayne	3,881	13.6%
				McNabney, Matthew C.	2,931	10.3%
	TOTAL	82,360		TOTAL	28,534	
Congressional District 7	Long, Billy*	67,012	62.4%	Williams, Genevieve	9,402	52.1%
	Byrne, Mary	14,069	13.1%	Reed, Steven L.	4,915	27.3%
	Canovi, Matt	9,538	8.9%	Lombardi-Olive, Camille	3,714	20.6%
	Evans, Matthew	5,346	5.0%			
	Batsche, Christopher	4,860	4.5%			
	Spencer, Lyndle	3,537	3.3%			
	Nelson, James	2,037	1.9%			
	Clay Bradham, Nathan	1,042	1.0%			
	TOTAL	107,441		TOTAL	18,031	
Congressional District 8	Smith, Jason*	65,450	67.5%	Cowell, Dave	22,314	100.0%
	Brown, Hal	15,342	15.8%			
	Mahn, Todd	11,564	11.9%			
	Smith, Phillip	4,602	4.7%			
	TOTAL	96,958		TOTAL	22,314	

Note: An asterisk (*) denotes incumbent.

MONTANA

One member At Large

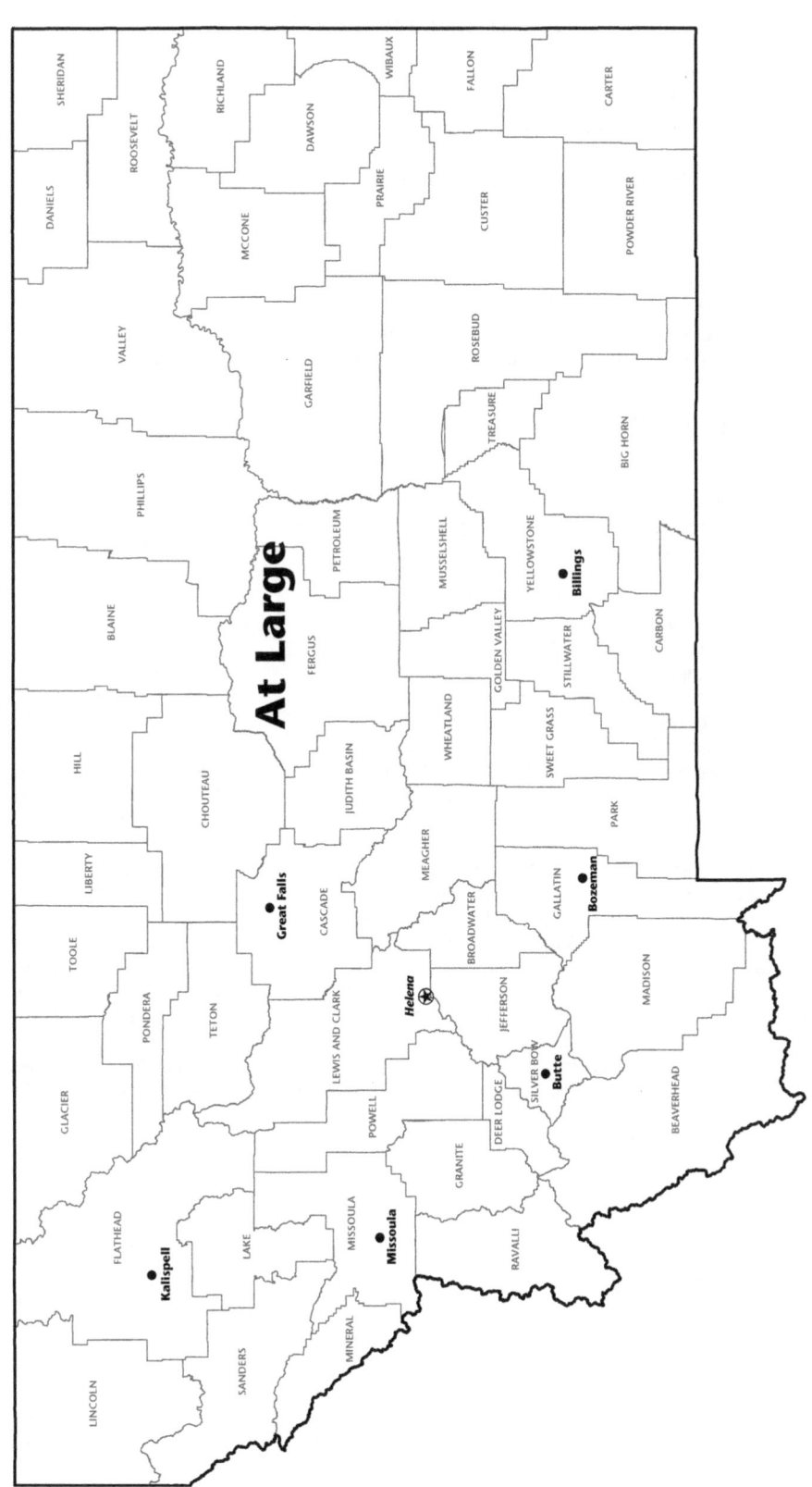

MONTANA

GOVERNOR
Steve Bullock (D). Re-elected 2016 to a four-year term. Previously elected 2012.

SENATORS (1 Democrat, 1 Republican)
Steve Daines (R). Elected 2014 to a six-year term.

Jon Tester (D). Re-elected 2012 to a six-year term. Previously elected 2006.

REPRESENTATIVE (1 Republican)
At Large. Greg Gianforte (R)

Note: Ryan Zinke was re-elected in 2016 but stepped down after the election to become secretary of the interior in the Trump administration. Greg Gianforte won a special election on May 25, 2017, to fill the vacancy.

POSTWAR VOTE FOR PRESIDENT

		Republican		Democratic				Total Vote		Major Vote	
Year	Total Vote	Vote	Candidate	Vote	Candidate	Other Vote	Rep.-Dem. Plurality	Rep.	Dem.	Rep.	Dem.
2016**	497,147	279,240	Trump, Donald J.	177,709	Clinton, Hillary Rodham	40,198	101,531 R	56.2%	35.7%	61.1%	38.9%
2012	484,048	267,928	Romney, W. Mitt	201,839	Obama, Barack H.*	14,281	66,089 R	55.4%	41.7%	57.0%	43.0%
2008	490,302	242,763	McCain, John S. III	231,667	Obama, Barack H.	15,872	11,096 R	49.5%	47.2%	51.2%	48.8%
2004	450,445	266,063	Bush, George W.*	173,710	Kerry, John F.	10,672	92,353 R	59.1%	38.6%	60.5%	39.5%
2000**	410,997	240,178	Bush, George W.	137,126	Gore, Albert Jr.	33,693	103,052 R	58.4%	33.4%	63.7%	36.3%
1996**	407,261	179,652	Dole, Robert "Bob"	167,922	Clinton, Bill*	59,687	11,730 R	44.1%	41.2%	51.7%	48.3%
1992**	410,611	144,207	Bush, George H.*	154,507	Clinton, Bill	111,897	10,300 D	35.1%	37.6%	48.3%	51.7%
1988	365,674	190,412	Bush, George H.	168,936	Dukakis, Michael S.	6,326	21,476 R	52.1%	46.2%	53.0%	47.0%
1984	384,377	232,450	Reagan, Ronald*	146,742	Mondale, Walter F.	5,185	85,708 R	60.5%	38.2%	61.3%	38.7%
1980**	363,952	206,814	Reagan, Ronald	118,032	Carter, Jimmy*	39,106	88,782 R	56.8%	32.4%	63.7%	36.3%
1976	328,734	173,703	Ford, Gerald R.*	149,259	Carter, Jimmy	5,772	24,444 R	52.8%	45.4%	53.8%	46.2%
1972	317,603	183,976	Nixon, Richard M.*	120,197	McGovern, George S.	13,430	63,779 R	57.9%	37.8%	60.5%	39.5%
1968**	274,404	138,835	Nixon, Richard M.	114,117	Humphrey, Hubert Horatio Jr.	21,452	24,718 R	50.6%	41.6%	54.9%	45.1%
1964	278,628	113,032	Goldwater, Barry M. Sr.	164,246	Johnson, Lyndon B.*	1,350	51,214 D	40.6%	58.9%	40.8%	59.2%
1960	277,579	141,841	Nixon, Richard M.	134,891	Kennedy, John F.	847	6,950 R	51.1%	48.6%	51.3%	48.7%
1956	271,171	154,933	Eisenhower, Dwight D.*	116,238	Stevenson, Adlai E. II		38,695 R	57.1%	42.9%	57.1%	42.9%
1952	265,037	157,394	Eisenhower, Dwight D.	106,213	Stevenson, Adlai E. II	1,430	51,181 R	59.4%	40.1%	59.7%	40.3%
1948	224,278	96,770	Dewey, Thomas E.	119,071	Truman, Harry S.*	8,437	22,301 D	43.1%	53.1%	44.8%	55.2%

Note: An asterisk (*) denotes incumbent. **In past elections, the other vote included: 2016 - 28,037 Libertarian (Gary Johnson); 2000 - 24,437 Green (Ralph Nader); 1996 - 55,229 Reform (Ross Perot); 1992 - 107,225 Independent (Perot); 1980 - 29,281 Independent (John Anderson); 1968 - 20,015 American Independent (George Wallace).

MONTANA

POSTWAR VOTE FOR GOVERNOR

Year	Total Vote	Republican Vote	Republican Candidate	Democratic Vote	Democratic Candidate	Other Vote	Rep.-Dem. Plurality	Percentage Total Vote Rep.	Dem.	Major Vote Rep.	Dem.
2016	509,360	236,115	Gianforte, Greg	255,933	Bullock, Steve*	17,312	19,818 D	46.4%	50.2%	48.0%	52.0%
2012	483,489	228,879	Hill, Rick	236,450	Bullock, Steve	18,160	7,571 D	47.3%	48.9%	49.2%	50.8%
2008	486,734	158,268	Brown, Roy	318,670	Schweitzer, Brian*	9,796	160,402 D	32.5%	65.5%	33.2%	66.8%
2004	446,146	205,313	Brown, Bob	225,016	Schweitzer, Brian	15,817	19,703 D	46.0%	50.4%	47.7%	52.3%
2000	410,192	209,135	Martz, Judy	193,131	O'Keefe, Mark	7,926	16,004 R	51.0%	47.1%	52.0%	48.0%
1996**	405,175	320,768	Racicot, Marc*	84,407	Jacobson, Judy		236,361 R	79.2%	20.8%	79.2%	20.8%
1992	407,842	209,401	Racicot, Marc	198,421	Bradley, Dorothy	20	10,980 R	51.3%	48.7%	51.3%	48.7%
1988	367,021	190,604	Stephens, Stan	169,313	Judge, Thomas L.	7,104	21,291 R	51.9%	46.1%	53.0%	47.0%
1984	378,970	100,070	Goodover, Pat M.	266,578	Schwinden, Ted*	12,322	166,508 D	26.4%	70.3%	27.3%	72.7%
1980	360,470	160,896	Ramirez, Jack	199,574	Schwinden, Ted		38,678 D	44.6%	55.4%	44.6%	55.4%
1976	316,720	115,848	Woodahl, Robert	195,420	Judge, Thomas L.*	5,452	79,572 D	36.6%	61.7%	37.2%	62.8%
1972	318,754	146,231	Smith, Ed	172,523	Judge, Thomas L.		26,292 D	45.9%	54.1%	45.9%	54.1%
1968	278,112	116,432	Babcock, Tim M.*	150,481	Anderson, Forrest H.	11,199	34,049 D	41.9%	54.1%	43.6%	56.4%
1964	280,975	144,113	Babcock, Tim M.	136,862	Renne, Roland		7,251 R	51.3%	48.7%	51.3%	48.7%
1960	279,881	154,230	Nutter, Donald G.	125,651	Cannon, Paul		28,579 R	55.1%	44.9%	55.1%	44.9%
1956	270,366	138,878	Aronson, John Hugo*	131,488	Olsen, Arnold		7,390 R	51.4%	48.6%	51.4%	48.6%
1952	263,792	134,423	Aronson, John Hugo	129,369	Bonner, John W.*		5,054 R	51.0%	49.0%	51.0%	49.0%
1948	222,964	97,792	Ford, Samuel C.*	124,267	Bonner, John W.	905	26,475 D	43.9%	55.7%	44.0%	56.0%

Note: An asterisk (*) denotes incumbent. **In 1996 the Democratic vote total included 7,936 absentee ballots cast for the party's initial gubernatorial candidate, Chet Blaylock, who died that October.

POSTWAR VOTE FOR SENATOR

Year	Total Vote	Republican Vote	Republican Candidate	Democratic Vote	Democratic Candidate	Other Vote	Rep.-Dem. Plurality	Percentage Total Vote Rep.	Dem.	Major Vote Rep.	Dem.
2014	369,826	213,709	Daines, Steve	148,184	Curtis, Amanda	7,933	65,525 R	57.8%	40.1%	59.1%	40.9%
2012	486,066	218,051	Rehberg, Dennis "Denny"	236,123	Tester, Jon*	31,892	18,072 D	44.9%	48.6%	48.0%	52.0%
2008	477,658	129,369	Kelleher, Bob	348,289	Baucus, Max S.*		218,920 D	27.1%	72.9%	27.1%	72.9%
2006	406,505	196,283	Burns, Conrad*	199,845	Tester, Jon	10,377	3,562 D	48.3%	49.2%	49.6%	50.4%
2002	326,537	103,611	Taylor, Mike	204,853	Baucus, Max S.*	18,073	101,242 D	31.7%	62.7%	33.6%	66.4%
2000	411,601	208,082	Burns, Conrad*	194,430	Schweitzer, Brian	9,089	13,652 R	50.6%	47.2%	51.7%	48.3%
1996	407,490	182,111	Rehberg, Dennis "Denny"	201,935	Baucus, Max S.*	23,444	19,824 D	44.7%	49.6%	47.4%	52.6%
1994	350,409	218,542	Burns, Conrad*	131,845	Mudd, Jack	22	86,697 R	62.4%	37.6%	62.4%	37.6%
1990	319,336	93,836	Kolstad, Allen C.	217,563	Baucus, Max S.*	7,937	123,727 D	29.4%	68.1%	30.1%	69.9%
1988	365,254	189,445	Burns, Conrad	175,809	Melcher, John*		13,636 R	51.9%	48.1%	51.9%	48.1%
1984	379,155	154,308	Cozzens, Chuck	215,704	Baucus, Max S.*	9,143	61,396 D	40.7%	56.9%	41.7%	58.3%
1982	321,062	133,789	Williams, Larry	174,861	Melcher, John*	12,412	41,072 D	41.7%	54.5%	43.3%	56.7%
1978	287,942	127,589	Williams, Larry	160,353	Baucus, Max S.		32,764 D	44.3%	55.7%	44.3%	55.7%
1976	321,445	115,213	Burger, Stanley C.	206,232	Melcher, John		91,019 D	35.8%	64.2%	35.8%	64.2%
1972	314,925	151,316	Hibbard, Henry S.	163,609	Metcalf, Lee*		12,293 D	48.0%	52.0%	48.0%	52.0%
1970	247,869	97,809	Wallace, Harold E.	150,060	Mansfield, Mike*		52,251 D	39.5%	60.5%	39.5%	60.5%
1966	259,863	121,697	Babcock, Tim M.	138,166	Metcalf, Lee*		16,469 D	46.8%	53.2%	46.8%	53.2%
1964	280,010	99,367	Blewett, Alex	180,643	Mansfield, Mike*		81,276 D	35.5%	64.5%	35.5%	64.5%
1960	276,612	136,281	Fjare, Orvin B.	140,331	Metcalf, Lee		4,050 D	49.3%	50.7%	49.3%	50.7%
1958	229,483	54,573	Welch, Lou W.	174,910	Mansfield, Mike*		120,337 D	23.8%	76.2%	23.8%	76.2%
1954	227,454	112,863	D'Ewart, Wesley A.	114,591	Murray, James E.*		1,728 D	49.6%	50.4%	49.6%	50.4%
1952	262,297	127,360	Ecton, Zales N.*	133,109	Mansfield, Mike	1,828	5,749 D	48.6%	50.7%	48.9%	51.1%
1948	221,003	94,458	Davis, Tom J.	125,193	Murray, James E.*	1,352	30,735 D	42.7%	56.6%	43.0%	57.0%
1946	190,566	101,901	Ecton, Zales N.	86,476	Erickson, Leif	2,189	15,425 R	53.5%	45.4%	54.1%	45.9%

Note: An asterisk (*) denotes incumbent.

MONTANA

PRESIDENT 2016

2010 Census Population	County	Total Vote	Republican (Trump)	Democratic (Clinton)	Other	Rep.-Dem. Plurality		Percentage			
								Total Vote		Major Vote	
								Rep.	Dem.	Rep.	Dem.
9,246	BEAVERHEAD	4,849	3,353	1,143	353	2,210 R		69.1%	23.6%	74.6%	25.4%
12,865	BIG HORN	4,237	1,853	2,094	290	241 D		43.7%	49.4%	46.9%	53.1%
6,491	BLAINE	2,684	1,268	1,202	214	66 R		47.2%	44.8%	51.3%	48.7%
5,612	BROADWATER	3,133	2,348	573	212	1,775 R		74.9%	18.3%	80.4%	19.6%
10,078	CARBON	5,991	3,748	1,828	415	1,920 R		62.6%	30.5%	67.2%	32.8%
1,160	CARTER	786	678	70	38	608 R		86.3%	8.9%	90.6%	9.4%
81,327	CASCADE	34,571	19,632	12,175	2,764	7,457 R		56.8%	35.2%	61.7%	38.3%
5,813	CHOUTEAU	2,603	1,679	732	192	947 R		64.5%	28.1%	69.6%	30.4%
11,699	CUSTER	5,185	3,657	1,176	352	2,481 R		70.5%	22.7%	75.7%	24.3%
1,751	DANIELS	962	730	168	64	562 R		75.9%	17.5%	81.3%	18.7%
8,966	DAWSON	4,374	3,320	787	267	2,533 R		75.9%	18.0%	80.8%	19.2%
9,298	DEER LODGE	4,206	1,763	2,058	385	295 D		41.9%	48.9%	46.1%	53.9%
2,890	FALLON	1,484	1,279	154	51	1,125 R		86.2%	10.4%	89.3%	10.7%
11,586	FERGUS	5,840	4,269	1,202	369	3,067 R		73.1%	20.6%	78.0%	22.0%
90,928	FLATHEAD	46,571	30,240	13,293	3,038	16,947 R		64.9%	28.5%	69.5%	30.5%
89,513	GALLATIN	53,819	23,802	24,246	5,771	444 D		44.2%	45.1%	49.5%	50.5%
1,206	GARFIELD	718	653	34	31	619 R		90.9%	4.7%	95.1%	4.9%
13,399	GLACIER	5,075	1,620	3,121	334	1,501 D		31.9%	61.5%	34.2%	65.8%
884	GOLDEN VALLEY	474	365	71	38	294 R		77.0%	15.0%	83.7%	16.3%
3,079	GRANITE	1,777	1,192	472	113	720 R		67.1%	26.6%	71.6%	28.4%
16,096	HILL	6,445	3,478	2,371	596	1,107 R		54.0%	36.8%	59.5%	40.5%
11,406	JEFFERSON	6,714	4,177	1,998	539	2,179 R		62.2%	29.8%	67.6%	32.4%
2,072	JUDITH BASIN	1,208	872	235	101	637 R		72.2%	19.5%	78.8%	21.2%
28,746	LAKE	13,181	7,530	4,776	875	2,754 R		57.1%	36.2%	61.2%	38.8%
63,395	LEWIS AND CLARK	34,478	16,895	14,478	3,105	2,417 R		49.0%	42.0%	53.9%	46.1%
2,339	LIBERTY	961	698	206	57	492 R		72.6%	21.4%	77.2%	22.8%
19,687	LINCOLN	9,330	6,729	2,041	560	4,688 R		72.1%	21.9%	76.7%	23.3%
7,691	MADISON	4,778	3,297	1,180	301	2,117 R		69.0%	24.7%	73.6%	26.4%
1,734	MCCONE	1,060	862	154	44	708 R		81.3%	14.5%	84.8%	15.2%
1,891	MEAGHER	977	729	193	55	536 R		74.6%	19.8%	79.1%	20.9%
4,223	MINERAL	2,012	1,330	519	163	811 R		66.1%	25.8%	71.9%	28.1%
109,299	MISSOULA	59,203	22,250	31,543	5,410	9,293 D		37.6%	53.3%	41.4%	58.6%
4,538	MUSSELSHELL	2,441	1,967	332	142	1,635 R		80.6%	13.6%	85.6%	14.4%
15,636	PARK	9,359	4,980	3,595	784	1,385 R		53.2%	38.4%	58.1%	41.9%
494	PETROLEUM	322	278	30	14	248 R		86.3%	9.3%	90.3%	9.7%
4,253	PHILLIPS	2,171	1,723	318	130	1,405 R		79.4%	14.6%	84.4%	15.6%
6,153	PONDERA	2,723	1,799	738	186	1,061 R		66.1%	27.1%	70.9%	29.1%
1,743	POWDER RIVER	1,053	884	127	42	757 R		84.0%	12.1%	87.4%	12.6%
7,027	POWELL	2,794	2,029	551	214	1,478 R		72.6%	19.7%	78.6%	21.4%
1,179	PRAIRIE	689	556	100	33	456 R		80.7%	14.5%	84.8%	15.2%
40,212	RAVALLI	22,556	14,810	6,223	1,523	8,587 R		65.7%	27.6%	70.4%	29.6%
9,746	RICHLAND	4,871	3,908	671	292	3,237 R		80.2%	13.8%	85.3%	14.7%
10,425	ROOSEVELT	3,652	1,797	1,560	295	237 R		49.2%	42.7%	53.5%	46.5%
9,233	ROSEBUD	3,453	2,253	987	213	1,266 R		65.2%	28.6%	69.5%	30.5%
11,413	SANDERS	5,953	4,286	1,218	449	3,068 R		72.0%	20.5%	77.9%	22.1%
3,384	SHERIDAN	1,835	1,241	477	117	764 R		67.6%	26.0%	72.2%	27.8%
34,200	SILVER BOW	16,452	6,376	8,619	1,457	2,243 D		38.8%	52.4%	42.5%	57.5%
9,117	STILLWATER	4,873	3,661	908	304	2,753 R		75.1%	18.6%	80.1%	19.9%
3,651	SWEET GRASS	2,107	1,595	402	110	1,193 R		75.7%	19.1%	79.9%	20.1%
6,073	TETON	3,188	2,170	808	210	1,362 R		68.1%	25.3%	72.9%	27.1%
5,324	TOOLE	2,037	1,497	402	138	1,095 R		73.5%	19.7%	78.8%	21.2%
718	TREASURE	443	351	59	33	292 R		79.2%	13.3%	85.6%	14.4%
7,369	VALLEY	3,894	2,698	886	310	1,812 R		69.3%	22.7%	75.3%	24.7%
2,168	WHEATLAND	946	702	179	65	523 R		74.2%	18.9%	79.7%	20.3%
1,017	WIBAUX	541	463	55	23	408 R		85.6%	10.2%	89.4%	10.6%
147,972	YELLOWSTONE	69,108	40,920	22,171	6,017	18,749 R		59.2%	32.1%	64.9%	35.1%
989,415	TOTAL	497,147	279,240	177,709	40,198	101,531 R		56.2%	35.7%	61.1%	38.9%

MONTANA
GOVERNOR 2016

2010 Census Population	County	Total Vote	Republican (Gianforte)	Democratic (Bullock)	Other	Rep.-Dem. Plurality	Percentage Total Vote Rep.	Dem.	Percentage Major Vote Rep.	Dem.
9,246	BEAVERHEAD	5,019	2,880	1,989	150	891 R	57.4%	39.6%	59.1%	40.9%
12,865	BIG HORN	4,363	1,497	2,724	142	1,227 D	34.3%	62.4%	35.5%	64.5%
6,491	BLAINE	2,782	1,080	1,629	73	549 D	38.8%	58.6%	39.9%	60.1%
5,612	BROADWATER	3,224	1,827	1,282	115	545 R	56.7%	39.8%	58.8%	41.2%
10,078	CARBON	6,113	3,145	2,775	193	370 R	51.4%	45.4%	53.1%	46.9%
1,160	CARTER	794	650	128	16	522 R	81.9%	16.1%	83.5%	16.5%
81,327	CASCADE	35,454	15,393	19,019	1,042	3,626 D	43.4%	53.6%	44.7%	55.3%
5,813	CHOUTEAU	2,686	1,357	1,260	69	97 R	50.5%	46.9%	51.9%	48.1%
11,699	CUSTER	5,301	3,037	2,065	199	972 R	57.3%	39.0%	59.5%	40.5%
1,751	DANIELS	971	649	289	33	360 R	66.8%	29.8%	69.2%	30.8%
8,966	DAWSON	4,426	3,147	1,077	202	2,070 R	71.1%	24.3%	74.5%	25.5%
9,298	DEER LODGE	4,359	1,147	3,034	178	1,887 D	26.3%	69.6%	27.4%	72.6%
2,890	FALLON	1,477	1,062	368	47	694 R	71.9%	24.9%	74.3%	25.7%
11,586	FERGUS	6,020	3,657	2,176	187	1,481 R	60.7%	36.1%	62.7%	37.3%
90,928	FLATHEAD	47,452	26,384	19,202	1,866	7,182 R	55.6%	40.5%	57.9%	42.1%
89,513	GALLATIN	55,144	22,534	30,758	1,852	8,224 D	40.9%	55.8%	42.3%	57.7%
1,206	GARFIELD	732	603	114	15	489 R	82.4%	15.6%	84.1%	15.9%
13,399	GLACIER	5,207	1,276	3,799	132	2,523 D	24.5%	73.0%	25.1%	74.9%
884	GOLDEN VALLEY	489	308	166	15	142 R	63.0%	33.9%	65.0%	35.0%
3,079	GRANITE	1,826	979	790	57	189 R	53.6%	43.3%	55.3%	44.7%
16,096	HILL	6,652	2,642	3,811	199	1,169 D	39.7%	57.3%	40.9%	59.1%
11,406	JEFFERSON	6,891	3,602	3,086	203	516 R	52.3%	44.8%	53.9%	46.1%
2,072	JUDITH BASIN	1,236	721	485	30	236 R	58.3%	39.2%	59.8%	40.2%
28,746	LAKE	13,451	6,363	6,561	527	198 D	47.3%	48.8%	49.2%	50.8%
63,395	LEWIS AND CLARK	35,573	13,296	21,363	914	8,067 D	37.4%	60.1%	38.4%	61.6%
2,339	LIBERTY	978	573	378	27	195 R	58.6%	38.7%	60.3%	39.7%
19,687	LINCOLN	9,442	5,728	3,308	406	2,420 R	60.7%	35.0%	63.4%	36.6%
7,691	MADISON	4,877	2,745	1,982	150	763 R	56.3%	40.6%	58.1%	41.9%
1,734	MCCONE	1,070	798	248	24	550 R	74.6%	23.2%	76.3%	23.7%
1,891	MEAGHER	997	602	364	31	238 R	60.4%	36.5%	62.3%	37.7%
4,223	MINERAL	2,062	1,065	878	119	187 R	51.6%	42.6%	54.8%	45.2%
109,299	MISSOULA	60,858	19,078	39,717	2,063	20,639 D	31.3%	65.3%	32.4%	67.6%
4,538	MUSSELSHELL	2,465	1,599	741	125	858 R	64.9%	30.1%	68.3%	31.7%
15,636	PARK	9,550	4,134	5,066	350	932 D	43.3%	53.0%	44.9%	55.1%
494	PETROLEUM	331	247	74	10	173 R	74.6%	22.4%	76.9%	23.1%
4,253	PHILLIPS	2,231	1,693	493	45	1,200 R	75.9%	22.1%	77.4%	22.6%
6,153	PONDERA	2,801	1,423	1,310	68	113 R	50.8%	46.8%	52.1%	47.9%
1,743	POWDER RIVER	1,066	780	257	29	523 R	73.2%	24.1%	75.2%	24.8%
7,027	POWELL	2,847	1,639	1,103	105	536 R	57.6%	38.7%	59.8%	40.2%
1,179	PRAIRIE	701	501	173	27	328 R	71.5%	24.7%	74.3%	25.7%
40,212	RAVALLI	23,006	12,713	9,455	838	3,258 R	55.3%	41.1%	57.3%	42.7%
9,746	RICHLAND	4,863	3,577	1,085	201	2,492 R	73.6%	22.3%	76.7%	23.3%
10,425	ROOSEVELT	3,727	1,525	2,039	163	514 D	40.9%	54.7%	42.8%	57.2%
9,233	ROSEBUD	3,546	2,018	1,430	98	588 R	56.9%	40.3%	58.5%	41.5%
11,413	SANDERS	6,039	3,470	2,267	302	1,203 R	57.5%	37.5%	60.5%	39.5%
3,384	SHERIDAN	1,883	1,033	773	77	260 R	54.9%	41.1%	57.2%	42.8%
34,200	SILVER BOW	17,041	4,512	12,007	522	7,495 D	26.5%	70.5%	27.3%	72.7%
9,117	STILLWATER	4,945	3,036	1,748	161	1,288 R	61.4%	35.3%	63.5%	36.5%
3,651	SWEET GRASS	2,148	1,385	706	57	679 R	64.5%	32.9%	66.2%	33.8%
6,073	TETON	3,292	1,777	1,441	74	336 R	54.0%	43.8%	55.2%	44.8%
5,324	TOOLE	2,069	1,214	799	56	415 R	58.7%	38.6%	60.3%	39.7%
718	TREASURE	448	276	160	12	116 R	61.6%	35.7%	63.3%	36.7%
7,369	VALLEY	3,952	2,343	1,465	144	878 R	59.3%	37.1%	61.5%	38.5%
2,168	WHEATLAND	966	547	399	20	148 R	56.6%	41.3%	57.8%	42.2%
1,017	WIBAUX	545	381	143	21	238 R	69.9%	26.2%	72.7%	27.3%
147,972	YELLOWSTONE	70,972	34,467	33,974	2,531	493 R	48.6%	47.9%	50.4%	49.6%
989,415	TOTAL	509,360	236,115	255,933	17,312	19,818 D	46.4%	50.2%	48.0%	52.0%

MONTANA

HOUSE OF REPRESENTATIVES

CD	Year	Total Vote	Republican		Democratic		Other Vote	Rep.-Dem. Plurality	Percentage			
									Total Vote		Major Vote	
			Vote	Candidate	Vote	Candidate			Rep.	Dem.	Rep.	Dem.
At Large	2016	507,831	285,358	ZINKE, RYAN*	205,919	JUNEAU, DENISE	16,554	79,439 R	56.2%	40.5%	58.1%	41.9%
At Large	2014	367,963	203,871	ZINKE, RYAN	148,690	LEWIS, JOHN	15,402	55,181 R	55.4%	40.4%	57.8%	42.2%
At Large	2012	479,740	255,468	DAINES, STEVE	204,939	GILLAN, KIM	19,333	50,529 R	53.3%	42.7%	55.5%	44.5%
At Large	2010	360,341	217,696	REHBERG, DENNIS "DENNY"*	121,954	MCDONALD, DENNIS	20,691	95,742 R	60.4%	33.8%	64.1%	35.9%
At Large	2008	480,900	308,470	REHBERG, DENNIS "DENNY"*	155,930	DRISCOLL, JOHN	16,500	152,540 R	64.1%	32.4%	66.4%	33.6%
At Large	2006	406,134	239,124	REHBERG, DENNIS "DENNY"*	158,916	LINDEEN, MONICA	8,094	80,208 R	58.9%	39.1%	60.1%	39.9%
At Large	2004	444,230	286,076	REHBERG, DENNIS "DENNY"*	145,606	VELAZQUEZ, TRACY E.	12,548	140,470 R	64.4%	32.8%	66.3%	33.7%
At Large	2002	331,321	214,100	REHBERG, DENNIS "DENNY"*	108,233	KELLY, STEVE	8,988	105,867 R	64.6%	32.7%	66.4%	33.6%
At Large	2000	410,523	211,418	REHBERG, DENNIS "DENNY"	189,971	KEENAN, NANCY	9,134	21,447 R	51.5%	46.3%	52.7%	47.3%
At Large	1998	331,551	175,748	HILL, RICK*	147,073	DESCHAMPS, DUSTY	8,730	28,675 R	53.0%	44.4%	54.4%	45.6%
At Large	1996	404,426	211,975	HILL, RICK	174,516	YELLOWTAIL, BILL	17,935	37,459 R	52.4%	43.2%	54.8%	45.2%
At Large	1994	352,133	148,715	JAMISON, CY	171,372	WILLIAMS, JOHN PATRICK "PAT"*	32,046	22,657 D	42.2%	48.7%	46.5%	53.5%
At Large	1992	403,735	189,570	MARLENEE, RON*	203,711	WILLIAMS, JOHN PATRICK "PAT"*	10,454	14,141 D	47.0%	50.5%	48.2%	51.8%

Note: An asterisk (*) denotes incumbent.

MONTANA

GENERAL AND PRIMARY ELECTIONS

2016 GENERAL ELECTIONS: OTHER VOTES

President   Other vote was 28,037 Libertarian (Gary Johnson), 7,970 Green (Jill Stein), 2,297 Write-in (Evan McMullin), 1,570 American Delta (Roque De La Fuente), 324 Write-in (Scattered Write-in)

Governor   Other vote was 17,312 Libertarian (Ted Dunlap)

House   Other vote was:

   At Large   16,554 Libertarian (Rick Breckenridge)

2016 PRIMARY ELECTIONS: SUPPLEMENTARY INFORMATION

Primary   June 7, 2016   **Registration** (as of June 7, 2016)   648,764   No Party Registration

Primary Type   Open—Any registered voter could participate in the party primary of his or her choice.

	REPUBLICAN PRIMARIES			DEMOCRATIC PRIMARIES		
President	Trump, Donald J.	115,594	73.7%	Sanders, Bernard	65,156	51.6%
	Cruz, Ted	14,682	9.4%	Clinton, Hillary Rodham	55,805	44.2%
	Kasich, John R.	10,777	6.9%	No Preference	5,415	4.3%
	No Preference	7,369	4.7%			
	Rubio, Marco	5,192	3.3%			
	Bush, Jeb	3,274	2.1%			
	TOTAL	156,888		TOTAL	126,376	
Governor	Gianforte, Greg	111,348	76.3%	Bullock, Steve*	111,675	91.2%
	Nelson, Terry	34,600	23.7%	McChesney, Bill	10,744	8.8%
	TOTAL	145,948		TOTAL	122,419	
Congressional At Large	Zinke, Ryan*	144,660	100.0%	Juneau, Denise	112,821	100.0%
	TOTAL	144,660		TOTAL	112,821	

Note: An asterisk (*) denotes incumbent.

NEBRASKA

Congressional districts first established for elections held in 2012

3 members

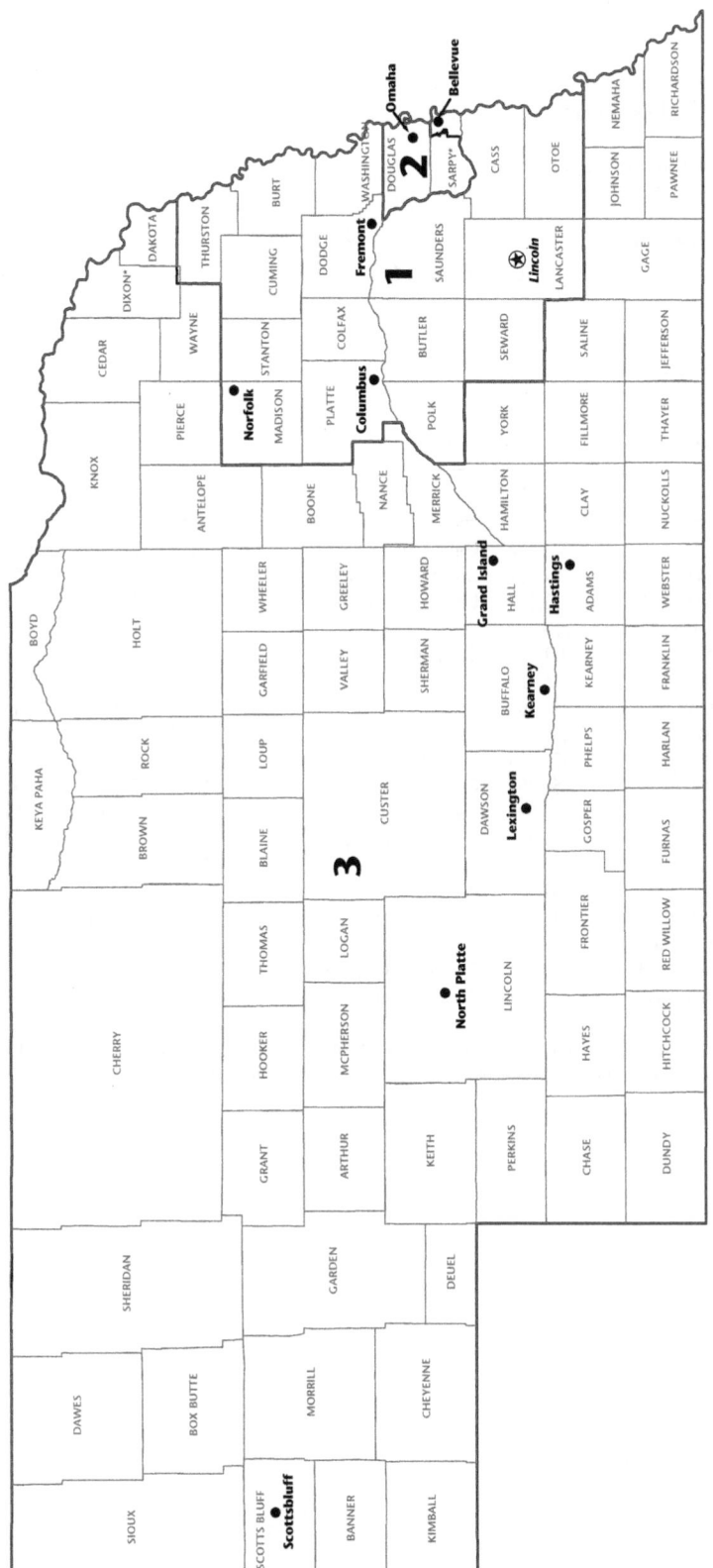

* Asterisk indicates a county whose boundaries include parts of two or more congressional districts.

NEBRASKA

GOVERNOR
Pete Ricketts (R). Elected 2014 to a four-year term.

SENATORS (2 Republicans)
Deb Fischer (R). Elected 2012 to a six-year term.

Ben Sasse (R). Elected 2014 to a six-year term.

REPRESENTATIVES (3 Republicans)
1. Jeff Fortenberry (R)　　　2. Don Bacon (R)　　　3. Adrian Smith (R)

POSTWAR VOTE FOR PRESIDENT

Year	Total Vote	Republican		Democratic		Other Vote	Rep.-Dem. Plurality	Percentage			
								Total Vote		Major Vote	
		Vote	Candidate	Vote	Candidate			Rep.	Dem.	Rep.	Dem.
2016**	844,227	495,961	Trump, Donald J.	284,494	Clinton, Hillary Rodham	63,772	211,467 R	58.7%	33.7%	63.5%	36.5%
2012	794,379	475,064	Romney, W. Mitt	302,081	Obama, Barack H.*	17,234	172,983 R	59.8%	38.0%	61.1%	38.9%
2008	801,281	452,979	McCain, John S. III	333,319	Obama, Barack H.	14,983	119,660 R	56.5%	41.6%	57.6%	42.4%
2004	778,186	512,814	Bush, George W.*	254,328	Kerry, John F.	11,044	258,486 R	65.9%	32.7%	66.8%	33.2%
2000**	697,019	433,862	Bush, George W.	231,780	Gore, Albert Jr.	31,377	202,082 R	62.2%	33.3%	65.2%	34.8%
1996**	677,415	363,467	Dole, Robert "Bob"	236,761	Clinton, Bill*	77,187	126,706 R	53.7%	35.0%	60.6%	39.4%
1992**	737,546	343,678	Bush, George H.*	216,864	Clinton, Bill	177,004	126,814 R	46.6%	29.4%	61.3%	38.7%
1988	661,465	397,956	Bush, George H.	259,235	Dukakis, Michael S.	4,274	138,721 R	60.2%	39.2%	60.6%	39.4%
1984	652,090	460,054	Reagan, Ronald*	187,866	Mondale, Walter F.	4,170	272,188 R	70.6%	28.8%	71.0%	29.0%
1980**	640,854	419,937	Reagan, Ronald	166,851	Carter, Jimmy*	54,066	253,086 R	65.5%	26.0%	71.6%	28.4%
1976	607,668	359,705	Ford, Gerald R.*	233,692	Carter, Jimmy	14,271	126,013 R	59.2%	38.5%	60.6%	39.4%
1972	576,289	406,298	Nixon, Richard M.*	169,991	McGovern, George S.		236,307 R	70.5%	29.5%	70.5%	29.5%
1968**	536,851	321,163	Nixon, Richard M.	170,784	Humphrey, Hubert Horatio Jr.	44,904	150,379 R	59.8%	31.8%	65.3%	34.7%
1964	584,154	276,847	Goldwater, Barry M. Sr.	307,307	Johnson, Lyndon B.*		30,460 D	47.4%	52.6%	47.4%	52.6%
1960	613,095	380,553	Nixon, Richard M.	232,542	Kennedy, John F.		148,011 R	62.1%	37.9%	62.1%	37.9%
1956	577,137	378,108	Eisenhower, Dwight D.*	199,029	Stevenson, Adlai E. II		179,079 R	65.5%	34.5%	65.5%	34.5%
1952	609,660	421,603	Eisenhower, Dwight D.	188,057	Stevenson, Adlai E. II		233,546 R	69.2%	30.8%	69.2%	30.8%
1948	488,940	264,774	Dewey, Thomas E.	224,165	Truman, Harry S.*	1	40,609 R	54.2%	45.8%	54.2%	45.8%

Note: An asterisk (*) denotes incumbent. **In past elections, the other vote included: 2016 - 38,946 Libertarian (Gary Johnson); 2000 - 24,540 Green (Ralph Nader); 1996 - 71,278 Reform (Ross Perot); 1992 - 174,104 Independent (Perot); 1980 - 44,993 Independent (John Anderson); 1968 - 44,904 American Independent (George Wallace).

NEBRASKA

POSTWAR VOTE FOR GOVERNOR

Year	Total Vote	Republican		Democratic		Other Vote	Rep.-Dem. Plurality	Percentage			
								Total Vote		Major Vote	
		Vote	Candidate	Vote	Candidate			Rep.	Dem.	Rep.	Dem.
2014	540,202	308,751	Ricketts, Pete	211,905	Hassebrook, Chuck	19,546	96,846 R	57.2%	39.2%	59.3%	40.7%
2010	487,988	360,645	Heineman, Dave*	127,343	Meister, Mike		233,302 R	73.9%	26.1%	73.9%	26.1%
2006	593,357	435,507	Heineman, Dave*	145,115	Hahn, David	12,735	290,392 R	73.4%	24.5%	75.0%	25.0%
2002	480,991	330,349	Johanns, Mike*	132,348	Dean, Stormy	18,294	198,001 R	68.7%	27.5%	71.4%	28.6%
1998	545,238	293,910	Johanns, Mike	250,678	Hoppner, Bill	650	43,232 R	53.9%	46.0%	54.0%	46.0%
1994	579,561	148,230	Spence, Gene	423,270	Nelson, Earl "Ben"*	8,061	275,040 D	25.6%	73.0%	25.9%	74.1%
1990	586,542	288,741	Orr, Kay*	292,771	Nelson, Earl "Ben"	5,030	4,030 D	49.2%	49.9%	49.7%	50.3%
1986	564,422	298,325	Orr, Kay	265,156	Boosalis, Helen	941	33,169 R	52.9%	47.0%	52.9%	47.1%
1982	547,902	270,203	Thone, Charles*	277,436	Kerrey, Bob	263	7,233 D	49.3%	50.6%	49.3%	50.7%
1978	492,423	275,473	Thone, Charles	216,754	Whelan, Gerald T.	196	58,719 R	55.9%	44.0%	56.0%	44.0%
1974	451,306	159,780	Marvel, Richard D.	267,012	Exon, J. James*	24,514	107,232 D	35.4%	59.2%	37.4%	62.6%
1970	461,619	201,994	Tiemann, Norbert T.*	248,552	Exon, J. James	11,073	46,558 D	43.8%	53.8%	44.8%	55.2%
1966**	486,396	299,245	Tiemann, Norbert T.	186,985	Sorensen, Philip C.	166	112,260 R	61.5%	38.4%	61.5%	38.5%
1964	578,090	231,029	Burney, Dwight W.	347,026	Morrison, Frank B.*	35	115,997 D	40.0%	60.0%	40.0%	60.0%
1962	464,585	221,885	Seaton, Fred A.	242,669	Morrison, Frank B.*	31	20,784 D	47.8%	52.2%	47.8%	52.2%
1960	598,971	287,302	Cooper, John R.	311,344	Morrison, Frank B.	325	24,042 D	48.0%	52.0%	48.0%	52.0%
1958	421,067	209,705	Anderson, Victor E.*	211,345	Brooks, Ralph G.	17	1,640 D	49.8%	50.2%	49.8%	50.2%
1956	567,916	308,285	Anderson, Victor E.*	228,048	Sorrell, Frank	31,583	80,237 R	54.3%	40.2%	57.5%	42.5%
1954	414,841	250,080	Anderson, Victor E.	164,753	Ritchie, William	8	85,327 R	60.3%	39.7%	60.3%	39.7%
1952	594,814	365,409	Crosby, Robert B.	229,400	Raecke, Walter R.	5	136,009 R	61.4%	38.6%	61.4%	38.6%
1950	449,728	247,089	Peterson, Val*	202,638	Raecke, Walter R.	1	44,451 R	54.9%	45.1%	54.9%	45.1%
1948	476,352	286,119	Peterson, Val*	190,214	Sorrell, Frank	19	95,905 R	60.1%	39.9%	60.1%	39.9%
1946	380,835	249,468	Peterson, Val	131,367	Sorrell, Frank		118,101 R	65.5%	34.5%	65.5%	34.5%

Note: An asterisk (*) denotes incumbent. **The term of office of Nebraska's governor was increased from two to four years effective with the 1966 election.

POSTWAR VOTE FOR SENATOR

Year	Total Vote	Republican		Democratic		Other Vote	Rep.-Dem. Plurality	Percentage			
								Total Vote		Major Vote	
		Vote	Candidate	Vote	Candidate			Rep.	Dem.	Rep.	Dem.
2014	540,337	347,636	Sasse, Ben	170,127	Domina, David A.	22,574	177,509 R	64.3%	31.5%	67.1%	32.9%
2012	788,572	455,593	Fischer, Deb	332,979	Kerrey, Bob		122,614 R	57.8%	42.2%	57.8%	42.2%
2008	792,511	455,854	Johanns, Mike	317,456	Kleeb, Scott	19,201	138,398 R	57.5%	40.1%	58.9%	41.1%
2006	592,316	213,928	Ricketts, Pete	378,388	Nelson, Earl "Ben"*		164,460 D	36.1%	63.9%	36.1%	63.9%
2002	480,217	397,438	Hagel, Chuck*	70,290	Matulka, Charlie A.	12,489	327,148 R	82.8%	14.6%	85.0%	15.0%
2000	692,344	337,967	Stenberg, Don	353,097	Nelson, Earl "Ben"	1,280	15,130 D	48.8%	51.0%	48.9%	51.1%
1996	676,789	379,933	Hagel, Chuck	281,904	Nelson, Earl "Ben"	14,952	98,029 R	56.1%	41.7%	57.4%	42.6%
1994	579,205	260,668	Stoney, Jan	317,297	Kerrey, Bob*	1,240	56,629 D	45.0%	54.8%	45.1%	54.9%
1990	593,828	243,013	Daub, Harold J.	349,779	Exon, J. James*	1,036	106,766 D	40.9%	58.9%	41.0%	59.0%
1988	667,860	278,250	Karnes, David	378,717	Kerrey, Bob	10,893	100,467 D	41.7%	56.7%	42.4%	57.6%
1984	639,668	307,147	Hoch, Nancy	332,217	Exon, J. James*	304	25,070 D	48.0%	51.9%	48.0%	52.0%
1982	545,647	155,760	Keck, Jim	363,350	Zorinsky, Edward*	26,537	207,590 D	28.5%	66.6%	30.0%	70.0%
1978	494,368	159,806	Shasteen, Donald	334,276	Exon, J. James	286	174,470 D	32.3%	67.6%	32.3%	67.7%
1976	598,314	284,284	McCollister, John Y.	313,809	Zorinsky, Edward	221	29,525 D	47.5%	52.4%	47.5%	52.5%
1972	568,580	301,841	Curtis, Carl T.*	265,922	Carpenter, Terry	817	35,919 R	53.1%	46.8%	53.2%	46.8%
1970	458,966	240,894	Hruska, Roman L.*	217,681	Morrison, Frank B.	391	23,213 R	52.5%	47.4%	52.5%	47.5%
1966	485,101	296,116	Curtis, Carl T.*	187,950	Morrison, Frank B.	1,035	108,166 R	61.0%	38.7%	61.2%	38.8%
1964	563,401	345,772	Hruska, Roman L.*	217,605	Arndt, Raymond W.	24	128,167 R	61.4%	38.6%	61.4%	38.6%
1960	598,743	352,748	Curtis, Carl T.*	245,837	Conrad, Robert B.	158	106,911 R	58.9%	41.1%	58.9%	41.1%
1958	417,385	232,227	Hruska, Roman L.	185,152	Morrison, Frank B.	6	47,075 R	55.6%	44.4%	55.6%	44.4%
1954	418,691	255,695	Curtis, Carl T.	162,990	Neville, Keith	6	92,705 R	61.1%	38.9%	61.1%	38.9%
1954S**	411,225	250,341	Hruska, Roman L.	160,881	Green, James F.	3	89,460 R	60.9%	39.1%	60.9%	39.1%
1952	591,749	408,971	Butler, Hugh*	164,660	Long, Stanley D.	18,118	244,311 R	69.1%	27.8%	71.3%	28.7%
1952S**	581,750	369,841	Griswold, Dwight	211,898	Ritchie, William	11	157,943 R	63.6%	36.4%	63.6%	36.4%
1948	471,895	267,575	Wherry, Kenneth S.*	204,320	Carpenter, Terry		63,255 R	56.7%	43.3%	56.7%	43.3%
1946	382,959	271,208	Butler, Hugh*	111,751	Mekota, John E.		159,457 R	70.8%	29.2%	70.8%	29.2%

Note: An asterisk (*) denotes incumbent. **One each of the 1952 and 1954 elections was for a short term to fill a vacancy.

NEBRASKA

PRESIDENT 2016

2010 Census Population	County	Total Vote	Republican (Trump)	Democratic (Clinton)	Other	Rep.-Dem. Plurality		Percentage Total Vote Rep.	Dem.	Major Vote Rep.	Dem.
31,364	ADAMS	13,513	9,287	3,302	924	5,985	R	68.7%	24.4%	73.8%	26.2%
6,685	ANTELOPE	3,281	2,732	383	166	2,349	R	83.3%	11.7%	87.7%	12.3%
460	ARTHUR	273	244	17	12	227	R	89.4%	6.2%	93.5%	6.5%
690	BANNER	402	357	19	26	338	R	88.8%	4.7%	94.9%	5.1%
478	BLAINE	317	276	30	11	246	R	87.1%	9.5%	90.2%	9.8%
5,505	BOONE	2,905	2,299	414	192	1,885	R	79.1%	14.3%	84.7%	15.3%
11,308	BOX BUTTE	4,924	3,617	965	342	2,652	R	73.5%	19.6%	78.9%	21.1%
2,099	BOYD	1,156	983	128	45	855	R	85.0%	11.1%	88.5%	11.5%
3,145	BROWN	1,597	1,385	153	59	1,232	R	86.7%	9.6%	90.1%	9.9%
46,102	BUFFALO	21,129	14,569	4,763	1,797	9,806	R	69.0%	22.5%	75.4%	24.6%
6,858	BURT	3,558	2,367	930	261	1,437	R	66.5%	26.1%	71.8%	28.2%
8,395	BUTLER	3,981	3,079	691	211	2,388	R	77.3%	17.4%	81.7%	18.3%
25,241	CASS	12,933	8,452	3,484	997	4,968	R	65.4%	26.9%	70.8%	29.2%
8,852	CEDAR	4,420	3,532	571	317	2,961	R	79.9%	12.9%	86.1%	13.9%
3,966	CHASE	1,898	1,648	171	79	1,477	R	86.8%	9.0%	90.6%	9.4%
5,713	CHERRY	3,118	2,623	317	178	2,306	R	84.1%	10.2%	89.2%	10.8%
9,998	CHEYENNE	4,711	3,665	711	335	2,954	R	77.8%	15.1%	83.8%	16.2%
6,542	CLAY	3,065	2,422	477	166	1,945	R	79.0%	15.6%	83.5%	16.5%
10,515	COLFAX	3,214	2,171	859	184	1,312	R	67.5%	26.7%	71.7%	28.3%
9,139	CUMING	4,074	3,122	719	233	2,403	R	76.6%	17.6%	81.3%	18.7%
10,939	CUSTER	5,652	4,695	641	316	4,054	R	83.1%	11.3%	88.0%	12.0%
21,006	DAKOTA	6,279	3,616	2,314	349	1,302	R	57.6%	36.9%	61.0%	39.0%
9,182	DAWES	3,676	2,632	801	243	1,831	R	71.6%	21.8%	76.7%	23.3%
24,326	DAWSON	8,635	5,984	2,136	515	3,848	R	69.3%	24.7%	73.7%	26.3%
1,941	DEUEL	984	809	120	55	689	R	82.2%	12.2%	87.1%	12.9%
6,000	DIXON	2,782	2,041	556	185	1,485	R	73.4%	20.0%	78.6%	21.4%
36,691	DODGE	15,529	9,933	4,544	1,052	5,389	R	64.0%	29.3%	68.6%	31.4%
517,110	DOUGLAS	240,433	108,077	113,798	18,558	5,721	D	45.0%	47.3%	48.7%	51.3%
2,008	DUNDY	953	823	89	41	734	R	86.4%	9.3%	90.2%	9.8%
5,890	FILLMORE	2,941	2,130	613	198	1,517	R	72.4%	20.8%	77.7%	22.3%
3,225	FRANKLIN	1,673	1,347	250	76	1,097	R	80.5%	14.9%	84.3%	15.7%
2,756	FRONTIER	1,328	1,110	161	57	949	R	83.6%	12.1%	87.3%	12.7%
4,959	FURNAS	2,340	1,921	304	115	1,617	R	82.1%	13.0%	86.3%	13.7%
22,311	GAGE	10,048	6,380	2,935	733	3,445	R	63.5%	29.2%	68.5%	31.5%
2,057	GARDEN	1,075	869	153	53	716	R	80.8%	14.2%	85.0%	15.0%
2,049	GARFIELD	980	821	121	38	700	R	83.8%	12.3%	87.2%	12.8%
2,044	GOSPER	1,010	794	166	50	628	R	78.6%	16.4%	82.7%	17.3%
614	GRANT	405	367	20	18	347	R	90.6%	4.9%	94.8%	5.2%
2,538	GREELEY	1,175	912	210	53	702	R	77.6%	17.9%	81.3%	18.7%
58,607	HALL	22,060	14,408	6,282	1,370	8,126	R	65.3%	28.5%	69.6%	30.4%
9,124	HAMILTON	5,004	3,783	878	343	2,905	R	75.6%	17.5%	81.2%	18.8%
3,423	HARLAN	1,832	1,496	254	82	1,242	R	81.7%	13.9%	85.5%	14.5%
967	HAYES	514	472	30	12	442	R	91.8%	5.8%	94.0%	6.0%
2,908	HITCHCOCK	1,468	1,232	161	75	1,071	R	83.9%	11.0%	88.4%	11.6%
10,435	HOLT	5,118	4,354	531	233	3,823	R	85.1%	10.4%	89.1%	10.9%
736	HOOKER	417	355	40	22	315	R	85.1%	9.6%	89.9%	10.1%
6,274	HOWARD	2,994	2,284	544	166	1,740	R	76.3%	18.2%	80.8%	19.2%
7,547	JEFFERSON	3,494	2,399	837	258	1,562	R	68.7%	24.0%	74.1%	25.9%
5,217	JOHNSON	2,089	1,355	563	171	792	R	64.9%	27.0%	70.6%	29.4%
6,489	KEARNEY	3,296	2,531	550	215	1,981	R	76.8%	16.7%	82.1%	17.9%
8,368	KEITH	4,034	3,235	571	228	2,664	R	80.2%	14.2%	85.0%	15.0%
824	KEYA PAHA	519	460	40	19	420	R	88.6%	7.7%	92.0%	8.0%
3,821	KIMBALL	1,677	1,330	230	117	1,100	R	79.3%	13.7%	85.3%	14.7%
8,701	KNOX	4,115	3,188	720	207	2,468	R	77.5%	17.5%	81.6%	18.4%
285,407	LANCASTER	136,223	61,588	61,898	12,737	310	D	45.2%	45.4%	49.9%	50.1%
36,288	LINCOLN	16,131	12,164	2,913	1,054	9,251	R	75.4%	18.1%	80.7%	19.3%
763	LOGAN	453	400	32	21	368	R	88.3%	7.1%	92.6%	7.4%
632	LOUP	385	323	48	14	275	R	83.9%	12.5%	87.1%	12.9%
34,876	MADISON	14,343	10,628	2,711	1,004	7,917	R	74.1%	18.9%	79.7%	20.3%
539	MCPHERSON	287	257	14	16	243	R	89.5%	4.9%	94.8%	5.2%

NEBRASKA

PRESIDENT 2016

2010 Census Population	County	Total Vote	Republican (Trump)	Democratic (Clinton)	Other	Rep.-Dem. Plurality	Percentage Total Vote Rep.	Dem.	Major Vote Rep.	Dem.
7,845	MERRICK	3,788	2,926	602	260	2,324 R	77.2%	15.9%	82.9%	17.1%
5,042	MORRILL	2,209	1,802	284	123	1,518 R	81.6%	12.9%	86.4%	13.6%
3,735	NANCE	1,621	1,261	281	79	980 R	77.8%	17.3%	81.8%	18.2%
7,248	NEMAHA	3,161	2,116	785	260	1,331 R	66.9%	24.8%	72.9%	27.1%
4,500	NUCKOLLS	2,205	1,726	353	126	1,373 R	78.3%	16.0%	83.0%	17.0%
15,740	OTOE	7,457	4,860	2,025	572	2,835 R	65.2%	27.2%	70.6%	29.4%
2,773	PAWNEE	1,327	974	279	74	695 R	73.4%	21.0%	77.7%	22.3%
2,970	PERKINS	1,455	1,217	161	77	1,056 R	83.6%	11.1%	88.3%	11.7%
9,188	PHELPS	4,695	3,849	572	274	3,277 R	82.0%	12.2%	87.1%	12.9%
7,266	PIERCE	3,630	3,052	382	196	2,670 R	84.1%	10.5%	88.9%	11.1%
32,237	PLATTE	14,433	10,965	2,646	822	8,319 R	76.0%	18.3%	80.6%	19.4%
5,406	POLK	2,582	2,028	413	141	1,615 R	78.5%	16.0%	83.1%	16.9%
11,055	RED WILLOW	5,170	4,258	645	267	3,613 R	82.4%	12.5%	86.8%	13.2%
8,363	RICHARDSON	3,805	2,769	818	218	1,951 R	72.8%	21.5%	77.2%	22.8%
1,526	ROCK	798	687	70	41	617 R	86.1%	8.8%	90.8%	9.2%
14,200	SALINE	5,136	3,004	1,733	399	1,271 R	58.5%	33.7%	63.4%	36.6%
158,840	SARPY	80,580	45,143	28,033	7,404	17,110 R	56.0%	34.8%	61.7%	38.3%
20,780	SAUNDERS	10,860	7,555	2,523	782	5,032 R	69.6%	23.2%	75.0%	25.0%
36,970	SCOTTS BLUFF	14,317	10,076	3,207	1,034	6,869 R	70.4%	22.4%	75.9%	24.1%
16,750	SEWARD	7,922	5,454	1,875	593	3,579 R	68.8%	23.7%	74.4%	25.6%
5,469	SHERIDAN	2,608	2,211	287	110	1,924 R	84.8%	11.0%	88.5%	11.5%
3,152	SHERMAN	1,573	1,150	340	83	810 R	73.1%	21.6%	77.2%	22.8%
1,311	SIOUX	736	616	81	39	535 R	83.7%	11.0%	88.4%	11.6%
6,129	STANTON	2,801	2,187	417	197	1,770 R	78.1%	14.9%	84.0%	16.0%
5,228	THAYER	2,690	2,051	499	140	1,552 R	76.2%	18.6%	80.4%	19.6%
647	THOMAS	393	344	30	19	314 R	87.5%	7.6%	92.0%	8.0%
6,940	THURSTON	2,088	1,043	919	126	124 R	50.0%	44.0%	53.2%	46.8%
4,260	VALLEY	2,205	1,780	339	86	1,441 R	80.7%	15.4%	84.0%	16.0%
20,234	WASHINGTON	10,832	7,424	2,623	785	4,801 R	68.5%	24.2%	73.9%	26.1%
9,595	WAYNE	3,776	2,693	835	248	1,858 R	71.3%	22.1%	76.3%	23.7%
3,812	WEBSTER	1,708	1,330	306	72	1,024 R	77.9%	17.9%	81.3%	18.7%
818	WHEELER	465	377	62	26	315 R	81.1%	13.3%	85.9%	14.1%
13,665	YORK	6,381	4,700	1,186	495	3,514 R	73.7%	18.6%	79.9%	20.1%
1,826,341	TOTAL	844,227	495,961	284,494	63,772	211,467 R	58.7%	33.7%	63.5%	36.5%

NEBRASKA

HOUSE OF REPRESENTATIVES

CD	Year	Total Vote	Republican Vote	Candidate	Democratic Vote	Candidate	Other Vote	Rep.-Dem. Plurality	Percentage Total Vote Rep.	Dem.	Major Vote Rep.	Dem.
1	2016	273,238	189,771	FORTENBERRY, JEFF*	83,467	WIK, DANIEL M.		106,304 R	69.5%	30.5%	69.5%	30.5%
1	2014	179,057	123,219	FORTENBERRY, JEFF*	55,838	CRAWFORD, DENNIS P.		67,381 R	68.8%	31.2%	68.8%	31.2%
1	2012	256,095	174,889	FORTENBERRY, JEFF*	81,206	REIMAN, KOREY L.		93,683 R	68.3%	31.7%	68.3%	31.7%
2	2016	288,308	141,066	BACON, DON	137,602	ASHFORD, BRAD*	9,640	3,464 R	48.9%	47.7%	50.6%	49.4%
2	2014	171,509	78,157	TERRY, LEE*	83,872	ASHFORD, BRAD	9,480	5,715 D	45.6%	48.9%	48.2%	51.8%
2	2012	263,731	133,964	TERRY, LEE*	129,767	EWING, JOHN W. JR.		4,197 R	50.8%	49.2%	50.8%	49.2%
3	2016	226,907	226,907	SMITH, ADRIAN*				226,907 R	100.0%		100.0%	
3	2014	184,964	139,440	SMITH, ADRIAN*	45,524	SULLIVAN, MARK		93,916 R	75.4%	24.6%	75.4%	24.6%
3	2012	252,689	187,423	SMITH, ADRIAN*	65,266	SULLIVAN, MARK		122,157 R	74.2%	25.8%	74.2%	25.8%
TOTAL	2016	788,453	557,744		221,069		9,640	336,675 R	70.7%	28.0%	73.0%	27.0%
TOTAL	2014	535,530	340,816		185,234		9,480	155,582 R	63.6%	34.6%	64.8%	35.2%
TOTAL	2012	772,515	496,276		276,239			220,037 R	64.2%	35.8%	64.2%	35.8%

Note: An asterisk (*) denotes incumbent.

NEBRASKA

GENERAL AND PRIMARY ELECTIONS

2016 GENERAL ELECTIONS: OTHER VOTES

President Other vote was 38,946 Libertarian (Gary Johnson), 16,051 Write-in (Scattered Write-In), 8,775 Green (Jill Stein)

House Other vote was:

CD 2 9,640 Libertarian (Steven Laird)

2016 PRIMARY ELECTIONS: SUPPLEMENTARY INFORMATION

Primary	May 10, 2016	**Registration** (as of May 10, 2016)	1,165,308	Republican	564,718
				Democratic	359,821
				Libertarian	7,414
				Nonpartisan	233,355

Primary Type Closed—Registered Democrats and Republicans could vote only in their party's primary. Voters registered as Nonpartisan could participate in either party's primary for the Senate and House (but not for governor).

	REPUBLICAN PRIMARIES			DEMOCRATIC PRIMARIES		
President	Trump, Donald J.	122,327	61.5%	Clinton, Hillary Rodham	42,692	53.1%
	Cruz, Ted	36,703	18.4%	Sanders, Bernard	37,744	46.9%
	Kasich, John R.	22,709	11.4%			
	Carson, Ben	10,016	5.0%			
	Rubio, Marco	7,233	3.6%			
	TOTAL	198,988		TOTAL	80,436	
Congressional District 1	Fortenberry, Jeff*	62,704	100.0%	Wik, Daniel M.	25,762	100.0%
	TOTAL	62,704		TOTAL	25,762	
Congressional District 2	Bacon, Don	32,328	66.0%	Ashford, Brad*	23,470	100.0%
	Maxwell, Chip	16,677	34.0%			
	TOTAL	49,005		TOTAL	23,470	
Congressional District 3	Smith, Adrian*	78,154	100.0%			
	TOTAL	78,154				

Note: An asterisk (*) denotes incumbent.

NEVADA

Congressional districts first established for elections held in 2012

4 members

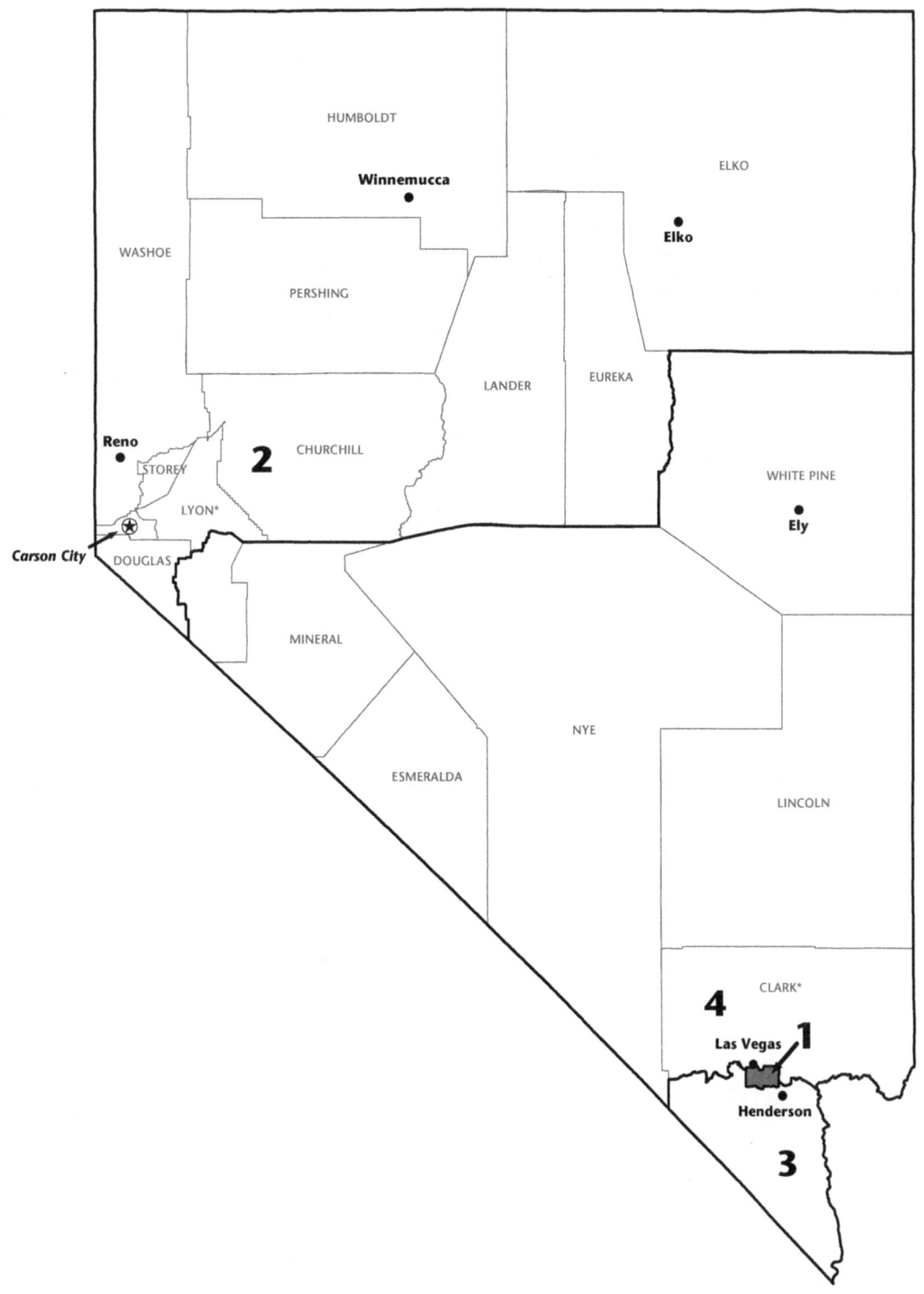

The city of Carson City is an independent city that is treated as a county equivalent; the label is included only for the city.

* Asterisk indicates a county whose boundaries include parts of two or more congressional districts.

NEVADA
Greater Las Vegas Area

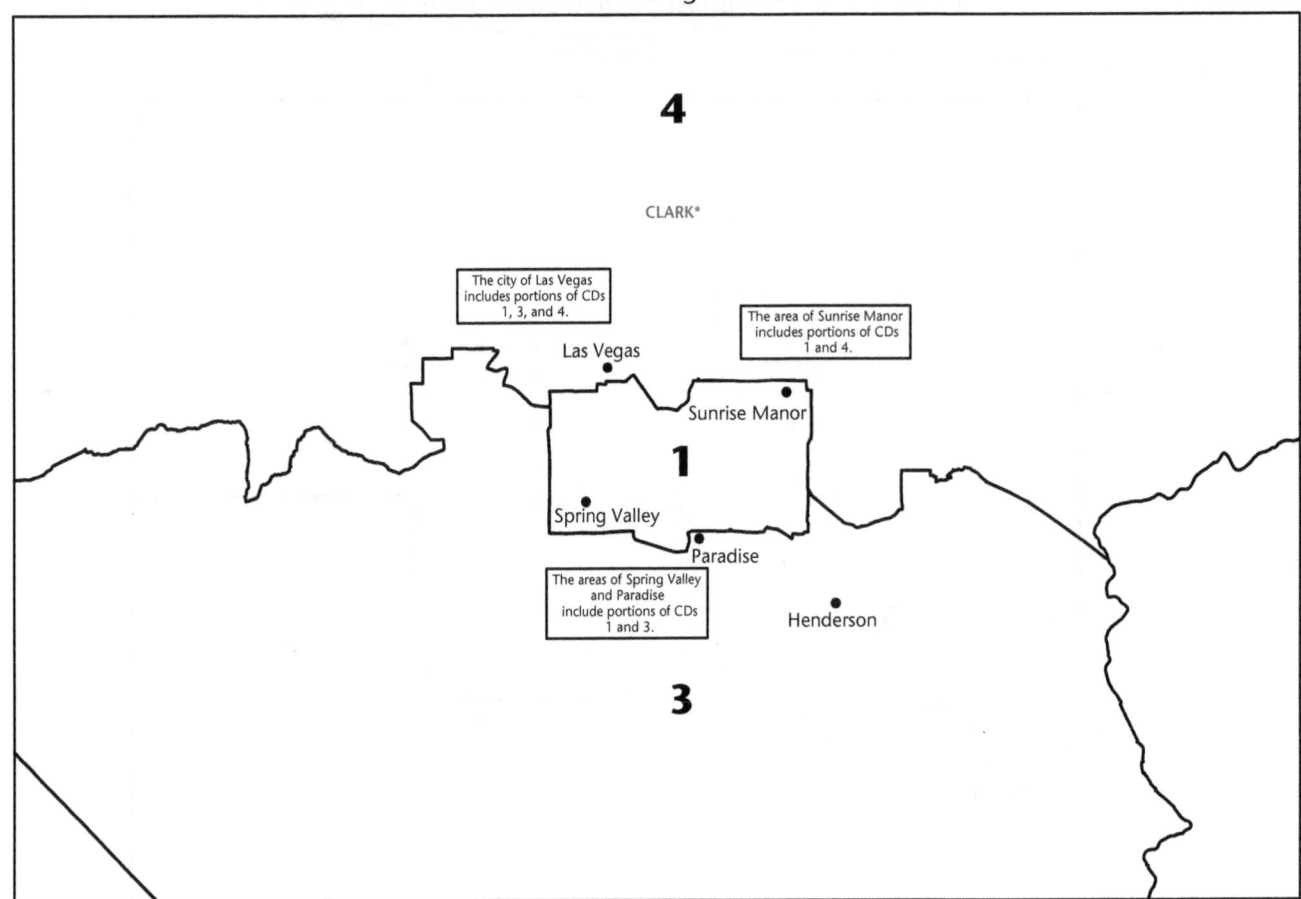

* Asterisk indicates a county whose boundaries include parts of two or more congressional districts.

NEVADA

GOVERNOR

Brian Sandoval (R). Re-elected 2014 to a four-year term. Previously elected 2010.

SENATORS (1 Republican, 1 Democrat)

Dean Heller (R). Elected 2012 to a six-year term. Sworn into office May 9, 2011, following the resignation of John Ensign (R), who was under investigation by the Senate Ethics Committee as to whether he tried to illegally cover up an extramarital affair with a former staff member.

Catherine Cortez Masto (D). Elected 2016 to a six-year term.

REPRESENTATIVES (1 Republican, 3 Democrats)

1. Dina Titus (D)
2. Mark Amodei (R)
3. Jacky Rosen (D)
4. Ruben Kihuen (D)

POSTWAR VOTE FOR PRESIDENT

Year	Total Vote	Republican		Democratic		Other Vote	Rep.-Dem. Plurality	Percentage			
								Total Vote		Major Vote	
		Vote	Candidate	Vote	Candidate			Rep.	Dem.	Rep.	Dem.
2016**	1,125,385	512,058	Trump, Donald J.	539,260	Clinton, Hillary Rodham	74,067	27,202 D	45.5%	47.9%	48.7%	51.3%
2012	1,014,918	463,567	Romney, W. Mitt	531,373	Obama, Barack H.*	19,978	67,806 D	45.7%	52.4%	46.6%	53.4%
2008	967,848	412,827	McCain, John S. III	533,736	Obama, Barack H.	21,285	120,909 D	42.7%	55.1%	43.6%	56.4%
2004	829,587	418,690	Bush, George W.*	397,190	Kerry, John F.	13,707	21,500 R	50.5%	47.9%	51.3%	48.7%
2000**	608,970	301,575	Bush, George W.	279,978	Gore, Albert Jr.	27,417	21,597 R	49.5%	46.0%	51.9%	48.1%
1996**	464,279	199,244	Dole, Robert "Bob"	203,974	Clinton, Bill*	61,061	4,730 D	42.9%	43.9%	49.4%	50.6%
1992**	506,318	175,828	Bush, George H.*	189,148	Clinton, Bill	141,342	13,320 D	34.7%	37.4%	48.2%	51.8%
1988	350,067	206,040	Bush, George H.	132,738	Dukakis, Michael S.	11,289	73,302 R	58.9%	37.9%	60.8%	39.2%
1984	286,667	188,770	Reagan, Ronald*	91,655	Mondale, Walter F.	6,242	97,115 R	65.8%	32.0%	67.3%	32.7%
1980**	247,885	155,017	Reagan, Ronald	66,666	Carter, Jimmy*	26,202	88,351 R	62.5%	26.9%	69.9%	30.1%
1976	201,876	101,273	Ford, Gerald R.*	92,479	Carter, Jimmy	8,124	8,794 R	50.2%	45.8%	52.3%	47.7%
1972	181,766	115,750	Nixon, Richard M.*	66,016	McGovern, George S.		49,734 R	63.7%	36.3%	63.7%	36.3%
1968**	154,218	73,188	Nixon, Richard M.	60,598	Humphrey, Hubert Horatio Jr.	20,432	12,590 R	47.5%	39.3%	54.7%	45.3%
1964	135,433	56,094	Goldwater, Barry M. Sr.	79,339	Johnson, Lyndon B.*		23,245 D	41.4%	58.6%	41.4%	58.6%
1960	107,267	52,387	Nixon, Richard M.	54,880	Kennedy, John F.		2,493 D	48.8%	51.2%	48.8%	51.2%
1956	96,689	56,049	Eisenhower, Dwight D.*	40,640	Stevenson, Adlai E. II		15,409 R	58.0%	42.0%	58.0%	42.0%
1952	82,190	50,502	Eisenhower, Dwight D.	31,688	Stevenson, Adlai E. II		18,814 R	61.4%	38.6%	61.4%	38.6%
1948	62,117	29,357	Dewey, Thomas E.	31,291	Truman, Harry S.*	1,469	1,934 D	47.3%	50.4%	48.4%	51.6%

Note: An asterisk (*) denotes incumbent. **In past elections, the other vote included: 2016 - 37,384 Libertarian (Gary Johnson); 2000 - 15,008 Green (Ralph Nader); 1996 - 43,986 Reform (Ross Perot); 1992 - 132,580 Independent (Perot); 1980 - 17,651 Independent (John Anderson); 1968 - 20,432 American Independent (George Wallace).

NEVADA

POSTWAR VOTE FOR GOVERNOR

Year	Total Vote	Republican		Democratic		Other Vote	Rep.-Dem. Plurality	Percentage			
								Total Vote		Major Vote	
		Vote	Candidate	Vote	Candidate			Rep.	Dem.	Rep.	Dem.
2014	547,349	386,340	Sandoval, Brian*	130,722	Goodman, Robert "Bob"	30,287	255,618 R	70.6%	23.9%	74.7%	25.3%
2010	716,529	382,350	Sandoval, Brian	298,171	Reid, Rory	36,008	84,179 R	53.4%	41.6%	56.2%	43.8%
2006	582,158	279,003	Gibbons, James A. "Jim"	255,684	Titus, Dina	47,471	23,319 R	47.9%	43.9%	52.2%	47.8%
2002	504,079	344,001	Guinn, Kenny*	110,935	Neal, Joe	49,143	233,066 R	68.2%	22.0%	75.6%	24.4%
1998	433,630	223,892	Guinn, Kenny	182,281	Jones, Jan Laverty	27,457	41,611 R	51.6%	42.0%	55.1%	44.9%
1994	379,676	156,875	Gibbons, James A. "Jim"	200,026	Miller, Robert J.*	22,775	43,151 D	41.3%	52.7%	44.0%	56.0%
1990	320,743	95,789	Gallaway, Jim	207,878	Miller, Robert J.*	17,076	112,089 D	29.9%	64.8%	31.5%	68.5%
1986	260,375	65,081	Cafferata, Patty	187,268	Bryan, Richard H.*	8,026	122,187 D	25.0%	71.9%	25.8%	74.2%
1982	239,751	100,104	List, Robert F.*	128,132	Bryan, Richard H.	11,515	28,028 D	41.8%	53.4%	43.9%	56.1%
1978	192,445	108,097	List, Robert F.	76,361	Rose, Robert E.	7,987	31,736 R	56.2%	39.7%	58.6%	41.4%
1974**	169,358	28,959	Crumpler, Shirley	114,114	O'Callaghan, Mike*	26,285	85,155 D	17.1%	67.4%	20.2%	79.8%
1970	146,991	64,400	Fike, Ed	70,697	O'Callaghan, Mike	11,894	6,297 D	43.8%	48.1%	47.7%	52.3%
1966	137,677	71,807	Laxalt, Paul	65,870	Sawyer, Grant*		5,937 R	52.2%	47.8%	52.2%	47.8%
1962	96,929	32,145	Gragson, Oran K.	64,784	Sawyer, Grant*		32,639 D	33.2%	66.8%	33.2%	66.8%
1958	84,889	34,025	Russell, Charles H.*	50,864	Sawyer, Grant		16,839 D	40.1%	59.9%	40.1%	59.9%
1954	78,462	41,665	Russell, Charles H.*	36,797	Pittman, Vail		4,868 R	53.1%	46.9%	53.1%	46.9%
1950	61,773	35,609	Russell, Charles H.	26,164	Pittman, Vail*		9,445 R	57.6%	42.4%	57.6%	42.4%
1946	49,902	21,247	Jepson, Melvin E.	28,655	Pittman, Vail		7,408 D	42.6%	57.4%	42.6%	57.4%

Note: An asterisk (*) denotes incumbent. **In past elections, the other vote included: 1974 - 26,285 Independent American (James Ray Houston).

POSTWAR VOTE FOR SENATOR

Year	Total Vote	Republican		Democratic		Other Vote	Rep.-Dem. Plurality	Percentage			
								Total Vote		Major Vote	
		Vote	Candidate	Vote	Candidate			Rep.	Dem.	Rep.	Dem.
2016	1,108,294	495,079	Heck, Joe	521,994	Masto, Catherine Cortez	91,221	26,915 D	44.7%	47.1%	48.7%	51.3%
2012	997,805	457,656	Heller, Dean*	446,080	Berkley, Shelley	94,069	11,576 R	45.9%	44.7%	50.6%	49.4%
2010	721,404	321,361	Angle, Sharron E.	362,785	Reid, Harry*	37,258	41,424 D	44.5%	50.3%	47.0%	53.0%
2006	582,572	322,501	Ensign, John*	238,796	Carter, Jack	21,275	83,705 R	55.4%	41.0%	57.5%	42.5%
2004	810,068	284,640	Ziser, Richard	494,805	Reid, Harry*	30,623	210,165 D	35.1%	61.1%	36.5%	63.5%
2000	600,250	330,687	Ensign, John	238,260	Bernstein, Ed	31,303	92,427 R	55.1%	39.7%	58.1%	41.9%
1998	435,790	208,222	Ensign, John	208,650	Reid, Harry*	18,918	428 D	47.8%	47.9%	49.9%	50.1%
1994	380,530	156,020	Furman, Hal	193,804	Bryan, Richard H.*	30,706	37,784 D	41.0%	50.9%	44.6%	55.4%
1992	495,887	199,413	Dahl, Demar	253,150	Reid, Harry*	43,324	53,737 D	40.2%	51.0%	44.1%	55.9%
1988	349,649	161,336	Hecht, Jacob Chic*	175,548	Bryan, Richard H.	12,765	14,212 D	46.1%	50.2%	47.9%	52.1%
1986	261,932	116,606	Santini, James	130,955	Reid, Harry	14,371	14,349 D	44.5%	50.0%	47.1%	52.9%
1982	240,394	120,377	Hecht, Jacob Chic	114,720	Cannon, Howard W.*	5,297	5,657 R	50.1%	47.7%	51.2%	48.8%
1980	246,436	144,224	Laxalt, Paul*	92,129	Gojack, Mary	10,083	52,095 R	58.5%	37.4%	61.0%	39.0%
1976	201,980	63,471	Towell, David	127,295	Cannon, Howard W.*	11,214	63,824 D	31.4%	63.0%	33.3%	66.7%
1974	169,473	79,605	Laxalt, Paul	78,981	Reid, Harry	10,887	624 R	47.0%	46.6%	50.2%	49.8%
1970	147,768	60,838	Raggio, William J.	85,187	Cannon, Howard W.*	1,743	24,349 D	41.2%	57.6%	41.7%	58.3%
1968	152,690	69,068	Fike, Ed	83,622	Bible, Alan Harvey*		14,554 D	45.2%	54.8%	45.2%	54.8%
1964	134,624	67,288	Laxalt, Paul	67,336	Cannon, Howard W.*		48 D	50.0%	50.0%	50.0%	50.0%
1962	97,192	33,749	Wright, William B.	63,443	Bible, Alan Harvey*		29,694 D	34.7%	65.3%	34.7%	65.3%
1958	84,492	35,760	Malone, George W.*	48,732	Cannon, Howard W.		12,972 D	42.3%	57.7%	42.3%	57.7%
1956	96,389	45,712	Young, Cliff	50,677	Bible, Alan Harvey*		4,965 D	47.4%	52.6%	47.4%	52.6%
1954S**	77,513	32,470	Brown, Ernest S.	45,043	Bible, Alan Harvey		12,573 D	41.9%	58.1%	41.9%	58.1%
1952	81,090	41,906	Malone, George W.*	39,184	Mechling, Thomas B.		2,722 R	51.7%	48.3%	51.7%	48.3%
1950	61,762	25,933	Marshall, George E.	35,829	McCarran, Patrick A.*		9,896 D	42.0%	58.0%	42.0%	58.0%
1946	50,354	27,801	Malone, George W.	22,553	Bunker, Berkeley L.		5,248 R	55.2%	44.8%	55.2%	44.8%

Note: An asterisk (*) denotes incumbent. **The 1954 election was for a short term to fill a vacancy.

NEVADA
PRESIDENT 2016

2010 Census Population	County	Total Vote	Republican (Trump)	Democratic (Clinton)	Other	Rep.-Dem. Plurality	Total Vote Rep.	Total Vote Dem.	Major Vote Rep.	Major Vote Dem.
55,274	CARSON CITY	25,016	13,125	9,610	2,281	3,515 R	52.5%	38.4%	57.7%	42.3%
24,877	CHURCHILL	10,938	7,830	2,210	898	5,620 R	71.6%	20.2%	78.0%	22.0%
1,951,269	CLARK	767,156	320,057	402,227	44,872	82,170 D	41.7%	52.4%	44.3%	55.7%
46,997	DOUGLAS	27,885	17,415	8,454	2,016	8,961 R	62.5%	30.3%	67.3%	32.7%
48,818	ELKO	18,559	13,551	3,401	1,607	10,150 R	73.0%	18.3%	79.9%	20.1%
783	ESMERALDA	423	329	65	29	264 R	77.8%	15.4%	83.5%	16.5%
1,987	EUREKA	854	723	74	57	649 R	84.7%	8.7%	90.7%	9.3%
16,528	HUMBOLDT	6,433	4,521	1,386	526	3,135 R	70.3%	21.5%	76.5%	23.5%
5,775	LANDER	2,413	1,828	403	182	1,425 R	75.8%	16.7%	81.9%	18.1%
5,345	LINCOLN	2,132	1,671	285	176	1,386 R	78.4%	13.4%	85.4%	14.6%
51,980	LYON	23,762	16,005	6,146	1,611	9,859 R	67.4%	25.9%	72.3%	27.7%
4,772	MINERAL	1,997	1,179	637	181	542 R	59.0%	31.9%	64.9%	35.1%
43,946	NYE	19,595	13,324	5,094	1,177	8,230 R	68.0%	26.0%	72.3%	27.7%
6,753	PERSHING	1,982	1,403	430	149	973 R	70.8%	21.7%	76.5%	23.5%
4,010	STOREY	2,558	1,616	752	190	864 R	63.2%	29.4%	68.2%	31.8%
421,407	WASHOE	209,909	94,758	97,379	17,772	2,621 D	45.1%	46.4%	49.3%	50.7%
10,030	WHITE PINE	3,773	2,723	707	343	2,016 R	72.2%	18.7%	79.4%	20.6%
2,700,551	TOTAL	1,125,385	512,058	539,260	74,067	27,202 D	45.5%	47.9%	48.7%	51.3%

NEVADA
SENATOR 2016

2010 Census Population	County	Total Vote	Republican (Heck)	Democratic (Masto)	Other	Rep.-Dem. Plurality	Total Vote Rep.	Total Vote Dem.	Major Vote Rep.	Major Vote Dem.
55,274	CARSON CITY	24,826	13,027	9,741	2,058	3,286 R	52.5%	39.2%	57.2%	42.8%
24,877	CHURCHILL	10,894	7,711	2,240	943	5,471 R	70.8%	20.6%	77.5%	22.5%
1,951,269	CLARK	753,243	303,734	386,179	63,330	82,445 D	40.3%	51.3%	44.0%	56.0%
46,997	DOUGLAS	27,650	17,587	8,410	1,653	9,177 R	63.6%	30.4%	67.7%	32.3%
48,818	ELKO	18,367	13,462	3,199	1,706	10,263 R	73.3%	17.4%	80.8%	19.2%
783	ESMERALDA	420	312	66	42	246 R	74.3%	15.7%	82.5%	17.5%
1,987	EUREKA	849	692	88	69	604 R	81.5%	10.4%	88.7%	11.3%
16,528	HUMBOLDT	6,384	4,397	1,406	581	2,991 R	68.9%	22.0%	75.8%	24.2%
5,775	LANDER	2,393	1,704	417	272	1,287 R	71.2%	17.4%	80.3%	19.7%
5,345	LINCOLN	2,121	1,609	315	197	1,294 R	75.9%	14.9%	83.6%	16.4%
51,980	LYON	23,578	15,231	6,323	2,024	8,908 R	64.6%	26.8%	70.7%	29.3%
4,772	MINERAL	1,988	1,141	627	220	514 R	57.4%	31.5%	64.5%	35.5%
43,946	NYE	19,360	11,611	5,253	2,496	6,358 R	60.0%	27.1%	68.9%	31.1%
6,753	PERSHING	1,972	1,286	466	220	820 R	65.2%	23.6%	73.4%	26.6%
4,010	STOREY	2,543	1,551	791	201	760 R	61.0%	31.1%	66.2%	33.8%
421,407	WASHOE	207,957	97,433	95,750	14,774	1,683 R	46.9%	46.0%	50.4%	49.6%
10,030	WHITE PINE	3,749	2,591	723	435	1,868 R	69.1%	19.3%	78.2%	21.8%
2,700,551	TOTAL	1,108,294	495,079	521,994	91,221	26,915 D	44.7%	47.1%	48.7%	51.3%

NEVADA

HOUSE OF REPRESENTATIVES

CD	Year	Total Vote	Republican		Democratic		Other Vote	Rep.-Dem. Plurality	Percentage			
									Total Vote		Major Vote	
			Vote	Candidate	Vote	Candidate			Rep.	Dem.	Rep.	Dem.
1	2016	188,352	54,174	PERRY, MARY	116,537	TITUS, DINA*	17,641	62,363 D	28.8%	61.9%	31.7%	68.3%
1	2014	80,299	30,413	TEIJEIRO, ANNETTE	45,643	TITUS, DINA*	4,243	15,230 D	37.9%	56.8%	40.0%	60.0%
1	2012	179,278	56,521	EDWARDS, CHRIS	113,967	TITUS, DINA	8,790	57,446 D	31.5%	63.6%	33.2%	66.8%
2	2016	313,336	182,676	AMODEI, MARK*	115,722	EVANS, H.D. "CHIP"	14,938	66,954 R	58.3%	36.9%	61.2%	38.8%
2	2014	186,210	122,402	AMODEI, MARK*	52,016	SPEES, KRISTEN	11,792	70,386 R	65.7%	27.9%	70.2%	29.8%
2	2012	281,449	162,213	AMODEI, MARK*	102,019	KOEPNICK, SAMUEL	17,217	60,194 R	57.6%	36.2%	61.4%	38.6%
3	2016	310,963	142,926	TARKANIAN, DANNY	146,869	ROSEN, JACKY	21,168	3,943 D	46.0%	47.2%	49.3%	50.7%
3	2014	145,719	88,528	HECK, JOE*	52,644	BILBRAY, ERIN	4,547	35,884 R	60.8%	36.1%	62.7%	37.3%
3	2012	272,523	137,244	HECK, JOE*	116,823	OCEGUERA, JOHN	18,456	20,421 R	50.4%	42.9%	54.0%	46.0%
4	2016	265,846	118,328	HARDY, CRESENT*	128,985	KIHUEN, RUBEN	18,533	10,657 D	44.5%	48.5%	47.8%	52.2%
4	2014	130,781	63,466	HARDY, CRESENT	59,844	HORSFORD, STEVEN A.*	7,471	3,622 R	48.5%	45.8%	51.5%	48.5%
4	2012	240,492	101,261	TARKANIAN, DANNY	120,501	HORSFORD, STEVEN A.	18,730	19,240 D	42.1%	50.1%	45.7%	54.3%
TOTAL	2016	1,078,497	498,104		508,113		72,280	10,009 D	46.2%	47.1%	49.5%	50.5%
TOTAL	2014	543,009	304,809		210,147		28,053	94,662 R	56.1%	38.7%	59.2%	40.8%
TOTAL	2012	973,742	457,239		453,310		63,193	3,929 R	47.0%	46.6%	50.2%	49.8%

Note: An asterisk (*) denotes incumbent.

NEVADA

GENERAL AND PRIMARY ELECTIONS

2016 GENERAL ELECTIONS: OTHER VOTES

President   Other vote was 37,384 Libertarian (Gary Johnson), 28,863 No Party ("None Of These Candidates"), 5,268 Constitution (Darrell Castle), 2,552 Independent (Roque De La Fuente)

Senate   Other vote was 42,257 No Party ("None Of These Candidates"), 17,128 Independent (Tom Jones), 14,208 Independent (Thomas Sawyer), 10,740 Independent (Tony Gumina), 6,888 Independent (Jarrod Williams)

House   Other vote was:

CD 1   13,897 Nonpartisan (Reuben D'Silva), 3,744 Independent American (Kamau Bakari)

CD 2   8,693 Independent American (John Everhart), 6,245 Independent (Drew Knight)

CD 3   11,602 Independent American (Warren Markowitz), 9,566 Independent (David Goossen)

CD 4   10,206 Libertarian (Steve Brown), 8,327 Independent (Mike Little)

2016 PRIMARY ELECTIONS: SUPPLEMENTARY INFORMATION

Presidential Caucus	February 20, 2016 (Democratic) February 23, 2016 (Republican)	**Registration** (as of May 24, 2016 – includes 237,355 inactive registrants)	1,535,222	Democratic	619,957
				Republican	516,753
				Independent American	70,210
				Libertarian	12,477
				Other	13,221
				Nonpartisan	302,604

Primary   June 14, 2016 (Congress)

Primary Type   Closed—Only registered Democrats and Republicans could vote in their party's primary.

NEVADA

GENERAL AND PRIMARY ELECTIONS

	REPUBLICAN PRIMARIES			DEMOCRATIC PRIMARIES		
Senator	Heck, Joe	74,524	64.9%	Masto, Catherine Cortez	81,971	80.6%
	Angle, Sharron E.	26,146	22.8%	Rheinhart, Allen	5,650	5.6%
	"None Of These Candidates"	3,903	3.4%	"None Of These Candidates"	5,501	5.4%
	Heck, Thomas "Sad Tom"	3,567	3.1%	O'Briant, Liddo Susan	4,842	4.8%
	Hamilton, Eddie	2,057	1.8%	Mahendra, Bobby	3,764	3.7%
	Davis, D'Nese	1,938	1.7%			
	Tarbell, William	1,179	1.0%			
	Leeds, Robert X.	662	0.6%			
	Preble, Juston	582	0.5%			
	Poliak, Carlo	279	0.2%			
	TOTAL	114,837		TOTAL	101,728	
Congressional District 1	Perry, Mary	2,588	25.0%	Titus, Dina*	15,556	82.4%
	Carlisle, Stephanie	2,563	24.8%	Solorio, Jose A.	1,775	9.4%
	Horne, Fred	1,911	18.5%	Boylan, Patrick	1,554	8.2%
	Miller, Jeff	1,459	14.1%			
	Johnston, Gary "Coach"	1,144	11.1%			
	Baker, Louis "Blulaker"	668	6.5%			
	TOTAL	10,333		TOTAL	18,885	
Congressional District 2	Amodei, Mark*	Unopposed		Evans, H.D. "Chip"	11,333	45.1%
				Shepherd, Rick	8,983	35.8%
				Alm, Vance	4,803	19.1%
				TOTAL	25,119	
Congressional District 3	Tarkanian, Danny	9,002	32.0%	Rosen, Jacky	14,221	62.2%
	Roberson, Michael	6,759	24.0%	Sbaih, Jesse	2,928	12.8%
	Fiore, Michele	5,124	18.2%	Michaels, Barry	2,219	9.7%
	Matthews, Andy	3,975	14.1%	Schiffman, Steven M.	1,237	5.4%
	Bowers, Kerry	1,569	5.6%	Singer, Alex Channing	1,208	5.3%
	Teijeiro, Annette	1,336	4.7%	Waite, Neil M.	1,055	4.6%
	Khal, Sami	381	1.4%			
	TOTAL	28,146		TOTAL	22,868	
Congressional District 4	Hardy, Cresent*	18,610	76.8%	Kihuen, Ruben	12,221	39.9%
	Monroe, Mike	4,336	17.9%	Flores, Lucy	7,854	25.7%
	Villines, Wayne J.	1,290	5.3%	Lee, Susie	6,407	20.9%
				Arberry, Morse Jr.	1,902	6.2%
				Smith, Rodney	869	2.8%
				Schaefer, Mike	773	2.5%
				Rolle, Dan	336	1.1%
				Casutt, Brandon	240	0.8%
	TOTAL	24,236		TOTAL	30,602	

Note: An asterisk (*) denotes incumbent.

NEW HAMPSHIRE

Congressional districts first established for elections held in 2012

2 members

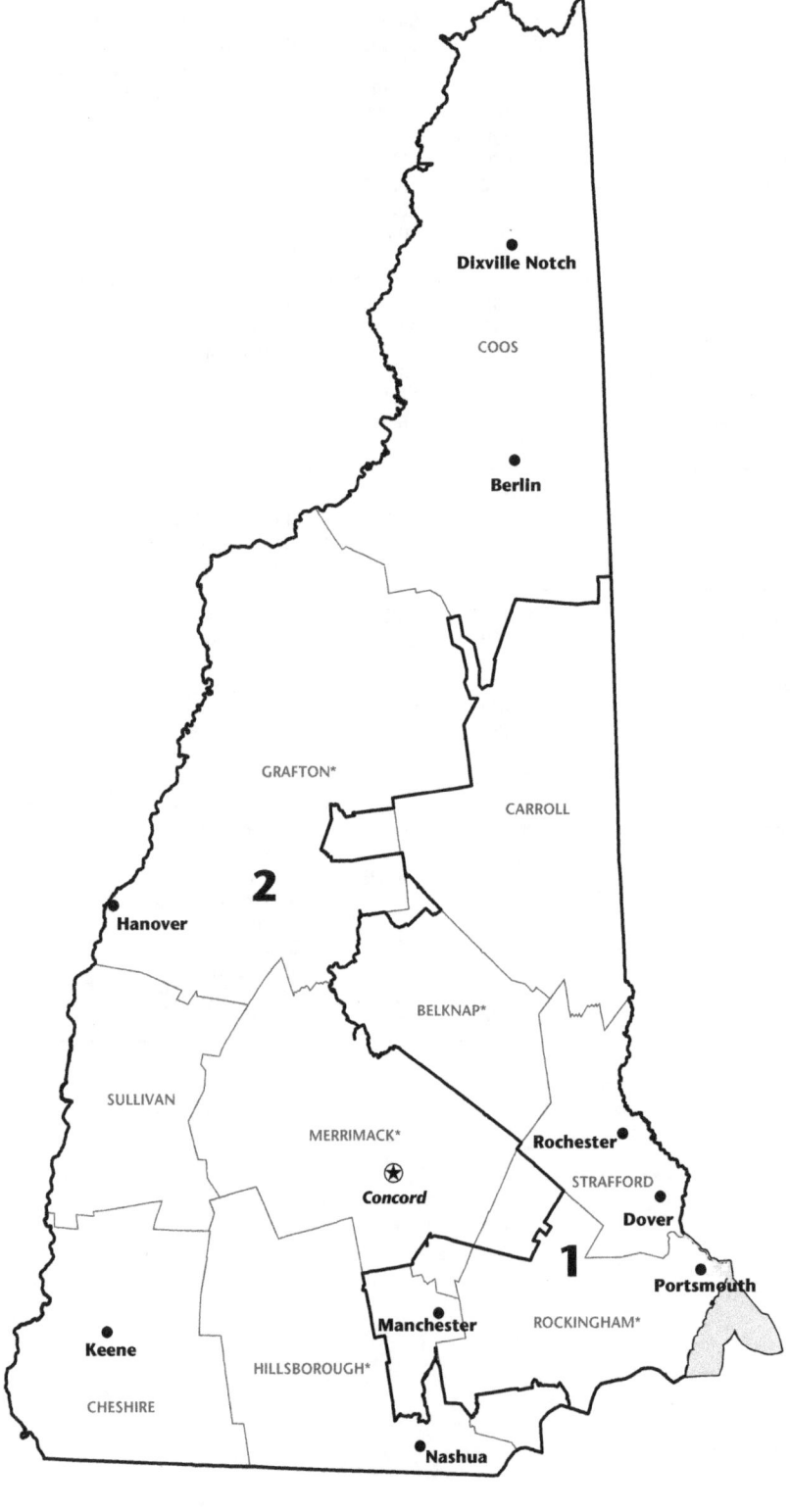

* Asterisk indicates a county whose boundaries include parts of two or more congressional districts.

NEW HAMPSHIRE

GOVERNOR

Chris Sununu (R). Elected 2016 to a two-year term.

SENATORS (2 Democrats)

Jeanne Shaheen (D). Re-elected 2014 to a six-year term. Previously elected 2008.

Maggie Hassan (D). Elected 2016 to a six-year term.

REPRESENTATIVES (2 Democrats)

1. Carol Shea-Porter (D)
2. Ann McLane Kuster (D)

POSTWAR VOTE FOR PRESIDENT

Year	Total Vote	Republican		Democratic		Other Vote	Rep.-Dem. Plurality	Percentage			
								Total Vote		Major Vote	
		Vote	Candidate	Vote	Candidate			Rep.	Dem.	Rep.	Dem.
2016**	744,296	345,790	Trump, Donald J.	348,526	Clinton, Hillary Rodham	49,980	2,736 D	46.5%	46.8%	49.8%	50.2%
2012	710,972	329,918	Romney, W. Mitt	369,561	Obama, Barack H.*	11,493	39,643 D	46.4%	52.0%	47.2%	52.8%
2008	710,970	316,534	McCain, John S. III	384,826	Obama, Barack H.	9,610	68,292 D	44.5%	54.1%	45.1%	54.9%
2004	677,738	331,237	Bush, George W.*	340,511	Kerry, John F.	5,990	9,274 D	48.9%	50.2%	49.3%	50.7%
2000**	569,081	273,559	Bush, George W.	266,348	Gore, Albert Jr.	29,174	7,211 R	48.1%	46.8%	50.7%	49.3%
1996**	499,175	196,532	Dole, Robert "Bob"	246,214	Clinton, Bill*	56,429	49,682 D	39.4%	49.3%	44.4%	55.6%
1992**	537,943	202,484	Bush, George H.*	209,040	Clinton, Bill	126,419	6,556 D	37.6%	38.9%	49.2%	50.8%
1988	451,074	281,537	Bush, George H.	163,696	Dukakis, Michael S.	5,841	117,841 R	62.4%	36.3%	63.2%	36.8%
1984	389,066	267,051	Reagan, Ronald*	120,395	Mondale, Walter F.	1,620	146,656 R	68.6%	30.9%	68.9%	31.1%
1980**	383,990	221,705	Reagan, Ronald	108,864	Carter, Jimmy*	53,421	112,841 R	57.7%	28.4%	67.1%	32.9%
1976	339,618	185,935	Ford, Gerald R.*	147,635	Carter, Jimmy	6,048	38,300 R	54.7%	43.5%	55.7%	44.3%
1972	334,055	213,724	Nixon, Richard M.*	116,435	McGovern, George S.	3,896	97,289 R	64.0%	34.9%	64.7%	35.3%
1968**	297,298	154,903	Nixon, Richard M.	130,589	Humphrey, Hubert Horatio Jr.	11,806	24,314 R	52.1%	43.9%	54.3%	45.7%
1964	288,093	104,029	Goldwater, Barry M. Sr.	184,064	Johnson, Lyndon B.*		80,035 D	36.1%	63.9%	36.1%	63.9%
1960	295,761	157,989	Nixon, Richard M.	137,772	Kennedy, John F.		20,217 R	53.4%	46.6%	53.4%	46.6%
1956	266,994	176,519	Eisenhower, Dwight D.*	90,364	Stevenson, Adlai E. II	111	86,155 R	66.1%	33.8%	66.1%	33.9%
1952	272,950	166,287	Eisenhower, Dwight D.	106,663	Stevenson, Adlai E. II		59,624 R	60.9%	39.1%	60.9%	39.1%
1948	231,440	121,299	Dewey, Thomas E.	107,995	Truman, Harry S.*	2,146	13,304 R	52.4%	46.7%	52.9%	47.1%

Note: An asterisk (*) denotes incumbent. **In past elections, the other vote included: 2016 - 30,777 Libertarian (Gary Johnson); 2000 - 22,198 Green (Ralph Nader); 1996 - 48,390 Reform (Ross Perot); 1992 - 121,337 Independent (Perot); 1980 - 49,693 Independent (John Anderson); 1968 - 11,173 American Independent (George Wallace).

NEW HAMPSHIRE

POSTWAR VOTE FOR GOVERNOR

Year	Total Vote	Republican		Democratic		Other Vote	Rep.-Dem. Plurality	Percentage			
								Total Vote		Major Vote	
		Vote	Candidate	Vote	Candidate			Rep.	Dem.	Rep.	Dem.
2016	724,863	354,040	Sununu, Chris	337,589	Van Ostern, Colin	33,234	16,451 R	48.8%	46.6%	51.2%	48.8%
2014	486,183	230,610	Havenstein, Walter "Walt"	254,666	Hassan, Maggie*	907	24,056 D	47.4%	52.4%	47.5%	52.5%
2012	693,877	295,026	Lamontagne, Ovide M.	378,934	Hassan, Maggie	19,917	83,908 D	42.5%	54.6%	43.8%	56.2%
2010	456,588	205,616	Stephen, John A.	240,346	Lynch, John*	10,626	34,730 D	45.0%	52.6%	46.1%	53.9%
2008	682,910	188,555	Kenney, Joseph D.	479,042	Lynch, John*	15,313	290,487 D	27.6%	70.1%	28.2%	71.8%
2006	403,679	104,288	Coburn, Jim	298,760	Lynch, John*	631	194,472 D	25.8%	74.0%	25.9%	74.1%
2004	667,020	325,981	Benson, Craig*	340,299	Lynch, John	740	14,318 D	48.9%	51.0%	48.9%	51.1%
2002	442,976	259,663	Benson, Craig	169,277	Fernald, Mark D.	14,036	90,386 R	58.6%	38.2%	60.5%	39.5%
2000	564,953	246,952	Humphrey, Gordon John	275,038	Shaheen, Jeanne*	42,963	28,086 D	43.7%	48.7%	47.3%	52.7%
1998	318,940	98,473	Lucas, Jay	210,769	Shaheen, Jeanne*	9,698	112,296 D	30.9%	66.1%	31.8%	68.2%
1996	497,040	196,321	Lamontagne, Ovide M.	284,175	Shaheen, Jeanne	16,544	87,854 D	39.5%	57.2%	40.9%	59.1%
1994	311,882	218,134	Merrill, Steve*	79,686	King, Wayne D.	14,062	138,448 R	69.9%	25.6%	73.2%	26.8%
1992	516,170	289,170	Merrill, Steve	206,232	Arnesen, Deborah A.	20,768	82,938 R	56.0%	40.0%	58.4%	41.6%
1990	295,018	177,773	Gregg, Judd*	101,923	Grandmaison, J. Joseph	15,322	75,850 R	60.3%	34.5%	63.6%	36.4%
1988	441,923	267,064	Gregg, Judd	172,543	McEachern, Paul*	2,316	94,521 R	60.4%	39.0%	60.8%	39.2%
1986	251,107	134,824	Sununu, John H.*	116,142	McEachern, Paul	141	18,682 R	53.7%	46.3%	53.7%	46.3%
1984	383,910	256,574	Sununu, John H.*	127,156	Spirou, Chris	180	129,418 R	66.8%	33.1%	66.9%	33.1%
1982	282,588	145,389	Sununu, John H.	132,317	Gallen, Hugh J.*	4,882	13,072 R	51.4%	46.8%	52.4%	47.6%
1980	384,031	156,178	Thomson, Meldrim Jr.	226,436	Gallen, Hugh J.*	1,417	70,258 D	40.7%	59.0%	40.8%	59.2%
1978	269,587	122,464	Thomson, Meldrim Jr.*	133,133	Gallen, Hugh J.	13,990	10,669 D	45.4%	49.4%	47.9%	52.1%
1976	342,669	197,589	Thomson, Meldrim Jr.*	145,015	Spanos, Harry V.	65	52,574 R	57.7%	42.3%	57.7%	42.3%
1974	226,665	115,933	Thomson, Meldrim Jr.*	110,591	Leonard, Richard W.	141	5,342 R	51.1%	48.8%	51.2%	48.8%
1972**	323,102	133,702	Thomson, Meldrim Jr.	126,107	Crowley, Roger J.	63,293	7,595 R	41.4%	39.0%	51.5%	48.5%
1970	222,441	102,298	Peterson, Walter R.*	98,098	Crowley, Roger J.	22,045	4,200 R	46.0%	44.1%	51.0%	49.0%
1968	285,342	149,902	Peterson, Walter R.	135,378	Bussiere, Emile R.	62	14,524 R	52.5%	47.4%	52.5%	47.5%
1966	233,642	107,259	Gregg, Hugh	125,882	King, John W.*	501	18,623 D	45.9%	53.9%	46.0%	54.0%
1964	285,863	94,824	Pillsbury, John	190,863	King, John W.*	176	96,039 D	33.2%	66.8%	33.2%	66.8%
1962	230,048	94,567	Pillsbury, John	135,481	King, John W.		40,914 D	41.1%	58.9%	41.1%	58.9%
1960	290,527	161,123	Powell, Wesley*	129,404	Boutin, Bernard L.		31,719 R	55.5%	44.5%	55.5%	44.5%
1958	206,745	106,790	Powell, Wesley	99,955	Boutin, Bernard L.		6,835 R	51.7%	48.3%	51.7%	48.3%
1956	258,695	141,578	Dwinell, Lane*	117,117	Shaw, John		24,461 R	54.7%	45.3%	54.7%	45.3%
1954	194,631	107,287	Dwinell, Lane	87,344	Shaw, John		19,943 R	55.1%	44.9%	55.1%	44.9%
1952	265,715	167,791	Gregg, Hugh	97,924	Craig, William H.		69,867 R	63.1%	36.9%	63.1%	36.9%
1950	191,239	108,907	Adams, Sherman*	82,258	Bingham, Robert P.	74	26,649 R	56.9%	43.0%	57.0%	43.0%
1948	222,571	116,212	Adams, Sherman	105,207	Hill, Herbert W.	1,152	11,005 R	52.2%	47.3%	52.5%	47.5%
1946	163,451	103,204	Dale, Charles M.	60,247	Keefe, F. Clyde		42,957 R	63.1%	36.9%	63.1%	36.9%

Note: An asterisk (*) denotes incumbent. **In past elections, the other vote included: 1972 - 63,199 Independent (Malcolm McLane).

NEW HAMPSHIRE

POSTWAR VOTE FOR SENATOR

Year	Total Vote	Republican		Democratic		Other Vote	Rep.-Dem. Plurality	Percentage			
								Total Vote		Major Vote	
		Vote	Candidate	Vote	Candidate			Rep.	Dem.	Rep.	Dem.
2016	739,140	353,632	Ayotte, Kelly*	354,649	Hassan, Maggie	30,859	1,017 D	47.8%	48.0%	49.9%	50.1%
2014	488,159	235,347	Brown, Scott P.	251,184	Shaheen, Jeanne*	1,628	15,837 D	48.2%	51.5%	48.4%	51.6%
2010	455,149	273,218	Ayotte, Kelly	167,545	Hodes, Paul W.	14,386	105,673 R	60.0%	36.8%	62.0%	38.0%
2008	694,787	314,403	Sununu, John E.*	358,438	Shaheen, Jeanne	21,946	44,035 D	45.3%	51.6%	46.7%	53.3%
2004	657,086	434,847	Gregg, Judd*	221,549	Haddock, Dorris R. "Granny D"	690	213,298 R	66.2%	33.7%	66.2%	33.8%
2002	447,135	227,229	Sununu, John E.	207,478	Shaheen, Jeanne	12,428	19,751 R	50.8%	46.4%	52.3%	47.7%
1998	314,956	213,477	Gregg, Judd*	88,883	Condodemetraky, George	12,596	124,594 R	67.8%	28.2%	70.6%	29.4%
1996	491,966	242,304	Smith, Robert C.*	227,397	Swett, Dick	22,265	14,907 R	49.3%	46.2%	51.6%	48.4%
1992	518,416	249,591	Gregg, Judd	234,982	Rauh, John	33,843	14,609 R	48.1%	45.3%	51.5%	48.5%
1990	291,393	189,792	Smith, Robert C.	91,299	Durkin, John A.	10,302	98,493 R	65.1%	31.3%	67.5%	32.5%
1986	244,797	154,090	Rudman, Warren B.*	79,225	Peabody, Endicott	11,482	74,865 R	62.9%	32.4%	66.0%	34.0%
1984	384,406	225,828	Humphrey, Gordon John*	157,447	D'Amours, Norman E.	1,131	68,381 R	58.7%	41.0%	58.9%	41.1%
1980	375,060	195,559	Rudman, Warren B.	179,455	Durkin, John A.*	46	16,104 R	52.1%	47.8%	52.1%	47.9%
1978	263,779	133,745	Humphrey, Gordon John	127,945	McIntyre, Thomas J.*	2,089	5,800 R	50.7%	48.5%	51.1%	48.9%
1975S	262,682	113,007	Wyman, Louis C.	140,778	Durkin, John A.	8,897	27,771 D	43.0%	53.6%	44.5%	55.5%
1974**	223,363	110,926	Wyman, Louis C.	110,924	Durkin, John A.	1,513	2 R	49.7%	49.7%	50.0%	50.0%
1972	324,354	139,852	Powell, Wesley	184,495	McIntyre, Thomas J.*	7	44,643 D	43.1%	56.9%	43.1%	56.9%
1968	286,989	170,163	Cotton, Norris R.*	116,816	King, John W.	10	53,347 R	59.3%	40.7%	59.3%	40.7%
1966	229,305	105,241	Thyng, Harrison R.	123,888	McIntyre, Thomas J.*	176	18,647 D	45.9%	54.0%	45.9%	54.1%
1962	224,479	134,035	Cotton, Norris R.*	90,444	Catalfo, Alfred Jr.		43,591 R	59.7%	40.3%	59.7%	40.3%
1962S	224,811	107,199	Bass, Perkins	117,612	McIntyre, Thomas J.		10,413 D	47.7%	52.3%	47.7%	52.3%
1960	287,545	173,521	Bridges, Styles*	114,024	Hill, Herbert W.		59,497 R	60.3%	39.7%	60.3%	39.7%
1956	251,943	161,424	Cotton, Norris R.*	90,519	Pickett, Laurence M.		70,905 R	64.1%	35.9%	64.1%	35.9%
1954	194,536	117,150	Bridges, Styles*	77,386	Morin, Gerard L.		39,764 R	60.2%	39.8%	60.2%	39.8%
1954S	189,558	114,068	Cotton, Norris R.	75,490	Betley, Stanley J.		38,578 R	60.2%	39.8%	60.2%	39.8%
1950	190,573	106,142	Tobey, Charles W.*	72,473	Kelley, Emmet J.	11,958	33,669 R	55.7%	38.0%	59.4%	40.6%
1948	222,898	129,600	Bridges, Styles*	91,760	Fortin, Alfred E.	1,538	37,840 R	58.1%	41.2%	58.5%	41.5%

Note: An asterisk (*) denotes incumbent. **Following the closely contested 1974 election, neither candidate was seated and the 1975 special election was held for the remaining years of that term. One each of the 1954 and 1962 elections was for a short term to fill a vacancy.

NEW HAMPSHIRE

PRESIDENT 2016

2010 Census Population	County	Total Vote	Republican (Trump)	Democratic (Clinton)	Other	Rep.-Dem. Plurality	Percentage			
							Total Vote		Major Vote	
							Rep.	Dem.	Rep.	Dem.
60,088	BELKNAP	35,045	19,315	13,517	2,213	5,798 R	55.1%	38.6%	58.8%	41.2%
47,818	CARROLL	29,616	14,635	12,987	1,994	1,648 R	49.4%	43.9%	53.0%	47.0%
77,117	CHESHIRE	41,895	16,876	22,064	2,955	5,188 D	40.3%	52.7%	43.3%	56.7%
33,055	COOS	15,627	7,952	6,563	1,112	1,389 R	50.9%	42.0%	54.8%	45.2%
89,118	GRAFTON	51,191	19,010	28,510	3,671	9,500 D	37.1%	55.7%	40.0%	60.0%
400,721	HILLSBOROUGH	214,157	100,013	99,589	14,555	424 R	46.7%	46.5%	50.1%	49.9%
146,445	MERRIMACK	83,648	37,674	40,198	5,776	2,524 D	45.0%	48.1%	48.4%	51.6%
295,223	ROCKINGHAM	181,434	90,447	79,994	10,993	10,453 R	49.9%	44.1%	53.1%	46.9%
123,143	STRAFFORD	69,000	29,072	34,894	5,034	5,822 D	42.1%	50.6%	45.4%	54.6%
43,742	SULLIVAN	22,683	10,796	10,210	1,677	586 R	47.6%	45.0%	51.4%	48.6%
1,316,470	TOTAL	744,296	345,790	348,526	49,980	2,736 D	46.5%	46.8%	49.8%	50.2%

NEW HAMPSHIRE

PRESIDENT 2016

2010 Census Population	City/Town	Total Vote	Republican (Trump)	Democratic (Clinton)	Other	Rep.-Dem. Plurality	Percentage			
							Total Vote		Major Vote	
							Rep.	Dem.	Rep.	Dem.
11,201	AMHERST	7,351	3,271	3,777	303	506 D	44.5%	51.4%	46.4%	53.6%
6,751	ATKINSON	4,460	2,595	1,671	194	924 R	58.2%	37.5%	60.8%	39.2%
8,576	BARRINGTON	5,222	2,469	2,375	378	94 R	47.3%	45.5%	51.0%	49.0%
21,203	BEDFORD	13,267	6,816	5,851	600	965 R	51.4%	44.1%	53.8%	46.2%
7,356	BELMONT	3,657	2,192	1,272	193	920 R	59.9%	34.8%	63.3%	36.7%
10,051	BERLIN	3,917	1,766	1,954	197	188 D	45.1%	49.9%	47.5%	52.5%
7,519	BOW	4,937	2,119	2,570	248	451 D	42.9%	52.1%	45.2%	54.8%
13,355	CLAREMONT	5,512	2,680	2,529	303	151 R	48.6%	45.9%	51.4%	48.6%
42,695	CONCORD	21,917	7,812	12,984	1,121	5,172 D	35.6%	59.2%	37.6%	62.4%
10,115	CONWAY	5,189	2,204	2,717	268	513 D	42.5%	52.4%	44.8%	55.2%
33,109	DERRY	16,913	9,237	6,825	851	2,412 R	54.6%	40.4%	57.5%	42.5%
29,987	DOVER	17,151	6,015	10,118	1,018	4,103 D	35.1%	59.0%	37.3%	62.7%
14,638	DURHAM	9,530	2,450	6,501	579	4,051 D	25.7%	68.2%	27.4%	72.6%
6,411	EPPING	3,959	2,117	1,625	217	492 R	53.5%	41.0%	56.6%	43.4%
14,306	EXETER	9,248	3,286	5,514	448	2,228 D	35.5%	59.6%	37.3%	62.7%
6,786	FARMINGTON	3,100	1,785	1,127	188	658 R	57.6%	36.4%	61.3%	38.7%
8,477	FRANKLIN	3,749	2,049	1,487	213	562 R	54.7%	39.7%	57.9%	42.1%
7,126	GILFORD	4,668	2,504	1,973	191	531 R	53.6%	42.3%	55.9%	44.1%
17,651	GOFFSTOWN	9,631	5,009	4,146	476	863 R	52.0%	43.0%	54.7%	45.3%
8,523	HAMPSTEAD	5,388	3,186	1,966	236	1,220 R	59.1%	36.5%	61.8%	38.2%
15,430	HAMPTON	10,161	4,802	4,953	406	151 D	47.3%	48.7%	49.2%	50.8%
11,260	HANOVER	7,727	926	6,561	240	5,635 D	12.0%	84.9%	12.4%	87.6%
7,684	HOLLIS	5,138	2,310	2,529	299	219 D	45.0%	49.2%	47.7%	52.3%
13,451	HOOKSETT	8,010	4,225	3,436	349	789 R	52.7%	42.9%	55.1%	44.9%
24,467	HUDSON	13,183	7,220	5,306	657	1,914 R	54.8%	40.2%	57.6%	42.4%
5,457	JAFFREY	2,789	1,284	1,311	194	27 D	46.0%	47.0%	49.5%	50.5%
23,409	KEENE	12,432	3,831	7,932	669	4,101 D	30.8%	63.8%	32.6%	67.4%
6,025	KINGSTON	3,689	2,081	1,422	186	659 R	56.4%	38.5%	59.4%	40.6%
15,951	LACONIA	8,023	4,303	3,303	417	1,000 R	53.6%	41.2%	56.6%	43.4%
13,151	LEBANON	7,092	1,841	4,898	353	3,057 D	26.0%	69.1%	27.3%	72.7%
8,271	LITCHFIELD	4,910	2,720	1,923	267	797 R	55.4%	39.2%	58.6%	41.4%
5,928	LITTLETON	2,833	1,436	1,241	156	195 R	50.7%	43.8%	53.6%	46.4%
24,129	LONDONDERRY	14,049	7,338	5,968	743	1,370 R	52.2%	42.5%	55.1%	44.9%
109,565	MANCHESTER	49,086	21,554	24,941	2,591	3,387 D	43.9%	50.8%	46.4%	53.6%
25,494	MERRIMACK TOWN	14,653	7,397	6,405	851	992 R	50.5%	43.7%	53.6%	46.4%
15,115	MILFORD	8,142	3,850	3,816	476	34 R	47.3%	46.9%	50.2%	49.8%
86,494	NASHUA	42,275	17,476	22,690	2,109	5,214 D	41.3%	53.7%	43.5%	56.5%
8,936	NEWMARKET	5,364	1,836	3,157	371	1,321 D	34.2%	58.9%	36.8%	63.2%
6,507	NEWPORT	2,904	1,665	1,085	154	580 R	57.3%	37.4%	60.5%	39.5%
12,897	PELHAM	7,653	4,624	2,719	310	1,905 R	60.4%	35.5%	63.0%	37.0%
7,115	PEMBROKE	3,946	1,919	1,810	217	109 R	48.6%	45.9%	51.5%	48.5%
6,284	PETERBOROUGH	3,892	1,179	2,487	226	1,308 D	30.3%	63.9%	32.2%	67.8%
7,609	PLAISTOW	4,399	2,531	1,672	196	859 R	57.5%	38.0%	60.2%	39.8%
6,990	PLYMOUTH	3,794	1,394	2,143	257	749 D	36.7%	56.5%	39.4%	60.6%
20,779	PORTSMOUTH	13,169	3,632	8,911	626	5,279 D	27.6%	67.7%	29.0%	71.0%
10,138	RAYMOND	5,348	3,151	1,921	276	1,230 R	58.9%	35.9%	62.1%	37.9%
29,752	ROCHESTER	14,935	7,789	6,267	879	1,522 R	52.2%	42.0%	55.4%	44.6%
28,776	SALEM	15,986	9,312	6,068	606	3,244 R	58.3%	38.0%	60.5%	39.5%
8,693	SEABROOK	4,494	2,743	1,595	156	1,148 R	61.0%	35.5%	63.2%	36.8%
11,766	SOMERSWORTH	5,312	2,389	2,643	280	254 D	45.0%	49.8%	47.5%	52.5%
7,230	SWANZEY	3,816	1,828	1,807	181	21 R	47.9%	47.4%	50.3%	49.7%
8,785	WEARE	5,042	2,957	1,734	351	1,223 R	58.6%	34.4%	63.0%	37.0%
13,592	WINDHAM	8,760	4,825	3,507	428	1,318 R	55.1%	40.0%	57.9%	42.1%
6,269	WOLFEBORO	4,244	2,176	1,871	197	305 R	51.3%	44.1%	53.8%	46.2%

NEW HAMPSHIRE

GOVERNOR 2016

2010 Census Population	County	Total Vote	Republican (Sununu)	Democratic (Van Ostern)	Other	Rep.-Dem. Plurality	Percentage			
							Total Vote		Major Vote	
							Rep.	Dem.	Rep.	Dem.
60,088	BELKNAP	34,364	18,798	14,069	1,497	4,729 R	54.7%	40.9%	57.2%	42.8%
47,818	CARROLL	28,879	15,192	12,503	1,184	2,689 R	52.6%	43.3%	54.9%	45.1%
77,117	CHESHIRE	40,494	17,107	21,471	1,916	4,364 D	42.2%	53.0%	44.3%	55.7%
33,055	COOS	15,183	7,424	7,006	753	418 R	48.9%	46.1%	51.4%	48.6%
89,118	GRAFTON	49,643	19,685	27,621	2,337	7,936 D	39.7%	55.6%	41.6%	58.4%
400,721	HILLSBOROUGH	208,868	103,811	95,231	9,826	8,580 R	49.7%	45.6%	52.2%	47.8%
146,445	MERRIMACK	81,957	37,295	41,195	3,467	3,900 D	45.5%	50.3%	47.5%	52.5%
295,223	ROCKINGHAM	176,371	94,385	74,076	7,910	20,309 R	53.5%	42.0%	56.0%	44.0%
123,143	STRAFFORD	67,043	29,578	34,173	3,292	4,595 D	44.1%	51.0%	46.4%	53.6%
43,742	SULLIVAN	22,061	10,765	10,244	1,052	521 R	48.8%	46.4%	51.2%	48.8%
1,316,470	TOTAL	724,863	354,040	337,589	33,234	16,451 R	48.8%	46.6%	51.2%	48.8%

2010 Census Population	City/Town	Total Vote	Republican (Sununu)	Democratic (Van Ostern)	Other	Rep.-Dem. Plurality	Percentage			
							Total Vote		Major Vote	
							Rep.	Dem.	Rep.	Dem.
11,201	AMHERST	7,410	3,751	3,384	275	367 R	50.6%	45.7%	52.6%	47.4%
6,751	ATKINSON	4,407	2,775	1,464	168	1,311 R	63.0%	33.2%	65.5%	34.5%
8,576	BARRINGTON	5,203	2,518	2,368	317	150 R	48.4%	45.5%	51.5%	48.5%
21,203	BEDFORD	13,405	7,911	5,087	407	2,824 R	59.0%	37.9%	60.9%	39.1%
7,356	BELMONT	3,635	2,045	1,411	179	634 R	56.3%	38.8%	59.2%	40.8%
10,051	BERLIN	3,901	1,639	2,054	208	415 D	42.0%	52.7%	44.4%	55.6%
7,519	BOW	5,013	2,412	2,446	155	34 D	48.1%	48.8%	49.7%	50.3%
13,355	CLAREMONT	5,476	2,627	2,554	295	73 R	48.0%	46.6%	50.7%	49.3%
42,695	CONCORD	21,960	7,800	13,296	864	5,496 D	35.5%	60.5%	37.0%	63.0%
10,115	CONWAY	5,064	2,321	2,481	262	160 D	45.8%	49.0%	48.3%	51.7%
33,109	DERRY	16,529	9,065	6,519	945	2,546 R	54.8%	39.4%	58.2%	41.8%
29,987	DOVER	16,992	6,564	9,710	718	3,146 D	38.6%	57.1%	40.3%	59.7%
14,638	DURHAM	9,109	2,913	5,896	300	2,983 D	32.0%	64.7%	33.1%	66.9%
6,411	EPPING	3,901	2,050	1,634	217	416 R	52.6%	41.9%	55.6%	44.4%
14,306	EXETER	8,703	3,386	4,939	378	1,553 D	38.9%	56.8%	40.7%	59.3%
6,786	FARMINGTON	3,046	1,656	1,206	184	450 R	54.4%	39.6%	57.9%	42.1%
8,477	FRANKLIN	3,767	1,861	1,675	231	186 R	49.4%	44.5%	52.6%	47.4%
7,126	GILFORD	4,636	2,552	1,909	175	643 R	55.0%	41.2%	57.2%	42.8%
17,651	GOFFSTOWN	9,541	5,088	4,067	386	1,021 R	53.3%	42.6%	55.6%	44.4%
8,523	HAMPSTEAD	5,347	3,243	1,864	240	1,379 R	60.7%	34.9%	63.5%	36.5%
15,430	HAMPTON	10,056	5,233	4,504	319	729 R	52.0%	44.8%	53.7%	46.3%
11,260	HANOVER	7,400	1,523	5,674	203	4,151 D	20.6%	76.7%	21.2%	78.8%
7,684	HOLLIS	5,111	2,671	2,257	183	414 R	52.3%	44.2%	54.2%	45.8%
13,451	HOOKSETT	7,948	4,331	3,327	290	1,004 R	54.5%	41.9%	56.6%	43.4%
24,467	HUDSON	12,895	7,157	5,100	638	2,057 R	55.5%	39.6%	58.4%	41.6%
5,457	JAFFREY	2,762	1,300	1,300	162	0 R	47.1%	47.1%	50.0%	50.0%
23,409	KEENE	12,079	4,070	7,491	518	3,421 D	33.7%	62.0%	35.2%	64.8%
6,025	KINGSTON	3,612	2,054	1,328	230	726 R	56.9%	36.8%	60.7%	39.3%
15,951	LACONIA	7,978	4,194	3,405	379	789 R	52.6%	42.7%	55.2%	44.8%
13,151	LEBANON	7,104	2,213	4,622	269	2,409 D	31.2%	65.1%	32.4%	67.6%
8,271	LITCHFIELD	4,810	2,772	1,851	187	921 R	57.6%	38.5%	60.0%	40.0%
5,928	LITTLETON	2,903	1,466	1,290	147	176 R	50.5%	44.4%	53.2%	46.8%
24,129	LONDONDERRY	13,835	7,668	5,536	631	2,132 R	55.4%	40.0%	58.1%	41.9%
109,565	MANCHESTER	48,418	21,881	24,063	2,474	2,182 D	45.2%	49.7%	47.6%	52.4%
25,494	MERRIMACK TOWN	14,820	7,867	6,329	624	1,538 R	53.1%	42.7%	55.4%	44.6%
15,115	MILFORD	8,069	3,920	3,658	491	262 R	48.6%	45.3%	51.7%	48.3%
86,494	NASHUA	41,673	18,316	21,328	2,029	3,012 D	44.0%	51.2%	46.2%	53.8%
8,936	NEWMARKET	5,335	2,080	2,968	287	888 D	39.0%	55.6%	41.2%	58.8%
6,507	NEWPORT	2,900	1,600	1,122	178	478 R	55.2%	38.7%	58.8%	41.2%
12,897	PELHAM	7,461	4,668	2,532	261	2,136 R	62.6%	33.9%	64.8%	35.2%

NEW HAMPSHIRE

GOVERNOR 2016

2010 Census Population	City/Town	Total Vote	Republican (Sununu)	Democratic (Van Ostern)	Other	Rep.-Dem. Plurality	Percentage			
							Total Vote		Major Vote	
							Rep.	Dem.	Rep.	Dem.
7,115	PEMBROKE	3,960	1,862	1,883	215	21 D	47.0%	47.6%	49.7%	50.3%
6,284	PETERBOROUGH	3,864	1,319	2,399	146	1,080 D	34.1%	62.1%	35.5%	64.5%
7,609	PLAISTOW	4,268	2,530	1,538	200	992 R	59.3%	36.0%	62.2%	37.8%
6,990	PLYMOUTH	3,720	1,433	2,069	218	636 D	38.5%	55.6%	40.9%	59.1%
20,779	PORTSMOUTH	12,988	4,422	8,107	459	3,685 D	34.0%	62.4%	35.3%	64.7%
10,138	RAYMOND	5,253	2,950	2,006	297	944 R	56.2%	38.2%	59.5%	40.5%
29,752	ROCHESTER	14,756	7,401	6,460	895	941 R	50.2%	43.8%	53.4%	46.6%
28,776	SALEM	15,589	9,343	5,516	730	3,827 R	59.9%	35.4%	62.9%	37.1%
8,693	SEABROOK	4,336	2,520	1,587	229	933 R	58.1%	36.6%	61.4%	38.6%
11,766	SOMERSWORTH	5,254	2,308	2,666	280	358 D	43.9%	50.7%	46.4%	53.6%
7,230	SWANZEY	3,769	1,802	1,763	204	39 R	47.8%	46.8%	50.5%	49.5%
8,785	WEARE	5,005	2,849	1,885	271	964 R	56.9%	37.7%	60.2%	39.8%
13,592	WINDHAM	8,730	5,447	2,998	285	2,449 R	62.4%	34.3%	64.5%	35.5%
6,269	WOLFEBORO	4,257	2,369	1,744	144	625 R	55.6%	41.0%	57.6%	42.4%

NEW HAMPSHIRE

SENATOR 2016

2010 Census Population	County	Total Vote	Republican (Ayotte)	Democratic (Hassan)	Other	Rep.-Dem. Plurality	Percentage			
							Total Vote		Major Vote	
							Rep.	Dem.	Rep.	Dem.
60,088	BELKNAP	34,836	18,710	14,743	1,383	3,967 R	53.7%	42.3%	55.9%	44.1%
47,818	CARROLL	29,348	14,838	13,431	1,079	1,407 R	50.6%	45.8%	52.5%	47.5%
77,117	CHESHIRE	41,472	16,741	22,809	1,922	6,068 D	40.4%	55.0%	42.3%	57.7%
33,055	COOS	15,493	7,539	7,340	614	199 R	48.7%	47.4%	50.7%	49.3%
89,118	GRAFTON	50,821	20,679	28,127	2,015	7,448 D	40.7%	55.3%	42.4%	57.6%
400,721	HILLSBOROUGH	213,053	105,156	98,727	9,170	6,429 R	49.4%	46.3%	51.6%	48.4%
146,445	MERRIMACK	82,982	38,540	41,412	3,030	2,872 D	46.4%	49.9%	48.2%	51.8%
295,223	ROCKINGHAM	180,250	91,361	81,343	7,546	10,018 R	50.7%	45.1%	52.9%	47.1%
123,143	STRAFFORD	68,442	29,419	36,023	3,000	6,604 D	43.0%	52.6%	45.0%	55.0%
43,742	SULLIVAN	22,443	10,649	10,694	1,100	45 D	47.4%	47.6%	49.9%	50.1%
1,316,470	TOTAL	739,140	353,632	354,649	30,859	1,017 D	47.8%	48.0%	49.9%	50.1%

2010 Census Population	City/Town	Total Vote	Republican (Ayotte)	Democratic (Hassan)	Other	Rep.-Dem. Plurality	Percentage			
							Total Vote		Major Vote	
							Rep.	Dem.	Rep.	Dem.
11,201	AMHERST	7,558	3,940	3,406	212	534 R	52.1%	45.1%	53.6%	46.4%
6,751	ATKINSON	4,477	2,644	1,679	154	965 R	59.1%	37.5%	61.2%	38.8%
8,576	BARRINGTON	5,293	2,539	2,498	256	41 R	48.0%	47.2%	50.4%	49.6%
21,203	BEDFORD	13,533	8,008	5,183	342	2,825 R	59.2%	38.3%	60.7%	39.3%
7,356	BELMONT	3,690	2,008	1,503	179	505 R	54.4%	40.7%	57.2%	42.8%
10,051	BERLIN	3,973	1,639	2,167	167	528 D	41.3%	54.5%	43.1%	56.9%
7,519	BOW	5,062	2,509	2,435	118	74 R	49.6%	48.1%	50.7%	49.3%
13,355	CLAREMONT	5,581	2,508	2,734	339	226 D	44.9%	49.0%	47.8%	52.2%
42,695	CONCORD	22,188	8,168	13,271	749	5,103 D	36.8%	59.8%	38.1%	61.9%
10,115	CONWAY	5,197	2,235	2,747	215	512 D	43.0%	52.9%	44.9%	55.1%
33,109	DERRY	16,920	8,721	7,211	988	1,510 R	51.5%	42.6%	54.7%	45.3%
29,987	DOVER	17,312	6,544	10,101	667	3,557 D	37.8%	58.3%	39.3%	60.7%
14,638	DURHAM	9,472	2,967	6,287	218	3,320 D	31.3%	66.4%	32.1%	67.9%
6,411	EPPING	3,977	2,018	1,744	215	274 R	50.7%	43.9%	53.6%	46.4%
14,306	EXETER	9,382	3,598	5,466	318	1,868 D	38.4%	58.3%	39.7%	60.3%

NEW HAMPSHIRE

SENATOR 2016

2010 Census Population	City/Town	Total Vote	Republican (Ayotte)	Democratic (Hassan)	Other	Rep.-Dem. Plurality	Percentage Total Vote Rep.	Dem.	Major Vote Rep.	Dem.
6,786	FARMINGTON	3,107	1,630	1,296	181	334 R	52.5%	41.7%	55.7%	44.3%
8,477	FRANKLIN	3,810	1,882	1,706	222	176 R	49.4%	44.8%	52.5%	47.5%
7,126	GILFORD	4,700	2,497	2,065	138	432 R	53.1%	43.9%	54.7%	45.3%
17,651	GOFFSTOWN	9,742	5,197	4,170	375	1,027 R	53.3%	42.8%	55.5%	44.5%
8,523	HAMPSTEAD	5,409	3,156	2,037	216	1,119 R	58.3%	37.7%	60.8%	39.2%
15,430	HAMPTON	10,244	4,997	4,954	293	43 R	48.8%	48.4%	50.2%	49.8%
11,260	HANOVER	7,761	1,646	5,992	123	4,346 D	21.2%	77.2%	21.6%	78.4%
7,684	HOLLIS	5,201	2,738	2,323	140	415 R	52.6%	44.7%	54.1%	45.9%
13,451	HOOKSETT	8,077	4,348	3,454	275	894 R	53.8%	42.8%	55.7%	44.3%
24,467	HUDSON	13,186	7,150	5,426	610	1,724 R	54.2%	41.1%	56.9%	43.1%
5,457	JAFFREY	2,828	1,313	1,363	152	50 D	46.4%	48.2%	49.1%	50.9%
23,409	KEENE	12,518	3,894	8,100	524	4,206 D	31.1%	64.7%	32.5%	67.5%
6,025	KINGSTON	3,697	2,000	1,492	205	508 R	54.1%	40.4%	57.3%	42.7%
15,951	LACONIA	8,097	4,070	3,690	337	380 R	50.3%	45.6%	52.4%	47.6%
13,151	LEBANON	7,227	2,176	4,801	250	2,625 D	30.1%	66.4%	31.2%	68.8%
8,271	LITCHFIELD	4,912	2,813	1,926	173	887 R	57.3%	39.2%	59.4%	40.6%
5,928	LITTLETON	2,914	1,541	1,250	123	291 R	52.9%	42.9%	55.2%	44.8%
24,129	LONDONDERRY	14,174	7,654	5,956	564	1,698 R	54.0%	42.0%	56.2%	43.8%
109,565	MANCHESTER	49,442	21,856	25,148	2,438	3,292 D	44.2%	50.9%	46.5%	53.5%
25,494	MERRIMACK TOWN	15,124	8,059	6,520	545	1,539 R	53.3%	43.1%	55.3%	44.7%
15,115	MILFORD	8,236	3,964	3,866	406	98 R	48.1%	46.9%	50.6%	49.4%
86,494	NASHUA	42,593	18,694	22,050	1,849	3,356 D	43.9%	51.8%	45.9%	54.1%
8,936	NEWMARKET	5,440	1,983	3,183	274	1,200 D	36.5%	58.5%	38.4%	61.6%
6,507	NEWPORT	2,938	1,555	1,203	180	352 R	52.9%	40.9%	56.4%	43.6%
12,897	PELHAM	7,655	4,433	2,892	330	1,541 R	57.9%	37.8%	60.5%	39.5%
7,115	PEMBROKE	4,011	1,910	1,908	193	2 R	47.6%	47.6%	50.0%	50.0%
6,284	PETERBOROUGH	3,954	1,362	2,450	142	1,088 D	34.4%	62.0%	35.7%	64.3%
7,609	PLAISTOW	4,361	2,339	1,779	243	560 R	53.6%	40.8%	56.8%	43.2%
6,990	PLYMOUTH	3,816	1,432	2,180	204	748 D	37.5%	57.1%	39.6%	60.4%
20,779	PORTSMOUTH	13,284	4,331	8,557	396	4,226 D	32.6%	64.4%	33.6%	66.4%
10,138	RAYMOND	5,369	2,931	2,153	285	778 R	54.6%	40.1%	57.7%	42.3%
29,752	ROCHESTER	15,028	7,236	6,926	866	310 R	48.2%	46.1%	51.1%	48.9%
28,776	SALEM	15,909	8,714	6,427	768	2,287 R	54.8%	40.4%	57.6%	42.4%
8,693	SEABROOK	4,436	2,341	1,875	220	466 R	52.8%	42.3%	55.5%	44.5%
11,766	SOMERSWORTH	5,348	2,258	2,818	272	560 D	42.2%	52.7%	44.5%	55.5%
7,230	SWANZEY	3,840	1,740	1,900	200	160 D	45.3%	49.5%	47.8%	52.2%
8,785	WEARE	5,083	2,886	1,932	265	954 R	56.8%	38.0%	59.9%	40.1%
13,592	WINDHAM	8,864	5,226	3,382	256	1,844 R	59.0%	38.2%	60.7%	39.3%
6,269	WOLFEBORO	4,313	2,308	1,862	143	446 R	53.5%	43.2%	55.3%	44.7%

NEW HAMPSHIRE

HOUSE OF REPRESENTATIVES

CD	Year	Total Vote	Republican Vote	Candidate	Democratic Vote	Candidate	Other Vote	Rep.-Dem. Plurality	Percentage Total Vote Rep.	Dem.	Major Vote Rep.	Dem.
1	2016	365,984	157,176	GUINTA, FRANK C. *	162,080	SHEA-PORTER, CAROL	46,728	4,904 D	42.9%	44.3%	49.2%	50.8%
1	2014	242,736	125,508	GUINTA, FRANK C.	116,769	SHEA-PORTER, CAROL *	459	8,739 R	51.7%	48.1%	51.8%	48.2%
1	2012	345,022	158,659	GUINTA, FRANK C. *	171,650	SHEA-PORTER, CAROL	14,713	12,991 D	46.0%	49.8%	48.0%	52.0%
2	2016	350,793	158,973	LAWRENCE, JAMES "JIM"	174,495	KUSTER, ANN MCLANE*	17,325	15,522 D	45.3%	49.7%	47.7%	52.3%
2	2014	238,184	106,871	GARCIA, MARILINDA	130,700	KUSTER, ANN MCLANE*	613	23,829 D	44.9%	54.9%	45.0%	55.0%
2	2012	337,394	152,977	BASS, CHARLES *	169,275	KUSTER, ANN MCLANE	15,142	16,298 D	45.3%	50.2%	47.5%	52.5%

NEW HAMPSHIRE

HOUSE OF REPRESENTATIVES

CD	Year	Total Vote	Republican Vote	Republican Candidate	Democratic Vote	Democratic Candidate	Other Vote	Rep.-Dem. Plurality	Total Vote Rep.	Total Vote Dem.	Major Vote Rep.	Major Vote Dem.
TOTAL	2016	716,777	316,149		336,575		64,053	20,426 D	44.1%	47.0%	48.4%	51.6%
TOTAL	2014	480,920	232,379		247,469		1,072	15,090 D	48.3%	51.5%	48.4%	51.6%
TOTAL	2012	682,416	311,636		340,925		29,855	29,289 D	45.7%	50.0%	47.8%	52.2%

Note: An asterisk (*) denotes incumbent.

NEW HAMPSHIRE

GENERAL AND PRIMARY ELECTIONS

2016 GENERAL ELECTIONS: OTHER VOTES

President   Other vote was 30,777 Libertarian (Gary Johnson), 6,496 Green (Jill Stein), 6,472 Write-in (Scattered Write-in), 4,493 Write-in (Bernard Sanders), 1,064 Write-in (Evan McMullin), 678 American Delta (Roque De La Fuente)

Governor   31,243 Libertarian (Max Abramson), 1,991 Write-in (Scattered Write-in)

Senate   17,742 Independent (Aaron Day), 12,597 Libertarian (Brian Chabot), 520 Write-in (Scattered Write-in)

House   Other vote was:

CD 1   34,735 Independent (Shawn O'Connor), 6,074 Independent (Brendan Kelly), 5,507 Libertarian (Robert Lombardo), 194 Write-in (Scattered Write-in), 163 Write-in (John Potucek), 55 Write-in (Richard Ashooh)

CD 2   17,088 Independent (John Babiarz), 237 Write-in (Scattered Write-in)

2016 PRIMARY ELECTIONS: SUPPLEMENTARY INFORMATION

Primary	February 9, 2016 (President) September 13, 2016 (Congress)	**Registration** (as of August 23, 2016)	916,652	Republican 293,307 Democratic 269,263 Undeclared 354,082

Primary Type   Semi-open—Registered Democrats and Republicans could vote only in their party's primary. "Undeclared" voters could participate in either party's primary, but must declare affiliation at the polls.

NEW HAMPSHIRE

GENERAL AND PRIMARY ELECTIONS

	REPUBLICAN PRIMARIES			DEMOCRATIC PRIMARIES		
President	Trump, Donald J.	100,735	35.2%	Sanders, Bernard	152,193	60.1%
	Kasich, John R.	44,932	15.7%	Clinton, Hillary Rodham	95,355	37.7%
	Cruz, Ted	33,244	11.6%	Write-In	3,475	1.4%
	Bush, Jeb	31,341	11.0%	O'Malley, Martin	667	0.3%
	Rubio, Marco	30,071	10.5%	Supreme, Vermin	268	0.1%
	Christie, Chris	21,089	7.4%	Thistle, David John	226	0.1%
	Fiorina, Carly	11,774	4.1%	Schwass, Graham	143	0.1%
	Carson, Ben	6,527	2.3%	Burke, Steve	108	
	Write-In	2,943	1.0%	De La Fuente, Roque "Rocky"	96	
	Paul, Rand	1,930	0.7%	Wolfe, John	54	

NEW HAMPSHIRE

GENERAL AND PRIMARY ELECTIONS

	REPUBLICAN PRIMARIES			DEMOCRATIC PRIMARIES		
	Huckabee, Mike	216	0.1%	Adams, Jon	53	
	Martin, Andy	202	0.1%	Kelso, Lloyd Thomas	46	
	Santorum, Rick	160	0.1%	Judd, Keith	44	
	Gilmore, James S. III	134		Elbot, Eric	36	
	Witz, Richard P. H.	104		Locke, Star	33	
	Pataki, George E.	79		French, William D.	29	
	Graham, Lindsey	73		Greenstein, Mark Stewart	29	
	Cullison, Brooks	56		O'Donnell, Edward T. Jr.	26	
	Cook, Timothy	55		Valentine, James	24	
	Jindal, Bobby	53		Lovitt, Robert	22	
	Lynch, Frank	47		Steinberg, Michael Alan	21	
	Robinson, Joe	44		McGaughey, Bill	19	
	Comley, Stephen Bradley Sr.	32		Hewes, Henry	18	
	Prag, Chomi	16		Sonnino, Edward	17	
	Dyas, J. Daniel Sr.	15		Lipscomb, Steven Roy	15	
	McCarthy, Stephen John	12		Sloan, Sam	15	
	Iwachiw, Walter N.	9		Hutton, Brock C.	14	
	Huey, Kevin Glenn	8		Moroz, Raymond Michael	8	
	Drozd, Matt	6		Weil, Richard Lyons	8	
	Mann, Robert L.	5				
	Messina, Peter	5				
	TOTAL	*285,917*		*TOTAL*	*253,062*	
Senator	Ayotte, Kelly*	86,676	78.6%	Hassan, Maggie	70,374	98.2%
	Rubens, Jim	19,156	17.4%	Write-In	1,322	1.8%
	Alciere, Tom	1,586	1.4%			
	Beloin, Gerard	1,255	1.1%			
	Emanuel, Stanley Michael	1,187	1.1%			
	Write-In	468	0.4%			
	TOTAL	*110,328*		*TOTAL*	*71,696*	
Governor	Sununu, Chris	34,194	30.6%	Van Ostern, Colin	37,759	51.4%
	Edelbut, Frank	33,161	29.6%	Marchand, Steve	18,285	24.9%
	Gatsas, Ted	22,961	20.5%	Connolly, Mark	14,878	20.3%
	Forrester, Jeanie	19,634	17.6%	Freeman, Ian	1,076	1.5%
	Lavoie, Jonathan	1,438	1.3%	Write-In	893	1.2%
	Write-In	477	0.4%	Dextraze, Derek	563	0.8%
	TOTAL	*111,865*		*TOTAL*	*73,454*	
Congressional District 1	Guinta, Frank C.*	26,400	46.5%	Shea-Porter, Carol	32,409	98.8%
	Ashooh, Richard	25,678	45.2%	Write-In	386	1.2%
	Callis, Michael	2,243	3.9%			
	Risley, Robert	1,347	2.4%			
	Gradert, Jamieson Hale	1,031	1.8%			
	Write-In	111	0.2%			
	TOTAL	*56,810*		*TOTAL*	*32,795*	
Congressional District 2	Lawrence, James "Jim"	17,180	39.7%	Kuster, Ann McLane*	36,683	99.3%
	Flanagan, Jack B.	12,046	27.8%	Write-In	249	0.7%
	Kelly, Walter	4,287	9.9%			
	Martin, Andy	3,145	7.3%			
	Estevez, Eric P.	2,443	5.6%			
	Mercer, Jay	2,113	4.9%			
	Newell, Casey	1,839	4.2%			
	Write-In	232	0.5%			
	TOTAL	*43,285*		*TOTAL*	*36,932*	

Note: An asterisk (*) denotes incumbent.

NEW JERSEY

Congressional districts first established for elections held in 2012

12 members

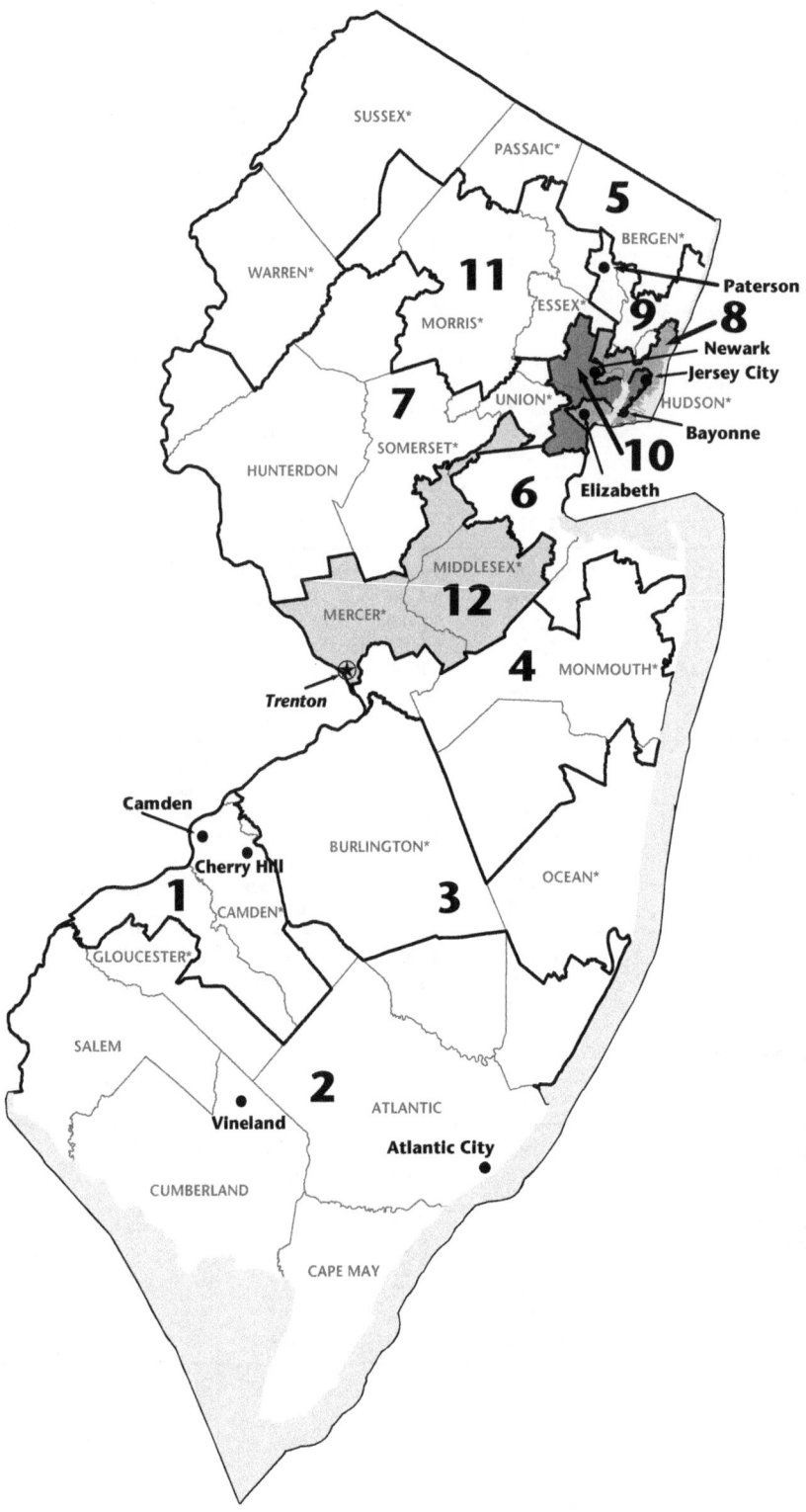

* Asterisk indicates a county whose boundaries include parts of two or more congressional districts.

NEW JERSEY
Northern New Jersey Gateway Area

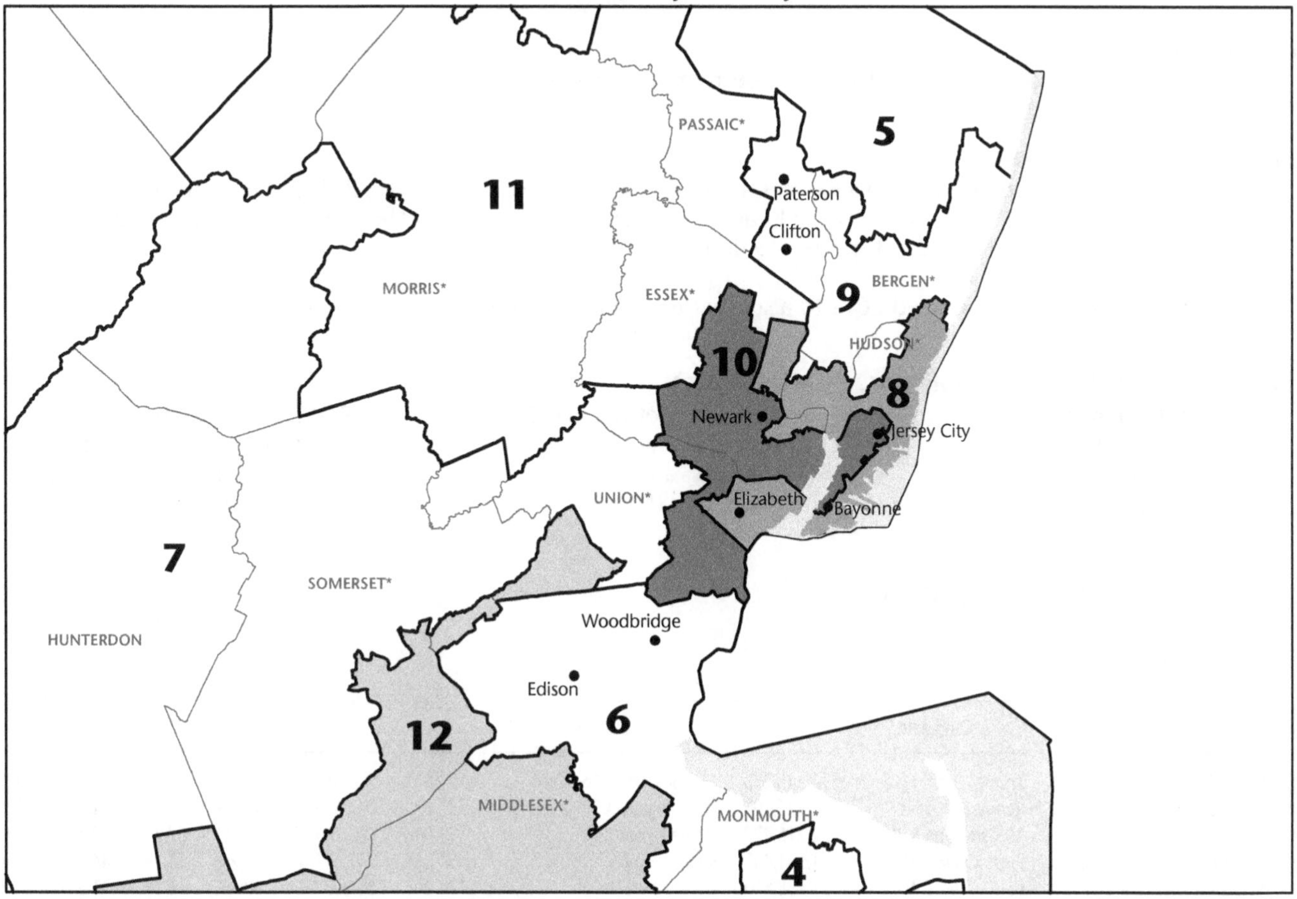

PASSAIC*

5

11

Paterson

Clifton

MORRIS*

ESSEX*

BERGEN*

9

HUDSON*

10

8

Newark

Jersey City

Elizabeth

Bayonne

UNION*

7

SOMERSET*

HUNTERDON

Woodbridge

Edison

12

6

MIDDLESEX*

MONMOUTH*

4

* Asterisk indicates a county whose boundaries include parts of two or more congressional districts.

NEW JERSEY

GOVERNOR

Chris Christie (R). Re-elected 2013 to a four-year term. Previously elected 2009.

SENATORS (2 Democrats)

Cory Booker (D). Re-elected 2014 to a six-year term. Previously elected October 16, 2013, to serve the remainder of the term vacated by the June 2013 death of Frank Lautenberg (D). Jeff Chiesa (R) had been appointed June 6, 2013, to fill the vacant seat until the October 2013 special election.

Robert Menendez (D). Re-elected 2012 to a six-year term. Previously elected 2006.

REPRESENTATIVES (5 Republicans, 7 Democrats)

1. Donald Norcross (D)
2. Frank A. LoBiondo (R)
3. Tom MacArthur (R)
4. Christopher H. Smith (R)
5. Joshua S. Gottheimer (D)
6. Frank Pallone (D)
7. Leonard Lance (R)
8. Albio Sires (D)
9. William J. Pascrell Jr. (D)
10. Donald M. Payne Jr. (D)
11. Rodney Frelinghuysen (R)
12. Bonnie Watson Coleman (D)

POSTWAR VOTE FOR PRESIDENT

| | | Republican | | Democratic | | | | Percentage | | | |
| | | | | | | Other | Rep.-Dem. | Total Vote | | Major Vote | |
Year	Total Vote	Vote	Candidate	Vote	Candidate	Vote	Plurality	Rep.	Dem.	Rep.	Dem.
2016**	3,874,046	1,601,933	Trump, Donald J.	2,148,278	Clinton, Hillary Rodham	123,835	546,345 D	41.4%	55.5%	42.7%	57.3%
2012	3,640,292	1,477,568	Romney, W. Mitt	2,125,101	Obama, Barack H.*	37,623	647,533 D	40.6%	58.4%	41.0%	59.0%
2008	3,868,237	1,613,207	McCain, John S. III	2,215,422	Obama, Barack H.	39,608	602,215 D	41.7%	57.3%	42.1%	57.9%
2004	3,611,691	1,670,003	Bush, George W.*	1,911,430	Kerry, John F.	30,258	241,427 D	46.2%	52.9%	46.6%	53.4%
2000**	3,187,226	1,284,173	Bush, George W.	1,788,850	Gore, Albert Jr.	114,203	504,677 D	40.3%	56.1%	41.8%	58.2%
1996**	3,075,807	1,103,078	Dole, Robert "Bob"	1,652,329	Clinton, Bill*	320,400	549,251 D	35.9%	53.7%	40.0%	60.0%
1992**	3,343,594	1,356,865	Bush, George H.*	1,436,206	Clinton, Bill	550,523	79,341 D	40.6%	43.0%	48.6%	51.4%
1988	3,099,553	1,743,192	Bush, George H.	1,320,352	Dukakis, Michael S.	36,009	422,840 R	56.2%	42.6%	56.9%	43.1%
1984	3,217,862	1,933,630	Reagan, Ronald*	1,261,323	Mondale, Walter F.	22,909	672,307 R	60.1%	39.2%	60.5%	39.5%
1980**	2,975,684	1,546,557	Reagan, Ronald	1,147,364	Carter, Jimmy*	281,763	399,193 R	52.0%	38.6%	57.4%	42.6%
1976	3,014,472	1,509,688	Ford, Gerald R.*	1,444,653	Carter, Jimmy	60,131	65,035 R	50.1%	47.9%	51.1%	48.9%
1972	2,997,229	1,845,502	Nixon, Richard M.*	1,102,211	McGovern, George S.	49,516	743,291 R	61.6%	36.8%	62.6%	37.4%
1968**	2,875,395	1,325,467	Nixon, Richard M.	1,264,206	Humphrey, Hubert Horatio Jr.	285,722	61,261 R	46.1%	44.0%	51.2%	48.8%
1964	2,847,663	964,174	Goldwater, Barry M. Sr.	1,868,231	Johnson, Lyndon B.*	15,258	904,057 D	33.9%	65.6%	34.0%	66.0%
1960	2,773,111	1,363,324	Nixon, Richard M.	1,385,415	Kennedy, John F.	24,372	22,091 D	49.2%	50.0%	49.6%	50.4%
1956	2,484,312	1,606,942	Eisenhower, Dwight D.*	850,337	Stevenson, Adlai E. II	27,033	756,605 R	64.7%	34.2%	65.4%	34.6%
1952	2,418,554	1,373,613	Eisenhower, Dwight D.	1,015,902	Stevenson, Adlai E. II	29,039	357,711 R	56.8%	42.0%	57.5%	42.5%
1948	1,949,555	981,124	Dewey, Thomas E.	895,455	Truman, Harry S.*	72,976	85,669 R	50.3%	45.9%	52.3%	47.7%

Note: An asterisk (*) denotes incumbent. **In past elections, the other vote included: 2016 - 72,477 Libertarian (Gary Johnson); 2000 - 94,554 Green (Ralph Nader); 1996 - 262,134 Reform (Ross Perot); 1992 - 521,829 Independent (Perot); 1980 - 234,632 Independent (John Anderson); 1968 - 262,187 American Independent (George Wallace).

NEW JERSEY

POSTWAR VOTE FOR GOVERNOR

Year	Total Vote	Republican		Democratic		Other Vote	Rep.-Dem. Plurality	Percentage			
								Total Vote		Major Vote	
		Vote	Candidate	Vote	Candidate			Rep.	Dem.	Rep.	Dem.
2013	2,120,866	1,278,932	Christie, Chris*	809,978	Buono, Barbara	31,956	468,954 R	60.3%	38.2%	61.2%	38.8%
2009	2,423,792	1,174,445	Christie, Chris	1,087,731	Corzine, Jon S.*	161,616	86,714 R	48.5%	44.9%	51.9%	48.1%
2005	2,290,099	985,271	Forrester, Doug	1,224,551	Corzine, Jon S.	80,277	239,280 D	43.0%	53.5%	44.6%	55.4%
2001	2,227,165	928,174	Schundler, Bret	1,256,853	McGreevey, James	42,138	328,679 D	41.7%	56.4%	42.5%	57.5%
1997	2,418,344	1,133,394	Whitman, Christine T.*	1,107,968	McGreevey, James	176,982	25,426 R	46.9%	45.8%	50.6%	49.4%
1993	2,505,964	1,236,124	Whitman, Christine T.	1,210,031	Florio, James J.*	59,809	26,093 R	49.3%	48.3%	50.5%	49.5%
1989	2,253,800	838,553	Courter, James A.	1,379,973	Florio, James J.	35,274	541,420 D	37.2%	61.2%	37.8%	62.2%
1985	1,972,624	1,372,631	Kean, Thomas H.*	578,402	Shapiro, Peter	21,591	794,229 R	69.6%	29.3%	70.4%	29.6%
1981	2,317,239	1,145,999	Kean, Thomas H.	1,144,202	Florio, James J.	27,038	1,797 R	49.5%	49.4%	50.0%	50.0%
1977	2,126,264	888,880	Bateman, Raymond H.	1,184,564	Byrne, Brendan T.*	52,820	295,684 D	41.8%	55.7%	42.9%	57.1%
1973	2,122,010	676,235	Sandman, Charles W.	1,414,613	Byrne, Brendan T.	31,162	738,378 D	31.9%	66.7%	32.3%	67.7%
1969	2,366,606	1,411,905	Cahill, William T.	911,003	Meyner, Robert B.	43,698	500,902 R	59.7%	38.5%	60.8%	39.2%
1965	2,229,583	915,996	Dumont, Wayne Jr.	1,279,568	Hughes, Richard J.*	34,019	363,572 D	41.1%	57.4%	41.7%	58.3%
1961	2,152,662	1,049,274	Mitchell, James P.	1,084,194	Hughes, Richard J.	19,194	34,920 D	48.7%	50.4%	49.2%	50.8%
1957	2,018,488	897,321	Forbes, Malcolm Stevenson Sr.	1,101,130	Meyner, Robert B.*	20,037	203,809 D	44.5%	54.6%	44.9%	55.1%
1953	1,810,812	809,068	Troast, Paul L.	962,710	Meyner, Robert B.	39,034	153,642 D	44.7%	53.2%	45.7%	54.3%
1949**	1,718,788	885,882	Driscoll, Alfred Eastlack*	810,022	Wene, Elmer H.	22,884	75,860 R	51.5%	47.1%	52.2%	47.8%
1946	1,414,527	807,378	Driscoll, Alfred Eastlack	585,960	Hansen, Lewis G.	21,189	221,418 R	57.1%	41.4%	57.9%	42.1%

Note: An asterisk (*) denotes incumbent. **The term of office of New Jersey's governor was increased from three to four years effective with the 1949 election.

POSTWAR VOTE FOR SENATOR

Year	Total Vote	Republican		Democratic		Other Vote	Rep.-Dem. Plurality	Percentage			
								Total Vote		Major Vote	
		Vote	Candidate	Vote	Candidate			Rep.	Dem.	Rep.	Dem.
2014	1,869,535	791,297	Bell, Jeffrey	1,043,866	Booker, Cory*	34,372	252,569 D	42.3%	55.8%	43.1%	56.9%
2013S**	1,348,659	593,684	Lonegan, Steven M.	740,742	Booker, Cory	14,233	147,058 D	44.0%	54.9%	44.5%	55.5%
2012	3,374,668	1,329,405	Kyrillos, Joe	1,985,783	Menendez, Robert*	59,480	656,378 D	39.4%	58.8%	40.1%	59.9%
2008	3,482,445	1,461,025	Zimmer, Dick	1,951,218	Lautenberg, Frank R.*	70,202	490,193 D	42.0%	56.0%	42.8%	57.2%
2006	2,250,070	997,775	Kean, Tom Jr.	1,200,843	Menendez, Robert*	51,452	203,068 D	44.3%	53.4%	45.4%	54.6%
2002	2,112,604	928,439	Forrester, Douglas R.	1,138,193	Lautenberg, Frank R.	45,972	209,754 D	43.9%	53.9%	44.9%	55.1%
2000	3,015,662	1,420,267	Franks, Bob	1,511,237	Corzine, Jon S.	84,158	90,970 D	47.1%	50.1%	48.4%	51.6%
1996	2,884,106	1,227,817	Zimmer, Dick	1,519,328	Torricelli, Robert G.	136,961	291,511 D	42.6%	52.7%	44.7%	55.3%
1994	2,054,887	966,244	Haytaian, Garabed	1,033,487	Lautenberg, Frank R.*	55,156	67,243 D	47.0%	50.3%	48.3%	51.7%
1990	1,938,454	918,874	Whitman, Christine T.	977,810	Bradley, Bill Warren*	41,770	58,936 D	47.4%	50.4%	48.4%	51.6%
1988	2,987,634	1,349,937	Dawkins, Peter M.	1,599,905	Lautenberg, Frank R.*	37,792	249,968 D	45.2%	53.6%	45.8%	54.2%
1984	3,096,456	1,080,100	Mochary, Mary V.	1,986,644	Bradley, Bill Warren*	29,712	906,544 D	34.9%	64.2%	35.2%	64.8%
1982	2,193,945	1,047,626	Fenwick, Millicent	1,117,549	Lautenberg, Frank R.	28,770	69,923 D	47.8%	50.9%	48.4%	51.6%
1978	1,957,515	844,200	Bell, Jeffrey	1,082,960	Bradley, Bill Warren	30,355	238,760 D	43.1%	55.3%	43.8%	56.2%
1976	2,771,387	1,054,505	Norcross, David F.	1,681,140	Williams, Harrison A. Jr.*	35,742	626,635 D	38.0%	60.7%	38.5%	61.5%
1972	2,791,907	1,743,854	Case, Clifford P.*	963,573	Kerbs, Paul J.	84,480	780,281 R	62.5%	34.5%	64.4%	35.6%
1970	2,142,105	903,026	Gross, Nelson G.	1,157,074	Williams, Harrison A. Jr.*	82,005	254,048 D	42.2%	54.0%	43.8%	56.2%
1966	2,130,688	1,278,843	Case, Clifford P.*	788,021	Wilentz, Warren W.	63,824	490,822 R	60.0%	37.0%	61.9%	38.1%
1964	2,709,575	1,011,280	Shanley, Bernard M.	1,677,515	Williams, Harrison A. Jr.*	20,780	666,235 D	37.3%	61.9%	37.6%	62.4%
1960	7,934,990	4,451,496	Case, Clifford P.*	3,454,155	Lord, Thorn	29,339	997,341 R	56.1%	43.5%	56.3%	43.7%
1958	1,881,329	882,287	Kean, Robert Winthrop	966,832	Williams, Harrison A. Jr.	32,210	84,545 D	46.9%	51.4%	47.7%	52.3%
1954	1,770,557	861,528	Case, Clifford P.*	858,158	Howell, Charles R.	50,871	3,370 R	48.7%	48.5%	50.1%	49.9%
1952	2,318,232	1,286,782	Smith, H. Alexander*	1,011,187	Alexander, Archibald S.	20,263	275,595 R	55.5%	43.6%	56.0%	44.0%
1948	1,869,882	934,720	Hendrickson, Robert C.	884,414	Alexander, Archibald S.	50,748	50,306 R	50.0%	47.3%	51.4%	48.6%
1946	1,367,155	799,808	Smith, H. Alexander*	548,458	Brunner, George E.	18,889	251,350 R	58.5%	40.1%	59.3%	40.7%

Note: An asterisk (*) denotes incumbent. **The 2013 election was for a short term to fill a vacancy.

NEW JERSEY

PRESIDENT 2016

2010 Census Population	County	Total Vote	Republican (Trump)	Democratic (Clinton)	Other	Rep.-Dem. Plurality	Percentage Total Vote Rep.	Dem.	Major Vote Rep.	Dem.
274,549	ATLANTIC	117,291	52,690	60,924	3,677	8,234 D	44.9%	51.9%	46.4%	53.6%
905,116	BERGEN	419,296	175,529	231,211	12,556	55,682 D	41.9%	55.1%	43.2%	56.8%
448,734	BURLINGTON	218,943	89,272	121,725	7,946	32,453 D	40.8%	55.6%	42.3%	57.7%
513,657	CAMDEN	226,592	72,631	146,717	7,244	74,086 D	32.1%	64.7%	33.1%	66.9%
97,265	CAPE MAY	48,722	28,446	18,750	1,526	9,696 R	58.4%	38.5%	60.3%	39.7%
156,898	CUMBERLAND	54,004	24,453	27,771	1,780	3,318 D	45.3%	51.4%	46.8%	53.2%
783,969	ESSEX	310,934	63,176	240,837	6,921	177,661 D	20.3%	77.5%	20.8%	79.2%
288,288	GLOUCESTER	139,542	67,544	66,870	5,128	674 R	48.4%	47.9%	50.3%	49.7%
634,266	HUDSON	219,375	49,043	163,917	6,415	114,874 D	22.4%	74.7%	23.0%	77.0%
128,349	HUNTERDON	70,836	38,712	28,898	3,226	9,814 R	54.7%	40.8%	57.3%	42.7%
366,513	MERCER	156,529	46,193	104,775	5,561	58,582 D	29.5%	66.9%	30.6%	69.4%
809,858	MIDDLESEX	326,102	122,953	193,044	10,105	70,091 D	37.7%	59.2%	38.9%	61.1%
630,380	MONMOUTH	314,377	166,723	137,181	10,473	29,542 R	53.0%	43.6%	54.9%	45.1%
492,276	MORRIS	250,416	126,071	115,249	9,096	10,822 R	50.3%	46.0%	52.2%	47.8%
576,567	OCEAN	274,362	179,079	87,150	8,133	91,929 R	65.3%	31.8%	67.3%	32.7%
501,226	PASSAIC	194,802	72,902	116,759	5,141	43,857 D	37.4%	59.9%	38.4%	61.6%
66,083	SALEM	29,494	16,381	11,904	1,209	4,477 R	55.5%	40.4%	57.9%	42.1%
323,444	SOMERSET	157,092	65,505	85,689	5,898	20,184 D	41.7%	54.5%	43.3%	56.7%
149,265	SUSSEX	74,126	46,658	24,212	3,256	22,446 R	62.9%	32.7%	65.8%	34.2%
536,499	UNION	221,975	68,114	147,414	6,447	79,300 D	30.7%	66.4%	31.6%	68.4%
108,692	WARREN	49,236	29,858	17,281	2,097	12,577 R	60.6%	35.1%	63.3%	36.7%
8,791,894	TOTAL	3,874,046	1,601,933	2,148,278	123,835	546,345 D	41.4%	55.5%	42.7%	57.3%

NEW JERSEY

HOUSE OF REPRESENTATIVES

CD	Year	Total Vote	Republican Vote	Candidate	Democratic Vote	Candidate	Other Vote	Rep.-Dem. Plurality	Total Vote Rep.	Dem.	Major Vote Rep.	Dem.
1	2016	305,473	112,388	PATTERSON, BOB	183,231	NORCROSS, DONALD*	9,854	70,843 D	36.8%	60.0%	38.0%	62.0%
1	2014	162,492	64,073	COBB, GARRY W.	93,315	NORCROSS, DONALD	5,104	29,242 D	39.4%	57.4%	40.7%	59.3%
1	2012	308,519	92,459	HORTON, GREGORY W.	210,470	ANDREWS, ROBERT E.*	5,590	118,011 D	30.0%	68.2%	30.5%	69.5%
2	2016	297,795	176,338	LOBIONDO, FRANK A.*	110,838	COLE, DAVID H.	10,619	65,500 R	59.2%	37.2%	61.4%	38.6%
2	2014	177,148	108,875	LOBIONDO, FRANK A.*	66,026	HUGHES, WILLIAM J. JR.	2,247	42,849 R	61.5%	37.3%	62.2%	37.8%
2	2012	289,072	166,679	LOBIONDO, FRANK A.*	116,463	SHOBER, CASSANDRA	5,930	50,216 R	57.7%	40.3%	58.9%	41.1%
3	2016	328,060	194,596	MACARTHUR, TOM*	127,526	LAVERGNE, FREDERICK JOHN	5,938	67,070 R	59.3%	38.9%	60.4%	39.6%
3	2014	186,103	100,471	MACARTHUR, TOM	82,537	BELGARD, AIMEE	3,095	17,934 R	54.0%	44.4%	54.9%	45.1%
3	2012	324,406	174,257	RUNYAN, JON*	145,509	ADLER, SHELLEY	4,640	28,748 R	53.7%	44.9%	54.5%	45.5%
4	2016	332,684	211,992	SMITH, CHRISTOPHER H.*	111,532	PHILLIPSON, LORNA	9,160	100,460 R	63.7%	33.5%	65.5%	34.5%
4	2014	174,849	118,826	SMITH, CHRISTOPHER H.*	54,415	SCOLAVINO, RUBEN	1,608	64,411 R	68.0%	31.1%	68.6%	31.4%
4	2012	306,249	195,146	SMITH, CHRISTOPHER H.*	107,992	FROELICH, BRIAN P.	3,111	87,154 R	63.7%	35.3%	64.4%	35.6%
5	2016	337,701	157,690	GARRETT, SCOTT*	172,587	GOTTHEIMER, JOSHUA S.	7,424	14,897 D	46.7%	51.1%	47.7%	52.3%
5	2014	188,921	104,678	GARRETT, SCOTT*	81,808	CHO, ROY	2,435	22,870 R	55.4%	43.3%	56.1%	43.9%
5	2012	304,377	167,503	GARRETT, SCOTT*	130,102	GUSSEN, ADAM	6,772	37,401 R	55.0%	42.7%	56.3%	43.7%
6	2016	263,435	91,908	SONNEK-SCHMELZ, BRENT	167,895	PALLONE, FRANK*	3,632	75,987 D	34.9%	63.7%	35.4%	64.6%
6	2014	120,457	46,891	WILKINSON, ANTHONY E.	72,190	PALLONE, FRANK*	1,376	25,299 D	38.9%	59.9%	39.4%	60.6%
6	2012	239,638	84,360	LITTLE, ANNA C.	151,782	PALLONE, FRANK*	3,496	67,422 D	35.2%	63.3%	35.7%	64.3%
7	2016	343,635	185,850	LANCE, LEONARD*	148,188	JACOB, PETER	9,597	37,662 R	54.1%	43.1%	55.6%	44.4%
7	2014	175,997	104,287	LANCE, LEONARD*	68,232	KOVACH, JANICE	3,478	36,055 R	59.3%	38.8%	60.4%	39.6%
7	2012	307,395	175,704	LANCE, LEONARD*	123,090	CHIVUKULA, UPENDRA J.	8,601	52,614 R	57.2%	40.0%	58.8%	41.2%

NEW JERSEY

HOUSE OF REPRESENTATIVES

			Republican		Democratic				Total Vote		Major Vote	
							Other	Rep.-Dem.	Percentage			
CD	Year	Total Vote	Vote	Candidate	Vote	Candidate	Vote	Plurality	Rep.	Dem.	Rep.	Dem.
8	2016	174,889	32,337	KHAN, AGHA	134,733	SIRES, ALBIO*	7,819	102,396 D	18.5%	77.0%	19.4%	80.6%
8	2014	79,518	15,141	TISCORNIA, JUDE ANTHONY	61,510	SIRES, ALBIO*	2,867	46,369 D	19.0%	77.4%	19.8%	80.2%
8	2012	167,800	31,767	KARCZEWSKI, MARIA	130,857	SIRES, ALBIO*	5,176	99,090 D	18.9%	78.0%	19.5%	80.5%
9	2016	233,242	65,376	CASTILLO, HECTOR L.	162,642	PASCRELL, WILLIAM J. JR.*	5,224	97,266 D	28.0%	69.7%	28.7%	71.3%
9	2014	120,459	36,246	PAUL, DIERDRE	82,498	PASCRELL, WILLIAM J. JR.*	1,715	46,252 D	30.1%	68.5%	30.5%	69.5%
9	2012	220,148	55,094	BOTEACH, SHMULEY	162,834	PASCRELL, WILLIAM J. JR.*	2,220	107,740 D	25.0%	74.0%	25.3%	74.7%
10	2016	222,771	26,450	PINCKNEY, DAVID H.	190,856	PAYNE, DONALD M. JR.*	5,465	164,406 D	11.9%	85.7%	12.2%	87.8%
10	2014	112,123	14,154	DENTLEY, YOLANDA	95,734	PAYNE, DONALD M. JR.*	2,235	81,580 D	12.6%	85.4%	12.9%	87.1%
10	2012	230,060	24,271	KELEMEN, BRIAN C.	201,435	PAYNE, DONALD M. JR.	4,354	177,164 D	10.5%	87.6%	10.8%	89.2%
11	2016	334,992	194,299	FRELINGHUYSEN, RODNEY*	130,162	WENZEL, JOSEPH M.	10,531	64,137 R	58.0%	38.9%	59.9%	40.1%
11	2014	174,932	109,455	FRELINGHUYSEN, RODNEY*	65,477	DUNEC, MARK S.		43,978 R	62.6%	37.4%	62.6%	37.4%
11	2012	309,899	182,239	FRELINGHUYSEN, RODNEY*	123,935	ARVANITES, JOHN	3,725	58,304 R	58.8%	40.0%	59.5%	40.5%
12	2016	288,634	92,407	UCCIO, STEVEN J.	181,430	COLEMAN, BONNIE WATSON*	14,797	89,023 D	32.0%	62.9%	33.7%	66.3%
12	2014	148,366	54,168	ECK, ALIETA	90,430	COLEMAN, BONNIE WATSON	3,768	36,262 D	36.5%	61.0%	37.5%	62.5%
12	2012	274,391	80,907	BECK, ERIC A.	189,938	HOLT, RUSH D.*	3,546	109,031 D	29.5%	69.2%	29.9%	70.1%
TOTAL	2016	3,463,311	1,541,631		1,821,620		100,060	279,989 D	44.5%	52.6%	45.8%	54.2%
TOTAL	2014	1,821,365	877,265		914,172		29,928	36,907 D	48.2%	50.2%	49.0%	51.0%
TOTAL	2012	3,281,954	1,430,386		1,794,407		57,161	364,021 D	43.6%	54.7%	44.4%	55.6%

Note: An asterisk (*) denotes incumbent.

NEW JERSEY

GENERAL AND PRIMARY ELECTIONS

2016 GENERAL ELECTIONS: OTHER VOTES

President   Other vote was 72,477 Libertarian (Gary Johnson), 37,772 Green (Jill Stein), 6,161 Constitution (Darrell Castle), 2,156 Socialist Workers (Alyson Kennedy), 1,838 American Delta (Roque De La Fuente), 1,749 Workers World (Monica Moorehead), 1,682 Socialism and Liberation (Gloria La Riva)

House   Other vote was:

CD 1   5,473 We Deserve Better (Scot John Tomaszewski), 2,410 Libertarian (William Sihr), 1,971 AmericanIndependents.Org (Mike Berman)

CD 2   3,773 Libertarian (John Ordille), 2,653 Make Government Work (James Keenan), 1,574 Representing the 99% (Steven Fenichel), 1,387 People's Independent Progressive (Eric Beechwood), 1,232 For Political Revolution (Gabriel Franco)

CD 3   5,938 Constitution (Lawrence Berlinski).

CD 4   5,840 Economic Growth (Hank Schroeder), 3,320 Libertarian (Jeremy Marcus)

CD 5   7,424 Libertarian (Claudio Belusic)

CD 6   1,912 Green (Rajit Malliah), 1,720 Libertarian (Judith Shamy)

CD 7   5,343 Libertarian (Dan O'Neill), 4,254 Conservative (Arthur Haussmann)

CD 8   4,381 Wake Up USA (Pablo Olivera), 3,438 Libertarian (Dan Delaney)

CD 9   3,327 Libertarian (Diego Rivera), 1,897 NSA Did 911 (Jeff Boss)

CD 10   3,719 Women of Power (Joanne Miller), 1,746 New Beginning's (Aaron Fraser)

CD 11   7,056 Financial Independence (Thomas Depasquale), 3,475 Libertarian (Jeff Hetrick)

CD 12   6,094 Legalize Monarchy (R. Forchion), 2,775 Teddy Roosevelt Progressive (Robert Shapiro), 2,482 Libertarian (Thomas Fitzpatrick), 2,135 Green (Steven Welzer), 1,311 We the People (Michael Bollentin)

NEW JERSEY

GENERAL AND PRIMARY ELECTIONS

2016 PRIMARY ELECTIONS: SUPPLEMENTARY INFORMATION

Primary	June 7, 2016	**Registration** (as of May 31, 2016)	5,552,475	Democratic	1,793,927
				Republican	1,086,925
				Libertarian	3,258
				Conservative	1,796
				Green	1,571
				U.S. Constitution	828
				Socialist	444
				Natural Law	396
				Reform	146
				Unaffiliated	2,663,184

Primary Type   Semi-open—Registered Democrats and Republicans could vote only in their party's primary. "Unaffiliated" voters could participate in either party's primary if they were willing to become a member of that party.

	REPUBLICAN PRIMARIES			DEMOCRATIC PRIMARIES		
President	Trump, Donald J.	360,212	80.4%	Clinton, Hillary Rodham	566,247	63.3%
	Kasich, John R.	59,866	13.4%	Sanders, Bernard	328,058	36.7%
	Cruz, Ted	27,874	6.2%			
	TOTAL	*447,952*		*TOTAL*	*894,305*	
Congressional District 1	Patterson, Bob	23,813	100.0%	Norcross, Donald*	56,753	70.3%
				Law, Alex	23,986	29.7%
	TOTAL	*23,813*		*TOTAL*	*80,739*	
Congressional District 2	LoBiondo, Frank A.*	39,913	100.0%	Cole, David H.	33,961	81.1%
				Rozzo, Costantino	7,932	18.9%
	TOTAL	*39,913*		*TOTAL*	*41,893*	
Congressional District 3	MacArthur, Tom*	46,264	100.0%	Lavergne, Frederick John	32,963	62.8%
				Keady, Jim	19,526	37.2%
	TOTAL	*46,264*		*TOTAL*	*52,489*	
Congressional District 4	Smith, Christopher H.*	41,789	92.0%	Phillipson, Lorna	40,528	100.0%
	MacDonald, Bruce C.	3,645	8.0%			
	TOTAL	*45,434*		*TOTAL*	*40,528*	
Congressional District 5	Garrett, Scott*	42,179	82.2%	Gottheimer, Joshua S.	43,250	100.0%
	Cino, Michael J.	4,884	9.5%			
	Vallorosi, Peter	4,252	8.3%			
	TOTAL	*51,315*		*TOTAL*	*43,250*	
Congressional District 6	Sonnek-Schmelz, Brent	17,856	100.0%	Pallone, Frank*	52,231	100.0%
	TOTAL	*17,856*		*TOTAL*	*52,231*	
Congressional District 7	Lance, Leonard*	31,807	53.9%	Jacob, Peter	46,152	100.0%
	Larsen, David	19,425	32.9%			
	Heard, Craig P.	7,774	13.2%			
	TOTAL	*59,006*		*TOTAL*	*46,152*	
Congressional District 8	Khan, Agha	4,679	100.0%	Sires, Albio*	45,988	86.9%
				Delgado, Eloy J.	6,933	13.1%
	TOTAL	*4,679*		*TOTAL*	*52,921*	
Congressional District 9	Castillo, Hector L.	12,757	100.0%	Pascrell, William J. Jr.*	47,671	100.0%
	TOTAL	*12,757*		*TOTAL*	*47,671*	

NEW JERSEY

NEW GENERAL AND PRIMARY ELECTIONS

	REPUBLICAN PRIMARIES			DEMOCRATIC PRIMARIES		
Congressional	Pinckney, David H.	3,395	100.0%	Payne, Donald M. Jr.*	75,175	100.0%
District 10	*TOTAL*	*3,395*		*TOTAL*	*75,175*	
Congressional	Frelinghuysen, Rodney*	44,618	76.2%	Wenzel, Joseph M.	34,688	70.4%
District 11	Van Glahn, Rick	13,909	23.8%	McFarlane, Richard	8,751	17.8%
				Brogowski, Lee Anne	5,799	11.8%
	TOTAL	*58,527*		*TOTAL*	*49,238*	
Congressional	Uccio, Steven J.	18,640	100.0%	Coleman, Bonnie Watson*	66,479	93.6%
District 12				Kucsma, Alexander J.	4,525	6.4%
	TOTAL	*18,640*		*TOTAL*	*71,004*	

Note: An asterisk (*) denotes incumbent.

NEW MEXICO

Congressional districts first established for elections held in 2012

3 members

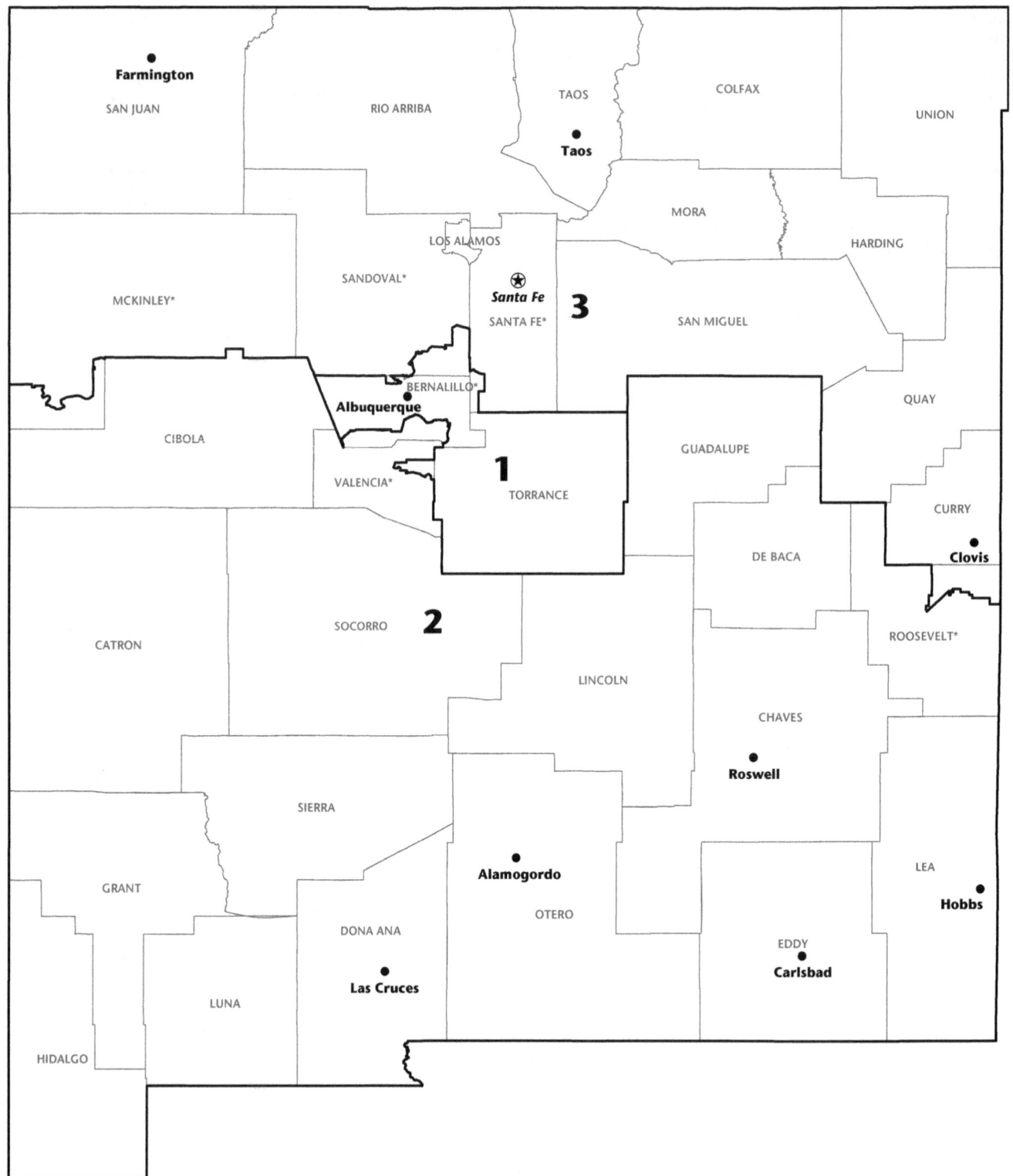

* Asterisk indicates a county whose boundaries include parts of two or more congressional districts.

NEW MEXICO

GOVERNOR
Susana Martinez (R). Re-elected 2014 to a four-year term. Previously elected 2010.

SENATORS (2 Democrats)
Martin Heinrich (D). Elected 2012 to a six-year term.

Tom Udall (D). Re-elected 2014 to a six-year term. Previously elected 2008.

REPRESENTATIVES (1 Republican, 2 Democrats)
1. Michelle Lujan Grisham (D)   2. Steve Pearce (R)   3. Ben Ray Lujan (D)

POSTWAR VOTE FOR PRESIDENT

| | | Republican | | Democratic | | Other | Rep.-Dem. | Percentage | | | |
| | | | | | | | | Total Vote | | Major Vote | |
Year	Total Vote	Vote	Candidate	Vote	Candidate	Vote	Plurality	Rep.	Dem.	Rep.	Dem.
2016**	798,319	319,667	Trump, Donald J.	385,234	Clinton, Hillary Rodham	93,418	65,567 D	40.0%	48.3%	45.3%	54.7%
2012	783,757	335,788	Romney, W. Mitt	415,335	Obama, Barack H.*	32,634	79,547 D	42.8%	53.0%	44.7%	55.3%
2008	830,158	346,832	McCain, John S. III	472,422	Obama, Barack H.	10,904	125,590 D	41.8%	56.9%	42.3%	57.7%
2004	756,304	376,930	Bush, George W.*	370,942	Kerry, John F.	8,432	5,988 R	49.8%	49.0%	50.4%	49.6%
2000**	598,605	286,417	Bush, George W.	286,783	Gore, Albert Jr.	25,405	366 D	47.8%	47.9%	50.0%	50.0%
1996**	556,074	232,751	Dole, Robert "Bob"	273,495	Clinton, Bill*	49,828	40,744 D	41.9%	49.2%	46.0%	54.0%
1992**	569,986	212,824	Bush, George H.*	261,617	Clinton, Bill	95,545	48,793 D	37.3%	45.9%	44.9%	55.1%
1988	521,287	270,341	Bush, George H.	244,497	Dukakis, Michael S.	6,449	25,844 R	51.9%	46.9%	52.5%	47.5%
1984	514,370	307,101	Reagan, Ronald*	201,769	Mondale, Walter F.	5,500	105,332 R	59.7%	39.2%	60.3%	39.7%
1980**	456,971	250,779	Reagan, Ronald	167,826	Carter, Jimmy*	38,366	82,953 R	54.9%	36.7%	59.9%	40.1%
1976	418,409	211,419	Ford, Gerald R.*	201,148	Carter, Jimmy	5,842	10,271 R	50.5%	48.1%	51.2%	48.8%
1972	386,241	235,606	Nixon, Richard M.*	141,084	McGovern, George S.	9,551	94,522 R	61.0%	36.5%	62.5%	37.5%
1968**	327,350	169,692	Nixon, Richard M.	130,081	Humphrey, Hubert Horatio Jr.	27,577	39,611 R	51.8%	39.7%	56.6%	43.4%
1964	328,645	132,838	Goldwater, Barry M. Sr.	194,015	Johnson, Lyndon B.*	1,792	61,177 D	40.4%	59.0%	40.6%	59.4%
1960	311,107	153,733	Nixon, Richard M.	156,027	Kennedy, John F.	1,347	2,294 D	49.4%	50.2%	49.6%	50.4%
1956	253,926	146,788	Eisenhower, Dwight D.*	106,098	Stevenson, Adlai E. II	1,040	40,690 R	57.8%	41.8%	58.0%	42.0%
1952	238,608	132,170	Eisenhower, Dwight D.	105,661	Stevenson, Adlai E. II	777	26,509 R	55.4%	44.3%	55.6%	44.4%
1948	187,063	80,303	Dewey, Thomas E.	105,464	Truman, Harry S.*	1,296	25,161 D	42.9%	56.4%	43.2%	56.8%

Note: An asterisk (*) denotes incumbent. **In past elections, the other vote included: 2016 - 74,541 Libertarian (Gary Johnson); 2000 - 21,251 Green (Ralph Nader); 1996 - 32,257 Reform (Ross Perot); 1992 - 91,895 Independent (Perot); 1980 - 29,459 Independent (John Anderson); 1968 - 25,737 American Independent (George Wallace).

NEW MEXICO

POSTWAR VOTE FOR GOVERNOR

Year	Total Vote	Republican		Democratic		Other Vote	Rep.-Dem. Plurality	Percentage			
		Vote	Candidate	Vote	Candidate			Total Vote		Major Vote	
								Rep.	Dem.	Rep.	Dem.
2014	512,805	293,443	Martinez, Susana*	219,362	King, Gary K.		74,081 R	57.2%	42.8%	57.2%	42.8%
2010	602,827	321,219	Martinez, Susana	280,614	Denish, Diane D.	994	40,605 R	53.3%	46.5%	53.4%	46.6%
2006	559,170	174,364	Dendahl, John	384,806	Richardson, Bill*		210,442 D	31.2%	68.8%	31.2%	68.8%
2002	484,233	189,074	Sanchez, John A.	268,693	Richardson, Bill	26,466	79,619 D	39.0%	55.5%	41.3%	58.7%
1998	498,703	271,948	Johnson, Gary E.*	226,755	Chavez, Martin J.		45,193 R	54.5%	45.5%	54.5%	45.5%
1994**	467,621	232,945	Johnson, Gary E.	186,686	King, Bruce*	47,990	46,259 R	49.8%	39.9%	55.5%	44.5%
1990	411,232	185,692	Bond, Frank	224,564	King, Bruce	976	38,872 D	45.2%	54.6%	45.3%	54.7%
1986	394,833	209,455	Carruthers, Garrey E.	185,378	Powell, Ray B.		24,077 R	53.0%	47.0%	53.0%	47.0%
1982	407,466	191,626	Irick, John B.	215,840	Anaya, Toney		24,214 D	47.0%	53.0%	47.0%	53.0%
1978	345,577	170,848	Skeen, Joseph R.	174,631	King, Bruce	98	3,783 D	49.4%	50.5%	49.5%	50.5%
1974	328,742	160,430	Skeen, Joseph R.	164,172	Apodaca, Jerry	4,140	3,742 D	48.8%	49.9%	49.4%	50.6%
1970**	290,375	134,640	Domenici, Peter V.	148,835	King, Bruce	6,900	14,195 D	46.4%	51.3%	47.5%	52.5%
1968	318,975	160,140	Cargo, David F.*	157,230	Chavez, Fabian	1,605	2,910 R	50.2%	49.3%	50.5%	49.5%
1966	260,232	134,625	Cargo, David F.	125,587	Lusk, T. E.	20	9,038 R	51.7%	48.3%	51.7%	48.3%
1964	318,042	126,540	Tucker, Merle H.	191,497	Campbell, Jack M.*	5	64,957 D	39.8%	60.2%	39.8%	60.2%
1962	247,135	116,184	Mechem, Edwin L.*	130,933	Campbell, Jack M.	18	14,749 D	47.0%	53.0%	47.0%	53.0%
1960	305,542	153,765	Mechem, Edwin L.	151,777	Burroughs, John*		1,988 R	50.3%	49.7%	50.3%	49.7%
1958	205,048	101,567	Mechem, Edwin L.*	103,481	Burroughs, John		1,914 D	49.5%	50.5%	49.5%	50.5%
1956	251,751	131,488	Mechem, Edwin L.	120,263	Simms, John F. Jr.*		11,225 R	52.2%	47.8%	52.2%	47.8%
1954	193,956	83,373	Stockton, Alvin	110,583	Simms, John F. Jr.		27,210 D	43.0%	57.0%	43.0%	57.0%
1952	240,150	129,116	Mechem, Edwin L.*	111,034	Grantham, Everett		18,082 R	53.8%	46.2%	53.8%	46.2%
1950	180,205	96,846	Mechem, Edwin L.	83,359	Miles, John E.		13,487 R	53.7%	46.3%	53.7%	46.3%
1948	189,992	86,023	Lujan, Manuel	103,969	Mabry, Thomas J.*		17,946 D	45.3%	54.7%	45.3%	54.7%
1946	132,630	62,575	Safford, Edward L.	70,055	Mabry, Thomas J.		7,480 D	47.2%	52.8%	47.2%	52.8%

Note: An asterisk (*) denotes incumbent. **In past elections, the other vote included: 1994 - 47,990 Green (Roberto Mondragon). The term of New Mexico's governor was increased from two to four years effective with the 1970 election.

POSTWAR VOTE FOR SENATOR

Year	Total Vote	Republican		Democratic		Other Vote	Rep.-Dem. Plurality	Percentage			
		Vote	Candidate	Vote	Candidate			Total Vote		Major Vote	
								Rep.	Dem.	Rep.	Dem.
2014	515,506	229,097	Weh, Allen	286,409	Udall, Tom*		57,312 D	44.4%	55.6%	44.4%	55.6%
2012	775,792	351,259	Wilson, Heather A.	395,717	Heinrich, Martin	28,816	44,458 D	45.3%	51.0%	47.0%	53.0%
2008	823,650	318,522	Pearce, Steve	505,128	Udall, Tom		186,606 D	38.7%	61.3%	38.7%	61.3%
2006	558,550	163,826	McCulloch, Allen	394,365	Bingaman, Jeff*	359	230,539 D	29.3%	70.6%	29.3%	70.7%
2002	483,340	314,301	Domenici, Peter V.*	169,039	Tristani, Gloria		145,262 R	65.0%	35.0%	65.0%	35.0%
2000	589,526	225,517	Redmond, Bill	363,744	Bingaman, Jeff*	265	138,227 D	38.3%	61.7%	38.3%	61.7%
1996	551,821	357,171	Domenici, Peter V.*	164,356	Trujillo, Art	30,294	192,815 R	64.7%	29.8%	68.5%	31.5%
1994	463,196	213,025	McMillan, Colin R.	249,989	Bingaman, Jeff*	182	36,964 D	46.0%	54.0%	46.0%	54.0%
1990	406,938	296,712	Domenici, Peter V.*	110,033	Benavides, Tom R.	193	186,679 R	72.9%	27.0%	72.9%	27.1%
1988	508,598	186,579	Valentine, William	321,983	Bingaman, Jeff*	36	135,404 D	36.7%	63.3%	36.7%	63.3%
1984	502,634	361,371	Domenici, Peter V.*	141,253	Pratt, Judith A.	10	220,118 R	71.9%	28.1%	71.9%	28.1%
1982	404,810	187,128	Schmitt, Harrison*	217,682	Bingaman, Jeff		30,554 D	46.2%	53.8%	46.2%	53.8%
1978	343,554	183,442	Domenici, Peter V.*	160,045	Anaya, Toney	67	23,397 R	53.4%	46.6%	53.4%	46.6%
1976	413,141	234,681	Schmitt, Harrison	176,382	Montoya, Joseph M.*	2,078	58,299 R	56.8%	42.7%	57.1%	42.9%
1972	378,330	204,253	Domenici, Peter V.	173,815	Daniels, Jack	262	30,438 R	54.0%	45.9%	54.0%	46.0%
1970	289,906	135,004	Carter, Anderson	151,486	Montoya, Joseph M.*	3,416	16,482 D	46.6%	52.3%	47.1%	52.9%
1966	258,203	120,988	Carter, Anderson	137,205	Anderson, Clinton P.*	10	16,217 D	46.9%	53.1%	46.9%	53.1%
1964	325,774	147,562	Mechem, Edwin L.	178,209	Montoya, Joseph M.	3	30,647 D	45.3%	54.7%	45.3%	54.7%
1960	300,551	109,897	Colwes, William	190,654	Anderson, Clinton P.*		80,757 D	36.6%	63.4%	36.6%	63.4%
1958	203,323	75,827	Atchley, Forrest S.	127,496	Chavez, Dennis*		51,669 D	37.3%	62.7%	37.3%	62.7%
1954	194,422	83,071	Mechem, Edwin L.	111,351	Anderson, Clinton P.*		28,280 D	42.7%	57.3%	42.7%	57.3%
1952	239,711	117,168	Hurley, Patrick J.	122,543	Chavez, Dennis*		5,375 D	48.9%	51.1%	48.9%	51.1%
1948	188,495	80,226	Hurley, Patrick J.	108,269	Anderson, Clinton P.		28,043 D	42.6%	57.4%	42.6%	57.4%
1946	133,282	64,632	Hurley, Patrick J.	68,650	Chavez, Dennis*		4,018 D	48.5%	51.5%	48.5%	51.5%

Note: An asterisk (*) denotes incumbent.

NEW MEXICO

PRESIDENT 2016

2010 Census Population	County	Total Vote	Republican (Trump)	Democratic (Clinton)	Other	Rep.-Dem. Plurality	Percentage Total Vote Rep.	Percentage Total Vote Dem.	Percentage Major Vote Rep.	Percentage Major Vote Dem.
662,564	BERNALILLO	274,662	94,698	143,417	36,547	48,719 D	34.5%	52.2%	39.8%	60.2%
3,725	CATRON	2,049	1,464	427	158	1,037 R	71.4%	20.8%	77.4%	22.6%
65,645	CHAVES	20,271	12,872	5,534	1,865	7,338 R	63.5%	27.3%	69.9%	30.1%
27,213	CIBOLA	8,063	3,195	3,741	1,127	546 D	39.6%	46.4%	46.1%	53.9%
13,750	COLFAX	5,332	2,585	2,129	618	456 R	48.5%	39.9%	54.8%	45.2%
48,376	CURRY	13,370	9,035	3,121	1,214	5,914 R	67.6%	23.3%	74.3%	25.7%
2,022	DE BACA	910	620	193	97	427 R	68.1%	21.2%	76.3%	23.7%
209,233	DONA ANA	70,648	25,374	37,947	7,327	12,573 D	35.9%	53.7%	40.1%	59.9%
53,829	EDDY	19,667	13,147	5,033	1,487	8,114 R	66.8%	25.6%	72.3%	27.7%
29,514	GRANT	12,811	5,288	6,276	1,247	988 D	41.3%	49.0%	45.7%	54.3%
4,687	GUADALUPE	1,827	595	970	262	375 D	32.6%	53.1%	38.0%	62.0%
695	HARDING	527	311	156	60	155 R	59.0%	29.6%	66.6%	33.4%
4,894	HIDALGO	1,872	910	784	178	126 R	48.6%	41.9%	53.7%	46.3%
64,727	LEA	17,712	12,495	3,930	1,287	8,565 R	70.5%	22.2%	76.1%	23.9%
20,497	LINCOLN	8,902	5,896	2,331	675	3,565 R	66.2%	26.2%	71.7%	28.3%
17,950	LOS ALAMOS	10,885	3,359	5,562	1,964	2,203 D	30.9%	51.1%	37.7%	62.3%
25,095	LUNA	7,295	3,478	3,195	622	283 R	47.7%	43.8%	52.1%	47.9%
71,492	MCKINLEY	21,703	5,104	13,576	3,023	8,472 D	23.5%	62.6%	27.3%	72.7%
4,881	MORA	2,441	665	1,536	240	871 D	27.2%	62.9%	30.2%	69.8%
63,797	OTERO	20,060	11,887	6,124	2,049	5,763 R	59.3%	30.5%	66.0%	34.0%
9,041	QUAY	3,572	2,212	1,017	343	1,195 R	61.9%	28.5%	68.5%	31.5%
40,246	RIO ARRIBA	14,878	3,599	9,592	1,687	5,993 D	24.2%	64.5%	27.3%	72.7%
19,846	ROOSEVELT	5,950	3,884	1,454	612	2,430 R	65.3%	24.4%	72.8%	27.2%
130,044	SAN JUAN	46,110	27,946	12,865	5,299	15,081 R	60.6%	27.9%	68.5%	31.5%
29,393	SAN MIGUEL	10,751	2,313	7,285	1,153	4,972 D	21.5%	67.8%	24.1%	75.9%
131,561	SANDOVAL	61,690	25,905	27,707	8,078	1,802 D	42.0%	44.9%	48.3%	51.7%
144,170	SANTA FE	71,434	14,332	50,793	6,309	36,461 D	20.1%	71.1%	22.0%	78.0%
11,988	SIERRA	5,181	3,010	1,612	559	1,398 R	58.1%	31.1%	65.1%	34.9%
17,866	SOCORRO	6,868	2,616	3,313	939	697 D	38.1%	48.2%	44.1%	55.9%
32,937	TAOS	15,260	2,727	10,668	1,865	7,941 D	17.9%	69.9%	20.4%	79.6%
16,383	TORRANCE	6,324	3,714	1,785	825	1,929 R	58.7%	28.2%	67.5%	32.5%
4,549	UNION	1,702	1,216	320	166	896 R	71.4%	18.8%	79.2%	20.8%
76,569	VALENCIA	27,592	13,215	10,841	3,536	2,374 R	47.9%	39.3%	54.9%	45.1%
2,059,179	TOTAL	798,319	319,667	385,234	93,418	65,567 D	40.0%	48.3%	45.3%	54.7%

NEW MEXICO

HOUSE OF REPRESENTATIVES

CD	Year	Total Vote	Republican Vote	Republican Candidate	Democratic Vote	Democratic Candidate	Other Vote	Rep.-Dem. Plurality	Total Vote Rep.	Total Vote Dem.	Major Vote Rep.	Major Vote Dem.
1	2016	277,967	96,879	PRIEM, RICHARD G.	181,088	GRISHAM, MICHELLE LUJAN *		84,209 D	34.9%	65.1%	34.9%	65.1%
1	2014	180,032	74,558	FRESE, MICHAEL H.	105,474	GRISHAM, MICHELLE LUJAN *		30,916 D	41.4%	58.6%	41.4%	58.6%
1	2012	275,856	112,473	ARNOLD-JONES, JANICE E.	162,924	GRISHAM, MICHELLE LUJAN	459	50,451 D	40.8%	59.1%	40.8%	59.2%
2	2016	228,817	143,515	PEARCE, STEVE *	85,232	SOULES, MERRIE LEE	70	58,283 R	62.7%	37.2%	62.7%	37.3%
2	2014	147,777	95,209	PEARCE, STEVE *	52,499	LARA, ROXANNE "ROCKY"	69	42,710 R	64.4%	35.5%	64.5%	35.5%
2	2012	225,515	133,180	PEARCE, STEVE *	92,162	ERHARD, EVELYN MADRID	173	41,018 R	59.1%	40.9%	59.1%	40.9%
3	2016	273,342	102,730	ROMERO, MICHAEL H.	170,612	LUJAN, BEN RAY *		67,882 D	37.6%	62.4%	37.6%	62.4%
3	2014	184,076	70,775	BYRD, JEFFERSON L.	113,249	LUJAN, BEN RAY *	52	42,474 D	38.4%	61.5%	38.5%	61.5%
3	2012	264,719	97,616	BYRD, JEFFERSON L.	167,103	LUJAN, BEN RAY *		69,487 D	36.9%	63.1%	36.9%	63.1%
TOTAL	2016	780,126	343,124		436,932		70	93,808 D	44.0%	56.0%	44.0%	56.0%
TOTAL	2014	511,885	240,542		271,222		121	30,680 D	47.0%	53.0%	47.0%	53.0%
TOTAL	2012	766,090	343,269		422,189		632	78,920 D	44.8%	55.1%	44.8%	55.2%

Note: An asterisk (*) denotes incumbent.

NEW MEXICO

GENERAL AND PRIMARY ELECTIONS

2016 GENERAL ELECTIONS: OTHER VOTES

President	Other vote was 74,541 Libertarian (Gary Johnson), 9,879 Green (Jill Stein), 5,825 Better For America (Evan McMullin), 1,514 Constitution (Darrell Castle), 1,184 Socialism and Liberation (Gloria La Riva), 475 American Delta (Roque De La Fuente)
House	Other vote was:
CD 2	70 Write-in (Jack McGrann)

2016 PRIMARY ELECTIONS: SUPPLEMENTARY INFORMATION

Primary	June 7, 2016	**Registration** (as of May 26, 2016)	1,233,916	Democratic Republican Other Declined to State	578,967 384,565 40,592 229,792

Primary Type Closed—Only registered Democrats and Republicans could vote in their party's primary.

	REPUBLICAN PRIMARIES			DEMOCRATIC PRIMARIES		
President	Trump, Donald J.	73,908	70.6%	Clinton, Hillary Rodham	111,334	51.5%
	Cruz, Ted	13,925	13.3%	Sanders, Bernard	104,741	48.5%
	Kasich, John R.	7,925	7.6%			
	Carson, Ben	3,830	3.7%			
	Bush, Jeb	3,531	3.4%			
	Fiorina, Carly	1,508	1.4%			
	TOTAL	*104,627*		*TOTAL*	*216,075*	
Congressional District 1	Priem, Richard G.	27,973	100.0%	Grisham, Michelle Lujan*	69,216	100.0%
	TOTAL	*27,973*		*TOTAL*	*69,216*	
Congressional District 2	Pearce, Steve*	36,722	100.0%	Soules, Merrie Lee	37,455	100.0%
	TOTAL	*36,722*		*TOTAL*	*37,455*	
Congressional District 3	Romero, Michael H.	17,025	62.0%	Lujan, Ben Ray*	76,789	100.0%
	Lucero, Michael Glenn	10,419	38.0%			
	TOTAL	*27,444*		*TOTAL*	*76,789*	

Note: An asterisk (*) denotes incumbent.

NEW YORK

Congressional districts first established for elections held in 2012

27 members

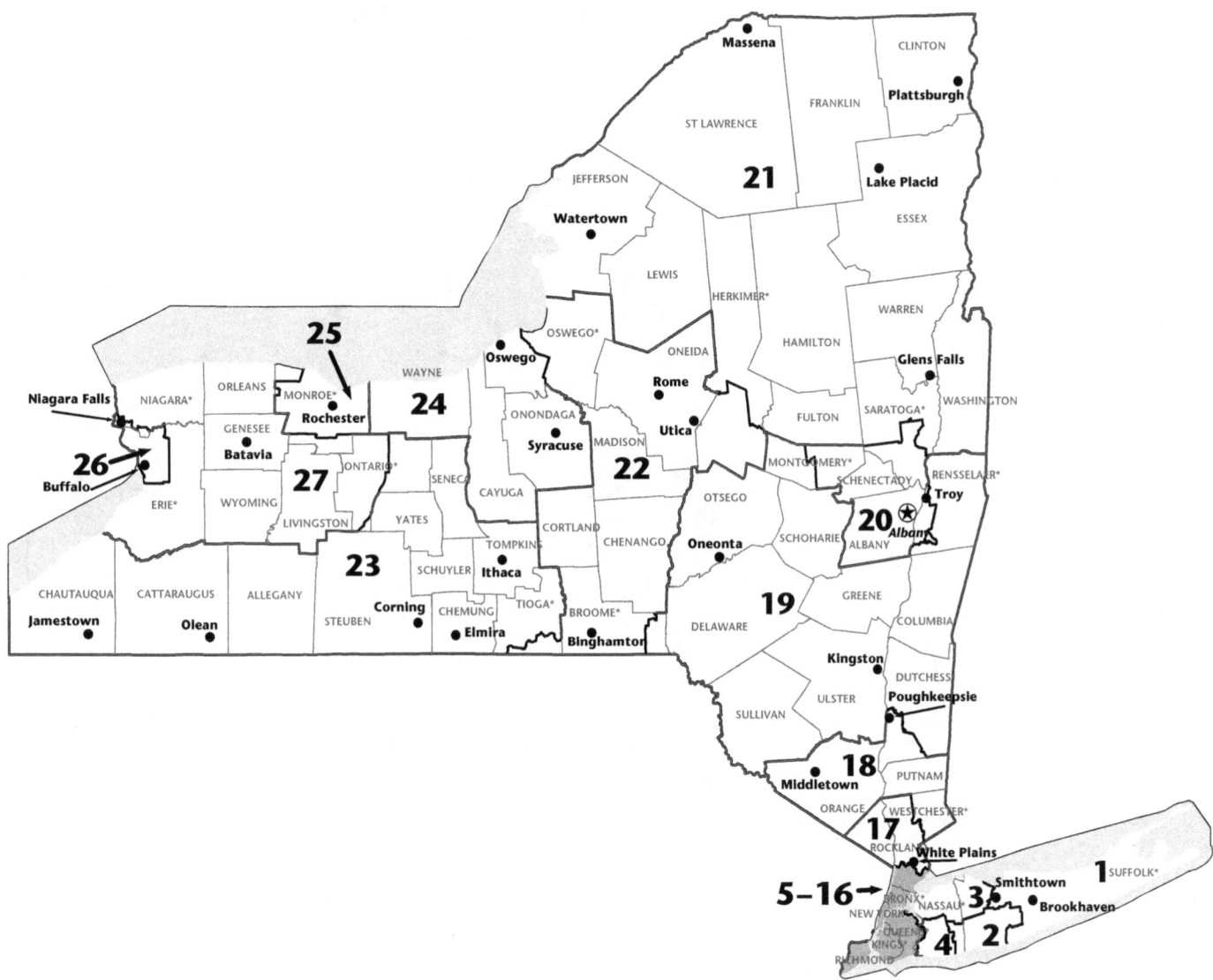

* Asterisk indicates a county whose boundaries include parts of two or more congressional districts.

NEW YORK
New York City Area

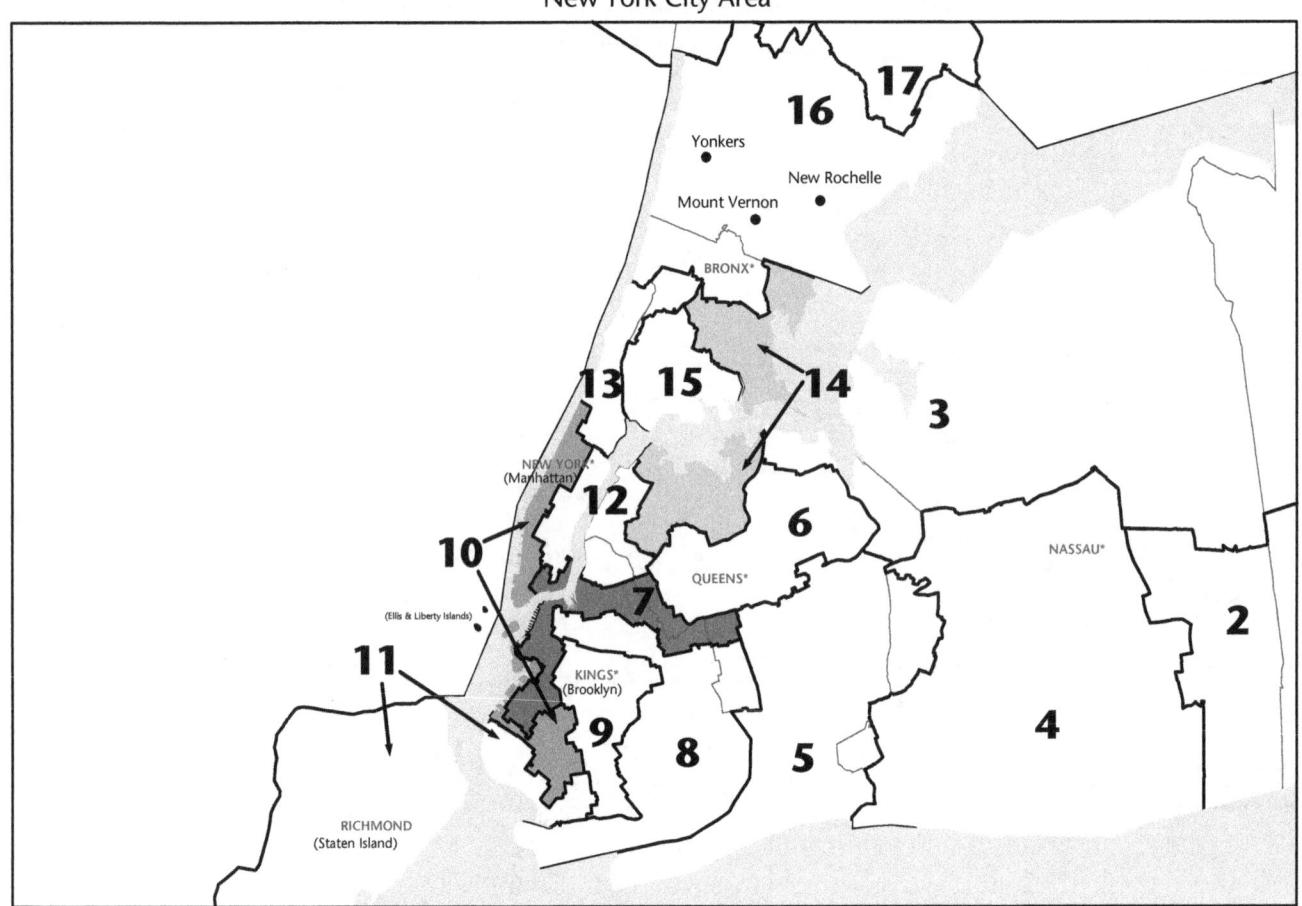

* Asterisk indicates a county whose boundaries include parts of two or more congressional districts.

NEW YORK

GOVERNOR

Andrew Cuomo (D). Re-elected 2014 to a four-year term. Previously elected 2010.

SENATORS (2 Democrats)

Kirsten E. Gillibrand (D). Re-elected 2012 to a six-year term. Previously elected 2010 to fill the remaining two years of the term vacated by Hillary Rodham Clinton (D), who resigned in January 2009 to become U.S. secretary of state. Gillibrand sworn in as senator January 27, 2009, shortly after the vacancy occurred.

Charles E. Schumer (D). Re-elected 2016 to a six-year term. Previously elected 2010, 2004, 1998.

REPRESENTATIVES (9 Republicans, 18 Democrats)

1. Lee M. Zeldin (R)
2. Peter T. King (R)
3. Thomas R. Suozzi (D)
4. Kathleen M. Rice (D)
5. Gregory W. Meeks (D)
6. Grace Meng (D)
7. Nydia Velazquez (D)
8. Hakeem Jeffries (D)
9. Yvette D. Clarke (D)
10. Jerrold Nadler (D)
11. Daniel Donovan (R)
12. Carolyn B. Maloney (D)
13. Adriano Espaillat (D)
14. Joseph Crowley (D)
15. José E. Serrano (D)
16. Eliot L. Engel (D)
17. Nita M. Lowey (D)
18. Sean Maloney (D)
19. John Faso (R)
20. Paul D. Tonko (D)
21. Elise Stefanik (R)
22. Claudia Tenney (R)
23. Thomas W. Reed II (R)
24. John M. Katko (R)
25. Louise M. Slaughter (D)
26. Brian M. Higgins (D)
27. Chris Collins (R)

POSTWAR VOTE FOR PRESIDENT

Year	Total Vote	Republican		Democratic		Other Vote	Rep.-Dem. Plurality	Percentage			
		Vote	Candidate	Vote	Candidate			Total Vote		Major Vote	
								Rep.	Dem.	Rep.	Dem.
2016**	7,721,442	2,819,533	Trump, Donald J.	4,556,118	Clinton, Hillary Rodham	345,791	1,736,585 D	36.5%	59.0%	38.2%	61.8%
2012	7,081,159	2,490,431	Romney, W. Mitt	4,485,741	Obama, Barack H.*	104,987	1,995,310 D	35.2%	63.3%	35.7%	64.3%
2008	7,640,931	2,752,771	McCain, John S. III	4,804,945	Obama, Barack H.	83,215	2,052,174 D	36.0%	62.9%	36.4%	63.6%
2004	7,391,036	2,962,567	Bush, George W.*	4,314,280	Kerry, John F.	114,189	1,351,713 D	40.1%	58.4%	40.7%	59.3%
2000**	6,821,999	2,403,374	Bush, George W.	4,107,697	Gore, Albert Jr.	310,928	1,704,323 D	35.2%	60.2%	36.9%	63.1%
1996**	6,316,129	1,933,492	Dole, Robert "Bob"	3,756,177	Clinton, Bill*	626,460	1,822,685 D	30.6%	59.5%	34.0%	66.0%
1992**	6,926,925	2,346,649	Bush, George H.*	3,444,450	Clinton, Bill	1,135,826	1,097,801 D	33.9%	49.7%	40.5%	59.5%
1988	6,485,683	3,081,871	Bush, George H.	3,347,882	Dukakis, Michael S.	55,930	266,011 D	47.5%	51.6%	47.9%	52.1%
1984	6,806,810	3,664,763	Reagan, Ronald*	3,119,609	Mondale, Walter F.	22,438	545,154 R	53.8%	45.8%	54.0%	46.0%
1980**	6,201,959	2,893,831	Reagan, Ronald	2,728,372	Carter, Jimmy*	579,756	165,459 R	46.7%	44.0%	51.5%	48.5%
1976	6,534,170	3,100,791	Ford, Gerald R.*	3,389,558	Carter, Jimmy	43,821	288,767 D	47.5%	51.9%	47.8%	52.2%
1972	7,165,919	4,192,778	Nixon, Richard M.*	2,951,084	McGovern, George S.	22,057	1,241,694 R	58.5%	41.2%	58.7%	41.3%
1968**	6,791,688	3,007,932	Nixon, Richard M.	3,378,470	Humphrey, Hubert Horatio Jr.	405,286	370,538 D	44.3%	49.7%	47.1%	52.9%
1964	7,166,275	2,243,559	Goldwater, Barry M. Sr.	4,913,102	Johnson, Lyndon B.*	9,614	2,669,543 D	31.3%	68.6%	31.3%	68.7%
1960	7,291,079	3,446,419	Nixon, Richard M.	3,830,085	Kennedy, John F.	14,575	383,666 D	47.3%	52.5%	47.4%	52.6%
1956	7,095,971	4,345,506	Eisenhower, Dwight D.*	2,747,944	Stevenson, Adlai E. II	2,521	1,597,562 R	61.2%	38.7%	61.3%	38.7%
1952	7,128,239	3,952,813	Eisenhower, Dwight D.	3,104,601	Stevenson, Adlai E. II	70,825	848,212 R	55.5%	43.6%	56.0%	44.0%
1948**	6,177,337	2,841,163	Dewey, Thomas E.	2,780,204	Truman, Harry S.*	555,970	60,959 R	46.0%	45.0%	50.5%	49.5%

Note: An asterisk (*) denotes incumbent. **In past elections, the other vote included: 2016 - 176,598 Libertarian (Gary Johnson); 2000 - 244,030 Green (Ralph Nader); 1996 - 503,458 Reform (Ross Perot); 1992 - 1,090,721 Independent (Perot); 1980 - 467,801 Independent (John Anderson); 1968 - 358,864 American Independent (George Wallace); 1948 - 509,559 Progressive (Henry Wallace).

NEW YORK

POSTWAR VOTE FOR GOVERNOR

Year	Total Vote	Republican		Democratic		Other Vote	Rep.-Dem. Plurality	Percentage			
								Total Vote		Major Vote	
		Vote	Candidate	Vote	Candidate			Rep.	Dem.	Rep.	Dem.
2014	3,819,086	1,537,077	Astorino, Rob	2,069,480	Cuomo, Andrew M.*	212,529	532,403 D	40.2%	54.2%	42.6%	57.4%
2010	4,658,825	1,548,184	Paladino, Carl	2,911,721	Cuomo, Andrew M.	198,920	1,363,537 D	33.2%	62.5%	34.7%	65.3%
2006	4,437,220	1,274,335	Faso, John	3,086,709	Spitzer, Eliot	76,176	1,812,374 D	28.7%	69.6%	29.2%	70.8%
2002**	4,579,078	2,262,255	Pataki, George E.*	1,534,064	McCall, H. Carl	782,759	728,191 R	49.4%	33.5%	59.6%	40.4%
1998	4,735,236	2,571,991	Pataki, George E.*	1,570,317	Vallone, Peter F.	592,928	1,001,674 R	54.3%	33.2%	62.1%	37.9%
1994	5,208,762	2,538,702	Pataki, George E.	2,364,904	Cuomo, Mario M.*	305,156	173,798 R	48.7%	45.4%	51.8%	48.2%
1990**	4,056,896	865,948	Rinfret, Pierre A.	2,157,087	Cuomo, Mario M.*	1,033,861	1,291,139 D	21.3%	53.2%	28.6%	71.4%
1986	4,294,124	1,363,810	O'Rourke, Andrew P.	2,775,229	Cuomo, Mario M.*	155,085	1,411,419 D	31.8%	64.6%	32.9%	67.1%
1982	5,254,891	2,494,827	Lehrman, Lew	2,675,213	Cuomo, Mario M.	84,851	180,386 D	47.5%	50.9%	48.3%	51.7%
1978	4,768,820	2,156,404	Duryea, Perry B.	2,429,272	Carey, Hugh L.*	183,144	272,868 D	45.2%	50.9%	47.0%	53.0%
1974	5,293,176	2,219,667	Wilson, Malcolm*	3,028,503	Carey, Hugh L.	45,006	808,836 D	41.9%	57.2%	42.3%	57.7%
1970	6,013,064	3,151,432	Rockefeller, Nelson A.*	2,421,426	Goldberg, Arthur J.	440,206	730,006 R	52.4%	40.3%	56.5%	43.5%
1966**	6,006,246	2,690,626	Rockefeller, Nelson A.*	2,298,363	O'Connor, Frank	1,017,257	392,263 R	44.8%	38.3%	53.9%	46.1%
1962	5,805,631	3,081,587	Rockefeller, Nelson A.*	2,552,418	Morgenthau, Robert M.	171,626	529,169 R	53.1%	44.0%	54.7%	45.3%
1958	5,712,665	3,126,929	Rockefeller, Nelson A.	2,553,895	Harriman, Averell*	31,841	573,034 R	54.7%	44.7%	55.0%	45.0%
1954	5,161,942	2,549,613	Ives, Irving M.	2,560,738	Harriman, Averell	51,591	11,125 D	49.4%	49.6%	49.9%	50.1%
1950	5,308,889	2,819,523	Dewey, Thomas E.*	2,246,855	Lynch, Walter A.	242,511	572,668 R	53.1%	42.3%	55.7%	44.3%
1946	4,964,552	2,825,633	Dewey, Thomas E.*	2,138,482	Mead, James M.	437	687,151 R	56.9%	43.1%	56.9%	43.1%

Note: An asterisk (*) denotes incumbent. **In past elections, the other vote included: 2002 - 654,016 Independence (B. Thomas Golisano); 1990 - 827,614 Conservative (Herbert I. London); 1966 - 510,023 Conservative (Paul L. Adams), 507,234 Liberal (Franklin Roosevelt Jr.).

POSTWAR VOTE FOR SENATOR

Year	Total Vote	Republican		Democratic		Other Vote	Rep.-Dem. Plurality	Percentage			
								Total Vote		Major Vote	
		Vote	Candidate	Vote	Candidate			Rep.	Dem.	Rep.	Dem.
2016	7,396,305	2,009,355	Long, Wendy	5,221,945	Schumer, Charles E.*	165,005	3,212,590 D	27.2%	70.6%	27.8%	72.2%
2012	6,679,678	1,758,702	Long, Wendy	4,822,330	Gillibrand, Kirsten E.*	98,646	3,063,628 D	26.3%	72.2%	26.7%	73.3%
2010	4,596,796	1,480,423	Townsend, Jay	3,047,880	Schumer, Charles E.*	68,493	1,567,457 D	32.2%	66.3%	32.7%	67.3%
2010S**	4,508,771	1,582,693	DioGuardi, Joseph J.	2,837,684	Gillibrand, Kirsten E.*	88,394	1,254,991 D	35.1%	62.9%	35.8%	64.2%
2006	4,490,053	1,392,189	Spencer, John	3,008,428	Clinton, Hillary Rodham*	89,436	1,616,239 D	31.0%	67.0%	31.6%	68.4%
2004	6,702,875	1,625,069	Mills, Howard D.	4,769,824	Schumer, Charles E.*	307,982	3,144,755 D	24.2%	71.2%	25.4%	74.6%
2000	6,779,839	2,915,730	Lazio, Rick A.	3,747,310	Clinton, Hillary Rodham	116,799	831,580 D	43.0%	55.3%	43.8%	56.2%
1998	4,670,805	2,058,988	D'Amato, Alfonse M.*	2,551,065	Schumer, Charles E.	60,752	492,077 D	44.1%	54.6%	44.7%	55.3%
1994	4,794,601	1,988,308	Castro, Bernadette	2,646,541	Moynihan, Daniel Patrick*	159,752	658,233 D	41.5%	55.2%	42.9%	57.1%
1992	6,458,826	3,166,994	D'Amato, Alfonse M.*	3,086,200	Abrams, Robert	205,632	80,794 R	49.0%	47.8%	50.6%	49.4%
1988	6,040,980	1,875,784	McMillan, Robert	4,048,649	Moynihan, Daniel Patrick*	116,547	2,172,865 D	31.1%	67.0%	31.7%	68.3%
1986	4,179,447	2,378,197	D'Amato, Alfonse M.*	1,723,216	Green, Mark J.	78,034	654,981 R	56.9%	41.2%	58.0%	42.0%
1982	4,967,729	1,696,766	Sullivan, Florence M.	3,232,146	Moynihan, Daniel Patrick*	38,817	1,535,380 D	34.2%	65.1%	34.4%	65.6%
1980**	6,014,914	2,699,652	D'Amato, Alfonse M.	2,618,661	Holtzman, Elizabeth	696,601	80,991 R	44.9%	43.5%	50.8%	49.2%
1976	6,319,755	2,836,633	Buckley, James L.*	3,422,594	Moynihan, Daniel Patrick	60,528	585,961 D	44.9%	54.2%	45.3%	54.7%
1974	5,163,600	2,340,188	Javits, Jacob K.*	1,973,781	Clark, Ramsey	849,631	366,407 R	45.3%	38.2%	54.2%	45.8%
1970**	5,904,782	1,434,472	Goodell, Charles E.*	2,171,232	Ottinger, Richard L.	2,299,078	736,760 D	24.3%	36.8%	39.8%	60.2%
1968**	6,574,415	3,269,772	Javits, Jacob K.*	2,150,695	O'Dwyer, Paul	1,153,948	1,119,077 R	49.7%	32.7%	60.3%	39.7%
1964	7,151,686	3,104,056	Keating, Kenneth B.*	3,823,749	Kennedy, Robert F.	223,881	719,693 D	43.4%	53.5%	44.8%	55.2%
1962	5,703,168	3,272,417	Javits, Jacob K.*	2,289,323	Donovan, James B.	141,428	983,094 R	57.4%	40.1%	58.8%	41.2%
1958	5,602,088	2,842,942	Keating, Kenneth B.	2,709,950	Hogan, Frank S.	49,196	132,992 R	50.7%	48.4%	51.2%	48.8%
1956	6,991,136	3,723,933	Javits, Jacob K.	3,265,159	Wagner, Robert Ferdinand	2,044	458,774 R	53.3%	46.7%	53.3%	46.7%
1952	6,980,259	3,853,934	Ives, Irving M.*	2,521,736	Cashmore, John	604,589	1,332,198 R	55.2%	36.1%	60.4%	39.6%
1950	5,228,403	2,367,353	Hanley, Joe R.	2,632,313	Lehman, Herbert H.*	228,737	264,960 D	45.3%	50.3%	47.4%	52.6%
1949S**	4,966,878	2,384,381	Dulles, John Foster	2,582,438	Lehman, Herbert H.	59	198,057 D	48.0%	52.0%	48.0%	52.0%
1946	4,867,564	2,559,365	Ives, Irving M.	2,308,112	Lehman, Herbert H.	87	251,253 R	52.6%	47.4%	52.6%	47.4%

Note: An asterisk (*) denotes incumbent. **In past elections, the other vote included: 1980 - 664,544 Liberal (Jacob K. Javits); 1970 - 2,288,190 Conservative (James L. Buckley); 1968 - 1,139,402 Conservative (Buckley). Buckley won the 1970 election with 38.8 percent of the total vote and a plurality of 116,958 votes. The 1949 election and one of the 2010 elections were for short terms to fill a vacancy.

NEW YORK

PRESIDENT 2016

2010 Census Population	County	Total Vote	Republican (Trump)	Democratic (Clinton)	Other	Rep.-Dem. Plurality		Percentage			
								Total Vote		Major Vote	
								Rep.	Dem.	Rep.	Dem.
304,204	ALBANY	139,818	47,808	83,071	8,939	35,263	D	34.2%	59.4%	36.5%	63.5%
48,946	ALLEGANY	18,692	12,525	4,882	1,285	7,643	R	67.0%	26.1%	72.0%	28.0%
1,385,108	BRONX	399,522	37,797	353,646	8,079	315,849	D	9.5%	88.5%	9.7%	90.3%
200,600	BROOME	86,072	40,943	39,212	5,917	1,731	R	47.6%	45.6%	51.1%	48.9%
80,317	CATTARAUGUS	31,161	19,692	9,497	1,972	10,195	R	63.2%	30.5%	67.5%	32.5%
80,026	CAYUGA	33,172	17,384	13,522	2,266	3,862	R	52.4%	40.8%	56.2%	43.8%
134,905	CHAUTAUQUA	54,234	31,594	19,091	3,549	12,503	R	58.3%	35.2%	62.3%	37.7%
88,830	CHEMUNG	36,119	20,097	13,757	2,265	6,340	R	55.6%	38.1%	59.4%	40.6%
50,477	CHENANGO	20,160	11,921	6,775	1,464	5,146	R	59.1%	33.6%	63.8%	36.2%
82,128	CLINTON	32,105	14,449	15,059	2,597	610	D	45.0%	46.9%	49.0%	51.0%
63,096	COLUMBIA	30,902	13,756	15,284	1,862	1,528	D	44.5%	49.5%	47.4%	52.6%
49,336	CORTLAND	20,244	9,900	8,771	1,573	1,129	R	48.9%	43.3%	53.0%	47.0%
47,980	DELAWARE	19,792	11,942	6,627	1,223	5,315	R	60.3%	33.5%	64.3%	35.7%
297,488	DUTCHESS	130,934	61,797	62,261	6,876	464	D	47.2%	47.6%	49.8%	50.2%
919,040	ERIE	423,625	188,303	215,456	19,866	27,153	D	44.5%	50.9%	46.6%	53.4%
39,370	ESSEX	17,218	7,958	7,762	1,498	196	R	46.2%	45.1%	50.6%	49.4%
51,599	FRANKLIN	16,952	8,221	7,297	1,434	924	R	48.5%	43.0%	53.0%	47.0%
55,531	FULTON	21,214	13,462	6,496	1,256	6,966	R	63.5%	30.6%	67.5%	32.5%
60,079	GENESEE	26,432	16,915	7,650	1,867	9,265	R	64.0%	28.9%	68.9%	31.1%
49,221	GREENE	22,050	13,073	7,405	1,572	5,668	R	59.3%	33.6%	63.8%	36.2%
4,836	HAMILTON	3,225	2,064	949	212	1,115	R	64.0%	29.4%	68.5%	31.5%
64,519	HERKIMER	26,255	16,699	8,083	1,473	8,616	R	63.6%	30.8%	67.4%	32.6%
116,229	JEFFERSON	38,236	21,763	13,809	2,664	7,954	R	56.9%	36.1%	61.2%	38.8%
2,504,700	KINGS	805,605	141,044	640,553	24,008	499,509	D	17.5%	79.5%	18.0%	82.0%
27,087	LEWIS	11,325	7,400	3,146	779	4,254	R	65.3%	27.8%	70.2%	29.8%
65,393	LIVINGSTON	30,031	17,290	10,697	2,044	6,593	R	57.6%	35.6%	61.8%	38.2%
73,442	MADISON	30,064	15,936	11,667	2,461	4,269	R	53.0%	38.8%	57.7%	42.3%
744,344	MONROE	347,790	136,582	188,592	22,616	52,010	D	39.3%	54.2%	42.0%	58.0%
50,219	MONTGOMERY	19,054	11,301	6,595	1,158	4,706	R	59.3%	34.6%	63.1%	36.9%
1,339,532	NASSAU	647,122	292,025	332,154	22,943	40,129	D	45.1%	51.3%	46.8%	53.2%
1,585,873	NEW YORK	668,940	64,930	579,013	24,997	514,083	D	9.7%	86.6%	10.1%	89.9%
216,469	NIAGARA	92,402	51,961	35,559	4,882	16,402	R	56.2%	38.5%	59.4%	40.6%
234,878	ONEIDA	91,009	51,437	33,743	5,829	17,694	R	56.5%	37.1%	60.4%	39.6%
467,026	ONONDAGA	208,440	83,649	112,337	12,454	28,688	D	40.1%	53.9%	42.7%	57.3%
107,931	ONTARIO	52,258	26,029	22,233	3,996	3,796	R	49.8%	42.5%	53.9%	46.1%
372,813	ORANGE	152,021	76,645	68,278	7,098	8,367	R	50.4%	44.9%	52.9%	47.1%
42,883	ORLEANS	16,380	10,936	4,470	974	6,466	R	66.8%	27.3%	71.0%	29.0%
122,109	OSWEGO	48,180	27,688	17,095	3,397	10,593	R	57.5%	35.5%	61.8%	38.2%
62,259	OTSEGO	25,668	13,308	10,451	1,909	2,857	R	51.8%	40.7%	56.0%	44.0%
99,710	PUTNAM	48,563	27,024	19,366	2,173	7,658	R	55.6%	39.9%	58.3%	41.7%
2,230,722	QUEENS	686,393	149,341	517,220	19,832	367,879	D	21.8%	75.4%	22.4%	77.6%
159,429	RENSSELAER	71,562	33,726	32,717	5,119	1,009	R	47.1%	45.7%	50.8%	49.2%
468,730	RICHMOND	180,960	101,437	74,143	5,380	27,294	R	56.1%	41.0%	57.8%	42.2%
311,687	ROCKLAND	135,091	60,911	69,342	4,838	8,431	D	45.1%	51.3%	46.8%	53.2%
219,607	SARATOGA	114,091	54,575	50,913	8,603	3,662	R	47.8%	44.6%	51.7%	48.3%
154,727	SCHENECTADY	67,279	28,953	33,747	4,579	4,794	D	43.0%	50.2%	46.2%	53.8%
32,749	SCHOHARIE	14,050	8,831	4,240	979	4,591	R	62.9%	30.2%	67.6%	32.4%
18,343	SCHUYLER	8,772	5,050	3,091	631	1,959	R	57.6%	35.2%	62.0%	38.0%
35,251	SENECA	13,980	7,236	5,697	1,047	1,539	R	51.8%	40.8%	55.9%	44.1%
111,944	ST. LAWRENCE	39,158	19,942	16,488	2,728	3,454	R	50.9%	42.1%	54.7%	45.3%
98,990	STEUBEN	42,002	26,831	12,526	2,645	14,305	R	63.9%	29.8%	68.2%	31.8%
1,493,350	SUFFOLK	681,254	350,570	303,951	26,733	46,619	R	51.5%	44.6%	53.6%	46.4%
77,547	SULLIVAN	29,955	15,931	12,568	1,456	3,363	R	53.2%	42.0%	55.9%	44.1%
51,125	TIOGA	22,299	13,260	7,526	1,513	5,734	R	59.5%	33.8%	63.8%	36.2%
101,564	TOMPKINS	42,678	10,371	28,890	3,417	18,519	D	24.3%	67.7%	26.4%	73.6%

NEW YORK

PRESIDENT 2016

2010 Census Population	County	Total Vote	Republican (Trump)	Democratic (Clinton)	Other	Rep.-Dem. Plurality	Percentage Total Vote Rep.	Dem.	Major Vote Rep.	Dem.
182,493	ULSTER	85,290	35,239	44,597	5,454	9,358 D	41.3%	52.3%	44.1%	55.9%
65,707	WARREN	31,408	15,751	13,091	2,566	2,660 R	50.1%	41.7%	54.6%	45.4%
63,216	WASHINGTON	24,528	13,610	9,098	1,820	4,512 R	55.5%	37.1%	59.9%	40.1%
93,772	WAYNE	39,687	23,380	13,473	2,834	9,907 R	58.9%	33.9%	63.4%	36.6%
949,113	WESTCHESTER	420,655	131,238	272,926	16,491	141,688 D	31.2%	64.9%	32.5%	67.5%
42,155	WYOMING	17,298	12,442	3,904	952	8,538 R	71.9%	22.6%	76.1%	23.9%
25,348	YATES	10,066	5,660	3,659	747	2,001 R	56.2%	36.4%	60.7%	39.3%
19,378,102	TOTAL	7,721,442	2,819,533	4,556,118	345,791	1,736,585 D	36.5%	59.0%	38.2%	61.8%

Note: Note: Candidates in New York can appear on the ballot line of more than one party. In the 2016 presidential election, the candidates received the following votes per party: Donald Trump - 2,527,141 (Republican), 292,392 (Conservative); Hillary Rodham Clinton - 4,379,783 (Democrat), 140,043 (Working Families), 36,292 (Women's Equality); Gary Johnson - 119,160 (Independence), 57,438 (Libertarian). New York City is comprised of five boroughs (or counties): Bronx, Kings, New York, Queens, and Richmond. The aggregate 2016 presidential vote for New York City was as follows: 2,741,420 TOTAL; 494,549 (18.0%) Republican (Trump); 2,164,575 (79.0%) Democratic (Clinton); 82,296 (3.0%) Other.

NEW YORK

SENATOR 2016

2010 Census Population	County	Total Vote	Republican (Long)	Democratic (Schumer)	Other	Rep.-Dem. Plurality	Percentage Total Vote Rep.	Dem.	Major Vote Rep.	Dem.
304,204	ALBANY	135,648	33,755	98,287	3,606	64,532 D	24.9%	72.5%	25.6%	74.4%
48,946	ALLEGANY	17,871	9,614	7,881	376	1,733 R	53.8%	44.1%	55.0%	45.0%
1,385,108	BRONX	375,741	25,905	344,113	5,723	318,208 D	6.9%	91.6%	7.0%	93.0%
200,600	BROOME	82,301	28,156	51,929	2,216	23,773 D	34.2%	63.1%	35.2%	64.8%
80,317	CATTARAUGUS	29,447	13,495	15,297	655	1,802 D	45.8%	51.9%	46.9%	53.1%
80,026	CAYUGA	31,999	11,536	19,796	667	8,260 D	36.1%	61.9%	36.8%	63.2%
134,905	CHAUTAUQUA	52,384	21,614	29,743	1,027	8,129 D	41.3%	56.8%	42.1%	57.9%
88,830	CHEMUNG	34,467	14,994	18,775	698	3,781 D	43.5%	54.5%	44.4%	55.6%
50,477	CHENANGO	19,152	8,463	10,111	578	1,648 D	44.2%	52.8%	45.6%	54.4%
82,128	CLINTON	30,556	10,802	18,955	799	8,153 D	35.4%	62.0%	36.3%	63.7%
63,096	COLUMBIA	29,843	10,101	18,893	849	8,792 D	33.8%	63.3%	34.8%	65.2%
49,336	CORTLAND	19,456	7,048	11,857	551	4,809 D	36.2%	60.9%	37.3%	62.7%
47,980	DELAWARE	19,028	8,932	9,635	461	703 D	46.9%	50.6%	48.1%	51.9%
297,488	DUTCHESS	124,639	48,934	72,659	3,046	23,725 D	39.3%	58.3%	40.2%	59.8%
919,040	ERIE	410,505	118,072	284,110	8,323	166,038 D	28.8%	69.2%	29.4%	70.6%
39,370	ESSEX	15,968	6,577	8,829	562	2,252 D	41.2%	55.3%	42.7%	57.3%
51,599	FRANKLIN	16,209	6,116	9,640	453	3,524 D	37.7%	59.5%	38.8%	61.2%
55,531	FULTON	19,995	9,357	10,237	401	880 D	46.8%	51.2%	47.8%	52.2%
60,079	GENESEE	25,189	12,245	12,343	601	98 D	48.6%	49.0%	49.8%	50.2%
49,221	GREENE	21,191	9,863	10,823	505	960 D	46.5%	51.1%	47.7%	52.3%
4,836	HAMILTON	3,074	1,572	1,444	58	128 R	51.1%	47.0%	52.1%	47.9%
64,519	HERKIMER	24,649	10,376	13,702	571	3,326 D	42.1%	55.6%	43.1%	56.9%
116,229	JEFFERSON	36,762	15,245	20,711	806	5,466 D	41.5%	56.3%	42.4%	57.6%
2,504,700	KINGS	767,137	83,820	659,982	23,335	576,162 D	10.9%	86.0%	11.3%	88.7%
27,087	LEWIS	10,779	5,106	5,492	181	386 D	47.4%	51.0%	48.2%	51.8%
65,393	LIVINGSTON	28,764	13,090	14,984	690	1,894 D	45.5%	52.1%	46.6%	53.4%
73,442	MADISON	28,827	11,363	16,706	758	5,343 D	39.4%	58.0%	40.5%	59.5%
744,344	MONROE	337,942	103,400	226,493	8,049	123,093 D	30.6%	67.0%	31.3%	68.7%
50,219	MONTGOMERY	18,121	7,332	10,357	432	3,025 D	40.5%	57.2%	41.4%	58.6%
1,339,532	NASSAU	622,973	210,823	403,274	8,876	192,451 D	33.8%	64.7%	34.3%	65.7%

NEW YORK

SENATOR 2016

2010 Census Population	County	Total Vote	Republican (Long)	Democratic (Schumer)	Other	Rep.-Dem. Plurality	Total Vote Rep.	Total Vote Dem.	Major Vote Rep.	Major Vote Dem.
1,585,873	NEW YORK	640,723	69,536	553,432	17,755	483,896 D	10.9%	86.4%	11.2%	88.8%
216,469	NIAGARA	87,501	33,662	52,114	1,725	18,452 D	38.5%	59.6%	39.2%	60.8%
234,878	ONEIDA	86,117	32,899	51,245	1,973	18,346 D	38.2%	59.5%	39.1%	60.9%
467,026	ONONDAGA	204,897	57,174	143,126	4,597	85,952 D	27.9%	69.9%	28.5%	71.5%
107,931	ONTARIO	50,598	20,344	29,001	1,253	8,657 D	40.2%	57.3%	41.2%	58.8%
372,813	ORANGE	146,099	55,727	87,368	3,004	31,641 D	38.1%	59.8%	38.9%	61.1%
42,883	ORLEANS	15,554	8,150	7,099	305	1,051 R	52.4%	45.6%	53.4%	46.6%
122,109	OSWEGO	46,059	18,780	26,172	1,107	7,392 D	40.8%	56.8%	41.8%	58.2%
62,259	OTSEGO	24,486	9,758	14,059	669	4,301 D	39.9%	57.4%	41.0%	59.0%
99,710	PUTNAM	46,143	20,588	24,635	920	4,047 D	44.6%	53.4%	45.5%	54.5%
2,230,722	QUEENS	654,848	99,252	541,334	14,262	442,082 D	15.2%	82.7%	15.5%	84.5%
159,429	RENSSELAER	69,402	23,577	43,897	1,928	20,320 D	34.0%	63.3%	34.9%	65.1%
468,730	RICHMOND	173,719	62,979	108,147	2,593	45,168 D	36.3%	62.3%	36.8%	63.2%
311,687	ROCKLAND	126,303	41,894	82,386	2,023	40,492 D	33.2%	65.2%	33.7%	66.3%
219,607	SARATOGA	110,757	42,709	65,362	2,686	22,653 D	38.6%	59.0%	39.5%	60.5%
154,727	SCHENECTADY	65,203	20,985	42,649	1,569	21,664 D	32.2%	65.4%	33.0%	67.0%
32,749	SCHOHARIE	13,615	6,606	6,721	288	115 D	48.5%	49.4%	49.6%	50.4%
18,343	SCHUYLER	8,346	4,026	4,075	245	49 D	48.2%	48.8%	49.7%	50.3%
35,251	SENECA	13,489	5,364	7,746	379	2,382 D	39.8%	57.4%	40.9%	59.1%
111,944	ST. LAWRENCE	37,298	13,633	22,755	910	9,122 D	36.6%	61.0%	37.5%	62.5%
98,990	STEUBEN	40,212	20,638	18,743	831	1,895 R	51.3%	46.6%	52.4%	47.6%
1,493,350	SUFFOLK	650,009	247,391	390,754	11,864	143,363 D	38.1%	60.1%	38.8%	61.2%
77,547	SULLIVAN	28,069	10,641	16,770	658	6,129 D	37.9%	59.7%	38.8%	61.2%
51,125	TIOGA	21,557	10,345	10,661	551	316 D	48.0%	49.5%	49.2%	50.8%
101,564	TOMPKINS	41,260	8,815	30,349	2,096	21,534 D	21.4%	73.6%	22.5%	77.5%
182,493	ULSTER	81,391	26,029	52,598	2,764	26,569 D	32.0%	64.6%	33.1%	66.9%
65,707	WARREN	30,035	11,164	17,885	986	6,721 D	37.2%	59.5%	38.4%	61.6%
63,216	WASHINGTON	23,726	9,787	13,246	693	3,459 D	41.3%	55.8%	42.5%	57.5%
93,772	WAYNE	38,499	17,929	19,704	866	1,775 D	46.6%	51.2%	47.6%	52.4%
949,113	WESTCHESTER	403,181	108,127	287,893	7,161	179,766 D	26.8%	71.4%	27.3%	72.7%
42,155	WYOMING	16,879	8,843	7,756	280	1,087 R	52.4%	46.0%	53.3%	46.7%
25,348	YATES	9,713	4,297	5,205	211	908 D	44.2%	53.6%	45.2%	54.8%
19,378,102	TOTAL	7,396,305	2,009,355	5,221,945	165,005	3,212,590 D	27.2%	70.6%	27.8%	72.2%

Note: Candidates in New York can appear on the ballot line of more than one party. In the 2016 Senate election, the candidates received the following votes per party: Charles E. Schumer - 4,784,218 (Democrat), 241,672 (Working Families), 150,654 (Independence), 45,401 (Women's Equality); Wendy Long - 1,723,920 (Republican), 267,622 (Conservative), 17,813 (Reform). New York City is composed of five boroughs (or counties): Bronx, Kings, New York, Queens, and Richmond. The aggregate 2016 Senate vote in New York City was as follows: 2,612,168 TOTAL; 2,207,008 (84.5%) Democratic (Schumer); 341,492 (13.1%) Republican (Long); 63,668 (2.4%) Other.

NEW YORK

HOUSE OF REPRESENTATIVES

CD	Year	Total Vote	Republican Vote	Republican Candidate	Democratic Vote	Democratic Candidate	Other Vote	Rep.-Dem. Plurality	Total Vote Rep.	Total Vote Dem.	Major Vote Rep.	Major Vote Dem.
1	2016	323,890	188,499	ZELDIN, LEE M.*	135,278	THRONE-HOLST, ANNA	113	53,221 R	58.2%	41.8%	58.2%	41.8%
1	2014	172,865	94,035	ZELDIN, LEE M.	78,722	BISHOP, TIMOTHY H.*	108	15,313 R	54.4%	45.5%	54.4%	45.6%
1	2012	278,659	132,304	ALTSCHULER, RANDY	146,179	BISHOP, TIMOTHY H.*	176	13,875 D	47.5%	52.5%	47.5%	52.5%
2	2016	292,595	181,506	KING, PETER T.*	110,938	GREGORY, DUWAYNE	151	70,568 R	62.0%	37.9%	62.1%	37.9%
2	2014	139,330	95,177	KING, PETER T.*	41,814	MAHER, PATRICIA M.	2,339	53,363 R	68.3%	30.0%	69.5%	30.5%
2	2012	242,943	142,309	KING, PETER T.*	100,545	FALCONE, VIVIANNE	89	41,764 R	58.6%	41.4%	58.6%	41.4%

NEW YORK

HOUSE OF REPRESENTATIVES

CD	Year	Total Vote	Republican Vote	Republican Candidate	Democratic Vote	Democratic Candidate	Other Vote	Rep.-Dem. Plurality	Total Vote Rep.	Total Vote Dem.	Major Vote Rep.	Major Vote Dem.
3	2016	324,254	152,304	MARTINS, JACK M.	171,775	SUOZZI, THOMAS R.	175	19,471 D	47.0%	53.0%	47.0%	53.0%
3	2014	164,375	74,269	LALLY, GRANT M.	90,032	ISRAEL, STEVE J.*	74	15,763 D	45.2%	54.8%	45.2%	54.8%
3	2012	273,171	113,203	LABATE, STEPHEN	157,880	ISRAEL, STEVE J.*	2,088	44,677 D	41.4%	57.8%	41.8%	58.2%
4	2016	313,000	126,438	GURFEIN, DAVID	186,423	RICE, KATHLEEN M.*	139	59,985 D	40.4%	59.6%	40.4%	59.6%
4	2014	170,099	80,127	BLAKEMAN, BRUCE	89,793	RICE, KATHLEEN M.	179	9,666 D	47.1%	52.8%	47.2%	52.8%
4	2012	265,300	85,693	BECKER, FRANCIS X. JR.	163,955	MCCARTHY, CAROLYN*	15,652	78,262 D	32.3%	61.8%	34.3%	65.7%
5	2016	233,853	30,312	O'REILLY, MICHAEL	199,815	MEEKS, GREGORY W.*	3,726	169,503 D	13.0%	85.4%	13.2%	86.8%
5	2014	79,821			75,712	MEEKS, GREGORY W.*	4,109	75,712 D		94.9%		100.0%
5	2012	187,141	17,875	JENNINGS, ALLAN JR.	167,836	MEEKS, GREGORY W.*	1,430	149,961 D	9.6%	89.7%	9.6%	90.4%
6	2016	189,433	50,617	MAIO, DANNIEL	136,506	MENG, GRACE*	2,310	85,889 D	26.7%	72.1%	27.1%	72.9%
6	2014	55,963			55,368	MENG, GRACE*	595	55,368 D		98.9%		100.0%
6	2012	164,374	50,846	HALLORAN, DANIEL	111,501	MENG, GRACE	2,027	60,655 D	30.9%	67.8%	31.3%	68.7%
7	2016	189,890	17,478	ROMAGUERA, ALLAN E.	172,146	VELAZQUEZ, NYDIA*	266	154,668 D	9.2%	90.7%	9.2%	90.8%
7	2014	63,812	5,713	FERNANDEZ, JOSE LUIS	56,593	VELAZQUEZ, NYDIA*	1,506	50,880 D	9.0%	88.7%	9.2%	90.8%
7	2012	152,111			143,930	VELAZQUEZ, NYDIA*	8,181	143,930 D		94.6%		100.0%
8	2016	230,203			214,595	JEFFRIES, HAKEEM*	15,608	214,595 D		93.2%		100.0%
8	2014	83,999			77,255	JEFFRIES, HAKEEM*	6,744	77,255 D		92.0%		100.0%
8	2012	204,207	17,650	BELLONE, ALAN	184,039	JEFFRIES, HAKEEM	2,518	166,389 D	8.6%	90.1%	8.8%	91.2%
9	2016	232,094			214,189	CLARKE, YVETTE D.*	17,905	214,189 D		92.3%		100.0%
9	2014	92,569			82,659	CLARKE, YVETTE D.*	9,910	82,659 D		89.3%		100.0%
9	2012	213,431	24,164	CAVANAGH, DANIEL	186,141	CLARKE, YVETTE D.*	3,126	161,977 D	11.3%	87.2%	11.5%	88.5%
10	2016	246,525	53,857	ROSENTHAL, PHILIP	192,371	NADLER, JERROLD*	297	138,514 D	21.8%	78.0%	21.9%	78.1%
10	2014	101,881			89,080	NADLER, JERROLD*	12,801	89,080 D		87.4%		100.0%
10	2012	205,349	39,413	CHAN, MICHAEL	165,743	NADLER, JERROLD*	193	126,330 D	19.2%	80.7%	19.2%	80.8%
11	2016	232,317	142,934	DONOVAN, DANIEL*	85,257	REICHARD, RICHARD	4,126	57,677 R	61.5%	36.7%	62.6%	37.4%
11	2014	107,363	58,886	GRIMM, MICHAEL G.*	45,244	RECCHIA JR., DOMENIC M.	3,233	13,642 R	54.8%	42.1%	56.6%	43.4%
11	2012	197,635	103,118	GRIMM, MICHAEL G.*	92,430	MURPHY, MARK	2,087	10,688 R	52.2%	46.8%	52.7%	47.3%
12	2016	294,071	49,399	ARDINI, ROBERT	244,358	MALONEY, CAROLYN B.*	314	194,959 D	16.8%	83.1%	16.8%	83.2%
12	2014	113,429	22,731	DI IORIO, NICHOLAS S. "NICK"	90,603	MALONEY, CAROLYN B.*	95	67,872 D	20.0%	79.9%	20.1%	79.9%
12	2012	241,426	46,841	WIGHT, CHRISTOPHER	194,370	MALONEY, CAROLYN B.*	215	147,529 D	19.4%	80.5%	19.4%	80.6%
13	2016	233,737	16,089	EVANS, TONY	207,194	ESPAILLAT, ADRIANO	10,454	191,105 D	6.9%	88.6%	7.2%	92.8%
13	2014	78,353			68,396	RANGEL, CHARLES B.*	9,957	68,396 D		87.3%		100.0%
13	2012	192,913	12,147	SCHLEY, CRAIG	175,016	RANGEL, CHARLES B.*	5,750	162,869 D	6.3%	90.7%	6.5%	93.5%
14	2016	178,323	30,545	SPOTORNO, FRANK	147,587	CROWLEY, JOSEPH*	191	117,042 D	17.1%	82.8%	17.1%	82.9%
14	2014	57,204			50,352	CROWLEY, JOSEPH*	6,852	50,352 D		88.0%		100.0%
14	2012	145,190	21,755	GIBBONS, WILLIAM JR.	120,761	CROWLEY, JOSEPH*	2,674	99,006 D	15.0%	83.2%	15.3%	84.7%
15	2016	174,036	6,129	VEGA, ALEJANDRO	165,688	SERRANO, JOSE E.*	2,219	159,559 D	3.5%	95.2%	3.6%	96.4%
15	2014	56,563			54,906	SERRANO, JOSE E.*	1,657	54,906 D		97.1%		100.0%
15	2012	157,115	4,427	DELLA VALLE, FRANK	152,661	SERRANO, JOSE E.*	27	148,234 D	2.8%	97.2%	2.8%	97.2%
16	2016	222,230			209,857	ENGEL, ELIOT L.*	12,373	209,857 D		94.4%		100.0%
16	2014	100,391			99,658	ENGEL, ELIOT L.*	733	99,658 D		99.3%		100.0%
16	2012	236,553	53,935	MCLAUGHLIN, JOSEPH	179,562	ENGEL, ELIOT L.*	3,056	125,627 D	22.8%	75.9%	23.1%	76.9%
17	2016	216,585			214,530	LOWEY, NITA M.*	2,055	214,530 D		99.1%		100.0%
17	2014	174,054	75,781	DAY, CHRIS	98,150	LOWEY, NITA M.*	123	22,369 D	43.5%	56.4%	43.6%	56.4%
17	2012	266,205	91,899	CARVIN, JOE	171,417	LOWEY, NITA M.*	2,889	79,518 D	34.5%	64.4%	34.9%	65.1%
18	2016	291,527	129,369	OLIVA, PHIL	162,060	MALONEY, SEAN*	98	32,691 D	44.4%	55.6%	44.4%	55.6%
18	2014	179,091	85,660	HAYWORTH, NAN	88,993	MALONEY, SEAN*	4,438	3,333 D	47.8%	49.7%	49.0%	51.0%
18	2012	277,063	133,049	HAYWORTH, NAN*	143,845	MALONEY, SEAN	169	10,796 D	48.0%	51.9%	48.1%	51.9%
19	2016	307,614	166,171	FASO, JOHN	141,224	TEACHOUT, ZEPHYR	219	24,947 R	54.0%	45.9%	54.1%	45.9%
19	2014	204,173	131,594	GIBSON, CHRISTOPHER P.*	72,470	ELDRIDGE, SEAN	109	59,124 R	64.5%	35.5%	64.5%	35.5%
19	2012	284,679	150,245	GIBSON, CHRISTOPHER P.*	134,295	SCHREIBMAN, JULIAN	139	15,950 R	52.8%	47.2%	52.8%	47.2%
20	2016	313,939	100,740	VITOLLO, FRANCIS	213,018	TONKO, PAUL D.*	181	112,278 D	32.1%	67.9%	32.1%	67.9%
20	2014	204,329	79,104	FISCHER, JIM	125,111	TONKO, PAUL D.*	114	46,007 D	38.7%	61.2%	38.7%	61.3%
20	2012	297,314	93,778	DIETERICH, ROBERT	203,401	TONKO, PAUL D.*	135	109,623 D	31.5%	68.4%	31.6%	68.4%

NEW YORK

HOUSE OF REPRESENTATIVES

			Republican		Democratic		Other Vote	Rep.-Dem. Plurality	Percentage			
									Total Vote		Major Vote	
CD	Year	Total Vote	Vote	Candidate	Vote	Candidate			Rep.	Dem.	Rep.	Dem.
21	2016	272,606	177,886	STEFANIK, ELISE*	82,161	DERRICK, MIKE	12,559	95,725 R	65.3%	30.1%	68.4%	31.6%
21	2014	174,668	96,226	STEFANIK, ELISE	59,063	WOOLF, AARON	19,379	37,163 R	55.1%	33.8%	62.0%	38.0%
21	2012	252,556	121,646	DOHENY, MATTHEW A.	126,631	OWENS, WILLIAM L. "BILL"*	4,279	4,985 D	48.2%	50.1%	49.0%	51.0%
22	2016	278,531	129,444	TENNEY, CLAUDIA	114,266	MYERS, KIM	34,821	15,178 R	46.5%	41.0%	53.1%	46.9%
22	2014	131,932	129,851	HANNA, RICHARD L.*			2,081	129,851 R	98.4%		100.0%	
22	2012	260,863	157,941	HANNA, RICHARD L.*	102,080	LAMB, DAN	842	55,861 R	60.5%	39.1%	60.7%	39.3%
23	2016	279,735	161,050	REED, THOMAS W. II*	118,584	PLUMB, JOHN	101	42,466 R	57.6%	42.4%	57.6%	42.4%
23	2014	183,481	113,130	REED, THOMAS W. II*	70,242	ROBERTSON, MARTHA	109	42,888 R	61.7%	38.3%	61.7%	38.3%
23	2012	265,282	137,669	REED, THOMAS W. II*	127,535	SHINAGAWA, NATE	78	10,134 R	51.9%	48.1%	51.9%	48.1%
24	2016	302,115	182,761	KATKO, JOHN M.*	119,040	DEACON, COLLEEN	314	63,721 R	60.5%	39.4%	60.6%	39.4%
24	2014	199,222	118,474	KATKO, JOHN M.	80,304	MAFFEI, DANIEL B.*	444	38,170 R	59.5%	40.3%	59.6%	40.4%
24	2012	292,988	127,054	BUERKLE, ANN MARIE*	143,044	MAFFEI, DANIEL B.	22,890	15,990 D	43.4%	48.8%	47.0%	53.0%
25	2016	325,831	142,650	ASSINI, MARK W.	182,950	SLAUGHTER, LOUISE M.*	231	40,300 D	43.8%	56.1%	43.8%	56.2%
25	2014	192,971	95,932	ASSINI, MARK W.	96,803	SLAUGHTER, LOUISE M.*	236	871 D	49.7%	50.2%	49.8%	50.2%
25	2012	313,452	133,389	BROOKS, MAGGIE	179,810	SLAUGHTER, LOUISE M.*	253	46,421 D	42.6%	57.4%	42.6%	57.4%
26	2016	288,679	73,377	SCHRATZ, SHELLY	215,289	HIGGINS, BRIAN M.*	13	141,912 D	25.4%	74.6%	25.4%	74.6%
26	2014	166,124	52,909	WEPPNER, KATHLEEN "KATHY"	113,210	HIGGINS, BRIAN M.*	5	60,301 D	31.8%	68.1%	31.9%	68.1%
26	2012	284,271	71,666	MADIGAN, MICHAEL H.	212,588	HIGGINS, BRIAN M.*	17	140,922 D	25.2%	74.8%	25.2%	74.8%
27	2016	328,809	220,885	COLLINS, CHRIS*	107,832	KASTENBAUM, DIANA	92	113,053 R	67.2%	32.8%	67.2%	32.8%
27	2014	203,645	144,675	COLLINS, CHRIS*	58,911	O'DONNELL, JIM	59	85,764 R	71.0%	28.9%	71.1%	28.9%
27	2012	317,534	161,220	COLLINS, CHRIS	156,219	HOCHUL, KATHY COURTNEY*	95	5,001 R	50.8%	49.2%	50.8%	49.2%
TOTAL	2016	7,116,422	2,530,440		4,464,931		121,051	1,934,491 D	35.6%	62.7%	36.2%	63.8%
TOTAL	2014	3,651,707	1,554,274		2,009,444		87,989	455,170 D	42.6%	55.0%	43.6%	56.4%
TOTAL	2012	6,469,725	2,245,236		4,143,414		81,075	1,898,178 D	34.7%	64.0%	35.1%	64.9%

Note: An asterisk (*) denotes incumbent. Votes received by each Democratic and Republican candidate on the ballot lines of other parties (Working Families, Conservative, Independence, Women's Equality, Reform) are included in their totals above.

NEW YORK

GENERAL AND PRIMARY ELECTIONS

2016 GENERAL ELECTIONS: OTHER VOTES

President — Other vote was 176,598 Libertarian (Gary Johnson), 107,935 Green (Jill Stein), 50,735 Write-in (Scattered Write-in) 10,397 Independent (Evan McMullin), 90 Veterans (Chris Keniston), 36 Socialist (Emidio Soltysik)

Senate — Other vote was 113,413 Green (Robin Wilson), 48,120 Libertarian (Alex Merced), 3,472 Write-in (Scattered Write-in)

House — Other vote was:

CD 1 — 113 Write-in (Scattered Write-in)
CD 2 — 151 Write-in (Scattered Write-in)
CD 3 — 175 Write-in (Scattered Write-in)
CD 4 — 139 Write-in (Scattered Write-in)
CD 5 — 3,587 Green (Frank Francois), 139 Write-in (Scattered Write-in)
CD 6 — 2,123 Haris Bhatti Party (Haris Bhatti), 187 Write-in (Scattered Write-in)
CD 7 — 266 Write-in (Scattered Write-in)
CD 8 — 15,401 Conservative (Daniel Cavanagh), 207 Write-in (Scattered Write-in)
CD 9 — 17,576 Conservative (Alan Bellone), 329 Write-in (Scattered Write-in)
CD 10 — 297 Write-in (Scattered Write-in)
CD 11 — 3,906 Green (Henry Bardel), 220 Write-in (Scattered Write-in)

NEW YORK

GENERAL AND PRIMARY ELECTIONS

2016 GENERAL ELECTIONS: OTHER VOTES

House   Other vote was:

CD 12   314 Write-in (Scattered Write-in)

CD 13   8,248 Green (Daniel Rivera), 1,877 Transparent Government (Scott Fenstermaker), 329 Write-in (Scattered Write-in)

CD 14   191 Write-in (Scattered Write-in)

CD 15   2,104 Conservative (Eduardo Ramirez), 115 Write-in (Scattered Write-in)

CD 16   11,825 People's Choice Congress (Derickson Lawrence) 548 Write-in (Scattered Write-in)

CD 17   2,055 Write-in (Scattered Write-in)

CD 18   98 Write-in (Scattered Write-in)

CD 19   219 Write-in (Scattered Write-in)

CD 20   181 Write-in (Scattered Write-in)

CD 21   12,452 Green (Matthew Funiciello), 107 Write-in (Scattered Write-in)

CD 22   34,638 Reform/Upstate Jobs Party (Martin Babinec), 183 Write-in (Scattered Write-in)

CD 23   101 Write-in (Scattered Write-in)

CD 24   314 Write-in (Scattered Write-in)

CD 25   231 Write-in (Scattered Write-in)

CD 26   13 Write-in (Scattered Write-in)

CD 27   92 Write-in (Scattered Write-in)

2016 PRIMARY ELECTIONS: SUPPLEMENTARY INFORMATION

| Primary | April 19, 2016 (President) June 28, 2016 (Congress) | **Registration** (as of April 1, 2016 – includes 998,094 inactive registrants) | 11,726,842 | Democratic Republican Independence Conservative Working Families Green Other Parties Unaffiliated | 5,792,497 2,731,688 475,566 159,355 48,344 26,271 7,646 2,485,475 |

Primary Type   Closed—Only registered Democrats and Republicans could vote in their party's primary.

	REPUBLICAN PRIMARIES			DEMOCRATIC PRIMARIES		
President	Trump, Donald J.	554,522	60.2%	Clinton, Hillary Rodham	1,133,980	58.0%
	Kasich, John R.	231,166	25.1%	Sanders, Bernard	820,256	42.0%
	Cruz, Ted	136,083	14.8%			
	TOTAL	921,771		TOTAL	1,954,236	
Senator	Long, Wendy	Unopposed		Schumer, Charles E.*	Unopposed	
Congressional District 1	Zeldin, Lee M.*	Unopposed		Throne-Holst, Anna	6,479	51.3%
				Calone, David L.	6,162	48.7%
				TOTAL	12,641	
Congressional District 2	King, Peter T.*	Unopposed		Gregory, DuWayne	Unopposed	
Congressional District 3	Martins, Jack M.	Unopposed		Suozzi, Thomas R.	7,142	35.1%
				Stern, Steve	4,475	22.0%
				Kaiman, Jon	4,394	21.6%
				Kaplan, Anna	3,311	16.3%
				Clarke, Jonathan C.	1,021	5.0%
				TOTAL	20,343	

NEW YORK

GENERAL AND PRIMARY ELECTIONS

	REPUBLICAN PRIMARIES			DEMOCRATIC PRIMARIES		
Congressional District 4	Gurfein, David	Unopposed		Rice, Kathleen M.*	Unopposed	
Congressional District 5	O'Reilly, Michael	Unopposed		Meeks, Gregory W.*	7,056	81.7%
				Mirza, Ali	1,579	18.3%
				TOTAL	8,635	
Congressional District 6	Maio, Danniel	Unopposed		Meng, Grace*	Unopposed	
Congressional District 7	Romaguera, Allan E.	Unopposed		Velazquez, Nydia*	10,162	61.7%
				Lee, Yungman	4,479	27.2%
				Kurzon, Jeff	1,736	10.5%
				Write-In	82	0.5%
				TOTAL	16,459	
Congressional District 8				Jeffries, Hakeem*	Unopposed	
Congressional District 9				Clarke, Yvette D.*	Unopposed	
Congressional District 10	Rosenthal, Philip	Unopposed		Nadler, Jerrold*	27,270	88.8%
				Rosenberg, Mikhail Oliver	3,206	10.4%
				Write-In	241	0.8%
				TOTAL	30,717	
Congressional District 11	Donovan, Daniel "Dan"*	Unopposed		Reichard, Richard	Unopposed	
Congressional District 12	Ardini, Robert	Unopposed		Maloney, Carolyn B.*	15,101	89.0%
				Lindner, Pete	1,654	9.8%
				Write-In	204	1.2%
				TOTAL	16,959	
Congressional District 13	Evans, Tony	Unopposed		Espaillat, Adriano	16,377	35.9%
				Wright, Keith L. T.	15,528	34.0%
				Williams, Clyde Edward Jr.	5,003	11.0%
				Powell, Adam C. IV	2,986	6.5%
				Linares, Guillermo	2,504	5.5%
				Johnson-Cook, Suzan D.	2,341	5.1%
				Gallagher, Michael	435	1.0%
				Sloan, Sam	227	0.5%
				Write-In	138	0.3%
				Caceres, Yohanny	116	0.3%
				TOTAL	45,655	
Congressional District 14	Spotorno, Frank	Unopposed		Crowley, Joseph*	Unopposed	
Congressional District 15	Vega, Alejandro	Unopposed		Serrano, Jose E.*	9,334	87.1%
				Baez, Leonel	1,127	10.5%
				Write-In	254	2.4%
				TOTAL	10,715	
Congressional District 16				Engel, Eliot L.*	Unopposed	
Congressional District 17				Lowey, Nita M.*	Unopposed	
Congressional District 18	Oliva, Phil	3,574	57.0%	Maloney, Sean*	Unopposed	
	Del Vecchio, Kenneth	2,696	43.0%			
	TOTAL	6,270				

NEW YORK

GENERAL AND PRIMARY ELECTIONS

	REPUBLICAN PRIMARIES			DEMOCRATIC PRIMARIES		
Congressional District 19	Faso, John	10,922	67.5%	Teachout, Zephyr	13,801	71.3%
	Heaney, Andrew	5,253	32.5%	Yandik, Will	5,561	28.7%
	TOTAL	*16,175*		*TOTAL*	*19,362*	
Congressional District 20	Vitollo, Francis	Unopposed		Tonko, Paul D.*	Unopposed	
Congressional District 21	Stefanik, Elise*	Unopposed		Derrick, Mike	Unopposed	
Congressional District 22	Tenney, Claudia	9,549	41.1%	Myers, Kim	Unopposed	
	Wells, Steven M.	7,985	34.3%			
	Phillips, George K.	5,716	24.6%			
	TOTAL	*23,250*				
Congressional District 23	Reed, Thomas W. II*	Unopposed		Plumb, John	Unopposed	
Congressional District 24	Katko, John M.*	Unopposed		Deacon, Colleen	6,517	49.9%
				Kingson, Eric	3,994	30.6%
				Williams, Steve	2,557	19.6%
				TOTAL	*13,068*	
Congressional District 25	Assini, Mark W.	Unopposed		Slaughter, Louise M.*	Unopposed	
Congressional District 26	Schratz, Shelly	Unopposed		Higgins, Brian M.*	Unopposed	
Congressional District 27	Collins, Chris*	Unopposed		Kastenbaum, Diana	Unopposed	

Note: An asterisk (*) denotes incumbent.

NORTH CAROLINA

Congressional districts first established for elections held in 2016

13 members

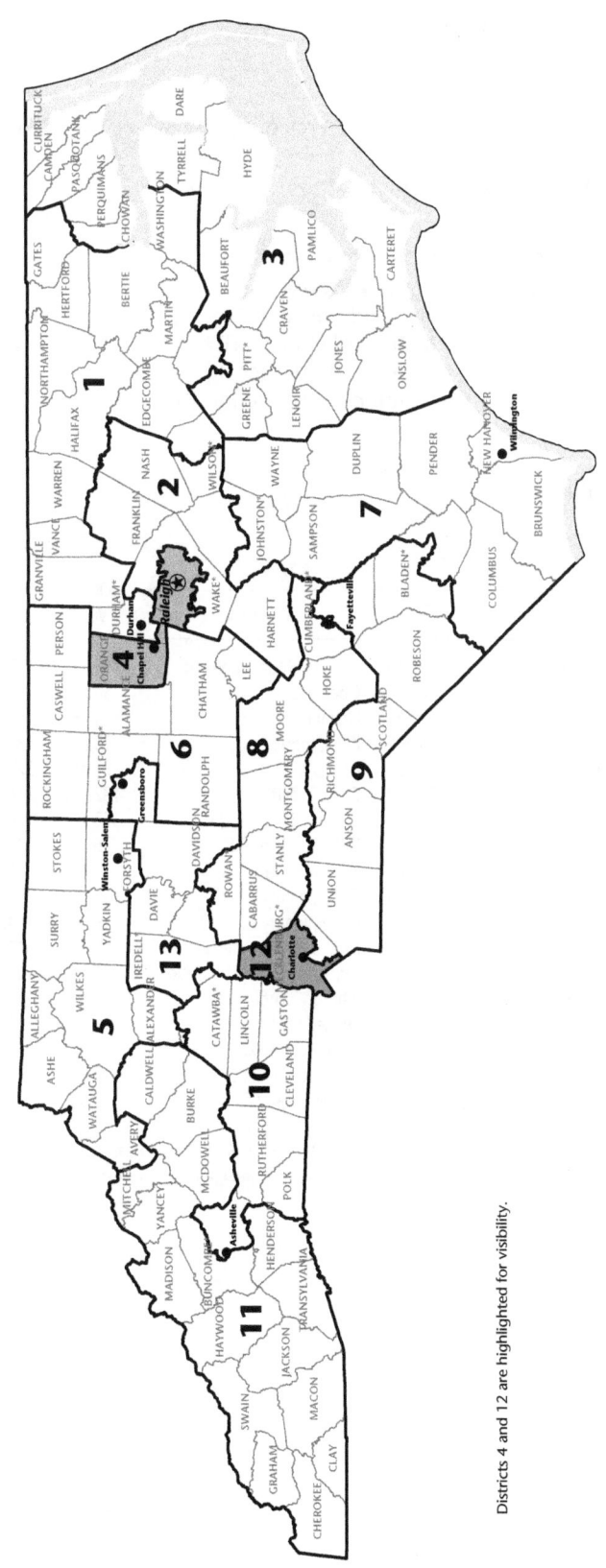

Districts 4 and 12 are highlighted for visibility.

* Asterisk indicates a county whose boundaries include parts of two or more congressional districts.

NORTH CAROLINA

GOVERNOR
Roy Cooper (D). Elected 2016 to a four-year term.

SENATORS (2 Republicans)
Richard Burr (R). Re-elected 2016 to a six-year term. Previously elected 2010, 2004.

Thom Tills (R). Elected 2014 to a six-year term.

REPRESENTATIVES (10 Republicans, 3 Democrats)
1. George K. "G.K." Butterfield (D)
2. George Holding (R)
3. Walter B. Jones Jr. (R)
4. David E. Price (D)
5. Virginia Ann Foxx (R)
6. Mark Walker (R)
7. David Rouzer (R)
8. Richard Hudson (R)
9. Robert Pittenger (R)
10. Patrick T. McHenry (R)
11. Mark Meadows (R)
12. Alma S. Adams (D)
13. Ted Budd (R)

POSTWAR VOTE FOR PRESIDENT

| | | Republican | | Democratic | | Other Vote | Rep.-Dem. Plurality | Percentage | | | |
| | | | | | | | | Total Vote | | Major Vote | |
Year	Total Vote	Vote	Candidate	Vote	Candidate			Rep.	Dem.	Rep.	Dem.
2016**	4,741,564	2,362,631	Trump, Donald J.	2,189,316	Clinton, Hillary Rodham	189,617	173,315 R	49.8%	46.2%	51.9%	48.1%
2012	4,505,372	2,270,395	Romney, W. Mitt	2,178,391	Obama, Barack H.*	56,586	92,004 R	50.4%	48.4%	51.0%	49.0%
2008	4,310,789	2,128,474	McCain, John S. III	2,142,651	Obama, Barack H.	39,664	14,177 D	49.4%	49.7%	49.8%	50.2%
2004	3,501,007	1,961,166	Bush, George W.*	1,525,849	Kerry, John F.	13,992	435,317 R	56.0%	43.6%	56.2%	43.8%
2000	2,911,262	1,631,163	Bush, George W.	1,257,692	Gore, Albert Jr.	22,407	373,471 R	56.0%	43.2%	56.5%	43.5%
1996**	2,515,807	1,225,938	Dole, Robert "Bob"	1,107,849	Clinton, Bill*	182,020	118,089 R	48.7%	44.0%	52.5%	47.5%
1992**	2,611,850	1,134,661	Bush, George H.*	1,114,042	Clinton, Bill	363,147	20,619 R	43.4%	42.7%	50.5%	49.5%
1988	2,134,370	1,237,258	Bush, George H.	890,167	Dukakis, Michael S.	6,945	347,091 R	58.0%	41.7%	58.2%	41.8%
1984	2,175,361	1,346,481	Reagan, Ronald*	824,287	Mondale, Walter F.	4,593	522,194 R	61.9%	37.9%	62.0%	38.0%
1980**	1,855,833	915,018	Reagan, Ronald	875,635	Carter, Jimmy*	65,180	39,383 R	49.3%	47.2%	51.1%	48.9%
1976	1,677,914	741,960	Ford, Gerald R.*	926,365	Carter, Jimmy	9,589	184,405 D	44.2%	55.2%	44.5%	55.5%
1972	1,518,612	1,054,889	Nixon, Richard M.*	438,705	McGovern, George S.	25,018	616,184 R	69.5%	28.9%	70.6%	29.4%
1968**	1,587,493	627,192	Nixon, Richard M.	464,113	Humphrey, Hubert Horatio Jr.	496,188	163,079 R	39.5%	29.2%	57.5%	42.5%
1964	1,424,983	624,844	Goldwater, Barry M. Sr.	800,139	Johnson, Lyndon B.*		175,295 D	43.8%	56.2%	43.8%	56.2%
1960	1,368,556	655,420	Nixon, Richard M.	713,136	Kennedy, John F.		57,716 D	47.9%	52.1%	47.9%	52.1%
1956	1,165,592	575,062	Eisenhower, Dwight D.*	590,530	Stevenson, Adlai E. II		15,468 D	49.3%	50.7%	49.3%	50.7%
1952	1,210,910	558,107	Eisenhower, Dwight D.	652,803	Stevenson, Adlai E. II		94,696 D	46.1%	53.9%	46.1%	53.9%
1948**	791,209	258,572	Dewey, Thomas E.	459,070	Truman, Harry S.*	73,567	200,498 D	32.7%	58.0%	36.0%	64.0%

Note: An asterisk (*) denotes incumbent. **In past elections, the other vote included: 2016 - 130,126 Libertarian (Gary Johnson); 1996 - 168,059 Reform (Ross Perot); 1992 - 357,864 Independent (Perot); 1980 - 52,800 Independent (John Anderson); 1968 - 496,188 American Independent (George Wallace, who finished second); 1948 - 69,652 States' Rights (Strom Thurmond).

NORTH CAROLINA

POSTWAR VOTE FOR GOVERNOR

| Year | Total Vote | Republican | | Democratic | | Other Vote | Rep.-Dem. Plurality | Percentage | | | |
| | | Vote | Candidate | Vote | Candidate | | | Total Vote | | Major Vote | |
								Rep.	Dem.	Rep.	Dem.
2016	4,711,014	2,298,880	McCrory, Pat*	2,309,157	Cooper, Roy	102,977	10,277 D	48.8%	49.0%	49.9%	50.1%
2012	4,468,295	2,440,707	McCrory, Pat	1,931,580	Dalton, Walter H.	96,008	509,127 R	54.6%	43.2%	55.8%	44.2%
2008	4,268,941	2,001,168	McCrory, Pat	2,146,189	Perdue, Bev	121,584	145,021 D	46.9%	50.3%	48.3%	51.7%
2004	3,486,688	1,495,021	Ballantine, Patrick J.	1,939,154	Easley, Mike*	52,513	444,133 D	42.9%	55.6%	43.5%	56.5%
2000	2,942,062	1,360,960	Vinroot, Richard	1,530,324	Easley, Mike	50,778	169,364 D	46.3%	52.0%	47.1%	52.9%
1996	2,566,185	1,097,053	Hayes, Robert "Robin"	1,436,638	Hunt, James B. Jr.*	32,494	339,585 D	42.8%	56.0%	43.3%	56.7%
1992	2,595,184	1,121,955	Gardner, James C.	1,368,246	Hunt, James B. Jr.	104,983	246,291 D	43.2%	52.7%	45.1%	54.9%
1988	2,180,205	1,222,338	Martin, James G.*	957,867	Jordan, Robert B.		264,471 R	56.1%	43.9%	56.1%	43.9%
1984	2,226,727	1,208,167	Martin, James G.	1,011,209	Edmisten, Rufus	7,351	196,958 R	54.3%	45.4%	54.4%	45.6%
1980	1,847,432	691,449	Lake, Beverly	1,143,145	Hunt, James B. Jr.*	12,838	451,696 D	37.4%	61.9%	37.7%	62.3%
1976	1,663,814	564,092	Flaherty, David T.	1,081,293	Hunt, James B. Jr.	18,429	517,201 D	33.9%	65.0%	34.3%	65.7%
1972	1,504,785	767,470	Holshouser, James E. Jr.	729,104	Bowles, Hargrove Skipper Jr.	8,211	38,366 R	51.0%	48.5%	51.3%	48.7%
1968	1,558,308	737,075	Gardner, James C.	821,233	Scott, Robert W.		84,158 D	47.3%	52.7%	47.3%	52.7%
1964	1,396,508	606,165	Gavin, Robert L.	790,343	Moore, Dan K.		184,178 D	43.4%	56.6%	43.4%	56.6%
1960	1,350,360	613,975	Gavin, Robert L.	735,248	Sanford, Terry	1,137	121,273 D	45.5%	54.4%	45.5%	54.5%
1956	1,135,859	375,379	Hayes, Kyle	760,480	Hodges, Luther H.		385,101 D	33.0%	67.0%	33.0%	67.0%
1952	1,179,635	383,329	Seawell, Herbert F. Jr.	796,306	Umstead, William B.		412,977 D	32.5%	67.5%	32.5%	67.5%
1948	780,525	206,166	Pritchard, George M.	570,995	Scott, W. Kerr	3,364	364,829 D	26.4%	73.2%	26.5%	73.5%

Note: An asterisk (*) denotes incumbent.

POSTWAR VOTE FOR SENATOR

| Year | Total Vote | Republican | | Democratic | | Other Vote | Rep.-Dem. Plurality | Percentage | | | |
| | | Vote | Candidate | Vote | Candidate | | | Total Vote | | Major Vote | |
								Rep.	Dem.	Rep.	Dem.
2016	4,691,133	2,395,376	Burr, Richard M.*	2,128,165	Ross, Deborah K.	167,592	267,211 R	51.1%	45.4%	53.0%	47.0%
2014	2,915,281	1,423,259	Tillis, Thom	1,377,651	Hagan, Kay*	114,371	45,608 R	48.8%	47.3%	50.8%	49.2%
2010	2,660,079	1,458,046	Burr, Richard M.*	1,145,074	Marshall, Elaine	56,959	312,972 R	54.8%	43.0%	56.0%	44.0%
2008	4,271,970	1,887,510	Dole, Elizabeth*	2,249,311	Hagan, Kay	135,149	361,801 D	44.2%	52.7%	45.6%	54.4%
2004	3,472,082	1,791,450	Burr, Richard M.	1,632,527	Bowles, Erskine B.	48,105	158,923 R	51.6%	47.0%	52.3%	47.7%
2002	2,331,181	1,248,664	Dole, Elizabeth	1,047,983	Bowles, Erskine B.	34,534	200,681 R	53.6%	45.0%	54.4%	45.6%
1998	2,012,143	945,943	Faircloth, Lauch*	1,029,237	Edwards, John	36,963	83,294 D	47.0%	51.2%	47.9%	52.1%
1996	2,556,456	1,345,833	Helms, Jesse*	1,173,875	Gantt, Harvey B.	36,748	171,958 R	52.6%	45.9%	53.4%	46.6%
1992	2,577,891	1,297,892	Faircloth, Lauch	1,194,015	Sanford, Terry*	85,984	103,877 R	50.3%	46.3%	52.1%	47.9%
1990	2,069,585	1,087,331	Helms, Jesse*	981,573	Gantt, Harvey B.	681	105,758 R	52.5%	47.4%	52.6%	47.4%
1986	1,591,330	767,668	Broyhill, James Thomas*	823,662	Sanford, Terry		55,994 D	48.2%	51.8%	48.2%	51.8%
1984	2,239,051	1,156,768	Helms, Jesse*	1,070,488	Hunt, James B. Jr.	11,795	86,280 R	51.7%	47.8%	51.9%	48.1%
1980	1,797,665	898,064	East, John P.	887,653	Morgan, Robert*	11,948	10,411 R	50.0%	49.4%	50.3%	49.7%
1978	1,135,814	619,151	Helms, Jesse*	516,663	Ingram, John		102,488 R	54.5%	45.5%	54.5%	45.5%
1974	1,020,367	377,618	Stevens, William E.	633,775	Morgan, Robert	8,974	256,157 D	37.0%	62.1%	37.3%	62.7%
1972	1,472,541	795,248	Helms, Jesse	677,293	Galifianakis, Nick		117,955 R	54.0%	46.0%	54.0%	46.0%
1968	1,437,340	566,934	Somers, Robert V.	870,406	Ervin, Sam James Jr.*		303,472 D	39.4%	60.6%	39.4%	60.6%
1966	901,978	400,502	Shallcross, John S.	501,440	Jordan, B. Everett*	36	100,938 D	44.4%	55.6%	44.4%	55.6%
1962	813,155	321,635	Greene, Claude L. Jr.	491,520	Ervin, Sam James Jr.*		169,885 D	39.6%	60.4%	39.6%	60.4%
1960	1,291,485	497,964	Hayes, Kyle	793,521	Jordan, B. Everett*		295,557 D	38.6%	61.4%	38.6%	61.4%
1958S**	616,469	184,977	Clarke, Richard C. Jr.	431,492	Jordan, B. Everett*		246,515 D	30.0%	70.0%	30.0%	70.0%
1956	1,098,828	367,475	Johnson, Joel A.	731,353	Ervin, Sam James Jr.*		363,878 D	33.4%	66.6%	33.4%	66.6%
1954	619,634	211,322	West, Paul C.	408,312	Scott, W. Kerr		196,990 D	34.1%	65.9%	34.1%	65.9%
1954S**	410,574			410,574	Ervin, Sam James Jr.*		410,574 D		100.0%		100.0%
1950	548,277	171,804	Leavitt, Halsey B.	376,473	Hoey, Clyde R.*		204,669 D	31.3%	68.7%	31.3%	68.7%
1950S**	544,924	177,753	Gavin, E. L.	364,912	Smith, Willis	2,259	187,159 D	32.6%	67.0%	32.8%	67.2%
1948	764,559	220,307	Wilkinson, John A.	540,762	Broughton, J. Melville*	3,490	320,455 D	28.8%	70.7%	28.9%	71.1%

Note: An asterisk (*) denotes incumbent. **One each of the 1950 and 1954 elections as well as the 1958 election were for short terms to fill vacancies. The Republican Party did not run a Senate candidate in the 1954 election for the short term.

NORTH CAROLINA

PRESIDENT 2016

2010 Census Population	County	Total Vote	Republican (Trump)	Democratic (Clinton)	Other	Rep.-Dem. Plurality	Percentage			
							Total Vote		Major Vote	
							Rep.	Dem.	Rep.	Dem.
151,131	ALAMANCE	71,157	38,815	29,833	2,509	8,982 R	54.5%	41.9%	56.5%	43.5%
37,198	ALEXANDER	18,271	13,893	3,767	611	10,126 R	76.0%	20.6%	78.7%	21.3%
11,155	ALLEGHANY	5,315	3,814	1,306	195	2,508 R	71.8%	24.6%	74.5%	25.5%
26,948	ANSON	10,545	4,506	5,859	180	1,353 D	42.7%	55.6%	43.5%	56.5%
27,281	ASHE	13,424	9,412	3,500	512	5,912 R	70.1%	26.1%	72.9%	27.1%
17,797	AVERY	8,249	6,298	1,689	262	4,609 R	76.3%	20.5%	78.9%	21.1%
47,759	BEAUFORT	23,938	14,543	8,764	631	5,779 R	60.8%	36.6%	62.4%	37.6%
21,282	BERTIE	9,347	3,456	5,778	113	2,322 D	37.0%	61.8%	37.4%	62.6%
35,190	BLADEN	15,897	8,550	7,058	289	1,492 R	53.8%	44.4%	54.8%	45.2%
107,431	BRUNSWICK	68,351	42,720	23,282	2,349	19,438 R	62.5%	34.1%	64.7%	35.3%
238,318	BUNCOMBE	138,947	55,716	75,452	7,779	19,736 D	40.1%	54.3%	42.5%	57.5%
90,912	BURKE	38,920	26,238	11,251	1,431	14,987 R	67.4%	28.9%	70.0%	30.0%
178,011	CABARRUS	93,289	53,819	35,521	3,949	18,298 R	57.7%	38.1%	60.2%	39.8%
83,029	CALDWELL	36,320	26,621	8,425	1,274	18,196 R	73.3%	23.2%	76.0%	24.0%
9,980	CAMDEN	5,006	3,546	1,274	186	2,272 R	70.8%	25.4%	73.6%	26.4%
66,469	CARTERET	37,781	26,569	9,939	1,273	16,630 R	70.3%	26.3%	72.8%	27.2%
23,719	CASWELL	11,070	6,026	4,792	252	1,234 R	54.4%	43.3%	55.7%	44.3%
154,358	CATAWBA	72,351	48,324	21,216	2,811	27,108 R	66.8%	29.3%	69.5%	30.5%
63,505	CHATHAM	39,849	17,105	21,065	1,679	3,960 D	42.9%	52.9%	44.8%	55.2%
27,444	CHEROKEE	14,181	10,844	2,860	477	7,984 R	76.5%	20.2%	79.1%	20.9%
14,793	CHOWAN	7,228	4,014	2,992	222	1,022 R	55.5%	41.4%	57.3%	42.7%
10,587	CLAY	6,010	4,437	1,367	206	3,070 R	73.8%	22.7%	76.4%	23.6%
98,078	CLEVELAND	44,673	28,479	14,964	1,230	13,515 R	63.7%	33.5%	65.6%	34.4%
58,098	COLUMBUS	23,732	14,272	9,063	397	5,209 R	60.1%	38.2%	61.2%	38.8%
103,505	CRAVEN	47,001	27,731	17,630	1,640	10,101 R	59.0%	37.5%	61.1%	38.9%
319,431	CUMBERLAND	127,506	51,265	71,605	4,636	20,340 D	40.2%	56.2%	41.7%	58.3%
23,547	CURRITUCK	12,669	9,163	2,913	593	6,250 R	72.3%	23.0%	75.9%	24.1%
33,920	DARE	19,609	11,460	7,222	927	4,238 R	58.4%	36.8%	61.3%	38.7%
162,878	DAVIDSON	74,856	54,317	18,109	2,430	36,208 R	72.6%	24.2%	75.0%	25.0%
41,240	DAVIE	21,756	15,602	5,270	884	10,332 R	71.7%	24.2%	74.8%	25.2%
58,505	DUPLIN	20,856	12,217	8,283	356	3,934 R	58.6%	39.7%	59.6%	40.4%
267,587	DURHAM	156,134	28,350	121,250	6,534	92,900 D	18.2%	77.7%	19.0%	81.0%
56,552	EDGECOMBE	24,886	8,261	16,224	401	7,963 D	33.2%	65.2%	33.7%	66.3%
350,670	FORSYTH	178,312	75,975	94,464	7,873	18,489 D	42.6%	53.0%	44.6%	55.4%
60,619	FRANKLIN	30,368	16,368	12,874	1,126	3,494 R	53.9%	42.4%	56.0%	44.0%
206,086	GASTON	96,431	61,798	31,177	3,456	30,621 R	64.1%	32.3%	66.5%	33.5%
12,197	GATES	5,392	2,874	2,385	133	489 R	53.3%	44.2%	54.6%	45.4%
8,861	GRAHAM	4,168	3,283	768	117	2,515 R	78.8%	18.4%	81.0%	19.0%
59,916	GRANVILLE	27,353	13,591	12,909	853	682 R	49.7%	47.2%	51.3%	48.7%
21,362	GREENE	8,095	4,374	3,605	116	769 R	54.0%	44.5%	54.8%	45.2%
488,406	GUILFORD	257,405	98,062	149,248	10,095	51,186 D	38.1%	58.0%	39.7%	60.3%
54,691	HALIFAX	25,167	9,031	15,748	388	6,717 D	35.9%	62.6%	36.4%	63.6%
114,678	HARNETT	46,065	27,614	16,737	1,714	10,877 R	59.9%	36.3%	62.3%	37.7%
59,036	HAYWOOD	30,727	18,929	10,473	1,325	8,456 R	61.6%	34.1%	64.4%	35.6%
106,740	HENDERSON	58,176	35,809	19,827	2,540	15,982 R	61.6%	34.1%	64.4%	35.6%
24,669	HERTFORD	10,186	3,099	6,910	177	3,811 D	30.4%	67.8%	31.0%	69.0%
46,952	HOKE	18,230	7,760	9,726	744	1,966 D	42.6%	53.4%	44.4%	55.6%
5,810	HYDE	2,304	1,288	965	51	323 R	55.9%	41.9%	57.2%	42.8%
159,437	IREDELL	82,567	54,754	24,734	3,079	30,020 R	66.3%	30.0%	68.9%	31.1%
40,271	JACKSON	18,713	9,870	7,713	1,130	2,157 R	52.7%	41.2%	56.1%	43.9%
168,878	JOHNSTON	85,909	54,372	28,362	3,175	26,010 R	63.3%	33.0%	65.7%	34.3%
10,153	JONES	5,135	2,974	2,065	96	909 R	57.9%	40.2%	59.0%	41.0%
57,866	LEE	25,084	13,712	10,469	903	3,243 R	54.7%	41.7%	56.7%	43.3%
59,495	LENOIR	26,807	13,613	12,634	560	979 R	50.8%	47.1%	51.9%	48.1%
78,265	LINCOLN	40,023	28,806	9,897	1,320	18,909 R	72.0%	24.7%	74.4%	25.6%
33,922	MACON	17,734	12,127	4,876	731	7,251 R	68.4%	27.5%	71.3%	28.7%
20,764	MADISON	11,269	6,783	3,926	560	2,857 R	60.2%	34.8%	63.3%	36.7%
24,505	MARTIN	11,964	5,897	5,846	221	51 R	49.3%	48.9%	50.2%	49.8%
44,996	MCDOWELL	19,875	14,568	4,667	640	9,901 R	73.3%	23.5%	75.7%	24.3%
919,628	MECKLENBURG	472,857	155,518	294,562	22,777	139,044 D	32.9%	62.3%	34.6%	65.4%

NORTH CAROLINA

PRESIDENT 2016

| 2010 Census Population | County | Total Vote | Republican (Trump) | Democratic (Clinton) | Other | Rep.-Dem. Plurality | Percentage | | | |
| | | | | | | | Total Vote | | Major Vote | |
							Rep.	Dem.	Rep.	Dem.
15,579	MITCHELL	8,096	6,282	1,596	218	4,686 R	77.6%	19.7%	79.7%	20.3%
27,798	MONTGOMERY	11,540	7,130	4,150	260	2,980 R	61.8%	36.0%	63.2%	36.8%
88,247	MOORE	48,692	30,490	16,329	1,873	14,161 R	62.6%	33.5%	65.1%	34.9%
95,840	NASH	47,665	23,319	23,235	1,111	84 R	48.9%	48.7%	50.1%	49.9%
202,667	NEW HANOVER	111,905	55,344	50,979	5,582	4,365 R	49.5%	45.6%	52.1%	47.9%
22,099	NORTHAMPTON	9,848	3,582	6,144	122	2,562 D	36.4%	62.4%	36.8%	63.2%
177,772	ONSLOW	57,135	37,122	17,514	2,499	19,608 R	65.0%	30.7%	67.9%	32.1%
133,801	ORANGE	82,340	18,557	59,923	3,860	41,366 D	22.5%	72.8%	23.6%	76.4%
13,144	PAMLICO	6,870	4,258	2,448	164	1,810 R	62.0%	35.6%	63.5%	36.5%
40,661	PASQUOTANK	17,391	8,180	8,615	596	435 D	47.0%	49.5%	48.7%	51.3%
52,217	PENDER	27,885	17,639	9,354	892	8,285 R	63.3%	33.5%	65.3%	34.7%
13,453	PERQUIMANS	6,708	4,177	2,319	212	1,858 R	62.3%	34.6%	64.3%	35.7%
39,464	PERSON	19,615	11,185	7,833	597	3,352 R	57.0%	39.9%	58.8%	41.2%
168,148	PITT	80,527	35,691	41,824	3,012	6,133 D	44.3%	51.9%	46.0%	54.0%
20,510	POLK	10,934	6,768	3,735	431	3,033 R	61.9%	34.2%	64.4%	35.6%
141,752	RANDOLPH	64,575	49,430	13,194	1,951	36,236 R	76.5%	20.4%	78.9%	21.1%
46,639	RICHMOND	19,328	10,383	8,501	444	1,882 R	53.7%	44.0%	55.0%	45.0%
134,168	ROBESON	40,858	20,762	19,016	1,080	1,746 R	50.8%	46.5%	52.2%	47.8%
93,643	ROCKINGHAM	42,278	26,830	14,228	1,220	12,602 R	63.5%	33.7%	65.3%	34.7%
138,428	ROWAN	64,369	42,810	19,400	2,159	23,410 R	66.5%	30.1%	68.8%	31.2%
67,810	RUTHERFORD	30,307	21,871	7,512	924	14,359 R	72.2%	24.8%	74.4%	25.6%
63,431	SAMPSON	25,928	14,838	10,547	543	4,291 R	57.2%	40.7%	58.5%	41.5%
36,157	SCOTLAND	13,928	6,256	7,319	353	1,063 D	44.9%	52.5%	46.1%	53.9%
60,585	STANLY	29,917	21,964	7,094	859	14,870 R	73.4%	23.7%	75.6%	24.4%
47,401	STOKES	22,550	17,116	4,665	769	12,451 R	75.9%	20.7%	78.6%	21.4%
73,673	SURRY	32,196	23,671	7,488	1,037	16,183 R	73.5%	23.3%	76.0%	24.0%
13,981	SWAIN	6,124	3,565	2,196	363	1,369 R	58.2%	35.9%	61.9%	38.1%
33,090	TRANSYLVANIA	17,869	10,520	6,558	791	3,962 R	58.9%	36.7%	61.6%	38.4%
4,407	TYRRELL	1,739	975	720	44	255 R	56.1%	41.4%	57.5%	42.5%
201,292	UNION	105,710	66,707	34,337	4,666	32,370 R	63.1%	32.5%	66.0%	34.0%
45,422	VANCE	19,977	7,332	12,229	416	4,897 D	36.7%	61.2%	37.5%	62.5%
900,993	WAKE	527,624	196,082	302,736	28,806	106,654 D	37.2%	57.4%	39.3%	60.7%
20,972	WARREN	9,842	3,214	6,413	215	3,199 D	32.7%	65.2%	33.4%	66.6%
13,228	WASHINGTON	6,165	2,564	3,510	91	946 D	41.6%	56.9%	42.2%	57.8%
51,079	WATAUGA	29,985	13,697	14,138	2,150	441 D	45.7%	47.2%	49.2%	50.8%
122,623	WAYNE	50,689	27,540	21,770	1,379	5,770 R	54.3%	42.9%	55.9%	44.1%
69,340	WILKES	31,296	23,752	6,638	906	17,114 R	75.9%	21.2%	78.2%	21.8%
81,234	WILSON	38,135	17,531	19,663	941	2,132 D	46.0%	51.6%	47.1%	52.9%
38,406	YADKIN	17,624	13,880	3,160	584	10,720 R	78.8%	17.9%	81.5%	18.5%
17,818	YANCEY	9,960	6,385	3,196	379	3,189 R	64.1%	32.1%	66.6%	33.4%
9,535,483	TOTAL	4,741,564	2,362,631	2,189,316	189,617	173,315 R	49.8%	46.2%	51.9%	48.1%

NORTH CAROLINA

GOVERNOR 2016

| 2010 Census Population | County | Total Vote | Republican (McCrory) | Democratic (Cooper) | Other | Rep.-Dem. Plurality | Percentage | | | |
| | | | | | | | Total Vote | | Major Vote | |
							Rep.	Dem.	Rep.	Dem.
151,131	ALAMANCE	70,816	37,501	32,032	1,283	5,469 R	53.0%	45.2%	53.9%	46.1%
37,198	ALEXANDER	18,283	13,248	4,648	387	8,600 R	72.5%	25.4%	74.0%	26.0%
11,155	ALLEGHANY	5,323	3,583	1,643	97	1,940 R	67.3%	30.9%	68.6%	31.4%
26,948	ANSON	10,474	4,511	5,851	112	1,340 D	43.1%	55.9%	43.5%	56.5%
27,281	ASHE	13,426	8,834	4,304	288	4,530 R	65.8%	32.1%	67.2%	32.8%

NORTH CAROLINA

GOVERNOR 2016

2010 Census Population	County	Total Vote	Republican (McCrory)	Democratic (Cooper)	Other	Rep.-Dem. Plurality		Total Vote Rep.	Total Vote Dem.	Major Vote Rep.	Major Vote Dem.
17,797	AVERY	8,189	6,023	1,978	188	4,045	R	73.5%	24.2%	75.3%	24.7%
47,759	BEAUFORT	23,787	14,610	8,855	322	5,755	R	61.4%	37.2%	62.3%	37.7%
21,282	BERTIE	9,264	3,700	5,504	60	1,804	D	39.9%	59.4%	40.2%	59.8%
35,190	BLADEN	15,764	8,312	7,263	189	1,049	R	52.7%	46.1%	53.4%	46.6%
107,431	BRUNSWICK	67,585	40,726	25,285	1,574	15,441	R	60.3%	37.4%	61.7%	38.3%
238,318	BUNCOMBE	138,045	51,874	81,877	4,294	30,003	D	37.6%	59.3%	38.8%	61.2%
90,912	BURKE	38,714	24,466	13,372	876	11,094	R	63.2%	34.5%	64.7%	35.3%
178,011	CABARRUS	92,889	52,530	37,918	2,441	14,612	R	56.6%	40.8%	58.1%	41.9%
83,029	CALDWELL	36,155	25,173	10,055	927	15,118	R	69.6%	27.8%	71.5%	28.5%
9,980	CAMDEN	4,903	3,410	1,361	132	2,049	R	69.5%	27.8%	71.5%	28.5%
66,469	CARTERET	37,572	26,095	10,687	790	15,408	R	69.5%	28.4%	70.9%	29.1%
23,719	CASWELL	10,953	5,762	5,035	156	727	R	52.6%	46.0%	53.4%	46.6%
154,358	CATAWBA	71,850	46,269	23,766	1,815	22,503	R	64.4%	33.1%	66.1%	33.9%
63,505	CHATHAM	39,868	17,052	22,097	719	5,045	D	42.8%	55.4%	43.6%	56.4%
27,444	CHEROKEE	13,867	9,717	3,712	438	6,005	R	70.1%	26.8%	72.4%	27.6%
14,793	CHOWAN	7,141	4,079	2,990	72	1,089	R	57.1%	41.9%	57.7%	42.3%
10,587	CLAY	5,875	4,029	1,690	156	2,339	R	68.6%	28.8%	70.4%	29.6%
98,078	CLEVELAND	44,402	27,548	16,114	740	11,434	R	62.0%	36.3%	63.1%	36.9%
58,098	COLUMBUS	23,367	13,740	9,316	311	4,424	R	58.8%	39.9%	59.6%	40.4%
103,505	CRAVEN	46,636	27,926	17,814	896	10,112	R	59.9%	38.2%	61.1%	38.9%
319,431	CUMBERLAND	126,120	52,762	70,449	2,909	17,687	D	41.8%	55.9%	42.8%	57.2%
23,547	CURRITUCK	12,372	8,851	3,156	365	5,695	R	71.5%	25.5%	73.7%	26.3%
33,920	DARE	19,305	10,702	8,086	517	2,616	R	55.4%	41.9%	57.0%	43.0%
162,878	DAVIDSON	74,481	50,860	21,945	1,676	28,915	R	68.3%	29.5%	69.9%	30.1%
41,240	DAVIE	21,667	14,721	6,438	508	8,283	R	67.9%	29.7%	69.6%	30.4%
58,505	DUPLIN	20,673	12,269	8,180	224	4,089	R	59.3%	39.6%	60.0%	40.0%
267,587	DURHAM	155,479	30,720	122,137	2,622	91,417	D	19.8%	78.6%	20.1%	79.9%
56,552	EDGECOMBE	24,766	8,389	16,162	215	7,773	D	33.9%	65.3%	34.2%	65.8%
350,670	FORSYTH	177,269	73,589	99,689	3,991	26,100	D	41.5%	56.2%	42.5%	57.5%
60,619	FRANKLIN	30,339	15,900	13,849	590	2,051	R	52.4%	45.6%	53.4%	46.6%
206,086	GASTON	95,860	60,006	33,708	2,146	26,298	R	62.6%	35.2%	64.0%	36.0%
12,197	GATES	5,291	2,875	2,338	78	537	R	54.3%	44.2%	55.2%	44.8%
8,861	GRAHAM	4,034	2,760	1,144	130	1,616	R	68.4%	28.4%	70.7%	29.3%
59,916	GRANVILLE	27,286	13,308	13,528	450	220	D	48.8%	49.6%	49.6%	50.4%
21,362	GREENE	8,052	4,383	3,602	67	781	R	54.4%	44.7%	54.9%	45.1%
488,406	GUILFORD	255,568	94,467	155,692	5,409	61,225	D	37.0%	60.9%	37.8%	62.2%
54,691	HALIFAX	25,042	8,830	16,021	191	7,191	D	35.3%	64.0%	35.5%	64.5%
114,678	HARNETT	45,829	27,122	17,666	1,041	9,456	R	59.2%	38.5%	60.6%	39.4%
59,036	HAYWOOD	30,450	16,625	12,864	961	3,761	R	54.6%	42.2%	56.4%	43.6%
106,740	HENDERSON	57,655	33,599	22,459	1,597	11,140	R	58.3%	39.0%	59.9%	40.1%
24,669	HERTFORD	9,999	3,243	6,681	75	3,438	D	32.4%	66.8%	32.7%	67.3%
46,952	HOKE	17,977	7,799	9,688	490	1,889	D	43.4%	53.9%	44.6%	55.4%
5,810	HYDE	2,293	1,257	1,011	25	246	R	54.8%	44.1%	55.4%	44.6%
159,437	IREDELL	81,927	50,923	28,585	2,419	22,338	R	62.2%	34.9%	64.0%	36.0%
40,271	JACKSON	18,584	8,782	9,205	597	423	D	47.3%	49.5%	48.8%	51.2%
168,878	JOHNSTON	85,670	52,921	31,182	1,567	21,739	R	61.8%	36.4%	62.9%	37.1%
10,153	JONES	5,108	2,998	2,050	60	948	R	58.7%	40.1%	59.4%	40.6%
57,866	LEE	24,930	13,017	11,369	544	1,648	R	52.2%	45.6%	53.4%	46.6%
59,495	LENOIR	26,620	13,882	12,458	280	1,424	R	52.1%	46.8%	52.7%	47.3%
78,265	LINCOLN	39,848	27,558	11,331	959	16,227	R	69.2%	28.4%	70.9%	29.1%
33,922	MACON	17,519	10,715	6,279	525	4,436	R	61.2%	35.8%	63.1%	36.9%
20,764	MADISON	11,163	6,049	4,796	318	1,253	R	54.2%	43.0%	55.8%	44.2%
24,505	MARTIN	11,886	6,015	5,783	88	232	R	50.6%	48.7%	51.0%	49.0%
44,996	MCDOWELL	19,643	13,049	6,022	572	7,027	R	66.4%	30.7%	68.4%	31.6%
919,628	MECKLENBURG	469,605	160,501	297,129	11,975	136,628	D	34.2%	63.3%	35.1%	64.9%
15,579	MITCHELL	8,019	5,822	1,998	199	3,824	R	72.6%	24.9%	74.5%	25.5%
27,798	MONTGOMERY	11,489	6,656	4,658	175	1,998	R	57.9%	40.5%	58.8%	41.2%
88,247	MOORE	48,473	29,688	17,794	991	11,894	R	61.2%	36.7%	62.5%	37.5%
95,840	NASH	47,638	22,486	24,646	506	2,160	D	47.2%	51.7%	47.7%	52.3%
202,667	NEW HANOVER	110,709	51,105	56,370	3,234	5,265	D	46.2%	50.9%	47.6%	52.4%

NORTH CAROLINA

GOVERNOR 2016

2010 Census Population	County	Total Vote	Republican (McCrory)	Democratic (Cooper)	Other	Rep.-Dem. Plurality	Percentage Total Vote Rep.	Dem.	Major Vote Rep.	Dem.
22,099	NORTHAMPTON	9,787	3,617	6,101	69	2,484 D	37.0%	62.3%	37.2%	62.8%
177,772	ONSLOW	56,340	36,688	17,994	1,658	18,694 R	65.1%	31.9%	67.1%	32.9%
133,801	ORANGE	81,989	19,153	61,344	1,492	42,191 D	23.4%	74.8%	23.8%	76.2%
13,144	PAMLICO	6,830	4,261	2,466	103	1,795 R	62.4%	36.1%	63.3%	36.7%
40,661	PASQUOTANK	17,180	8,071	8,774	335	703 D	47.0%	51.1%	47.9%	52.1%
52,217	PENDER	27,493	16,622	10,187	684	6,435 R	60.5%	37.1%	62.0%	38.0%
13,453	PERQUIMANS	6,592	4,160	2,356	76	1,804 R	63.1%	35.7%	63.8%	36.2%
39,464	PERSON	19,473	10,770	8,400	303	2,370 R	55.3%	43.1%	56.2%	43.8%
168,148	PITT	79,944	36,705	41,916	1,323	5,211 D	45.9%	52.4%	46.7%	53.3%
20,510	POLK	10,778	6,225	4,302	251	1,923 R	57.8%	39.9%	59.1%	40.9%
141,752	RANDOLPH	64,204	46,370	16,374	1,460	29,996 R	72.2%	25.5%	73.9%	26.1%
46,639	RICHMOND	19,103	9,844	8,948	311	896 R	51.5%	46.8%	52.4%	47.6%
134,168	ROBESON	40,223	21,305	18,536	382	2,769 R	53.0%	46.1%	53.5%	46.5%
93,643	ROCKINGHAM	42,015	24,831	16,334	850	8,497 R	59.1%	38.9%	60.3%	39.7%
138,428	ROWAN	64,073	40,812	21,631	1,630	19,181 R	63.7%	33.8%	65.4%	34.6%
67,810	RUTHERFORD	29,912	19,672	9,512	728	10,160 R	65.8%	31.8%	67.4%	32.6%
63,431	SAMPSON	25,766	14,935	10,566	265	4,369 R	58.0%	41.0%	58.6%	41.4%
36,157	SCOTLAND	13,631	6,091	7,351	189	1,260 D	44.7%	53.9%	45.3%	54.7%
60,585	STANLY	29,818	21,054	8,163	601	12,891 R	70.6%	27.4%	72.1%	27.9%
47,401	STOKES	22,467	15,726	6,177	564	9,549 R	70.0%	27.5%	71.8%	28.2%
73,673	SURRY	31,951	21,714	9,624	613	12,090 R	68.0%	30.1%	69.3%	30.7%
13,981	SWAIN	6,026	3,096	2,662	268	434 R	51.4%	44.2%	53.8%	46.2%
33,090	TRANSYLVANIA	17,676	9,549	7,598	529	1,951 R	54.0%	43.0%	55.7%	44.3%
4,407	TYRRELL	1,722	990	704	28	286 R	57.5%	40.9%	58.4%	41.6%
201,292	UNION	105,048	66,739	35,921	2,388	30,818 R	63.5%	34.2%	65.0%	35.0%
45,422	VANCE	19,849	7,381	12,267	201	4,886 D	37.2%	61.8%	37.6%	62.4%
900,993	WAKE	526,575	199,356	315,555	11,664	116,199 D	37.9%	59.9%	38.7%	61.3%
20,972	WARREN	9,789	3,218	6,469	102	3,251 D	32.9%	66.1%	33.2%	66.8%
13,228	WASHINGTON	6,104	2,665	3,386	53	721 D	43.7%	55.5%	44.0%	56.0%
51,079	WATAUGA	29,752	13,073	15,650	1,029	2,577 D	43.9%	52.6%	45.5%	54.5%
122,623	WAYNE	50,360	27,821	21,859	680	5,962 R	55.2%	43.4%	56.0%	44.0%
69,340	WILKES	31,148	22,246	8,280	622	13,966 R	71.4%	26.6%	72.9%	27.1%
81,234	WILSON	38,023	17,161	20,471	391	3,310 D	45.1%	53.8%	45.6%	54.4%
38,406	YADKIN	17,581	13,192	4,033	356	9,159 R	75.0%	22.9%	76.6%	23.4%
17,818	YANCEY	10,006	5,845	3,931	230	1,914 R	58.4%	39.3%	59.8%	40.2%
9,535,483	TOTAL	4,711,014	2,298,880	2,309,157	102,977	10,277 D	48.8%	49.0%	49.9%	50.1%

NORTH CAROLINA

SENATOR 2016

2010 Census Population	County	Total Vote	Republican (Burr)	Democratic (Ross)	Other	Rep.-Dem. Plurality	Percentage Total Vote Rep.	Dem.	Major Vote Rep.	Dem.
151,131	ALAMANCE	70,621	39,380	28,873	2,368	10,507 R	55.8%	40.9%	57.7%	42.3%
37,198	ALEXANDER	18,095	13,271	3,895	929	9,376 R	73.3%	21.5%	77.3%	22.7%
11,155	ALLEGHANY	5,286	3,720	1,337	229	2,383 R	70.4%	25.3%	73.6%	26.4%
26,948	ANSON	10,426	4,383	5,793	250	1,410 D	42.0%	55.6%	43.1%	56.9%
27,281	ASHE	13,339	9,253	3,575	511	5,678 R	69.4%	26.8%	72.1%	27.9%
17,797	AVERY	8,094	6,071	1,705	318	4,366 R	75.0%	21.1%	78.1%	21.9%
47,759	BEAUFORT	23,619	14,313	8,436	870	5,877 R	60.6%	35.7%	62.9%	37.1%
21,282	BERTIE	9,183	3,446	5,590	147	2,144 D	37.5%	60.9%	38.1%	61.9%
35,190	BLADEN	15,635	8,242	6,999	394	1,243 R	52.7%	44.8%	54.1%	45.9%
107,431	BRUNSWICK	67,306	42,112	22,370	2,824	19,742 R	62.6%	33.2%	65.3%	34.7%

NORTH CAROLINA

SENATOR 2016

2010 Census Population	County	Total Vote	Republican (Burr)	Democratic (Ross)	Other	Rep.-Dem. Plurality	Percentage Total Vote Rep.	Dem.	Major Vote Rep.	Dem.
238,318	BUNCOMBE	137,516	56,086	75,897	5,533	19,811 D	40.8%	55.2%	42.5%	57.5%
90,912	BURKE	38,408	25,165	11,471	1,772	13,694 R	65.5%	29.9%	68.7%	31.3%
178,011	CABARRUS	92,371	53,723	34,266	4,382	19,457 R	58.2%	37.1%	61.1%	38.9%
83,029	CALDWELL	35,917	25,532	8,538	1,847	16,994 R	71.1%	23.8%	74.9%	25.1%
9,980	CAMDEN	4,860	3,401	1,279	180	2,122 R	70.0%	26.3%	72.7%	27.3%
66,469	CARTERET	37,388	26,189	9,668	1,531	16,521 R	70.0%	25.9%	73.0%	27.0%
23,719	CASWELL	10,937	5,991	4,671	275	1,320 R	54.8%	42.7%	56.2%	43.8%
154,358	CATAWBA	71,437	47,232	20,744	3,461	26,488 R	66.1%	29.0%	69.5%	30.5%
63,505	CHATHAM	39,701	18,049	20,530	1,122	2,481 D	45.5%	51.7%	46.8%	53.2%
27,444	CHEROKEE	13,815	10,116	3,210	489	6,906 R	73.2%	23.2%	75.9%	24.1%
14,793	CHOWAN	7,041	4,027	2,881	133	1,146 R	57.2%	40.9%	58.3%	41.7%
10,587	CLAY	5,857	4,183	1,482	192	2,701 R	71.4%	25.3%	73.8%	26.2%
98,078	CLEVELAND	44,121	27,491	15,025	1,605	12,466 R	62.3%	34.1%	64.7%	35.3%
58,098	COLUMBUS	23,228	13,637	8,841	750	4,796 R	58.7%	38.1%	60.7%	39.3%
103,505	CRAVEN	46,474	27,741	16,955	1,778	10,786 R	59.7%	36.5%	62.1%	37.9%
319,431	CUMBERLAND	125,901	51,902	69,733	4,266	17,831 D	41.2%	55.4%	42.7%	57.3%
23,547	CURRITUCK	12,337	8,921	2,999	417	5,922 R	72.3%	24.3%	74.8%	25.2%
33,920	DARE	19,209	11,393	7,226	590	4,167 R	59.3%	37.6%	61.2%	38.8%
162,878	DAVIDSON	74,151	53,535	17,753	2,863	35,782 R	72.2%	23.9%	75.1%	24.9%
41,240	DAVIE	21,614	15,568	5,117	929	10,451 R	72.0%	23.7%	75.3%	24.7%
58,505	DUPLIN	20,557	12,002	8,013	542	3,989 R	58.4%	39.0%	60.0%	40.0%
267,587	DURHAM	155,240	33,718	117,884	3,638	84,166 D	21.7%	75.9%	22.2%	77.8%
56,552	EDGECOMBE	24,645	8,353	15,847	445	7,494 D	33.9%	64.3%	34.5%	65.5%
350,670	FORSYTH	177,213	82,004	89,666	5,543	7,662 D	46.3%	50.6%	47.8%	52.2%
60,619	FRANKLIN	30,197	16,279	12,880	1,038	3,399 R	53.9%	42.7%	55.8%	44.2%
206,086	GASTON	95,268	60,298	30,582	4,388	29,716 R	63.3%	32.1%	66.3%	33.7%
12,197	GATES	5,266	2,821	2,316	129	505 R	53.6%	44.0%	54.9%	45.1%
8,861	GRAHAM	3,981	2,935	872	174	2,063 R	73.7%	21.9%	77.1%	22.9%
59,916	GRANVILLE	27,163	13,580	12,758	825	822 R	50.0%	47.0%	51.6%	48.4%
21,362	GREENE	8,000	4,280	3,518	202	762 R	53.5%	44.0%	54.9%	45.1%
488,406	GUILFORD	254,932	103,341	143,914	7,677	40,573 D	40.5%	56.5%	41.8%	58.2%
54,691	HALIFAX	25,001	8,983	15,601	417	6,618 D	35.9%	62.4%	36.5%	63.5%
114,678	HARNETT	45,765	27,305	16,821	1,639	10,484 R	59.7%	36.8%	61.9%	38.1%
59,036	HAYWOOD	30,297	17,873	10,953	1,471	6,920 R	59.0%	36.2%	62.0%	38.0%
106,740	HENDERSON	57,508	35,486	19,793	2,229	15,693 R	61.7%	34.4%	64.2%	35.8%
24,669	HERTFORD	9,950	3,116	6,714	120	3,598 D	31.3%	67.5%	31.7%	68.3%
46,952	HOKE	17,953	7,669	9,561	723	1,892 D	42.7%	53.3%	44.5%	55.5%
5,810	HYDE	2,270	1,244	949	77	295 R	54.8%	41.8%	56.7%	43.3%
159,437	IREDELL	81,560	53,125	24,187	4,248	28,938 R	65.1%	29.7%	68.7%	31.3%
40,271	JACKSON	18,499	9,628	8,014	857	1,614 R	52.0%	43.3%	54.6%	45.4%
168,878	JOHNSTON	85,244	53,977	28,279	2,988	25,698 R	63.3%	33.2%	65.6%	34.4%
10,153	JONES	5,069	2,911	2,001	157	910 R	57.4%	39.5%	59.3%	40.7%
57,866	LEE	24,791	13,535	10,392	864	3,143 R	54.6%	41.9%	56.6%	43.4%
59,495	LENOIR	26,455	13,518	12,297	640	1,221 R	51.1%	46.5%	52.4%	47.6%
78,265	LINCOLN	39,580	27,867	9,798	1,915	18,069 R	70.4%	24.8%	74.0%	26.0%
33,922	MACON	17,469	11,357	5,367	745	5,990 R	65.0%	30.7%	67.9%	32.1%
20,764	MADISON	11,062	6,286	4,271	505	2,015 R	56.8%	38.6%	59.5%	40.5%
24,505	MARTIN	11,818	5,825	5,678	315	147 R	49.3%	48.0%	50.6%	49.4%
44,996	MCDOWELL	19,532	13,671	4,901	960	8,770 R	70.0%	25.1%	73.6%	26.4%
919,628	MECKLENBURG	467,547	173,272	277,020	17,255	103,748 D	37.1%	59.2%	38.5%	61.5%
15,579	MITCHELL	7,942	5,951	1,714	277	4,237 R	74.9%	21.6%	77.6%	22.4%
27,798	MONTGOMERY	11,440	6,838	4,206	396	2,632 R	59.8%	36.8%	61.9%	38.1%
88,247	MOORE	48,339	30,724	16,059	1,556	14,665 R	63.6%	33.2%	65.7%	34.3%
95,840	NASH	47,476	23,450	23,093	933	357 R	49.4%	48.6%	50.4%	49.6%
202,667	NEW HANOVER	110,215	56,153	48,994	5,068	7,159 R	50.9%	44.5%	53.4%	46.6%
22,099	NORTHAMPTON	9,724	3,511	6,065	148	2,554 D	36.1%	62.4%	36.7%	63.3%
177,772	ONSLOW	56,116	36,180	17,029	2,907	19,151 R	64.5%	30.3%	68.0%	32.0%
133,801	ORANGE	81,816	21,884	57,877	2,055	35,993 D	26.7%	70.7%	27.4%	72.6%
13,144	PAMLICO	6,780	4,200	2,374	206	1,826 R	61.9%	35.0%	63.9%	36.1%
40,661	PASQUOTANK	17,105	8,083	8,579	443	496 D	47.3%	50.2%	48.5%	51.5%

NORTH CAROLINA
SENATOR 2016

2010 Census Population	County	Total Vote	Republican (Burr)	Democratic (Ross)	Other	Rep.-Dem. Plurality	Total Vote Rep.	Total Vote Dem.	Major Vote Rep.	Major Vote Dem.
52,217	PENDER	27,428	17,180	9,087	1,161	8,093 R	62.6%	33.1%	65.4%	34.6%
13,453	PERQUIMANS	6,565	4,153	2,281	131	1,872 R	63.3%	34.7%	64.5%	35.5%
39,464	PERSON	19,363	11,033	7,765	565	3,268 R	57.0%	40.1%	58.7%	41.3%
168,148	PITT	79,647	37,150	40,062	2,435	2,912 D	46.6%	50.3%	48.1%	51.9%
20,510	POLK	10,715	6,362	3,970	383	2,392 R	59.4%	37.1%	61.6%	38.4%
141,752	RANDOLPH	63,988	48,048	13,208	2,732	34,840 R	75.1%	20.6%	78.4%	21.6%
46,639	RICHMOND	18,866	9,732	8,430	704	1,302 R	51.6%	44.7%	53.6%	46.4%
134,168	ROBESON	39,650	19,792	19,053	805	739 R	49.9%	48.1%	51.0%	49.0%
93,643	ROCKINGHAM	41,888	26,157	14,193	1,538	11,964 R	62.4%	33.9%	64.8%	35.2%
138,428	ROWAN	63,679	41,230	19,227	3,222	22,003 R	64.7%	30.2%	68.2%	31.8%
67,810	RUTHERFORD	29,758	20,366	8,240	1,152	12,126 R	68.4%	27.7%	71.2%	28.8%
63,431	SAMPSON	25,617	14,819	10,269	529	4,550 R	57.8%	40.1%	59.1%	40.9%
36,157	SCOTLAND	13,561	6,113	7,161	287	1,048 D	45.1%	52.8%	46.1%	53.9%
60,585	STANLY	29,646	20,831	7,255	1,560	13,576 R	70.3%	24.5%	74.2%	25.8%
47,401	STOKES	22,447	16,698	4,774	975	11,924 R	74.4%	21.3%	77.8%	22.2%
73,673	SURRY	31,814	23,143	7,509	1,162	15,634 R	72.7%	23.6%	75.5%	24.5%
13,981	SWAIN	5,992	3,323	2,320	349	1,003 R	55.5%	38.7%	58.9%	41.1%
33,090	TRANSYLVANIA	17,665	10,221	6,749	695	3,472 R	57.9%	38.2%	60.2%	39.8%
4,407	TYRRELL	1,707	941	695	71	246 R	55.1%	40.7%	57.5%	42.5%
201,292	UNION	104,394	67,893	32,116	4,385	35,777 R	65.0%	30.8%	67.9%	32.1%
45,422	VANCE	19,762	7,362	12,056	344	4,694 D	37.3%	61.0%	37.9%	62.1%
900,993	WAKE	524,609	217,789	290,286	16,534	72,497 D	41.5%	55.3%	42.9%	57.1%
20,972	WARREN	9,775	3,258	6,336	181	3,078 D	33.3%	64.8%	34.0%	66.0%
13,228	WASHINGTON	6,081	2,534	3,392	155	858 D	41.7%	55.8%	42.8%	57.2%
51,079	WATAUGA	29,524	14,259	13,837	1,428	422 R	48.3%	46.9%	50.8%	49.2%
122,623	WAYNE	50,104	27,530	21,286	1,288	6,244 R	54.9%	42.5%	56.4%	43.6%
69,340	WILKES	30,918	22,852	6,749	1,317	16,103 R	73.9%	21.8%	77.2%	22.8%
81,234	WILSON	37,870	17,641	19,435	794	1,794 D	46.6%	51.3%	47.6%	52.4%
38,406	YADKIN	17,535	13,704	3,162	669	10,542 R	78.2%	18.0%	81.3%	18.7%
17,818	YANCEY	9,893	5,956	3,566	371	2,390 R	60.2%	36.0%	62.5%	37.5%
9,535,483	TOTAL	4,691,133	2,395,376	2,128,165	167,592	267,211 R	51.1%	45.4%	53.0%	47.0%

NORTH CAROLINA
HOUSE OF REPRESENTATIVES

CD	Year	Total Vote	Republican Vote	Republican Candidate	Democratic Vote	Democratic Candidate	Other Vote	Rep.-Dem. Plurality	Total Vote Rep.	Total Vote Dem.	Major Vote Rep.	Major Vote Dem.
1	2016**	350,699	101,567	DEW, H. POWELL JR.	240,661	BUTTERFIELD, GEORGE K. "G.K."*	8,471	139,094 D	29.0%	68.6%	29.7%	70.3%
1	2014	210,323	55,990	RICH, ARTHUR	154,333	BUTTERFIELD, GEORGE K. "G.K."*		98,343 D	26.6%	73.4%	26.6%	73.4%
1	2012	338,066	77,288	DILAURO, PETE	254,644	BUTTERFIELD, GEORGE K. "G.K."*	6,134	177,356 D	22.9%	75.3%	23.3%	76.7%
2	2016**	390,567	221,485	HOLDING, GEORGE*	169,082	MCNEIL, JOHN P.		52,403 R	56.7%	43.3%	56.7%	43.3%
2	2014	207,607	122,128	ELLMERS, RENEE*	85,479	AIKEN, CLAY		36,649 R	58.8%	41.2%	58.8%	41.2%
2	2012	311,397	174,066	ELLMERS, RENEE*	128,973	WILKINS, STEVE	8,358	45,093 R	55.9%	41.4%	57.4%	42.6%
3	2016**	323,701	217,531	JONES, WALTER B. JR.*	106,170	REEVES, ERNEST TYRONE		111,361 R	67.2%	32.8%	67.2%	32.8%
3	2014	205,597	139,415	JONES, WALTER B. JR.*	66,182	ADAME, MARSHALL		73,233 R	67.8%	32.2%	67.8%	32.2%
3	2012	309,885	195,571	JONES, WALTER B. JR.*	114,314	ANDERSON, ERIK		81,257 R	63.1%	36.9%	63.1%	36.9%
4	2016**	409,541	130,161	GOOGE, SUE	279,380	PRICE, DAVID E.*		149,219 D	31.8%	68.2%	31.8%	68.2%
4	2014	227,362	57,416	WRIGHT, PAUL	169,946	PRICE, DAVID E.*		112,530 D	25.3%	74.7%	25.3%	74.7%
4	2012	348,485	88,951	D'ANNUNZIO, TIM	259,534	PRICE, DAVID E.*		170,583 D	25.5%	74.5%	25.5%	74.5%
5	2016**	355,512	207,625	FOXX, VIRGINIA ANN*	147,887	BRANNON, JOSHUA "JOSH"		59,738 R	58.4%	41.6%	58.4%	41.6%
5	2014	228,252	139,279	FOXX, VIRGINIA ANN*	88,973	BRANNON, JOSHUA "JOSH"		50,306 R	61.0%	39.0%	61.0%	39.0%
5	2012	349,197	200,945	FOXX, VIRGINIA ANN*	148,252	MOTSINGER, ELISABETH		52,693 R	57.5%	42.5%	57.5%	42.5%

NORTH CAROLINA

HOUSE OF REPRESENTATIVES

CD	Year	Total Vote	Republican Vote	Republican Candidate	Democratic Vote	Democratic Candidate	Other Vote	Rep.-Dem. Plurality	Total Vote Rep.	Total Vote Dem.	Major Vote Rep.	Major Vote Dem.
6	2016**	351,150	207,983	WALKER, MARK*	143,167	GLIDEWELL, POWELL WATKINS "PETE" III		64,816 R	59.2%	40.8%	59.2%	40.8%
6	2014	251,070	147,312	WALKER, MARK	103,758	FJELD, LAURA		43,554 R	58.7%	41.3%	58.7%	41.3%
6	2012	364,583	222,116	COBLE, HOWARD*	142,467	FORIEST, TONY		79,649 R	60.9%	39.1%	60.9%	39.1%
7	2016**	347,706	211,801	ROUZER, DAVID*	135,905	CASTEEN, J. WESLEY		75,896 R	60.9%	39.1%	60.9%	39.1%
7	2014	226,504	134,431	ROUZER, DAVID	84,054	BARFIELD JR., JONATHAN	8,019	50,377 R	59.4%	37.1%	61.5%	38.5%
7	2012	336,736	168,041	ROUZER, DAVID	168,695	MCINTYRE, MIKE*		654 D	49.9%	50.1%	49.9%	50.1%
8	2016**	323,045	189,863	HUDSON, RICHARD*	133,182	MILLS, THOMAS		56,681 R	58.8%	41.2%	58.8%	41.2%
8	2014	187,422	121,568	HUDSON, RICHARD*	65,854	BLUE, ANTONIO		55,714 R	64.9%	35.1%	64.9%	35.1%
8	2012	302,280	160,695	HUDSON, RICHARD	137,139	KISSELL, LARRY*	4,446	23,556 R	53.2%	45.4%	54.0%	46.0%
9	2016**	332,493	193,452	PITTENGER, ROBERT*	139,041	CANO, CHRISTIAN		54,411 R	58.2%	41.8%	58.2%	41.8%
9	2014	173,668	163,080	PITTENGER, ROBERT*			10,588	163,080 R	93.9%		100.0%	
9	2012	375,690	194,537	PITTENGER, ROBERT	171,503	ROBERTS, JENNIFER	9,650	23,034 R	51.8%	45.7%	53.1%	46.9%
10	2016**	349,744	220,825	MCHENRY, PATRICK T.*	128,919	MILLARD, ANDY		91,906 R	63.1%	36.9%	63.1%	36.9%
10	2014	218,796	133,504	MCHENRY, PATRICK T.*	85,292	MACQUEEN IV, TATE		48,212 R	61.0%	39.0%	61.0%	39.0%
10	2012	334,849	190,826	MCHENRY, PATRICK T.*	144,023	KEEVER, PATRICIA R. "PATSY"		46,803 R	57.0%	43.0%	57.0%	43.0%
11	2016**	359,508	230,405	MEADOWS, MARK*	129,103	BRYSON, FREDERICK "RICK"		101,302 R	64.1%	35.9%	64.1%	35.9%
11	2014	230,024	144,682	MEADOWS, MARK*	85,342	HILL, THOMAS		59,340 R	62.9%	37.1%	62.9%	37.1%
11	2012	331,426	190,319	MEADOWS, MARK	141,107	ROGERS, HAYDEN		49,212 R	57.4%	42.6%	57.4%	42.6%
12	2016**	349,300	115,185	THREATT, LEON	234,115	ADAMS, ALMA S.*		118,930 D	33.0%	67.0%	33.0%	67.0%
12	2014	172,664	42,568	COAKLEY, VINCE	130,096	ADAMS, ALMA S.		87,528 D	24.7%	75.3%	24.7%	75.3%
12	2012	310,908	63,317	BROSCH, JACK	247,591	WATT, MELVIN*		184,274 D	20.4%	79.6%	20.4%	79.6%
13	2016**	355,492	199,443	BUDD, TED	156,049	DAVIS, BRUCE		43,394 R	56.1%	43.9%	56.1%	43.9%
13	2014	268,709	153,991	HOLDING, GEORGE*	114,718	CLEARY, BRENDA		39,273 R	57.3%	42.7%	57.3%	42.7%
13	2012	370,610	210,495	HOLDING, GEORGE	160,115	MALONE, CHARLES		50,380 R	56.8%	43.2%	56.8%	43.2%
TOTAL	2016	4,598,458	2,447,326		2,142,661		8,471	304,665 R	53.2%	46.6%	53.3%	46.7%
TOTAL	2014	2,807,998	1,555,364		1,234,027		18,607	321,337 R	55.4%	43.9%	55.8%	44.2%
TOTAL	2012	4,384,112	2,137,167		2,218,357		28,588	81,190 D	48.7%	50.6%	49.1%	50.9%

Note: An asterisk (*) denotes incumbent. **Due to mid-decade redistricting, boundaries for all districts are not comparable to those used in the 2012 and 2014 races.

NORTH CAROLINA

GENERAL AND PRIMARY ELECTIONS

2016 GENERAL ELECTIONS: OTHER VOTES

President Other vote was 130,126 Libertarian (Gary Johnson), 47,386 Write-in (Scattered Write-In), 12,105 Write-in (Jill Stein)

Governor Other vote was 102,977 Libertarian (Lon Cecil)

Senate Other vote was 167,592 Libertarian (Sean Haugh)

House Other vote was:

CD 1 8,471 Libertarian (J.J. Summerell)

NORTH CAROLINA

GENERAL AND PRIMARY ELECTIONS

2016 PRIMARY ELECTIONS: SUPPLEMENTARY INFORMATION

Primary	March 15, 2016 (President) June 7, 2016 (Congress)	**Registration** (as of June 7, 2016)	6,585,796	Democratic Republican Libertarian Unaffiliated	2,650,659 2,007,168 27,673 1,900,296

Primary Type Semi-open—Registered Democrats and Republicans could vote only in their party's primary. Unaffiliated voters could participate in the primary of any recognized party. However, if a voter cast a ballot in one party's primary, he or she could not participate in the runoff of another party.

	REPUBLICAN PRIMARIES			DEMOCRATIC PRIMARIES		
President	Trump, Donald J.	462,413	40.2%	Clinton, Hillary Rodham	622,915	54.5%
	Cruz, Ted	422,621	36.8%	Sanders, Bernard	467,018	40.9%
	Kasich, John R.	145,659	12.7%	No Preference	37,485	3.3%
	Rubio, Marco	88,907	7.7%	O'Malley, Martin	12,122	1.1%
	Carson, Ben	11,019	1.0%	De La Fuente, Roque "Rocky"	3,376	0.3%
	No Preference	6,081	0.5%			
	Bush, Jeb	3,893	0.3%			
	Huckabee, Mike	3,071	0.3%			
	Paul, Rand	2,753	0.2%			
	Christie, Chris	1,256	0.1%			
	Fiorina, Carly	929	0.1%			
	Santorum, Rick	663	0.1%			
	Gilmore, James S. III	265				
	TOTAL	*1,149,530*		*TOTAL*	*1,142,916*	
Senator	Burr, Richard M.*	627,263	61.4%	Ross, Deborah K.	614,414	62.3%
	Brannon, Greg	257,296	25.2%	Rey, Chris	162,869	16.5%
	Wright, Paul	86,933	8.5%	Griffin, Kevin D.	115,618	11.7%
	Holmquist, Larry	50,500	4.9%	Reeves, Ernest Tyrone	93,005	9.4%
	TOTAL	*1,021,992*		*TOTAL*	*985,906*	
Governor	McCrory, Pat*	876,885	81.7%	Cooper, Roy	710,658	68.7%
	Brawley, C. Robert	113,638	10.6%	Spaulding, Ken	323,774	31.3%
	Moss, Charles Kenneth	82,132	7.7%			
	TOTAL	*1,072,655*		*TOTAL*	*1,034,432*	
Congressional District 1	Dew, H. Powell Jr.	Unopposed		Butterfield, George K. "G.K."*	Unopposed	
Congressional District 2	Holding, George*	17,084	53.4%	McNeil, John P.	7,613	46.1%
	Ellmers, Renee*	7,552	23.6%	Watson, Jane	3,875	23.5%
	Brannon, Greg	7,359	23.0%	Hight, Steven E.	1,870	11.3%
				Sanyal, Arunava "Ron"	1,761	10.7%
				Brewington, Elton R.	1,387	8.4%
	TOTAL	*31,995*		*TOTAL*	*16,506*	
Congressional District 3	Jones, Walter B. Jr.*	15,799	64.9%	Reeves, Ernest Tyrone	6,456	54.7%
	Law, Phil	4,946	20.3%	Hurst, David Allan	5,351	45.3%
	Griffin, Taylor	3,610	14.8%			
	TOTAL	*24,355*		*TOTAL*	*11,807*	
Congressional District 4	Googe, Sue	10,947	71.3%	Price, David E.*	Unopposed	
	Kimball, Teiji	4,399	28.7%			
	TOTAL	*15,346*				
Congressional District 5	Foxx, Virginia Ann*	17,162	67.9%	Brannon, Joshua "Josh"	7,430	47.7%
	Curran, Patricia "Pattie"	8,098	32.1%	Wallin, Charlie	4,184	26.9%
				Roberts, Jim	3,959	25.4%
	TOTAL	*25,260*		*TOTAL*	*15,573*	

NORTH CAROLINA

GENERAL AND PRIMARY ELECTIONS

	REPUBLICAN PRIMARIES			DEMOCRATIC PRIMARIES		
Congressional District 6	Walker, Mark*	16,859	77.9%	Glidewell, Powell Watkins "Pete" III	Unopposed	
	Hardin, Chris	4,777	22.1%			
	TOTAL	21,636				
Congressional District 7	Rouzer, David*	Unopposed		Casteen, J. Wesley	Unopposed	
Congressional District 8	Hudson, Richard*	16,375	64.6%	Mills, Thomas	Unopposed	
	D'Annunzio, Tim	8,982	35.4%			
	TOTAL	25,357				
Congressional District 9	Pittenger, Robert*	9,299	35.0%	Cano, Christian	Unopposed	
	Harris, Mark	9,165	34.4%			
	Johnson, Todd	8,142	30.6%			
	TOTAL	26,606				
Congressional District 10	McHenry, Patrick T.*	14,817	78.4%	Millard, Andy	Unopposed	
	Gregory, Jeff	2,277	12.1%			
	Baker, Jeffrey	905	4.8%			
	Wiley, Albert L.	896	4.7%			
	TOTAL	18,895				
Congressional District 11	Meadows, Mark*	Unopposed		Bryson, Frederick "Rick"	9,695	50.7%
				Hill, Thomas	9,440	49.3%
				TOTAL	19,135	
Congressional District 12	Threatt, Leon	3,495	41.8%	Adams, Alma S.*	12,400	42.5%
	Wright, Paul	2,894	34.6%	Graham, Malcolm	8,428	28.9%
	Duffie, Ryan	1,973	23.6%	Cotham, Patricia "Tricia"	6,165	21.1%
				Cunningham, Carla D.	1,255	4.3%
				Henley, Gardenia M.	444	1.5%
				Moore, Rodney W.	245	0.8%
				Miller, Rick	235	0.8%
	TOTAL	8,362		TOTAL	29,172	
Congressional District 13	Budd, Ted	6,340	20.0%	Davis, Bruce	4,709	25.7%
	Blust, John Marshall	3,308	10.4%	Isner, Bob	4,597	25.1%
	Henning, Hank	3,289	10.4%	Coker, Adam	4,125	22.5%
	Howard, Julia Craven	3,254	10.3%	Ferguson, Mazie	2,963	16.2%
	McCall, Matthew J.	2,872	9.1%	Griffin, Kevin D.	1,946	10.6%
	Brock, Andrew C.	2,803	8.8%			
	Walser, Jason A.	2,319	7.3%			
	Barrett, Dan	2,296	7.2%			
	Warren, Harry	1,266	4.0%			
	Robinson, Vernon L.	970	3.1%			
	Daly, Kay	889	2.8%			
	Rouco, George	773	2.4%			
	Snyder, Jim	436	1.4%			
	Shoaf, Farren Kent	404	1.3%			
	Gant, Chad A.	198	0.6%			
	Thompson, David W.	147	0.5%			
	Feather, Kathleen "Kathy"	142	0.4%			
	TOTAL	31,706		TOTAL	18,340	

Note: An asterisk (*) denotes incumbent.

NORTH DAKOTA

One member At Large

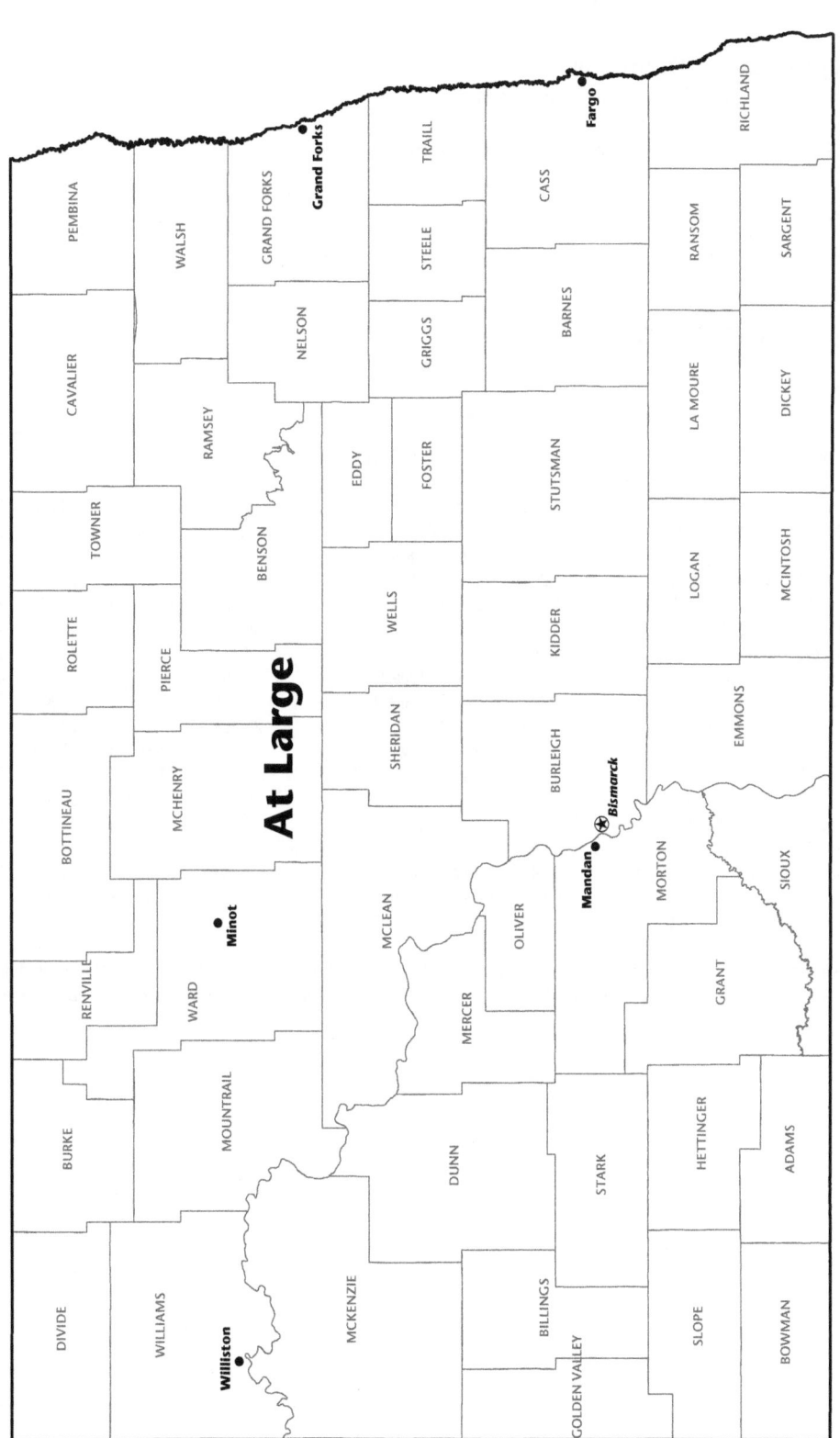

NORTH DAKOTA

GOVERNOR
Doug Burgum (R). Elected 2016 to a four-year term.

SENATORS (1 Republican, 1 Democrat)
Heidi Heitkamp (D). Elected 2012 to a six-year term.

John Hoeven (R). Re-elected 2016 to a six-year term. Previously elected 2010.

REPRESENTATIVES (1 Republican)
At Large. Kevin Cramer (R)

POSTWAR VOTE FOR PRESIDENT

| | | Republican | | Democratic | | | | Percentage | | | |
| | | | | | | | | Total Vote | | Major Vote | |
Year	Total Vote	Vote	Candidate	Vote	Candidate	Other Vote	Rep.-Dem. Plurality	Rep.	Dem.	Rep.	Dem.
2016**	344,360	216,794	Trump, Donald J.	93,758	Clinton, Hillary Rodham	33,808	123,036 R	63.0%	27.2%	69.8%	30.2%
2012	322,627	188,163	Romney, W. Mitt	124,827	Obama, Barack H.*	9,637	63,336 R	58.3%	38.7%	60.1%	39.9%
2008	316,621	168,601	McCain, John S. III	141,278	Obama, Barack H.	6,742	27,323 R	53.3%	44.6%	54.4%	45.6%
2004	312,833	196,651	Bush, George W.*	111,052	Kerry, John F.	5,130	85,599 R	62.9%	35.5%	63.9%	36.1%
2000**	288,256	174,852	Bush, George W.	95,284	Gore, Albert Jr.	18,120	79,568 R	60.7%	33.1%	64.7%	35.3%
1996**	266,411	125,050	Dole, Robert "Bob"	106,905	Clinton, Bill*	34,456	18,145 R	46.9%	40.1%	53.9%	46.1%
1992**	308,133	136,244	Bush, George H.*	99,168	Clinton, Bill	72,721	37,076 R	44.2%	32.2%	57.9%	42.1%
1988	297,261	166,559	Bush, George H.	127,739	Dukakis, Michael S.	2,963	38,820 R	56.0%	43.0%	56.6%	43.4%
1984	308,971	200,336	Reagan, Ronald*	104,429	Mondale, Walter F.	4,206	95,907 R	64.8%	33.8%	65.7%	34.3%
1980**	301,545	193,695	Reagan, Ronald	79,189	Carter, Jimmy*	28,661	114,506 R	64.2%	26.3%	71.0%	29.0%
1976	297,188	153,470	Ford, Gerald R.*	136,078	Carter, Jimmy	7,640	17,392 R	51.6%	45.8%	53.0%	47.0%
1972	280,514	174,109	Nixon, Richard M.*	100,384	McGovern, George S.	6,021	73,725 R	62.1%	35.8%	63.4%	36.6%
1968**	247,882	138,669	Nixon, Richard M.	94,769	Humphrey, Hubert Horatio Jr.	14,444	43,900 R	55.9%	38.2%	59.4%	40.6%
1964	258,389	108,207	Goldwater, Barry M. Sr.	149,784	Johnson, Lyndon B.*	398	41,577 D	41.9%	58.0%	41.9%	58.1%
1960	278,431	154,310	Nixon, Richard M.	123,963	Kennedy, John F.	158	30,347 R	55.4%	44.5%	55.5%	44.5%
1956	253,991	156,766	Eisenhower, Dwight D.*	96,742	Stevenson, Adlai E. II	483	60,024 R	61.7%	38.1%	61.8%	38.2%
1952	270,127	191,712	Eisenhower, Dwight D.	76,694	Stevenson, Adlai E. II	1,721	115,018 R	71.0%	28.4%	71.4%	28.6%
1948	220,716	115,139	Dewey, Thomas E.	95,812	Truman, Harry S.*	9,765	19,327 R	52.2%	43.4%	54.6%	45.4%

Note: An asterisk (*) denotes incumbent. **In past elections, the other vote included: 2016 - 21,434 Libertarian (Gary Johnson); 2000 - 9,486 Green (Ralph Nader); 1996 - 32,515 Reform (Ross Perot); 1992 - 71,084 Independent (Perot); 1980 - 23,640 Independent (John Anderson); 1968 - 14,244 American Independent (George Wallace).

NORTH DAKOTA

POSTWAR VOTE FOR GOVERNOR

Year	Total Vote	Republican Vote	Republican Candidate	Democratic Vote	Democratic Candidate	Other Vote	Rep.-Dem. Plurality	Total Vote Rep.	Total Vote Dem.	Major Vote Rep.	Major Vote Dem.
2016	339,601	259,863	Burgum, Doug	65,855	Nelson, Marvin E.	13,883	194,008 R	76.5%	19.4%	79.8%	20.2%
2012	317,812	200,526	Dalrymple, Jack*	109,047	Taylor, Ryan M.	8,239	91,479 R	63.1%	34.3%	64.8%	35.2%
2008	315,692	235,009	Hoeven, John*	74,279	Mathern, Tim	6,404	160,730 R	74.4%	23.5%	76.0%	24.0%
2004	309,873	220,803	Hoeven, John*	84,877	Satrom, Joe	4,193	135,926 R	71.3%	27.4%	72.2%	27.8%
2000	289,412	159,255	Hoeven, John	130,144	Heitkamp, Heidi	13	29,111 R	55.0%	45.0%	55.0%	45.0%
1996	264,298	174,937	Schafer, Edward T.*	89,349	Kaldor, Lee	12	85,588 R	66.2%	33.8%	66.2%	33.8%
1992	304,861	176,398	Schafer, Edward T.	123,845	Spaeth, Nicholas	4,618	52,553 R	57.9%	40.6%	58.8%	41.2%
1988	299,080	119,986	Mallberg, Leon L.	179,094	Sinner, George A.*		59,108 D	40.1%	59.9%	40.1%	59.9%
1984	314,382	140,460	Olson, Allen I.	173,922	Sinner, George A.		33,462 D	44.7%	55.3%	44.7%	55.3%
1980	302,621	162,230	Olson, Allen I.	140,391	Link, Arthur A.*		21,839 R	53.6%	46.4%	53.6%	46.4%
1976	297,249	138,321	Elkin, Richard	153,309	Link, Arthur A.*	5,619	14,988 D	46.5%	51.6%	47.4%	52.6%
1972	281,931	138,032	Davis, John E.	143,899	Link, Arthur A.		5,867 D	49.0%	51.0%	49.0%	51.0%
1968	247,998	108,380	McCarney, Robert P.	135,955	Guy, William L.*	3,663	27,575 D	43.7%	54.8%	44.4%	55.6%
1964**	262,661	116,247	Halcrow, Don	146,414	Guy, William L.*		30,167 D	44.3%	55.7%	44.3%	55.7%
1962	228,509	113,251	Andrews, Mark	115,258	Guy, William L.*		2,007 D	49.6%	50.4%	49.6%	50.4%
1960	275,375	122,486	Dahl, C. P.	136,148	Guy, William L.	16,741	13,662 D	44.5%	49.4%	47.4%	52.6%
1958	210,599	111,836	Davis, John E.*	98,763	Lord, John F.		13,073 R	53.1%	46.9%	53.1%	46.9%
1956	252,435	147,566	Davis, John E.	104,869	Warner, Wallace E.		42,697 R	58.5%	41.5%	58.5%	41.5%
1954	193,501	124,253	Brunsdale, Norman*	69,248	Bymers, Cornelius		55,005 R	64.2%	35.8%	64.2%	35.8%
1952	253,934	199,944	Brunsdale, Norman*	53,990	Johnson, Ole S.		145,954 R	78.7%	21.3%	78.7%	21.3%
1950	183,772	121,822	Brunsdale, Norman	61,950	Byerly, Clyde G.		59,872 R	66.3%	33.7%	66.3%	33.7%
1948	214,958	131,764	Aandahl, Fred G.*	80,655	Henry, Howard	2,539	51,109 R	61.3%	37.5%	62.0%	38.0%
1946	169,391	116,672	Aandahl, Fred G.*	52,719	Burdick, Quentin N.		63,953 R	68.9%	31.1%	68.9%	31.1%

Note: An asterisk (*) denotes incumbent. **The term of office of North Dakota's governor was increased from two to four years effective with the 1964 election.

POSTWAR VOTE FOR SENATOR

Year	Total Vote	Republican Vote	Republican Candidate	Democratic Vote	Democratic Candidate	Other Vote	Rep.-Dem. Plurality	Total Vote Rep.	Total Vote Dem.	Major Vote Rep.	Major Vote Dem.
2016	342,501	268,788	Hoeven, John*	58,116	Glassheim, Eliot	15,597	210,672 R	78.5%	17.0%	82.2%	17.8%
2012	320,851	158,282	Berg, Rick	161,163	Heitkamp, Heidi	1,406	2,881 D	49.3%	50.2%	49.5%	50.5%
2010	238,812	181,689	Hoeven, John	52,955	Potter, Tracy	4,168	128,734 R	76.1%	22.2%	77.4%	22.6%
2006	218,152	64,417	Grotberg, Dwight	150,146	Conrad, Kent*	3,589	85,729 D	29.5%	68.8%	30.0%	70.0%
2004	310,696	98,553	Liffrig, Mike G.	212,143	Dorgan, Byron L.*		113,590 D	31.7%	68.3%	31.7%	68.3%
2000	287,539	111,069	Sand, Duane	176,470	Conrad, Kent*		65,401 D	38.6%	61.4%	38.6%	61.4%
1998	213,358	75,013	Nalewaja, Donna	134,747	Dorgan, Byron L.*	3,598	59,734 D	35.2%	63.2%	35.8%	64.2%
1994	236,547	99,390	Clayburg, Ben	137,157	Conrad, Kent*		37,767 D	42.0%	58.0%	42.0%	58.0%
1992	303,957	118,162	Sydness, Steve	179,347	Dorgan, Byron L.	6,448	61,185 D	38.9%	59.0%	39.7%	60.3%
1992S**	163,311	55,194	Dalrymple, Jack	103,246	Conrad, Kent*	4,871	48,052 D	33.8%	63.2%	34.8%	65.2%
1988	289,170	112,937	Striden, Earl	171,899	Burdick, Quentin N.*	4,334	58,962 D	39.1%	59.4%	39.6%	60.4%
1986	288,998	141,797	Andrews, Mark*	143,932	Conrad, Kent	3,269	2,135 D	49.1%	49.8%	49.6%	50.4%
1982	262,465	89,304	Knorr, Gene	164,873	Burdick, Quentin N.*	8,288	75,569 D	34.0%	62.8%	35.1%	64.9%
1980	299,272	210,347	Andrews, Mark	86,658	Johanneson, Kent	2,267	123,689 R	70.3%	29.0%	70.8%	29.2%
1976	283,062	103,466	Stroup, Richard	175,772	Burdick, Quentin N.*	3,824	72,306 D	36.6%	62.1%	37.1%	62.9%
1974	235,661	114,117	Young, Milton R.*	113,931	Guy, William L.	7,613	186 R	48.4%	48.3%	50.0%	50.0%
1970	219,560	82,996	Kleppe, Tom	134,519	Burdick, Quentin N.*	2,045	51,523 D	37.8%	61.3%	38.2%	61.8%
1968	239,776	154,968	Young, Milton R.*	80,815	Lashkowitz, Herschel	3,993	74,153 R	64.6%	33.7%	65.7%	34.3%
1964	258,945	109,681	Kleppe, Tom	149,264	Burdick, Quentin N.*		39,583 D	42.4%	57.6%	42.4%	57.6%
1962	223,737	135,705	Young, Milton R.*	88,032	Lanier, William		47,673 R	60.7%	39.3%	60.7%	39.3%
1960S**	210,349	103,475	Davis, John E.	104,593	Burdick, Quentin N.	2,281	1,118 D	49.2%	49.7%	49.7%	50.3%
1958	204,635	117,070	Langer, William*	84,892	Vendsel, Raymond	2,673	32,178 R	57.2%	41.5%	58.0%	42.0%
1956	244,161	155,305	Young, Milton R.*	87,919	Burdick, Quentin N.	937	67,386 R	63.6%	36.0%	63.9%	36.1%
1952**	237,995	157,907	Langer, William*	55,347	Morrison, Harold A.	24,741	102,560 R	66.3%	23.3%	74.0%	26.0%
1950	186,716	126,209	Young, Milton R.*	60,507	O'Brien, Harry		65,702 R	67.6%	32.4%	67.6%	32.4%
1946**	165,382	88,210	Langer, William*	38,368	Larson, Abner B.	38,804	49,842 R	53.3%	23.2%	69.7%	30.3%
1946S**	136,852	75,998	Young, Milton R.*	37,507	Lanier, William	23,347	38,491 R	55.5%	27.4%	67.0%	33.0%

Note: An asterisk (*) denotes incumbent. **In past elections, the other vote included: 1952 - 24,741 Independent (Fred G. Aandahl); 1946 - 38,804 Independent (Arthur E. Thompson, who finished second); 1946 Special - 20,848 Independent (Gerald P. Nye). One of the 1992 elections was for a short term to fill a vacancy and the special election was held in December. The 1946 and 1960 special elections were held in June for short terms to fill vacancies.

NORTH DAKOTA

PRESIDENT 2016

2010 Census Population	County	Total Vote	Republican (Trump)	Democratic (Clinton)	Other	Rep.-Dem. Plurality	Percentage			
							Total Vote		Major Vote	
							Rep.	Dem.	Rep.	Dem.
2,343	ADAMS	1,218	909	216	93	693 R	74.6%	17.7%	80.8%	19.2%
11,066	BARNES	5,344	3,160	1,597	587	1,563 R	59.1%	29.9%	66.4%	33.6%
6,660	BENSON	2,011	929	842	240	87 R	46.2%	41.9%	52.5%	47.5%
783	BILLINGS	605	495	59	51	436 R	81.8%	9.8%	89.4%	10.6%
6,429	BOTTINEAU	3,494	2,494	736	264	1,758 R	71.4%	21.1%	77.2%	22.8%
3,151	BOWMAN	1,787	1,446	227	114	1,219 R	80.9%	12.7%	86.4%	13.6%
1,968	BURKE	1,052	895	119	38	776 R	85.1%	11.3%	88.3%	11.7%
81,308	BURLEIGH	47,979	32,532	10,881	4,566	21,651 R	67.8%	22.7%	74.9%	25.1%
149,778	CASS	80,821	39,816	31,361	9,644	8,455 R	49.3%	38.8%	55.9%	44.1%
3,993	CAVALIER	2,006	1,357	476	173	881 R	67.6%	23.7%	74.0%	26.0%
5,289	DICKEY	2,407	1,667	554	186	1,113 R	69.3%	23.0%	75.1%	24.9%
2,071	DIVIDE	1,219	867	245	107	622 R	71.1%	20.1%	78.0%	22.0%
3,536	DUNN	2,243	1,771	358	114	1,413 R	79.0%	16.0%	83.2%	16.8%
2,385	EDDY	1,231	791	355	85	436 R	64.3%	28.8%	69.0%	31.0%
3,550	EMMONS	1,981	1,677	215	89	1,462 R	84.7%	10.9%	88.6%	11.4%
3,343	FOSTER	1,719	1,241	347	131	894 R	72.2%	20.2%	78.1%	21.9%
1,680	GOLDEN VALLEY	957	796	99	62	697 R	83.2%	10.3%	88.9%	11.1%
66,861	GRAND FORKS	30,365	16,340	10,851	3,174	5,489 R	53.8%	35.7%	60.1%	39.9%
2,394	GRANT	1,381	1,108	185	88	923 R	80.2%	13.4%	85.7%	14.3%
2,420	GRIGGS	1,265	847	298	120	549 R	67.0%	23.6%	74.0%	26.0%
2,477	HETTINGER	1,296	1,050	168	78	882 R	81.0%	13.0%	86.2%	13.8%
2,435	KIDDER	1,376	1,111	179	86	932 R	80.7%	13.0%	86.1%	13.9%
4,139	LA MOURE	2,151	1,481	502	168	979 R	68.9%	23.3%	74.7%	25.3%
1,990	LOGAN	1,067	888	114	65	774 R	83.2%	10.7%	88.6%	11.4%
5,395	MCHENRY	2,820	2,050	490	280	1,560 R	72.7%	17.4%	80.7%	19.3%
2,809	MCINTOSH	1,446	1,100	235	111	865 R	76.1%	16.3%	82.4%	17.6%
6,360	MCKENZIE	4,672	3,670	698	304	2,972 R	78.6%	14.9%	84.0%	16.0%
8,962	MCLEAN	5,315	3,860	1,081	374	2,779 R	72.6%	20.3%	78.1%	21.9%
8,424	MERCER	4,682	3,759	621	302	3,138 R	80.3%	13.3%	85.8%	14.2%
27,471	MORTON	15,832	11,336	3,080	1,416	8,256 R	71.6%	19.5%	78.6%	21.4%
7,673	MOUNTRAIL	4,106	2,582	1,220	304	1,362 R	62.9%	29.7%	67.9%	32.1%
3,126	NELSON	1,717	1,025	536	156	489 R	59.7%	31.2%	65.7%	34.3%
1,846	OLIVER	1,017	830	119	68	711 R	81.6%	11.7%	87.5%	12.5%
7,413	PEMBINA	3,153	2,208	681	264	1,527 R	70.0%	21.6%	76.4%	23.6%
4,357	PIERCE	2,071	1,437	431	203	1,006 R	69.4%	20.8%	76.9%	23.1%
11,451	RAMSEY	5,305	3,217	1,505	583	1,712 R	60.6%	28.4%	68.1%	31.9%
5,457	RANSOM	2,359	1,210	838	311	372 R	51.3%	35.5%	59.1%	40.9%
2,470	RENVILLE	1,293	993	201	99	792 R	76.8%	15.5%	83.2%	16.8%
16,321	RICHLAND	7,592	4,767	2,064	761	2,703 R	62.8%	27.2%	69.8%	30.2%
13,937	ROLETTE	3,755	1,217	2,099	439	882 D	32.4%	55.9%	36.7%	63.3%
3,829	SARGENT	1,997	1,088	694	215	394 R	54.5%	34.8%	61.1%	38.9%
1,321	SHERIDAN	787	650	95	42	555 R	82.6%	12.1%	87.2%	12.8%
4,153	SIOUX	1,232	260	758	214	498 D	21.1%	61.5%	25.5%	74.5%
727	SLOPE	430	362	43	25	319 R	84.2%	10.0%	89.4%	10.6%
24,199	STARK	12,322	9,755	1,753	814	8,002 R	79.2%	14.2%	84.8%	15.2%
1,975	STEELE	999	538	361	100	177 R	53.9%	36.1%	59.8%	40.2%
21,100	STUTSMAN	10,155	6,718	2,498	939	4,220 R	66.2%	24.6%	72.9%	27.1%
2,246	TOWNER	1,157	733	305	119	428 R	63.4%	26.4%	70.6%	29.4%
8,121	TRAILL	3,933	2,265	1,241	427	1,024 R	57.6%	31.6%	64.6%	35.4%
11,119	WALSH	4,636	2,995	1,167	474	1,828 R	64.6%	25.2%	72.0%	28.0%
61,675	WARD	27,412	18,636	5,806	2,970	12,830 R	68.0%	21.2%	76.2%	23.8%
4,207	WELLS	2,383	1,796	419	168	1,377 R	75.4%	17.6%	81.1%	18.9%
22,398	WILLIAMS	12,807	10,069	1,735	1,003	8,334 R	78.6%	13.5%	85.3%	14.7%
672,591	TOTAL	344,360	216,794	93,758	33,808	123,036 R	63.0%	27.2%	69.8%	30.2%

NORTH DAKOTA

GOVERNOR 2016

2010 Census Population	County	Total Vote	Republican (Burgum)	Democratic (Nelson)	Other	Rep.-Dem. Plurality	Percentage			
							Total Vote		Major Vote	
							Rep.	Dem.	Rep.	Dem.
2,343	ADAMS	1,217	1,049	135	33	914 R	86.2%	11.1%	88.6%	11.4%
11,066	BARNES	5,327	4,217	917	193	3,300 R	79.2%	17.2%	82.1%	17.9%
6,660	BENSON	2,007	1,109	817	81	292 R	55.3%	40.7%	57.6%	42.4%
783	BILLINGS	607	537	48	22	489 R	88.5%	7.9%	91.8%	8.2%
6,429	BOTTINEAU	3,471	2,768	595	108	2,173 R	79.7%	17.1%	82.3%	17.7%
3,151	BOWMAN	1,792	1,577	178	37	1,399 R	88.0%	9.9%	89.9%	10.1%
1,968	BURKE	1,046	905	122	19	783 R	86.5%	11.7%	88.1%	11.9%
81,308	BURLEIGH	47,392	37,790	7,821	1,781	29,969 R	79.7%	16.5%	82.9%	17.1%
149,778	CASS	79,466	57,024	18,559	3,883	38,465 R	71.8%	23.4%	75.4%	24.6%
3,993	CAVALIER	2,014	1,598	374	42	1,224 R	79.3%	18.6%	81.0%	19.0%
5,289	DICKEY	2,405	1,945	404	56	1,541 R	80.9%	16.8%	82.8%	17.2%
2,071	DIVIDE	1,212	939	232	41	707 R	77.5%	19.1%	80.2%	19.8%
3,536	DUNN	2,216	1,860	302	54	1,558 R	83.9%	13.6%	86.0%	14.0%
2,385	EDDY	1,236	716	489	31	227 R	57.9%	39.6%	59.4%	40.6%
3,550	EMMONS	1,973	1,738	185	50	1,553 R	88.1%	9.4%	90.4%	9.6%
3,343	FOSTER	1,738	1,397	286	55	1,111 R	80.4%	16.5%	83.0%	17.0%
1,680	GOLDEN VALLEY	951	795	128	28	667 R	83.6%	13.5%	86.1%	13.9%
66,861	GRAND FORKS	29,222	20,458	7,392	1,372	13,066 R	70.0%	25.3%	73.5%	26.5%
2,394	GRANT	1,394	1,209	152	33	1,057 R	86.7%	10.9%	88.8%	11.2%
2,420	GRIGGS	1,273	961	278	34	683 R	75.5%	21.8%	77.6%	22.4%
2,477	HETTINGER	1,287	1,104	143	40	961 R	85.8%	11.1%	88.5%	11.5%
2,435	KIDDER	1,385	1,167	178	40	989 R	84.3%	12.9%	86.8%	13.2%
4,139	LA MOURE	2,165	1,748	368	49	1,380 R	80.7%	17.0%	82.6%	17.4%
1,990	LOGAN	1,090	964	96	30	868 R	88.4%	8.8%	90.9%	9.1%
5,395	MCHENRY	2,853	2,335	427	91	1,908 R	81.8%	15.0%	84.5%	15.5%
2,809	MCINTOSH	1,459	1,253	174	32	1,079 R	85.9%	11.9%	87.8%	12.2%
6,360	MCKENZIE	4,594	3,889	563	142	3,326 R	84.7%	12.3%	87.4%	12.6%
8,962	MCLEAN	5,310	4,239	918	153	3,321 R	79.8%	17.3%	82.2%	17.8%
8,424	MERCER	4,624	3,954	552	118	3,402 R	85.5%	11.9%	87.7%	12.3%
27,471	MORTON	15,615	12,589	2,411	615	10,178 R	80.6%	15.4%	83.9%	16.1%
7,673	MOUNTRAIL	4,059	2,759	1,125	175	1,634 R	68.0%	27.7%	71.0%	29.0%
3,126	NELSON	1,744	1,185	500	59	685 R	67.9%	28.7%	70.3%	29.7%
1,846	OLIVER	1,021	890	105	26	785 R	87.2%	10.3%	89.4%	10.6%
7,413	PEMBINA	3,171	2,556	513	102	2,043 R	80.6%	16.2%	83.3%	16.7%
4,357	PIERCE	2,078	1,641	394	43	1,247 R	79.0%	19.0%	80.6%	19.4%
11,451	RAMSEY	5,331	4,004	1,111	216	2,893 R	75.1%	20.8%	78.3%	21.7%
5,457	RANSOM	2,358	1,722	546	90	1,176 R	73.0%	23.2%	75.9%	24.1%
2,470	RENVILLE	1,273	1,076	161	36	915 R	84.5%	12.6%	87.0%	13.0%
16,321	RICHLAND	7,503	5,867	1,332	304	4,535 R	78.2%	17.8%	81.5%	18.5%
13,937	ROLETTE	3,754	1,240	2,383	131	1,143 D	33.0%	63.5%	34.2%	65.8%
3,829	SARGENT	2,014	1,464	493	57	971 R	72.7%	24.5%	74.8%	25.2%
1,321	SHERIDAN	786	678	86	22	592 R	86.3%	10.9%	88.7%	11.3%
4,153	SIOUX	1,201	438	684	79	246 D	36.5%	57.0%	39.0%	61.0%
727	SLOPE	428	376	41	11	335 R	87.9%	9.6%	90.2%	9.8%
24,199	STARK	12,051	10,354	1,307	390	9,047 R	85.9%	10.8%	88.8%	11.2%
1,975	STEELE	1,029	766	231	32	535 R	74.4%	22.4%	76.8%	23.2%
21,100	STUTSMAN	9,884	7,953	1,574	357	6,379 R	80.5%	15.9%	83.5%	16.5%
2,246	TOWNER	1,171	841	303	27	538 R	71.8%	25.9%	73.5%	26.5%
8,121	TRAILL	3,939	2,994	793	152	2,201 R	76.0%	20.1%	79.1%	20.9%
11,119	WALSH	4,682	3,613	787	282	2,826 R	77.2%	16.8%	82.1%	17.9%
61,675	WARD	26,930	21,223	4,335	1,372	16,888 R	78.8%	16.1%	83.0%	17.0%
4,207	WELLS	2,383	1,970	355	58	1,615 R	82.7%	14.9%	84.7%	15.3%
22,398	WILLIAMS	12,470	10,419	1,452	599	8,967 R	83.6%	11.6%	87.8%	12.2%
672,591	TOTAL	339,601	259,863	65,855	13,883	194,008 R	76.5%	19.4%	79.8%	20.2%

Note: Democratic candidates in North Dakota appear on the ballot for the Democratic-Nonpartisan League Party.

NORTH DAKOTA
SENATOR 2016

2010 Census Population	County	Total Vote	Republican (Hoeven)	Democratic (Glassheim)	Other	Rep.-Dem. Plurality	Percentage Total Vote Rep.	Dem.	Major Vote Rep.	Dem.
2,343	ADAMS	1,223	1,067	114	42	953 R	87.2%	9.3%	90.3%	9.7%
11,066	BARNES	5,338	4,302	835	201	3,467 R	80.6%	15.6%	83.7%	16.3%
6,660	BENSON	2,022	1,340	574	108	766 R	66.3%	28.4%	70.0%	30.0%
783	BILLINGS	605	543	43	19	500 R	89.8%	7.1%	92.7%	7.3%
6,429	BOTTINEAU	3,499	2,998	383	118	2,615 R	85.7%	10.9%	88.7%	11.3%
3,151	BOWMAN	1,794	1,605	136	53	1,469 R	89.5%	7.6%	92.2%	7.8%
1,968	BURKE	1,055	970	66	19	904 R	91.9%	6.3%	93.6%	6.4%
81,308	BURLEIGH	47,831	38,830	6,904	2,097	31,926 R	81.2%	14.4%	84.9%	15.1%
149,778	CASS	79,822	57,151	18,268	4,403	38,883 R	71.6%	22.9%	75.8%	24.2%
3,993	CAVALIER	2,048	1,707	290	51	1,417 R	83.3%	14.2%	85.5%	14.5%
5,289	DICKEY	2,431	2,022	335	74	1,687 R	83.2%	13.8%	85.8%	14.2%
2,071	DIVIDE	1,230	1,039	140	51	899 R	84.5%	11.4%	88.1%	11.9%
3,536	DUNN	2,233	1,909	251	73	1,658 R	85.5%	11.2%	88.4%	11.6%
2,385	EDDY	1,226	962	219	45	743 R	78.5%	17.9%	81.5%	18.5%
3,550	EMMONS	1,978	1,774	136	68	1,638 R	89.7%	6.9%	92.9%	7.1%
3,343	FOSTER	1,743	1,491	170	82	1,321 R	85.5%	9.8%	89.8%	10.2%
1,680	GOLDEN VALLEY	956	857	62	37	795 R	89.6%	6.5%	93.3%	6.7%
66,861	GRAND FORKS	29,840	20,860	7,714	1,266	13,146 R	69.9%	25.9%	73.0%	27.0%
2,394	GRANT	1,406	1,251	108	47	1,143 R	89.0%	7.7%	92.1%	7.9%
2,420	GRIGGS	1,281	1,046	194	41	852 R	81.7%	15.1%	84.4%	15.6%
2,477	HETTINGER	1,296	1,160	88	48	1,072 R	89.5%	6.8%	92.9%	7.1%
2,435	KIDDER	1,398	1,224	117	57	1,107 R	87.6%	8.4%	91.3%	8.7%
4,139	LA MOURE	2,182	1,818	292	72	1,526 R	83.3%	13.4%	86.2%	13.8%
1,990	LOGAN	1,092	989	72	31	917 R	90.6%	6.6%	93.2%	6.8%
5,395	MCHENRY	2,856	2,433	296	127	2,137 R	85.2%	10.4%	89.2%	10.8%
2,809	MCINTOSH	1,473	1,327	110	36	1,217 R	90.1%	7.5%	92.3%	7.7%
6,360	MCKENZIE	4,605	3,903	494	208	3,409 R	84.8%	10.7%	88.8%	11.2%
8,962	MCLEAN	5,336	4,391	732	213	3,659 R	82.3%	13.7%	85.7%	14.3%
8,424	MERCER	4,677	4,041	470	166	3,571 R	86.4%	10.0%	89.6%	10.4%
27,471	MORTON	15,756	12,963	2,104	689	10,859 R	82.3%	13.4%	86.0%	14.0%
7,673	MOUNTRAIL	4,083	2,980	892	211	2,088 R	73.0%	21.8%	77.0%	23.0%
3,126	NELSON	1,750	1,343	323	84	1,020 R	76.7%	18.5%	80.6%	19.4%
1,846	OLIVER	1,025	915	74	36	841 R	89.3%	7.2%	92.5%	7.5%
7,413	PEMBINA	3,184	2,644	453	87	2,191 R	83.0%	14.2%	85.4%	14.6%
4,357	PIERCE	2,094	1,816	225	53	1,591 R	86.7%	10.7%	89.0%	11.0%
11,451	RAMSEY	5,368	4,291	869	208	3,422 R	79.9%	16.2%	83.2%	16.8%
5,457	RANSOM	2,368	1,793	463	112	1,330 R	75.7%	19.6%	79.5%	20.5%
2,470	RENVILLE	1,293	1,140	104	49	1,036 R	88.2%	8.0%	91.6%	8.4%
16,321	RICHLAND	7,562	6,074	1,117	371	4,957 R	80.3%	14.8%	84.5%	15.5%
13,937	ROLETTE	3,726	1,801	1,701	224	100 R	48.3%	45.7%	51.4%	48.6%
3,829	SARGENT	2,024	1,513	423	88	1,090 R	74.8%	20.9%	78.2%	21.8%
1,321	SHERIDAN	792	703	60	29	643 R	88.8%	7.6%	92.1%	7.9%
4,153	SIOUX	1,192	426	633	133	207 D	35.7%	53.1%	40.2%	59.8%
727	SLOPE	428	388	25	15	363 R	90.7%	5.8%	93.9%	6.1%
24,199	STARK	12,200	10,635	1,101	464	9,534 R	87.2%	9.0%	90.6%	9.4%
1,975	STEELE	1,032	791	204	37	587 R	76.6%	19.8%	79.5%	20.5%
21,100	STUTSMAN	10,087	8,392	1,329	366	7,063 R	83.2%	13.2%	86.3%	13.7%
2,246	TOWNER	1,177	952	179	46	773 R	80.9%	15.2%	84.2%	15.8%
8,121	TRAILL	3,958	3,062	747	149	2,315 R	77.4%	18.9%	80.4%	19.6%
11,119	WALSH	4,708	3,788	749	171	3,039 R	80.5%	15.9%	83.5%	16.5%
61,675	WARD	27,225	22,538	3,309	1,378	19,229 R	82.8%	12.2%	87.2%	12.8%
4,207	WELLS	2,397	2,080	239	78	1,841 R	86.8%	10.0%	89.7%	10.3%
22,398	WILLIAMS	12,596	10,750	1,180	666	9,570 R	85.3%	9.4%	90.1%	9.9%
672,591	TOTAL	342,501	268,788	58,116	15,597	210,672 R	78.5%	17.0%	82.2%	17.8%

Note: Democratic candidates in North Dakota appear on the ballot for the Democratic-Nonpartisan League Party.

NORTH DAKOTA

HOUSE OF REPRESENTATIVES

| | | | Republican | | Democratic | | Other | Rep.-Dem. | Percentage | | | |
| | | | | | | | | | Total Vote | | Major Vote | |
CD	Year	Total Vote	Vote	Candidate	Vote	Candidate	Vote	Plurality	Rep.	Dem.	Rep.	Dem.
At Large	2016	338,459	233,980	CRAMER, KEVIN*	80,377	IRON EYES, CHASE	24,102	153,603 R	69.1%	23.7%	74.4%	25.6%
At Large	2014	248,670	138,100	CRAMER, KEVIN*	95,678	SINNER, GEORGE	14,892	42,422 R	55.5%	38.5%	59.1%	40.9%
At Large	2012	316,071	173,433	CRAMER, KEVIN	131,869	GULLESON, PAM	10,769	41,564 R	54.9%	41.7%	56.8%	43.2%
At Large	2010	237,137	129,802	BERG, RICK	106,542	POMEROY, EARL*	793	23,260 R	54.7%	44.9%	54.9%	45.1%
At Large	2008	313,965	119,388	SAND, DUANE	194,577	POMEROY, EARL*		75,189 D	38.0%	62.0%	38.0%	62.0%
At Large	2006	217,621	74,687	MECHTEL, MATT	142,934	POMEROY, EARL*		68,247 D	34.3%	65.7%	34.3%	65.7%
At Large	2004	310,814	125,684	SAND, DUANE	185,130	POMEROY, EARL*		59,446 D	40.4%	59.6%	40.4%	59.6%
At Large	2002	231,030	109,957	CLAYBURGH, RICK	121,073	POMEROY, EARL*		11,116 D	47.6%	52.4%	47.6%	52.4%
At Large	2000	285,658	127,251	DORSO, JOHN	151,173	POMEROY, EARL*	7,234	23,922 D	44.5%	52.9%	45.7%	54.3%
At Large	1998	212,888	87,511	CRAMER, KEVIN	119,668	POMEROY, EARL*	5,709	32,157 D	41.1%	56.2%	42.2%	57.8%
At Large	1996	263,010	113,684	CRAMER, KEVIN	144,833	POMEROY, EARL*	4,493	31,149 D	43.2%	55.1%	44.0%	56.0%
At Large	1994	235,389	105,988	PORTER, GARY	123,134	POMEROY, EARL*	6,267	17,146 D	45.0%	52.3%	46.3%	53.7%
At Large	1992	297,898	117,442	KORSMO, JOHN T.	169,273	POMEROY, EARL	11,183	51,831 D	39.4%	56.8%	41.0%	59.0%
At Large	1990	233,979	81,443	SCHAFER, EDWARD T.	152,530	DORGAN, BYRON L.*	6	71,087 D	34.8%	65.2%	34.8%	65.2%
At Large	1988	299,982	84,475	SYDNESS, STEVE	212,583	DORGAN, BYRON L.*	2,924	128,108 D	28.2%	70.9%	28.4%	71.6%
At Large	1986	286,361	66,989	VINJE, SYVER	216,258	DORGAN, BYRON L.*	3,114	149,269 D	23.4%	75.5%	23.7%	76.3%
At Large	1984	308,729	65,761	ALTENBURG, LOIS I.	242,968	DORGAN, BYRON L.*		177,207 D	21.3%	78.7%	21.3%	78.7%
At Large	1982	260,499	72,241	JONES, KENT	186,534	DORGAN, BYRON L.*	1,724	114,293 D	27.7%	71.6%	27.9%	72.1%
At Large	1980	293,076	124,707	SMYKOWSKI, JIM	166,437	DORGAN, BYRON L.	1,932	41,730 D	42.6%	56.8%	42.8%	57.2%
At Large	1978	220,348	147,746	ANDREWS, MARK*	68,016	HAGEN, BRUCE	4,586	79,730 R	67.1%	30.9%	68.5%	31.5%
At Large	1976	289,881	181,018	ANDREWS, MARK*	104,263	OMDAHL, LLOYD B.	4,600	76,755 R	62.4%	36.0%	63.5%	36.5%
At Large	1974	233,688	130,184	ANDREWS, MARK*	103,504	DORGAN, BYRON L.		26,680 R	55.7%	44.3%	55.7%	44.3%
At Large	1972	268,721	195,360	ANDREWS, MARK*	72,850	ISTA, RICHARD	511	122,510 R	72.7%	27.1%	72.8%	27.2%

Note: An asterisk (*) denotes incumbent. Democratic candidates in North Dakota appear on the ballot for the Democratic-Nonpartisan League Party. North Dakota had two House seats prior to 1972.

NORTH DAKOTA

GENERAL AND PRIMARY ELECTIONS

2016 GENERAL ELECTIONS: OTHER VOTES

President   Other vote was 21,434 Libertarian (Gary Johnson), 6,397 Write-in (Scattered Write-In), 3,780 Green (Jill Stein), 1,833 Constitution (Darrell Castle), 364 Independent (Roque De La Fuente)

Governor   Other vote was 13,230 Libertarian (Marty Riske), 653 Write-in (Scattered Write-in)

Senate   Other vote was 10,556 Libertarian (Robert Marquette), 4,675 Independent (James Germalic), 366 Write-in (Scattered Write-in)

House   Other vote was:

At Large   23,528 Libertarian (Robert Seaman), 574 Write-in (Scattered Write-in)

2016 PRIMARY ELECTIONS: SUPPLEMENTARY INFORMATION

Presidential Caucus*   June 7, 2016 (Democratic)   **Registration**   No Party Registration
                                                            (No Formal Registration)

Primary   June 14, 2016 (Congress)

Primary Type   Open—Any person of voting age (18 years old at the time of the primary election) could participate in the primary of either party.

*Note: The Republican Party did not select a presidential candidate at their caucus held April 1–3, 2016, but instead selected unpledged delegates.

NORTH DAKOTA

GENERAL AND PRIMARY ELECTIONS

	REPUBLICAN PRIMARIES			DEMOCRATIC PRIMARIES		
Senator	Hoeven, John*	103,677	99.6%	Glassheim, Eliot	17,243	99.7%
	Write-In	445	0.4%	Write-In	48	0.3%
	TOTAL	104,122		TOTAL	17,291	
Governor	Burgum, Doug	68,042	59.5%	Nelson, Marvin E.	17,278	99.7%
	Stenehjem, Wayne	44,158	38.6%	Write-In	59	0.3%
	Sorum, Paul	2,164	1.9%			
	Write-In	51				
	TOTAL	114,415		TOTAL	17,337	
Congressional At Large	Cramer, Kevin*	96,357	99.1%	Iron Eyes, Chase	17,063	99.7%
	Write-In	919	0.9%	Write-In	59	0.3%
	TOTAL	97,276		TOTAL	17,122	

Note: An asterisk (*) denotes incumbent.

OHIO

Congressional districts first established for elections held in 2012

16 members

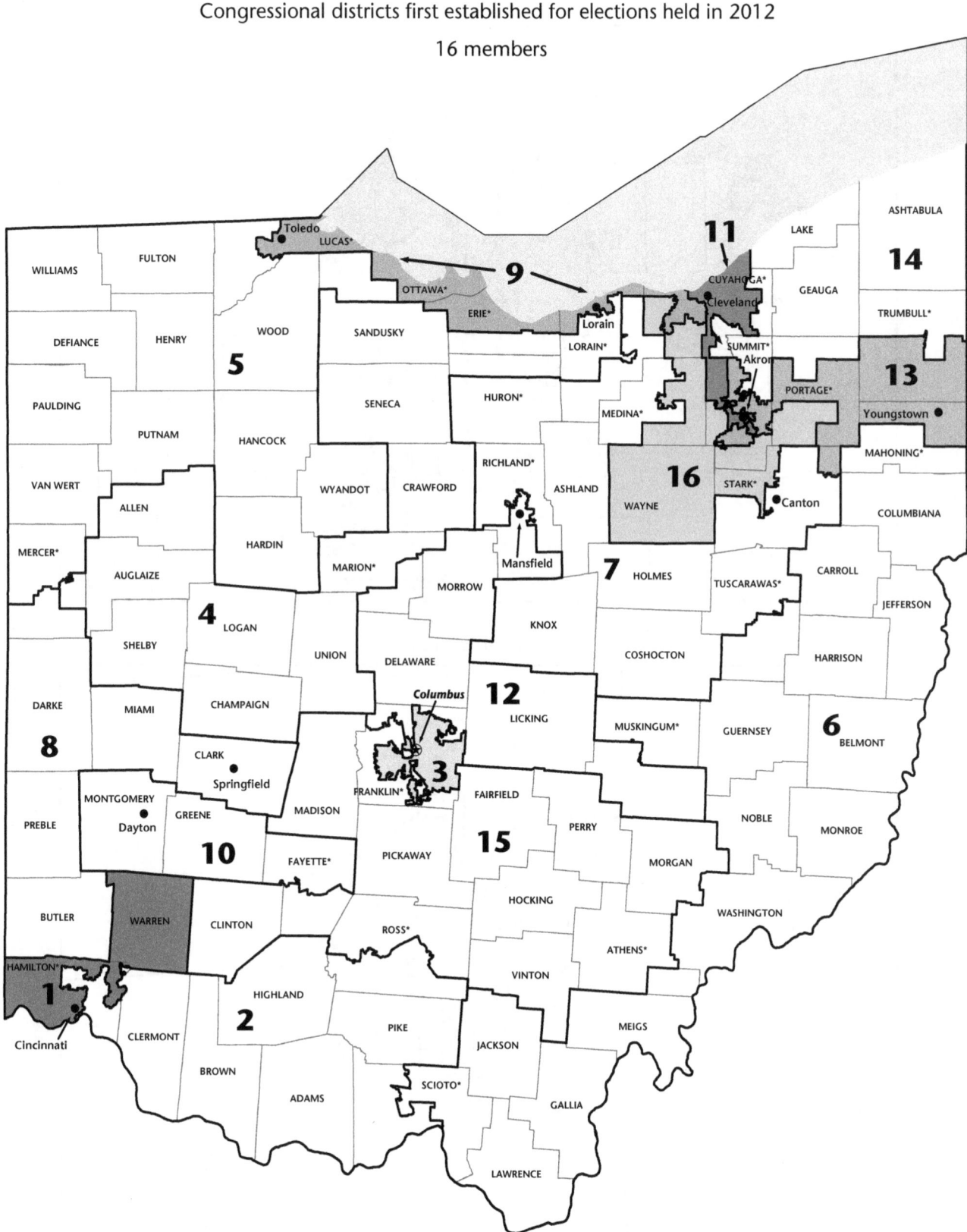

* Asterisk indicates a county whose boundaries include parts of two or more congressional districts.

364

OHIO
Cleveland Area

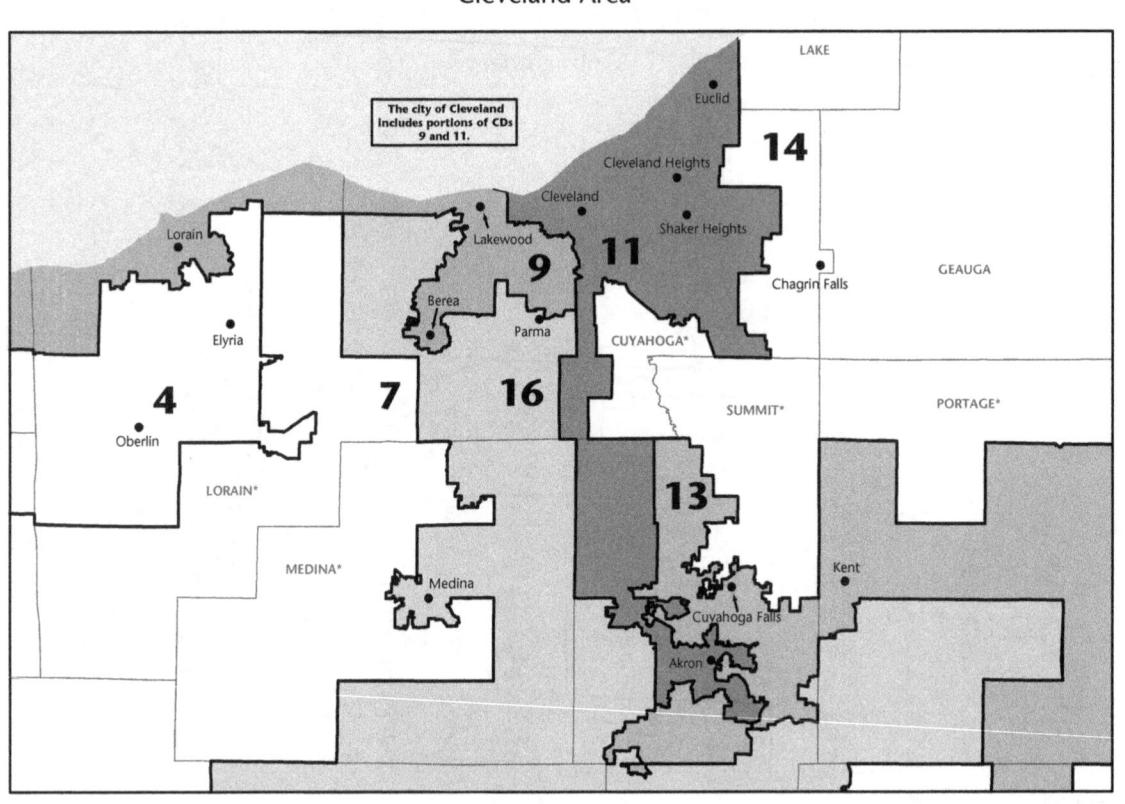

Columbus Area

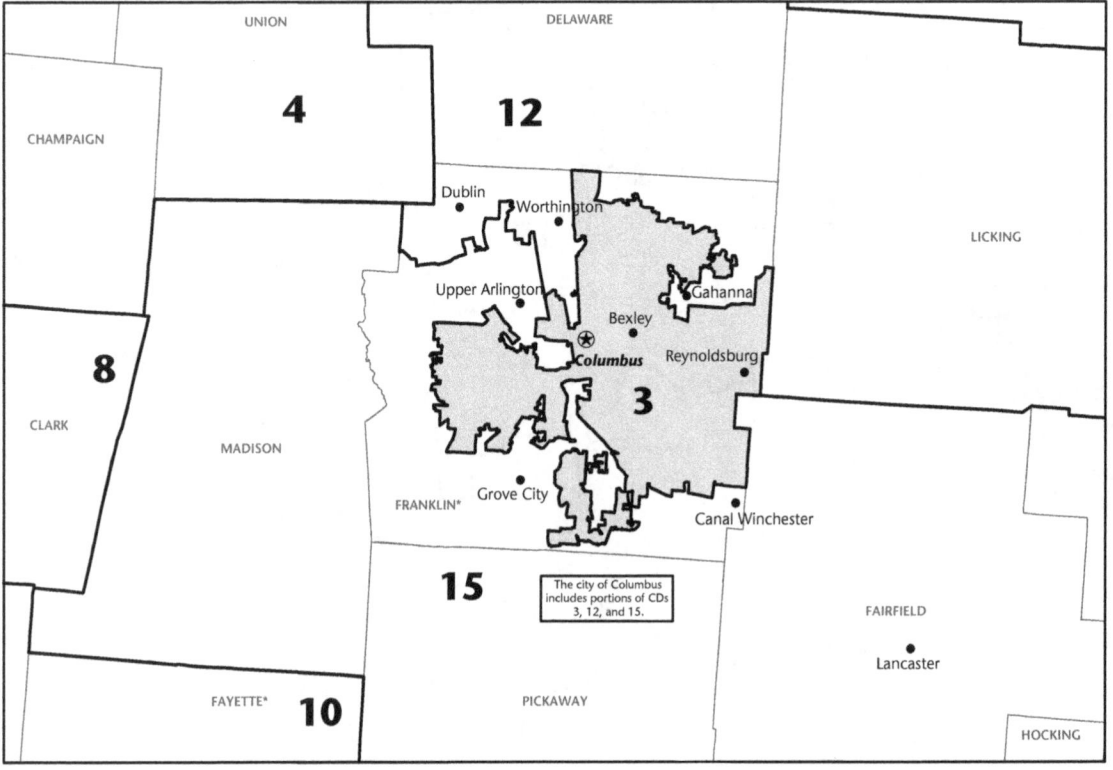

* Asterisk indicates a county whose boundaries include parts of two or more congressional districts.

OHIO

GOVERNOR

John Kasich (R). Re-elected 2014 to a four-year term. Previously elected 2010.

SENATORS (1 Republican, 1 Democrat)

Sherrod Brown (D). Re-elected 2012 to a six-year term. Previously elected 2006.

Rob Portman (R). Re-elected 2016 to a six-year term. Previously elected 2010.

REPRESENTATIVES (12 Republicans, 4 Democrats)

1. Steve Chabot (R)
2. Brad Wenstrup (R)
3. Joyce Beatty (D)
4. Jim Jordan (R)
5. Bob Latta (R)
6. Bill Johnson (R)
7. Bob Gibbs (R)
8. Warren Davidson (R)
9. Marcy Kaptur (D)
10. Michael R. Turner (R)
11. Marcia L. Fudge (D)
12. Pat Tiberi (R)
13. Tim Ryan (D)
14. David Joyce (R)
15. Steve Stivers (R)
16. Jim Renacci (R)

POSTWAR VOTE FOR PRESIDENT

| | | Republican | | Democratic | | Other | Rep.-Dem. | Percentage | | | |
| | | | | | | | | Total Vote | | Major Vote | |
Year	Total Vote	Vote	Candidate	Vote	Candidate	Vote	Plurality	Rep.	Dem.	Rep.	Dem.
2016**	5,496,487	2,841,005	Trump, Donald J.	2,394,164	Clinton, Hillary Rodham	261,318	446,841 R	51.7%	43.6%	54.3%	45.7%
2012	5,580,840	2,661,433	Romney, W. Mitt	2,827,710	Obama, Barack H.*	91,697	166,277 D	47.7%	50.7%	48.5%	51.5%
2008	5,708,350	2,677,820	McCain, John S. III	2,940,044	Obama, Barack H.	90,486	262,224 D	46.9%	51.5%	47.7%	52.3%
2004	5,627,908	2,859,768	Bush, George W.*	2,741,167	Kerry, John F.	26,973	118,601 R	50.8%	48.7%	51.1%	48.9%
2000**	4,701,998	2,350,363	Bush, George W.	2,183,628	Gore, Albert Jr.	168,007	166,735 R	50.0%	46.4%	51.8%	48.2%
1996**	4,534,434	1,859,883	Dole, Robert "Bob"	2,148,222	Clinton, Bill*	526,329	288,339 D	41.0%	47.4%	46.4%	53.6%
1992**	4,939,967	1,894,310	Bush, George H.*	1,984,942	Clinton, Bill	1,060,715	90,632 D	38.3%	40.2%	48.8%	51.2%
1988	4,393,699	2,416,549	Bush, George H.	1,939,629	Dukakis, Michael S.	37,521	476,920 R	55.0%	44.1%	55.5%	44.5%
1984	4,547,619	2,678,560	Reagan, Ronald*	1,825,440	Mondale, Walter F.	43,619	853,120 R	58.9%	40.1%	59.5%	40.5%
1980**	4,283,603	2,206,545	Reagan, Ronald	1,752,414	Carter, Jimmy*	324,644	454,131 R	51.5%	40.9%	55.7%	44.3%
1976	4,111,873	2,000,505	Ford, Gerald R.*	2,011,621	Carter, Jimmy	99,747	11,116 D	48.7%	48.9%	49.9%	50.1%
1972	4,094,787	2,441,827	Nixon, Richard M.*	1,558,889	McGovern, George S.	94,071	882,938 R	59.6%	38.1%	61.0%	39.0%
1968**	3,959,698	1,791,014	Nixon, Richard M.	1,700,586	Humphrey, Hubert Horatio Jr.	468,098	90,428 R	45.2%	42.9%	51.3%	48.7%
1964	3,969,196	1,470,865	Goldwater, Barry M. Sr.	2,498,331	Johnson, Lyndon B.*		1,027,466 D	37.1%	62.9%	37.1%	62.9%
1960	4,161,859	2,217,611	Nixon, Richard M.	1,944,248	Kennedy, John F.		273,363 R	53.3%	46.7%	53.3%	46.7%
1956	3,702,265	2,262,610	Eisenhower, Dwight D.*	1,439,655	Stevenson, Adlai E. II		822,955 R	61.1%	38.9%	61.1%	38.9%
1952	3,700,758	2,100,391	Eisenhower, Dwight D.	1,600,367	Stevenson, Adlai E. II		500,024 R	56.8%	43.2%	56.8%	43.2%
1948	2,936,071	1,445,684	Dewey, Thomas E.	1,452,791	Truman, Harry S.*	37,596	7,107 D	49.2%	49.5%	49.9%	50.1%

Note: An asterisk (*) denotes incumbent. **In past elections, the other vote included: 2016 - 174,498 Libertarian (Gary Johnson); 2000 - 117,799 Green (Ralph Nader); 1996 - 483,207 Reform (Ross Perot); 1992 - 1,036,426 Independent (Perot); 1980 - 254,472 Independent (John Anderson); 1968 - 467,495 American Independent (George Wallace).

OHIO

POSTWAR VOTE FOR GOVERNOR

Year	Total Vote	Republican		Democratic		Other Vote	Rep.-Dem. Plurality	Percentage			
								Total Vote		Major Vote	
		Vote	Candidate	Vote	Candidate			Rep.	Dem.	Rep.	Dem.
2014	3,055,913	1,944,848	Kasich, John R.*	1,009,359	FitzGerald, Ed	101,706	935,489 R	63.6%	33.0%	65.8%	34.2%
2010	3,852,469	1,889,186	Kasich, John R.	1,812,059	Strickland, Ted*	151,224	77,127 R	49.0%	47.0%	51.0%	49.0%
2006	4,022,754	1,474,285	Blackwell, J. Kenneth	2,435,384	Strickland, Ted	113,085	961,099 D	36.6%	60.5%	37.7%	62.3%
2002	3,228,992	1,865,007	Taft, Robert Alphonso*	1,236,924	Hagan, Timothy	127,061	628,083 R	57.8%	38.3%	60.1%	39.9%
1998	3,354,213	1,678,721	Taft, Robert Alphonso	1,498,956	Fisher, Lee	176,536	179,765 R	50.0%	44.7%	52.8%	47.2%
1994	3,346,238	2,401,572	Voinovich, George*	835,849	Burch, Robert L.	108,817	1,565,723 R	71.8%	25.0%	74.2%	25.8%
1990	3,482,650	1,938,103	Voinovich, George	1,544,416	Celebrezze, Anthony J.	131	393,687 R	55.7%	44.3%	55.7%	44.3%
1986	3,066,611	1,207,264	Rhodes, James A.	1,858,372	Celeste, Richard F.*	975	651,108 D	39.4%	60.6%	39.4%	60.6%
1982	3,356,791	1,303,962	Brown, Clarence J. Jr.	1,981,952	Celeste, Richard F.	70,877	677,990 D	38.8%	59.0%	39.7%	60.3%
1978	2,843,351	1,402,167	Rhodes, James A.*	1,354,631	Celeste, Richard F.	86,553	47,536 R	49.3%	47.6%	50.9%	49.1%
1974	3,072,010	1,493,679	Rhodes, James A.	1,482,191	Gilligan, John J.*	96,140	11,488 R	48.6%	48.2%	50.2%	49.8%
1970	3,184,131	1,382,657	Cloud, Roger	1,725,560	Gilligan, John J.	75,914	342,903 D	43.4%	54.2%	44.5%	55.5%
1966	2,887,331	1,795,277	Rhodes, James A.*	1,092,054	Reams, Henry Frazier "Frazier" Jr.		703,223 R	62.2%	37.8%	62.2%	37.8%
1962	3,116,953	1,836,432	Rhodes, James A.	1,280,521	Disalle, Michael V.*		555,911 R	58.9%	41.1%	58.9%	41.1%
1958**	3,284,134	1,414,874	O'Neill, C. William*	1,869,260	Disalle, Michael V.		454,386 D	43.1%	56.9%	43.1%	56.9%
1956	3,542,091	1,984,988	O'Neill, C. William	1,557,103	Disalle, Michael V.		427,885 R	56.0%	44.0%	56.0%	44.0%
1954	2,597,790	1,192,528	Rhodes, James A.	1,405,262	Lausche, Frank J.*		212,734 D	45.9%	54.1%	45.9%	54.1%
1952	3,605,168	1,590,058	Taft, Charles P.	2,015,110	Lausche, Frank J.*		425,052 D	44.1%	55.9%	44.1%	55.9%
1950	2,892,819	1,370,570	Ebright, Don H.	1,522,249	Lausche, Frank J.*		151,679 D	47.4%	52.6%	47.4%	52.6%
1948	3,018,289	1,398,514	Herbert, Thomas J.*	1,619,775	Lausche, Frank J.		221,261 D	46.3%	53.7%	46.3%	53.7%
1946	2,303,750	1,166,550	Herbert, Thomas J.	1,125,997	Lausche, Frank J.*	11,203	40,553 R	50.6%	48.9%	50.9%	49.1%

Note: An asterisk (*) denotes incumbent. **The term of office of Ohio's governor was increased from two to four years effective with the 1958 election.

POSTWAR VOTE FOR SENATOR

Year	Total Vote	Republican		Democratic		Other Vote	Rep.-Dem. Plurality	Percentage			
								Total Vote		Major Vote	
		Vote	Candidate	Vote	Candidate			Rep.	Dem.	Rep.	Dem.
2016	5,374,164	3,118,567	Portman, Rob*	1,996,908	Strickland, Ted	258,689	1,121,659 R	58.0%	37.2%	61.0%	39.0%
2012	5,449,114	2,435,740	Mandel, Josh	2,762,757	Brown, Sherrod*	250,617	327,017 D	44.7%	50.7%	46.9%	53.1%
2010	3,815,098	2,168,742	Portman, Rob	1,503,297	Fisher, Lee	143,059	665,445 R	56.8%	39.4%	59.1%	40.9%
2006	4,019,236	1,761,037	DeWine, Michael "Mike"*	2,257,369	Brown, Sherrod	830	496,332 D	43.8%	56.2%	43.8%	56.2%
2004	5,426,196	3,464,651	Voinovich, George*	1,961,249	Fingerhut, Eric D.	296	1,503,402 R	63.9%	36.1%	63.9%	36.1%
2000	4,448,801	2,665,512	DeWine, Michael "Mike"*	1,595,066	Celeste, Theodore S.	188,223	1,070,446 R	59.9%	35.9%	62.6%	37.4%
1998	3,404,351	1,922,087	Voinovich, George	1,482,054	Boyle, Mary O.	210	440,033 R	56.5%	43.5%	56.5%	43.5%
1994	3,436,884	1,836,556	DeWine, Michael "Mike"	1,348,213	Hyatt, Joel	252,115	488,343 R	53.4%	39.2%	57.7%	42.3%
1992	4,793,953	2,028,300	DeWine, Michael "Mike"	2,444,419	Glenn, John H.*	321,234	416,119 D	42.3%	51.0%	45.3%	54.7%
1988	4,352,905	1,872,716	Voinovich, George	2,480,038	Metzenbaum, Howard M.*	151	607,322 D	43.0%	57.0%	43.0%	57.0%
1986	3,121,188	1,171,893	Kindness, Thomas N.	1,949,208	Glenn, John H.*	87	777,315 D	37.5%	62.5%	37.5%	62.5%
1982	3,395,463	1,396,790	Pfeifer, Paul E.	1,923,767	Metzenbaum, Howard M.*	74,906	526,977 D	41.1%	56.7%	42.1%	57.9%
1980	4,027,303	1,137,695	Betts, James E.	2,770,786	Glenn, John H.*	118,822	1,633,091 D	28.2%	68.8%	29.1%	70.9%
1976	3,920,613	1,823,774	Taft, Robert Alphonso*	1,941,113	Metzenbaum, Howard M.	155,726	117,339 D	46.5%	49.5%	48.4%	51.6%
1974	2,987,951	918,133	Perk, Ralph J.	1,930,670	Glenn, John H.	139,148	1,012,537 D	30.7%	64.6%	32.2%	67.8%
1970	3,151,274	1,565,682	Taft, Robert Alphonso	1,495,262	Metzenbaum, Howard M.	90,330	70,420 R	49.7%	47.4%	51.2%	48.8%
1968	3,743,121	1,928,964	Saxbe, William B.	1,814,152	Gilligan, John J.	5	114,812 R	51.5%	48.5%	51.5%	48.5%
1964	3,830,389	1,906,781	Taft, Robert Alphonso	1,923,608	Young, Stephen M.*		16,827 D	49.8%	50.2%	49.8%	50.2%
1962	2,995,105	1,151,292	Briley, John Marshall	1,843,813	Lausche, Frank J.*		692,521 D	38.4%	61.6%	38.4%	61.6%
1958	3,149,410	1,497,199	Bricker, John W.*	1,652,211	Young, Stephen M.		155,012 D	47.5%	52.5%	47.5%	52.5%
1956	3,525,499	1,660,910	Bender, George H.*	1,864,589	Lausche, Frank J.		203,679 D	47.1%	52.9%	47.1%	52.9%
1954S**	2,512,773	1,257,874	Bender, George H.	1,254,899	Burke, Thomas A.		2,975 R	50.1%	49.9%	50.1%	49.9%
1952	3,442,291	1,878,961	Bricker, John W.*	1,563,330	Disalle, Michael V.		315,631 R	54.6%	45.4%	54.6%	45.4%
1950	2,860,102	1,645,643	Taft, Robert Alphonso*	1,214,459	Ferguson, Joseph T.		431,184 R	57.5%	42.5%	57.5%	42.5%
1946	2,237,269	1,275,774	Bricker, John W.	947,610	Huffman, James W.	13,885	328,164 R	57.0%	42.4%	57.4%	42.6%
1946S**	2,123,526	1,193,942	Taft, Kingsley A.	929,584	Webber, Henry P.		264,358 R	56.2%	43.8%	56.2%	43.8%

Note: An asterisk (*) denotes incumbent. **One of the 1946 elections and the 1954 election were for short terms to fill a vacancy.

OHIO

PRESIDENT 2016

2010 Census Population	County	Total Vote	Republican (Trump)	Democratic (Clinton)	Other	Rep.-Dem. Plurality	Percentage Total Vote Rep.	Dem.	Major Vote Rep.	Dem.
28,550	ADAMS	11,359	8,659	2,326	374	6,333 R	76.2%	20.5%	78.8%	21.2%
106,331	ALLEN	45,894	30,487	13,294	2,113	17,193 R	66.4%	29.0%	69.6%	30.4%
53,139	ASHLAND	24,590	17,493	5,740	1,357	11,753 R	71.1%	23.3%	75.3%	24.7%
101,497	ASHTABULA	40,867	23,318	15,577	1,972	7,741 R	57.1%	38.1%	60.0%	40.0%
64,757	ATHENS	29,443	11,354	16,370	1,719	5,016 D	38.6%	55.6%	41.0%	59.0%
45,949	AUGLAIZE	23,627	18,658	3,980	989	14,678 R	79.0%	16.8%	82.4%	17.6%
70,400	BELMONT	31,122	21,108	8,785	1,229	12,323 R	67.8%	28.2%	70.6%	29.4%
44,846	BROWN	19,607	14,573	4,353	681	10,220 R	74.3%	22.2%	77.0%	23.0%
368,130	BUTLER	173,839	106,976	58,642	8,221	48,334 R	61.5%	33.7%	64.6%	35.4%
28,836	CARROLL	13,074	9,254	3,154	666	6,100 R	70.8%	24.1%	74.6%	25.4%
40,097	CHAMPAIGN	18,104	12,631	4,594	879	8,037 R	69.8%	25.4%	73.3%	26.7%
138,333	CLARK	61,429	35,205	23,328	2,896	11,877 R	57.3%	38.0%	60.1%	39.9%
197,363	CLERMONT	99,121	67,518	26,715	4,888	40,803 R	68.1%	27.0%	71.7%	28.3%
42,040	CLINTON	18,675	13,838	4,066	771	9,772 R	74.1%	21.8%	77.3%	22.7%
107,841	COLUMBIANA	46,201	31,676	12,432	2,093	19,244 R	68.6%	26.9%	71.8%	28.2%
36,901	COSHOCTON	15,552	10,785	4,013	754	6,772 R	69.3%	25.8%	72.9%	27.1%
43,784	CRAWFORD	19,236	13,611	4,625	1,000	8,986 R	70.8%	24.0%	74.6%	25.4%
1,280,122	CUYAHOGA	603,815	184,211	398,271	21,333	214,060 D	30.5%	66.0%	31.6%	68.4%
52,959	DARKE	25,491	20,012	4,470	1,009	15,542 R	78.5%	17.5%	81.7%	18.3%
39,037	DEFIANCE	18,193	11,688	5,368	1,137	6,320 R	64.2%	29.5%	68.5%	31.5%
174,214	DELAWARE	103,860	57,568	40,872	5,420	16,696 R	55.4%	39.4%	58.5%	41.5%
77,079	ERIE	37,578	19,648	16,057	1,873	3,591 R	52.3%	42.7%	55.0%	45.0%
146,156	FAIRFIELD	72,912	44,314	24,881	3,717	19,433 R	60.8%	34.1%	64.0%	36.0%
29,030	FAYETTE	11,163	7,995	2,739	429	5,256 R	71.6%	24.5%	74.5%	25.5%
1,163,414	FRANKLIN	581,129	199,331	351,198	30,600	151,867 D	34.3%	60.4%	36.2%	63.8%
42,698	FULTON	21,229	13,709	6,069	1,451	7,640 R	64.6%	28.6%	69.3%	30.7%
30,934	GALLIA	12,938	9,822	2,628	488	7,194 R	75.9%	20.3%	78.9%	21.1%
93,389	GEAUGA	49,941	30,227	17,569	2,145	12,658 R	60.5%	35.2%	63.2%	36.8%
161,573	GREENE	81,858	48,540	28,943	4,375	19,597 R	59.3%	35.4%	62.6%	37.4%
40,087	GUERNSEY	16,557	11,445	4,359	753	7,086 R	69.1%	26.3%	72.4%	27.6%
802,374	HAMILTON	409,107	173,665	215,719	19,723	42,054 D	42.4%	52.7%	44.6%	55.4%
74,782	HANCOCK	36,021	24,183	9,609	2,229	14,574 R	67.1%	26.7%	71.6%	28.4%
32,058	HARDIN	12,298	8,717	2,920	661	5,797 R	70.9%	23.7%	74.9%	25.1%
15,864	HARRISON	7,079	5,098	1,688	293	3,410 R	72.0%	23.8%	75.1%	24.9%
28,215	HENRY	13,932	9,301	3,756	875	5,545 R	66.8%	27.0%	71.2%	28.8%
43,589	HIGHLAND	18,501	14,020	3,773	708	10,247 R	75.8%	20.4%	78.8%	21.2%
29,380	HOCKING	12,838	8,497	3,775	566	4,722 R	66.2%	29.4%	69.2%	30.8%
42,366	HOLMES	11,054	8,720	1,788	546	6,932 R	78.9%	16.2%	83.0%	17.0%
59,626	HURON	24,834	16,226	7,192	1,416	9,034 R	65.3%	29.0%	69.3%	30.7%
33,225	JACKSON	13,693	9,949	3,226	518	6,723 R	72.7%	23.6%	75.5%	24.5%
69,709	JEFFERSON	32,201	21,117	9,675	1,409	11,442 R	65.6%	30.0%	68.6%	31.4%
60,921	KNOX	28,687	19,131	8,171	1,385	10,960 R	66.7%	28.5%	70.1%	29.9%
230,041	LAKE	116,246	64,255	46,397	5,594	17,858 R	55.3%	39.9%	58.1%	41.9%
62,450	LAWRENCE	26,607	18,689	6,974	944	11,715 R	70.2%	26.2%	72.8%	27.2%
166,492	LICKING	82,761	51,241	27,376	4,144	23,865 R	61.9%	33.1%	65.2%	34.8%
45,858	LOGAN	21,571	15,957	4,647	967	11,310 R	74.0%	21.5%	77.4%	22.6%
301,356	LORAIN	140,562	66,818	66,949	6,795	131 D	47.5%	47.6%	50.0%	50.0%
441,815	LUCAS	197,556	75,698	110,833	11,025	35,135 D	38.3%	56.1%	40.6%	59.4%
43,435	MADISON	17,290	11,631	4,779	880	6,852 R	67.3%	27.6%	70.9%	29.1%
238,823	MAHONING	115,072	53,616	57,381	4,075	3,765 D	46.6%	49.9%	48.3%	51.7%
66,501	MARION	26,322	16,961	7,928	1,433	9,033 R	64.4%	30.1%	68.1%	31.9%
172,332	MEDINA	91,373	54,810	32,182	4,381	22,628 R	60.0%	35.2%	63.0%	37.0%
23,770	MEIGS	9,985	7,309	2,260	416	5,049 R	73.2%	22.6%	76.4%	23.6%
40,814	MERCER	21,726	17,506	3,384	836	14,122 R	80.6%	15.6%	83.8%	16.2%
102,506	MIAMI	52,734	37,079	13,120	2,535	23,959 R	70.3%	24.9%	73.9%	26.1%
14,642	MONROE	6,795	4,868	1,662	265	3,206 R	71.6%	24.5%	74.5%	25.5%
535,153	MONTGOMERY	258,301	123,909	122,016	12,376	1,893 R	48.0%	47.2%	50.4%	49.6%
15,054	MORGAN	6,443	4,431	1,736	276	2,695 R	68.8%	26.9%	71.9%	28.1%
34,827	MORROW	16,548	11,948	3,761	839	8,187 R	72.2%	22.7%	76.1%	23.9%
86,074	MUSKINGUM	36,991	24,056	11,123	1,812	12,933 R	65.0%	30.1%	68.4%	31.6%

OHIO

PRESIDENT 2016

2010 Census Population	County	Total Vote	Republican (Trump)	Democratic (Clinton)	Other	Rep.-Dem. Plurality		Percentage			
								Total Vote		Major Vote	
								Rep.	Dem.	Rep.	Dem.
14,645	NOBLE	6,013	4,549	1,221	243	3,328	R	75.7%	20.3%	78.8%	21.2%
41,428	OTTAWA	22,218	12,653	8,285	1,280	4,368	R	56.9%	37.3%	60.4%	39.6%
19,614	PAULDING	9,047	6,500	2,093	454	4,407	R	71.8%	23.1%	75.6%	24.4%
36,058	PERRY	14,995	10,228	4,138	629	6,090	R	68.2%	27.6%	71.2%	28.8%
55,698	PICKAWAY	24,745	17,076	6,529	1,140	10,547	R	69.0%	26.4%	72.3%	27.7%
28,709	PIKE	11,879	7,902	3,539	438	4,363	R	66.5%	29.8%	69.1%	30.9%
161,419	PORTAGE	76,139	39,971	32,397	3,771	7,574	R	52.5%	42.5%	55.2%	44.8%
42,270	PREBLE	20,565	15,446	4,325	794	11,121	R	75.1%	21.0%	78.1%	21.9%
34,499	PUTNAM	18,767	14,961	2,922	884	12,039	R	79.7%	15.6%	83.7%	16.3%
124,475	RICHLAND	55,214	36,590	16,085	2,539	20,505	R	66.3%	29.1%	69.5%	30.5%
78,064	ROSS	30,380	18,652	10,356	1,372	8,296	R	61.4%	34.1%	64.3%	35.7%
60,944	SANDUSKY	28,044	16,316	9,929	1,799	6,387	R	58.2%	35.4%	62.2%	37.8%
79,499	SCIOTO	30,784	20,550	9,132	1,102	11,418	R	66.8%	29.7%	69.2%	30.8%
56,745	SENECA	23,987	14,825	7,404	1,758	7,421	R	61.8%	30.9%	66.7%	33.3%
49,423	SHELBY	23,740	18,590	4,243	907	14,347	R	78.3%	17.9%	81.4%	18.6%
375,586	STARK	175,239	98,388	68,146	8,705	30,242	R	56.1%	38.9%	59.1%	40.9%
541,781	SUMMIT	257,979	112,026	134,256	11,697	22,230	D	43.4%	52.0%	45.5%	54.5%
210,312	TRUMBULL	96,029	49,024	43,014	3,991	6,010	R	51.1%	44.8%	53.3%	46.7%
92,582	TUSCARAWAS	41,289	26,918	12,188	2,183	14,730	R	65.2%	29.5%	68.8%	31.2%
52,300	UNION	27,429	18,096	7,718	1,615	10,378	R	66.0%	28.1%	70.1%	29.9%
28,744	VAN WERT	13,770	10,469	2,697	604	7,772	R	76.0%	19.6%	79.5%	20.5%
13,435	VINTON	5,502	3,883	1,351	268	2,532	R	70.6%	24.6%	74.2%	25.8%
212,693	WARREN	117,267	77,643	33,730	5,894	43,913	R	66.2%	28.8%	69.7%	30.3%
61,778	WASHINGTON	29,840	20,514	8,026	1,300	12,488	R	68.7%	26.9%	71.9%	28.1%
114,520	WAYNE	49,853	32,270	15,031	2,552	17,239	R	64.7%	30.2%	68.2%	31.8%
37,642	WILLIAMS	17,308	11,939	4,358	1,011	7,581	R	69.0%	25.2%	73.3%	26.7%
125,488	WOOD	64,341	32,498	27,318	4,525	5,180	R	50.5%	42.5%	54.3%	45.7%
22,615	WYANDOT	10,592	7,468	2,515	609	4,953	R	70.5%	23.7%	74.8%	25.2%
11,536,504	TOTAL	5,496,487	2,841,005	2,394,164	261,318	446,841	R	51.7%	43.6%	54.3%	45.7%

OHIO

SENATOR 2016

2010 Census Population	County	Total Vote	Republican (Portman)	Democratic (Strickland)	Other	Rep.-Dem. Plurality		Percentage			
								Total Vote		Major Vote	
								Rep.	Dem.	Rep.	Dem.
28,550	ADAMS	11,125	8,489	2,181	455	6,308	R	76.3%	19.6%	79.6%	20.4%
106,331	ALLEN	45,047	32,085	10,900	2,062	21,185	R	71.2%	24.2%	74.6%	25.4%
53,139	ASHLAND	23,944	17,410	5,083	1,451	12,327	R	72.7%	21.2%	77.4%	22.6%
101,497	ASHTABULA	40,393	23,443	14,097	2,853	9,346	R	58.0%	34.9%	62.4%	37.6%
64,757	ATHENS	27,943	11,247	15,077	1,619	3,830	D	40.2%	54.0%	42.7%	57.3%
45,949	AUGLAIZE	23,374	19,414	3,044	916	16,370	R	83.1%	13.0%	86.4%	13.6%
70,400	BELMONT	30,625	19,712	9,305	1,608	10,407	R	64.4%	30.4%	67.9%	32.1%
44,846	BROWN	19,174	14,824	3,490	860	11,334	R	77.3%	18.2%	80.9%	19.1%
368,130	BUTLER	169,772	117,597	45,307	6,868	72,290	R	69.3%	26.7%	72.2%	27.8%
28,836	CARROLL	12,752	9,011	2,851	890	6,160	R	70.7%	22.4%	76.0%	24.0%
40,097	CHAMPAIGN	17,955	13,100	3,796	1,059	9,304	R	73.0%	21.1%	77.5%	22.5%
138,333	CLARK	60,967	39,651	18,384	2,932	21,267	R	65.0%	30.2%	68.3%	31.7%
197,363	CLERMONT	98,091	74,623	19,062	4,406	55,561	R	76.1%	19.4%	79.7%	20.3%
42,040	CLINTON	18,389	14,311	3,342	736	10,969	R	77.8%	18.2%	81.1%	18.9%
107,841	COLUMBIANA	44,798	30,416	11,609	2,773	18,807	R	67.9%	25.9%	72.4%	27.6%

OHIO

SENATOR 2016

2010 Census Population	County	Total Vote	Republican (Portman)	Democratic (Strickland)	Other	Rep.-Dem. Plurality	Percentage			
							Total Vote		Major Vote	
							Rep.	Dem.	Rep.	Dem.
36,901	COSHOCTON	15,340	10,923	3,565	852	7,358 R	71.2%	23.2%	75.4%	24.6%
43,784	CRAWFORD	18,949	13,741	4,113	1,095	9,628 R	72.5%	21.7%	77.0%	23.0%
1,280,122	CUYAHOGA	578,376	222,125	327,680	28,571	105,555 D	38.4%	56.7%	40.4%	59.6%
52,959	DARKE	25,073	20,524	3,500	1,049	17,024 R	81.9%	14.0%	85.4%	14.6%
39,037	DEFIANCE	17,732	11,899	4,908	925	6,991 R	67.1%	27.7%	70.8%	29.2%
174,214	DELAWARE	102,906	69,886	29,801	3,219	40,085 R	67.9%	29.0%	70.1%	29.9%
77,079	ERIE	37,042	21,268	13,610	2,164	7,658 R	57.4%	36.7%	61.0%	39.0%
146,156	FAIRFIELD	71,856	47,649	21,073	3,134	26,576 R	66.3%	29.3%	69.3%	30.7%
29,030	FAYETTE	11,003	8,097	2,442	464	5,655 R	73.6%	22.2%	76.8%	23.2%
1,163,414	FRANKLIN	568,135	252,178	292,165	23,792	39,987 D	44.4%	51.4%	46.3%	53.7%
42,698	FULTON	20,858	14,605	5,210	1,043	9,395 R	70.0%	25.0%	73.7%	26.3%
30,934	GALLIA	12,667	8,613	3,523	531	5,090 R	68.0%	27.8%	71.0%	29.0%
93,389	GEAUGA	49,514	33,807	13,458	2,249	20,349 R	68.3%	27.2%	71.5%	28.5%
161,573	GREENE	81,385	55,612	22,383	3,390	33,229 R	68.3%	27.5%	71.3%	28.7%
40,087	GUERNSEY	16,219	11,639	3,836	744	7,803 R	71.8%	23.7%	75.2%	24.8%
802,374	HAMILTON	402,470	216,298	170,427	15,745	45,871 R	53.7%	42.3%	55.9%	44.1%
74,782	HANCOCK	35,425	25,928	7,761	1,736	18,167 R	73.2%	21.9%	77.0%	23.0%
32,058	HARDIN	12,028	8,852	2,505	671	6,347 R	73.6%	20.8%	77.9%	22.1%
15,864	HARRISON	6,976	4,780	1,823	373	2,957 R	68.5%	26.1%	72.4%	27.6%
28,215	HENRY	13,758	9,976	3,110	672	6,866 R	72.5%	22.6%	76.2%	23.8%
43,589	HIGHLAND	18,201	13,866	3,521	814	10,345 R	76.2%	19.3%	79.7%	20.3%
29,380	HOCKING	12,648	8,246	3,753	649	4,493 R	65.2%	29.7%	68.7%	31.3%
42,366	HOLMES	10,947	8,851	1,575	521	7,276 R	80.9%	14.4%	84.9%	15.1%
59,626	HURON	24,304	16,493	6,094	1,717	10,399 R	67.9%	25.1%	73.0%	27.0%
33,225	JACKSON	13,455	9,310	3,574	571	5,736 R	69.2%	26.6%	72.3%	27.7%
69,709	JEFFERSON	31,339	18,957	10,437	1,945	8,520 R	60.5%	33.3%	64.5%	35.5%
60,921	KNOX	28,501	19,775	7,214	1,512	12,561 R	69.4%	25.3%	73.3%	26.7%
230,041	LAKE	111,918	68,348	37,594	5,976	30,754 R	61.1%	33.6%	64.5%	35.5%
62,450	LAWRENCE	25,794	16,363	8,269	1,162	8,094 R	63.4%	32.1%	66.4%	33.6%
166,492	LICKING	81,904	54,495	23,345	4,064	31,150 R	66.5%	28.5%	70.0%	30.0%
45,858	LOGAN	21,406	16,772	3,556	1,078	13,216 R	78.4%	16.6%	82.5%	17.5%
301,356	LORAIN	137,346	73,531	56,032	7,783	17,499 R	53.5%	40.8%	56.8%	43.2%
441,815	LUCAS	192,294	87,961	95,425	8,908	7,464 D	45.7%	49.6%	48.0%	52.0%
43,435	MADISON	17,151	12,351	3,895	905	8,456 R	72.0%	22.7%	76.0%	24.0%
238,823	MAHONING	112,304	55,620	51,211	5,473	4,409 R	49.5%	45.6%	52.1%	47.9%
66,501	MARION	25,848	17,058	7,094	1,696	9,964 R	66.0%	27.4%	70.6%	29.4%
172,332	MEDINA	89,228	58,835	25,744	4,649	33,091 R	65.9%	28.9%	69.6%	30.4%
23,770	MEIGS	9,580	6,415	2,756	409	3,659 R	67.0%	28.8%	69.9%	30.1%
40,814	MERCER	21,442	17,812	2,919	711	14,893 R	83.1%	13.6%	85.9%	14.1%
102,506	MIAMI	52,119	40,745	9,202	2,172	31,543 R	78.2%	17.7%	81.6%	18.4%
14,642	MONROE	6,622	3,981	2,270	371	1,711 R	60.1%	34.3%	63.7%	36.3%
535,153	MONTGOMERY	253,824	144,700	98,101	11,023	46,599 R	57.0%	38.6%	59.6%	40.4%
15,054	MORGAN	6,317	4,336	1,691	290	2,645 R	68.6%	26.8%	71.9%	28.1%
34,827	MORROW	16,369	11,957	3,453	959	8,504 R	73.0%	21.1%	77.6%	22.4%
86,074	MUSKINGUM	36,469	25,944	8,871	1,654	17,073 R	71.1%	24.3%	74.5%	25.5%
14,645	NOBLE	5,758	4,259	1,228	271	3,031 R	74.0%	21.3%	77.6%	22.4%
41,428	OTTAWA	21,773	14,097	6,608	1,068	7,489 R	64.7%	30.3%	68.1%	31.9%
19,614	PAULDING	8,866	5,743	2,576	547	3,167 R	64.8%	29.1%	69.0%	31.0%
36,058	PERRY	14,913	10,011	4,066	836	5,945 R	67.1%	27.3%	71.1%	28.9%
55,698	PICKAWAY	24,412	17,387	5,943	1,082	11,444 R	71.2%	24.3%	74.5%	25.5%
28,709	PIKE	11,675	7,354	3,839	482	3,515 R	63.0%	32.9%	65.7%	34.3%
161,419	PORTAGE	73,541	41,313	27,492	4,736	13,821 R	56.2%	37.4%	60.0%	40.0%
42,270	PREBLE	20,316	15,900	3,424	992	12,476 R	78.3%	16.9%	82.3%	17.7%
34,499	PUTNAM	18,533	15,326	2,538	669	12,788 R	82.7%	13.7%	85.8%	14.2%
124,475	RICHLAND	54,484	36,357	15,078	3,049	21,279 R	66.7%	27.7%	70.7%	29.3%
78,064	ROSS	29,793	19,018	9,384	1,391	9,634 R	63.8%	31.5%	67.0%	33.0%
60,944	SANDUSKY	27,619	18,075	7,715	1,829	10,360 R	65.4%	27.9%	70.1%	29.9%
79,499	SCIOTO	30,661	19,336	10,271	1,054	9,065 R	63.1%	33.5%	65.3%	34.7%
56,745	SENECA	23,530	16,097	6,154	1,279	9,943 R	68.4%	26.2%	72.3%	27.7%
49,423	SHELBY	23,486	19,370	3,163	953	16,207 R	82.5%	13.5%	86.0%	14.0%

OHIO

SENATOR 2016

2010 Census Population	County	Total Vote	Republican (Portman)	Democratic (Strickland)	Other	Rep.-Dem. Plurality	Total Vote Rep.	Total Vote Dem.	Major Vote Rep.	Major Vote Dem.
375,586	STARK	172,436	104,011	58,440	9,985	45,571 R	60.3%	33.9%	64.0%	36.0%
541,781	SUMMIT	249,596	123,025	112,591	13,980	10,434 R	49.3%	45.1%	52.2%	47.8%
210,312	TRUMBULL	93,861	50,252	38,576	5,033	11,676 R	53.5%	41.1%	56.6%	43.4%
92,582	TUSCARAWAS	40,546	27,032	11,147	2,367	15,885 R	66.7%	27.5%	70.8%	29.2%
52,300	UNION	27,045	19,868	5,976	1,201	13,892 R	73.5%	22.1%	76.9%	23.1%
28,744	VAN WERT	13,406	9,782	2,727	897	7,055 R	73.0%	20.3%	78.2%	21.8%
13,435	VINTON	5,332	3,478	1,546	308	1,932 R	65.2%	29.0%	69.2%	30.8%
212,693	WARREN	114,657	85,848	23,827	4,982	62,021 R	74.9%	20.8%	78.3%	21.7%
61,778	WASHINGTON	29,028	18,078	9,676	1,274	8,402 R	62.3%	33.3%	65.1%	34.9%
114,520	WAYNE	49,025	33,604	12,697	2,724	20,907 R	68.5%	25.9%	72.6%	27.4%
37,642	WILLIAMS	16,973	12,224	3,692	1,057	8,532 R	72.0%	21.8%	76.8%	23.2%
125,488	WOOD	63,168	37,532	22,393	3,243	15,139 R	59.4%	35.4%	62.6%	37.4%
22,615	WYANDOT	10,340	7,735	2,124	481	5,611 R	74.8%	20.5%	78.5%	21.5%
11,536,504	TOTAL	5,374,164	3,118,567	1,996,908	258,689	1,121,659 R	58.0%	37.2%	61.0%	39.0%

OHIO

HOUSE OF REPRESENTATIVES

CD	Year	Total Vote	Republican Vote	Republican Candidate	Democratic Vote	Democratic Candidate	Other Vote	Rep.-Dem. Plurality	Total Vote Rep.	Total Vote Dem.	Major Vote Rep.	Major Vote Dem.
1	2016	354,788	210,014	CHABOT, STEVE*	144,644	YOUNG, MICHELE	130	65,370 R	59.2%	40.8%	59.2%	40.8%
1	2014	197,383	124,779	CHABOT, STEVE*	72,604	KUNDRATA, FRED		52,175 R	63.2%	36.8%	63.2%	36.8%
1	2012	349,716	201,907	CHABOT, STEVE*	131,490	SINNARD, JEFF	16,319	70,417 R	57.7%	37.6%	60.6%	39.4%
2	2016	340,279	221,193	WENSTRUP, BRAD*	111,694	SMITH, WILLIAM	7,392	109,499 R	65.0%	32.8%	66.4%	33.6%
2	2014	201,111	132,658	WENSTRUP, BRAD*	68,453	TYSZKIEWICZ, MAREK		64,205 R	66.0%	34.0%	66.0%	34.0%
2	2012	331,381	194,299	WENSTRUP, BRAD	137,082	SMITH, WILLIAM		57,217 R	58.6%	41.4%	58.6%	41.4%
3	2016	291,351	91,560	ADAMS, JOHN	199,791	BEATTY, JOYCE*		108,231 D	31.4%	68.6%	31.4%	68.6%
3	2014	143,261	51,475	ADAMS, JOHN	91,769	BEATTY, JOYCE*	17	40,294 D	35.9%	64.1%	35.9%	64.1%
3	2012	295,938	77,903	LONG, CHRIS	201,921	BEATTY, JOYCE	16,114	124,018 D	26.3%	68.2%	27.8%	72.2%
4	2016	309,208	210,227	JORDAN, JIM*	98,981	GARRETT, JANET		111,246 R	68.0%	32.0%	68.0%	32.0%
4	2014	186,072	125,907	JORDAN, JIM*	60,165	GARRETT, JANET		65,742 R	67.7%	32.3%	67.7%	32.3%
4	2012	312,998	182,643	JORDAN, JIM*	114,214	SLONE, JIM	16,141	68,429 R	58.4%	36.5%	61.5%	38.5%
5	2016	344,991	244,599	LATTA, BOB*	100,392	NEU, JAMES JR.		144,207 R	70.9%	29.1%	70.9%	29.1%
5	2014	202,300	134,449	LATTA, BOB*	58,507	FRY, ROBERT	9,344	75,942 R	66.5%	28.9%	69.7%	30.3%
5	2012	351,878	201,514	LATTA, BOB*	137,806	ZIMMANN, ANGELA	12,558	63,708 R	57.3%	39.2%	59.4%	40.6%
6	2016	302,755	213,975	JOHNSON, BILL*	88,780	LORENTZ, MICHAEL L.		125,195 R	70.7%	29.3%	70.7%	29.3%
6	2014	190,652	111,026	JOHNSON, BILL*	73,561	GARRISON, JENNIFER	6,065	37,465 R	58.2%	38.6%	60.1%	39.9%
6	2012	308,980	164,536	JOHNSON, BILL*	144,444	WILSON, CHARLES A. JR.		20,092 R	53.3%	46.7%	53.3%	46.7%
7	2016	309,553	198,221	GIBBS, BOB*	89,638	RICH, ROY	21,694	108,583 R	64.0%	29.0%	68.9%	31.1%
7	2014	143,959	143,959	GIBBS, BOB*				143,959 R	100.0%		100.0%	
7	2012	315,812	178,104	GIBBS, BOB*	137,708	HEALY-ABRAMS, JOYCE		40,396 R	56.4%	43.6%	56.4%	43.6%
8	2016	325,506	223,833	DAVIDSON, WARREN	87,794	FOUGHT, STEVEN	13,879	136,039 R	68.8%	27.0%	71.8%	28.2%
8	2014	188,330	126,539	BOEHNER, JOHN A.*	51,534	POETTER, TOM	10,257	75,005 R	67.2%	27.4%	71.1%	28.9%
8	2012	246,442	246,380	BOEHNER, JOHN A.*			62	246,380 R	100.0%		100.0%	
9	2016	282,398	88,427	LARSON, DONALD P.	193,966	KAPTUR, MARCY*	5	105,539 D	31.3%	68.7%	31.3%	68.7%
9	2014	160,715	51,704	MAY, RICHARD	108,870	KAPTUR, MARCY*	141	57,166 D	32.2%	67.7%	32.2%	67.8%
9	2012	298,166	68,666	WURZELBACHER, SAMUEL	217,775	KAPTUR, MARCY*	11,725	149,109 D	23.0%	73.0%	24.0%	76.0%

OHIO

HOUSE OF REPRESENTATIVES

CD	Year	Total Vote	Republican Vote	Republican Candidate	Democratic Vote	Democratic Candidate	Other Vote	Rep.-Dem. Plurality	Total Vote Rep.	Total Vote Dem.	Major Vote Rep.	Major Vote Dem.
10	2016	336,602	215,724	TURNER, MICHAEL R.*	109,981	KLEPINGER, ROBERT	10,897	105,743 R	64.1%	32.7%	66.2%	33.8%
10	2014	200,606	130,752	TURNER, MICHAEL R.*	63,249	KLEPINGER, ROBERT	6,605	67,503 R	65.2%	31.5%	67.4%	32.6%
10	2012	349,671	208,201	TURNER, MICHAEL R.*	131,097	NEUHARDT, SHAREN SWARTZ	10,373	77,104 R	59.5%	37.5%	61.4%	38.6%
11	2016	302,686	59,769	GOLDSTEIN, BEVERLY A.	242,917	FUDGE, MARCIA L.*		183,148 D	19.7%	80.3%	19.7%	80.3%
11	2014	172,566	35,461	ZETZER, MARK	137,105	FUDGE, MARCIA L.*		101,644 D	20.5%	79.5%	20.5%	79.5%
11	2012	258,378			258,378	FUDGE, MARCIA L.*		258,378 D		100.0%		100.0%
12	2016	377,534	251,266	TIBERI, PAT*	112,638	ALBERTSON, ED	13,630	138,628 R	66.6%	29.8%	69.0%	31.0%
12	2014	221,081	150,573	TIBERI, PAT*	61,360	TIBBS, DAVID ARTHUR	9,148	89,213 R	68.1%	27.8%	71.0%	29.0%
12	2012	368,488	233,874	TIBERI, PAT*	134,614	REESE, JIM		99,260 R	63.5%	36.5%	63.5%	36.5%
13	2016	308,004	99,377	MORCKEL, RICHARD A.	208,610	RYAN, TIM*	17	109,233 D	32.3%	67.7%	32.3%	67.7%
13	2014	175,549	55,233	PEKAREK, THOMAS	120,230	RYAN, TIM*	86	64,997 D	31.5%	68.5%	31.5%	68.5%
13	2012	323,612	88,120	AGANA, MARISHA	235,492	RYAN, TIM*		147,372 D	27.2%	72.8%	27.2%	72.8%
14	2016	350,269	219,191	JOYCE, DAVID*	130,907	WAGER, MICHAEL	171	88,284 R	62.6%	37.4%	62.6%	37.4%
14	2014	214,580	135,736	JOYCE, DAVID*	70,856	WAGER, MICHAEL	7,988	64,880 R	63.3%	33.0%	65.7%	34.3%
14	2012	339,884	183,660	JOYCE, DAVID	131,638	BLANCHARD, DALE VIRGIL	24,586	52,022 R	54.0%	38.7%	58.2%	41.8%
15	2016	336,807	222,847	STIVERS, STEVE*	113,960	WHARTON, SCOTT		108,887 R	66.2%	33.8%	66.2%	33.8%
15	2014	194,621	128,496	STIVERS, STEVE*	66,125	WHARTON, SCOTT		62,371 R	66.0%	34.0%	66.0%	34.0%
15	2012	333,465	205,277	STIVERS, STEVE*	128,188	LANG, PAT		77,089 R	61.6%	38.4%	61.6%	38.4%
16	2016	345,624	225,794	RENACCI, JIM*	119,830	MUNDY, KEITH		105,964 R	65.3%	34.7%	65.3%	34.7%
16	2014	207,375	132,176	RENACCI, JIM*	75,199	CROSSLAND, PETE		56,977 R	63.7%	36.3%	63.7%	36.3%
16	2012	355,771	185,167	RENACCI, JIM*	170,604	SUTTON, BETTY		14,563 R	52.0%	48.0%	52.0%	48.0%
TOTAL	2016	5,218,355	2,996,017		2,154,523		67,815	841,494 R	57.4%	41.3%	58.2%	41.8%
TOTAL	2014	3,000,161	1,770,923		1,179,587		49,651	591,336 R	59.0%	39.3%	60.0%	40.0%
TOTAL	2012	5,140,580	2,620,251		2,412,451		107,878	207,800 R	51.0%	46.9%	52.1%	47.9%

Note: An asterisk (*) denotes incumbent.

OHIO

GENERAL AND PRIMARY ELECTIONS

2016 GENERAL ELECTIONS: OTHER VOTES

President Other vote was 174,498 Libertarian (Gary Johnson), 46,271 Green (Jill Stein), 24,235 No Party (Richard Duncan), 12,574 Write-in (Evan McMullin), 1,887 Write-in (Darrell Castle), 1,853 Write-in (Scattered Write-in)

Senate Other vote was 93,041 Independent (Thomas Connors), 88,246 Green (Joseph DeMare), 77,291 Independent (Scott Rupert), 111 Write-in (James Stahl)

House Other vote was:

CD 1 114 Write-in (Shalom Keller), 16 Write-in (Kiumars Kiani)
CD 2 7,392 Write-in (Janet Everhard)
CD 7 21,694 Independent (Dan Phillip)
CD 8 13,879 Green (Derrick Hendricks)
CD 9 5 Write-in (George Skalsky)
CD 10 10,890 Independent (Thomas McMasters), 7 Write-in (David Harlow)
CD 12 13,474 Green (Joe Manchik), 156 Write-in (John Baumeister)
CD 13 17 Write-in (Calvin Hill)
CD 14 171 Write-in (Andrew Jarvi)

OHIO

GENERAL AND PRIMARY ELECTIONS

2016 PRIMARY ELECTIONS: SUPPLEMENTARY INFORMATION

Primary	March 15, 2016	**Registration** (as of March 15, 2016)	7,563,184	No Party Registration

Primary Type Open—Any registered voter could participate in the primary of either party. However, records are kept of voter participation in recent primaries, and voters who cast a ballot in one party's primary could be challenged if they attempted to participate in the other party's primary. They could be asked to sign an affidavit affirming the fact that they were voting in the opposing party's primary and would become identified with that party because of their primary ballot cast.

	REPUBLICAN PRIMARIES			DEMOCRATIC PRIMARIES		
President	Kasich, John R.	933,886	47.0%	Clinton, Hillary Rodham	696,681	56.1%
	Trump, Donald J.	713,404	35.9%	Sanders, Bernard	535,395	43.1%
	Cruz, Ted	264,640	13.3%	De La Fuente, Roque "Rocky"	9,402	0.8%
	Rubio, Marco	46,478	2.3%			
	Carson, Ben	14,351	0.7%			
	Bush, Jeb	5,398	0.3%			
	Huckabee, Mike	4,941	0.2%			
	Christie, Chris	2,430	0.1%			
	Fiorina, Carly	2,112	0.1%			
	Santorum, Rick	1,320	0.1%			
	TOTAL	*1,988,960*		*TOTAL*	*1,241,478*	
Senator	Portman, Rob*	1,336,686	82.2%	Strickland, Ted	742,676	65.0%
	Eckhart, Don Elijah	290,268	17.8%	Sittenfeld, P.G.	254,232	22.3%
				Prather, Kelli	144,945	12.7%
	TOTAL	*1,626,954*		*TOTAL*	*1,141,853*	
Congressional District 1	Chabot, Steve*	101,026	100.0%	Young, Michele	39,535	68.0%
				Kundrata, Fred	11,944	20.5%
				Berns, Jim	6,693	11.5%
	TOTAL	*101,026*		*TOTAL*	*58,172*	
Congressional District 2	Wenstrup, Brad*	101,765	84.9%	Smith, William	19,422	41.7%
	Lewis, Jim	18,136	15.1%	Richards, Ronny	13,976	30.0%
				Hurley, Russ	13,154	28.3%
	TOTAL	*119,901*		*TOTAL*	*46,552*	
Congressional District 3	Adams, John	36,851	100.0%	Beatty, Joyce*	79,893	100.0%
	TOTAL	*36,851*		*TOTAL*	*79,893*	
Congressional District 4	Jordan, Jim*	109,743	100.0%	Garrett, Janet	29,679	66.7%
				Johnson, Daniel	11,314	25.4%
				Dennerll, Norbert G. Jr.	3,480	7.8%
	TOTAL	*109,743*		*TOTAL*	*44,473*	
Congressional District 5	Latta, Bob*	119,907	100.0%	Neu, James Jr.	44,005	100.0%
	TOTAL	*119,907*		*TOTAL*	*44,005*	
Congressional District 6	Johnson, Bill*	102,187	100.0%	Lorentz, Michael L.	20,649	100.0%
	TOTAL	*102,187*		*TOTAL*	*20,649*	
Congressional District 7	Gibbs, Bob*	80,853	74.7%	Rich, Roy	43,683	100.0%
	Robertson, Terry	27,453	25.3%			
	TOTAL	*108,306*		*TOTAL*	*43,683*	

OHIO

GENERAL AND PRIMARY ELECTIONS

	REPUBLICAN PRIMARIES			DEMOCRATIC PRIMARIES		
Congressional District 8	Davidson, Warren	42,701	32.2%	Foister, Corey	33,165	100.0%
	Derickson, Timothy S.	31,685	23.9%			
	Beagle, Bill	26,049	19.6%			
	Spurlino, Jim	9,602	7.2%			
	Winteregg, J.D.	5,375	4.1%			
	George, Scott	3,094	2.3%			
	King, Terri	2,970	2.2%			
	White, Kevin F.	2,384	1.8%			
	Smith, Michael	2,009	1.5%			
	Ashworth, Matthew	1,637	1.2%			
	Robbins, John W.	1,579	1.2%			
	Haemmerle, Eric J.	1,386	1.0%			
	Wooley, George S.	1,045	0.8%			
	Meer, Edward R.	633	0.5%			
	Matvey, Joseph	548	0.4%			
	TOTAL	*132,697*		*TOTAL*	*33,165*	
Congressional District 9	Larson, Donald P.	20,859	44.3%	Kaptur, Marcy*	80,065	100.0%
	Kraus, Steven W.	16,966	36.0%			
	Lieske, Joel	9,262	19.7%			
	TOTAL	*47,087*		*TOTAL*	*80,065*	
Congressional District 10	Turner, Mike R.*	108,235	100.0%	Klepinger, Robert	51,854	100.0%
	TOTAL	*108,235*		*TOTAL*	*51,854*	
Congressional District 11	Goldstein, Beverly A.	23,290	100.0%	Fudge, Marcia L.*	109,706	100.0%
	TOTAL	*23,290*		*TOTAL*	*109,706*	
Congressional District 12	Tiberi, Pat*	128,173	100.0%	Albertson, Ed	48,537	100.0%
	TOTAL	*128,173*		*TOTAL*	*48,537*	
Congressional District 13	Morckel, Richard A.	50,750	100.0%	Ryan, Tim*	88,154	89.3%
				Luchansky, John Stephen	10,578	10.7%
	TOTAL	*50,750*		*TOTAL*	*98,732*	
Congressional District 14	Joyce, David*	79,919	64.5%	Wager, Michael	36,796	66.6%
	Lynch, Matt	44,004	35.5%	Mackey, Alfred	18,442	33.4%
	TOTAL	*123,923*		*TOTAL*	*55,238*	
Congressional District 15	Stivers, Steve*	106,410	100.0%	Wharton, Scott	48,477	100.0%
	TOTAL	*106,410*		*TOTAL*	*48,477*	
Congressional District 16	Renacci, Jim*	107,039	100.0%	Mundy, Keith	48,907	100.0%
	TOTAL	*107,039*		*TOTAL*	*48,907*	

Note: An asterisk (*) denotes incumbent.

OKLAHOMA

Congressional districts first established for elections held in 2012

5 members

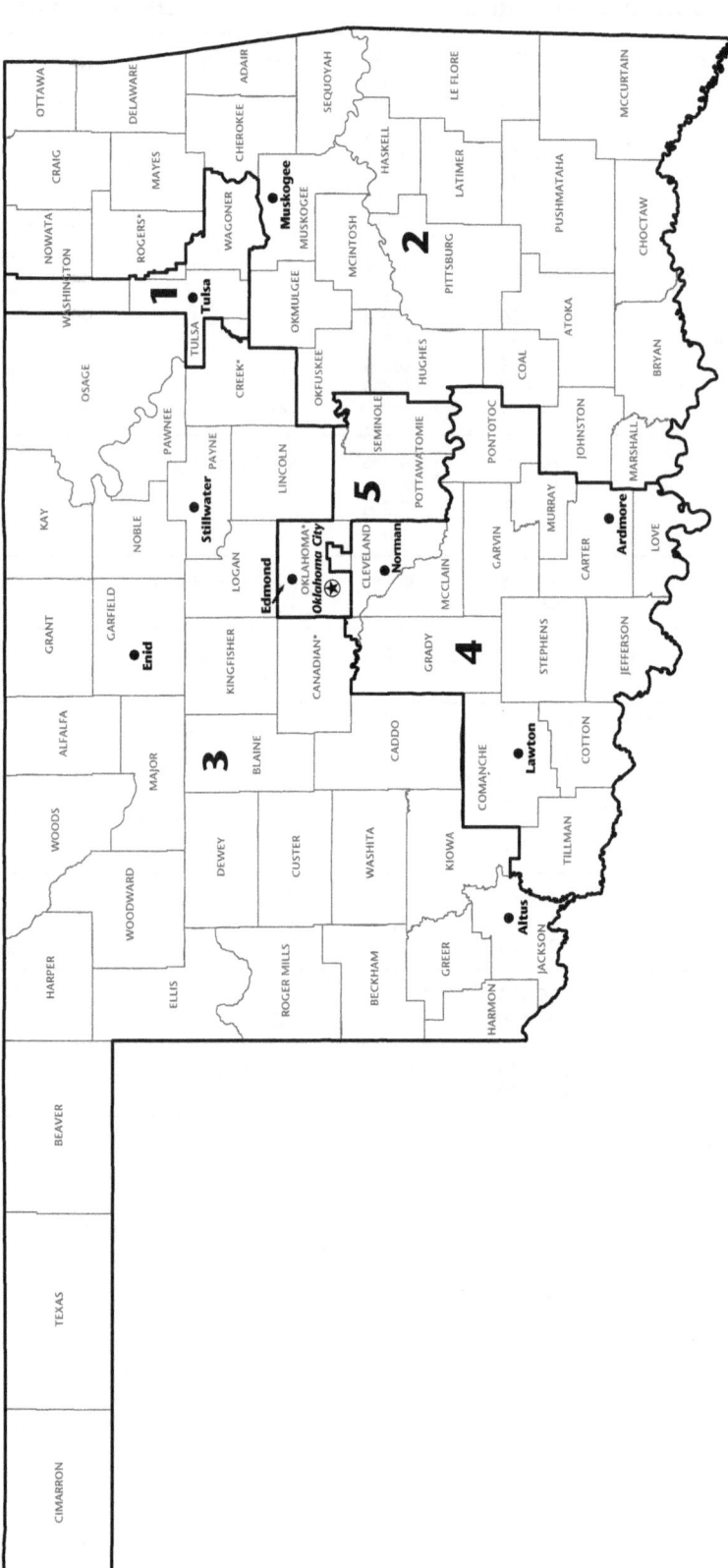

* Asterisk indicates a county whose boundaries include parts of two or more congressional districts.

OKLAHOMA

GOVERNOR
Mary Fallin (R). Re-elected 2014 to a four-year term. Previously elected 2010.

SENATORS (2 Republicans)
James M. Inhofe (R). Re-elected 2014 to a six-year term. Previously elected 2008, 2002, 1996, and 1994 to fill out the remaining two years of the term vacated when David L. Boren (D) resigned in November 1994 to become president of the University of Oklahoma.

James Lankford (R). Re-elected 2016 to a six-year term. Previously elected 2014 to complete the final two years of the term vacated by Tom Coburn (R), who resigned January 3, 2015, after the recurrence of prostate cancer.

REPRESENTATIVES (5 Republicans)
1. Jim Bridenstine (R)
2. Markwayne Mullin (R)
3. Frank D. Lucas (R)
4. Thomas J. Cole (R)
5. Steve D. Russell (R)

POSTWAR VOTE FOR PRESIDENT

Year	Total Vote	Republican		Democratic		Other Vote	Rep.-Dem. Plurality	Percentage			
								Total Vote		Major Vote	
		Vote	Candidate	Vote	Candidate			Rep.	Dem.	Rep.	Dem.
2016**	1,452,992	949,136	Trump, Donald J.	420,375	Clinton, Hillary Rodham	83,481	528,761 R	65.3%	28.9%	69.3%	30.7%
2012	1,334,872	891,325	Romney, W. Mitt	443,547	Obama, Barack H.*		447,778 R	66.8%	33.2%	66.8%	33.2%
2008	1,462,661	960,165	McCain, John S. III	502,496	Obama, Barack H.		457,669 R	65.6%	34.4%	65.6%	34.4%
2004	1,463,758	959,792	Bush, George W.*	503,966	Kerry, John F.		455,826 R	65.6%	34.4%	65.6%	34.4%
2000	1,234,229	744,337	Bush, George W.	474,276	Gore, Albert Jr.	15,616	270,061 R	60.3%	38.4%	61.1%	38.9%
1996**	1,206,713	582,315	Dole, Robert "Bob"	488,105	Clinton, Bill*	136,293	94,210 R	48.3%	40.4%	54.4%	45.6%
1992**	1,390,359	592,929	Bush, George H.*	473,066	Clinton, Bill	324,364	119,863 R	42.6%	34.0%	55.6%	44.4%
1988	1,171,036	678,367	Bush, George H.	483,423	Dukakis, Michael S.	9,246	194,944 R	57.9%	41.3%	58.4%	41.6%
1984	1,255,676	861,530	Reagan, Ronald*	385,080	Mondale, Walter F.	9,066	476,450 R	68.6%	30.7%	69.1%	30.9%
1980**	1,149,708	695,570	Reagan, Ronald	402,026	Carter, Jimmy*	52,112	293,544 R	60.5%	35.0%	63.4%	36.6%
1976	1,092,251	545,708	Ford, Gerald R.*	532,442	Carter, Jimmy	14,101	13,266 R	50.0%	48.7%	50.6%	49.4%
1972	1,029,900	759,025	Nixon, Richard M.*	247,147	McGovern, George S.	23,728	511,878 R	73.7%	24.0%	75.4%	24.6%
1968**	943,086	449,697	Nixon, Richard M.	301,658	Humphrey, Hubert Horatio Jr.	191,731	148,039 R	47.7%	32.0%	59.9%	40.1%
1964	932,499	412,665	Goldwater, Barry M. Sr.	519,834	Johnson, Lyndon B.*		107,169 D	44.3%	55.7%	44.3%	55.7%
1960	903,150	533,039	Nixon, Richard M.	370,111	Kennedy, John F.		162,928 R	59.0%	41.0%	59.0%	41.0%
1956	859,350	473,769	Eisenhower, Dwight D.*	385,581	Stevenson, Adlai E. II		88,188 R	55.1%	44.9%	55.1%	44.9%
1952	948,984	518,045	Eisenhower, Dwight D.	430,939	Stevenson, Adlai E. II		87,106 R	54.6%	45.4%	54.6%	45.4%
1948	721,599	268,817	Dewey, Thomas E.	452,782	Truman, Harry S.*		183,965 D	37.3%	62.7%	37.3%	62.7%

Note: An asterisk (*) denotes incumbent. **In past elections, the other vote included: 2016 - 83,481 Libertarian (Gary Johnson); 1996 - 130,788 Reform (Ross Perot); 1992 - 319,878 Independent (Perot); 1980 - 38,284 Independent (John Anderson); 1968 - 191,731 American Independent (George Wallace).

OKLAHOMA

POSTWAR VOTE FOR GOVERNOR

Year	Total Vote	Republican		Democratic		Other Vote	Rep.-Dem. Plurality	Percentage			
								Total Vote		Major Vote	
		Vote	Candidate	Vote	Candidate			Rep.	Dem.	Rep.	Dem.
2014	824,831	460,298	Fallin, Mary*	338,239	Dorman, Joe	26,294	122,059 R	55.8%	41.0%	57.6%	42.4%
2010	1,034,767	625,506	Fallin, Mary	409,261	Askins, Jari		216,245 R	60.4%	39.6%	60.4%	39.6%
2006	926,462	310,327	Istook, Ernest J.	616,135	Henry, Brad*		305,808 D	33.5%	66.5%	33.5%	66.5%
2002**	1,035,620	441,277	Largent, Steve	448,143	Henry, Brad	146,200	6,866 D	42.6%	43.3%	49.6%	50.4%
1998	873,585	505,498	Keating, Frank*	357,552	Boyd, Laura	10,535	147,946 R	57.9%	40.9%	58.6%	41.4%
1994**	995,012	466,740	Keating, Frank	294,936	Mildren, Jack	233,336	171,804 R	46.9%	29.6%	61.3%	38.7%
1990	911,314	297,584	Price, Bill	523,196	Walters, David	90,534	225,612 D	32.7%	57.4%	36.3%	63.7%
1986	909,925	431,762	Bellmon, Henry Louis	405,295	Walters, David	72,868	26,467 R	47.5%	44.5%	51.6%	48.4%
1982	883,130	332,207	Daxon, Tom	548,159	Nigh, George*	2,764	215,952 D	37.6%	62.1%	37.7%	62.3%
1978	777,414	367,055	Shotts, Ron	402,240	Nigh, George	8,119	35,185 D	47.2%	51.7%	47.7%	52.3%
1974	804,842	290,459	Inhofe, James M.	514,383	Boren, David L.		223,924 D	36.1%	63.9%	36.1%	63.9%
1970	698,790	336,157	Bartlett, Dewey F.*	338,338	Hall, David	24,295	2,181 D	48.1%	48.4%	49.8%	50.2%
1966	677,258	377,078	Bartlett, Dewey F.	296,328	Moore, Preston J.	3,852	80,750 R	55.7%	43.8%	56.0%	44.0%
1962	709,763	392,316	Bellmon, Henry Louis	315,357	Atkinson, W. P.	2,090	76,959 R	55.3%	44.4%	55.4%	44.6%
1958	538,839	107,495	Ferguson, Phil	399,504	Edmondson, J. Howard	31,840	292,009 D	19.9%	74.1%	21.2%	78.8%
1954	609,194	251,808	Sparks, Reuben K.	357,386	Gary, Raymond		105,578 D	41.3%	58.7%	41.3%	58.7%
1950	644,276	313,205	Ferguson, Jo O.	329,308	Murray, Johnston	1,763	16,103 D	48.6%	51.1%	48.7%	51.3%
1946	494,599	227,426	Flynn, Olney F.	259,491	Turner, Roy J.	7,682	32,065 D	46.0%	52.5%	46.7%	53.3%

Note: An asterisk (*) denotes incumbent. **In past elections, the other vote included: 2002 - 146,200 Independent (Gary L. Richardson); 1994 - 233,336 Independent (Wes Watkins).

POSTWAR VOTE FOR SENATOR

Year	Total Vote	Republican		Democratic		Other Vote	Rep.-Dem. Plurality	Percentage			
								Total Vote		Major Vote	
		Vote	Candidate	Vote	Candidate			Rep.	Dem.	Rep.	Dem.
2016	1,448,047	980,892	Lankford, James*	355,911	Workman, Mike	111,244	624,981 R	67.7%	24.6%	73.4%	26.6%
2014	820,733	558,166	Inhofe, James M.*	234,307	Silverstein, Matthew Benjamin "Matt"	28,260	323,859 R	68.0%	28.5%	70.4%	29.6%
2014S**	820,890	557,002	Lankford, James	237,923	Johnson, Connie	25,965	319,079 R	67.9%	29.0%	70.1%	29.9%
2010	1,017,151	718,482	Coburn, Tom*	265,814	Rogers, Jim	32,855	452,668 R	70.6%	26.1%	73.0%	27.0%
2008	1,346,819	763,375	Inhofe, James M.*	527,736	Rice, Andrew	55,708	235,639 R	56.7%	39.2%	59.1%	40.9%
2004	1,446,846	763,433	Coburn, Tom	596,750	Carson, Brad	86,663	166,683 R	52.8%	41.2%	56.1%	43.9%
2002	1,018,424	583,579	Inhofe, James M.*	369,789	Walters, David	65,056	213,790 R	57.3%	36.3%	61.2%	38.8%
1998	859,713	570,682	Nickles, Don*	268,898	Carroll, Don E.	20,133	301,784 R	66.4%	31.3%	68.0%	32.0%
1996	1,183,150	670,610	Inhofe, James M.*	474,162	Boren, Jim	38,378	196,448 R	56.7%	40.1%	58.6%	41.4%
1994S**	982,430	542,390	Inhofe, James M.	392,488	McCurdy, Dave	47,552	149,902 R	55.2%	40.0%	58.0%	42.0%
1992	1,294,423	757,876	Nickles, Don*	494,350	Lewis, Steve	42,197	263,526 R	58.5%	38.2%	60.5%	39.5%
1990	884,498	148,814	Jones, Stephen	735,684	Boren, David L.*		586,870 D	16.8%	83.2%	16.8%	83.2%
1986	893,666	493,436	Nickles, Don*	400,230	Jones, James R.		93,206 R	55.2%	44.8%	55.2%	44.8%
1984	1,197,937	280,638	Crozier, Will E. Bill	906,131	Boren, David L.*	11,168	625,493 D	23.4%	75.6%	23.6%	76.4%
1980	1,098,294	587,252	Nickles, Don	478,283	Coats, Andrew	32,759	108,969 R	53.5%	43.5%	55.1%	44.9%
1978	754,264	247,857	Kamm, Robert B.	493,953	Boren, David L.	12,454	246,096 D	32.9%	65.5%	33.4%	66.6%
1974	791,809	390,997	Bellmon, Henry Louis*	387,162	Edmondson, Ed	13,650	3,835 R	49.4%	48.9%	50.2%	49.8%
1972	1,005,148	516,934	Bartlett, Dewey F.	478,212	Edmondson, Ed	10,002	38,722 R	51.4%	47.6%	51.9%	48.1%
1968	909,119	470,120	Bellmon, Henry Louis	419,658	Monroney, Almer Stillwell Mike*	19,341	50,462 R	51.7%	46.2%	52.8%	47.2%
1966	638,742	295,585	Patterson, Pat J.	343,157	Harris, Fred R.*		47,572 D	46.3%	53.7%	46.3%	53.7%
1964S**	912,174	445,392	Wilkinson, Bud	466,782	Harris, Fred R.		21,390 D	48.8%	51.2%	48.8%	51.2%
1962	664,712	307,966	Crawford, B. Hayden	353,890	Monroney, Almer Stillwell Mike*	2,856	45,924 D	46.3%	53.2%	46.5%	53.5%
1960	864,475	385,646	Crawford, B. Hayden	474,116	Kerr, Robert Samuel Sr.*	4,713	88,470 D	44.6%	54.8%	44.9%	55.1%
1956	831,142	371,146	McKeever, Douglas	459,996	Monroney, Almer Stillwell Mike*		88,850 D	44.7%	55.3%	44.7%	55.3%
1954	600,120	262,013	Mock, Fred M.	335,127	Kerr, Robert Samuel Sr.*	2,980	73,114 D	43.7%	55.8%	43.9%	56.1%
1950	631,177	285,224	Alexander, W. H.	345,953	Monroney, Almer Stillwell Mike		60,729 D	45.2%	54.8%	45.2%	54.8%
1948	708,931	265,169	Rizley, Ross	441,654	Kerr, Robert Samuel Sr.	2,108	176,485 D	37.4%	62.3%	37.5%	62.5%

Note: An asterisk (*) denotes incumbent. **The 1964, 1994, and 2014 elections were for short terms to fill vacancies.

OKLAHOMA

PRESIDENT 2016

2010 Census Population	County	Total Vote	Republican (Trump)	Democratic (Clinton)	Other	Rep.-Dem. Plurality		Percentage			
								Total Vote		Major Vote	
								Rep.	Dem.	Rep.	Dem.
22,683	ADAIR	6,513	4,787	1,382	344	3,405 R		73.5%	21.2%	77.6%	22.4%
5,642	ALFALFA	2,258	1,933	216	109	1,717 R		85.6%	9.6%	89.9%	10.1%
14,182	ATOKA	5,018	4,084	795	139	3,289 R		81.4%	15.8%	83.7%	16.3%
5,636	BEAVER	2,243	1,993	176	74	1,817 R		88.9%	7.8%	91.9%	8.1%
22,119	BECKHAM	7,552	6,308	960	284	5,348 R		83.5%	12.7%	86.8%	13.2%
11,943	BLAINE	3,793	2,884	711	198	2,173 R		76.0%	18.7%	80.2%	19.8%
42,416	BRYAN	13,818	10,478	2,804	536	7,674 R		75.8%	20.3%	78.9%	21.1%
29,600	CADDO	9,348	6,482	2,420	446	4,062 R		69.3%	25.9%	72.8%	27.2%
115,541	CANADIAN	55,278	39,986	11,674	3,618	28,312 R		72.3%	21.1%	77.4%	22.6%
47,557	CARTER	18,534	13,752	4,002	780	9,750 R		74.2%	21.6%	77.5%	22.5%
46,987	CHEROKEE	16,490	9,994	5,456	1,040	4,538 R		60.6%	33.1%	64.7%	35.3%
15,205	CHOCTAW	5,426	4,206	1,067	153	3,139 R		77.5%	19.7%	79.8%	20.2%
2,475	CIMARRON	1,079	963	71	45	892 R		89.2%	6.6%	93.1%	6.9%
255,755	CLEVELAND	109,450	62,538	38,829	8,083	23,709 R		57.1%	35.5%	61.7%	38.3%
5,925	COAL	2,399	1,898	411	90	1,487 R		79.1%	17.1%	82.2%	17.8%
124,098	COMANCHE	32,564	19,183	11,463	1,918	7,720 R		58.9%	35.2%	62.6%	37.4%
6,193	COTTON	2,602	2,054	424	124	1,630 R		78.9%	16.3%	82.9%	17.1%
15,029	CRAIG	5,785	4,283	1,252	250	3,031 R		74.0%	21.6%	77.4%	22.6%
69,967	CREEK	28,830	21,575	5,841	1,414	15,734 R		74.8%	20.3%	78.7%	21.3%
27,469	CUSTER	10,541	7,826	2,104	611	5,722 R		74.2%	20.0%	78.8%	21.2%
41,487	DELAWARE	15,716	11,826	3,311	579	8,515 R		75.2%	21.1%	78.1%	21.9%
4,810	DEWEY	2,248	1,965	222	61	1,743 R		87.4%	9.9%	89.8%	10.2%
4,151	ELLIS	1,827	1,611	155	61	1,456 R		88.2%	8.5%	91.2%	8.8%
60,580	GARFIELD	21,710	16,009	4,397	1,304	11,612 R		73.7%	20.3%	78.5%	21.5%
27,576	GARVIN	10,546	8,253	1,855	438	6,398 R		78.3%	17.6%	81.6%	18.4%
52,431	GRADY	22,286	17,316	3,882	1,088	13,434 R		77.7%	17.4%	81.7%	18.3%
4,527	GRANT	2,201	1,827	288	86	1,539 R		83.0%	13.1%	86.4%	13.6%
6,239	GREER	1,896	1,482	323	91	1,159 R		78.2%	17.0%	82.1%	17.9%
2,922	HARMON	977	715	225	37	490 R		73.2%	23.0%	76.1%	23.9%
3,685	HARPER	1,499	1,318	134	47	1,184 R		87.9%	8.9%	90.8%	9.2%
12,769	HASKELL	4,738	3,701	882	155	2,819 R		78.1%	18.6%	80.8%	19.2%
14,003	HUGHES	4,526	3,388	961	177	2,427 R		74.9%	21.2%	77.9%	22.1%
26,446	JACKSON	7,806	5,969	1,473	364	4,496 R		76.5%	18.9%	80.2%	19.8%
6,472	JEFFERSON	2,350	1,910	365	75	1,545 R		81.3%	15.5%	84.0%	16.0%
10,957	JOHNSTON	4,018	3,093	786	139	2,307 R		77.0%	19.6%	79.7%	20.3%
46,562	KAY	16,803	12,172	3,738	893	8,434 R		72.4%	22.2%	76.5%	23.5%
15,034	KINGFISHER	6,131	5,156	786	189	4,370 R		84.1%	12.8%	86.8%	13.2%
9,446	KIOWA	3,493	2,596	767	130	1,829 R		74.3%	22.0%	77.2%	22.8%
11,154	LATIMER	4,056	3,100	797	159	2,303 R		76.4%	19.6%	79.5%	20.5%
50,384	LE FLORE	17,221	13,362	3,250	609	10,112 R		77.6%	18.9%	80.4%	19.6%
34,273	LINCOLN	14,025	10,854	2,430	741	8,424 R		77.4%	17.3%	81.7%	18.3%
41,848	LOGAN	18,979	13,633	4,248	1,098	9,385 R		71.8%	22.4%	76.2%	23.8%
9,423	LOVE	3,789	2,922	735	132	2,187 R		77.1%	19.4%	79.9%	20.1%
7,527	MAJOR	3,407	2,948	310	149	2,638 R		86.5%	9.1%	90.5%	9.5%
15,840	MARSHALL	5,492	4,206	1,096	190	3,110 R		76.6%	20.0%	79.3%	20.7%
41,259	MAYES	15,717	11,555	3,423	739	8,132 R		73.5%	21.8%	77.1%	22.9%
34,506	MCCLAIN	16,858	13,169	2,894	795	10,275 R		78.1%	17.2%	82.0%	18.0%
33,151	MCCURTAIN	10,726	8,656	1,802	268	6,854 R		80.7%	16.8%	82.8%	17.2%
20,252	MCINTOSH	7,963	5,505	2,123	335	3,382 R		69.1%	26.7%	72.2%	27.8%
13,488	MURRAY	5,528	4,175	1,087	266	3,088 R		75.5%	19.7%	79.3%	20.7%
70,990	MUSKOGEE	24,216	15,043	7,977	1,196	7,066 R		62.1%	32.9%	65.3%	34.7%
11,561	NOBLE	4,878	3,715	901	262	2,814 R		76.2%	18.5%	80.5%	19.5%
10,536	NOWATA	4,237	3,321	742	174	2,579 R		78.4%	17.5%	81.7%	18.3%
12,191	OKFUSKEE	3,943	2,800	943	200	1,857 R		71.0%	23.9%	74.8%	25.2%
718,633	OKLAHOMA	273,942	141,569	112,813	19,560	28,756 R		51.7%	41.2%	55.7%	44.3%
40,069	OKMULGEE	13,949	8,944	4,385	620	4,559 R		64.1%	31.4%	67.1%	32.9%
47,472	OSAGE	18,966	12,577	5,597	792	6,980 R		66.3%	29.5%	69.2%	30.8%
31,848	OTTAWA	10,690	7,631	2,584	475	5,047 R		71.4%	24.2%	74.7%	25.3%
16,577	PAWNEE	6,364	4,729	1,344	291	3,385 R		74.3%	21.1%	77.9%	22.1%
77,350	PAYNE	27,760	16,651	8,788	2,321	7,863 R		60.0%	31.7%	65.5%	34.5%

OKLAHOMA

PRESIDENT 2016

2010 Census Population	County	Total Vote	Republican (Trump)	Democratic (Clinton)	Other	Rep.-Dem. Plurality	Percentage			
							Total Vote		Major Vote	
							Rep.	Dem.	Rep.	Dem.
45,837	PITTSBURG	17,271	12,753	3,711	807	9,042 R	73.8%	21.5%	77.5%	22.5%
37,492	PONTOTOC	14,831	10,431	3,637	763	6,794 R	70.3%	24.5%	74.1%	25.9%
69,442	POTTAWATOMIE	25,452	17,848	6,015	1,589	11,833 R	70.1%	23.6%	74.8%	25.2%
11,572	PUSHMATAHA	4,483	3,581	748	154	2,833 R	79.9%	16.7%	82.7%	17.3%
3,647	ROGER MILLS	1,759	1,547	151	61	1,396 R	87.9%	8.6%	91.1%	8.9%
86,905	ROGERS	40,862	30,913	7,902	2,047	23,011 R	75.7%	19.3%	79.6%	20.4%
25,482	SEMINOLE	8,037	5,613	2,071	353	3,542 R	69.8%	25.8%	73.0%	27.0%
42,391	SEQUOYAH	14,437	10,888	3,061	488	7,827 R	75.4%	21.2%	78.1%	21.9%
45,048	STEPHENS	17,904	14,182	3,086	636	11,096 R	79.2%	17.2%	82.1%	17.9%
20,640	TEXAS	5,780	4,621	858	301	3,763 R	79.9%	14.8%	84.3%	15.7%
7,992	TILLMAN	2,706	1,944	657	105	1,287 R	71.8%	24.3%	74.7%	25.3%
603,403	TULSA	247,054	144,258	87,847	14,949	56,411 R	58.4%	35.6%	62.2%	37.8%
73,085	WAGONER	31,300	23,005	6,723	1,572	16,282 R	73.5%	21.5%	77.4%	22.6%
50,976	WASHINGTON	22,224	15,825	5,048	1,351	10,777 R	71.2%	22.7%	75.8%	24.2%
11,629	WASHITA	4,631	3,854	588	189	3,266 R	83.2%	12.7%	86.8%	13.2%
8,878	WOODS	3,668	2,947	522	199	2,425 R	80.3%	14.2%	85.0%	15.0%
20,081	WOODWARD	7,595	6,347	873	375	5,474 R	83.6%	11.5%	87.9%	12.1%
3,751,351	TOTAL	1,452,992	949,136	420,375	83,481	528,761 R	65.3%	28.9%	69.3%	30.7%

OKLAHOMA

SENATOR 2016

2010 Census Population	County	Total Vote	Republican (Lankford)	Democratic (Workman)	Other	Rep.-Dem. Plurality	Percentage			
							Total Vote		Major Vote	
							Rep.	Dem.	Rep.	Dem.
22,683	ADAIR	6,466	4,576	1,552	338	3,024 R	70.8%	24.0%	74.7%	25.3%
5,642	ALFALFA	2,262	1,982	169	111	1,813 R	87.6%	7.5%	92.1%	7.9%
14,182	ATOKA	4,922	3,441	1,185	296	2,256 R	69.9%	24.1%	74.4%	25.6%
5,636	BEAVER	2,222	1,940	169	113	1,771 R	87.3%	7.6%	92.0%	8.0%
22,119	BECKHAM	7,540	6,305	870	365	5,435 R	83.6%	11.5%	87.9%	12.1%
11,943	BLAINE	3,797	3,041	551	205	2,490 R	80.1%	14.5%	84.7%	15.3%
42,416	BRYAN	13,584	9,566	2,965	1,053	6,601 R	70.4%	21.8%	76.3%	23.7%
29,600	CADDO	9,343	6,894	1,971	478	4,923 R	73.8%	21.1%	77.8%	22.2%
115,541	CANADIAN	55,275	42,127	8,987	4,161	33,140 R	76.2%	16.3%	82.4%	17.6%
47,557	CARTER	18,378	12,935	4,030	1,413	8,905 R	70.4%	21.9%	76.2%	23.8%
46,987	CHEROKEE	16,436	9,898	5,267	1,271	4,631 R	60.2%	32.0%	65.3%	34.7%
15,205	CHOCTAW	5,315	3,694	1,279	342	2,415 R	69.5%	24.1%	74.3%	25.7%
2,475	CIMARRON	1,063	903	77	83	826 R	84.9%	7.2%	92.1%	7.9%
255,755	CLEVELAND	109,612	67,796	29,105	12,711	38,691 R	61.9%	26.6%	70.0%	30.0%
5,925	COAL	2,307	1,525	613	169	912 R	66.1%	26.6%	71.3%	28.7%
124,098	COMANCHE	32,444	20,022	9,653	2,769	10,369 R	61.7%	29.8%	67.5%	32.5%
6,193	COTTON	2,575	2,011	387	177	1,624 R	78.1%	15.0%	83.9%	16.1%
15,029	CRAIG	5,725	4,195	1,226	304	2,969 R	73.3%	21.4%	77.4%	22.6%
69,967	CREEK	28,603	21,506	5,229	1,868	16,277 R	75.2%	18.3%	80.4%	19.6%
27,469	CUSTER	10,544	8,317	1,628	599	6,689 R	78.9%	15.4%	83.6%	16.4%
41,487	DELAWARE	15,577	11,382	3,301	894	8,081 R	73.1%	21.2%	77.5%	22.5%
4,810	DEWEY	2,240	1,979	185	76	1,794 R	88.3%	8.3%	91.5%	8.5%
4,151	ELLIS	1,827	1,615	135	77	1,480 R	88.4%	7.4%	92.3%	7.7%
60,580	GARFIELD	21,690	16,776	3,401	1,513	13,375 R	77.3%	15.7%	83.1%	16.9%
27,576	GARVIN	10,500	8,170	1,684	646	6,486 R	77.8%	16.0%	82.9%	17.1%

OKLAHOMA
SENATOR 2016

2010 Census Population	County	Total Vote	Republican (Lankford)	Democratic (Workman)	Other	Rep.-Dem. Plurality	Percentage Total Vote Rep.	Dem.	Major Vote Rep.	Dem.
52,431	GRADY	22,248	17,667	3,218	1,363	14,449 R	79.4%	14.5%	84.6%	15.4%
4,527	GRANT	2,187	1,863	205	119	1,658 R	85.2%	9.4%	90.1%	9.9%
6,239	GREER	1,880	1,466	317	97	1,149 R	78.0%	16.9%	82.2%	17.8%
2,922	HARMON	958	736	186	36	550 R	76.8%	19.4%	79.8%	20.2%
3,685	HARPER	1,509	1,354	97	58	1,257 R	89.7%	6.4%	93.3%	6.7%
12,769	HASKELL	4,669	3,368	1,094	207	2,274 R	72.1%	23.4%	75.5%	24.5%
14,003	HUGHES	4,501	3,379	889	233	2,490 R	75.1%	19.8%	79.2%	20.8%
26,446	JACKSON	7,756	6,064	1,229	463	4,835 R	78.2%	15.8%	83.1%	16.9%
6,472	JEFFERSON	2,291	1,711	434	146	1,277 R	74.7%	18.9%	79.8%	20.2%
10,957	JOHNSTON	3,917	2,636	999	282	1,637 R	67.3%	25.5%	72.5%	27.5%
46,562	KAY	16,719	12,310	3,145	1,264	9,165 R	73.6%	18.8%	79.7%	20.3%
15,034	KINGFISHER	6,123	5,323	524	276	4,799 R	86.9%	8.6%	91.0%	9.0%
9,446	KIOWA	3,483	2,717	635	131	2,082 R	78.0%	18.2%	81.1%	18.9%
11,154	LATIMER	3,997	2,803	966	228	1,837 R	70.1%	24.2%	74.4%	25.6%
50,384	LE FLORE	16,865	11,611	4,049	1,205	7,562 R	68.8%	24.0%	74.1%	25.9%
34,273	LINCOLN	14,063	11,215	2,007	841	9,208 R	79.7%	14.3%	84.8%	15.2%
41,848	LOGAN	18,995	14,234	3,319	1,442	10,915 R	74.9%	17.5%	81.1%	18.9%
9,423	LOVE	3,719	2,600	855	264	1,745 R	69.9%	23.0%	75.3%	24.7%
7,527	MAJOR	3,405	3,032	226	147	2,806 R	89.0%	6.6%	93.1%	6.9%
15,840	MARSHALL	5,427	3,824	1,197	406	2,627 R	70.5%	22.1%	76.2%	23.8%
41,259	MAYES	15,641	11,306	3,409	926	7,897 R	72.3%	21.8%	76.8%	23.2%
34,506	MCCLAIN	16,862	13,434	2,388	1,040	11,046 R	79.7%	14.2%	84.9%	15.1%
33,151	MCCURTAIN	10,375	7,330	2,321	724	5,009 R	70.7%	22.4%	76.0%	24.0%
20,252	MCINTOSH	7,904	5,299	2,163	442	3,136 R	67.0%	27.4%	71.0%	29.0%
13,488	MURRAY	5,495	4,162	999	334	3,163 R	75.7%	18.2%	80.6%	19.4%
70,990	MUSKOGEE	24,074	15,144	7,472	1,458	7,672 R	62.9%	31.0%	67.0%	33.0%
11,561	NOBLE	4,849	3,819	759	271	3,060 R	78.8%	15.7%	83.4%	16.6%
10,536	NOWATA	4,212	3,115	845	252	2,270 R	74.0%	20.1%	78.7%	21.3%
12,191	OKFUSKEE	3,921	2,795	906	220	1,889 R	71.3%	23.1%	75.5%	24.5%
718,633	OKLAHOMA	274,314	160,491	89,222	24,601	71,269 R	58.5%	32.5%	64.3%	35.7%
40,069	OKMULGEE	13,893	8,936	4,064	893	4,872 R	64.3%	29.3%	68.7%	31.3%
47,472	OSAGE	18,886	12,469	5,142	1,275	7,327 R	66.0%	27.2%	70.8%	29.2%
31,848	OTTAWA	10,571	6,970	2,792	809	4,178 R	65.9%	26.4%	71.4%	28.6%
16,577	PAWNEE	6,336	4,661	1,242	433	3,419 R	73.6%	19.6%	79.0%	21.0%
77,350	PAYNE	27,813	18,275	6,932	2,606	11,343 R	65.7%	24.9%	72.5%	27.5%
45,837	PITTSBURG	17,140	11,888	4,138	1,114	7,750 R	69.4%	24.1%	74.2%	25.8%
37,492	PONTOTOC	14,757	10,173	3,549	1,035	6,624 R	68.9%	24.0%	74.1%	25.9%
69,442	POTTAWATOMIE	25,499	19,184	4,647	1,668	14,537 R	75.2%	18.2%	80.5%	19.5%
11,572	PUSHMATAHA	4,341	3,061	971	309	2,090 R	70.5%	22.4%	75.9%	24.1%
3,647	ROGER MILLS	1,747	1,537	144	66	1,393 R	88.0%	8.2%	91.4%	8.6%
86,905	ROGERS	40,773	31,194	6,862	2,717	24,332 R	76.5%	16.8%	82.0%	18.0%
25,482	SEMINOLE	8,049	5,897	1,672	480	4,225 R	73.3%	20.8%	77.9%	22.1%
42,391	SEQUOYAH	14,128	9,458	3,640	1,030	5,818 R	66.9%	25.8%	72.2%	27.8%
45,048	STEPHENS	17,823	14,102	2,780	941	11,322 R	79.1%	15.6%	83.5%	16.5%
20,640	TEXAS	5,750	4,526	769	455	3,757 R	78.7%	13.4%	85.5%	14.5%
7,992	TILLMAN	2,669	1,941	577	151	1,364 R	72.7%	21.6%	77.1%	22.9%
603,403	TULSA	246,208	154,406	72,350	19,452	82,056 R	62.7%	29.4%	68.1%	31.9%
73,085	WAGONER	31,065	23,039	6,037	1,989	17,002 R	74.2%	19.4%	79.2%	20.8%
50,976	WASHINGTON	22,182	16,445	4,223	1,514	12,222 R	74.1%	19.0%	79.6%	20.4%
11,629	WASHITA	4,616	3,885	528	203	3,357 R	84.2%	11.4%	88.0%	12.0%
8,878	WOODS	3,644	3,040	404	200	2,636 R	83.4%	11.1%	88.3%	11.7%
20,081	WOODWARD	7,551	6,401	754	396	5,647 R	84.8%	10.0%	89.5%	10.5%
3,751,351	TOTAL	1,448,047	980,892	355,911	111,244	624,981 R	67.7%	24.6%	73.4%	26.6%

OKLAHOMA

HOUSE OF REPRESENTATIVES

CD	Year	Total Vote	Republican Vote	Republican Candidate	Democratic Vote	Democratic Candidate	Other Vote	Rep.-Dem. Plurality		Percentage Total Vote Rep.	Dem.	Major Vote Rep.	Dem.
1	2016		Unopposed	BRIDENSTINE, JIM*					R				
1	2014		Unopposed	BRIDENSTINE, JIM*					R				
1	2012	285,312	181,084	BRIDENSTINE, JIM	91,421	OLSON, JOHN	12,807	89,663	R	63.5%	32.0%	66.5%	33.5%
2	2016	268,870	189,839	MULLIN, MARKWAYNE*	62,387	HARRIS-TILL, JOSHUA	16,644	127,452	R	70.6%	23.2%	75.3%	24.7%
2	2014	158,407	110,925	MULLIN, MARKWAYNE*	38,964	EVERETT, EARL E.	8,518	71,961	R	70.0%	24.6%	74.0%	26.0%
2	2012	250,612	143,701	MULLIN, MARKWAYNE	96,081	WALLACE, ROB	10,830	47,620	R	57.3%	38.3%	59.9%	40.1%
3	2016	290,615	227,525	LUCAS, FRANK D.*	63,090	ROBBINS, FRANKIE		164,435	R	78.3%	21.7%	78.3%	21.7%
3	2014	169,605	133,335	LUCAS, FRANK D.*	36,270	ROBBINS, FRANKIE		97,065	R	78.6%	21.4%	78.6%	21.4%
3	2012	268,003	201,744	LUCAS, FRANK D.*	53,472	MURRAY, TIMOTHY RAY	12,787	148,272	R	75.3%	20.0%	79.0%	21.0%
4	2016	293,189	204,143	COLE, THOMAS J.*	76,472	OWEN, CHRISTINA	12,574	127,671	R	69.6%	26.1%	72.7%	27.3%
4	2014	166,268	117,721	COLE, THOMAS J.*	40,998	SMITH, BERT	7,549	76,723	R	70.8%	24.7%	74.2%	25.8%
4	2012	260,331	176,740	COLE, THOMAS J.*	71,846	BEBO, DONNA MARIE	11,745	104,894	R	67.9%	27.6%	71.1%	28.9%
5	2016	280,570	160,184	RUSSELL, STEVE D.*	103,273	MCAFFREY, AL	17,113	56,911	R	57.1%	36.8%	60.8%	39.2%
5	2014	159,133	95,632	RUSSELL, STEVE D.	57,790	MCAFFREY, AL	5,711	37,842	R	60.1%	36.3%	62.3%	37.7%
5	2012	261,677	153,603	LANKFORD, JAMES*	97,504	GUILD, TOM	10,570	56,099	R	58.7%	37.3%	61.2%	38.8%
TOTAL	2016	1,133,244	781,691		305,222		46,331	476,469	R	69.0%	26.9%	71.9%	28.1%
TOTAL	2014	653,413	457,613		174,022		21,778	283,591	R	70.0%	26.6%	72.4%	27.6%
TOTAL	2012	1,325,935	856,872		410,324		58,739	446,548	R	64.6%	30.9%	67.6%	32.4%

Note: An asterisk (*) denotes incumbent.

OKLAHOMA

GENERAL AND PRIMARY ELECTIONS

2016 GENERAL ELECTIONS: OTHER VOTES

President Other vote was 83,481 Libertarian (Gary Johnson)

Senate Other vote was 43,421 Libertarian (Robert Murphy), 40,405 Independent (Sean Braddy), 27,418 Independent (Mark Beard)

House Other vote was:

CD 2 16,644 Independent (John McCarthy)
CD 4 12,574 Libertarian (Sevier White)
CD 5 17,113 Libertarian (Zachary Knight)

2016 PRIMARY ELECTIONS: SUPPLEMENTARY INFORMATION

Primary March 1, 2016 (President) June 28, 2016 (Congress)

Registration (as of June 30, 2016) 2,054,087

Republican 931,181
Democratic 839,482
Libertarian 823
Independent 282,601

Primary Runoff August 23, 2016

Primary Type Semi-Open—Only registered Democrats and Republicans could vote in their party's primary. Independent voters could vote in the Democratic primary.

OKLAHOMA

GENERAL AND PRIMARY ELECTIONS

	REPUBLICAN PRIMARIES			DEMOCRATIC PRIMARIES		
President	Cruz, Ted	158,078	34.4%	Sanders, Bernard	174,228	51.9%
	Trump, Donald J.	130,267	28.3%	Clinton, Hillary Rodham	139,443	41.5%
	Rubio, Marco	119,633	26.0%	O'Malley, Martin	7,672	2.3%
	Carson, Ben	28,601	6.2%	Judd, Keith	4,386	1.3%
	Kasich, John R.	16,524	3.6%	Steinberg, Michael Alan	4,171	1.2%
	Bush, Jeb	2,091	0.5%	Locke, Star	3,458	1.0%
	Paul, Rand	1,666	0.4%	De La Fuente, Roque "Rocky"	2,485	0.7%
	Huckabee, Mike	1,308	0.3%			
	Fiorina, Carly	610	0.1%			
	Christie, Chris	545	0.1%			
	Santorum, Rick	375	0.1%			
	Graham, Lindsey	224				
	TOTAL	459,922		TOTAL	335,843	
Senator	Lankford, James*	Unopposed		Workman, Mike	Unopposed	
Congressional District 1	Bridenstine, Jim*	50,595	80.8%			
	Atkinson, Tom	10,056	16.0%			
	Rogers, Evelyn L.	2,004	3.2%			
	TOTAL	62,655				
Congressional District 2	Mullin, Markwayne*	20,065	63.4%	Harris-Till, Joshua	31,681	60.0%
	Jackson, Jarrin	11,580	36.6%	Schiefelbein, Paul E.	21,152	40.0%
	TOTAL	31,645		TOTAL	52,833	
Congressional District 3	Lucas, Frank D.*	42,027	77.9%	Robbins, Frankie	Unopposed	
	Brown, Desiree	11,891	22.1%			
	TOTAL	53,918				
Congressional District 4	Cole, Tom*	28,813	71.4%	Owen, Christina	16,314	62.2%
	Taylor, James	7,398	18.3%	Smith, Bert	9,922	37.8%
	Roberts, Shawn M.	4,151	10.3%			
	TOTAL	40,362		TOTAL	26,236	
Congressional District 5	Russell, Steve D.*	27,436	80.3%	McAffrey, Al	10,013	36.8%
	Volpe, Frank	6,721	19.7%	Guild, Tom	10,000	36.8%
				Leonard, Leona	7,190	26.4%
	TOTAL	34,157		TOTAL	27,203	
				PRIMARY RUNOFF		
				McAffrey, Al	8,032	50.1%
				Guild, Tom	7,988	49.9%
				TOTAL	16,020	

Note: An asterisk (*) denotes incumbent. A runoff was triggered if the leading candidate received less than 50 percent of the primary vote.

OREGON

Congressional districts first established for elections held in 2012

5 members

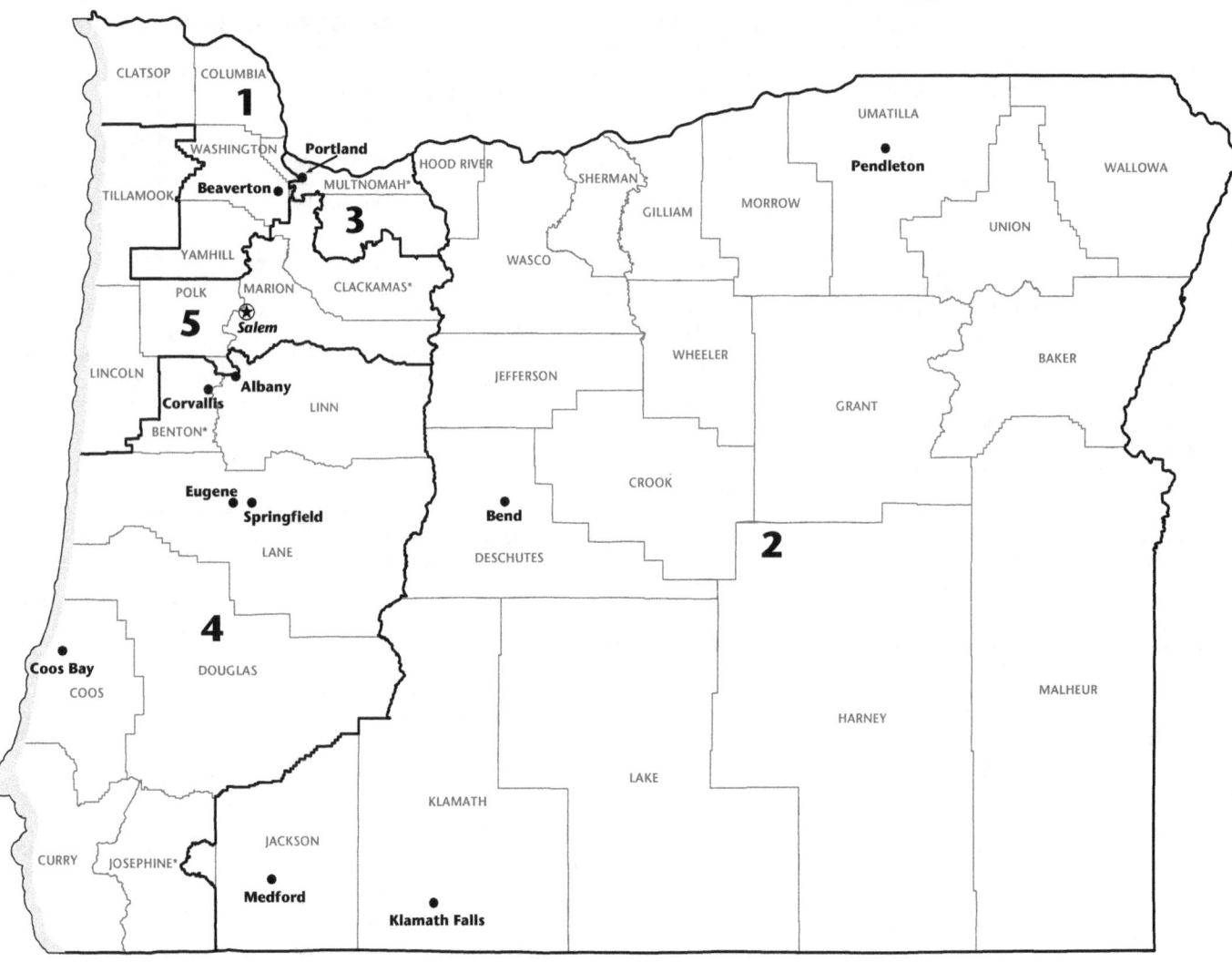

* Asterisk indicates a county whose boundaries include parts of two or more congressional districts.

OREGON

GOVERNOR
Kate Brown (D). Elected 2016, after having assumed the governorship to complete the remaining two years of the term vacated by the resignation February 18, 2015, of John Kitzhaber (D), who left office under an ethics cloud involving conflict of interest charges spawned by his fiancée.

SENATORS (2 Democrats)
Jeff Merkley (D). Re-elected 2014 to a six-year term. Previously elected 2008.

Ron Wyden (D). Re-elected 2016 to a six-year term. Previously elected 2010, 2004, 1998, and in a special election January 30, 1996, to serve the remaining three years of the term vacated when Senator Robert W. Packwood (R) resigned in October 1995.

REPRESENTATIVES (1 Republican, 4 Democrats)
1. Suzanne Bonamici (D)
2. Greg Walden (R)
3. Earl Blumenauer (D)
4. Peter A. DeFazio (D)
5. Kurt Schrader (D)

POSTWAR VOTE FOR PRESIDENT

		Republican		Democratic		Other Vote	Rep.-Dem. Plurality	Total Vote		Major Vote	
Year	Total Vote	Vote	Candidate	Vote	Candidate			Rep.	Dem.	Rep.	Dem.
2016**	2,001,336	782,403	Trump, Donald J.	1,002,106	Clinton, Hillary Rodham	216,827	219,703 D	39.1%	50.1%	43.8%	56.2%
2012	1,789,270	754,175	Romney, W. Mitt	970,488	Obama, Barack H.*	64,607	216,313 D	42.1%	54.2%	43.7%	56.3%
2008	1,827,864	738,475	McCain, John S. III	1,037,291	Obama, Barack H.	52,098	298,816 D	40.4%	56.7%	41.6%	58.4%
2004	1,836,782	866,831	Bush, George W.*	943,163	Kerry, John F.	26,788	76,332 D	47.2%	51.3%	47.9%	52.1%
2000**	1,533,968	713,577	Bush, George W.	720,342	Gore, Albert Jr.	100,049	6,765 D	46.5%	47.0%	49.8%	50.2%
1996**	1,377,760	538,152	Dole, Robert "Bob"	649,641	Clinton, Bill*	189,967	111,489 D	39.1%	47.2%	45.3%	54.7%
1992**	1,462,643	475,757	Bush, George H.*	621,314	Clinton, Bill	365,572	145,557 D	32.5%	42.5%	43.4%	56.6%
1988	1,201,694	560,126	Bush, George H.	616,206	Dukakis, Michael S.	25,362	56,080 D	46.6%	51.3%	47.6%	52.4%
1984	1,226,527	685,700	Reagan, Ronald*	536,479	Mondale, Walter F.	4,348	149,221 R	55.9%	43.7%	56.1%	43.9%
1980**	1,181,516	571,044	Reagan, Ronald	456,890	Carter, Jimmy*	153,582	114,154 R	48.3%	38.7%	55.6%	44.4%
1976	1,029,876	492,120	Ford, Gerald R.*	490,407	Carter, Jimmy	47,349	1,713 R	47.8%	47.6%	50.1%	49.9%
1972	927,946	486,686	Nixon, Richard M.*	392,760	McGovern, George S.	48,500	93,926 R	52.4%	42.3%	55.3%	44.7%
1968**	819,622	408,433	Nixon, Richard M.	358,866	Humphrey, Hubert Horatio Jr.	52,323	49,567 R	49.8%	43.8%	53.2%	46.8%
1964	786,305	282,779	Goldwater, Barry M. Sr.	501,017	Johnson, Lyndon B.*	2,509	218,238 D	36.0%	63.7%	36.1%	63.9%
1960	776,421	408,060	Nixon, Richard M.	367,402	Kennedy, John F.	959	40,658 R	52.6%	47.3%	52.6%	47.4%
1956	736,132	406,393	Eisenhower, Dwight D.*	329,204	Stevenson, Adlai E. II	535	77,189 R	55.2%	44.7%	55.2%	44.8%
1952	695,059	420,815	Eisenhower, Dwight D.	270,579	Stevenson, Adlai E. II	3,665	150,236 R	60.5%	38.9%	60.9%	39.1%
1948	524,080	260,904	Dewey, Thomas E.	243,147	Truman, Harry S.*	20,029	17,757 R	49.8%	46.4%	51.8%	48.2%

Note: An asterisk (*) denotes incumbent. **In past elections, the other vote included: 2016 - 94,231 Libertarian (Gary Johnson); 2000 - 77,357 Green (Ralph Nader); 1996 - 121,221 Reform (Ross Perot); 1992 - 354,091 Independent (Perot); 1980 - 112,389 Independent (John Anderson); 1968 - 49,683 American Independent (George Wallace).

OREGON

POSTWAR VOTE FOR GOVERNOR

Year	Total Vote	Republican Vote	Republican Candidate	Democratic Vote	Democratic Candidate	Other Vote	Rep.-Dem. Plurality		Percentage Total Vote Rep.	Total Vote Dem.	Major Vote Rep.	Major Vote Dem.
2016S**	1,944,807	844,372	Pierce, Bud	985,022	Brown, Kate*	115,413	140,650	D	43.4%	50.6%	46.2%	53.8%
2014	1,469,717	648,542	Richardson, Dennis	733,230	Kitzhaber, John*	87,945	84,688	D	44.1%	49.9%	46.9%	53.1%
2010	1,453,548	694,287	Dudley, Chris	716,525	Kitzhaber, John	42,736	22,238	D	47.8%	49.3%	49.2%	50.8%
2006	1,379,475	589,748	Saxton, Ron	699,786	Kulongoski, Ted*	89,941	110,038	D	42.8%	50.7%	45.7%	54.3%
2002	1,260,497	581,785	Mannix, Kevin L.	618,004	Kulongoski, Ted	60,708	36,219	D	46.2%	49.0%	48.5%	51.5%
1998	1,113,098	334,001	Sizemore, Bill	717,061	Kitzhaber, John*	62,036	383,060	D	30.0%	64.4%	31.8%	68.2%
1994	1,221,010	517,874	Smith, Denny	622,083	Kitzhaber, John	81,053	104,209	D	42.4%	50.9%	45.4%	54.6%
1990**	1,112,847	444,646	Frohnmayer, Dave	508,749	Roberts, Barbara	159,452	64,103	D	40.0%	45.7%	46.6%	53.4%
1986	1,059,630	506,986	Paulus, Norma	549,456	Goldschmidt, Neil	3,188	42,470	D	47.8%	51.9%	48.0%	52.0%
1982	1,042,009	639,841	Atiyeh, Victor*	374,316	Kulongoski, Ted	27,852	265,525	R	61.4%	35.9%	63.1%	36.9%
1978	911,143	498,452	Atiyeh, Victor	409,411	Straub, Robert W.*	3,280	89,041	D	54.7%	44.9%	54.9%	45.1%
1974	770,574	324,751	Atiyeh, Victor	444,812	Straub, Robert W.	1,011	120,061	D	42.1%	57.7%	42.2%	57.8%
1970	666,394	369,964	McCall, Tom*	293,892	Straub, Robert W.	2,538	76,072	R	55.5%	44.1%	55.7%	44.3%
1966	682,862	377,346	McCall, Tom	305,008	Straub, Robert W.	508	72,338	R	55.3%	44.7%	55.3%	44.7%
1962	637,407	345,497	Hatfield, Mark O.*	265,359	Thornton, Robert Y.	26,551	80,138	R	54.2%	41.6%	56.6%	43.4%
1958	599,994	331,900	Hatfield, Mark O.	267,934	Holmes, Robert D.*	160	63,966	R	55.3%	44.7%	55.3%	44.7%
1956S**	731,279	361,840	Smith, Elmo E.	369,439	Holmes, Robert D.		7,599	D	49.5%	50.5%	49.5%	50.5%
1954	566,701	322,522	Patterson, Paul	244,179	Carson, Joseph K. Jr.		78,343	R	56.9%	43.1%	56.9%	43.1%
1950	505,910	334,160	McKay, Douglas*	171,750	Flegal, Austin F.		162,410	R	66.1%	33.9%	66.1%	33.9%
1948S**	509,624	271,295	McKay, Douglas	226,949	Wallace, Lew	11,380	44,346	R	53.2%	44.5%	54.5%	45.5%
1946	344,155	237,681	Snell, Earl*	106,474	Donaugh, Carl C.		131,207	R	69.1%	30.9%	69.1%	30.9%

Note: An asterisk (*) denotes incumbent. **In past elections, the other vote included: 1990 - 144,062 Independent (Al Mobley). The 1948, 1956, and 2016 elections were for short terms to fill a vacancy.

POSTWAR VOTE FOR SENATOR

Year	Total Vote	Republican Vote	Republican Candidate	Democratic Vote	Democratic Candidate	Other Vote	Rep.-Dem. Plurality		Percentage Total Vote Rep.	Total Vote Dem.	Major Vote Rep.	Major Vote Dem.
2016	1,952,478	651,106	Callahan, Mark	1,105,119	Wyden, Ron*	196,253	454,013	D	33.3%	56.6%	37.1%	62.9%
2014	1,461,618	538,847	Wehby, Monica	814,537	Merkley, Jeff*	108,234	275,690	D	36.9%	55.7%	39.8%	60.2%
2010	1,442,588	566,199	Huffman, Jim	825,507	Wyden, Ron*	50,882	259,308	D	39.2%	57.2%	40.7%	59.3%
2008	1,767,504	805,159	Smith, Gordon H.*	864,392	Merkley, Jeff	97,953	59,233	D	45.6%	48.9%	48.2%	51.8%
2004	1,780,550	565,254	King, Al	1,128,728	Wyden, Ron*	86,568	563,474	D	31.7%	63.4%	33.4%	66.6%
2002	1,267,221	712,287	Smith, Gordon H.*	501,898	Bradbury, Bill	53,036	210,389	R	56.2%	39.6%	58.7%	41.3%
1998	1,117,747	377,739	Lim, John	682,425	Wyden, Ron*	57,583	304,686	D	33.8%	61.1%	35.6%	64.4%
1996	1,360,230	677,336	Smith, Gordon H.*	624,370	Bruggere, Tom	58,524	52,966	R	49.8%	45.9%	52.0%	48.0%
1996S**	1,196,608	553,519	Smith, Gordon H.	571,739	Wyden, Ron	71,350	18,220	D	46.3%	47.8%	49.2%	50.8%
1992	1,376,033	717,455	Packwood, Robert W.*	639,851	Aucoin, Les	18,727	77,604	R	52.1%	46.5%	52.9%	47.1%
1990	1,099,255	590,095	Hatfield, Mark O.*	507,743	Lonsdale, Harry	1,417	82,352	R	53.7%	46.2%	53.8%	46.2%
1986	1,042,555	656,317	Packwood, Robert W.*	375,735	Bauman, Rick	10,503	280,582	R	63.0%	36.0%	63.6%	36.4%
1984	1,214,735	808,152	Hatfield, Mark O.*	406,122	Hendriksen, Margie	461	402,030	R	66.5%	33.4%	66.6%	33.4%
1980	1,140,494	594,290	Packwood, Robert W.*	501,963	Kulongoski, Ted	44,241	92,327	R	52.1%	44.0%	54.2%	45.8%
1978	892,518	550,165	Hatfield, Mark O.*	341,616	Cook, Vernon	737	208,549	R	61.6%	38.3%	61.7%	38.3%
1974	766,414	420,984	Packwood, Robert W.*	338,591	Roberts, Betty	6,839	82,393	R	54.9%	44.2%	55.4%	44.6%
1972	920,833	494,671	Hatfield, Mark O.*	425,036	Morse, Wayne L.	1,126	69,635	R	53.7%	46.2%	53.8%	46.2%
1968	814,176	408,646	Packwood, Robert W.	405,353	Morse, Wayne L.*	177	3,293	R	50.2%	49.8%	50.2%	49.8%
1966	685,067	354,391	Hatfield, Mark O.	330,374	Duncan, Robert B.	302	24,017	R	51.7%	48.2%	51.8%	48.2%
1962	636,558	291,587	Unander, Sig	344,716	Morse, Wayne L.*	255	53,129	D	45.8%	54.2%	45.8%	54.2%
1960	755,875	343,009	Smith, Elmo E.	412,757	Neuberger, Maurine B.*	109	69,748	D	45.4%	54.6%	45.4%	54.6%
1956	732,254	335,405	McKay, Douglas	396,849	Morse, Wayne L.*		61,444	D	45.8%	54.2%	45.8%	54.2%
1954	569,088	283,313	Cordon, Guy*	285,775	Neuberger, Richard L.		2,462	D	49.8%	50.2%	49.8%	50.2%
1950	503,455	376,510	Morse, Wayne L.*	116,780	Latourette, Howard	10,165	259,730	R	74.8%	23.2%	76.3%	23.7%
1948	498,570	299,295	Cordon, Guy*	199,275	Wilson, Manley J.		100,020	R	60.0%	40.0%	60.0%	40.0%

Note: An asterisk (*) denotes incumbent. **The January 1996 election was for a short term to fill a vacancy.

OREGON

PRESIDENT 2016

2010 Census Population	County	Total Vote	Republican (Trump)	Democratic (Clinton)	Other	Rep.-Dem. Plurality		Percentage			
								Total Vote		Major Vote	
								Rep.	Dem.	Rep.	Dem.
16,134	BAKER	8,779	6,218	1,797	764	4,421	R	70.8%	20.5%	77.6%	22.4%
85,579	BENTON	48,753	13,445	29,193	6,115	15,748	D	27.6%	59.9%	31.5%	68.5%
375,992	CLACKAMAS	214,039	88,392	102,095	23,552	13,703	D	41.3%	47.7%	46.4%	53.6%
37,039	CLATSOP	19,664	8,138	9,252	2,274	1,114	D	41.4%	47.1%	46.8%	53.2%
49,351	COLUMBIA	26,618	13,217	10,167	3,234	3,050	R	49.7%	38.2%	56.5%	43.5%
63,043	COOS	31,313	17,865	10,448	3,000	7,417	R	57.1%	33.4%	63.1%	36.9%
20,978	CROOK	12,172	8,511	2,637	1,024	5,874	R	69.9%	21.7%	76.3%	23.7%
22,364	CURRY	12,611	7,212	4,300	1,099	2,912	R	57.2%	34.1%	62.6%	37.4%
157,733	DESCHUTES	98,557	45,692	42,444	10,421	3,248	R	46.4%	43.1%	51.8%	48.2%
107,667	DOUGLAS	53,521	34,582	14,096	4,843	20,486	R	64.6%	26.3%	71.0%	29.0%
1,871	GILLIAM	1,019	671	239	109	432	R	65.8%	23.5%	73.7%	26.3%
7,445	GRANT	4,340	3,210	739	391	2,471	R	74.0%	17.0%	81.3%	18.7%
7,422	HARNEY	3,974	2,912	683	379	2,229	R	73.3%	17.2%	81.0%	19.0%
22,346	HOOD RIVER	10,910	3,272	6,510	1,128	3,238	D	30.0%	59.7%	33.4%	66.6%
203,206	JACKSON	109,327	53,870	44,447	11,010	9,423	R	49.3%	40.7%	54.8%	45.2%
21,720	JEFFERSON	9,459	5,483	2,980	996	2,503	R	58.0%	31.5%	64.8%	35.2%
82,713	JOSEPHINE	44,560	26,923	13,453	4,184	13,470	R	60.4%	30.2%	66.7%	33.3%
66,380	KLAMATH	30,507	20,435	7,210	2,862	13,225	R	67.0%	23.6%	73.9%	26.1%
7,895	LAKE	3,930	3,022	639	269	2,383	R	76.9%	16.3%	82.5%	17.5%
351,715	LANE	191,950	67,141	102,753	22,056	35,612	D	35.0%	53.5%	39.5%	60.5%
46,034	LINCOLN	25,256	10,039	12,501	2,716	2,462	D	39.7%	49.5%	44.5%	55.5%
116,672	LINN	58,719	33,488	17,995	7,236	15,493	R	57.0%	30.6%	65.0%	35.0%
31,313	MALHEUR	10,435	7,194	2,246	995	4,948	R	68.9%	21.5%	76.2%	23.8%
315,335	MARION	136,840	63,377	57,788	15,675	5,589	R	46.3%	42.2%	52.3%	47.7%
11,173	MORROW	4,167	2,721	1,017	429	1,704	R	65.3%	24.4%	72.8%	27.2%
735,334	MULTNOMAH	399,103	67,954	292,561	38,588	224,607	D	17.0%	73.3%	18.8%	81.2%
75,403	POLK	40,295	18,940	16,420	4,935	2,520	R	47.0%	40.7%	53.6%	46.4%
1,765	SHERMAN	1,017	732	202	83	530	R	72.0%	19.9%	78.4%	21.6%
25,250	TILLAMOOK	13,803	6,538	5,768	1,497	770	R	47.4%	41.8%	53.1%	46.9%
75,889	UMATILLA	27,597	17,059	7,673	2,865	9,386	R	61.8%	27.8%	69.0%	31.0%
25,748	UNION	12,968	8,431	3,249	1,288	5,182	R	65.0%	25.1%	72.2%	27.8%
7,008	WALLOWA	4,366	2,848	1,116	402	1,732	R	65.2%	25.6%	71.8%	28.2%
25,213	WASCO	11,964	5,833	4,781	1,350	1,052	R	48.8%	40.0%	55.0%	45.0%
529,710	WASHINGTON	269,232	83,197	153,251	32,784	70,054	D	30.9%	56.9%	35.2%	64.8%
1,441	WHEELER	818	591	155	72	436	R	72.2%	18.9%	79.2%	20.8%
99,193	YAMHILL	48,753	23,250	19,301	6,202	3,949	R	47.7%	39.6%	54.6%	45.4%
3,831,074	TOTAL	2,001,336	782,403	1,002,106	216,827	219,703	D	39.1%	50.1%	43.8%	56.2%

OREGON

GOVERNOR 2016

2010 Census Population	County	Total Vote	Republican (Pierce)	Democratic (Brown)	Other	Rep.-Dem. Plurality		Percentage			
								Total Vote		Major Vote	
								Rep.	Dem.	Rep.	Dem.
16,134	BAKER	8,691	6,069	2,047	575	4,022	R	69.8%	23.6%	74.8%	25.2%
85,579	BENTON	47,308	16,543	28,043	2,722	11,500	D	35.0%	59.3%	37.1%	62.9%
375,992	CLACKAMAS	208,647	100,882	96,735	11,030	4,147	R	48.4%	46.4%	51.0%	49.0%
37,039	CLATSOP	19,198	8,425	9,667	1,106	1,242	D	43.9%	50.4%	46.6%	53.4%
49,351	COLUMBIA	25,993	12,925	11,020	2,048	1,905	R	49.7%	42.4%	54.0%	46.0%
63,043	COOS	30,719	16,889	11,500	2,330	5,389	R	55.0%	37.4%	59.5%	40.5%
20,978	CROOK	12,040	8,232	2,990	818	5,242	R	68.4%	24.8%	73.4%	26.6%
22,364	CURRY	12,251	6,410	4,947	894	1,463	R	52.3%	40.4%	56.4%	43.6%
157,733	DESCHUTES	95,980	47,824	42,298	5,858	5,526	R	49.8%	44.1%	53.1%	46.9%
107,667	DOUGLAS	52,643	32,647	15,878	4,118	16,769	R	62.0%	30.2%	67.3%	32.7%

OREGON

GOVERNOR 2016

2010 Census Population	County	Total Vote	Republican (Pierce)	Democratic (Brown)	Other	Rep.-Dem. Plurality		Percentage			
								Total Vote		Major Vote	
								Rep.	Dem.	Rep.	Dem.
1,871	GILLIAM	1,027	694	277	56	417	R	67.6%	27.0%	71.5%	28.5%
7,445	GRANT	4,271	3,093	904	274	2,189	R	72.4%	21.2%	77.4%	22.6%
7,422	HARNEY	3,944	2,770	886	288	1,884	R	70.2%	22.5%	75.8%	24.2%
22,346	HOOD RIVER	10,679	3,672	6,441	566	2,769	D	34.4%	60.3%	36.3%	63.7%
203,206	JACKSON	105,973	52,259	46,803	6,911	5,456	R	49.3%	44.2%	52.8%	47.2%
21,720	JEFFERSON	9,294	5,484	3,169	641	2,315	R	59.0%	34.1%	63.4%	36.6%
82,713	JOSEPHINE	43,396	24,078	15,139	4,179	8,939	R	55.5%	34.9%	61.4%	38.6%
66,380	KLAMATH	29,971	19,211	8,420	2,340	10,791	R	64.1%	28.1%	69.5%	30.5%
7,895	LAKE	3,860	2,794	762	304	2,032	R	72.4%	19.7%	78.6%	21.4%
351,715	LANE	186,651	72,208	103,226	11,217	31,018	D	38.7%	55.3%	41.2%	58.8%
46,034	LINCOLN	24,868	10,084	13,212	1,572	3,128	D	40.6%	53.1%	43.3%	56.7%
116,672	LINN	57,599	34,539	19,156	3,904	15,383	R	60.0%	33.3%	64.3%	35.7%
31,313	MALHEUR	10,213	6,966	2,436	811	4,530	R	68.2%	23.9%	74.1%	25.9%
315,335	MARION	134,908	72,752	55,748	6,408	17,004	R	53.9%	41.3%	56.6%	43.4%
11,173	MORROW	4,130	2,682	1,152	296	1,530	R	64.9%	27.9%	70.0%	30.0%
735,334	MULTNOMAH	382,942	84,139	279,210	19,593	195,071	D	22.0%	72.9%	23.2%	76.8%
75,403	POLK	39,764	21,847	15,960	1,957	5,887	R	54.9%	40.1%	57.8%	42.2%
1,765	SHERMAN	993	721	234	38	487	R	72.6%	23.6%	75.5%	24.5%
25,250	TILLAMOOK	13,540	6,599	6,152	789	447	R	48.7%	45.4%	51.8%	48.2%
75,889	UMATILLA	26,841	16,269	8,541	2,031	7,728	R	60.6%	31.8%	65.6%	34.4%
25,748	UNION	12,754	8,561	3,410	783	5,151	R	67.1%	26.7%	71.5%	28.5%
7,008	WALLOWA	4,311	2,837	1,253	221	1,584	R	65.8%	29.1%	69.4%	30.6%
25,213	WASCO	11,694	5,874	5,057	763	817	R	50.2%	43.2%	53.7%	46.3%
529,710	WASHINGTON	260,547	102,282	143,278	14,987	40,996	D	39.3%	55.0%	41.7%	58.3%
1,441	WHEELER	820	575	194	51	381	R	70.1%	23.7%	74.8%	25.2%
99,193	YAMHILL	47,586	25,773	18,882	2,931	6,891	R	54.2%	39.7%	57.7%	42.3%
3,831,074	TOTAL	1,946,046	845,609	985,027	115,410	139,418	D	43.5%	50.6%	46.2%	53.8%

OREGON

SENATOR 2016

2010 Census Population	County	Total Vote	Republican (Callahan)	Democratic (Wyden)	Other	Rep.-Dem. Plurality		Percentage			
								Total Vote		Major Vote	
								Rep.	Dem.	Rep.	Dem.
16,134	BAKER	8,679	4,654	3,348	677	1,306	R	53.6%	38.6%	58.2%	41.8%
85,579	BENTON	47,597	12,998	29,007	5,592	16,009	D	27.3%	60.9%	30.9%	69.1%
375,992	CLACKAMAS	209,173	78,099	113,152	17,922	35,053	D	37.3%	54.1%	40.8%	59.2%
37,039	CLATSOP	19,273	6,201	11,143	1,929	4,942	D	32.2%	57.8%	35.8%	64.2%
49,351	COLUMBIA	26,109	10,123	13,064	2,922	2,941	D	38.8%	50.0%	43.7%	56.3%
63,043	COOS	30,759	14,086	13,468	3,205	618	R	45.8%	43.8%	51.1%	48.9%
20,978	CROOK	11,997	6,254	4,840	903	1,414	R	52.1%	40.3%	56.4%	43.6%
22,364	CURRY	12,297	5,633	5,395	1,269	238	R	45.8%	43.9%	51.1%	48.9%
157,733	DESCHUTES	96,489	36,041	52,098	8,350	16,057	D	37.4%	54.0%	40.9%	59.1%
107,667	DOUGLAS	52,404	27,634	19,832	4,938	7,802	R	52.7%	37.8%	58.2%	41.8%
1,871	GILLIAM	1,019	442	507	70	65	D	43.4%	49.8%	46.6%	53.4%
7,445	GRANT	4,239	2,277	1,631	331	646	R	53.7%	38.5%	58.3%	41.7%
7,422	HARNEY	3,914	2,070	1,540	304	530	R	52.9%	39.3%	57.3%	42.7%
22,346	HOOD RIVER	10,729	2,646	6,967	1,116	4,321	D	24.7%	64.9%	27.5%	72.5%
203,206	JACKSON	106,468	42,336	53,474	10,658	11,138	D	39.8%	50.2%	44.2%	55.8%

OREGON

SENATOR 2016

2010 Census Population	County	Total Vote	Republican (Callahan)	Democratic (Wyden)	Other	Rep.-Dem. Plurality	Percentage			
							Total Vote		Major Vote	
							Rep.	Dem.	Rep.	Dem.
21,720	JEFFERSON	9,319	3,967	4,517	835	550 D	42.6%	48.5%	46.8%	53.2%
82,713	JOSEPHINE	43,510	20,767	18,463	4,280	2,304 R	47.7%	42.4%	52.9%	47.1%
66,380	KLAMATH	29,999	14,808	12,342	2,849	2,466 R	49.4%	41.1%	54.5%	45.5%
7,895	LAKE	3,868	2,227	1,363	278	864 R	57.6%	35.2%	62.0%	38.0%
351,715	LANE	187,296	56,716	110,836	19,744	54,120 D	30.3%	59.2%	33.8%	66.2%
46,034	LINCOLN	24,925	7,725	14,512	2,688	6,787 D	31.0%	58.2%	34.7%	65.3%
116,672	LINN	57,146	26,991	23,908	6,247	3,083 R	47.2%	41.8%	53.0%	47.0%
31,313	MALHEUR	10,188	6,045	3,082	1,061	2,963 R	59.3%	30.3%	66.2%	33.8%
315,335	MARION	133,827	55,351	66,269	12,207	10,918 D	41.4%	49.5%	45.5%	54.5%
11,173	MORROW	4,127	1,978	1,719	430	259 R	47.9%	41.7%	53.5%	46.5%
735,334	MULTNOMAH	386,684	56,395	285,058	45,231	228,663 D	14.6%	73.7%	16.5%	83.5%
75,403	POLK	39,565	16,693	19,250	3,622	2,557 D	42.2%	48.7%	46.4%	53.6%
1,765	SHERMAN	999	498	440	61	58 R	49.8%	44.0%	53.1%	46.9%
25,250	TILLAMOOK	13,563	5,100	7,187	1,276	2,087 D	37.6%	53.0%	41.5%	58.5%
75,889	UMATILLA	26,905	12,899	11,279	2,727	1,620 R	47.9%	41.9%	53.4%	46.6%
25,748	UNION	12,721	6,372	5,302	1,047	1,070 R	50.1%	41.7%	54.6%	45.4%
7,008	WALLOWA	4,308	2,238	1,767	303	471 R	51.9%	41.0%	55.9%	44.1%
25,213	WASCO	11,740	4,124	6,512	1,104	2,388 D	35.1%	55.5%	38.8%	61.2%
529,710	WASHINGTON	262,243	78,184	158,685	25,374	80,501 D	29.8%	60.5%	33.0%	67.0%
1,441	WHEELER	803	384	355	64	29 R	47.8%	44.2%	52.0%	48.0%
99,193	YAMHILL	47,596	20,150	22,807	4,639	2,657 D	42.3%	47.9%	46.9%	53.1%
3,831,074	TOTAL	1,952,478	651,106	1,105,119	196,253	454,013 D	33.3%	56.6%	37.1%	62.9%

OREGON

HOUSE OF REPRESENTATIVES

CD	Year	Total Vote	Republican		Democratic		Other Vote	Rep.-Dem. Plurality	Percentage			
			Vote	Candidate	Vote	Candidate			Total Vote		Major Vote	
									Rep.	Dem.	Rep.	Dem.
1	2016	378,095	139,756	HEINRICH, BRIAN J.	225,391	BONAMICI, SUZANNE*	12,948	85,635 D	37.0%	59.6%	38.3%	61.7%
1	2014	279,253	96,245	YATES, JASON	160,038	BONAMICI, SUZANNE*	22,970	63,793 D	34.5%	57.3%	37.6%	62.4%
1	2012	331,980	109,699	MORGAN, DELINDA	197,845	BONAMICI, SUZANNE*	24,436	88,146 D	33.0%	59.6%	35.7%	64.3%
2	2016	380,739	272,952	WALDEN, GREG*	106,640	CRARY, JAMES "JIM"	1,147	166,312 R	71.7%	28.0%	71.9%	28.1%
2	2014	287,425	202,374	WALDEN, GREG*	73,785	CHRISTOFFERSON, AELEA	11,266	128,589 R	70.4%	25.7%	73.3%	26.7%
2	2012	332,255	228,043	WALDEN, GREG*	96,741	SEGERS, JOYCE B.	7,471	131,302 R	68.6%	29.1%	70.2%	29.8%
3	2016	382,355			274,687	BLUMENAUER, EARL*	107,668	274,687 D		71.8%		100.0%
3	2014	292,757	57,424	BUCHAL, JAMES	211,748	BLUMENAUER, EARL*	23,585	154,324 D	19.6%	72.3%	21.3%	78.7%
3	2012	355,875	70,325	GREEN, RONALD	264,979	BLUMENAUER, EARL*	20,571	194,654 D	19.8%	74.5%	21.0%	79.0%
4	2016	397,568	157,743	ROBINSON, ART	220,628	DEFAZIO, PETER A.*	19,197	62,885 D	39.7%	55.5%	41.7%	58.3%
4	2014	310,179	116,534	ROBINSON, ART	181,624	DEFAZIO, PETER A.*	12,021	65,090 D	37.6%	58.6%	39.1%	60.9%
4	2012	360,088	140,549	ROBINSON, ART	212,866	DEFAZIO, PETER A.*	6,673	72,317 D	39.0%	59.1%	39.8%	60.2%
5	2016	373,108	160,443	WILLIS, COLM	199,505	SCHRADER, KURT*	13,160	39,062 D	43.0%	53.5%	44.6%	55.4%
5	2014	281,088	110,332	SMITH, TOOTIE	150,944	SCHRADER, KURT*	19,812	40,612 D	39.3%	53.7%	42.2%	57.8%
5	2012	327,970	139,223	THOMPSON, FRED	177,229	SCHRADER, KURT*	11,518	38,006 D	42.4%	54.0%	44.0%	56.0%
TOTAL	2016	1,911,865	730,894		1,026,851		154,120	295,957 D	38.2%	53.7%	41.6%	58.4%
TOTAL	2014	1,450,702	582,909		778,139		89,654	195,230 D	40.2%	53.6%	42.8%	57.2%
TOTAL	2012	1,708,168	687,839		949,660		70,669	261,821 D	40.3%	55.6%	42.0%	58.0%

Note: An asterisk (*) denotes incumbent.

OREGON

GENERAL AND PRIMARY ELECTIONS

2016 GENERAL ELECTIONS: OTHER VOTES

President   Other vote was 94,231 Libertarian (Gary Johnson), 72,594 Write-in (Scattered Write-in), 50,002 Green (Jill Stein)

Governor   Other vote was 47,481 Independent Party of Oregon (Cliff Thomason), 45,191 Libertarian (James Foster), 19,400 Constitution (Donald Auer), 3,338 Write-in (Scattered Write-in)

Senate   Other vote was 61,915 Working Families (Shanti Lewallen), 59,516 Independent (Steven Reynolds), 48,823 Progressive (Eric Navickas), 23,941 Libertarian (James Lindsay), 2,058 Write-in (Scattered Write-in)

House   Other vote was:

CD 1   12,257 Libertarian (Sheahan Kyle), 691 Write-in (Scattered Write-in)
CD 2   1,147 Write-in (Scattered Write-in)
CD 3   78,154 Independent (David Walker), 27,978 Progressive (Delk David), 1,536 Write-in (Scattered Write-in)
CD 4   12,194 Pacific Green (Michael Beilstein), 6,527 Libertarian (Gil Guthrie), 476 Write-in (Scattered Write-in)
CD 5   12,542 Pacific Green (Marvin Sandnes), 618 Write-in (Scattered Write-in)

2016 PRIMARY ELECTIONS: SUPPLEMENTARY INFORMATION

Primary May 17, 2016   **Registration** (as of April 30, 2016)   2,298,420

Democratic	956,300
Republican	688,133
Independent Party	104,555
Libertarian	15,780
Working Families	9,738
Pacific Green	6,569
Constitution	3,463
Progressive	1,348
Americans Elect	496
Other	18,450
Non-Affiliated	493,588

Primary Type   Closed—Only registered Democrats and Republicans could vote in their party's primary.

	REPUBLICAN PRIMARIES			DEMOCRATIC PRIMARIES		
President	Trump, Donald J.	252,748	64.2%	Sanders, Bernard	360,829	56.2%
	Cruz, Ted	65,513	16.6%	Clinton, Hillary Rodham	269,846	42.1%
	Kasich, John R.	62,248	15.8%	Write-In	10,920	1.7%
	Write-In	13,411	3.4%			
	TOTAL	393,920		TOTAL	641,595	
Senator	Callahan, Mark	123,473	38.2%	Wyden, Ron*	501,903	83.2%
	Carpenter, Sam	104,494	32.4%	Stine, Kevin H.	78,287	13.0%
	Stewart, Faye	57,399	17.8%	Weaver, Paul	20,346	3.4%
	Laschober, Dan	34,157	10.6%	Write-In	2,740	0.5%
	Write-In	3,357	1.0%			
	TOTAL	322,880		TOTAL	603,276	
Governor	Pierce, Bud	171,158	47.7%	Brown, Kate*	494,890	83.0%
	Alley, Allen	103,388	28.8%	Bell, Julian	49,313	8.3%
	Cuff, Bruce A.	41,598	11.6%	Stauffer, Dave	16,108	2.7%
	Niemeyer, Bob	35,669	9.9%	Johnson, Steve	13,363	2.2%
	Forthan, Bob Leonard	4,290	1.2%	Forsythe, Kevin M.	10,147	1.7%
	Write-In	3,020	0.8%	Write-In	6,595	1.1%
				Chance, Chet	5,636	0.9%
	TOTAL	359,123		TOTAL	596,052	

OREGON

GENERAL AND PRIMARY ELECTIONS

	REPUBLICAN PRIMARIES			DEMOCRATIC PRIMARIES		
Congressional District 1	Heinrich, Brian J.	19,290	48.4%	Bonamici, Suzanne*	99,153	89.7%
	Delgado Morgan, Delinda	10,640	26.7%	Woodley, Shabba	10,961	9.9%
	Burgess, Jonathan E.	9,127	22.9%	Write-In	375	0.3%
	Write-In	768	1.9%			
	TOTAL	*39,825*		*TOTAL*	*110,489*	
Congressional District 2	Walden, Greg*	85,039	79.9%	Crary, James "Jim"	53,484	97.6%
	Romero, Paul J. Jr.	21,099	19.8%	Write-In	1,295	2.4%
	Write-In	238	0.2%			
	TOTAL	*106,376*		*TOTAL*	*54,779*	
Congressional District 3	Write-In,	2,160	90.9%	Blumenauer, Earl*	144,706	98.3%
	Walker, David (Write-in)	217	9.1%	Write-In	2,511	1.7%
	TOTAL	*2,377*		*TOTAL*	*147,217*	
Congressional District 4	Robinson, Art	55,557	67.3%	DeFazio, Peter A.*	113,816	91.6%
	Perkins, Jo Rae	26,375	31.9%	McKinney, Joseph	9,894	8.0%
	Write-In	620	0.8%	Write-In	601	0.5%
	TOTAL	*82,552*		*TOTAL*	*124,311*	
Congressional District 5	Willis, Colm	40,568	57.6%	Schrader, Kurt*	72,634	71.7%
	West, Ben	14,696	20.8%	McTeague, Dave	28,184	27.8%
	Allan, Seth	10,779	15.3%	Write-In	549	0.5%
	Rainey, Earl D.	3,783	5.4%			
	Write-In	665	0.9%			
	TOTAL	*70,491*		*TOTAL*	*101,367*	

Note: An asterisk (*) denotes incumbent. No Republican candidate filed to run in the CD 3 elections. All votes in that district were write-ins.

PENNSYLVANIA

Congressional districts first established for elections held in 2012

18 members

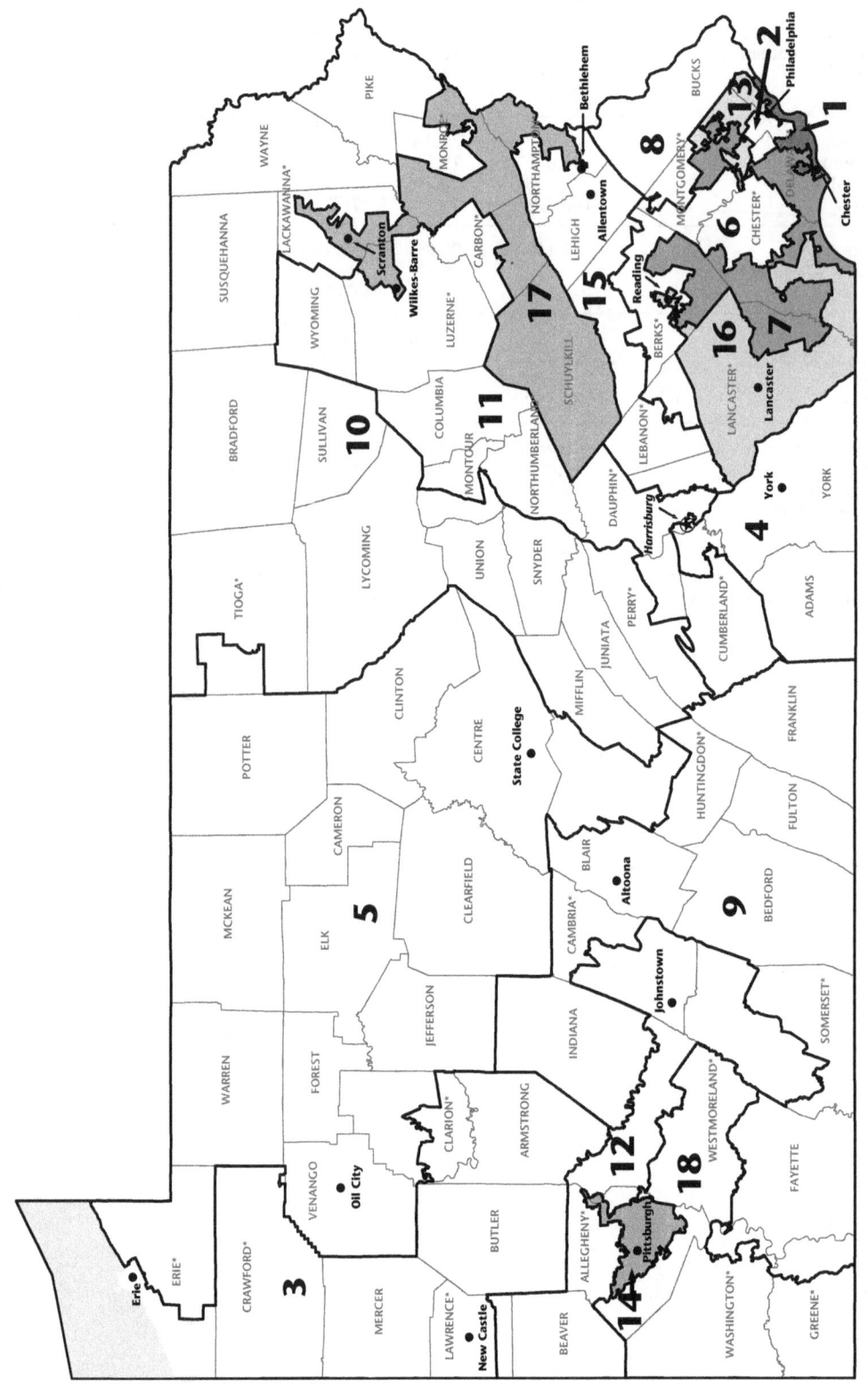

The city of Philadelphia is coextensive with the county of Philadelphia.

* Asterisk indicates a county whose boundaries include parts of two or more congressional districts.

PENNSYLVANIA
Greater Pittsburgh Area

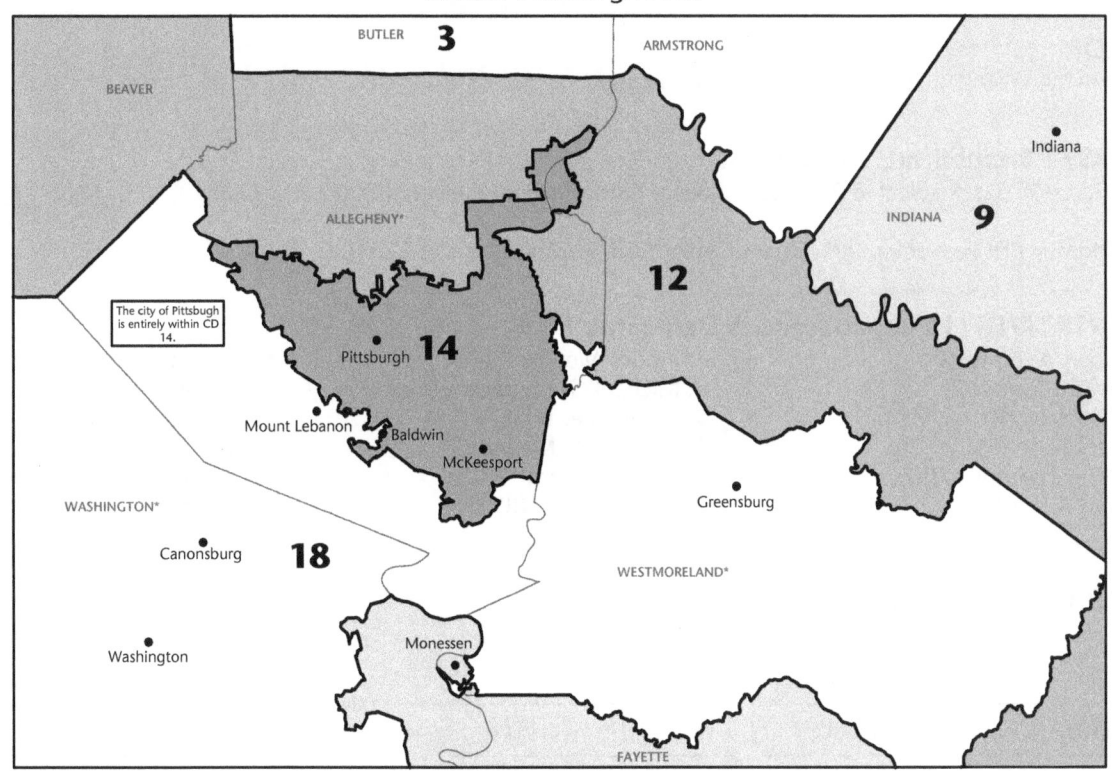

Greater Philadelphia Area

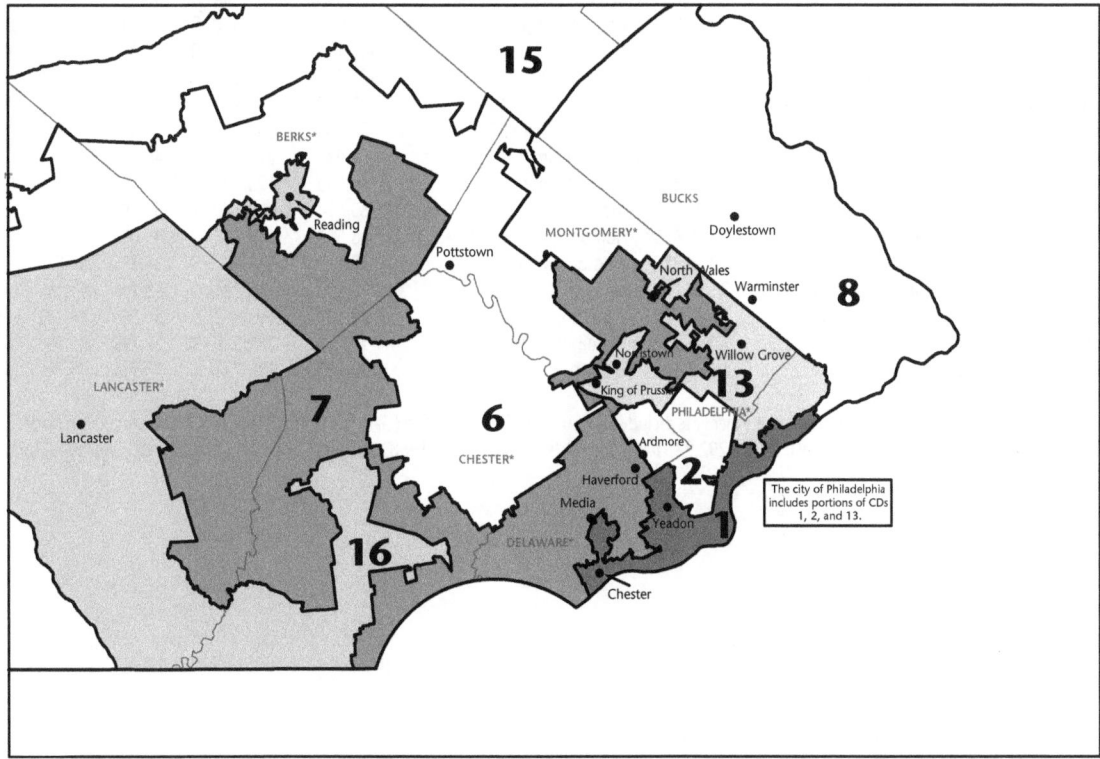

* Asterisk indicates a county whose boundaries include parts of two or more congressional districts.

PENNSYLVANIA

GOVERNOR
Thomas W. Wolf (D). Elected 2014 to a four-year term.

SENATORS (1 Republican, 1 Democrat)
Bob Casey Jr. (D). Re-elected 2012 to a six-year term. Previously elected 2006.

Pat Toomey (R). Re-elected 2016 to a six-year term. Previously elected 2010.

REPRESENTATIVES (13 Republicans, 5 Democrats)

1. Robert A. Brady (D)
2. Dwight Evans (D)
3. Mike Kelly (R)
4. Scott Perry (R)
5. Glenn Thompson (R)
6. Ryan A. Costello (R)
7. Patrick Meehan (R)
8. Michael G. Fitzpatrick (R)
9. Bill Shuster (R)
10. Thomas A. Marino (R)
11. Lou Barletta (R)
12. Keith Rothfus (R)
13. Brendan F. Boyle (D)
14. Mike Doyle (D)
15. Charlie W. Dent (R)
16. Lloyd K. Smucker (R)
17. Matt Cartwright (D)
18. Timothy Murphy (R)

POSTWAR VOTE FOR PRESIDENT

		Republican		Democratic		Other Vote	Rep.-Dem. Plurality	Percentage			
								Total Vote		Major Vote	
Year	Total Vote	Vote	Candidate	Vote	Candidate			Rep.	Dem.	Rep.	Dem.
2016**	6,165,478	2,970,733	Trump, Donald J.	2,926,441	Clinton, Hillary Rodham	268,304	44,292 R	48.2%	47.5%	50.4%	49.6%
2012	5,753,670	2,680,434	Romney, W. Mitt	2,990,274	Obama, Barack H.*	82,962	309,840 D	46.6%	52.0%	47.3%	52.7%
2008	6,013,272	2,655,885	McCain, John S. III	3,276,363	Obama, Barack H.	81,024	620,478 D	44.2%	54.5%	44.8%	55.2%
2004	5,769,590	2,793,847	Bush, George W.*	2,938,095	Kerry, John F.	37,648	144,248 D	48.4%	50.9%	48.7%	51.3%
2000**	4,913,119	2,281,127	Bush, George W.	2,485,967	Gore, Albert Jr.	146,025	204,840 D	46.4%	50.6%	47.9%	52.1%
1996**	4,506,118	1,801,169	Dole, Robert "Bob"	2,215,819	Clinton, Bill*	489,130	414,650 D	40.0%	49.2%	44.8%	55.2%
1992**	4,959,810	1,791,841	Bush, George H.*	2,239,164	Clinton, Bill	928,805	447,323 D	36.1%	45.1%	44.5%	55.5%
1988	4,536,251	2,300,087	Bush, George H.	2,194,944	Dukakis, Michael S.	41,220	105,143 R	50.7%	48.4%	51.2%	48.8%
1984	4,844,903	2,584,323	Reagan, Ronald*	2,228,131	Mondale, Walter F.	32,449	356,192 R	53.3%	46.0%	53.7%	46.3%
1980**	4,561,501	2,261,872	Reagan, Ronald	1,937,540	Carter, Jimmy*	362,089	324,332 R	49.6%	42.5%	53.9%	46.1%
1976	4,620,787	2,205,604	Ford, Gerald R.*	2,328,677	Carter, Jimmy	86,506	123,073 D	47.7%	50.4%	48.6%	51.4%
1972	4,592,106	2,714,521	Nixon, Richard M.*	1,796,951	McGovern, George S.	80,634	917,570 R	59.1%	39.1%	60.2%	39.8%
1968**	4,747,928	2,090,017	Nixon, Richard M.	2,259,405	Humphrey, Hubert Horatio Jr.	398,506	169,388 D	44.0%	47.6%	48.1%	51.9%
1964	4,822,690	1,673,657	Goldwater, Barry M. Sr.	3,130,954	Johnson, Lyndon B.*	18,079	1,457,297 D	34.7%	64.9%	34.8%	65.2%
1960	5,006,541	2,439,956	Nixon, Richard M.	2,556,282	Kennedy, John F.	10,303	116,326 D	48.7%	51.1%	48.8%	51.2%
1956	4,576,503	2,585,252	Eisenhower, Dwight D.*	1,981,769	Stevenson, Adlai E. II	9,482	603,483 R	56.5%	43.3%	56.6%	43.4%
1952	4,580,969	2,415,789	Eisenhower, Dwight D.	2,146,269	Stevenson, Adlai E. II	18,911	269,520 R	52.7%	46.9%	53.0%	47.0%
1948	3,735,348	1,902,197	Dewey, Thomas E.	1,752,426	Truman, Harry S.*	80,725	149,771 R	50.9%	46.9%	52.0%	48.0%

Note: An asterisk (*) denotes incumbent. **In past elections, the other vote included: 2016 - 146,715 Libertarian (Gary Johnson); 2000 - 103,392 Green (Ralph Nader); 1996 - 430,984 Reform (Ross Perot); 1992 - 902,667 Independent (Perot); 1980 - 292,921 Independent (John Anderson); 1968 - 378,582 American Independent (George Wallace).

PENNSYLVANIA

POSTWAR VOTE FOR GOVERNOR

Year	Total Vote	Republican Vote	Republican Candidate	Democratic Vote	Democratic Candidate	Other Vote	Rep.-Dem. Plurality	Total Vote Rep.	Total Vote Dem.	Major Vote Rep.	Major Vote Dem.
2014	3,495,866	1,575,511	Corbett, Tom*	1,920,355	Wolf, Thomas W.		344,844 D	45.1%	54.9%	45.1%	54.9%
2010	3,989,102	2,172,763	Corbett, Tom	1,814,788	Onorato, Dan	1,551	357,975 R	54.5%	45.5%	54.5%	45.5%
2006	4,096,077	1,622,135	Swann, Lynn	2,470,517	Rendell, Edward G.*	3,425	848,382 D	39.6%	60.3%	39.6%	60.4%
2002	3,583,179	1,589,408	Fisher, Mike	1,913,235	Rendell, Edward G.	80,536	323,827 D	44.4%	53.4%	45.4%	54.6%
1998**	3,025,152	1,736,844	Ridge, Thomas J.*	938,745	Itkin, Ivan	349,563	798,099 R	57.4%	31.0%	64.9%	35.1%
1994**	3,588,526	1,627,976	Ridge, Thomas J.	1,433,099	Singel, Mark S.	527,451	194,877 R	45.4%	39.9%	53.2%	46.8%
1990	3,052,760	987,516	Hafer, Barbara	2,065,244	Casey, Robert*		1,077,728 D	32.3%	67.7%	32.3%	67.7%
1986	3,388,275	1,638,268	Scranton, William W.	1,717,484	Casey, Robert	32,523	79,216 D	48.4%	50.7%	48.8%	51.2%
1982	3,683,985	1,872,784	Thornburgh, Richard*	1,772,353	Ertel, Allen E.	38,848	100,431 R	50.8%	48.1%	51.4%	48.6%
1978	3,741,969	1,966,042	Thornburgh, Richard	1,737,888	Flaherty, Peter	38,039	228,154 R	52.5%	46.4%	53.1%	46.9%
1974	3,491,234	1,578,917	Lewis, Andrew L.	1,878,252	Shapp, Milton J.*	34,065	299,335 D	45.2%	53.8%	45.7%	54.3%
1970	3,700,060	1,542,854	Broderick, Raymond	2,043,029	Shapp, Milton J.*	114,177	500,175 D	41.7%	55.2%	43.0%	57.0%
1966	4,050,668	2,110,349	Shafer, Raymond P.	1,868,719	Shapp, Milton J.	71,600	241,630 R	52.1%	46.1%	53.0%	47.0%
1962	4,378,042	2,424,918	Scranton, William W.	1,938,627	Dilworth, Richardson	14,497	486,291 R	55.4%	44.3%	55.6%	44.4%
1958	3,986,918	1,948,769	McGonigle, Arthur T.	2,024,852	Lawrence, David L.	13,297	76,083 D	48.9%	50.8%	49.0%	51.0%
1954	3,720,457	1,717,070	Wood, Lloyd H.	1,996,266	Leader, George M.	7,121	279,196 D	46.2%	53.7%	46.2%	53.8%
1950	3,540,059	1,796,119	Fine, John S.	1,710,355	Dilworth, Richardson	33,585	85,764 R	50.7%	48.3%	51.2%	48.8%
1946	3,123,994	1,828,462	Duff, James H.	1,270,947	Rice, John S.	24,585	557,515 R	58.5%	40.7%	59.0%	41.0%

Note: An asterisk (*) denotes incumbent. **In past elections, the other vote included: 1998 - 315,761 Constitutional (Peg Luksik); 1994 - 460,269 Constitutional (Luksik).

POSTWAR VOTE FOR SENATOR

Year	Total Vote	Republican Vote	Republican Candidate	Democratic Vote	Democratic Candidate	Other Vote	Rep.-Dem. Plurality	Total Vote Rep.	Total Vote Dem.	Major Vote Rep.	Major Vote Dem.
2016	6,051,856	2,951,702	Toomey, Pat*	2,865,012	McGinty, Katie A.	235,142	86,690 R	48.8%	47.3%	50.7%	49.3%
2012	5,629,491	2,509,132	Smith, Tom	3,021,364	Casey, Bob Jr.*	98,995	512,232 D	44.6%	53.7%	45.4%	54.6%
2010	3,977,661	2,028,945	Toomey, Pat	1,948,716	Sestak, Joe		80,229 R	51.0%	49.0%	51.0%	49.0%
2006	4,081,043	1,684,778	Santorum, Rick*	2,392,984	Casey, Bob Jr.	3,281	708,206 D	41.3%	58.6%	41.3%	58.7%
2004	5,559,105	2,925,080	Specter, Arlen*	2,334,126	Hoeffel, Joseph M.	299,899	590,954 R	52.6%	42.0%	55.6%	44.4%
2000	4,735,504	2,481,962	Santorum, Rick*	2,154,908	Klink, Ron	98,634	327,054 R	52.4%	45.5%	53.5%	46.5%
1998	2,957,772	1,814,180	Specter, Arlen*	1,028,839	Lloyd, Bill	114,753	785,341 R	61.3%	34.8%	63.8%	36.2%
1994	3,513,361	1,735,691	Santorum, Rick	1,648,481	Wofford, Harris*	129,189	87,210 R	49.4%	46.9%	51.3%	48.7%
1992	4,802,410	2,358,125	Specter, Arlen*	2,224,966	Yeakel, Lynn	219,319	133,159 R	49.1%	46.3%	51.5%	48.5%
1991S**	3,382,746	1,521,986	Thornburgh, Richard	1,860,760	Wofford, Harris*		338,774 D	45.0%	55.0%	45.0%	55.0%
1988	4,366,598	2,901,715	Heinz, Henry John III*	1,416,764	Vignola, Joseph C.	48,119	1,484,951 R	66.5%	32.4%	67.2%	32.8%
1986	3,378,226	1,906,537	Specter, Arlen*	1,448,219	Edgar, Robert W.	23,470	458,318 R	56.4%	42.9%	56.8%	43.2%
1982	3,604,108	2,136,418	Heinz, Henry John III*	1,412,965	Wecht, Cyril H.	54,725	723,453 R	59.3%	39.2%	60.2%	39.8%
1980	4,418,042	2,230,404	Specter, Arlen	2,122,391	Flaherty, Peter	65,247	108,013 R	50.5%	48.0%	51.2%	48.8%
1976	4,546,353	2,381,891	Heinz, Henry John III	2,126,977	Green, William J. III	37,485	254,914 R	52.4%	46.8%	52.8%	47.2%
1974	3,477,812	1,843,317	Schweiker, Richard S.*	1,596,121	Flaherty, Peter	38,374	247,196 R	53.0%	45.9%	53.6%	46.4%
1970	3,644,305	1,874,106	Scott, Hugh*	1,653,774	Sesler, William G.	116,425	220,332 R	51.4%	45.4%	53.1%	46.9%
1968	4,624,218	2,399,762	Schweiker, Richard S.	2,117,662	Clark, Joseph S.*	106,794	282,100 R	51.9%	45.8%	53.1%	46.9%
1964	4,803,835	2,429,858	Scott, Hugh*	2,359,223	Blatt, Genevieve	14,754	70,635 R	50.6%	49.1%	50.7%	49.3%
1962	4,383,475	2,134,649	Van Zandt, James E.	2,238,383	Clark, Joseph S.*	10,443	103,734 D	48.7%	51.1%	48.8%	51.2%
1958	3,988,622	2,042,586	Scott, Hugh	1,929,821	Leader, George M.	16,215	112,765 R	51.2%	48.4%	51.4%	48.6%
1956	4,529,874	2,250,671	Duff, James H.*	2,268,641	Clark, Joseph S.	10,562	17,970 D	49.7%	50.1%	49.8%	50.2%
1952	4,519,761	2,331,034	Martin, Edward*	2,168,546	Bard, Guy Kurtz	20,181	162,488 R	51.6%	48.0%	51.8%	48.2%
1950	3,548,703	1,820,400	Duff, James H.	1,694,076	Myers, Francis J.*	34,227	126,324 R	51.3%	47.7%	51.8%	48.2%
1946	3,127,860	1,853,458	Martin, Edward	1,245,338	Guffey, Joseph F.*	29,064	608,120 R	59.3%	39.8%	59.8%	40.2%

Note: An asterisk (*) denotes incumbent. **The 1991 election was for a short term to fill a vacancy.

PENNSYLVANIA

PRESIDENT 2016

2010 Census Population	County	Total Vote	Republican (Trump)	Democratic (Clinton)	Other	Rep.-Dem. Plurality		Percentage			
								Total Vote		Major Vote	
								Rep.	Dem.	Rep.	Dem.
101,407	ADAMS	47,489	31,423	14,219	1,847	17,204	R	66.2%	29.9%	68.8%	31.2%
1,223,348	ALLEGHENY	650,114	259,480	367,617	23,017	108,137	D	39.9%	56.5%	41.4%	58.6%
68,941	ARMSTRONG	31,618	23,484	7,178	956	16,306	R	74.3%	22.7%	76.6%	23.4%
170,539	BEAVER	83,571	48,167	32,531	2,873	15,636	R	57.6%	38.9%	59.7%	40.3%
49,762	BEDFORD	23,637	19,552	3,645	440	15,907	R	82.7%	15.4%	84.3%	15.7%
411,442	BERKS	183,065	96,626	78,437	8,002	18,189	R	52.8%	42.8%	55.2%	44.8%
127,089	BLAIR	54,909	39,135	13,958	1,816	25,177	R	71.3%	25.4%	73.7%	26.3%
62,622	BRADFORD	25,708	18,141	6,369	1,198	11,772	R	70.6%	24.8%	74.0%	26.0%
625,249	BUCKS	344,297	164,361	167,060	12,876	2,699	D	47.7%	48.5%	49.6%	50.4%
183,862	BUTLER	97,071	64,428	28,584	4,059	35,844	R	66.4%	29.4%	69.3%	30.7%
143,679	CAMBRIA	63,072	42,258	18,867	1,947	23,391	R	67.0%	29.9%	69.1%	30.9%
5,085	CAMERON	2,186	1,589	531	66	1,058	R	72.7%	24.3%	75.0%	25.0%
65,249	CARBON	28,776	18,743	8,936	1,097	9,807	R	65.1%	31.1%	67.7%	32.3%
153,990	CENTRE	76,148	35,274	37,088	3,786	1,814	D	46.3%	48.7%	48.7%	51.3%
498,886	CHESTER	268,800	116,114	141,682	11,004	25,568	D	43.2%	52.7%	45.0%	55.0%
39,988	CLARION	17,535	12,576	4,273	686	8,303	R	71.7%	24.4%	74.6%	25.4%
81,642	CLEARFIELD	34,271	24,932	8,200	1,139	16,732	R	72.7%	23.9%	75.3%	24.7%
39,238	CLINTON	15,394	10,022	4,744	628	5,278	R	65.1%	30.8%	67.9%	32.1%
67,295	COLUMBIA	28,228	18,004	8,934	1,290	9,070	R	63.8%	31.6%	66.8%	33.2%
88,765	CRAWFORD	37,492	24,987	10,971	1,534	14,016	R	66.6%	29.3%	69.5%	30.5%
235,406	CUMBERLAND	121,617	69,076	47,085	5,456	21,991	R	56.8%	38.7%	59.5%	40.5%
268,100	DAUPHIN	130,872	60,863	64,706	5,303	3,843	D	46.5%	49.4%	48.5%	51.5%
558,979	DELAWARE	297,634	110,667	177,402	9,565	66,735	D	37.2%	59.6%	38.4%	61.6%
31,946	ELK	14,426	10,025	3,853	548	6,172	R	69.5%	26.7%	72.2%	27.8%
280,566	ERIE	123,679	60,069	58,112	5,498	1,957	R	48.6%	47.0%	50.8%	49.2%
136,606	FAYETTE	53,767	34,590	17,946	1,231	16,644	R	64.3%	33.4%	65.8%	34.2%
7,716	FOREST	2,401	1,683	626	92	1,057	R	70.1%	26.1%	72.9%	27.1%
149,618	FRANKLIN	69,731	49,768	17,465	2,498	32,303	R	71.4%	25.0%	74.0%	26.0%
14,845	FULTON	6,771	5,694	912	165	4,782	R	84.1%	13.5%	86.2%	13.8%
38,686	GREENE	15,764	10,849	4,482	433	6,367	R	68.8%	28.4%	70.8%	29.2%
45,913	HUNTINGDON	19,706	14,494	4,539	673	9,955	R	73.6%	23.0%	76.2%	23.8%
88,880	INDIANA	37,770	24,888	11,528	1,354	13,360	R	65.9%	30.5%	68.3%	31.7%
45,200	JEFFERSON	19,478	15,192	3,650	636	11,542	R	78.0%	18.7%	80.6%	19.4%
24,636	JUNIATA	10,454	8,273	1,821	360	6,452	R	79.1%	17.4%	82.0%	18.0%
214,437	LACKAWANNA	103,456	48,384	51,983	3,089	3,599	D	46.8%	50.2%	48.2%	51.8%
519,445	LANCASTER	241,112	137,914	91,093	12,105	46,821	R	57.2%	37.8%	60.2%	39.8%
91,108	LAWRENCE	40,753	25,428	14,009	1,316	11,419	R	62.4%	34.4%	64.5%	35.5%
133,568	LEBANON	61,845	40,525	18,953	2,367	21,572	R	65.5%	30.6%	68.1%	31.9%
349,497	LEHIGH	160,993	73,690	81,324	5,979	7,634	D	45.8%	50.5%	47.5%	52.5%
320,918	LUZERNE	134,983	78,688	52,451	3,844	26,237	R	58.3%	38.9%	60.0%	40.0%
116,111	LYCOMING	50,565	35,627	13,020	1,918	22,607	R	70.5%	25.7%	73.2%	26.8%
43,450	MCKEAN	16,296	11,635	4,025	636	7,610	R	71.4%	24.7%	74.3%	25.7%
116,638	MERCER	52,309	31,544	18,733	2,032	12,811	R	60.3%	35.8%	62.7%	37.3%
46,682	MIFFLIN	18,601	14,094	3,877	630	10,217	R	75.8%	20.8%	78.4%	21.6%
169,842	MONROE	69,752	33,386	33,918	2,448	532	D	47.9%	48.6%	49.6%	50.4%
799,874	MONTGOMERY	434,687	162,731	256,082	15,874	93,351	D	37.4%	58.9%	38.9%	61.1%
18,267	MONTOUR	8,556	5,288	2,857	411	2,431	R	61.8%	33.4%	64.9%	35.1%
297,735	NORTHAMPTON	143,519	71,736	66,272	5,511	5,464	R	50.0%	46.2%	52.0%	48.0%
94,528	NORTHUMBERLAND	36,622	25,427	9,788	1,407	15,639	R	69.4%	26.7%	72.2%	27.8%
45,969	PERRY	21,158	15,616	4,632	910	10,984	R	73.8%	21.9%	77.1%	22.9%
1,526,006	PHILADELPHIA	707,631	108,748	584,025	14,858	475,277	D	15.4%	82.5%	15.7%	84.3%
57,369	PIKE	26,101	16,056	9,256	789	6,800	R	61.5%	35.5%	63.4%	36.6%
17,457	POTTER	7,784	6,251	1,302	231	4,949	R	80.3%	16.7%	82.8%	17.2%
148,289	SCHUYLKILL	62,869	44,001	16,770	2,098	27,231	R	70.0%	26.7%	72.4%	27.6%
39,702	SNYDER	16,363	11,725	4,002	636	7,723	R	71.7%	24.5%	74.6%	25.4%
77,742	SOMERSET	35,773	27,379	7,376	1,018	20,003	R	76.5%	20.6%	78.8%	21.2%
6,428	SULLIVAN	3,136	2,291	750	95	1,541	R	73.1%	23.9%	75.3%	24.7%
43,356	SUSQUEHANNA	18,863	12,891	5,123	849	7,768	R	68.3%	27.2%	71.6%	28.4%
41,981	TIOGA	18,325	13,614	3,901	810	9,713	R	74.3%	21.3%	77.7%	22.3%
44,947	UNION	17,468	10,622	6,180	666	4,442	R	60.8%	35.4%	63.2%	36.8%

PENNSYLVANIA

PRESIDENT 2016

2010 Census Population	County	Total Vote	Republican (Trump)	Democratic (Clinton)	Other	Rep.-Dem. Plurality	Percentage			
							Total Vote		Major Vote	
							Rep.	Dem.	Rep.	Dem.
54,984	VENANGO	23,348	16,021	6,309	1,018	9,712 R	68.6%	27.0%	71.7%	28.3%
41,815	WARREN	18,434	12,477	5,145	812	7,332 R	67.7%	27.9%	70.8%	29.2%
207,820	WASHINGTON	101,450	61,386	36,322	3,742	25,064 R	60.5%	35.8%	62.8%	37.2%
52,822	WAYNE	24,018	16,244	7,008	766	9,236 R	67.6%	29.2%	69.9%	30.1%
365,169	WESTMORELAND	182,051	116,522	59,669	5,860	56,853 R	64.0%	32.8%	66.1%	33.9%
28,276	WYOMING	13,144	8,837	3,811	496	5,026 R	67.2%	29.0%	69.9%	30.1%
434,972	YORK	205,986	128,528	68,524	8,934	60,004 R	62.4%	33.3%	65.2%	34.8%
	Votes Not Reported by County				50,076					
12,702,379	TOTAL	6,165,478	2,970,733	2,926,441	268,304	44,292 R	48.2%	47.5%	50.4%	49.6%

PENNSYLVANIA

SENATOR 2016

2010 Census Population	County	Total Vote	Republican (Toomey)	Democratic (McGinty)	Other	Rep.-Dem. Plurality	Percentage			
							Total Vote		Major Vote	
							Rep.	Dem.	Rep.	Dem.
101,407	ADAMS	47,503	30,492	14,593	2,418	15,899 R	64.2%	30.7%	67.6%	32.4%
1,223,348	ALLEGHENY	647,026	261,316	357,450	28,260	96,134 D	40.4%	55.2%	42.2%	57.8%
68,941	ARMSTRONG	31,400	20,793	8,387	2,220	12,406 R	66.2%	26.7%	71.3%	28.7%
170,539	BEAVER	83,321	44,000	34,263	5,058	9,737 R	52.8%	41.1%	56.2%	43.8%
49,762	BEDFORD	23,439	17,739	4,356	1,344	13,383 R	75.7%	18.6%	80.3%	19.7%
411,442	BERKS	179,413	95,466	77,028	6,919	18,438 R	53.2%	42.9%	55.3%	44.7%
127,089	BLAIR	54,790	36,533	15,107	3,150	21,426 R	66.7%	27.6%	70.7%	29.3%
62,622	BRADFORD	25,559	16,574	6,985	2,000	9,589 R	64.8%	27.3%	70.4%	29.6%
625,249	BUCKS	339,452	175,898	157,709	5,845	18,189 R	51.8%	46.5%	52.7%	47.3%
183,862	BUTLER	96,605	62,425	28,715	5,465	33,710 R	64.6%	29.7%	68.5%	31.5%
143,679	CAMBRIA	62,728	36,948	21,894	3,886	15,054 R	58.9%	34.9%	62.8%	37.2%
5,085	CAMERON	2,154	1,390	593	171	797 R	64.5%	27.5%	70.1%	29.9%
65,249	CARBON	28,216	16,360	10,086	1,770	6,274 R	58.0%	35.7%	61.9%	38.1%
153,990	CENTRE	76,392	36,527	35,487	4,378	1,040 R	47.8%	46.5%	50.7%	49.3%
498,886	CHESTER	270,802	133,662	127,552	9,588	6,110 R	49.4%	47.1%	51.2%	48.8%
39,988	CLARION	17,445	11,310	4,931	1,204	6,379 R	64.8%	28.3%	69.6%	30.4%
81,642	CLEARFIELD	34,011	22,128	9,454	2,429	12,674 R	65.1%	27.8%	70.1%	29.9%
39,238	CLINTON	15,165	8,702	5,511	952	3,191 R	57.4%	36.3%	61.2%	38.8%
67,295	COLUMBIA	28,102	16,292	9,819	1,991	6,473 R	58.0%	34.9%	62.4%	37.6%
88,765	CRAWFORD	37,259	24,472	11,047	1,740	13,425 R	65.7%	29.6%	68.9%	31.1%
235,406	CUMBERLAND	121,943	71,638	44,796	5,509	26,842 R	58.7%	36.7%	61.5%	38.5%
268,100	DAUPHIN	128,674	63,740	62,551	2,383	1,189 R	49.5%	48.6%	50.5%	49.5%
558,979	DELAWARE	293,625	126,300	163,377	3,948	37,077 D	43.0%	55.6%	43.6%	56.4%
31,946	ELK	14,323	8,703	4,509	1,111	4,194 R	60.8%	31.5%	65.9%	34.1%
280,566	ERIE	122,724	60,948	56,846	4,930	4,102 R	49.7%	46.3%	51.7%	48.3%
136,606	FAYETTE	53,204	29,699	20,547	2,958	9,152 R	55.8%	38.6%	59.1%	40.9%
7,716	FOREST	2,374	1,502	708	164	794 R	63.3%	29.8%	68.0%	32.0%
149,618	FRANKLIN	69,794	48,658	17,827	3,309	30,831 R	69.7%	25.5%	73.2%	26.8%
14,845	FULTON	6,731	5,456	1,025	250	4,431 R	81.1%	15.2%	84.2%	15.8%
38,686	GREENE	15,414	8,826	5,692	896	3,134 R	57.3%	36.9%	60.8%	39.2%
45,913	HUNTINGDON	19,589	13,078	5,105	1,406	7,973 R	66.8%	26.1%	71.9%	28.1%
88,880	INDIANA	37,792	22,245	12,592	2,955	9,653 R	58.9%	33.3%	63.9%	36.1%
45,200	JEFFERSON	19,317	13,706	4,160	1,451	9,546 R	71.0%	21.5%	76.7%	23.3%
24,636	JUNIATA	10,422	7,657	2,153	612	5,504 R	73.5%	20.7%	78.1%	21.9%
214,437	LACKAWANNA	101,910	40,519	53,936	7,455	13,417 D	39.8%	52.9%	42.9%	57.1%

PENNSYLVANIA

SENATOR 2016

2010 Census Population	County	Total Vote	Republican (Toomey)	Democratic (McGinty)	Other	Rep.-Dem. Plurality	Percentage Total Vote Rep.	Total Vote Dem.	Major Vote Rep.	Major Vote Dem.
519,445	LANCASTER	242,605	142,774	89,922	9,909	52,852 R	58.9%	37.1%	61.4%	38.6%
91,108	LAWRENCE	40,280	22,674	15,289	2,317	7,385 R	56.3%	38.0%	59.7%	40.3%
133,568	LEBANON	61,525	39,386	19,079	3,060	20,307 R	64.0%	31.0%	67.4%	32.6%
349,497	LEHIGH	160,075	76,216	77,232	6,627	1,016 D	47.6%	48.2%	49.7%	50.3%
320,918	LUZERNE	131,678	66,551	56,477	8,650	10,074 R	50.5%	42.9%	54.1%	45.9%
116,111	LYCOMING	50,567	33,015	14,187	3,365	18,828 R	65.3%	28.1%	69.9%	30.1%
43,450	MCKEAN	16,122	11,530	3,987	605	7,543 R	71.5%	24.7%	74.3%	25.7%
116,638	MERCER	51,806	30,567	19,193	2,046	11,374 R	59.0%	37.0%	61.4%	38.6%
46,682	MIFFLIN	18,213	13,089	4,031	1,093	9,058 R	71.9%	22.1%	76.5%	23.5%
169,842	MONROE	66,791	30,743	34,280	1,768	3,537 D	46.0%	51.3%	47.3%	52.7%
799,874	MONTGOMERY	432,358	189,574	237,353	5,431	47,779 D	43.8%	54.9%	44.4%	55.6%
18,267	MONTOUR	8,550	5,066	2,898	586	2,168 R	59.3%	33.9%	63.6%	36.4%
297,735	NORTHAMPTON	139,889	72,172	64,151	3,566	8,021 R	51.6%	45.9%	52.9%	47.1%
94,528	NORTHUMBERLAND	35,535	21,826	11,117	2,592	10,709 R	61.4%	31.3%	66.3%	33.7%
45,969	PERRY	21,091	14,898	4,962	1,231	9,936 R	70.6%	23.5%	75.0%	25.0%
1,526,006	PHILADELPHIA	685,165	116,714	560,421	8,030	443,707 D	17.0%	81.8%	17.2%	82.8%
57,369	PIKE	25,634	15,192	9,329	1,113	5,863 R	59.3%	36.4%	62.0%	38.0%
17,457	POTTER	7,700	5,990	1,387	323	4,603 R	77.8%	18.0%	81.2%	18.8%
148,289	SCHUYLKILL	62,128	37,757	19,539	4,832	18,218 R	60.8%	31.4%	65.9%	34.1%
39,702	SNYDER	16,282	10,867	4,299	1,116	6,568 R	66.7%	26.4%	71.7%	28.3%
77,742	SOMERSET	35,733	25,470	8,340	1,923	17,130 R	71.3%	23.3%	75.3%	24.7%
6,428	SULLIVAN	3,093	2,020	867	206	1,153 R	65.3%	28.0%	70.0%	30.0%
43,356	SUSQUEHANNA	19,247	11,996	5,535	1,716	6,461 R	62.3%	28.8%	68.4%	31.6%
41,981	TIOGA	18,174	13,418	3,992	764	9,426 R	73.8%	22.0%	77.1%	22.9%
44,947	UNION	17,501	10,568	6,092	841	4,476 R	60.4%	34.8%	63.4%	36.6%
54,984	VENANGO	23,208	14,581	6,989	1,638	7,592 R	62.8%	30.1%	67.6%	32.4%
41,815	WARREN	18,212	12,130	5,124	958	7,006 R	66.6%	28.1%	70.3%	29.7%
207,820	WASHINGTON	100,909	56,952	38,133	5,824	18,819 R	56.4%	37.8%	59.9%	40.1%
52,822	WAYNE	23,828	14,538	7,487	1,803	7,051 R	61.0%	31.4%	66.0%	34.0%
365,169	WESTMORELAND	180,258	107,532	62,981	9,745	44,551 R	59.7%	34.9%	63.1%	36.9%
28,276	WYOMING	13,066	7,844	4,154	1,068	3,690 R	60.0%	31.8%	65.4%	34.6%
434,972	YORK	206,015	126,350	69,394	10,271	56,956 R	61.3%	33.7%	64.5%	35.5%
12,702,379	TOTAL	6,051,856	2,951,702	2,865,012	235,142	86,690 R	48.8%	47.3%	50.7%	49.3%

PENNSYLVANIA

HOUSE OF REPRESENTATIVES

CD	Year	Total Vote	Republican Vote	Republican Candidate	Democratic Vote	Democratic Candidate	Other Vote	Rep.-Dem. Plurality	Total Vote Rep.	Total Vote Dem.	Major Vote Rep.	Major Vote Dem.
1	2016	299,010	53,219	WILLIAMS, DEBORAH L.	245,791	BRADY, ROBERT A.*		192,572 D	17.8%	82.2%	17.8%	82.2%
1	2014	158,441	27,193	RATH, MEGAN ANN	131,248	BRADY, ROBERT A.*		104,055 D	17.2%	82.8%	17.2%	82.8%
1	2012	277,102	41,708	FEATHERMAN, JOHN J.	235,394	BRADY, ROBERT A.*		193,686 D	15.1%	84.9%	15.1%	84.9%
2	2016	357,645	35,131	JONES, JAMES A.	322,514	EVANS, DWIGHT		287,383 D	9.8%	90.2%	9.8%	90.2%
2	2014	206,538	25,397	JAMES, ARMOND	181,141	FATTAH, CHAKA*		155,744 D	12.3%	87.7%	12.3%	87.7%
2	2012	356,386	33,381	MANSFIELD, ROBERT	318,176	FATTAH, CHAKA*	4,829	284,795 D	9.4%	89.3%	9.5%	90.5%
3	2016	244,893	244,893	KELLY, MIKE*				244,893 R	100.0%		100.0%	
3	2014	187,790	113,859	KELLY, MIKE*	73,931	LAVALLEE, DANIEL		39,928 R	60.6%	39.4%	60.6%	39.4%
3	2012	302,514	165,826	KELLY, MIKE*	123,933	EATON, MISSA	12,755	41,893 R	54.8%	41.0%	57.2%	42.8%
4	2016	334,000	220,628	PERRY, SCOTT*	113,372	BURKHOLDER, JOSHUA T.		107,256 R	66.1%	33.9%	66.1%	33.9%
4	2014	197,340	147,090	PERRY, SCOTT*	50,250	THOMPSON, LINDA DELIAH		96,840 R	74.5%	25.5%	74.5%	25.5%
4	2012	303,980	181,603	PERRY, SCOTT	104,643	PERKINSON, HARRY	17,734	76,960 R	59.7%	34.4%	63.4%	36.6%

PENNSYLVANIA

HOUSE OF REPRESENTATIVES

CD	Year	Total Vote	Republican Vote	Republican Candidate	Democratic Vote	Democratic Candidate	Other Vote	Rep.-Dem. Plurality	Total Vote Rep.	Total Vote Dem.	Major Vote Rep.	Major Vote Dem.
5	2016	307,843	206,761	THOMPSON, GLENN*	101,082	TAYLOR, KERITH STRANO		105,679 R	67.2%	32.8%	67.2%	32.8%
5	2014	180,857	115,018	THOMPSON, GLENN*	65,839	TAYLOR, KERITH STRANO		49,179 R	63.6%	36.4%	63.6%	36.4%
5	2012	282,465	177,740	THOMPSON, GLENN*	104,725	DUMAS, CHARLES		73,015 R	62.9%	37.1%	62.9%	37.1%
6	2016	362,469	207,469	COSTELLO, RYAN A.*	155,000	PARRISH, MICHAEL D.		52,469 R	57.2%	42.8%	57.2%	42.8%
6	2014	212,544	119,643	COSTELLO, RYAN A.	92,901	TRIVEDI, MANAN		26,742 R	56.3%	43.7%	56.3%	43.7%
6	2012	335,528	191,725	GERLACH, JAMES W.*	143,803	TRIVEDI, MANAN		47,922 R	57.1%	42.9%	57.1%	42.9%
7	2016	379,502	225,678	MEEHAN, PATRICK*	153,824	BALCHUNIS, MARY ELLEN		71,854 R	59.5%	40.5%	59.5%	40.5%
7	2014	235,125	145,869	MEEHAN, PATRICK*	89,256	BALCHUNIS, MARY ELLEN		56,613 R	62.0%	38.0%	62.0%	38.0%
7	2012	353,451	209,942	MEEHAN, PATRICK*	143,509	BADEY, GEORGE		66,433 R	59.4%	40.6%	59.4%	40.6%
8	2016	380,818	207,263	FITZPATRICK, BRIAN K.	173,555	SANTARSIERO, STEVEN J.		33,708 R	54.4%	45.6%	54.4%	45.6%
8	2014	222,498	137,731	FITZPATRICK, MICHAEL G.*	84,767	STROUSE, KEVIN		52,964 R	61.9%	38.1%	61.9%	38.1%
8	2012	352,238	199,379	FITZPATRICK, MICHAEL G.*	152,859	BOOCKVAR, KATHY		46,520 R	56.6%	43.4%	56.6%	43.4%
9	2016	294,565	186,580	SHUSTER, BILL*	107,985	ARTHUR HALVORSON		78,595 R	63.3%	36.7%	63.3%	36.7%
9	2014	173,317	110,094	SHUSTER, BILL*	63,223	HARTZOK, ALANNA K.		46,871 R	63.5%	36.5%	63.5%	36.5%
9	2012	274,305	169,177	SHUSTER, BILL*	105,128	RAMSBURG, KAREN		64,049 R	61.7%	38.3%	61.7%	38.3%
10	2016	301,105	211,282	MARINO, THOMAS A.*	89,823	MOLESEVICH, MICHAEL M.		121,459 R	70.2%	29.8%	70.2%	29.8%
10	2014	180,322	112,851	MARINO, THOMAS A.*	44,737	BRION, SCOTT F.	22,734	68,114 R	62.6%	24.8%	71.6%	28.4%
10	2012	273,790	179,563	MARINO, THOMAS A.*	94,227	SCOLLO, PHILLIP		85,336 R	65.6%	34.4%	65.6%	34.4%
11	2016	313,221	199,421	BARLETTA, LOU*	113,800	MARSICANO, MICHAEL PAUL		85,621 R	63.7%	36.3%	63.7%	36.3%
11	2014	184,692	122,464	BARLETTA, LOU*	62,228	OSTROWSKI, ANDY J.		60,236 R	66.3%	33.7%	66.3%	33.7%
11	2012	285,198	166,967	BARLETTA, LOU*	118,231	STILP, GENE		48,736 R	58.5%	41.5%	58.5%	41.5%
12	2016	359,204	221,851	ROTHFUS, KEITH*	137,353	MCCLELLAND, ERIN		84,498 R	61.8%	38.2%	61.8%	38.2%
12	2014	215,921	127,993	ROTHFUS, KEITH*	87,928	MCCLELLAND, ERIN		40,065 R	59.3%	40.7%	59.3%	40.7%
12	2012	338,941	175,352	ROTHFUS, KEITH	163,589	CRITZ, MARK S.*		11,763 R	51.7%	48.3%	51.7%	48.3%
13	2016	239,316			239,316	BOYLE, BRENDAN F.*		239,316 D		100.0%		100.0%
13	2014	184,150	60,549	ADCOCK, CARSON DEE	123,601	BOYLE, BRENDAN F.		63,052 D	32.9%	67.1%	32.9%	67.1%
13	2012	303,819	93,918	ROONEY, JOE	209,901	SCHWARTZ, ALLYSON Y.*		115,983 D	30.9%	69.1%	30.9%	69.1%
14	2016	343,292	87,999	MCALLISTER, LEONARD FRANCIS JR.	255,293	DOYLE, MIKE*		167,294 D	25.6%	74.4%	25.6%	74.4%
14	2014	148,351			148,351	DOYLE, MIKE*		148,351 D		100.0%		100.0%
14	2012	327,634	75,702	LESSMANN, HANS	251,932	DOYLE, MIKE*		176,230 D	23.1%	76.9%	23.1%	76.9%
15	2016	326,474	190,618	DENT, CHARLIE W.*	124,129	DAUGHERTY, RICK	11,727	66,489 R	58.4%	38.0%	60.6%	39.4%
15	2014	128,285	128,285	DENT, CHARLIE W.*				128,285 R	100.0%		100.0%	
15	2012	297,724	168,960	DENT, CHARLIE W.*	128,764	DAUGHERTY, RICK		40,196 R	56.8%	43.2%	56.8%	43.2%
16	2016	313,773	168,669	SMUCKER, LLOYD K.	134,586	HARTMAN, CHRISTINA M.	10,518	34,083 R	53.8%	42.9%	55.6%	44.4%
16	2014	176,235	101,722	PITTS, JOSEPH R.*	74,513	HOUGHTON, THOMAS D.		27,209 R	57.7%	42.3%	57.7%	42.3%
16	2012	284,781	156,192	PITTS, JOSEPH R.*	111,185	STRADER, ARYANNA	17,404	45,007 R	54.8%	39.0%	58.4%	41.6%
17	2016	293,164	135,430	CONNOLLY, MATTHEW DONALD "MATT"	157,734	CARTWRIGHT, MATT*		22,304 D	46.2%	53.8%	46.2%	53.8%
17	2014	165,051	71,371	MOYLAN III, DAVID J.	93,680	CARTWRIGHT, MATT*		22,309 D	43.2%	56.8%	43.2%	56.8%
17	2012	267,601	106,208	CUMMINGS, LAUREEN	161,393	CARTWRIGHT, MATT		55,185 D	39.7%	60.3%	39.7%	60.3%
18	2016	293,684	293,684	MURPHY, TIMOTHY*				293,684 R	100.0%		100.0%	
18	2014	166,076	166,076	MURPHY, TIMOTHY*				166,076 R	100.0%		100.0%	
18	2012	338,873	216,727	MURPHY, TIMOTHY*	122,146	MAGGI, LARRY		94,581 R	64.0%	36.0%	64.0%	36.0%
TOTAL	2016	5,743,978	3,096,576		2,625,157		22,245	471,419 R	53.9%	45.7%	55.2%	45.9%
TOTAL	2014	3,323,533	1,833,205		1,467,594		22,734	365,611 R	55.2%	44.2%	55.5%	44.5%
TOTAL	2012	5,556,330	2,710,070		2,793,538		52,722	83,468 D	48.8%	50.3%	49.2%	50.8%

Note: An asterisk (*) denotes incumbent.

PENNSYLVANIA

GENERAL AND PRIMARY ELECTIONS

2016 GENERAL ELECTIONS: OTHER VOTES

President Other vote was 146,715 Libertarian (Gary Johnson), 49,941 Green (Jill Stein), 37,544 Write-in (Scattered Write-in) 21,572 Constitution (Darrell Castle), 6,472 Write-in (Evan McMullin), 6,060 Write-in (Bernard Sanders)

Senate Other vote was 235,142 Libertarian (Edward Clifford)

House Other vote was:

CD 15 11,727 Libertarian (Paul Rizzo)
CD 16 10,518 Libertarian (Shawn House)

2016 PRIMARY ELECTIONS: SUPPLEMENTARY INFORMATION

Primary	April 26, 2016	**Registration** (as of April 26, 2016)	8,273,703	Democratic Republican Other	4,062,187 3,126,166 1,085,350

Primary Type Closed—Only registered Democrats and Republicans could vote in their party's primary.

	REPUBLICAN PRIMARIES			DEMOCRATIC PRIMARIES		
President	Trump, Donald J.	902,593	56.6%	Clinton, Hillary Rodham	935,107	55.6%
	Cruz, Ted	345,506	21.7%	Sanders, Bernard	731,881	43.5%
	Kasich, John R.	310,003	19.4%	De La Fuente, Roque "Rocky"	14,439	0.9%
	Carson, Ben	14,842	0.9%			
	Rubio, Marco	11,954	0.7%			
	Bush, Jeb	9,577	0.6%			
	TOTAL	*1,594,475*		*TOTAL*	*1,681,427*	
Senator	Toomey, Pat*	1,342,941	100.0%	McGinty, Katie A.	669,774	42.5%
				Sestak, Joe	513,221	32.6%
				Fetterman, John K.	307,090	19.5%
				Vodvarka, Joseph John	85,837	5.4%
	TOTAL	*1,342,941*		*TOTAL*	*1,575,922*	
Congressional District 1	Williams, Deborah L. *TOTAL*	19,042 *19,042*	100.0%	Brady, Robert A.* *TOTAL*	108,233 *108,233*	100.0%
Congressional District 2	Jones, James A.	11,838	100.0%	Evans, Dwight	75,515	42.3%
				Fattah, Chaka*	61,518	34.4%
				Gordon, Brian Anthony	23,655	13.2%
				Muroff, Daniel R.	18,016	10.1%
	TOTAL	*11,838*		*TOTAL*	*178,704*	
Congressional District 3	Kelly, Mike* *TOTAL*	88,964 *88,964*	100.0%			
Congressional District 4	Perry, Scott* *TOTAL*	100,552 *100,552*	100.0%			
Congressional District 5	Thompson, Glenn* *TOTAL*	89,000 *89,000*	100.0%	Taylor, Kerith Strano *TOTAL*	56,696 *56,696*	100.0%
Congressional District 6	Costello, Ryan A.* *TOTAL*	88,349 *88,349*	100.0%	Parrish, Michael D. *TOTAL*	62,732 *62,732*	100.0%

PENNSYLVANIA

GENERAL AND PRIMARY ELECTIONS

	REPUBLICAN PRIMARIES			DEMOCRATIC PRIMARIES		
Congressional District 7	Meehan, Patrick*	86,178	76.4%	Balchunis, Mary Ellen	52,792	74.0%
	Casacio, Stanley "Stan"	26,674	23.6%	Golderer, William	18,509	26.0%
	TOTAL	*112,852*		*TOTAL*	*71,301*	
Congressional District 8	Fitzpatrick, Brian K.	74,150	78.4%	Santarsiero, Steven J.	50,416	59.8%
	Warren, Andrew L.	11,828	12.5%	Naughton, Shaughnessy	33,864	40.2%
	Duome, Marc	8,641	9.1%			
	TOTAL	*94,619*		*TOTAL*	*84,280*	
Congressional District 9	Shuster, Bill*	49,393	50.6%			
	Halvorson, Arthur L. "Art"	48,166	49.4%			
	TOTAL	*97,559*				
Congressional District 10	Marino, Thomas A.*	95,321	100.0%			
	TOTAL	*95,321*				
Congressional District 11	Barletta, Lou*	92,342	100.0%	Marsicano, Michael Paul	58,117	100.0%
	TOTAL	*92,342*		*TOTAL*	*58,117*	
Congressional District 12	Rothfus, Keith*	87,270	100.0%	McClelland, Erin	73,326	100.0%
	TOTAL	*87,270*		*TOTAL*	*73,326*	
Congressional District 13				Boyle, Brendan F.*	90,512	100.0%
				TOTAL	*90,512*	
Congressional District 14				Doyle, Mike*	103,710	76.6%
				Brooks, Janis C.	31,659	23.4%
				TOTAL	*135,369*	
Congressional District 15	Dent, Charlie W.*	75,821	100.0%	Daugherty, Rick	59,475	100.0%
	TOTAL	*75,821*		*TOTAL*	*59,475*	
Congressional District 16	Smucker, Lloyd K.	49,716	54.1%	Hartman, Christina M.	51,588	100.0%
	Beiler, Chester Omar "Chet"	42,246	45.9%			
	TOTAL	*91,962*		*TOTAL*	*51,588*	
Congressional District 17	Connolly, Matthew Donald "Matt"	34,263	62.7%	Cartwright, Matt*	73,648	100.0%
	Geissinger, Glenn A.	20,399	37.3%			
	TOTAL	*54,662*		*TOTAL*	*73,648*	
Congressional District 18	Murphy, Timothy*	88,266	100.0%			
	TOTAL	*88,266*				

Note: An asterisk (*) denotes incumbent.

RHODE ISLAND

Congressional districts first established for elections held in 2012

2 members

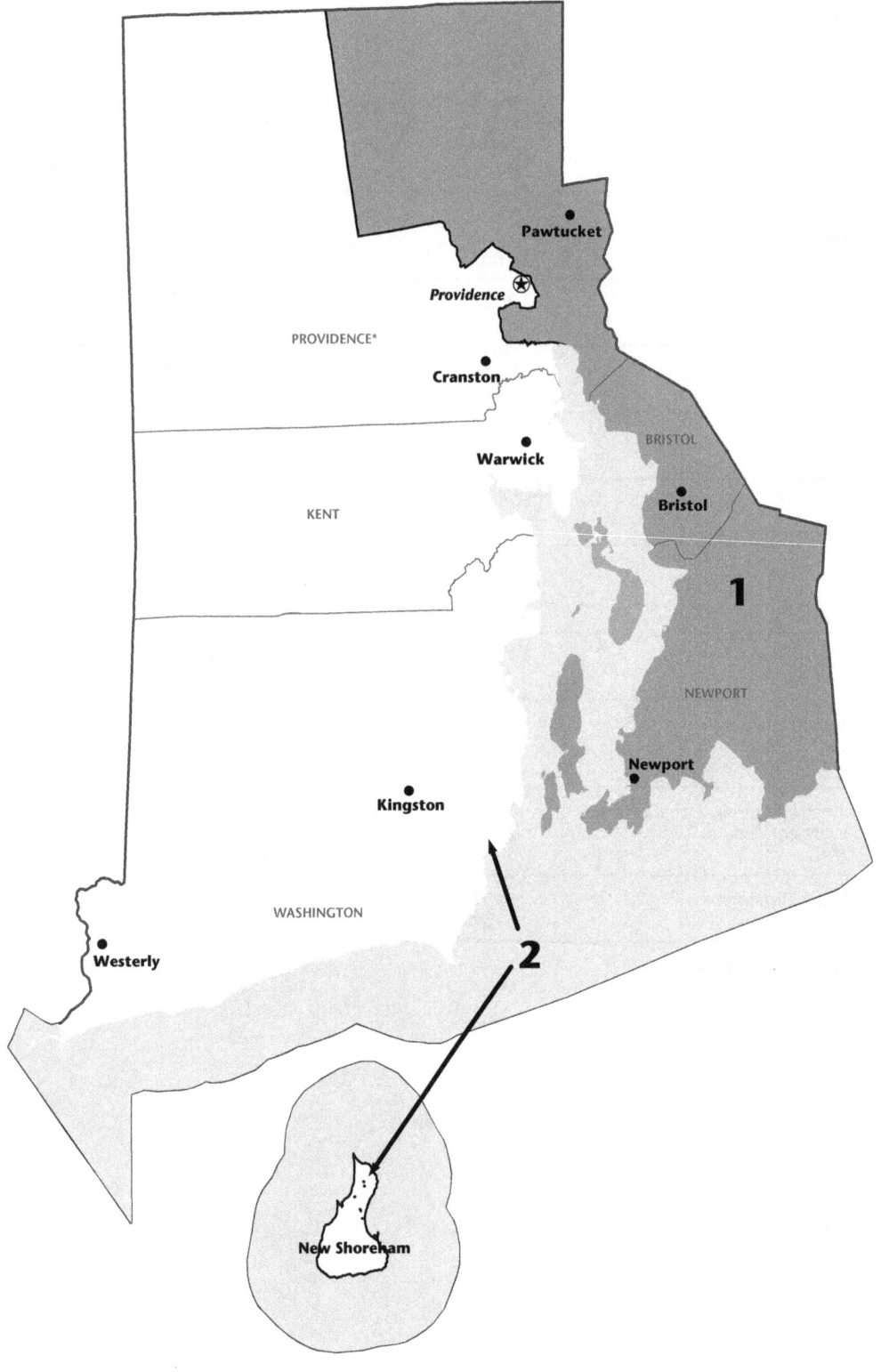

* Asterisk indicates a county whose boundaries include parts of two or more congressional districts.

RHODE ISLAND

GOVERNOR
Gina Raimondo (D). Elected 2014 to a four-year term.

SENATORS (2 Democrats)
Jack F. Reed (D). Re-elected 2014 to a six-year term. Previously elected 2008, 2002, 1996.

Sheldon Whitehouse (D). Re-elected 2012 to a six-year term. Previously elected 2006.

REPRESENTATIVES (2 Democrats)
1. David N. Cicilline (D)   2. James R. Langevin (D)

POSTWAR VOTE FOR PRESIDENT

| Year | Total Vote | Republican | | Democratic | | Other Vote | Rep.-Dem. Plurality | Percentage | | | |
| | | Vote | Candidate | Vote | Candidate | | | Total Vote | | Major Vote | |
								Rep.	Dem.	Rep.	Dem.
2016**	464,144	180,543	Trump, Donald J.	252,525	Clinton, Hillary Rodham	31,076	71,982 D	38.9%	54.4%	41.7%	58.3%
2012	446,049	157,204	Romney, W. Mitt	279,677	Obama, Barack H.*	9,168	122,473 D	35.2%	62.7%	36.0%	64.0%
2008	471,766	165,391	McCain, John S. III	296,571	Obama, Barack H.	9,804	131,180 D	35.1%	62.9%	35.8%	64.2%
2004	437,134	169,046	Bush, George W.*	259,760	Kerry, John F.	8,328	90,714 D	38.7%	59.4%	39.4%	60.6%
2000**	409,047	130,555	Bush, George W.	249,508	Gore, Albert Jr.	28,984	118,953 D	31.9%	61.0%	34.4%	65.6%
1996**	390,284	104,683	Dole, Robert "Bob"	233,050	Clinton, Bill*	52,551	128,367 D	26.8%	59.7%	31.0%	69.0%
1992**	453,477	131,601	Bush, George H.*	213,299	Clinton, Bill	108,577	81,698 D	29.0%	47.0%	38.2%	61.8%
1988	404,620	177,761	Bush, George H.	225,123	Dukakis, Michael S.	1,736	47,362 D	43.9%	55.6%	44.1%	55.9%
1984	410,492	212,080	Reagan, Ronald*	197,106	Mondale, Walter F.	1,306	14,974 R	51.7%	48.0%	51.8%	48.2%
1980**	416,072	154,793	Reagan, Ronald	198,342	Carter, Jimmy*	62,937	43,549 D	37.2%	47.7%	43.8%	56.2%
1976	411,170	181,249	Ford, Gerald R.*	227,636	Carter, Jimmy	2,285	46,387 D	44.1%	55.4%	44.3%	55.7%
1972	415,808	220,383	Nixon, Richard M.*	194,645	McGovern, George S.	780	25,738 R	53.0%	46.8%	53.1%	46.9%
1968**	385,000	122,359	Nixon, Richard M.	246,518	Humphrey, Hubert Horatio Jr.	16,123	124,159 D	31.8%	64.0%	33.2%	66.8%
1964	390,091	74,615	Goldwater, Barry M. Sr.	315,463	Johnson, Lyndon B.*	13	240,848 D	19.1%	80.9%	19.1%	80.9%
1960	405,535	147,502	Nixon, Richard M.	258,032	Kennedy, John F.	1	110,530 D	36.4%	63.6%	36.4%	63.6%
1956	387,609	225,819	Eisenhower, Dwight D.*	161,790	Stevenson, Adlai E. II		64,029 R	58.3%	41.7%	58.3%	41.7%
1952	414,498	210,935	Eisenhower, Dwight D.	203,293	Stevenson, Adlai E. II	270	7,642 R	50.9%	49.0%	50.9%	49.1%
1948	327,702	135,787	Dewey, Thomas E.	188,736	Truman, Harry S.*	3,179	52,949 D	41.4%	57.6%	41.8%	58.2%

Note: An asterisk (*) denotes incumbent. **In past elections, the other vote included: 2016 - 14,746 Libertarian (Gary Johnson); 2000 - 25,052 Green (Ralph Nader); 1996 - 43,723 Reform (Ross Perot); 1992 - 105,045 Independent (Perot); 1980 - 59,819 Independent (John Anderson); 1968 - 15,678 American Independent (George Wallace).

RHODE ISLAND

POSTWAR VOTE FOR GOVERNOR

Year	Total Vote	Republican Vote	Candidate	Democratic Vote	Candidate	Other Vote	Rep.-Dem. Plurality	Total Vote Rep.	Total Vote Dem.	Major Vote Rep.	Major Vote Dem.
2014**	324,055	117,428	Fung, Allan	131,899	Raimondo, Gina	74,728	14,471 D	36.2%	40.7%	47.1%	52.9%
2010**	342,545	114,911	Robitaille, John F.	78,896	Caprio, Frank T.	148,738	36,015 R	33.5%	23.0%	59.3%	40.7%
2006	387,010	197,366	Carcieri, Donald L.*	189,562	Fogarty, Charles J.	82	7,804 R	51.0%	49.0%	51.0%	49.0%
2002	332,655	181,827	Carcieri, Donald L.	150,229	York, Myrth	599	31,598 R	54.7%	45.2%	54.8%	45.2%
1998	306,383	156,180	Almond, Lincoln C.*	129,105	York, Myrth	21,098	27,075 R	51.0%	42.1%	54.7%	45.3%
1994**	361,377	171,194	Almond, Lincoln C.	157,361	York, Myrth	32,822	13,833 R	47.4%	43.5%	52.1%	47.9%
1992	424,818	145,590	Leonard, Elizabeth Ann	261,484	Sundlun, Bruce G.*	17,744	115,894 D	34.3%	61.6%	35.8%	64.2%
1990	356,672	92,177	Diprete, Edward*	264,411	Sundlun, Bruce G.	84	172,234 D	25.8%	74.1%	25.8%	74.2%
1988	400,516	203,550	Diprete, Edward*	196,936	Sundlun, Bruce G.	30	6,614 R	50.8%	49.2%	50.8%	49.2%
1986	322,724	208,822	Diprete, Edward*	104,508	Sundlun, Bruce G.	9,394	104,314 R	64.7%	32.4%	66.6%	33.4%
1984	408,375	245,059	Diprete, Edward	163,311	Solomon, Anthony J.	5	81,748 R	60.0%	40.0%	60.0%	40.0%
1982	337,259	79,602	Marzullo, Vincent	247,208	Garrahy, J. Joseph*	10,449	167,606 D	23.6%	73.3%	24.4%	75.6%
1980	405,916	106,729	Cianci, Vincent A.	299,174	Garrahy, J. Joseph*	13	192,445 D	26.3%	73.7%	26.3%	73.7%
1978	314,363	96,596	Almond, Lincoln C.	197,386	Garrahy, J. Joseph*	20,381	100,790 D	30.7%	62.8%	32.9%	67.1%
1976	398,683	178,254	Taft, James L.	218,561	Garrahy, J. Joseph	1,868	40,307 D	44.7%	54.8%	44.9%	55.1%
1974	321,660	69,224	Nugent, James W.	252,436	Noel, Philip W.*		183,212 D	21.5%	78.5%	21.5%	78.5%
1972	412,866	194,315	DeSimone, Herbert F.	216,953	Noel, Philip W.	1,598	22,638 D	47.1%	52.5%	47.2%	52.8%
1970	346,342	171,549	DeSimone, Herbert F.	173,420	Licht, Frank*	1,373	1,871 D	49.5%	50.1%	49.7%	50.3%
1968	383,725	187,958	Chafee, John H.*	195,766	Licht, Frank	1	7,808 D	49.0%	51.0%	49.0%	51.0%
1966	332,064	210,202	Chafee, John H.*	121,862	Hobbs, Horace E.		88,340 R	63.3%	36.7%	63.3%	36.7%
1964	391,668	239,501	Chafee, John H.*	152,165	Gallogly, Edward P.	2	87,336 R	61.1%	38.9%	61.1%	38.9%
1962	327,506	163,952	Chafee, John H.	163,554	Notte, John A. Jr.*		398 R	50.1%	49.9%	50.1%	49.9%
1960	401,362	174,044	Del Sesto, Christopher*	227,318	Notte, John A. Jr.		53,274 D	43.4%	56.6%	43.4%	56.6%
1958	346,780	176,505	Del Sesto, Christopher	170,275	Roberts, Dennis J.*		6,230 R	50.9%	49.1%	50.9%	49.1%
1956	383,919	191,604	Del Sesto, Christopher	192,315	Roberts, Dennis J.*		711 D	49.9%	50.1%	49.9%	50.1%
1954	328,670	137,131	Lewis, Dean J.	189,595	Roberts, Dennis J.*	1,944	52,464 D	41.7%	57.7%	42.0%	58.0%
1952	409,689	194,102	Archambault, Raoul	215,587	Roberts, Dennis J.*		21,485 D	47.4%	52.6%	47.4%	52.6%
1950	296,808	120,683	Lachapelle, Eugene J.	176,125	Roberts, Dennis J.		55,442 D	40.7%	59.3%	40.7%	59.3%
1948	323,863	124,441	Ruerat, Albert P.	198,056	Pastore, John O.*	1,366	73,615 D	38.4%	61.2%	38.6%	61.4%
1946	275,341	126,456	Murphy, John G.	148,885	Pastore, John O.*		22,429 D	45.9%	54.1%	45.9%	54.1%

Note: An asterisk (*) denotes incumbent. **In past elections, the other vote included: 2014 - 69,278 Moderate (Robert J. Healey Jr.); 2010 - 123,571 Independent (Lincoln Chafee, who was elected with 36.1 percent of the total vote and a plurality of 8,660 votes). The term of office of Rhode Island's governor was increased from two to four years effective with the 1994 election.

POSTWAR VOTE FOR SENATOR

Year	Total Vote	Republican Vote	Candidate	Democratic Vote	Candidate	Other Vote	Rep.-Dem. Plurality	Total Vote Rep.	Total Vote Dem.	Major Vote Rep.	Major Vote Dem.
2014	316,898	92,684	Zaccaria, Mark S.	223,675	Reed, Jack F.*	539	130,991 D	29.2%	70.6%	29.3%	70.7%
2012	418,189	146,222	Hinckley, Barry	271,034	Whitehouse, Sheldon*	933	124,812 D	35.0%	64.8%	35.0%	65.0%
2008	438,812	116,174	Tingle, Robert G.	320,644	Reed, Jack F.*	1,994	204,470 D	26.5%	73.1%	26.6%	73.4%
2006	385,451	179,001	Chafee, Lincoln D.*	206,110	Whitehouse, Sheldon	340	27,109 D	46.4%	53.5%	46.5%	53.5%
2002	323,912	69,881	Tingle, Robert G.	253,922	Reed, Jack F.*	109	184,041 D	21.6%	78.4%	21.6%	78.4%
2000	391,537	222,588	Chafee, Lincoln D.*	161,023	Weygand, Robert A.	7,926	61,565 R	56.8%	41.1%	58.0%	42.0%
1996	363,371	127,368	Mayer, Nancy J.	230,676	Reed, Jack F.	5,327	103,308 D	35.1%	63.5%	35.6%	64.4%
1994	345,388	222,856	Chafee, John H.*	122,532	Kushner, Linda J.		100,324 R	64.5%	35.5%	64.5%	35.5%
1990	364,062	138,947	Schneider, Claudine	225,105	Pell, Claiborne*	10	86,158 D	38.2%	61.8%	38.2%	61.8%
1988	397,996	217,273	Chafee, John H.*	180,717	Licht, Richard A.	6	36,556 R	54.6%	45.4%	54.6%	45.4%
1984	395,285	108,492	Leonard, Barbara	286,780	Pell, Claiborne*	13	178,288 D	27.4%	72.6%	27.4%	72.6%
1982	342,779	175,495	Chafee, John H.*	167,283	Michaelson, Julius C.	1	8,212 R	51.2%	48.8%	51.2%	48.8%
1978	305,618	76,061	Reynolds, James G.	229,557	Pell, Claiborne*		153,496 D	24.9%	75.1%	24.9%	75.1%
1976	398,906	230,329	Chafee, John H.*	167,665	Lorber, Richard P.	912	62,664 R	57.7%	42.0%	57.9%	42.1%
1972	413,432	188,990	Chafee, John H.	221,942	Pell, Claiborne*	2,500	32,952 D	45.7%	53.7%	46.0%	54.0%
1970	341,222	107,351	McLaughlin, John	230,469	Pastore, John O.*	3,402	123,118 D	31.5%	67.5%	31.8%	68.2%
1966	324,173	104,838	Briggs, Ruth M.	219,331	Pell, Claiborne*	4	114,493 D	32.3%	67.7%	32.3%	67.7%
1964	386,322	66,715	Lagueux, Ronald R.	319,607	Pastore, John O.*		252,892 D	17.3%	82.7%	17.3%	82.7%
1960	399,983	124,408	Archambault, Raoul	275,575	Pell, Claiborne		151,167 D	31.1%	68.9%	31.1%	68.9%
1958	344,519	122,353	Ewing, Bayard	222,166	Pastore, John O.*		99,813 D	35.5%	64.5%	35.5%	64.5%
1954	326,624	132,970	Sundlun, Walter I.	193,654	Green, Theodore Francis*		60,684 D	40.7%	59.3%	40.7%	59.3%
1952	410,978	185,850	Ewing, Bayard	225,128	Pastore, John O.*		39,278 D	45.2%	54.8%	45.2%	54.8%
1950S**	299,410	114,890	Levy, Austin T.	184,520	Pastore, John O.		69,630 D	38.4%	61.6%	38.4%	61.6%
1948	320,952	130,668	Hazard, Thomas P.	190,284	Green, Theodore Francis*		59,616 D	40.7%	59.3%	40.7%	59.3%
1946	273,528	122,780	Dyer, W. Gurnee	150,748	McGrath, J. Howard		27,968 D	44.9%	55.1%	44.9%	55.1%

Note: An asterisk (*) denotes incumbent. **The 1950 election was for a short term to fill a vacancy.

RHODE ISLAND

PRESIDENT 2016

2010 Census Population	County	Total Vote	Republican (Trump)	Democratic (Clinton)	Other	Rep.-Dem. Plurality	Total Vote Rep.	Total Vote Dem.	Major Vote Rep.	Major Vote Dem.
49,875	BRISTOL	25,475	8,965	14,609	1,901	5,644 D	35.2%	57.3%	38.0%	62.0%
166,158	KENT	81,453	37,736	37,788	5,929	52 D	46.3%	46.4%	50.0%	50.0%
82,888	NEWPORT	41,045	15,077	22,851	3,117	7,774 D	36.7%	55.7%	39.8%	60.2%
626,667	PROVIDENCE	248,452	90,881	142,879	14,692	51,998 D	36.6%	57.5%	38.9%	61.1%
126,979	WASHINGTON	66,369	27,230	33,741	5,398	6,511 D	41.0%	50.8%	44.7%	55.3%
	Votes Not Reported by County	1,350	654	657	39	3 D	48.4%	48.7%	49.9%	50.1%
1,052,567	TOTAL	464,144	180,543	252,525	31,076	71,982 D	38.9%	54.4%	41.7%	58.3%

2010 Census Population	City/Town	Total Vote	Republican (Trump)	Democratic (Clinton)	Other	Rep.-Dem. Plurality	Total Vote Rep.	Total Vote Dem.	Major Vote Rep.	Major Vote Dem.
16,310	BARRINGTON	9,758	2,898	6,153	707	3,255 D	29.7%	63.1%	32.0%	68.0%
22,954	BRISTOL TOWN	10,665	4,080	5,771	814	1,691 D	38.3%	54.1%	41.4%	58.6%
15,955	BURRILLVILLE	7,270	4,139	2,558	573	1,581 R	56.9%	35.2%	61.8%	38.2%
19,376	CENTRAL FALLS	4,236	657	3,394	185	2,737 D	15.5%	80.1%	16.2%	83.8%
7,827	CHARLESTOWN	4,443	1,906	2,207	330	301 D	42.9%	49.7%	46.3%	53.7%
35,014	COVENTRY	17,514	9,199	7,032	1,283	2,167 R	52.5%	40.2%	56.7%	43.3%
80,387	CRANSTON	36,796	15,934	18,763	2,099	2,829 D	43.3%	51.0%	45.9%	54.1%
33,506	CUMBERLAND	17,237	7,444	8,655	1,138	1,211 D	43.2%	50.2%	46.2%	53.8%
13,146	EAST GREENWICH	7,689	3,122	4,019	548	897 D	40.6%	52.3%	43.7%	56.3%
47,037	EAST PROVIDENCE	20,410	7,134	11,904	1,372	4,770 D	35.0%	58.3%	37.5%	62.5%
6,425	EXETER	3,586	1,820	1,471	295	349 R	50.8%	41.0%	55.3%	44.7%
4,606	FOSTER	2,534	1,374	967	193	407 R	54.2%	38.2%	58.7%	41.3%
9,746	GLOCESTER	5,263	2,914	1,977	372	937 R	55.4%	37.6%	59.6%	40.4%
8,188	HOPKINTON	4,226	2,135	1,766	325	369 R	50.5%	41.8%	54.7%	45.3%
5,405	JAMESTOWN	3,563	1,148	2,172	243	1,024 D	32.2%	61.0%	34.6%	65.4%
28,769	JOHNSTON	13,844	7,563	5,652	629	1,911 R	54.6%	40.8%	57.2%	42.8%
21,105	LINCOLN	11,408	5,410	5,279	719	131 R	47.4%	46.3%	50.6%	49.4%
3,492	LITTLE COMPTON	2,186	821	1,165	200	344 D	37.6%	53.3%	41.3%	58.7%
16,150	MIDDLETOWN	7,557	2,745	4,248	564	1,503 D	36.3%	56.2%	39.3%	60.7%
15,868	NARRAGANSETT	8,077	3,292	4,214	571	922 D	40.8%	52.2%	43.9%	56.1%
1,051	NEW SHOREHAM	891	214	609	68	395 D	24.0%	68.4%	26.0%	74.0%
24,672	NEWPORT CITY	9,658	2,644	6,287	727	3,643 D	27.4%	65.1%	29.6%	70.4%
26,486	NORTH KINGSTOWN	15,256	6,147	7,793	1,316	1,646 D	40.3%	51.1%	44.1%	55.9%
32,078	NORTH PROVIDENCE	15,511	6,936	7,760	815	824 D	44.7%	50.0%	47.2%	52.8%
11,967	NORTH SMITHFIELD	6,251	3,242	2,570	439	672 R	51.9%	41.1%	55.8%	44.2%
71,148	PAWTUCKET	23,001	6,221	15,574	1,206	9,353 D	27.0%	67.7%	28.5%	71.5%
17,389	PORTSMOUTH	9,658	3,922	4,945	791	1,023 D	40.6%	51.2%	44.2%	55.8%
178,042	PROVIDENCE CITY	55,639	7,682	45,053	2,904	37,371 D	13.8%	81.0%	14.6%	85.4%
7,708	RICHMOND	4,127	2,058	1,713	356	345 R	49.9%	41.5%	54.6%	45.4%
10,329	SCITUATE	6,005	3,536	2,045	424	1,491 R	58.9%	34.1%	63.4%	36.6%
21,430	SMITHFIELD	10,378	5,254	4,402	722	852 R	50.6%	42.4%	54.4%	45.6%
30,639	SOUTH KINGSTOWN	14,617	4,627	8,677	1,313	4,050 D	31.7%	59.4%	34.8%	65.2%
15,780	TIVERTON	8,423	3,797	4,034	592	237 D	45.1%	47.9%	48.5%	51.5%
10,611	WARREN	5,052	1,987	2,685	380	698 D	39.3%	53.1%	42.5%	57.5%
82,672	WARWICK	41,440	18,338	20,038	3,064	1,700 D	44.3%	48.4%	47.8%	52.2%
6,135	WEST GREENWICH	3,374	1,953	1,159	262	794 R	57.9%	34.4%	62.8%	37.2%
29,191	WEST WARWICK	12,036	5,724	5,540	772	184 R	47.6%	46.0%	50.8%	49.2%
22,787	WESTERLY	11,146	5,031	5,291	824	260 D	45.1%	47.5%	48.7%	51.3%
41,186	WOONSOCKET	12,691	5,442	6,346	903	904 D	42.9%	50.0%	46.2%	53.8%

RHODE ISLAND

HOUSE OF REPRESENTATIVES

CD	Year	Total Vote	Republican Vote	Republican Candidate	Democratic Vote	Democratic Candidate	Other Vote	Rep.-Dem. Plurality	Total Vote Rep.	Total Vote Dem.	Major Vote Rep.	Major Vote Dem.
1	2016	202,371	71,023	TAUB, H. RUSSELL	130,534	CICILLINE, DAVID N.*	814	59,511 D	35.1%	64.5%	35.2%	64.8%
1	2014	146,353	58,877	LYNCH, CORMICK	87,060	CICILLINE, DAVID N.*	416	28,183 D	40.2%	59.5%	40.3%	59.7%
1	2012	205,115	83,737	DOHERTY, BRENDAN P.	108,612	CICILLINE, DAVID N.*	12,766	24,875 D	40.8%	53.0%	43.5%	56.5%
2	2016	229,148	70,301	REIS, RHUE	133,108	LANGEVIN, JAMES R.*	25,739	62,807 D	30.7%	58.1%	34.6%	65.4%
2	2014	169,904	63,844	REIS, RHUE	105,716	LANGEVIN, JAMES R.*	344	41,872 D	37.6%	62.2%	37.7%	62.3%
2	2012	222,660	78,189	RILEY, MICHAEL G.	124,067	LANGEVIN, JAMES R.*	20,404	45,878 D	35.1%	55.7%	38.7%	61.3%
TOTAL	2016	431,519	141,324		263,642		26,553	122,318 D	32.8%	61.1%	34.9%	65.1%
TOTAL	2014	316,257	122,721		192,776		760	70,055 D	38.8%	61.0%	38.9%	61.1%
TOTAL	2012	427,775	161,926		232,679		33,170	70,753 D	37.9%	54.4%	41.0%	59.0%

Note: An asterisk (*) denotes incumbent.

RHODE ISLAND

GENERAL AND PRIMARY ELECTIONS

2016 GENERAL ELECTIONS: OTHER VOTES

President Other vote was 14,746 Libertarian (Gary Johnson) 6,718 Write-in (Scattered Write-In), 6,220 Green (Jill Stein), 2,205 Write-in (Bernard Sanders), 671 American Delta (Roque De La Fuente), 516 Write-in (Evan McMullin)

House Other vote was:

CD 1 814 Write-in (Scattered Write-in)

CD 2 16,253 Independent (Jeffrey Johnson), 8,942 Independent (Salvatore Caiozzo), 544 Write-in (Scattered Write-in)

2016 PRIMARY ELECTIONS: SUPPLEMENTARY INFORMATION

Primary April 26, 2016 (President) September 13, 2016 (Congress)

Registration (as of August 14, 2016) 770,214

Democratic 309,112
Republican 92,713
Moderate 2,544
Unaffiliated 365,845

Primary Type Semi-open—Registered Democrats and Republicans could vote only in their party's primary. Unaffiliated voters could participate in either party's primary.

REPUBLICAN PRIMARIES			DEMOCRATIC PRIMARIES		
President	Trump, Donald J.	39,221	63.7%	Sanders, Bernard	66,993	54.7%
	Kasich, John R.	14,963	24.3%	Clinton, Hillary Rodham	52,749	43.1%
	Cruz, Ted	6,416	10.4%	Uncommitted	1,662	1.4%
	Uncommitted	417	0.7%	Write-In	673	0.5%
	Rubio, Marco	382	0.6%	Stewart, Mark	236	0.2%
	Write-In	215	0.3%	De La Fuente, Roque "Rocky"	145	0.1%
	TOTAL	61,614		TOTAL	122,458	
Congressional District 1	Taub, H. Russell	629	100.0%	Cicilline, David N.*	24,136	67.6%
				Young, Christopher F.	11,594	32.4%
	TOTAL	629		TOTAL	35,730	
Congressional District 2	Reis, Rhue	641	100.0%	Langevin, James R.*	16,334	64.4%
				Archer, Steven	4,768	18.8%
				Hamilton, John D.	4,272	16.8%
	TOTAL	641		TOTAL	25,374	

Note: An asterisk (*) denotes incumbent.

SOUTH CAROLINA

Congressional districts first established for elections held in 2012

7 members

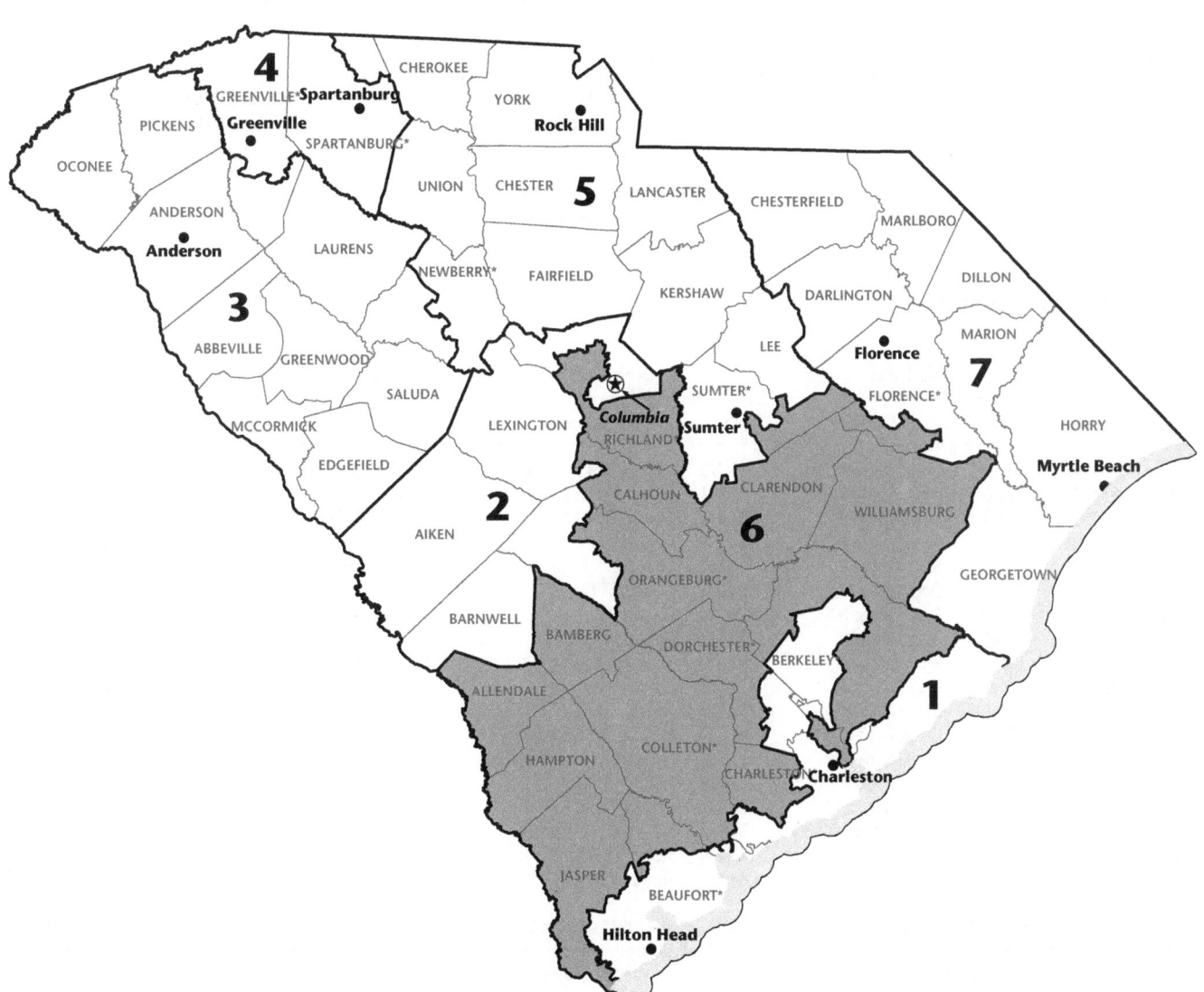

* Asterisk indicates a county whose boundaries include parts of two or more congressional districts.

SOUTH CAROLINA

GOVERNOR

Henry McMaster (R). Sworn in January 24, 2017, to complete the remainder of the term vacated by the resignation of Nikki R. Haley to become U.S. ambassador to the United Nations.

SENATORS (2 Republicans)

Lindsey Graham (R). Re-elected 2014 to a six-year term. Previously elected 2008, 2002.

Tim Scott (R). Elected 2014 to a six-year term. Initially sworn in on January 3, 2013, to fill the vacancy created by the resignation of Jim DeMint (R), who resigned two days earlier to become president of the Heritage Foundation.

REPRESENTATIVES (6 Republicans, 1 Democrat)

1. Mark Sanford (R)
2. Joe Wilson (R)
3. Jeff Duncan (R)
4. Trey Gowdy (R)
5. Ralph Norman (R)
6. James E. Clyburn (D)
7. Tom Rice (R)

Note: In CD 5, Mick Mulvaney (R) won re-election in 2016, but resigned in February 2017 to become the director of Office of Management and Budget (OMB) in the Trump administration. Ralph Norman (R) won a special election June 20, 2017, to fill the vacancy.

POSTWAR VOTE FOR PRESIDENT

| | | Republican | | Democratic | | | | Percentage | | | |
| | | | | | | | | Total Vote | | Major Vote | |
Year	Total Vote	Vote	Candidate	Vote	Candidate	Other Vote	Rep.-Dem. Plurality	Rep.	Dem.	Rep.	Dem.
2016**	2,103,027	1,155,389	Trump, Donald J.	855,373	Clinton, Hillary Rodham	92,265	300,016 R	54.9%	40.7%	57.5%	42.5%
2012	1,964,118	1,071,645	Romney, W. Mitt	865,941	Obama, Barack H.*	26,532	205,704 R	54.6%	44.1%	55.3%	44.7%
2008	1,920,969	1,034,896	McCain, John S. III	862,449	Obama, Barack H.	23,624	172,447 R	53.9%	44.9%	54.5%	45.5%
2004	1,617,730	937,974	Bush, George W.*	661,699	Kerry, John F.	18,057	276,275 R	58.0%	40.9%	58.6%	41.4%
2000**	1,382,717	785,937	Bush, George W.	565,561	Gore, Albert Jr.	31,219	220,376 R	56.8%	40.9%	58.2%	41.8%
1996**	1,151,689	573,458	Dole, Robert "Bob"	506,283	Clinton, Bill*	71,948	67,175 R	49.8%	44.0%	53.1%	46.9%
1992**	1,202,527	577,507	Bush, George H.*	479,514	Clinton, Bill	145,506	97,993 R	48.0%	39.9%	54.6%	45.4%
1988	986,009	606,443	Bush, George H.	370,554	Dukakis, Michael S.	9,012	235,889 R	61.5%	37.6%	62.1%	37.9%
1984	968,529	615,539	Reagan, Ronald*	344,459	Mondale, Walter F.	8,531	271,080 R	63.6%	35.6%	64.1%	35.9%
1980**	894,071	441,841	Reagan, Ronald	430,385	Carter, Jimmy*	21,845	11,456 R	49.4%	48.1%	50.7%	49.3%
1976	802,583	346,149	Ford, Gerald R.*	450,807	Carter, Jimmy	5,627	104,658 D	43.1%	56.2%	43.4%	56.6%
1972	673,960	477,044	Nixon, Richard M.*	186,824	McGovern, George S.	10,092	290,220 R	70.8%	27.7%	71.9%	28.1%
1968**	666,978	254,062	Nixon, Richard M.	197,486	Humphrey, Hubert Horatio Jr.	215,430	56,576 R	38.1%	29.6%	56.3%	43.7%
1964	524,779	309,048	Goldwater, Barry M. Sr.	215,723	Johnson, Lyndon B.*	8	93,325 R	58.9%	41.1%	58.9%	41.1%
1960	386,688	188,558	Nixon, Richard M.	198,129	Kennedy, John F.	1	9,571 D	48.8%	51.2%	48.8%	51.2%
1956**	300,583	75,700	Eisenhower, Dwight D.*	136,372	Stevenson, Adlai E. II	88,511	60,672 D	25.2%	45.4%	35.7%	64.3%
1952	341,087	168,082	Eisenhower, Dwight D.	173,004	Stevenson, Adlai E. II	1	4,922 D	49.3%	50.7%	49.3%	50.7%
1948**	142,571	5,386	Dewey, Thomas E.	34,423	Truman, Harry S.*	102,762	29,037 D	3.8%	24.1%	13.5%	86.5%

Note: An asterisk (*) denotes incumbent. **In past elections, the other vote included: 2016 - 49,204 Libertarian (Gary Johnson); 2000 - 20,200 Green (Ralph Nader); 1996 - 64,386 Reform (Ross Perot); 1992 - 138,872 Independent (Perot); 1980 - 14,153 Independent (John Anderson); 1968 - 215,430 American Independent (George Wallace, who finished second); 1956 - 88,509 Uncommitted States' Rights electors, which placed second; 1948 - 102,607 States' Rights (Strom Thurmond, who won South Carolina with 72.0 percent of the total vote and a plurality of 68,184 votes).

SOUTH CAROLINA

POSTWAR VOTE FOR GOVERNOR

Year	Total Vote	Republican		Democratic		Other Vote	Rep.-Dem. Plurality	Percentage			
								Total Vote		Major Vote	
		Vote	Candidate	Vote	Candidate			Rep.	Dem.	Rep.	Dem.
2014	1,246,301	696,645	Haley, Nikki R.*	516,166	Sheheen, Vincent A.	33,490	180,479 R	55.9%	41.4%	57.4%	42.6%
2010	1,344,198	690,525	Haley, Nikki R.	630,534	Sheheen, Vincent A.	23,139	59,991 R	51.4%	46.9%	52.3%	47.7%
2006	1,091,952	601,868	Sanford, Marshall Clement "Mark" Jr.*	489,076	Moore, Tommy	1,008	112,792 R	55.1%	44.8%	55.2%	44.8%
2002	1,107,725	585,422	Sanford, Marshall Clement "Mark" Jr.	521,140	Hodges, James H.*	1,163	64,282 R	52.8%	47.0%	52.9%	47.1%
1998	1,070,869	484,088	Beasley, David*	570,070	Hodges, James H.	16,711	85,982 D	45.2%	53.2%	45.9%	54.1%
1994	933,850	470,756	Beasley, David	447,002	Theodore, Nick A.	16,092	23,754 R	50.4%	47.9%	51.3%	48.7%
1990	760,965	528,831	Campbell, Carroll*	212,034	Mitchell, Theo	20,100	316,797 R	69.5%	27.9%	71.4%	28.6%
1986	753,751	384,565	Campbell, Carroll	361,325	Daniel, Mike	7,861	23,240 R	51.0%	47.9%	51.6%	48.4%
1982	671,625	202,806	Workman, W. D. III	468,819	Riley, Richard W.*		266,013 D	30.2%	69.8%	30.2%	69.8%
1978	627,182	236,946	Young, Edward L.	384,898	Riley, Richard W.	5,338	147,952 D	37.8%	61.4%	38.1%	61.9%
1974	523,199	266,109	Edwards, James B.	248,938	Dorn, W.J. Bryan	8,152	17,171 R	50.9%	47.6%	51.7%	48.3%
1970	484,257	221,233	Watson, Albert W.	249,951	West, John C.	13,073	28,718 D	45.7%	51.6%	47.0%	53.0%
1966	439,942	184,088	Rogers, Joseph O. Jr.	255,854	McNair, Robert E.*		71,766 D	41.8%	58.2%	41.8%	58.2%
1962	253,721			253,704	Russell, Donald S.	17	253,704 D		100.0%		100.0%
1958	77,740			77,714	Hollings, Ernest F.	26	77,714 D		100.0%		100.0%
1954	214,212			214,204	Timmerman, George Bell	8	214,204 D		100.0%		100.0%
1950	50,642			50,633	Byrnes, James F.	9	50,633 D		100.0%		100.0%
1946	26,520			26,520	Thurmond, James Strom		26,520 D		100.0%		100.0%

Note: An asterisk (*) denotes incumbent. The Republican Party did not run a candidate in the gubernatorial elections of 1946, 1950, 1954, 1958, and 1962.

POSTWAR VOTE FOR SENATOR

Year	Total Vote	Republican		Democratic		Other Vote	Rep.-Dem. Plurality	Percentage			
								Total Vote		Major Vote	
		Vote	Candidate	Vote	Candidate			Rep.	Dem.	Rep.	Dem.
2016	2,049,893	1,241,609	Scott, Tim*	757,022	Dixon, Thomas	51,262	484,587 R	60.6%	36.9%	62.1%	37.9%
2014	1,240,075	672,941	Graham, Lindsey*	480,933	Hutto, C. Bradley "Brad"	86,201	192,008 R	54.3%	38.8%	58.3%	41.7%
2014S**	1,238,982	757,215	Scott, Tim*	459,583	Dickerson, Joyce	22,184	297,632 R	61.1%	37.1%	62.2%	37.8%
2010	1,318,794	810,771	DeMint, James W. "Jim"*	364,598	Greene, Alvin M.	143,425	446,173 R	61.5%	27.6%	69.0%	31.0%
2008	1,871,431	1,076,534	Graham, Lindsey*	790,621	Conley, Bob	4,276	285,913 R	57.5%	42.2%	57.7%	42.3%
2004	1,597,221	857,167	DeMint, James W. "Jim"	704,384	Tenenbaum, Inez M.	35,670	152,783 R	53.7%	44.1%	54.9%	45.1%
2002	1,102,948	600,010	Graham, Lindsey	487,359	Sanders, Alex	15,579	112,651 R	54.4%	44.2%	55.2%	44.8%
1998	1,068,367	488,132	Inglis, Robert D.	562,791	Hollings, Ernest F.*	17,444	74,659 D	45.7%	52.7%	46.4%	53.6%
1996	1,161,372	619,859	Thurmond, James Strom*	510,951	Close, Elliott	30,562	108,908 R	53.4%	44.0%	54.8%	45.2%
1992	1,180,438	554,175	Hartnett, Thomas F.	591,030	Hollings, Ernest F.*	35,233	36,855 D	46.9%	50.1%	48.4%	51.6%
1990	750,716	482,032	Thurmond, James Strom*	244,112	Cunningham, Bob	24,572	237,920 R	64.2%	32.5%	66.4%	33.6%
1986	737,962	262,886	McMaster, Henry D.	465,500	Hollings, Ernest F.*	9,576	202,614 D	35.6%	63.1%	36.1%	63.9%
1984	965,130	644,815	Thurmond, James Strom*	306,982	Purvis, Melvin	13,333	337,833 R	66.8%	31.8%	67.7%	32.3%
1980	870,594	257,946	Mays, Marshall T.	612,554	Hollings, Ernest F.*	94	354,608 D	29.6%	70.4%	29.6%	70.4%
1978	632,852	351,733	Thurmond, James Strom*	281,119	Ravenel, Charles D.		70,614 R	55.6%	44.4%	55.6%	44.4%
1974	512,397	146,645	Bush, Gwenfred	356,126	Hollings, Ernest F.*	9,626	209,481 D	28.6%	69.5%	29.2%	70.8%
1972	672,246	426,601	Thurmond, James Strom*	245,457	Zeigler, Eugene N.	188	181,144 R	63.5%	36.5%	63.5%	36.5%
1968	652,855	248,780	Parker, Marshall	404,060	Hollings, Ernest F.*	15	155,280 D	38.1%	61.9%	38.1%	61.9%
1966	436,252	271,297	Thurmond, James Strom*	164,955	Morrah, Bradley		106,342 R	62.2%	37.8%	62.2%	37.8%
1966S**	435,822	212,032	Parker, Marshall	223,790	Hollings, Ernest F.		11,758 D	48.7%	51.3%	48.7%	51.3%
1962	312,647	133,930	Workman, W. D. III	178,712	Johnston, Olin D.*	5	44,782 D	42.8%	57.2%	42.8%	57.2%
1960	330,266			330,164	Thurmond, James Strom*	102	330,164 D		100.0%		100.0%
1956	279,845	49,695	Crawford, L. P.	230,150	Johnston, Olin D.*		180,455 D	17.8%	82.2%	17.8%	82.2%
1956S**	245,371			245,371	Thurmond, James Strom		245,371 D		100.0%		100.0%
1954**	226,967			83,525	Brown, Edgar A.	143,442	83,525 D#		36.8%		100.0%
1950	50,277			50,240	Johnston, Olin D.*	37	50,240 D		99.9%		100.0%
1948	135,998			135,998	Maybank, Burnet R.*		135,998 D		100.0%		100.0%

Note: An asterisk (*) denotes incumbent. A pound sign (#) in the plurality column indicates that the winner in 1954 was an Independent Democrat. **In past elections, the other vote included: 1954 - 143,442 Independent Democratic (Strom Thurmond). Thurmond ran as a write-in candidate and won with 63.1 percent of the total vote and a plurality of 59,917 votes. One each of the 1956, 1966, and 2014 elections was for a short term to fill a vacancy. The Republican Party did not run a Senate candidate in 1948, 1950, 1954, 1956 (for the short term), and 1960.

SOUTH CAROLINA

PRESIDENT 2016

2010 Census Population	County	Total Vote	Republican (Trump)	Democratic (Clinton)	Other	Rep.-Dem. Plurality	Percentage Total Vote Rep.	Dem.	Major Vote Rep.	Dem.
25,417	ABBEVILLE	10,775	6,763	3,741	271	3,022 R	62.8%	34.7%	64.4%	35.6%
160,099	AIKEN	74,851	46,025	25,455	3,371	20,570 R	61.5%	34.0%	64.4%	35.6%
10,419	ALLENDALE	3,592	789	2,735	68	1,946 D	22.0%	76.1%	22.4%	77.6%
187,126	ANDERSON	80,483	56,232	21,097	3,154	35,135 R	69.9%	26.2%	72.7%	27.3%
15,987	BAMBERG	6,214	2,204	3,898	112	1,694 D	35.5%	62.7%	36.1%	63.9%
22,621	BARNWELL	9,485	4,889	4,400	196	489 R	51.5%	46.4%	52.6%	47.4%
162,233	BEAUFORT	78,524	42,922	32,138	3,464	10,784 R	54.7%	40.9%	57.2%	42.8%
177,843	BERKELEY	79,517	44,587	30,705	4,225	13,882 R	56.1%	38.6%	59.2%	40.8%
15,175	CALHOUN	7,549	3,787	3,573	189	214 R	50.2%	47.3%	51.5%	48.5%
350,209	CHARLESTON	176,345	75,443	89,299	11,603	13,856 D	42.8%	50.6%	45.8%	54.2%
55,342	CHEROKEE	21,759	15,167	6,092	500	9,075 R	69.7%	28.0%	71.3%	28.7%
33,140	CHESTER	14,192	7,265	6,579	348	686 R	51.2%	46.4%	52.5%	47.5%
46,734	CHESTERFIELD	16,581	9,312	6,858	411	2,454 R	56.2%	41.4%	57.6%	42.4%
34,971	CLARENDON	15,395	7,386	7,732	277	346 D	48.0%	50.2%	48.9%	51.1%
38,892	COLLETON	17,251	9,091	7,627	533	1,464 R	52.7%	44.2%	54.4%	45.6%
68,681	DARLINGTON	29,674	14,989	13,888	797	1,101 R	50.5%	46.8%	51.9%	48.1%
32,062	DILLON	11,698	5,637	5,834	227	197 D	48.2%	49.9%	49.1%	50.9%
136,555	DORCHESTER	62,567	34,987	24,055	3,525	10,932 R	55.9%	38.4%	59.3%	40.7%
26,985	EDGEFIELD	11,644	6,842	4,491	311	2,351 R	58.8%	38.6%	60.4%	39.6%
23,956	FAIRFIELD	11,267	4,027	6,945	295	2,918 D	35.7%	61.6%	36.7%	63.3%
136,885	FLORENCE	57,931	29,573	26,710	1,648	2,863 R	51.0%	46.1%	52.5%	47.5%
60,158	GEORGETOWN	31,657	17,389	13,310	958	4,079 R	54.9%	42.0%	56.6%	43.4%
451,225	GREENVILLE	215,165	127,832	74,483	12,850	53,349 R	59.4%	34.6%	63.2%	36.8%
69,661	GREENWOOD	28,763	16,961	10,711	1,091	6,250 R	59.0%	37.2%	61.3%	38.7%
21,090	HAMPTON	8,806	3,488	5,170	148	1,682 D	39.6%	58.7%	40.3%	59.7%
269,291	HORRY	132,920	89,288	39,410	4,222	49,878 R	67.2%	29.6%	69.4%	30.6%
24,777	JASPER	11,427	5,187	5,956	284	769 D	45.4%	52.1%	46.5%	53.5%
61,697	KERSHAW	28,995	17,542	10,330	1,123	7,212 R	60.5%	35.6%	62.9%	37.1%
76,652	LANCASTER	38,938	23,719	13,812	1,407	9,907 R	60.9%	35.5%	63.2%	36.8%
66,537	LAURENS	26,566	16,816	8,889	861	7,927 R	63.3%	33.5%	65.4%	34.6%
19,220	LEE	8,156	2,803	5,199	154	2,396 D	34.4%	63.7%	35.0%	65.0%
262,391	LEXINGTON	122,093	80,026	35,230	6,837	44,796 R	65.5%	28.9%	69.4%	30.6%
33,062	MARION	14,276	5,444	8,569	263	3,125 D	38.1%	60.0%	38.8%	61.2%
28,933	MARLBORO	10,389	4,267	5,954	168	1,687 D	41.1%	57.3%	41.7%	58.3%
10,233	MCCORMICK	5,216	2,652	2,479	85	173 R	50.8%	47.5%	51.7%	48.3%
37,508	NEWBERRY	16,807	10,017	6,217	573	3,800 R	59.6%	37.0%	61.7%	38.3%
74,273	OCONEE	33,635	24,178	7,998	1,459	16,180 R	71.9%	23.8%	75.1%	24.9%
92,501	ORANGEBURG	38,910	11,931	26,318	661	14,387 D	30.7%	67.6%	31.2%	68.8%
119,224	PICKENS	49,049	36,236	10,354	2,459	25,882 R	73.9%	21.1%	77.8%	22.2%
384,504	RICHLAND	168,722	52,469	108,000	8,253	55,531 D	31.1%	64.0%	32.7%	67.3%
19,875	SALUDA	8,564	5,526	2,813	225	2,713 R	64.5%	32.8%	66.3%	33.7%
284,307	SPARTANBURG	121,090	76,277	39,997	4,816	36,280 R	63.0%	33.0%	65.6%	34.4%
107,456	SUMTER	44,086	18,745	24,047	1,294	5,302 D	42.5%	54.5%	43.8%	56.2%
28,961	UNION	12,092	7,061	4,729	302	2,332 R	58.4%	39.1%	59.9%	40.1%
34,423	WILLIAMSBURG	15,054	4,864	9,953	237	5,089 D	32.3%	66.1%	32.8%	67.2%
226,073	YORK	114,357	66,754	41,593	6,010	25,161 R	58.4%	36.4%	61.6%	38.4%
4,625,364	TOTAL	2,103,027	1,155,389	855,373	92,265	300,016 R	54.9%	40.7%	57.5%	42.5%

SOUTH CAROLINA

SENATOR 2016

2010 Census Population	County	Total Vote	Republican (Scott)	Democratic (Dixon)	Other	Rep.-Dem. Plurality	Total Vote Rep.	Total Vote Dem.	Major Vote Rep.	Major Vote Dem.
25,417	ABBEVILLE	10,470	6,669	3,570	231	3,099 R	63.7%	34.1%	65.1%	34.9%
160,099	AIKEN	73,170	47,318	23,681	2,171	23,637 R	64.7%	32.4%	66.6%	33.4%
10,419	ALLENDALE	3,395	796	2,544	55	1,748 D	23.4%	74.9%	23.8%	76.2%
187,126	ANDERSON	78,415	57,675	18,648	2,092	39,027 R	73.6%	23.8%	75.6%	24.4%
15,987	BAMBERG	6,073	2,159	3,825	89	1,666 D	35.6%	63.0%	36.1%	63.9%
22,621	BARNWELL	9,187	4,793	4,228	166	565 R	52.2%	46.0%	53.1%	46.9%
162,233	BEAUFORT	76,293	48,125	26,619	1,549	21,506 R	63.1%	34.9%	64.4%	35.6%
177,843	BERKELEY	77,710	50,423	25,435	1,852	24,988 R	64.9%	32.7%	66.5%	33.5%
15,175	CALHOUN	7,388	3,834	3,365	189	469 R	51.9%	45.5%	53.3%	46.7%
350,209	CHARLESTON	172,925	97,219	71,631	4,075	25,588 R	56.2%	41.4%	57.6%	42.4%
55,342	CHEROKEE	21,020	14,565	5,901	554	8,664 R	69.3%	28.1%	71.2%	28.8%
33,140	CHESTER	13,614	6,649	6,578	387	71 R	48.8%	48.3%	50.3%	49.7%
46,734	CHESTERFIELD	16,016	8,895	6,783	338	2,112 R	55.5%	42.4%	56.7%	43.3%
34,971	CLARENDON	14,934	7,477	7,214	243	263 R	50.1%	48.3%	50.9%	49.1%
38,892	COLLETON	16,495	9,427	6,710	358	2,717 R	57.2%	40.7%	58.4%	41.6%
68,681	DARLINGTON	28,882	15,261	13,066	555	2,195 R	52.8%	45.2%	53.9%	46.1%
32,062	DILLON	10,921	5,743	4,969	209	774 R	52.6%	45.5%	53.6%	46.4%
136,555	DORCHESTER	61,362	39,918	20,009	1,435	19,909 R	65.1%	32.6%	66.6%	33.4%
26,985	EDGEFIELD	11,256	6,662	4,320	274	2,342 R	59.2%	38.4%	60.7%	39.3%
23,956	FAIRFIELD	10,832	4,265	6,342	225	2,077 D	39.4%	58.5%	40.2%	59.8%
136,885	FLORENCE	56,744	31,449	24,330	965	7,119 R	55.4%	42.9%	56.4%	43.6%
60,158	GEORGETOWN	31,052	18,737	11,882	433	6,855 R	60.3%	38.3%	61.2%	38.8%
451,225	GREENVILLE	211,013	141,731	63,441	5,841	78,290 R	67.2%	30.1%	69.1%	30.9%
69,661	GREENWOOD	27,969	17,568	9,797	604	7,771 R	62.8%	35.0%	64.2%	35.8%
21,090	HAMPTON	8,299	3,265	4,831	203	1,566 D	39.3%	58.2%	40.3%	59.7%
269,291	HORRY	128,542	90,641	35,038	2,863	55,603 R	70.5%	27.3%	72.1%	27.9%
24,777	JASPER	10,601	5,152	5,201	248	49 D	48.6%	49.1%	49.8%	50.2%
61,697	KERSHAW	28,226	17,949	9,486	791	8,463 R	63.6%	33.6%	65.4%	34.6%
76,652	LANCASTER	37,621	23,199	13,350	1,072	9,849 R	61.7%	35.5%	63.5%	36.5%
66,537	LAURENS	25,625	17,051	7,793	781	9,258 R	66.5%	30.4%	68.6%	31.4%
19,220	LEE	7,868	2,727	4,998	143	2,271 D	34.7%	63.5%	35.3%	64.7%
262,391	LEXINGTON	119,676	85,385	29,995	4,296	55,390 R	71.3%	25.1%	74.0%	26.0%
33,062	MARION	13,586	5,500	7,915	171	2,415 D	40.5%	58.3%	41.0%	59.0%
28,933	MARLBORO	10,015	4,132	5,717	166	1,585 D	41.3%	57.1%	42.0%	58.0%
10,233	MCCORMICK	5,019	2,699	2,241	79	458 R	53.8%	44.7%	54.6%	45.4%
37,508	NEWBERRY	16,308	10,048	5,772	488	4,276 R	61.6%	35.4%	63.5%	36.5%
74,273	OCONEE	32,747	25,248	6,722	777	18,526 R	77.1%	20.5%	79.0%	21.0%
92,501	ORANGEBURG	38,153	12,256	25,384	513	13,128 D	32.1%	66.5%	32.6%	67.4%
119,224	PICKENS	48,028	37,726	8,858	1,444	28,868 R	78.6%	18.4%	81.0%	19.0%
384,504	RICHLAND	165,408	66,736	95,045	3,627	28,309 D	40.3%	57.5%	41.3%	58.7%
19,875	SALUDA	8,343	5,443	2,691	209	2,752 R	65.2%	32.3%	66.9%	33.1%
284,307	SPARTANBURG	118,122	79,487	35,239	3,396	44,248 R	67.3%	29.8%	69.3%	30.7%
107,456	SUMTER	43,173	19,462	22,916	795	3,454 D	45.1%	53.1%	45.9%	54.1%
28,961	UNION	11,599	6,727	4,514	358	2,213 R	58.0%	38.9%	59.8%	40.2%
34,423	WILLIAMSBURG	14,473	5,138	9,179	156	4,041 D	35.5%	63.4%	35.9%	64.1%
226,073	YORK	111,325	68,280	39,249	3,796	29,031 R	61.3%	35.3%	63.5%	36.5%
4,625,364	TOTAL	2,049,893	1,241,609	757,022	51,262	484,587 R	60.6%	36.9%	62.1%	37.9%

Note: Candidates in South Carolina can appear on the ballot line of more than one party. Thomas Dixon received the following vote: 704,540 (Democratic), 37,610 (Working Families), 14,872 (Green).

SOUTH CAROLINA

HOUSE OF REPRESENTATIVES

CD	Year	Total Vote	Republican		Democratic		Other Vote	Rep.-Dem. Plurality	Percentage			
			Vote	Candidate	Vote	Candidate			Total Vote		Major Vote	
									Rep.	Dem.	Rep.	Dem.
1	2016	325,170	190,410	SANFORD, MARK*	119,779	CHERNY, DIMITRI	14,981	70,631 R	58.6%	36.8%	61.4%	38.6%
1	2014	127,815	119,392	SANFORD, MARK*			8,423	119,392 R	93.4%		100.0%	
1	2012	290,013	179,908	SCOTT, TIM*	103,557	ROSE, BOBBIE G.	6,548	76,351 R	62.0%	35.7%	63.5%	36.5%
2	2016	304,996	183,746	WILSON, JOE*	109,452	BJORN, ARIK	11,798	74,294 R	60.2%	35.9%	62.7%	37.3%
2	2014	194,808	121,649	WILSON, JOE*	68,719	BLACK, PHIL	4,440	52,930 R	62.4%	35.3%	63.9%	36.1%
2	2012	203,718	196,116	WILSON, JOE*			7,602	196,116 R	96.3%		100.0%	
3	2016	272,481	198,431	DUNCAN, JEFF*	73,766	CLEVELAND, HOSEA	284	124,665 R	72.8%	27.1%	72.9%	27.1%
3	2014	164,009	116,741	DUNCAN, JEFF*	47,181	MULLIS, BARBARA JO	87	69,560 R	71.2%	28.8%	71.2%	28.8%
3	2012	254,763	169,512	DUNCAN, JEFF*	84,735	DOYLE, BRIAN RYAN B.	516	84,777 R	66.5%	33.3%	66.7%	33.3%
4	2016	295,670	198,648	GOWDY, TREY*	91,676	FEDALEI, CHRISTOPHER	5,346	106,972 R	67.2%	31.0%	68.4%	31.6%
4	2014	149,049	126,452	GOWDY, TREY*			22,597	126,452 R	84.8%		100.0%	
4	2012	266,884	173,201	GOWDY, TREY*	89,964	MORROW, DEB	3,719	83,237 R	64.9%	33.7%	65.8%	34.2%
5	2016	299,731	175,909	MULVANEY, MICK*	115,437	PERSON, FRANCIS "FRAN"	6,435	60,472 R	59.1%	38.8%	60.4%	39.6%
5	2014	175,145	103,078	MULVANEY, MICK*	71,985	ADAMS, TOM A.	82	31,093 R	58.9%	41.1%	58.9%	41.1%
5	2012	278,003	154,324	MULVANEY, MICK*	123,443	KNOTT, JOYCE	236	30,881 R	55.5%	44.4%	55.6%	44.4%
6	2016	253,901	70,099	STERLING, LAURA	177,947	CLYBURN, JAMES E.*	5,855	107,848 D	27.6%	70.1%	28.3%	71.7%
6	2014	173,432	44,311	CULLER, ANTHONY	125,747	CLYBURN, JAMES E.*	3,374	81,436 D	25.5%	72.5%	26.1%	73.9%
6	2012	233,615			218,717	CLYBURN, JAMES E.*	14,898	218,717 D		93.6%		100.0%
7	2016	289,463	176,468	RICE, TOM*	112,744	HYMAN, MAL	251	63,724 R	61.0%	38.9%	61.0%	39.0%
7	2014	171,524	102,833	RICE, TOM*	68,576	TINUBU, GLORIA BROMELL	115	34,257 R	60.0%	40.0%	60.0%	40.0%
7	2012	275,738	153,068	RICE, TOM	122,389	TINUBU, GLORIA BROMELL	281	30,679 R	55.5%	44.4%	55.6%	44.4%
TOTAL	2016	2,039,462	1,193,711		800,801		44,950	392,910 R	58.5%	39.3%	59.8%	40.2%
TOTAL	2014	1,155,782	734,456		382,208		39,118	352,248 R	63.5%	33.1%	65.8%	34.2%
TOTAL	2012	1,802,734	1,026,129		742,805		33,800	283,324 R	56.9%	41.2%	58.0%	42.0%

Note: An asterisk (*) denotes incumbent. Some Democratic candidates received votes on additional ballot lines for the Working Families Party and the Green Party. These votes are included in their totals above.

SOUTH CAROLINA

GENERAL AND PRIMARY ELECTIONS

2016 GENERAL ELECTIONS: OTHER VOTES

President Other vote was 49,204 Libertarian (Gary Johnson), 21,016 Independent (Evan McMullin), 13,034 Green (Jill Stein), 5,765 Constitution (Darrell Castle), 3,246 American (Peter Skewes)

Senate Other vote was 37,482 Libertarian (Bill Bledsoe), 11,923 Independent (Rebel Scarborough), 1,857 Write-in (Scattered Write-in)

House Other vote was:

CD 1 11,614 Libertarian (Michael Grier), 2,774 American (Albert Travison), 593 Write-in (Scattered Write-in)
CD 2 11,444 American (George McCain, Jr.), 354 Write-in (Scattered Write-in)
CD 3 284 Write-in (Scattered Write-in)
CD 4 5,103 Constitution (Michael Chandler), 243 Write-in (Scattered Write-in)
CD 5 6,239 American (Rudy Barnes), 196 Write-in (Scattered Write-in)
CD 6 3,131 Libertarian (Rich Piotrowski), 2,499 Green (Price Mallory), 225 Write-in (Scattered Write-in)
CD 7 251 Write-in (Scattered Write-in)

SOUTH CAROLINA

GENERAL AND PRIMARY ELECTIONS

2016 PRIMARY ELECTIONS: SUPPLEMENTARY INFORMATION

Primary	February 20, 2016 (Republican President) February 27, 2016 (Democratic President) June 14, 2016 (Congress)	**Registration** (as of June 14, 2016)	3,022,826	No Party Registration

Primary Type Open—Any registered voter could participate in either the Democratic or Republican primary, although any voter who participated in one party's primary could not vote in a runoff of the other party.

	REPUBLICAN PRIMARIES			DEMOCRATIC PRIMARIES		
President	Trump, Donald J.	240,882	32.5%	Clinton, Hillary Rodham	272,379	73.4%
	Rubio, Marco	166,565	22.5%	Sanders, Bernard	96,498	26.0%
	Cruz, Ted	165,417	22.3%	Wilson, Willie	1,314	0.4%
	Bush, Jeb	58,056	7.8%	O'Malley, Martin	713	0.2%
	Kasich, John R.	56,410	7.6%			
	Carson, Ben	53,551	7.2%			
	TOTAL	740,881		TOTAL	370,904	
Senator	Scott, Tim*	Unopposed		Dixon, Thomas	Unopposed	
Congressional District 1	Sanford, Mark*	21,299	55.6%	Cherny, Dimitri	Unopposed	
	Horne, Jenny	17,001	44.4%			
	TOTAL	38,300				
Congressional District 2	Wilson, Joe*	Unopposed		Bjorn, Arik	9,681	50.1%
				Black, Phil	9,636	49.9%
				TOTAL	19,317	
Congressional District 3	Duncan, Jeff*	Unopposed		Cleveland, Hosea	Unopposed	
Congressional District 4	Gowdy, Trey*	Unopposed		Fedalei, Christopher	Unopposed	
Congressional District 5	Mulvaney, Mick*	22,603	78.3%	Person, Francis "Fran"	Unopposed	
	Craig, Ray	6,280	21.7%			
	TOTAL	28,883				
Congressional District 6	Sterling, Laura	Unopposed		Clyburn, James E.*	Unopposed	
Congressional District 7	Rice, Tom*	Unopposed		Hyman, Mal	Unopposed	

Note: An asterisk (*) denotes incumbent.

SOUTH DAKOTA

One member At Large

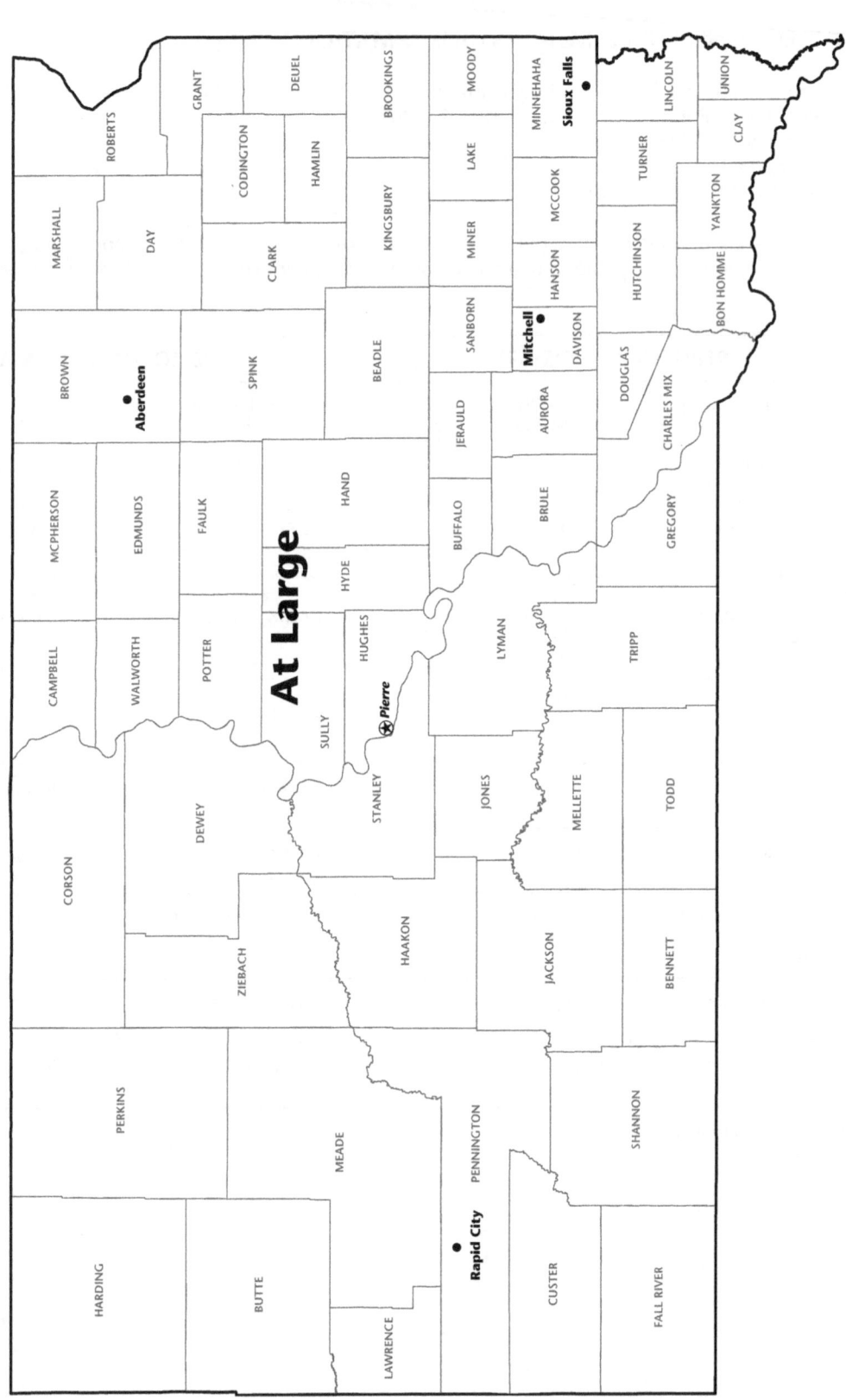

SOUTH DAKOTA

GOVERNOR

Dennis Daugaard (R). Re-elected 2014 to a four-year term. Previously elected 2010.

SENATORS (2 Republicans)

Mike Rounds (R). Elected 2014 to a six-year term.

John Thune (R). Re-elected 2016 to a six-year term. Previously elected 2010, 2004.

REPRESENTATIVE (1 Republican)

At Large. Kristi Noem (R)

POSTWAR VOTE FOR PRESIDENT

| Year | Total Vote | Republican | | Democratic | | Other Vote | Rep.-Dem. Plurality | Percentage | | | |
| | | Vote | Candidate | Vote | Candidate | | | Total Vote | | Major Vote | |
								Rep.	Dem.	Rep.	Dem.
2016**	370,093	227,721	Trump, Donald J.	117,458	Clinton, Hillary Rodham	24,914	110,263 R	61.5%	31.7%	66.0%	34.0%
2012	363,815	210,610	Romney, W. Mitt	145,039	Obama, Barack H.*	8,166	65,571 R	57.9%	39.9%	59.2%	40.8%
2008	381,975	203,054	McCain, John S. III	170,924	Obama, Barack H.	7,997	32,130 R	53.2%	44.7%	54.3%	45.7%
2004	388,215	232,584	Bush, George W.*	149,244	Kerry, John F.	6,387	83,340 R	59.9%	38.4%	60.9%	39.1%
2000	316,269	190,700	Bush, George W.	118,804	Gore, Albert Jr.	6,765	71,896 R	60.3%	37.6%	61.6%	38.4%
1996**	323,826	150,543	Dole, Robert "Bob"	139,333	Clinton, Bill*	33,950	11,210 R	46.5%	43.0%	51.9%	48.1%
1992**	336,254	136,718	Bush, George H.*	124,888	Clinton, Bill	74,648	11,830 R	40.7%	37.1%	52.3%	47.7%
1988	312,991	165,415	Bush, George H.	145,560	Dukakis, Michael S.	2,016	19,855 R	52.8%	46.5%	53.2%	46.8%
1984	317,867	200,267	Reagan, Ronald*	116,113	Mondale, Walter F.	1,487	84,154 R	63.0%	36.5%	63.3%	36.7%
1980**	327,703	198,343	Reagan, Ronald	103,855	Carter, Jimmy*	25,505	94,488 R	60.5%	31.7%	65.6%	34.4%
1976	300,678	151,505	Ford, Gerald R.*	147,068	Carter, Jimmy	2,105	4,437 R	50.4%	48.9%	50.7%	49.3%
1972	307,415	166,476	Nixon, Richard M.*	139,945	McGovern, George S.	994	26,531 R	54.2%	45.5%	54.3%	45.7%
1968**	281,264	149,841	Nixon, Richard M.	118,023	Humphrey, Hubert Horatio Jr.	13,400	31,818 R	53.3%	42.0%	55.9%	44.1%
1964	293,118	130,108	Goldwater, Barry M. Sr.	163,010	Johnson, Lyndon B.*		32,902 D	44.4%	55.6%	44.4%	55.6%
1960	306,487	178,417	Nixon, Richard M.	128,070	Kennedy, John F.		50,347 R	58.2%	41.8%	58.2%	41.8%
1956	293,857	171,569	Eisenhower, Dwight D.*	122,288	Stevenson, Adlai E. II		49,281 R	58.4%	41.6%	58.4%	41.6%
1952	294,283	203,857	Eisenhower, Dwight D.	90,426	Stevenson, Adlai E. II		113,431 R	69.3%	30.7%	69.3%	30.7%
1948	250,105	129,651	Dewey, Thomas E.	117,653	Truman, Harry S.*	2,801	11,998 R	51.8%	47.0%	52.4%	47.6%

Note: An asterisk (*) denotes incumbent. **In past elections, the other vote included: 2016 - 20,850 Libertarian (Gary Johnson); 1996 - 31,250 Reform (Ross Perot); 1992 - 73,295 Independent (Perot); 1980 - 21,431 Independent (John Anderson); 1968 - 13,400 American Independent (George Wallace).

SOUTH DAKOTA

POSTWAR VOTE FOR GOVERNOR

Year	Total Vote	Republican Vote	Republican Candidate	Democratic Vote	Democratic Candidate	Other Vote	Rep.-Dem. Plurality	Total Vote Rep.	Total Vote Dem.	Major Vote Rep.	Major Vote Dem.
2014	277,403	195,477	Daugaard, Dennis*	70,549	Wismer, Susan	11,377	124,928 R	70.5%	25.4%	73.5%	26.5%
2010	317,083	195,046	Daugaard, Dennis	122,037	Heidepriem, Scott		73,009 R	61.5%	38.5%	61.5%	38.5%
2006	335,508	206,990	Rounds, Mike*	121,226	Billion, Jack	7,292	85,764 R	61.7%	36.1%	63.1%	36.9%
2002	334,559	189,920	Rounds, Mike	140,263	Abbott, Jim	4,376	49,657 R	56.8%	41.9%	57.5%	42.5%
1998	260,187	166,621	Janklow, William J.*	85,473	Hunhoff, Bernie	8,093	81,148 R	64.0%	32.9%	66.1%	33.9%
1994	311,613	172,515	Janklow, William J.	126,273	Beddow, Jim	12,825	46,242 R	55.4%	40.5%	57.7%	42.3%
1990	256,723	151,198	Mickelson, George S.*	105,525	Samuelson, Bob L.		45,673 R	58.9%	41.1%	58.9%	41.1%
1986	294,441	152,543	Mickelson, George S.	141,898	Herseth, R. Lars		10,645 R	51.8%	48.2%	51.8%	48.2%
1982	278,565	197,429	Janklow, William J.*	81,136	O'Connor, Michael J.		116,293 R	70.9%	29.1%	70.9%	29.1%
1978	259,795	147,116	Janklow, William J.	112,679	McKellips, Roger		34,437 R	56.6%	43.4%	56.6%	43.4%
1974**	278,228	129,077	Olson, John E.	149,151	Kneip, Richard F.*		20,074 D	46.4%	53.6%	46.4%	53.6%
1972	308,177	123,165	Thompson, Carveth	185,012	Kneip, Richard F.*		61,847 D	40.0%	60.0%	40.0%	60.0%
1970	239,963	108,347	Farrar, Frank	131,616	Kneip, Richard F.		23,269 D	45.2%	54.8%	45.2%	54.8%
1968	276,906	159,646	Farrar, Frank	117,260	Chamerlin, Robert		42,386 R	57.7%	42.3%	57.7%	42.3%
1966	228,214	131,710	Boe, Nils A.*	96,504	Chamerlin, Robert		35,206 R	57.7%	42.3%	57.7%	42.3%
1964	290,570	150,151	Boe, Nils A.	140,419	Lindley, John F.		9,732 R	51.7%	48.3%	51.7%	48.3%
1962	256,120	143,682	Gubbrud, Archie M.*	112,438	Herseth, Ralph		31,244 R	56.1%	43.9%	56.1%	43.9%
1960	304,625	154,530	Gubbrud, Archie M.	150,095	Herseth, Ralph*		4,435 R	50.7%	49.3%	50.7%	49.3%
1958	258,281	125,520	Saunders, Phil	132,761	Herseth, Ralph		7,241 D	48.6%	51.4%	48.6%	51.4%
1956	292,017	158,819	Foss, Joe*	133,198	Herseth, Ralph		25,621 R	54.4%	45.6%	54.4%	45.6%
1954	236,255	133,878	Foss, Joe	102,377	Martin, Ed C.		31,501 R	56.7%	43.3%	56.7%	43.3%
1952	289,514	203,102	Anderson, Sigurd*	86,412	Iverson, Sherman A.		116,690 R	70.2%	29.8%	70.2%	29.8%
1950	253,316	154,254	Anderson, Sigurd	99,062	Robbie, Joe		55,192 R	60.9%	39.1%	60.9%	39.1%
1948	245,372	149,883	Mickelson, George T.*	95,489	Volz, Harold J.		54,394 R	61.1%	38.9%	61.1%	38.9%
1946	162,292	108,998	Mickelson, George T.	53,294	Haeder, Richard		55,704 R	67.2%	32.8%	67.2%	32.8%

Note: An asterisk (*) denotes incumbent. **The term of office of South Dakota's governor was increased from two to four years effective with the 1974 election.

POSTWAR VOTE FOR SENATOR

Year	Total Vote	Republican Vote	Republican Candidate	Democratic Vote	Democratic Candidate	Other Vote	Rep.-Dem. Plurality	Total Vote Rep.	Total Vote Dem.	Major Vote Rep.	Major Vote Dem.
2016	369,656	265,516	Thune, John*	104,140	Williams, Jay		161,376 R	71.8%	28.2%	71.8%	28.2%
2014	279,412	140,741	Rounds, Mike	82,456	Weiland, Rick	56,215	58,285 R	50.4%	29.5%	63.1%	36.9%
2010	227,947	227,947	Thune, John*				227,947 R	100.0%		100.0%	
2008	380,673	142,784	Dykstra, Joel	237,889	Johnson, Timothy P.*		95,105 D	37.5%	62.5%	37.5%	62.5%
2004	391,188	197,848	Thune, John	193,340	Daschle, Thomas A.*		4,508 R	50.6%	49.4%	50.6%	49.4%
2002	337,508	166,957	Thune, John	167,481	Johnson, Timothy P.*	3,070	524 D	49.5%	49.6%	49.9%	50.1%
1998	262,111	95,431	Schmidt, Ron	162,884	Daschle, Thomas A.*	3,796	67,453 D	36.4%	62.1%	36.9%	63.1%
1996	324,487	157,954	Pressler, Larry*	166,533	Johnson, Timothy P.		8,579 D	48.7%	51.3%	48.7%	51.3%
1992	334,495	108,733	Haar, Charlene	217,095	Daschle, Thomas A.*	8,667	108,362 D	32.5%	64.9%	33.4%	66.6%
1990	258,976	135,682	Pressler, Larry*	116,727	Muenster, Ted	6,567	18,955 R	52.4%	45.1%	53.8%	46.2%
1986	295,830	143,173	Abdnor, James*	152,657	Daschle, Thomas A.		9,484 D	48.4%	51.6%	48.4%	51.6%
1984	315,713	235,176	Pressler, Larry*	80,537	Cunningham, George V.		154,639 R	74.5%	25.5%	74.5%	25.5%
1980	327,478	190,594	Abdnor, James	129,018	McGovern, George S.*	7,866	61,576 R	58.2%	39.4%	59.6%	40.4%
1978	255,599	170,832	Pressler, Larry	84,767	Barnett, Don		86,065 R	66.8%	33.2%	66.8%	33.2%
1974	278,884	130,955	Thorsness, Leo K.	147,929	McGovern, George S.*		16,974 D	47.0%	53.0%	47.0%	53.0%
1972	306,386	131,613	Hirsch, Robert W.	174,773	Abourezk, James George*		43,160 D	43.0%	57.0%	43.0%	57.0%
1968	279,912	120,951	Gubbrud, Archie M.	158,961	McGovern, George S.*		38,010 D	43.2%	56.8%	43.2%	56.8%
1966	227,080	150,517	Mundt, Karl E.*	76,563	Wright, Donn H.		73,954 R	66.3%	33.7%	66.3%	33.7%
1962	254,319	126,861	Bottum, Joe*	127,458	McGovern, George S.		597 D	49.9%	50.1%	49.9%	50.1%
1960	305,442	160,181	Mundt, Karl E.*	145,261	McGovern, George S.		14,920 R	52.4%	47.6%	52.4%	47.6%
1956	290,622	147,621	Case, Francis*	143,001	Holum, Kenneth		4,620 R	50.8%	49.2%	50.8%	49.2%
1954	235,745	135,071	Mundt, Karl E.*	100,674	Holum, Kenneth		34,397 R	57.3%	42.7%	57.3%	42.7%
1950	251,362	160,670	Case, Francis	90,692	Engel, John A.		69,978 R	63.9%	36.1%	63.9%	36.1%
1948	242,833	144,084	Mundt, Karl E.	98,749	Engel, John A.		45,335 R	59.3%	40.7%	59.3%	40.7%

Note: An asterisk (*) denotes incumbent. The Democratic Party did not run a Senate candidate in the 2010 election.

SOUTH DAKOTA
PRESIDENT 2016

2010 Census Population	County	Total Vote	Republican (Trump)	Democratic (Clinton)	Other	Rep.-Dem. Plurality	Total Vote Rep.	Dem.	Major Vote Rep.	Dem.
2,710	AURORA	1,407	974	340	93	634 R	69.2%	24.2%	74.1%	25.9%
17,398	BEADLE	6,772	4,455	1,912	405	2,543 R	65.8%	28.2%	70.0%	30.0%
3,431	BENNETT	1,149	666	412	71	254 R	58.0%	35.9%	61.8%	38.2%
7,070	BON HOMME	2,974	2,105	704	165	1,401 R	70.8%	23.7%	74.9%	25.1%
31,965	BROOKINGS	12,680	6,748	4,879	1,053	1,869 R	53.2%	38.5%	58.0%	42.0%
36,531	BROWN	16,114	9,613	5,452	1,049	4,161 R	59.7%	33.8%	63.8%	36.2%
5,255	BRULE	2,288	1,565	571	152	994 R	68.4%	25.0%	73.3%	26.7%
1,912	BUFFALO	490	171	296	23	125 D	34.9%	60.4%	36.6%	63.4%
10,110	BUTTE	4,351	3,357	696	298	2,661 R	77.2%	16.0%	82.8%	17.2%
1,466	CAMPBELL	831	704	105	22	599 R	84.7%	12.6%	87.0%	13.0%
9,129	CHARLES MIX	3,433	2,382	935	116	1,447 R	69.4%	27.2%	71.8%	28.2%
3,691	CLARK	1,657	1,139	398	120	741 R	68.7%	24.0%	74.1%	25.9%
13,864	CLAY	5,069	2,109	2,608	352	499 D	41.6%	51.5%	44.7%	55.3%
27,227	CODINGTON	11,669	7,764	3,174	731	4,590 R	66.5%	27.2%	71.0%	29.0%
4,050	CORSON	1,175	588	535	52	53 R	50.0%	45.5%	52.4%	47.6%
8,216	CUSTER	4,721	3,293	1,121	307	2,172 R	69.8%	23.7%	74.6%	25.4%
19,504	DAVISON	7,952	5,157	2,355	440	2,802 R	64.9%	29.6%	68.7%	31.4%
5,710	DAY	2,747	1,627	974	146	653 R	59.2%	35.5%	62.6%	37.5%
4,364	DEUEL	2,080	1,366	570	144	796 R	65.7%	27.4%	70.6%	29.4%
5,301	DEWEY	1,708	723	888	97	165 D	42.3%	52.0%	44.9%	55.1%
3,002	DOUGLAS	1,605	1,338	214	53	1,124 R	83.4%	13.3%	86.2%	13.8%
4,071	EDMUNDS	1,918	1,433	380	105	1,053 R	74.7%	19.8%	79.0%	21.0%
7,094	FALL RIVER	3,563	2,511	821	231	1,690 R	70.5%	23.0%	75.4%	24.6%
2,364	FAULK	1,118	858	204	56	654 R	76.7%	18.3%	80.8%	19.2%
7,356	GRANT	3,564	2,382	971	211	1,411 R	66.8%	27.2%	71.0%	29.0%
4,271	GREGORY	2,091	1,600	391	100	1,209 R	76.5%	18.7%	80.4%	19.6%
1,937	HAAKON	1,044	936	77	31	859 R	89.7%	7.4%	92.4%	7.6%
5,903	HAMLIN	2,762	2,051	555	156	1,496 R	74.3%	20.1%	78.7%	21.3%
3,431	HAND	1,818	1,391	334	93	1,057 R	76.5%	18.4%	80.6%	19.4%
3,331	HANSON	2,006	1,497	424	85	1,073 R	74.6%	21.1%	77.9%	22.1%
1,255	HARDING	770	695	38	37	657 R	90.3%	4.9%	94.8%	5.2%
17,022	HUGHES	8,175	5,174	2,450	551	2,724 R	63.3%	30.0%	67.9%	32.1%
7,343	HUTCHINSON	3,365	2,517	692	156	1,825 R	74.8%	20.6%	78.4%	21.6%
1,420	HYDE	690	543	125	22	418 R	78.7%	18.1%	81.3%	18.7%
3,031	JACKSON	1,095	722	323	50	399 R	65.9%	29.5%	69.1%	30.9%
2,071	JERAULD	967	648	264	55	384 R	67.0%	27.3%	71.1%	29.0%
1,006	JONES	558	450	69	39	381 R	80.7%	12.4%	86.7%	13.3%
5,148	KINGSBURY	2,551	1,680	703	168	977 R	65.9%	27.6%	70.5%	29.5%
11,200	LAKE	6,786	4,038	2,314	434	1,724 R	59.5%	34.1%	63.6%	36.4%
24,097	LAWRENCE	11,842	7,411	3,356	1,075	4,055 R	62.6%	28.3%	68.8%	31.2%
44,828	LINCOLN	25,231	15,499	8,076	1,656	7,423 R	61.4%	32.0%	65.7%	34.3%
3,755	LYMAN	1,421	977	369	75	608 R	68.8%	26.0%	72.6%	27.4%
4,656	MARSHALL	1,947	1,056	754	137	302 R	54.2%	38.7%	58.3%	41.7%
5,618	MCCOOK	2,587	1,794	623	170	1,171 R	69.4%	24.1%	74.2%	25.8%
2,459	MCPHERSON	1,137	892	192	53	700 R	78.5%	16.9%	82.3%	17.7%
25,434	MEADE	11,621	8,441	2,223	957	6,218 R	72.6%	19.1%	79.2%	20.9%
2,048	MELLETTE	683	402	238	43	164 R	58.9%	34.9%	62.8%	37.2%
2,389	MINER	1,064	706	281	77	425 R	66.4%	26.4%	71.5%	28.5%
169,468	MINNEHAHA	78,263	42,043	30,610	5,610	11,433 R	53.7%	39.1%	57.9%	42.1%
6,486	MOODY	2,933	1,731	1,043	159	688 R	59.0%	35.6%	62.4%	37.6%
13,586	OGLALA LAKOTA	2,905	241	2,510	154	2,269 D	8.3%	86.4%	8.8%	91.2%
100,948	PENNINGTON	47,743	29,804	14,074	3,865	15,730 R	62.4%	29.5%	67.9%	32.1%
2,982	PERKINS	1,606	1,333	188	85	1,145 R	83.0%	11.7%	87.6%	12.4%
2,329	POTTER	1,337	1,071	215	51	856 R	80.1%	16.1%	83.3%	16.7%
10,149	ROBERTS	3,889	2,144	1,540	205	604 R	55.1%	39.6%	58.2%	41.8%
2,355	SANBORN	1,123	819	241	63	578 R	72.9%	21.5%	77.3%	22.7%
6,415	SPINK	2,951	1,854	919	178	935 R	62.8%	31.1%	66.9%	33.1%
2,966	STANLEY	1,567	1,148	329	90	819 R	73.3%	21.0%	77.7%	22.3%
1,373	SULLY	861	679	137	45	542 R	78.9%	15.9%	83.2%	16.8%
9,612	TODD	2,125	487	1,505	133	1,018 D	22.9%	70.8%	24.5%	75.6%

SOUTH DAKOTA

PRESIDENT 2016

2010 Census Population	County	Total Vote	Republican (Trump)	Democratic (Clinton)	Other	Rep.-Dem. Plurality	Percentage			
							Total Vote		Major Vote	
							Rep.	Dem.	Rep.	Dem.
5,644	TRIPP	2,630	2,069	462	99	1,607 R	78.7%	17.6%	81.8%	18.3%
8,347	TURNER	4,150	2,937	961	252	1,976 R	70.8%	23.2%	75.4%	24.7%
14,399	UNION	7,897	5,290	2,227	380	3,063 R	67.0%	28.2%	70.4%	29.6%
5,438	WALWORTH	2,477	1,896	457	124	1,439 R	76.5%	18.5%	80.6%	19.4%
22,438	YANKTON	9,623	5,659	3,301	663	2,358 R	58.8%	34.3%	63.2%	36.8%
2,801	ZIEBACH	767	368	353	46	15 R	48.0%	46.0%	51.0%	49.0%
814,180	TOTAL	370,093	227,721	117,458	24,914	110,263 R	61.5%	31.7%	66.0%	34.0%

SOUTH DAKOTA

SENATE 2016

2010 Census Population	County	Total Vote	Republican (Thune)	Democratic (Williams)	Other	Rep.-Dem. Plurality	Percentage			
							Total Vote		Major Vote	
							Rep.	Dem.	Rep.	Dem.
2,710	AURORA	1,416	1,073	343		730 R	75.8%	24.2%	75.8%	24.2%
17,398	BEADLE	6,858	5,049	1,809		3,240 R	73.6%	26.4%	73.6%	26.4%
3,431	BENNETT	1,140	758	382		376 R	66.5%	33.5%	66.5%	33.5%
7,070	BON HOMME	3,023	2,253	770		1,483 R	74.5%	25.5%	74.5%	25.5%
31,965	BROOKINGS	12,764	8,817	3,947		4,870 R	69.1%	30.9%	69.1%	30.9%
36,531	BROWN	16,164	11,371	4,793		6,578 R	70.3%	29.7%	70.3%	29.7%
5,255	BRULE	2,300	1,746	554		1,192 R	75.9%	24.1%	75.9%	24.1%
1,912	BUFFALO	489	232	257		25 D	47.4%	52.6%	47.4%	52.6%
10,110	BUTTE	4,304	3,546	758		2,788 R	82.4%	17.6%	82.4%	17.6%
1,466	CAMPBELL	827	740	87		653 R	89.5%	10.5%	89.5%	10.5%
9,129	CHARLES MIX	3,425	2,484	941		1,543 R	72.5%	27.5%	72.5%	27.5%
3,691	CLARK	1,677	1,269	408		861 R	75.7%	24.3%	75.7%	24.3%
13,864	CLAY	5,084	2,923	2,161		762 R	57.5%	42.5%	57.5%	42.5%
27,227	CODINGTON	11,743	8,740	3,003		5,737 R	74.4%	25.6%	74.4%	25.6%
4,050	CORSON	1,154	680	474		206 R	58.9%	41.1%	58.9%	41.1%
8,216	CUSTER	4,707	3,530	1,177		2,353 R	75.0%	25.0%	75.0%	25.0%
19,504	DAVISON	8,007	6,017	1,990		4,027 R	75.1%	24.9%	75.1%	24.9%
5,710	DAY	2,777	1,815	962		853 R	65.4%	34.6%	65.4%	34.6%
4,364	DEUEL	2,097	1,563	534		1,029 R	74.5%	25.5%	74.5%	25.5%
5,301	DEWEY	1,695	862	833		29 R	50.9%	49.1%	50.9%	49.1%
3,002	DOUGLAS	1,605	1,377	228		1,149 R	85.8%	14.2%	85.8%	14.2%
4,071	EDMUNDS	1,913	1,517	396		1,121 R	79.3%	20.7%	79.3%	20.7%
7,094	FALL RIVER	3,539	2,671	868		1,803 R	75.5%	24.5%	75.5%	24.5%
2,364	FAULK	1,131	925	206		719 R	81.8%	18.2%	81.8%	18.2%
7,356	GRANT	3,595	2,705	890		1,815 R	75.2%	24.8%	75.2%	24.8%
4,271	GREGORY	2,097	1,671	426		1,245 R	79.7%	20.3%	79.7%	20.3%
1,937	HAAKON	1,040	956	84		872 R	91.9%	8.1%	91.9%	8.1%
5,903	HAMLIN	2,789	2,253	536		1,717 R	80.8%	19.2%	80.8%	19.2%
3,431	HAND	1,852	1,517	335		1,182 R	81.9%	18.1%	81.9%	18.1%
3,331	HANSON	1,963	1,512	451		1,061 R	77.0%	23.0%	77.0%	23.0%
1,255	HARDING	758	684	74		610 R	90.2%	9.8%	90.2%	9.8%
17,022	HUGHES	8,230	6,339	1,891		4,448 R	77.0%	23.0%	77.0%	23.0%
7,343	HUTCHINSON	3,388	2,779	609		2,170 R	82.0%	18.0%	82.0%	18.0%
1,420	HYDE	691	567	124		443 R	82.1%	17.9%	82.1%	17.9%
3,031	JACKSON	1,080	771	309		462 R	71.4%	28.6%	71.4%	28.6%
2,071	JERAULD	981	720	261		459 R	73.4%	26.6%	73.4%	26.6%
1,006	JONES	561	494	67		427 R	88.1%	11.9%	88.1%	11.9%
5,148	KINGSBURY	2,573	1,899	674		1,225 R	73.8%	26.2%	73.8%	26.2%
11,200	LAKE	6,708	4,677	2,031		2,646 R	69.7%	30.3%	69.7%	30.3%
24,097	LAWRENCE	11,833	8,566	3,267		5,299 R	72.4%	27.6%	72.4%	27.6%

SOUTH DAKOTA

SENATE 2016

2010 Census Population	County	Total Vote	Republican (Thune)	Democratic (Williams)	Other	Rep.-Dem. Plurality	Total Vote Rep.	Total Vote Dem.	Major Vote Rep.	Major Vote Dem.
44,828	LINCOLN	25,307	19,264	6,043		13,221 R	76.1%	23.9%	76.1%	23.9%
3,755	LYMAN	1,429	1,051	378		673 R	73.5%	26.5%	73.5%	26.5%
4,656	MARSHALL	1,970	1,341	629		712 R	68.1%	31.9%	68.1%	31.9%
5,618	MCCOOK	2,620	2,021	599		1,422 R	77.1%	22.9%	77.1%	22.9%
2,459	MCPHERSON	1,174	1,009	165		844 R	85.9%	14.1%	85.9%	14.1%
25,434	MEADE	11,546	9,198	2,348		6,850 R	79.7%	20.3%	79.7%	20.3%
2,048	MELLETTE	688	464	224		240 R	67.4%	32.6%	67.4%	32.6%
2,389	MINER	1,091	807	284		523 R	74.0%	26.0%	74.0%	26.0%
169,468	MINNEHAHA	77,853	52,494	25,359		27,135 R	67.4%	32.6%	67.4%	32.6%
6,486	MOODY	2,953	1,983	970		1,013 R	67.2%	32.8%	67.2%	32.8%
13,586	OGLALA LAKOTA	2,872	655	2,217		1,562 D	22.8%	77.2%	22.8%	77.2%
100,948	PENNINGTON	47,174	33,967	13,207		20,760 R	72.0%	28.0%	72.0%	28.0%
2,982	PERKINS	1,605	1,374	231		1,143 R	85.6%	14.4%	85.6%	14.4%
2,329	POTTER	1,340	1,087	253		834 R	81.1%	18.9%	81.1%	18.9%
10,149	ROBERTS	3,926	2,550	1,376		1,174 R	65.0%	35.0%	65.0%	35.0%
2,355	SANBORN	1,133	889	244		645 R	78.5%	21.5%	78.5%	21.5%
6,415	SPINK	2,993	2,177	816		1,361 R	72.7%	27.3%	72.7%	27.3%
2,966	STANLEY	1,557	1,254	303		951 R	80.5%	19.5%	80.5%	19.5%
1,373	SULLY	854	718	136		582 R	84.1%	15.9%	84.1%	15.9%
9,612	TODD	2,100	724	1,376		652 D	34.5%	65.5%	34.5%	65.5%
5,644	TRIPP	2,626	2,134	492		1,642 R	81.3%	18.7%	81.3%	18.7%
8,347	TURNER	4,160	3,289	871		2,418 R	79.1%	20.9%	79.1%	20.9%
14,399	UNION	7,853	6,060	1,793		4,267 R	77.2%	22.8%	77.2%	22.8%
5,438	WALWORTH	2,457	1,975	482		1,493 R	80.4%	19.6%	80.4%	19.6%
22,438	YANKTON	9,631	6,542	3,089		3,453 R	67.9%	32.1%	67.9%	32.1%
2,801	ZIEBACH	766	421	345		76 R	55.0%	45.0%	55.0%	45.0%
814,180	TOTAL	369,656	265,516	104,140		161,376 R	71.8%	28.2%	71.8%	28.2%

SOUTH DAKOTA

HOUSE OF REPRESENTATIVES

CD	Year	Total Vote	Republican Vote	Republican Candidate	Democratic Vote	Democratic Candidate	Other Vote	Rep.-Dem. Plurality	Total Vote Rep.	Total Vote Dem.	Major Vote Rep.	Major Vote Dem.
At Large	2016	369,973	237,163	NOEM, KRISTI*	132,810	HAWKS, PAULA		104,353 R	64.1%	35.9%	64.1%	35.9%
At Large	2014	276,319	183,834	NOEM, KRISTI*	92,485	ROBINSON, CORINNA		91,349 R	66.5%	33.5%	66.5%	33.5%
At Large	2012	361,429	207,640	NOEM, KRISTI*	153,789	VARILEK, MATT		53,851 R	57.4%	42.6%	57.4%	42.6%
At Large	2010	319,426	153,703	NOEM, KRISTI	146,589	SANDLIN, STEPHANIE HERSETH*	19,134	7,114 R	48.1%	45.9%	51.2%	48.8%
At Large	2008	379,007	122,966	LIEN, CHRIS	256,041	SANDLIN, STEPHANIE HERSETH*		133,075 D	32.4%	67.6%	32.4%	67.6%
At Large	2006	333,562	97,864	WHALEN, BRUCE W.	230,468	SANDLIN, STEPHANIE HERSETH*	5,230	132,604 D	29.3%	69.1%	29.8%	70.2%
At Large	2004	389,468	178,823	DIEDRICH, LARRY W.	207,837	SANDLIN, STEPHANIE HERSETH*	2,808	29,014 D	45.9%	53.4%	46.2%	53.8%
At Large	2002	336,807	180,023	JANKLOW, WILLIAM J.	153,656	SANDLIN, STEPHANIE HERSETH	3,128	26,367 R	53.4%	45.6%	54.0%	46.0%
At Large	2000	314,761	231,083	THUNE, JOHN*	78,321	HOHN, CURT	5,357	152,762 R	73.4%	24.9%	74.7%	25.3%
At Large	1998	258,590	194,157	THUNE, JOHN*	64,433	MOSER, JEFF		129,724 R	75.1%	24.9%	75.1%	24.9%
At Large	1996	323,203	186,393	THUNE, JOHN	119,547	WEILAND, RICK	17,263	66,846 R	57.7%	37.0%	60.9%	39.1%
At Large	1994	305,922	112,054	BERKHOUT, JAN	183,036	JOHNSON, TIMOTHY P.*	10,832	70,982 D	36.6%	59.8%	38.0%	62.0%
At Large	1992	332,902	89,375	TIMMER, JOHN	230,070	JOHNSON, TIMOTHY P.*	13,457	140,695 D	26.8%	69.1%	28.0%	72.0%
At Large	1990	257,298	83,484	FRANKENFELD, DON	173,814	JOHNSON, TIMOTHY P.*		90,330 D	32.4%	67.6%	32.4%	67.6%
At Large	1988	311,916	88,157	VOLK, DAVID	223,759	JOHNSON, TIMOTHY P.*		135,602 D	28.3%	71.7%	28.3%	71.7%
At Large	1986	289,723	118,261	BELL, DALE	171,462	JOHNSON, TIMOTHY P.		53,201 D	40.8%	59.2%	40.8%	59.2%
At Large	1984	316,222	134,821	BELL, DALE	181,401	DASCHLE, THOMAS A.*		46,580 D	42.6%	57.4%	42.6%	57.4%
At Large	1982	275,652	133,530	ROBERTS, CLINT*	142,122	DASCHLE, THOMAS A.*		8,592 D	48.4%	51.6%	48.4%	51.6%

Note: An asterisk (*) denotes incumbent.

SOUTH DAKOTA

GENERAL AND PRIMARY ELECTIONS

2016 GENERAL ELECTIONS: OTHER VOTES

President   Other vote was 20,850 Libertarian (Gary Johnson), 4,064 Constitution (Darrell Castle)

2016 PRIMARY ELECTIONS: SUPPLEMENTARY INFORMATION

Primary	June 7, 2016	**Registration** (as of June 7, 2016 – includes 53,512 inactive registrants)	578,010	Republican Democratic Constitution Other No Party Affiliation/ Independent	243,523 168,301 504 2,131 243,523

Primary Type   Republicans held a "closed" primary, with only registered Republicans allowed to vote in it. Democrats held a "semi-open" primary, with registered Democrats, independents, and other voters not affiliated with a recognized political party eligible to cast a Democratic primary ballot.

	REPUBLICAN PRIMARIES			DEMOCRATIC PRIMARIES		
President	Trump, Donald J.	44,867	67.1%	Clinton, Hillary Rodham	27,047	51.0%
	Cruz, Ted	11,352	17.0%	Sanders, Bernard	25,959	49.0%
	Kasich, John R.	10,660	15.9%			
	TOTAL	*66,879*		*TOTAL*	*53,006*	
Senator	Thune, John*	Unopposed		Williams, Jay	Unopposed	
Congressional At Large	Noem, Kristi*	Unopposed		Hawks, Paula	Unopposed	

Note: An asterisk (*) denotes incumbent.

TENNESSEE
Congressional districts first established for elections held in 2012
9 members

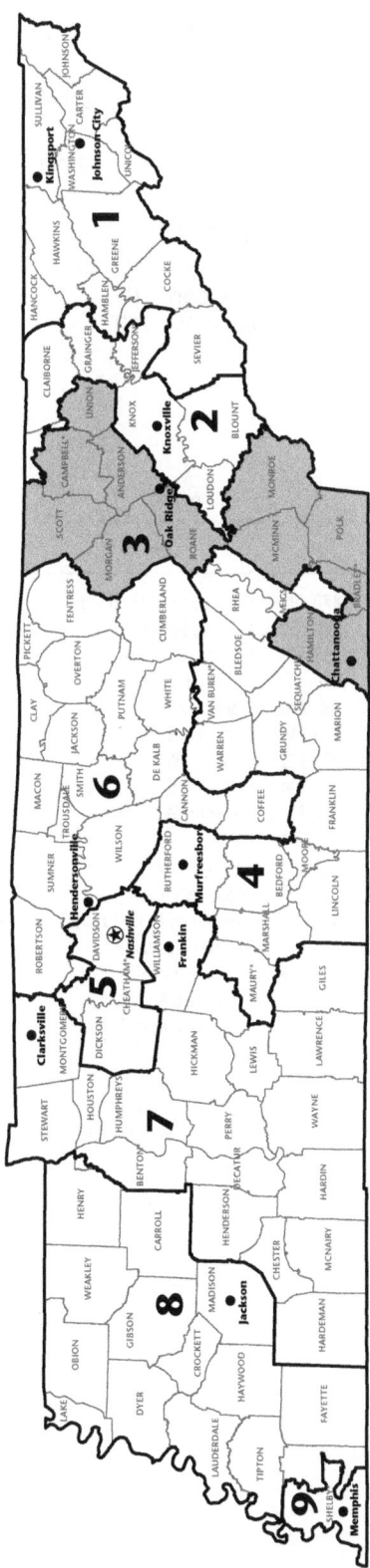

* Asterisk indicates a county whose boundaries include parts of two or more congressional districts.

TENNESSEE

GOVERNOR
Bill Haslam (R). Re-elected 2014 to a four-year term. Previously elected 2010.

SENATORS (2 Republicans)
Lamar Alexander (R). Re-elected 2014 to a six-year term. Previously elected 2008, 2002.

Bob Corker (R). Re-elected 2012 to a six-year term. Previously elected 2006.

REPRESENTATIVES (7 Republicans, 2 Democrats)
1. Phil Roe (R)
2. John J. Duncan Jr. (R)
3. Chuck Fleischmann (R)
4. Scott DesJarlais (R)
5. Jim Cooper (D)
6. Diane Black (R)
7. Marsha Blackburn (R)
8. David Kustoff (R)
9. Steven I. Cohen (D)

POSTWAR VOTE FOR PRESIDENT

| | | Republican | | Democratic | | Other Vote | Rep.-Dem. Plurality | Percentage | | | |
| | | | | | | | | Total Vote | | Major Vote | |
Year	Total Vote	Vote	Candidate	Vote	Candidate			Rep.	Dem.	Rep.	Dem.
2016**	2,508,027	1,522,925	Trump, Donald J.	870,695	Clinton, Hillary Rodham	114,407	652,230 R	60.7%	34.7%	63.6%	36.4%
2012	2,458,577	1,462,330	Romney, W. Mitt	960,709	Obama, Barack H.*	35,538	501,621 R	59.5%	39.1%	60.4%	39.6%
2008	2,599,749	1,479,178	McCain, John S. III	1,087,437	Obama, Barack H.	33,134	391,741 R	56.9%	41.8%	57.6%	42.4%
2004	2,437,319	1,384,375	Bush, George W.*	1,036,477	Kerry, John F.	16,467	347,898 R	56.8%	42.5%	57.2%	42.8%
2000**	2,076,181	1,061,949	Bush, George W.	981,720	Gore, Albert Jr.	32,512	80,229 R	51.1%	47.3%	52.0%	48.0%
1996**	1,894,105	863,530	Dole, Robert "Bob"	909,146	Clinton, Bill*	121,429	45,616 D	45.6%	48.0%	48.7%	51.3%
1992**	1,982,638	841,300	Bush, George H.*	933,521	Clinton, Bill	207,817	92,221 D	42.4%	47.1%	47.4%	52.6%
1988	1,636,250	947,233	Bush, George H.	679,794	Dukakis, Michael S.	9,223	267,439 R	57.9%	41.5%	58.2%	41.8%
1984	1,711,994	990,212	Reagan, Ronald*	711,714	Mondale, Walter F.	10,068	278,498 R	57.8%	41.6%	58.2%	41.8%
1980**	1,617,616	787,761	Reagan, Ronald	783,051	Carter, Jimmy*	46,804	4,710 R	48.7%	48.4%	50.1%	49.9%
1976	1,476,345	633,969	Ford, Gerald R.*	825,879	Carter, Jimmy	16,497	191,910 D	42.9%	55.9%	43.4%	56.6%
1972	1,201,182	813,147	Nixon, Richard M.*	357,293	McGovern, George S.	30,742	455,854 R	67.7%	29.7%	69.5%	30.5%
1968**	1,248,617	472,592	Nixon, Richard M.	351,233	Humphrey, Hubert Horatio Jr.	424,792	121,359 R	37.8%	28.1%	57.4%	42.6%
1964	1,143,946	508,965	Goldwater, Barry M. Sr.	634,947	Johnson, Lyndon B.*	34	125,982 D	44.5%	55.5%	44.5%	55.5%
1960	1,051,792	556,577	Nixon, Richard M.	481,453	Kennedy, John F.	13,762	75,124 R	52.9%	45.8%	53.6%	46.4%
1956	939,404	462,288	Eisenhower, Dwight D.*	456,507	Stevenson, Adlai E. II	20,609	5,781 R	49.2%	48.6%	50.3%	49.7%
1952	892,553	446,147	Eisenhower, Dwight D.	443,710	Stevenson, Adlai E. II	2,696	2,437 R	50.0%	49.7%	50.1%	49.9%
1948**	550,283	202,914	Dewey, Thomas E.	270,402	Truman, Harry S.*	76,967	67,488 D	36.9%	49.1%	42.9%	57.1%

Note: An asterisk (*) denotes incumbent. **In past elections, the other vote included: 2016 - 70,397 Libertarian (Gary Johnson); 2000 - 19,781 Green (Ralph Nader); 1996 - 105,918 Reform (Ross Perot); 1992 - 199,968 Independent (Perot); 1980 - 35,991 Independent (John Anderson); 1968 - 424,792 American Independent (George Wallace, who finished second); 1948 - 73,815 States' Rights (Strom Thurmond).

TENNESSEE

POSTWAR VOTE FOR GOVERNOR

		Republican		Democratic		Other Vote	Rep.-Dem. Plurality	Percentage Total Vote		Major Vote	
Year	Total Vote	Vote	Candidate	Vote	Candidate			Rep.	Dem.	Rep.	Dem.
2014	1,353,728	951,796	Haslam, Bill*	309,237	Brown, Charles V. "Charlie"	92,695	642,559 R	70.3%	22.8%	75.5%	24.5%
2010	1,601,549	1,041,545	Haslam, Bill	529,851	McWherter, Mike	30,153	511,694 R	65.0%	33.1%	66.3%	33.7%
2006	1,818,549	540,853	Bryson, Jim	1,247,491	Bredesen, Phil*	30,205	706,638 D	29.7%	68.6%	30.2%	69.8%
2002	1,653,167	786,803	Hilleary, Van	837,284	Bredesen, Phil	29,080	50,481 D	47.6%	50.6%	48.4%	51.6%
1998	976,236	669,973	Sundquist, Don*	287,750	Hooker, John Jay Jr.	18,513	382,223 R	68.6%	29.5%	70.0%	30.0%
1994	1,487,124	807,107	Sundquist, Don	664,243	Bredesen, Phil	15,774	142,864 R	54.3%	44.7%	54.9%	45.1%
1990	790,441	289,348	Henry, Dwight	480,885	McWherter, Ned*	20,208	191,537 D	36.6%	60.8%	37.6%	62.4%
1986	1,210,339	553,449	Dunn, Winfield	656,602	McWherter, Ned	288	103,153 D	45.7%	54.2%	45.7%	54.3%
1982	1,238,927	737,963	Alexander, Lamar*	500,937	Tyree, Randy	27	237,026 R	59.6%	40.4%	59.6%	40.4%
1978	1,189,695	661,959	Alexander, Lamar	523,495	Butcher, Jake	4,241	138,464 R	55.6%	44.0%	55.8%	44.2%
1974	1,040,714	455,467	Alexander, Lamar	576,833	Blanton, L. Ray	8,414	121,366 D	43.8%	55.4%	44.1%	55.9%
1970	1,108,247	575,777	Dunn, Winfield	509,521	Hooker, John Jay Jr.	22,949	66,256 R	52.0%	46.0%	53.1%	46.9%
1966	656,566			532,998	Ellington, Buford	123,568	532,998 D		81.2%		100.0%
1962**	620,758	99,884	Patty, Hubert D.	315,648	Clement, Frank G.	205,226	215,764 D	16.1%	50.8%	24.0%	76.0%
1958**	432,545	35,938	Wall, Thomas P.	248,874	Ellington, Buford	147,733	212,936 D	8.3%	57.5%	12.6%	87.4%
1954**	322,586			281,291	Clement, Frank G.*	41,295	281,291 D		87.2%		100.0%
1952	806,771	166,377	Witt, R. Beecher	640,290	Clement, Frank G.	104	473,913 D	20.6%	79.4%	20.6%	79.4%
1950**	236,194			184,437	Browning, Gordon*	51,757	184,437 D		78.1%		100.0%
1948	543,881	179,957	Acuff, Roy	363,903	Browning, Gordon	21	183,946 D	33.1%	66.9%	33.1%	66.9%
1946	229,456	73,222	Lowe, W. O.	149,937	McCord, James N.*	6,297	76,715 D	31.9%	65.3%	32.8%	67.2%

Note: An asterisk (*) denotes incumbent. **In past elections, the other vote included: 1962 - 203,765 Independent (William R. Anderson, who finished second); 1958 - 136,399 Independent (Jim Nance McCord, who finished second); 1954 - 39,574 Independent (John R. Neal, who finished second); 1950 - 51,757 Independent (Neal, who finished second). The Republican Party did not run a gubernatorial candidate in 1950, 1954, and 1966. The term of office of Tennessee's governor was increased from two to four years effective with the 1954 election.

POSTWAR VOTE FOR SENATOR

		Republican		Democratic		Other Vote	Rep.-Dem. Plurality	Percentage Total Vote		Major Vote	
Year	Total Vote	Vote	Candidate	Vote	Candidate			Rep.	Dem.	Rep.	Dem.
2014	1,366,628	850,087	Alexander, Lamar*	437,848	Ball, Gordon	78,693	412,239 R	62.2%	32.0%	66.0%	34.0%
2012	2,321,477	1,506,443	Corker, Bob*	705,882	Clayton, Mark E.	109,152	800,561 R	64.9%	30.4%	68.1%	31.9%
2008	2,424,585	1,579,477	Alexander, Lamar*	767,236	Tuke, Robert D.	77,872	812,241 R	65.1%	31.6%	67.3%	32.7%
2006	1,833,695	929,911	Corker, Bob	879,976	Ford, Harold E. Jr.	23,808	49,935 R	50.7%	48.0%	51.4%	48.6%
2002	1,642,421	891,420	Alexander, Lamar	728,295	Clement, Robert Nelson	22,706	163,125 R	54.3%	44.3%	55.0%	45.0%
2000	1,928,613	1,255,444	Frist, William H.*	621,152	Clark, Jeff	52,017	634,292 R	65.1%	32.2%	66.9%	33.1%
1996	1,778,664	1,091,554	Thompson, Fred*	654,937	Houston, Gordon J.	32,173	436,617 R	61.4%	36.8%	62.5%	37.5%
1994	1,480,391	834,226	Frist, William H.	623,164	Sasser, James R.*	23,001	211,062 R	56.4%	42.1%	57.2%	42.8%
1994S**	1,465,862	885,998	Thompson, Fred	565,930	Cooper, Jim	13,934	320,068 R	60.4%	38.6%	61.0%	39.0%
1990	783,922	233,703	Hawkins, William R.	530,898	Gore, Albert Jr.*	19,321	297,195 D	29.8%	67.7%	30.6%	69.4%
1988	1,567,181	541,033	Anderson, Bill	1,020,061	Sasser, James R.*	6,087	479,028 D	34.5%	65.1%	34.7%	65.3%
1984	1,648,036	557,016	Ashe, Victor	1,000,607	Gore, Albert Jr.	90,413	443,591 D	33.8%	60.7%	35.8%	64.2%
1982	1,259,785	479,642	Beard, Robin L.	780,113	Sasser, James R.*	30	300,471 D	38.1%	61.9%	38.1%	61.9%
1978	1,157,094	642,644	Baker, Howard H. Jr.*	466,228	Eskind, Jane	48,222	176,416 R	55.5%	40.3%	58.0%	42.0%
1976	1,432,046	673,231	Brock, William E.*	751,180	Sasser, James R.	7,635	77,949 D	47.0%	52.5%	47.3%	52.7%
1972	1,164,195	716,539	Baker, Howard H. Jr.*	440,599	Blanton, L. Ray	7,057	275,940 R	61.5%	37.8%	61.9%	38.1%
1970	1,097,041	562,645	Brock, William E.	519,858	Gore, Albert Sr.*	14,538	42,787 R	51.3%	47.4%	52.0%	48.0%
1966	866,961	483,063	Baker, Howard H. Jr.*	383,843	Clement, Frank G.	55	99,220 R	55.7%	44.3%	55.7%	44.3%
1964	1,064,018	493,475	Kuykendall, Daniel H.	570,542	Gore, Albert Sr.*	1	77,067 D	46.4%	53.6%	46.4%	53.6%
1964S**	1,091,093	517,330	Baker, Howard H. Jr.	568,905	Bass, Ross	4,858	51,575 D	47.4%	52.1%	47.6%	52.4%
1960	828,519	234,053	Frazier, A. Bradley	594,460	Kefauver, Estes	6	360,407 D	28.2%	71.7%	28.2%	71.8%
1958	401,666	76,371	Atkins, Hobart F.	317,324	Gore, Albert Sr.*	7,971	240,953 D	19.0%	79.0%	19.4%	80.6%
1954	356,094	106,971	Wall, Tom	249,121	Kefauver, Estes*	2	142,150 D	30.0%	70.0%	30.0%	70.0%
1952	735,219	153,479	Atkins, Hobart F.	545,432	Gore, Albert Sr.	36,308	391,953 D	20.9%	74.2%	22.0%	78.0%
1948	499,138	166,947	Reece, B. Carroll	326,062	Kefauver, Estes	6,129	159,115 D	33.4%	65.3%	33.9%	66.1%
1946	218,713	57,237	Ladd, W. B.	145,654	McKellar, Kenneth D.*	15,822	88,417 D	26.2%	66.6%	28.2%	71.8%

Note: An asterisk (*) denotes incumbent. **One each of the 1964 and 1994 elections was for a short term to fill a vacancy.

TENNESSEE

PRESIDENT 2016

2010 Census Population	County	Total Vote	Republican (Trump)	Democratic (Clinton)	Other	Rep.-Dem. Plurality	Percentage Total Vote Rep.	Dem.	Major Vote Rep.	Dem.
75,129	ANDERSON	29,881	19,212	9,013	1,656	10,199 R	64.3%	30.2%	68.1%	31.9%
45,058	BEDFORD	15,355	11,486	3,395	474	8,091 R	74.8%	22.1%	77.2%	22.8%
16,489	BENTON	6,328	4,716	1,474	138	3,242 R	74.5%	23.3%	76.2%	23.8%
12,876	BLEDSOE	4,664	3,622	897	145	2,725 R	77.7%	19.2%	80.2%	19.8%
123,010	BLOUNT	52,208	37,443	12,100	2,665	25,343 R	71.7%	23.2%	75.6%	24.4%
98,963	BRADLEY	38,666	29,768	7,070	1,828	22,698 R	77.0%	18.3%	80.8%	19.2%
40,716	CAMPBELL	12,532	9,870	2,248	414	7,622 R	78.8%	17.9%	81.4%	18.6%
13,801	CANNON	5,314	4,007	1,127	180	2,880 R	75.4%	21.2%	78.0%	22.0%
28,522	CARROLL	10,384	7,756	2,327	301	5,429 R	74.7%	22.4%	76.9%	23.1%
57,424	CARTER	21,084	16,898	3,453	733	13,445 R	80.1%	16.4%	83.0%	17.0%
39,105	CHEATHAM	15,924	11,297	3,878	749	7,419 R	70.9%	24.4%	74.4%	25.6%
17,131	CHESTER	6,507	5,081	1,243	183	3,838 R	78.1%	19.1%	80.3%	19.7%
32,213	CLAIBORNE	10,740	8,602	1,832	306	6,770 R	80.1%	17.1%	82.4%	17.6%
7,861	CLAY	2,920	2,141	707	72	1,434 R	73.3%	24.2%	75.2%	24.8%
35,662	COCKE	12,126	9,791	1,981	354	7,810 R	80.7%	16.3%	83.2%	16.8%
52,796	COFFEE	19,971	14,417	4,743	811	9,674 R	72.2%	23.7%	75.2%	24.8%
14,586	CROCKETT	5,397	3,982	1,303	112	2,679 R	73.8%	24.1%	75.3%	24.7%
56,053	CUMBERLAND	26,360	20,413	5,202	745	15,211 R	77.4%	19.7%	79.7%	20.3%
626,681	DAVIDSON	249,068	84,550	148,864	15,654	64,314 D	33.9%	59.8%	36.2%	63.8%
11,757	DECATUR	4,592	3,588	894	110	2,694 R	78.1%	19.5%	80.1%	19.9%
18,723	DEKALB	6,955	5,171	1,569	215	3,602 R	74.3%	22.6%	76.7%	23.3%
49,666	DICKSON	18,699	13,233	4,722	744	8,511 R	70.8%	25.3%	73.7%	26.3%
38,335	DYER	13,336	10,180	2,816	340	7,364 R	76.3%	21.1%	78.3%	21.7%
38,413	FAYETTE	19,394	13,055	5,874	465	7,181 R	67.3%	30.3%	69.0%	31.0%
17,959	FENTRESS	7,333	6,038	1,100	195	4,938 R	82.3%	15.0%	84.6%	15.4%
41,052	FRANKLIN	16,404	11,532	4,374	498	7,158 R	70.3%	26.7%	72.5%	27.5%
49,683	GIBSON	19,547	13,786	5,258	503	8,528 R	70.5%	26.9%	72.4%	27.6%
29,485	GILES	11,137	7,970	2,917	250	5,053 R	71.6%	26.2%	73.2%	26.8%
22,657	GRAINGER	8,008	6,626	1,154	228	5,472 R	82.7%	14.4%	85.2%	14.8%
68,831	GREENE	23,583	18,562	4,216	805	14,346 R	78.7%	17.9%	81.5%	18.5%
13,703	GRUNDY	4,763	3,636	999	128	2,637 R	76.3%	21.0%	78.4%	21.6%
62,544	HAMBLEN	20,692	15,857	4,075	760	11,782 R	76.6%	19.7%	79.6%	20.4%
336,463	HAMILTON	142,408	78,733	55,316	8,359	23,417 R	55.3%	38.8%	58.7%	41.3%
6,819	HANCOCK	2,231	1,843	322	66	1,521 R	82.6%	14.4%	85.1%	14.9%
27,253	HARDEMAN	9,273	4,919	4,185	169	734 R	53.0%	45.1%	54.0%	46.0%
26,026	HARDIN	9,949	8,012	1,622	315	6,390 R	80.5%	16.3%	83.2%	16.8%
56,833	HAWKINS	20,774	16,648	3,507	619	13,141 R	80.1%	16.9%	82.6%	17.4%
18,787	HAYWOOD	6,834	3,013	3,711	110	698 D	44.1%	54.3%	44.8%	55.2%
27,769	HENDERSON	10,217	8,138	1,800	279	6,338 R	79.7%	17.6%	81.9%	18.1%
32,330	HENRY	12,945	9,508	3,063	374	6,445 R	73.4%	23.7%	75.6%	24.4%
24,690	HICKMAN	7,813	5,695	1,824	294	3,871 R	72.9%	23.3%	75.7%	24.3%
8,426	HOUSTON	3,168	2,182	866	120	1,316 R	68.9%	27.3%	71.6%	28.4%
18,538	HUMPHREYS	7,153	4,930	1,967	256	2,963 R	68.9%	27.5%	71.5%	28.5%
11,638	JACKSON	4,466	3,236	1,129	101	2,107 R	72.5%	25.3%	74.1%	25.9%
51,407	JEFFERSON	19,072	14,776	3,494	802	11,282 R	77.5%	18.3%	80.9%	19.1%
18,244	JOHNSON	6,579	5,410	988	181	4,422 R	82.2%	15.0%	84.6%	15.4%
432,226	KNOX	180,697	105,767	62,878	12,052	42,889 R	58.5%	34.8%	62.7%	37.3%
7,832	LAKE	1,970	1,357	577	36	780 R	68.9%	29.3%	70.2%	29.8%
27,815	LAUDERDALE	8,087	4,884	3,056	147	1,828 R	60.4%	37.8%	61.5%	38.5%
41,869	LAWRENCE	15,666	12,420	2,821	425	9,599 R	79.3%	18.0%	81.5%	18.5%
12,161	LEWIS	4,622	3,585	890	147	2,695 R	77.6%	19.3%	80.1%	19.9%
33,361	LINCOLN	13,348	10,398	2,554	396	7,844 R	77.9%	19.1%	80.3%	19.7%
48,556	LOUDON	23,391	17,610	4,919	862	12,691 R	75.3%	21.0%	78.2%	21.8%
22,248	MACON	7,504	6,263	1,072	169	5,191 R	83.5%	14.3%	85.4%	14.6%
98,294	MADISON	38,120	21,335	15,448	1,337	5,887 R	56.0%	40.5%	58.0%	42.0%
28,237	MARION	10,862	7,696	2,832	334	4,864 R	70.9%	26.1%	73.1%	26.9%
30,617	MARSHALL	11,455	8,184	2,852	419	5,332 R	71.4%	24.9%	74.2%	25.8%
80,956	MAURY	35,369	23,799	10,038	1,532	13,761 R	67.3%	28.4%	70.3%	29.7%
52,266	MCMINN	18,755	14,691	3,510	554	11,181 R	78.3%	18.7%	80.7%	19.3%
26,075	MCNAIRY	10,038	7,841	1,848	349	5,993 R	78.1%	18.4%	80.9%	19.1%

TENNESSEE

PRESIDENT 2016

2010 Census Population	County	Total Vote	Republican (Trump)	Democratic (Clinton)	Other	Rep.-Dem. Plurality	Total Vote Rep.	Total Vote Dem.	Major Vote Rep.	Major Vote Dem.
11,753	MEIGS	4,320	3,342	856	122	2,486 R	77.4%	19.8%	79.6%	20.4%
44,519	MONROE	17,093	13,374	3,186	533	10,188 R	78.2%	18.6%	80.8%	19.2%
172,331	MONTGOMERY	57,620	32,341	21,699	3,580	10,642 R	56.1%	37.7%	59.8%	40.2%
6,362	MOORE	2,926	2,325	496	105	1,829 R	79.5%	17.0%	82.4%	17.6%
21,987	MORGAN	6,705	5,441	1,054	210	4,387 R	81.1%	15.7%	83.8%	16.2%
31,807	OBION	12,249	9,526	2,426	297	7,100 R	77.8%	19.8%	79.7%	20.3%
22,083	OVERTON	8,229	6,059	1,945	225	4,114 R	73.6%	23.6%	75.7%	24.3%
7,915	PERRY	2,855	2,167	597	91	1,570 R	75.9%	20.9%	78.4%	21.6%
5,077	PICKETT	2,615	2,021	536	58	1,485 R	77.3%	20.5%	79.0%	21.0%
16,825	POLK	6,520	5,097	1,252	171	3,845 R	78.2%	19.2%	80.3%	19.7%
72,321	PUTNAM	27,212	19,002	6,851	1,359	12,151 R	69.8%	25.2%	73.5%	26.5%
31,809	RHEA	11,062	8,660	1,942	460	6,718 R	78.3%	17.6%	81.7%	18.3%
54,181	ROANE	21,669	15,880	4,837	952	11,043 R	73.3%	22.3%	76.7%	23.3%
66,283	ROBERTSON	27,113	19,410	6,637	1,066	12,773 R	71.6%	24.5%	74.5%	25.5%
262,604	RUTHERFORD	107,436	64,515	36,706	6,215	27,809 R	60.0%	34.2%	63.7%	36.3%
22,228	SCOTT	7,123	6,044	934	145	5,110 R	84.9%	13.1%	86.6%	13.4%
14,112	SEQUATCHIE	5,694	4,441	1,053	200	3,388 R	78.0%	18.5%	80.8%	19.2%
89,889	SEVIER	36,312	28,629	6,297	1,386	22,332 R	78.8%	17.3%	82.0%	18.0%
927,644	SHELBY	337,383	116,344	208,992	12,047	92,648 D	34.5%	61.9%	35.8%	64.2%
19,166	SMITH	7,436	5,494	1,689	253	3,805 R	73.9%	22.7%	76.5%	23.5%
13,324	STEWART	5,299	3,864	1,222	213	2,642 R	72.9%	23.1%	76.0%	24.0%
156,823	SULLIVAN	62,278	46,979	12,578	2,721	34,401 R	75.4%	20.2%	78.9%	21.1%
160,645	SUMNER	71,505	50,129	18,161	3,215	31,968 R	70.1%	25.4%	73.4%	26.6%
61,081	TIPTON	23,481	16,910	5,785	786	11,125 R	72.0%	24.6%	74.5%	25.5%
7,870	TROUSDALE	3,160	2,103	946	111	1,157 R	66.6%	29.9%	69.0%	31.0%
18,313	UNICOI	7,195	5,671	1,262	262	4,409 R	78.8%	17.5%	81.8%	18.2%
19,109	UNION	6,247	5,053	1,012	182	4,041 R	80.9%	16.2%	83.3%	16.7%
5,548	VAN BUREN	2,419	1,820	539	60	1,281 R	75.2%	22.3%	77.2%	22.8%
39,839	WARREN	13,612	9,540	3,535	537	6,005 R	70.1%	26.0%	73.0%	27.0%
122,979	WASHINGTON	49,750	34,252	13,024	2,474	21,228 R	68.8%	26.2%	72.5%	27.5%
17,021	WAYNE	5,857	5,036	717	104	4,319 R	86.0%	12.2%	87.5%	12.5%
35,021	WEAKLEY	12,184	9,008	2,772	404	6,236 R	73.9%	22.8%	76.5%	23.5%
25,841	WHITE	9,825	7,671	1,845	309	5,826 R	78.1%	18.8%	80.6%	19.4%
183,182	WILLIAMSON	106,271	68,212	31,013	7,046	37,199 R	64.2%	29.2%	68.7%	31.3%
113,993	WILSON	56,734	39,406	14,385	2,943	25,021 R	69.5%	25.4%	73.3%	26.7%
6,346,105	TOTAL	2,508,027	1,522,925	870,695	114,407	652,230 R	60.7%	34.7%	63.6%	36.4%

TENNESSEE

HOUSE OF REPRESENTATIVES

CD	Year	Total Vote	Republican Vote	Republican Candidate	Democratic Vote	Democratic Candidate	Other Vote	Rep.-Dem. Plurality	Total Vote Rep.	Total Vote Dem.	Major Vote Rep.	Major Vote Dem.
1	2016	253,025	198,293	ROE, PHIL*	39,024	BOHMS, ALAN	15,708	159,269 R	78.4%	15.4%	83.6%	16.4%
1	2014	139,470	115,533	ROE, PHIL*			23,937	115,533 R	82.8%		100.0%	
1	2012	239,672	182,252	ROE, PHIL*	47,663	WOODRUFF, ALAN	9,757	134,589 R	76.0%	19.9%	79.3%	20.7%
2	2016	280,856	212,455	DUNCAN, JOHN J. JR.*	68,401	STARR, STUART		144,054 R	75.6%	24.4%	75.6%	24.4%
2	2014	166,751	120,883	DUNCAN, JOHN J. JR.*	37,612	SCOTT, BOB	8,256	83,271 R	72.5%	22.6%	76.3%	23.7%
2	2012	264,505	196,894	DUNCAN, JOHN J. JR.*	54,522	GOODALE, TROY	13,089	142,372 R	74.4%	20.6%	78.3%	21.7%
3	2016	266,006	176,613	FLEISCHMANN, CHUCK*	76,727	SHEKARI, MELODY	12,666	99,886 R	66.4%	28.8%	69.7%	30.3%
3	2014	156,097	97,344	FLEISCHMANN, CHUCK*	53,983	HEADRICK, MARY M.	4,770	43,361 R	62.4%	34.6%	64.3%	35.7%
3	2012	256,909	157,830	FLEISCHMANN, CHUCK*	91,094	HEADRICK, MARY M.	7,985	66,736 R	61.4%	35.5%	63.4%	36.6%

TENNESSEE

HOUSE OF REPRESENTATIVES

CD	Year	Total Vote	Republican		Democratic		Other Vote	Rep.-Dem. Plurality	Percentage			
									Total Vote		Major Vote	
			Vote	Candidate	Vote	Candidate			Rep.	Dem.	Rep.	Dem.
4	2016	254,937	165,796	DESJARLAIS, SCOTT*	89,141	REYNOLDS, STEVEN		76,655 R	65.0%	35.0%	65.0%	35.0%
4	2014	145,418	84,815	DESJARLAIS, SCOTT*	51,357	SHERRELL, LENDA	9,246	33,458 R	58.3%	35.3%	62.3%	37.7%
4	2012	230,590	128,568	DESJARLAIS, SCOTT*	102,022	STEWART, ERIC		26,546 R	55.8%	44.2%	55.8%	44.2%
5	2016	273,544	102,433	SNYDER, STACY RIES	171,111	COOPER, JIM*		68,678 D	37.4%	62.6%	37.4%	62.6%
5	2014	154,276	55,078	RIES, BOB	96,148	COOPER, JIM*	3,050	41,070 D	35.7%	62.3%	36.4%	63.6%
5	2012	263,095	86,240	STAATS, BRAD	171,621	COOPER, JIM*	5,234	85,381 D	32.8%	65.2%	33.4%	66.6%
6	2016	284,490	202,234	BLACK, DIANE*	61,995	KENT, DAVID W.	20,261	140,239 R	71.1%	21.8%	76.5%	23.5%
6	2014	162,097	115,231	BLACK, DIANE*	37,232	POWERS, AMOS SCOTT	9,634	77,999 R	71.1%	23.0%	75.6%	24.4%
6	2012	241,241	184,383	BLACK, DIANE*			56,858	184,383 R	76.4%		100.0%	
7	2016	277,513	200,407	BLACKBURN, MARSHA*	65,226	CHANDLER, THARON	11,880	135,181 R	72.2%	23.5%	75.4%	24.6%
7	2014	157,907	110,534	BLACKBURN, MARSHA*	42,280	CRAMER, DANIEL N.	5,093	68,254 R	70.0%	26.8%	72.3%	27.7%
7	2012	257,306	182,730	BLACKBURN, MARSHA*	61,679	AMOUZOUVIK, CREDO	12,897	121,051 R	71.0%	24.0%	74.8%	25.2%
8	2016	282,733	194,386	KUSTOFF, DAVID	70,925	HOBSON, RICKEY	17,422	123,461 R	68.8%	25.1%	73.3%	26.7%
8	2014	172,595	122,255	FINCHER, STEPHEN LEE*	42,433	BRADLEY, WES	7,907	79,822 R	70.8%	24.6%	74.2%	25.8%
8	2012	279,422	190,923	FINCHER, STEPHEN LEE*	79,490	DIXON, TIMOTHY	9,009	111,433 R	68.3%	28.4%	70.6%	29.4%
9	2016	217,957	41,123	ALBERSON, FLOYD WAYNE	171,631	COHEN, STEPHEN I.*	5,203	130,508 D	18.9%	78.7%	19.3%	80.7%
9	2014	116,550	27,173	BERGMANN, CHARLOTTE	87,376	COHEN, STEPHEN I.*	2,001	60,203 D	23.3%	75.0%	23.7%	76.3%
9	2012	250,987	59,742	FLINN, GEORGE S. "JR."	188,422	COHEN, STEPHEN I.*	2,823	128,680 D	23.8%	75.1%	24.1%	75.9%
TOTAL	2016	2,391,061	1,493,740		814,181		83,140	679,559 R	62.5%	34.1%	64.7%	35.3%
TOTAL	2014	1,371,161	848,846		448,421		73,894	400,425 R	61.9%	32.7%	65.4%	34.6%
TOTAL	2012	2,283,727	1,369,562		796,513		117,652	573,049 R	60.0%	34.9%	63.2%	36.8%

Note: An asterisk (*) denotes incumbent.

TENNESSEE

GENERAL AND PRIMARY ELECTIONS

2016 GENERAL ELECTIONS: OTHER VOTES

President   Other vote was 70,397 Libertarian (Gary Johnson), 15,993 Independent (Jill Stein), 11,991 Write-in (Evan McMullin), 7,276 Independent (Mike Smith), 4,075 Independent (Roque De La Fuente), 2,877 Independent (Alyson Kennedy), 1,798 Write-in (Scattered Write-in)

House   Other vote was:

CD 1   15,702 Independent (Robert Franklin), 6 Write-in (Paul Krane)

CD 3   5,098 Independent (Rick Tyler), 5,075 Independent (Cassandra Mitchell), 2,493 Independent (Topher Kersting)

CD 6   20,261 Independent (David Ross)

CD 7   11,880 Independent (Leonard Ladner)

CD 8   6,442 Independent (Shelia Godwin), 4,057 Independent (James Hart), 2,497 Independent (Adrian Montague), 1,981 Independent (Karen Talley-Lane)

CD 9   5,203 Independent (Paul Cook)

TENNESSEE

GENERAL AND PRIMARY ELECTIONS

2016 PRIMARY ELECTIONS: SUPPLEMENTARY INFORMATION

Primary	March 1, 2016 (President) August 4, 2016 (Congress)	**Registration** (as of June 30, 2016 – includes 654,057 inactive registrants)	3,972,539	No Party Registration

Primary Type   Open—Any registered voter could participate in either the Democratic or the Republican primary, but must declare affiliation with that party at the polls.

	REPUBLICAN PRIMARIES			DEMOCRATIC PRIMARIES		
President	Trump, Donald J.	333,180	38.9%	Clinton, Hillary Rodham	245,930	66.1%
	Cruz, Ted	211,471	24.7%	Sanders, Bernard	120,800	32.5%
	Rubio, Marco	181,274	21.2%	Uncommitted	3,467	0.9%
	Carson, Ben	64,951	7.6%	O'Malley, Martin	2,025	0.5%
	Kasich, John R.	45,301	5.3%			
	Bush, Jeb	9,551	1.1%			
	Huckabee, Mike	2,415	0.3%			
	Paul, Rand	2,350	0.3%			
	Uncommitted	1,849	0.2%			
	Christie, Chris	1,256	0.1%			
	Fiorina, Carly	715	0.1%			
	Santorum, Rick	710	0.1%			
	Gilmore, James S. III	267				
	Graham, Lindsey	253				
	Pataki, George E.	186				
	TOTAL	*855,729*		*TOTAL*	*372,222*	
Congressional District 1	Roe, Phil*	35,350	82.2%	Bohms, Alan	4,161	100.0%
	Tribble, Clint	7,673	17.8%			
	TOTAL	*43,023*		*TOTAL*	*4,161*	
Congressional District 2	Duncan, John J. Jr.*	28,806	100.0%	Starr, Stuart	7,851	100.0%
	TOTAL	*28,806*		*TOTAL*	*7,851*	
Congressional District 3	Fleischmann, Chuck*	31,964	83.9%	Shekari, Melody	8,660	53.9%
	Smith, Geoffery Suhmer	3,076	8.1%	Friedman, Michael	5,329	33.2%
	Levene, Allan	3,059	8.0%	Love, George Ryan	2,070	12.9%
	TOTAL	*38,099*		*TOTAL*	*16,059*	
Congressional District 4	DesJarlais, Scott*	24,211	52.1%	Reynolds, Steven	11,511	100.0%
	Starrett, Grant	20,138	43.3%			
	Persley, Erran	1,615	3.5%			
	Faparusi Sr., Oluyomi "Fapas"	493	1.1%			
	TOTAL	*46,457*		*TOTAL*	*11,511*	
Congressional District 5	Snyder, Stacy Ries	7,666	50.8%	Cooper, Jim*	32,103	100.0%
	Smith, John "Big John"	4,295	28.5%			
	Ball, Jody	3,124	20.7%			
	TOTAL	*15,085*		*TOTAL*	*32,103*	
Congressional District 6	Black, Diane*	33,215	63.7%	Kent, David W.	7,551	67.0%
	Carr, Joe	16,665	31.9%	Matheson, Flo	3,714	33.0%
	Strong, Donald	1,354	2.6%			
	Hay, Tommy N.	945	1.8%			
	TOTAL	*52,179*		*TOTAL*	*11,265*	
Congressional District 7	Blackburn, Marsha*	38,490	100.0%	Chandler, Tharon	9,956	100.0%
	TOTAL	*38,490*		*TOTAL*	*9,956*	

TENNESSEE

GENERAL AND PRIMARY ELECTIONS

	REPUBLICAN PRIMARIES			DEMOCRATIC PRIMARIES		
Congressional District 8	Kustoff, David	16,889	27.4%	Hobson, Rickey	7,774	54.8%
	Flinn, George S. Jr.	14,200	23.1%	Frye, Gregory Alan	6,413	45.2%
	Luttrell, Mark H. Jr.	10,878	17.7%			
	Kelsey, Brian	7,942	12.9%			
	Greer, Brad	6,819	11.1%			
	Leatherwood, Tom	2,620	4.3%			
	Baker, Hunter	1,014	1.6%			
	Atkins, Ken	410	0.7%			
	Honeycutt, Raymond	231	0.4%			
	Howell, George B.	211	0.3%			
	Wharton, David	131	0.2%			
	Bault, Dave	109	0.2%			
	Maldonado, David J.	76	0.1%			
	TOTAL	*61,530*		*TOTAL*	*14,187*	
Congressional District 9	Alberson, Wayne	8,381	100.0%	Cohen, Stephen I.*	35,645	85.5%
				Ford, Justin	4,165	10.0%
				Williams, M. LaTroy	1,452	3.5%
				Crim, Larry	406	1.0%
	TOTAL	*8,381*		*TOTAL*	*41,668*	

Note: An asterisk (*) denotes incumbent.

TEXAS
Congressional districts first established for elections held in 2012
36 members

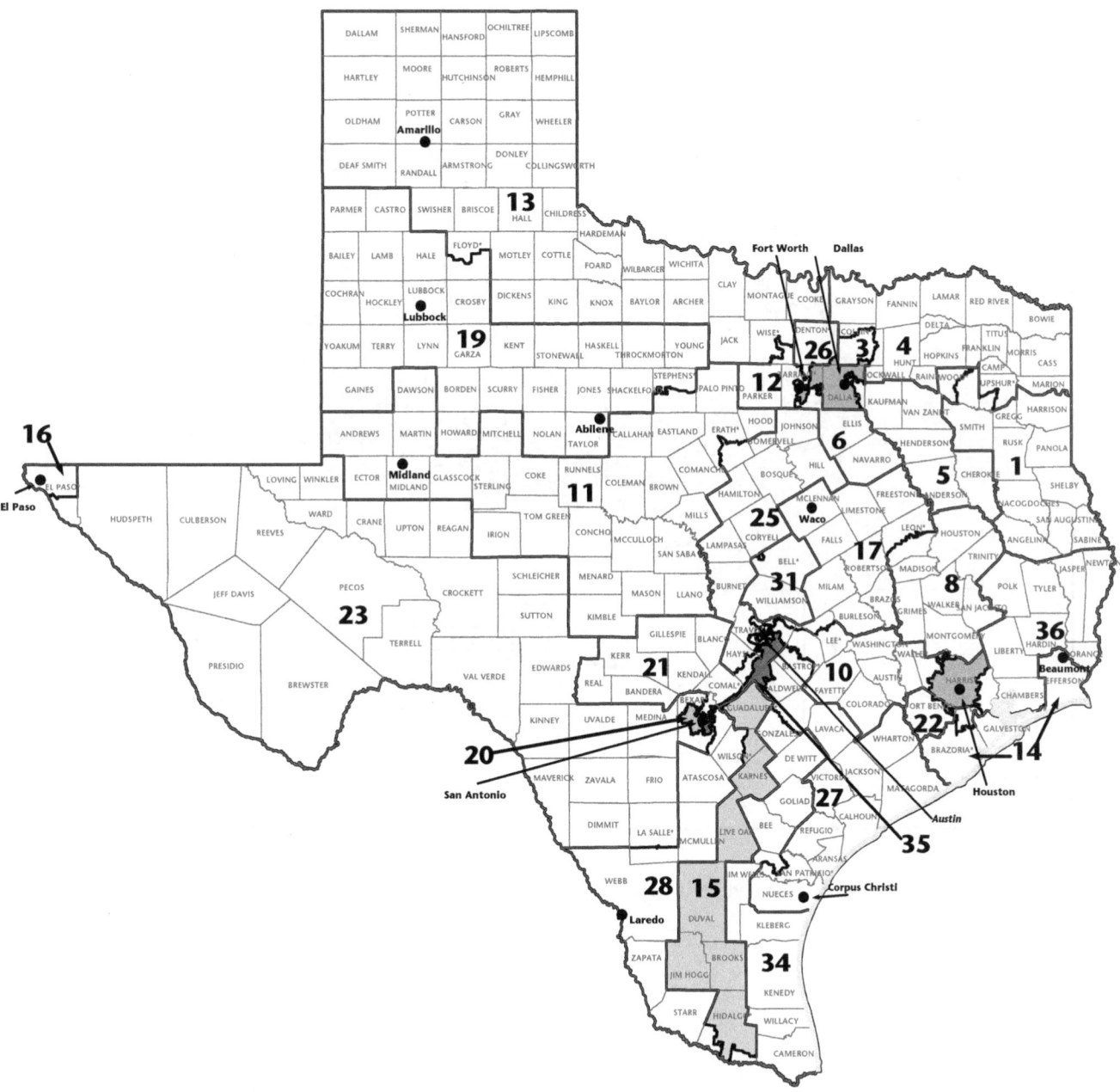

* Asterisk indicates a county whose boundaries include parts of two or more congressional districts.

TEXAS

Greater Dallas–Fort Worth Area

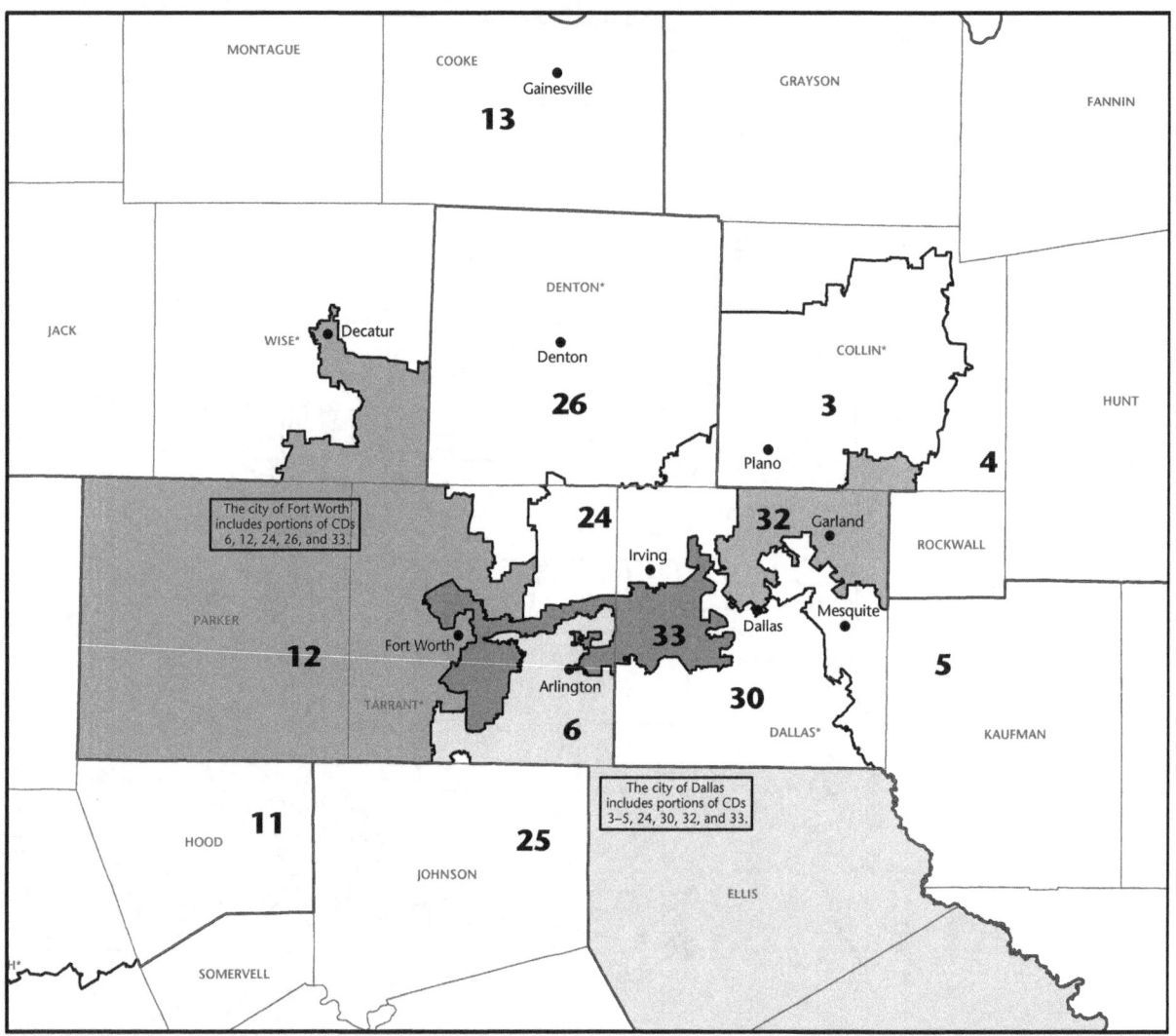

* Asterisk indicates a county whose boundaries include parts of two or more congressional districts.

TEXAS
Greater Houston Area

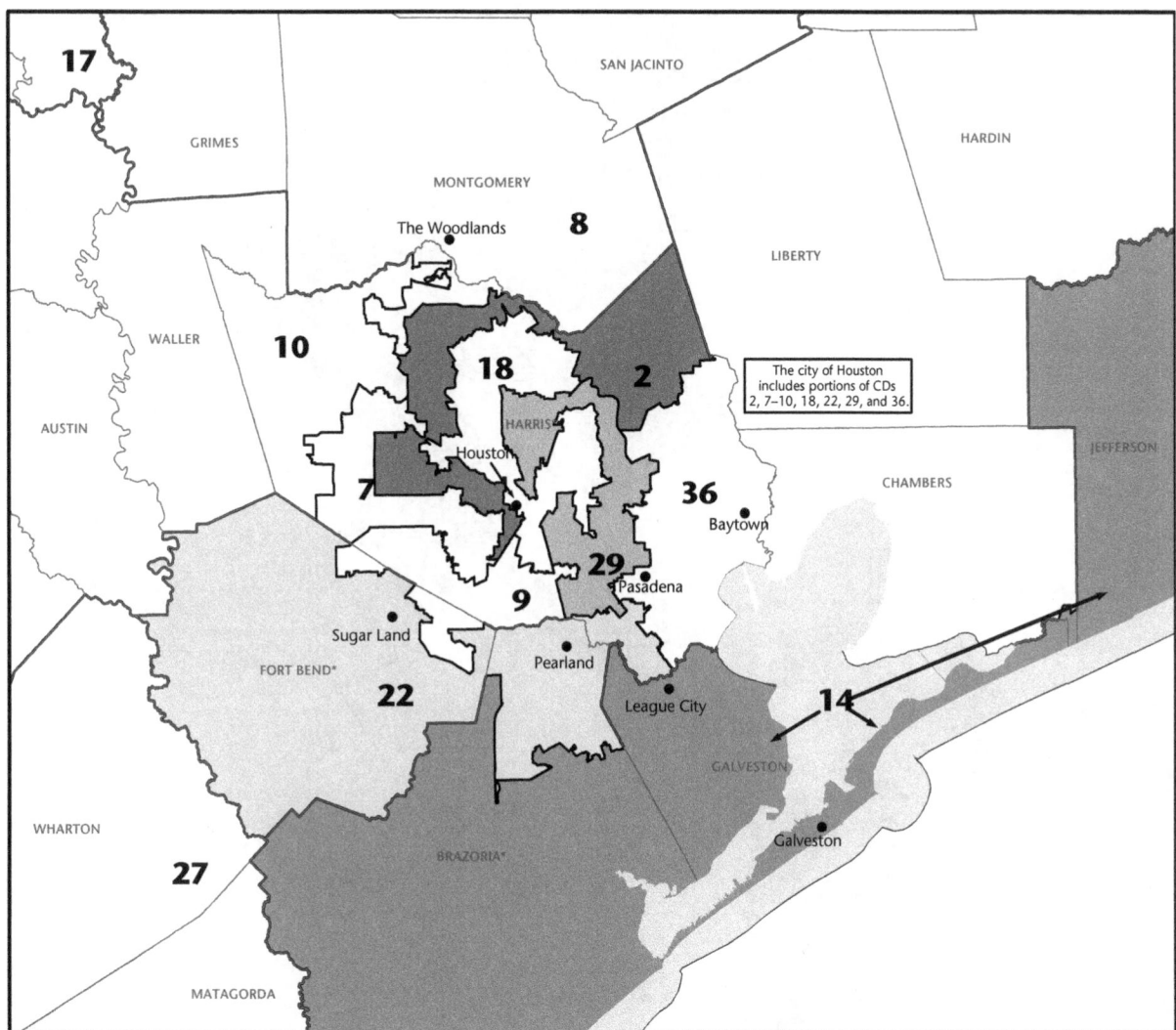

* Asterisk indicates a county whose boundaries include parts of two or more congressional districts.

TEXAS

Greater San Antonio, Austin Areas

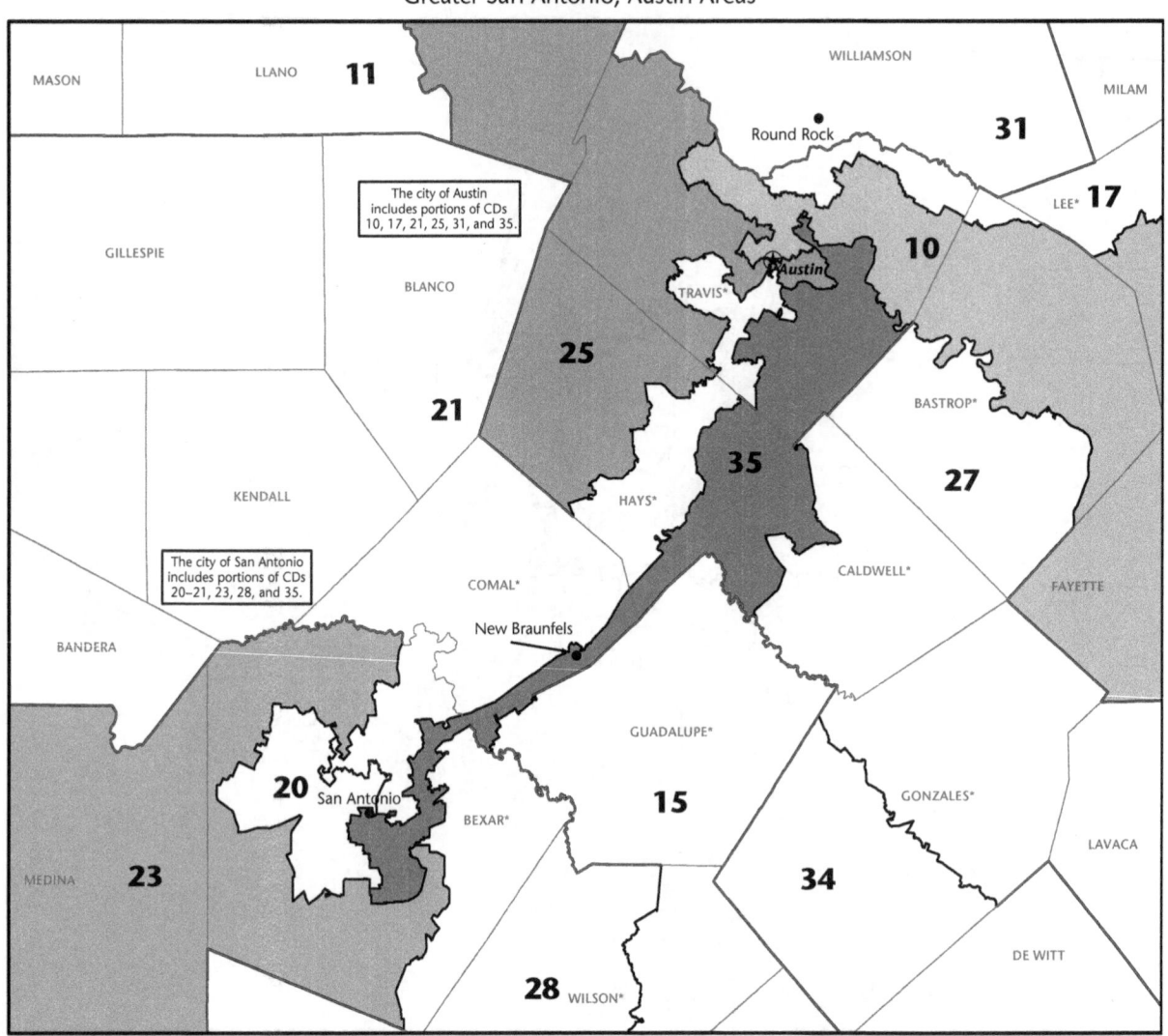

Within the map:

MASON · LLANO · **11** · WILLIAMSON · MILAM

Round Rock

31

LEE* · **17**

GILLESPIE

The city of Austin includes portions of CDs 10, 17, 21, 25, 31, and 35.

BLANCO

10

TRAVIS* · *Austin*

25

BASTROP*

21

35

KENDALL

HAYS*

27

The city of San Antonio includes portions of CDs 20–21, 23, 28, and 35.

COMAL*

CALDWELL*

FAYETTE

BANDERA

New Braunfels

GUADALUPE*

20 · San Antonio

15

GONZALES*

BEXAR*

MEDINA · **23**

34

LAVACA

DE WITT

28 · WILSON*

* Asterisk indicates a county whose boundaries include parts of two or more congressional districts.

TEXAS

GOVERNOR
Greg Abbott (R). Elected 2014 to a four-year term.

SENATORS (2 Republicans)
John Cornyn (R). Re-elected 2014 to a six-year term. Previously elected 2008, 2002.

Ted Cruz (R). Elected 2012 to a six-year term.

REPRESENTATIVES (25 Republicans, 11 Democrats)
1. Louie Gohmert (R)
2. Ted Poe (R)
3. Sam Johnson (R)
4. John Ratcliffe (R)
5. Jeb Hensarling (R)
6. Joe L. Barton (R)
7. John Culberson (R)
8. Kevin Brady (R)
9. Al Green (D)
10. Michael T. McCaul (R)
11. K. Michael Conaway (R)
12. Kay Granger (R)
13. William M. Thornberry (R)
14. Randy Weber (R)
15. Vicente Gonzalez (D)
16. Beto O'Rourke (D)
17. Bill Flores (R)
18. Sheila Jackson Lee (D)
19. Jodey Arrington (R)
20. Joaquin Castro (D)
21. Lamar Smith (R)
22. Pete Olson (R)
23. Will Hurd (R)
24. Kenny Marchant (R)
25. Roger Williams (R)
26. Michael C. Burgess (R)
27. R. Blake Farenthold (R)
28. Henry Cuellar (D)
29. Gene Green (D)
30. Eddie Bernice Johnson (D)
31. John R. Carter (R)
32. Pete Sessions (R)
33. Marc A. Veasey (D)
34. Filemon Vela (D)
35. Lloyd Doggett (D)
36. Brian Babin (R)

POSTWAR VOTE FOR PRESIDENT

		Republican		Democratic		Other	Rep.-Dem.	Total Vote		Major Vote	
Year	Total Vote	Vote	Candidate	Vote	Candidate	Vote	Plurality	Rep.	Dem.	Rep.	Dem.
2016**	8,969,226	4,685,047	Trump, Donald J.	3,877,868	Clinton, Hillary Rodham	406,311	807,179 R	52.2%	43.2%	54.7%	45.3%
2012	7,993,851	4,569,843	Romney, W. Mitt	3,308,124	Obama, Barack H.*	115,884	1,261,719 R	57.2%	41.4%	58.0%	42.0%
2008	8,077,795	4,479,328	McCain, John S. III	3,528,633	Obama, Barack H.	69,834	950,695 R	55.5%	43.7%	55.9%	44.1%
2004	7,410,765	4,526,917	Bush, George W.*	2,832,704	Kerry, John F.	51,144	1,694,213 R	61.1%	38.2%	61.5%	38.5%
2000**	6,407,637	3,799,639	Bush, George W.	2,433,746	Gore, Albert Jr.	174,252	1,365,893 R	59.3%	38.0%	61.0%	39.0%
1996**	5,611,644	2,736,167	Dole, Robert "Bob"	2,459,683	Clinton, Bill*	415,794	276,484 R	48.8%	43.8%	52.7%	47.3%
1992**	6,154,018	2,496,071	Bush, George H.*	2,281,815	Clinton, Bill	1,376,132	214,256 R	40.6%	37.1%	52.2%	47.8%
1988	5,427,410	3,036,829	Bush, George H.	2,352,748	Dukakis, Michael S.	37,833	684,081 R	56.0%	43.3%	56.3%	43.7%
1984	5,397,571	3,433,428	Reagan, Ronald*	1,949,276	Mondale, Walter F.	14,867	1,484,152 R	63.6%	36.1%	63.8%	36.2%
1980**	4,541,636	2,510,705	Reagan, Ronald	1,881,147	Carter, Jimmy*	149,784	629,558 R	55.3%	41.4%	57.2%	42.8%
1976	4,071,884	1,953,300	Ford, Gerald R.*	2,082,319	Carter, Jimmy	36,265	129,019 D	48.0%	51.1%	48.4%	51.6%
1972	3,471,285	2,298,896	Nixon, Richard M.*	1,154,293	McGovern, George S.	18,096	1,144,603 R	66.2%	33.3%	66.6%	33.4%
1968**	3,079,216	1,227,844	Nixon, Richard M.	1,266,804	Humphrey, Hubert Horatio Jr.	584,568	38,960 D	39.9%	41.1%	49.2%	50.8%
1964	2,626,811	958,566	Goldwater, Barry M. Sr.	1,663,185	Johnson, Lyndon B.*	5,060	704,619 D	36.5%	63.3%	36.6%	63.4%
1960	2,311,084	1,121,310	Nixon, Richard M.	1,167,567	Kennedy, John F.	22,207	46,257 D	48.5%	50.5%	49.0%	51.0%
1956	1,955,168	1,080,619	Eisenhower, Dwight D.*	859,958	Stevenson, Adlai E. II	14,591	220,661 R	55.3%	44.0%	55.7%	44.3%
1952	2,075,946	1,102,878	Eisenhower, Dwight D.	969,228	Stevenson, Adlai E. II	3,840	133,650 R	53.1%	46.7%	53.2%	46.8%
1948**	1,249,577	303,467	Dewey, Thomas E.	824,235	Truman, Harry S.*	121,875	520,768 D	24.3%	66.0%	26.9%	73.1%

Note: An asterisk (*) denotes incumbent. **In past elections, the other vote included: 2016 - 283,492 Libertarian (Gary Johnson); 2000 - 137,994 Green (Ralph Nader); 1996 - 378,537 Reform (Ross Perot); 1992 - 1,354,781 Independent (Perot); 1980 - 111,613 Independent (John Anderson); 1968 - 584,269 American Independent (George Wallace); 1948 - 113,920 States' Rights (Strom Thurmond).

TEXAS

POSTWAR VOTE FOR GOVERNOR

Year	Total Vote	Republican Vote	Republican Candidate	Democratic Vote	Democratic Candidate	Other Vote	Rep.-Dem. Plurality		Total Vote Rep.	Total Vote Dem.	Major Vote Rep.	Major Vote Dem.
2014	4,718,268	2,796,547	Abbott, Greg	1,835,596	Davis, Wendy R.	86,125	960,951	R	59.3%	38.9%	60.4%	39.6%
2010	4,979,870	2,737,481	Perry, Rick*	2,106,395	White, Bill	135,994	631,086	R	55.0%	42.3%	56.5%	43.5%
2006**	4,399,116	1,716,792	Perry, Rick*	1,310,337	Bell, Chris	1,371,987	406,455	R	39.0%	29.8%	56.7%	43.3%
2002	4,553,987	2,632,591	Perry, Rick*	1,819,798	Sanchez, Tony	101,598	812,793	R	57.8%	40.0%	59.1%	40.9%
1998	3,738,483	2,551,454	Bush, George W.*	1,165,444	Mauro, Garry	21,585	1,386,010	R	68.2%	31.2%	68.6%	31.4%
1994	4,396,242	2,350,994	Bush, George W.	2,016,928	Richards, Ann*	28,320	334,066	R	53.5%	45.9%	53.8%	46.2%
1990	3,892,487	1,826,231	Williams, Clayton	1,925,670	Richards, Ann	140,586	99,439	D	46.9%	49.5%	48.7%	51.3%
1986	3,441,460	1,813,779	Clements, William P.	1,584,515	White, Mark*	43,166	229,264	R	52.7%	46.0%	53.4%	46.6%
1982	3,191,091	1,465,937	Clements, William P.*	1,697,870	White, Mark	27,284	231,933	D	45.9%	53.2%	46.3%	53.7%
1978	2,369,764	1,183,839	Clements, William P.	1,166,979	Hill, John	18,946	16,860	R	50.0%	49.2%	50.4%	49.6%
1974**	1,654,957	514,725	Granberry, Jim	1,016,334	Briscoe, Dolph*	123,898	501,609	D	31.1%	61.4%	33.6%	66.4%
1972	3,410,071	1,534,060	Grover, Henry C.	1,633,913	Briscoe, Dolph	242,098	99,853	D	45.0%	47.9%	48.4%	51.6%
1970	2,235,855	1,037,723	Eggers, Paul W.	1,197,736	Smith, Preston*	396	160,013	D	46.4%	53.6%	46.4%	53.6%
1968	2,916,508	1,254,331	Eggers, Paul W.	1,662,019	Smith, Preston	158	407,688	D	43.0%	57.0%	43.0%	57.0%
1966	1,425,861	368,025	Kennerly, T. E.	1,037,517	Connally, John B.*	20,319	669,492	D	25.8%	72.8%	26.2%	73.8%
1964	2,544,753	661,675	Crichton, Jack	1,877,793	Connally, John B.*	5,285	1,216,118	D	26.0%	73.8%	26.1%	73.9%
1962	1,569,181	715,025	Cox, Jack	847,036	Connally, John B.	7,120	132,011	D	45.6%	54.0%	45.8%	54.2%
1960	2,250,718	612,963	Steger, William	1,637,755	Daniel, Price*		1,024,792	D	27.2%	72.8%	27.2%	72.8%
1958	789,133	94,098	Mayer, Edwin S.	695,035	Daniel, Price*		600,937	D	11.9%	88.1%	11.9%	88.1%
1956	1,826,242	271,088	Bryant, William R.	1,433,051	Daniel, Price	122,103	1,161,963	D	14.8%	78.5%	15.9%	84.1%
1954	636,892	66,154	Adams, Tod R.	569,533	Shivers, Allan*	1,205	503,379	D	10.4%	89.4%	10.4%	89.6%
1952	1,890,535			1,853,863	Shivers, Allan*	36,672	1,853,863	D		98.1%		100.0%
1950	407,138	39,793	Currie, Ralph W.	367,345	Shivers, Allan*		327,552	D	9.8%	90.2%	9.8%	90.2%
1948	1,208,860	177,399	Lane, Alvin H.	1,024,160	Jester, Beauford H.*	7,301	846,761	D	14.7%	84.7%	14.8%	85.2%
1946	378,784	33,277	Nolte, Eugene Jr.	345,507	Jester, Beauford H.		312,230	D	8.8%	91.2%	8.8%	91.2%

Note: An asterisk (*) denotes incumbent. **In past elections, the other vote included: 2006 - 796,851 Independent (Carole Keeton Strayhorn); 547,674 Independent (Richard "Kinky" Friedman). The term of office of Texas's governor was increased from two to four years effective with the 1974 election. The Republican Party did not run a candidate in the 1952 gubernatorial election.

TEXAS

POSTWAR VOTE FOR SENATOR

Year	Total Vote	Republican Vote	Republican Candidate	Democratic Vote	Democratic Candidate	Other Vote	Rep.-Dem. Plurality		Total Vote Rep.	Total Vote Dem.	Major Vote Rep.	Major Vote Dem.
2014	4,648,358	2,861,531	Cornyn, John*	1,597,387	Alameel, David	189,440	1,264,144	R	61.6%	34.4%	64.2%	35.8%
2012	7,864,822	4,440,137	Cruz, Ted	3,194,927	Sadler, Paul	229,758	1,245,210	R	56.5%	40.6%	58.2%	41.8%
2008	7,912,075	4,337,469	Cornyn, John*	3,389,365	Noriega, Richard J. "Rick"	185,241	948,104	R	54.8%	42.8%	56.1%	43.9%
2006	4,314,663	2,661,789	Hutchison, Kay Bailey*	1,555,202	Radnofsky, Barbara Ann	97,672	1,106,587	R	61.7%	36.0%	63.1%	36.9%
2002	4,514,012	2,496,243	Cornyn, John	1,955,758	Kirk, Ron	62,011	540,485	R	55.3%	43.3%	56.1%	43.9%
2000	6,276,652	4,082,091	Hutchison, Kay Bailey*	2,030,315	Kelly, Gene	164,246	2,051,776	R	65.0%	32.3%	66.8%	33.2%
1996	5,527,441	3,027,680	Gramm, W. Phil*	2,428,776	Morales, Victor M.	70,985	598,904	R	54.8%	43.9%	55.5%	44.5%
1994	4,279,940	2,604,218	Hutchison, Kay Bailey*	1,639,615	Mattox, Jim	36,107	964,603	R	60.8%	38.3%	61.4%	38.6%
1993S**	1,765,254	1,188,716	Hutchison, Kay Bailey	576,538	Krueger, Robert*		612,178	R	67.3%	32.7%	67.3%	32.7%
1990	3,822,157	2,302,357	Gramm, W. Phil*	1,429,986	Parmer, Hugh	89,814	872,371	R	60.2%	37.4%	61.7%	38.3%
1988	5,323,606	2,129,228	Boulter, E. Beau	3,149,806	Bentsen, Lloyd M. Jr.*	44,572	1,020,578	D	40.0%	59.2%	40.3%	59.7%
1984	5,319,178	3,116,348	Gramm, W. Phil	2,202,557	Doggett, Lloyd	273	913,791	R	58.6%	41.4%	58.6%	41.4%
1982	3,103,167	1,256,759	Collins, James M.	1,818,223	Bentsen, Lloyd M. Jr.*	28,185	561,464	D	40.5%	58.6%	40.9%	59.1%
1978	2,312,540	1,151,376	Tower, John G.*	1,139,149	Krueger, Robert	22,015	12,227	R	49.8%	49.3%	50.3%	49.7%
1976	3,874,516	1,636,370	Steelman, Alan	2,199,956	Bentsen, Lloyd M. Jr.*	38,190	563,586	D	42.2%	56.8%	42.7%	57.3%
1972	3,413,918	1,822,877	Tower, John G.*	1,511,985	Sanders, Barefoot	79,056	310,892	R	53.4%	44.3%	54.7%	45.3%
1970	2,231,671	1,035,794	Bush, George H.	1,194,069	Bentsen, Lloyd M. Jr.	1,808	158,275	D	46.4%	53.5%	46.5%	53.5%
1966	1,493,182	842,501	Tower, John G.*	643,855	Carr, Waggoner	6,826	198,646	R	56.4%	43.1%	56.7%	43.3%
1964	2,603,856	1,134,337	Bush, George H.	1,463,958	Yarborough, Ralph*	5,561	329,621	D	43.6%	56.2%	43.7%	56.3%
1961S**	886,091	448,217	Tower, John G.	437,874	Blakley, William A.*		10,343	R	50.6%	49.4%	50.6%	49.4%
1960	2,253,764	926,653	Tower, John G.	1,306,605	Johnson, Lyndon B.*	20,506	379,952	D	41.1%	58.0%	41.5%	58.5%
1958	787,128	185,926	Whittenburg, Roy	587,030	Yarborough, Ralph*	14,172	401,104	D	23.6%	74.6%	24.1%	75.9%
1957S**	957,298				Yarborough, Ralph	875,338		D				
1954	636,475	94,131	Watson, Carlos G.	539,319	Johnson, Lyndon B.*	3,025	445,188	D	14.8%	84.7%	14.9%	85.1%
1952	1,894,671			1,894,671	Daniel, Price		1,894,671	D		100.0%		100.0%
1948	1,061,363	349,665	Porter, Jack	702,785	Johnson, Lyndon B.	8,913	353,120	D	32.9%	66.2%	33.2%	66.8%
1946	380,550	43,619	Sells, Murray C.	336,931	Connally, Tom T.*		293,312	D	11.5%	88.5%	11.5%	88.5%

Note: An asterisk (*) denotes incumbent. **The June 1993 election was for a short term to fill a vacancy; the vote above was for the special election runoff. The April 1957 and May 1961 elections were also for short terms to fill vacancies. Although neither vote was held with official party designations, the 1961 vote above reflected the result of a runoff between unofficial party candidates. In 1957 there was a single ballot without a runoff and Democrat Ralph Yarborough polled 364,605 votes (38.1 percent of the total vote) and won the election with a 73,802-vote plurality over Democrat Martin Dies. The Republican Party did not run a candidate in the 1952 Senate election.

TEXAS

PRESIDENT 2016

2010 Census Population	County	Total Vote	Republican (Trump)	Democratic (Clinton)	Other	Rep.-Dem. Plurality	Percentage Total Vote Rep.	Dem.	Major Vote Rep.	Dem.
58,458	ANDERSON	16,977	13,201	3,369	407	9,832 R	77.8%	19.8%	79.7%	20.3%
14,786	ANDREWS	4,943	3,927	836	180	3,091 R	79.4%	16.9%	82.4%	17.6%
86,771	ANGELINA	29,911	21,668	7,538	705	14,130 R	72.4%	25.2%	74.2%	25.8%
23,158	ARANSAS	10,512	7,740	2,465	307	5,275 R	73.6%	23.4%	75.8%	24.2%
9,054	ARCHER	4,283	3,786	394	103	3,392 R	88.4%	9.2%	90.6%	9.4%
1,901	ARMSTRONG	1,021	924	70	27	854 R	90.5%	6.9%	93.0%	7.0%
44,911	ATASCOSA	13,672	8,618	4,651	403	3,967 R	63.0%	34.0%	64.9%	35.1%
28,417	AUSTIN	12,275	9,637	2,320	318	7,317 R	78.5%	18.9%	80.6%	19.4%
7,165	BAILEY	1,793	1,344	397	52	947 R	75.0%	22.1%	77.2%	22.8%
20,485	BANDERA	10,218	8,163	1,726	329	6,437 R	79.9%	16.9%	82.5%	17.5%
74,171	BASTROP	28,454	16,328	10,569	1,557	5,759 R	57.4%	37.1%	60.7%	39.3%
3,726	BAYLOR	1,499	1,267	191	41	1,076 R	84.5%	12.7%	86.9%	13.1%
31,861	BEE	8,485	4,744	3,444	297	1,300 R	55.9%	40.6%	57.9%	42.1%
310,235	BELL	94,994	51,998	37,801	5,195	14,197 R	54.7%	39.8%	57.9%	42.1%
1,714,773	BEXAR	589,645	240,333	319,550	29,762	79,217 D	40.8%	54.2%	42.9%	57.1%
10,497	BLANCO	5,685	4,212	1,244	229	2,968 R	74.1%	21.9%	77.2%	22.8%
641	BORDEN	365	330	31	4	299 R	90.4%	8.5%	91.4%	8.6%
18,212	BOSQUE	7,838	6,339	1,278	221	5,061 R	80.9%	16.3%	83.2%	16.8%
92,565	BOWIE	34,602	24,924	8,838	840	16,086 R	72.0%	25.5%	73.8%	26.2%
313,166	BRAZORIA	121,181	72,791	43,200	5,190	29,591 R	60.1%	35.6%	62.8%	37.2%
194,851	BRAZOS	67,211	38,738	23,121	5,352	15,617 R	57.6%	34.4%	62.6%	37.4%
9,232	BREWSTER	4,252	2,077	1,873	302	204 R	48.8%	44.0%	52.6%	47.4%
1,637	BRISCOE	736	625	91	20	534 R	84.9%	12.4%	87.3%	12.7%
7,223	BROOKS	2,596	613	1,937	46	1,324 D	23.6%	74.6%	24.0%	76.0%
38,106	BROWN	14,026	12,017	1,621	388	10,396 R	85.7%	11.6%	88.1%	11.9%
17,187	BURLESON	6,960	5,316	1,491	153	3,825 R	76.4%	21.4%	78.1%	21.9%
42,750	BURNET	19,204	14,638	3,797	769	10,841 R	76.2%	19.8%	79.4%	20.6%
38,066	CALDWELL	12,092	6,691	4,795	606	1,896 R	55.3%	39.7%	58.3%	41.7%
21,381	CALHOUN	6,965	4,638	2,118	209	2,520 R	66.6%	30.4%	68.7%	31.3%
13,544	CALLAHAN	5,579	4,865	569	145	4,296 R	87.2%	10.2%	89.5%	10.5%
406,220	CAMERON	92,079	29,472	59,402	3,205	29,930 D	32.0%	64.5%	33.2%	66.8%
12,401	CAMP	4,542	3,201	1,260	81	1,941 R	70.5%	27.7%	71.8%	28.2%
6,182	CARSON	2,964	2,620	249	95	2,371 R	88.4%	8.4%	91.3%	8.7%
30,464	CASS	12,344	9,726	2,391	227	7,335 R	78.8%	19.4%	80.3%	19.7%
8,062	CASTRO	1,997	1,414	526	57	888 R	70.8%	26.3%	72.9%	27.1%
35,096	CHAMBERS	16,786	13,339	2,948	499	10,391 R	79.5%	17.6%	81.9%	18.1%
50,845	CHEROKEE	16,790	12,919	3,469	402	9,450 R	76.9%	20.7%	78.8%	21.2%
7,041	CHILDRESS	2,084	1,802	253	29	1,549 R	86.5%	12.1%	87.7%	12.3%
10,752	CLAY	5,018	4,377	536	105	3,841 R	87.2%	10.7%	89.1%	10.9%
3,127	COCHRAN	901	679	190	32	489 R	75.4%	21.1%	78.1%	21.9%
3,320	COKE	1,423	1,265	140	18	1,125 R	88.9%	9.8%	90.0%	10.0%
8,895	COLEMAN	3,643	3,177	388	78	2,789 R	87.2%	10.7%	89.1%	10.9%
782,341	COLLIN	361,419	201,014	140,624	19,781	60,390 R	55.6%	38.9%	58.8%	41.2%
3,057	COLLINGSWORTH	1,156	983	145	28	838 R	85.0%	12.5%	87.1%	12.9%
20,874	COLORADO	8,513	6,325	1,987	201	4,338 R	74.3%	23.3%	76.1%	23.9%
108,472	COMAL	62,178	45,136	14,238	2,804	30,898 R	72.6%	22.9%	76.0%	24.0%
13,974	COMANCHE	5,237	4,333	789	115	3,544 R	82.7%	15.1%	84.6%	15.4%
4,087	CONCHO	1,068	885	148	35	737 R	82.9%	13.9%	85.7%	14.3%
38,437	COOKE	15,955	13,181	2,352	422	10,829 R	82.6%	14.7%	84.9%	15.1%
75,388	CORYELL	18,253	12,225	5,064	964	7,161 R	67.0%	27.7%	70.7%	29.3%
1,505	COTTLE	612	506	92	14	414 R	82.7%	15.0%	84.6%	15.4%
4,375	CRANE	1,384	1,049	299	36	750 R	75.8%	21.6%	77.8%	22.2%
3,719	CROCKETT	1,395	980	372	43	608 R	70.3%	26.7%	72.5%	27.5%
6,059	CROSBY	1,728	1,181	468	79	713 R	68.3%	27.1%	71.6%	28.4%
2,398	CULBERSON	767	280	454	33	174 D	36.5%	59.2%	38.1%	61.9%
6,703	DALLAM	1,544	1,261	222	61	1,039 R	81.7%	14.4%	85.0%	15.0%
2,368,139	DALLAS	758,973	262,945	461,080	34,948	198,135 D	34.6%	60.8%	36.3%	63.7%
13,833	DAWSON	3,563	2,636	835	92	1,801 R	74.0%	23.4%	75.9%	24.1%
20,097	DE WITT	6,843	5,519	1,163	161	4,356 R	80.7%	17.0%	82.6%	17.4%
19,372	DEAF SMITH	4,216	2,911	1,185	120	1,726 R	69.0%	28.1%	71.1%	28.9%

TEXAS

PRESIDENT 2016

2010 Census Population	County	Total Vote	Republican (Trump)	Democratic (Clinton)	Other	Rep.-Dem. Plurality	Percentage			
							Total Vote		Major Vote	
							Rep.	Dem.	Rep.	Dem.
5,231	DELTA	2,472	1,836	400	236	1,436 R	74.3%	16.2%	82.1%	17.9%
662,614	DENTON	298,455	170,603	110,890	16,962	59,713 R	57.2%	37.2%	60.6%	39.4%
2,444	DICKENS	909	755	128	26	627 R	83.1%	14.1%	85.5%	14.5%
9,996	DIMMIT	3,225	974	2,173	78	1,199 D	30.2%	67.4%	31.0%	69.0%
3,677	DONLEY	1,465	1,225	191	49	1,034 R	83.6%	13.0%	86.5%	13.5%
11,782	DUVAL	4,168	1,316	2,783	69	1,467 D	31.6%	66.8%	32.1%	67.9%
18,583	EASTLAND	6,963	6,011	776	176	5,235 R	86.3%	11.1%	88.6%	11.4%
137,130	ECTOR	36,530	25,020	10,249	1,261	14,771 R	68.5%	28.1%	70.9%	29.1%
2,002	EDWARDS	1,073	746	303	24	443 R	69.5%	28.2%	71.1%	28.9%
800,647	EL PASO	214,324	55,512	147,843	10,969	92,331 D	25.9%	69.0%	27.3%	72.7%
149,610	ELLIS	63,357	44,941	16,253	2,163	28,688 R	70.9%	25.7%	73.4%	26.6%
37,890	ERATH	13,893	11,210	2,160	523	9,050 R	80.7%	15.5%	83.8%	16.2%
17,866	FALLS	5,248	3,441	1,684	123	1,757 R	65.6%	32.1%	67.1%	32.9%
33,915	FANNIN	12,044	9,548	2,132	364	7,416 R	79.3%	17.7%	81.7%	18.3%
24,554	FAYETTE	11,174	8,743	2,144	287	6,599 R	78.2%	19.2%	80.3%	19.7%
3,974	FISHER	1,729	1,265	403	61	862 R	73.2%	23.3%	75.8%	24.2%
6,446	FLOYD	1,959	1,474	435	50	1,039 R	75.2%	22.2%	77.2%	22.8%
1,336	FOARD	513	383	113	17	270 R	74.7%	22.0%	77.2%	22.8%
585,375	FORT BEND	262,066	117,291	134,686	10,089	17,395 D	44.8%	51.4%	46.5%	53.5%
10,605	FRANKLIN	4,380	3,585	665	130	2,920 R	81.8%	15.2%	84.4%	15.6%
19,816	FREESTONE	7,684	6,026	1,471	187	4,555 R	78.4%	19.1%	80.4%	19.6%
17,217	FRIO	4,400	1,856	2,444	100	588 D	42.2%	55.5%	43.2%	56.8%
17,526	GAINES	4,620	3,907	597	116	3,310 R	84.6%	12.9%	86.7%	13.3%
291,309	GALVESTON	122,903	73,757	43,658	5,488	30,099 R	60.0%	35.5%	62.8%	37.2%
6,461	GARZA	1,484	1,225	230	29	995 R	82.5%	15.5%	84.2%	15.8%
24,837	GILLESPIE	13,214	10,446	2,288	480	8,158 R	79.1%	17.3%	82.0%	18.0%
1,226	GLASSCOCK	604	553	34	17	519 R	91.6%	5.6%	94.2%	5.8%
7,210	GOLIAD	3,708	2,620	973	115	1,647 R	70.7%	26.2%	72.9%	27.1%
19,807	GONZALES	6,334	4,587	1,571	176	3,016 R	72.4%	24.8%	74.5%	25.5%
22,535	GRAY	7,405	6,500	701	204	5,799 R	87.8%	9.5%	90.3%	9.7%
120,877	GRAYSON	47,416	35,325	10,301	1,790	25,024 R	74.5%	21.7%	77.4%	22.6%
121,730	GREGG	41,749	28,764	11,677	1,308	17,087 R	68.9%	28.0%	71.1%	28.9%
26,604	GRIMES	9,533	7,065	2,194	274	4,871 R	74.1%	23.0%	76.3%	23.7%
131,533	GUADALUPE	57,822	36,632	18,391	2,799	18,241 R	63.4%	31.8%	66.6%	33.4%
36,273	HALE	8,858	6,366	2,101	391	4,265 R	71.9%	23.7%	75.2%	24.8%
3,353	HALL	1,091	893	164	34	729 R	81.9%	15.0%	84.5%	15.5%
8,517	HAMILTON	3,620	3,060	479	81	2,581 R	84.5%	13.2%	86.5%	13.5%
5,613	HANSFORD	1,947	1,730	171	46	1,559 R	88.9%	8.8%	91.0%	9.0%
4,139	HARDEMAN	1,513	1,207	249	57	958 R	79.8%	16.5%	82.9%	17.1%
54,635	HARDIN	22,780	19,606	2,780	394	16,826 R	86.1%	12.2%	87.6%	12.4%
4,092,459	HARRIS	1,312,112	545,955	707,914	58,243	161,959 D	41.6%	54.0%	43.5%	56.5%
65,631	HARRISON	26,548	18,749	7,151	648	11,598 R	70.6%	26.9%	72.4%	27.6%
6,062	HARTLEY	1,952	1,730	173	49	1,557 R	88.6%	8.9%	90.9%	9.1%
5,899	HASKELL	1,770	1,403	314	53	1,089 R	79.3%	17.7%	81.7%	18.3%
157,107	HAYS	72,164	33,826	33,224	5,114	602 R	46.9%	46.0%	50.4%	49.6%
3,807	HEMPHILL	1,695	1,462	181	52	1,281 R	86.3%	10.7%	89.0%	11.0%
78,532	HENDERSON	30,045	23,650	5,669	726	17,981 R	78.7%	18.9%	80.7%	19.3%
774,769	HIDALGO	173,437	48,642	118,809	5,986	70,167 D	28.0%	68.5%	29.0%	71.0%
35,089	HILL	12,970	10,108	2,547	315	7,561 R	77.9%	19.6%	79.9%	20.1%
22,935	HOCKLEY	7,311	5,809	1,260	242	4,549 R	79.5%	17.2%	82.2%	17.8%
51,182	HOOD	26,262	21,382	4,008	872	17,374 R	81.4%	15.3%	84.2%	15.8%
35,161	HOPKINS	13,538	10,707	2,510	321	8,197 R	79.1%	18.5%	81.0%	19.0%
23,732	HOUSTON	8,353	6,205	1,978	170	4,227 R	74.3%	23.7%	75.8%	24.2%
35,012	HOWARD	8,723	6,637	1,770	316	4,867 R	76.1%	20.3%	78.9%	21.1%
3,476	HUDSPETH	871	503	324	44	179 R	57.7%	37.2%	60.8%	39.2%
86,129	HUNT	31,554	23,910	6,396	1,248	17,514 R	75.8%	20.3%	78.9%	21.1%
22,150	HUTCHINSON	8,155	7,042	854	259	6,188 R	86.4%	10.5%	89.2%	10.8%
1,599	IRION	766	660	90	16	570 R	86.2%	11.7%	88.0%	12.0%
9,044	JACK	3,350	2,973	314	63	2,659 R	88.7%	9.4%	90.4%	9.6%
14,075	JACKSON	5,302	4,266	904	132	3,362 R	80.5%	17.1%	82.5%	17.5%

TEXAS

PRESIDENT 2016

2010 Census Population	County	Total Vote	Republican (Trump)	Democratic (Clinton)	Other	Rep.-Dem. Plurality	Percentage			
							Total Vote		Major Vote	
							Rep.	Dem.	Rep.	Dem.
35,710	JASPER	13,419	10,609	2,590	220	8,019 R	79.1%	19.3%	80.4%	19.6%
2,342	JEFF DAVIS	1,191	695	422	74	273 R	58.4%	35.4%	62.2%	37.8%
252,273	JEFFERSON	87,618	42,862	42,443	2,313	419 R	48.9%	48.4%	50.2%	49.8%
5,300	JIM HOGG	2,119	430	1,635	54	1,205 D	20.3%	77.2%	20.8%	79.2%
40,838	JIM WELLS	12,379	5,420	6,694	265	1,274 D	43.8%	54.1%	44.7%	55.3%
150,934	JOHNSON	57,606	44,382	10,988	2,236	33,394 R	77.0%	19.1%	80.2%	19.8%
20,202	JONES	5,960	4,819	936	205	3,883 R	80.9%	15.7%	83.7%	16.3%
14,824	KARNES	4,198	2,965	1,145	88	1,820 R	70.6%	27.3%	72.1%	27.9%
103,350	KAUFMAN	41,265	29,587	10,278	1,400	19,309 R	71.7%	24.9%	74.2%	25.8%
33,410	KENDALL	20,120	15,700	3,643	777	12,057 R	78.0%	18.1%	81.2%	18.8%
416	KENEDY	186	84	99	3	15 D	45.2%	53.2%	45.9%	54.1%
808	KENT	434	360	59	15	301 R	82.9%	13.6%	85.9%	14.1%
49,625	KERR	23,297	17,727	4,681	889	13,046 R	76.1%	20.1%	79.1%	20.9%
4,607	KIMBLE	1,952	1,697	206	49	1,491 R	86.9%	10.6%	89.2%	10.8%
286	KING	159	149	5	5	144 R	93.7%	3.1%	96.8%	3.2%
3,598	KINNEY	1,430	936	458	36	478 R	65.5%	32.0%	67.1%	32.9%
32,061	KLEBERG	9,512	4,367	4,716	429	349 D	45.9%	49.6%	48.1%	51.9%
3,719	KNOX	1,367	1,078	247	42	831 R	78.9%	18.1%	81.4%	18.6%
6,886	LA SALLE	2,059	872	1,129	58	257 D	42.4%	54.8%	43.6%	56.4%
49,793	LAMAR	18,611	14,561	3,583	467	10,978 R	78.2%	19.3%	80.3%	19.7%
13,977	LAMB	3,995	3,111	771	113	2,340 R	77.9%	19.3%	80.1%	19.9%
19,677	LAMPASAS	8,205	6,385	1,483	337	4,902 R	77.8%	18.1%	81.2%	18.8%
19,263	LAVACA	8,661	7,347	1,170	144	6,177 R	84.8%	13.5%	86.3%	13.7%
16,612	LEE	6,535	4,997	1,372	166	3,625 R	76.5%	21.0%	78.5%	21.5%
16,801	LEON	7,439	6,391	909	139	5,482 R	85.9%	12.2%	87.5%	12.5%
75,643	LIBERTY	24,267	18,892	4,862	513	14,030 R	77.9%	20.0%	79.5%	20.5%
23,384	LIMESTONE	7,739	5,796	1,778	165	4,018 R	74.9%	23.0%	76.5%	23.5%
3,302	LIPSCOMB	1,332	1,159	135	38	1,024 R	87.0%	10.1%	89.6%	10.4%
11,531	LIVE OAK	4,302	3,464	742	96	2,722 R	80.5%	17.2%	82.4%	17.6%
19,301	LLANO	10,447	8,299	1,825	323	6,474 R	79.4%	17.5%	82.0%	18.0%
82	LOVING	65	58	4	3	54 R	89.2%	6.2%	93.5%	6.5%
278,831	LUBBOCK	99,013	65,651	28,023	5,339	37,628 R	66.3%	28.3%	70.1%	29.9%
5,915	LYNN	2,009	1,546	403	60	1,143 R	77.0%	20.1%	79.3%	20.7%
13,664	MADISON	4,289	3,351	881	57	2,470 R	78.1%	20.5%	79.2%	20.8%
10,546	MARION	4,238	2,983	1,165	90	1,818 R	70.4%	27.5%	71.9%	28.1%
4,799	MARTIN	1,762	1,455	266	41	1,189 R	82.6%	15.1%	84.5%	15.5%
4,012	MASON	2,057	1,656	354	47	1,302 R	80.5%	17.2%	82.4%	17.6%
36,702	MATAGORDA	12,196	8,366	3,500	330	4,866 R	68.6%	28.7%	70.5%	29.5%
54,258	MAVERICK	13,588	2,816	10,397	375	7,581 D	20.7%	76.5%	21.3%	78.7%
8,283	MCCULLOCH	3,103	2,552	482	69	2,070 R	82.2%	15.5%	84.1%	15.9%
234,906	MCLENNAN	79,075	48,260	27,063	3,752	21,197 R	61.0%	34.2%	64.1%	35.9%
707	MCMULLEN	499	454	40	5	414 R	91.0%	8.0%	91.9%	8.1%
46,006	MEDINA	17,246	12,085	4,634	527	7,451 R	70.1%	26.9%	72.3%	27.7%
2,242	MENARD	864	682	154	28	528 R	78.9%	17.8%	81.6%	18.4%
136,872	MIDLAND	49,212	36,973	10,025	2,214	26,948 R	75.1%	20.4%	78.7%	21.3%
24,757	MILAM	8,664	6,364	2,051	249	4,313 R	73.5%	23.7%	75.6%	24.4%
4,936	MILLS	2,245	1,951	243	51	1,708 R	86.9%	10.8%	88.9%	11.1%
9,403	MITCHELL	2,196	1,780	354	62	1,426 R	81.1%	16.1%	83.4%	16.6%
19,719	MONTAGUE	8,604	7,526	885	193	6,641 R	87.5%	10.3%	89.5%	10.5%
455,746	MONTGOMERY	204,632	150,314	45,835	8,483	104,479 R	73.5%	22.4%	76.6%	23.4%
21,904	MOORE	5,284	3,977	1,098	209	2,879 R	75.3%	20.8%	78.4%	21.6%
12,934	MORRIS	4,973	3,446	1,425	102	2,021 R	69.3%	28.7%	70.7%	29.3%
1,210	MOTLEY	615	566	40	9	526 R	92.0%	6.5%	93.4%	6.6%
64,524	NACOGDOCHES	22,622	14,771	6,846	1,005	7,925 R	65.3%	30.3%	68.3%	31.7%
47,735	NAVARRO	16,433	11,994	4,002	437	7,992 R	73.0%	24.4%	75.0%	25.0%
14,445	NEWTON	5,534	4,288	1,156	90	3,132 R	77.5%	20.9%	78.8%	21.2%
15,216	NOLAN	4,857	3,552	1,029	276	2,523 R	73.1%	21.2%	77.5%	22.5%
340,223	NUECES	104,405	50,766	49,198	4,441	1,568 R	48.6%	47.1%	50.8%	49.2%
10,223	OCHILTREE	3,002	2,628	274	100	2,354 R	87.5%	9.1%	90.6%	9.4%
2,052	OLDHAM	948	850	78	20	772 R	89.7%	8.2%	91.6%	8.4%

TEXAS

PRESIDENT 2016

2010 Census Population	County	Total Vote	Republican (Trump)	Democratic (Clinton)	Other	Rep.-Dem. Plurality	Percentage Total Vote Rep.	Total Vote Dem.	Major Vote Rep.	Major Vote Dem.
81,837	ORANGE	32,000	25,513	5,735	752	19,778 R	79.7%	17.9%	81.6%	18.4%
28,111	PALO PINTO	10,270	8,284	1,708	278	6,576 R	80.7%	16.6%	82.9%	17.1%
23,796	PANOLA	10,416	8,445	1,835	136	6,610 R	81.1%	17.6%	82.1%	17.9%
116,927	PARKER	56,817	46,473	8,344	2,000	38,129 R	81.8%	14.7%	84.8%	15.2%
10,269	PARMER	2,466	1,915	485	66	1,430 R	77.7%	19.7%	79.8%	20.2%
15,507	PECOS	4,185	2,468	1,554	163	914 R	59.0%	37.1%	61.4%	38.6%
45,413	POLK	19,852	15,176	4,187	489	10,989 R	76.4%	21.1%	78.4%	21.6%
121,073	POTTER	28,651	19,630	7,657	1,364	11,973 R	68.5%	26.7%	71.9%	28.1%
7,818	PRESIDIO	2,208	652	1,458	98	806 D	29.5%	66.0%	30.9%	69.1%
10,914	RAINS	4,701	3,968	628	105	3,340 R	84.4%	13.4%	86.3%	13.7%
120,725	RANDALL	54,305	43,462	8,367	2,476	35,095 R	80.0%	15.4%	83.9%	16.1%
3,367	REAGAN	904	709	167	28	542 R	78.4%	18.5%	80.9%	19.1%
3,309	REAL	1,681	1,382	262	37	1,120 R	82.2%	15.6%	84.1%	15.9%
12,860	RED RIVER	5,161	3,926	1,149	86	2,777 R	76.1%	22.3%	77.4%	22.6%
13,783	REEVES	3,184	1,417	1,659	108	242 D	44.5%	52.1%	46.1%	53.9%
7,383	REFUGIO	2,948	1,830	1,034	84	796 R	62.1%	35.1%	63.9%	36.1%
929	ROBERTS	554	524	20	10	504 R	94.6%	3.6%	96.3%	3.7%
16,622	ROBERTSON	7,035	4,668	2,203	164	2,465 R	66.4%	31.3%	67.9%	32.1%
78,337	ROCKWALL	39,948	28,451	9,655	1,842	18,796 R	71.2%	24.2%	74.7%	25.3%
10,501	RUNNELS	3,782	3,250	453	79	2,797 R	85.9%	12.0%	87.8%	12.2%
53,330	RUSK	18,994	14,675	3,935	384	10,740 R	77.3%	20.7%	78.9%	21.1%
10,834	SABINE	4,651	3,998	614	39	3,384 R	86.0%	13.2%	86.7%	13.3%
8,865	SAN AUGUSTINE	3,569	2,622	910	37	1,712 R	73.5%	25.5%	74.2%	25.8%
26,384	SAN JACINTO	10,343	8,059	2,038	246	6,021 R	77.9%	19.7%	79.8%	20.2%
64,804	SAN PATRICIO	21,656	13,030	7,871	755	5,159 R	60.2%	36.3%	62.3%	37.7%
6,131	SAN SABA	2,357	2,025	293	39	1,732 R	85.9%	12.4%	87.4%	12.6%
3,461	SCHLEICHER	1,059	821	208	30	613 R	77.5%	19.6%	79.8%	20.2%
16,921	SCURRY	5,289	4,410	733	146	3,677 R	83.4%	13.9%	85.7%	14.3%
3,378	SHACKELFORD	1,504	1,378	103	23	1,275 R	91.6%	6.8%	93.0%	7.0%
25,448	SHELBY	9,086	7,179	1,758	149	5,421 R	79.0%	19.3%	80.3%	19.7%
3,034	SHERMAN	935	807	96	32	711 R	86.3%	10.3%	89.4%	10.6%
209,714	SMITH	84,768	58,930	22,300	3,538	36,630 R	69.5%	26.3%	72.5%	27.5%
8,490	SOMERVELL	3,897	3,206	541	150	2,665 R	82.3%	13.9%	85.6%	14.4%
60,968	STARR	11,740	2,224	9,289	227	7,065 D	18.9%	79.1%	19.3%	80.7%
9,630	STEPHENS	3,461	3,034	348	79	2,686 R	87.7%	10.1%	89.7%	10.3%
1,143	STERLING	633	549	70	14	479 R	86.7%	11.1%	88.7%	11.3%
1,490	STONEWALL	701	555	135	11	420 R	79.2%	19.3%	80.4%	19.6%
4,128	SUTTON	1,417	1,075	313	29	762 R	75.9%	22.1%	77.4%	22.6%
7,854	SWISHER	2,204	1,671	462	71	1,209 R	75.8%	21.0%	78.3%	21.7%
1,809,034	TARRANT	668,513	345,921	288,392	34,200	57,529 R	51.7%	43.1%	54.5%	45.5%
131,506	TAYLOR	45,759	33,250	10,085	2,424	23,165 R	72.7%	22.0%	76.7%	23.3%
984	TERRELL	438	288	140	10	148 R	65.8%	32.0%	67.3%	32.7%
12,651	TERRY	3,355	2,459	753	143	1,706 R	73.3%	22.4%	76.6%	23.4%
1,641	THROCKMORTON	808	715	84	9	631 R	88.5%	10.4%	89.5%	10.5%
32,334	TITUS	9,419	6,511	2,597	311	3,914 R	69.1%	27.6%	71.5%	28.5%
110,224	TOM GREEN	38,479	27,494	9,173	1,812	18,321 R	71.5%	23.8%	75.0%	25.0%
1,024,266	TRAVIS	468,720	127,209	308,260	33,251	181,051 D	27.1%	65.8%	29.2%	70.8%
14,585	TRINITY	5,985	4,737	1,154	94	3,583 R	79.1%	19.3%	80.4%	19.6%
21,766	TYLER	8,016	6,624	1,248	144	5,376 R	82.6%	15.6%	84.1%	15.9%
39,309	UPSHUR	16,013	13,209	2,380	424	10,829 R	82.5%	14.9%	84.7%	15.3%
3,355	UPTON	1,347	1,007	286	54	721 R	74.8%	21.2%	77.9%	22.1%
26,405	UVALDE	8,964	4,835	3,867	262	968 R	53.9%	43.1%	55.6%	44.4%
48,879	VAL VERDE	13,617	5,890	6,964	763	1,074 D	43.3%	51.1%	45.8%	54.2%
52,579	VAN ZANDT	21,890	18,473	2,799	618	15,674 R	84.4%	12.8%	86.8%	13.2%
86,793	VICTORIA	31,123	21,275	8,866	982	12,409 R	68.4%	28.5%	70.6%	29.4%
67,861	WALKER	19,796	12,884	6,091	821	6,793 R	65.1%	30.8%	67.9%	32.1%
43,205	WALLER	16,784	10,531	5,748	505	4,783 R	62.7%	34.2%	64.7%	35.3%
10,658	WARD	3,445	2,547	783	115	1,764 R	73.9%	22.7%	76.5%	23.5%
33,718	WASHINGTON	14,828	10,945	3,382	501	7,563 R	73.8%	22.8%	76.4%	23.6%
250,304	WEBB	56,905	12,947	42,307	1,651	29,360 D	22.8%	74.3%	23.4%	76.6%

TEXAS
PRESIDENT 2016

2010 Census Population	County	Total Vote	Republican (Trump)	Democratic (Clinton)	Other	Rep.-Dem. Plurality	Total Vote Rep.	Total Vote Dem.	Major Vote Rep.	Major Vote Dem.
41,280	WHARTON	14,732	10,149	4,238	345	5,911 R	68.9%	28.8%	70.5%	29.5%
5,410	WHEELER	2,306	2,087	194	25	1,893 R	90.5%	8.4%	91.5%	8.5%
131,500	WICHITA	38,119	27,631	8,770	1,718	18,861 R	72.5%	23.0%	75.9%	24.1%
13,535	WILBARGER	4,105	3,166	809	130	2,357 R	77.1%	19.7%	79.6%	20.4%
22,134	WILLACY	5,095	1,547	3,422	126	1,875 D	30.4%	67.2%	31.1%	68.9%
422,679	WILLIAMSON	203,081	104,175	84,468	14,438	19,707 R	51.3%	41.6%	55.2%	44.8%
42,918	WILSON	19,432	13,998	4,790	644	9,208 R	72.0%	24.7%	74.5%	25.5%
7,110	WINKLER	1,876	1,403	420	53	983 R	74.8%	22.4%	77.0%	23.0%
59,127	WISE	24,776	20,670	3,412	694	17,258 R	83.4%	13.8%	85.8%	14.2%
41,964	WOOD	18,727	15,700	2,630	397	13,070 R	83.8%	14.0%	85.7%	14.3%
7,879	YOAKUM	2,303	1,797	426	80	1,371 R	78.0%	18.5%	80.8%	19.2%
18,550	YOUNG	7,707	6,601	876	230	5,725 R	85.6%	11.4%	88.3%	11.7%
14,018	ZAPATA	3,142	1,029	2,063	50	1,034 D	32.7%	65.7%	33.3%	66.7%
11,677	ZAVALA	3,396	694	2,636	66	1,942 D	20.4%	77.6%	20.8%	79.2%
25,145,561	TOTAL	8,969,226	4,685,047	3,877,868	406,311	807,179 R	52.2%	43.2%	54.7%	45.3%

TEXAS
HOUSE OF REPRESENTATIVES

CD	Year	Total Vote	Republican Vote	Republican Candidate	Democratic Vote	Democratic Candidate	Other Vote	Rep.-Dem. Plurality	Total Vote Rep.	Total Vote Dem.	Major Vote Rep.	Major Vote Dem.
1	2016	260,409	192,434	GOHMERT, LOUIS*	62,847	MCKELLAR, SHIRLEY J.	5,128	129,587 R	73.9%	24.1%	75.4%	24.6%
1	2014	148,560	115,084	GOHMERT, LOUIS*	33,476	MCKELLAR, SHIRLEY J.		81,608 R	77.5%	22.5%	77.5%	22.5%
1	2012	249,658	178,322	GOHMERT, LOUIS*	67,222	MCKELLAR, SHIRLEY J.	4,114	111,100 R	71.4%	26.9%	72.6%	27.4%
2	2016	278,236	168,692	POE, TED*	100,231	BRYAN, PAT	9,313	68,461 R	60.6%	36.0%	62.7%	37.3%
2	2014	150,026	101,936	POE, TED*	44,462	LETSOS, NIKO	3,628	57,474 R	67.9%	29.6%	69.6%	30.4%
2	2012	246,328	159,664	POE, TED*	80,512	DOUGHERTY, JIM	6,152	79,152 R	64.8%	32.7%	66.5%	33.5%
3	2016	316,467	193,684	JOHNSON, SAM*	109,420	BELL, ADAM	13,363	84,264 R	61.2%	34.6%	63.9%	36.1%
3	2014	138,280	113,404	JOHNSON, SAM*			24,876	113,404 R	82.0%		100.0%	
3	2012	187,180	187,180	JOHNSON, SAM*				187,180 R	100.0%		100.0%	
4	2016	246,220	216,643	RATCLIFFE, JOHN*			29,577	216,643 R	88.0%		100.0%	
4	2014	115,085	115,085	RATCLIFFE, JOHN				115,085 R	100.0%		100.0%	
4	2012	250,343	182,679	HALL, RALPH M.*	60,214	HATHCOX, VALINDA	7,450	122,465 R	73.0%	24.1%	75.2%	24.8%
5	2016	192,875	155,469	HENSARLING, JEB*			37,406	155,469 R	80.6%		100.0%	
5	2014	104,262	88,998	HENSARLING, JEB*			15,264	88,998 R	85.4%		100.0%	
5	2012	208,230	134,091	HENSARLING, JEB*	69,178	MROSKO, LINDA S.	4,961	64,913 R	64.4%	33.2%	66.0%	34.0%
6	2016	273,296	159,444	BARTON, JOE L.*	106,667	WOOLRIDGE, RUBY FAYE	7,185	52,777 R	58.3%	39.0%	59.9%	40.1%
6	2014	150,996	92,334	BARTON, JOE L.*	55,027	COZAD, DAVID E.	3,635	37,307 R	61.1%	36.4%	62.7%	37.3%
6	2012	249,936	145,019	BARTON, JOE L.*	98,053	SANDERS, KENNETH	6,864	46,966 R	58.0%	39.2%	59.7%	40.3%
7	2016	255,533	143,542	CULBERSON, JOHN*	111,991	CARGAS, JAMES		31,551 R	56.2%	43.8%	56.2%	43.8%
7	2014	143,219	90,606	CULBERSON, JOHN*	49,478	CARGAS, JAMES	3,135	41,128 R	63.3%	34.5%	64.7%	35.3%
7	2012	234,837	142,793	CULBERSON, JOHN*	85,553	CARGAS, JAMES	6,491	57,240 R	60.8%	36.4%	62.5%	37.5%
8	2016	236,379	236,379	BRADY, KEVIN*				236,379 R	100.0%		100.0%	
8	2014	140,013	125,066	BRADY, KEVIN*			14,947	125,066 R	89.3%		100.0%	
8	2012	251,052	194,043	BRADY, KEVIN*	51,051	BURNS, NEIL	5,958	142,992 R	77.3%	20.3%	79.2%	20.8%
9	2016	188,523	36,491	MARTIN, JEFF	152,032	GREEN, AL*		115,541 D	19.4%	80.6%	19.4%	80.6%
9	2014	86,003			78,109	GREEN, AL*	7,894	78,109 D		90.8%		100.0%
9	2012	183,566	36,139	MUELLER, STEVE	144,075	GREEN, AL*	3,352	107,936 D	19.7%	78.5%	20.1%	79.9%

TEXAS

HOUSE OF REPRESENTATIVES

			Republican		Democratic		Other	Rep.-Dem.	Total Vote		Major Vote	
									Percentage			
CD	Year	Total Vote	Vote	Candidate	Vote	Candidate	Vote	Plurality	Rep.	Dem.	Rep.	Dem.
10	2016	312,600	179,221	MCCAUL, MICHAEL T.*	120,170	CADIEN, TAWANA W.	13,209	59,051 R	57.3%	38.4%	59.9%	40.1%
10	2014	176,460	109,726	MCCAUL, MICHAEL T.*	60,243	CADIEN, TAWANA W.	6,491	49,483 R	62.2%	34.1%	64.6%	35.4%
10	2012	264,019	159,783	MCCAUL, MICHAEL T.*	95,710	CADIEN, TAWANA W.	8,526	64,073 R	60.5%	36.3%	62.5%	37.5%
11	2016	225,548	201,871	CONAWAY, K. MICHAEL*			23,677	201,871 R	89.5%		100.0%	
11	2014	119,574	107,939	CONAWAY, K. MICHAEL*			11,635	107,939 R	90.3%		100.0%	
11	2012	226,023	177,742	CONAWAY, K. MICHAEL*	41,970	RILEY, JIM	6,311	135,772 R	78.6%	18.6%	80.9%	19.1%
12	2016	283,115	196,482	GRANGER, KAY*	76,029	BRADSHAW, BILL	10,604	120,453 R	69.4%	26.9%	72.1%	27.9%
12	2014	158,730	113,186	GRANGER, KAY*	41,757	GREENE, MARK	3,787	71,429 R	71.3%	26.3%	73.1%	26.9%
12	2012	247,712	175,649	GRANGER, KAY*	66,080	ROBINSON, DAVE	5,983	109,569 R	70.9%	26.7%	72.7%	27.3%
13	2016	221,242	199,050	THORNBERRY, WILLIAM M.*			22,192	199,050 R	90.0%		100.0%	
13	2014	131,451	110,842	THORNBERRY, WILLIAM M.*	16,822	MINTER, MIKE G.	3,787	94,020 R	84.3%	12.8%	86.8%	13.2%
13	2012	206,388	187,775	THORNBERRY, WILLIAM M.*			18,613	187,775 R	91.0%		100.0%	
14	2016	259,685	160,631	WEBER, RANDY*	99,054	COLE, MICHAEL K.		61,577 R	61.9%	38.1%	61.9%	38.1%
14	2014	145,698	90,116	WEBER, RANDY*	52,545	BROWN, DONALD G.	3,037	37,571 R	61.9%	36.1%	63.2%	36.8%
14	2012	245,839	131,460	WEBER, RANDY	109,697	LAMPSON, NICK	4,682	21,763 R	53.5%	44.6%	54.5%	45.5%
15	2016	177,479	66,877	WESTLEY, TIM	101,712	GONZALEZ, VICENTE	8,890	34,835 D	37.7%	57.3%	39.7%	60.3%
15	2014	90,184	39,016	ZAMORA, EDDIE	48,708	HINOJOSA, RUBÉN*	2,460	9,692 D	43.3%	54.0%	44.5%	55.5%
15	2012	146,661	54,056	BRUEGGEMANN, DALE A.	89,296	HINOJOSA, RUBÉN*	3,309	35,240 D	36.9%	60.9%	37.7%	62.3%
16	2016	175,229			150,228	O'ROURKE, BETO*	25,001	150,228 D		85.7%		100.0%
16	2014	73,105	21,324	ROEN, COREY DEAN	49,338	O'ROURKE, BETO*	2,443	28,014 D	29.2%	67.5%	30.2%	69.8%
16	2012	155,005	51,043	CARRASCO, BARBARA	101,403	O'ROURKE, BETO	2,559	50,360 D	32.9%	65.4%	33.5%	66.5%
17	2016	245,728	149,417	FLORES, BILL*	86,603	MATTA, WILLIAM	9,708	62,814 R	60.8%	35.2%	63.3%	36.7%
17	2014	132,865	85,807	FLORES, BILL*	43,049	HAYNES, NICK	4,009	42,758 R	64.6%	32.4%	66.6%	33.4%
17	2012	179,262	143,284	FLORES, BILL*			35,978	143,284 R	79.9%		100.0%	
18	2016	204,308	48,306	BARTLEY, LORI	150,157	JACKSON LEE, SHEILA*	5,845	101,851 D	23.6%	73.5%	24.3%	75.7%
18	2014	106,010	26,249	SEIBERT, SEAN	76,097	JACKSON LEE, SHEILA*	3,664	49,848 D	24.8%	71.8%	25.6%	74.4%
18	2012	194,932	44,015	SEIBERT, SEAN	146,223	JACKSON LEE, SHEILA*	4,694	102,208 D	22.6%	75.0%	23.1%	76.9%
19	2016	203,475	176,314	ARRINGTON, JODEY			27,161	176,314 R	86.7%		100.0%	
19	2014	116,818	90,160	NEUGEBAUER, RANDY*	21,458	MARCHBANKS, JAMES NEAL	5,200	68,702 R	77.2%	18.4%	80.8%	19.2%
19	2012	192,063	163,239	NEUGEBAUER, RANDY*			28,824	163,239 R	85.0%		100.0%	
20	2016	187,669			149,640	CASTRO, JOAQUIN*	38,029	149,640 D		79.7%		100.0%
20	2014	87,964			66,554	CASTRO, JOAQUIN*	21,410	66,554 D		75.7%		100.0%
20	2012	186,177	62,376	ROSA, DAVID	119,032	CASTRO, JOAQUIN	4,769	56,656 D	33.5%	63.9%	34.4%	65.6%
21	2016	356,031	202,967	SMITH, LAMAR*	129,765	WAKELY, TOM	23,299	73,202 R	57.0%	36.4%	61.0%	39.0%
21	2014	188,996	135,660	SMITH, LAMAR*			53,336	135,660 R	71.8%		100.0%	
21	2012	308,865	187,015	SMITH, LAMAR*	109,326	DUVAL, CANDACE E.	12,524	77,689 R	60.5%	35.4%	63.1%	36.9%
22	2016	305,543	181,864	OLSON, PETE*	123,679	GIBSON, MARK		58,185 R	59.5%	40.5%	59.5%	40.5%
22	2014	151,566	100,861	OLSON, PETE*	47,844	BRISCOE, FRANK	2,861	53,017 R	66.5%	31.6%	67.8%	32.2%
22	2012	250,911	160,668	OLSON, PETE*	80,203	ROGERS, KESHA	10,040	80,465 R	64.0%	32.0%	66.7%	33.3%
23	2016	228,965	110,577	HURD, WILL*	107,526	GALLEGO, PETE P.	10,862	3,051 R	48.3%	47.0%	50.7%	49.3%
23	2014	115,429	57,459	HURD, WILL	55,037	GALLEGO, PETE P.*	2,933	2,422 R	49.8%	47.7%	51.1%	48.9%
23	2012	192,169	87,547	CANSECO, FRANCISCO "QUICO"*	96,676	GALLEGO, PETE P.	7,946	9,129 D	45.6%	50.3%	47.5%	52.5%
24	2016	275,635	154,845	MARCHANT, KENNY E.*	108,389	MCDOWELL, JAN	12,401	46,456 R	56.2%	39.3%	58.8%	41.2%
24	2014	144,073	93,712	MARCHANT, KENNY E.*	46,548	MCGEHEARTY, PATRICK F.	3,813	47,164 R	65.0%	32.3%	66.8%	33.2%
24	2012	243,489	148,586	MARCHANT, KENNY E.*	87,645	RUSK, TIM	7,258	60,941 R	61.0%	36.0%	62.9%	37.1%
25	2016	310,196	180,988	WILLIAMS, ROGER*	117,073	THOMAS, KATHI	12,135	63,915 R	58.3%	37.7%	60.7%	39.3%
25	2014	177,883	107,120	WILLIAMS, ROGER*	64,463	MONTOYA, MARCO	6,300	42,657 R	60.2%	36.2%	62.4%	37.6%
25	2012	263,932	154,245	WILLIAMS, ROGER	98,827	HENDERSON, ELAINE M.	10,860	55,418 R	58.4%	37.4%	60.9%	39.1%
26	2016	319,080	211,730	BURGESS, MICHAEL C.*	94,507	MAUCK, ERIC	12,843	117,223 R	66.4%	29.6%	69.1%	30.9%
26	2014	141,470	116,944	BURGESS, MICHAEL C.*			24,526	116,944 R	82.7%		100.0%	
26	2012	258,723	176,642	BURGESS, MICHAEL C.*	74,237	SANCHEZ, DAVID	7,844	102,405 R	68.3%	28.7%	70.4%	29.6%
27	2016	230,580	142,251	FARENTHOLD, R. BLAKE*	88,329	BARRERA, RAUL "ROY"		53,922 R	61.7%	38.3%	61.7%	38.3%
27	2014	131,047	83,342	FARENTHOLD, R. BLAKE*	44,152	REED, WESLEY C.	3,553	39,190 R	63.6%	33.7%	65.4%	34.6%
27	2012	212,651	120,684	FARENTHOLD, R. BLAKE*	83,395	HARRISON, ROSE MEZA	8,572	37,289 R	56.8%	39.2%	59.1%	40.9%

TEXAS

HOUSE OF REPRESENTATIVES

CD	Year	Total Vote	Republican		Democratic		Other Vote	Rep.-Dem. Plurality	Percentage			
			Vote	Candidate	Vote	Candidate			Total Vote		Major Vote	
									Rep.	Dem.	Rep.	Dem.
28	2016	184,442	57,740	HARDIN, ZEFFEN	122,086	CUELLAR, HENRY	4,616	64,346 D	31.3%	66.2%	32.1%	67.9%
28	2014	76,136			62,508	CUELLAR, HENRY*	13,628	62,508 D		82.1%		100.0%
28	2012	165,645	49,309	HAYWARD, WILLIAM R.	112,456	CUELLAR, HENRY*	3,880	63,147 D	29.8%	67.9%	30.5%	69.5%
29	2016	131,982	31,646	GARZA, JULIO	95,649	GREEN, GENE*	4,687	64,003 D	24.0%	72.5%	24.9%	75.1%
29	2014	46,143			41,321	GREEN, GENE*	4,822	41,321 D		89.5%		100.0%
29	2012	95,611			86,053	GREEN, GENE*	9,558	86,053 D		90.0%		100.0%
30	2016	218,826	41,518	LINGERFELT, CHARLES	170,502	JOHNSON, EDDIE B.*	6,806	128,984 D	19.0%	77.9%	19.6%	80.4%
30	2014	105,793			93,041	JOHNSON, EDDIE B.*	12,752	93,041 D		87.9%		100.0%
30	2012	217,014	41,222	WASHINGTON, TRAVIS	171,059	JOHNSON, EDDIE B.*	4,733	129,837 D	19.0%	78.8%	19.4%	80.6%
31	2016	284,588	166,060	CARTER, JOHN*	103,852	CLARK, MIKE	14,676	62,208 R	58.4%	36.5%	61.5%	38.5%
31	2014	143,028	91,607	CARTER, JOHN*	45,715	MINOR, LOUIE	5,706	45,892 R	64.0%	32.0%	66.7%	33.3%
31	2012	237,187	145,348	CARTER, JOHN*	82,977	WYMAN, STEPHEN M.	8,862	62,371 R	61.3%	35.0%	63.7%	36.3%
32	2016	229,171	162,868	SESSIONS, PETE*			66,303	162,868 R	71.1%		100.0%	
32	2014	156,096	96,495	SESSIONS, PETE*	55,325	PEREZ, FRANK	4,276	41,170 R	61.8%	35.4%	63.6%	36.4%
32	2012	251,636	146,653	SESSIONS, PETE*	99,288	MCGOVERN, KATHERINE SAVERS	5,695	47,365 R	58.3%	39.5%	59.6%	40.4%
33	2016	126,369	33,222	MITCHELL, M. MARK	93,147	VEASEY, MARC*		59,925 D	26.3%	73.7%	26.3%	73.7%
33	2014	50,592			43,769	VEASEY, MARC*	6,823	43,769 D		86.5%		100.0%
33	2012	117,375	30,252	BRADLEY, CHUCK	85,114	VEASEY, MARC	2,009	54,862 D	25.8%	72.5%	26.2%	73.8%
34	2016	166,961	62,323	GONZALEZ, REY JR.	104,638	VELA, FILEMON*		42,315 D	37.3%	62.7%	37.3%	62.7%
34	2014	79,877	30,811	SMITH, LARRY S.	47,503	VELA, FILEMON*	1,563	16,692 D	38.6%	59.5%	39.3%	60.7%
34	2012	144,778	52,448	BRADSHAW, JESSICA PUENTE	89,606	VELA, FILEMON	2,724	37,158 D	36.2%	61.9%	36.9%	63.1%
35	2016	197,576	62,384	NARVAIZ, SUSAN	124,612	DOGGETT, LLOYD*	10,580	62,228 D	31.6%	63.1%	33.4%	66.6%
35	2014	96,225	32,040	NARVAIZ, SUSAN	60,124	DOGGETT, LLOYD*	4,061	28,084 D	33.3%	62.5%	34.8%	65.2%
35	2012	165,179	52,894	NARVAIZ, SUSAN	105,626	DOGGETT, LLOYD*	6,659	52,732 D	32.0%	63.9%	33.4%	66.6%
36	2016	218,565	193,675	BABIN, BRIAN*			24,890	193,675 R	88.6%		100.0%	
36	2014	133,842	101,663	BABIN, BRIAN*	29,543	COLE, MICHAEL K.	2,636	72,120 R	76.0%	22.1%	77.5%	22.5%
36	2012	233,832	165,405	STOCKMAN, STEVE	62,143	MARTIN, MAX	6,284	103,262 R	70.7%	26.6%	72.7%	27.3%
TOTAL	2016	8,528,526	4,877,605		3,160,535		490,386	1,717,070 R	57.2%	37.1%	60.7%	39.3%
TOTAL	2014	4,453,499	2,684,592		1,474,016		294,891	1,210,576 R	60.3%	33.1%	64.6%	35.4%
TOTAL	2012	7,664,208	4,429,270		2,949,900		285,038	1,479,370 R	57.8%	38.5%	60.0%	40.0%

Note: An asterisk (*) denotes incumbent.

TEXAS

GENERAL AND PRIMARY ELECTIONS

2016 GENERAL ELECTIONS: OTHER VOTES

President   Other vote was 283,492 Libertarian (Gary Johnson), 71,558 Green (Jill Stein), 42,366 Write-in (Evan McMullin), 4,634 Write-in (Scattered Write-in), 4,261 Write-in (Darrell Castle)

House   Other vote was:

CD 1   5,062 Libertarian (Phil Gray), 66 Write-in (Renee Culler)

CD 2   6,429 Green (Joshua Darr), 2,884 Libertarian (James Veasaw)

CD 3   10,448 Libertarian (Scott Jameson), 2,915 Green (Paul Blair)

CD 4   29,577 Libertarian (Cody Wommack)

CD 5   37,406 Libertarian (Ken Ashby)

CD 6   7,185 Green (Darrel Smith)

CD 10   13,209 Libertarian (Bill Kelsey)

CD 11   23,677 Libertarian (Nicholas Landholt)

CD 12   10,604 Libertarian (Ed Colliver)

TEXAS

GENERAL AND PRIMARY ELECTIONS

House	Other vote was:
CD 13	14,725 Libertarian (Calvin Deweese), 7,467 Green (H. Tomlinson)
CD 15	5,448 Green (Vanessa Tijerina), 3,442 Libertarian (Ross Leone)
CD 16	17,491 Libertarian (Jaime Perez), 7,510 Green (Mary Gourdoux)
CD 17	9,708 Libertarian (Clark Patterson)
CD 18	5,845 Green (Thomas Kleven)
CD 19	17,376 Libertarian (Troy Bonar), 9,785 Green (Mark Lawson)
CD 20	29,055 Libertarian (Jeffrey Blunt), 8,974 Green (Paul Pipkin)
CD 21	14,735 Libertarian (Mark Loewe), 8,564 Green (Antonio Diaz)
CD 23	10,862 Libertarian (Ruben Corvalan)
CD 24	8,625 Libertarian (Mike Kolls), 3,776 Green (Kevin McCormick)
CD 25	12,135 Libertarian (Loren Schneiderman)
CD 26	12,843 Libertarian (Mark Boler)
CD 28	4,616 Green (Michael Cary)
CD 29	3,234 Libertarian (Nazirite Perez)
CD 30	4,753 Libertarian (Jarrett Woods), 2,053 Green (Thom Prentice)
CD 31	14,676 Libertarian (Scott Ballard)
CD 32	43,490 Libertarian (Ed Rankin), 22,813 Green (Gary Stuard)
CD 35	6,504 Libertarian (Rhett Smith), 4,076 Green (Scott Trimble)
CD 36	24,890 Green (Hal Ridley)

2016 PRIMARY ELECTIONS: SUPPLEMENTARY INFORMATION

Primary	March 1, 2016	**Registration** (as of March 1, 2016)	14,238,436	No Party Registration
Primary Runoff	May 24, 2016			

Primary Type   Open—Any registered voter could participate in the Democratic or Republican primary, although if he or she voted in the primary of one party, he or she could not vote in the runoff of the other party.

	REPUBLICAN PRIMARIES			DEMOCRATIC PRIMARIES		
President	Cruz, Ted	1,241,118	43.8%	Clinton, Hillary Rodham	936,004	65.2%
	Trump, Donald J.	758,762	26.8%	Sanders, Bernard	476,547	33.2%
	Rubio, Marco	503,055	17.7%	De La Fuente, Roque "Rocky"	8,429	0.6%
	Kasich, John R.	120,473	4.2%	O'Malley, Martin	5,364	0.4%
	Carson, Ben	117,969	4.2%	Wilson, Willie	3,254	0.2%
	Bush, Jeb	35,420	1.2%	Judd, Keith	2,569	0.2%
	Uncommitted	29,609	1.0%	Hawes, Calvis L.	2,017	0.1%
	Paul, Rand	8,000	0.3%	Locke, Star	1,711	0.1%
	Huckabee, Mike	6,226	0.2%			
	Gray, Elizabeth	5,449	0.2%			
	Christie, Chris	3,448	0.1%			
	Fiorina, Carly	3,247	0.1%			
	Santorum, Rick	2,006	0.1%			
	Graham, Lindsey	1,706	0.1%			
	TOTAL	*2,836,488*		*TOTAL*	*1,435,895*	
Congressional District 1	Gohmert, Louis*	96,313	81.9%	McKellar, Shirley J.	17,139	100.0%
	Winston, Simon	16,335	13.9%			
	Culler, Anthony	4,879	4.2%			
	TOTAL	*117,527*		*TOTAL*	*17,139*	
Congressional District 2	Poe, Ted*	75,404	100.0%	Bryan, Pat	25,814	100.0%
	TOTAL	*75,404*		*TOTAL*	*25,814*	

TEXAS

GENERAL AND PRIMARY ELECTIONS

	REPUBLICAN PRIMARIES			DEMOCRATIC PRIMARIES		
Congressional District 3	Johnson, Sam*	65,451	74.6%	Bell, Adam	14,270	60.3%
	Slavens, John Calvin	10,043	11.5%	Filak, Michael A.	9,395	39.7%
	Thurgood, Keith L.	7,173	8.2%			
	Cornette, David	5,037	5.7%			
	TOTAL	87,704		TOTAL	23,665	
Congressional District 4	Ratcliffe, John*	77,254	68.0%			
	Gigliotti, Lou	23,939	21.1%			
	Hall, Ralph M.	12,353	10.9%			
	TOTAL	113,546				
Congressional District 5	Hensarling, Jeb*	73,143	100.0%			
	TOTAL	73,143				
Congressional District 6	Barton, Joe L.*	55,285	68.6%	Woolridge, Ruby Faye	23,294	69.7%
	Fowler, Steven	17,960	22.3%	Roseman, Jeffrey	5,993	17.9%
	Baker, Collin	7,292	9.1%	Jaquess, Don	4,132	12.4%
	TOTAL	80,537		TOTAL	33,419	
Congressional District 7	Culberson, John*	44,290	57.3%	Cargas, James	24,190	100.0%
	Lloyd, James	19,217	24.9%			
	Espinoza, Maria	13,793	17.8%			
	TOTAL	77,300		TOTAL	24,190	
Congressional District 8	Brady, Kevin*	65,059	53.4%			
	Toth, Steve	45,436	37.3%			
	McMichael, Craig	6,050	5.0%			
	Dean, Andre	5,233	4.3%			
	TOTAL	121,778				
Congressional District 9	Martin, Jeff	11,696	100.0%	Green, Al*	44,487	100.0%
	TOTAL	11,696		TOTAL	44,487	
Congressional District 10	McCaul, Michael T.*	76,646	100.0%	Cadien, Tawana W.	22,660	51.9%
				Gallaher, Scot B.	20,961	48.1%
	TOTAL	76,646		TOTAL	43,621	
Congressional District 11	Conaway, Mike*	101,056	100.0%			
	TOTAL	101,056				
Congressional District 12	Granger, Kay*	87,329	100.0%	Bradshaw, Bill	25,839	100.0%
	TOTAL	87,329		TOTAL	25,839	
Congressional District 13	Thornberry, Mac*	98,033	100.0%			
	TOTAL	98,033				
Congressional District 14	Weber, Randy*	57,869	84.0%	Cole, Michael K.	28,731	100.0%
	Casey, Keith	10,988	16.0%			
	TOTAL	68,857		TOTAL	28,731	
Congressional District 15	Westley, Tim	13,164	45.0%	Gonzalez, Vicente	22,151	42.2%
	Villarreal, Ruben O.	9,349	32.0%	Palacios, Juan "Sonny" Jr.	9,913	18.9%
	Salinas, Xavier	6,734	23.0%	Elizondo, Dolly	8,888	16.9%
				Quintanilla, Joel	6,152	11.7%
				Ramirez, Ruben Ramon	3,149	6.0%
				Sweeten, Rance G. "Randy"	2,224	4.2%
	TOTAL	29,247		TOTAL	52,477	
	PRIMARY RUNOFF			**PRIMARY RUNOFF**		
	Westley, Tim	1,384	50.5%	Gonzalez, Vicente	16,071	65.7%
	Villarreal, Ruben O.	1,355	49.5%	Palacios, Juan "Sonny" Jr.	8,379	34.3%
	TOTAL	2,739		TOTAL	24,450	

TEXAS

GENERAL AND PRIMARY ELECTIONS

	REPUBLICAN PRIMARIES			DEMOCRATIC PRIMARIES		
Congressional District 16				O'Rourke, Beto*	40,051	85.6%
				Mendoza, Ben E. "Buddy"	6,749	14.4%
				TOTAL	*46,800*	
Congressional District 17	Flores, Bill*	60,502	72.4%	Matta, William	27,639	100.0%
	Patterson, Ralph	15,411	18.4%			
	Sims, Kaleb	7,634	9.1%			
	TOTAL	*83,547*		*TOTAL*	*27,639*	
Congressional District 18	Bartley, Lori	5,691	33.7%	Jackson Lee, Sheila*	46,113	100.0%
	Gonzales, Reggie	5,587	33.1%			
	Fisher, Sharon J.	4,414	26.1%			
	Pate, Ava	1,204	7.1%			
	TOTAL	*16,896*		*TOTAL*	*46,113*	
	PRIMARY RUNOFF					
	Bartley, Lori	1,491	57.6%			
	Gonzales, Reggie	1,096	42.4%			
	TOTAL	*2,587*				
Congressional District 19	Robertson, Glen	27,868	26.8%			
	Arrington, Jodey	27,013	25.9%			
	Starr, Michael Bob	22,303	21.4%			
	May, Donald R.	9,616	9.2%			
	Garrett, Greg	8,309	8.0%			
	Corley, Jason	2,558	2.5%			
	Warren, DeRenda	2,323	2.2%			
	Parrish, Don	2,197	2.1%			
	Key, John C.	1,959	1.9%			
	TOTAL	*104,146*				
	PRIMARY RUNOFF					
	Arrington, Jodey	25,322	53.7%			
	Robertson, Glen	21,832	46.3%			
	TOTAL	*47,154*				
Congressional District 20				Castro, Joaquin*	42,163	100.0%
				TOTAL	*42,163*	
Congressional District 21	Smith, Lamar*	69,866	60.1%	Wakely, Tom	29,632	59.0%
	McCall, Matt	33,624	28.9%	Vakil, Tejas	20,595	41.0%
	Phelps, Todd	6,597	5.7%			
	Murphy, John	6,200	5.3%			
	TOTAL	*116,287*		*TOTAL*	*50,227*	
Congressional District 22	Olson, Pete*	73,375	100.0%	Gibson, Mark	23,084	76.2%
				Hassan, Ahmad	7,226	23.8%
	TOTAL	*73,375*		*TOTAL*	*30,310*	
Congressional District 23	Hurd, Will*	39,870	82.2%	Gallego, Pete P.	43,223	88.4%
	Peterson, William "Hart"	8,628	17.8%	Keenen, Lee	5,688	11.6%
	TOTAL	*48,498*		*TOTAL*	*48,911*	
Congressional District 24	Marchant, Kenny E.*	67,412	100.0%	McDowell, Jan	27,803	100.0%
	TOTAL	*67,412*		*TOTAL*	*27,803*	
Congressional District 25	Williams, Roger*	83,965	100.0%	Thomas, Kathi	44,633	100.0%
	TOTAL	*83,965*		*TOTAL*	*44,633*	
Congressional District 26	Burgess, Michael C.*	73,607	79.4%	Mauck, Eric	24,816	100.0%
	Krause, Joel A.	13,201	14.2%			
	Beebe, Micah	5,942	6.4%			
	TOTAL	*92,750*		*TOTAL*	*24,816*	

TEXAS

GENERAL AND PRIMARY ELECTIONS

	REPUBLICAN PRIMARIES			DEMOCRATIC PRIMARIES		
Congressional District 27	Farenthold, Blake*	42,195	55.9%	Barrera, Raul "Roy"	15,939	50.3%
	Deeb, Gregg	33,280	44.1%	Madrigal, Reynaldo "Ray"	11,157	35.2%
				Raasch, Wayne	4,570	14.4%
	TOTAL	75,475		TOTAL	31,666	
Congressional District 28	Hardin, Zeffen	21,614	100.0%	Cuellar, Henry*	49,993	89.8%
				Hayward, William R.	5,683	10.2%
	TOTAL	21,614		TOTAL	55,676	
Congressional District 29	Garza, Julio	7,421	59.1%	Green, Gene*	17,814	57.4%
	Schafranek, Robert	5,139	40.9%	Garcia, Adrian	11,972	38.6%
				Garcia, Dominique M.	1,224	3.9%
	TOTAL	12,560		TOTAL	31,010	
Congressional District 30	Lingerfelt, Charles	14,234	100.0%	Johnson, Eddie B.*	44,527	69.4%
				Caraway, Barbara Mallory	15,273	23.8%
				Vance, Brandon J.	4,339	6.8%
	TOTAL	14,234		TOTAL	64,139	
Congressional District 31	Carter, John*	62,817	71.3%	Clark, Mike	28,002	100.0%
	Sweeney, Mike	25,306	28.7%			
	TOTAL	88,123		TOTAL	28,002	
Congressional District 32	Sessions, Pete*	49,813	61.4%			
	Ramsland, Russ	19,203	23.7%			
	Brown, Paul	9,488	11.7%			
	Roughneen, Cherie Myint	2,601	3.2%			
	TOTAL	81,105				
Congressional District 33	Mitchell, M. Mark	6,411	52.4%	Veasey, Marc*	20,526	63.4%
	Chadwick, Bruce	5,831	47.6%	Quintanilla, Carlos	11,846	36.6%
	TOTAL	12,242		TOTAL	32,372	
Congressional District 34	Gonzalez, Rey Jr.	12,532	50.6%	Vela, Filemon*	41,414	100.0%
	Vaden, William R. "Willie"	12,253	49.4%			
	TOTAL	24,785		TOTAL	41,414	
Congressional District 35	Narvaiz, Susan	22,549	100.0%	Doggett, Lloyd*	41,189	100.0%
	TOTAL	22,549		TOTAL	41,189	
Congressional District 36	Babin, Brian*	80,649	100.0%			
	TOTAL	80,649				

Note: An asterisk (*) denotes incumbent. A runoff was triggered if the leading vote-getter in the primary received less than a majority of the primary vote.

UTAH

Congressional districts first established for elections held in 2012

4 members

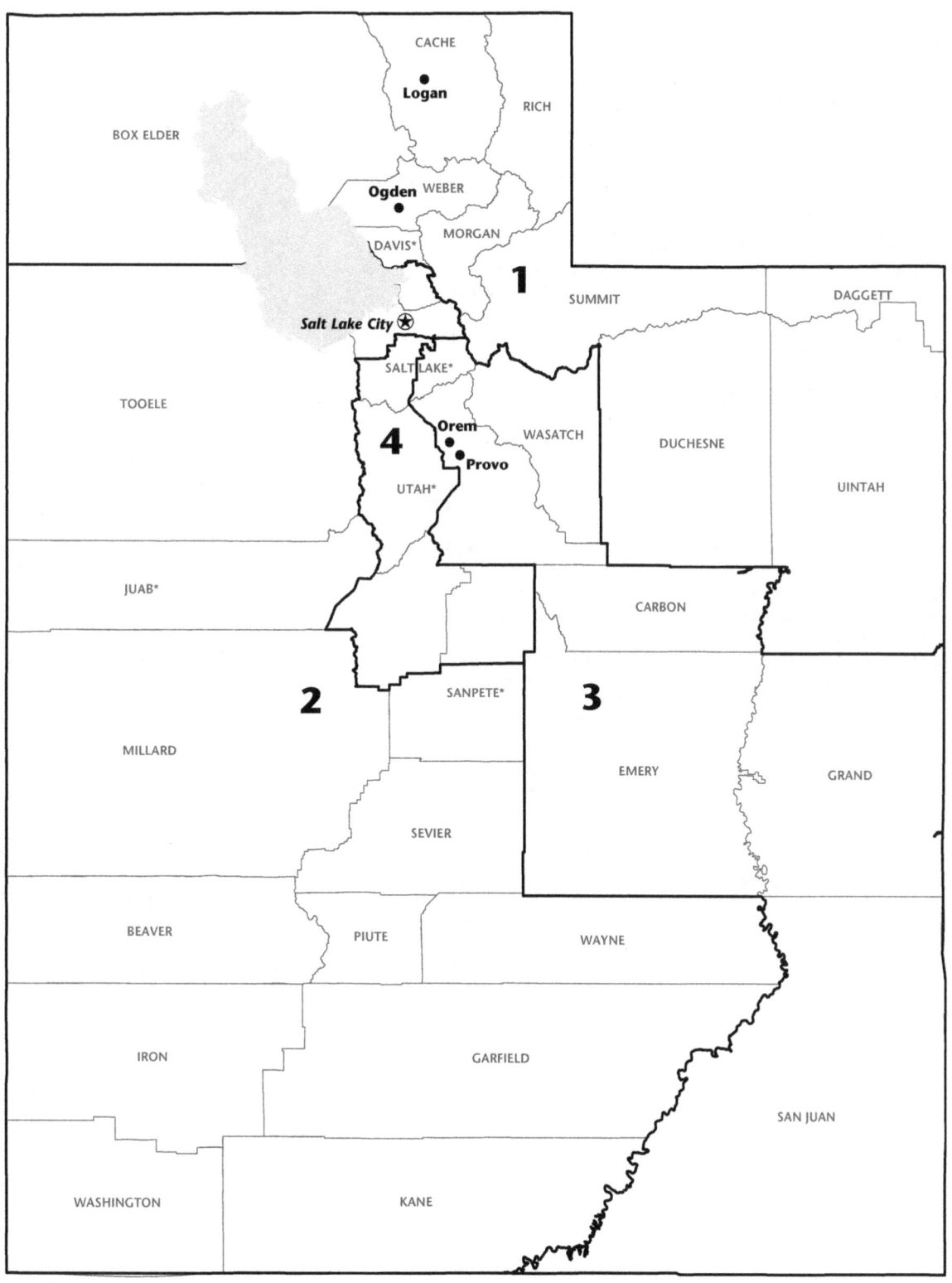

* Asterisk indicates a county whose boundaries include parts of two or more congressional districts.

UTAH

GOVERNOR

Gary R. Herbert (R). Re-elected 2016 to a four-year term. Previously elected 2014, and 2010 to remaining two years of term vacated by resignation of Jon Huntsman Jr. (R) to become ambassador to China. Herbert sworn in as governor August 11, 2009.

SENATORS (2 Republicans)

Orrin G. Hatch (R). Re-elected 2012 to a six-year term. Previously elected 2006, 2000, 1994, 1988, 1982, 1976.

Mike Lee (R). Re-elected 2016 to a six-year term. Previously elected 2010.

REPRESENTATIVES (4 Republicans)

1. Robert "Rob" Bishop (R)
2. Chris Stewart (R)
3. Vacancy (R)
4. Mia B. Love (R)

Note: Jason Chaffetz (R) was re-elected in 2016 in CD 3, but resigned June 30, 2017.

POSTWAR VOTE FOR PRESIDENT

Year	Total Vote	Republican		Democratic		Other Vote	Rep.-Dem. Plurality	Percentage			
								Total Vote		Major Vote	
		Vote	Candidate	Vote	Candidate			Rep.	Dem.	Rep.	Dem.
2016**	1,131,430	515,231	Trump, Donald J.	310,676	Clinton, Hillary Rodham	305,523	204,555 R	45.5%	27.5%	62.4%	37.6%
2012	1,017,440	740,600	Romney, W. Mitt	251,813	Obama, Barack H.*	25,027	488,787 R	72.8%	24.7%	74.6%	25.4%
2008	952,370	596,030	McCain, John S. III	327,670	Obama, Barack H.	28,670	268,360 R	62.6%	34.4%	64.5%	35.5%
2004	927,844	663,742	Bush, George W.*	241,199	Kerry, John F.	22,903	422,543 R	71.5%	26.0%	73.3%	26.7%
2000**	770,754	515,096	Bush, George W.	203,053	Gore, Albert Jr.	52,605	312,043 R	66.8%	26.3%	71.7%	28.3%
1996**	665,629	361,911	Dole, Robert "Bob"	221,633	Clinton, Bill*	82,085	140,278 R	54.4%	33.3%	62.0%	38.0%
1992**	743,999	322,632	Bush, George H.*	183,429	Clinton, Bill	237,938	139,203 R	43.4%	24.7%	63.8%	36.2%
1988	647,008	428,442	Bush, George H.	207,343	Dukakis, Michael S.	11,223	221,099 R	66.2%	32.0%	67.4%	32.6%
1984	629,656	469,105	Reagan, Ronald*	155,369	Mondale, Walter F.	5,182	313,736 R	74.5%	24.7%	75.1%	24.9%
1980**	604,222	439,687	Reagan, Ronald	124,266	Carter, Jimmy*	40,269	315,421 R	72.8%	20.6%	78.0%	22.0%
1976	541,198	337,908	Ford, Gerald R.*	182,110	Carter, Jimmy	21,180	155,798 R	62.4%	33.6%	65.0%	35.0%
1972	478,476	323,643	Nixon, Richard M.*	126,284	McGovern, George S.	28,549	197,359 R	67.6%	26.4%	71.9%	28.1%
1968**	422,568	238,728	Nixon, Richard M.	156,665	Humphrey, Hubert Horatio Jr.	27,175	82,063 R	56.5%	37.1%	60.4%	39.6%
1964	401,413	181,785	Goldwater, Barry M. Sr.	219,628	Johnson, Lyndon B.*		37,843 D	45.3%	54.7%	45.3%	54.7%
1960	374,709	205,361	Nixon, Richard M.	169,248	Kennedy, John F.	100	36,113 R	54.8%	45.2%	54.8%	45.2%
1956	333,995	215,631	Eisenhower, Dwight D.*	118,364	Stevenson, Adlai E. II		97,267 R	64.6%	35.4%	64.6%	35.4%
1952	329,554	194,190	Eisenhower, Dwight D.	135,364	Stevenson, Adlai E. II		58,826 R	58.9%	41.1%	58.9%	41.1%
1948	276,306	124,402	Dewey, Thomas E.	149,151	Truman, Harry S.*	2,753	24,749 D	45.0%	54.0%	45.5%	54.5%

Note: An asterisk (*) denotes incumbent. **In past elections, the other vote included: 2016 - 243,690 Unaffiliated (Evan McMullin), 39,608 Libertarian (Gary Johnson), 2000 - 35,850 Green (Ralph Nader); 1996 - 66,461 Reform (Ross Perot); 1992 - 203,400 Independent (Perot, who finished second); 1980 - 30,284 Independent (John Anderson); 1968 - 26,906 American Independent (George Wallace).

UTAH

POSTWAR VOTE FOR GOVERNOR

Year	Total Vote	Republican Vote	Republican Candidate	Democratic Vote	Democratic Candidate	Other Vote	Rep.-Dem. Plurality	Total Vote Rep.	Total Vote Dem.	Major Vote Rep.	Major Vote Dem.
2016	1,125,035	750,850	Herbert, Gary R.*	323,349	Weinholtz, Mike	50,836	427,501 R	66.7%	28.7%	69.9%	30.1%
2012	1,006,524	688,592	Herbert, Gary R.*	277,622	Cooke, Peter S.	40,310	410,970 R	68.4%	27.6%	71.3%	28.7%
2010S**	643,307	412,151	Herbert, Gary R.*	205,246	Corroon, Peter	25,910	206,905 R	64.1%	31.9%	66.8%	33.2%
2008	945,525	734,049	Huntsman, Jon Jr.*	186,503	Springmeyer, Bob	24,973	547,546 R	77.6%	19.7%	79.7%	20.3%
2004	919,960	531,190	Huntsman, Jon Jr.	380,359	Matheson, Scot Jr.	8,411	150,831 R	57.7%	41.3%	58.3%	41.7%
2000	761,806	424,837	Leavitt, Mike O.*	321,979	Orton, Bill	14,990	102,858 R	55.8%	42.3%	56.9%	43.1%
1996	671,879	503,693	Leavitt, Mike O.*	156,616	Bradley, Jim	11,570	347,077 R	75.0%	23.3%	76.3%	23.7%
1992**	762,549	321,713	Leavitt, Mike O.	177,181	Hanson, Stewart	263,655	144,532 R	42.2%	23.2%	64.5%	35.5%
1988**	649,114	260,462	Bangerter, Norman H.*	249,321	Wilson, Ted	139,331	11,141 R	40.1%	38.4%	51.1%	48.9%
1984	629,619	351,792	Bangerter, Norman H.	275,669	Owens, Wayne	2,158	76,123 R	55.9%	43.8%	56.1%	43.9%
1980	600,019	266,578	Wright, Bob	330,974	Matheson, Scott M.*	2,467	64,396 D	44.4%	55.2%	44.6%	55.4%
1976	539,649	248,027	Romney, Vernon B.	280,706	Matheson, Scott M.	10,916	32,679 D	46.0%	52.0%	46.9%	53.1%
1972	476,447	144,449	Strike, Nicholas L.	331,998	Rampton, Calvin L.*		187,549 D	30.3%	69.7%	30.3%	69.7%
1968	421,012	131,729	Buehner, Carl W.	289,283	Rampton, Calvin L.*		157,554 D	31.3%	68.7%	31.3%	68.7%
1964	398,256	171,300	Melich, Mitchell	226,956	Rampton, Calvin L.		55,656 D	43.0%	57.0%	43.0%	57.0%
1960	371,489	195,634	Clyde, George Dewey*	175,855	Barlocker, William A.		19,779 R	52.7%	47.3%	52.7%	47.3%
1956**	332,889	127,164	Clyde, George Dewey	111,297	Romney, L. C.	94,428	15,867 R	38.2%	33.4%	53.3%	46.7%
1952	327,704	180,516	Lee, J. Bracken*	147,188	Glade, Earl J.		33,328 R	55.1%	44.9%	55.1%	44.9%
1948	275,067	151,253	Lee, J. Bracken	123,814	Maw, Herbert B.*		27,439 R	55.0%	45.0%	55.0%	45.0%

Note: An asterisk (*) denotes incumbent. **In past elections, the other vote included: 1992 - 255,753 Independent (Merrill Cook, who finished second); 1988 - 136,651 Independent (Cook); 1956 - 94,428 Independent (J. Bracken Lee). The 2010 election was for a short term to fill a vacancy.

POSTWAR VOTE FOR SENATOR

Year	Total Vote	Republican Vote	Republican Candidate	Democratic Vote	Democratic Candidate	Other Vote	Rep.-Dem. Plurality	Total Vote Rep.	Total Vote Dem.	Major Vote Rep.	Major Vote Dem.
2016	1,115,608	760,241	Lee, Mike*	301,860	Snow, Misty K.	53,507	458,381 R	68.1%	27.1%	71.6%	28.4%
2012	1,006,901	657,608	Hatch, Orrin G.*	301,873	Howell, Scott N.	47,420	355,735 R	65.3%	30.0%	68.5%	31.5%
2010	633,829	390,179	Lee, Mike	207,685	Granato, Sam	35,965	182,494 R	61.6%	32.8%	65.3%	34.7%
2006	571,252	356,238	Hatch, Orrin G.*	177,459	Ashdown, Pete	37,555	178,779 R	62.4%	31.1%	66.7%	33.3%
2004	911,726	626,640	Bennett, Robert F.*	258,955	Van Dam, R. Paul	26,131	367,685 R	68.7%	28.4%	70.8%	29.2%
2000	769,704	504,803	Hatch, Orrin G.*	242,569	Howell, Scott N.	22,332	262,234 R	65.6%	31.5%	67.5%	32.5%
1998	494,909	316,652	Bennett, Robert F.*	163,172	Leckman, Scott	15,085	153,480 R	64.0%	33.0%	66.0%	34.0%
1994	519,323	357,297	Hatch, Orrin G.*	146,938	Shea, Patrick A.	15,088	210,359 R	68.8%	28.3%	70.9%	29.1%
1992	758,479	420,069	Bennett, Robert F.	301,228	Owens, Wayne	37,182	118,841 R	55.4%	39.7%	58.2%	41.8%
1988	640,702	430,089	Hatch, Orrin G.*	203,364	Moss, Brian	7,249	226,725 R	67.1%	31.7%	67.9%	32.1%
1986	435,111	314,608	Garn, E. J.*	115,523	Oliver, Craig	4,980	199,085 R	72.3%	26.6%	73.1%	26.9%
1982	530,802	309,332	Hatch, Orrin G.*	219,482	Wilson, Ted	1,988	89,850 R	58.3%	41.3%	58.5%	41.5%
1980	594,298	437,675	Garn, E. J.*	151,454	Berman, Dan	5,169	286,221 R	73.6%	25.5%	74.3%	25.7%
1976	540,108	290,221	Hatch, Orrin G.	241,948	Moss, Frank E.*	7,939	48,273 R	53.7%	44.8%	54.5%	45.5%
1974	420,642	210,299	Garn, E. J.	185,377	Owens, Wayne	24,966	24,922 R	50.0%	44.1%	53.1%	46.9%
1970	374,303	159,004	Burton, Laurence J.	210,207	Moss, Frank E.*	5,092	51,203 D	42.5%	56.2%	43.1%	56.9%
1968	419,262	225,075	Bennett, Wallace F.*	192,168	Weilenmann, Milton	2,019	32,907 R	53.7%	45.8%	53.9%	46.1%
1964	397,384	169,562	Wilkinson, Ernest L.	227,822	Moss, Frank E.*		58,260 D	42.7%	57.3%	42.7%	57.3%
1962	318,411	166,755	Bennett, Wallace F.*	151,656	King, David S.		15,099 R	52.4%	47.6%	52.4%	47.6%
1958**	291,311	101,471	Watkins, Arthur V.*	112,827	Moss, Frank E.	77,013	11,356 D	34.8%	38.7%	47.4%	52.6%
1956	330,381	178,261	Bennett, Wallace F.*	152,120	Hopkin, Alonzo F.		26,141 R	54.0%	46.0%	54.0%	46.0%
1952	327,033	177,435	Watkins, Arthur V.*	149,598	Granger, Walter K.		27,837 R	54.3%	45.7%	54.3%	45.7%
1950	264,440	142,427	Bennett, Wallace F.	121,198	Thomas, Elbert D.*	815	21,229 R	53.9%	45.8%	54.0%	46.0%
1946	197,399	101,142	Watkins, Arthur V.	96,257	Murdock, Abe*		4,885 R	51.2%	48.8%	51.2%	48.8%

Note: An asterisk (*) denotes incumbent. **In past elections, the other vote included: 1958 - 77,013 Independent (J. Bracken Lee).

UTAH

PRESIDENT 2016

2010 Census Population	County	Total Vote	Republican (Trump)	Democratic (Clinton)	Other	Rep.-Dem. Plurality	Percentage			
							Total Vote		Major Vote	
							Rep.	Dem.	Rep.	Dem.
6,629	BEAVER	2,491	1,838	264	389	1,515 R	73.8%	10.6%	87.4%	12.6%
49,975	BOX ELDER	19,735	12,230	2,282	5,223	7,973 R	62.0%	11.6%	84.3%	15.7%
112,656	CACHE	46,157	21,139	8,563	16,455	7,444 R	45.8%	18.6%	71.2%	28.8%
21,403	CARBON	7,952	5,275	1,717	960	3,558 R	66.3%	21.6%	75.4%	24.6%
1,059	DAGGETT	474	331	77	66	254 R	69.8%	16.2%	81.1%	18.9%
306,479	DAVIS	138,411	62,219	28,776	47,416	22,484 R	45.0%	20.8%	68.4%	31.6%
18,607	DUCHESNE	6,942	5,508	500	934	4,778 R	79.3%	7.2%	91.7%	8.3%
10,976	EMERY	4,289	3,425	380	484	3,045 R	79.9%	8.9%	90.0%	10.0%
5,172	GARFIELD	2,344	1,606	358	380	1,248 R	68.5%	15.3%	81.8%	18.2%
9,225	GRAND	4,533	1,975	1,960	598	15 R	43.6%	43.2%	50.2%	49.8%
46,163	IRON	17,654	11,561	2,450	3,643	8,809 R	65.5%	13.9%	82.5%	17.5%
10,246	JUAB	4,177	2,827	442	908	2,065 R	67.7%	10.6%	86.5%	13.5%
7,125	KANE	3,505	2,265	741	499	1,524 R	64.6%	21.1%	75.3%	24.7%
12,503	MILLARD	5,242	3,860	431	951	3,141 R	73.6%	8.2%	90.0%	10.0%
9,469	MORGAN	5,192	3,188	577	1427	1,990 R	61.4%	11.1%	84.7%	15.3%
1,556	PIUTE	729	626	47	56	579 R	85.9%	6.4%	93.0%	7.0%
2,264	RICH	1,109	797	104	208	623 R	71.9%	9.4%	88.5%	11.5%
1,029,655	SALT LAKE	418,868	138,043	175,863	104,962	37,820 D	33.0%	42.0%	44.0%	56.0%
14,746	SAN JUAN	5,447	2,645	2,042	760	603 R	48.6%	37.5%	56.4%	43.6%
27,822	SANPETE	10,164	6,673	1,061	2,430	4,635 R	65.7%	10.4%	86.3%	13.7%
20,802	SEVIER	8,654	6,740	695	1219	5,824 R	77.9%	8.0%	90.7%	9.3%
36,324	SUMMIT	20,641	7,333	10,503	2,805	3,170 D	35.5%	50.9%	41.1%	58.9%
58,218	TOOELE	21,829	11,169	4,573	6,087	6,400 R	51.2%	20.9%	71.0%	29.0%
32,588	UINTAH	12,797	9,810	995	1992	8,314 R	76.7%	7.8%	90.8%	9.2%
516,564	UTAH	201,551	102,182	28,522	70,847	41,650 R	50.7%	14.2%	78.2%	21.8%
23,530	WASATCH	12,120	6,115	3,063	2,942	3,052 R	50.5%	25.3%	66.6%	33.4%
138,115	WASHINGTON	61,963	42,650	10,288	9,025	32,362 R	68.8%	16.6%	80.6%	19.4%
2,778	WAYNE	1,421	966	271	184	695 R	68.0%	19.1%	78.1%	21.9%
231,236	WEBER	85,039	40,235	23,131	21,673	17,104 R	47.3%	27.2%	63.5%	36.5%
2,763,885	TOTAL	1,131,430	515,231	310,676	305,523	204,555 R	45.5%	27.5%	62.4%	37.6%

UTAH

GOVERNOR 2016

2010 Census Population	County	Total Vote	Republican (Herbert)	Democratic (Weinholtz)	Other	Rep.-Dem. Plurality	Percentage			
							Total Vote		Major Vote	
							Rep.	Dem.	Rep.	Dem.
6,629	BEAVER	2,466	2,033	324	109	1,709 R	82.4%	13.1%	86.3%	13.7%
49,975	BOX ELDER	19,640	16,084	2,564	992	13,520 R	81.9%	13.1%	86.3%	13.7%
112,656	CACHE	45,847	34,553	9,025	2,269	25,528 R	75.4%	19.7%	79.3%	20.7%
21,403	CARBON	7,930	5,574	2,034	322	3,540 R	70.3%	25.6%	73.3%	26.7%
1,059	DAGGETT	472	351	104	17	247 R	74.4%	22.0%	77.1%	22.9%
306,479	DAVIS	138,581	101,402	30,720	6,459	70,682 R	73.2%	22.2%	76.7%	23.3%
18,607	DUCHESNE	6,922	5,837	715	370	5,122 R	84.3%	10.3%	89.1%	10.9%
10,976	EMERY	4,264	3,638	483	143	3,155 R	85.3%	11.3%	88.3%	11.7%
5,172	GARFIELD	2,339	1,888	378	73	1,510 R	80.7%	16.2%	83.3%	16.7%
9,225	GRAND	4,539	2,266	2,067	206	199 R	49.9%	45.5%	52.3%	47.7%
46,163	IRON	17,466	13,646	2,597	1,223	11,049 R	78.1%	14.9%	84.0%	16.0%
10,246	JUAB	4,136	3,483	487	166	2,996 R	84.2%	11.8%	87.7%	12.3%
7,125	KANE	3,469	2,589	729	151	1,860 R	74.6%	21.0%	78.0%	22.0%
12,503	MILLARD	5,213	4,455	534	224	3,921 R	85.5%	10.2%	89.3%	10.7%
9,469	MORGAN	5,172	4,304	629	239	3,675 R	83.2%	12.2%	87.2%	12.8%

UTAH
GOVERNOR 2016

2010 Census Population	County	Total Vote	Republican (Herbert)	Democratic (Weinholtz)	Other	Rep.-Dem. Plurality	Total Vote Rep.	Total Vote Dem.	Major Vote Rep.	Major Vote Dem.
1,556	PIUTE	715	630	54	31	576 R	88.1%	7.6%	92.1%	7.9%
2,264	RICH	1,114	948	122	44	826 R	85.1%	11.0%	88.6%	11.4%
1,029,655	SALT LAKE	416,827	218,570	181,462	16,795	37,108 R	52.4%	43.5%	54.6%	45.4%
14,746	SAN JUAN	5,441	3,188	1,975	278	1,213 R	58.6%	36.3%	61.7%	38.3%
27,822	SANPETE	10,177	8,701	1,033	443	7,668 R	85.5%	10.2%	89.4%	10.6%
20,802	SEVIER	8,583	7,305	903	375	6,402 R	85.1%	10.5%	89.0%	11.0%
36,324	SUMMIT	20,461	9,595	10,162	704	567 D	46.9%	49.7%	48.6%	51.4%
58,218	TOOELE	21,697	15,030	5,425	1,242	9,605 R	69.3%	25.0%	73.5%	26.5%
32,588	UINTAH	12,712	10,697	1,388	627	9,309 R	84.1%	10.9%	88.5%	11.5%
516,564	UTAH	199,749	162,178	28,469	9,102	133,709 R	81.2%	14.3%	85.1%	14.9%
23,530	WASATCH	12,108	8,552	3,125	431	5,427 R	70.6%	25.8%	73.2%	26.8%
138,115	WASHINGTON	61,151	47,202	10,565	3,384	36,637 R	77.2%	17.3%	81.7%	18.3%
2,778	WAYNE	1,416	1,108	275	33	833 R	78.2%	19.4%	80.1%	19.9%
231,236	WEBER	84,428	55,043	25,001	4,384	30,042 R	65.2%	29.6%	68.8%	31.2%
2,763,885	TOTAL	1,125,035	750,850	323,349	50,836	427,501 R	66.7%	28.7%	69.9%	30.1%

UTAH
SENATOR 2016

2010 Census Population	County	Total Vote	Republican (Lee)	Democratic (Snow)	Other	Rep.-Dem. Plurality	Total Vote Rep.	Total Vote Dem.	Major Vote Rep.	Major Vote Dem.
6,629	BEAVER	2,442	2,075	295	72	1,780 R	85.0%	12.1%	87.6%	12.4%
49,975	BOX ELDER	19,494	16,240	2,328	926	13,912 R	83.3%	11.9%	87.5%	12.5%
112,656	CACHE	45,527	35,209	8,378	1,940	26,831 R	77.3%	18.4%	80.8%	19.2%
21,403	CARBON	7,835	5,607	1,882	346	3,725 R	71.6%	24.0%	74.9%	25.1%
1,059	DAGGETT	461	340	95	26	245 R	73.8%	20.6%	78.2%	21.8%
306,479	DAVIS	138,148	102,865	28,459	6,824	74,406 R	74.5%	20.6%	78.3%	21.7%
18,607	DUCHESNE	6,886	6,047	621	218	5,426 R	87.8%	9.0%	90.7%	9.3%
10,976	EMERY	4,245	3,648	461	136	3,187 R	85.9%	10.9%	88.8%	11.2%
5,172	GARFIELD	2,336	1,903	361	72	1,542 R	81.5%	15.5%	84.1%	15.9%
9,225	GRAND	4,549	2,258	2,032	259	226 R	49.6%	44.7%	52.6%	47.4%
46,163	IRON	17,481	14,239	2,567	675	11,672 R	81.5%	14.7%	84.7%	15.3%
10,246	JUAB	4,163	3,574	448	141	3,126 R	85.9%	10.8%	88.9%	11.1%
7,125	KANE	3,466	2,568	752	146	1,816 R	74.1%	21.7%	77.3%	22.7%
12,503	MILLARD	5,186	4,575	469	142	4,106 R	88.2%	9.0%	90.7%	9.3%
9,469	MORGAN	5,163	4,378	595	190	3,783 R	84.8%	11.5%	88.0%	12.0%
1,556	PIUTE	712	640	54	18	586 R	89.9%	7.6%	92.2%	7.8%
2,264	RICH	1,107	970	110	27	860 R	87.6%	9.9%	89.8%	10.2%
1,029,655	SALT LAKE	411,338	220,652	168,403	22,283	52,249 R	53.6%	40.9%	56.7%	43.3%
14,746	SAN JUAN	5,418	3,243	1,947	228	1,296 R	59.9%	35.9%	62.5%	37.5%
27,822	SANPETE	10,069	8,583	1,128	358	7,455 R	85.2%	11.2%	88.4%	11.6%
20,802	SEVIER	8,564	7,438	836	290	6,602 R	86.9%	9.8%	89.9%	10.1%
36,324	SUMMIT	20,189	9,409	9,610	1,170	201 D	46.6%	47.6%	49.5%	50.5%
58,218	TOOELE	21,482	15,325	4,959	1,198	10,366 R	71.3%	23.1%	75.6%	24.4%
32,588	UINTAH	12,702	10,989	1,232	481	9,757 R	86.5%	9.7%	89.9%	10.1%
516,564	UTAH	198,832	164,401	26,246	8,185	138,155 R	82.7%	13.2%	86.2%	13.8%
23,530	WASATCH	11,880	8,464	2,898	518	5,566 R	71.2%	24.4%	74.5%	25.5%
138,115	WASHINGTON	60,856	48,244	10,220	2,392	38,024 R	79.3%	16.8%	82.5%	17.5%
2,778	WAYNE	1,413	1,079	260	74	819 R	76.4%	18.4%	80.6%	19.4%
231,236	WEBER	83,664	55,278	24,214	4,172	31,064 R	66.1%	28.9%	69.5%	30.5%
2,763,885	TOTAL	1,115,608	760,241	301,860	53,507	458,381 R	68.1%	27.1%	71.6%	28.4%

UTAH

HOUSE OF REPRESENTATIVES

| | | | Republican | | Democratic | | | | Percentage | | | |
| | | | | | | | | | Total Vote | | Major Vote | |
CD	Year	Total Vote	Vote	Candidate	Vote	Candidate	Other Vote	Rep.-Dem. Plurality	Rep.	Dem.	Rep.	Dem.
1	2016	277,455	182,928	BISHOP, ROBERT "ROB"*	73,381	CLEMENS, PETER C.	21,146	109,547 R	65.9%	26.4%	71.4%	28.6%
1	2014	130,034	84,231	BISHOP, ROBERT "ROB"*	36,422	MCALEER, DONNA M.	9,381	47,809 R	64.8%	28.0%	69.8%	30.2%
1	2012	245,528	175,487	BISHOP, ROBERT "ROB"*	60,611	MCALEER, DONNA M.	9,430	114,876 R	71.5%	24.7%	74.3%	25.7%
2	2016	276,841	170,542	STEWART, CHRIS*	93,780	ALBARRAN, CHARLENE	12,519	76,762 R	61.6%	33.9%	64.5%	35.5%
2	2014	146,188	88,915	STEWART, CHRIS*	47,585	ROBLES, LUZ	9,688	41,330 R	60.8%	32.6%	65.1%	34.9%
2	2012	248,545	154,523	STEWART, CHRIS	83,176	SEEGMILLER, JAY	10,846	71,347 R	62.2%	33.5%	65.0%	35.0%
3	2016	285,305	209,589	CHAFFETZ, JASON*	75,716	TRYON, STEPHEN		133,873 R	73.5%	26.5%	73.5%	26.5%
3	2014	142,580	102,952	CHAFFETZ, JASON*	32,059	WONNACOTT, BRIAN	7,569	70,893 R	72.2%	22.5%	76.3%	23.7%
3	2012	259,547	198,828	CHAFFETZ, JASON*	60,719	SIMONSEN, SOREN D.		138,109 R	76.6%	23.4%	76.6%	23.4%
4	2016	274,569	147,597	LOVE, MIA B.*	113,413	OWENS, DOUG	13,559	34,184 R	53.8%	41.3%	56.5%	43.5%
4	2014	147,168	74,936	LOVE, MIA B.	67,425	OWENS, DOUG	4,807	7,511 R	50.9%	45.8%	52.6%	47.4%
4	2012	245,277	119,035	LOVE, MIA B.	119,803	MATHESON, JIM*	6,439	768 D	48.5%	48.8%	49.8%	50.2%
TOTAL	2016	1,114,170	710,656		356,290		47,224	354,366 R	63.8%	32.0%	66.6%	33.4%
TOTAL	2014	565,970	351,034		183,491		31,445	167,543 R	62.0%	32.4%	65.7%	34.3%
TOTAL	2012	998,897	647,873		324,309		26,715	323,564 R	64.9%	32.5%	66.6%	33.4%

Note: An asterisk (*) denotes incumbent.

UTAH

GENERAL AND PRIMARY ELECTIONS

2016 GENERAL ELECTIONS: OTHER VOTES

President   Other vote was 243,690 Unaffiliated (Evan McMullin), 39,608 Libertarian (Gary Johnson), 9,438 Unaffiliated (Jill Stein), 8,032 Constitution (Darrell Castle), 2,752 Independent American (Rocky Giordani), 883 Unaffiliated (Roque De La Fuente), 544 Unaffiliated (Monica Moorehead), 521 Unaffiliated (Alyson Kennedy), 55 Write-in (Scattered Write-in)

Governor   34,827 Libertarian (Brian Kamerath), 15,912 Independent American (Dell Schanze), 97 Write-in (L.S. Brown)

Senate   27,340 Independent American (Stoney Fonua), 26,167 Unaffiliated (Bill Barron)

House   Other vote was:

CD 1   16,296 Libertarian (Craig Bowden), 4,850 Unaffiliated (Chadwick Fairbanks)
CD 2   12,519 Constitution (Paul McCollaum)
CD 4   13,559 Constitution (Collin Simonsen)

2016 PRIMARY ELECTIONS: SUPPLEMENTARY INFORMATION

Presidential Caucus   March 22, 2016   **Registration** (as of June 27, 2016 – includes 207,611 inactive registrants)   1,474,206

Republican	699,005
Democratic	160,277
Independent American	13,871
Libertarian	9,660
Constitution	4,542
Unaffiliated	586,851

Primary   June 28, 2016

Primary Type   Semi-Open—Registered Democrats and unaffiliated voters could participate in the Democratic primary. Only registered Republicans could vote in the Republican primary.

UTAH

GENERAL AND PRIMARY ELECTIONS

	REPUBLICAN PRIMARIES			DEMOCRATIC PRIMARIES		
Senator	Lee, Mike*	Unopposed		Snow, Misty K.	28,928	59.4%
				Swinton, Jonathan	19,774	40.6%
				TOTAL	*48,702*	
Governor	Herbert, Gary R.*	176,866	71.7%	Weinholtz, Mike	Unopposed	
	Johnson, Jonathan	69,663	28.3%			
	TOTAL	*246,529*				
Congressional District 1	Bishop, Robert "Rob"*	Unopposed		Clemens, Peter C.	Unopposed	
Congressional District 2	Stewart, Chris*	Unopposed		Albarran, Charlene	Unopposed	
Congressional District 3	Chaffetz, Jason*	47,439	78.6%	Tryon, Stephen	Unopposed	
	Teng, Chia-Chi	12,922	21.4%			
	TOTAL	*60,361*				
Congressional District 4	Love, Mia B.*	Unopposed		Owens, Doug	Unopposed	

Note: An asterisk (*) denotes incumbent.

VERMONT

One member At Large

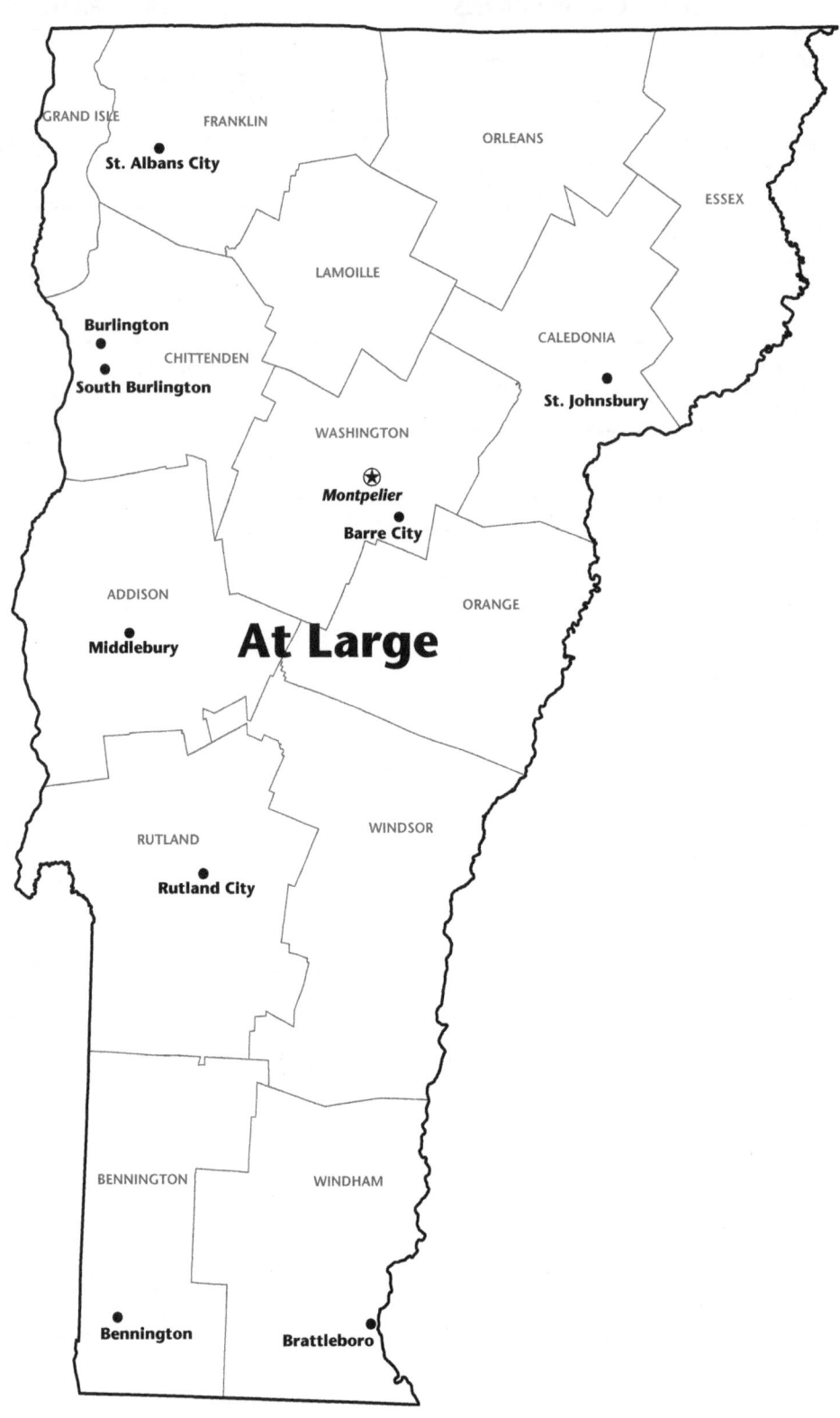

VERMONT

GOVERNOR
Phil Scott (R). Elected 2016 to a four-year term.

SENATORS (1 Democrat, 1 Independent)
Patrick J. Leahy (D). Re-elected 2016 to a six-year term. Previously elected 2010, 2004, 1998, 1992, 1986, 1980, 1974.

Bernard Sanders (Ind.). Re-elected 2012 to a six-year term. Previously elected 2006.

REPRESENTATIVE (1 Democrat)
At Large. Peter Welch (D)

POSTWAR VOTE FOR PRESIDENT

| | | Republican | | Democratic | | | | Percentage | | | |
| | | | | | | Other Vote | Rep.-Dem. Plurality | Total Vote | | Major Vote | |
Year	Total Vote	Vote	Candidate	Vote	Candidate			Rep.	Dem.	Rep.	Dem.
2016**	315,067	95,369	Trump, Donald J.	178,573	Clinton, Hillary Rodham	41,125	83,204 D	30.3%	56.7%	34.8%	65.2%
2012	299,290	92,698	Romney, W. Mitt	199,239	Obama, Barack H.*	7,353	106,541 D	31.0%	66.6%	31.8%	68.2%
2008	325,046	98,974	McCain, John S. III	219,262	Obama, Barack H.	6,810	120,288 D	30.4%	67.5%	31.1%	68.9%
2004	312,309	121,180	Bush, George W.*	184,067	Kerry, John F.	7,062	62,887 D	38.8%	58.9%	39.7%	60.3%
2000**	294,308	119,775	Bush, George W.	149,022	Gore, Albert Jr.	25,511	29,247 D	40.7%	50.6%	44.6%	55.4%
1996**	258,449	80,352	Dole, Robert "Bob"	137,894	Clinton, Bill*	40,203	57,542 D	31.1%	53.4%	36.8%	63.2%
1992**	289,701	88,122	Bush, George H.*	133,592	Clinton, Bill	67,987	45,470 D	30.4%	46.1%	39.7%	60.3%
1988	243,328	124,331	Bush, George H.	115,776	Dukakis, Michael S.	3,221	8,555 R	51.1%	47.6%	51.8%	48.2%
1984	234,561	135,865	Reagan, Ronald*	95,730	Mondale, Walter F.	2,966	40,135 R	57.9%	40.8%	58.7%	41.3%
1980**	213,299	94,628	Reagan, Ronald	81,952	Carter, Jimmy*	36,719	12,676 R	44.4%	38.4%	53.6%	46.4%
1976	187,765	102,085	Ford, Gerald R.*	80,954	Carter, Jimmy	4,726	21,131 R	54.4%	43.1%	55.8%	44.2%
1972	186,947	117,149	Nixon, Richard M.*	68,174	McGovern, George S.	1,624	48,975 R	62.7%	36.5%	63.2%	36.8%
1968**	161,404	85,142	Nixon, Richard M.	70,255	Humphrey, Hubert Horatio Jr.	6,007	14,887 R	52.8%	43.5%	54.8%	45.2%
1964	163,089	54,942	Goldwater, Barry M. Sr.	108,127	Johnson, Lyndon B.*	20	53,185 D	33.7%	66.3%	33.7%	66.3%
1960	167,324	98,131	Nixon, Richard M.	69,186	Kennedy, John F.	7	28,945 R	58.6%	41.3%	58.6%	41.4%
1956	152,978	110,390	Eisenhower, Dwight D.*	42,549	Stevenson, Adlai E. II	39	67,841 R	72.2%	27.8%	72.2%	27.8%
1952	153,557	109,717	Eisenhower, Dwight D.	43,355	Stevenson, Adlai E. II	485	66,362 R	71.5%	28.2%	71.7%	28.3%
1948	123,382	75,926	Dewey, Thomas E.	45,557	Truman, Harry S.*	1,899	30,369 R	61.5%	36.9%	62.5%	37.5%

Note: An asterisk (*) denotes incumbent. **In past elections, the other vote included: 2016 - 10,078 Libertarian (Gary Johnson); 2000 - 20,374 Green (Ralph Nader); 1996 - 31,024 Reform (Ross Perot); 1992 - 65,991 Independent (Perot); 1980 - 31,761 Independent (John Anderson); 1968 - 5,104 American Independent (George Wallace).

VERMONT

POSTWAR VOTE FOR GOVERNOR

Year	Total Vote	Republican Vote	Republican Candidate	Democratic Vote	Democratic Candidate	Other Vote	Rep.-Dem. Plurality	Percentage Total Vote Rep.	Dem.	Major Vote Rep.	Dem.
2016	315,295	166,817	Scott, Phil	139,253	Minter, Sue	9,225	27,564 R	52.9%	44.2%	54.5%	45.5%
2014**	193,087	87,075	Milne, Scott	89,509	Shumlin, Peter*	16,503	2,434 D	45.1%	46.4%	49.3%	50.7%
2012	295,261	110,940	Brock, Randy	170,598	Shumlin, Peter*	13,723	59,658 D	37.6%	57.8%	39.4%	60.6%
2010**	241,605	115,212	Dubie, Brian E.	119,543	Shumlin, Peter	6,850	4,331 D	47.7%	49.5%	49.1%	50.9%
2008**	319,085	170,492	Douglas, Jim*	69,534	Symington, Gaye	79,059	100,958 R	53.4%	21.8%	71.0%	29.0%
2006	262,524	148,014	Douglas, Jim*	108,090	Parker, Scudder	6,420	39,924 R	56.4%	41.2%	57.8%	42.2%
2004	309,285	181,540	Douglas, Jim*	117,327	Clavell, Peter	10,418	64,213 R	58.7%	37.9%	60.7%	39.3%
2002**	230,161	103,436	Douglas, Jim	97,565	Racine, Doug	29,160	5,871 R	44.9%	42.4%	51.5%	48.5%
2000	293,473	111,359	Dwyer, Ruth	148,059	Dean, Howard B.*	34,055	36,700 D	37.9%	50.5%	42.9%	57.1%
1998	218,120	89,726	Dwyer, Ruth	121,425	Dean, Howard B.*	6,969	31,699 D	41.1%	55.7%	42.5%	57.5%
1996	254,648	57,161	Gropper, John L.	179,544	Dean, Howard B.*	17,943	122,383 D	22.4%	70.5%	24.1%	75.9%
1994	212,046	40,292	Kelley, David F.	145,661	Dean, Howard B.*	26,093	105,369 D	19.0%	68.7%	21.7%	78.3%
1992	285,728	65,837	McClaughry, John	213,523	Dean, Howard B.*	6,368	147,686 D	23.0%	74.7%	23.6%	76.4%
1990	211,422	109,540	Snelling, Richard A.	97,321	Welch, Peter	4,561	12,219 R	51.8%	46.0%	53.0%	47.0%
1988	242,879	105,191	Bernhardt, Michael	134,438	Kunin, Madeline*	3,250	29,247 D	43.3%	55.4%	43.9%	56.1%
1986**	196,716	75,162	Smith, Peter	92,379	Kunin, Madeline*	29,175	17,217 D	38.2%	47.0%	44.9%	55.1%
1984	233,753	113,264	Easton, John J.	116,938	Kunin, Madeline	3,551	3,674 D	48.5%	50.0%	49.2%	50.8%
1982	169,251	93,111	Snelling, Richard A.*	74,394	Kunin, Madeline	1,746	18,717 R	55.0%	44.0%	55.6%	44.4%
1980	210,381	123,229	Snelling, Richard A.*	77,363	Diamond, M. Jerome	9,789	45,866 R	58.6%	36.8%	61.4%	38.6%
1978	124,482	78,181	Snelling, Richard A.*	42,482	Granai, Edwin C.	3,819	35,699 R	62.8%	34.1%	64.8%	35.2%
1976	185,929	99,268	Snelling, Richard A.	75,262	Hackel, Stella B.	11,399	24,006 R	53.4%	40.5%	56.9%	43.1%
1974	141,156	53,672	Kennedy, Walter L.	79,842	Salmon, Thomas P.*	7,642	26,170 D	38.0%	56.6%	40.2%	59.8%
1972	189,237	82,491	Hackett, Luther F.	104,533	Salmon, Thomas P.	2,213	22,042 D	43.6%	55.2%	44.1%	55.9%
1970	153,528	87,458	Davis, Deane C.*	66,028	O'Brien, Leo	42	21,430 R	57.0%	43.0%	57.0%	43.0%
1968	161,089	89,387	Davis, Deane C.	71,656	Daley, John J.	46	17,731 R	55.5%	44.5%	55.5%	44.5%
1966	136,262	57,577	Snelling, Richard A.	78,669	Hoff, Philip H.*	16	21,092 D	42.3%	57.7%	42.3%	57.7%
1964	164,199	57,576	Foote, Ralph A.	106,611	Hoff, Philip H.*	12	49,035 D	35.1%	64.9%	35.1%	64.9%
1962	121,422	60,035	Keyser, F. Ray Jr.*	61,383	Hoff, Philip H.	4	1,348 D	49.4%	50.6%	49.4%	50.6%
1960	164,632	92,861	Keyser, F. Ray Jr.	71,755	Niquette, Russell F.	16	21,106 R	56.4%	43.6%	56.4%	43.6%
1958	123,728	62,222	Stafford, Robert T.	61,503	Leddy, Bernard J.	3	719 R	50.3%	49.7%	50.3%	49.7%
1956	153,809	88,379	Johnson, Joseph B.*	65,420	Branon, E. Frank	10	22,959 R	57.5%	42.5%	57.5%	42.5%
1954	114,360	59,778	Johnson, Joseph B.	54,554	Branon, E. Frank	28	5,224 R	52.3%	47.7%	52.3%	47.7%
1952	150,836	78,338	Emerson, Lee Earl*	60,051	Larrow, Robert W.	12,447	18,287 R	51.9%	39.8%	56.6%	43.4%
1950	87,155	64,915	Emerson, Lee Earl	22,227	Moran, J. Edward	13	42,688 R	74.5%	25.5%	74.5%	25.5%
1948	120,183	86,394	Gibson, Ernest Willard Jr.*	33,588	Ryan, Charles F.	201	52,806 R	71.9%	27.9%	72.0%	28.0%
1946	72,044	57,849	Gibson, Ernest Willard Jr.	14,096	Coburn, Berthold C.	99	43,753 R	80.3%	19.6%	80.4%	19.6%

Note: An asterisk (*) denotes incumbent. **In past elections, the other vote included: 2008 - 69,791 Independent (Anthony Pollina, who finished second); 1986 - 28,430 Independent (Bernard Sanders). In 1986, 2002, 2010, and 2014, in the absence of a majority of the total vote for any candidate, the State Legislature elected the governor — Democrat Madeleine M. Kunin in January 1987, Republican Jim Douglas in January 2003, and Democrat Peter Shumlin in January 2011 and January 2015.

VERMONT

POSTWAR VOTE FOR SENATOR

Year	Total Vote	Republican Vote	Republican Candidate	Democratic Vote	Democratic Candidate	Other Vote	Rep.-Dem. Plurality		Total Vote Rep.	Total Vote Dem.	Major Vote Rep.	Major Vote Dem.
2016	313,809	103,637	Milne, Scott	192,243	Leahy, Patrick J.*	17,929	88,606	D	33.0%	61.3%	35.0%	65.0%
2012**	294,267	73,198	MacGovern, John			221,069	73,198	R#	24.9%		100.0%	
2010	235,178	72,699	Britton, Len	151,281	Leahy, Patrick J.*	11,198	78,582	D	30.9%	64.3%	32.5%	67.5%
2006**	262,419	84,924	Tarrant, Richard			177,495	84,924	R#	32.4%		100.0%	
2004	307,208	75,398	McMullen, Jack	216,972	Leahy, Patrick J.*	14,838	141,574	D	24.5%	70.6%	25.8%	74.2%
2000	288,500	189,133	Jeffords, James M.*	73,352	Flanagan, Ed	26,015	115,781	R	65.6%	25.4%	72.1%	27.9%
1998	214,036	48,051	Tuttle, Fred	154,567	Leahy, Patrick J.*	11,418	106,516	D	22.4%	72.2%	23.7%	76.3%
1994	211,672	106,505	Jeffords, James M.*	85,868	Backus, Jan	19,299	20,637	R	50.3%	40.6%	55.4%	44.6%
1992	285,739	123,854	Douglas, Jim	154,762	Leahy, Patrick J.*	7,123	30,908	D	43.3%	54.2%	44.5%	55.5%
1988	240,108	163,183	Jeffords, James M.	71,460	Gray, William	5,465	91,723	R	68.0%	29.8%	69.5%	30.5%
1986	196,532	67,798	Snelling, Richard A.	124,123	Leahy, Patrick J.*	4,611	56,325	D	34.5%	63.2%	35.3%	64.7%
1982	168,003	84,450	Stafford, Robert T.*	79,340	Guest, James A.	4,213	5,110	R	50.3%	47.2%	51.6%	48.4%
1980	209,124	101,421	Ledbetter, Stewart M.	104,176	Leahy, Patrick J.*	3,527	2,755	D	48.5%	49.8%	49.3%	50.7%
1976	189,046	94,481	Stafford, Robert T.*	85,682	Salmon, Thomas P.	8,883	8,799	R	50.0%	45.3%	52.4%	47.6%
1974	142,772	66,223	Mallary, Richard W.	70,629	Leahy, Patrick J.	5,920	4,406	D	46.4%	49.5%	48.4%	51.6%
1972S**	71,348	45,888	Stafford, Robert T.*	23,842	Major, Randolph T.	1,618	22,046	R	64.3%	33.4%	65.8%	34.2%
1970	154,899	91,198	Prouty, Winston L.*	62,271	Hoff, Philip H.	1,430	28,927	R	58.9%	40.2%	59.4%	40.6%
1968**	157,375	157,154	Aiken, George David*			221	157,154	R	99.9%		100.0%	
1964	164,350	87,879	Prouty, Winston L.*	76,457	Fayette, Frederick J.	14	11,422	R	53.5%	46.5%	53.5%	46.5%
1962	121,571	81,241	Aiken, George David*	40,134	Johnson, W. Robert	196	41,107	R	66.8%	33.0%	66.9%	33.1%
1958	124,442	64,900	Prouty, Winston L.	59,536	Fayette, Frederick J.	6	5,364	R	52.2%	47.8%	52.2%	47.8%
1956	155,289	103,101	Aiken, George David*	52,184	O'Shea, Bernard G.	4	50,917	R	66.4%	33.6%	66.4%	33.6%
1952	154,052	111,406	Flanders, Ralph E.*	42,630	Johnston, Allan R.	16	68,776	R	72.3%	27.7%	72.3%	27.7%
1950	89,171	69,543	Aiken, George David*	19,608	Bigelow, James E.	20	49,935	R	78.0%	22.0%	78.0%	22.0%
1946	73,340	54,729	Flanders, Ralph E.	18,594	McDevitt, Charles P.	17	36,135	R	74.6%	25.4%	74.6%	25.4%

Note: An asterisk (*) denotes incumbent. A pound sign (#) indicates that the winner was an independent. **In past elections, the other vote included: 2012 - 209,053 Independent (Bernard Sanders, who received 71.0 percent of the total vote and was re-elected with a plurality of 135,855 votes); 2006 - 171,638 Independent (Bernard Sanders, who received 65.4 percent of the total vote and was elected with a plurality of 86,714 votes). Sanders also won the Democratic primary in 2006 and 2012, but declined the nomination each time in order to run as an independent. The Democratic Party did not run a candidate in the 2006 or 2012 Senate election. The January 1972 election was for a short term to fill a vacancy. In 1968 the Republican candidate (George D. Aiken) won both major party nominations.

VERMONT

PRESIDENT 2016

2010 Census Population	County	Total Vote	Republican (Trump)	Democratic (Clinton)	Other	Rep.-Dem. Plurality		Total Vote Rep.	Total Vote Dem.	Major Vote Rep.	Major Vote Dem.
36,821	ADDISON	19,031	5,297	11,219	2,515	5,922	D	27.8%	59.0%	32.1%	67.9%
37,125	BENNINGTON	17,381	5,925	9,539	1,917	3,614	D	34.1%	54.9%	38.3%	61.7%
31,227	CALEDONIA	14,074	5,534	6,445	2,095	911	D	39.3%	45.8%	46.2%	53.8%
156,545	CHITTENDEN	83,416	18,601	54,814	10,001	36,213	D	22.3%	65.7%	25.3%	74.7%
6,306	ESSEX	2,925	1,506	1,019	400	487	R	51.5%	34.8%	59.6%	40.4%
47,746	FRANKLIN	21,411	8,752	9,351	3,308	599	D	40.9%	43.7%	48.3%	51.7%
6,970	GRAND ISLE	4,109	1,487	2,094	528	607	D	36.2%	51.0%	41.5%	58.5%
24,475	LAMOILLE	12,762	3,570	7,241	1,951	3,671	D	28.0%	56.7%	33.0%	67.0%
28,936	ORANGE	14,649	5,007	7,541	2,101	2,534	D	34.2%	51.5%	39.9%	60.1%
27,231	ORLEANS	12,046	5,159	5,185	1,702	26	D	42.8%	43.0%	49.9%	50.1%
61,642	RUTLAND	29,615	12,479	13,635	3,501	1,156	D	42.1%	46.0%	47.8%	52.2%
59,534	WASHINGTON	31,086	7,993	18,594	4,499	10,601	D	25.7%	59.8%	30.1%	69.9%
44,513	WINDHAM	22,634	5,454	14,340	2,840	8,886	D	24.1%	63.4%	27.6%	72.4%
56,670	WINDSOR	29,928	8,605	17,556	3,767	8,951	D	28.8%	58.7%	32.9%	67.1%
625,741	TOTAL	315,067	95,369	178,573	41,125	83,204	D	30.3%	56.7%	34.8%	65.2%

VERMONT

PRESIDENT 2016

2010 Census Population	City/Town	Total Vote	Republican (Trump)	Democratic (Clinton)	Other	Rep.-Dem. Plurality		Percentage			
								Total Vote		Major Vote	
								Rep.	Dem.	Rep.	Dem.
9,052	BARRE CITY	3,216	1,091	1,653	472	562	D	33.9%	51.4%	39.8%	60.2%
7,924	BARRE TOWN	4,168	1,862	1,760	546	102	R	44.7%	42.2%	51.4%	48.6%
15,764	BENNINGTON	6,025	1,949	3,361	715	1,412	D	32.3%	55.8%	36.7%	63.3%
12,046	BRATTLEBORO	5,937	859	4,347	731	3,488	D	14.5%	73.2%	16.5%	83.5%
42,417	BURLINGTON	18,937	2,082	14,519	2,336	12,437	D	11.0%	76.7%	12.5%	87.5%
17,067	COLCHESTER	7,763	2,425	4,483	855	2,058	D	31.2%	57.7%	35.1%	64.9%
4,621	DERBY	2,182	1,004	885	293	119	R	46.0%	40.6%	53.1%	46.9%
19,587	ESSEX	2,925	1,506	1,019	400	487	R	51.5%	34.8%	59.6%	40.4%
9,952	HARTFORD	5,137	1,303	3,190	644	1,887	D	25.4%	62.1%	29.0%	71.0%
5,009	JERICHO	3,325	890	2,017	418	1,127	D	26.8%	60.7%	30.6%	69.4%
5,981	LYNDON	2,062	883	827	352	56	R	42.8%	40.1%	51.6%	48.4%
4,391	MANCHESTER	2,393	706	1,452	235	746	D	29.5%	60.7%	32.7%	67.3%
8,496	MIDDLEBURY	3,667	595	2,682	390	2,087	D	16.2%	73.1%	18.2%	81.8%
10,352	MILTON	5,070	2,085	2,260	725	175	D	41.1%	44.6%	48.0%	52.0%
7,855	MONTPELIER	4,771	492	3,698	581	3,206	D	10.3%	77.5%	11.7%	88.3%
5,227	MORRISTOWN	2,707	741	1,550	416	809	D	27.4%	57.3%	32.3%	67.7%
6,207	NORTHFIELD	2,147	708	1,113	326	405	D	33.0%	51.8%	38.9%	61.1%
4,778	RANDOLPH	2,254	737	1,160	357	423	D	32.7%	51.5%	38.9%	61.1%
4,081	RICHMOND	2,524	515	1,694	315	1,179	D	20.4%	67.1%	23.3%	76.7%
5,282	ROCKINGHAM	2,155	576	1,315	264	739	D	26.7%	61.0%	30.5%	69.5%
16,495	RUTLAND CITY	7,097	2,734	3,495	868	761	D	38.5%	49.2%	43.9%	56.1%
4,054	RUTLAND TOWN	2,298	979	1,064	255	85	D	42.6%	46.3%	47.9%	52.1%
7,144	SHELBURNE	4,786	941	3,390	455	2,449	D	19.7%	70.8%	21.7%	78.3%
17,904	SOUTH BURLINGTON	10,400	2,059	7,246	1,095	5,187	D	19.8%	69.7%	22.1%	77.9%
9,373	SPRINGFIELD	3,953	1,510	1,873	570	363	D	38.2%	47.4%	44.6%	55.4%
6,918	ST. ALBANS CITY	2,505	807	1,287	411	480	D	32.2%	51.4%	38.5%	61.5%
5,999	ST. ALBANS TOWN	3,114	1,268	1,416	430	148	D	40.7%	45.5%	47.2%	52.8%
7,603	ST. JOHNSBURY	3,010	1,110	1,469	431	359	D	36.9%	48.8%	43.0%	57.0%
4,314	STOWE	2,841	559	1,974	308	1,415	D	19.7%	69.5%	22.1%	77.9%
6,427	SWANTON	2,670	1,192	1,101	377	91	R	44.6%	41.2%	52.0%	48.0%
5,064	WATERBURY	3,040	592	2,035	413	1,443	D	19.5%	66.9%	22.5%	77.5%
8,698	WILLISTON	5,602	1,481	3,508	613	2,027	D	26.4%	62.6%	29.7%	70.3%
7,267	WINOOSKI	3,068	536	2,105	427	1,569	D	17.5%	68.6%	20.3%	79.7%
3,048	WOODSTOCK	1,880	372	1,319	189	947	D	19.8%	70.2%	22.0%	78.0%

VERMONT

GOVERNOR 2016

2010 Census Population	County	Total Vote	Republican (Scott)	Democratic (Minter)	Other	Rep.-Dem. Plurality		Percentage			
								Total Vote		Major Vote	
								Rep.	Dem.	Rep.	Dem.
36,821	ADDISON	19,140	10,101	8,576	463	1,525	R	52.8%	44.8%	54.1%	45.9%
37,125	BENNINGTON	17,320	8,551	8,140	629	411	R	49.4%	47.0%	51.2%	48.8%
31,227	CALEDONIA	14,201	9,221	4,494	486	4,727	R	64.9%	31.6%	67.2%	32.8%
156,545	CHITTENDEN	83,223	38,277	42,993	1,953	4,716	D	46.0%	51.7%	47.1%	52.9%
6,306	ESSEX	2,907	2,056	736	115	1,320	R	70.7%	25.3%	73.6%	26.4%
47,746	FRANKLIN	21,522	14,512	6,425	585	8,087	R	67.4%	29.9%	69.3%	30.7%
6,970	GRAND ISLE	4,040	2,615	1,422	103	1,193	R	63.1%	34.3%	64.8%	35.2%
24,475	LAMOILLE	12,770	7,222	5,242	306	1,980	R	56.6%	41.0%	57.9%	42.1%
28,936	ORANGE	14,740	8,459	5,901	380	2,558	R	57.4%	40.0%	58.9%	41.1%
27,231	ORLEANS	12,068	8,291	3,299	478	4,992	R	68.7%	27.3%	71.5%	28.5%
61,642	RUTLAND	29,594	18,443	10,155	996	8,288	R	62.3%	34.3%	64.5%	35.5%
59,534	WASHINGTON	31,416	16,977	13,756	683	3,221	R	54.0%	43.8%	55.2%	44.8%
44,513	WINDHAM	22,406	8,084	13,372	950	5,288	D	36.1%	59.7%	37.7%	62.3%
56,670	WINDSOR	29,848	14,008	14,742	1,098	734	D	46.9%	49.4%	48.7%	51.3%
625,741	TOTAL	315,295	166,817	139,253	9,225	27,564	R	52.9%	44.2%	54.5%	45.5%

VERMONT

GOVERNOR 2016

2010 Census Population	City/Town	Total Vote	Republican (Scott)	Democratic (Minter)	Other	Rep.-Dem. Plurality		Percentage Total Vote Rep.	Dem.	Major Vote Rep.	Dem.
9,052	BARRE CITY	3,244	2,115	1,043	86	1,072	R	65.2%	32.2%	67.0%	33.0%
7,924	BARRE TOWN	4,253	3,282	909	62	2,373	R	77.2%	21.4%	78.3%	21.7%
15,764	BENNINGTON	6,012	2,646	3,117	249	471	D	44.0%	51.8%	45.9%	54.1%
12,046	BRATTLEBORO	5,846	1,321	4,286	239	2,965	D	22.6%	73.3%	23.6%	76.4%
42,417	BURLINGTON	18,613	5,028	12,946	639	7,918	D	27.0%	69.6%	28.0%	72.0%
17,067	COLCHESTER	7,850	4,478	3,184	188	1,294	R	57.0%	40.6%	58.4%	41.6%
4,621	DERBY	2,184	1,591	527	66	1,064	R	72.8%	24.1%	75.1%	24.9%
19,587	ESSEX	11,234	6,169	4,864	201	1,305	R	54.9%	43.3%	55.9%	44.1%
9,952	HARTFORD	5,107	2,151	2,773	183	622	D	42.1%	54.3%	43.7%	56.3%
5,009	JERICHO	3,309	1,702	1,548	59	154	R	51.4%	46.8%	52.4%	47.6%
5,981	LYNDON	2,051	1,410	572	69	838	R	68.7%	27.9%	71.1%	28.9%
4,391	MANCHESTER	2,380	1,231	1,084	65	147	R	51.7%	45.5%	53.2%	46.8%
8,496	MIDDLEBURY	3,651	1,351	2,212	88	861	D	37.0%	60.6%	37.9%	62.1%
10,352	MILTON	5,102	3,493	1,484	125	2,009	R	68.5%	29.1%	70.2%	29.8%
7,855	MONTPELIER	4,782	1,515	3,172	95	1,657	D	31.7%	66.3%	32.3%	67.7%
5,227	MORRISTOWN	2,738	1,566	1,095	77	471	R	57.2%	40.0%	58.9%	41.1%
6,207	NORTHFIELD	2,224	1,463	718	43	745	R	65.8%	32.3%	67.1%	32.9%
4,778	RANDOLPH	2,267	1,337	867	63	470	R	59.0%	38.2%	60.7%	39.3%
4,081	RICHMOND	2,538	1,173	1,302	63	129	D	46.2%	51.3%	47.4%	52.6%
5,282	ROCKINGHAM	2,134	809	1,227	98	418	D	37.9%	57.5%	39.7%	60.3%
16,495	RUTLAND CITY	7,069	4,190	2,611	268	1,579	R	59.3%	36.9%	61.6%	38.4%
4,054	RUTLAND TOWN	2,295	1,519	732	44	787	R	66.2%	31.9%	67.5%	32.5%
7,144	SHELBURNE	4,793	2,177	2,540	76	363	D	45.4%	53.0%	46.2%	53.8%
17,904	SOUTH BURLINGTON	10,385	4,609	5,586	190	977	D	44.4%	53.8%	45.2%	54.8%
9,373	SPRINGFIELD	3,924	2,161	1,578	185	583	R	55.1%	40.2%	57.8%	42.2%
6,918	ST. ALBANS CITY	2,511	1,469	976	66	493	R	58.5%	38.9%	60.1%	39.9%
5,999	ST. ALBANS TOWN	3,129	2,154	903	72	1,251	R	68.8%	28.9%	70.5%	29.5%
7,603	ST. JOHNSBURY	3,015	1,869	1,034	112	835	R	62.0%	34.3%	64.4%	35.6%
4,314	STOWE	2,796	1,372	1,421	3	49	D	49.1%	50.8%	49.1%	50.9%
6,427	SWANTON	2,681	1,867	730	84	1,137	R	69.6%	27.2%	71.9%	28.1%
5,064	WATERBURY	3,067	1,552	1,465	50	87	R	50.6%	47.8%	51.4%	48.6%
8,698	WILLISTON	5,619	3,153	2,371	95	782	R	56.1%	42.2%	57.1%	42.9%
7,267	WINOOSKI	3,034	1,057	1,885	92	828	D	34.8%	62.1%	35.9%	64.1%
3,048	WOODSTOCK	1,894	792	1,048	54	256	D	41.8%	55.3%	43.0%	57.0%

VERMONT

SENATOR 2016

2010 Census Population	County	Total Vote	Republican (Milne)	Democratic (Leahy)	Other	Rep.-Dem. Plurality		Percentage Total Vote Rep.	Dem.	Major Vote Rep.	Dem.
36,821	ADDISON	19,029	6,294	11,882	853	5,588	D	33.1%	62.4%	34.6%	65.4%
37,125	BENNINGTON	17,249	5,527	10,246	1,476	4,719	D	32.0%	59.4%	35.0%	65.0%
31,227	CALEDONIA	14,074	5,910	7,348	816	1,438	D	42.0%	52.2%	44.6%	55.4%
156,545	CHITTENDEN	82,848	21,654	57,338	3,856	35,684	D	26.1%	69.2%	27.4%	72.6%
6,306	ESSEX	2,891	1,356	1,324	211	32	R	46.9%	45.8%	50.6%	49.4%
47,746	FRANKLIN	21,478	8,526	11,948	1,004	3,422	D	39.7%	55.6%	41.6%	58.4%
6,970	GRAND ISLE	4,110	1,556	2,363	191	807	D	37.9%	57.5%	39.7%	60.3%
24,475	LAMOILLE	12,767	4,163	7,902	702	3,739	D	32.6%	61.9%	34.5%	65.5%
28,936	ORANGE	14,650	5,823	8,073	754	2,250	D	39.7%	55.1%	41.9%	58.1%
27,231	ORLEANS	11,973	5,199	6,033	741	834	D	43.4%	50.4%	46.3%	53.7%
61,642	RUTLAND	29,458	12,492	15,404	1,562	2,912	D	42.4%	52.3%	44.8%	55.2%
59,534	WASHINGTON	31,184	9,914	19,628	1,642	9,714	D	31.8%	62.9%	33.6%	66.4%
44,513	WINDHAM	22,301	5,410	14,720	2,171	9,310	D	24.3%	66.0%	26.9%	73.1%
56,670	WINDSOR	29,797	9,813	18,034	1,950	8,221	D	32.9%	60.5%	35.2%	64.8%
625,741	*TOTAL*	313,809	103,637	192,243	17,929	88,606	D	33.0%	61.3%	35.0%	65.0%

VERMONT

SENATOR 2016

2010 Census Population	City/Town	Total Vote	Republican (Milne)	Democratic (Leahy)	Other	Rep.-Dem. Plurality	Total Vote Rep.	Total Vote Dem.	Major Vote Rep.	Major Vote Dem.
9,052	BARRE CITY	3,240	1,279	1,784	177	505 D	39.5%	55.1%	41.8%	58.2%
7,924	BARRE TOWN	4,240	2,225	1,875	140	350 R	52.5%	44.2%	54.3%	45.7%
15,764	BENNINGTON	5,988	1,654	3,751	583	2,097 D	27.6%	62.6%	30.6%	69.4%
12,046	BRATTLEBORO	5,811	873	4,347	591	3,474 D	15.0%	74.8%	16.7%	83.3%
42,417	BURLINGTON	18,520	2,540	14,644	1,336	12,104 D	13.7%	79.1%	14.8%	85.2%
17,067	COLCHESTER	7,830	2,556	4,937	337	2,381 D	32.6%	63.1%	34.1%	65.9%
4,621	DERBY	2,180	980	1,073	127	93 D	45.0%	49.2%	47.7%	52.3%
19,587	ESSEX	11,187	3,528	7,282	377	3,754 D	31.5%	65.1%	32.6%	67.4%
9,952	HARTFORD	5,121	1,611	3,220	290	1,609 D	31.5%	62.9%	33.3%	66.7%
5,009	JERICHO	3,294	1,062	2,115	117	1,053 D	32.2%	64.2%	33.4%	66.6%
5,981	LYNDON	2,046	927	986	133	59 D	45.3%	48.2%	48.5%	51.5%
4,391	MANCHESTER	2,375	827	1,404	144	577 D	34.8%	59.1%	37.1%	62.9%
8,496	MIDDLEBURY	3,629	800	2,663	166	1,863 D	22.0%	73.4%	23.1%	76.9%
10,352	MILTON	5,009	2,171	2,662	176	491 D	43.3%	53.1%	44.9%	55.1%
7,855	MONTPELIER	4,753	728	3,767	258	3,039 D	15.3%	79.3%	16.2%	83.8%
5,227	MORRISTOWN	2,717	870	1,702	145	832 D	32.0%	62.6%	33.8%	66.2%
6,207	NORTHFIELD	2,200	837	1,235	128	398 D	38.0%	56.1%	40.4%	59.6%
4,778	RANDOLPH	2,258	857	1,272	129	415 D	38.0%	56.3%	40.3%	59.7%
4,081	RICHMOND	2,527	660	1,763	104	1,103 D	26.1%	69.8%	27.2%	72.8%
5,282	ROCKINGHAM	2,127	504	1,401	222	897 D	23.7%	65.9%	26.5%	73.5%
16,495	RUTLAND CITY	7,020	2,698	3,908	414	1,210 D	38.4%	55.7%	40.8%	59.2%
4,054	RUTLAND TOWN	2,284	1,024	1,179	81	155 D	44.8%	51.6%	46.5%	53.5%
7,144	SHELBURNE	4,807	1,214	3,459	134	2,245 D	25.3%	72.0%	26.0%	74.0%
17,904	SOUTH BURLINGTON	10,343	2,552	7,360	431	4,808 D	24.7%	71.2%	25.7%	74.3%
9,373	SPRINGFIELD	3,899	1,455	2,067	377	612 D	37.3%	53.0%	41.3%	58.7%
6,918	ST. ALBANS CITY	2,504	773	1,584	147	811 D	30.9%	63.3%	32.8%	67.2%
5,999	ST. ALBANS TOWN	3,130	1,229	1,777	124	548 D	39.3%	56.8%	40.9%	59.1%
7,603	ST. JOHNSBURY	2,985	1,174	1,623	188	449 D	39.3%	54.4%	42.0%	58.0%
4,314	STOWE	2,851	791	1,950	110	1,159 D	27.7%	68.4%	28.9%	71.1%
6,427	SWANTON	2,677	1,126	1,436	115	310 D	42.1%	53.6%	44.0%	56.0%
5,064	WATERBURY	3,026	780	2,120	126	1,340 D	25.8%	70.1%	26.9%	73.1%
8,698	WILLISTON	5,603	1,754	3,669	180	1,915 D	31.3%	65.5%	32.3%	67.7%
7,267	WINOOSKI	3,006	606	2,180	220	1,574 D	20.2%	72.5%	21.8%	78.2%
3,048	WOODSTOCK	1,893	564	1,261	68	697 D	29.8%	66.6%	30.9%	69.1%
316,397						0				

VERMONT

HOUSE OF REPRESENTATIVES

CD	Year	Total Vote	Republican Vote	Republican Candidate	Democratic Vote	Democratic Candidate	Other Vote	Rep.-Dem. Plurality	Total Vote Rep.	Total Vote Dem.	Major Vote Rep.	Major Vote Dem.
At Large	2016	295,334			264,414	WELCH, PETER*	30,920	264,414 D		89.5%		100.0%
At Large	2014	191,504	59,432	DONKA, MARK	123,349	WELCH, PETER*	8,723	63,917 D	31.0%	64.4%	32.5%	67.5%
At Large	2012	289,931	67,543	DONKA, MARK	208,600	WELCH, PETER*	13,788	141,057 D	23.3%	71.9%	24.5%	75.5%
At Large	2010	238,521	76,403	BEAUDRY, PAUL D.	154,006	WELCH, PETER*	8,112	77,603 D	32.0%	64.6%	33.2%	66.8%
At Large	2008	298,151			248,203	WELCH, PETER*	49,948	248,203 D		83.2%		100.0%
At Large	2006	262,726	117,023	RAINVILLE, MARTHA	139,815	WELCH, PETER	5,888	22,792 D	44.5%	53.2%	45.6%	54.4%
At Large	2004	305,008	74,271	PARKE, GREG	21,684	DROWN, LARRY	209,053	52,587 R#	24.4%	7.1%	77.4%	22.6%
At Large	2002	225,476	72,813	MEUB, WILLIAM			152,663	72,813 R#	32.3%		100.0%	
At Large	2000	283,366	51,977	KERIN, KAREN ANN	14,918	DIAMONDSTONE, PETE	216,471	37,059 R#	18.3%	5.3%	77.7%	22.3%
At Large	1998	215,133	70,740	CANDON, MARK			144,393	70,740 R#	32.9%		100.0%	
At Large	1996	254,706	83,021	SWEETSER, SUSAN W.	23,830	LONG, JACK	147,855	59,191 R#	32.6%	9.4%	77.7%	22.3%
At Large	1994	211,449	98,523	CARROLL, JOHN			112,926	98,523 R#	46.6%		100.0%	
At Large	1992	281,626	86,901	PHILBIN, TIMOTHY	22,279	YOUNG, LEWIS E.	172,446	64,622 R#	30.9%	7.9%	79.6%	20.4%
At Large	1990	209,856	82,938	SMITH, PETER*	6,315	SANDOVAL, DOLORES	120,603	76,623 R#	39.5%	3.0%	92.9%	7.1%
At Large	1988	240,131	98,937	SMITH, PETER	45,330	POIRIER, PAUL N.	95,864	53,607 R	41.2%	18.9%	68.6%	31.4%

VERMONT

HOUSE OF REPRESENTATIVES

CD	Year	Total Vote	Republican		Democratic		Other Vote	Rep.-Dem. Plurality	Percentage			
									Total Vote		Major Vote	
			Vote	Candidate	Vote	Candidate			Rep.	Dem.	Rep.	Dem.
At Large	1986	188,954	168,403	JEFFORDS, JAMES M.*			20,551	168,403 R	89.1%		100.0%	
At Large	1984	226,297	148,025	JEFFORDS, JAMES M.*	60,360	POLLINA, ANTHONY	17,912	87,665 R	65.4%	26.7%	71.0%	29.0%
At Large	1982	164,951	114,191	JEFFORDS, JAMES M.*	38,296	KAPLAN, MARK A.	12,464	75,895 R	69.2%	23.2%	74.9%	25.1%
At Large	1980	194,697	154,274	JEFFORDS, JAMES M.*			40,423	154,274 R	79.2%		100.0%	
At Large	1978	120,502	90,688	JEFFORDS, JAMES M.*	23,228	DIETZ, S. MARIE	6,586	67,460 R	75.3%	19.3%	79.6%	20.4%
At Large	1976	184,783	124,458	JEFFORDS, JAMES M.*	60,202	BURGESS, JOHN A.	123	64,256 R	67.4%	32.6%	67.4%	32.6%
At Large	1974	140,899	74,561	JEFFORDS, JAMES M.	56,342	CAIN, FRANCIS J.	9,996	18,219 R	52.9%	40.0%	57.0%	43.0%
At Large	1972	186,028	120,924	MALLARY, RICHARD W.	65,062	MEYER, WILLIAM H.	42	55,862 R	65.0%	35.0%	65.0%	35.0%
At Large	1970	152,557	103,806	STAFFORD, ROBERT T.*	44,415	O'SHEA, BERNARD G.	4,336	59,391 R	68.0%	29.1%	70.0%	30.0%
At Large	1968	157,133	156,956	STAFFORD, ROBERT T.*			177	156,956 R	99.9%		100.0%	
At Large	1966	135,748	89,097	STAFFORD, ROBERT T.*	46,643	RYAN, WILLIAM J.	8	42,454 R	65.6%	34.4%	65.6%	34.4%
At Large	1964	163,452	92,252	STAFFORD, ROBERT T.*	71,193	O'SHEA, BERNARD G.	7	21,059 R	56.4%	43.6%	56.4%	43.6%
At Large	1962	121,381	68,822	STAFFORD, ROBERT T.*	52,535	REYNOLDS, HAROLD	24	16,287 R	56.7%	43.3%	56.7%	43.3%
At Large	1960	166,035	94,905	STAFFORD, ROBERT T.	71,111	MEYER, WILLIAM H.*	19	23,794 R	57.2%	42.8%	57.2%	42.8%
At Large	1958	122,702	59,536	ARTHUR, HAROLD J.	63,131	MEYER, WILLIAM H.	35	3,595 D	48.5%	51.5%	48.5%	51.5%
At Large	1956	154,536	103,736	PROUTY, WINSTON L.*	50,797	ST. AMOUR, CAMILLE	3	52,939 R	67.1%	32.9%	67.1%	32.9%
At Large	1954	114,289	70,143	PROUTY, WINSTON L.*	44,141	BOYLAN, JOHN J.	5	26,002 R	61.4%	38.6%	61.4%	38.6%
At Large	1952	153,060	109,871	PROUTY, WINSTON L.*	43,187	COMINGS, HERBERT B.	2	66,684 R	71.8%	28.2%	71.8%	28.2%
At Large	1950	88,851	65,248	PROUTY, WINSTON L.	22,709	COMINGS, HERBERT B.	894	42,539 R	73.4%	25.6%	74.2%	25.8%
At Large	1948	121,968	74,076	PLUMLEY, CHARLES A.*	47,767	READY, ROBERT W.	125	26,309 R	60.7%	39.2%	60.8%	39.2%
At Large	1946	73,066	46,985	PLUMLEY, CHARLES A.*	26,056	CALDBECK, MATTHEW J.	25	20,929 R	64.3%	35.7%	64.3%	35.7%

Note: An asterisk (*) denotes incumbent. A pound sign (#) indicates that the winner was an independent (Bernard Sanders).

VERMONT

GENERAL AND PRIMARY ELECTIONS

2016 GENERAL ELECTIONS: OTHER VOTES

President Other vote was 18,218 Write-in (Bernard Sanders), 10,078 Libertarian (Gary Johnson), 6,758 Green (Jill Stein), 4,042 Write-in (Scattered Write-in), 1,063 Independent (Roque De La Fuente), 639 Write-in (Evan McMullin), 327 Liberty Union (Gloria La Riva)

Governor 8,912 Liberty Union (Bill Lee), 313 Write-in (Scattered Write-in)

Senate 9,156 Marijuana (Cris Ericson), 5,223 Independent (Jerry Trudell), 3,241 Liberty Union (Pete Diamondstone), 309 Write-in (Scattered Write-in)

House Other vote was:

  At Large 29,410 Liberty Union (Erica Clawson), 1,510 Write-in (Scattered Write-in)

2016 PRIMARY ELECTIONS: SUPPLEMENTARY INFORMATION

Primary March 1, 2016 (President) August 9, 2016 (Congress) **Registration** (as of August 9, 2016) 453,405 No Party Registration

Primary Type Open—Any registered voter could participate in the primary of any recognized party.

VERMONT

GENERAL AND PRIMARY ELECTIONS

	REPUBLICAN PRIMARIES			DEMOCRATIC PRIMARIES		
President	Trump, Donald J.	19,974	32.5%	Sanders, Bernard	115,900	86.0%
	Kasich, John R.	18,534	30.2%	Clinton, Hillary Rodham	18,338	13.6%
	Rubio, Marco	11,781	19.2%	O'Malley, Martin	282	0.2%
	Cruz, Ted	5,932	9.7%	Write-in	238	0.2%
	Carson, Ben	2,551	4.2%	De La Fuente, Roque "Rocky"	80	0.1%
	Bush, Jeb	1,106	1.8%			
	Paul, Rand	423	0.7%			
	Write-in	390	0.6%			
	Christie, Chris	361	0.6%			
	Fiorina, Carly	212	0.3%			
	Santorum, Rick	164	0.3%			
	TOTAL	61,428		TOTAL	134,838	
Senator	Milne, Scott	37,782	96.9%	Leahy, Patrick J.*	62,249	88.6%
	Write-In	1,223	3.1%	Ericson, Cris	7,596	10.8%
				Write-In	424	0.6%
	TOTAL	39,005		TOTAL	70,269	
Governor	Scott, Phil	27,728	60.3%	Minter, Sue	36,046	50.4%
	Lisman, Bruce M.	18,113	39.4%	Dunne, Matt	26,706	37.3%
	Write-In	114	0.2%	Galbraith, Peter	6,611	9.2%
				Write-In	1,328	1.9%
				Ericson, Cris	537	0.8%
				Paige, H. Brooke	361	0.5%
	TOTAL	45,955		TOTAL	71,589	
Congressional At Large	Welch, Peter	2,093	61.1%	Welch, Peter*	67,285	99.5%
	Write-In	1,335	38.9%	Write-In	345	0.5%
	TOTAL	3,428		TOTAL	67,630	

Note: An asterisk (*) denotes incumbent.

VIRGINIA

Congressional districts first established for elections held in 2016

11 members

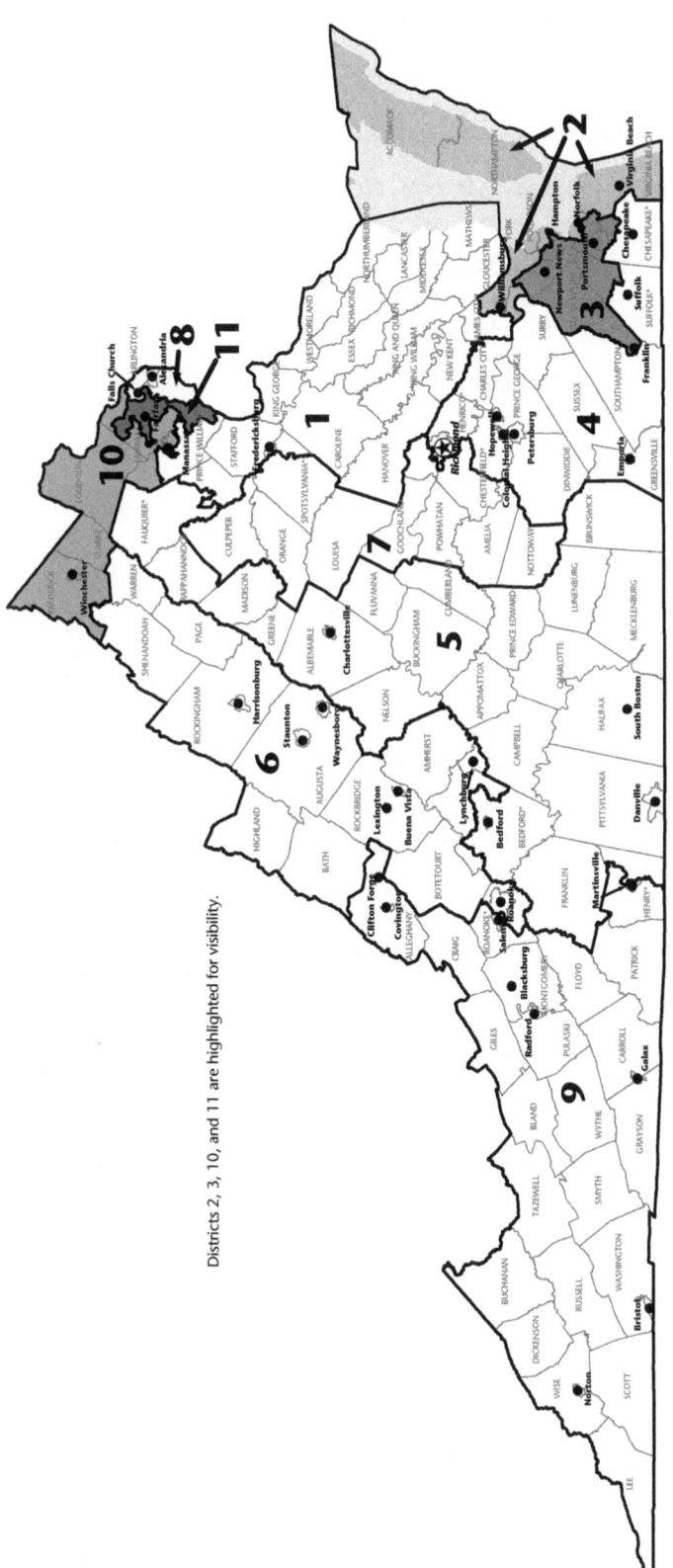

Districts 2, 3, 10, and 11 are highlighted for visibility.

Independent cities are treated as county equivalents; in most cases labels are included only for the city.

* Asterisk indicates a county whose boundaries include parts of two or more congressional districts.

VIRGINIA

GOVERNOR
Terry R. McAuliffe (D). Elected 2013 to a four-year term.

SENATORS (2 Democrats)
Tim Kaine (D). Elected 2012 to a six-year term.

Mark R. Warner (D). Re-elected 2014 to a six-year term. Previously elected 2008.

REPRESENTATIVES (7 Republicans, 4 Democrats)
1. Robert J. "Bob" Wittman (R)
2. Scott W. Taylor (R)
3. Robert C. Bobby Scott (D)
4. Donald McEachin (D)
5. Tom Garrett (R)
6. Bob Goodlatte (R)
7. Dave Brat (R)
8. Donald S. Beyer Jr. (D)
9. H. Morgan Griffith (R)
10. Barbara Comstock (R)
11. Gerald E. "Gerry" Connolly (D)

POSTWAR VOTE FOR PRESIDENT

| | | Republican | | Democratic | | | | Total Vote | | Major Vote | |
| | | | | | | Other | Rep.-Dem. | Percentage | | | |
Year	Total Vote	Vote	Candidate	Vote	Candidate	Vote	Plurality	Rep.	Dem.	Rep.	Dem.
2016**	3,982,752	1,769,443	Trump, Donald J.	1,981,473	Clinton, Hillary Rodham	231,836	212,030 D	44.4%	49.8%	47.2%	52.8%
2012	3,854,489	1,822,522	Romney, W. Mitt	1,971,820	Obama, Barack H.*	60,147	149,298 D	47.3%	51.2%	48.0%	52.0%
2008	3,723,260	1,725,005	McCain, John S. III	1,959,532	Obama, Barack H.	38,723	234,527 D	46.3%	52.6%	46.8%	53.2%
2004	3,198,367	1,716,959	Bush, George W.*	1,454,742	Kerry, John F.	26,666	262,217 R	53.7%	45.5%	54.1%	45.9%
2000**	2,739,447	1,437,490	Bush, George W.	1,217,290	Gore, Albert Jr.	84,667	220,200 R	52.5%	44.4%	54.1%	45.9%
1996**	2,416,642	1,138,350	Dole, Robert "Bob"	1,091,060	Clinton, Bill*	187,232	47,290 R	47.1%	45.1%	51.1%	48.9%
1992**	2,558,665	1,150,517	Bush, George H.*	1,038,650	Clinton, Bill	369,498	111,867 R	45.0%	40.6%	52.6%	47.4%
1988	2,191,609	1,309,162	Bush, George H.	859,799	Dukakis, Michael S.	22,648	449,363 R	59.7%	39.2%	60.4%	39.6%
1984	2,146,635	1,337,078	Reagan, Ronald*	796,250	Mondale, Walter F.	13,307	540,828 R	62.3%	37.1%	62.7%	37.3%
1980**	1,866,032	989,609	Reagan, Ronald	752,174	Carter, Jimmy*	124,249	237,435 R	53.0%	40.3%	56.8%	43.2%
1976	1,697,094	836,554	Ford, Gerald R.*	813,896	Carter, Jimmy	46,644	22,658 R	49.3%	48.0%	50.7%	49.3%
1972	1,457,019	988,493	Nixon, Richard M.*	438,887	McGovern, George S.	29,639	549,606 R	67.8%	30.1%	69.3%	30.7%
1968**	1,361,491	590,319	Nixon, Richard M.	442,387	Humphrey, Hubert Horatio Jr.	328,785	147,932 R	43.4%	32.5%	57.2%	42.8%
1964	1,042,267	481,334	Goldwater, Barry M. Sr.	558,038	Johnson, Lyndon B.*	2,895	76,704 D	46.2%	53.5%	46.3%	53.7%
1960	771,449	404,521	Nixon, Richard M.	362,327	Kennedy, John F.	4,601	42,194 R	52.4%	47.0%	52.8%	47.2%
1956	697,978	386,459	Eisenhower, Dwight D.*	267,760	Stevenson, Adlai E. II	43,759	118,699 R	55.4%	38.4%	59.1%	40.9%
1952	619,689	349,037	Eisenhower, Dwight D.	268,677	Stevenson, Adlai E. II	1,975	80,360 R	56.3%	43.4%	56.5%	43.5%
1948**	419,256	172,070	Dewey, Thomas E.	200,786	Truman, Harry S.*	46,400	28,716 D	41.0%	47.9%	46.1%	53.9%

Note: An asterisk (*) denotes incumbent. **In past elections, the other vote included: 2016 - 118,274 Libertarian (Gary Johnson); 2000 - 59,398 Green (Ralph Nader); 1996 - 159,861 Reform (Ross Perot); 1992 - 348,639 Independent (Perot); 1980 - 95,418 Independent (John Anderson); 1968 - 321,833 American Independent (George Wallace); 1948 - 43,393 States' Rights (Strom Thurmond).

VIRGINIA

POSTWAR VOTE FOR GOVERNOR

Year	Total Vote	Republican Vote	Republican Candidate	Democratic Vote	Democratic Candidate	Other Vote	Rep.-Dem. Plurality	Total Vote Rep.	Total Vote Dem.	Major Vote Rep.	Major Vote Dem.
2013	2,241,071	1,013,354	Cuccinelli, Ken	1,069,789	McAuliffe, Terry R.	157,928	56,435 D	45.2%	47.7%	48.6%	51.4%
2009	1,985,103	1,163,651	McDonnell, Robert F.	818,950	Deeds, R. Creigh	2,502	344,701 R	58.6%	41.3%	58.7%	41.3%
2005	1,983,778	912,327	Kilgore, Jerry W.	1,025,942	Kaine, Tim	45,509	113,615 D	46.0%	51.7%	47.1%	52.9%
2001	1,886,721	887,234	Earley, Mark	984,177	Warner, Mark R.	15,310	96,943 D	47.0%	52.2%	47.4%	52.6%
1997	1,736,314	969,062	Gilmore, James S. III	738,971	Beyer, Donald S. Jr.	28,281	230,091 R	55.8%	42.6%	56.7%	43.3%
1993	1,793,916	1,045,319	Allen, George F.	733,527	Terry, Mary Sue	15,070	311,792 R	58.3%	40.9%	58.8%	41.2%
1989	1,789,078	890,195	Coleman, J. Marshall	896,936	Wilder, L. Douglas	1,947	6,741 D	49.8%	50.1%	49.8%	50.2%
1985	1,343,240	601,649	Durrette, Wyatt B.	741,438	Baliles, Gerald L.	153	139,789 D	44.8%	55.2%	44.8%	55.2%
1981	1,420,638	659,398	Coleman, J. Marshall	760,384	Robb, Charles S.	856	100,986 D	46.4%	53.5%	46.4%	53.6%
1977	1,250,940	699,302	Dalton, John N.	541,319	Howell, Henry	10,319	157,983 R	55.9%	43.3%	56.4%	43.6%
1973**	1,035,495	525,075	Godwin, Mills E. Jr.			510,420	525,075 R	50.7%		100.0%	
1969	915,764	480,869	Holton, Linwood	415,695	Battle, William C.	19,200	65,174 R	52.5%	45.4%	53.6%	46.4%
1965**	562,789	212,207	Holton, Linwood	269,526	Godwin, Mills E. Jr.	81,056	57,319 D	37.7%	47.9%	44.1%	55.9%
1961	394,490	142,567	Pearson, H. Clyde	251,861	Harrison, Albertis S. Jr.	62	109,294 D	36.1%	63.8%	36.1%	63.9%
1957	517,655	188,628	Dalton, Ted	326,921	Almond, J. Lindsay Jr.	2,106	138,293 D	36.4%	63.2%	36.6%	63.4%
1953	414,025	183,328	Dalton, Ted	226,998	Stanley, Thomas B.	3,699	43,670 D	44.3%	54.8%	44.7%	55.3%
1949	262,350	71,991	Johnson, Walter	184,772	Battle, John S.	5,587	112,781 D	27.4%	70.4%	28.0%	72.0%
1945	164,741	52,386	Landreth, S. Lloyd	112,355	Tuck, William M.		59,969 D	31.8%	68.2%	31.8%	68.2%

Note: An asterisk (*) denotes incumbent. **In past elections, the other vote included: 1973 - 510,103 Independent (Henry Howell); 1965 - 75,307 Conservative (William J. Story Jr.). The plurality is the difference between the Republican and Democratic vote. The Democratic Party did not run a candidate in the 1973 gubernatorial election.

POSTWAR VOTE FOR SENATOR

Year	Total Vote	Republican Vote	Republican Candidate	Democratic Vote	Democratic Candidate	Other Vote	Rep.-Dem. Plurality	Total Vote Rep.	Total Vote Dem.	Major Vote Rep.	Major Vote Dem.
2014	2,184,473	1,055,940	Gillespie, Edward W. "Ed"	1,073,667	Warner, Mark R.*	54,866	17,727 D	48.3%	49.1%	49.6%	50.4%
2012	3,802,196	1,785,542	Allen, George F.	2,010,067	Kaine, Tim	6,587	224,525 D	47.0%	52.9%	47.0%	53.0%
2008	3,643,294	1,228,830	Gilmore, James S. III	2,369,327	Warner, Mark R.	45,137	1,140,497 D	33.7%	65.0%	34.2%	65.8%
2006	2,370,445	1,166,277	Allen, George F.*	1,175,606	Webb, Jim H. Jr.	28,562	9,329 D	49.2%	49.6%	49.8%	50.2%
2002	1,489,422	1,229,894	Warner, John W.*			259,528	1,229,894 R	82.6%		100.0%	
2000	2,718,301	1,420,460	Allen, George F.	1,296,093	Robb, Charles S.*	1,748	124,367 R	52.3%	47.7%	52.3%	47.7%
1996	2,354,715	1,235,744	Warner, John W.*	1,115,982	Warner, Mark R.	2,989	119,762 R	52.5%	47.4%	52.5%	47.5%
1994**	2,057,463	882,213	North, Oliver L.	938,376	Robb, Charles S.*	236,874	56,163 D	42.9%	45.6%	48.5%	51.5%
1990**	1,083,660	876,782	Warner, John W.*			206,878	876,782 R	80.9%		100.0%	
1988	2,068,897	593,652	Dawkins, Maurice A.	1,474,086	Robb, Charles S.	1,159	880,434 D	28.7%	71.2%	28.7%	71.3%
1984	2,007,487	1,406,194	Warner, John W.*	601,142	Harrison, Edythe C.	151	805,052 R	70.0%	29.9%	70.1%	29.9%
1982	1,415,622	724,571	Trible, Paul	690,839	Davis, Richard	212	33,732 R	51.2%	48.8%	51.2%	48.8%
1978	1,222,256	613,232	Warner, John W.	608,511	Miller, Andrew P.	513	4,721 R	50.2%	49.8%	50.2%	49.8%
1976**	1,557,500			596,009	Zumwalt, Elmo R.	961,491	596,009 D#		38.3%		100.0%
1972	1,396,268	718,337	Scott, William L.	643,963	Spong, William B.*	33,968	74,374 R	51.4%	46.1%	52.7%	47.3%
1970**	946,751	145,031	Garland, Ray L.	295,057	Rawlings, George C.	506,663	150,026 D#	15.3%	31.2%	33.0%	67.0%
1966	733,879	245,681	Ould, James P. Jr.	429,855	Spong, William B.	58,343	184,174 D	33.5%	58.6%	36.4%	63.6%
1966S**	729,839	272,804	Traylor, Lawrence M.	389,028	Byrd, Harry Flood Jr.*	68,007	116,224 D	37.4%	53.3%	41.2%	58.8%
1964**	928,363	176,624	May, Richard A.	592,260	Byrd, Harry F.*	159,479	415,636 D	19.0%	63.8%	23.0%	77.0%
1960**	622,820			506,169	Robertson, A. Willis*	116,651	506,169 D		81.3%		100.0%
1958**	457,640			317,221	Byrd, Harry F.*	140,419	317,221 D		69.3%		100.0%
1954**	306,447			244,844	Robertson, A. Willis*	61,603	244,844 D		79.9%		100.0%
1952**	543,516			398,677	Byrd, Harry F.*	144,839	398,677 D		73.4%		100.0%
1948	386,998	119,366	Woods, Robert H.	253,865	Robertson, A. Willis*	13,767	134,499 D	30.8%	65.6%	32.0%	68.0%
1946	252,863	77,005	Parsons, Lester S.	163,960	Byrd, Harry F.*	11,898	86,955 D	30.5%	64.8%	32.0%	68.0%
1946S**	248,962	72,253	Woods, Robert H.	169,680	Robertson, A. Willis	7,029	97,427 D	29.0%	68.2%	29.9%	70.1%

Note: An asterisk (*) denotes incumbent. A pound sign (#) indicates that winner was an independent. **In past elections, the other vote included: 1994 - 235,324 Independent (J. Marshall Coleman); 1990 - 196,755 Independent (Nancy Spannaus, who finished second); 1976 - 890,778 Independent (Harry Flood Byrd Jr., who won the election with 57.2 percent of the total vote and a plurality of 294,769 votes); 1970 - 506,633 Independent (Harry Flood Byrd Jr., who won the election with 53.5 percent of the total vote and a plurality of 211,576 votes); 1964 - 95,526 Independent (James W. Respess); 1960 - 88,718 Independent Democrat (Stuart D. Baker, who finished second); 1958 - 120,224 Independent (Louis Wensel, who finished second); 1954 - 32,681 Independent Democrat (Charles William Lewis Jr., who finished second); 1952 - 69,133 Independent Democrat (H. M. Vise Sr., who finished second); 67,281 Social Democrat (Clarke T. Robb). One each of the 1946 and 1966 elections was for a short term to fill a vacancy. The Democratic Party did not run a candidate in the Senate elections of 1990 and 2002. The Republican Party did not run a candidate in the Senate elections of 1952, 1954, 1958, 1960, and 1976.

VIRGINIA

PRESIDENT 2016

2010 Census Population	County/City	Total Vote	Republican (Trump)	Democratic (Clinton)	Other	Rep.-Dem. Plurality	Percentage — Total Vote Rep.	Dem.	Percentage — Major Vote Rep.	Dem.
33,164	ACCOMACK	15,818	8,583	6,740	495	1,843 R	54.3%	42.6%	56.0%	44.0%
98,970	ALBEMARLE	56,726	19,259	33,345	4,122	14,086 D	34.0%	58.8%	36.6%	63.4%
16,250	ALLEGHANY	7,325	4,874	2,166	285	2,708 R	66.5%	29.6%	69.2%	30.8%
12,690	AMELIA	7,040	4,708	2,128	204	2,580 R	66.9%	30.2%	68.9%	31.1%
32,353	AMHERST	15,396	9,719	5,057	620	4,662 R	63.1%	32.8%	65.8%	34.2%
14,973	APPOMATTOX	7,997	5,715	2,023	259	3,692 R	71.5%	25.3%	73.9%	26.1%
207,627	ARLINGTON	121,339	20,186	92,016	9,137	71,830 D	16.6%	75.8%	18.0%	82.0%
73,750	AUGUSTA	36,343	26,163	8,177	2,003	17,986 R	72.0%	22.5%	76.2%	23.8%
4,731	BATH	2,253	1,548	603	102	945 R	68.7%	26.8%	72.0%	28.0%
68,676	BEDFORD	42,525	30,659	9,768	2,098	20,891 R	72.1%	23.0%	75.8%	24.2%
6,824	BLAND	3,139	2,573	453	113	2,120 R	82.0%	14.4%	85.0%	15.0%
33,148	BOTETOURT	18,739	13,375	4,494	870	8,881 R	71.4%	24.0%	74.9%	25.1%
17,434	BRUNSWICK	7,669	3,046	4,481	142	1,435 D	39.7%	58.4%	40.5%	59.5%
24,098	BUCHANAN	9,247	7,296	1,721	230	5,575 R	78.9%	18.6%	80.9%	19.1%
17,146	BUCKINGHAM	7,289	3,950	3,128	211	822 R	54.2%	42.9%	55.8%	44.2%
54,842	CAMPBELL	27,535	19,551	6,664	1,320	12,887 R	71.0%	24.2%	74.6%	25.4%
28,545	CAROLINE	14,248	7,147	6,432	669	715 R	50.2%	45.1%	52.6%	47.4%
30,042	CARROLL	13,655	10,663	2,559	433	8,104 R	78.1%	18.7%	80.6%	19.4%
7,256	CHARLES CITY	4,107	1,476	2,496	135	1,020 D	35.9%	60.8%	37.2%	62.8%
12,586	CHARLOTTE	5,807	3,479	2,155	173	1,324 R	59.9%	37.1%	61.8%	38.2%
316,236	CHESTERFIELD	176,362	85,045	81,074	10,243	3,971 R	48.2%	46.0%	51.2%	48.8%
14,034	CLARKE	8,213	4,661	3,051	501	1,610 R	56.8%	37.1%	60.4%	39.6%
5,190	CRAIG	2,791	2,140	541	110	1,599 R	76.7%	19.4%	79.8%	20.2%
46,689	CULPEPER	22,218	13,349	7,759	1,110	5,590 R	60.1%	34.9%	63.2%	36.8%
10,052	CUMBERLAND	4,906	2,697	2,036	173	661 R	55.0%	41.5%	57.0%	43.0%
15,903	DICKENSON	6,440	4,932	1,335	173	3,597 R	76.6%	20.7%	78.7%	21.3%
28,001	DINWIDDIE	13,575	7,447	5,765	363	1,682 R	54.9%	42.5%	56.4%	43.6%
11,151	ESSEX	5,372	2,657	2,542	173	115 R	49.5%	47.3%	51.1%	48.9%
1,081,726	FAIRFAX	551,183	157,710	355,133	38,340	197,423 D	28.6%	64.4%	30.8%	69.2%
65,203	FAUQUIER	37,460	22,127	12,971	2,362	9,156 R	59.1%	34.6%	63.0%	37.0%
15,279	FLOYD	8,050	5,293	2,300	457	2,993 R	65.8%	28.6%	69.7%	30.3%
25,691	FLUVANNA	13,592	7,025	5,760	807	1,265 R	51.7%	42.4%	54.9%	45.1%
56,159	FRANKLIN	26,971	18,569	7,257	1,145	11,312 R	68.8%	26.9%	71.9%	28.1%
78,305	FREDERICK	40,440	26,083	11,932	2,425	14,151 R	64.5%	29.5%	68.6%	31.4%
17,286	GILES	8,212	5,910	1,950	352	3,960 R	72.0%	23.7%	75.2%	24.8%
36,858	GLOUCESTER	19,619	13,096	5,404	1,119	7,692 R	66.8%	27.5%	70.8%	29.2%
21,717	GOOCHLAND	14,037	8,384	4,889	764	3,495 R	59.7%	34.8%	63.2%	36.8%
15,533	GRAYSON	7,285	5,592	1,407	286	4,185 R	76.8%	19.3%	79.9%	20.1%
18,403	GREENE	9,607	5,945	2,924	738	3,021 R	61.9%	30.4%	67.0%	33.0%
12,243	GREENSVILLE	4,363	1,737	2,558	68	821 D	39.8%	58.6%	40.4%	59.6%
36,241	HALIFAX	16,994	9,704	6,897	393	2,807 R	57.1%	40.6%	58.5%	41.5%
99,863	HANOVER	62,723	39,630	19,382	3,711	20,248 R	63.2%	30.9%	67.2%	32.8%
306,935	HENRICO	163,536	59,857	93,935	9,744	34,078 D	36.6%	57.4%	38.9%	61.1%
54,151	HENRY	24,091	15,208	8,198	685	7,010 R	63.1%	34.0%	65.0%	35.0%
2,321	HIGHLAND	1,391	958	371	62	587 R	68.9%	26.7%	72.1%	27.9%
35,270	ISLE OF WIGHT	21,075	12,204	7,881	990	4,323 R	57.9%	37.4%	60.8%	39.2%
67,009	JAMES CITY	43,169	21,306	19,105	2,758	2,201 R	49.4%	44.3%	52.7%	47.3%
6,945	KING AND QUEEN	3,690	2,099	1,468	123	631 R	56.9%	39.8%	58.8%	41.2%
23,584	KING GEORGE	12,050	7,341	4,007	702	3,334 R	60.9%	33.3%	64.7%	35.3%
15,935	KING WILLIAM	9,146	5,975	2,760	411	3,215 R	65.3%	30.2%	68.4%	31.6%
11,391	LANCASTER	6,645	3,523	2,869	253	654 R	53.0%	43.2%	55.1%	44.9%
25,587	LEE	9,399	7,543	1,627	229	5,916 R	80.3%	17.3%	82.3%	17.7%
312,311	LOUDOUN	183,050	69,949	100,795	12,306	30,846 D	38.2%	55.1%	41.0%	59.0%
33,153	LOUISA	17,612	10,528	6,212	872	4,316 R	59.8%	35.3%	62.9%	37.1%
12,914	LUNENBURG	5,586	3,204	2,227	155	977 R	57.4%	39.9%	59.0%	41.0%
13,308	MADISON	6,979	4,419	2,203	357	2,216 R	63.3%	31.6%	66.7%	33.3%
8,978	MATHEWS	5,311	3,517	1,563	231	1,954 R	66.2%	29.4%	69.2%	30.8%
32,727	MECKLENBURG	14,945	8,288	6,285	372	2,003 R	55.5%	42.1%	56.9%	43.1%
10,959	MIDDLESEX	6,017	3,670	2,108	239	1,562 R	61.0%	35.0%	63.5%	36.5%
94,392	MONTGOMERY	43,031	19,459	20,021	3,551	562 D	45.2%	46.5%	49.3%	50.7%

VIRGINIA

PRESIDENT 2016

2010 Census Population	County/City	Total Vote	Republican (Trump)	Democratic (Clinton)	Other	Rep.-Dem. Plurality	Percentage Total Vote Rep.	Dem.	Major Vote Rep.	Dem.
15,020	NELSON	8,311	4,154	3,689	468	465 R	50.0%	44.4%	53.0%	47.0%
18,429	NEW KENT	12,233	8,118	3,546	569	4,572 R	66.4%	29.0%	69.6%	30.4%
12,389	NORTHAMPTON	6,168	2,686	3,255	227	569 D	43.5%	52.8%	45.2%	54.8%
12,330	NORTHUMBERLAND	7,397	4,302	2,852	243	1,450 R	58.2%	38.6%	60.1%	39.9%
15,853	NOTTOWAY	6,744	3,712	2,829	203	883 R	55.0%	41.9%	56.7%	43.3%
33,481	ORANGE	17,267	10,521	5,957	789	4,564 R	60.9%	34.5%	63.8%	36.2%
24,042	PAGE	10,740	7,831	2,514	395	5,317 R	72.9%	23.4%	75.7%	24.3%
18,490	PATRICK	8,525	6,454	1,768	303	4,686 R	75.7%	20.7%	78.5%	21.5%
63,506	PITTSYLVANIA	31,598	21,554	9,199	845	12,355 R	68.2%	29.1%	70.1%	29.9%
28,046	POWHATAN	16,888	11,885	4,060	943	7,825 R	70.4%	24.0%	74.5%	25.5%
23,368	PRINCE EDWARD	9,143	4,101	4,591	451	490 D	44.9%	50.2%	47.2%	52.8%
35,725	PRINCE GEORGE	16,184	9,157	6,419	608	2,738 R	56.6%	39.7%	58.8%	41.2%
402,002	PRINCE WILLIAM	196,442	71,721	113,144	11,577	41,423 D	36.5%	57.6%	38.8%	61.2%
34,872	PULASKI	15,165	10,322	4,172	671	6,150 R	68.1%	27.5%	71.2%	28.8%
7,373	RAPPAHANNOCK	4,483	2,539	1,747	197	792 R	56.6%	39.0%	59.2%	40.8%
9,254	RICHMOND	3,661	2,213	1,347	101	866 R	60.4%	36.8%	62.2%	37.8%
92,376	ROANOKE	51,489	31,408	17,200	2,881	14,208 R	61.0%	33.4%	64.6%	35.4%
22,307	ROCKBRIDGE	10,795	6,680	3,508	607	3,172 R	61.9%	32.5%	65.6%	34.4%
76,314	ROCKINGHAM	37,487	25,990	9,366	2,131	16,624 R	69.3%	25.0%	73.5%	26.5%
28,897	RUSSELL	12,246	9,521	2,330	395	7,191 R	77.7%	19.0%	80.3%	19.7%
23,177	SCOTT	10,100	8,247	1,581	272	6,666 R	81.7%	15.7%	83.9%	16.1%
41,993	SHENANDOAH	20,508	14,094	5,273	1,141	8,821 R	68.7%	25.7%	72.8%	27.2%
32,208	SMYTH	12,890	9,750	2,665	475	7,085 R	75.6%	20.7%	78.5%	21.5%
18,570	SOUTHAMPTON	8,872	5,035	3,595	242	1,440 R	56.8%	40.5%	58.3%	41.7%
122,397	SPOTSYLVANIA	62,549	34,623	24,207	3,719	10,416 R	55.4%	38.7%	58.9%	41.1%
128,961	STAFFORD	65,934	33,868	27,908	4,158	5,960 R	51.4%	42.3%	54.8%	45.2%
7,058	SURRY	4,228	1,819	2,272	137	453 D	43.0%	53.7%	44.5%	55.5%
12,087	SUSSEX	5,044	2,055	2,879	110	824 D	40.7%	57.1%	41.6%	58.4%
45,078	TAZEWELL	18,566	15,168	2,895	503	12,273 R	81.7%	15.6%	84.0%	16.0%
37,575	WARREN	17,951	11,773	5,169	1,009	6,604 R	65.6%	28.8%	69.5%	30.5%
54,876	WASHINGTON	25,846	19,320	5,553	973	13,767 R	74.8%	21.5%	77.7%	22.3%
17,454	WESTMORELAND	8,574	4,448	3,836	290	612 R	51.9%	44.7%	53.7%	46.3%
41,452	WISE	15,163	12,086	2,701	376	9,385 R	79.7%	17.8%	81.7%	18.3%
29,235	WYTHE	13,328	10,046	2,770	512	7,276 R	75.4%	20.8%	78.4%	21.6%
65,464	YORK	34,113	18,837	12,999	2,277	5,838 R	55.2%	38.1%	59.2%	40.8%
	Independent Cities									
139,966	ALEXANDRIA	75,762	13,285	57,242	5,235	43,957 D	17.5%	75.6%	18.8%	81.2%
17,835	BRISTOL	7,027	4,892	1,835	300	3,057 R	69.6%	26.1%	72.7%	27.3%
6,650	BUENA VISTA	2,407	1,430	693	284	737 R	59.4%	28.8%	67.4%	32.6%
43,475	CHARLOTTESVILLE	22,467	2,960	17,901	1,606	14,941 D	13.2%	79.7%	14.2%	85.8%
222,209	CHESAPEAKE	112,662	54,047	52,627	5,988	1,420 R	48.0%	46.7%	50.7%	49.3%
17,411	COLONIAL HEIGHTS	8,457	5,681	2,367	409	3,314 R	67.2%	28.0%	70.6%	29.4%
5,961	COVINGTON	2,382	1,349	914	119	435 R	56.6%	38.4%	59.6%	40.4%
43,055	DANVILLE	18,940	7,303	11,059	578	3,756 D	38.6%	58.4%	39.8%	60.2%
5,927	EMPORIA	2,366	789	1,530	47	741 D	33.3%	64.7%	34.0%	66.0%
22,565	FAIRFAX CITY	12,028	3,702	7,367	959	3,665 D	30.8%	61.2%	33.4%	66.6%
12,332	FALLS CHURCH	7,757	1,324	5,819	614	4,495 D	17.1%	75.0%	18.5%	81.5%
8,582	FRANKLIN CITY	4,061	1,421	2,519	121	1,098 D	35.0%	62.0%	36.1%	63.9%
24,286	FREDERICKSBURG	11,257	3,744	6,707	806	2,963 D	33.3%	59.6%	35.8%	64.2%
7,042	GALAX	2,376	1,603	681	92	922 R	67.5%	28.7%	70.2%	29.8%
137,436	HAMPTON	62,277	17,902	41,312	3,063	23,410 D	28.7%	66.3%	30.2%	69.8%
48,914	HARRISONBURG	17,987	6,262	10,212	1,513	3,950 D	34.8%	56.8%	38.0%	62.0%
22,591	HOPEWELL	9,008	3,885	4,724	399	839 D	43.1%	52.4%	45.1%	54.9%
7,042	LEXINGTON	2,465	766	1,514	185	748 D	31.1%	61.4%	33.6%	66.4%
75,568	LYNCHBURG	35,657	17,982	14,792	2,883	3,190 R	50.4%	41.5%	54.9%	45.1%
37,821	MANASSAS	15,411	5,953	8,423	1,035	2,470 D	38.6%	54.7%	41.4%	58.6%
14,273	MANASSAS PARK	5,232	1,733	3,204	295	1,471 D	33.1%	61.2%	35.1%	64.9%
13,821	MARTINSVILLE	5,907	2,149	3,533	225	1,384 D	36.4%	59.8%	37.8%	62.2%
180,719	NEWPORT NEWS	75,637	25,468	45,618	4,551	20,150 D	33.7%	60.3%	35.8%	64.2%
242,803	NORFOLK CITY	83,385	21,552	57,023	4,810	35,471 D	25.8%	68.4%	27.4%	72.6%

VIRGINIA

PRESIDENT 2016

2010 Census Population	County/City	Total Vote	Republican (Trump)	Democratic (Clinton)	Other	Rep.-Dem. Plurality	Total Vote Rep.	Total Vote Dem.	Major Vote Rep.	Major Vote Dem.
3,958	NORTON	1,460	1,021	383	56	638 R	69.9%	26.2%	72.7%	27.3%
32,420	PETERSBURG	13,786	1,451	12,021	314	10,570 D	10.5%	87.2%	10.8%	89.2%
12,150	POQUOSON	7,177	5,092	1,601	484	3,491 R	70.9%	22.3%	76.1%	23.9%
95,535	PORTSMOUTH	43,261	12,795	28,497	1,969	15,702 D	29.6%	65.9%	31.0%	69.0%
16,408	RADFORD	6,082	2,638	2,925	519	287 D	43.4%	48.1%	47.4%	52.6%
204,214	RICHMOND CITY	103,406	15,581	81,259	6,566	65,678 D	15.1%	78.6%	16.1%	83.9%
97,032	ROANOKE CITY	39,466	14,789	22,286	2,391	7,497 D	37.5%	56.5%	39.9%	60.1%
24,802	SALEM	12,225	7,226	4,202	797	3,024 R	59.1%	34.4%	63.2%	36.8%
23,746	STAUNTON	11,255	5,133	5,333	789	200 D	45.6%	47.4%	49.0%	51.0%
84,585	SUFFOLK	43,240	18,006	23,280	1,954	5,274 D	41.6%	53.8%	43.6%	56.4%
437,994	VIRGINIA BEACH	203,019	98,224	91,032	13,763	7,192 R	48.4%	44.8%	51.9%	48.1%
21,006	WAYNESBORO	9,204	4,801	3,764	639	1,037 R	52.2%	40.9%	56.1%	43.9%
14,068	WILLIAMSBURG	7,626	1,925	5,206	495	3,281 D	25.2%	68.3%	27.0%	73.0%
26,203	WINCHESTER	10,665	4,790	5,164	711	374 D	44.9%	48.4%	48.1%	51.9%
	TOTAL	*3,982,752*	*1,769,443*	*1,981,473*	*231,836*	*212,030 D*	*44.4%*	*49.8%*	*47.2%*	*52.8%*

VIRGINIA

HOUSE OF REPRESENTATIVES

CD	Year	Total Vote	Rep. Vote	Republican Candidate	Dem. Vote	Democratic Candidate	Other Vote	Rep.-Dem. Plurality	Total Vote Rep.	Total Vote Dem.	Major Vote Rep.	Major Vote Dem.
1	2016	384,655	230,213	WITTMAN, ROBERT J. "ROB"*	140,785	ROWE, MATT	13,657	89,428 R	59.8%	36.6%	62.1%	37.9%
1	2014	209,621	131,861	WITTMAN, ROBERT J. "ROB"*	72,059	MOSHER, NORMAN "NORM"	5,701	59,802 R	62.9%	34.4%	64.7%	35.3%
1	2012	356,806	200,845	WITTMAN, ROBERT J. "ROB"*	147,036	COOK, ADAM M.	8,925	53,809 R	56.3%	41.2%	57.7%	42.3%
2	2016	310,640	190,475	TAYLOR, SCOTT	119,440	BROWN, SHAUN DENISE	725	71,035 R	61.3%	38.4%	61.5%	38.5%
2	2014	173,060	101,558	RIGELL, E. SCOTT*	71,178	PATRICK, SUZANNE	324	30,380 R	58.7%	41.1%	58.8%	41.2%
2	2012	309,222	166,231	RIGELL, E. SCOTT*	142,548	HIRSCHBIEL, PAUL O. JR.	443	23,683 R	53.8%	46.1%	53.8%	46.2%
3	2016	312,371	103,289	WILLIAMS, MARTIN "MARTY"	208,337	SCOTT, ROBERT C. "BOBBY"*	745	105,048 D	33.1%	66.7%	33.1%	66.9%
3	2014	147,402			139,197	SCOTT, ROBERT C. "BOBBY"*	8,205	139,197 D		94.4%		100.0%
3	2012	318,936	58,931	LONGO, DEAN J.	259,199	SCOTT, ROBERT C. "BOBBY"*	806	200,268 D	18.5%	81.3%	18.5%	81.5%
4	2016	346,699	145,731	WADE, MIKE	200,136	MCEACHIN, A. DONALD	832	54,405 D	42.0%	57.7%	42.1%	57.9%
4	2014	200,638	120,684	FORBES, J. RANDY*	75,270	FAUSZ, ELLIOTT	4,684	45,414 R	60.2%	37.5%	61.6%	38.4%
4	2012	350,046	199,292	FORBES, J. RANDY*	150,190	WARD, ELLA P.	564	49,102 R	56.9%	42.9%	57.0%	43.0%
5	2016**	356,765	207,758	GARRETT, TOM	148,339	DITTMAR, JANE	668	59,419 R	58.2%	41.6%	58.3%	41.7%
5	2014	204,945	124,735	HURT, ROBERT*	73,482	GAUGHAN, WALTER LAWRENCE	6,728	51,253 R	60.9%	35.9%	62.9%	37.1%
5	2012	348,111	193,009	HURT, ROBERT*	149,214	DOUGLASS, JOHN WADE	5,888	43,795 R	55.4%	42.9%	56.4%	43.6%
6	2016**	338,456	225,471	GOODLATTE, ROBERT W. "BOB"*	112,170	DEGNER, KAI	815	113,301 R	66.6%	33.1%	66.8%	33.2%
6	2014	179,708	133,898	GOODLATTE, ROBERT W. "BOB"*			45,810	133,898 R	74.5%		100.0%	
6	2012	323,893	211,278	GOODLATTE, ROBERT W. "BOB"*	111,949	SCHMOOKLER, ANDY	666	99,329 R	65.2%	34.6%	65.4%	34.6%
7	2016	379,209	218,057	BRAT, DAVID*	160,159	BEDELL, EILEEN	993	57,898 R	57.5%	42.2%	57.7%	42.3%
7	2014	243,351	148,026	BRAT, DAVID	89,914	TRAMMELL, JOHN K. "JACK"	5,411	58,112 R	60.8%	36.9%	62.2%	37.8%
7	2012	381,909	222,983	CANTOR, ERIC I.*	158,012	POWELL, E. WAYNE	914	64,971 R	58.4%	41.4%	58.5%	41.5%
8	2016**	360,687	98,387	HERNICK, CHARLES ALAN	246,653	BEYER, DONALD S. JR.*	15,647	148,266 D	27.3%	68.4%	28.5%	71.5%
8	2014	203,076	63,810	EDMOND, MICAH	128,102	BEYER, DONALD S. JR.	11,164	64,292 D	31.4%	63.1%	33.2%	66.8%
8	2012	351,187	107,370	MURRAY, J. PATRICK	226,847	MORAN, JAMES P. JR.*	16,970	119,477 D	30.6%	64.6%	32.1%	67.9%
9	2016**	310,327	212,838	GRIFFITH, H. MORGAN*	87,877	KITTS, DEREK	9,612	124,961 R	68.6%	28.3%	70.8%	29.2%
9	2014	162,815	117,465	GRIFFITH, H. MORGAN*			45,350	117,465 R	72.1%		100.0%	
9	2012	301,658	184,882	GRIFFITH, H. MORGAN*	116,400	FLACCAVENTO, ANTHONY J.	376	68,482 R	61.3%	38.6%	61.4%	38.6%

VIRGINIA

HOUSE OF REPRESENTATIVES

			Republican		Democratic				Total Vote		Major Vote	
CD	Year	Total Vote	Vote	Candidate	Vote	Candidate	Other Vote	Rep.-Dem. Plurality	Rep.	Dem.	Rep.	Dem.
10	2016**	400,117	210,791	COMSTOCK, BARBARA*	187,712	BENNETT, LUANN	1,614	23,079 R	52.7%	46.9%	52.9%	47.1%
10	2014	222,910	125,914	COMSTOCK, BARBARA	89,957	FOUST, JOHN	7,039	35,957 R	56.5%	40.4%	58.3%	41.7%
10	2012	366,444	214,038	WOLF, FRANK R.*	142,024	CABRAL, KRISTIN A.	10,382	72,014 R	58.4%	38.8%	60.1%	39.9%
11	2016**	282,322			247,818	CONNOLLY, GERALD E. "GERRY"*	34,504	247,818 D		87.8%		100.0%
11	2014	187,787	75,796	SCHOLTE, SUZANNE	106,780	CONNOLLY, GERALD E. "GERRY"*	5,211	30,984 D	40.4%	56.9%	41.5%	58.5%
11	2012	332,243	117,902	PERKINS, CHRIS S.	202,606	CONNOLLY, GERALD E. "GERRY"*	11,735	84,704 D	35.5%	61.0%	36.8%	63.2%
TOTAL	2016	3,782,248	1,843,010		1,859,426		79,812	16,416 D	48.7%	49.2%	49.8%	50.2%
TOTAL	2014	2,135,313	1,143,747		845,939		145,627	297,808 R	53.6%	39.6%	57.5%	42.5%
TOTAL	2012	3,740,455	1,876,761		1,806,025		57,669	70,736 R	50.2%	48.3%	51.0%	49.0%

Note: An asterisk (*) denotes incumbent. **Due to mid-decade redistricting, boundaries for all districts except CD 5, 6, 8, 9, 10, and 11 are not comparable to those used in the 2012 and 2014 races.

VIRGINIA

GENERAL AND PRIMARY ELECTIONS

2016 GENERAL ELECTIONS: OTHER VOTES

President Other vote was 118,274 Libertarian (Gary Johnson), 54,054 Independent (Evan McMullin), 31,870 Write-in (Scattered Write-Ins), 27,638 Green (Jill Stein)

House Other vote was:

CD 1   12,866 Independent (Glenda Parker), 791 Write-in (Scattered Write-in)
CD 2   725 Write-in (Scattered Write-in)
CD 3   745 Write-in (Scattered Write-in)
CD 4   832 Write-in (Scattered Write-in)
CD 5   668 Write-in (Scattered Write-in)
CD 6   815 Write-in (Scattered Write-in)
CD 7   993 Write-in (Scattered Write-in)
CD 8   14,664 Independent (Julio Garcia), 983 Write-in (Scattered Write-in)
CD 9   9,050 Independent (Janice Boyd), 562 Write-in (Scattered Write-in)
CD 10 1,614 Write-in (Scattered Write-in)
CD 11 34,504 Write-in (Scattered Write-in)

2016 PRIMARY ELECTIONS: SUPPLEMENTARY INFORMATION

Primary March 1, 2016 (President) June 14, 2016 (Congress)   **Registration** (as of June 1, 2016 – includes 515,620 inactive registrants)   5,354,785   No Party Registration

Primary Type Open—Any registered voter could participate in the primary of either party.

VIRGINIA

GENERAL AND PRIMARY ELECTIONS

	REPUBLICAN PRIMARIES			DEMOCRATIC PRIMARIES		
President	Trump, Donald J.	356,896	34.8%	Clinton, Hillary Rodham	504,791	64.3%
	Rubio, Marco	327,936	32.0%	Sanders, Bernard	276,387	35.2%
	Cruz, Ted	171,162	16.7%	O'Malley, Martin	3,930	0.5%
	Kasich, John R.	97,791	9.5%	Write-In	82	
	Carson, Ben	60,237	5.9%			
	Bush, Jeb	3,645	0.4%			
	Paul, Rand	2,920	0.3%			
	Huckabee, Mike	1,459	0.1%			
	Christie, Chris	1,102	0.1%			
	Fiorina, Carly	914	0.1%			
	Gilmore, James S. III	653	0.1%			
	Graham, Lindsey	444				
	Santorum, Rick	399				
	Write-In	59				
	TOTAL	*1,025,617*		*TOTAL*	*785,190*	
Congressional District 1	Wittman, Robert J. "Rob"*	Unopposed		Rowe, Matt	Unopposed	
Congressional District 2	Taylor, Scott W.	21,406	52.5%	Brown, Shaun Denise	Unopposed	
	Forbes, J. Randy*	16,552	40.6%			
	Cardwell, C. Pat	2,773	6.8%			
	Write-In	6				
	TOTAL	*40,737*				
Congressional District 3	Williams, Martin "Marty"	Unopposed		Scott, Robert C. "Bobby"*	Unopposed	
Congressional District 4	Wade, Mike	4,987	64.0%	McEachin, A. Donald	11,851	75.3%
	Gonzalez, Jackee	2,801	36.0%	Ward, Ella P.	3,867	24.6%
	Write-In	1		Write-In	10	0.1%
	TOTAL	*7,789*		*TOTAL*	*15,728*	
Congressional District 5	Garrett, Tom	Unopposed		Dittmar, Jane	Unopposed	
Congressional District 6	Goodlatte, Robert W. "Bob"*	18,993	77.9%	Degner, Kai	Unopposed	
	Griego, Harry	5,383	22.1%			
	TOTAL	*24,376*				
Congressional District 7	Brat, David*	Unopposed		Bedell, Eileen	Unopposed	
Congressional District 8	Hernick, Charles Alan	Unopposed		Beyer, Donald S. Jr.*	Unopposed	
Congressional District 9	Griffith, H. Morgan*	Unopposed		Kitts, Derek	Unopposed	
Congressional District 10	Comstock, Barbara*	Unopposed		Bennett, LuAnn	Unopposed	
Congressional District 11				Connolly, Gerald E. "Gerry"*	Unopposed	

Note: An asterisk (*) denotes incumbent.

WASHINGTON

Congressional districts first established for elections held in 2012
10 members

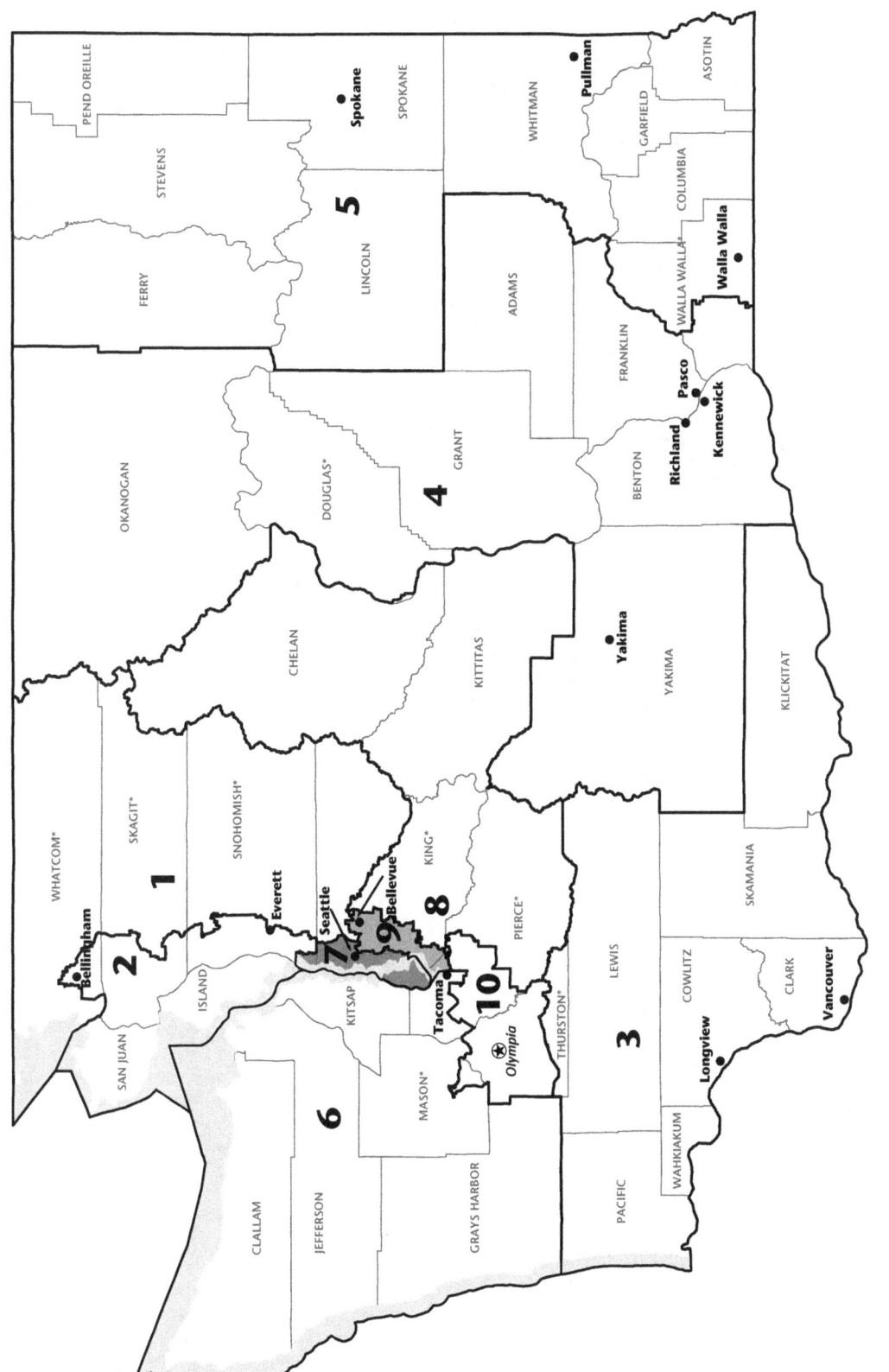

WASHINGTON
Seattle Area

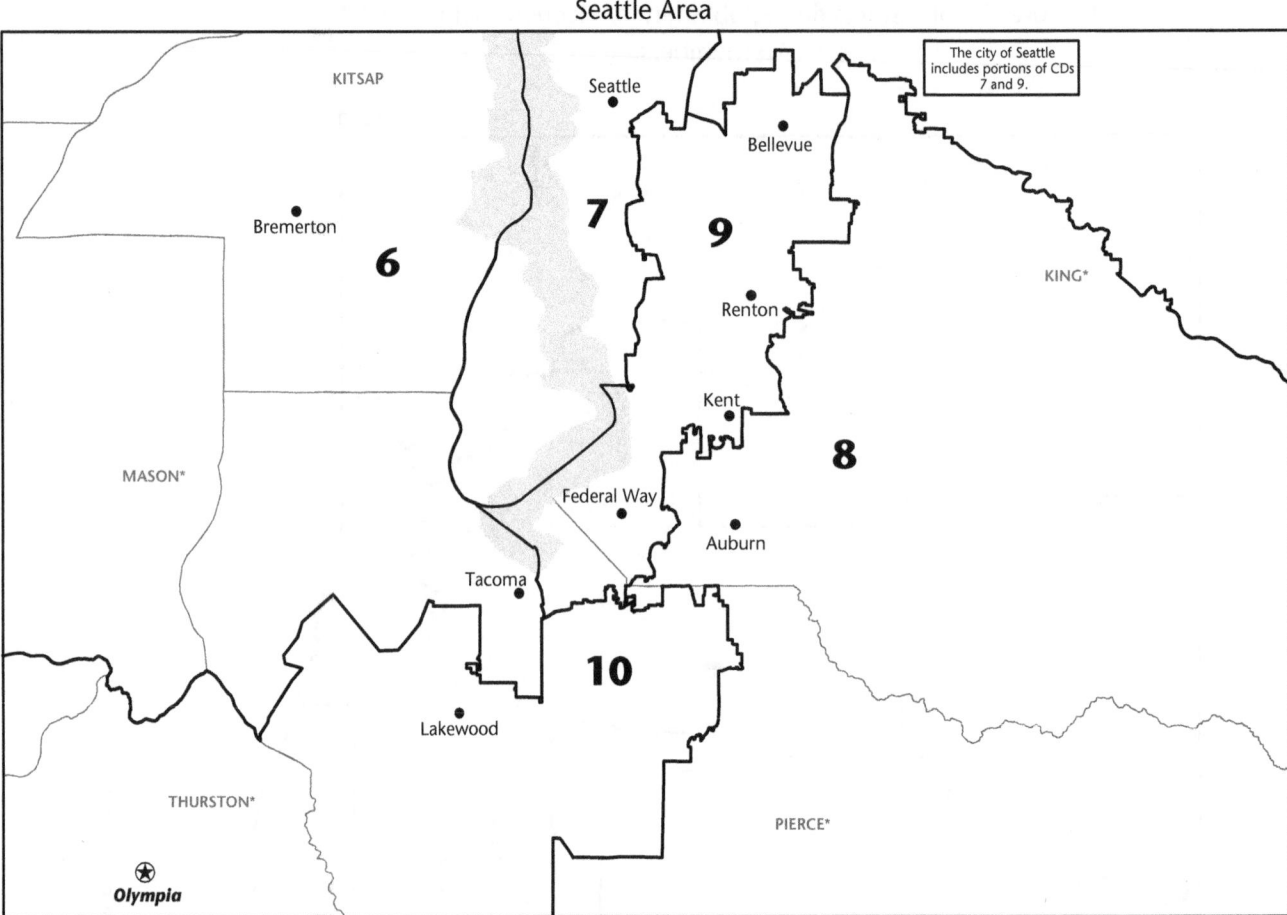

* Asterisk indicates a county whose boundaries include parts of two or more congressional districts.

WASHINGTON

GOVERNOR

Jay Inslee (D). Re-elected 2016 to a four-year term. Previously elected 2012.

SENATORS (2 Democrats)

Maria Cantwell (D). Re-elected 2012 to a six-year term. Previously elected 2006, 2000.

Patty Murray (D). Re-elected 2016 to a six-year term. Previously elected 2010, 2004, 1998, 1992.

REPRESENTATIVES (4 Republicans, 6 Democrats)

1. Suzan DelBene (D)
2. Rick Larsen (D)
3. Jaime Herrera Beutler (R)
4. Dan Newhouse (R)
5. Cathy McMorris Rodgers (R)
6. Derek Kilmer (D)
7. Pramila Jayapal (D)
8. David George "Dave" Reichert (R)
9. Adam Smith (D)
10. Denny Heck (D)

POSTWAR VOTE FOR PRESIDENT

Year	Total Vote	Republican Vote	Republican Candidate	Democratic Vote	Democratic Candidate	Other Vote	Rep.-Dem. Plurality	Total Vote Rep.	Total Vote Dem.	Major Vote Rep.	Major Vote Dem.
2016**	3,317,019	1,221,747	Trump, Donald J.	1,742,718	Clinton, Hillary Rodham	352,554	520,971 D	36.8%	52.5%	41.2%	58.8%
2012	3,125,516	1,290,670	Romney, W. Mitt	1,755,396	Obama, Barack H.*	79,450	464,726 D	41.3%	56.2%	42.4%	57.6%
2008	3,036,878	1,229,216	McCain, John S. III	1,750,848	Obama, Barack H.	56,814	521,632 D	40.5%	57.7%	41.2%	58.8%
2004	2,859,084	1,304,894	Bush, George W.*	1,510,201	Kerry, John F.	43,989	205,307 D	45.6%	52.8%	46.4%	53.6%
2000**	2,487,433	1,108,864	Bush, George W.	1,247,652	Gore, Albert Jr.	130,917	138,788 D	44.6%	50.2%	47.1%	52.9%
1996**	2,253,837	840,712	Dole, Robert "Bob"	1,123,323	Clinton, Bill*	289,802	282,611 D	37.3%	49.8%	42.8%	57.2%
1992**	2,288,230	731,234	Bush, George H.*	993,037	Clinton, Bill	563,959	261,803 D	32.0%	43.4%	42.4%	57.6%
1988	1,865,253	903,835	Bush, George H.	933,516	Dukakis, Michael S.	27,902	29,681 D	48.5%	50.0%	49.2%	50.8%
1984	1,883,910	1,051,670	Reagan, Ronald*	807,352	Mondale, Walter F.	24,888	244,318 R	55.8%	42.9%	56.6%	43.4%
1980**	1,742,394	865,244	Reagan, Ronald	650,193	Carter, Jimmy*	226,957	215,051 R	49.7%	37.3%	57.1%	42.9%
1976	1,555,534	777,732	Ford, Gerald R.*	717,323	Carter, Jimmy	60,479	60,409 R	50.0%	46.1%	52.0%	48.0%
1972	1,470,847	837,135	Nixon, Richard M.*	568,334	McGovern, George S.	65,378	268,801 R	56.9%	38.6%	59.6%	40.4%
1968**	1,304,281	588,510	Nixon, Richard M.	616,037	Humphrey, Hubert Horatio Jr.	99,734	27,527 D	45.1%	47.2%	48.9%	51.1%
1964	1,258,556	470,366	Goldwater, Barry M. Sr.	779,881	Johnson, Lyndon B.*	8,309	309,515 D	37.4%	62.0%	37.6%	62.4%
1960	1,241,572	629,273	Nixon, Richard M.	599,298	Kennedy, John F.	13,001	29,975 R	50.7%	48.3%	51.2%	48.8%
1956	1,150,889	620,430	Eisenhower, Dwight D.*	523,002	Stevenson, Adlai E. II	7,457	97,428 R	53.9%	45.4%	54.3%	45.7%
1952	1,102,708	599,107	Eisenhower, Dwight D.	492,845	Stevenson, Adlai E. II	10,756	106,262 R	54.3%	44.7%	54.9%	45.1%
1948	905,058	386,314	Dewey, Thomas E.	476,165	Truman, Harry S.*	42,579	89,851 D	42.7%	52.6%	44.8%	55.2%

Note: An asterisk (*) denotes incumbent. **In past elections, the other vote included: 2016 - 160,879 Libertarian (Gary Johnson); 2000 - 103,002 Green (Ralph Nader); 1996 - 201,003 Reform (Ross Perot); 1992 - 541,780 Independent (Perot); 1980 - 185,073 Independent (John Anderson); 1968 - 96,990 American Independent (George Wallace).

WASHINGTON

POSTWAR VOTE FOR GOVERNOR

Year	Total Vote	Republican		Democratic		Other Vote	Rep.-Dem. Plurality	Percentage			
		Vote	Candidate	Vote	Candidate			Total Vote		Major Vote	
								Rep.	Dem.	Rep.	Dem.
2016	3,245,282	1,476,346	Bryant, Bill	1,760,520	Inslee, Jay*	8,416	284,174 D	45.5%	54.2%	45.6%	54.4%
2012	3,071,047	1,488,245	McKenna, Rob	1,582,802	Inslee, Jay		94,557 D	48.5%	51.5%	48.5%	51.5%
2008	3,002,862	1,404,124	Rossi, Dino	1,598,738	Gregoire, Christine*		194,614 D	46.8%	53.2%	46.8%	53.2%
2004**	2,810,058	1,373,232	Rossi, Dino	1,373,361	Gregoire, Christine	63,465	129 D	48.9%	48.9%	50.0%	50.0%
2000	2,469,852	980,060	Carlson, John	1,441,973	Locke, Gary*	47,819	461,913 D	39.7%	58.4%	40.5%	59.5%
1996	2,237,030	940,538	Craswell, Ellen	1,296,492	Locke, Gary		355,954 D	42.0%	58.0%	42.0%	58.0%
1992	2,270,826	1,086,216	Eikenberry, Ken	1,184,315	Lowry, Mike	295	98,099 D	47.8%	52.2%	47.8%	52.2%
1988	1,874,929	708,481	Williams, Bob	1,166,448	Gardner, Booth*		457,967 D	37.8%	62.2%	37.8%	62.2%
1984	1,888,987	881,994	Spellman, John D.*	1,006,993	Gardner, Booth		124,999 D	46.7%	53.3%	46.7%	53.3%
1980	1,730,896	981,083	Spellman, John D.	749,813	McDermott, James A.		231,270 R	56.7%	43.3%	56.7%	43.3%
1976	1,546,380	687,039	Spellman, John D.	821,797	Ray, Dixy Lee	37,544	134,758 D	44.4%	53.1%	45.5%	54.5%
1972	1,472,542	747,825	Evans, Daniel J.*	630,613	Rosellini, Albert D.	94,104	117,212 R	50.8%	42.8%	54.3%	45.7%
1968	1,265,354	692,377	Evans, Daniel J.*	560,262	O'Connell, John J.	12,715	132,115 R	54.7%	44.3%	55.3%	44.7%
1964	1,250,274	697,256	Evans, Daniel J.	548,692	Rosellini, Albert D.*	4,326	148,564 R	55.8%	43.9%	56.0%	44.0%
1960	1,215,748	594,122	Andrews, Lloyd J.	611,987	Rosellini, Albert D.*	9,639	17,865 D	48.9%	50.3%	49.3%	50.7%
1956	1,128,977	508,041	Anderson, Emmett T.	616,773	Rosellini, Albert D.	4,163	108,732 D	45.0%	54.6%	45.2%	54.8%
1952	1,078,497	567,822	Langlie, Arthur B.*	510,675	Mitchell, Hugh B.		57,147 R	52.6%	47.4%	52.6%	47.4%
1948	883,141	445,958	Langlie, Arthur B.	417,035	Wallgren, Monrad C.*	20,148	28,923 R	50.5%	47.2%	51.7%	48.3%

Note: An asterisk (*) denotes incumbent. **In 2004, the initial official vote count put Republican Dino Rossi ahead by 261 votes. A machine recount reduced Rossi's margin to 42 votes. A subsequent manual recount gave Democrat Christine Gregoire the election by a margin of 129 votes (see above), and she was inaugurated governor.

POSTWAR VOTE FOR SENATOR

Year	Total Vote	Republican		Democratic		Other Vote	Rep.-Dem. Plurality	Percentage			
		Vote	Candidate	Vote	Candidate			Total Vote		Major Vote	
								Rep.	Dem.	Rep.	Dem.
2016	3,243,317	1,329,338	Vance, Chris	1,913,979	Murray, Patty*		584,641 D	41.0%	59.0%	41.0%	59.0%
2012	3,069,417	1,213,924	Baumgartner, Michael	1,855,493	Cantwell, Maria*		641,569 D	39.5%	60.5%	39.5%	60.5%
2010	2,511,094	1,196,164	Rossi, Dino	1,314,930	Murray, Patty*		118,766 D	47.6%	52.4%	47.6%	52.4%
2006	2,083,734	832,106	McGavick, Mike	1,184,659	Cantwell, Maria*	66,969	352,553 D	39.9%	56.9%	41.3%	58.7%
2004	2,818,651	1,204,584	Nethercutt, George R.	1,549,708	Murray, Patty*	64,359	345,124 D	42.7%	55.0%	43.7%	56.3%
2000	2,461,379	1,197,208	Gorton, Slade*	1,199,437	Cantwell, Maria	64,734	2,229 D	48.6%	48.7%	50.0%	50.0%
1998	1,888,561	785,377	Smith, Linda	1,103,184	Murray, Patty*		317,807 D	41.6%	58.4%	41.6%	58.4%
1994	1,700,173	947,821	Gorton, Slade*	752,352	Sims, Ron		195,469 R	55.7%	44.3%	55.7%	44.3%
1992	2,219,162	1,020,829	Chandler, Rod	1,197,973	Murray, Patty	360	177,144 D	46.0%	54.0%	46.0%	54.0%
1988	1,848,542	944,359	Gorton, Slade	904,183	Lowry, Mike		40,176 R	51.1%	48.9%	51.1%	48.9%
1986	1,337,367	650,931	Gorton, Slade*	677,471	Adams, Brock	8,965	26,540 D	48.7%	50.7%	49.0%	51.0%
1983S**	1,213,307	672,326	Evans, Daniel J.*	540,981	Lowry, Mike		131,345 R	55.4%	44.6%	55.4%	44.6%
1982	1,368,476	332,273	Jewett, Doug	943,655	Jackson, Henry M.*	92,548	611,382 D	24.3%	69.0%	26.0%	74.0%
1980	1,728,369	936,317	Gorton, Slade	792,052	Magnuson, Warren G.*		144,265 R	54.2%	45.8%	54.2%	45.8%
1976	1,491,111	361,546	Brown, George M.	1,071,219	Jackson, Henry M.*	58,346	709,673 D	24.2%	71.8%	25.2%	74.8%
1974	1,007,847	363,626	Metcalf, Jack	611,811	Magnuson, Warren G.*	32,410	248,185 D	36.1%	60.7%	37.3%	62.7%
1970	1,066,807	170,790	Elicker, Charles W.	879,385	Jackson, Henry M.*	16,632	708,595 D	16.0%	82.4%	16.3%	83.7%
1968	1,236,063	435,894	Metcalf, Jack	796,183	Magnuson, Warren G.*	3,986	360,289 D	35.3%	64.4%	35.4%	64.6%
1964	1,213,088	337,138	Andrews, Lloyd J.	875,950	Jackson, Henry M.*		538,812 D	27.8%	72.2%	27.8%	72.2%
1962	943,229	446,204	Christensen, Richard G.	491,365	Magnuson, Warren G.*	5,660	45,161 D	47.3%	52.1%	47.6%	52.4%
1958	886,822	278,271	Bantz, William B.	597,040	Jackson, Henry M.*	11,511	318,769 D	31.4%	67.3%	31.8%	68.2%
1956	1,122,217	436,652	Langlie, Arthur B.	685,565	Magnuson, Warren G.*		248,913 D	38.9%	61.1%	38.9%	61.1%
1952	1,058,735	460,884	Cain, Harry P.*	595,288	Jackson, Henry M.	2,563	134,404 D	43.5%	56.2%	43.6%	56.4%
1950	744,783	342,464	Williams, Walter	397,719	Magnuson, Warren G.*	4,600	55,255 D	46.0%	53.4%	46.3%	53.7%
1946	660,342	358,847	Cain, Harry P.	298,683	Mitchell, Hugh B.	2,812	60,164 R	54.3%	45.2%	54.6%	45.4%

Note: An asterisk (*) denotes incumbent. **The 1983 election was for a short term to fill a vacancy.

WASHINGTON

PRESIDENT 2016

2010 Census Population	County	Total Vote	Republican (Trump)	Democratic (Clinton)	Other	Rep.-Dem. Plurality	Percentage Total Vote Rep.	Dem.	Major Vote Rep.	Dem.
18,728	ADAMS	4,782	3,083	1,299	400	1,784 R	64.5%	27.2%	70.4%	29.6%
21,623	ASOTIN	9,974	5,741	3,134	1,099	2,607 R	57.6%	31.4%	64.7%	35.3%
175,177	BENTON	83,592	47,194	26,360	10,038	20,834 R	56.5%	31.5%	64.2%	35.8%
72,453	CHELAN	34,433	18,114	13,032	3,287	5,082 R	52.6%	37.8%	58.2%	41.8%
71,404	CLALLAM	40,533	18,794	17,677	4,062	1,117 R	46.4%	43.6%	51.5%	48.5%
425,363	CLARK	208,485	92,441	92,757	23,287	316 D	44.3%	44.5%	49.9%	50.1%
4,078	COLUMBIA	2,229	1,497	526	206	971 R	67.2%	23.6%	74.0%	26.0%
102,410	COWLITZ	47,142	24,185	17,908	5,049	6,277 R	51.3%	38.0%	57.5%	42.5%
38,431	DOUGLAS	15,901	9,603	4,918	1,380	4,685 R	60.4%	30.9%	66.1%	33.9%
7,551	FERRY	3,687	2,202	1,098	387	1,104 R	59.7%	29.8%	66.7%	33.3%
78,163	FRANKLIN	24,614	13,206	8,886	2,522	4,320 R	53.7%	36.1%	59.8%	40.2%
2,266	GARFIELD	1,246	851	279	116	572 R	68.3%	22.4%	75.3%	24.7%
89,120	GRANT	29,258	18,518	7,810	2,930	10,708 R	63.3%	26.7%	70.3%	29.7%
72,797	GRAYS HARBOR	29,301	14,067	12,020	3,214	2,047 R	48.0%	41.0%	53.9%	46.1%
78,506	ISLAND	44,273	18,465	20,960	4,848	2,495 D	41.7%	47.3%	46.8%	53.2%
29,872	JEFFERSON	20,879	6,037	12,656	2,186	6,619 D	28.9%	60.6%	32.3%	67.7%
1,931,249	KING	1,028,450	216,339	718,322	93,789	501,983 D	21.0%	69.8%	23.1%	76.9%
251,133	KITSAP	128,770	49,018	63,156	16,596	14,138 D	38.1%	49.0%	43.7%	56.3%
40,915	KITTITAS	19,615	10,100	7,489	2,026	2,611 R	51.5%	38.2%	57.4%	42.6%
20,318	KLICKITAT	11,074	5,789	4,194	1,091	1,595 R	52.3%	37.9%	58.0%	42.0%
75,455	LEWIS	35,199	21,992	9,654	3,553	12,338 R	62.5%	27.4%	69.5%	30.5%
10,570	LINCOLN	5,861	4,108	1,244	509	2,864 R	70.1%	21.2%	76.8%	23.2%
60,699	MASON	29,003	13,677	11,993	3,333	1,684 R	47.2%	41.4%	53.3%	46.7%
41,120	OKANOGAN	17,556	9,610	6,298	1,648	3,312 R	54.7%	35.9%	60.4%	39.6%
20,920	PACIFIC	10,972	5,360	4,620	992	740 R	48.9%	42.1%	53.7%	46.3%
13,001	PEND OREILLE	7,016	4,373	1,934	709	2,439 R	62.3%	27.6%	69.3%	30.7%
795,225	PIERCE	360,017	146,824	172,538	40,655	25,714 D	40.8%	47.9%	46.0%	54.0%
15,769	SAN JUAN	11,134	2,688	7,172	1,274	4,484 D	24.1%	64.4%	27.3%	72.7%
116,901	SKAGIT	58,059	24,736	26,690	6,633	1,954 D	42.6%	46.0%	48.1%	51.9%
11,066	SKAMANIA	5,829	2,928	2,232	669	696 R	50.2%	38.3%	56.7%	43.3%
713,335	SNOHOMISH	354,734	128,255	185,227	41,252	56,972 D	36.2%	52.2%	40.9%	59.1%
471,221	SPOKANE	236,050	113,435	93,767	28,848	19,668 R	48.1%	39.7%	54.7%	45.3%
43,531	STEVENS	23,395	15,161	5,767	2,467	9,394 R	64.8%	24.7%	72.4%	27.6%
252,264	THURSTON	134,191	48,624	68,798	16,769	20,174 D	36.2%	51.3%	41.4%	58.6%
3,978	WAHKIAKUM	2,429	1,344	832	253	512 R	55.3%	34.3%	61.8%	38.2%
58,781	WALLA WALLA	26,228	13,651	9,694	2,883	3,957 R	52.0%	37.0%	58.5%	41.5%
201,140	WHATCOM	113,339	40,599	60,340	12,400	19,741 D	35.8%	53.2%	40.2%	59.8%
44,776	WHITMAN	18,028	7,403	8,146	2,479	743 D	41.1%	45.2%	47.6%	52.4%
243,231	YAKIMA	79,741	41,735	31,291	6,715	10,444 R	52.3%	39.2%	57.2%	42.8%
6,724,540	TOTAL	3,317,019	1,221,747	1,742,718	352,554	520,971 D	36.8%	52.5%	41.2%	58.8%

WASHINGTON

GOVERNOR 2016

2010 Census Population	County	Total Vote	Republican (Bryant)	Democratic (Inslee)	Other	Rep.-Dem. Plurality	Percentage Total Vote Rep.	Dem.	Major Vote Rep.	Dem.
18,728	ADAMS	4,696	3,151	1,533	12	1,618 R	67.1%	32.6%	67.3%	32.7%
21,623	ASOTIN	9,771	5,609	4,149	13	1,460 R	57.4%	42.5%	57.5%	42.5%
175,177	BENTON	82,030	50,730	31,128	172	19,602 R	61.8%	37.9%	62.0%	38.0%
72,453	CHELAN	33,865	19,934	13,866	65	6,068 R	58.9%	40.9%	59.0%	41.0%
71,404	CLALLAM	39,602	20,108	19,354	140	754 R	50.8%	48.9%	51.0%	49.0%

WASHINGTON

GOVERNOR 2016

2010 Census Population	County	Total Vote	Republican (Bryant)	Democratic (Inslee)	Other	Rep.-Dem. Plurality	Percentage			
							Total Vote		Major Vote	
							Rep.	Dem.	Rep.	Dem.
425,363	CLARK	200,379	103,787	96,032	560	7,755 R	51.8%	47.9%	51.9%	48.1%
4,078	COLUMBIA	2,184	1,491	688	5	803 R	68.3%	31.5%	68.4%	31.6%
102,410	COWLITZ	45,833	26,116	19,593	124	6,523 R	57.0%	42.7%	57.1%	42.9%
38,431	DOUGLAS	15,666	10,197	5,441	28	4,756 R	65.1%	34.7%	65.2%	34.8%
7,551	FERRY	3,621	2,252	1,360	9	892 R	62.2%	37.6%	62.3%	37.7%
78,163	FRANKLIN	24,163	14,387	9,731	45	4,656 R	59.5%	40.3%	59.7%	40.3%
2,266	GARFIELD	1,248	875	370	3	505 R	70.1%	29.6%	70.3%	29.7%
89,120	GRANT	28,742	19,401	9,242	99	10,159 R	67.5%	32.2%	67.7%	32.3%
72,797	GRAYS HARBOR	28,988	14,843	14,038	107	805 R	51.2%	48.4%	51.4%	48.6%
78,506	ISLAND	43,455	21,560	21,797	98	237 D	49.6%	50.2%	49.7%	50.3%
29,872	JEFFERSON	20,538	7,049	13,399	90	6,350 D	34.3%	65.2%	34.5%	65.5%
1,931,249	KING	1,001,594	321,242	677,943	2,409	356,701 D	32.1%	67.7%	32.2%	67.8%
251,133	KITSAP	126,522	59,762	66,392	368	6,630 D	47.2%	52.5%	47.4%	52.6%
40,915	KITTITAS	19,163	11,139	7,984	40	3,155 R	58.1%	41.7%	58.2%	41.8%
20,318	KLICKITAT	10,801	6,260	4,517	24	1,743 R	58.0%	41.8%	58.1%	41.9%
75,455	LEWIS	34,788	23,539	11,163	86	12,376 R	67.7%	32.1%	67.8%	32.2%
10,570	LINCOLN	5,787	4,160	1,616	11	2,544 R	71.9%	27.9%	72.0%	28.0%
60,699	MASON	28,584	15,365	13,126	93	2,239 R	53.8%	45.9%	53.9%	46.1%
41,120	OKANOGAN	17,270	9,794	7,437	39	2,357 R	56.7%	43.1%	56.8%	43.2%
20,920	PACIFIC	10,778	5,428	5,313	37	115 R	50.4%	49.3%	50.5%	49.5%
13,001	PEND OREILLE	6,904	4,364	2,520	20	1,844 R	63.2%	36.5%	63.4%	36.6%
795,225	PIERCE	354,065	176,287	176,825	953	538 D	49.8%	49.9%	49.9%	50.1%
15,769	SAN JUAN	10,900	3,356	7,509	35	4,153 D	30.8%	68.9%	30.9%	69.1%
116,901	SKAGIT	57,147	28,701	28,273	173	428 R	50.2%	49.5%	50.4%	49.6%
11,066	SKAMANIA	5,583	3,094	2,476	13	618 R	55.4%	44.3%	55.5%	44.5%
713,335	SNOHOMISH	350,251	166,770	182,544	937	15,774 D	47.6%	52.1%	47.7%	52.3%
471,221	SPOKANE	231,093	124,576	106,009	508	18,567 R	53.9%	45.9%	54.0%	46.0%
43,531	STEVENS	23,044	15,851	7,148	45	8,703 R	68.8%	31.0%	68.9%	31.1%
252,264	THURSTON	131,408	59,014	71,835	559	12,821 D	44.9%	54.7%	45.1%	54.9%
3,978	WAHKIAKUM	2,359	1,413	941	5	472 R	59.9%	39.9%	60.0%	40.0%
58,781	WALLA WALLA	25,629	14,880	10,705	44	4,175 R	58.1%	41.8%	58.2%	41.8%
201,140	WHATCOM	110,957	47,953	62,634	370	14,681 D	43.2%	56.4%	43.4%	56.6%
44,776	WHITMAN	17,662	8,892	8,727	43	165 R	50.3%	49.4%	50.5%	49.5%
243,231	YAKIMA	78,212	43,016	35,162	34	7,854 R	55.0%	45.0%	55.0%	45.0%
6,724,540	TOTAL	3,245,282	1,476,346	1,760,520	8,416	284,174 D	45.5%	54.2%	45.6%	54.4%

WASHINGTON

SENATOR 2016

2010 Census Population	County	Total Vote	Republican (Vance)	Democratic (Murray)	Other	Rep.-Dem. Plurality	Percentage			
							Total Vote		Major Vote	
							Rep.	Dem.	Rep.	Dem.
18,728	ADAMS	4,677	2,818	1,859		959 R	60.3%	39.7%	60.3%	39.7%
21,623	ASOTIN	9,745	5,497	4,248		1,249 R	56.4%	43.6%	56.4%	43.6%
175,177	BENTON	82,077	46,397	35,680		10,717 R	56.5%	43.5%	56.5%	43.5%
72,453	CHELAN	33,732	18,146	15,586		2,560 R	53.8%	46.2%	53.8%	46.2%
71,404	CLALLAM	39,504	18,955	20,549		1,594 D	48.0%	52.0%	48.0%	52.0%
425,363	CLARK	200,559	97,637	102,922		5,285 D	48.7%	51.3%	48.7%	51.3%
4,078	COLUMBIA	2,193	1,339	854		485 R	61.1%	38.9%	61.1%	38.9%
102,410	COWLITZ	45,919	23,031	22,888		143 R	50.2%	49.8%	50.2%	49.8%
38,431	DOUGLAS	15,655	9,333	6,322		3,011 R	59.6%	40.4%	59.6%	40.4%
7,551	FERRY	3,619	2,099	1,520		579 R	58.0%	42.0%	58.0%	42.0%

WASHINGTON

SENATOR 2016

2010 Census Population	County	Total Vote	Republican (Vance)	Democratic (Murray)	Other	Rep.-Dem. Plurality	Percentage			
							Total Vote		Major Vote	
							Rep.	Dem.	Rep.	Dem.
78,163	FRANKLIN	23,963	13,197	10,766		2,431 R	55.1%	44.9%	55.1%	44.9%
2,266	GARFIELD	1,257	771	486		285 R	61.3%	38.7%	61.3%	38.7%
89,120	GRANT	28,733	18,404	10,329		8,075 R	64.1%	35.9%	64.1%	35.9%
72,797	GRAYS HARBOR	28,916	13,483	15,433		1,950 D	46.6%	53.4%	46.6%	53.4%
78,506	ISLAND	43,456	19,761	23,695		3,934 D	45.5%	54.5%	45.5%	54.5%
29,872	JEFFERSON	20,506	6,408	14,098		7,690 D	31.2%	68.8%	31.2%	68.8%
1,931,249	KING	1,001,523	273,410	728,113		454,703 D	27.3%	72.7%	27.3%	72.7%
251,133	KITSAP	126,530	54,746	71,784		17,038 D	43.3%	56.7%	43.3%	56.7%
40,915	KITTITAS	19,122	10,292	8,830		1,462 R	53.8%	46.2%	53.8%	46.2%
20,318	KLICKITAT	10,813	5,692	5,121		571 R	52.6%	47.4%	52.6%	47.4%
75,455	LEWIS	34,585	21,319	13,266		8,053 R	61.6%	38.4%	61.6%	38.4%
10,570	LINCOLN	5,780	3,837	1,943		1,894 R	66.4%	33.6%	66.4%	33.6%
60,699	MASON	28,525	13,677	14,848		1,171 D	47.9%	52.1%	47.9%	52.1%
41,120	OKANOGAN	17,255	9,160	8,095		1,065 R	53.1%	46.9%	53.1%	46.9%
20,920	PACIFIC	10,770	4,819	5,951		1,132 D	44.7%	55.3%	44.7%	55.3%
13,001	PEND OREILLE	6,868	4,093	2,775		1,318 R	59.6%	40.4%	59.6%	40.4%
795,225	PIERCE	353,815	157,644	196,171		38,527 D	44.6%	55.4%	44.6%	55.4%
15,769	SAN JUAN	10,880	3,091	7,789		4,698 D	28.4%	71.6%	28.4%	71.6%
116,901	SKAGIT	57,172	26,600	30,572		3,972 D	46.5%	53.5%	46.5%	53.5%
11,066	SKAMANIA	5,633	2,945	2,688		257 R	52.3%	47.7%	52.3%	47.7%
713,335	SNOHOMISH	350,240	148,325	201,915		53,590 D	42.3%	57.7%	42.3%	57.7%
471,221	SPOKANE	230,914	117,197	113,717		3,480 R	50.8%	49.2%	50.8%	49.2%
43,531	STEVENS	22,980	14,830	8,150		6,680 R	64.5%	35.5%	64.5%	35.5%
252,264	THURSTON	130,781	52,623	78,158		25,535 D	40.2%	59.8%	40.2%	59.8%
3,978	WAHKIAKUM	2,346	1,217	1,129		88 R	51.9%	48.1%	51.9%	48.1%
58,781	WALLA WALLA	25,614	12,969	12,645		324 R	50.6%	49.4%	50.6%	49.4%
201,140	WHATCOM	110,754	44,924	65,830		20,906 D	40.6%	59.4%	40.6%	59.4%
44,776	WHITMAN	17,567	8,040	9,527		1,487 D	45.8%	54.2%	45.8%	54.2%
243,231	YAKIMA	78,339	40,612	37,727		2,885 R	51.8%	48.2%	51.8%	48.2%
6,724,540	TOTAL	3,243,317	1,329,338	1,913,979		584,641 D	41.0%	59.0%	41.0%	59.0%

WASHINGTON

HOUSE OF REPRESENTATIVES

CD	Year	Total Vote	Republican		Democratic		Other Vote	Rep.-Dem. Plurality	Percentage			
			Vote	Candidate	Vote	Candidate			Total Vote		Major Vote	
									Rep.	Dem.	Rep.	Dem.
1	2016	349,398	155,779	SUTHERLAND, ROBERT	193,619	DELBENE, SUZAN*		37,840 D	44.6%	55.4%	44.6%	55.4%
1	2014	225,579	101,428	CELIS, PEDRO	124,151	DELBENE, SUZAN*		22,723 D	45.0%	55.0%	45.0%	55.0%
1	2012	328,212	151,187	KOSTER, JOHN	177,025	DELBENE, SUZAN*		25,838 D	46.1%	53.9%	46.1%	53.9%
2	2016	325,408	117,094	HENNEMANN, MARC	208,314	LARSEN, RICK*		91,220 D	36.0%	64.0%	36.0%	64.0%
2	2014	201,691	79,518	GUILLOT, B.J.	122,173	LARSEN, RICK*		42,655 D	39.4%	60.6%	39.4%	60.6%
2	2012	302,291	117,465	MATTHEWS, DAN	184,826	LARSEN, RICK*		67,361 D	38.9%	61.1%	38.9%	61.1%
3	2016	313,277	193,457	BEUTLER, JAIME HERRERA*	119,820	MOELLER, JIM		73,637 R	61.8%	38.2%	61.8%	38.2%
3	2014	202,814	124,796	BEUTLER, JAIME HERRERA*	78,018	DINGETHAL, BOB		46,778 R	61.5%	38.5%	61.5%	38.5%
3	2012	293,884	177,446	BEUTLER, JAIME HERRERA*	116,438	HAUGEN, JON T.		61,008 R	60.4%	39.6%	60.4%	39.6%
4	2016**	229,919	132,517	NEWHOUSE, DAN M.*			97,402	132,517 R	57.6%		100.0%	
4	2014	153,079	77,772	NEWHOUSE, DAN M.			75,307	77,772 R	50.8%		100.0%	
4	2012	233,689	154,749	HASTINGS, DOC*	78,940	BAECHLER, MARY		75,809 R	66.2%	33.8%	66.2%	33.8%
5	2016	323,534	192,959	RODGERS, CATHY MCMORRIS*	130,575	PAKOOTAS, JOSEPH "JOE"		62,384 R	59.6%	40.4%	59.6%	40.4%
5	2014	223,242	135,470	RODGERS, CATHY MCMORRIS*	87,772	PAKOOTAS, JOSEPH "JOE"		47,698 R	60.7%	39.3%	60.7%	39.3%
5	2012	308,578	191,066	RODGERS, CATHY MCMORRIS*	117,512	COWAN, RICH		73,554 R	61.9%	38.1%	61.9%	38.1%

WASHINGTON

HOUSE OF REPRESENTATIVES

CD	Year	Total Vote	Republican Vote	Republican Candidate	Democratic Vote	Democratic Candidate	Other Vote	Rep.-Dem. Plurality	Total Vote Rep.	Total Vote Dem.	Major Vote Rep.	Major Vote Dem.
6	2016	327,834	126,116	BLOOM, TODD	201,718	KILMER, DEREK*		75,602 D	38.5%	61.5%	38.5%	61.5%
6	2014	224,290	83,025	MCCLENDON, MARTIN "MARTY"	141,265	KILMER, DEREK*		58,240 D	37.0%	63.0%	37.0%	63.0%
6	2012	316,386	129,725	DRISCOLL, BILL	186,661	KILMER, DEREK		56,936 D	41.0%	59.0%	41.0%	59.0%
7	2016**	378,754			212,010	JAYAPAL, PRAMILA	166,744	212,010 D		56.0%		100.0%
7	2014	251,875	47,921	KELLER, CRAIG	203,954	MCDERMOTT, JAMES A.*		156,033 D	19.0%	81.0%	19.0%	81.0%
7	2012	374,580	76,212	BEMIS, RON	298,368	MCDERMOTT, JAMES A.*		222,156 D	20.3%	79.7%	20.3%	79.7%
8	2016	320,865	193,145	REICHERT, DAVID GEORGE "DAVE"*	127,720	VENTRELLA, TONY		65,425 R	60.2%	39.8%	60.2%	39.8%
8	2014	198,744	125,741	REICHERT, DAVID GEORGE "DAVE"*	73,003	RITCHIE, JASON		52,738 R	63.3%	36.7%	63.3%	36.7%
8	2012	302,090	180,204	REICHERT, DAVID GEORGE "DAVE"*	121,886	PORTERFIELD, KAREN		58,318 R	59.7%	40.3%	59.7%	40.3%
9	2016	281,482	76,317	BASLER, DOUG	205,165	SMITH, ADAM*		128,848 D	27.1%	72.9%	27.1%	72.9%
9	2014	166,794	48,662	BASLER, DOUG	118,132	SMITH, ADAM*		69,470 D	29.2%	70.8%	29.2%	70.8%
9	2012	268,139	76,105	POSTMA, JAMES	192,034	SMITH, ADAM*		115,929 D	28.4%	71.6%	28.4%	71.6%
10	2016	290,564	120,104	POSTMA, JAMES	170,460	HECK, DENNY*		50,356 D	41.3%	58.7%	41.3%	58.7%
10	2014	181,492	82,213	MCDONALD, JOYCE	99,279	HECK, DENNY*		17,066 D	45.3%	54.7%	45.3%	54.7%
10	2012	278,417	115,381	MURI, RICHARD	163,036	HECK, DENNY		47,655 D	41.4%	58.6%	41.4%	58.6%
TOTAL	2016	3,141,035	1,307,488		1,569,401		264,146	261,913 D	41.6%	50.0%	45.4%	54.6%
TOTAL	2014	2,029,600	906,546		1,047,747		75,307	141,201 D	44.7%	51.6%	46.4%	53.6%
TOTAL	2012	3,006,266	1,369,540		1,636,726			267,186 D	45.6%	54.4%	45.6%	54.4%

Note: An asterisk (*) denotes incumbent. ** In Washington's jungle primary, the top two vote recipients in CD 4 (Dan Newhouse and Clint Didier) were both Republicans, and in CD 7 (Pramila Jayapal and Brady Walkinshaw) were both Democrats. Didier and Walkinshaw are listed here as other candidates and recieved the full count of other votes.

WASHINGTON

GENERAL AND PRIMARY ELECTIONS

2016 GENERAL ELECTIONS: OTHER VOTES

President   Other vote was 160,879 Libertarian (Gary Johnson), 107,805 Write-in (Scattered Write-In), 58,417 Green (Jill Stein), 17,623 Constitution (Darrell Castle), 4,307 Socialist Workers (Alyson Kennedy), 3,523 Peace and Freedom (Gloria La Riva)

Governor   8,416 Write-in (Scattered Write-in)

Senate
House   Other vote was:

CD 4   97,402 Republican (Clint Didier)
CD 7   166,744 Democrat (Brady Walkinshaw)

2016 PRIMARY ELECTIONS: SUPPLEMENTARY INFORMATION

Primary	May 24, 2016 (President) August 2, 2016 (Congress)	**Registration** (as of August 2, 2016 – includes 616,967 inactive registrants)	4,719,721	No Party Registration

Primary Type   Open—Any registered voter could participate in the primary, and below the presidential level candidates of all parties ran together on the same ballot. The top two vote-getters advanced to the November general election.

WASHINGTON

GENERAL AND PRIMARY ELECTIONS

	REPUBLICAN PRIMARIES			DEMOCRATIC PRIMARIES		
President	Trump, Donald J.	455,023	75.5%	Clinton, Hillary Rodham	420,461	52.4%
	Cruz, Ted	65,172	10.8%	Sanders, Bernard	382,293	47.6%
	Kasich, John R.	58,954	9.8%			
	Carson, Ben	23,849	4.0%			
	TOTAL	*602,998*		*TOTAL*	*802,754*	

ALL-PARTY PRIMARIES

Senator	Murray, Patty* (Democrat)#	745,421	53.8%
	Vance, Chris (Republican)#	381,004	27.5%
	Makus, Eric John (Republican)	57,825	4.2%
	Cornell, Philip L. (Democrat)	46,460	3.4%
	Nazarino, Scott (Republican)	41,542	3.0%
	Luke, Mike (Libertarian)	20,988	1.5%
	Said, Mohammad (Democrat)	13,362	1.0%
	Lands, Donna Rae (Conservative)	11,472	0.8%
	Cummings, Ted (Independent)	11,028	0.8%
	Wright, Sam (Human Rights)	10,751	0.8%
	Mover, Uncle (Republican)	8,569	0.6%
	Teuton, Jeremy (System Reboot)	7,991	0.6%
	Amundson, Thor (Democrat)	7,906	0.6%
	Jackson, Chuck (Independent)	6,318	0.5%
	Churchill, Pano (Lincoln Caucus)	5,150	0.4%
	Haller, Zach (Independent)	5,092	0.4%
	Tsimerman, Alex (Standupamerica)	4,117	0.3%
	TOTAL	*1,384,996*	
Governor	Inslee, Jay* (Democrat)#	687,412	49.3%
	Bryant, Bill (Republican)#	534,519	38.3%
	Hirt, Bill (Republican)	48,382	3.5%
	O'Rourke, Patrick (Democrat)	40,572	2.9%
	Rubenstein, Steve (Independent)	22,582	1.6%
	Deal, James Robert (Democrat)	14,623	1.0%
	Dodds, Johnathan (Democrat)	14,152	1.0%
	Goodspaceguy (Republican)	13,191	0.9%
	Martin, Mary (Socialist Workers Party)	10,374	0.7%
	Blomstrom, David (Fifth Republic Party)	4,512	0.3%
	Joubert, Christian Pierre (Holistic Party)	4,103	0.3%
	TOTAL	*1,394,422*	
Congressional District 1	DelBene, Suzan* (Democrat)#	77,756	53.5%
	Sutherland, Robert (Republican)#	44,970	31.0%
	Orlinski, John (Republican)	13,694	9.4%
	Stafne, Scott (Libertarian)	4,601	3.2%
	Storms, Alex (Independent)	4,194	2.9%
	TOTAL	*145,215*	
Congressional District 2	Larsen, Rick* (Democrat)#	71,955	51.8%
	Hennemann, Marc (Republican)#	44,822	32.3%
	Lapointe, Mike (Democrat)	14,697	10.6%
	Luke, Brian (Libertarian)	4,771	3.4%
	Illonummi, Kari (Independent)	2,628	1.9%
	TOTAL	*138,873*	
Congressional District 3	Beutler, Jaime Herrera* (Republican)#	70,142	55.5%
	Moeller, Jim (Democrat)#	30,848	24.4%
	McDevitt, David (Democrat)	12,896	10.2%
	Marx, Angela (Democrat)	4,851	3.8%
	Arthur, Kathleen (Democrat)	4,296	3.4%
	Worthington, L.A. "Worthy" (No Party Affiliation)	3,402	2.7%
	TOTAL	*126,435*	

WASHINGTON

GENERAL AND PRIMARY ELECTIONS

ALL-PARTY PRIMARIES

Congressional District 4	Newhouse, Dan M.* (Republican)#	44,720	45.8%
	Didier, Clint (Republican)#	26,892	27.5%
	McKinley, Doug (Democrat)	21,678	22.2%
	Malan, John "The Man" (Democrat)	2,320	2.4%
	Jakeman, Glenn (Republican)	2,090	2.1%
	TOTAL	97,700	
Congressional District 5	Rodgers, Cathy McMorris* (Republican)#	60,184	42.2%
	Pakootas, Joseph "Joe" (Democrat)#	44,999	31.5%
	Wilson, Dave (Independent)	18,993	13.3%
	Horne, Tom (Republican)	15,830	11.1%
	McGee, Krystol (Libertarian)	2,678	1.9%
	TOTAL	142,684	
Congressional District 6	Kilmer, Derek* (Democrat)#	87,311	58.4%
	Bloom, Todd (Republican)#	36,659	24.5%
	Brodhead, Stephan Andrew (Republican)	12,269	8.2%
	Coverdale, Mike (No Party Affiliation)	7,223	4.8%
	Nuchims, Paul (Democrat)	3,318	2.2%
	Vega, Tyler Myles (Green)	2,803	1.9%
	TOTAL	149,583	
Congressional District 7	Jayapal, Pramila (Democrat)#	82,753	42.1%
	Walkinshaw, Brady Piñero (Democrat)#	41,773	21.3%
	McDermott, Joe (Democrat)	37,495	19.1%
	Keller, Craig (Republican)	16,058	8.2%
	Sutherland, Scott (Republican)	9,008	4.6%
	Jhaveri, Arun (Democrat)	3,389	1.7%
	Regier, Leslie (No Party Affiliation)	2,592	1.3%
	Rivers, Donovan (Democrat)	2,379	1.2%
	Cooper, Carl (No Party Affiliation)	1,056	0.5%
	TOTAL	196,503	
Congressional District 8	Reichert, David George "Dave"* (Republican)#	73,600	56.8%
	Ventrella, Tony (Democrat)#	22,035	17.0%
	Ramos, Santiago (Democrat)	17,900	13.8%
	Skold, Alida (Democrat)	10,825	8.4%
	Arnold, Keith (Independent)	3,153	2.4%
	Walsh, Margaret M. (We R Independent Party)	2,024	1.6%
	TOTAL	129,537	
Congressional District 9	Smith, Adam* (Democrat)#	67,100	56.3%
	Basler, Doug (Republican)#	27,848	23.4%
	Wineberry, Jesse (Democrat)	17,613	14.8%
	Smith, Daniel (Democrat)	3,935	3.3%
	Flener, Jeary (No Party Affiliation)	2,733	2.3%
	TOTAL	119,229	
Congressional District 10	Heck, Denny* (Democrat)#	58,865	46.5%
	Postma, James (Republican)#	46,473	36.7%
	Ferguson, Jennifer (Democrat)	16,750	13.2%
	Boyce, Richard (No Party Affiliation)	4,411	3.5%
	TOTAL	126,499	

Note: An asterisk (*) denotes incumbent. A pound sign (#) next to the top 2 candidates in each primary indicates that they qualified for the general election. For offices besides president, Washington held an all-party primary, in which candidates of all parties ran together on a single ballot. The top two vote-getters, regardless of party, advanced to the November general election. Candidates identified themselves on the ballot as "preferring" a particular party (or independent, non-party status), whether or not they were a member of that party or were supported by that party.

WEST VIRGINIA

Congressional districts first established for elections held in 2012

3 members

WEST VIRGINIA

GOVERNOR

Jim Justice (R). Elected 2016 to a four-year term. (Justice was elected as a Democrat in 2016 but became a Republican on August 3, 2017.)

SENATORS (1 Republican, 1 Democrat)

Shelley Moore Capito (R). Elected 2014 to a six-year term.

Joe Manchin III (D). Re-elected 2012 to a six-year term. Previously elected 2010 to fill the remaining two years of the term vacated by the death of Robert C. Byrd (D) in June 2010. Carte Goodwin (D) was appointed to fill the vacancy until the special election could be held in November 2010.

REPRESENTATIVES (3 Republicans)

1. David McKinley (R)
2. Alex X. Mooney (R)
3. Evan Jenkins (R)

POSTWAR VOTE FOR PRESIDENT

Year	Total Vote	Republican		Democratic		Other Vote	Rep.-Dem. Plurality	Percentage			
								Total Vote		Major Vote	
		Vote	Candidate	Vote	Candidate			Rep.	Dem.	Rep.	Dem.
2016**	714,423	489,371	Trump, Donald J.	188,794	Clinton, Hillary Rodham	36,258	300,577 R	68.5%	26.4%	72.2%	27.8%
2012	670,438	417,655	Romney, W. Mitt	238,269	Obama, Barack H.*	14,514	179,386 R	62.3%	35.5%	63.7%	36.3%
2008	713,451	397,466	McCain, John S. III	303,857	Obama, Barack H.	12,128	93,609 R	55.7%	42.6%	56.7%	43.3%
2004	755,887	423,778	Bush, George W.*	326,541	Kerry, John F.	5,568	97,237 R	56.1%	43.2%	56.5%	43.5%
2000**	648,124	336,475	Bush, George W.	295,497	Gore, Albert Jr.	16,152	40,978 R	51.9%	45.6%	53.2%	46.8%
1996**	636,459	233,946	Dole, Robert "Bob"	327,812	Clinton, Bill*	74,701	93,866 D	36.8%	51.5%	41.6%	58.4%
1992**	683,762	241,974	Bush, George H.*	331,001	Clinton, Bill	110,787	89,027 D	35.4%	48.4%	42.2%	57.8%
1988	653,311	310,065	Bush, George H.	341,016	Dukakis, Michael S.	2,230	30,951 D	47.5%	52.2%	47.6%	52.4%
1984	735,742	405,483	Reagan, Ronald*	328,125	Mondale, Walter F.	2,134	77,358 R	55.1%	44.6%	55.3%	44.7%
1980**	737,715	334,206	Reagan, Ronald	367,462	Carter, Jimmy*	36,047	33,256 D	45.3%	49.8%	47.6%	52.4%
1976	750,964	314,760	Ford, Gerald R.*	435,914	Carter, Jimmy	290	121,154 D	41.9%	58.0%	41.9%	58.1%
1972	762,399	484,964	Nixon, Richard M.*	277,435	McGovern, George S.		207,529 R	63.6%	36.4%	63.6%	36.4%
1968**	754,206	307,555	Nixon, Richard M.	374,091	Humphrey, Hubert Horatio Jr.	72,560	66,536 D	40.8%	49.6%	45.1%	54.9%
1964	792,040	253,953	Goldwater, Barry M. Sr.	538,087	Johnson, Lyndon B.*		284,134 D	32.1%	67.9%	32.1%	67.9%
1960	837,781	395,995	Nixon, Richard M.	441,786	Kennedy, John F.		45,791 D	47.3%	52.7%	47.3%	52.7%
1956	830,831	449,297	Eisenhower, Dwight D.*	381,534	Stevenson, Adlai E. II		67,763 R	54.1%	45.9%	54.1%	45.9%
1952	873,548	419,970	Eisenhower, Dwight D.	453,578	Stevenson, Adlai E. II		33,608 D	48.1%	51.9%	48.1%	51.9%
1948	748,750	316,251	Dewey, Thomas E.	429,188	Truman, Harry S.*	3,311	112,937 D	42.2%	57.3%	42.4%	57.6%

Note: An asterisk (*) denotes incumbent. **In past elections, the other vote included: 2016 - 23,004 Libertarian (Gary Johnson); 2000 - 10,680 Green (Ralph Nader); 1996 - 71,639 Reform (Ross Perot); 1992 - 108,829 Independent (Perot); 1980 - 31,691 Independent (John Anderson); 1968 - 72,560 American Independent (George Wallace).

WEST VIRGINIA

POSTWAR VOTE FOR GOVERNOR

		Republican		Democratic		Other	Rep.-Dem.	Total Vote		Major Vote	
Year	Total Vote	Vote	Candidate	Vote	Candidate	Vote	Plurality	Rep.	Dem.	Rep.	Dem.
2016	713,879	301,987	Cole, Bill	350,408	Justice, Jim	61,484	48,421 D	42.3%	49.1%	46.3%	53.7%
2012	664,455	303,291	Maloney, Bill	335,468	Tomblin, Earl Ray*	25,696	32,177 D	45.6%	50.5%	47.5%	52.5%
2011S**	301,084	141,656	Maloney, Bill	149,202	Tomblin, Earl Ray*	10,226	7,546 D	47.0%	49.6%	48.7%	51.3%
2008	706,046	181,612	Weeks, Russ	492,697	Manchin, Joe III*	31,737	311,085 D	25.7%	69.8%	26.9%	73.1%
2004	744,433	253,131	Warner, Monty	472,758	Manchin, Joe III	18,544	219,627 D	34.0%	63.5%	34.9%	65.1%
2000	648,047	305,926	Underwood, Cecil H.*	324,822	Wise, Robert Ellsworth	17,299	18,896 D	47.2%	50.1%	48.5%	51.5%
1996	628,559	324,518	Underwood, Cecil H.	287,870	Pritt, Charlotte	16,171	36,648 R	51.6%	45.8%	53.0%	47.0%
1992	657,193	240,390	Benedict, Cleveland K.	368,302	Caperton, Gaston*	48,501	127,912 D	36.6%	56.0%	39.5%	60.5%
1988	649,593	267,172	Moore, Arch A. Jr.*	382,421	Caperton, Gaston		115,249 D	41.1%	58.9%	41.1%	58.9%
1984	741,502	394,937	Moore, Arch A. Jr.	346,565	See, Clyde M.		48,372 R	53.3%	46.7%	53.3%	46.7%
1980	742,150	337,240	Moore, Arch A. Jr.	401,863	Rockefeller, John D. IV*	3,047	64,623 D	45.4%	54.1%	45.6%	54.4%
1976	749,270	253,420	Underwood, Cecil H.	495,661	Rockefeller, John D. IV	189	242,241 D	33.8%	66.2%	33.8%	66.2%
1972	774,279	423,817	Moore, Arch A. Jr.*	350,462	Rockefeller, John D. IV		73,355 R	54.7%	45.3%	54.7%	45.3%
1968	743,845	378,315	Moore, Arch A. Jr.	365,530	Sprouse, James M.		12,785 R	50.9%	49.1%	50.9%	49.1%
1964	788,582	355,559	Underwood, Cecil H.	433,023	Smith, Hulett		77,464 D	45.1%	54.9%	45.1%	54.9%
1960	827,420	380,665	Neely, Harold E.	446,755	Barron, W. W.		66,090 D	46.0%	54.0%	46.0%	54.0%
1956	817,623	440,502	Underwood, Cecil H.	377,121	Mollohan, Robert H.		63,381 R	53.9%	46.1%	53.9%	46.1%
1952	882,527	427,629	Holt, Rush D.	454,898	Marland, William C.		27,269 D	48.5%	51.5%	48.5%	51.5%
1948	768,061	329,309	Boreman, Herbert S.	438,752	Patteson, Okey L.		109,443 D	42.9%	57.1%	42.9%	57.1%

Note: An asterisk (*) denotes incumbent. **The 2011 election was for a short term to fill a vacancy.

POSTWAR VOTE FOR SENATOR

		Republican		Democratic		Other	Rep.-Dem.	Total Vote		Major Vote	
Year	Total Vote	Vote	Candidate	Vote	Candidate	Vote	Plurality	Rep.	Dem.	Rep.	Dem.
2014	453,659	281,820	Capito, Shelley Moore	156,360	Tennant, Natalie E.	15,479	125,460 R	62.1%	34.5%	64.3%	35.7%
2012	660,212	240,787	Raese, John R.	399,908	Manchin, Joe III*	19,517	159,121 D	36.5%	60.6%	37.6%	62.4%
2010S**	529,948	230,013	Raese, John R.	283,358	Manchin, Joe III	16,577	53,345 D	43.4%	53.5%	44.8%	55.2%
2008	702,308	254,629	Wolfe, Jay	447,560	Rockefeller, John D. IV*	119	192,931 D	36.3%	63.7%	36.3%	63.7%
2006	459,884	155,043	Raese, John R.	296,276	Byrd, Robert C.*	8,565	141,233 D	33.7%	64.4%	34.4%	65.6%
2002	436,183	160,902	Wolfe, M. Jay	275,281	Rockefeller, John D. IV*		114,379 D	36.9%	63.1%	36.9%	63.1%
2000	603,477	121,635	Gallaher, David T.	469,215	Byrd, Robert C.*	12,627	347,580 D	20.2%	77.8%	20.6%	79.4%
1996	595,614	139,088	Burks, Betty A.	456,526	Rockefeller, John D. IV*		317,438 D	23.4%	76.6%	23.4%	76.6%
1994	420,936	130,441	Klos, Stan	290,495	Byrd, Robert C.*		160,054 D	31.0%	69.0%	31.0%	69.0%
1990	404,305	128,071	Yoder, John	276,234	Rockefeller, John D. IV*		148,163 D	31.7%	68.3%	31.7%	68.3%
1988	634,547	223,564	Wolfe, M. Jay	410,983	Byrd, Robert C.*		187,419 D	35.2%	64.8%	35.2%	64.8%
1984	722,212	344,680	Raese, John R.	374,233	Rockefeller, John D. IV	3,299	29,553 D	47.7%	51.8%	47.9%	52.1%
1982	565,314	173,910	Benedict, Cleveland K.	387,170	Byrd, Robert C.*	4,234	213,260 D	30.8%	68.5%	31.0%	69.0%
1978	493,351	244,317	Moore, Arch A. Jr.	249,034	Randolph, Jennings*		4,717 D	49.5%	50.5%	49.5%	50.5%
1976	566,790			566,423	Byrd, Robert C.*	367	566,423 D		99.9%		100.0%
1972	731,841	245,531	Leonard, Louise	486,310	Randolph, Jennings*		240,779 D	33.5%	66.5%	33.5%	66.5%
1970	445,623	99,658	Dodson, Elmer H.	345,965	Byrd, Robert C.*		246,307 D	22.4%	77.6%	22.4%	77.6%
1966	491,216	198,891	Love, Francis J.	292,325	Randolph, Jennings*		93,434 D	40.5%	59.5%	40.5%	59.5%
1964	761,087	246,072	Benedict, Cooper P.	515,015	Byrd, Robert C.*		268,943 D	32.3%	67.7%	32.3%	67.7%
1960	828,292	369,935	Underwood, Cecil H.	458,355	Randolph, Jennings*	2	88,420 D	44.7%	55.3%	44.7%	55.3%
1958	644,917	263,172	Revercomb, Chapman*	381,745	Byrd, Robert C.		118,573 D	40.8%	59.2%	40.8%	59.2%
1958S**	630,677	256,510	Hoblitzell, John D. Jr.*	374,167	Randolph, Jennings		117,657 D	40.7%	59.3%	40.7%	59.3%
1956S**	805,174	432,123	Revercomb, Chapman	373,051	Marland, William C.		59,072 R	53.7%	46.3%	53.7%	46.3%
1954	593,329	268,066	Sweeney, Thomas	325,263	Neely, Matthew M.*		57,197 D	45.2%	54.8%	45.2%	54.8%
1952	876,573	406,554	Revercomb, Chapman	470,019	Kilgore, Harley M.*		63,465 D	46.4%	53.6%	46.4%	53.6%
1948	763,888	328,534	Revercomb, Chapman*	435,354	Neely, Matthew M.		106,820 D	43.0%	57.0%	43.0%	57.0%
1946	542,768	269,617	Sweeney, Thomas	273,151	Kilgore, Harley M.*		3,534 D	49.7%	50.3%	49.7%	50.3%

Note: An asterisk (*) denotes incumbent. **The 1956 election, one of the 1958 elections, and the 2010 election were for short terms to fill a vacancy. The Republican Party did not run a candidate in the 1976 Senate election.

WEST VIRGINIA

PRESIDENT 2016

2010 Census Population	County	Total Vote	Republican (Trump)	Democratic (Clinton)	Other	Rep.-Dem. Plurality	Percentage			
							Total Vote		Major Vote	
							Rep.	Dem.	Rep.	Dem.
16,589	BARBOUR	6,054	4,527	1,222	305	3,305 R	74.8%	20.2%	78.7%	21.3%
104,169	BERKELEY	42,850	28,244	12,321	2,285	15,923 R	65.9%	28.8%	69.6%	30.4%
24,629	BOONE	8,683	6,504	1,790	389	4,714 R	74.9%	20.6%	78.4%	21.6%
14,523	BRAXTON	5,090	3,537	1,321	232	2,216 R	69.5%	26.0%	72.8%	27.2%
24,069	BROOKE	9,613	6,625	2,568	420	4,057 R	68.9%	26.7%	72.1%	27.9%
96,319	CABELL	33,085	19,850	11,447	1,788	8,403 R	60.0%	34.6%	63.4%	36.6%
7,627	CALHOUN	2,617	2,035	456	126	1,579 R	77.8%	17.4%	81.7%	18.3%
9,386	CLAY	2,972	2,300	568	104	1,732 R	77.4%	19.1%	80.2%	19.8%
8,202	DODDRIDGE	2,840	2,358	362	120	1,996 R	83.0%	12.7%	86.7%	13.3%
46,039	FAYETTE	15,337	10,357	4,290	690	6,067 R	67.5%	28.0%	70.7%	29.3%
8,693	GILMER	2,543	1,896	545	102	1,351 R	74.6%	21.4%	77.7%	22.3%
11,937	GRANT	4,956	4,346	512	98	3,834 R	87.7%	10.3%	89.5%	10.5%
35,480	GREENBRIER	14,066	9,556	3,765	745	5,791 R	67.9%	26.8%	71.7%	28.3%
23,964	HAMPSHIRE	8,608	6,692	1,580	336	5,112 R	77.7%	18.4%	80.9%	19.1%
30,676	HANCOCK	12,702	8,909	3,262	531	5,647 R	70.1%	25.7%	73.2%	26.8%
14,025	HARDY	5,643	4,274	1,155	214	3,119 R	75.7%	20.5%	78.7%	21.3%
69,099	HARRISON	27,960	18,750	7,694	1,516	11,056 R	67.1%	27.5%	70.9%	29.1%
29,211	JACKSON	12,187	9,020	2,663	504	6,357 R	74.0%	21.9%	77.2%	22.8%
53,498	JEFFERSON	24,147	13,204	9,518	1,425	3,686 R	54.7%	39.4%	58.1%	41.9%
193,063	KANAWHA	75,690	43,850	28,263	3,577	15,587 R	57.9%	37.3%	60.8%	39.2%
16,372	LEWIS	6,928	5,274	1,347	307	3,927 R	76.1%	19.4%	79.7%	20.3%
21,720	LINCOLN	7,066	5,307	1,459	300	3,848 R	75.1%	20.6%	78.4%	21.6%
36,743	LOGAN	12,359	9,897	2,092	370	7,805 R	80.1%	16.9%	82.6%	17.4%
56,418	MARION	23,029	14,668	6,964	1,397	7,704 R	63.7%	30.2%	67.8%	32.2%
33,107	MARSHALL	13,216	9,666	2,918	632	6,748 R	73.1%	22.1%	76.8%	23.2%
27,324	MASON	10,186	7,654	2,081	451	5,573 R	75.1%	20.4%	78.6%	21.4%
22,113	MCDOWELL	6,203	4,629	1,438	136	3,191 R	74.6%	23.2%	76.3%	23.7%
62,264	MERCER	22,982	17,404	4,704	874	12,700 R	75.7%	20.5%	78.7%	21.3%
28,212	MINERAL	11,564	9,070	2,050	444	7,020 R	78.4%	17.7%	81.6%	18.4%
26,839	MINGO	9,510	7,911	1,370	229	6,541 R	83.2%	14.4%	85.2%	14.8%
96,189	MONONGALIA	36,048	18,432	14,699	2,917	3,733 R	51.1%	40.8%	55.6%	44.4%
13,502	MONROE	5,805	4,443	1,111	251	3,332 R	76.5%	19.1%	80.0%	20.0%
17,541	MORGAN	7,654	5,732	1,573	349	4,159 R	74.9%	20.6%	78.5%	21.5%
26,233	NICHOLAS	9,491	7,251	1,840	400	5,411 R	76.4%	19.4%	79.8%	20.2%
44,443	OHIO	17,938	11,139	5,493	1,306	5,646 R	62.1%	30.6%	67.0%	33.0%
7,695	PENDLETON	3,225	2,398	729	98	1,669 R	74.4%	22.6%	76.7%	23.3%
7,605	PLEASANTS	3,150	2,358	621	171	1,737 R	74.9%	19.7%	79.2%	20.8%
8,719	POCAHONTAS	3,646	2,496	928	222	1,568 R	68.5%	25.5%	72.9%	27.1%
33,520	PRESTON	12,659	9,538	2,470	651	7,068 R	75.3%	19.5%	79.4%	20.6%
55,486	PUTNAM	24,893	17,788	5,884	1,221	11,904 R	71.5%	23.6%	75.1%	24.9%
78,859	RALEIGH	29,618	22,048	6,443	1,127	15,605 R	74.4%	21.8%	77.4%	22.6%
29,405	RANDOLPH	10,876	7,629	2,735	512	4,894 R	70.1%	25.1%	73.6%	26.4%
10,449	RITCHIE	4,075	3,405	496	174	2,909 R	83.6%	12.2%	87.3%	12.7%
14,926	ROANE	5,247	3,781	1,222	244	2,559 R	72.1%	23.3%	75.6%	24.4%
13,927	SUMMERS	4,862	3,455	1,190	217	2,265 R	71.1%	24.5%	74.4%	25.6%
16,895	TAYLOR	6,538	4,733	1,491	314	3,242 R	72.4%	22.8%	76.0%	24.0%
7,141	TUCKER	3,475	2,565	751	159	1,814 R	73.8%	21.6%	77.4%	22.6%
9,208	TYLER	3,654	2,996	507	151	2,489 R	82.0%	13.9%	85.5%	14.5%
24,254	UPSHUR	9,218	7,005	1,766	447	5,239 R	76.0%	19.2%	79.9%	20.1%
42,481	WAYNE	15,182	11,152	3,357	673	7,795 R	73.5%	22.1%	76.9%	23.1%
9,154	WEBSTER	2,978	2,302	556	120	1,746 R	77.3%	18.7%	80.5%	19.5%
16,583	WETZEL	6,265	4,519	1,359	387	3,160 R	72.1%	21.7%	76.9%	23.1%
5,717	WIRT	2,422	1,911	386	125	1,525 R	78.9%	15.9%	83.2%	16.8%
86,956	WOOD	35,615	25,434	8,400	1,781	17,034 R	71.4%	23.6%	75.2%	24.8%
23,796	WYOMING	7,831	6,547	1,062	222	5,485 R	83.6%	13.6%	86.0%	14.0%
	Votes Not Reported by County				1,372					
1,852,994	TOTAL	714,423	489,371	188,794	36,258	300,577 R	68.5%	26.4%	72.2%	27.8%

WEST VIRGINIA

GOVERNOR 2016

2010 Census Population	County	Total Vote	Republican (Cole)	Democratic (Justice)	Other	Rep.-Dem. Plurality	Percentage Total Vote Rep.	Dem.	Major Vote Rep.	Dem.
16,589	BARBOUR	6,096	2,928	2,701	467	227 R	48.0%	44.3%	52.0%	48.0%
104,169	BERKELEY	41,852	23,103	14,879	3,870	8,224 R	55.2%	35.6%	60.8%	39.2%
24,629	BOONE	8,796	2,622	5,649	525	3,027 D	29.8%	64.2%	31.7%	68.3%
14,523	BRAXTON	5,041	1,765	2,959	317	1,194 D	35.0%	58.7%	37.4%	62.6%
24,069	BROOKE	9,453	4,087	4,570	796	483 D	43.2%	48.3%	47.2%	52.8%
96,319	CABELL	33,324	12,065	18,148	3,111	6,083 D	36.2%	54.5%	39.9%	60.1%
7,627	CALHOUN	2,615	1,157	1,193	265	36 D	44.2%	45.6%	49.2%	50.8%
9,386	CLAY	3,028	1,138	1,683	207	545 D	37.6%	55.6%	40.3%	59.7%
8,202	DODDRIDGE	2,856	1,739	905	212	834 R	60.9%	31.7%	65.8%	34.2%
46,039	FAYETTE	15,519	4,560	9,631	1,328	5,071 D	29.4%	62.1%	32.1%	67.9%
8,693	GILMER	2,565	1,116	1,195	254	79 D	43.5%	46.6%	48.3%	51.7%
11,937	GRANT	4,753	3,203	1,313	237	1,890 R	67.4%	27.6%	70.9%	29.1%
35,480	GREENBRIER	14,182	4,361	8,589	1,232	4,228 D	30.8%	60.6%	33.7%	66.3%
23,964	HAMPSHIRE	8,430	5,239	2,537	654	2,702 R	62.1%	30.1%	67.4%	32.6%
30,676	HANCOCK	12,433	5,992	5,322	1,119	670 R	48.2%	42.8%	53.0%	47.0%
14,025	HARDY	5,562	3,015	2,237	310	778 R	54.2%	40.2%	57.4%	42.6%
69,099	HARRISON	28,279	11,916	14,317	2,046	2,401 D	42.1%	50.6%	45.4%	54.6%
29,211	JACKSON	12,291	5,122	6,200	969	1,078 D	41.7%	50.4%	45.2%	54.8%
53,498	JEFFERSON	23,834	11,599	9,588	2,647	2,011 R	48.7%	40.2%	54.7%	45.3%
193,063	KANAWHA	76,396	23,849	44,756	7,791	20,907 D	31.2%	58.6%	34.8%	65.2%
16,372	LEWIS	6,967	3,294	3,222	451	72 R	47.3%	46.2%	50.6%	49.4%
21,720	LINCOLN	7,184	2,534	4,141	509	1,607 D	35.3%	57.7%	38.0%	62.0%
36,743	LOGAN	12,214	4,497	6,781	936	2,284 D	36.8%	55.5%	39.9%	60.1%
56,418	MARION	23,176	8,952	12,158	2,066	3,206 D	38.6%	52.5%	42.4%	57.6%
33,107	MARSHALL	13,125	5,696	6,491	938	795 D	43.4%	49.5%	46.7%	53.3%
27,324	MASON	10,257	4,062	5,566	629	1,504 D	39.6%	54.3%	42.2%	57.8%
22,113	MCDOWELL	6,167	2,493	3,459	215	966 D	40.4%	56.1%	41.9%	58.1%
62,264	MERCER	23,146	12,662	9,323	1,161	3,339 R	54.7%	40.3%	57.6%	42.4%
28,212	MINERAL	11,447	7,047	3,485	915	3,562 R	61.6%	30.4%	66.9%	33.1%
26,839	MINGO	9,416	3,699	5,168	549	1,469 D	39.3%	54.9%	41.7%	58.3%
96,189	MONONGALIA	36,163	14,343	16,016	5,804	1,673 D	39.7%	44.3%	47.2%	52.8%
13,502	MONROE	5,868	2,562	2,797	509	235 D	43.7%	47.7%	47.8%	52.2%
17,541	MORGAN	7,431	4,764	1,929	738	2,835 R	64.1%	26.0%	71.2%	28.8%
26,233	NICHOLAS	9,630	3,358	5,780	492	2,422 D	34.9%	60.0%	36.7%	63.3%
44,443	OHIO	18,021	8,048	8,377	1,596	329 D	44.7%	46.5%	49.0%	51.0%
7,695	PENDLETON	3,159	1,568	1,335	256	233 R	49.6%	42.3%	54.0%	46.0%
7,605	PLEASANTS	3,173	1,288	1,713	172	425 D	40.6%	54.0%	42.9%	57.1%
8,719	POCAHONTAS	3,680	1,227	1,975	478	748 D	33.3%	53.7%	38.3%	61.7%
33,520	PRESTON	12,520	6,575	3,964	1,981	2,611 R	52.5%	31.7%	62.4%	37.6%
55,486	PUTNAM	25,169	9,956	13,410	1,803	3,454 D	39.6%	53.3%	42.6%	57.4%
78,859	RALEIGH	29,830	11,140	16,841	1,849	5,701 D	37.3%	56.5%	39.8%	60.2%
29,405	RANDOLPH	10,957	4,500	5,120	1,337	620 D	41.1%	46.8%	46.8%	53.2%
10,449	RITCHIE	4,054	2,523	1,284	247	1,239 R	62.2%	31.7%	66.3%	33.7%
14,926	ROANE	5,308	2,090	2,794	424	704 D	39.4%	52.6%	42.8%	57.2%
13,927	SUMMERS	4,940	1,793	2,727	420	934 D	36.3%	55.2%	39.7%	60.3%
16,895	TAYLOR	6,611	3,102	3,005	504	97 R	46.9%	45.5%	50.8%	49.2%
7,141	TUCKER	3,478	1,609	1,481	388	128 R	46.3%	42.6%	52.1%	47.9%
9,208	TYLER	3,662	1,969	1,449	244	520 R	53.8%	39.6%	57.6%	42.4%
24,254	UPSHUR	9,194	4,716	3,726	752	990 R	51.3%	40.5%	55.9%	44.1%
42,481	WAYNE	15,341	5,824	8,558	959	2,734 D	38.0%	55.8%	40.5%	59.5%
9,154	WEBSTER	2,998	1,269	1,474	255	205 D	42.3%	49.2%	46.3%	53.7%
16,583	WETZEL	6,282	2,545	3,234	503	689 D	40.5%	51.5%	44.0%	56.0%
5,717	WIRT	2,430	1,106	1,171	153	65 D	45.5%	48.2%	48.6%	51.4%
86,956	WOOD	35,726	15,959	17,240	2,527	1,281 D	44.7%	48.3%	48.1%	51.9%
23,796	WYOMING	7,850	2,641	4,842	367	2,201 D	33.6%	61.7%	35.3%	64.7%
1,852,994	TOTAL	713,879	301,987	350,408	61,484	48,421 D	42.3%	49.1%	46.3%	53.7%

WEST VIRGINIA

HOUSE OF REPRESENTATIVES

| | | | Republican | | Democratic | | Other | Rep.-Dem. | Percentage | | | |
| | | | | | | | | | Total Vote | | Major Vote | |
CD	Year	Total Vote	Vote	Candidate	Vote	Candidate	Vote	Plurality	Rep.	Dem.	Rep.	Dem.
1	2016	237,003	163,469	MCKINLEY, DAVID*	73,534	MANYPENNY, MIKE		89,935 R	69.0%	31.0%	69.0%	31.0%
1	2014	144,600	92,491	MCKINLEY, DAVID*	52,109	GAINER, GLEN B. III		40,382 R	64.0%	36.0%	64.0%	36.0%
1	2012	214,151	133,809	MCKINLEY, DAVID*	80,342	THORN, SUE		53,467 R	62.5%	37.5%	62.5%	37.5%
2	2016	242,014	140,807	MOONEY, ALEX X.*	101,207	HUNT, MARK		39,600 R	58.2%	41.8%	58.2%	41.8%
2	2014	154,238	72,619	MOONEY, ALEX X.	67,687	CASEY, NICK	13,932	4,932 R	47.1%	43.9%	51.8%	48.2%
2	2012	226,766	158,206	CAPITO, SHELLEY MOORE*	68,560	SWINT, HOWARD		89,646 R	69.8%	30.2%	69.8%	30.2%
3	2016	207,332	140,741	JENKINS, EVAN*	49,708	DETCH, MATT	16,883	91,033 R	67.9%	24.0%	73.9%	26.1%
3	2014	140,401	77,713	JENKINS, EVAN	62,688	RAHALL, NICK J. II*		15,025 R	55.4%	44.6%	55.4%	44.6%
3	2012	200,437	92,238	SNUFFER, RICK	108,199	RAHALL, NICK J. II*		15,961 D	46.0%	54.0%	46.0%	54.0%
TOTAL	2016	686,349	445,017		224,449		16,883	220,568 R	64.8%	32.7%	66.5%	33.5%
TOTAL	2014	439,239	242,823		182,484		13,932	60,339 R	55.3%	41.5%	57.1%	42.9%
TOTAL	2012	641,354	384,253		257,101			127,152 R	59.9%	40.1%	59.9%	40.1%

Note: An asterisk (*) denotes incumbent.

WEST VIRGINIA

GENERAL AND PRIMARY ELECTIONS

2016 GENERAL ELECTIONS: OTHER VOTES

President   Other vote was 23,004 Libertarian (Gary Johnson), 8,075 Green (Jill Stein), 3,807 Constitution (Darrell Castle), 1,104 Write-in (Evan McMullin), 268 Write-in (Scattered Write-in)

Governor   42,068 Mountain (Charlotte Pritt), 15,354 Libertarian (David Moran), 4,041 Constitution (Phil Hudok), 14 Write-in (Ras Ible), 7 Write-in (Quinton Caldwell)

House   Other vote was:

CD 3   16,883 Libertarian (Zane Lawhorn)

2016 PRIMARY ELECTIONS: SUPPLEMENTARY INFORMATION

Primary	May 10, 2016	**Registration** (as of April 19, 2016)	1,248,208	Democratic	577,338
				Republican	378,238
				Libertarian	3,398
				Mountain	1,656
				Other	30,987
				No Party	256,591

Primary Type   Semi-Open—Registered Democrats and registered Republicans could vote only in their party's primary. Those voters registered with no party could participate in either the Democratic or the Republican primary.

WEST VIRGINIA

GENERAL AND PRIMARY ELECTIONS

	REPUBLICAN PRIMARIES			DEMOCRATIC PRIMARIES		
President	Trump, Donald J.	157,238	77.1%	Sanders, Bernard	124,700	51.4%
	Cruz, Ted	18,301	9.0%	Clinton, Hillary Rodham	86,914	35.8%
	Kasich, John R.	13,721	6.7%	Farrell, Paul T. Jr.	21,694	8.9%
	Carson, Ben	4,421	2.2%	Judd, Keith	4,460	1.8%
	Rubio, Marco	2,908	1.4%	O'Malley, Martin	3,796	1.6%
	Bush, Jeb	2,305	1.1%	De La Fuente, Roque "Rocky"	975	0.4%
	Paul, Rand	1,798	0.9%			
	Huckabee, Mike	1,780	0.9%			
	Christie, Chris	727	0.4%			
	Fiorina, Carly	659	0.3%			
	Hall, David E.	203	0.1%			
	TOTAL	*204,061*		*TOTAL*	*242,539*	
Governor	Cole, Bill	161,127	100.0%	Justice, Jim	132,704	51.4%
				Goodwin, Booth	65,416	25.3%
				Kessler, Jeffrey V.	60,230	23.3%
	TOTAL	*161,127*		*TOTAL*	*258,350*	
Congressional District 1	McKinley, David*	61,217	100.0%	Manypenny, Mike	60,911	100.0%
	TOTAL	*61,217*		*TOTAL*	*60,911*	
Congressional District 2	Mooney, Alex X.*	45,543	73.0%	Hunt, Mark	21,296	29.1%
	Savitt, Marc	16,849	27.0%	Simpson, Cory	19,180	26.2%
				Payne, Tom	15,250	20.8%
				Peyton, Harvey D.	11,143	15.2%
				Wilson, Robert "Robin" Jr.	6,344	8.7%
	TOTAL	*62,392*		*TOTAL*	*73,213*	
Congressional District 3	Jenkins, Evan*	41,162	100.0%	Detch, Matt	53,703	100.0%
	TOTAL	*41,162*		*TOTAL*	*53,703*	

Note: An asterisk (*) denotes incumbent.

486

WISCONSIN

Congressional districts first established for elections held in 2012

8 members

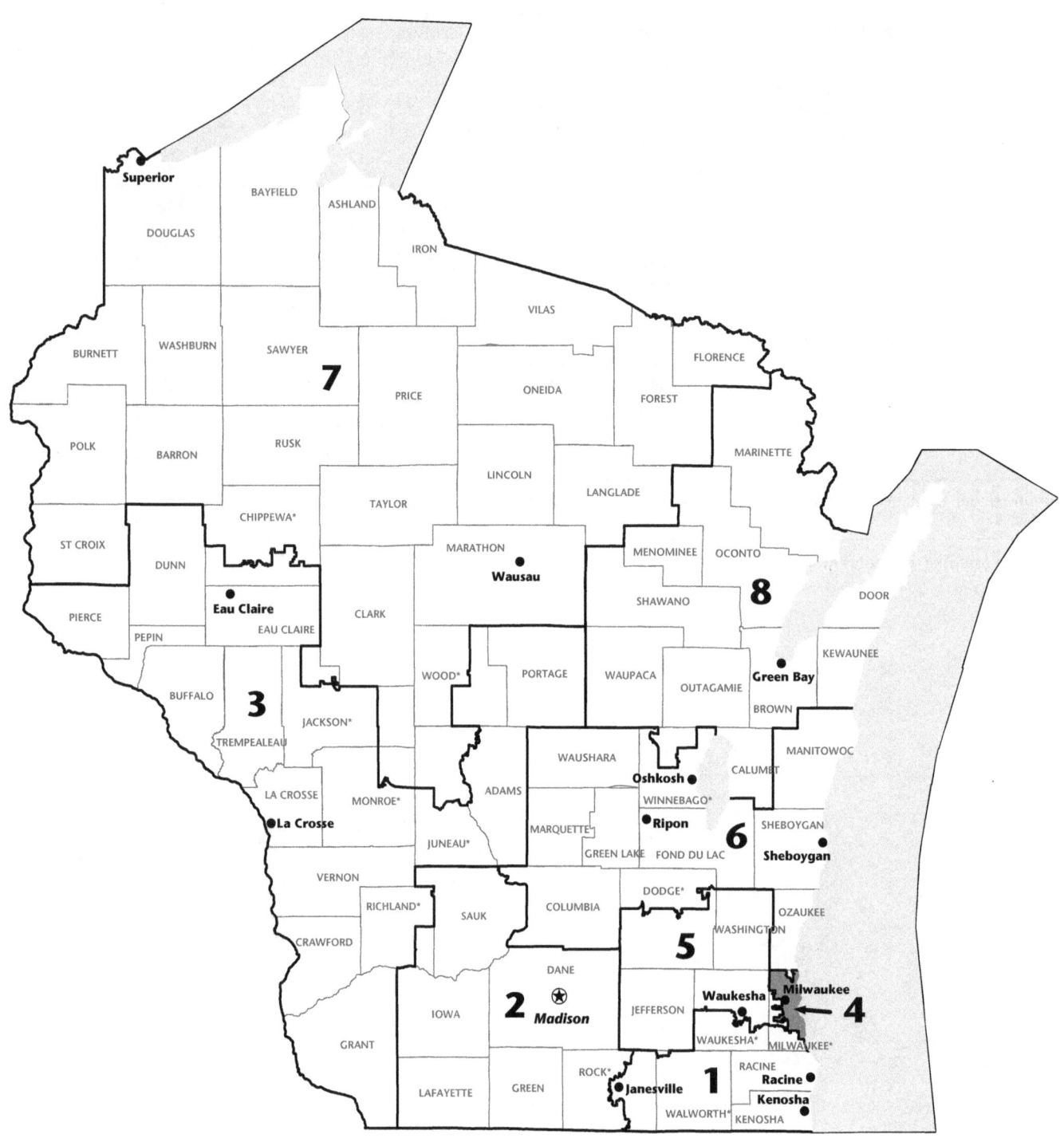

* Asterisk indicates a county whose boundaries include parts of two or more congressional districts.

WISCONSIN

GOVERNOR

Scott Walker (R). Re-elected 2014 to a four-year term. Previously elected 2010. Won special recall election June 5, 2012, to remain in office.

SENATORS (1 Republican, 1 Democrat)

Tammy Baldwin (D). Elected 2012 to a six-year term.

Ron Johnson (R). Re-elected 2016 to a six-year term. Previously elected 2010.

REPRESENTATIVES (5 Republicans, 3 Democrats)

1. Paul D. Ryan (R)
2. Mark Pocan (D)
3. Ron Kind (D)
4. Gwen Moore (D)
5. F. James Sensenbrenner Jr. (R)
6. Glenn Grothman (R)
7. Sean P. Duffy (R)
8. Mike Gallagher (R)

POSTWAR VOTE FOR PRESIDENT

		Republican		Democratic				Total Vote		Major Vote	
Year	Total Vote	Vote	Candidate	Vote	Candidate	Other Vote	Rep.-Dem. Plurality	Rep.	Dem.	Rep.	Dem.
2016**	2,976,150	1,405,284	Trump, Donald J.	1,382,536	Clinton, Hillary Rodham	188,330	22,748 R	47.2%	46.5%	50.4%	49.6%
2012	3,068,434	1,407,966	Romney, W. Mitt	1,620,985	Obama, Barack H.*	39,483	213,019 D	45.9%	52.8%	46.5%	53.5%
2008	2,983,417	1,262,393	McCain, John S. III	1,677,211	Obama, Barack H.	43,813	414,818 D	42.3%	56.2%	42.9%	57.1%
2004	2,997,007	1,478,120	Bush, George W.*	1,489,504	Kerry, John F.	29,383	11,384 D	49.3%	49.7%	49.8%	50.2%
2000**	2,598,607	1,237,279	Bush, George W.	1,242,987	Gore, Albert Jr.	118,341	5,708 D	47.6%	47.8%	49.9%	50.1%
1996**	2,196,169	845,029	Dole, Robert "Bob"	1,071,971	Clinton, Bill*	279,169	226,942 D	38.5%	48.8%	44.1%	55.9%
1992**	2,531,114	930,855	Bush, George H.*	1,041,066	Clinton, Bill	559,193	110,211 D	36.8%	41.1%	47.2%	52.8%
1988	2,191,608	1,047,499	Bush, George H.	1,126,794	Dukakis, Michael S.	17,315	79,295 D	47.8%	51.4%	48.2%	51.8%
1984	2,211,689	1,198,584	Reagan, Ronald*	995,740	Mondale, Walter F.	17,365	202,844 R	54.2%	45.0%	54.6%	45.4%
1980**	2,273,221	1,088,845	Reagan, Ronald	981,584	Carter, Jimmy*	202,792	107,261 R	47.9%	43.2%	52.6%	47.4%
1976	2,104,175	1,004,987	Ford, Gerald R.*	1,040,232	Carter, Jimmy	58,956	35,245 D	47.8%	49.4%	49.1%	50.9%
1972	1,852,890	989,430	Nixon, Richard M.*	810,174	McGovern, George S.	53,286	179,256 R	53.4%	43.7%	55.0%	45.0%
1968**	1,691,538	809,997	Nixon, Richard M.	748,804	Humphrey, Hubert Horatio Jr.	132,737	61,193 R	47.9%	44.3%	52.0%	48.0%
1964	1,691,815	638,495	Goldwater, Barry M. Sr.	1,050,424	Johnson, Lyndon B.*	2,896	411,929 D	37.7%	62.1%	37.8%	62.2%
1960	1,729,082	895,175	Nixon, Richard M.	830,805	Kennedy, John F.	3,102	64,370 R	51.8%	48.0%	51.9%	48.1%
1956	1,550,558	954,844	Eisenhower, Dwight D.*	586,768	Stevenson, Adlai E. II	8,946	368,076 R	61.6%	37.8%	61.9%	38.1%
1952	1,607,370	979,744	Eisenhower, Dwight D.	622,175	Stevenson, Adlai E. II	5,451	357,569 R	61.0%	38.7%	61.2%	38.8%
1948	1,276,800	590,959	Dewey, Thomas E.	647,310	Truman, Harry S.*	38,531	56,351 D	46.3%	50.7%	47.7%	52.3%

Note: An asterisk (*) denotes incumbent. **In past elections, the other vote included: 2016 - 106,674 Libertarian (Gary Johnson); 2000 - 94,070 Green (Ralph Nader); 1996 - 227,339 Reform (Ross Perot); 1992 - 544,479 Independent (Perot); 1980 - 160,657 Independent (John Anderson); 1968 - 127,835 American Independent (George Wallace).

WISCONSIN

POSTWAR VOTE FOR GOVERNOR

Year	Total Vote	Republican Vote	Candidate	Democratic Vote	Candidate	Other Vote	Rep.-Dem. Plurality	Total Vote Rep.	Dem.	Major Vote Rep.	Dem.
2014	2,410,314	1,259,706	Walker, Scott*	1,122,913	Burke, Mary	27,695	136,793 R	52.3%	46.6%	52.9%	47.1%
2012S**	2,516,065	1,335,585	Walker, Scott*	1,164,480	Barrett, Thomas M.	16,000	171,105 R	53.1%	46.3%	53.4%	46.6%
2010	2,160,832	1,128,941	Walker, Scott	1,004,303	Barrett, Thomas M.	27,588	124,638 R	52.2%	46.5%	52.9%	47.1%
2006	2,161,700	979,427	Green, Mark	1,139,115	Doyle, James E.*	43,158	159,688 D	45.3%	52.7%	46.2%	53.8%
2002**	1,775,349	734,779	McCallum, Scott*	800,515	Doyle, James E.	240,055	65,736 D	41.4%	45.1%	47.9%	52.1%
1998	1,756,014	1,047,716	Thompson, Tommy G.*	679,553	Garvey, Ed	28,745	368,163 R	59.7%	38.7%	60.7%	39.3%
1994	1,563,835	1,051,326	Thompson, Tommy G.*	482,850	Chvala, Chuck	29,659	568,476 R	67.2%	30.9%	68.5%	31.5%
1990	1,379,727	802,321	Thompson, Tommy G.*	576,280	Loftus, Thomas	1,126	226,041 R	58.2%	41.8%	58.2%	41.8%
1986	1,526,960	805,090	Thompson, Tommy G.	705,578	Earl, Anthony S.*	16,292	99,512 R	52.7%	46.2%	53.3%	46.7%
1982	1,580,344	662,838	Kohler, Terry J.	896,812	Earl, Anthony S.	20,694	233,974 D	41.9%	56.7%	42.5%	57.5%
1978	1,500,996	816,056	Dreyfus, Lee S.	673,813	Schreiber, Martin J.*	11,127	142,243 R	54.4%	44.9%	54.8%	45.2%
1974	1,181,976	497,195	Dyke, William D.	628,639	Lucey, Patrick J.*	56,142	131,444 D	42.1%	53.2%	44.2%	55.8%
1970**	1,343,160	602,617	Olson, Jack B.	728,403	Lucey, Patrick J.	12,140	125,786 D	44.9%	54.2%	45.3%	54.7%
1968	1,689,738	893,463	Knowles, Warren P.*	791,100	Lafollette, Bronson C.	5,175	102,363 R	52.9%	46.8%	53.0%	47.0%
1966	1,170,173	626,041	Knowles, Warren P.*	539,258	Lucey, Patrick J.	4,874	86,783 R	53.5%	46.1%	53.7%	46.3%
1964	1,694,887	856,779	Knowles, Warren P.	837,901	Reynolds, John W.*	207	18,878 R	50.6%	49.4%	50.6%	49.4%
1962	1,265,900	625,536	Kuehn, Philip G.	637,491	Reynolds, John W.	2,873	11,955 D	49.4%	50.4%	49.5%	50.5%
1960	1,728,009	837,123	Kuehn, Philip G.	890,868	Nelson, Gaylord Anton*	18	53,745 D	48.4%	51.6%	48.4%	51.6%
1958	1,202,219	556,391	Thomson, Vernon W.*	644,296	Nelson, Gaylord Anton	1,532	87,905 D	46.3%	53.6%	46.3%	53.7%
1956	1,557,788	808,273	Thomson, Vernon W.	749,421	Proxmire, William	94	58,852 R	51.9%	48.1%	51.9%	48.1%
1954	1,158,666	596,158	Kohler, Walter J. Jr.*	560,747	Proxmire, William	1,761	35,411 R	51.5%	48.4%	51.5%	48.5%
1952	1,615,214	1,009,171	Kohler, Walter J. Jr.*	601,844	Proxmire, William	4,199	407,327 R	62.5%	37.3%	62.6%	37.4%
1950	1,138,148	605,649	Kohler, Walter J. Jr.	525,319	Thompson, Carl W.	7,180	80,330 R	53.2%	46.2%	53.6%	46.4%
1948	1,266,139	684,839	Rennebohm, Oscar*	558,497	Thompson, Carl W.	22,803	126,342 R	54.1%	44.1%	55.1%	44.9%
1946	1,040,444	621,970	Goodland, Walter S.*	406,499	Hoan, Daniel W.	11,975	215,471 R	59.8%	39.1%	60.5%	39.5%

Note: An asterisk (*) denotes incumbent. **The 2012 Wisconsin gubernatorial contest was a special recall election held in June 2012. Governor Scott Walker retained his office. In past elections, the other vote included: 2002 - 185,455 Libertarian (Ed Thompson). The term of office of Wisconsin's governor was increased from two to four years effective with the 1970 election.

POSTWAR VOTE FOR SENATOR

Year	Total Vote	Republican Vote	Candidate	Democratic Vote	Candidate	Other Vote	Rep.-Dem. Plurality	Total Vote Rep.	Dem.	Major Vote Rep.	Dem.
2016	2,948,741	1,479,471	Johnson, Ron*	1,380,335	Feingold, Russell D.	88,935	99,136 R	50.2%	46.8%	51.7%	48.3%
2012	3,009,411	1,380,126	Thompson, Tommy G.	1,547,104	Baldwin, Tammy	82,181	166,978 D	45.9%	51.4%	47.1%	52.9%
2010	2,171,331	1,125,999	Johnson, Ron	1,020,958	Feingold, Russell D.*	24,374	105,041 R	51.9%	47.0%	52.4%	47.6%
2006	2,138,297	630,299	Lorge, Robert Gerald	1,439,214	Kohl, Herbert H.*	68,784	808,915 D	29.5%	67.3%	30.5%	69.5%
2004	2,949,743	1,301,183	Michels, Tim	1,632,697	Feingold, Russell D.*	15,863	331,514 D	44.1%	55.4%	44.4%	55.6%
2000	2,540,083	940,744	Gillespie, John	1,563,238	Kohl, Herbert H.*	36,101	622,494 D	37.0%	61.5%	37.6%	62.4%
1998	1,760,836	852,272	Neumann, Mark W.	890,059	Feingold, Russell D.*	18,505	37,787 D	48.4%	50.5%	48.9%	51.1%
1994	1,565,628	636,989	Welch, Robert T.	912,662	Kohl, Herbert H.*	15,977	275,673 D	40.7%	58.3%	41.1%	58.9%
1992	2,455,124	1,129,599	Kasten, Robert W.*	1,290,662	Feingold, Russell D.	34,863	161,063 D	46.0%	52.6%	46.7%	53.3%
1988	2,168,190	1,030,440	Engeleiter, Susan	1,128,625	Kohl, Herbert H.	9,125	98,185 D	47.5%	52.1%	47.7%	52.3%
1986	1,483,174	754,573	Kasten, Robert W.*	702,963	Garvey, Ed	25,638	51,610 R	50.9%	47.4%	51.8%	48.2%
1982	1,544,981	527,355	McCallum, Scott	983,311	Proxmire, William*	34,315	455,956 D	34.1%	63.6%	34.9%	65.1%
1980	2,204,202	1,106,311	Kasten, Robert W.	1,065,487	Nelson, Gaylord Anton*	32,404	40,824 R	50.2%	48.3%	50.9%	49.1%
1976	1,935,183	521,902	York, Stanley	1,396,970	Proxmire, William*	16,311	875,068 D	27.0%	72.2%	27.2%	72.8%
1974	1,199,495	429,327	Petri, Thomas E.	740,700	Nelson, Gaylord Anton*	29,468	311,373 D	35.8%	61.8%	36.7%	63.3%
1970	1,338,967	381,297	Erickson, John E.	948,445	Proxmire, William*	9,225	567,148 D	28.5%	70.8%	28.7%	71.3%
1968	1,654,861	633,910	Leonard, Jerris	1,020,931	Nelson, Gaylord Anton*	20	387,021 D	38.3%	61.7%	38.3%	61.7%
1964	1,673,776	780,116	Renk, Wilbur N.	892,013	Proxmire, William*	1,647	111,897 D	46.6%	53.3%	46.7%	53.3%
1962	1,260,168	594,846	Wiley, Alexander*	662,342	Nelson, Gaylord Anton	2,980	67,496 D	47.2%	52.6%	47.3%	52.7%
1958	1,194,678	510,398	Steinle, Roland J.	682,440	Proxmire, William*	1,840	172,042 D	42.7%	57.1%	42.8%	57.2%
1957S**	772,620	312,931	Kohler, Walter J. Jr.	435,985	Proxmire, William	23,704	123,054 D	40.5%	56.4%	41.8%	58.2%
1956	1,523,356	892,473	Wiley, Alexander*	627,903	Maier, Henry W.	2,980	264,570 R	58.6%	41.2%	58.7%	41.3%
1952	1,605,228	870,444	McCarthy, Joseph R.*	731,402	Fairchild, Thomas E.	3,382	139,042 R	54.2%	45.6%	54.3%	45.7%
1950	1,116,135	595,283	Wiley, Alexander*	515,539	Fairchild, Thomas E.	5,313	79,744 R	53.3%	46.2%	53.6%	46.4%
1946	1,014,594	620,430	McCarthy, Joseph R.	378,772	McMurray, Howard J.	15,392	241,658 R	61.2%	37.3%	62.1%	37.9%

Note: An asterisk (*) denotes incumbent. **The August 1957 election was for a short term to fill a vacancy.

WISCONSIN
PRESIDENT 2016

2010 Census Population	County	Total Vote	Republican (Trump)	Democratic (Clinton)	Other	Rep.-Dem. Plurality	Total Vote Rep.	Dem.	Major Vote Rep.	Dem.
20,875	ADAMS	10,130	5,966	3,745	419	2,221 R	58.9%	37.0%	61.4%	38.6%
16,157	ASHLAND	8,032	3,303	4,226	503	923 D	41.1%	52.6%	43.9%	56.1%
45,870	BARRON	22,671	13,614	7,889	1,168	5,725 R	60.1%	34.8%	63.3%	36.7%
15,014	BAYFIELD	9,612	4,124	4,953	535	829 D	42.9%	51.5%	45.4%	54.6%
248,007	BROWN	129,011	67,210	53,382	8,419	13,828 R	52.1%	41.4%	55.7%	44.3%
13,587	BUFFALO	6,981	4,048	2,525	408	1,523 R	58.0%	36.2%	61.6%	38.4%
15,457	BURNETT	8,738	5,410	2,949	379	2,461 R	61.9%	33.7%	64.7%	35.3%
48,971	CALUMET	26,595	15,367	9,642	1,586	5,725 R	57.8%	36.3%	61.4%	38.6%
62,415	CHIPPEWA	31,568	17,916	11,887	1,765	6,029 R	56.8%	37.7%	60.1%	39.9%
34,690	CLARK	13,673	8,652	4,221	800	4,431 R	63.3%	30.9%	67.2%	32.8%
56,833	COLUMBIA	29,698	14,163	13,528	2,007	635 R	47.7%	45.6%	51.1%	48.9%
16,644	CRAWFORD	7,728	3,836	3,419	473	417 R	49.6%	44.2%	52.9%	47.1%
488,073	DANE	309,354	71,275	217,697	20,382	146,422 D	23.0%	70.4%	24.7%	75.3%
88,759	DODGE	43,078	26,635	13,968	2,475	12,667 R	61.8%	32.4%	65.6%	34.4%
27,785	DOOR	17,592	8,580	8,014	998	566 R	48.8%	45.6%	51.7%	48.3%
44,159	DOUGLAS	22,536	9,661	11,357	1,518	1,696 D	42.9%	50.4%	46.0%	54.0%
43,857	DUNN	22,106	11,486	9,034	1,586	2,452 R	52.0%	40.9%	56.0%	44.0%
98,736	EAU CLAIRE	55,025	23,331	27,340	4,354	4,009 D	42.4%	49.7%	46.0%	54.0%
4,423	FLORENCE	2,656	1,898	665	93	1,233 R	71.5%	25.0%	74.1%	25.9%
101,633	FOND DU LAC	51,796	31,022	17,387	3,387	13,635 R	59.9%	33.6%	64.1%	35.9%
9,304	FOREST	4,545	2,787	1,579	179	1,208 R	61.3%	34.7%	63.8%	36.2%
51,208	GRANT	24,368	12,350	10,051	1,967	2,299 R	50.7%	41.2%	55.1%	44.9%
36,842	GREEN	18,985	8,693	9,122	1,170	429 D	45.8%	48.0%	48.8%	51.2%
19,051	GREEN LAKE	9,416	6,216	2,693	507	3,523 R	66.0%	28.6%	69.8%	30.2%
23,687	IOWA	12,275	4,809	6,669	797	1,860 D	39.2%	54.3%	41.9%	58.1%
5,916	IRON	3,513	2,081	1,275	157	806 R	59.2%	36.3%	62.0%	38.0%
20,449	JACKSON	9,267	4,906	3,818	543	1,088 R	52.9%	41.2%	56.2%	43.8%
83,686	JEFFERSON	43,109	23,417	16,569	3,123	6,848 R	54.3%	38.4%	58.6%	41.4%
26,664	JUNEAU	11,735	7,130	4,073	532	3,057 R	60.8%	34.7%	63.6%	36.4%
166,426	KENOSHA	76,304	36,037	35,799	4,468	238 R	47.2%	46.9%	50.2%	49.8%
20,574	KEWAUNEE	10,767	6,618	3,627	522	2,991 R	61.5%	33.7%	64.6%	35.4%
114,638	LA CROSSE	63,674	26,378	32,406	4,890	6,028 D	41.4%	50.9%	44.9%	55.1%
16,836	LAFAYETTE	7,662	3,977	3,288	397	689 R	51.9%	42.9%	54.7%	45.3%
19,977	LANGLADE	10,186	6,478	3,250	458	3,228 R	63.6%	31.9%	66.6%	33.4%
28,743	LINCOLN	14,712	8,401	5,371	940	3,030 R	57.1%	36.5%	61.0%	39.0%
81,442	MANITOWOC	40,786	23,244	14,538	3,004	8,706 R	57.0%	35.6%	61.5%	38.5%
134,063	MARATHON	69,518	39,014	26,481	4,023	12,533 R	56.1%	38.1%	59.6%	40.4%
41,749	MARINETTE	20,343	13,122	6,409	812	6,713 R	64.5%	31.5%	67.2%	32.8%
15,404	MARQUETTE	7,891	4,709	2,808	374	1,901 R	59.7%	35.6%	62.6%	37.4%
4,232	MENOMINEE	1,308	267	1,002	39	735 D	20.4%	76.6%	21.0%	79.0%
947,735	MILWAUKEE	441,053	126,069	288,822	26,162	162,753 D	28.6%	65.5%	30.4%	69.6%
44,673	MONROE	19,699	11,356	7,052	1,291	4,304 R	57.6%	35.8%	61.7%	38.3%
37,660	OCONTO	20,206	13,345	5,940	921	7,405 R	66.0%	29.4%	69.2%	30.8%
35,998	ONEIDA	21,531	12,132	8,109	1,290	4,023 R	56.3%	37.7%	59.9%	40.1%
176,695	OUTAGAMIE	93,933	49,879	38,068	5,986	11,811 R	53.1%	40.5%	56.7%	43.3%
86,395	OZAUKEE	54,560	30,464	20,170	3,926	10,294 R	55.8%	37.0%	60.2%	39.8%
7,469	PEPIN	3,735	2,206	1,344	185	862 R	59.1%	36.0%	62.1%	37.9%
41,019	PIERCE	21,376	11,272	8,399	1,705	2,873 R	52.7%	39.3%	57.3%	42.7%
44,205	POLK	22,745	13,810	7,565	1,370	6,245 R	60.7%	33.3%	64.6%	35.4%
70,019	PORTAGE	38,589	17,305	18,529	2,755	1,224 D	44.8%	48.0%	48.3%	51.7%
14,159	PRICE	7,568	4,559	2,667	342	1,892 R	60.2%	35.2%	63.1%	36.9%
195,408	RACINE	94,302	46,681	42,641	4,980	4,040 R	49.5%	45.2%	52.3%	47.7%
18,021	RICHLAND	8,069	4,013	3,569	487	444 R	49.7%	44.2%	52.9%	47.1%
160,331	ROCK	76,074	31,493	39,339	5,242	7,846 D	41.4%	51.7%	44.5%	55.5%
14,755	RUSK	7,088	4,564	2,171	353	2,393 R	64.4%	30.6%	67.8%	32.2%
61,976	SAUK	31,357	14,799	14,690	1,868	109 R	47.2%	46.8%	50.2%	49.8%
16,557	SAWYER	9,137	5,185	3,503	449	1,682 R	56.7%	38.3%	59.7%	40.3%
41,949	SHAWANO	19,810	12,769	6,068	973	6,701 R	64.5%	30.6%	67.8%	32.2%
115,507	SHEBOYGAN	59,767	32,514	23,000	4,253	9,514 R	54.4%	38.5%	58.6%	41.4%
84,345	ST. CROIX	47,507	26,222	17,482	3,803	8,740 R	55.2%	36.8%	60.0%	40.0%

WISCONSIN

PRESIDENT 2016

2010 Census Population	County	Total Vote	Republican (Trump)	Democratic (Clinton)	Other	Rep.-Dem. Plurality	Percentage — Total Vote — Rep.	Dem.	Percentage — Major Vote — Rep.	Dem.
20,689	TAYLOR	9,471	6,579	2,393	499	4,186 R	69.5%	25.3%	73.3%	26.7%
28,816	TREMPEALEAU	13,687	7,366	5,636	685	1,730 R	53.8%	41.2%	56.7%	43.3%
29,773	VERNON	14,275	7,004	6,371	900	633 R	49.1%	44.6%	52.4%	47.6%
21,430	VILAS	13,611	8,166	4,770	675	3,396 R	60.0%	35.0%	63.1%	36.9%
102,228	WALWORTH	51,391	28,863	18,710	3,818	10,153 R	56.2%	36.4%	60.7%	39.3%
15,911	WASHBURN	9,193	5,436	3,282	475	2,154 R	59.1%	35.7%	62.4%	37.6%
131,887	WASHINGTON	76,757	51,740	20,852	4,165	30,888 R	67.4%	27.2%	71.3%	28.7%
389,891	WAUKESHA	237,593	142,543	79,224	15,826	63,319 R	60.0%	33.3%	64.3%	35.7%
52,410	WAUPACA	26,095	16,209	8,451	1,435	7,758 R	62.1%	32.4%	65.7%	34.3%
24,496	WAUSHARA	12,074	7,667	3,791	616	3,876 R	63.5%	31.4%	66.9%	33.1%
166,994	WINNEBAGO	87,135	43,445	37,047	6,643	6,398 R	49.9%	42.5%	54.0%	46.0%
74,749	WOOD	37,818	21,498	14,225	2,095	7,273 R	56.8%	37.6%	60.2%	39.8%
5,686,986	TOTAL	2,976,150	1,405,284	1,382,536	188,330	22,748 R	47.2%	46.5%	50.4%	49.6%

WISCONSIN

SENATOR 2016

2010 Census Population	County	Total Vote	Republican (Johnson)	Democratic (Feingold)	Other	Rep.-Dem. Plurality	Percentage — Total Vote — Rep.	Dem.	Percentage — Major Vote — Rep.	Dem.
20,875	ADAMS	10,032	5,446	4,093	493	1,353 R	54.3%	40.8%	57.1%	42.9%
16,157	ASHLAND	7,907	3,214	4,452	241	1,238 D	40.6%	56.3%	41.9%	58.1%
45,870	BARRON	22,350	12,893	8,699	758	4,194 R	57.7%	38.9%	59.7%	40.3%
15,014	BAYFIELD	9,445	4,020	5,162	263	1,142 D	42.6%	54.7%	43.8%	56.2%
248,007	BROWN	127,438	71,760	51,008	4,670	20,752 R	56.3%	40.0%	58.5%	41.5%
13,587	BUFFALO	6,883	3,851	2,746	286	1,105 R	55.9%	39.9%	58.4%	41.6%
15,457	BURNETT	8,599	5,198	3,143	258	2,055 R	60.4%	36.6%	62.3%	37.7%
48,971	CALUMET	26,619	16,485	9,197	937	7,288 R	61.9%	34.6%	64.2%	35.8%
62,415	CHIPPEWA	31,324	17,339	12,661	1,324	4,678 R	55.4%	40.4%	57.8%	42.2%
34,690	CLARK	13,515	8,084	4,779	652	3,305 R	59.8%	35.4%	62.8%	37.2%
56,833	COLUMBIA	29,467	13,557	15,057	853	1,500 D	46.0%	51.1%	47.4%	52.6%
16,644	CRAWFORD	7,651	3,671	3,708	272	37 D	48.0%	48.5%	49.7%	50.3%
488,073	DANE	306,960	80,670	220,344	5,946	139,674 D	26.3%	71.8%	26.8%	73.2%
88,759	DODGE	43,166	27,078	14,760	1,328	12,318 R	62.7%	34.2%	64.7%	35.3%
27,785	DOOR	17,558	9,295	7,671	592	1,624 R	52.9%	43.7%	54.8%	45.2%
44,159	DOUGLAS	22,052	9,364	11,893	795	2,529 D	42.5%	53.9%	44.1%	55.9%
43,857	DUNN	21,812	11,425	9,491	896	1,934 R	52.4%	43.5%	54.6%	45.4%
98,736	EAU CLAIRE	54,160	24,650	27,527	1,983	2,877 D	45.5%	50.8%	47.2%	52.8%
4,423	FLORENCE	2,614	1,770	759	85	1,011 R	67.7%	29.0%	70.0%	30.0%
101,633	FOND DU LAC	51,329	32,464	17,131	1,734	15,333 R	63.2%	33.4%	65.5%	34.5%
9,304	FOREST	4,443	2,589	1,651	203	938 R	58.3%	37.2%	61.1%	38.9%
51,208	GRANT	23,932	12,197	10,926	809	1,271 R	51.0%	45.7%	52.7%	47.3%
36,842	GREEN	18,852	8,106	10,207	539	2,101 D	43.0%	54.1%	44.3%	55.7%
19,051	GREEN LAKE	9,319	6,215	2,774	330	3,441 R	66.7%	29.8%	69.1%	30.9%
23,687	IOWA	12,206	4,679	7,226	301	2,547 D	38.3%	59.2%	39.3%	60.7%
5,916	IRON	3,402	1,949	1,361	92	588 R	57.3%	40.0%	58.9%	41.1%
20,449	JACKSON	9,155	4,615	4,096	444	519 R	50.4%	44.7%	53.0%	47.0%
83,686	JEFFERSON	42,334	23,902	17,149	1,283	6,753 R	56.5%	40.5%	58.2%	41.8%
26,664	JUNEAU	11,549	6,441	4,697	411	1,744 R	55.8%	40.7%	57.8%	42.2%
166,426	KENOSHA	75,900	37,540	35,670	2,690	1,870 R	49.5%	47.0%	51.3%	48.7%

WISCONSIN

SENATOR 2016

2010 Census Population	County	Total Vote	Republican (Johnson)	Democratic (Feingold)	Other	Rep.-Dem. Plurality	Percentage			
							Total Vote		Major Vote	
							Rep.	Dem.	Rep.	Dem.
20,574	KEWAUNEE	10,763	6,678	3,697	388	2,981 R	62.0%	34.3%	64.4%	35.6%
114,638	LA CROSSE	62,697	27,694	32,903	2,100	5,209 D	44.2%	52.5%	45.7%	54.3%
16,836	LAFAYETTE	7,594	3,659	3,757	178	98 D	48.2%	49.5%	49.3%	50.7%
19,977	LANGLADE	9,889	6,007	3,465	417	2,542 R	60.7%	35.0%	63.4%	36.6%
28,743	LINCOLN	14,564	8,031	5,785	748	2,246 R	55.1%	39.7%	58.1%	41.9%
81,442	MANITOWOC	39,881	23,769	14,299	1,813	9,470 R	59.6%	35.9%	62.4%	37.6%
134,063	MARATHON	68,937	38,570	27,812	2,555	10,758 R	55.9%	40.3%	58.1%	41.9%
41,749	MARINETTE	19,872	12,597	6,502	773	6,095 R	63.4%	32.7%	66.0%	34.0%
15,404	MARQUETTE	7,804	4,357	3,190	257	1,167 R	55.8%	40.9%	57.7%	42.3%
4,232	MENOMINEE	1,231	303	844	84	541 D	24.6%	68.6%	26.4%	73.6%
947,735	MILWAUKEE	434,714	147,922	276,556	10,236	128,634 D	34.0%	63.6%	34.8%	65.2%
44,673	MONROE	19,426	10,797	7,673	956	3,124 R	55.6%	39.5%	58.5%	41.5%
37,660	OCONTO	19,810	13,004	6,061	745	6,943 R	65.6%	30.6%	68.2%	31.8%
35,998	ONEIDA	21,273	12,047	8,293	933	3,754 R	56.6%	39.0%	59.2%	40.8%
176,695	OUTAGAMIE	93,768	53,252	37,067	3,449	16,185 R	56.8%	39.5%	59.0%	41.0%
86,395	OZAUKEE	54,677	35,456	18,159	1,062	17,297 R	64.8%	33.2%	66.1%	33.9%
7,469	PEPIN	3,699	2,097	1,491	111	606 R	56.7%	40.3%	58.4%	41.6%
41,019	PIERCE	20,879	11,418	8,646	815	2,772 R	54.7%	41.4%	56.9%	43.1%
44,205	POLK	22,379	13,535	8,094	750	5,441 R	60.5%	36.2%	62.6%	37.4%
70,019	PORTAGE	37,952	17,547	18,985	1,420	1,438 D	46.2%	50.0%	48.0%	52.0%
14,159	PRICE	7,551	4,282	2,955	314	1,327 R	56.7%	39.1%	59.2%	40.8%
195,408	RACINE	93,773	49,682	41,606	2,485	8,076 R	53.0%	44.4%	54.4%	45.6%
18,021	RICHLAND	7,981	3,837	3,905	239	68 D	48.1%	48.9%	49.6%	50.4%
160,331	ROCK	75,353	30,487	42,437	2,429	11,950 D	40.5%	56.3%	41.8%	58.2%
14,755	RUSK	6,993	4,229	2,443	321	1,786 R	60.5%	34.9%	63.4%	36.6%
61,976	SAUK	31,387	14,127	16,323	937	2,196 D	45.0%	52.0%	46.4%	53.6%
16,557	SAWYER	8,930	5,154	3,507	269	1,647 R	57.7%	39.3%	59.5%	40.5%
41,949	SHAWANO	19,666	12,794	6,114	758	6,680 R	65.1%	31.1%	67.7%	32.3%
115,507	SHEBOYGAN	59,521	35,146	22,441	1,934	12,705 R	59.0%	37.7%	61.0%	39.0%
84,345	ST. CROIX	46,700	27,406	17,713	1,581	9,693 R	58.7%	37.9%	60.7%	39.3%
20,689	TAYLOR	9,390	6,177	2,828	385	3,349 R	65.8%	30.1%	68.6%	31.4%
28,816	TREMPEALEAU	13,550	7,081	5,963	506	1,118 R	52.3%	44.0%	54.3%	45.7%
29,773	VERNON	14,121	6,712	6,887	522	175 D	47.5%	48.8%	49.4%	50.6%
21,430	VILAS	13,492	8,247	4,820	425	3,427 R	61.1%	35.7%	63.1%	36.9%
102,228	WALWORTH	50,855	30,786	18,358	1,711	12,428 R	60.5%	36.1%	62.6%	37.4%
15,911	WASHBURN	9,024	5,250	3,508	266	1,742 R	58.2%	38.9%	59.9%	40.1%
131,887	WASHINGTON	77,461	55,961	19,831	1,669	36,130 R	72.2%	25.6%	73.8%	26.2%
389,891	WAUKESHA	237,651	161,351	71,779	4,521	89,572 R	67.9%	30.2%	69.2%	30.8%
52,410	WAUPACA	25,727	16,208	8,514	1,005	7,694 R	63.0%	33.1%	65.6%	34.4%
24,496	WAUSHARA	11,904	7,579	3,834	491	3,745 R	63.7%	32.2%	66.4%	33.6%
166,994	WINNEBAGO	86,286	46,843	36,077	3,366	10,766 R	54.3%	41.8%	56.5%	43.5%
74,749	WOOD	37,643	20,925	15,175	1,543	5,750 R	55.6%	40.3%	58.0%	42.0%
5,686,986	TOTAL	2,948,741	1,479,471	1,380,335	88,935	99,136 R	50.2%	46.8%	51.7%	48.3%

WISCONSIN

HOUSE OF REPRESENTATIVES

CD	Year	Total Vote	Republican Vote	Republican Candidate	Democratic Vote	Democratic Candidate	Other Vote	Rep.-Dem. Plurality	Total Vote Rep.	Total Vote Dem.	Major Vote Rep.	Major Vote Dem.
1	2016	354,245	230,072	RYAN, PAUL D.*	107,003	SOLEN, RYAN	17,170	123,069 R	64.9%	30.2%	68.3%	31.7%
1	2014	288,170	182,316	RYAN, PAUL D.*	105,552	ZERBAN, ROB	302	76,764 R	63.3%	36.6%	63.3%	36.7%
1	2012	365,058	200,423	RYAN, PAUL D.*	158,414	ZEBRAN, ROB	6,221	42,009 R	54.9%	43.4%	55.9%	44.1%
2	2016	398,060	124,044	THERON, PETER	273,537	POCAN, MARK*	479	149,493 D	31.2%	68.7%	31.2%	68.8%
2	2014	328,847	103,619	THERON, PETER	224,920	POCAN, MARK*	308	121,301 D	31.5%	68.4%	31.5%	68.5%
2	2012	390,898	124,683	LEE, CHAD	265,422	POCAN, MARK	793	140,739 D	31.9%	67.9%	32.0%	68.0%
3	2016	260,370			257,401	KIND, RON*	2,969	257,401 D		98.9%		100.0%
3	2014	275,161	119,540	KURTZ, TONY	155,368	KIND, RON*	253	35,828 D	43.4%	56.5%	43.5%	56.5%
3	2012	339,764	121,713	BOLAND, RAY	217,712	KIND, RON*	339	95,999 D	35.8%	64.1%	35.9%	64.1%
4	2016	286,909			220,181	MOORE, GWEN*	66,728	220,181 D		76.7%		100.0%
4	2014	254,892	68,490	SEBRING, DAN	179,045	MOORE, GWEN*	7,357	110,555 D	26.9%	70.2%	27.7%	72.3%
4	2012	325,788	80,787	SEBRING, DAN	235,257	MOORE, GWEN	9,744	154,470 D	24.8%	72.2%	25.6%	74.4%
5	2016	390,844	260,706	SENSENBRENNER, F. JAMES JR.*	114,477	PENEBAKER, KHARY	15,661	146,229 R	66.7%	29.3%	69.5%	30.5%
5	2014	332,826	231,160	SENSENBRENNER, F. JAMES JR.*	101,190	ROCKWOOD, CHRIS B.	476	129,970 R	69.5%	30.4%	69.6%	30.4%
5	2012	369,664	250,335	SENSENBRENNER, F. JAMES JR.*	118,478	HEASTER, DAVE	851	131,857 R	67.7%	32.1%	67.9%	32.1%
6	2016	357,183	204,147	GROTHMAN, GLENN S.*	133,072	LLOYD, SARAH	19,964	71,075 R	57.2%	37.3%	60.5%	39.5%
6	2014	299,033	169,767	GROTHMAN, GLENN S.	122,212	HARRIS, MARK L.	7,054	47,555 R	56.8%	40.9%	58.1%	41.9%
6	2012	359,745	223,460	PETRI, THOMAS E.*	135,921	KALLAS, JOSEPH C.	364	87,539 R	62.1%	37.8%	62.2%	37.8%
7	2016	362,271	223,418	DUFFY, SEAN*	138,643	HOEFT, MARY	210	84,775 R	61.7%	38.3%	61.7%	38.3%
7	2014	286,603	169,891	DUFFY, SEAN*	112,949	WESTLUND, KELLY	3,763	56,942 R	59.3%	39.4%	60.1%	39.9%
7	2012	359,669	201,720	DUFFY, SEAN*	157,524	KREITLOW, PAT	425	44,196 R	56.1%	43.8%	56.2%	43.8%
8	2016	363,780	227,892	GALLAGHER, MIKE	135,682	NELSON, TOM	206	92,210 R	62.6%	37.3%	62.7%	37.3%
8	2014	290,048	188,553	RIBBLE, REID J.*	101,345	GRUETT, RON	150	87,208 R	65.0%	34.9%	65.0%	35.0%
8	2012	355,464	198,874	RIBBLE, REID J.*	156,287	WALL, JAMIE	303	42,587 R	55.9%	44.0%	56.0%	44.0%
TOTAL	2016	2,773,662	1,270,279		1,379,996		123,387	109,717 D	45.8%	49.8%	47.9%	52.1%
TOTAL	2014	2,355,580	1,233,336		1,102,581		19,663	130,755 R	52.4%	46.8%	52.8%	47.2%
TOTAL	2012	2,866,050	1,401,995		1,445,015		19,040	43,020 D	48.9%	50.4%	49.2%	50.8%

Note: An asterisk (*) denotes incumbent.

WISCONSIN

GENERAL AND PRIMARY ELECTIONS

2016 GENERAL ELECTIONS: OTHER VOTES

President   Other vote was 106,674 Libertarian (Gary Johnson), 31,072 Green (Jill Stein), 23,295 Write-in (Scattered Write-in), 12,162 Constitution (Darrell Castle), 11,855 Write-in (Evan McMullin), 1,770 Workers World (Monica Moorehead), 1,502 Independent (Roque De La Fuente)

Senate   87,531 Libertarian (Phillip Anderson), 1,396 Write-in (Scattered Write-in), 8 Write-in (John Schiess)

House   Other vote was:

CD 1   9,429 Trump Conservative (Spencer Zimmerman), 7,486 Libertarian (Jason Lebeck), 255 Write-in (Scattered Write-in)

CD 2   479 Write-in (Scattered Write-in)

CD 3   2,800 Write-in (Scattered Write-in), 169 Write-in (Ryan Peterson)

CD 4   33,494 Independent (Robert Raymond), 32,183 Libertarian (Andy Craig), 1,051 Write-in (Scattered Write-in)

CD 5   15,324 Libertarian (John Arndt), 337 Write-in (Scattered Write-in)

CD 6   19,716 Independent (Jeff Dahlke), 248 Write-in (Scattered Write-in)

CD 7   210 Write-in (Scattered Write-in)

CD 8   188 Write-in (Scattered Write-in), 16 Write-in (Wendy Gribben), 2 Write-in (Jerry Kobishop)

WISCONSIN

GENERAL AND PRIMARY ELECTIONS

2016 PRIMARY ELECTIONS: SUPPLEMENTARY INFORMATION

Primary	April 5, 2016 (President) August 9, 2016 (Congress)	**Registration** (as of August 1, 2016)	3,492,577	No Party Registration

Primary Type   Open—Any registered voter could participate in the party primary of his or her choice.

	REPUBLICAN PRIMARIES			DEMOCRATIC PRIMARIES		
President	Cruz, Ted	533,079	48.2%	Sanders, Bernard	570,192	56.6%
	Trump, Donald J.	387,295	35.0%	Clinton, Hillary Rodham	433,739	43.0%
	Kasich, John R.	155,902	14.1%	O'Malley, Martin	1,732	0.2%
	Rubio, Marco	10,591	1.0%	Uninstructed Delegation	1,488	0.1%
	Carson, Ben	5,660	0.5%	Write-In	431	
	Bush, Jeb	3,054	0.3%	De La Fuente, Roque "Rocky"	18	
	Paul, Rand	2,519	0.2%			
	Uninstructed Delegation	2,281	0.2%			
	Huckabee, Mike	1,424	0.1%			
	Write-In	1,381	0.1%			
	Christie, Chris	1,191	0.1%			
	Fiorina, Carly	772	0.1%			
	Santorum, Rick	511				
	Gilmore, James S. III	245				
	Williams, Victor	39				
	TOTAL	*1,105,944*		*TOTAL*	*1,007,600*	
Senator	Johnson, Ron*	248,754	99.5%	Feingold, Russell D.	303,791	90.1%
	Write-In	1,225	0.5%	Harbach, Scott	33,096	9.8%
				Write-In	189	0.1%
	TOTAL	*249,979*		*TOTAL*	*337,076*	
Congressional District 1	Ryan, Paul D.*	57,364	84.1%	Solen, Ryan	14,639	58.9%
	Nehlen, Paul	10,864	15.9%	Breu, Tom	10,142	40.8%
	Write-In	15		Write-In	86	0.3%
	TOTAL	*68,243*		*TOTAL*	*24,867*	
Congressional District 2	Theron, Peter	12,866	99.4%	Pocan, Mark*	71,461	99.5%
	Write-In	79	0.6%	Write-In	395	0.5%
	TOTAL	*12,945*		*TOTAL*	*71,856*	
Congressional District 3	Write-In	361	100.0%	Kind, Ron*	33,320	81.2%
				Buchholz, Myron	7,689	18.7%
				Write-In	7	
	TOTAL	*361*		*TOTAL*	*41,016*	
Congressional District 4	Write-In	228	100.0%	Moore, Gwen*	55,256	84.5%
				George, Gary R.	10,013	15.3%
				Write-In	128	0.2%
	TOTAL	*228*		*TOTAL*	*65,397*	
Congressional District 5	Sensenbrenner, F. James Jr.*	34,203	99.7%	Penebaker, Khary	19,353	99.4%
	Write-In	100	0.3%	Write-In	115	0.6%
	TOTAL	*34,303*		*TOTAL*	*19,468*	
Congressional District 6	Grothman, Glenn S.*	29,795	99.6%	Lloyd, Sarah	19,652	75.1%
	Write-In	105	0.4%	Slattery, W. Michael	6,459	24.7%
				Write-In	43	0.2%
	TOTAL	*29,900*		*TOTAL*	*26,154*	

WISCONSIN

GENERAL AND PRIMARY ELECTIONS

	REPUBLICAN PRIMARIES			DEMOCRATIC PRIMARIES		
Congressional District 7	Duffy, Sean*	29,501	89.4%	Hoeft, Mary	27,289	80.6%
	Raihala, Don	3,456	10.5%	Lewis, Joel	6,531	19.3%
	Write-In	24	0.1%	Write-In	50	0.1%
	TOTAL	32,981		TOTAL	33,870	
Congressional District 8	Gallagher, Mike	40,322	74.5%	Nelson, Tom	20,914	99.9%
	Lasee, Frank	10,705	19.8%	Write-In	28	0.1%
	McNulty, Terry	3,109	5.7%			
	Write-In	16				
	TOTAL	54,152		TOTAL	20,942	

Note: An asterisk (*) denotes incumbent.

WYOMING

One member At Large

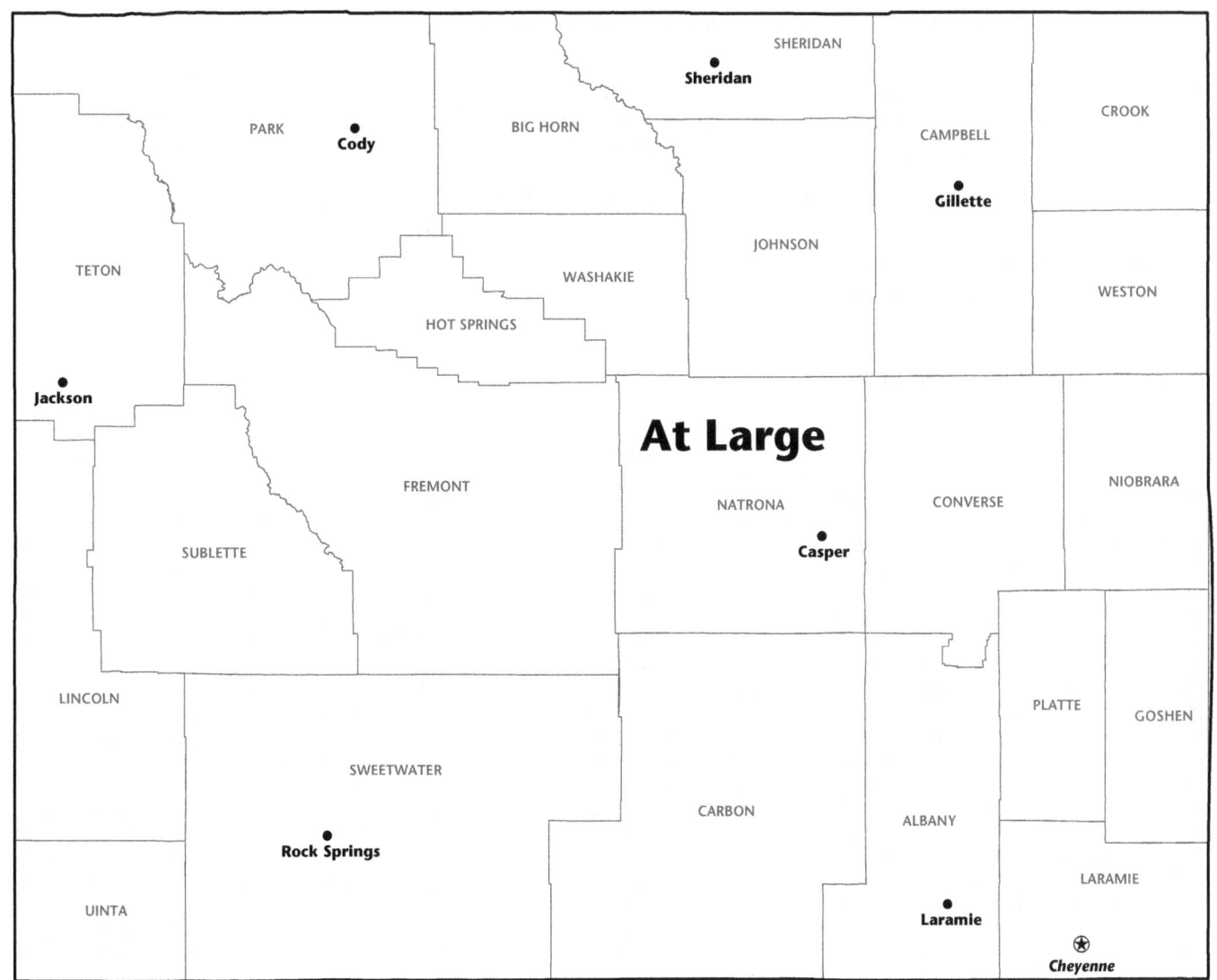

WYOMING

GOVERNOR

Matt Mead (R). Re-elected 2014 to a four-year term. Previously elected 2010.

SENATORS (2 Republicans)

John Barrasso (R). Re-elected 2012 to a six-year term. Previously elected 2008 to complete the remaining four years of the term vacated by the June 2007 death of Senator Craig Thomas (R); sworn in as Thomas's successor June 25, 2007.

Michael B. Enzi (R). Re-elected 2014 to a six-year term. Previously elected 2008, 2002, 1996.

REPRESENTATIVE (1 Republican)

At Large. Elizabeth "Liz" Cheney (R)

POSTWAR VOTE FOR PRESIDENT

| Year | Total Vote | Republican | | Democratic | | Other Vote | Rep.-Dem. Plurality | Percentage | | | |
| | | Vote | Candidate | Vote | Candidate | | | Total Vote | | Major Vote | |
								Rep.	Dem.	Rep.	Dem.
2016**	255,849	174,419	Trump, Donald J.	55,973	Clinton, Hillary Rodham	25,457	118,446 R	68.2%	21.9%	75.7%	24.3%
2012	249,061	170,962	Romney, W. Mitt	69,286	Obama, Barack H.*	8,813	101,676 R	68.6%	27.8%	71.2%	28.8%
2008	254,658	164,958	McCain, John S. III	82,868	Obama, Barack H.	6,832	82,090 R	64.8%	32.5%	66.6%	33.4%
2004	243,428	167,629	Bush, George W.*	70,776	Kerry, John F.	5,023	96,853 R	68.9%	29.1%	70.3%	29.7%
2000**	218,351	147,947	Bush, George W.	60,481	Gore, Albert Jr.	9,923	87,466 R	67.8%	27.7%	71.0%	29.0%
1996**	211,571	105,388	Dole, Robert "Bob"	77,934	Clinton, Bill*	28,249	27,454 R	49.8%	36.8%	57.5%	42.5%
1992**	200,598	79,347	Bush, George H.*	68,160	Clinton, Bill	53,091	11,187 R	39.6%	34.0%	53.8%	46.2%
1988	176,551	106,867	Bush, George H.	67,113	Dukakis, Michael S.	2,571	39,754 R	60.5%	38.0%	61.4%	38.6%
1984	188,968	133,241	Reagan, Ronald*	53,370	Mondale, Walter F.	2,357	79,871 R	70.5%	28.2%	71.4%	28.6%
1980**	176,713	110,700	Reagan, Ronald	49,427	Carter, Jimmy*	16,586	61,273 R	62.6%	28.0%	69.1%	30.9%
1976	156,343	92,717	Ford, Gerald R.*	62,239	Carter, Jimmy	1,387	30,478 R	59.3%	39.8%	59.8%	40.2%
1972	145,570	100,464	Nixon, Richard M.*	44,358	McGovern, George S.	748	56,106 R	69.0%	30.5%	69.4%	30.6%
1968**	127,205	70,927	Nixon, Richard M.	45,173	Humphrey, Hubert Horatio Jr.	11,105	25,754 R	55.8%	35.5%	61.1%	38.9%
1964	142,716	61,998	Goldwater, Barry M. Sr.	80,718	Johnson, Lyndon B.*		18,720 D	43.4%	56.6%	43.4%	56.6%
1960	140,782	77,451	Nixon, Richard M.	63,331	Kennedy, John F.		14,120 R	55.0%	45.0%	55.0%	45.0%
1956	124,127	74,573	Eisenhower, Dwight D.*	49,554	Stevenson, Adlai E. II		25,019 R	60.1%	39.9%	60.1%	39.9%
1952	129,253	81,049	Eisenhower, Dwight D.	47,934	Stevenson, Adlai E. II	270	33,115 R	62.7%	37.1%	62.8%	37.2%
1948	101,425	47,947	Dewey, Thomas E.	52,354	Truman, Harry S.*	1,124	4,407 D	47.3%	51.6%	47.8%	52.2%

Note: An asterisk (*) denotes incumbent. **In past elections, the other vote included: 2016 - 13,287 Libertarian (Gary Johnson); 2000 - 4,625 Green (Ralph Nader); 1996 - 25,928 Reform (Ross Perot); 1992 - 51,263 Independent (Perot); 1980 - 12,072 Independent (John Anderson); 1968 - 11,105 American Independent (George Wallace).

WYOMING

POSTWAR VOTE FOR GOVERNOR

Year	Total Vote	Republican Vote	Republican Candidate	Democratic Vote	Democratic Candidate	Other Vote	Rep.-Dem. Plurality	Total Vote Rep.	Total Vote Dem.	Major Vote Rep.	Major Vote Dem.
2014	167,877	99,700	Mead, Matt*	45,752	Gosar, Peter	22,425	53,948 R	59.4%	27.3%	68.5%	31.5%
2010	188,463	123,780	Mead, Matt	43,240	Petersen, Leslie	21,443	80,540 R	65.7%	22.9%	74.1%	25.9%
2006	193,892	58,100	Hunkins, Ray	135,516	Freudenthal, Dave*	276	77,416 D	30.0%	69.9%	30.0%	70.0%
2002	185,459	88,873	Bebout, Eli	92,662	Freudenthal, Dave	3,924	3,789 D	47.9%	50.0%	49.0%	51.0%
1998	174,888	97,235	Geringer, Jim*	70,754	Vinich, John P.	6,899	26,481 R	55.6%	40.5%	57.9%	42.1%
1994	200,990	118,016	Geringer, Jim	80,747	Karpan, Kathy	2,227	37,269 R	58.7%	40.2%	59.4%	40.6%
1990	160,109	55,471	Mead, Mary	104,638	Sullivan, Mike*		49,167 D	34.6%	65.4%	34.6%	65.4%
1986	164,720	75,841	Simpson, Peter	88,879	Sullivan, Mike		13,038 D	46.0%	54.0%	46.0%	54.0%
1982	168,555	62,128	Morton, Warren A.	106,427	Herschler, Ed*		44,299 D	36.9%	63.1%	36.9%	63.1%
1978	137,567	67,595	Ostlund, John C.	69,972	Herschler, Ed*		2,377 D	49.1%	50.9%	49.1%	50.9%
1974	128,386	56,645	Jones, Dick	71,741	Herschler, Ed		15,096 D	44.1%	55.9%	44.1%	55.9%
1970	118,257	74,249	Hathaway, Stanley K.*	44,008	Rooney, John J.		30,241 R	62.8%	37.2%	62.8%	37.2%
1966	120,873	65,624	Hathaway, Stanley K.	55,249	Wilkerson, Ernest		10,375 R	54.3%	45.7%	54.3%	45.7%
1962	119,268	64,970	Hansen, Clifford P.	54,298	Gage, Jack R.*		10,672 R	54.5%	45.5%	54.5%	45.5%
1958	112,537	52,488	Simpson, Milward L.*	55,070	Hickey, John J.	4,979	2,582 D	46.6%	48.9%	48.8%	51.2%
1954	111,438	56,275	Simpson, Milward L.	55,163	Jack, William		1,112 R	50.5%	49.5%	50.5%	49.5%
1950	96,959	54,441	Barrett, Frank A.	42,518	McIntyre, John J.		11,923 R	56.1%	43.9%	56.1%	43.9%
1946	81,353	38,333	Wright, Earl	43,020	Hunt, Lester C.*		4,687 D	47.1%	52.9%	47.1%	52.9%

Note: An asterisk (*) denotes incumbent.

POSTWAR VOTE FOR SENATOR

Year	Total Vote	Republican Vote	Republican Candidate	Democratic Vote	Democratic Candidate	Other Vote	Rep.-Dem. Plurality	Total Vote Rep.	Total Vote Dem.	Major Vote Rep.	Major Vote Dem.
2014	168,390	121,554	Enzi, Michael B.*	29,377	Hardy, Charles E. "Charlie"	17,459	92,177 R	72.2%	17.4%	80.5%	19.5%
2012	244,862	185,250	Barrasso, John*	53,019	Chestnut, Tim	6,593	132,231 R	75.7%	21.7%	77.7%	22.3%
2008	249,946	189,046	Enzi, Michael B.*	60,631	Rothfuss, Chris	269	128,415 R	75.6%	24.3%	75.7%	24.3%
2008S**	249,558	183,063	Barrasso, John*	66,202	Carter, Nick	293	116,861 R	73.4%	26.5%	73.4%	26.6%
2006	193,136	135,174	Thomas, Craig*	57,671	Groutage, Dale	291	77,503 R	70.0%	29.9%	70.1%	29.9%
2002	183,280	133,710	Enzi, Michael B.*	49,570	Corcoran, Joyce Jansa		84,140 R	73.0%	27.0%	73.0%	27.0%
2000	213,659	157,622	Thomas, Craig*	47,087	Logan, Mel	8,950	110,535 R	73.8%	22.0%	77.0%	23.0%
1996	211,077	114,116	Enzi, Michael B.	89,103	Karpan, Kathy	7,858	25,013 R	54.1%	42.2%	56.2%	43.8%
1994	201,710	118,754	Thomas, Craig	79,287	Sullivan, Mike	3,669	39,467 R	58.9%	39.3%	60.0%	40.0%
1990	157,632	100,784	Simpson, Alan K.*	56,848	Helling, Kathy		43,936 R	63.9%	36.1%	63.9%	36.1%
1988	180,964	91,143	Wallop, Malcolm*	89,821	Vinich, John P.		1,322 R	50.4%	49.6%	50.4%	49.6%
1984	186,898	146,373	Simpson, Alan K.*	40,525	Ryan, Victor A.		105,848 R	78.3%	21.7%	78.3%	21.7%
1982	167,191	94,725	Wallop, Malcolm*	72,466	McDaniel, Rodger		22,259 R	56.7%	43.3%	56.7%	43.3%
1978	133,364	82,908	Simpson, Alan K.	50,456	Whitaker, Raymond B.		32,452 R	62.2%	37.8%	62.2%	37.8%
1976	155,368	84,810	Wallop, Malcolm	70,558	McGee, Gale*		14,252 R	54.6%	45.4%	54.6%	45.4%
1972	142,067	101,314	Hansen, Clifford P.*	40,753	Vinich, Mike		60,561 R	71.3%	28.7%	71.3%	28.7%
1970	120,486	53,279	Wold, John S.	67,207	McGee, Gale*		13,928 D	44.2%	55.8%	44.2%	55.8%
1966	122,689	63,548	Hansen, Clifford P.	59,141	Roncalio, Teno		4,407 R	51.8%	48.2%	51.8%	48.2%
1964	141,670	65,185	Wold, John S.	76,485	McGee, Gale*		11,300 D	46.0%	54.0%	46.0%	54.0%
1962S**	119,372	69,043	Simpson, Milward L.	50,329	Hickey, John J.*		18,714 R	57.8%	42.2%	57.8%	42.2%
1960	138,550	78,103	Thomson, E. Keith	60,447	Whitaker, Raymond B.		17,656 R	56.4%	43.6%	56.4%	43.6%
1958	114,157	56,122	Barrett, Frank A.*	58,035	McGee, Gale		1,913 D	49.2%	50.8%	49.2%	50.8%
1954	112,252	54,407	Harrison, William Henry	57,845	O'Mahoney, Joseph C.*		3,438 D	48.5%	51.5%	48.5%	51.5%
1952	130,097	67,176	Barrett, Frank A.	62,921	O'Mahoney, Joseph C.*		4,255 R	51.6%	48.4%	51.6%	48.4%
1948	101,480	43,527	Robertson, Edward V.*	57,953	Hunt, Lester C.		14,426 D	42.9%	57.1%	42.9%	57.1%
1946	81,557	35,714	Henderson, Harry B.	45,843	O'Mahoney, Joseph C.*		10,129 D	43.8%	56.2%	43.8%	56.2%

Note: An asterisk (*) denotes incumbent. **The 1962 election and one of the 2008 elections were for short terms to fill a vacancy.

WYOMING

PRESIDENT 2016

2010 Census Population	County	Total Vote	Republican (Trump)	Democratic (Clinton)	Other	Rep.-Dem. Plurality		Total Vote Rep.	Total Vote Dem.	Major Vote Rep.	Major Vote Dem.
36,299	ALBANY	17,060	7,602	6,890	2,568	712	R	44.6%	40.4%	52.5%	47.5%
11,668	BIG HORN	5,317	4,067	604	646	3,463	R	76.5%	11.4%	87.1%	12.9%
46,133	CAMPBELL	18,199	15,778	1,324	1,097	14,454	R	86.7%	7.3%	92.3%	7.7%
15,885	CARBON	6,374	4,409	1,279	686	3,130	R	69.2%	20.1%	77.5%	22.5%
13,833	CONVERSE	6,654	5,520	668	466	4,852	R	83.0%	10.0%	89.2%	10.8%
7,083	CROOK	3,826	3,348	273	205	3,075	R	87.5%	7.1%	92.5%	7.5%
40,123	FREMONT	17,023	11,167	4,200	1,656	6,967	R	65.6%	24.7%	72.7%	27.3%
13,249	GOSHEN	5,796	4,418	924	454	3,494	R	76.2%	15.9%	82.7%	17.3%
4,812	HOT SPRINGS	2,586	1,939	400	247	1,539	R	75.0%	15.5%	82.9%	17.1%
8,569	JOHNSON	4,417	3,477	638	302	2,839	R	78.7%	14.4%	84.5%	15.5%
91,738	LARAMIE	40,969	24,847	11,573	4,549	13,274	R	60.6%	28.2%	68.2%	31.8%
18,106	LINCOLN	8,875	6,779	1,105	991	5,674	R	76.4%	12.5%	86.0%	14.0%
75,450	NATRONA	33,348	23,552	6,577	3,219	16,975	R	70.6%	19.7%	78.2%	21.8%
2,484	NIOBRARA	1,314	1,116	115	83	1,001	R	84.9%	8.8%	90.7%	9.3%
28,205	PARK	15,095	11,115	2,535	1,445	8,580	R	73.6%	16.8%	81.4%	18.6%
8,667	PLATTE	4,529	3,437	719	373	2,718	R	75.9%	15.9%	82.7%	17.3%
29,116	SHERIDAN	14,510	10,266	2,927	1,317	7,339	R	70.8%	20.2%	77.8%	22.2%
10,247	SUBLETTE	4,390	3,409	644	337	2,765	R	77.7%	14.7%	84.1%	15.9%
43,806	SWEETWATER	17,130	12,154	3,231	1,745	8,923	R	71.0%	18.9%	79.0%	21.0%
21,294	TETON	12,627	3,921	7,314	1,392	3,393	D	31.1%	57.9%	34.9%	65.1%
21,118	UINTA	8,470	6,154	1,202	1,114	4,952	R	72.7%	14.2%	83.7%	16.3%
8,533	WASHAKIE	3,814	2,911	532	371	2,379	R	76.3%	13.9%	84.5%	15.5%
7,208	WESTON	3,526	3,033	299	194	2,734	R	86.0%	8.5%	91.0%	9.0%
563,626	TOTAL	255,849	174,419	55,973	25,457	118,446	R	68.2%	21.9%	75.7%	24.3%

WYOMING

HOUSE OF REPRESENTATIVES

CD	Year	Total Vote	Republican Vote	Republican Candidate	Democratic Vote	Democratic Candidate	Other Vote	Rep.-Dem. Plurality		Total Vote Rep.	Total Vote Dem.	Major Vote Rep.	Major Vote Dem.
At Large	2016	251,776	156,176	CHENEY, ELIZABETH "LIZ"	75,466	GREENE, RYAN	20,134	80,710	R	62.0%	30.0%	67.4%	32.6%
At Large	2014	165,100	113,038	LUMMIS, CYNTHIA M.*	37,803	GRAYSON, RICHARD	14,259	75,235	R	68.5%	22.9%	74.9%	25.1%
At Large	2012	241,621	166,452	LUMMIS, CYNTHIA M.*	57,573	HENRICHSEN, CHRIS	17,596	108,879	R	68.9%	23.8%	74.3%	25.7%
At Large	2010	186,969	131,661	LUMMIS, CYNTHIA M.*	45,768	WENDT, DAVID	9,540	85,893	R	70.4%	24.5%	74.2%	25.8%
At Large	2008	249,395	131,244	LUMMIS, CYNTHIA M.	106,758	TRAUNER, GARY	11,393	24,486	R	52.6%	42.8%	55.1%	44.9%
At Large	2006	193,369	93,336	CUBIN, BARBARA*	92,324	TRAUNER, GARY	7,709	1,012	R	48.3%	47.7%	50.3%	49.7%
At Large	2004	239,034	132,107	CUBIN, BARBARA*	99,989	LADD, TED	6,938	32,118	R	55.3%	41.8%	56.9%	43.1%
At Large	2002	182,152	110,229	CUBIN, BARBARA*	65,961	AKIN, RON	5,962	44,268	R	60.5%	36.2%	62.6%	37.4%
At Large	2000	212,312	141,848	CUBIN, BARBARA*	60,638	GREEN, MICHAEL ALLEN	9,826	81,210	R	66.8%	28.6%	70.1%	29.9%
At Large	1998	174,219	100,687	CUBIN, BARBARA*	67,399	FARRIS, SCOTT	6,133	33,288	R	57.8%	38.7%	59.9%	40.1%
At Large	1996	209,983	116,004	CUBIN, BARBARA*	85,724	MAXFIELD, PETE	8,255	30,280	R	55.2%	40.8%	57.5%	42.5%
At Large	1994	196,197	104,426	CUBIN, BARBARA	81,022	SCHUSTER, BOB	10,749	23,404	R	53.2%	41.3%	56.3%	43.7%
At Large	1992	196,977	113,882	THOMAS, CRAIG*	77,418	HERSCHLER, JON	5,677	36,464	R	57.8%	39.3%	59.5%	40.5%
At Large	1990	158,055	87,078	THOMAS, CRAIG	70,977	MAXFIELD, PETE		16,101	R	55.1%	44.9%	55.1%	44.9%
At Large	1988	177,651	118,350	CHENEY, RICHARD*	56,527	SHARRATT, BRYAN	2,774	61,823	R	66.6%	31.8%	67.7%	32.3%
At Large	1986	159,787	111,007	CHENEY, RICHARD*	48,780	GILMORE, RICK		62,227	R	69.5%	30.5%	69.5%	30.5%
At Large	1984	187,904	138,234	CHENEY, RICHARD*	45,857	MCFADDEN, HUGH B.	3,813	92,377	R	73.6%	24.4%	75.1%	24.9%
At Large	1982	159,277	113,236	CHENEY, RICHARD*	46,041	HOMMEL, THEODORE H.		67,195	R	71.1%	28.9%	71.1%	28.9%
At Large	1980	169,699	116,361	CHENEY, RICHARD*	53,338	ROGERS, JIM		63,023	R	68.6%	31.4%	68.6%	31.4%
At Large	1978	129,377	75,855	CHENEY, RICHARD	53,522	BAGLEY, BILL		22,333	R	58.6%	41.4%	58.6%	41.4%
At Large	1976	151,868	66,147	HART, LARRY	85,721	RONCALIO, TENO*		19,574	D	43.6%	56.4%	43.6%	56.4%
At Large	1974	126,933	57,499	STROOCK, TOM	69,434	RONCALIO, TENO*		11,935	D	45.3%	54.7%	45.3%	54.7%
At Large	1972	146,299	70,667	KIDD, WILLIAM	75,632	RONCALIO, TENO*		4,965	D	48.3%	51.7%	48.3%	51.7%
At Large	1970	116,304	57,848	ROBERTS, HARRY	58,456	RONCALIO, TENO*		608	D	49.7%	50.3%	49.7%	50.3%
At Large	1968	123,313	77,363	WOLD, JOHN S.	45,950	LINFORD, VELMA		31,413	R	62.7%	37.3%	62.7%	37.3%
At Large	1966	120,426	62,984	HARRISON, WILLIAM HENRY	57,442	CHRISTIAN, AL		5,542	R	52.3%	47.7%	52.3%	47.7%
At Large	1964	139,175	68,482	HARRISON, WILLIAM HENRY	70,693	RONCALIO, TENO*		2,211	D	49.2%	50.8%	49.2%	50.8%

WYOMING

HOUSE OF REPRESENTATIVES

			Republican		Democratic		Other Vote	Rep.-Dem. Plurality	Percentage			
									Total Vote		Major Vote	
CD	Year	Total Vote	Vote	Candidate	Vote	Candidate			Rep.	Dem.	Rep.	Dem.
At Large	1962	116,474	71,489	HARRISON, WILLIAM HENRY*	44,985	MANKUS, LOUIS A.		26,504 R	61.4%	38.6%	61.4%	38.6%
At Large	1960	134,331	70,241	HARRISON, WILLIAM HENRY	64,090	ARMSTRONG, HEPBURN T.		6,151 R	52.3%	47.7%	52.3%	47.7%
At Large	1958	111,780	59,894	THOMSON, E. KEITH*	51,886	WHITAKER, RAYMOND B.		8,008 R	53.6%	46.4%	53.6%	46.4%
At Large	1956	120,128	69,903	THOMSON, E. KEITH*	50,225	O'CALLAGHAN, JERRY A.		19,678 R	58.2%	41.8%	58.2%	41.8%
At Large	1954	108,771	61,111	THOMSON, E. KEITH	47,660	TULLY, SAM		13,451 R	56.2%	43.8%	56.2%	43.8%
At Large	1952	126,720	76,161	HARRISON, WILLIAM HENRY*	50,559	ROSS, ROBERT R. JR.		25,602 R	60.1%	39.9%	60.1%	39.9%
At Large	1950	93,348	50,865	HARRISON, WILLIAM HENRY	42,483	CLARK, JOHN B.		8,382 R	54.5%	45.5%	54.5%	45.5%
At Large	1948	97,464	50,218	BARRETT, FRANK A.*	47,246	FLANNERY, L. G.		2,972 R	51.5%	48.5%	51.5%	48.5%
At Large	1946	79,438	44,482	BARRETT, FRANK A.*	34,956	MCINTYRE, JOHN J.		9,526 R	56.0%	44.0%	56.0%	44.0%

Note: An asterisk (*) denotes incumbent.

WYOMING

GENERAL AND PRIMARY ELECTIONS

2016 GENERAL ELECTIONS: OTHER VOTES

President   Other vote was 13,287 Libertarian (Gary Johnson), 6,904 Write-in (Scattered Write-in), 2,515 Independent (Jill Stein), 2,042 Constitution (Darrell Castle), 709 Independent (Roque De La Fuente)

House   Other vote was:

At Large   10,362 Constitution (Daniel Cummings), 9,033 Libertarian (Lawrence Struempf), 739 Write-in (Scattered Write-in)

2016 PRIMARY ELECTIONS: SUPPLEMENTARY INFORMATION

Presidential Caucus	March 12, 2016 (Republican) April 9, 2016 (Democratic)	**Registration** (as of August 16, 2016)	210,465	Republican Democratic Libertarian Constitution Other Unaffiliated	144,211 42,427 1,138 332 29 22,328	

Primary   August 16, 2016 (Congress)

Primary Type   Semi Open—Only registered Democrats and Republicans could vote in their party's primary, although on primary day, any new voter could register with the party of his or her choice and any previously registered voter could participate in another party's primary by changing his or her registration to that party.

	REPUBLICAN PRIMARIES			DEMOCRATIC PRIMARIES		
Congressional At Large	Cheney, Elizabeth "Liz"	35,043	39.8%	Greene, Ryan	10,955	57.9%
	Christensen, Leland	19,330	21.9%	Hardy, Charles E. "Charlie"	7,868	41.6%
	Stubson, Tim	15,524	17.6%	Write-In	113	0.6%
	Smith, Darin	13,381	15.2%			
	Konsmo, Mike	1,363	1.5%			
	Senteney, Jason Adam	976	1.1%			
	Rammell, Rex	890	1.0%			
	Paad, Paul	886	1.0%			
	Beaudry, Heath	534	0.6%			
	Write-In	155	0.2%			
	TOTAL	88,082		TOTAL	18,936	

Note: An asterisk (*) denotes incumbent.

DISTRICT OF COLUMBIA

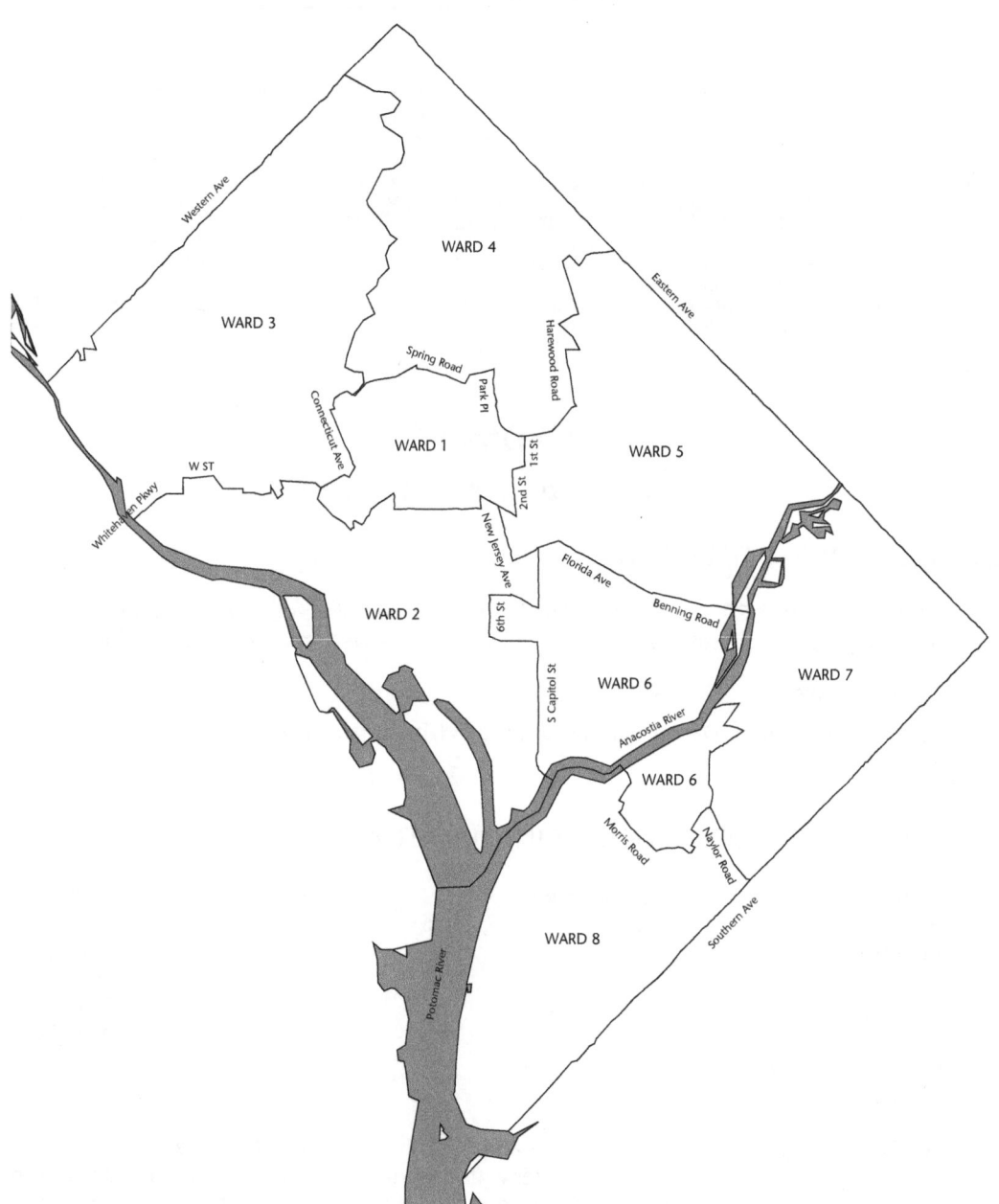

DISTRICT OF COLUMBIA

DELEGATE

Elaine Holmes Norton (D). Re-elected 2016 to a two-year term. Previously elected 2014, 2012, 2010, 2008, 2006, 2004, 2002, 2000, 1998, 1996, 1994, 1992, 1990.

POSTWAR VOTE FOR PRESIDENT

Year	Total Vote	Republican Vote	Republican Candidate	Democratic Vote	Democratic Candidate	Other Vote	Rep.-Dem. Plurality	Total Vote Rep.	Total Vote Dem.	Major Vote Rep.	Major Vote Dem.
2016**	311,268	12,723	Trump, Donald J.	282,830	Clinton, Hillary Rodham	15,715	270,107 D	4.1%	90.9%	4.3%	95.7%
2012	293,764	21,381	Romney, W. Mitt	267,070	Obama, Barack H.*	5,313	245,689 D	7.3%	90.9%	7.4%	92.6%
2008	265,853	17,367	McCain, John S. III	245,800	Obama, Barack H.	2,686	228,433 D	6.5%	92.5%	6.6%	93.4%
2004	227,586	21,256	Bush, George W.*	202,970	Kerry, John F.	3,360	181,714 D	9.3%	89.2%	9.5%	90.5%
2000**	201,894	18,073	Bush, George W.	171,923	Gore, Albert Jr.	11,898	153,850 D	9.0%	85.2%	9.5%	90.5%
1996**	185,726	17,339	Dole, Robert "Bob"	158,220	Clinton, Bill*	10,167	140,881 D	9.3%	85.2%	9.9%	90.1%
1992**	227,572	20,698	Bush, George H.*	192,619	Clinton, Bill	14,255	171,921 D	9.1%	84.6%	9.7%	90.3%
1988	192,877	27,590	Bush, George H.	159,407	Dukakis, Michael S.	5,880	131,817 D	14.3%	82.6%	14.8%	85.2%
1984	211,288	29,009	Reagan, Ronald*	180,408	Mondale, Walter F.	1,871	151,399 D	13.7%	85.4%	13.9%	86.1%
1980**	175,237	23,545	Reagan, Ronald	131,113	Carter, Jimmy*	20,579	107,568 D	13.4%	74.8%	15.2%	84.8%
1976	168,830	27,873	Ford, Gerald R.*	137,818	Carter, Jimmy	3,139	109,945 D	16.5%	81.6%	16.8%	83.2%
1972	163,421	35,226	Nixon, Richard M.*	127,627	McGovern, George S.	568	92,401 D	21.6%	78.1%	21.6%	78.4%
1968	170,578	31,012	Nixon, Richard M.	139,566	Humphrey, Hubert Horatio Jr.		108,554 D	18.2%	81.8%	18.2%	81.8%
1964**			Goldwater, Barry M. Sr.		Johnson, Lyndon B.*						

Note: An asterisk (*) denotes incumbent. **In past elections, the other vote included: 2016 - 4,906 Libertarian (Gary Johnson); 2000 - 10,576 Green (Ralph Nader); 1996 - 3,611 Reform (Ross Perot); 1992 - 9,681 Independent (Perot); 1980 - 16,337 Independent (John Anderson). Under the Twenty-third Amendment to the Constitution, the District of Columbia could choose presidential electors beginning with the 1964 election.

POSTWAR VOTE FOR DELEGATE

Year	Total Vote	Republican Vote	Republican Candidate	Democratic Vote	Democratic Candidate	Other Vote	Rep.-Dem. Plurality	Total Vote Rep.	Total Vote Dem.	Major Vote Rep.	Major Vote Dem.
2012	278,563			246,664	Norton, Eleanor Holmes*	31,899	246,664 D		88.5%		100.0%
2010	132,656	8,109	Smith, Missy Reilly	117,990	Norton, Eleanor Holmes*	6,557	109,881 D	6.1%	88.9%	6.4%	93.6%
2008	247,741			228,376	Norton, Eleanor Holmes*	19,095	228,376 D		92.3%		100.0%
2006	114,777			111,726	Norton, Eleanor Holmes*	3,051	111,726 D		97.3%		100.0%
2004	221,213	18,296	Monroe, Michael Andrew	202,027	Norton, Eleanor Holmes*	890	183,731 D	8.3%	91.3%	8.3%	91.7%
2002	128,233			119,268	Norton, Eleanor Holmes*	8,965	119,628 D		93.0%		100.0%
2000	175,631	10,258	Wolterbeek, Edward	158,824	Norton, Eleanor Holmes*	6,549	148,566 D	5.8%	90.4%	6.1%	93.9%
1998	136,359	8,610	Wolterbeek, Edward	122,228	Norton, Eleanor Holmes*	5,221	113,618 D	6.3%	89.6%	6.6%	93.4%
1996	149,998	11,306	Simonds, Sprague	134,996	Norton, Eleanor Holmes*	3,696	123,690 D	7.5%	90.0%	7.7%	92.3%
1994	173,664	13,828	Saltz, Donald	154,988	Norton, Eleanor Holmes*	4,848	141,160 D	8.0%	89.2%	8.2%	91.8%
1992	196,574	20,108	Emerson, Susan	166,808	Norton, Eleanor Holmes*	9,838	146700 D	10.2%	84.8%	10.8%	89.2%
1990	159,627	41,999	Singleton, Harry M.	98,442	Norton, Eleanor Holmes*	19,186	56,443 D	26.3%	61.7%	29.9%	70.1%
1988	170,933	22,936	Reed, William	121,817	Fauntroy, Walter E.*	26180	98,881 D	13.4%	71.3%	15.8%	84.2%
1986	126,855	17,643	King, Mary L.H.	101,604	Fauntroy, Walter E.*	7,608	83,961 D	13.9%	80.1%	14.8%	85.2%
1984	161,771			154,583	Fauntroy, Walter E.*	7,188	154,583 D		95.6%		100.0%
1982	112,543	17,242	West, John	93,422	Fauntroy, Walter E.*	1,879	76,180 D	15.3%	83.0%	15.6%	84.4%
1980	151,046	21,245	Roehr, Robert J.	112,339	Fauntroy, Walter E.*	17,462	91,094 D	14.1%	74.4%	15.9%	84.1%
1978	96,306	11,677	Champion, Jackson R.	76,557	Fauntroy, Walter E.*	8,072	64,880 D	12.1%	79.5%	13.2%	86.8%
1976	159,790	21,699	Hall, Daniel L.	123,464	Fauntroy, Walter E.*	14,627	101,765 D	13.6%	77.3%	14.9%	85.1%
1974	104,014	9,166	Phillips, William R.	66,337	Fauntroy, Walter E.*	28,511	57,171 D	8.8%	63.8%	12.1%	87.9%
1972	159,612	39,487	Chin-Lee, William	95,300	Fauntroy, Walter E.*	24,825	55,813 D	24.7%	59.7%	29.3%	70.7%
1971S**	116,635	29,249	Nevius, John A.	68,166	Fauntroy, Walter E.	19,220	38,917 D	25.1%	58.4%	30.0%	70.0%

Note: An asterisk (*) denotes incumbent. **The 1971 election was held in March for a short term until the end of the 92nd Congress.

DISTRICT OF COLUMBIA

PRESIDENT 2016

2010 Census Population	Ward	Total Vote	Republican (Trump)	Democratic (Clinton)	Other	Rep.-Dem. Plurality	Percentage			
							Total Vote		Major Vote	
							Rep.	Dem.	Rep.	Dem.
76,197	Ward 1	40,529	1,066	37,490	1,973	36,424 D	2.6%	92.5%	2.8%	97.2%
79,915	Ward 2	33,161	2,304	28,714	2,143	26,410 D	6.9%	86.6%	7.4%	92.6%
77,152	Ward 3	42,582	3,323	36,475	2,784	33,152 D	7.8%	85.7%	8.3%	91.7%
75,773	Ward 4	40,997	1,358	37,962	1,677	36,604 D	3.3%	92.6%	3.5%	96.5%
74,308	Ward 5	39,928	1,141	37,021	1,766	35,880 D	2.9%	92.7%	3.0%	97.0%
76,598	Ward 6	51,687	2,506	45,540	3,641	43,034 D	4.8%	88.1%	5.2%	94.8%
71,068	Ward 7	33,292	547	31,784	961	31,237 D	1.6%	95.5%	1.7%	98.3%
70,712	Ward 8	29,092	478	27,844	770	27,366 D	1.6%	95.7%	1.7%	98.3%
601,723	TOTAL	311,268	12,723	282,830	15,715	270,107 D	4.1%	90.9%	4.3%	95.7%

DISTRICT OF COLUMBIA

GENERAL AND PRIMARY ELECTIONS

2016 GENERAL ELECTIONS: OTHER VOTES

President Other vote was 6,551 Write-in (Scattered Write-in), 4,906 Libertarian (Gary Johnson), 4,258 Green (Jill Stein)

2016 PRIMARY ELECTIONS: SUPPLEMENTARY INFORMATION

Presidential Caucus	March 12, 2016 (Republican)	**Registration** (as of April 30, 2016)	434,961	Democratic	330,679
				Republican	27,387
				Statehood Green	3,407
				Other	1,895
				No Party Affiliation	71,593
Primary	June 14, 2016 (Democratic Presidential and Congress)				

Primary Type Closed—Only registered Democrats and Republicans could vote in their party's primary.

REPUBLICAN PRIMARIES	DEMOCRATIC PRIMARIES		
President			
	Clinton, Hillary Rodham	76,704	78.5%
	Sanders, Bernard	20,361	20.8%
	Write-In	485	0.5%
	De La Fuente, Roque "Rocky"	213	0.2%
	TOTAL	97,763	

Note: An asterisk (*) denotes incumbent.